Global Marketing

Foreign Entry, Market Development & Strategy Implementation

first canadian edition

Michael R. **Czinkota**
Georgetown University

Ilkka A. **Ronkainen**
Georgetown University

Carlyle **Farrell**
Ryerson University

Ronald **McTavish**
Brock University

NELSON EDUCATION

Global Marketing, First Canadian Edition
by Michael R. Czinkota, Ilkka A. Ronkainen, Carlyle Farrell, Ron McTavish

Associate Vice President, Editorial Director:
Evelyn Veitch

Editor-in-Chief, Higher Education:
Anne Williams

Acquisitions Editor:
Amie Plourde

Marketing Manager:
Kathaleen McCormick

Developmental Editor:
Toni Chahley

Photo Researcher and Permissions Coordinator:
Julie Pratt

Content Production Managers:
Carrie McGregor/Karri Yano

Production Service:
Graphic World Inc.

Copy Editor:
Margaret Crammond

Proofreader:
Graphic World Inc.

Indexer:
Graphic World Inc.

Manufacturing Coordinator:
Joanne McNeill

Design Director:
Ken Phipps

Managing Designer:
Katherine Strain

Interior Design:
Peter Papayanakis

Cover Design:
William Bache

Cover Image:
Giles Caldicott/Getty Images

Compositor:
Graphic World Inc.

Printer:
Courier

Adapted from *International Marketing,* Eighth Edition, © 2007, and *International Marketing,* Seventh Edition, © 2004, by Michael R. Czinkota and Ilkka A. Ronkainen, by Thomson South-West, a part of The Thomson Corporation.

Printed and bound in The United States
1 2 3 4 11 10 09 08

For more information contact Nelson Education Ltd., 1120 Birchmount Road, Toronto, Ontario, M1K 5G4. Or you can visit our Internet site at http://www.nelson.com

Library and Archives Canada Cataloguing in Publication Data

Global marketing : foreign entry, market development & strategy implementation / Michael R. Czinkota . . . [et al.]. -- 1st Canadian ed.

Includes index.
ISBN 978-0-17-610406-1

1. Export marketing. 2. Export marketing—Canada. I. Czinkota, Michael R. International marketing. II. Czinkota, Michael R.

HF1416.G555 2008 658.8′4 C2008-900962-2

To Ilona and Margaret Victoria—MRC
To Susan, Sonna, and Alex—IAR
To Buelah and Dominick—CF
To my wife Jo—RM

Preface

It is our pleasure to present the first Canadian edition of *Global Marketing*. This text is written specifically for a Canadian audience and builds on the track record of excellence established by *International Marketing*, which is now in its eighth edition. We have made significant changes to the text that cater to the needs of Canadian students and professors. We have also changed the title of the text to *Global Marketing* to reflect our view that Canadian companies are competing in an integrated global marketing environment. Canadian companies and institutions have been used as examples throughout the text to increase the relevance of the material to Canadian students. We have also presented the unique challenges faced by small and medium-sized companies in Canada as they compete for market share in international markets. Each chapter of the text opens with a discussion of Canadian firms and institutions engaged in the global economy—the challenges they face and the successes they have achieved. Most of the chapters include In More Detail boxes, which provide students with further explanation of key technical terms or additional information on a topic of relevance to global marketers.

The first Canadian edition has been completely reorganized. It now consists of 17 chapters and is more streamlined. For example, global product decisions are now discussed in one chapter. The same applies to global pricing, distribution, and promotion strategy. Given the importance of services to the Canadian economy, we have also added a new chapter on global services. Recognizing the importance of one-on-one relationships in global marketing, we have written two entirely new chapters in this important area, one on personal selling and sales management, the other on international negotiations. In the latter, we discuss the practical, step-by-step stages of negotiations in different cultural environments and provide guidelines for effective global negotiating practice. New material on global outsourcing has also been included. In addition, the chapter on research has been substantially rewritten. The discussion of global research now takes the reader through the sequential steps in completing a typical international research project. Also included is a new appendix that describes a few of the more commonly used techniques of data analysis. In addition, we have thoroughly overhauled the chapter on strategic planning to incorporate a detailed discussion of key issues facing Canadian firms setting their internationalization strategies. We have also substantially revised the chapter on international trade and have sought to provide students with a more solid theoretical base for discussion of issues such as protectionism, free trade, and government involvement in promoting trade and investment flows. New material has also been added on the measurement of political risk and global terrorism, and an entirely new chapter on the future of global marketing concludes the text. In this final chapter we discuss a variety of factors that will have an impact on global marketing in the future, and we point to the emergence of new competitive forces with which Canadian companies will have to contend.

Here are the key reasons why this book is special:

- We write about both the theory and the application of global marketing. Based on our personal research record and business experience, we can offer research insights from around the globe and show how corporations are adjusting to the marketplace realities of today.
- We acknowledge and give clear examples of how the world has changed in an era of terrorism, hostility, and distrust. We look at the marketing repercussions of these changes on people management, sourcing policies, cargo security, inventory management, and port utilization. However, we also draw on our work with corporations to find new forms of collaboration and network building without compromising safety or security.

- We address the concerns of emerging and developing marketing venues throughout the text. We present the issue of under-served markets, with a total population of four billion, and also suggest how these people and countries can take on a greater role as contributors to marketing efforts in mainstream markets.
- We cover the full spectrum of global marketing, from start-up operations to the formation of virtual alliances. We offer a thorough discussion of the operations of multinational corporations, but also present a specific focus on the activities of small and medium-sized firms, which are increasingly major players in the international market.
- We examine global marketing from a truly Canadian perspective. By addressing, confronting, and analyzing the existence of different environments, expectations, and market conditions, we highlight the need for awareness, sensitivity, and adaptation.
- We also address the growing interaction between government and business. Because of our policy experience, we know how businesses work with governments and what role governmental considerations can play for the global marketer. This policy orientation greatly contributes to the managerial relevance of this book.
- We fully incorporate the important societal dimensions of diversity, environmental concern, ethics, and economic transformation.

Personal Support

Most important, we personally stand behind our product and we will work hard to delight you. Should you have any questions or comments on this book, you can contact us, talk to us, and receive feedback from us.

Michael R. Czinkota
(202) 687-4204
Czinkotm@msb.edu

Ilkka A. Ronkainen
(202) 687-3788
Ronkaii@msb.edu

Carlyle Farrell
(416) 979-5000
farrellc@ryerson.ca

Ron McTavish
(905) 688-5550
rmctavish@brocku.ca

Organization

The text is designed primarily for the advanced undergraduate student with prior exposure to the marketing field. Because of its in-depth coverage, it also presents an excellent challenge for graduate instruction and executive education.

The text is divided into six parts. The first part provides an overview of global marketing. Part II examines the global marketing environment. This second part provides a comprehensive discussion of the legal and political environment, the role of culture in global marketing, and the importance of the economic environment. The third part of the text addresses the issues of foreign market entry analysis and strategic planning. Strategic planning in a global marketing environment is discussed along with the issues involved in conducting global marketing research. Modes of entry open to the global marketer are also discussed in this part of the text. Part IV is devoted to global marketing strategy. Global product, distribution, pricing, and promotion strategies are discussed in this part. We also discuss selling and sales management. Part V is concerned with the implementation of global marketing strategy and focuses on the organization and management of foreign operations and the important topic of international negotiations. The sixth and final part of the text presents a discussion of the future of global marketing.

Key Features of the First Canadian Edition

Chapter 1 provides the reader with an up-to-date discussion of the evolution of the term "global marketing" and how the concept differs from other terms such as "international marketing" and "multi-domestic marketing." This chapter also provides a discussion of the globalization of the Canadian economy and the anti-globalization movement in Canada.

Chapter 2 presents students with a comprehensive discussion of the major theories of international trade and investment, including Porter's diamond of competitive advantage, Dunning's OLI framework, and transaction cost analysis. The chapter also provides a review of Canada's trade and investment performance and highlights the importance of international trade organizations in resolving disputes between Canada and its major trading partners, such as the softwood lumber dispute with the United States.

Chapter 3 provides the reader with a discussion of what is meant by the term "Canadian culture" and introduces a number of analytical frameworks within which the culture of various countries may be discussed. Hofstede's framework is introduced, for example, and students are able to visualize where Canada falls on the various dimensions of this framework. Alternative models of cultural analysis such as the Kluckhohn-Strodtbeck (KS) framework and Gannon's metaphors are also presented.

Chapter 4 discusses the economic environment and its importance to global marketers. Up-to-date information on regional integration and the challenges it presents to global marketers are discussed. Marketing to consumers at the base of the income pyramid is also discussed, along with the innovative approach adopted by a Canadian company in accessing this market. The role of the Export Development Corporation in assisting Canadian companies to penetrate infrastructure markets around the globe is also highlighted in this chapter.

Chapter 5 is concerned with the legal and political environment. The chapter discusses embargoes and sanctions and presents the legal authority for the imposition of sanctions by the Canadian government. The chapter also profiles the political and legal challenges faced by Canadian firms doing business around the globe and presents the reader with an approach to the quantification of political risk. The chapter also contains a new section on the impact of terrorism on the activities of the global marketer.

Chapter 6 is concerned with the key area of strategic planning. In this thoroughly revised chapter, emphasis is placed on the internationalization issues facing Canadian firms in an increasingly globalized world. Key questions are addressed, such as when to internationalize, what markets to target, what competitive strategies to adopt, and how markets are to be entered. The chapter also stresses the importance of the firm's core strategies in shaping the direction of global strategy. Also discussed in the chapter are issues of global marketing strategy and implementation, such as the location of the firm's value-added activities, and responding to competitive moves.

Chapter 7 examines the issue of global marketing research. This chapter is completely reorganized around the steps in the marketing research process and contains new examples of how Canadian firms are using research to gain a competitive advantage in the global marketplace. The role of Canadian organizations such as International Trade Canada in facilitating this process is discussed. The chapter also contains a new appendix describing several of the more commonly used data analysis techniques.

Chapter 8 is concerned with foreign market entry strategies. The chapter profiles the approach used by Canadian companies in penetrating foreign markets and provides new material on strategic options for market expansion. The chapter also contains up to date information on the largest Canadian firms by global revenue and recent data on Canada's ranking on the foreign direct investment confidence index.

Chapter 9 examines global product strategies. The chapter explores the factors to be considered in the decision to adapt a product to global markets and illustrates how Canadian companies have risen to the challenge. The chapter also explores the problem of counterfeiting in international markets and examines the work of organizations such as the Canadian Anti-Counterfeiting Network in protecting Canadian firms doing business abroad. The chapter also provides new material on brand changeover strategies that may be used by the global marketer, and it presents recent data on Canada's most valuable brands.

Chapter 10 is an entirely rewritten chapter on international services marketing. Reflecting the importance of services to the Canadian economy, this chapter features Canadian success stories in global service marketing not previously published, and it discusses effective implementation of global marketing strategies in this area. The role of the Internet in opening up new horizons for service marketers is also explored.

Chapter 11 is concerned with global pricing strategies. The chapter introduces new material on the influence of head-office control on global pricing strategies and examines the role of Canadian institutions such as Export Development Canada and the Canadian Commercial Corporation in providing export financing to Canadian exporters.

Chapter 12 explores global distribution strategies. The chapter examines the critical issue of finding suitable intermediaries in international markets and highlights the innovative approach of one Canadian firm in the health care field in addressing this problem. The chapter also introduces new material on the strategic options open to the firm to address the problem of parallel distribution and also incorporates new information on the important topic of global outsourcing.

Chapter 13 is focused on global advertising and sales promotion. The chapter contains a new discussion of the impact of culture on advertising style and provides new material on the modification of global advertising campaigns to local markets. The chapter also provides more recent data on advertising expenditure by some of Canada's largest firms.

Chapter 14 is an entirely new chapter written to give full recognition to the importance of face-to-face contact and persuasion in global marketing. The chapter examines the step-by-step process of global selling, then reviews the problems of managing an international sales force, such as selecting, training, and motivating the sales force. Canadian examples are used throughout. The chapter also features a detailed discussion of sales-force automation and reviews the problems of Canadian expatriates working abroad.

Chapter 15 reviews the range of organizational options available to Canadian companies as they expand their international operations. Firms can choose from a variety of structures ranging from a simple home-based operation handling exports orders to a fully-fledged global operation. Discussion of implementing an appropriate structure and setting up effective control mechanisms form the essence of this chapter.

Chapter 16 is a completely new chapter focusing on how international trade deals are negotiated in diverse cultural environments in different countries. The chapter has a strong practical flavour. A step-by-step review of the global negotiation process is provided, as well as practical guidelines for effective negotiating practice in foreign countries; emphasis is placed on the importance to negotiators of securing agreement on even the smallest contract details.

Chapter 17 is also an entirely new chapter. It reviews a host of factors—financial, technological, demographic, market—and assesses their likely impact on the future of global marketing, including individual program elements (product, price, promotion, distribution). The chapter also reviews global marketing as a career option for Canadian students and suggests different ways to enter it. The chapter concludes with a review of recent global competitive trends and asks if Canadian companies are prepared to meet these challenges.

Innovative Learning Tools

Contemporary Realism

Each chapter opens with and contains several The Global Marketplace boxes. These focus on real marketing situations and are intended to help students understand and absorb the presented materials. Most chapters also contain one or more In More Detail boxes. These provide the student with additional insight into key technical concepts or are used to amplify a point presented in the main body of the text.

Research Emphasis

A special effort has been made to provide current research information and data from around the world. Chapter notes are augmented by lists of relevant recommended readings incorporating the latest research findings. These materials enable the instructor and the student to go beyond the text whenever time permits.

Internet Focus

Chapters now make specific reference to how the Internet, electronic commerce, and the World Wide Web affect global marketing. We highlight how the ways of reaching customers and suppliers have changed given the new technology. We also explain the enhanced ability of firms to position themselves internationally in competition with other larger players. Whenever appropriate, we direct readers to Internet resources that can be useful in updating information. Each chapter also provides several Internet questions in order to offer training opportunities that make use of the Internet.

Geography

This edition contains several full-color maps, covering the social, economic, and political features of the world. In addition, several chapters have maps particularly designed for this book, which integrate the materials discussed in the text and reflect a truly "global" perspective. These maps enable the instructor to visually demonstrate concepts such as political blocs and socioeconomic variables.

Cases

Following each part of the text is a variety of cases. More than 70 percent of the cases are new to the first Canadian edition, and they present students with real business situations in a global context. All cases address the activities of actual or former companies and cover a broad geographic spectrum, including countries such as Poland, Japan, and China.

Ancillary Package

The **Instructor's Resource CD-ROM** includes:

- An **Instructor's Manual** with a chapter outline, chapter objectives, suggestions for teaching, key terms and definitions, questions for discussion with answers, Internet exercises with answers, and teaching notes for all of the cases in the textbook. The Canadian adaptation of the Instructor's Manual is authored by Lee Li of York University.
- A **PowerPoint Presentation**, including charts, tables, figures, and other visual aids. The Canadian adaptation of the PowerPoint Presentation is authored by Greg Libitz of St. Lawrence College.
- A **Test Bank** containing interactive quizzes, in both Word as well as **ExamView – Computerized Testing Software**. This software is free to instructors who adopt the text. The Canadian adaptation of the Test Bank is authored by Zahra Ladha of the University of British Columbia.

Acknowledgments

We wish to thank the reviewers of this first Canadian edition. We are indebted to these individuals for their insightful and thorough review of multiple drafts of this new text and their objective and timely responses to our requests for guidance. These reviewers, our colleagues at institutions across Canada, must be singled out for our most sincere gratitude as this first Canadian edition goes to press.

James Coughlin
Sir Sandford Fleming College

Sheila Ross
Southern Alberta Institute of Technology

F.H. Rolf Seringhaus
Wilfrid Laurier University

Miguel Morales
St. Mary's University

Elena Skliarenko
Seneca College

David Stewart
Memorial University

Nicolas Papadopoulos
Carleton University

We also wish to thank our publisher, Nelson Education Ltd., for their unflagging support of this undertaking and their willingness to allocate the resources necessary to see it through to completion. Evelyn Veitch, Amie Plourde, and Toni Chahley must be singled out for their contribution and commitment to this effort. Veronica Visentin, who left the company to pursue other interests, made a significant contribution to the earlier stages of this project and also has our gratitude.

We would also like to thank the many Canadian companies who have been willing to discuss their international experiences with us, thereby deepening our understanding of the practicalities—and hazards—of global marketing. In addition, when we have found it necessary to consult bodies such as Industry Canada, Export Development Canada, and others during the writing of the text, we have experienced nothing but the fullest degree of cooperation.

We are also indebted to Aahona Banerjee for her research assistance and to the many undergraduate students in international marketing at Ryerson University who provided invaluable feedback on the concepts presented in this text. A debt of gratitude is also owed to Brock University students and to the university for its support of various international and export-related activities that contributed to the shaping of the text.

Finally, we wish to thank members of our families for their encouragement, understanding, and support during the many months that were needed to bring this text to fruition.

Carlyle Farrell
Ron McTavish
Toronto and St. Catharines
October 2007

About the Authors

Michael R. Czinkota teaches international marketing and business at the Graduate School and the Robert Emmett McDonough School of Business at Georgetown University. He has held professorial appointments at universities in Asia, Australia, Europe, and the Americas.

Dr. Czinkota served in the U.S. government as Deputy Assistant Secretary of Commerce. He also served as head of the U.S. Delegation to the OECD Industry Committee in Paris and as senior advisor for Export Controls.

Dr. Czinkota's background includes eight years of private-sector business experience as a partner in a fur-trading firm and in an advertising agency. His research has been supported by the U.S. government, the National Science Foundation, the Organization of American States, and the American Management Association. He was listed as one of the three most published contributors to international business research in the *Journal of International Business Studies,* and has written several books, including *Best Practices in International Marketing* and *Mastering Global Markets* (Thomson).

Dr. Czinkota served on the Global Advisory Board of the American Marketing Association, the Global Council of the American Management Association, and the Board of Governors of the Academy of Marketing Science. He is on the editorial boards of the *Journal of the Academy of Marketing Science,* the *Journal of International Marketing,* and the *Asian Journal of Marketing*. For his work in international business and trade policy, he was named a Distinguished Fellow of the Academy of Marketing Science, a Fellow of the Chartered Institute of Marketing, and a Fellow of the Royal Society of Arts in the United Kingdom. He has been awarded honorary degrees from the Universidad Pontificia Madre y Maestra in the Dominican Republic and the Universidad del Pacifico in Lima, Peru.

Dr. Czinkota serves on several corporate boards and has worked with corporations such as AT&T, IBM, GE, Nestlé, and US WEST. He advises the Executive Office of the President of the United States, the United Nations, and the World Trade Organization. Dr. Czinkota is often asked to testify before the United States Congress.

Dr. Czinkota was born and raised in Germany and educated in Austria, Scotland, Spain, and the United States. He studied law and business administration at the University of Erlangen-Nürnberg and was awarded a two-year Fulbright Scholarship. He holds an MBA in international business and a Ph.D. in logistics from The Ohio State University.

Ilkka A. Ronkainen is a member of the faculty of marketing and international business at the School of Business at Georgetown University. From 1981 to 1986 he served as Associate Director and from 1986 to 1987 as Chairman of the National Center for Export-Import Studies. Currently, he directs Georgetown University's Hong Kong Program.

Dr. Ronkainen serves as docent of international marketing at the Helsinki School of Economics. He was visiting professor at HSE during the 1997–88 and 1991–92 academic years and continues to teach in its Executive MBA, International MBA, and International BBA programs. He is currently the chairholder at the Saastamoinen Foundation Professorship in International Marketing.

Dr. Ronkainen holds a Ph.D. and a master's degree from the University of South Carolina as well as an M.S. (Economics) degree from the Helsinki School of Economics.

Dr. Ronkainen has published extensively in academic journals and the trade press. He is a coauthor of a number of international business and marketing texts, including Best *Practices in International Marketing* and *Mastering Global Markets* (Thomson). He serves on the review boards of the *Journal of Business Research, International Marketing Review,* and the *Journal of Travel Research,* and has reviewed for the *Journal of International Marketing* and the *Journal of International Business Studies.* He served as the North American coordinator for the European Marketing Academy, 1984–90. He was a member of the board of the Washington International Trade Association from 1981 to 1986 and started the association's newsletter, *Trade Trends.*

Dr. Ronkainen has served as a consultant to a wide range of U.S. and international institutions. He has worked with entities such as IBM, the Rand Organization, and the Organization of American States. He maintains close relations with a number of Finnish companies and their internationalization and educational efforts.

Carlyle Farrell is an Associate Professor and Interim Chair of the Global Management Studies Department in the Ted Rogers School of Management at Ryerson University. Dr. Farrell teaches international marketing at the undergraduate and graduate levels and conducts research in the areas of brand globalization, export promotion, international channel relations, and Third World multinationals. He has published in a range of academic journals including the *Atlantic Economic Journal*, the *Journal of Food Products Marketing*, the *Journal of Teaching in International Business*, and the *International Journal of Medical Marketing*. Dr. Farrell is the recipient of the Ryerson University Best New Scholar award for 2006 and is a frequent media commentator on international trade issues. He holds a B.Sc. degree from the University of the West Indies, an M.Sc. from the University of Guelph, and a Ph.D. from the University of Manitoba.

Professor Farrell has over 15 years of private-sector experience as a consultant and senior executive. As an international marketing consultant, he has worked on assignments in over 20 countries across Europe, Africa, South America, and the Caribbean. Dr. Farrell's clients have included Rabobank International, the United Nations Food and Agriculture Organization, Industry Canada, the Ontario Ministry of Agriculture and Food, the Dominica Export Import Agency, the World Bank, Inter American Development Bank, African Development Bank, efoodmanager AG, and numerous other small and medium-sized companies. He has also served as president of the Canadian subsidiary of a U.S.-based e-commerce firm, where he had full P&L responsibility and was instrumental in building the company's brand in the Canadian marketplace. Dr. Farrell has also served as manager of a food manufacturing company in the Caribbean, where he was responsible for executing the strategic vision for this start-up enterprise and crafting its domestic and regional marketing strategies.

Ronald (Ron) McTavish is Professor Emeritus, Department of Marketing, International Business and Strategy, Brock University, and formerly Dean of the Faculty of Business at Brock. He previously spent several years as Professor of Marketing at the John Molson School of Business in Montreal where he served as Director of the International Aviation MBA Program. He also served as Professor in the Faculty of Business Administration at Memorial University of Newfoundland.

Dr. McTavish has extensive international experience, including appointments at 12 university business schools worldwide. After several years as Associate Professor of Marketing at Strathclyde University in Scotland, he held visiting positions at the University of Nigeria, Pace University (New York), the Chinese University of Hong Kong, the University of the West Indies, Bond University (Australia), the University of Porto (Portugal), and Sultan Qaboos University (Oman). He holds a Ph.D. and a master's degree from the University of Strathclyde, and an honours degree in Economics from London University, England.

He has published extensively in academic journals including the *European Journal of Marketing*, *Long Range Planning*, the *International Journal of Bank Marketing*, the *International Journal of Business Studies*, the *Journal of Global Marketing*, and the *Journal of Macromarketing*. He has coauthored four books in the marketing area and contributed to a number of others, and has twice won best paper awards at Administrative Sciences Association of Canada conferences. He has a special interest in the export behaviour of small and medium-sized Canadian businesses and is engaged in a longitudinal study of this behaviour in the Niagara region. Previous papers reporting on this study were published by the Niagara Economic Development Corporation in 1996 and 2004.

Dr. McTavish has worked as consultant to various Canadian and international companies and organizations. These include the Royal Bank of Canada, Mobil Oil (Canada), the Institute of Canadian Bankers, Smorgon Fibre Containers (Australia), ESAB (Sweden), Walton Solomon Consultants (Nigeria), the Howden Group (U.K.), and the Weir Group (U.K.). His activities in the Middle East, Africa, and Hong Kong included emphasis on strategic export development, working in collaboration with local agencies such as the Jamaica Exporters' Association and the Oman Chamber of Commerce and Industry.

Brief Contents

Part 1
Overview of Global Marketing

Part 2
The Global Market Environment

Part 3
Foreign Market Entry Analysis and Planning

Part 4
Global Marketing Strategy

Part 5

The Implementation of Global Marketing Strategy

Part 6

Looking Ahead

Contents

Part 1

Overview of Global Marketing

Chapter 4 The Economic Environment 93

Chapter 5 The Global Political and Legal Environments 131

Chapter 7 Global Marketing Research 205

Chapter 8 Foreign Market Entry Strategies 237

Part 4
Global Marketing Strategy

Chapter 9 Product Strategies and Global Brand Management 297

Chapter 10 International Services Marketing 333

Chapter 14 Management of the Global Sales Force 481

Part 4 Cases Polar-adidas 516

Nova Scotia 521

Starwood Hotels & Resorts Worldwide Inc.: Cross-Marketing Strategies 525

Chapter 16 International Negotiations 581

Part 5 Cases Importing Industry Specific Software: How American Are Canadians? 601

Teleflex Canada: A Culture of Innovation 604

Part 6 Looking Ahead

Chapter 17 The Future of Global Marketing 615

Part 1

Overview of Global Marketing

Part 1 sets the stage for the text by providing an overview of the concept of global marketing and its importance to Canadian firms. Globalization, its forms, and its drivers are discussed in this part, along with the perspective of the anti-globalization movement. Part 1 also addresses the issue of the international trade environment within which firms must plan and implement global marketing activities. International trade agreements and protectionism are discussed, and the implications for global marketers are developed. A number of international trade and investment theories that provide a basis for understanding current debates surrounding globalization, trade liberalization, and government efforts to attract foreign investment are also presented.

Chapter 1

The Global Marketing Imperative

The Global MARKETPLACE 1.1

The Triumph of Free Enterprise and Global Markets

Today might be called the triumph of free enterprise and global markets. There is proof that market economies are more efficient than planned economies. More and more governments around the world are encouraging market-based activities, eschewing protectionist policies, and actively seeking to participate in the global economy. We are witnessing the abolition of state monopolies, the opening of national economies to world markets, and the ongoing introduction and enforcement of rules to ensure competitive market outcomes. Canadian companies such as Bombardier, Research In Motion, the Royal Bank, and Scotiabank are active participants in this new global environment and are continually exploring new market opportunities abroad. These leading Canadian firms now maintain manufacturing and service delivery operations outside of Canada and serve millions of consumers in both developed and emerging markets around the world. The Royal Bank, for example, now services its corporate and investment banking clients in the U.S. through RBC Capital Markets with offices in New York, Houston, San Francisco, and other major American cities. Scotiabank, on the other hand, announced in early 2007 that it had acquired a 10 percent stake in Puerto Rico's First Bancorp—a move which consolidates its position as one of the major financial services companies in that part of the world. The bank is now operative in 25 countries in that region and serves more than 2 million customers.

© Qilai Shen/epa/Corbis

It is not just developed countries that are seeking to participate more fully in global markets. Even China with its strong communist roots is slowly embracing free enterprise and moving toward a more liberalized economy. China's 1.3 billion consumers now constitute an attractive market for Western products, and firms around the world have been positioning themselves to serve this growing appetite for consumer products. For example, IKEA, the Swedish furniture company, has opened a 43,000-square-metre retail store in Beijing to capitalize on this unprecedented marketing opportunity.[1] Key sectors of the Chinese economy such as banking and telecommunications are also being opened up to foreign competition. China's deregulation of these sectors has allowed Canada's Scotiabank to purchase a minority stake in Xi'an City Commercial Bank jointly with International Financial Corporation. Scotiabank is now one of a handful of foreign banks with an investment in a Chinese financial services company.[2]

To understand this global marketing imperative we must recognize that the fastest globalizing nations have enjoyed rates of economic growth up to 50 percent higher than those that have integrated into the world economy more slowly.[3] Linked to this growth, these same countries have also achieved relatively more gains in political freedom and greater increases in life expectancy, literacy rates, and their overall standard of living.

Firms have benefited substantially from the expansion of global marketing activities. With wider market reach and many more customers, firms in the global marketplace produce more and do so more efficiently than do their domestic-only counterparts. As a result, international firms simultaneously achieve lower costs and higher profits both at home and abroad. Market diversification and the stability arising from firms' lack of dependence on any particular geographic market are other positive effects. Firms also learn from their competitors and can recruit and develop the best talent from all over the world. The cumulative effect of all these dimensions is significant. Research has shown that firms of all sizes and in all industries engaged in international markets outperformed their strictly domestic counterparts. They grow more than twice as fast in sales and earn significantly higher returns on equity and assets.[4]

Workers also benefit from global marketing activities. International firms of all sizes pay significantly higher wages than domestic-only firms. Due to their greater profitability and longevity, workplace security is also substantially greater for employees working for global firms than for those working for local firms.[5] Compelled by global media scrutiny, international firms have also become greater practitioners of social responsibility—much to the benefit of their employees around the world. In fact, in many developing countries the global corporation is expected to be proactive in defending the rights of workers.

Consumers are the greatest beneficiaries of all in the victory of free enterprise and global markets. They are offered an unprecedented degree of product availability and choice. Furthermore, due to international competition, the prices of these products are usually low and offer a better quality and quantity of life to a broad spectrum of individuals. Rising incomes have increased consumers' purchasing power. For the first time in history, international goods and services are within the reach of consumers in developing and emerging countries and are no longer the exclusive preserve of the elite in the developed world.

Yet, in spite of all these achievements, global marketing faces challenges. Many practitioners refuse to participate in the international market—judging either the market to be too dangerous or themselves too unprepared. Marketing globally has also created social and ethical issues for many firms as they seek to balance the profit motive with social and ethical concerns of stakeholders at home and abroad. The anti-globalization movement has also raised important questions about the long-term viability of globalization and its impact on the poor. No wonder many people are left confused and skeptical. Given that the public in general does not have a great deal of interest in international and trade matters, there is a pressing need for an analysis of the transformational and uplifting capabilities of global market forces.

Sources:

1. *Financial Post,* "IKEA opens flagship store in Beijing, biggest outside home base in Sweden. April 11, 2006.
2. Scotiabank website, **http://www.scotiabank.com/cda/content/0,1608,CID9902_LIDen,00.html** (accessed February 19, 2007).
3. Global Business Policy Council, *Globalization Ledger* (Washington, DC: A.T. Kearney, 2000), Introduction.
4. Charles Taylor and Witold Henisz, *U.S. Manufacturers in the Global Market Place* (New York: The Conference Board, 1994), Report 1058.
5. J. David Richardson and Karin Rindal, *Why Exports Matter: More!* Washington, DC: The Institute for International Economics and the Manufacturing Institute, 1996.

Adapted from Michael R. Czinkota and Ilkka Ronkainen, "An International Marketing Manifesto," *Journal of International Marketing,* Winter 2003. Adapted with the permission of the American Marketing Association.

You are about to begin an exciting, important, and necessary task: the exploration of **global marketing.** Global marketing is exciting because it combines the science and the art of business with many other disciplines. Economics, anthropology, cultural studies, geography, history, languages, jurisprudence, statistics, demographics, and many other fields combine to help you explore and understand the global marketplace. Different business environments and approaches to marketing will stimulate your intellectual curiosity and enable you to absorb and understand new phenomena. Global marketing has been compared by many who have been active in the field to the task of mountain climbing: challenging, arduous, and exhilarating.

An understanding of global marketing is important because the world is becoming increasingly integrated and companies can no longer focus narrowly on their home country market. For example, consumer trends originating in one country may quickly spread to other countries around the world, creating new marketing opportunities for globally oriented companies. Similarly, competitive threats may now arise from companies located down the street or halfway around the world. Also, political and economic instability in foreign countries can impact consumer confidence and markets at home as well as in potentially lucrative export markets. Forces shaping the global marketplace cannot be ignored. Increasingly, we all are living up to the claim of the Greek philosopher Socrates, who stated, "I am a citizen, not of Athens or Greece, but of the world." Global marketing takes place all around us every day, has a major effect on our lives, and offers new opportunities and challenges, as The Global Marketplace 1.1 shows. After reading through this book and observing global marketing phenomena, you will see what happens, understand what happens, and, at some time in the future, perhaps even make it happen. All of this is much better than standing by and wondering what happened.

Global marketing is necessary because, from a national standpoint, economic isolationism is not sustainable in the long run. Failure to participate in the global marketplace assures a nation of declining economic capability and its citizens of a decrease in their standard of living. Countries such as North Korea provide evidence of the hardships which may follow from economic isolationism. Successful global marketing holds the promise of an improved quality of life, a better society, more efficient business transactions, and, as some have stated, even a more peaceful world.

This chapter is designed to increase your awareness of what global marketing is all about. It defines what is meant by the term "global marketing" and discusses related concepts such as **multi-domestic marketing**. The chapter also discusses the phenomenon of **globalization** and examines the key factors that drive the trend. The merits of globalization are heavily debated, and this chapter presents both the pro- and the anti-"globalist" perspectives on the debate. The globalization of the Canadian economy is also discussed in this chapter along with the impact of the trend on poorer nations. Both the opportunities and the threats that result from the global marketplace are highlighted in this chapter, and the need for a global marketing approach on the part of individuals and institutions is emphasized.

Global Marketing Defined

In brief, global marketing refers to the planning, coordination, and integration of marketing activities across multiple country markets. Several aspects of this definition need to be examined. Firstly, global marketing refers to marketing activities that take place across national borders and outside of the firm's home country. The fact that global marketing activities cross national borders serves to distinguish them from traditional domestic marketing initiatives. In global marketing, the firm is no longer dealing with a familiar set of cultural, social, economic, political, and market conditions but must now adjust to an environment that is decidedly different from its home country. Language, consumer needs, and buyer behaviour may well be different, and there may be obstacles to market entry and regulatory restrictions on the operations of foreign firms. Gaining access to local distribution networks and finding strategic partners may also prove to be challenging, as may coordinating the implementation of marketing activities across multiple countries.

Global marketers are concerned with issues such as the following:

- What countries would be best suited for the products and services offered by our company?
- Should we enter foreign markets by exporting, foreign direct investment, or perhaps a more loosely structured strategic alliance? (See In More Detail 1.1.)
- How do consumers in foreign markets make purchase decisions, and are the products and services offered by our firm consistent with their needs?

In More Detail 1.1

SELECTED APPROACHES TO FOREIGN MARKET ENTRY

Global marketers may enter foreign markets using a variety of approaches. While these are discussed in more detail in Chapter 8, two approaches, foreign direct investment and strategic alliances, may be mentioned here.

Foreign Direct Investment (FDI) FDI refers to capital inflows from abroad that are used to create or expand a company's long-term interest in an enterprise.

Strategic Alliances Strategic alliances are networks of companies that collaborate in the achievement of specific, mutually beneficial corporate objectives. Alliances can take forms ranging from information cooperation in the market development area to joint ownership of worldwide operations. Companies form strategic alliances as a way of developing new markets and sharing the risk of foreign market entry.

- How should we price, promote, and distribute our products in foreign markets bearing in mind the cultural, social, political, and economic differences from our home country?
- In what countries should we source our raw materials and intermediate inputs in order to be price competitive in global markets?
- What competitive threats are we likely to face in foreign markets as well as in our home market?
- What elements of our marketing strategy can we successfully standardize?
- How can our firm coordinate and integrate its marketing activities across foreign countries?

Traditional domestic marketing is not concerned with the issues cited above. The "liability of foreignness" adds an additional layer of complexity and risk to the firm's marketing decisions.

The second point that should be noted about the definition of global marketing is that the firm is pursuing marketing activities in multiple countries outside of its home market. Of course, involvement in global marketing does not mean that a firm must sell its products in every country, or even every region, of the world. With such a strict criterion not even large multinational companies such as Coca-Cola, Bombardier, and Nike would qualify. In fact, research has shown that the vast majority of large firms generate most of their sales in their home region; that is, they do not have the breadth of coverage in all markets around the world to be considered truly "global."[1] Despite the above research finding, global marketing does require that firms operate in multiple countries simultaneously, and this necessitates coordination and integration of marketing activities across these various country markets. This coordination and integration may be in terms of the sale of a standardized product with the same brand name in every country market in which the firm operates, or the company may choose to introduce this standardized product with a uniform advertising campaign that uses similar advertising appeals in all country markets. Pricing strategies across national markets may be harmonized, and the timing of product introductions across these markets may also be coordinated. Coordination and integration of marketing strategy with an emphasis on standardization are central tenets of global marketing. In essence, the global marketer does not "see" a large number of national markets but a single global market to be segmented and targeted irrespective of national borders.

It should be clearly understood that despite the above unique characteristics, global marketing very much retains the basic marketing principles of "satisfaction" and "exchange." In other words, the basic principles of marketing still apply, but their application, complexity, and intensity may vary substantially. It is in the global marketing field where one can observe most closely the role of marketing as a key agent of societal change and as a key instrument for the development of socially responsive business strategy. When we look, for example, at the emerging market economies of China, India, and Russia, we can see the many new challenges confronting global marketing. How does the marketing concept fit into these societies? How can marketing contribute to economic development and the improvement of society? How should distribution systems be organized? How can we get the price mechanism to work? Similarly, in the areas of social responsibility and ethics, the global marketer is faced with culturally diverse environments with differing expectations and often inconsistent legal systems when it comes to monitoring environmental pollution, maintaining safe working conditions, copying technology or trademarks, or paying bribes.[2] In addition, the long-term repercussions of marketing actions need to be understood and evaluated in terms of their societal impact. These are just a few of the issues that the global marketer needs to address. The capability to master these challenges successfully affords a company the potential for new opportunities and high rewards.

Global marketing is concerned with transactions between parties. While this is also true of domestic marketing, the transactions that take place in global marketing are between entities in different countries. This adds an additional layer of complexity to global marketing activities. We should also note that those who do not participate in the transactions are still exposed to global marketing and subject to its changing influences. The global marketer is part of the exchange, recognizes the changing nature of transactions, and adjusts to a constantly moving target subject to shifts in the business environment.

The need for adjusting, for comprehending change, and for successfully carrying out transactions highlights the fact that global marketing is as much art as science. To achieve success in the art of global marketing, it is necessary to be firmly grounded in its scientific aspects. Only then will individual consumers, policymakers, and business executives be able to incorporate global marketing considerations into their thinking and planning. Only then will they be able to consider international issues and repercussions, and make decisions based on a sound analysis of these considerations.

If all of these issues are integrated into each decision made by individuals and by firms, global markets can become a source of growth, profit, needs satisfaction, and quality of life that would not have existed had individuals and firms limited themselves to domestic activities. The purpose of this book is to aid in this decision process.

Evolution of the Concept

The term "global marketing" was popularized by Theodore Levitt in the 1980s.[3] Levitt argued that markets are becoming more global with a convergence of cultural and national preferences. This convergence toward commonality meant that companies could service country markets with standardized products and a uniform marketing strategy. In fact it made sense for them to so. Corporations did not need to adapt to national differences; instead, they could cater to the convergence of national preferences around the world and in the process exploit the **economies of scale** that would allow them to become more competitive. As a firm expanded its output, cost per unit would decline, allowing the firm to be more price competitive in the markets that it serves.

Before the concept of global marketing was recognized, marketers interested in pursuing opportunities abroad would attempt to extend their domestic marketing strategies to the targeted foreign markets. There was little attempt to adjust to the nuances of each foreign market by adapting the firm's marketing strategy to cater to the unique needs of consumers in foreign countries. Companies pursuing this approach tended to view international sales as secondary to their core domestic operation and, therefore, would expend little intellectual or financial effort to reach and develop these foreign markets.

The growing recognition that foreign markets are different from the home market subsequently led some companies to adopt a country-by-country or multi-domestic strategy, in which each country organization operated as a profit centre. The firm would develop and implement a unique marketing strategy for each country in which it did business. Each of the firm's country organizations, whether they were subsidiaries or divisions, would market a range of different products and services targeted to different customer segments, utilizing different marketing strategies with little or no coordination of operations between countries (Exhibit 1.2). A Canadian company's subsidiary in Mexico, for example, would develop and implement its own marketing strategy for that country without regard to what the firm was attempting to accomplish in other Latin American countries or in other parts of the world.

However, as national markets became increasingly similar and scale economies became increasingly important, the inefficiencies of duplicating product development and manufacturing in each country became more apparent and the pressure to leverage resources and coordinate activities across borders gained urgency. Similarly, the increasing number

Exhibit 1.2 The Evolution of Global Marketing

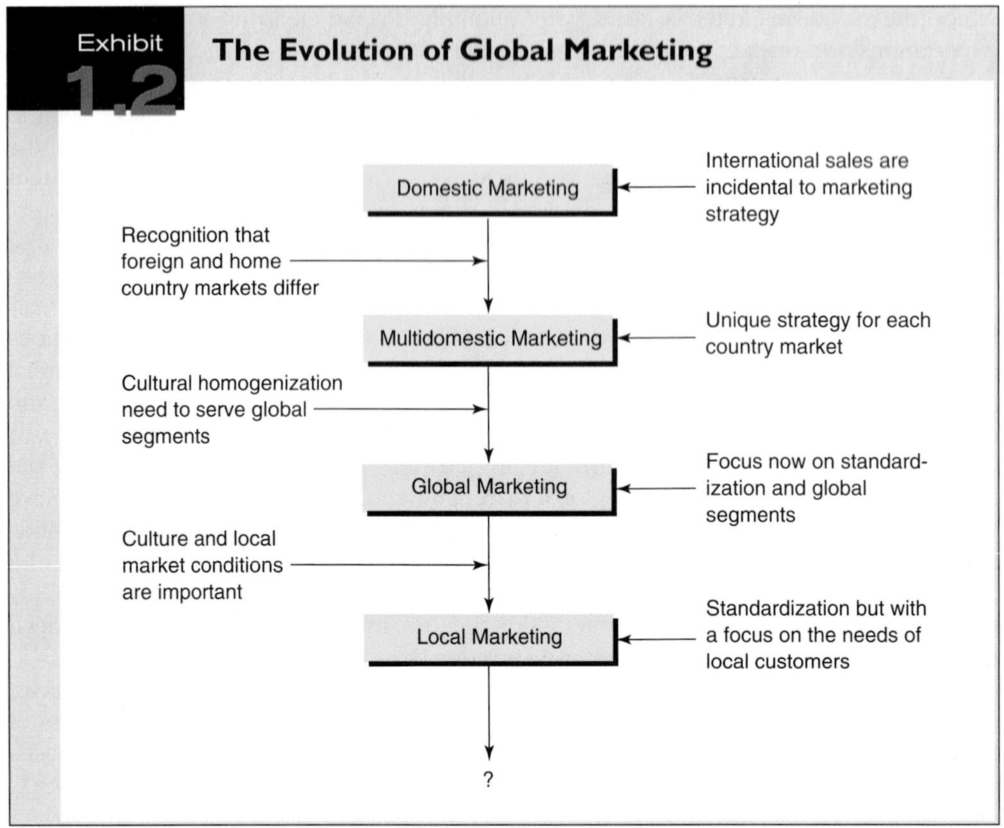

of customers operating globally, as well as the same or similar competitors faced throughout the major markets, added to the need for strategy integration. Global marketing was born out of this recognition of the potential advantages of strategy integration across country markets. To achieve integration, however, meant that the global marketer was not concerned with adapting the marketing mix to the local market. This ran counter to the marketing orientation stressed in domestic marketing.

It should be noted that by the late 1980s marketers began to recognize that country and cultural differences could not be ignored in strategy development. An understanding of the local environment and consumers was important to success even as the firm pursued a global marketing strategy.[4] The marketing orientation is still relevant and applicable and requires an understanding of each national market. The new mantra became "Think global, act local." Companies attempted to "act local' in a number of ways such as reformulating global products to suit local tastes, working more intensely with local companies that understood the local consumer, and by acquiring, improving, and re-launching local brands.[5] This recognition of the importance of culture and local market conditions gave rise to the concept of "**glocal marketing**," which reflects the need for balance between global marketing, with its focus on standardization, and local marketing, with its focus on adaptation to country differences.[6]

Readers should also note that the terms global marketing and **international marketing** are often used interchangeably. The two terms are, however, significantly different. International marketing is an older term focused on issues surrounding foreign market entry and local marketing—issues that are also covered in this text.[7] The term global marketing as defined above is used consistently throughout the remainder of this text.

Globalization

Globalization refers to the increased integration of the world's economies. There are strong global linkages binding firms, institutions, and individuals in countries around the world. This integration was first recognized during the worldwide oil crisis of 1970, and since that time these linkages have continued to strengthen. A drought in Brazil and its effects on coffee production and prices are felt in Canada and indeed around the world. The sudden decline of the Mexican peso reverberated throughout Poland, Hungary, and the Czech Republic. The "Asian meltdown" of the 1990s spawned uncertainty and affected businesses on every continent. The Argentine financial crisis of 2002 not only instigated domestic economic hardships of historic proportions, but it also created a financial and political domino—or, in this case, tango—effect throughout Latin America and required major intervention by the International Monetary Fund (IMF), a supranational organization concerned with maintaining global financial stability.

This integration has also become more apparent on an individual level. Communication has built new international bridges, be it through music or international programs transmitted by CNN. New products have attained international appeal and encouraged similar activities around the world—where many of us wear jeans, dance to soca and reggae, and eat kebabs, curry, and sushi. Transportation linkages let individuals from different countries see and meet each other with unprecedented ease. Common cultural pressures result in similar social phenomena and behaviour—for example, more dual-income families are emerging around the world, which leads to more frequent, but also more stressful, shopping.[8]

Globalization has also resulted in a re-orientation of corporate processes, which opens up entirely new horizons. Never before has it been so easy to gather, manipulate, analyze, and disseminate information—but never before has the pressure been so great to do so. Ongoing global technological innovation in marketing has direct effects on the efficiency and effectiveness of all business activities. Products can be produced more quickly, obtained less expensively from sources around the world, distributed at lower cost, and customized to meet diverse clients' needs. As an example, only a decade ago, it would have been thought impossible for a firm to produce parts for a car in more than one country, assemble the car in yet another country, and sell it in still other nations. Today, such global investment strategies coupled with production and distribution sharing are becoming a matter of routine. Of course, these changes increase the level of global competition, which in turn makes it an ongoing effort if one wants to stay in a leadership position.

Advances in Internet technology also allow firms to separate their activities by content and context. Firms can operate in a "**marketspace**," where buyers and sellers transact online, rather than in a traditional marketplace. In this way, firms may keep the content while changing the context of a transaction.[9] For example, a newspaper can now be distributed globally online rather than house-to-house on paper, thereby allowing outreach to entirely new customer groups. This is not to say that all internationally oriented firms are effective at using such technologies for global expansion. Research suggests that Canadian and U.S. exporters, for example, have not yet fully embraced Internet technologies for transactions across national borders.[10]

Globalization has also spawned a significant increase in investment. The level of global investment is at an unprecedented high and these shifts in financial flows have had major effects. These flows have resulted in the buildup of international debt by governments, affected the international value of currencies, provided foreign capital for firms, and triggered major foreign direct investment activities. All these developments make us more and more dependent on one another. This interdependence, however, is not stable. On almost a daily basis, realignments taking place on both micro and macro levels make past trade orientations at least partially obsolete.

Not only is the environment changing, but the pace of change is accelerating as well. The first office computers emerged in the mid 1980s; today, home computers have become commonplace and mobile computing is being adopted at an accelerating pace. E-mail was introduced to a mass market only in the 1990s; today, many college students hardly ever send personal notes using a stamp and envelope.[11]

Many marketing managers have to deal with the opportunities and the consequences of globalization. Even the biggest companies in the largest home markets cannot survive on domestic sales alone if they are in global industries such as cars, banking, consumer electronics, entertainment, pharmaceuticals, publishing, travel services, or home appliances. They have to be in all major markets to compete or even to survive.

Globalization reflects a business orientation based on the belief that the world is becoming more homogeneous and that distinctions between national markets are not only fading but, for some products, will eventually disappear. As a result, companies need to globalize their international strategy by formulating it across markets to take advantage of underlying market, cost, environmental, and competitive factors. This has meant, for example, that Chinese companies (in categories ranging from auto parts and appliances to telecommunications) have entered the main markets of the world, such as Europe and North America, to become global powerhouses. Having a global presence ensures viability against other players in the home market as well.

Forms of Globalization

Generally we make a distinction between two forms of globalization: the globalization of markets and the globalization of production (Exhibit 1.3). The globalization of markets refers to the convergence of consumer tastes around the world as recognized by Levitt. Teenagers in Lusaka, Tokyo, and Toronto all demonstrate similar tastes in brand-name running shoes and MP3 players. Global brands such as Nike and Apple are able to capitalize on this phenomenon with standardized products and marketing campaigns. Globalization of production, on the other hand, refers to the ability of firms to shift their manufacturing operations to countries around the world to take advantage of lower wage rates and government incentives. A Canadian manufacturer may service global markets with products produced in a facility located in Mexico City, Toronto, or Mumbai, depending on the relative costs associated with doing business in each locale. Firms may shift production to any part of the world to take advantage of cost savings in various countries.

Globalization Drivers

Both external and internal factors will create favourable conditions for development of strategy and resource allocation on a global basis.[12] These drivers of globalization can be divided into market, cost, environmental, and competitive factors (Exhibit 1.4).

Market Factors

The world customer identified by Ernst Dichter more than 40 years ago has gained new meaning today.[13] For example, Kenichi Ohmae has identified consumers in the **triad** of North America, Europe, and the Asia-Pacific region, whom marketers can treat as a single

Exhibit 1.3 The Forms of Globalization

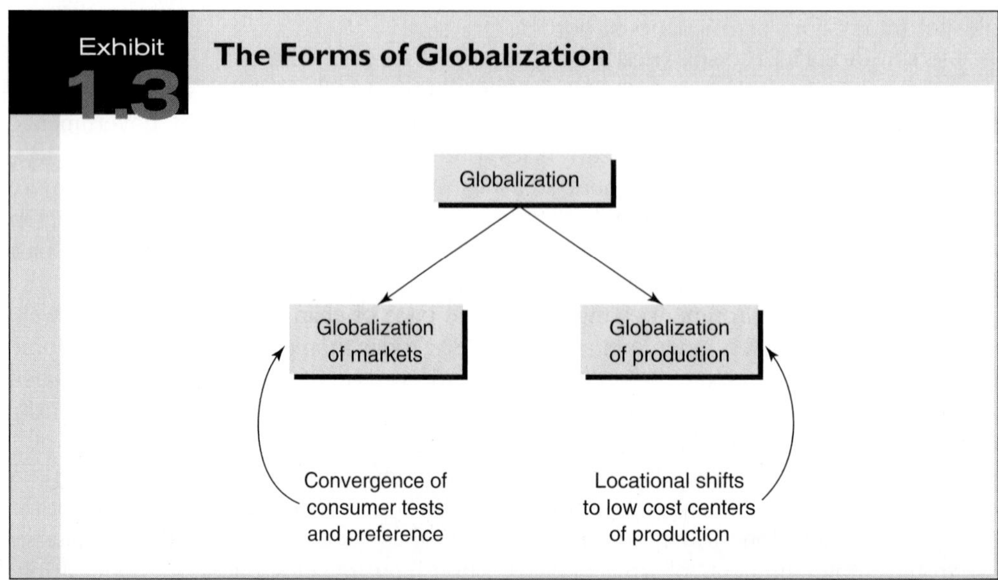

Exhibit 1.4 **The Drivers of Globalization**

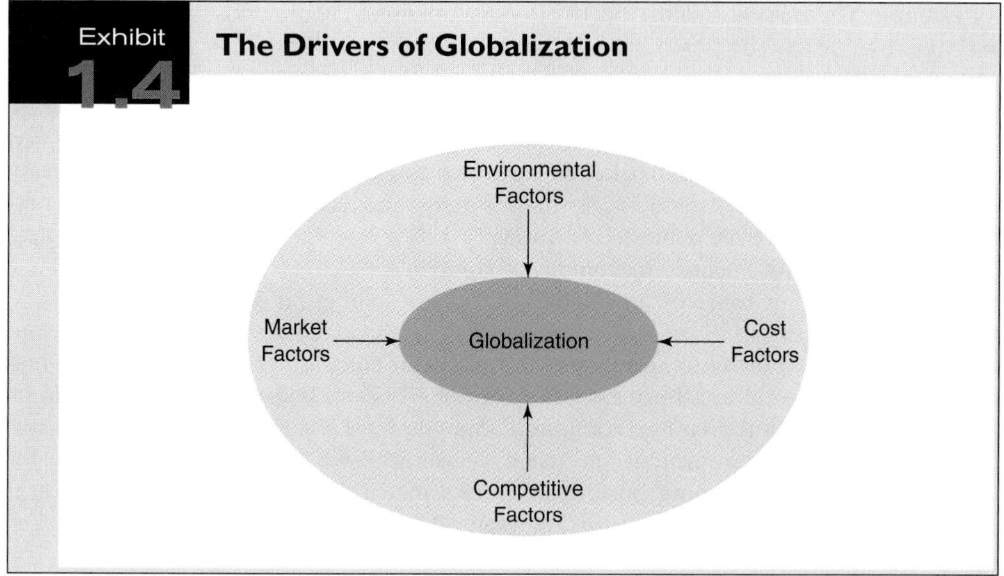

market with similar consumption habits.[14] Over a billion in number, these consumers have similar educational backgrounds, income levels, lifestyles, use of leisure time, and aspirations. One reason given for the similarities in their demand is a level of purchasing power (10 times greater than that of less developed countries or even emerging economies) that translates into higher diffusion rates for certain products. Another reason is that developed infrastructures—diffusion of telecommunication and common platforms such as Microsoft Windows and the Internet—lead to attractive markets for other goods and services. Products can be designed to meet similar demand conditions throughout the triad. These similarities also enhance the transferability of other marketing elements.

At the same time, channels of distribution are becoming more global; that is, a growing number of retailers are now showing great flexibility in their strategies for entering new geographic markets.[15] Some are already world powers (e.g., Benetton), whereas others are pursuing aggressive growth (e.g., IKEA). Also noteworthy are cross-border retail alliances, which expand the presence of retailers to new markets quite rapidly. The presence of global and regional channels makes it even more necessary for the marketer to rationalize marketing efforts.

Cost Factors

Avoiding cost inefficiencies and duplication of effort are two of the most powerful globalization drivers. A single-country approach may not be large enough for the local business to achieve all possible economies of scale and **economies of scope** as well as synergies, especially given the dramatic changes in the marketplace (see In More Detail 1.2). Take,

In More Detail 1.2

ECONOMIES OF SCALE VS. ECONOMIES OF SCOPE

Economies of scale refers to the reduction in per unit cost of production as the firm expands its level of production. Longer production runs and increased output translates into lower cost per unit. The firm which is able to exploit these scale economies may be more price competitive in global markets as it faces a lower per unit cost structure than competing firms. Economies of scope, on the other hand, refers to reduced cost per unit as the firm spreads its total costs (production, marketing, and R & D) over a larger number of brands, product lines, or target markets.

for example, pharmaceuticals. In the 1970s, developing a new drug cost about $16 million and took four years. The drug could be produced in Canada, Britain, or the United States and eventually exported. Now, developing a drug costs as much as $500 million and takes as long as 12 years, with competitive efforts close behind.[16] For the leading companies, annual R & D budgets can run to $5 billion. Only global products for global markets can support that much risk.[17] Size has become a major asset, which partly explains the many mergers and acquisitions in industries such as aerospace, pharmaceuticals, and telecommunications. In the heavily contested consumer goods sectors, launching a new brand may cost as much as $100 million, meaning that companies such as Unilever and Procter & Gamble are not going to necessarily spend precious resources on one-country projects.

In many cases, expanded market participation and activity concentration can accelerate the accumulation of learning and experience. General Electric's philosophy is to be first or second in the world in a business or to get out. This can be seen, for example, in its global effort to develop premium computed tomography (CT), a diagnostic scanning system. GE swapped its consumer electronics business with the French Thomson for Thomson's diagnostic imaging business. At the same time, GE established GE Medical Systems Asia in Tokyo, anchored on Yokogawa Medical Systems, which is 75 percent owned by GE.

Environmental Factors

As will be shown in Chapter 2, government barriers have fallen dramatically in the last several years and this has further facilitated the globalization of markets and the activities of marketers within them. For example, the forces pushing toward a pan-European market are very powerful: The increasing wealth and mobility of European consumers (favoured by relaxed immigration controls), the accelerating flow of information across borders, the introduction of new products where local preferences are not well established, and the common currency are powerful pan-European forces.[18] Also, the resulting removal of physical, fiscal, and technical barriers is indicative of the changes that are taking place around the world on a greater scale.

At the same time, rapid technological evolution is contributing to the process. For example, Ford Motor Company is able to accomplish its globalization efforts by using new communications methods, such as teleconferencing, intranet, and CAD/CAM links, as well as travel, to manage the complex task of linking and coordinating car companies on different continents.[19] Newly emerging markets will benefit from advanced communications by being able to leapfrog stages of economic development. Places that until recently were incommunicado in China, Vietnam, Hungary, or Brazil are rapidly acquiring state-of-the-art telecommunications, especially in mobile telephony, that will let them foster both internal and external development.[20]

Competitive Factors

Many industries are already dominated by global competitors that are trying to take advantage of the three sets of factors mentioned earlier. To remain competitive, the marketer may have to be the first to do something or to be able to match or preempt competitors' moves. Products are now introduced, upgraded, and distributed at rates unimaginable a decade ago. Without a global network, a marketer may run the risk of seeing carefully researched ideas picked off by other global players. This is what Procter & Gamble and Unilever did to Kao's Attack concentrated detergent, which they mimicked and introduced into the United States and Europe before Kao could react. Even with a global network, companies' innovative products are continuously under threat from global competitors. For example, Apple's hugely popular iPod media player, with an estimated 25 percent of worldwide sales and a commanding lead in the U.S., Japan, and Western Europe, has been targeted by Microsoft with Zune, its own innovative product offering.[21]

With the triad markets often both flat in terms of growth and fiercely competitive, many global marketers are looking for new markets and for new product categories for growth. The Swiss firm Nestlé, for example, is setting its sights on consumer markets in fast-growing Asia, especially China, and has diversified into pharmaceuticals by acquiring Alcon and by becoming a major shareholder in the world's number-one cosmetics company, the French L'Oréal. The firm has acquired Ralston Purina and has become the leading manufacturer of pet food; similarly, through its acquisition of Perrier, it has become a leader in the bottled water market. The firm's flagship Maggi Noodle Soup has been tremendously successful in India, and the company has invested over $100 million to build a coffee-processing plant in Russia. Nestlé was founded in 1866 to market baby formula.[22]

Market presence may be necessary to execute global strategies and to prevent others from having undue advantage in unchallenged markets. Caterpillar faced mounting global competition from Komatsu but found out that strengthening its products and operations was not enough to meet the challenge. Although Japan was a small part of the world market, as a secure home base (no serious competitors), it generated 80 percent of Komatsu's cash flow. To put a check on its major global competitor's market share and cash flow, Caterpillar formed a heavy-equipment joint venture with Mitsubishi to serve the Japanese market.[23] Similarly, when Unilever tried to acquire Richardson-Vicks in the United States, Procter & Gamble saw this as a threat to its home market position and outbid its archrival for the company. International Paper prevented Finland's United Paper Mills from acquiring Champion International to protect its market position as the leading papermaker in North America and the world.

The Outcome

The four globalization drivers have affected countries and industrial sectors differently. While some industries are truly globally contested, such as paper and soft drinks, some others, such as government procurement, are still quite closed and will gradually become more open. Commodities and manufactured goods are already in a "globalized" state, while many consumer goods are accelerating toward more globalization. Similarly, the leading trading nations of the world display far more openness than low-income countries, thus advancing the state of globalization in general. The expansion of the global trade arena is summarized in Exhibit 1.5. The size of the market estimated to be global in the 21st century is well over $21 billion, boosted by new sectors and markets that will become available. For example, while financially unattractive in the short to medium

Exhibit 1.5 The Global Landscape by Industry and Market

Industry

Country	Commodities and scale-driven goods	Consumer goods and locally delivered goods and services	Government services
Triad*	Established arena Globalized in 1980s		
Emerging countries†	Growing arena Globally contestable today		
Low-income countries‡	Closed arena Still blocked or lacking significant opportunity		

Global ← → Local

More globalized ↑ ↓ Less globalized

* 30 OECD countries from North America, Western Europe, and Asia; Japan and Australia included
† 70 Countries with middle income per capita, plus China and India
‡ 100 Countries of small absolute size and low income per capita

Source: Adapted and updated from Jane Fraser and Jeremy Oppenheim, "What's New about Globalization," *The McKinsey Quarterly* 33, no. 2 (1997): 173; and Jagdish N. Sheth and Atul Parkatiyar, "The Antecedents and Consequences of Integrated Global Marketing," *International Marketing Review* 18, no. 1 (2001): 16–29.

term, low-income markets may be beneficial in learning the business climate, developing relationships, and building brands for the future. Hewlett-Packard, through its e-Inclusion initiative, is looking at speech interfaces for the Internet, solar applications, and cheap devices that connect with the Web.[24]

Leading companies by their very actions drive the globalization process. Except for the opportunistic behaviour of companies such as Coca-Cola, there is no structural reason why soft drinks should be at a more advanced stage of globalization than beer and spirits, which remain more local. Similarly, Nike and Reebok have driven their businesses in a global direction by creating global brands, a global customer segment, and a global supply chain. By creating a single online trading exchange for all their parts and suppliers, General Motors, Ford, and DaimlerChrysler created a worldwide market of $240 billion in automotive components.[25]

Globalization of the Canadian Economy

Canada is one of the most globalized countries in the world. In a recent research project Canada was ranked third most globalized country in the world behind the United States and Sweden (Exhibit 1.6). Canada's overall globalization index was computed as 6.37, second highest in the group of 80 countries studied. The research project, authored by Axel Dreher, measures overall globalization on three dimensions: economic integration, social integration, and political integration.[26] The globalization index and its three subindexes range from 0 to 10, with increasing values denoting greater globalization. The economic integration dimension examines factors such as the trade and investment flows between countries and the extent to which the country uses policy measures to restrict these flows. Canada scores 5.17 on this dimension, ahead of the United States and Japan but behind the U.K., Germany, Singapore, Sweden, and Switzerland. Social integration reflects the flow and the movement of ideas, people, and information, and here Canada scores 6.56 but trails the U.S., which scored 6.9 on this measure. The final dimension of the globalization index is political integration, which captures the diffusion of government policies around the world. On this dimension Canada scores 7.61 but again trails the U.S. as well as France and Sweden.

There is little doubt that Canada is fully integrated into the global economy. Canadian firms are aggressively pursuing international markets and have involved themselves in

Exhibit 1.6 **Globalization by Country**

Rank	Selected Countries	Overall Globalization Index
1	United States	6.48
2	**Canada**	**6.37**
3	Sweden	6.20
4	Denmark	5.75
5	Finland	5.73
6	Luxembourg	5.71
21	Japan	4.64
30	USSR	3.74
52	China	3.04
56	Mexico	2.91
122	Haiti	0.94
123	Rwanda	0.92

Source: Table 2: Ratings of Globalization. On p. 21 in Dreher (2006) Does Globalization Affect Growth? Evidence from a New Index of Globalization, *Applied Economics* 38, 1091–1110, Taylor & Francis. Reprinted by permission of the publisher (Taylor & Francis Ltd., **http://www.informaworld.com**) and the author.

The Global MARKETPLACE 1.2

Caron's Farm

With a 40,000-tap sugar bush, Jean-Pierre and Lise Caron have one of Canada's largest maple farms. They've been syrup producers for 20 years, but today, they're on the verge of bankruptcy. They're also on the Quebec Federation of Maple Syrup Producers most wanted list, accused of violating the federation's strict quota system by selling behind its back—on the black market. The Carons are now appealing a fine worth more than their entire farm, located in Squatec, Que., a heavily forested area between the St. Lawrence Seaway and northern New Brunswick. "We're not happy at all, we don't have the right to speak up," says Lise Caron. "Producers in all the other provinces can export, but in Quebec we have a quota. I have a problem with that."

It's not the first time the federation has been to court. The marketing board, which represents all of Quebec's 7,300 maple syrup producers and manages their bulk sales, has in recent years charged at least 200 others for similar violations. Many have appealed, unsuccessfully. But the Carons' $735,000 fine is the biggest ever, and their case, the first of its type to go as far as the Quebec Superior Court, could set a precedent for the province's $178-million industry—which makes up 93 percent of Canadian maple syrup production and 80 percent of production worldwide. "One thing I'm sure of is that many other producers are waiting for the outcome of this case," says the Carons' lawyer, Nancy Lajoie.

Though maple syrup accounts for just 2 percent of Quebec agriculture, 50 percent of all complaints received by the Régie des marchés agricoles et alimentaires du Quebec, the tribunal overseeing collective marketing in the province, are about the maple syrup federation's regulations. According to some in the industry, it's these rules that are forcing producers like the Carons to choose between the black market and bankruptcy. And their case may affect more than maple syrup. Lajoie is also contesting the impartiality of the Régie, which had previously ruled in favour of the Carons' fine. If they win, it could mean changes for how the Régie operates. And since the Régie's affairs affect most Quebec farmers—83 percent of the province's agricultural production uses collective marketing—the $6-billion agriculture business in the province may never be the same again.

Source: Andrea Jezovit, "A Sticky Situation: Quebec's Maple Syrup Situation," *Canadian Business*, January 29, 2007, http://www.canadianbusiness.com/managing/strategy/article.jsp?content=20070129_84941_84941 (accessed March 13, 2007).

several cross-border deals. Canadian fund manager Caisse de depot et placement du Quebec is pursuing acquisitions in China's banking sector, and Waterloo's Research In Motion is a dominant global player in the personal digital assistant market. Scotiabank, as noted earlier, has invested in a local Chinese bank, and Tim Hortons is aggressively attempting to build a presence in the U.S. market. Despite these laudable efforts, however, one must recognize that some Canadian firms still face restrictions in terms of their participation in global markets. The case of Caron's farm, a Quebec-based maple syrup producer, illustrates this point (see The Global Marketplace 1.2).

The Anti-Globalization Movement

The globalization trend has drawn its fair share of critics over the years. Anti-globalists have expressed concerns about the impact of the trend on the poor, on the environment, and on national sovereignty. At the World Trade Organization (WTO) meeting in Seattle in December 1999, protestors vented their anger, which spilled out into the street in a spate of looting and rioting. The objective of the 50,000-strong protest, including thousands of Canadians who made the trip from British Columbia,[27] was clearly to disrupt the meeting and signal their opposition to trade liberalization and the free flow of capital. The World Economic Forum in Davos, Switzerland, in February 2000 also served as a flash point for anti-globalization protests. On this occasion, a McDonald's restaurant, an ever-present symbol of globalization to many, was trashed by angry protestors. This was followed, in September of the same year, by yet another protest at the joint IMF-World

Exhibit 1.7 **Anti-Globalization Protests in Lausanne, Switzerland, during the 2003 G8 Meeting**

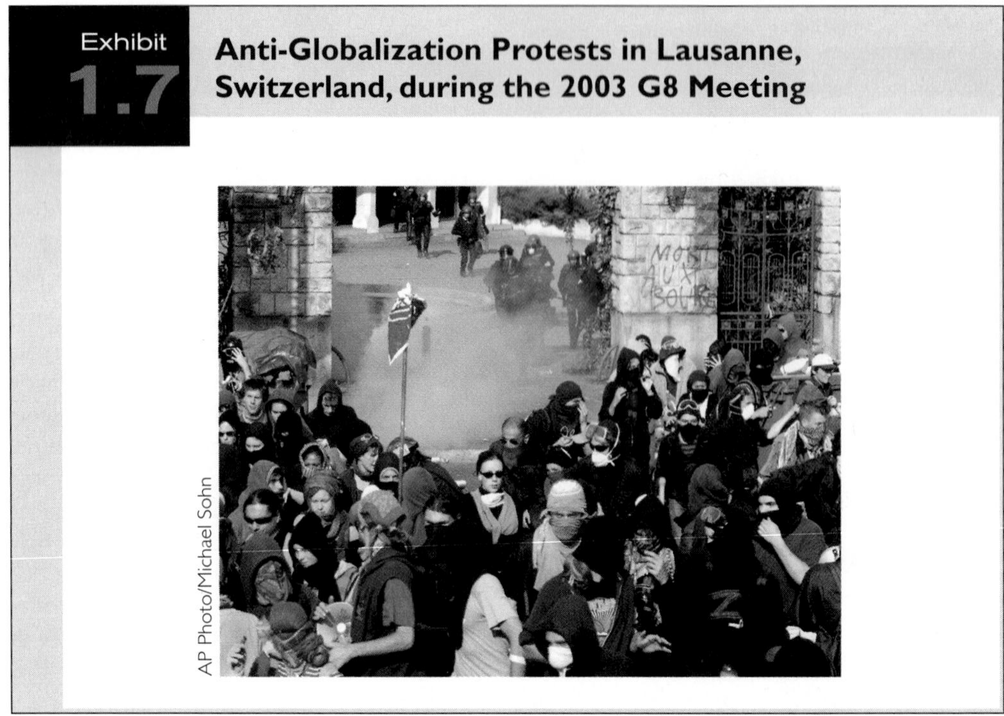

AP Photo/Michael Sohn

Bank meeting in Prague, Czech Republic. This protest also turned violent, but the low point was to occur a year later in Genoa, Italy, when a protestor was shot and killed by police at the G8 meeting.

Canada has also been the scene of several anti-globalization protests since the watershed event in Seattle in 1999. In November 2000 protestors gathered in Montreal, Quebec, to register their objections at the G20 meeting taking place in that city. The following year the protests moved to Quebec City, Quebec, for the Summit of the Americas meeting, and a year later protests took place in Calgary, Alberta, and Ottawa, Ontario, at the G8 meetings. In July 2003 protestors once again convened in Montreal, Quebec, for the mini-ministerial meeting of the WTO. Hundreds were arrested during this protest, which also saw the trashing of Burger King and GAP stores. Vandalism, mass arrests, and police use of tear gas and pepper spray have become regular occurrences at anti-globalization protests in Canada.[28]

There is little doubt that the violence and protests that have come to be associated with the anti-globalization movement make headlines around the world. There are some who argue, however, that those who engage in and promote violence at international meetings do not represent the anti-globalization movement. It is important to recognize that the anti-globalization movement is not monolithic. The movement encompasses groups that follow diverse agendas and espouse differing tactics. Some members advocate anarchy and are fundamentally opposed to any form of authority, arguing that it is undesirable and should be eliminated. Other members of the movement are nationalists and speak of the preeminence of the nation, while others may be socialists or eco-socialists.[29] The concerns of these groups are also heterogeneous, ranging from concern for the poor in developing countries, to the environment, to the proliferation of sweatshops, to feminism, to migration. While some groups raise valid and important issues, it is clear that the tactics of others are meant to enflame passions and detract from reasoned debate.

Opportunities and Challenges in Global Marketing

To prosper in a world of abrupt changes and discontinuities, of newly emerging forces and dangers, of unforeseen influences from abroad, firms need to prepare themselves and develop active responses. New strategies need to be envisioned, new plans need to be made, and the way of doing business needs to be changed. The way to obtain and retain leadership, economically, politically, or morally, is, as the examples of Rome, Constantinople, and London have amply demonstrated, not through passivity but rather through a continuous, alert adaptation to the changing world environment. To help a country remain a player in the world economy, governments, firms, and individuals need to respond aggressively with innovation, process improvements, and creativity.[30]

The growth of global business activities offers increased opportunities. International activities can be crucial to a firm's survival and growth. By transferring knowledge around the globe, an international firm can build and strengthen its competitive position. Firms that heavily depend on long production runs can expand their activities far beyond their domestic markets and benefit from reaching many more customers. Market saturation can be avoided by lengthening or rejuvenating product life cycles in other countries. Production sites once were inflexible, but now plants can be shifted from one country to another and suppliers can be found on every continent. Cooperative agreements can be formed that enable all parties to bring their major strengths to the table and emerge with better products, services, and ideas than they could produce on their own. In addition, research has found that multinational corporations face a lower risk of insolvency and pay higher wages than do domestic companies.[31] At the same time, global marketing enables consumers all over the world to find greater varieties of products at lower prices and to improve their lifestyles and comfort.

International opportunities require careful exploration. What is needed is an awareness of global developments, an understanding of their meaning, and a development of capabilities to adjust to change. Firms must adapt to the global marketplace if they are to be successful. One key facet of the marketing concept is adaptation to the environment, particularly the market. Even though many executives understand the need for such an adaptation in their domestic market, they often believe that international customers are just like the ones the firm deals with at home. It is here that many firms commit grave mistakes that lead to inefficiency, lack of consumer acceptance, and sometimes even corporate failure.

Firms increasingly understand that many of the key difficulties encountered in doing business globally are marketing problems. Judging by corporate needs, a background in global marketing is highly desirable for business students seeking employment, not only for today but also for long-term career plans.

Many firms do not participate in the global market. Often, managers believe that global marketing should only be carried out by large multinational corporations. It is true that there are some very large players from many countries active in the world market. But smaller firms are major players, too. For example, 85 percent of Canadian exporters were small businesses employing less than 100 employees. These small enterprises accounted for 20 percent of the total value of Canada's goods and services exports. Small business exporters reported average sales of $2.3 million in 2002. Medium-sized Canadian firms, that is, those with between 100 and 499 employees, accounted for 15 percent of total Canadian exports and had an average export sales volume of just under $12 million.[32] It should be noted that the situation is even more dramatic in a country such as Germany, where 50 percent of that nation's exports are created by firms with 19 or fewer employees.[33]

Those firms and industries that are not participating in the world market have to recognize that in today's trade environment, isolation has become impossible. Willing or unwilling, firms are becoming participants in global business affairs. Even if not by choice, most firms and individuals are affected directly or indirectly by economic and political developments that occur in the international marketplace. Those firms that refuse to participate are relegated to reacting to the global marketplace and therefore are unprepared for harsh competition from abroad.

Some industries have recognized the need for international adjustments. Farmers understand the need for high productivity in light of stiff international competition. Car producers, computer makers, and firms in other technologically advanced industries have learned to forge global relationships to stay in the race. Firms in the steel, textile, and leather sectors have shifted production, and perhaps even adjusted their core business, in response to overwhelming onslaughts from abroad. Other industries in some countries have been caught unawares and have been unable to adjust. The result is the extinction of firms or entire industries, such as VCRs in the United States and coal mining and steel smelting in other countries.

Goals of This Book

This book aims to make you a better, more successful participant in the global marketplace by providing information about what is going on in international markets and by helping you to translate knowledge into successful business transactions. By learning about both theory and practice, you can obtain a good conceptual understanding of the field of global marketing as well as become firmly grounded in the realities of the global marketplace. Therefore, this book approaches global marketing in the way the manager of a firm does, reflecting different levels of international involvement and a keen awareness of the uncontrollable elements of the business environment.

Firms differ widely in their international activities and needs, depending on their level of experience, resources, and capabilities. For the firm that is just beginning to enter the global market, the level of knowledge about international complexities is low, the demand on time is high, expectations about success are uncertain, and the international environment is often inflexible. Conversely, for a multinational firm that is globally oriented and employs thousands of people on each continent, much more leeway exists in terms of resource availability, experience, and information. In addition, the multinational firm has the option of responding creatively to the environment by shifting resources or even shaping the environment itself. For example, the heads of large corporations have access to government ministers to plead their case for a change in policy, an alternative that is rarely afforded to smaller firms. To become a large international corporation, however, a firm usually has to start out small. Similarly, to direct far-flung global operations, managers first have to learn the basics. This text therefore provides the perspectives of both the large and the small firm in the global marketplace.

The book discusses in detail the beginning internationalization of the firm. The emphasis is on the needs of those who are starting out and the operational questions that are crucial to success. Some basic yet essential issues are addressed: What is the difference between domestic and global marketing? Does the applicability of marketing principles change when they are transferred to the global environment? How do marketers find out whether there is a market for a product abroad without spending a fortune in time and money on research? How can the firm promote its products in foreign markets? How do marketers find and evaluate a foreign distributor, and how do they make sure that their firm gets paid? How can marketers minimize government red tape yet take advantage of any governmental programs that are of use to them? These questions are addressed both conceptually and empirically.

The text also provides details on alternative foreign market entry strategies open to both large and small firms and provides the basis for the selection of an approach that is optimal for the firm given its resources and international expertise. The need for a detailed analysis of the global marketing opportunity is stressed in the text and students are provided with the tools to understand and evaluate the macro environment within which the allocation of marketing resources takes place. The text also provides readers with an understanding of the elements of global marketing strategy and how such strategies are formulated and implemented.

We expect that this approach to global marketing will permit you not only to master another academic subject, but also to become well versed in both the operational and the strategic aspects of the field. The result should be a better understanding of how the global market works and the capability to participate in the global marketing imperative.

Key Terms

economies of scale (p. 7)
economies of scope (p. 11)
foreign direct investment (p. 6)
globalization (p. 5)
global marketing (p. 4)
glocal marketing (p. 8)
international marketing (p. 8)
marketspace (p. 9)
multi-domestic marketing (p. 5)
strategic alliances (p. 6)
triad (p. 10)

Questions for Discussion

1. Do you think that the globalization trend will eventually run out of steam?
2. How should firms balance the benefits of standardization with the importance of satisfying the needs of consumers in various country markets?
3. Is it beneficial for nations to become dependent on one another?
4. Can you think of examples of global marketing contributing to world peace?
5. Describe some opportunities and challenges in global marketing created by new advances in information technology.

Internet Exercises

1. Visit the website of the World Economic Forum at **http://www.weforum.org/en/index.htm.** What is the mandate of this organization? Why do you believe that this organization's meetings would attract anti-globalization protestors?
2. Visit the Scotiabank website at **http://www.scotiabank.com/cda/index/0,,LIDen_SID15,00.html** and identify the foreign markets in which this bank is active. Why do you believe that Scotiabank is active in so few markets in Europe and the Middle East?

Recommended Readings

Freidman, Thomas L. *The Lexus and the Olive Tree: Understanding Globalization*. New York: Farrar Straus Giroux, 1999.

Mishkin, Frederic S. *The Next Great Globalization*. Princeton, NJ: Princeton University Press, 2006.

Saul, John Ralston. *The Collapse of Globalism and the Reinvention of the World*. Toronto: Viking Canada, 2005.

Notes

1. A. Rugman and A. Verbeke, "A Perspective on Regional and Global Strategies of Multinational Enterprises," Journal of International Business 35 (2004): 3–18.
2. Robert W. Armstrong and Jill Sweeney, "Industrial Type, Culture, Mode of Entry, and Perceptions of International Marketing Ethics Problems: A Cross-Culture Comparison," Journal of Business Ethics 13, no. 10 (1994):775–85.
3. T. Levitt, "The Globalization of Markets," Harvard Business Review (May–June 1983): 92–102.
4. Y. Wind, "The Myth of Globalization," The Journal of Consumer Marketing 3, no. 2 (1986).
5. R. Tedlow and R. Abdelal, "Theodore Levitt's The Globalization of Markets—An Evaluation after Two Decades," chapter 2 in The Global Market: Developing a Strategy to Manage Across Borders, ed. John Quelch and Rohit Deshpande (San Francisco: Jossey-Bass, 2004).
6. G. Svensson, "Beyond Global Marketing and the Globalization of Marketing Activities," Management Decision 40, no. 5/6 (2002).
7. J. Johansson, "Global Marketing: Research on Foreign Entry, Local Marketing, Global Management," in Handbook of Marketing, ed. Barton A. Weitz and Robin Wenley (London: Sage Publications, 2003).
8. Eugene H. Fram and Riad Ajami, "Globalization of Markets and Shopping Stress: Cross-Country Comparisons," Business Horizons (January–February 1994): 17–23.
9. John J. Sviokla and Jeffrey F. Rayport, "Mapping the Marketspace: Information Technology and the New Marketing Environment," Harvard Business School Bulletin 71 (June 1995): 49–51.
10. C. Farrell and M. Han, "Integrating the Internet into International Marketing Strategy: A Conceptual Model," Proceedings International Business Division, ASAC, 2004.
11. Michael R. Czinkota and Sarah McCue, The STAT-USA Companion to International Business, (Washington, DC: U.S. Dept. of Commerce, 2001), 16.
12. This section draws from George S. Yip, Total Global Strategy II (Upper Saddle River, NJ: Prentice Hall, 2002), chapters 1 and 2; Jagdish N. Sheth and Atul Parvatiyar, "The Antecedents and Consequences of Integrated Global Marketing," International Marketing Review 18, no. 1 (2001): 16–29; George S. Yip, "Global Strategy ... In a World of Nations?" Sloan Management Review 31 (Fall 1989): 29–41; and Susan P. Douglas and C. Samuel Craig, "Evolution of Global Marketing Strategy: Scale, Scope, and Synergy," Columbia Journal of World Business 24 (Fall 1989): 47–58.
13. Ernst Dichter, "The World Customer," Harvard Business Review 40 (July–August 1962): 113–22.
14. Kenichi Ohmae, The Invisible Continent: Four Strategic Imperatives of the New Economy (New York: Harper Business, 2001), chapter 1; Kenichi Ohmae, The Borderless World: Power and Strategy in the Interlinked Economy (New York: Harper Business, 1999), chapter 1; and Kenichi Ohmae, Triad Power: The Coming Shape of Global Competition (New York: Free Press, 1985), 22–27.
15. Luciano Catoni, Nora Förisdal Larssen, James Nayor, and Andrea Zocchi, "Travel Tips for Retailers," The McKinsey Quarterly 38 (no. 3, 2002): 88–98.
16. Some observers may argue that this figure is conservative. Studies have suggested that development costs may well exceed US$800 million when all costs from initial investment to marketing are considered. Despite these significant costs, only 21.5 percent of drugs which enter Phase 1 human trials are actually brought to market (see R. Frank, "New Estimates of Drug Development Costs," Journal of Health Economics 22 (2003): 325–30).
17. Catherine George and J. Michael Pearson, "Riding the Pharma Roller Coaster," The McKinsey Quarterly 38, no. 4 (2002): 89–98.

18. Stuart Crainer, "And the New Economy Winner Is ... Europe," Strategy and Business 6 (2nd quarter 2001): 40–47.

19. Suzy Wetlaufer, "Driving Change: An Interview with Ford Motor Company's Jacques Nasser," Harvard Business Review 77 (March–April 1999): 76–88.

20. "Telecommunications," The Economist, April 4, 2002, 102.

21. "Microsoft's 'Zune' to take on iPod" Reuters, July 22, 2006, **http://edition.cnn.com/2006/BUSINESS/07/21/microsoft.ipod.reut/** (accessed July 24, 2006).

22. "Oligopoly profile: Nestlé." Oligopoly Watch, August 18, 2003, **http://www.oligopolywatch.com/2003/08/18.html** (accessed July 25, 2006).

23. Jordan D. Lewis, Trusted Partners: How Companies Build Mutual Trust and Win Together (New York: The Free Press, 2000), 157.

24. Cait Murphy, "The Hunt for Globalization That Works," Fortune, October 28, 2002, 67–72.

25. "3 Big Carmakers to Create Net Site for Buying Parts," The Washington Post, February 26, 2000, E1, E8.

26. A. Dreher, "Does Globalization Affect Growth: Evidence from a New Index of Globalization," Applied Economics 38, no. 10 (2006): 1091–1110.

27. CBC website **http://www.cbc.ca/news/story/1999/11/30/bc_talks991130.html** (accessed February 20, 2007).

28. Anti-Globalization's Disappearing Act. **http://www.dominionpaper.ca/environment/2003/08/08/antiglobal.html** (accessed February 20, 2007).

29. Wikipedia, "Anti-globalization" **http://en.wikipedia.org/wiki/Anti-globalization_movement** (accessed July 25, 2006).

30. Peter R. Dickson and Michael R. Czinkota, "How the U.S. Can Be Number One Again: Resurrecting the Industrial Policy Debate," The Columbia Journal of World Business 31, no. 3 (Fall 1996): 76–87.

31. Howard Lewis III and J. David Richardson, Why Global Commitment Really Matters (Washington, DC: Institute for International Economics, 2001).

32. Industry Canada website **http://strategis.ic.gc.ca/epic/site/sbrp-rppe.nsf/en/rd02042e.html** (accessed February 20, 2007).

33. Cognetics, Cambridge, MA, 1993.

Chapter 2

International Trade Policy and Trade Institutions

The Global MARKETPLACE 2.1

Trade as the Engine of Growth

Pascal Lamy, Director General of the World Trade Organization (WTO), noted that all drivers of economic growth must be activated if the international community is to respond to global challenges such as poverty, natural disasters, and political instability. International trade is an important engine of economic growth that can assist in generating the prosperity that is crucial to addressing such global challenges. International trade enhances the global allocation of resources and increases world output and factor productivity. Trade allows nations to specialize in the areas of economic activity they are best suited to, leading to welfare gains and overall development. Progress in stimulating international trade through negotiated reductions in transparent tariffs has been exceptionally good. With the notable exception of agricultural products, the record of trade policymakers in reducing global protectionism over successive rounds of multilateral negotiations has been outstanding. These reductions in global tariffs have resulted in significant increases in merchandise trade since the late 1940s. That said, tariffs on agricultural products continue to be stubbornly high and account for 61 percent of the welfare loss that arises from trade distortion. Also, a number of countries continue to utilize non-tariff barriers such as licensing requirements and health and safety regulations to protect their domestic industries and restrict international market access.

Tariff and non-tariff barriers are used by numerous countries to protect their agricultural sectors from the forces of international competition. Canada, through its system of supply management and the operations of the Canadian Wheat Board, has instituted measures that restrict international trade flows in agricultural products and protect local producers from foreign competition and international market fluctuations. The United States and the European Union also implement protectionist policies in this sector. Interestingly, it is not only developed countries that enact measures to limit market access. Increasingly we find developing countries utilizing protectionist measures to restrict imports from other developing nations. Continued work will be required to improve international market access for all countries and ensure that the gains from trade are equitably shared.

Sources: Lamy P. "Trade is Fundamental Tool in the Fight Against Poverty." Address to the Trade and Development Board of UNCTAD, October 6, 2005, http://www.wto.org/english/news_e/sppl_e/sppl05_e.htm; Lamy P. "The WTO Needs Your Scrutiny" Address to the Steering Committee of the Parliamentary Conference on the WTO. September 22–23, 2005, http://www.wto.org/english/news_e/sppl_e/sppl02_e.htm.

International trade is of central importance to governments, firms, and individuals. As indicated in The Global Marketplace 2.1, international trade allows countries to specialize in those areas of economic activity to which their resources and skills are best suited. This specialization allows for more efficient use of the country's resources and increased domestic production and productivity. International trade is also an indispensable source of tax revenue for government treasuries. These tax revenues may be used to support social programs such as education and health as well as infrastructure development. While it is private-sector firms that are primarily engaged in international trade, domestic governments and supranational organizations such as the World Trade Organization (WTO) are heavily involved in the formulation and implementation of the regulatory and policy framework that governs the actions of private-sector firms in international markets. For the global corporation, the international trade environment has a bearing on foreign market entry decisions and the implementation of global marketing strategy. This chapter examines the framework of international trade policies and regulations as well as the institutions charged with their development and implementation.

The chapter begins with a discussion of the theoretical foundation for international trade. Beginning with the early classical writers, the discussion traces the development of international trade theory and the foundations for modern arguments for trade liberalization. The discussion of international trade theory is followed by a comprehensive analysis of the major transnational institutions involved in the development and monitoring of the international trade policy environment. These institutions include the World Trade Organization (WTO), World Bank, International Monetary Fund (IMF), and the United Nations Conference on Trade and Development (UNCTAD). It is important to recognize that changes in the policies and institutions that govern international trade have a profound effect on the strategic decisions made by the global marketer. These changes can result in countries or entire regions becoming more (or less) attractive for the global marketer and can have a significant impact on the ease of market entry and the ability of the firm to operate effectively in the foreign jurisdiction. The chapter explores some of the arguments that are used by national governments to justify restrictions on trade and the forms such protectionist measures may take. Approaches used by governments to promote domestic exports are also examined, followed by a review of Canada's trade and investment performance and that of its major trading partners. Finally, the chapter concludes with some observations on the implementation of national trade and investment policies.

Theoretical Foundation for International Trade

Why do countries engage in international trade? Why doesn't Canada produce all of the goods and services consumed by its citizens? What factors determine the composition and pattern of a nation's trade? Why do some countries such as the United States operate with trade deficits while other countries such as China and Canada operate with significant trade surpluses? The fact that international trade occurs suggests immediately that countries must derive some benefits from the process of exchange. In this section we examine a number of theories that have been espoused to explain why countries engage in international trade and how they benefit. The theories proposed offer a firm-level as well as a country-level perspective in explaining what is to be gained by engaging in international trade.

Mercantilism

From 1500 to 1750 **mercantilism** was the dominant economic philosophy[1] that drove national approaches to international trade and wealth accumulation. Mercantilist doctrine held that a nation's wealth is measured by its stock of precious metals ("specie"). World resources were viewed as static and, therefore, in any international transaction one country's gain was another country's loss. Economic activity was viewed as a **zero-sum game**; in other words, for one party to win the other must lose. This approach led to a focus on the accumulation of precious metals and the maintenance of a strong army, navy, and merchant marine to enforce the state's power in a hostile environment. The focus on precious metals also led to the regulation of individual activity, as uncontrolled individual initiative was seen as inconsistent with the accumulation of precious metals by the state.

Mercantilists viewed the economic system as consisting of three components: a manufacturing sector, an agricultural sector, and the foreign colonies.[2] Government policies were designed to stimulate exports and curtail imports in order to produce a positive **balance of trade**. Balance of trade is the difference between a country's exports and imports. The colonies were seen as a source of cheap raw materials and agricultural products, as well as potential markets for manufactured goods. Exports were subsidized while imports were subject to high tariffs and quotas—two policy measures which restrict international trade. The only exception to these tariffs and quotas was raw materials that were to be imported for further processing. Raw materials were subject to low tariffs or were imported free of all duties. Mercantilist philosophy also extended to the implementation of domestic economic policy. Policies that kept wages low were pursued. At the time, labour was viewed as the most significant factor of production, and low labour costs translated into increased competitiveness in export markets. Population growth was also emphasized in order to contain wage pressures.

The Theory of Absolute Advantage

Adam Smith pointed out flaws in the mercantilist philosophy.[3] Smith, in his theory of **absolute advantage**, showed that international trade was not a zero-sum game as argued by proponents of mercantilism.[4] Smith showed that a country should specialize in the production of what it could produce more efficiently than its prospective trading partners, and trade with those countries for all other products it wished to consume. At the time, these classical writers held to the **labour theory of value**, which states that commodities should be valued in terms of the amount of labour embodied in their production. According to Smith, countries should specialize in those products requiring the fewest units of labour; in other words, they should produce products in which they have an absolute advantage. The country should export these products while importing all others. Each country should follow a similar approach, manufacturing and exporting those products for which they have an absolute advantage and importing all other products required for domestic consumption. By doing so, all parties to the international trade transaction would benefit. This notion that trade is not a zero-sum game is at the root of much of the current discussion of trade liberalization.

In More Detail 2.1

AN EXAMPLE OF ABSOLUTE ADVANTAGE

Consider, for example, that Canada and Indonesia produce two products: corn and textiles. We assume that the labour theory of value holds.

	Labour Requirement		Price Ratios
	Corn (hrs/bu)	*Textiles (hrs/m)*	in Autarky
Canada	5	10	1:2
Indonesia	6	3	1:0.5

In this hypothetical example, Canada requires 5 hours of labour to produce a bushel of corn but 10 hours of labour to produce a metre of cloth. Indonesia, on the other hand, requires 6 hours of labour to produce a bushel of corn but only 3 hours of labour to produce a metre of cloth. In this simple two-country, two-commodity framework, the price ratios in **autarky**, that is, in the absence of trade, are shown as 1:2 for Canada and 1:0.5 for Indonesia. Canada has an absolute advantage in the production of corn since less labour is required to produce corn (5 hours) compared to Indonesia (6 hours). Indonesia, on the other hand, has an absolute advantage in the production of textiles since less labour is required to produce a metre of cloth (3 hours) compared to Canada (10 hours). This difference in absolute advantage, according to Smith, constitutes the basis for trade. With trade, Canada would be able to acquire textiles from Indonesia for fewer hours of labour than would be required if the textiles were produced at home. Similarly, Indonesia would benefit from importing corn from Canada since this commodity could be acquired for fewer units of labour than would be required to produce it in Indonesia. Both countries would therefore benefit, proving that trade is in fact a positive-sum game.

In More Detail 2.2

AN EXAMPLE OF COMPARATIVE ADVANTAGE

In this purely hypothetical example, Canada has an absolute advantage in the production of both corn and textiles. Less labour is required to produce corn in Canada than in Indonesia, giving Canada an absolute advantage over Indonesia in that commodity. Similarly, less labour is required to produce textiles in Canada than in Indonesia, again giving Canada an absolute advantage in that product. According to Adam Smith, there would be no basis for trade in this situation. Canada would not benefit from trade with Indonesia in either product.

	Labour Requirement		Price Ratios
	Corn (hrs/bu)	Textiles (hrs/m)	in Autarky
Canada	1	3	1:3
Indonesia	8	4	1:0.5

Ricardo pointed out, however, that trade would still occur in the above situation where one country had an absolute advantage in both products. In this example, Canada is seen to be relatively more efficient in the production of corn than textiles since fewer units of labour are required for the production of the former. Indonesia, on the other hand, is seen to be relatively more efficient in the production of textiles than corn. According to Ricardo, Canada would benefit by specializing in the production of corn and importing textiles from Indonesia. Indonesia would benefit by specializing in the production of textiles and importing corn from Canada. Both countries would benefit from trade even though Canada has an absolute advantage in the production of both products.

The Theory of Comparative Advantage

David Ricardo, in his seminal text *The Principles of Political Economy and Taxation* (1817), argued that it was possible for a country to gain from international trade even when it did not possess an absolute advantage. Ricardo illustrated that a country would benefit from trade if it possessed a **comparative advantage**. Such a comparative advantage would exist provided there was a difference in the relative labour requirements for the production of a particular product. A country, such as Canada, should carefully evaluate those products it can produce most efficiently, that is, with the fewest resources, and concentrate on the production of those products. Ricardo's work builds on that of Adam Smith in showing that trade is not a zero-sum game but goes further by illustrating that trade gains do not depend on countries possessing an absolute advantage.

The Heckscher-Ohlin Model

Two Swedish economists, Eli Heckscher and Bertil Ohlin, built on the concept of comparative advantage by investigating the importance of a country's relative factor endowments on the gains from trade. The notion of relative factor endowments is easily understood. Countries such as India or China have a higher endowment of labour than countries such as Canada and the United States. The former countries are less well endowed with capital when compared to Canada and the U.S. The Heckscher-Ohlin model assumes that different products have different factor intensities, which means that they require relatively more capital or more labour to manufacture. The production of steel, for example, would require relatively more capital than the production of cloth. Also, some countries such as India and China possess relatively more labour than capital, while for other countries the opposite is true. Given these differences, handmade clothing (a labour-intensive product) is likely to be cheaper in a country such as India with its abundance of labour than in Canada where labour is relatively less abundant. These differences in country resource endowments and factor intensities, according to the Heckscher-Ohlin model, result in price differences that drive countries to trade with each other.

A major conclusion of the Heckscher-Ohlin model is that a country will export the products that use most intensely its most abundant factor of production. Such a country, on the other hand, will import those products which use most intensely its least abundant factor of production. Given Canada's abundance of natural resources, the Heckscher-

Ohlin model may well explain that country's dominance in certain export markets such as wheat, oil, and hydroelectric power. It should be noted, however, that empirical support for the Heckscher-Ohlin model has not been conclusive (see In More Detail 2.3).

The Product Cycle Theory

In 1966 Raymond Vernon proposed the product cycle theory.[5] The theory was developed to account for the failure of the Heckscher-Ohlin model to explain international trade patterns.[6] Vernon's theory assumes that an advanced country such as Canada would produce products which catered to high-income countries and which were relatively labour saving and capital using. According to Vernon's theory, the life cycle of a product is divided into three stages (see Exhibit 2.1). In the first stage the product is produced only in Canada. The product is new and innovative, and firms producing the product are assumed to want to market it in Canada where demand is strongest and consumer response can be adequately gauged. In the first stage of the cycle, global marketing does not take place.

In the second stage of the product cycle, Canadian firms begin to export the product to other advanced countries such as the U.S. and those in Western Europe. In this second or maturity product stage, Canadian firms adopt mass production techniques and begin to exploit economies of scale. As sales in other developed country markets increase, Canadian firms may wish to investigate the possibilities of production in other advanced, high-income countries. Assuming a favourable cost situation, the initial surge in Canadian exports of the product is tempered as foreign production, in the U.S. and Western Europe, expands, and world markets are supplied with product from these non-Canadian facilities. Vernon also raised the possibility that the product may begin to flow into the Canadian market (the country that originated the innovation) from U.S. and Western European plants.

The standardized product stage is the third and final stage of Vernon's product cycle theory. At this stage, manufacture of the product shifts to developing countries. The product is no longer considered new and innovative, manufacturing processes are now well known, and there is widespread consumer acceptance. Driven by low labour costs, production now takes place in developing countries such as Mexico, India, and China, with the advanced countries such as Canada, the U.S., and those in Western Europe becoming largely importers of the product. According to the product cycle theory, therefore, com-

In More Detail 2.3

THE LEONTIEF PARADOX

In 1953 Wassily Leontief provided an empirical test of the Heckscher-Ohlin model. Using a device known as an input-output table, and U.S. data from 1947, Leontief modelled a scenario whereby the United States simultaneously reduced its imports and exports by $1 million each. The input-output table allowed Leontief to determine the amount of capital and labour that would be released from producing exports, and the amount of capital (K) and labour (L) that would be required to produce those products that were no longer imported. The ratios of capital to labour $(K/L)_x$ for exports and capital to labour for imports $(K/L)_m$ may then be compared. The metric $(K/L)_m$ / $(K/L)_x$ is known as the **Leontief statistic**. Given that the United States is an advanced capital-rich country, one would expect, according to the Heckscher-Ohlin model, a value of less than one for the Leontief statistic. The value computed by Leontief for the United States was in fact 1.3, a totally surprising result. Over the years many analysts have attempted to explain the Leontief paradox. Some economists have argued that countries have a preference for products that are produced with the factor that is most abundant in that country. This is called **own intensity preference**. The United States, for example, would have a preference for products produced with capital, leading to a reversal of the demand patterns predicted by the Heckscher-Ohlin model. A higher preference for capital-intensive goods in the U.S. would bid up the price of those goods, making the U.S. more competitive in labour-intensive products. Conversely, countries with an abundance of labour would display a greater preference for labour-intensive products. The Leontief paradox raises interesting questions for the product strategy of global companies entering developing country markets.

Exhibit 2.1 **The International Product Life Cycle**

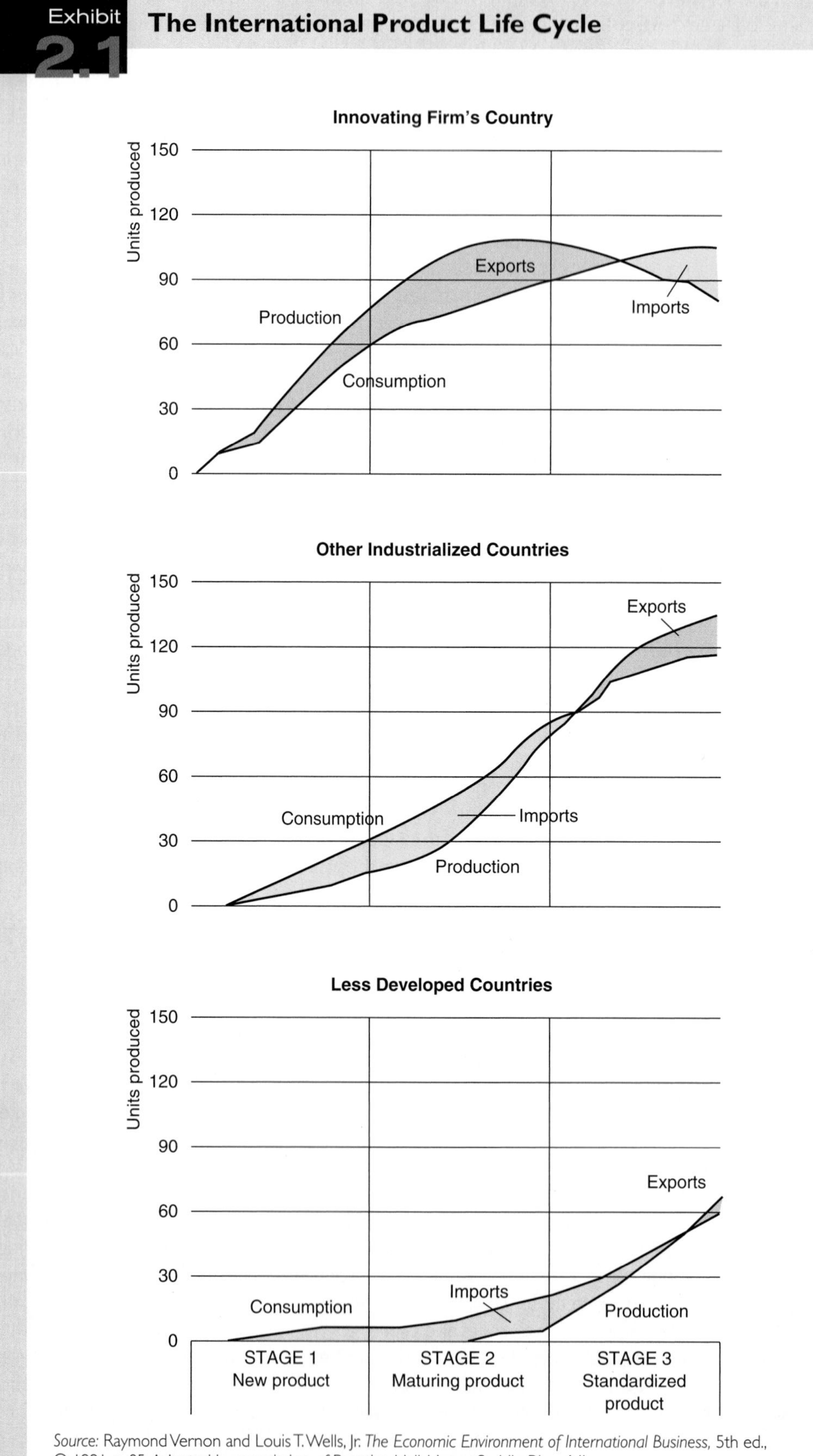

Source: Raymond Vernon and Louis T. Wells, Jr. *The Economic Environment of International Business,* 5th ed., © 1991, p. 85. Adapted by permission of Prentice Hall, Upper Saddle River, NJ.

parative advantage is not static but shifts over time as the product moves through the three stages. In the early stages, production is confined to developed countries with their capital-intensive manufacturing techniques and sophisticated consumers. In the final stage of the cycle, comparative advantage shifts to developing countries with an emphasis on labour-intensive production methods. Comparative advantage is dynamic and not static as assumed in earlier theories.

The Linder Theory

The theories discussed to this point have examined comparative advantage and the pattern of trade by emphasizing the supply side. A theory proposed by Staffan Linder in 1961 departed from this tradition by attempting to explain trade patterns by examining consumer demand.[7] Linder proposed that tastes and preferences of consumers would be a function of income levels. Countries with high per capita income levels would, therefore, be expected to exhibit a certain pattern of tastes and preferences—that is, toward higher quality, higher priced, and more sophisticated products. According to the Linder theory, countries should be expected to trade most intensely with countries with similar levels of per capita income and less intensely with countries with dissimilar levels of per capita income. The Linder theory has also been dubbed the **country similarity theory**. It should be noted that the Linder theory was developed to explain the pattern of trade in manufactured (not agricultural) products.

It should also be pointed out that empirical support for the Linder theory has been mixed. One would expect, based on the theory, that the greater the difference in per capita income levels between countries, the less intensely those countries would trade. Trade intensity and income should be negatively correlated. Several studies have in fact found such a negative relationship.[8] Some analysts, however, dismiss these results as spurious given that countries with similar income levels also tend to be geographically and culturally close.[9] The negative correlation observed in supporting studies may well reflect merely the impact of this geographic and cultural "distance."

Krugman's Model of International Trade

Paul Krugman has proposed a model based on product differentiation. This model and those proposed by a number of other related writers constitute what has been described as the **new trade theory**. Krugman's model incorporates **monopolistic competition**

In More Detail 2.4

AN EXAMPLE OF THE COUNTRY SIMILARITY THEORY

Country X, with a certain level of income, may exhibit a demand pattern that includes only products Q1, Q2, Q3, Q4, and Q5. Consumers are not interested in consuming any other products and as a result domestic firms would confine their activities to the production of these five products. We may view Q1 and Q2 as being relatively low-quality products, with Q3, Q4, and Q5 being of progressively higher quality (see Exhibit 2.2).

Country Y, with a higher per capita income than country X, will exhibit a different demand pattern. Consumers in Y, because of their higher income and more sophisticated tastes, may demand products Q3, Q4, Q5, Q6, and Q7. Again, product quality and sophistication increases from Q3 to Q7. Firms in Y do not produce Q1 and Q2 because there is no demand in that country for such low-quality products. Similarly, Q6 and Q7 are higher quality products not purchased by lower income consumers in country X. Linder hypothesized that international trade between X and Y would involve only products with overlapping demands, i.e., Q3, Q4, and Q5. A third country, Z, with even higher per capita income than Y, may exhibit a demand pattern restricted to products Q5, Q6, Q7, Q8, and Q9. Product quality and sophistication again increase from Q5 to Q9. This third country would trade products Q5, Q6, and Q7 with Y but will only trade product Q5 with X.

Exhibit 2.2 **Country Similarity Theory**

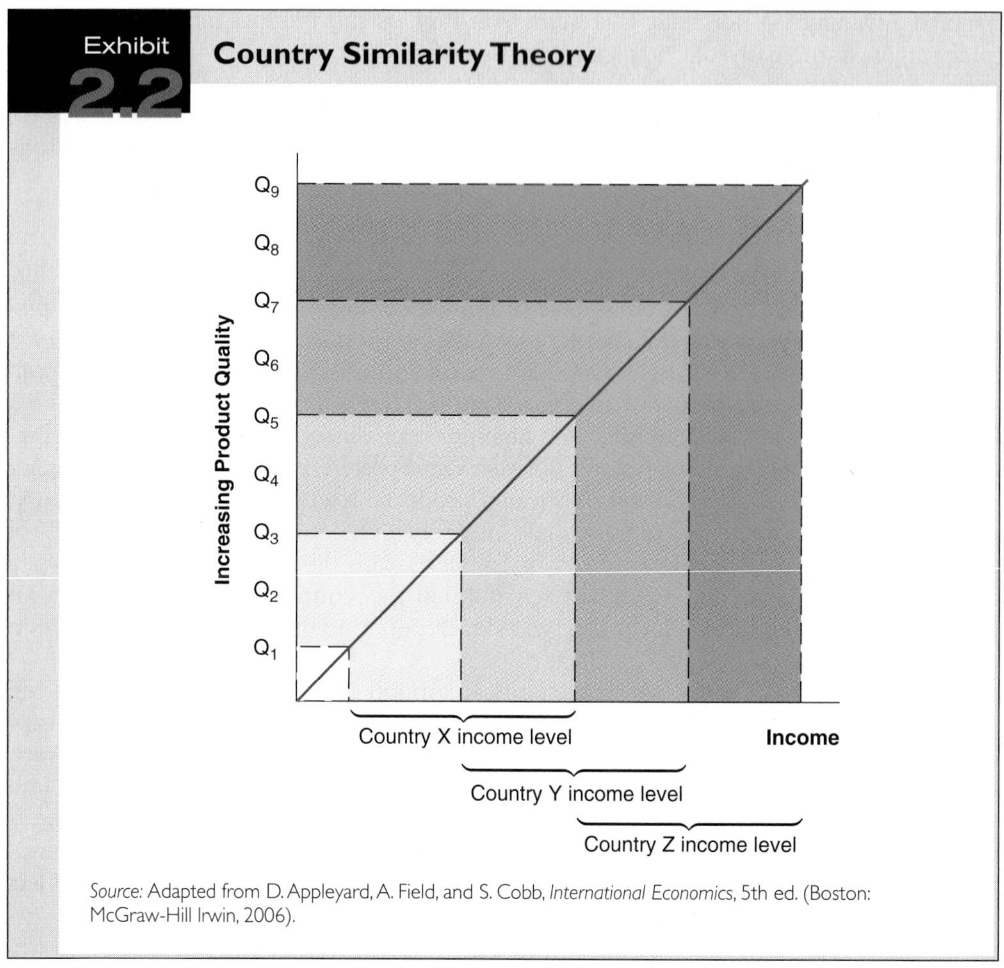

Source: Adapted from D. Appleyard, A. Field, and S. Cobb, *International Economics*, 5th ed. (Boston: McGraw-Hill Irwin, 2006).

and economies of scale, two characteristics not included consistently in earlier theoretical frameworks. Under monopolistic competition, firms produce differentiated products, and consumer brand loyalty is, therefore, possible. As two countries enter an international trading relationship, the size of the overall market expands, allowing firms in each country to increase production and exploit economies of scale. Production costs for all products are reduced, and consumers in both countries now have access to a wider range of products. According to Krugman's model, international trade has the effect of increasing incomes, expanding overall output, and increasing the range of products available to consumers.

The Diamond of National Advantage

Proposed by Michael Porter of Harvard University, the diamond of national advantage builds on the concept of comparative advantage by postulating that a country's competitive advantage in international markets is driven by four factors (see Exhibit 2.3). These factors are as follows:

1. Factor conditions, i.e., the country's endowment of factors of production, such as a skilled labour force, energy, and other natural resources
2. Demand conditions, or the existence of a domestic base of knowledgeable and sophisticated consumers who can drive product innovation and quality standards
3. Supporting industries, i.e., a cadre of firms providing professional services germane to the company's domain of expertise

Exhibit 2.3 **The Diamond of National Advantage**

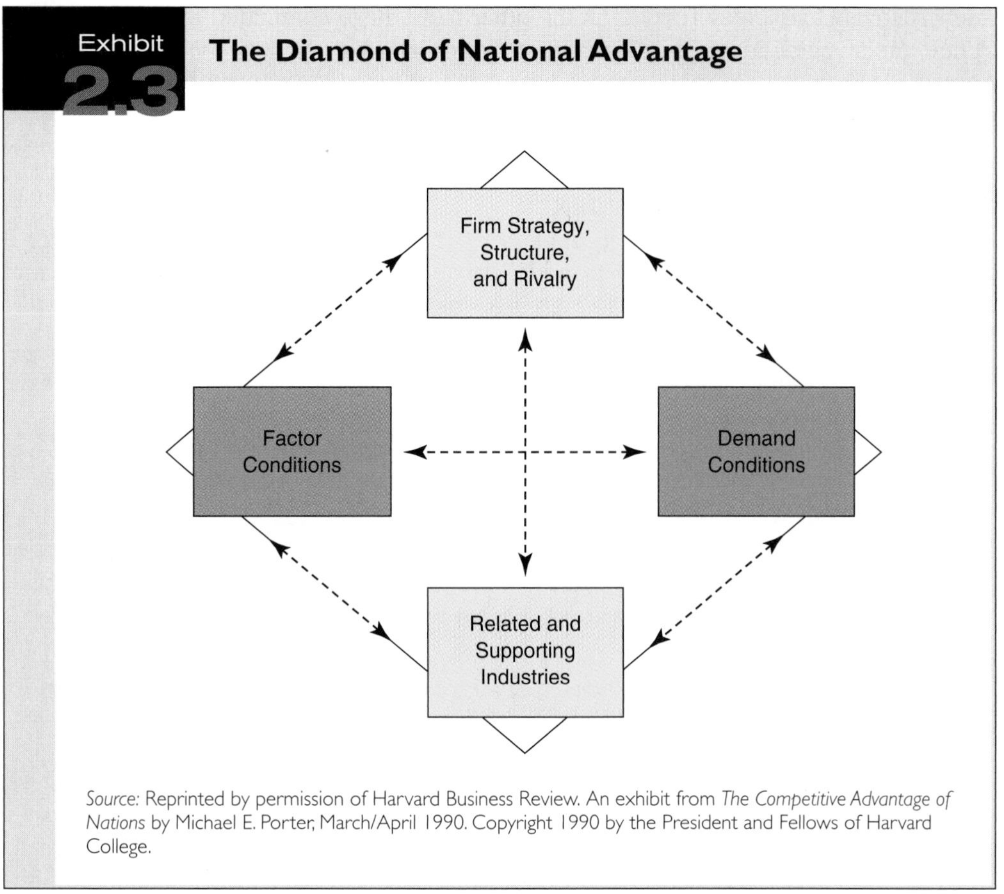

Source: Reprinted by permission of Harvard Business Review. An exhibit from *The Competitive Advantage of Nations* by Michael E. Porter, March/April 1990. Copyright 1990 by the President and Fellows of Harvard College.

4. Firm strategy, structure, and rivalry, which drive productive efficiency and competitiveness among domestic companies, making them stronger participants in international markets

Porter's notion of national competitive advantage is a dynamic one, and countries can change their competitive position over time by focusing on the four factors and their interrelationships. Moreover, countries can maintain their competitive advantage in specific industries over long periods of time irrespective of the impact of labour costs. In the product cycle theory discussed above, more attractive labour costs in developing countries eventually resulted in a movement of manufacturing operations abroad. In contrast, Porter's model suggests that astute business strategy, the benefit of supporting industries, and the demands of domestic consumers may well negate the impact of lower wage rates. Porter's model has been used to explain the tendency for "clustering" in high-technology industries, that is, the tendency for firms in that sector to locate in the same geographic areas such as Waterloo, Ontario, or Silicon Valley in California.

Models of International Investment

Global marketing activities may in some cases require the firm to undertake strategic investments in one or more foreign countries. Decisions must be made as to where to locate manufacturing operations in order to best serve target markets and the optimal number of facilities around the world that will allow the firm to achieve that objective. In many instances these decisions result in net gains for some countries and net losses for others. For example, Hershey, the global candy marketer, operated a manufacturing plant in Smith Falls, Ontario, since 1962. This plant has now been closed and the operation relocated to more cost-effective facilities in Mexico.[10] Some 600 people in Ontario have lost their jobs as a result of Hershey's investment decisions. Major Japanese auto manufacturers such as Honda and Toyota, on the other hand, have committed millions of dollars in new capital spending to this Canadian province as a way of better serving their North American customers.[11] Several theories have been proposed to explain how these investment decisions are made.

Dunning's OLI Framework

Dunning has proposed a model to explain the foreign investment decisions of global firms. His so-called eclectic, or OLI, model draws on several strands of economics and argues that three factors drive the foreign investment decisions of the firm:

1. *Ownership advantages*. The ownership of foreign production facilities conveys an advantage on firms over competitors that do not own such facilities. These competitors may attempt to serve global markets via other approaches in which they do not have access to resources, such as cheap foreign labour, or are unable to exercise control over key resources. Without ownership of the foreign assets, these approaches may, however, put them at a competitive disadvantage in international markets.
2. *Location advantages*. Location decisions may provide the firm with several important advantages such as the ability to shift production, sales, and profits to low-tax jurisdictions; take advantage of government manufacturing incentives; or benefit from a stable industrial relations climate.
3. *Internalization advantages*. Here Dunning has argued that for a firm to undertake foreign investment it must be more profitable for the firm to operate the overseas business itself when compared to its other options. The firm's other options may include licensing its technology or business model to another firm in the foreign market or entering into a management contract with some other entity to operate on its behalf in the foreign market. Licensing arrangements would involve allowing another firm to use its intellectual property for a fee. Engaging in foreign production on its own allows the firm to internalize its management skills, technology, and capital assets.

Transactions Cost Analysis

This model attempts to explain the foreign investment behaviour of the firm by examining the individual transactions in which it is engaged. Firms are engaged in numerous types of transactions associated with functions such as purchasing of raw materials and the marketing of its final products. Transaction costs are generally classified as being search costs (e.g., costs associated with finding suitable input suppliers, agents, and distributors), contracting costs (that is, the cost associated with negotiating and drawing up contracts between the firm and its suppliers and market intermediaries), monitoring costs (that is, the cost of monitoring contractual agreements), and enforcement costs (that is, the cost of enforcing contractual agreements). There is a transaction cost associated with each function from manufacturing to marketing that the firm undertakes. Transaction costs will vary depending on whether the firm chooses to internalize or externalize the various functions it performs, that depending on whether the firm opts to use its own internal resources to perform the function or decides to outsource it to a third party. Transaction costs will also vary depending on the foreign market in question. Transaction costs are likely to be much higher for a Canadian firm doing business in the Middle East than they would be for the same Canadian firm doing business in the U.S., given language and other cultural similarities and common approaches to doing business.

Transactions cost analysis attempts to explain the foreign investment behaviour of the firm. Firms seek to minimize transaction costs in their efforts to expand and market globally. Firms will only opt to undertake direct foreign investment and control foreign production assets if they minimize transaction costs in doing so. If outsourcing production and making use of external market intermediaries result in lower transaction costs for the firm, then it is unlikely that the firm will engage in foreign production. Companies such as Honda and Toyota have made the decision that investment in Ontario results in lower transaction costs in this particular market. Hershey, on the other hand, has determined that its transaction costs will be minimized by exporting to Ontario from its new plant location in Mexico.

Transnational Institutions Affecting World Trade

The World Trade Organization

The World Trade Organization (WTO) has its origins in the General Agreement on Tariffs and Trade (GATT), to which it became the successor organization in January of 1995. In order to better understand the emergence of the WTO, a brief review of the GATT is appropriate. The GATT has been called "a remarkable success story of a postwar international organization that was never intended to become one."[12] The GATT grew out of a failed attempt to create an international trade organization at the 1947 United Nations conference on trade and employment in Havana, Cuba. This attempt, while not successful, resulted in the establishment of a forum for multilateral trade negotiations that would endure for several decades. The GATT sets out rules for non-discrimination, transparent procedures, and settlement of disputes in international trade.

Over time, the GATT evolved into an institution that sponsored successive rounds of international trade negotiations with a key focus on the reduction of prevailing high tariffs (see Exhibit 2.5). The Uruguay Round was the final round of the GATT and saw the participation of some 123 countries over a period of 8 years. This contrasts with the 23 original participants at the 1947 Havana meeting.

Early in its existence, the GATT achieved the liberalization of trade in 50,000 products, amounting to two-thirds of the value of the trade among its participants. In subsequent years, special GATT negotiations such as the Kennedy Round and the Tokyo Round further reduced trade barriers and developed improved dispute-settlement mechanisms,

Exhibit 2.4 **Church House, London 1946**

The inaugural session of the Preparatory Committee charged with creating an international trade organization.

UN/DPI Photo by Marcel Bolomey

Exhibit 2.5 The Evolution of Multilateral Trade Negotiations

Round and Location	No. of Participants	Year	Comments
1 (Havana Cuba)	23	1947	Establishment of GATT and tariff reductions.
2 (Annecy, France)	38	1949	Further tariff reductions.
3 (Torquay, U.K.)	38	1950	Further tariff reductions.
4	–	–	This round of negotiations was skipped.
5 Dillon Round (Geneva, Switzerland)		1960	Rounds of negotiations now given a name.
6 Kennedy Round, (Geneva, Switzerland)	60	1964-67	Expansion of tariff reductions and new trade rules established on antidumping measures.
7 Tokyo Round (Tokyo, Japan)	102	1973-79	Significant tariff reductions and a series of agreements on non-tariff barriers. These were signed only by some participants and are known as the Tokyo codes. No agreement on agriculture reform or safeguard measures.
8 (Uruguay Round)	123	1986-94	Last round of GATT. WTO created.

Source: WTO, The Multilateral Trading System: 50 Years of Achievement, **http://www.wto.org/english/thewto_e/minist_e/min98_e/slide_e/slideshow_index.htm.**

better provisions dealing with subsidies, and a more explicit definition of rules for import controls. In spite of, or perhaps because of, these impressive gains, the GATT became less effective over time. Duties had already been drastically reduced, and further reductions were unlikely to have a major impact on world trade. Most imports now either enter Canada and other member countries duty free or are subject to low tariffs.

Tariffs are no longer the impediment to trade that they once were. Many nations have, however, developed new tools for managing and distorting trade flows. These are called **non-tariff barriers**, and they were not covered under the GATT rules. Examples of non-tariff barriers are "voluntary agreements" to restrain trade and bilateral or multilateral special trade agreements, such as the Multifibre Arrangement, which restricts trade in textiles and apparel (see In More Detail 2.5).

After many years of often contentious negotiations, the Uruguay Round accord was finally ratified in January of 1995. As part of this ratification a new institution, the World

In More Detail 2.5

TRADE IN TEXTILES AND CLOTHING

The Multifibre Arrangement (MFA) regulated trade in textiles and clothing from 1974 to 1994. The MFA was essentially a framework of bilateral agreements or unilateral actions which established quotas for the import of textiles and clothing. These quotas, imposed by countries that believed their domestic industry would be harmed by import surges, were clearly inconsistent with GATT principles of fair treatment for all member countries. The MFA was replaced by the Agreement on Textiles and Clothing (ATC) in 1995, at the conclusion of the Uruguay round of negotiations. The ATC set out a transition program for the integration of textiles and clothing products into GATT rules, and the phased enlargement of import quotas by increasing growth rates at each stage until import restrictions were eliminated. The ATC also provided for new safeguard provisions to protect the domestic industries of importing countries during the transition phase. The ATC expired on January 1, 2005.

Source: WTO, "Textiles: Back in the Mainstream," http://www.wto.org/english/thewto_e_whatis_e/tif_e/agrm5_e.htm.

Trade Organization, was created. The WTO is now the umbrella organization responsible for overseeing the implementation of all the multilateral agreements negotiated in the Uruguay Round and those that will be negotiated in the future. The GATT has ceased to exist as a separate institution and has become part of WTO, which is also responsible for the General Agreement on Trade in Services (GATS), agreements on trade-related aspects of intellectual property rights (TRIPS), and trade-related investment measures (TRIMS). The WTO now consists of 149 members, including China, which was officially admitted in 2001, and Saudi Arabia, which joined in 2005.

The WTO makes major contributions to improved trade and investment flows around the world. Because of the nature of the organization, a successful WTO may well infringe on the sovereignty of nations. For example, more streamlined dispute settlements mean that decisions are made more quickly and nations in violation of international trade rules are confronted more often. Negative WTO decisions affecting large trading nations are likely to be received with resentment. Some governments intend to broaden the mandate of the WTO to also deal with social causes and issues such as labour laws, competition, and emigration freedoms. Since many nations fear that social causes can be used to devise new rules of protectionism against their exports, the addition of such issues may become a key reason for divisiveness and dissent within the WTO.[13] Outside groups such as non-governmental organizations and special interest alliances believe that international trade and the WTO represent a threat to their causes.

In 2001, a new round of international trade negotiations was initiated. Because the agreement to do so was reached in the city of Doha (Qatar), the negotiations are now called the Doha Round. The aim of the Doha Round was to further hasten implementation of liberalization, specifically to help impoverished and developing nations. In addition, the goal was to expand the role of the WTO to encompass more of the trade activities where there were insufficient rules for their definition and structure. This was due to either purposeful exclusion of governments in earlier negotiations or due to new technology changing the global marketplace. Examples include trade in agricultural goods, anti-dumping regulations, and electronic commerce.

The Doha Round has been dubbed the "developing country round" and clearly focuses on agriculture—a sector of critical importance to less-developed countries. The round is ambitious given that the agriculture sector has not benefited from the 50 years of negotiated tariff reductions that have clearly improved trade in industrial products. These negotiations centre on export subsidies, domestic subsidies, and tariffs. The round has targeted 2013 for the elimination of export subsidies on agricultural products and is expecting major reductions in domestic agricultural support from the European Union, the U.S., and Japan. The Doha Round has also emphasized safeguard measures for developing countries to protect their markets from import surges and declining commodity prices.

Exhibit 2.6 **Softwood Lumber for Export**

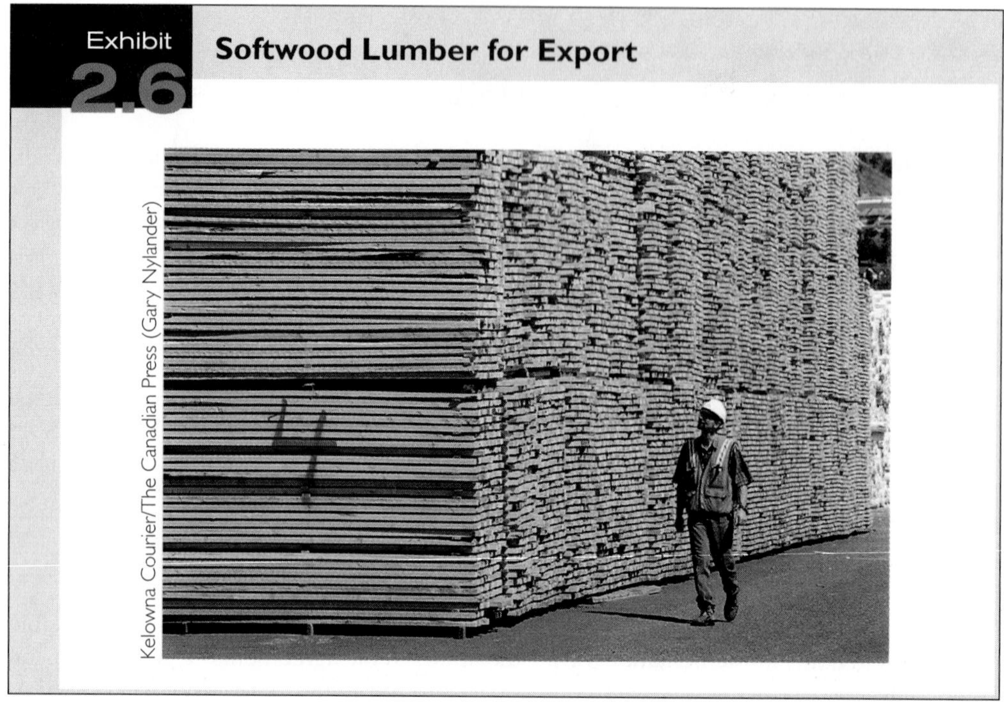

Kelowna Courier/The Canadian Press (Gary Nylander)

The International Monetary Fund

The International Monetary Fund (IMF) was conceived in 1944 at an international conference held at Bretton Woods in New Hampshire.[14] The goal of the conference was to chart a course for the development of an economic framework that would allow the 44 participant countries to avoid a repeat of the failed economic policies that precipitated the Great Depression. These policy measures, which included competitive devaluations, restrictions on imports, and restrictions on the sale of foreign exchange, did not have the desired impact of protecting countries from a slowdown in economic activity in the major developed nations. Instead, these measures resulted in an accelerated reduction in global output and increased levels of unemployment.

Today, the IMF plays a critical role in ensuring the stability and smooth operation of the global monetary system, that is, the system of international payments and exchange rates that allows countries to engage in international trade. To accomplish this role, the IMF provides member countries with policy advice and technical assistance to guard against severe macroeconomic imbalances such as ballooning current account and trade deficits in the U.S., currency crises in Asian markets, and deflation in Japan. The IMF also provides temporary financing to deal with short-term balance-of-payments problems in member countries (see In More Detail 2.6).

The IMF is funded by member subscriptions. Upon joining the IMF, countries are required to pay 25 percent of their quota in **special drawing rights** (SDRs) or hard currencies such as Japanese yen or U.S. dollars. SDRs are an international reserve asset introduced by the IMF in 1969. The remaining 75 percent of the country's quota may be paid in the member country's own currency as required by the fund to support its short-term interventions around the globe. These funds provide countries with protection against temporary fluctuations in the value of their currency.

The World Bank

The World Bank, the official name of which is the International Bank for Reconstruction and Development, has had success similar to the IMF.[15] It was initially formed in 1944 to aid countries suffering from the destruction of war. After successfully completing this

The Global MARKETPLACE 2.2

The WTO and the Softwood Lumber Dispute

The WTO provides both the policy framework within which global trade takes place and a mechanism through which disputes between members may be settled. While the WTO provides a consistent framework for dispute resolution, problems may still arise due to the existence of bilateral and regional trade agreements between countries. This situation is evidenced by the softwood lumber dispute between Canada and the United States. This dispute has been ongoing for many years and has seen rulings by the WTO pitted against rulings from the North American Free Trade Agreement (NAFTA)—a regional agreement between Canada, Mexico, and the United States.

Softwood lumber is one of Canada's most significant exports to the United States. Roughly 22 billion board feet of lumber were shipped to the U.S. in 2005. U.S. producers are unable to meet domestic demand; as a result, the housing industry has turned to Canada, which now supplies one-third of the lumber used in the United States. The Coalition for Fair Lumber Imports (CFLI) has, for over 20 years, sought protection for U.S. lumber producers from Canadian imports. The CFLI has launched a series of legal challenges over the years claiming that certain provinces subsidize lumber exports and that these exports threaten to cause the U.S. lumber industry material injury.

In May 2001 the U.S. International Trade Commission (USITC), in a unanimous ruling, agreed that Canadian softwood lumber exports had not materially injured the U.S. industry but that there was a threat of material injury. Canadian softwood lumber exports were deemed by the commission to be subsidized and dumped on the U.S. market. The USITC decision followed an investigation by the U.S. Department of Commerce (USDOC) into whether federal and provincial government forest management policies constituted a subsidy for Canadian exporters and whether Canadian firms were dumping lumber on the U.S. market. The USDOC found that Canadian exports were subsidized and that Canadian exporters did sell their products in the U.S. below fair-market value. As a result, the U.S. imposed countervailing duties.

In August 2001, Canada requested WTO consultation on the subsidy issue and, in February 2002, requested a NAFTA panel review of the U.S. dumping allegations. The U.S. imposed anti-dumping and countervailing duties on Canadian lumber in May 2002 and has since collected some $5 billion from Canadian exporters. A series of challenges under both NAFTA and the WTO ensued. In August 2005 an Extraordinary Challenge Committee of NAFTA agreed with Canada that the USITC's original "threat of material injury" decision was flawed and did not provide a basis for anti-dumping and countervail actions by the U.S. The WTO, however, ruled that the U.S. had complied with its international obligations when duties were levied. Canada has argued that the NAFTA panel ruling should supersede the WTO decision, while U.S. negotiators have argued for the preeminence of the WTO's authority in the matter.

Sources: **http://www.dfait-maeci.gc.ca/trade/eicb/softwood/intro-en.asp**, Softwood Lumber, Export and Import Controls, Department of Foreign Affairs and International Trade. Reproduced with the permission of Her Majesty the Queen in Right of Canada, represented by the Minister of International Trade, 2008. For a more detailed chronology of the softwood lumber dispute, see: **http://www.dfait-maeci.gc.ca/eicb/softwood/chrono-en.asp**.

In More Detail 2.6

BALANCE OF PAYMENTS

The **balance of payments** is an accounting statement that summarizes economic transactions between one country and other countries with which it does business. In Canada, balance-of-payments statistics are published quarterly by Statistics Canada. The statement is divided into three accounts:

The Current Account Records imports and exports of goods and services, income, and official transfers. Data for 2004 indicate that Canada had receipts of $536 billion, payments of $507 billion, and a current account surplus of $29 billion.

The Capital Account Records transfers of goods and financial assets as people enter and leave Canada. In 2004 capital account net flows were $4.4 billion.

The Financial Account Records Canada's public and private investments and lending. In 2004 net flows to the financial account were –$26.9 billion.

Source: Data sources include Statistics Canada Table 376-0001 and 376-0002.

process, it took on the task of aiding world development. With more and more new nations emerging from the colonial fold of the world powers of the early 20th century, the World Bank has made major efforts to assist fledgling economies in their attempts to participate in a modern economic trade framework. More recently, it has begun to participate actively with the IMF to resolve the debt problems of the developing world and is also playing a major role in bringing a market economy to the former members of the Eastern bloc.

Despite these accomplishments, a major debate surrounds the effectiveness of the World Bank's expenditures. In the 1970s and 1980s, a substantial amount of money was invested in infrastructure projects in developing countries, based on the expectation that such investment would rapidly propel the economies of these nations forward. In retrospect, it appears that a large portion of these funds was squandered by corrupt regimes, and many large projects have turned into white elephants that produced little in terms of economic progress. In addition, some projects have had serious negative side effects for the recipient nations. For example, the highway through the rain forest in Brazil has resulted in the migration of people to the area and has upset the very fragile ecological balance. The World Bank is now trying to re-orient its outlook, focusing more on institution building and the development of human capital through investments in education and health.

The United Nations

A number of United Nations organizations also play a central role in shaping the international trade environment. The United Nations Conference on Trade and Development (UNCTAD)[16] is one such organization. UNCTAD had its origins in the early 1960s as developing countries became increasingly concerned about their role in international trade. UNCTAD works with the governments of developing countries to prepare them for international trade negotiations with the developed world. This role is particularly valuable within the context of multilateral trade negotiations where complex issues are discussed. UNCTAD works with developing countries in the collection and analysis of international trade data and the formulation of consistent negotiation positions in multilateral talks with developed countries. The first meeting was held in Geneva in 1964, and it was agreed that a permanent secretariat would be established, with meetings scheduled every four years. There are 192 member countries of UNCTAD, including Canada, Japan, Germany, and the United States.

The International Trade Center (ITC) is the international cooperation arm of UNCTAD and the WTO. Established in 1964, the ITC's mandate is to assist firms in developing countries and countries in transition with their integration into the multilateral trading system. Unlike the WTO and UNCTAD, which operate at a more macro level, the ITC works at the level of the individual firm to ensure that international trade rules are understood and that firms in developing countries and countries in transition are positioned to take advantage of the market-access opportunities that flow from multilateral trade negotiations.

International Trade Policy and Protectionism

Multilateral trade negotiations under GATT/WTO have been relatively successful in removing the most transparent barriers to international trade. That said, national governments continue to institute policy measures designed to protect sensitive industries or provide a competitive advantage to favoured industries. Canada's system of supply management is a case in point. The Canadian government, while committed to the principles of free trade and multilateralism, has steadfastly refused to make concessions on the protection of Canada's dairy and poultry industries. The European Union and the United States have also been resolute in their protection of the agriculture sector. Despite the plethora of theoretical and empirical studies documenting the gains from free trade, national governments have instituted policy measures designed to protect specific industries.

Arguments for Protection

Arguments designed to support such interventions have generally focused on a few key issues and have been adopted by both developed and developing countries.

The Infant Industry Argument

This position is credited to Alexander Hamilton, the first U.S. Secretary of the Treasury, and dates back to 1791. Hamilton noted that the manufacturing sectors of newly independent countries had the potential to become first-class international players if they could be accorded a period of protection from direct competition. If exposed to competition from manufacturers in more mature economies, it would be difficult for these fledgling industries to survive and prosper. This argument has been adopted by many countries around the world and in fact underpinned much of the import substitution policies pursued by Latin American countries in the 1950s and 1960s. Even today, countries such as Japan have been successful at instituting policy measures designed to shield key industries such as metal fabrication from foreign competition.

The Employment Argument

This position views the protection of domestic industry from the standpoint of maintaining employment levels in key sectors. It is not uncommon for industry associations or individual firms to petition domestic governments for protection from foreign competition. The Canadian wine industry provides an excellent example.[17] In the late 1980s just prior to the execution of the Canada–U.S. free trade agreement there was a considerable degree of concern that thousands of jobs would be lost in the Canadian wine industry as a result of free trade with the United States. Proponents of the Canadian wine industry lobbied federal and provincial government officials for "temporary" protection from U.S. competition. They argued that the industry needed time to adjust to the new competitive realities as cheaper and better quality California grapes would soon flood the Canadian market, forcing thousands of grape growers out of work. Canadian growers had historically been protected by provincial government taxes imposed on U.S. imports.

The National Security Argument

Since the terrorist attack on the World Trade Center on September 11, 2001, the national security argument has been effectively used to restrict international trade and investment. Interestingly, this argument has also been used in Canada and not only in the United States. China Minmetals, a corporation owned by the Chinese government, provides an example. In 2004 China Minmetals offered to purchase Noranda Inc., one of Canada's preeminent mining companies, for $7 billion. Objections to the deal came from several quarters and included arguments that the takeover posed a risk to Canada's national security.[18] The prospect that Canadian natural resources could be exported to China in the face of resource deficits at home did not resonate with Canadian lawmakers. The takeover bid eventually failed. The United States government faced a similar dilemma in the wake of a bid valued at US$18.5 billion from China National Offshore Oil Company (CNOOC) for Unocal, a major U.S. oil company. Significant concerns were raised by U.S. lawmakers who clearly favoured a competing bid from Chevron.[19] Many of these concerns revolved around the national security issue and the prospect of a former communist country controlling shipments of a strategic natural resource to the U.S. market.

Forms of Protectionism

Protectionism refers to measures adopted by national governments to unduly restrict trade and foreign investment. National governments use various policy measures to restrict trade and investment flows and protect domestic industries. These measures include tariffs, quotas, voluntary export restrictions, and quality standards.

Tariffs

A **tariff** is a tax imposed by a domestic government on an internationally traded product. A tariff may be imposed on a product that is being exported from a country (an **export tariff**) or a product that is being transshipped from one country to another (a **transit tariff**). Most tariffs are levied on imports and are called **import tariffs**. Tariffs generate revenues for the domestic government that levies them and may be assessed as a percentage of the market value of the imported product (an **ad valorem tariff**) or as a specific dollar amount on each unit of the product that enters, leaves, or is transshipped through the country (a **specific tariff**). In some instances, tariffs may have both ad valorem and specific components; these are referred to as **compound tariffs**.

Tariffs may be imposed to protect domestic industry. Should country A impose a tariff on steel imports from country B, the effect will be to raise the price of foreign steel in A and reduce the demand. This reduction in demand for foreign steel will provide an opportunity for steel manufacturers in A to sell more of their product in the domestic market. As noted previously, tariffs are at historically low levels as a result of successive rounds of multilateral trade negotiations.

Quotas

A **quota** is a quantitative restriction on the volume of a product that can be imported into a country over a specified time period. Quotas are a form of non-tariff barrier (NTB) used by countries to restrict free trade and protect domestic industries. The impact of a quota is that it restricts availability of the foreign product in the domestic market—a result that favours domestic producers. There are various forms of quotas used by national governments.

Absolute Quotas

Absolute quotas place a strict limit on the volume of imports coming into a country. In extreme circumstances, the allowable volume of imports may be set to zero and is referred to as an **embargo**. Embargos are rarely used by national governments. Under the Foreign Assistance Act of 1961, the United States has maintained an embargo against Cuba for over 40 years. With the exception of food and medicine, U.S. corporations are prohibited from engaging in international trade with the tiny Caribbean island.

Tariff Rate Quotas (TRQs)

As a result of negotiations under the Uruguay Round of GATT, most countries have agreed to replace quotas with their tariff equivalent. Such tariff rate quotas impose a low tariff level on an initial quantity of imported product. Once this volume of imports is reached, the tariff rate imposed on additional volumes escalates markedly. Canada's system of supply management, for example, restricts imports of sensitive dairy and poultry products by using tariff rate quotas in order to protect domestic producers from foreign competition.

Voluntary Export Restraints (VERs)

VERs are essentially promises by one country—say, China—to limit exports of a product to some pre-specified volume or pre-specified percentage of the overall size of the foreign market. China has, for example, agreed to limit exports of textiles to the European Union and the United States in order to not harm European and American clothing manufacturers. The Chinese government has agreed to impose export tariffs on its own manufacturers to stem the surge in textile exports to U.S. and European markets following termination of the Agreement on Textiles and Clothing on January 1, 2005. This voluntary restraint measure is designed to avert the re-imposition of quotas by the U.S. and European governments under WTO safeguard provisions.[20]

Exchange Controls

National governments may restrict imports and protect domestic industry by instituting exchange controls. Exchange controls limit the amount of foreign currency that importers can purchase, thereby impeding their ability to transact with foreign exporters. Most international transactions require the exporting firm be paid in a currency other than the importer's domestic currency. Export prices may, for example, be quoted in euros or U.S. dollars, necessitating that the importing firm pay for the goods received in one of these "hard" currencies. If the domestic importer is unable to convert local currency to a hard currency, it is unlikely that the import transaction would be consummated. It should be noted that exchange controls also affect the operation of multinational firms with overseas sales subsidiaries. These operations rely on the free convertibility of local currency to hard currency in order to remit profits to the parent firm on an ongoing basis.

National governments also have the option of controlling not only the amount of foreign currency that can be purchased but also the rate of exchange. Domestic firms engaged in exporting may, for example, be accorded a very favourable rate while importers face a much less favourable rate. Importing firms made to purchase foreign exchange from the central bank at unfavourable rates will be forced to raise the prices of the imported goods, leading to a reduction in the quantity demanded on the local market.

Exchange controls are often invoked in times of economic and political crisis. For example, controls were instituted in Venezuela in 2003 in the wake of civil unrest in that country that interrupted receipt of revenues from oil exports. Oil is Venezuela's main source of foreign exchange. All firms and institutions in Venezuela interested in purchasing foreign exchange must register with the Commission of Foreign Exchange Administration (otherwise known as CADIVI, or the Comisión de Administración de Divisas). Importers now face increasing difficulty in securing foreign exchange because CADIVI authorizes purchases based on the tariff code of the good imported. Luxury items and those produced by domestic firms the government wishes to protect are now excluded.[21]

Restricted Access to Local Distribution

National governments may also protect domestic industries by restricting access to normal channels of distribution for foreign firms. While market entry may not be impeded, if the foreign firm encounters problems in reaching the final consumer or can only do so at a high cost, domestic firms are effectively protected. In Thailand, a foreign financial institution operating as a subsidiary may only open four offices in the country, and only one of these offices may be in the capital city of Bangkok.[22] Similarly, Japan's *keiretsu* system makes it extremely difficult for foreign firms to operate in that country. The *keiretsu* system involves tightly knit corporate and cultural relationships between Japanese manufacturers, wholesalers, and retailers. Foreign companies often experience difficulty in penetrating markets controlled by *keiretsu* partners. Japanese banks are also at the centre of the *keiretsu* system, as are major corporations such as Mitsubishi, Mitsui, and Sumitomo.

Product Standards

National governments may impose product quality or testing standards on foreign goods entering a country. Canada requires bilingual labelling on food products entering the country, Taiwan mandates strict purity testing of imported fruit juices, and Malaysia requires testing of all imported meat and poultry to ensure that they have been prepared in accordance with Islamic practice. These standards have the effect of making it more difficult for imported products to enter the market. Governments argue that the standards imposed are required to protect the health and safety of its citizens, while exporters claim that they are protectionist measures designed to restrict sales of foreign products.

Lack of Intellectual Property Protection

Governments may also discourage imports and protect local industries by their failure to offer intellectual property (IP) protection to foreign firms. A lack of IP protection may be a serious disincentive for firms to engage in international trade in certain countries.

Investment Barriers

Government restrictions on ownership are not uncommon. In industries such as airlines, broadcasting, financial services, and defense contracting, governments may impose severe restrictions on foreign ownership. Arab-owned Dubai Ports World recently transferred its ownership of six U.S. ports to a U.S.-owned entity in the wake of security concerns expressed by the U.S. government.[23] Canada restricts foreign ownership of financial institutions, and Indonesia limits foreign ownership of broadcast media.

Government Export Promotion

As noted above, national governments seek to protect domestic industry from foreign competition by restricting imports and investment. In many instances domestic policies are also implemented by national governments to actively encourage exports. Government **export promotion** may be defined as public policy measures that actually or potentially enhance exporting activity at the company, industry, or national level.[24] Foreign market entry involves significant risks for the exporting firm. The essential objective of government export promotion programs is to reduce the risks inherent in participation in international markets.[25] Government export promotion activities may take several forms:

1. *Provision of market intelligence.* One of the major constraints companies face in global marketing is gaining access to timely information on foreign markets. This is particularly true of small and medium-sized companies, which often lack the resources to conduct primary research on the opportunities and risks that exist outside of their national borders. National governments may opt to conduct this research and share the results with domestic exporters thereby facilitating foreign market entry. The Ontario Ministry of Food, for example, routinely commissions industry studies of overseas markets of interest to the province's exporters. Studies have examined the Caribbean, Mexican, and U.S. markets.
2. *Export subsidies.* National governments may provide an export subsidy to domestic firms in order to increase their competitiveness in international markets. Export subsidies may take many forms, such as the elimination or reduction of corporate taxes on export revenues, exemption of duties on imported raw materials destined for export manufacturing, and favourable interest rates. Export subsidies distort international trade by conferring an artificial advantage on favoured firms. The WTO has ruled that Brazil's aerospace subsidies to regional jet maker, Embraer, are illegal.[26] The program, Pro-Ex, provides Embraer with a lower interest rate when financing the foreign sale of its regional jets. Embraer is alleged to have received some US$4.5 billion in government subsidies. It should be noted that the Canadian government has also been cited for its subsidies to jet manufacturer Bombardier,

Exhibit 2.7 **CRJ700 Aircraft, Assembled at the Mirabel, Québec Facility**

Bombardier Inc.

administered through its Technology Partnership Canada (TPC) program. TPC was an agency of Industry Canada that provided funding for strategic research and development in areas such as aerospace and defense technologies.[27]

3. *Export financing.* Export financing is an often-used form of export promotion. Many governments support their exporters with direct loans, loan guarantees, and other forms of financial assistance. Export credit insurance may be all the assistance domestic firms require to become involved in foreign markets. In some situations, the credit worthiness of the foreign buyer may be questionable or unknown, and credit insurance may serve to shift the risk of loss to the national government, thereby facilitating the export sale.

   A significant number of governments provide export financing and insurance services. The United States Export-Import Bank, for example, provides assistance to exporters in the form of direct loans and loan guarantees. Export Development Canada provides a similar set of financing options for Canadian exporters, while the Columbian Government Trade Bureau provides working capital to eligible exporters in that country. Similar agencies exist in countries such as Australia (Export Finance and Insurance Corporation), the United Kingdom (Exports Credit Guarantee Department), and Hong Kong (Hong Kong Export Credit Insurance Corporation).

4. *Foreign trade zones.* Governments may spur export development by the creation of **foreign trade zones.** These are geographic areas in a country within which companies receive preferential treatment of their imported raw materials and exports of their finished products. A firm may, for example, import component parts into a foreign trade zone duty free. The components are assembled within the foreign trade zone and subsequently shipped to markets overseas. Tight controls are maintained to ensure that finished products from these zones do not enter the domestic market. Numerous countries maintain foreign trade zones. The Mexican **maquiladora** system is an example. Maquiladoras are factories located within a foreign trade zone on the border with the United States (Exhibit 2.8). Raw materials

Exhibit 2.8 **Maquiladoras on the U.S.-Mexican Border**

Spencer Grant/Photo Edit

imported by maquiladoras attract no customs duty from the Mexican government, and capital equipment used by these factories may also be imported free of duties. There are roughly 2,800 maquiladoras in operation in Mexico, employing some 1.1 million people. Foreign trade zones operate in several other countries around the world, including China and Mauritius.

International Trade and Investment Performance

A nation's set of domestic policies will invariably result in either optimal or sub-optimal trade and investment performance. Measures implemented in the home country will either spur on domestic firms to seek out new foreign markets and investment opportunities outside their national borders or will hinder their global competitiveness. A nation's domestic policies may also serve to attract investment capital from abroad or discourage foreign multinationals from establishing plants and creating jobs in that country. Trade and investment performance are important outcome variables that result from domestic government policy.

International Trade Performance

Canada is a trading nation. International trade is extremely important to the Canadian economy. In 2003 Canada's trade in goods represented over 60 percent of gross domestic product. This degree of trade dependence is high relative to Canada's major trading partners such as the United States and Japan. As shown Exhibit 2.9, among Canada's major trading partners only China exhibits an equally high degree of dependence on international markets.

The United States is Canada's largest trading partner. In 2005, 84 percent of Canada's total exports were shipped to the U.S. Interestingly, the next most significant export market for Canada was Japan, which accounted for only 2 percent of Canada's exports in 2005 (Exhibit 2.10). Canada's exports are heavily concentrated in the automotive, energy, and natural-resource sectors. Exhibit 2.11 shows details of Canada's export composition in 2005. Automotive products (which include passenger vehicles, trucks, and automotive parts), petroleum products, and lumber accounted for over 35 percent of Canada's total exports in that year. Aerospace products, electrical equipment, and metals also figure significantly in the overall export picture.

It should also be noted that most of Canada's imports (roughly 57 percent) were shipped from the United States (Exhibit 2.12). China is the next most significant source of imports, but this country accounted for only 8 percent of the total value of goods imported into Canada. Exhibit 2.13 provides an appreciation of the breadth of Canada's imports.

Exhibit 2.9 **Merchandise Trade as a Percentage of Gross Domestic Product, 2006**

Country	Percentage
Canada	60
China	66
Japan	28
United Kingdom	45
United States	22

Source: Data generated from World Development Indicators 2006. Available online at http://ddp-ext.worldbank.org/ext/DDPQQ/member.do?method=getMembers&userid=1&queryID=135.

Exhibit 2.10 Canada's Major Export Markets, 2005

Country	Share of Total Exports (%)
United States	84
Japan	2.1
United Kingdom	1.9
China	1.6
Germany	0.7
Mexico	0.7
France	0.6
South Korea	0.6
Belgium	0.5
Netherlands	0.5

Source: Strategis Industry Canada, January 2006, **http://www.strategis.gc.ca/sc_mrkti/tdst/engdoc/tr_homep.html.** Reproduced with the permission of the Minister of Public Works and Government Services, 2008.

Exhibit 2.11 Composition of Canada's Exports, 2005

Product Category	Exports
Motor vehicles for passenger transport (other than buses/public transport)	$45,317,357,293
Liquefied petroleum or hydrocarbon gases	$38,193,590,838
Crude petroleum oils and oils obtained from bituminous minerals	$29,926,770,542
Motor vehicle parts (excl. body, chassis, and engines)	$16,231,756,791
Trucks and other vehicles for the transport of goods	$12,027,617,887
Preparations of non-crude petroleum oils and oils obtained from bituminous minerals	$11,690,320,628
Lumber (thickness >6mm)	$10,566,972,926
Helicopters, airplanes, and spacecraft	$7,466,548,024
Unwrought aluminum	$5,398,010,177
Newsprint – in rolls or sheets	$5,263,927,404
Chemical woodpulp – soda or sulphate	$5,022,475,738
Electrical apparatus for telephonic line use (incl. telephones and modems)	$4,504,436,339
Furniture – other than for medical, surgical, or dental use	$4,193,848,137
Uncoated paper and paperboard for writing, printing, or graphic uses	$4,154,869,602
Gold	$4,083,910,371
Polymers of ethylene in primary forms	$3,938,661,930
Spark-ignition reciprocating or rotary internal combustion piston engines	$3,675,733,319
Turbo-jets, turbo-propellers, and other gas turbines	$3,533,490,715
Particle board of wood or other ligneous material	$3,461,549,111
Medicaments – put up in measured doses or packed for retail use	$3,386,712,748
Coal and solid fuels manufactured from coal	$3,188,401,599
Electrical energy	$3,121,611,779
Electronic integrated circuits and microassemblies	$2,994,978,013
Mineral or chemical fertilizers, potassic	$2,767,832,878
Wheat	$2,707,912,580
Subtotal	$236,819,297,369
Others	$198,834,583,995
Total (all products)	$435,653,881,364

Source: Compiled from Strategis Industry Canada database: **http://www.strategis.gc.ca/sc_mrkti/tdst/engdoc/tr_homep.html.** Reproduced with the permission of the Minister of Public Works and Government Services, 2008.

Exhibit 2.12 Canada's Major Import Markets, 2005

Country	Share of Total Imports (%)
United States	57.0
China	7.8
Japan	3.8
Mexico	3.8
Germany	2.7
United Kingdom	2.7
Norway	1.6
South Korea	1.4
France	1.3
Italy	1.2

Source: Strategis Industry Canada, January 2006: **http://www.strategis.gc.ca/sc_mrkti/tdst/engdoc/tr_homep.html.** Reproduced with the permission of the Minister of Public Works and Government Services, 2008.

Exhibit 2.13 Composition of Canada's Imports, 2005

Product Category	Imports
Motor vehicles for passenger transport (other than buses/public transport)	$24,299,301,470
Motor vehicle parts (excl. body, chassis, and engines)	$24,225,947,336
Crude petroleum oils and oils obtained from bituminous minerals	$21,925,304,708
Computers and computer peripherals	$10,174,593,202
Trucks and other vehicles for the transport of goods	$9,338,718,137
Medicaments – put up in measured doses or packed for retail use	$7,265,215,859
Spark-ignition reciprocating or rotary internal combustion piston engines	$5,837,037,998
Preparations of non-crude petroleum oils and oils obtained from bituminous minerals	$5,798,362,908
Electronic integrated circuits and microassemblies	$4,769,161,690
Liquefied petroleum or hydrocarbon gases	$3,921,496,848
Parts and accessories for computers and other office machinery	$3,558,887,839
Turbo-jets, turbo-propellers and other gas turbines	$3,468,988,576
Transmission apparatus for TV/radio broadcasting	$3,289,319,029
Parts for engines	$3,096,614,731
Seats	$3,043,690,921
Tractors	$2,976,153,732
Helicopters, airplanes, and spacecraft	$2,975,249,375
Parts of helicopters, airplanes, balloons, dirigibles, and spacecraft	$2,973,818,512
Electrical apparatus for telephonic line use (incl. telephones and modems)	$2,737,646,224
Insulated wire, cable, and other insulated electric conductors, optical fibre cables	$2,733,437,963
Taps, cocks, valves, and similar appliances for pipes, boiler shells, tanks, vats, and the like	$2,676,060,260
Self-propelled bulldozers, scrapers, graders, levellers, shovel loaders, taping machines, and the like	$2,660,595,749
New pneumatic tires of rubber	$2,394,979,915
Furniture – other than for medical, surgical, or dental use	$2,236,086,054
Apparatus for switching or protecting electrical circuits – voltage not exceeding 1000 volts	$2,210,803,530
Subtotal	$160,587,472,566
Others	$218,989,136,707
Total (all products)	$379,576,609,273

Source: Compiled from data on the Strategis Industry Canada website: **http://www.strategis.gc.ca/sc_mrkti/tdst/engdoc/tr_homep.html.** Reproduced with the permission of the Minister of Public Works and Government Services, 2008.

Exhibit 2.14

Canada's Balance of Merchandise Trade, 2000–2004 ($m)

Import/Export	2000	2001	2002	2003	2004
Total merchandise exports	$429,372	$420,730	$414,056	$400,175	$429,134
Total merchandise imports	$362,337	$350,071	$356,759	$342,608	$363,076
Trade balance	$67,035	$70,659	$57,297	$57,567	$66,058

Source: "Canada's Balance of Merchandise Trade, 2000–2004 ($m)," data is adapted from the Statistics Canada CANSIM database, **http://cansim2.statcan.ca,** Table number 228-0003.

The data indicate that imports are concentrated in areas such as automotive products, computers, prescription medicines, and petroleum products.

Canada operates with an overall trade surplus, meaning that more goods and services are exported to other countries than are imported from other countries. Exhibit 2.14 shows Canada's net merchandise trade position over the period 2000–2004. In 2004, Canada exported $66 billion more goods than it imported. This is a positive sign for the Canadian economy. Statistics Canada data on merchandise trade suggest a less positive picture, however, for the United States. In 2004, Canada exported roughly $350 billion in merchandise to the United States but imported only $250 billion from that country. This represents a sizable trade deficit with this trading partner. The situation is significantly more striking when the U.S. trade position with all countries is considered.

In 2005 the U.S. trade deficit approached US$800 billion, up from just over US$400 billion in 2001 (Exhibit 2.15). When the U.S. trade deficit data are further disaggregated, it becomes clear that the trade imbalance with China is a major component of the overall deficit. In 2005, China accounted for US$200 billion of the total U.S. deficit of $766 billion, or 26 percent. Canada accounted for US$76 billion of the U.S trade deficit, while all countries of the European Union accounted for US$122 billion. U.S. trade with Mexico in 2005 resulted in a deficit of over US$50 billion (Exhibit 2.16).

Trade deficits have a major impact on a country and its citizens. Trade deficits indicate that a country, in its international activities, is consuming more than it is producing. One key way to reduce trade deficits is to increase exports. Such an approach is highly beneficial for several reasons. For example, exports support the creation of jobs and can become a major contributor to economic growth. This fact became particularly evident during the economic slowdown of the 1990s, when export growth accounted for most of the domestic economic growth in Canada and the United States, and produced most new employment.

Equally important is the fact that, through exporting, firms can achieve economies of scale. By broadening its market reach and serving customers abroad, a firm can produce

Exhibit 2.15

United States' Balance of Merchandise Trade, 2001–2005 ($m)

Import/Export	2001	2002	2003	2004	2005
Total merchandise exports	$729,100,317,849	$693,103,192,211	$723,743,176,992	$817,935,848,814	$904,379,818,171
Total merchandise imports	$1,140,999,396,002	$1,161,365,969,084	$1,259,395,643,106	$1,469,670,757,223	$1,670,940,374,952
Trade balance	−$411,899,078,153	−$468,262,776,873	−$535,652,466,114	−$651,734,908,409	−$766,560,556,781

Source: U.S. Census Bureau, retrieved from Industry Canada website.

Exhibit 2.16 **U.S. Trade Deficit by Country/Region, 2005**

Country	Trade Deficit (US$ m)
Russia	−$13,569
Middle East	−$31,288
Mexico	−$50,149
Latin America (excluding Mexico)	−$50,691
Canada	**−$76,450**
European Union	−$122,427
China	**−$201,626**
Total deficit	−$766,561

Source: U.S. Census Bureau, retrieved from Industry Canada website.

more and do so more efficiently. As a result, the firm may achieve lower costs and higher profits both at home and abroad. Through exporting, the firm also benefits from market diversification. It can take advantage of different growth rates in different markets and gain stability by not being overly dependent on any particular market. Exporting also lets the firm learn from the competition, makes the firm sensitive to different demand structures and cultural dimensions, and proves its ability to survive in a less-familiar environment in spite of higher transaction costs. All these lessons can make the firm a stronger competitor at home.

It should also be noted that imports may have a positive longer-term effect that cannot be discounted. With imports, firms become exposed to new competition, which may offer new approaches, better processes, or better products and services. In order to maintain their market share, domestic firms are forced to compete more effectively by improving their own products and activities. Consumers in turn receive more choices when it comes to their selection. The competitive pressures exerted by imports also work to keep quality high and prices low.

International Investment Performance

International marketing activities consist not only of trade but of a spectrum of involvement, much of which results in international direct investment activities. Such investment activities can be crucial to a firm's success in new and growing markets. UNCTAD's *World Investment Report* for 2005 indicates that world foreign direct investment (FDI) inflows stood at US$648 billion in 2004—a 2 percent increase over 2003 levels. Inflows to developing countries increased by 40 percent between 2003 and 2004, while inflows for developed countries posted a decrease of some 14 percent. In 2004 the U.S. was the top recipient of FDI ($96 billion), followed by the U.K. ($80 billion) and China ($61 billion). Inflows into Canada were negligible by comparison. Global FDI outflows amounted to some $730 billion in 2004, with almost 50 percent of these outflows originating in just 3 countries—the U.S., the U.K., and Luxembourg. The worldwide stock of FDI stood at US$9 trillion in 2004.[28]

Net positive foreign direct investment provides evidence that companies abroad are finding opportunities to participate in the country and judge the potential returns in that country to be higher than in other parts of the world. Net negative direct investment flows suggest that domestic firms are expanding aggressively into foreign markets. An examination of the data on Canada's investment position indicates that the latter is the case (Exhibit 2.17). Over the period 2000–2004, Canadian firms invested more abroad than was received in FDI.

Much of Canada's inflow of foreign investment comes from the United States. In fact, for decades the United States was the leading foreign direct investor in the world. The

Exhibit 2.17

Canada's Investment Position, 2000–2004 ($m)

Capital	2000	2001	2002	2003	2004
Direct investment abroad	$356,506	$399,253	$433,364	$403,444	$445,063
Foreign direct investment	$319,116	$340,429	$354,122	$354,465	$365,675
Net position	($37,390)	($58,824)	($79,242)	($48,979)	($79,388)

Source: Adapted from the Statistics Canada CANSIM database, **http://cansim2.statcan.ca**, Table number 376-0054.

extent of foreign direct investment will be different for various industries. Foreign direct investment tends to be concentrated in specific sectors where the foreign investors believe they are able to contribute the best and benefit the most from their investment.

Implementation of International Trade and Investment Policy

From an international perspective, trade and investment negotiations must continue. In doing, so, trade and investment policy can take either a multilateral or bilateral approach. **Bilateral negotiations** are carried out mainly between two nations, while **multilateral negotiations** are carried out among a number of nations. The approach can also be broad, covering a wide variety of products, services, or investments, or it can be narrow in that it focuses on specific problems.

In order to address narrowly defined trade issues, bilateral negotiations and a specific approach seem quite appealing. Very specific problems can be discussed and resolved expediently. However, to be successful on a global scale, negotiations need to produce winners. Narrowly based bilateral negotiations require that there be, for each issue, a clearly identified winner and loser. Therefore, such negotiations have less chance for long-term success, because no one wants to be the loser. This suggests that multilateral negotiations on a broad scale, where concessions can be traded off among countries, might make it possible for all participants to emerge and declare themselves as winners. The difficulty lies in devising enough incentives to bring the appropriate and desirable partners to the bargaining table.

Policymakers must be willing to trade off short-term achievements for long-term goals. All too often, measures that would be beneficial in the long term are sacrificed to short-term expediency to avoid temporary pain and the resulting political cost. Given the increasing links among nations and their economies, however, such adjustments are inevitable. In the recent past, trade and investment volume continued to grow for everyone. Conflicts were minimized, and adjustment possibilities were increased substantially. As trade and investment policies must be implemented in an increasingly competitive environment, however, conflicts are likely to increase significantly. Thoughtful economic coordination will therefore be required among the leading trading nations. Such coordination will result to some degree in the loss of national sovereignty.

New mechanisms to evaluate restraint measures will also need to be designed. The beneficiaries of trade and investment restraints are usually clearly defined and have much to gain, whereas the losers are much less visible. This will make coalition building a key issue. The total cost of policy measures affecting trade and investment flows must be assessed, must be communicated, and must be taken into consideration before such measures are implemented. The affected parties need to be concerned and to join forces. The voices of retailers, consumers, wholesalers, and manufacturers all need to be heard. Only then will policymakers be sufficiently responsive in setting policy objectives that increase opportunities for firms and choice for consumers.

Summary

Since 1945, the Western nations have made concerted efforts to improve the trade environment and expand trade activities. In order for them to do so, various multinational organizations, such as the WTO, the IMF, and the World Bank, were founded. Many of these organizations have been very successful in their mission, yet new realities of the trade environment demand new types of action. Excellent progress has been made on the more transparent barriers to trade, and the world economy has witnessed an expansion of trade as a result. However, new approaches are required to deal with the non-tariff barriers used by so many countries to restrict market access and protect domestic industries.

Canada is a trade-dependent nation, an active participant in the global economy, and a strong supporter of the multilateral trade framework. However, numerous countries and regions, including Canada, the U.S., the European Union, China, and Japan, have instituted measures to protect sensitive industries. These protectionist measures have served to restrain trade and investment flows. The emergence of countries such as China will require a comprehensive review of international trade policy. Clearly the significant trade deficit the U.S. has incurred with China also needs to be monitored. Some policymakers intend to enhance trade performance by threatening the world with increasing protectionism. The danger of such a policy lies in the fact that world trade would shrink and standards of living would decline. Protectionism cannot, in the long run, prevent adjustment or increase productivity and competitiveness. It is therefore important to improve the capability of firms to compete internationally and to provide an international trade framework that facilitates global marketing activities.

Key Terms

absolute advantage (p. 23)
ad valorem tariff (p. 38)
autarky (p. 23)
balance of payments (p. 35)
balance of trade (p. 23)
bilateral negotiations (p. 47)
comparative advantage (p. 24)
compound tariffs (p. 38)
country similarity theory (p. 27)
embargo (p. 38)
export promotion (p. 40)
export tariff (p. 38)
foreign trade zones (p. 41)
import tariffs (p. 38)
labour theory of value (p. 23)
Leontief statistic (p. 25)
maquiladora (p. 41)
mercantilism (p. 22)
monopolistic competition (p. 27)
multilateral negotiations (p. 47)
new trade theory (p. 27)
non-tariff barriers (p. 32)
own intensity preference (p. 25)
protectionism (p. 37)
quota (p. 38)
special drawing rights (p. 34)
specie-flow mechanism (p. 49)
specific tariff (p. 38)
tariff (p. 38)
trade deficits (p. 45)
transit tariff (p. 38)
zero-sum game (p. 22)

Questions for Discussion

1. Why is international trade important to a nation?
2. Discuss the role of "voluntary" import restraints in international marketing.
3. What is meant by multilateral negotiations?
4. How have consumer demands changed international trade?
5. Discuss the impact of import restrictions on consumers.
6. Does foreign direct investment have an effect on trade?

Internet Exercises

1. Visit the website of the WTO at http://www.wto.org/index.htm and determine the objectives of following agreements: the General Agreement on Trade in Services (GATS), agreements on trade-related aspects of intellectual property rights (TRIPS), and the trade-related investment measures (TRIMS).
2. Visit Industry Canada's Strategis website at http://strategis.gc.ca/sc_mrkti/tdst/engdoc/tr_homep.html and determine (a) the dollar value of Canada's exports to its three most important export markets for the most recent year for which data are available and (b) the dollar value of Canada's imports from its three most important import markets for the most recent year for which data are available.

Recommended Readings

Albaum, G., J. Strandskov, and E. Duerr. *International Marketing and Export Management.* 4th ed. Harlow, UK: Pearson Education, 2002.

Appleyard, D., A. Field, and S. Cobb. *International Economics.* 5th ed. Boston: McGraw-Hill Irwin, 2006.

Business Guide to the World Trading System. 2nd ed. Geneva: International Trade Centre UNCTAD/WTO, 2000.

Das, Bhagirath Lal. *An Introduction to the WTO Agreements.* New York: St. Martin's Press, 1998.

Finger, Michael J. *Institutions and Trade Policy.* Northampton, MA: Edward Elgar, 2002.

Letterman, Gregory G. *Basics of Multilateral Institutions and Multinational Organizations: Economics and Commerce.* Ardsley, NY: Transnational, 2002.

McCue, Sarah S. *Trade Secrets: The Export Answer Book.* 3rd ed. Detroit, MI: Wayne State University Press, 2001.

Messerlin, Patrick A. *Measuring the Costs of Protection in Europe: European Commerical Policy in the 2000s.* Washington, DC: Institute for International Economics, 2001.

Seringhaus R., and P. Rosson. *Government Export Promotion: A Global Perspective.* London and New York: Routledge, 1990.

Notes

1. The use of the term "philosophy" does not suggest that writers of this era used a consistent set of methodological approaches or upheld a common set of principles. In fact economic historians note that the intellectual efforts of the mercantilists were largely uncoordinated. See, for example, M. Blaug, *Economic Theory in Retrospect*, 4th ed. (London: Cambridge University Press, 1985).
2. D.R. Appleyard, A.J. Field, and S.L. Cobb, *International Economics*, 5th ed. (New York: McGraw-Hill Irwin, 2006).
3. Adam Smith, *An Inquiry into the Nature and Causes of the Wealth of Nations,* Vol. 11, Liberty Classics, ed. R.H. Campbell, A.S. Skinner, and W.E. Todd (New York: Oxford University Press, 1976).
4. Adam Smith was not the only classical writer to challenge the mercantilist doctrine. Thomas Mun and David Hume took issue with the notion that mercantilist policies could be pursued indefinitely. Hume, in his **specie-flow mechanism**, noted that the accumulation of specie by one country via a trade surplus would lead to an increase in the money supply and force an increase in wages and prices. This would eventually choke off the country's international competitiveness and reverse the positive balance of trade. Hume's argument assumes full employment and a fixed positive relationship between the quantity of money in circulation and prices. The specie flow mechanism also rests on the assumption that the demand for the traded good is price elastic and therefore an increase in price results in a reduction in total expenditure.
5. Raymond Vernon, "International Investment and International Trade in the Product Cycle," *Quarterly Journal of Economics* 80, no. 2 (1966): 190–207.
6. The product cycle theory builds on earlier work by Michael Posner in 1961 who proposed the imitation lag hypothesis. According to this hypothesis there is a time lag between the introduction of a new product in one country (A) and its production in another country (B). Some time is required for firms in B to acquire the technology and work out any problems in the manufacturing process (i.e., the imitation lag). Posner also proposed another lag, a demand lag, that took account of the time required for consumers in B to embrace the product and be convinced of its value added. The net lag is the difference between the imitation and demand lags and represents the period during which A will export to B.
7. S.B. Linder, *An Essay on Trade and Transformation* (New York: John Wiley and Sons, 1961).
8. See for example N. Fortune, "Some Determinants of Trade in Finished Manufactures," *Swedish Journal of Economics* (September 1971): 311–17; and J. W. Sailors, U. Qureshi, and E.W. Cross, "An Empirical Verification of Linder's Trade Thesis," *Southern Economic Journal* (October 1973): 262–68.
9. See for example T. Kennedy and R. McHugh, "An Intertemporal Test and Rejection of the Linder Hypothesis," *Southern Economic Journal* 46, no. 3 (1980): 898.
10. Ontario chocolate factory end feared, **http://money.canoe.ca/News/Sectors/Consumer/2007/02/17/pf-3639994.html** (accessed February 18, 2007).
11. Toyota to build 100,000 vehicles per year in Woodstock, Ont., starting 2008 **http://www.cbc.ca/cp/business/050630/b0630102.html** (accessed February 21, 2007).
12. Thomas R. Graham, "Global Trade: War and Peace," *Foreign Policy* (Spring 1983): 126–37.
13. M. Czinkota, "The World Trade Organization—Perspectives and Prospects," *Journal of International Marketing* 3, no. 1 (1995): 85–92.
14. See the IMF website at: **http://www.imf.org/external/index.htm** for additional information.
15. For further details on this institution, see the World Bank website at **http://www.worldbank.org/.**
16. See UNCTAD website at **http://www.unctad.org/Templates/Startpage.asp?intItemID=2068&lang=1.**
17. CBC video archives **http://archives.cbc.ca/IDC-1-69-1041-5825/life_society/canada_wine/clip4.**
18. See op-ed to *The Globe and Mail* by Anne Golden of the Conference Board of Canada. **http://www.conferenceboard.ca/press/2005/OpEds/041201_FDI_Op-ed.asp.**
19. Leslie Wayne and David Barboza, "Unocal Deal: A Lot More Than Money Is at Issue," *New York Times* **http://www.truthout.org/cgi-bin/artman/exec/view.cgi/37/12139.**
20. McGregor R., "Short-Term Pain for Long-term Textiles Gain." *Financial Times.*
21. G. Baena, "How to Make Business in Venezuela under the Foreign Exchange Control Regime," **http://www.bomchilgroup.org/venmar04.html.**
22. Government of Thailand Financial Sector Master Plan, **http://www.thailandoutlook.com/thailandoutlook1/download/government/Fin_MasterPlan-29-Mar-04.pdf.**
23. BBC News, "Dubai firm to 'transfer' US ports," March 10, 2006, **http://news.bbc.co.uk/1/hi/business/4791512.stm.**
24. R. Seringhaus and P. Rosson, *Government Export Promotion: A Global Perspective* (London and New York: Routledge, 1990).

25. T. Wilkinson, "Entrepreneurial Climate and U.S. State Foreign Offices as Predictors of Export Success," *Journal of Small Business Management* 41, no. 4 (January 2006): 99–113.

26. CBC News. WTO rules on subsidy dispute between Brazil, Canada, August 3, 1999, **http://www.cbc.ca/story/business/national/1999/08/03/bombardier990803.html.**

27. See TPC website for further details, **http://tpc-ptc.ic.gc.ca/epic/internet/intpc-ptc.nsf/en/Home.**

28. UNCTAD, *World Investment Report: Transnational Corporations and the Internationalization of R&D* (New York and Geneva: United Nations, 2005).

Starbucks in Ireland

"Since opening our first store in London six years ago, we have been very pleased with the enthusiastic reception we have received. We very much hope to be as welcomed by customers in Northern Ireland."[1]

—Cliff Burrows
Managing Director, Starbucks Coffee Company (UK)

Starbucks Corporation is the No.1 specialty coffee shop in the world[2] [Exhibits 1 and 2]. Since its inception in 1971, Starbucks grew rapidly by selling Italian style espresso coffee, primarily in the U.S. However, the saturation of the U.S. market in the mid-1990s forced it to pursue international expansion for future growth. The company started its global expansion by entering into the Asian market, covering among others, Japan and China. After successfully winning over the traditionally tea drinking countries in Asia, in the late 1990s, Starbucks forayed into Europe and captured many profitable markets. Looking for more emerging markets, in 2005, Starbucks came to Ireland, where many well-established and reputed coffee chains were already present. Analysts opined that although Starbucks had successfully gained market share in many countries, following the same success in a highly competitive and mature market like Ireland would be difficult.

Case Study Reference No. MES0040

This case was written by Priti Krishnan, under the direction of Sumit Kumar Chaudhuri, ICFAI Business School Case Development Centre. It is intended to be used as the basis for class discussion rather than to illustrate either effective or ineffective handling of a management situation. This case was compiled from published sources.

Related Products Availability
Teaching Note
Structured Assignment

Phone : 91(40) 23435387 - 91
Fax : 91(40) 23435386
E-mail : info@ibscdc.org
Distributed and Printed by IBS-CDC, India
www.ibscdc.org

Learning to Lead

Starbucks' Foray into Foreign Markets

Starbucks Corporation was founded by three coffee lovers – Jerry Baldwin, Gordon Bowker, and Ziev Siegl in 1971. Initially, Starbucks was only a local coffee roasting plant that sold Italian style espresso beverages, pastries, and confections as well as accessories and equipments related to coffee. Until 1982, that continued to be their core business. The same year, Howard Schultz (chairman of Starbucks) joined Starbucks as part of its marketing team. During a usual trip to Italy, Schultz was inspired by the rich tradition of espresso bars in the country. On his return, he persuaded Starbucks' owners, that in 1984 the first espresso coffee store of Starbucks was opened, which turned out to be a huge success. In 1985, Schultz left Starbucks to open his own espresso coffee bar, 'Il Giornale', which sold coffee beverages prepared from Starbucks coffee beans. In 1987, he, along with David Olsen, purchased Starbucks for $3.8 million and changed its name to Starbucks Corporation.[3]

Since then, Starbucks has grown rapidly from 17 stores to 9,671 in 2005.[4] The company believes that its uniqueness is that it not only provides high quality products but also offers the 'Starbucks Experience' [Box 1]. Howard Schultz, chairman of Starbucks, said, "You get more than the finest coffee when you visit a Starbucks—you get great people, first-rate music, and a comfortable and upbeat meeting place. We establish the value of buying a product at Starbucks by our uncompromising quality and by building a personal relationship with each of our customers. Starbucks is rekindling America's love affair with coffee, bringing romance and fresh flavor back to the brew."[5]

Over the years, Starbucks built its presence predominantly in the U.S. Until 2004, Starbucks has opened nearly 7000 stores in the U.S. [Refer to Exhibit 2] and plans to increase the same to 10,000.[6] However, with much of the U.S. market being saturated with more than 3 stores per 100,000 residents[7] (calculated to be the 'saturation point') [Exhibit 3], Dan Geiman, an analyst with McAdams Wright Ragen,[8] said, "That number's looking a little bit conserva-

Exhibit 1 Starbucks Net Revenues from 1994 to 2004

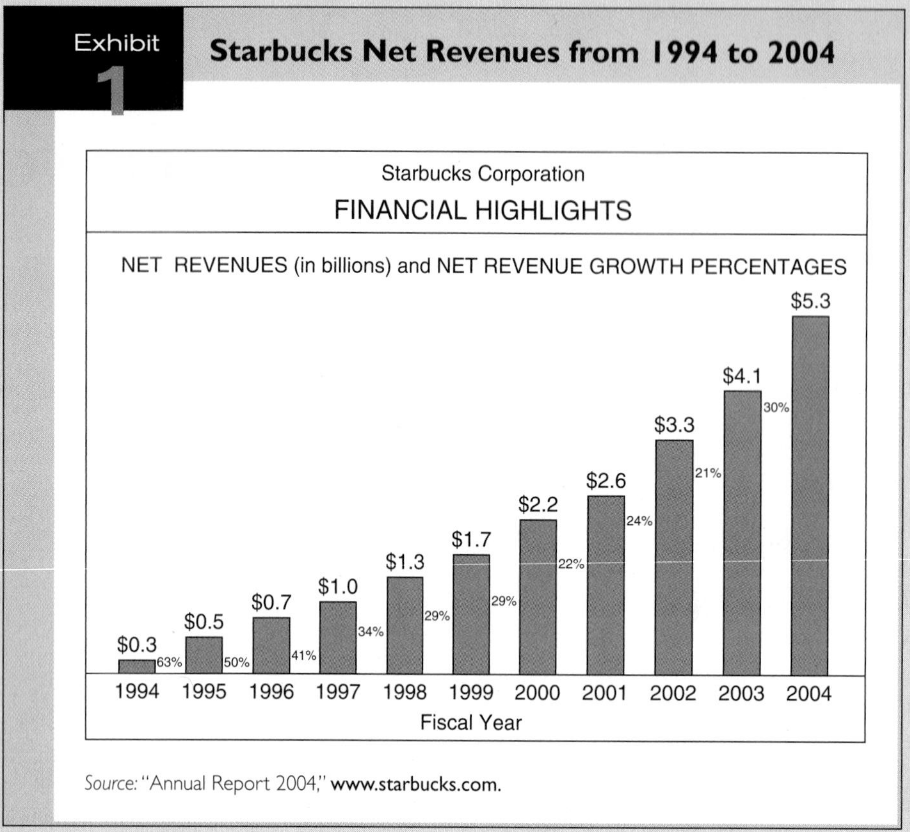

Source: "Annual Report 2004," **www.starbucks.com.**

tive at this point."[9] Under such conditions, Starbucks considered expanding its operations internationally.

The first international expansion of Starbucks was in 1987 when the company opened its operations in Vancouver, Canada. Despite foraying into foreign countries, until 1995, Starbucks' marketing efforts were primarily concentrated in the U.S. Following saturation of the U.S. market in 1996, Starbucks started considering international expansion seriously to become "a great, enduring company with the most recognized and respected brand in the world."[10] The same year, it entered Japan. Through joint ventures with local operators, Star-

Exhibit 2 Starbucks Stores in U.S. and Worldwide

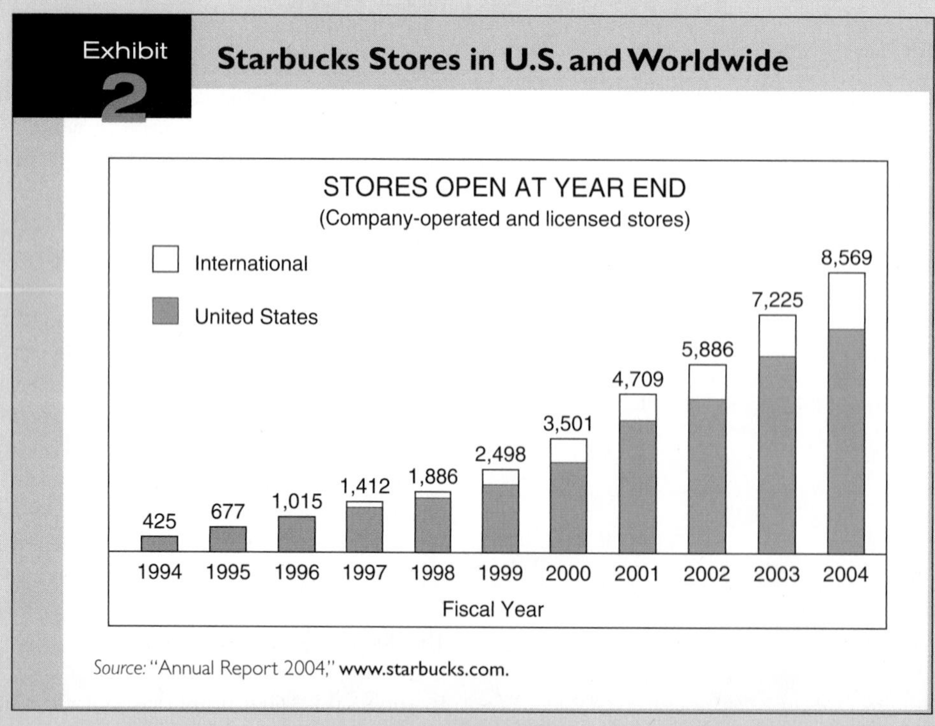

Source: "Annual Report 2004," **www.starbucks.com.**

Box 1 The Starbucks Experience

Starbucks believes that the 'Starbucks Experience,' which is about providing a comfortable and buoyant ambience to its customers, has enabled it to connect with millions of customers worldwide. The company provides facilities like patio seating inside and outside the store, laptop ports and playing area for children. People visit the stores (apart from drinking coffee) to meet friends, listen to music, and relax.

Source: Compiled By ICFAI Business School Case Development Center from **www.galpinastonmartin.com**

bucks introduced its coffee and 'Starbucks experience' into Japan, which is considered to be a traditionally tea-drinking country. Although critics had warned Starbucks about the probable reluctance from the Japanese towards the company's no-smoking policy and take-out coffee culture, by 2002, Starbucks had successfully captured the Japanese market by opening 368 outlets.[11] Howard Schultz said, "Almost six years after we opened here [Japan], this is the best-performing market on a unit level for Starbucks in the world. It's also the second largest in the world [after the U.S.]. When we came here in August of 1996, we underestimated the size of the market just like we did in America. So we're sitting here today with approximately 360 stores, and we're opening two new stores a week in Japan. We'll have 500 stores by September 2003, heading toward 1,000."[12]

The expansion strategy of Starbucks focused mainly in new countries where consumers were already habituated to drink tea or coffee. In 1999, Starbucks brought its coffee concept into China, though in a measured way. Like Japan, China too is known for its strong inclination towards tea. Having learned this, Starbucks first introduced its coffee in the big hotels and restaurants of Beijing before it opened its own cafés. By 2002, Starbucks had established 25 stores in Beijing with 70% of its consumers being locals.[13] Witnessing Starbucks' success, many competitors sprang up in China and opened similar cafés.

Starbucks embraced global expansion with the aim of providing the "Starbucks Experience" in as many countries as possible. However, as Europe had a well-established café culture, the company first targeted Asia. Schultz said, "The decision was made to go to Asia first because we felt that the maturity of the coffee market in Europe was very strong and was not going to change much over the years. The Asian market was in its developmental stage and we had an opportunity to position Starbucks as a leader in a new industry."[14]

In 1998, Starbucks entered Europe through the acquisition of Seattle Coffee Company (a U.K. retailer having 64 cafés across the country).[15] Although in the U.K. the company attained success, the main challenge confronting Starbucks was to establish itself in other countries of Europe that were known for their strong coffee culture and loyal customers. Analysts opined that due to such factors the chances of Starbucks succeeding in Europe (excluding U.K.) was limited. Barry Sine, an analyst at H.D Brous & Co said, "Starbucks is an American imitation of a European concept. To try to sell that back to the Europeans, that's a real marketing challenge."[16] In 2001, Starbucks opened its first store in Europe at Zurich. Thereafter it grew rapidly by opening its outlets in Austria, Germany, Spain, and Greece. Although Starbucks proved to be a success in most parts of Europe, it faced problems

Exhibit 3 Saturation of the U.S. Market

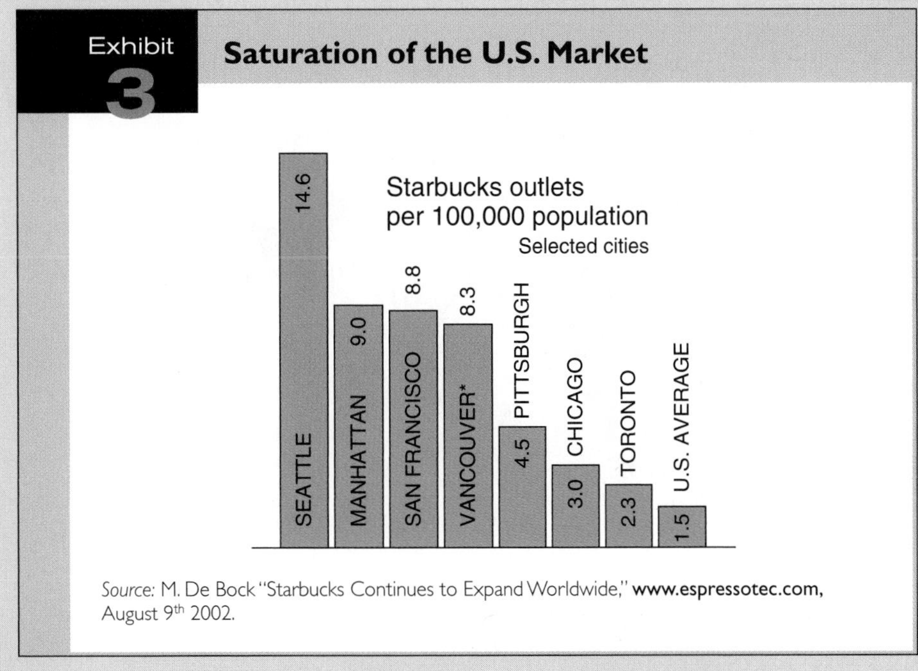

Source: M. De Bock "Starbucks Continues to Expand Worldwide," **www.espressotec.com**, August 9th 2002.

in France and Italy, where there were strong associations of local coffee owners who thwarted any kind of foreign influence in their businesses. Commenting on the company's chances in Europe, analysts at Salomon Smith Barney[17] wrote, "The Asian market could support more sites than North America in the long-term. Europe may have similar potential, although individual countries such as Italy and France may prove tough to crack."[18]

The global expansion of Starbucks that started with Japan continued at a rapid pace covering the Pacific Rim, Middle East, and the United Kingdom [Exhibit 4]. Although the company faced anti-globalization sentiments across the world, its overseas businesses became a key driver for its overall growth, contributing mainly to its success and profitability. Howard Schultz said, "Our international business is now really contributing significantly to the growth and profitability of our company."[19] By 2005, the company had its presence in 36 countries outside the U.S.[20] Starbucks stated that through its unique 'Starbucks Experience' it has been able to transcend barriers of language and culture. Audrey Lincoff, public affairs director at Starbucks, said, "The success we have enjoyed as we have entered new international markets is a validation of the worldwide acceptance of the Starbucks brand, and demonstrates that we are in the early days of our growth and development."[21]

Having acquired most of the major markets in Europe, Starbucks focused on the next most highly developed market close to the U.K. Yvonne Neeson, brand manager, Bewleys[22] said, "Now, when you go into an Irish garage forecourt and get a decent bean-to-cup, and compare it to what you get in an English garage … you can see that Ireland is a pretty sophisticated coffee market."[23]

Expansion Strategies in Ireland

In 2005, Starbucks launched itself into another tea-drinking country, Ireland. Although Starbucks outlets (that were operating under licensing agreements) were already present in Ireland at the headquarters of Royal Bank of Scotland and at Microsoft in Dublin, the first company owned outlet was opened on July 28th, 2005 in the Dundrum Town Center at South Dublin. After a month, the company introduced its second store in College Green, Northern Ireland. Expressing optimism about the opportunities for Starbucks' high quality coffee in Ireland, Howard Schultz said, "The Company's two Irish stores were among the fastest growing new stores we've opened in all Europe. The pent-up demand at the first two stores has probably inflated the level of traction. But this is a very dynamic opportunity for us here."[24] As it was reported that sales of specialty coffee shops in Ireland had increased from € 21.8 million to € 40.1 million between 1999 and 2004,[25] analysts felt that the Irish market could prove to be profitable for Starbucks.

Exhibit 4 **International Expansion of Starbucks**

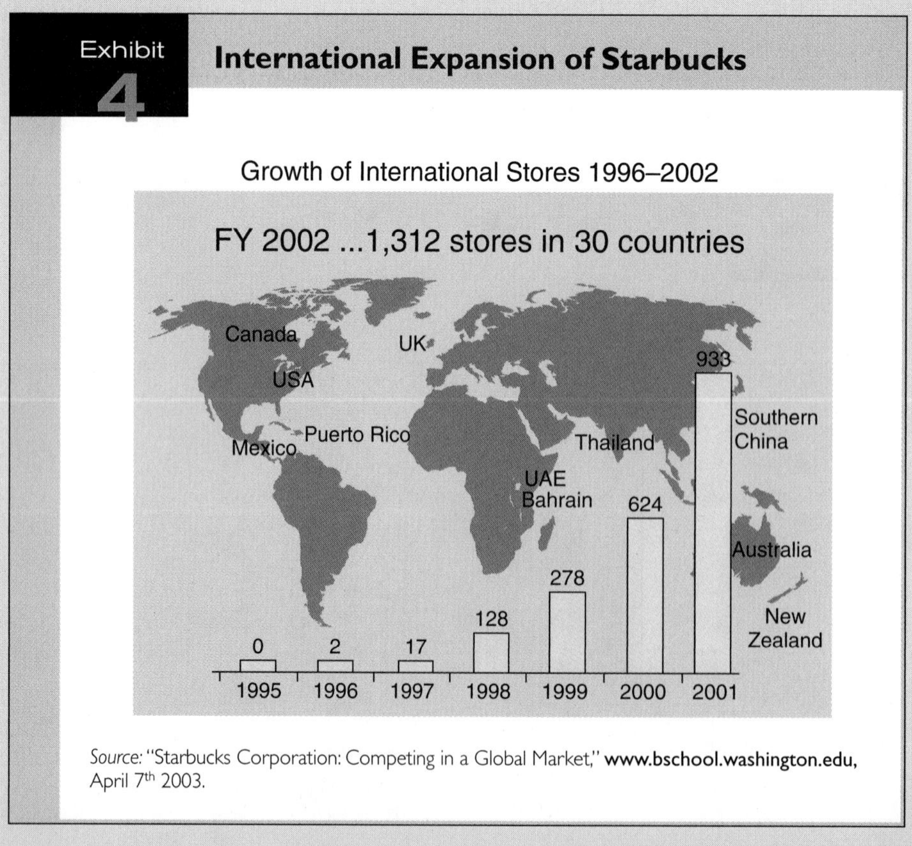

Source: "Starbucks Corporation: Competing in a Global Market," **www.bschool.washington.edu**, April 7th 2003.

Exhibit 5 Competitive Scenario of Specialty Coffee Chains Market in Ireland

Area of Ireland: 27,135 sq mi (70,280 sq km)
Population of Ireland (2005): 4,015,676

NAME OF COFFEE CHAIN	NUMBER OF STORES IN IRELAND
Insomnia Cafe	20
Café Sci	10
Costa Coffee	10
Gloria Jean's Coffees	5
Starbucks	2

Compiled by ICFAI Business School Case Development Center.

Globally, Starbucks is known as a company that clusters the market with too many outlets. The company believes that by doing so it can dominate a market. Following the same strategy, in Ireland, Starbucks plans to launch 29 coffee stores,[26] of which six are expected to be in Dublin by mid-2006.[27] Taking advantage of the ban on smoking introduced in Ireland in 2004, Starbucks believed that its stores in Ireland could successfully be an alternative to the traditional public houses. Ever since the company started its business, it has followed a no-smoking policy. Howard Schultz said, "We were told it would be a death sentence for our company. In Europe, in Japan and China it has turned out to be just the opposite."[28]

Although Starbucks acquires market share in international markets through joint ventures, due to the small size of local coffee chains in Ireland, the company called off its plans of expanding through acquisitions. "The strategy simply doesn't make sense here as most of the café sizes are too small for Starbucks' format."[29] While that meant Starbucks had to expand through its own stores, some analysts observed that intense competition for retail outlets in Ireland, which results in high rents, might slow down Starbucks expansion plans. "Starbucks are really finding it difficult to secure the right property. There is so much competition for these outlets and rents are extremely high."[30]

However, a few experts opined that as Starbucks is a well-marketed brand and holds strong brand recognition, it was only a matter of time before Starbucks could establish itself in Ireland. John Sheridan, a director with Merrion Capital Group[31] stockbrokers and a former director of Insomnia, Starbucks' main competitor in Ireland, said, "The Irish are well travelled and everyone would have heard of Starbucks. That will be in their favour."[32]

In a few years time, Starbucks plans to open an outlet in every big shopping center in Dublin. While Ireland is an attractive market for Starbucks, analysts predict stiff competition for Starbucks as it enters a highly competitive market [Exhibit 5]. Jim Corbett, Bewley's managing director, said Starbucks would have "no shortage of competition. The Irish market is more developed than many that Starbucks already operates in, in terms of the quality of the product, the pricing, the range. This is not virgin territory."[33]

A Competitive Existence

The Irish coffee house market is highly competitive with many well-established coffee chains. The primary among them are Café Sol, Gloria Jean's Coffees, Costa Coffee and Insomnia. While Insomnia Café is the leading premium coffee and sandwich retail chain of Ireland, Costa Coffee is a well-known U.K.-based brand. Across Ireland, Insomnia Café and Costa Coffee have 20 and 10 outlets, respectively.

Gloria Jean's Coffees on the other hand, is a rapidly expanding brand in Ireland. In Australia, the company built a strong market share by establishing 278 cafes against 45 from Starbucks.[34] Analysts expect Gloria to follow the same success in Ireland. Noeleen Duffy, Managing Director of Glorjean Ltd., Cork, said, "There has been a fantastic response to Gloria Jean's Coffees in Ireland. The café market is highly competitive and Gloria

Jean's success is due to the unique combination of high quality products, specialised service and the relaxed environment we offer our customers."[35]

Given the number of coffee chains in Ireland and the strength of their loyal customers, Starbucks' competitors stated that they were not threatened by the company's entry into Ireland. Bobby Kerr, Chief Executive Officer of Insomnia, said, "We know Starbucks. We respect them, but we don't fear them. They're coming into a very developed market. It's not like a whole new dawn, which they may have experienced in other markets. And we have 20 sites. So far they've got one."[36]

On the contrary, analysts opine that with two outlets and a third one of Starbucks likely to be opened in January 2006, the impact the company would have in an already competitive market is difficult to predict. It is observed that although Starbucks has experienced an excellent growth record worldwide, the challenges facing Starbucks in as competitive a market as Dublin could test the company's capability to survive in Ireland.

"The core of the company's success remains its ability to grow in its most mature markets."[37]

Notes

1. "Starbucks Coffee Breaks Into NI Market", **www.highbeam.com,** March 19th 2004
2. "Starbucks Corporation," **www.hoovers.com**
3. Wang, Meng "Exporting a North American Concept to Asia: Starbucks in China", **www.highbeam.com,** May 1st 2005
4. Boyer, Tom "Starbucks Pours Out Another Steaming Quarter", **www.highbeam.com,** July 28th 2005
5. "Company Profile," **www.starbucks.com,** August 2005
6. Kurlantzick, Joshua "Serving up Success," **www.entrepreneur.com,** November 2003
7. M. De. Bock "Starbucks Continues to Expand Worldwide," **www.espressotec.com,** August 9th 2002
8. McAdams Wright Ragen is a brokerage firm located in Seattle. Founded in January 1999, the firm offers its services to retail and institutional investors.
9. **www.mfbank.com**
10. Moffett, Michael, and Ramaswamy, Kannan "Planet Starbucks (B): Caffeinating the World," **www.thunderbird.edu**
11. Holmes, Stanley et al "Planet Starbucks", **www.businessweek.com,** September 9th 2002
12. "Planet Starbucks (B): Caffeinating the World," op.cit.
13. Ibid.
14. Ibid.
15. Ibid.
16. Weber, Gretchen "What's Brewing Overseas," **www.workforce.com,** February 2005
17. Smith Barney is a part of the Citigroup Global Markets Inc, which is a financial firm offering services like brokerage, investment banking and asset management to companies, goverments and individuals globally.
18. Ernst, Steve "Starbucks: Europe, Asia next," **www.bizjournal.com,** June 2nd 2002
19. Brown, John M., and Jenny Wiggins "Coffee Empire Expands Reach by Pressing Its Luck in Ireland," **www.ft.com,** December 15th 2005
20. "Full Transcript of Starbucks' 4Q05 Conference Call — Prepared Remarks (SBUX)," **www.retailstockblog.com**
21. Anderson, Rick "Starbucks: Just Getting Started," **www.alternet.org,** June 27th 2003
22. Bewleys is Ireland's market leader in ground coffee. It was founded in 1840.
23. "BSA Confronts the Big Issue," **www.coffee-house.org.uk,** July/August 2005
24. "Coffee Empire Expands Reach by Pressing Its Luck in Ireland," op.cit.
25. Ibid.
26. "Starbucks Café Chains Plans to Launch in Ireland this Year," **www.irishtimes.com**
27. Friemann, Gretchen "Expansion of Starbucks Thwarted by Intense Competition for Sites," **www.ireland.com,** November 2nd 2005
28. "Coffee Empire Expands Reach by Pressing Its Luck in Ireland," op.cit.
29. "Expansion of Starbucks Thwarted by Intense Competition for Sites," op.cit.
30. Ibid.
31. Founded in 1999, Merrion Capital Group is a stockbroking and corporate finance company located in Ireland.
32. "Coffee Empire Expands Reach by Pressing Its Luck in Ireland," op.cit.
33. Ibid.
34. Keene, Conor "Gloria Jean's to Take on Starbucks in Bid for Domination of Irish Market," **www.irishexaminer.com,** July 22nd 2005
35. "Gloria Jean's Coffees Rapid Growth in Ireland", **www.gloriajeanscoffees.com,** June 30th 2005
36. O'Mahony, Catherine "Insomnia wide awake", **www.archives.tcm.ie,** August 28th 2005
37. "Starbucks Pours Out Another Steaming Quarter," op.cit.

Parker Pen Company

Parker Pen Company, the manufacturer of writing instruments based in Janesville, Wisconsin, has always been one of the world's best-known companies in its field. George Safford Parker had patented his first fountain pen in 1889, and founded Parker Pen Company in 1892, marketing Parker pens as the best writing instruments. The idea of pens as status symbols dates back to the 1920s, when a Parker Pen manager argued that if people bought cars as status symbols, they could purchase high-priced pens as ones as well. As the business expanded its product line, market presence was also increased. In 1903, Parker's first overseas distributorship was established in Scandinavia through a shopkeeper in Copenhagen. In 1953, Parker Pen opened a 226,000-square-foot state-of-the-art facility in Janesville and manufacturing plants in France and Mexico. International marketing activities extended the company to 154 countries by the 1980s.

In early 1984, the company launched a global marketing campaign in which everything was to have "one look, one voice," and with all planning to take place at headquarters. Everything connected with the selling effort was to be standardized. This was a grand experiment of a widely debated concept. A number of international companies were eager to learn from Parker's experiences.

Results became evident quickly. In February 1985, the globalization experiment was ended, and most of the masterminds of the strategy either left the company or were fired.

Globalization

Globalization is a business initiative based on the conviction that the world is becoming more homogeneous and that distinctions between national markets are not only fading but, for some products, they will eventually disappear. Some products, such as Coca-Cola and Levi's, have already proven the existence of universal appeal. Coke's "one sight, one sound, one sell" approach is a legend in the world of global marketers. Other companies have some products that can be "world products," and some that cannot and should not be. For example, if cultural and competitive differences are less important than their similarities, a single advertising approach can exploit these similarities to stimulate sales everywhere, and at far lower cost than if campaigns were developed for each individual market.

Compared with the multidomestic approach, globalization differs in these three basic ways:

1. The global approach looks for similarities between markets. The multidomestic approach ignores similarities.
2. The global approach actively seeks homogeneity in products, image, marketing, and advertising message. The multidomestic approach produces unnecessary differences from market to market.
3. The global approach asks, "Should this product or process be for world consumption?" The multidomestic approach, relying solely on local autonomy, never asks the question.

Globalization requires many internal modifications as well. Changes in philosophy concerning local autonomy, concern for local operating results rather than corporate performance, and local strategies designed for local—rather than global—competitors are all delicate issues to be solved. By design, globalization calls for centralized decision-making; therefore, the "not-invented-here" syndrome becomes a problem. This can be solved by involving those having to implement the globalization strategy at every possible stage as well as keeping lines of communication open.

Globalization at Parker Pen Company

In January 1982, James R. Peterson became the president and CEO of Parker Pen. At that time, the company was struggling, and global marketing was one of the key measures to be used to revive the company. While at

Sources: This case was prepared by Ilkka A. Ronkainen for discussion purposes and not to exemplify correct or incorrect decision-making. The case draws facts from Neal McChristy, "Pens: The Ultimate Writing Experience," *Office Solutions,* 18 (number 10, 2001): 31–34; Joseph M. Winski and Laurel Wentz, "Parker Pen: What Went Wrong?" *Advertising Age,* June 2, 1986, 1, 60–61, 71; and Lori Kesler, "Parker Rebuilds a Quality Image," *Advertising Age,* March 21, 1988, 49. For the Parker Pen story, see **http://www. parkerpen.com.** For a comprehensive discussion on globalization, see George S. Yip, *Total Global Strategy II,* (Upper Saddle River, NJ: Prentice-Hall, 2002).

R. J. Reynolds, Peterson had been impressed with the industry's success with globalization. He wanted for Parker Pen nothing less than the writing instrument equivalent of the Marlboro man.

For the previous few years, a weak dollar had lulled Parker Pen into a false sense of security. About 80 percent of the company's sales were abroad, which meant that when local currency profits were translated into dollars, big profits were recorded.

The market was changing, however. The Japanese had started marketing inexpensive disposable pens with considerable success through mass marketers. Brands such as Paper Mate, Bic, Pilot, and Pentel each had greater sales, causing Parker's overall market share to plummet to 6 percent. Parker Pen, meanwhile, stayed with its previous strategy and continued marketing its top-of-the-line pens through department stores and stationery stores. Even in this segment, Parker Pen's market share was eroding because of the efforts of A. T. Cross Company and Montblanc of Germany.

Subsidiaries enjoyed a high degree of autonomy in marketing operations, which resulted in broad and diverse product lines and 40 different advertising agencies handling the Parker Pen account worldwide.

When the dollar's value skyrocketed in the 1980s, Parker's profits plunged and the loss of market share became painfully evident.

Peterson moved quickly upon his arrival. He trimmed the payroll, chopped the product line to 100 (from 500), consolidated manufacturing operations, and ordered an overhaul of the main plant to make it a state-of-the-art facility. Ogilvy & Mather was hired to take sole control of Parker Pen advertising worldwide. The logic behind going with one agency instead of the 40 formerly employed was cost savings and the ability to coordinate strategies on a worldwide basis. Among the many agencies terminated was Lowe Howard-Spink in London, which had produced some of the best advertising for Parker Pen's most profitable subsidiary. The immediate impact was a noticeable decline in employee morale and some expressed bitterness at the subsidiary being dictated to although it had been cross-subsidizing the American operations over the years.

A decision was also made to go aggressively after the low end of the market. The company would sell an upscale line called Premier, mainly as a positioning device. The biggest profits were to come from a roller-ball pen called Vector, selling for $2.98. Plans were drawn to sell an even cheaper pen called Itala—a disposable pen never thought possible at Parker.

Three new managers, to be known as Group Marketing, were brought in. All three had extensive marketing experience, most of it in international markets. Richard Swart, who became Marketing Vice President for writing instruments, had handled 3M's image advertising worldwide and taught company managers the ins and outs of marketing planning. Jack Marks became head of writing instruments advertising. At Gillette, he had orchestrated the worldwide marketing of Silkience hair-care products. Carlos Del Nero, brought in to be Parker's manager of global marketing planning, had gained broad international experience at Fisher-Price. The concept of marketing by centralized direction was approved.

The idea of selling pens the same way everywhere did not sit well with many Parker subsidiaries and distributors. Pens were indeed the same, but markets, they believed, were different: France and Italy fancied expensive fountain pens; Scandinavia was a ballpoint market. In some markets, Parker could assume an above-the-fray stance; in others it had to get into the trenches and compete on price. Nonetheless, headquarters communicated to them all:

Advertising for Parker Pens (no matter model or mode) will be based on a common creative strategy and positioning. The worldwide advertising theme, "Make Your Mark With Parker," has been adopted. It will utilize similar graphic layout and photography. It will utilize an agreed-upon typeface. It will utilize the approved Parker logo/ design. It will be adapted from centrally supplied materials.

Swart insisted that the directives were to be used only as "starting points" and that they allowed for ample local flexibility. The subsidiaries perceived them differently. The U.K. subsidiary, especially, fought the scheme all the way. Ogilvy & Mather London strongly opposed the "one world, one brand, one advertisement" dictum. Conflict arose, with Swart allegedly shouting at one of the meetings: "Yours is not to reason why; yours is to implement." Local flexibility in advertising was out of the question (see Exhibit 1).

The London-created "Make Your Mark" campaign was launched in October 1984. Except for language, it was essentially the same: long copy, horizontal layout, illustrations in precisely the same place, the Parker logo at the bottom, and the tag line or local equivalent in the lower right-hand corner. Swart once went to the extreme of suggesting that Parker ads avoid long copy and use just one big picture.

Problems arose on the manufacturing side. The new $15 million plant broke down repeatedly. Costs soared, and the factory turned out defective products in unacceptable numbers. In addition, the new marketing approach started causing problems. Although Parker never abandoned its high-end position in foreign markets, its concentration on low-priced, mass distribution products in the United States caused dilution of its image and ultimately losses of $22 million in 1985. Conflict was evident internally, and the board of directors began to turn against the concept of globalization.

In January 1985, Peterson resigned. Del Nero left the company in April; Swart was fired in May, Marks in June.

Exhibit 1 Ads for Parker's Global Campaign

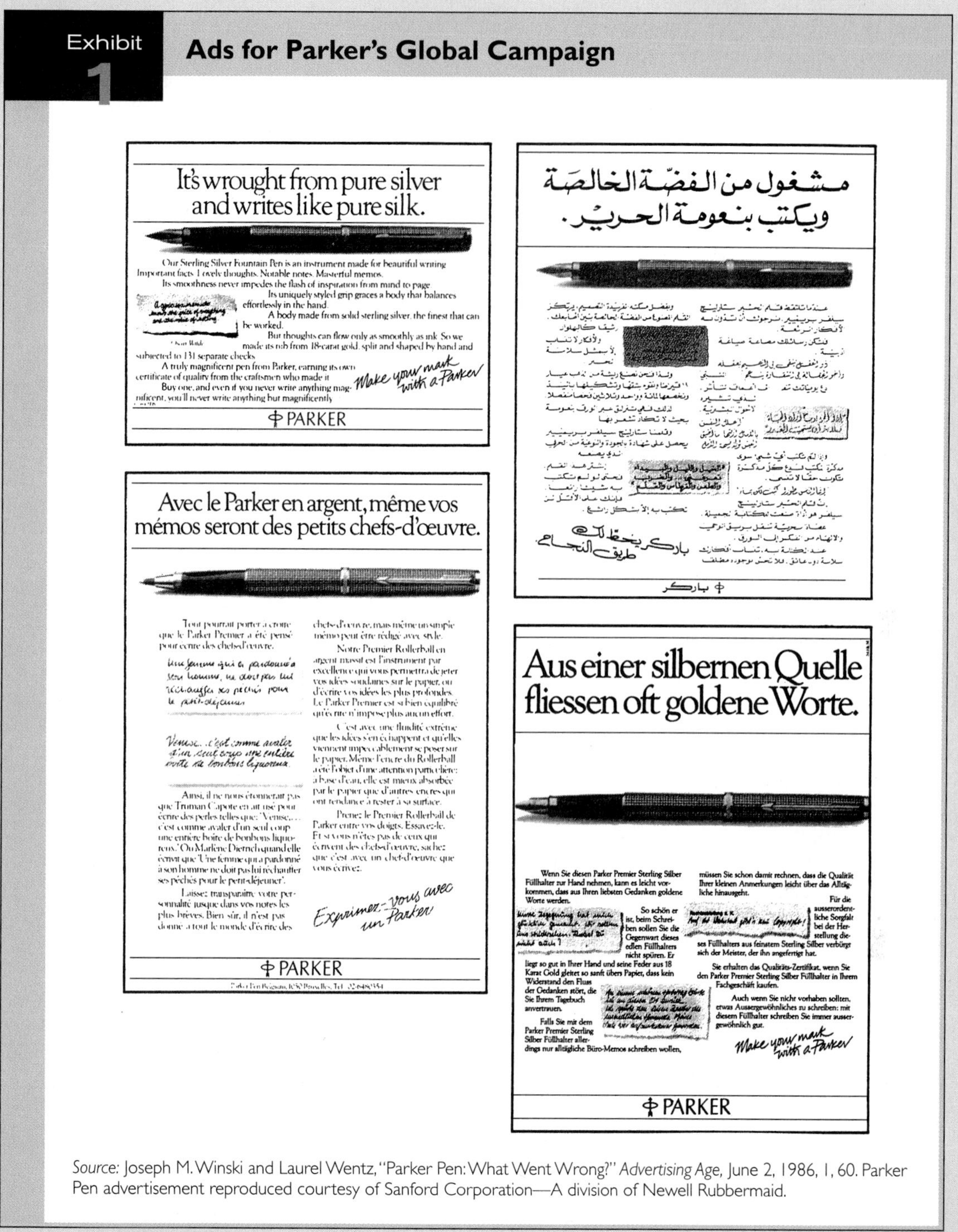

Source: Joseph M. Winski and Laurel Wentz, "Parker Pen: What Went Wrong?" *Advertising Age,* June 2, 1986, 1, 60. Parker Pen advertisement reproduced courtesy of Sanford Corporation—A division of Newell Rubbermaid.

When Michael Fromstein became CEO of the company, he assembled the company's country managers in Janesville and announced: "Global marketing is dead. You are free again."

Epilogue

After nearly a century in Janesville, Wisconsin, the Writing Instrument Group was acquired for $100 million in 1986 in a leveraged management buyout by Parker U.K. managers and investors. Headquarters were moved to Newhaven, England, and the privately-held company returned to many of its old traditions of innovation and quality. Advertising was returned to Lowe.

In 1993, the company was acquired by Gillette and made part of the company's Stationery Products Group, and in 2000, Newell Rubbermaid acquired the business including the Paper Mate, Parker, Waterman, and Liquid Paper brands to make their Office Products Group the world leader in writing instruments with 3,000 different products.

Questions For Discussion

1. Was the proposed globalization strategy for Parker Pen flawed or merely plagued by implementation challenges?
2. What marketing miscalculations were made by the advocates of globalization at Parker Pen?
3. Parker Pen has since become part of two major global-brand powerhouses. What are the benefits and drawbacks of being part of a larger entity in the global marketing environment?

Part 2

The Global Market Environment

Chapter

Part 2 of this text is devoted to the cultural, economic, and political environments that shape the design and implementation of the firm's global marketing strategy. The need for cultural literacy is emphasized, approaches to cultural analytics are discussed, and practical suggestions for using culture to strategic advantage in global markets are presented. Part 2 of the text also stresses the importance of economic variables to global marketing decisions and, in particular, the selection of appropriate country target markets. Important considerations in the implementation of global marketing strategy are the political and legal systems in the home and host countries. The impact of these on global marketing decisions is also discussed in this part.

Chapter 3

The Role of Culture in Global Marketing

The Global MARKETPLACE 3.1

Transferring Cultural Values

Koei Canada is a wholly owned subsidiary of Japan-based Koei Co. The company, a video-game developer, operates from offices in downtown Toronto, Canada, and employs roughly 30 people. Koei Canada develops games for personal computers as well as home and hand-held game consoles. The company's software development team is currently engaged in the development of Fatal Inertia, a futuristic aerial combat racing game that will be released for Sony PlayStation3 and Xbox 360 consoles. Titles already released by the company include Romance of the Three Kingdoms, the Dynasty Warriors series, and Crimson Sea.

When Koei Co. established its production studio in Canada, it attempted to infuse Japanese culture into its new subsidiary's operations. Three times a week, employees at the company begin their day standing at their desks, greeting their boss with a collective "Good morning." The morning greeting is followed by a briefing on business events by the company's manager. This ritual is common practice in Japan and is termed *chorei.* The practice is, however, not a part of Western culture. Also alien to Westerners is Koei Co.'s decision to have its software programmers in Toronto log into a digital clock to ensure punctuality, and work sitting together in an open room without cubicles. The company's practice of having female employees of the Toronto office serve tea to guests of senior executives has also raised eyebrows among some Canadian staffers. At the end of every year, employees of Koei Canada are also expected to participate in "*o soji,*" a cleanup of the office by everyone from senior managers to secretaries. While Koei Canada has been given free rein in terms of creative content, attempts to impose Japanese culture on Westerners is likely to make employee retention difficult. The problem of transferring cultural values from home to host country is one that many more companies will face as they explore global market opportunities.

Sources: Koei Canada website: **http://www.koeicanada.ca/home.html;** and Phred Dvorak, "A Firm's Culture Can Get Lost in Translation When It's Exported," *The Wall Street Journal Online,* **http://www.goinglobal.com/hot_topics/general_dvorak_culture.asp** (accessed February 23, 2007).

The ever-increasing level of world trade, opening of markets, enhanced purchasing power of customers, and intensifying competition all have allowed and even forced marketers to expand their operations. As The Global Marketplace 3.1 shows, the challenge for the global marketing manager is to handle cultural differences that exist around the world. Cultural values, attitudes, and customs may not translate readily from one country to another. These values, attitudes, and customs, of course, influence behavioural patterns that govern human interaction. These influences occur on two levels: first, as they relate to customer behaviour and, second, as they affect the implementation of marketing programs within individual markets and across markets.

For years, marketers have been heralding the arrival of the global customer, an individual or entity that would both think and purchase alike the world or region over.[1] These universal needs could then be translated into marketing programs that would exploit these similarities. However, if this approach were based on the premise of standardization, a critical and fatal mistake would be made. Overseas success is very much a function of cultural adaptability, patience, flexibility, and tolerance for others' beliefs.[2]

To take advantage of global markets or global segments, marketers are required to have or attain a thorough understanding of what drives customer behaviour in different markets, and to detect the extent to which similarities exist or can be achieved through marketing efforts. This requires **cultural literacy** on the part of the global marketing manager, meaning that the manager has acquired enough detailed knowledge of the culture of the target market to be able to function effectively.

In expanding their presence, marketers will acquire not only new customers but new partners as well. These essential partners, whose efforts are necessary for market development and penetration, include agents, distributors, other facilitating agents (such as advertising agencies and law firms), and, in many cases, governments. Expansion will also mean new employees or strategic alliance partners whose motivations will either make or break marketing programs. Thus, understanding the "hot buttons" and "turnoffs" of these groups becomes critical. Companies located in multicultural cities such as Toronto are more likely to have employees who were born outside of Canada and whose native language is neither English nor French. Their domestic customers are also more likely to have been born outside of Canada, and their suppliers may well be firms owned by individuals who are not Canadians. The cultural values these groups bring to any business transaction will clearly affect the success of the firm's global marketing efforts.

In the past, marketing managers who did not want to worry about the cultural challenge could simply decide not to do so and concentrate on domestic markets. In today's business environment, a company has no choice but to face international competition. In this new environment, believing that concern about culture and its elements is a waste of time often proves to be disastrous. Cultural understanding allows marketers to determine when adaptation may be necessary and when commonalities allow for regional or global approaches. Understanding culture is critical not only in terms of getting strategies right but also for ensuring that implementation by local operations is effective.

Cultural differences often are the subject of anecdotes, and business blunders may provide a good laugh. **Cultural diversity** must be recognized not simply as a fact of life but as a positive benefit. Differing perspectives that result from cultural diversity may actually suggest better solutions to challenges shared across borders. Cultural competence must be recognized as a key management skill.[3] Adjustments will have to be made to accommodate the extraordinary variety in customer preferences and work practices by cultivating the ability to detect similarities and to allow for differences. Ideally, this means that successful ideas can be transferred across borders for efficiency and adapted to local conditions for effectiveness. For example, in one of his regular trips to company headquarters in Switzerland, the general manager of Nestlé Thailand was briefed on a promotion for a cold coffee concoction called Nescafé Shake. The Thai group swiftly adopted and adapted the idea. It designed plastic containers to mix the drink and invented a dance, the Shake, to popularize the product.[4] Cultural incompetence, however, can easily jeopardize millions of dollars in wasted negotiations, potential purchases, sales and contracts, and customer relations. Furthermore, the internal efficiency of a firm may be weakened if managers, employees, and intermediaries are not "on the same wavelength."

The intent of this chapter is first to analyze the concept of culture and its various elements and then to provide suggestions for meeting the cultural challenge.

Culture Defined

Culture gives an individual an anchoring point—an identity—as well as codes of conduct. Of the more than 160 definitions of culture analyzed by Alfred Kroeber and Clyde Kluckhohn, some conceive of culture as separating humans from non-humans, some define it as communicable knowledge, and some see it as the sum of historical achievements produced by humanity's social life.[5] All the definitions have common elements: culture is learned, shared, and transmitted from one generation to the next. Culture is primarily passed on by parents to their children but is also conveyed by social organizations, special-interest groups, governments, schools, and religious institutions. Common ways of thinking and behaving that are developed are then reinforced through social pressure. Geert Hofstede calls this the "collective programming of the mind."[6] Culture is also multidimensional, consisting of a number of common elements that are interdependent. Changes occurring in one of the dimensions will affect the others as well.

For the purposes of this text, **culture** is defined as an integrated system of learned behaviour patterns that are distinguishing characteristics of the members of any given society. It includes everything that a group thinks, says, does, and makes—its customs, language, material artifacts, and shared systems of attitudes and feelings.[7] The definition therefore encompasses a wide variety of elements, from the materialistic to the spiritual. Culture is inherently conservative, resisting change and fostering continuity. Every person is **encultured** into a particular culture, learning the "right way" of doing things. Problems may arise when a person encultured in one culture has to adjust to another one. The process of **acculturation**, adjusting and adapting to a specific culture other than one's own, is one of the keys to success in international operations.

Edward T. Hall, who has conducted some of the most valuable studies on the effects of culture on business, makes a distinction between high and low context cultures.[8] In **high context cultures**, such as Japan and Saudi Arabia, context is at least as important as what is actually said. The speaker and the listener rely on a common understanding of the context. In **low context cultures**, however, most of the information is contained explicitly in the words. Canadians and Americans engage in low context communications (see Exhibit 3.1). Unless we are aware of this basic difference, messages and intentions can easily be misunderstood.

Hall's analysis has several important implications for the global marketer, from understanding and influencing consumer behaviour and conducting marketing research to negotiating contracts with foreign market intermediaries and conducting performance appraisals of host country staff. For example, the use of personal selling techniques in a high context culture such as Japan requires significant cultural literacy if the customer's true reaction to the product offering is to be accurately gauged. Japanese customers may not wish to articulate directly their true feelings about the product or the company's value proposition—especially when these perceptions are extremely negative. Similarly, conducting marketing research to support a new product launch will require that the researcher be able to "read between the lines," as respondents may not be forthright in expressing their concerns. An incorrect interpretation could lead the firm to make costly errors.

Likewise, negotiations with foreign suppliers, partners, and intermediaries may well prove to be difficult if context is ignored. Expectations of the relationship may not be expressed directly in a high context culture, and this may slow the pace of negotiations or lead to implementation problems if a deal is in fact reached. Problems may also surface in the area of performance appraisals. If performance appraisals of marketing personnel are to be centrally guided or conducted in a multinational corporation, those involved must be acutely aware of cultural nuances. One of the interesting differences is that the Canadian and U.S. systems emphasize the individual's development and accomplishments, whereas the Japanese system focuses on the group within which the individual works. In North America, criticism is more direct and is recorded formally, whereas in

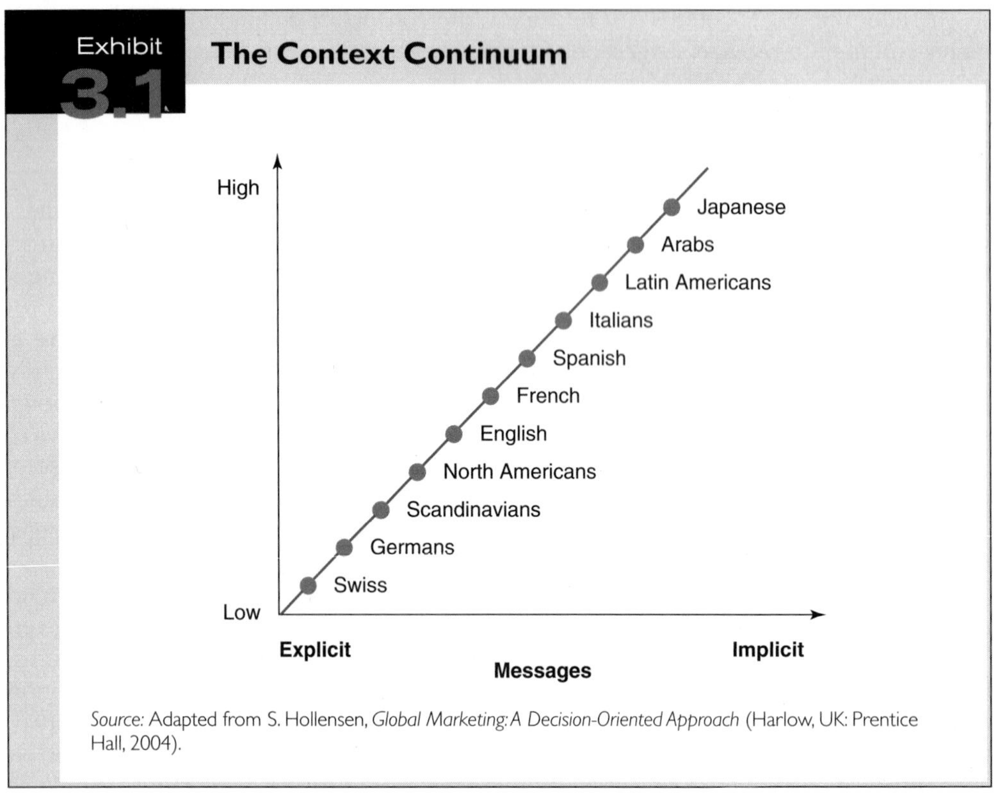

Source: Adapted from S. Hollensen, *Global Marketing: A Decision-Oriented Approach* (Harlow, UK: Prentice Hall, 2004).

Japan it is more subtle and verbal. Furthermore, what is not said can carry more meaning than what is actually said.

Few cultures today are as homogeneous as those of Japan and Saudi Arabia. Elsewhere, intra-cultural differences based on nationality, religion, race, or geographic areas have resulted in the emergence of distinct subcultures. The global marketing manager's task is to distinguish relevant cross-cultural and intra-cultural differences and then to isolate potential opportunities and problems. On the other hand, borrowing and interaction between national cultures will lead to greater understanding, which in turn may lead to the development of more effective global marketing strategies. In this context the global marketer is afforded the opportunity to act as a **change agent** by introducing new products, new ideas, or new practices, thereby influencing consumer preferences. Although this may consist of no more than shifting consumption from one product brand to another, it may lead to massive social change in the manner of consumption, the type of products consumed, and social organization. For better or worse, the global expansion of North American fast-food outlets has changed eating habits and the social context within which meals are shared with friends. This is especially true among younger people.

The example of Kentucky Fried Chicken (KFC) in India illustrates the need for cultural literacy and the difficulties marketers may have in entering culturally complex markets. Even though the company opened its outlets in two of India's most cosmopolitan cities (Bangalore and New Delhi), it found itself the target of protests by a wide range of opponents. KFC could have alleviated or eliminated some of the anti-Western passions by taking a series of preparatory steps. First, rather than opting for more direct control, KFC should have allied with local partners for advice and support. Second, KFC should have tried to appear more Indian rather than using high-profile advertising with Western ideas. Indians are quite ambivalent toward foreign culture, and ideas usable elsewhere do not always work well in India. Finally, KFC should have planned for reaction by competition that came from small restaurants with political clout at the local level.[9]

In some cases, the global marketer may be accused of "cultural imperialism," especially if the changes brought about are dramatic or if culture-specific adaptations in the marketing approach are not made. This has been a problem especially for many U.S. companies that have entered foreign markets. Particularly for countries such as Canada, with its prox-

Exhibit 3.2 McDonald's New Drive-thru in Beijing, China

AP Photo/Ng Han Guan

imity to the U.S., the issue of Americanization and cultural imperialism is a flashpoint for heated debate replete with calls for the protection of Canadian culture (see In More Detail 3.1). The Canadian federal government has spent millions of dollars to protect Canada's cultural sovereignty, with significant resources devoted to the Canadian Broadcasting Corporation (CBC) and the National Film Board.

In More Detail 3.1

WHAT IS CANADIAN CULTURE?

Canadian culture is a product of its history and geography. British, French, Aboriginal, and American influences have shaped what is now described as Canadian culture. The British conquest of Quebec in 1759 resulted in a significant French-speaking population coming under British rule. Later in the century, migration from Britain's 13 colonies in North America resulted in strong British and American influences in Canada. These 13 colonies would eventually proclaim their independence from Britain in 1776 and become the United States of America. Even before these migratory influences, however, Aboriginal peoples had inhabited the geographic region now called Canada for thousands of years, preserving and passing down their traditions from one generation to another. Aboriginal peoples have had contact with Europeans in Canada since A.D. 1000 and contributed significantly to the culture and economic development of the early European colonies. Aboriginal peoples have played a significant role in shaping Canada's unique cultural identity.

Most French-speaking Canadians reside in the province of Quebec. The Quebec Act of 1774 ensures that Francophone culture and language survives in a predominantly English-speaking Canada. Bilingualism, one of the foundations of Canadian culture, is mandated by federal laws and policies, although most Canadians are de facto unilingual. In fact only 18 percent of Canadians speak both French and English. Official bilingualism dates back to Canadian Confederation in 1867. Multiculturalism, another cornerstone of Canadian culture, is enshrined in the Canadian Charter of Rights and Freedoms. Multiculturalism, defined as an ideology that advocates equal status for cultural groups within a society, was first adopted by Canada as official policy and subsequently embraced by other English-speaking countries in the European Union. Tolerance of diverse cultures has come to define Canadian cultural identity.

Some observers view Canada as a country that consists of a number of regional, Aboriginal, and ethnic subcultures, while others see the country as consisting of a distinct French culture and a distinct English culture. Whichever perspective is taken, Canadians are viewed around the world as peacemakers, anti-imperialistic and strongly in favour of equity and multilateralism.

Sources: Wikipedia, Culture of Canada, **http://en.wikipedia.org/wiki/Canadian_culture** (accessed February 23, 2007); Wikipedia, Bilingualism in Canada, **http://en.wikipedia.org/wiki/Bilingualism_in_Canada** (accessed February 23, 2007); Wikipedia, Multiculturalism, **http://en.wikipedia.org/wiki/Multiculturalism** (accessed February 23, 2007).

Exhibit 3.3 **Fête Nationale du Québec**

Jean Heguy/First Light

The worst scenario for marketers is when they are accused of pushing Western behaviours and values—along with products and promotions—into other cultures, which can result in consumer boycotts and even destruction of property. McDonald's, KFC, Coca-Cola, Disney, and Pepsi, for example, have all drawn the ire of anti-American demonstrators for being icons of globalization.

Canada is at the forefront of the promotion of cultural diversity. This is not surprising given that Canada has been a major consumer of American culture for decades. According to Concordia University professor Mary Vipond, almost every Canadian city and town had a movie theatre by 1914 and almost 60 percent of the content consisted of American films. By the mid 1920s, Canadians were purchasing U.S. magazines and spending much of their leisure time listening to American radio stations. The spread of American culture to Canada

The Global MARKETPLACE 3.2

In Defence of Chinese Cultural Values?

Pirates of the Caribbean: Dead Man's Chest took in over $130 million in its opening weekend in North American cinemas. The film surpassed *Spider-Man,* the 2002 blockbuster, which grossed $115 million in its opening weekend. While the film has also sold out in several international markets, the Chinese government has reportedly banned its screening in China.

The ban resulted from the film's supernatural and other objectionable content, including ghosts, skulls, a vicious octopus, and portrayals of cannibalism. China routinely censors foreign films that may be viewed as compromising Chinese culture—films which offend Chinese aesthetics, values, and religious beliefs.

The ban has angered many people, both Chinese and Westerners. Some see the censorship as a defence of Chinese cultural values and an attempt to avoid negative Western influences. Others view the government's action as a blatant act of protectionism with little to do with protecting national culture.

Source: AP.

Exhibit 3.4 A Scene from Pirates of the Caribbean: Dead Man's Chest

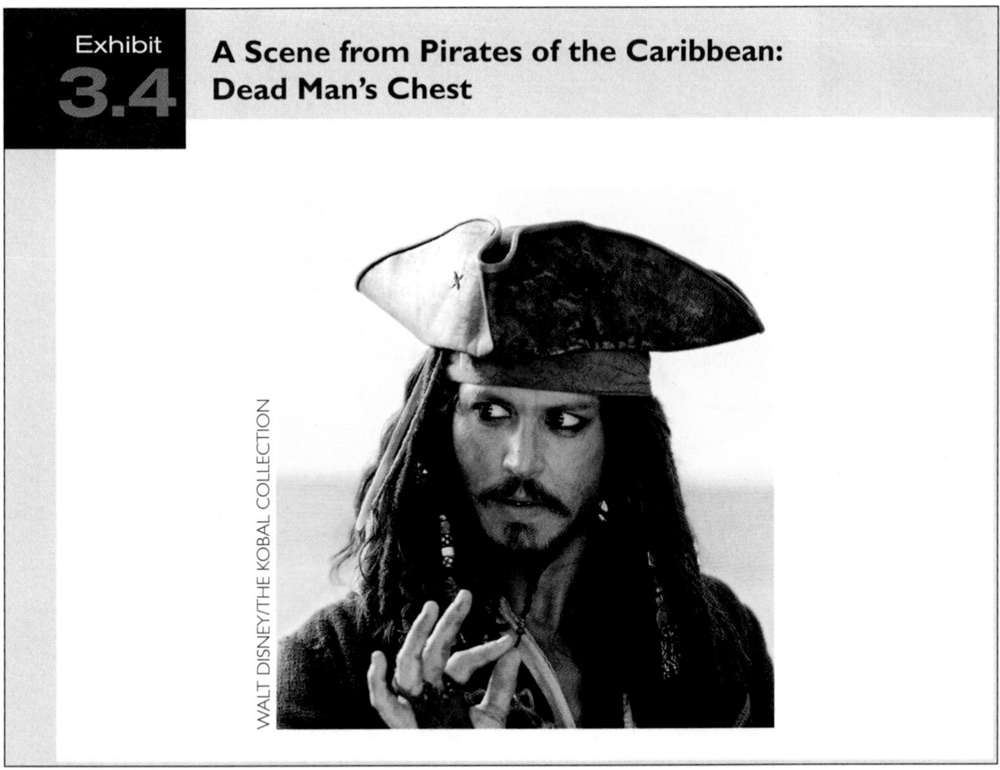
WALT DISNEY/THE KOBAL COLLECTION

is easily understood when one considers the countries' proximity and the proportion of English speakers in each. Canadians, however, value cultural diversity and have fought vigorously against U.S. cultural imperialism. In fact, Canada became the first nation to ratify the Convention on the Protection and Promotion of the Diversity of Cultural Expressions adopted by UNESCO in October, 2005.[10]

The Elements of Culture

Culture is a multi-dimensional construct. Exhibit 3.5 shows the elements that are traditionally[11] considered to comprise culture. The sensitivity and adaptation to these elements by an international firm depends on the firm's level of involvement in the market—for example, licensing versus direct investment—and the product or service marketed. Naturally, some products and services or management practices require very little adjustment, whereas others have to be adapted dramatically.

Language

Language has been described as the mirror of culture. Language itself is multidimensional by nature. This is true not only of the spoken word but also of what can be called the nonverbal language of international business. Messages are conveyed by the words used, by the way the words are spoken (for example, tone of voice), and by nonverbal means such as gestures, body position, and eye contact.

Very often, mastery of the language is required before a person is acculturated to a culture other than his or her own. Language mastery must go beyond technical competency, because every language has words and phrases that can be readily understood only in context. Such phrases are carriers of culture; they represent special ways a culture has developed to view some aspect of human existence.

Language capability serves four distinct roles in global marketing.[12] Language is important in information gathering and evaluation efforts. Rather than rely completely on the

Exhibit 3.5 **The Elements of Culture**

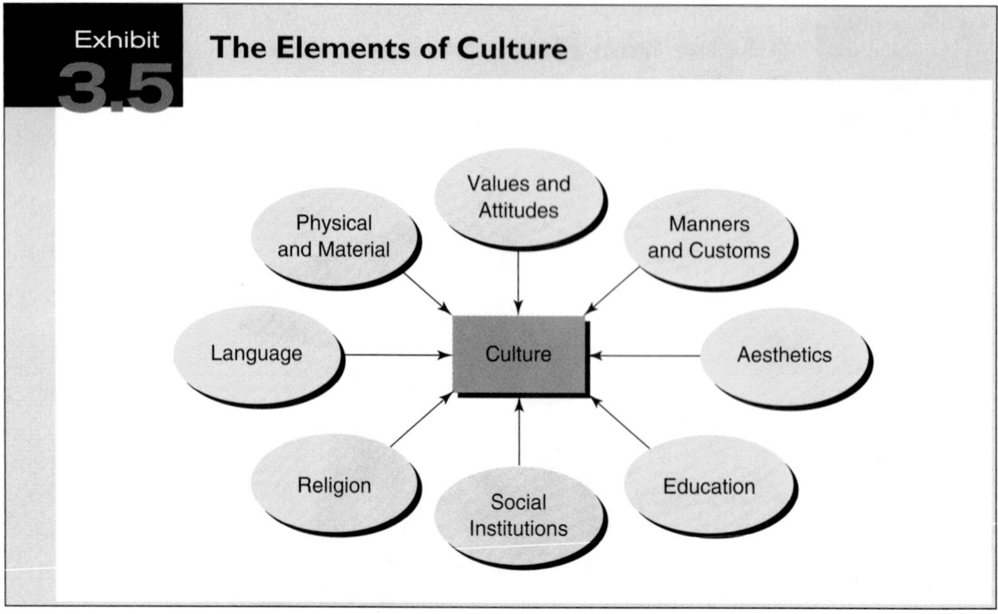

opinions of others, the manager is able to see and hear personally what is going on. People are far more comfortable speaking their own language, and this should be treated as an advantage. The best intelligence on a market is gathered by becoming part of the market rather than by observing it from the outside. For example, local managers of a multinational corporation should be the firm's primary source of political information to assess potential risk. Second, language provides access to local society. Although English may be widely spoken, and may even be the official company language, speaking the local language may make a dramatic difference. For example, firms that translate promotional materials and information are seen as being serious about doing business in the country. Third, language capability is increasingly important in company communications, whether within the corporate family or with channel members. Imagine the difficulties encountered by a country manager who must communicate with employees through an interpreter. Finally, language provides more than the ability to communicate; it extends beyond mechanics to the interpretation of contexts.

The manager's command of the national language(s) in a market must be greater than simple word recognition. Consider, for example, how dramatically different English terms can be when used in Canada, Australia, the United Kingdom, or the United States. In Australia the word "root," when used as a verb, is slang for having sex, whereas in Canada and the U.S. it has no such connotation. In negotiations, for U.S. delegates "tabling a proposal" means that they want to delay a decision, whereas their British counterparts understand the expression to mean that immediate action is to be taken. If the British promise something "by the end of the day," this does not mean within 24 hours, but rather when they have completed the job. Additionally, they may say that negotiations "bombed," meaning that they were a success; to a Canadian or U.S. manager, this could convey exactly the opposite message. Similar challenges occur with other languages and markets. Swedish is spoken as a mother tongue by 8 percent of the population in Finland, where it has idioms that are not well understood by Swedes. Goodyear has identified five different terms for the word "tires" in the Spanish-speaking Americas: *cauchos* in Venezuela, *cubiertas* in Argentina, *gomas* in Puerto Rico, *neumaticos* in Chile, and *llantas* in most of the other countries in the region.[13]

Difficulties with language usually arise through carelessness, which is manifested in a number of translation blunders. The old saying "If you want to kill a message, translate it," is true. A classic example involves GM and its "Body by Fisher" theme; when translated into Flemish, this became "Corpse by Fisher." There is also the danger of sound-alikes. For example, IBM's series 44 computers had a different number classification in Japan than in any other market because the Japanese word for four *(shih)* also sounds like the word for death. The danger of using a translingual homonym also exists; that is, an innocent English word may have a strong aural resemblance to a word not used in polite company in another country. Examples in French-speaking areas include Pet milk products and a toothpaste called Cue. A French firm trying to sell pâté to a Baltimore importer experienced a problem with the brand name Tartex, which sounded like a shoe polish. Kellogg renamed Bran Buds in Sweden, where the brand name translated roughly to "burned farmer." In some cases, adjustments may not have to be dramatic to work. For example, elevator marketer Kone wanted to ensure the correct pronunciation of its name, so it added an acute accent (Koné) to its name in French-speaking countries to avoid controversy.

An advertising campaign presented by Electrolux highlights the difficulties in transferring advertising campaigns between markets. Electrolux's theme in marketing its vacuum cleaners, "Nothing Sucks Like an Electrolux," is interpreted literally in the United Kingdom, but in Canada and the United States, the slang implications would interfere with the intended message. In a Lucky Goldstar ad, adaptation into Arabic was carried out without considering that Arabic reads from right to left. As a result, the creative concept in this execution was destroyed.

The role of language extends beyond that of a communications medium. Linguistic diversity often is an indicator of other types of diversity. In Quebec, the French language has always been a major consideration of most francophone governments because it is one of the clear manifestations of the identity of the province that separates it from the English-speaking provinces. The Charter of the French Language states that the rights of the francophone collectivity are, among others, the right of consumers to be informed and served in French. In trying to maintain their linguistic identity, the Quebec government has tried to ban the use of any foreign term or expression wherever an officially approved French equivalent exists (e.g., *la mercatique,* not *le brainstorming*).[14] This applies also to websites that bear the ".fr" designation; they have to be in the French language. Similarly, the Hong Kong government is promoting the use of Cantonese rather than English as the language of commerce.

Despite the fact that English is encountered daily by those on the Internet, the "e" in e-business does not mean "English." In a survey, European users highlighted the need to bridge the culture gap. One third of the senior managers said they will not tolerate English online, while less than 20 percent of the German middle managers and less than 50 percent of the French ones believe they can use English well. Fully three-quarters of those surveyed considered that being forced to use non-localized content on the Internet had a negative impact on productivity.[15] A truly global portal works only if online functions are provided in a multilingual and multicultural format.

Dealing with the language problem invariably requires the use of local assistance. A good local advertising agency and a good local market research firm can prevent many problems. When translation is required, as when communicating with suppliers or customers, care should be taken in selecting the translator or translation software. One of the simplest methods of control is **translation–back-translation**—the translating of a foreign language version back to the original language by a different person from the one who made the first translation. This approach may, however, only help to detect omissions and blunders. To assess the quality of the translation, a complete evaluation with testing of the message's impact is necessary.[16] In essence, this means that global marketers should never translate words but emotion, which then, in turn, may well lead to the use of completely different words.

Language also has to be understood in its historic context. In Germany, Nokia launched an advertising campaign for the interchangeable covers for its portable phones using the theme *Jedem das Seine* ("to each his own"). The campaign was withdrawn after the American Jewish Congress pointed out that the same slogan was found on the entry portal to Buchenwald, a Nazi-era concentration camp.[17] The Indian division of Cadbury Schweppes incensed Hindu society by running an advertisement comparing its Temptations chocolate to war-torn Kashmir. The ad carried the tag line, "I'm good. I'm tempting.

I'm too good to share. What am I? Cadbury's Temptations or Kashmir?" The ad featured a map of Kashmir to highlight the point, and it also first appeared on August 15th, Indian Independence Day.[18]

Nonverbal Language

Managers must analyze and become familiar with the hidden language of foreign cultures.[19] Five key topics—time, space, material possessions, friendship patterns, and business agreements—offer a starting point from which managers can begin to acquire the understanding necessary to do business in foreign countries. In many parts of the world, time is flexible and not seen as a limited commodity; people come late to appointments or may not come at all. In Hong Kong, for example, it is futile to set exact meeting times, because getting from one place to another may take minutes or hours depending on the traffic. Showing indignation or impatience at such behaviour would astonish an Arab, Latin American, Asian, or someone from the Caribbean.

In some countries, extended social acquaintance and the establishment of appropriate personal rapport are essential to conducting business. The feeling is that one should know one's business partner on a personal level before transactions can occur. Therefore, rushing straight to business will not be rewarded, because deals are made not only on the basis of the best product or price, but also on the entity or person deemed most trustworthy. Contracts may be bound on handshakes, not lengthy and complex agreements—a fact that makes some, especially Western, businesspeople uneasy.

Individuals vary in the amount of space they want separating them from others. Arabs and Latin Americans like to stand close to people they are talking with. If a Canadian executive, who may not be comfortable at such close range, backs away from an Arab, this might incorrectly be taken as a negative reaction. Also, Westerners are often taken aback by the more physical nature of affection between Slavs—for example, being kissed by a business partner, regardless of sex.

International body language must be included in the nonverbal language of international business. For example, a Canadian manager may, after successful completion of negotiations, impulsively give a finger-and-thumb "OK" sign. In southern France, the manager will have indicated that the sale is worthless, and in Japan, that a little bribe has been asked for; the gesture is grossly insulting to Brazilians. An interesting exercise is to compare and contrast the conversation styles of different nationalities. Northern Europeans are quite reserved in using their hands and maintain a good amount of personal space, whereas Southern Europeans involve their bodies to a far greater degree in making a point.

Religion

In most cultures, people find in religion a reason for being and legitimacy in the belief that they are part of a larger context. To define religion requires the inclusion of the supernatural and the existence of a higher power. Religion defines the ideals for life, which in turn are reflected in the values and attitudes of societies and individuals. Such values and attitudes shape the behaviour and practices of institutions and members of cultures.

Religion has an impact on global marketing that is seen in a culture's values and attitudes toward entrepreneurship, consumption, and social organization. The impact will vary depending on the strength of the dominant religious tenets. While religion's impact may be quite indirect in Protestant Northern Europe, its impact in countries where Islamic fundamentalism is on the rise (such as Algeria) may be profound.

Religion provides the basis for transcultural similarities under shared beliefs and behaviour. The impact of these similarities will be assessed in terms of the dominant religions of the world: Christianity, Islam, Hinduism, Buddhism, and Confucianism (see Exhibit 3.6). Other religions may have smaller numbers of followers, such as Judaism with 14 million followers around the world, but their impact is still significant due to the many centuries during which they have influenced world history. While some countries may

Exhibit 3.6 **Religions of the World: A Part of Culture**

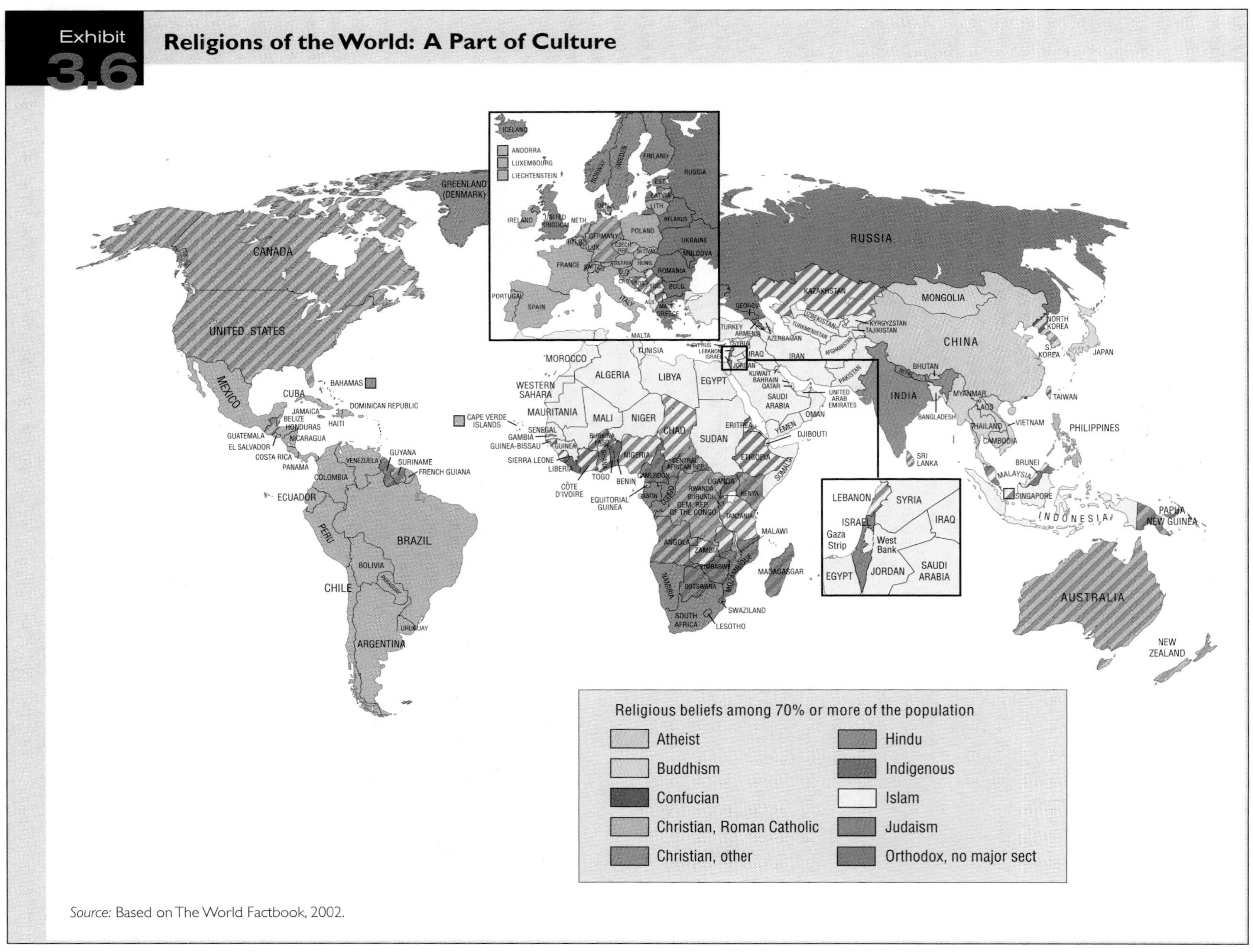

Source: Based on The World Factbook, 2002.

officially have secularism, such as Marxism-Leninism, as a state belief (for example, China, Vietnam, and Cuba), traditional religious beliefs still remain a powerful force in shaping behaviour. Global marketing managers must be aware of the differences not only among the major religions but also within them. The impact of these divisions may range from hostility, as in Sri Lanka, to barely perceptible but long-standing suspicion, as in many European countries where Protestant and Catholic are the main divisions. With some religions, such as Hinduism, people may be divided into groups that determine their status and to a large extent their ability to consume.

Christianity has the largest following among world religions, with more than 2 billion adherents. While there are many significant groups within Christianity, the major ones are Catholicism and Protestantism. A prominent difference between the two of them is their attitude toward making money. While Catholicism has questioned it, the Protestant ethic has emphasized the importance of work and the accumulation of wealth for the glory of God. At the same time, frugality is stressed, and the residual accumulation of wealth from hard work forms the foundation for investment. It has been proposed that this was the basis for the development of capitalism in the Western world and for the rise of predominantly Protestant countries to world economic leadership in the 20th century.

Major holidays are often tied to religion. Holidays will be observed differently from one culture to another, and the same holiday may have different connotations. Most Christian cultures observe Christmas and exchange gifts on either December 24 or 25. One exception is the Dutch, who exchange gifts on St. Nicholas Day, December 6. Tandy Corporation, in its first year in the Netherlands, targeted its major Christmas promotion for the third week of December with less than satisfactory results. The global marketing manager must see to it that local holidays are taken into account in the scheduling of events ranging from fact-finding missions to marketing programs.

Islam, which reaches from the west coast of Africa to the Philippines and across a wide band that includes Tanzania, central Asia, western China, India, and Malaysia, has more than 1.2 billion followers.[20] Islam is also a significant minority religion in many parts of the world, including Europe. It plays a pervasive role in the life of its followers, referred to as Muslims, through the sharia (law of Islam). This is most obvious in the five stated daily periods of prayer, fasting during the holy month of Ramadan, and the pilgrimage to Mecca, Islam's holy city. While Islam is supportive of entrepreneurship, it nevertheless strongly discourages acts that may be interpreted as exploitation. Islam also lacks discrimination, except for those outside the religion. Some have argued that Islam's basic fatalism (that is, nothing happens without the will of Allah) and traditionalism have deterred economic development in countries observing the religion.

The role of women in business is tied to religion, especially in the Middle East, where women are not able to function as they would in the West. The effects of this are numerous; for example, a firm may be limited in its use of female managers or personnel in these areas, and women's role as consumers and influencers in the consumption process may be different. Except for food purchases, men make the final purchase decisions.[21] Access to women in Islamic countries may only be possible through the use of female sales personnel, direct marketing, and women's specialty shops.[22]

Religion affects the marketing of products and service delivery. When beef or poultry is exported to an Islamic country, the animal must be killed in the halal method and certified appropriately. Recognition of religious restrictions on products (for example, alcoholic beverages) can reveal opportunities, as evidenced by successful launches of several nonalcoholic beverages in the Middle East. Other restrictions may call for innovative solutions. A challenge for the Swedish firm that had the primary responsibility for building a traffic system to Mecca was that non-Muslims are not allowed access to the city. The solution was to use closed-circuit television to supervise the work. Further, given that Islam considers interest payments usury, bankers and Muslim scholars have worked to create interest-free banking products that rely on lease agreements, mutual funds, and other methods to avoid paying interest.[23]

Hinduism has 860 million followers, mainly in India, Nepal, Malaysia, Guyana, Suriname, and Sri Lanka. In addition to being a religion, it is also a way of life predicated on the caste, or class, to which one is born. While the caste system has produced social stability, its impact on business can be quite negative. For example, if one cannot rise above one's caste, individual effort is hampered. Problems in work-force integration and coordination may become quite severe. Furthermore, the drive for business success may not be forthcoming because of the fact that followers place value mostly on spiritual rather than materialistic achievement.

The family is an important element in Hindu society, with extended families being the norm. The extended family structure will have an impact on the purchasing power and consumption of Hindu families. Market researchers, in particular, must take this into account in assessing market potential and consumption patterns.

Buddhism, which extends its influence throughout Asia from Sri Lanka to Japan, has 360 million followers. Although it evolved from Hinduism, it has no caste system. Life is seen as an existence of suffering, with achieving nirvana, a state marked by an absence of desire, as the solution to suffering. The emphasis in Buddhism is on spiritual achievement rather than worldly goods.

Confucianism has over 150 million followers throughout Asia, especially among the Chinese, and has been characterized as a code of conduct rather than a religion. However, its teachings that stress loyalty and relationships have been broadly adopted. Loyalty to central authority and placing the good of a group before that of the individual may explain the economic success of Japan, South Korea, Singapore, and the Republic of China. It also has led to cultural misunderstandings: in Western societies there has been a perception that the subordination of the individual to the common good has resulted in the sacrifice of human rights. The emphasis on relationships is very evident when developing business ties in Asia. The preparatory stage may take years before the needed level of understanding is reached and actual business transactions can take place.

Values and Attitudes

Values are shared beliefs or group norms that have been internalized by individuals.[24] Attitudes are evaluations of alternatives based on these values. The Japanese culture raises an almost invisible—yet often unscalable—wall against all *gaijin,* foreigners. Many middle-aged bureaucrats and company officials, for example, are **consumer ethnocentric**; that is, they feel that buying foreign products is unpatriotic, or even morally wrong. The resistance therefore is not so much against foreign products as it is against those who produce and market them. As a result, foreign-based corporations have had difficulty in hiring university graduates or mid-career personnel because of bias against foreign employers. Dealing in China and with the Chinese, the global marketing manager will have to realize that marketing has more to do with cooperation than competition. The Chinese believe that one should build the relationship first and, if that is successful, transactions will follow. The relationship, or *guanxi,* is a set of exchanges of favours to establish trust.[25]

The more rooted in central beliefs (such as religion) that values and attitudes are, the more cautiously the global marketing manager has to move. Attitude toward change is basically positive in industrialized countries, whereas in more tradition-bound societies, change is viewed with great suspicion, especially when it comes from a foreign entity. These situations call for thorough research, most likely a localized approach, and a major commitment at the top level for a considerable period of time. For example, Procter & Gamble has made impressive inroads with its products by adopting a long-term, Japanese-style view of profits. The company has gained some 20 percent of the detergent market and made Pampers a household word among Japanese mothers. The struggle toward such rewards can require foreign companies to take big losses for five years or more.

To counter the perceived negative influence of Mattel's Barbie and Ken dolls on Iranian values, a government agency affiliated with Iran's Ministry of Education is marketing its own Dara and Sara dolls. The new products, a brother and sister, are modeled on Iranian schoolbook characters. Sara is dressed in a white head scarf covering black or brown curls. A popular outfit is a full-length, flower-dotted chador, which covers the doll from

Exhibit 3.7 **Iranian Dolls Dara and Sara**

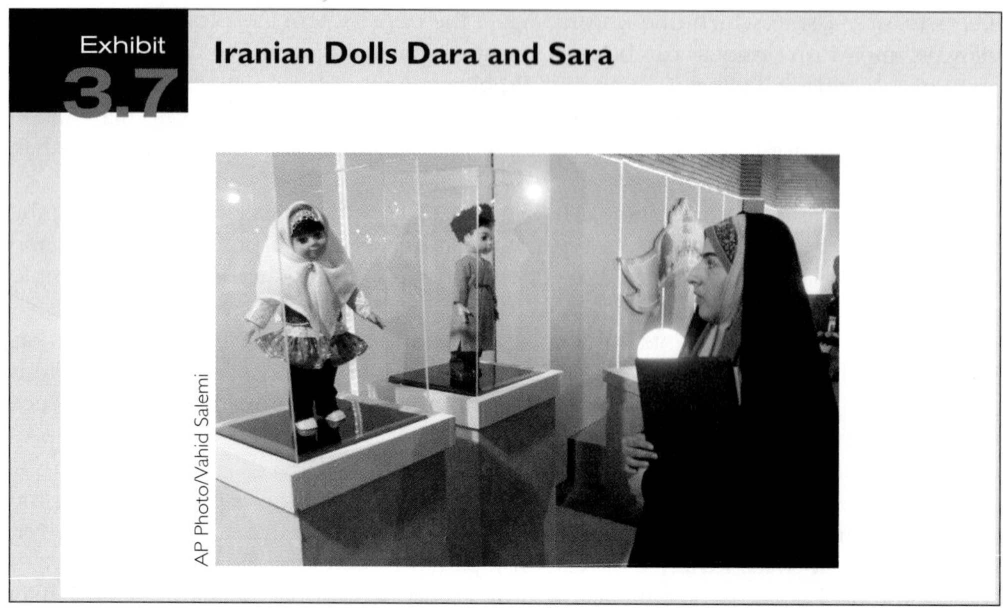

AP Photo/Vahid Salemi

head to toe. One toy seller explained that playing with Mattel's golden-haired, skimpily dressed Barbie may lead girls to grow up into women who reject Iranian values.[26]

Cultural attitudes are not always a deterrent to foreign business practices or foreign goods. Japanese youth, for instance, display extremely positive attitudes toward Western goods, from popular music to Nike sneakers to Louis Vuitton haute couture to Starbucks lattes. Even in Japan's recovering economy, global brands are able to charge premium prices if they are able to tap into cultural attitudes that revere imported goods. Similarly, attitudes of North American youth toward Japanese "cool" have increased the popularity of authentic Japanese *manga* (comics) and animated cartoons. Pokémon cards, Hello Kitty merchandise, and Sony's tiny MiniDisc players are examples of Japanese products that caught on in North America almost as quickly as in Japan.[27] It should be recognized, however, that while products that hit the right cultural buttons can be huge successes in foreign markets, not all top brands will translate easily from one culture to another. Some analysts, for example, have expressed concern that the Tim Hortons brand may not fare as well in the United States as it does in Canada.[28] While the company has been able to capitalize on the emotional appeal of the legendary Canadian hockey player in its home market, this may not resonate with mainstream Americans. The Disneyland concept worked well in Tokyo but has had a tougher time in Paris. One of the main reasons was that while the Japanese have positive attitudes toward American pop culture, the Europeans are quite content with their own cultural values and traditions.[29]

Manners and Customs

Changes occurring in manners and customs must be carefully monitored, especially in cases that seem to indicate narrowing of cultural differences between peoples. Understanding manners and customs is especially important in negotiations because interpretations based on one's own frame of reference may lead to a totally incorrect conclusion. To negotiate effectively abroad, one needs to read correctly all types of communication. North American executives often interpret inaction and silence as a negative sign, so Japanese executives tend to expect their North American counterparts to lower prices or sweeten the deal if they just say as little as possible. Even a simple agreement may take days to negotiate in the Middle East, because the Arab party may want to talk about unrelated issues or do something else for a while. There is a perception that Canadian executives are swayed by equity and fair play, and abrasive style of Russian negotiators and their usual last-minute requests for changes may cause astonishment and concern on the part of ill-prepared negotiators. Further, consider the reaction of a U.S. businessperson if a Finnish counterpart were to propose continuing negotiations in the sauna. Preparation is needed not only in the business sense but in a cultural sense as well. Some of the potential areas in which marketers may not be prepared include (1) insufficient understanding of different ways of thinking; (2) insufficient attention to the necessity of saving face; (3) insufficient knowledge and appreciation of the host country—history, culture, government, and image of foreigners; (4) insufficient recognition of the decision-making process and the role of personal relations and personalities; and (5) insufficient allocation of time for negotiations.[30]

One instance when preparation and sensitivity are called for is in the area of gift giving. Exhibit 3.8 provides examples of what to give and when. Gifts are an important part of relationship management during visits and a way of recognizing partners during holidays. Care should be taken with the way the gift is wrapped; for example, it should be in appropriately coloured paper. If delivered in person, the actual giving has to be executed correctly; in China, this is done by extending the gift to the recipient using both hands.[31]

Managers must be concerned with differences in the ways products are used. For example, General Foods' Tang is positioned as a breakfast drink in the United States; in France, where orange juice is not usually consumed at breakfast, Tang is positioned as a refreshment. The questions that the global marketer must ask are, "What are we selling?" "What are the use benefits we should be providing?" and "Who or what are we competing against?" Care should be taken not to assume cross-border similarities even if many of the indicators converge. For example, a jam producer noted that the Brazilian market seemed to hold significant potential because per capita jelly and jam consumption was one-tenth that of Argentina, clearly a difference not justified by obvious factors. However, Argentines consume jam at tea time, a custom that does not exist in Brazil. Furthermore, Argentina's climate and soil favour growing wheat, leading it to consume three times the amount of bread Brazil does.[32]

Many Western companies have stumbled in Japan because they did not learn enough about the distinctive habits of Japanese consumers. Purveyors of soup should know that the Japanese drink it mainly for breakfast. Johnson & Johnson had relatively little success selling baby powder in Japan until research was conducted on use conditions. In their small homes, mothers fear that the powder will fly around and get into their spotlessly clean kitchens. The company now sells baby powder in flat boxes with powder puffs so

Exhibit 3.8 Gifts: When and What to Give

China	India	Japan	Mexico	Saudi Arabia
Chinese New Year (January or February)	Hindu Diwali festival (October or November)	Oseibo (January 1)	Christmas/New Year (December/January)	Id al-Fitr (December or January)
✔ Modest gifts such as coffee-table books, ties, pens	✔ Sweets, nuts, and fruit; elephant carvings; candle holders	✔ Scotch, brandy, Americana, round fruit such as melons	✔ Desk clocks, fine pens, gold lighters	✔ Fine compasses to determine direction for prayer, cashmere
X Clocks, anything from Taiwan	X Leather objects, snake images	X Gifts that come in sets of four or nine	X Sterling silver items, logo gifts, food baskets	X Pork and pigskin, liquor

✔ recommended
X to be avoided

Source: Kate Murphy, "Gifts without Gaffes for Global Clients," *Business Week* (December 6, 1999), 153.

that mothers can apply it sparingly. Adults will not use it at all. They wash and rinse themselves before soaking in hot baths; powder would make them feel dirty again.

Package sizes and labels must be adapted in many countries to suit the needs of the particular culture. In Mexico, for example, Campbell's sells soup in cans large enough to serve four or five because families are generally large. In Britain, where consumers are more accustomed to ready-to-serve soups, Campbell's prints "one can makes two" on its condensed soup labels to ensure that shoppers understand how to use it.

In Canada, men buy diamond engagement rings for their fiancées. This custom is not global, however. In Germany, for example, young women tend to buy diamond rings for themselves. This precludes the use of global advertising campaigns by a company such as Birks.

Managers must be careful of myths and legends. One candy company was ready to launch a new peanut-packed chocolate bar in Japan, aimed at giving teenagers quick energy while they crammed for exams. The company then learned about a Japanese folk legend that eating chocolate with peanuts can cause nosebleed. The launch never took place. Approaches that might rarely be taken in Canada, the United States, or Europe could be recommended in other regions; for example, Conrad Hotels (the international arm of Hilton) experienced low initial occupancy rates at its Hong Kong facility until the firm brought in a feng shui advisor. These traditional consultants are used extensively by Hong Kong businesses for building location and interior design recommendations that will, it is hoped, create optimum harmony (and thus prosperity). In Conrad's case, the suggestion was to move a piece of sculpture outside of the hotel's lobby because one of the characters in the statue looked like it was trying to run out of the hotel.[33] Meticulous research plays a major role in avoiding these types of problems. Marketing research is discussed in Chapter 7.

Material Elements

Material culture results from technology and is directly related to the way a society organizes its economic activity. The level of material culture can be a segmentation variable if the degree of industrialization of the market is used as a basis. For companies selling industrial goods, this can provide a convenient starting point. In developing countries, demand may be highest for basic energy-generating products. In fully developed markets, timesaving home appliances may be more in demand.

While the level of material culture is often a good indicator of potential demand, goods sometimes discover unexpectedly rich markets due to the informal economy at work in developing nations. In Kenya, for example, where most of the country's 30 million people live on less than a dollar a day, more than 770,000 have signed up for mobile phone service during the last two years; wireless providers are scrambling to keep up with demand. Leapfrogging older technologies, mobile phones are especially attractive to Kenya's thousands of small-business entrepreneurs—market stall owners, taxi drivers, and even hustlers who sell on the sidewalks. For most, income goes unreported, creating an invisible wealth on the streets. Mobile phones outnumber fixed lines in Kenya, as well as in Uganda, Venezuela, Cambodia, South Korea, and Chile. This development is attractive for marketers as well, given the expense of laying land lines.

Technological advances have probably been the major cause of cultural change in many countries. For example, the increase in leisure time so characteristic in Western cultures has been a direct result of technological development. Increasingly, consumers are seeking more diverse products—including convenience items—as a way of satisfying their demand for a higher quality of life and more leisure time. For example, a 1999 Gallup survey in China found that 44 percent of the respondents were saving to buy electronic items and appliances, second only to saving for a rainy day.[34] Marketers able to tailor and market their products to fit the new lifestyle, especially in emerging markets, stand to reap the benefits. Consumers around the world are showing greater acceptance of equipment for personal use, reflected in increased sales of mobile phones and small computers as well as increased Internet use.

The Global MARKETPLACE 3.3

Soup: Now It's M'm-M'm-Global!

In the late 1990s, Campbell Soup Company aimed to generate half of its revenues outside the U.S. by the 21st century. This turned out to be an ambitious goal: its foreign sales were only a quarter of the total in 2000. Adding to the challenge is the fact that prepared food may be one of the toughest products to sell overseas. It is not as universal or as easily marketed as soap or soft drinks, given regional taste preferences. While an average Pole consumes five bowls of soup a week, 98 percent of Polish soups are homemade.

Campbell has managed to overcome some cultural obstacles in selected countries. In Poland, Campbell advertises to working mothers looking for convenience. Says Lee Andrews, Campbell's new-product manager in Warsaw, "We can't shove a can in their faces and replace Mom."

However, in many regions, Campbell is trying to cook more like her. This means creating new products that appeal to distinctly regional tastes. The approach has been to use test kitchens and taste-testing with consumers. Results have included fiery cream of poblano soup in Mexico as well as watercress and duck-gizzard soup for China. Cream of pumpkin has become Australia's top-selling canned soup.

Asia has traditionally accounted for only 2 percent of Campbell's worldwide sales, but the region—China, in particular—is being targeted as the area with the strongest growth potential. In new markets, Campbell typically launches a basic meat or chicken broth, which consumers can doctor with meats, vegetables, and spices. Later, more sophisticated soups are brought on line. In China, the real competition comes from homemade soup, which accounts for over 99 percent of all consumption. With this in mind, Campbell's prices have been kept at an attractive level and the product promoted on convenience.

Japan comes in at number two as a soup consumer (after the United States). Campbell teamed with Nakano Vinegar Co., Ltd., to learn the subtle ins and outs of marketing to the Japanese. For example, fish-based products were immediately added to the line. To cater better to local market needs, grassroots research plays a significant role. Campbell has a staff that eats in five restaurants every day. They order soup and then report as fully as possible on the taste, the spices used, and any ingredients they can identify. They describe appearance, texture, colour, consistency—even what garnishes are used. These mystery shoppers also interview people and browse store shelves to determine what is popular.

Local ingredients may count, but Campbell draws the line on some Asian favourites. Dog soup is out, as is shark's fin, since most species are endangered. For most other options, including snake, for example, the company keeps an open mind.

Campbell is also finding that ethnic foods are growing in popularity around the world. With its emphasis on vegetables, Asian cuisine benefits from a healthy image in Europe and North America. This means that some new products being presently developed for the Asian consumer may become global favourites in no time.

At the same time, the company has made a strategic shift, acknowledging that, outside the U.S., cultural preferences for dry soups are well entrenched. While Campbell is succeeding in developing canned soups for local tastes, its acquisition of dry soup makers like the Anglo-Dutch Unilever will help it become a truly global soup company.

Sources: "A Fine Kettle of Fish," *World Trade*, October 2001, 74–76; "Campbell Soup Creates a Stake in the European Market with Recent Acquisition," *The Philadelphia Inquirer*, January 30, 2001, A3; "Souping Up Campbell's," *Business Week*, November 3, 1997, 70–72; Linda Grant, "Stirring It Up at Campbell," *Fortune*, May 13, 1996, 80–86; "Ethnic Food Whets Appetites in Europe, Enticing Producers to Add Foreign Fare," *The Wall Street Journal*, November 1, 1993, B5A; "Hmmm, Could Use a Little More Snake," *Business Week*, March 15, 1993, 53; "Canned and Delivered," *Business China*, November 16, 1992, 12; and **http://www.campbellsoup.com.**

With technological advancement we have witnessed a significant degree of **cultural convergence**. Advances such as the Internet have spurred communication and the spread of Western—primarily U.S.—ideas. Young people from Hong Kong to Zambia wear T-shirts embossed with the names of their favourite NBA stars or hip-hop artists. This, however, does not suggest that these young people wish to do away with their own cultures and be Americans. There is little evidence that nation-states wish to move toward some type of generic, Western-dominated culture.[35] There is simultaneously convergence and divergence of national cultures as nations are exposed to Western influences but also seek to preserve their own cultures and identities.

Material culture—mainly the degree to which it exists and how much it is esteemed—will have an impact on marketing decisions. Many exporters do not understand the degree to which Canadian and U.S. consumers are package-conscious; for example, cans must be shiny and beautiful. On the other hand, packaging problems may arise in other countries due to lack of certain materials, different specifications when the material is available, different line-fill machinery, and immense differences in quality and consistency of printing ink, especially in South America and other parts of the Third World. Even the ability of media to reach target audiences will be affected by ownership of radios, television sets, and personal computers.

Aesthetics

Each culture makes a clear statement concerning good taste, as expressed in the arts and in the particular symbolism of colours, form, and music. What is and what is not acceptable may vary dramatically, even in otherwise highly similar markets. Sex in advertising is an example. In an apparent attempt to preserve the purity of Japanese womanhood, Japanese advertisers frequently turn to blonde, blue-eyed foreign models to make the point. In introducing the shower soap Fa from the European market to the North American market, Henkel also extended its European advertising campaign to the new market. The main difference was to have the young woman in the waves don a bathing suit rather than be portrayed naked, as in the German original.

Colour is often used as a mechanism for brand identification, feature reinforcement, and differentiation. In international markets, colours have more symbolic value than in domestic markets. Black, for instance, is considered the colour of mourning in Canada, the United States, and Europe, whereas white has the same symbolic value in Japan and most of the Far East. A British bank interested in expanding its operations to Singapore wanted to use blue and green as its identification colours. A consulting firm was quick to tell the client that green is associated with death there. Although the bank insisted on its original choice of colours, the green was changed to an acceptable shade.[36] Similarly, music used in broadcast advertisements is often adjusted to reflect regional differences.

Global firms have to take into consideration local tastes and concerns in designing their facilities. They may have a general policy of uniformity in building or office space design, but local tastes may often warrant modifications. Respecting local cultural traditions may also generate goodwill toward the global marketer. For example, McDonald's painstakingly renovated a seventeenth-century building for its third outlet in Moscow.

Education

Education, either formal or informal, plays a major role in the passing on and sharing of culture. Educational levels of a culture can be assessed using literacy rates and enrollment in secondary or higher education, information that is available from secondary data sources. International firms also need to know about the qualitative aspects of education, namely, varying emphases on particular skills, and the overall level of the education provided. Japan and the Republic of Korea, for example, emphasize the sciences, especially engineering, to a greater degree than do Western countries.

Educational levels will have an impact on various business functions. Training programs for a production facility will have to take the educational backgrounds of trainees into account. For example, a high level of illiteracy will suggest the use of visual aids rather than printed manuals. Local recruiting for sales jobs will be affected by the availability of suitably trained personnel. In some cases, global firms routinely send locally recruited personnel to headquarters for training.

The global marketing manager may also have to be prepared to fight obstacles in recruiting a suitable sales force or support personnel. For example, the Japanese culture places a premium on loyalty, and employees consider themselves to be members of the corporate family. If a foreign firm decides to leave Japan, employees may find themselves stranded mid-career, unable to find a place in the Japanese business system. University graduates are therefore reluctant to join all but the largest and most well known of foreign firms.[37]

If technology is marketed, the level of sophistication of the product will depend on the educational level of future users. Product adaptation decisions are often influenced by the extent to which targeted customers are able to use the product or service properly.

Social Institutions

Social institutions affect the ways in which people relate to each other. The family unit, which in Western industrialized countries consists of parents and children, in a number of cultures is extended to include grandparents and other relatives. This will have an impact on consumption patterns and must be taken into account, for example, when conducting market research. The concept of kinship, or blood relations between individuals, is defined in a very broad way in societies such as those in sub-Saharan Africa. Family relations and a strong obligation to family are important factors to be considered in human resource management in those regions. Understanding tribal politics in countries such as Nigeria may help the manager avoid unnecessary complications in executing business transactions.

The division of a particular population into classes is termed **social stratification**. Stratification ranges from the situation in Northern Europe, where most people are members of the middle class, to highly stratified societies such as India, in which the higher strata control most of the buying power and decision-making positions.

An important part of the socialization process of consumers worldwide is **reference groups**. These groups provide the values and attitudes that become influential in shaping behaviour. Primary reference groups include the family, coworkers, and other intimate groupings, whereas secondary groups are social organizations in which less-continuous interaction takes place, such as professional associations and trade organizations. Besides socialization, reference groups develop an individual's concept of self, which manifests itself, for example, through the use of products. Reference groups also provide a baseline for compliance with group norms through either conforming to or avoiding certain behaviours.

Social organization also determines the roles of managers and subordinates and the way they relate to one another. In some cultures, managers and subordinates are separated explicitly and implicitly by various boundaries ranging from social class differences to separate office facilities. In others, cooperation is elicited through equality. The fitting of an organizational culture for internal marketing purposes to the larger context of a national culture has to be executed with care. Changes that are too dramatic may cause disruption of productivity or, at the minimum, suspicion.

While Western business practice has developed impersonal structures for channelling power and influence through reliance on laws and contracts, the Chinese emphasize getting on the good side of someone and storing up political capital with him or her. Things can get done without this capital, or *guanxi,* only if one invests enormous personal energy, is willing to offend even trusted associates, and is prepared to see it all melt away at a moment's notice.[38] For the Chinese, contracts form a useful agenda and a symbol of progress, but obligations come from relationships. McDonald's found this out in Beijing, where it was evicted from a central building after only 2 years despite having a 20-year contract. The incomer had a strong *guanxi,* whereas McDonald's had not kept its relationships in good repair.[39]

Cultural Literacy and Ethnocentricity

To be effective, global marketing managers need to develop cultural literacy. Ethnocentricity or the belief that one's culture is superior to that of others must be resisted. Cultural literacy will allow the manager to better understand the motivations and actions of consumers, foreign market intermediaries, and government officials—insights that would facilitate adaptation and commercial success. If managers approach international markets with the attitude of "That's how we do it back home, therefore it must also be good enough for these people," the results are likely to be disastrous. How then is cultural literacy developed?

Sources of Cultural Knowledge

The concept of cultural knowledge is broad and multifaceted. **Cultural knowledge** can be defined by the way it is acquired. Objective or **factual information** is obtained from others through communication, research, and education. **Experiential knowledge**, on the other hand, can be acquired only by being involved in a culture other than one's own.[40] A summary of the types of knowledge needed by the global marketing manager is provided in Exhibit 3.9. Both factual and experiential information can be general or country-specific. In fact, the more a manager becomes involved in the international arena, the more he or she is able to develop a metaknowledge, that is, ground rules that apply to a great extent whether in Kuala Lumpur, Malaysia, or Asunción, Paraguay. Market-specific knowledge does not necessarily travel well; the general variables on which the information is based do.

In a survey on how to acquire international expertise, managers ranked eight factors in terms of their importance, as shown in Exhibit 3.10. These managers emphasized the experiential acquisition of knowledge. Written materials were indicated to play an important but supplementary role, very often providing general or country-specific information before operational decisions must be made. Interestingly, many of today's international managers have pre-career experience in government, the armed forces, or missionary service. Although the survey emphasized travel, a one-time trip to London with a stay at a large hotel and scheduled sightseeing tours does not contribute to cultural knowledge in a significant way. Travel that involves meetings with company personnel, intermediaries, facilitating agents, customers, and government officials, on the other hand, does contribute.

From the corporate point of view, the development of a global capability requires experience acquisition in more involved ways. This translates into foreign assignments and networking across borders, for instance, through the use of multi-country, multicultural teams to develop strategies and programs. At Nestlé, for example, managers are shuffled around a region (such as Asia or Latin America) at four- to five-year intervals and may have tours at headquarters for two to three years between such assignments. This allows these managers to pick up ideas and tools to be used in markets where they have

Exhibit 3.9 Types of International Information

Source of Information	Type of Information: General	Type of Information: Country-Specific
Objective	Examples: • Impact of GDP • Regional integration	Examples: • Tariff barriers • Government regulations
Experiential	Example: • Corporate adjustment to internationalization	Examples: • Product acceptance • Program appropriateness

Exhibit 3.10

Managers' Rankings of Factors Involved in Acquiring International Expertise

Factor	Considered Critical	Considered Important
1. Assignments overseas	85%	9%
2. Business travel	83	17
3. Training programs	28	57
4. Non-business travel	28	54
5. Reading	22	72
6. Graduate courses	13	52
7. Pre-career activities	9	50
8. Undergraduate courses	0.5	48

Source: Data collected by authors from 110 executives by questionnaire, February 2003. Original study by Stephen J. Kobrin, *International Expertise in American Business* (New York: Institute of International Education, 1984), 38.

not been used or where they have not been necessary up to now. In Thailand, where supermarkets are revolutionizing consumer-goods marketing, techniques perfected elsewhere in the Nestlé system are being put to effective use. These experiences will then, in turn, be used to develop newly emerging markets in the same region, such as Vietnam.

Facilitators who specialize in advising clients on the cultural dimensions of marketing are available as well. Their task is not only to avoid cultural mistakes but also to add culture as an ingredient of success in the program. Blunders that could have been avoided with factual information about a foreign market are generally inexcusable. A manager who travels to Taipei without first obtaining a visa and is therefore turned back has no one else to blame. Other oversights may lead to more costly mistakes.

International business success requires not only comprehensive fact finding and preparation, but also an ability to understand and fully appreciate the nuances of different cultural traits and patterns. Gaining this **interpretive knowledge** requires "getting one's feet wet" over a sufficient length of time.

Cross-Cultural Training

The increase in overall international activity of firms has increased the need for cultural sensitivity training at all levels of the organization. Today's training must take into consideration not only outsiders to the firm but interaction within the corporate family as well. However inconsequential the degree of interaction may seem, it can still cause problems if proper understanding is lacking. Consider, for example, the date 11/12/03 on a message; a European will interpret this as the 11th of December, but in the United States it is the 12th of November.

Some companies try to avoid the training problem by hiring only nationals or well-travelled executives for their international operations. This makes sense for the management of overseas operations but will not solve the training need, especially if transfers to a culture unfamiliar to the manager are likely. International experience may not necessarily transfer from one market to another.

To foster cultural sensitivity and acceptance of new ways of doing things within the organization, management must institute internal education programs. These programs may include (1) culture-specific information (e.g., data covering other countries, such as videopacks and CultureGrams), (2) cultural general information (e.g., values, practices, and assumptions of countries other than one's own), and (3) self-specific information (e.g., identifying one's own cultural paradigm, including values, assumptions, and perceptions about others).[41] In addition, many companies use mentoring, whereby an individual is assigned to someone who is experienced and who will spend the required time squiring and explaining. Talks given by returnees and by visiting lecturers hired specifically for the task round out the formal part of training.[42]

The objective of formal training programs is to foster the four critical characteristics of preparedness, sensitivity, patience, and flexibility in managers and other personnel. These programs vary dramatically in terms of their rigour, involvement, and, of course, cost.[43] In the 1990s, Korean firms embarked on a mission of *segyehwa*, or globalization, which meant preparing the managers and employees who would be in charge of implementing the program. At Kumho Group, the chairman required all airline and tire-maker employees to spend an hour each morning studying a language or learning about foreign cultures. Cards taped up in bathrooms taught a new phrase in English or Japanese each day.

Environmental briefings and cultural orientation programs are types of **area studies** programs. These programs provide factual preparation for a manager to operate in, or work with people from, a particular country. Area studies should be a basic prerequisite for other types of training programs. Alone, they serve little practical purpose because they do not really get the manager's feet wet. Other, more involved programs contribute the context in which to put facts so that they can be properly understood.

When time is available, managers can be trained extensively in language. This may be required if an exotic language is involved. **Sensitivity training** focuses on enhancing a manager's flexibility in situations that are quite different from those at home. The approach is based on the assumption that understanding and accepting oneself is critical to understanding a person from another culture.

Finally, training may involve **field experience**, which exposes a manager to a different cultural environment for a limited amount of time. Although the expense of placing and maintaining an expatriate is high (and, therefore, the cost of failure is high), field experience is rarely used in training. One field experience technique that has been suggested when the training process needs to be rigorous is the host-family surrogate. This technique places a trainee (and possibly his or her family) in a domestically located family of the nationality to which they are assigned.[44]

Regardless of the degree of training, preparation, and positive personal characteristics, a manager will always remain foreign. A manager should never rely on his or her own judgment when local managers can be consulted. In many instances, a manager should have an interpreter present at negotiations, especially if the manager is not completely bilingual. Overconfidence in one's language capabilities can create problems.

Cultural Analysis

How can the global marketing manager better understand and explain differences in culture? It has been argued by Hofstede that differences in culture can be accounted for by four major dimensions of culture.[45] Hofstede's work was motivated by the need to understand why motivational concepts worked well in some societies but not in others. Hofstede based his analysis on a comprehensive survey of IBM employees in over 70 countries from 1967 to 1973. Data from over 100,000 questionnaires were used in the analysis. Hofstede's dimensions consist of the following:

1. *Individualism.* This dimension reflects the extent to which people in the society are focused on individual achievement as opposed to that of the group. In highly individualistic societies, individuals learn to act for themselves and are not oriented to working as part of a group. In less individualistic or more collectivist societies, the achievement of the group is emphasized and individual initiative and decision making is downplayed.
2. *Power distance.* Power distance reflects the extent to which people accept inequality in society. In societies with a high degree of power distance, significant differences in wealth and education are accepted more readily. In low power distance societies, power is more widely distributed among citizens and wealth is more equitably shared. In such societies individuals will expect to be given more of a say in an organization's decision making and to participate fully in its profits.

3. *Uncertainty avoidance.* This dimension reflects the extent to which individuals in the society expect to be guided by formal rules and regulations. High uncertainty avoidance will tend to exist in societies that have a low tolerance for risk taking and entrepreneurship. Individuals in these societies seek out plans, policies, and regulations to guide and justify their actions. They are less likely to engage in actions where the payoff and the consequences are unknown.
4. *Masculinity.* This dimension reflects the extent to which the society is focused on achievement, success, performance, and competition ("masculine" values) as opposed to a focus on developing and maintaining caring, nurturing relationships ("feminine" values).

Hofstede subsequently added a fifth dimension, "time," to distinguish cultural differences. This dimension reflects a society's long-term versus short-term orientation.[46] All the high-scoring countries, reflective of a long-term orientation, are Asian (e.g., China, Hong Kong, Taiwan, Japan, and South Korea), while most Western countries (such as the United States and Britain) have low scores, indicative of a short-term focus. Some have argued that this cultural dimension may explain the Japanese marketing success based on market-share (rather than short-term profit) motivation in market development.

Exhibits 3.11 and 3.12 present a summary of where Canada and several other countries fall on the power distance and individualism scales (Exhibit 3.11) and the uncertainty

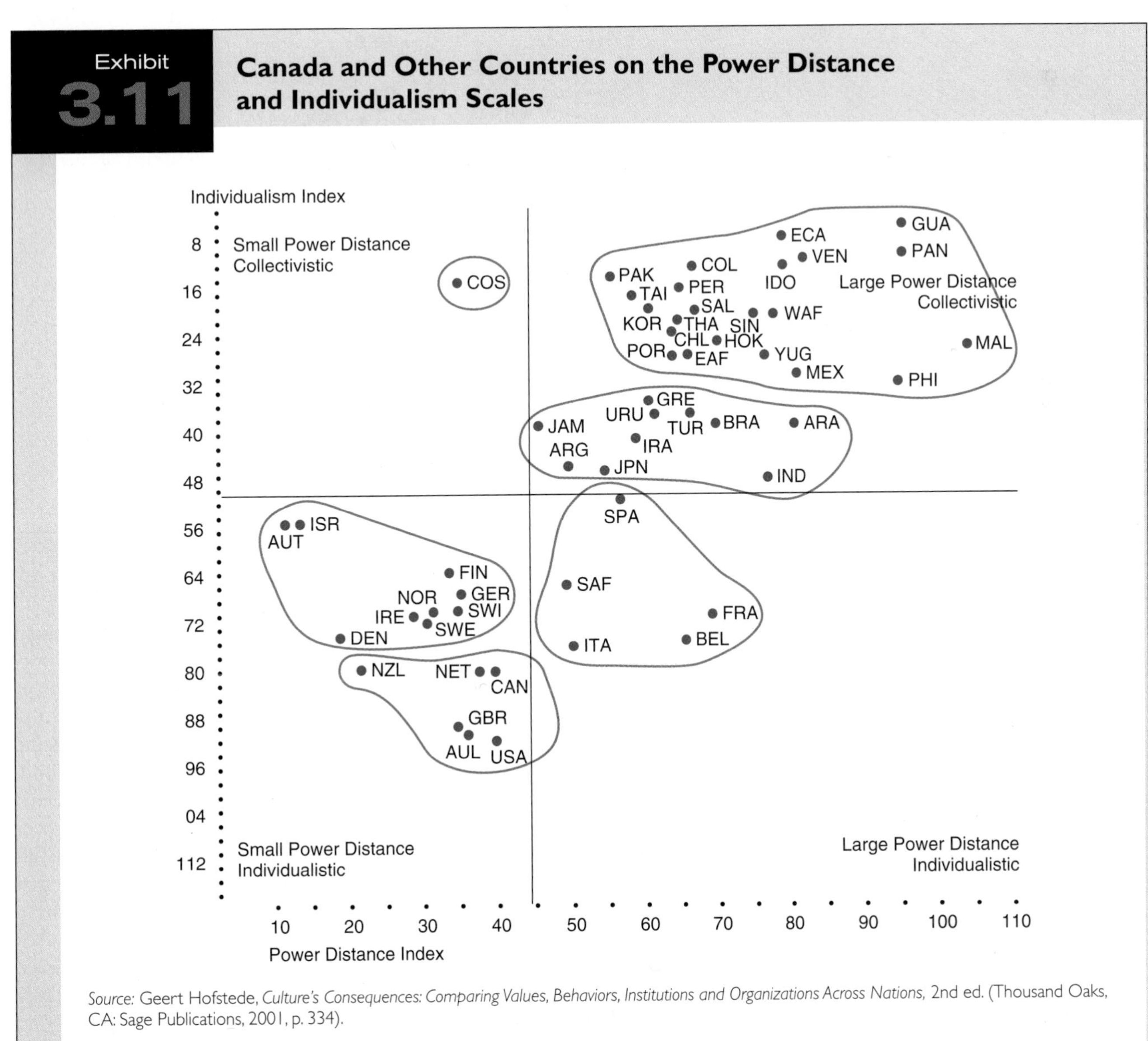

Exhibit 3.11 Canada and Other Countries on the Power Distance and Individualism Scales

Source: Geert Hofstede, *Culture's Consequences: Comparing Values, Behaviors, Institutions and Organizations Across Nations,* 2nd ed. (Thousand Oaks, CA: Sage Publications, 2001, p. 334).

Canada and Other Countries on the Uncertainty, Avoidance, and Masculinity Scales

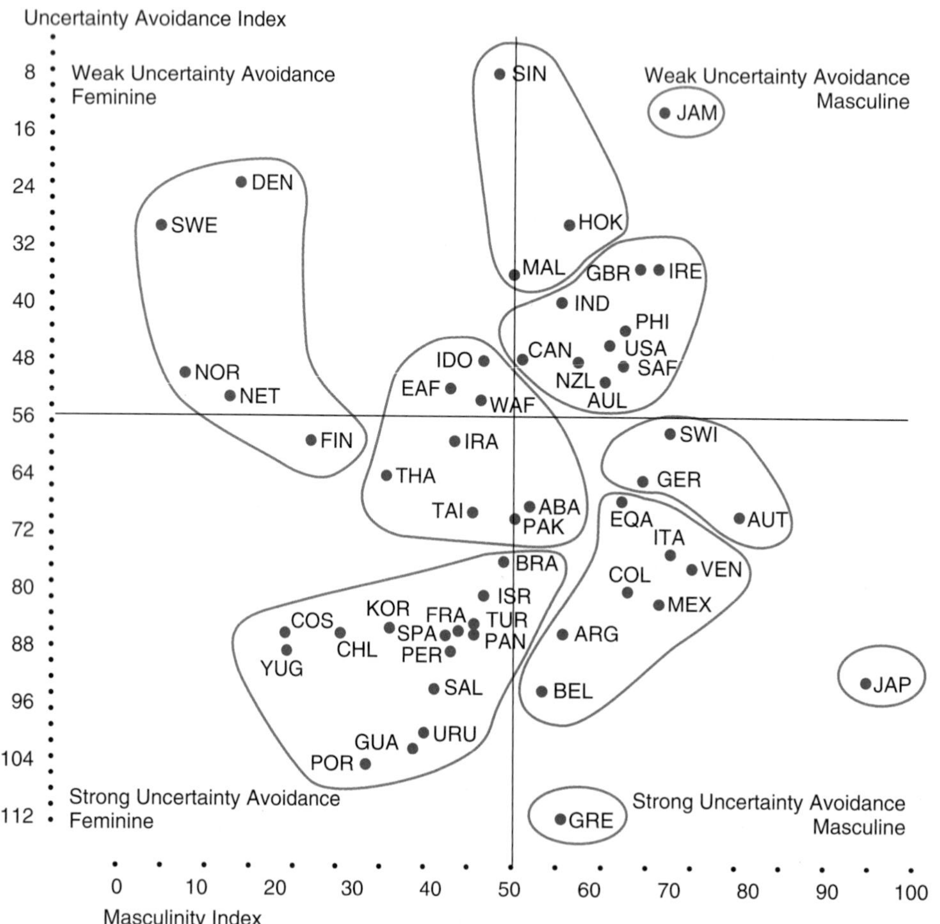

Source: Geert Hofstede, *Culture's Consequences: Comparing Values, Behaviors, Institutions and Organizations Across Nations,* 2nd ed. (Thousand Oaks, CA: Sage Publications, 2001, p. 334).

avoidance and masculinity scales (Exhibit 3.12). The cultural similarity between Canada, the United States, and Great Britain is clearly evident.

Knowledge of a target market's position on these dimensions will help the marketer design a strategy for optimal results. Marketers want to elicit a specific, common, and favourable response from their target markets. Cultural analysis can also provide specific guidelines for marketing-mix development. Since countries such as Canada, New Zealand, the United Kingdom, and the United States highly regard individualism, promotional appeals should be relevant to the individual. Also, in order to incorporate the lower power distance within the market, copy should be informal and friendly.[47] In opposite situations such as Pakistan and Taiwan, marketing communications have to emphasize that the new product is socially accepted. However, if the product is imported, it can sometimes utilize global or foreign cultural positioning. For example, individualism is often used for imported products but almost never for domestic ones.[48] Similarly, channel choice is affected by cultural factors. Firms in societies emphasizing individualism are more likely to choose channel partners based on objective criteria, whereas firms at the opposite end would prefer to deal with other firms whose representatives they consider to be friends.[49]

When negotiating in Germany, one can expect a counterpart who is thorough, systematic, very well prepared, but also rather dogmatic and therefore lacking in flexibility and compromise. Great emphasis is placed on efficiency. In Mexico, however, the counterpart may prefer to address problems on a personal and private basis rather than on a business level. This means more emphasis on socializing and conveying one's humanity, sincerity, loyalty, and friendship. Also, the differences in pace and business practices of the region have to be accepted. Boeing found in its annual study on world aviation safety that countries with both low individualism and substantial power distances had accident rates 2.6 times greater than at the other end of the scale. These findings will naturally have an impact on training and service operations of airlines.

Communication about the innovation takes place through the physical product itself (samples) or through a new policy in the company. If a new practice, such as quality circles or pan-regional planning, is in question, results may be communicated in reports or through word of mouth by the participating employees. Communication content depends on the following factors: the product's or policy's relative advantage over existing alternatives; compatibility with established behavioural patterns; complexity, or the degree to which the product or process is perceived as difficult to understand and use; trialability, or the degree to which it may be experimented with and not incur major risk; and observability, which is the extent to which the consequences of the innovation are visible.

Before the product or policy is evaluated, information about it will be compared with existing beliefs about the circumstances surrounding the situation. Distortion will occur as a result of selective attention, exposure, and retention. As examples, anything foreign may be seen in a negative light, another multinational company's efforts may have failed, or the government may implicitly discourage the proposed activity. Additional information may then be sought from any of the input sources or from opinion leaders in the market.

Adoption tendency refers to the likelihood that the product or process will be accepted. Examples of this are advertising in the People's Republic of China and equity joint ventures with Western participants in Russia, both unheard of a few years ago. If an innovation clears the hurdles, it may be adopted and slowly diffused into the entire market. A global marketing manager has two basic choices: adapt company offerings and methods to those in the market or try to change market conditions to fit company programs. In Japan, a number of Western companies have run into obstructions in the Japanese distribution system, where great value is placed on established relationships; everything is done on the basis of favouring the familiar and fearing the unfamiliar. In most cases, this problem is solved by joint venturing with a major Japanese entity that has established contacts. On occasion, when the company's approach is compatible with the central beliefs of a culture,

In More Detail 3.2

ALTERNATIVE MODELS OF CULTURAL ANALYSIS

In addition to Hofstede's framework, the global manager may use alternative models to explain cultural differences.

Kluckhohn-Strodtbeck (KS) Framework The KS framework examines cultural differences from the standpoint of whether people in the society believe that they are in control of their environment; whether they are future oriented or focused on the past; whether they can be trusted to act freely and responsibly; whether the society is more interested in material well-being as opposed to the attainment of spiritual goals; whether people believe that we are collectively responsible for each other's welfare; and whether people prefer to conduct their affairs in private or in public.

Gannon's Metaphors Gannon argued that cultures can be described by a single descriptive metaphor that encapsulates a holistic mental image of how people from that culture think and behave. German culture may be characterized by the classical symphony—the embodiment of precision, coordination, and individual skill. American football can be used to characterize U.S. culture, given its emphasis on competition, the desire for individual glory, and strong leaders calling and directing the team's strategy. Although these metaphors are simplistic generalizations, they may assist global marketing managers in orienting their thinking.

the company may be able to change existing customs rather than adjust to them. Initially, Procter & Gamble's traditional hard-selling style in television commercials jolted most Japanese viewers, who were accustomed to more subtle approaches. Now the ads are being imitated by Japanese competitors. However, this should not be interpreted to mean that Japanese advertising will necessarily adapt to the influence of Western approaches. The emphasis in Japan is still on who speaks rather than on what is spoken. That is why, for example, Japan is a market where Procter & Gamble's company name is presented along with the brand name of the product in the marketing communication for a brand, rather than using only the product's brand name, which is the customary treatment in the North American and European markets.[50]

Adjusting to cultural differences requires putting one's own cultural values aside. James E. Lee proposes that the natural **self-reference criterion**—the unconscious reference to one's own cultural values—is the root of most international business problems.[51] However, recognizing and admitting this are often quite difficult. The following analytical approach is recommended to reduce the influence of one's own cultural values:

1. Define the problem or goal in terms of domestic cultural traits, habits, or norms.
2. Define the problem or goal in terms of foreign cultural traits, habits, or norms. Make no value judgments.
3. Isolate the self-reference criterion influence in the problem and examine it carefully to see how it complicates the problem.
4. Re-define the problem without the self-reference criterion influence and solve for the optimal goal situation.

This approach can be applied to product introduction. If Maple Leaf Foods wants to introduce bacon into markets where breakfast is traditionally not eaten, managers must consider very carefully how to instill this new behaviour.

Analytical procedures require constant monitoring of changes caused by outside events as well as the changes caused by the business entity itself. Controlling ethnocentricism can be achieved only by acknowledging it and properly adjusting to its possible effects in managerial decision making. The international manager needs to be prepared and able to put that preparedness to effective use.[52]

Cultural Rules for Success In Global Marketing

Culture should not be viewed as a challenge but as an opportunity that can be exploited. As has been shown in this chapter, this requires an understanding of the differences and their fundamental determinants. Differences can quite easily be dismissed as indicators of inferiority or approaches to be changed; however, the opposite may actually be the case. Best practice knows no one particular origin, nor should it acknowledge boundaries. The following rules serve as a summary of how culture and its appreciation may provide a tool to ensure marketing success.

- *Embrace local culture.* Many corporate credos include a promise to be the best possible corporate citizens in every community where they operate. For example, in 3M's plant near Bangkok, Thailand, a Buddhist shrine, wreathed in flowers, pays homage to the spirits that Thais believe took care of the land prior to the plant's arrival. Showing sensitivity to local customs helps local acceptance and builds employee morale. It also contributes to a deeper understanding of the market and keeps the marketer from inadvertently doing something to alienate constituents.
- *Build relationships.* Each market has its own unique set of constituents who need to be identified and nurtured. Establishing and nurturing local ties at the various stages of the market-development cycle develop relationships that can be invaluable in expansion and countering political risk. 3M started its preparations for entering the China market soon after President Nixon's historic visit in 1972. For 10 years, company officials visited Beijing and entertained visits of Chinese officials to company headquarters in Minneapolis-St. Paul.

Such efforts paid off in 1984, when the Chinese government made 3M the first wholly owned venture in the market. Many such emerging markets require long-term commitment on the part of the marketer.

- *Employ locals to gain cultural knowledge.* The single best way to understand a market is to grow with it by developing human resources and business partnerships along the way. Of the 7,500 3M employees in Asia, few are from North America. As a matter of fact, of the 34,000 3M employees outside of North America, fewer than 1 percent are expatriates. The rest are locals who know local customs and the purchasing habits of their compatriots. In every way possible, locals are made equals with their North American counterparts. For example, grants are made available for 3M employees to engage in the product-development process with concept and idea development.
- *Help employees understand you.* Employing locals will give a marketer a valuable asset in market development, that is, in acculturation. However, these employees also need their own process of adjustment (i.e., "corporatization") to be effective. At any given time, some of 3M's Asian technicians are in the United States, where they learn the latest product and process advances while gaining insight into how the company works. Also, they are able to develop personal ties with people who may work with them. Furthermore, they often contribute by infusing their insights into company plans. Similar schemes are in place for distributors. Distributor advisory councils allow intermediaries to share their views with the company.
- *Adapt products and processes to local markets.* Nowhere is commitment to local markets as evident as in its product offering. Global, regional, and purely local products are called for, and constant and consistent product-development efforts on a market-by-market basis are warranted to find the next global success. When Asian sales of 3M's famous Scotch-Brite cleaning pads were languishing, company researchers interviewed housewives and domestic help to determine why. They found that, traditionally, floors are scrubbed with the help of the rough shells of coconuts. 3M responded by making its cleaning pads brown and shaping them like a foot. In China, a big seller for 3M is a composite to fill tooth cavities. In North America, dentists pack a soft material into the cavity and blast it with a special beam of light, making it as hard as enamel in a matter of seconds. In China, dentists cannot afford this technology. The solution was an air-drying composite that hardens in a matter of minutes, but at a reasonable expense to the dental customer.
- *Coordinate by region.* The transfer of best practice is critical, especially in areas that have cultural similarities. When 3M designers in Singapore discovered that customers used its Nomad household mats in their cars, they spread the word to their counterparts throughout Asia. The company encourages its product managers from different parts of Asia to hold regular periodic meetings and share insights and strategies. The goal of this cross-pollination is to come up with regional programs and "Asianize," or even globalize, a product more quickly. Joint endeavours build cross-border esprit de corps, especially when managers may have their own markets' interests primarily at heart.[53]

Summary

Culture is one of the most challenging uncontrollable elements of the global marketplace. This system of learned behaviour patterns characteristic of the members of a given society is constantly shaped by a set of dynamic variables: language, religion, values and attitudes, manners and customs, aesthetics, technology, education, and social institutions. An international manager, to cope with this system, needs both factual and interpretive knowledge of culture. To some extent, the factual can be learned; the interpretation comes only through experience.

The most complicated problems in dealing with the cultural environment stem from the fact that we cannot learn culture—we have to live it. Two schools of thought exist in the business world on how to deal with cultural diversity. One is that business is business the world around, following the model of Pepsi and McDonald's. In some cases, globalization is a fact of life; however, cultural differences are still far from converging.

The other school proposes that companies must tailor business approaches to individual cultures. Setting up policies and procedures in each country has been compared to an organ transplant; the critical question centres on acceptance or rejection. The major challenge to the global marketing manager is to make sure that rejection is not a result of cultural myopia or even blindness.

The internationally successful companies all share an important quality: patience. They have not rushed into situations but rather have built their operations carefully by following the most basic business principles. These principles are to know your challenger, know your audience, and know your customer.

Key Terms

acculturation (p. 65)
area studies (p. 84)
change agent (p. 66)
consumer ethnocentric (p. 75)
cultural convergence (p. 80)
cultural diversity (p. 64)
cultural knowledge (p. 82)
cultural literacy (p. 64)
cultural universals (p. 91)
culture (p. 65)
encultured (p. 65)
experiential knowledge (p. 82)
factual information (p. 82)
field experience (p. 84)
high context cultures (p. 65)
interpretive knowledge (p. 83)
low context cultures (p. 65)
reference groups (p. 81)
self-reference criterion (p. 88)
sensitivity training (p. 84)
social stratification (p. 81)
translation–back-translation (p. 71)

Questions for Discussion

1. Comment on the assumption, "If people are serious about doing business with you, they will speak English."
2. You are on your first business visit to Germany. You feel confident about your ability to speak the language (you studied German in school and have taken a refresher course), and you decide to use it. During introductions, you want to break the ice by asking, *"Wie geht's?"* and insisting that everyone call you by your first name. Speculate as to the reaction.
3. What can a company do to culturally sensitize its staff?
4. What can be learned about a culture from reading and attending to factual materials? Given the tremendous increase in international marketing activities, where will companies in a relatively early stage of the internationalization process find the personnel to handle the new challenges?
5. Management at a Canadian food company trying to market tomato paste in the Middle East did not know that, translated into Arabic, tomato paste is "tomato glue." How could they have known in time to avoid problems?
6. Give examples of how the self-reference criterion might be manifested.

Internet Exercises

1. Use the Google search engine at **http://www.google.ca/** to identify three Canadian companies that offer cross-cultural training. Are there significant differences in the services they offer?
2. Visit the website of the Canadian Broadcasting Corporation (CBC) at **http://www.cbc.radio-canada.ca/home.asp.** Given the services the CBC provides, how effective do you believe the organization is in protecting Canada's cultural sovereignty?

Recommended Readings

Axtell, Roger E. *Do's and Taboos around the World.* New York: John Wiley & Sons, 1993.

Brislin, R.W., W.J. Lonner, and R.M. Thorndike, *Cross-Cultural Research Methods.* New York: John Wiley & Sons, 1973.

Copeland, Lennie, and L. Griggs. *Going International: How to Make Friends and Deal Effectively in the Global Marketplace.* New York: Random House, 1990.

Elashmawi, Farid, and Phillip R. Harris. *Multicultural Management 2000: Essential Cultural Insights for Global Business Success.* Houston, TX: Gulf, 1998.

Hall, Edward T., and Mildred Reed Hall. *Understanding Cultural Differences.* Yarmouth, ME: Intercultural Press, 1990.

Hoecklin, Lisa. *Managing Cultural Differences.* Workingham, UK: Addison-Wesley, 1995.

Hofstede, Geert. *Culture's Consequences.* London: Sage Publications, 1981.

Kenna, Peggy, and Sondra Lacy. *Business Japan: Understanding Japanese Business Culture.* Lincolnwood, IL: NTC, 1994.

Lewis, Richard D. *When Cultures Collide.* London: Nicholas Brealey Publishing, 2000.

Marx, Elizabeth. *Breaking through Culture Shock: What You Need to Succeed in International Business.* London: Nicholas Brealey Publishing, 1999.

O'Hara-Devereux, Mary, and Robert Johansen. *Global Work: Bridging Distance, Culture, and Time.* San Francisco: Jossey-Bass Publishers, 1994.

Parker, Barbara. *Globalization and Business Practice: Managing across Boundaries.* London: Sage Publications, 1999.

Terpstra, Vern, and K. David. *The Cultural Environment of International Business.* Cincinnati, OH: South-Western, 1992.

Trompenaars, Fons, and Charles Hampden-Turner. *Riding the Waves of Culture.* New York: Irwin, 1998.

Notes

1. Ernest Dichter, "The World Consumer," *Harvard Business Review* 40 (July–August 1962): 113–22; and Kenichi Ohmae, *Triad Power—The Coming Shape of Global Competition* (New York: The Free Press, 1985), 22–27.
2. "Rule No. 1: Don't Diss the Locals," *Business Week*, May 15, 1995, 8.
3. Mary O'Hara-Devereaux and Robert Johansen, *Global Work: Bridging Distance, Culture, and Time* (San Francisco: Jossey-Bass Publishers, 1994), 11.
4. Carla Rapoport, "Nestlé's Brand Building Machine," *Fortune*, September 19, 1994, 147–56.
5. Alfred Kroeber and Clyde Kluckhohn, *Culture: A Critical Review of Concepts and Definitions* (New York: Random House, 1985), 11.
6. Geert Hofstede, "National Cultures Revisited," *Asia-Pacific Journal of Management* 1 (September 1984): 22–24.
7. Robert L. Kohls, *Survival Kit for Overseas Living* (Chicago: Intercultural Press, 1979), 3.
8. Edward T. Hall, *Beyond Culture* (Garden City, NY: Anchor Press, 1976), 15.
9. Marita von Oldenborgh, "What's Next for India?" *International Business*, January 1996, 44–47; and Ravi Vijh, "Think Global, Act Indian," *Export Today*, June 1996, 27–28.
10. See UNESCO website, **http://portal.unesco.org** for additional details.
11. One author has identified as many as 73 **cultural universals** or key elements that help us to understand why and how cultures differ. See George P. Murdoch, "The Common Denominator of Cultures," in *The Science of Man in the World*, ed. Ralph Linton (New York: Columbia University Press, 1945), 123–42.
12. David A. Ricks, *Blunders in International Business* (Malden, MA: Blackwell Publishers, 2000), chap. 1.
13. David A. Hanni, John K. Ryans, and Ivan R. Vernon, "Coordinating International Advertising: The Goodyear Case Revisited for Latin America," *Journal of International Marketing* 3, no. 2 (1995): 83–98.
14. "France: Mind Your Language," *The Economist*, March 23, 1996, 70–71.
15. Rory Cowan, "The e Does Not Stand for English," *Global Business*, March 2000, L/22.
16. Margareta Bowen, "Business Translation," *Jerome Quarterly* 8 (August–September 1993): 5–9.
17. "Nokia Veti Pois Mainoskampanjansa," *Uutislehti 100*, June 15, 1998, 5.
18. "Sticky Issue," *The Economist*, August 24, 2002, 51.
19. Edward T. Hall, "The Silent Language of Overseas Business," *Harvard Business Review* 38 (May–June 1960): 87–96.
20. *World Almanac and the Book of Facts* (Mahwah, NJ: Funk & Wagnalls, 1995), 734.
21. Nora Fitzgerald, "Oceans Apart, but Closer than You Think," *World Trade*, February 1996, 58.
22. Mushtaq Luqmami, Zahir A. Quraeshi, and Linda Delene, "Marketing in Islamic Countries: A Viewpoint," *MSU Business Topics* 23 (Summer 1980): 17–24.
23. "Islamic Banking: Faith and Creativity," *The New York Times*, April 8, 1994, D1, D6.
24. Roger D. Blackwell, Paul W. Miniard, and James F. Engel, *Consumer Behavior* (Mason, OH: Thomson, 2001), chap. 10.
25. Y. Wong and T. Leung, *Guanxi: Relationship Marketing in a Chinese Context* (New York: Haworth Press, 2001).
26. "Iran Unveils Islamic Twin Dolls to Fight Culture War," *AP Worldstream*, March 5, 2002.
27. Douglas McGray, "Japan's Gross National Cool," *Foreign Policy*, May/June 2002, 44.
28. Robert Thompson, "Say When," *Financial Post Business*, March 2006, 32.
29. Earl P. Spencer, "EuroDisney—What Happened?" *Journal of International Marketing* 3, no. 3 (1995): 103–14.
30. Sergey Frank, "Global Negotiations: Vive Les Differences!" *Sales & Marketing Management* 144 (May 1992): 64–69.
31. See, for example, Terri Morrison, *Kiss, Bow, or Shake Hands: How to Do Business in Sixty Countries* (Holbrook, MA: Adams Media, 1994); or Roger Axtell, *Do's and Taboos around the World* (New York: John Wiley & Sons, 1993).
32. James A. Gingrich, "Five Rules for Winning Emerging Market Consumers," *Strategy and Business* (2nd quarter, 1999): 68–76.
33. "Feng Shui Man Orders Sculpture out of the Hotel," *South China Morning Post*, July 27, 1992, 4.
34. The results of the Gallup study are available in "What the Chinese Want," *Fortune*, October 11, 1999, 229–34.
35. E. Christopher, "Cultural Convergence: A Reality or Merely Wishful Thinking," *Journal of Asia Entrepreneurship and Sustainability* 1, no. 11 (2005).
36. Joe Agnew, "Cultural Differences Probed to Create Product Identity," *Marketing News*, October 24, 1986, 22.
37. Joseph A. McKinney, "Joint Ventures of United States Firms in Japan: A Survey," *Venture Japan* 1, no. 2 (1988): 14–19.
38. Peter MacInnis, "Guanxi or Contract: A Way to Understand and Predict Conflict between Chinese and Western Senior Managers in China-Based Joint Ventures," in *Multinational Business Management and Internationalization of Business Enterprises*, ed. Daniel E. McCarthy and Stanley J. Hille, 345–51 (Nanjing, China: Nanjing University Press, 1993).
39. Tim Ambler, "Reflections in China: Re-Orienting Images of Marketing," *Marketing Management* 4 (Summer 1995): 23–30.
40. James H. Sood and Patrick Adams, "Model of Management Learning Styles as a Predictor of Export Behavior and Performance," *Journal of Business Research* 12 (June 1984): 169–82.
41. W. Chan Kim and R. A. Mauborgne, "Cross-Cultural Strategies," *Journal of Business Strategy* 7 (Spring 1987): 28–37.
42. Mauricio Lorence, "Assignment USA: The Japanese Solution," *Sales & Marketing Management* 144 (October 1992): 60–66.

43. Rosalie Tung, "Selection and Training of Personnel for Overseas Assignments," *Columbia Journal of World Business* 16 (Spring 1981): 68–78.

44. Simcha Ronen, "Training the International Assignee," in *Training and Career Development,* ed. I. Goldstein, 426–40 (San Francisco: Jossey-Bass, 1989).

45. Geert Hofstede, Culture's Consequences: International Differences in Work-Related Values (Beverly Hills, CA: Sage Publications, 1984).

46. Geert Hofstede and Michael H. Bond, "The Confucius Connection: From Cultural Roots to Economic Growth," *Organizational Dynamics* 16 (Spring 1988): 4–21.

47. Sudhir H. Kale, "Culture-Specific Marketing Communications: An Analytical Approach," *International Marketing Review* 8, no. 2 (1991): 18–30.

48. Hong Cheng and John C. Schweitzer, "Cultural Values Reflected in Chinese and U.S. Television Commercials," *Journal of Advertising Research* 36 (May/June 1996): 27–45.

49. Sudhir H. Kale, "Distribution Channel Relationships in Diverse Cultures," *International Marketing Review* 8, no. 3 (1991): 31–45.

50. "Exploring Differences in Japan, U.S. Culture," *Advertising Age International,* September 18, 1995, I-8.

51. James A. Lee, "Cultural Analysis in Overseas Operations," *Harvard Business Review* 44 (March–April 1966): 106–14.

52. Peter B. Fitzpatrick and Alan S. Zimmerman, *Essentials of Export Marketing* (New York: American Management Organization, 1985), 16.

53. 3M examples are adopted from John R. Engen, "Far Eastern Front," *World Trade,* December 1994, 20–24.

Chapter 4

The Economic Environment

The Global MARKETPLACE 4.1

Markets at the Bottom of the Income Pyramid

Marketers are facing a challenging time at the start of the 21st century: domestic markets are not experiencing growth, and many of the promising international markets have been struck by recession or by financial crises. The time may have come to consider the 4 billion people in the world who live in poverty, subsisting on less than $1,500 a year, as potential customers. Despite initial skepticism, marketers are finding that they can make profits while at the same time having a positive effect on the sustainable livelihoods of these people. However, these new ventures will require radical departures from the traditional business models; for example, new partnerships (ranging from local governments to nonprofits) and new pricing structures (allowing customers to rent or lease rather than buy).

The World Economic Pyramid

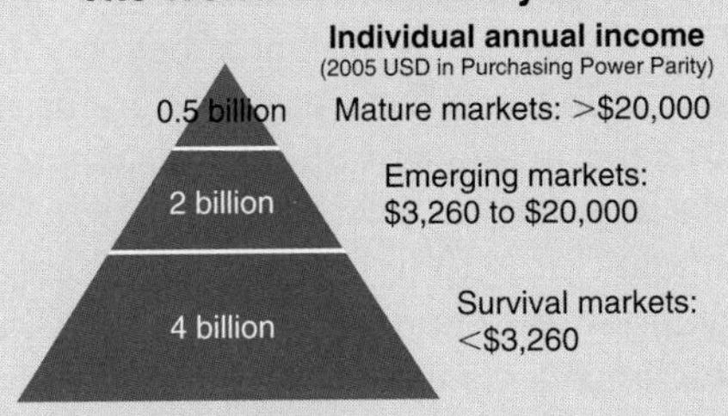

Most companies focus on mature and emerging markets, while the huge market of 4 billion people living on less than $3,260 a year goes largely untapped.

Source: Reprinted with permission from World Resources Institute, http://www.wri.org.

Druide Laboratories Inc. of Pointe-Claire, Quebec, has recognized the opportunity to use alternative business models to access markets at the bottom of the income pyramid. Partnered with a local Afghan businessman and with funding from the Canadian International Development Agency, a federal government agency, Druide has established an operation in Afghanistan to produce and market liquid laundry and body soap in that country. The company, Florance, was established in 2006 and employs 14 Afghan men and women.

The company produces 4,000 bottles of soap per day, which are marketed across Afghanistan. The approach allows Druide Laboratories to access a market segment that would not ordinarily be able to afford its products.

In penetrating subsistence markets, the first order of business is to learn about the needs, aspirations, and habits of targeted populations for whom traditional intelligence gathering may not be the most effective. Hewlett-Packard has an initiative called World e-Inclusion, which, working with a range of global and local partners, aims to sell, lease, or donate a billion dollars' worth of satellite-powered computer products and services to markets in Africa, Asia, Eastern Europe, Latin America, and the

Middle East. To engage with beta communities in Senegal, Hewlett-Packard partnered with Joko, Inc., a company founded by revered Senegalese pop star Youssou N'Dour.

In the product area, marketers must combine advanced technology with local insights. Hindustan Lever (part of Unilever) learned that low-income Indians, usually forced to settle for low-quality products, wanted to buy high-end detergents and personal care products but could not afford them in the quantities available. In response, the company developed extremely low-cost packaging material and other innovations that allowed for a product priced in pennies instead of the $4 to $15 price of the regular containers. The same brand is on all of the product forms, regardless of packaging. Because these consumers do not shop at supermarkets, Lever employs local residents with pushcarts who take small quantities of the sachets to kiosks.

Coca-Cola has introduced "Project Mission" in Botswana to launch a drink to combat anemia, blindness, and other afflictions common in poorer parts of the world. The drink, called Vitango, is like the company's Hi-C orange-flavoured drink, but it contains 12 vitamins and minerals chronically lacking in the diets of people in developing countries. The project satisfies multiple objectives for the Coca-Cola company. First, it could help boost sales at a time when global sales of carbonated drinks are slowing, and, second, it will help in establishing relationships with governments and other local constituents that will serve as a positive platform for brand Coca-Cola.

HOANG DINH NAM/AFP/Getty Images

Due to economic and physical isolation of poor communities, providing access can lead to a thriving business. In Bangladesh (with income levels of $200), GrameenPhone Ltd. leases access to wireless phones to villagers. Every phone is used by an average of 100 people and generates $90 in revenue a month—two or three times the revenues generated by wealthier users who own their phones in urban areas. Similarly, the Jhai Foundation, an American-Lao foundation, is helping villagers in Laos with Internet access. The first step, however, was to develop an inexpensive and robust computer. The computer has no moving parts and very few delicate ones. Instead of a hard disk, it relies on flash-memory chips, and instead of an energy-guzzling glass cathode-ray tube, its screen is a liquid-crystal display.

The emergence of these markets presents a great opportunity for global marketers. It also creates a chance for business, government, and civil society to unite in a common cause to help the aspiring poor to join the world market economy.

Sources: "Making the Web Worldwide," *The Economist*, September 28, 2002, 76; C.K. Prahalad and Stuart L. Hart, "The Fortune at the Bottom of the Pyramid," *Strategy and Business*, 1st quarter, 2002, 35–47; "Drinks for Developing Countries," *The Washington Post*, November 27, 2001, B1, B6; Dana James, "B2-4B Spells Profits," *Marketing News*, November 5, 2001, 1, 11–12; CIDA INC website, Combating unemployment in Afghanistan, **http://www.acdi-cida.gc.ca/CIDAWEB/acdicida.nsf/En/NAT-130111834-M5N** (accessed February 25, 2007).

In the development and implementation of global marketing strategy, one must consider the economic environment. The economic environment is beyond the control of the global marketer but plays a central role in the selection of foreign markets and will ultimately determine the contribution of that market to the firm's sales revenues. The level of interest rates set by central banks around the world has an impact on business investment, consumer spending, and economic growth in key markets. Foreign exchange rates, or the price of a country's currency in terms of some other, also adjust in sympathy with interest rates and can have a dramatic impact on the demand for imported products. The global marketer has no control over these relationships but must factor them into the foreign market entry decision. These economic relationships must also be used on an ongoing basis when deciding on the allocation of marketing resources to specific country markets or even deciding that it is time to exit a particular market.

Economic Factors in Assessing Foreign Markets

The assessment of a foreign market environment should start with the evaluation of economic variables relating to the size and nature of the markets. Because of the large number of worthwhile alternatives, initial screening of markets should be done efficiently yet effectively. The analysis should make use of a wide array of economic criteria to establish a preliminary estimate of market potential. One of the most basic characterizations of the world economy is provided in Exhibit 4.1, which incorporates many of the economic variables pertinent to marketers.

The **Group of Five**—listed in Exhibit 4.1 as the United States, Britain, France, Germany, and Japan—consists of the major industrialized countries of the world. This group is often expanded to the **Group of Seven** (by adding Italy and Canada) and to the **Group of Ten** (by adding Sweden, the Netherlands, and Belgium). It may also be expanded to encompass the members of the Organization for Economic Cooperation and Development (OECD), which consists of 30 countries, including Western Europe, the United States, Australia, Canada, Czech Republic, Hungary, Japan, Mexico, New Zealand, Poland, Slovakia, South Korea, and Turkey.

Important among the middle-income developing countries are the newly industrialized countries (NICs), which include Singapore, Taiwan, Korea, Hong Kong, Brazil, and Mexico (some propose adding Malaysia and the Philippines to the list as well). Some of these NICs will earn a new acronym, RIC (rapidly industrializing country). Over the past 20 years,

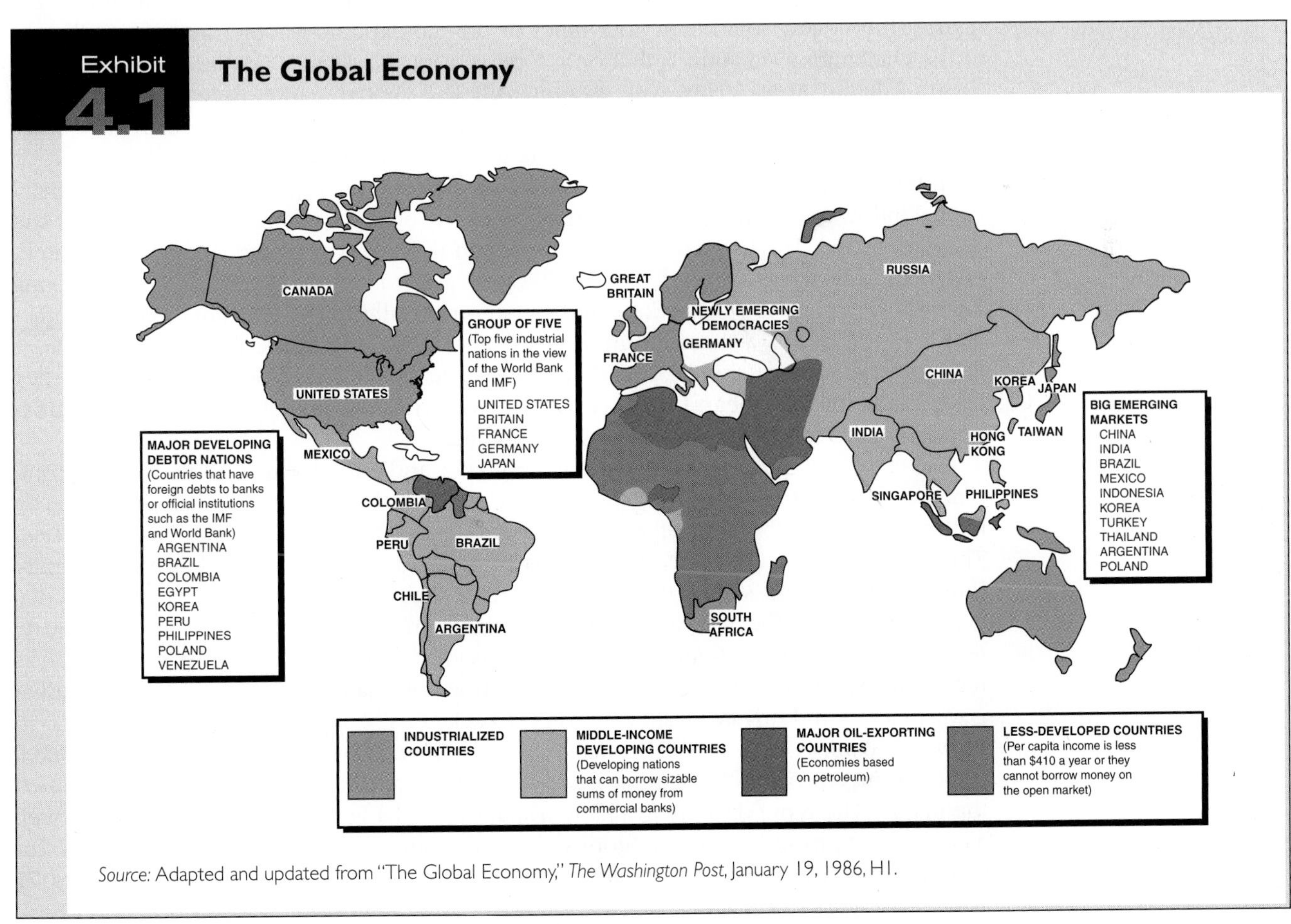

Exhibit 4.1 The Global Economy

Source: Adapted and updated from "The Global Economy," *The Washington Post*, January 19, 1986, H1.

Singapore has served as a hub, providing critical financial and managerial services to the Southeast Asian markets. Singapore has successfully attracted foreign investment, mostly regional corporate headquarters and knowledge-intensive industries, and has served as one of the main gateways for Asian trade. Its exports have reached well over 300 percent of GDP.[1]

The major oil-exporting countries, in particular the 11 members of the Organization of Petroleum Exporting Countries (OPEC) and countries such as Trinidad and Russia, are dependent on the price of oil for their world market participation. The 11 members of OPEC are Algeria, Indonesia, Iran, Iraq, Kuwait, Libya, Nigeria, Qatar, Saudi Arabia, UAE, and Venezuela. Canada is not a member of OPEC, but oil and gas exports are a major contributor to the economy of the western province of Alberta. Created in 1960, OPEC's mission is to coordinate petroleum policies among its members in order to stabilize prices, ensure a regular supply to consuming countries, and generate a fair return on capital to those investing in the oil industry.[2] A relatively high dollar price per barrel works very much in favour of OPEC member countries and other oil-exporting nations.

Many of the emerging economies are dependent on the success of their ongoing market development efforts to industrialize. China became the second-largest exporter of textiles to the United States after it began increasing production in the 1980s. Despite an image of hopeless poverty, India has over 200 million middle-class consumers and is rapidly embracing new technologies and industries. A special group in this category consists of the countries saddled with a major debt burden, such as Egypt and Peru. The degree and form of their participation in the world market will largely depend on how the debt issue is solved with the governments of the major industrialized countries and the multilateral and commercial banks.

In less-developed countries, debt problems make market development difficult. Africa, the poorest continent, owes the rest of the world $375 billion, an amount equal to three-quarters of its GNP and nearly four times its annual exports. Another factor contributing to the challenging situation is that only 1 percent of the world's private investment goes to sub-Saharan Africa.[3] However, as shown in The Global Marketplace 4.1, these countries, which constitute the majority of the world's population, may also provide a large potential market opportunity for marketers in the 21st century.[4]

In the former centrally planned economies, dramatic changes are under way. A hefty capital inflow will be key to modernizing the newly emerging democracies of Central and Eastern Europe. They are crippled by $60 billion in foreign debt and decades of communist misrule. Desperately needed will be Western technology, management, and marketing know-how to provide better jobs and put more locally made and imported consumer goods in the shops. Within the groups, prospects vary: the future for countries such as Hungary, the Czech Republic, and Poland looks far better than it does for Russia, as they have joined the **European Union (EU)**.[5] The top world economies as measured by gross domestic product (GDP) are shown in Exhibit 4.2.

Classifications of markets will vary by originator and intended use. Marketers will combine economic variables to fit their planning purposes by using those that relate directly to the product and/or service the company markets, such as the consumer's ability to buy. The discussion that follows is designed to summarize a set of criteria that helps identify foreign markets and screen the most opportune ones for future entry. The factors discussed will assist the global marketing manager in the ongoing decisions to allocate resources to specific national markets. Discussed are variables on which information is readily available from secondary sources such as international organizations, individual governments, and private organizations or associations.

World Bank and United Nations publications and individual countries' *Statistical Abstracts* may provide the starting point for market investigations. The more developed the market, the more data are available. Data are available on past developments as well as on projections of broader categories such as population and income. Euromonitor, for example, publishes *World Consumer Income & Expenditure Patterns*, which covers 71 countries around the world.

Market Characteristics

The main dimensions of a market can be captured by considering variables such as those relating to the population and its various characteristics, infrastructure, geographical features of the environment, and foreign involvement in the economy.

Population

The total world population stood at 6.6 billion in early 2007. The number of people in a particular market provides one of the most basic indicators of market size and is, in itself, indicative of the potential demand for certain staple items that have universal appeal and are generally affordable. As indicated by the data in Exhibit 4.3, population is not evenly divided among the major regions of the world; Asia holds over half the world's population.

These population figures can be analyzed in terms of marketing implications by noting that the addition of two countries will bring the population of the EU up to almost half a billion people. The two largest entities in Asia, China and India, constitute nearly 70 percent of Asia's population. The greatest population densities are also to be found in Europe, providing the global marketer with a strategically located centre of operation and ready access to the major markets of the world. The U.S., which has a population 10 times the size of Canada, continues to provide Canadian marketers with a large and geographically close target market.

Population figures themselves must be broken down into meaningful categories in order for the global marketer to take better advantage of them. Because market entry decisions may lie in the future, it is worthwhile to analyze population projections in the areas of interest and focus on their possible implications. Exhibit 4.3 includes United Nations projections that point to a population explosion, but mainly in the developing countries. Northern Europe will show nearly zero population growth for the next 30 years, whereas the population of Africa will triple. Even in the low- or zero-growth markets, the news is not necessarily bad for the global marketer. Those in the 25 to 45 age group, whose numbers are increasing, are among the most affluent consumers of all, having formed family units and started to consume household goods in large quantities as they reach the peak of their personal earnings potential. Early in this century, they are expected to start spending more on leisure goods and health care and related services.[6]

To influence population growth patterns, governments will have to undertake, with the help of private enterprise, quite different social marketing tasks. These will range from promoting and providing incentives for larger families (in Scandinavia, for example) to increased family planning efforts (in Thailand, for example). Regardless of the outcome of such government programs, current trends will further accelerate the division of world markets into the haves and the have-nots. More adjustment capability will be required on the part of companies that want to market in the developing countries because of lower purchasing power of individuals and increasing government participation in the marketing of basic products. However, as the life expectancy in a market extends and new target markets become available, marketers may be able to extend their products' life cycles by marketing them abroad.

Depending on the marketer's interest, population figures can be classified to show specific characteristics of their respective markets. Age distribution and life expectancy correlate heavily with the level of development of the market. Industrialized countries, with their increasing median age and a larger share of the population above 65, will open unique opportunities for global marketers with new products and services. For example, Kimberly-Clark markets its Depend line of incontinence products both in Europe and North America.

An important variable for the global marketer is the size of the household. A **household** describes all the persons, both related and unrelated, who occupy a housing unit.[7] Within the EU, the average household size has shrunk from 2.9 to 2.7 persons in the last 25 years and is expected to decline further.[8] Based on 2005 data, average household size

Economic Strength

Top World Economies (GDP in million dollars U.S.)

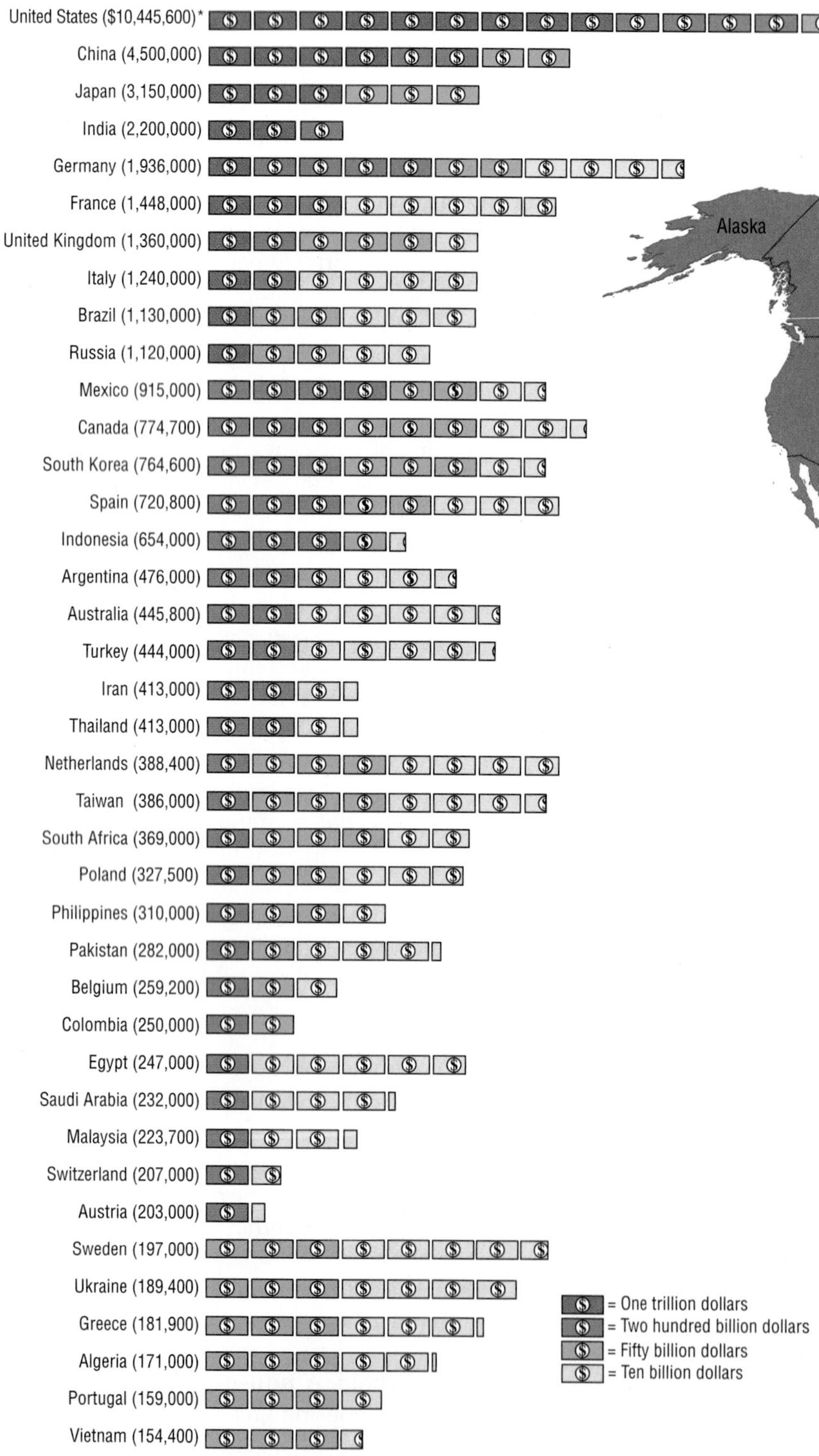

United States ($10,445,600)*
China (4,500,000)
Japan (3,150,000)
India (2,200,000)
Germany (1,936,000)
France (1,448,000)
United Kingdom (1,360,000)
Italy (1,240,000)
Brazil (1,130,000)
Russia (1,120,000)
Mexico (915,000)
Canada (774,700)
South Korea (764,600)
Spain (720,800)
Indonesia (654,000)
Argentina (476,000)
Australia (445,800)
Turkey (444,000)
Iran (413,000)
Thailand (413,000)
Netherlands (388,400)
Taiwan (386,000)
South Africa (369,000)
Poland (327,500)
Philippines (310,000)
Pakistan (282,000)
Belgium (259,200)
Colombia (250,000)
Egypt (247,000)
Saudi Arabia (232,000)
Malaysia (223,700)
Switzerland (207,000)
Austria (203,000)
Sweden (197,000)
Ukraine (189,400)
Greece (181,900)
Algeria (171,000)
Portugal (159,000)
Vietnam (154,400)

= One trillion dollars
= Two hundred billion dollars
= Fifty billion dollars
= Ten billion dollars

GREENLAND (DENMARK)
Alaska
CANADA
UNITED STATES
BERMUDA
MEXICO
CUBA
BAHAMAS
DOMINICAN REPUBLIC
PUERTO RICO
JAMAICA
HONDURAS
HAITI
GUATEMALA
EL SALVADOR
NICARAGUA
COSTA RICA
PANAMA
VENEZUELA
GUYANA
SURINAME
FRENCH GUIANA
COLOMBIA
ECUADOR
BRAZIL
PERU
BOLIVIA
CHILE
PARAGUAY
ARGENTINA
URUGUAY

GDP per head $
17,500
15,000
12,000
10,000
7,500
5,000
2,500
1,000

No current data available

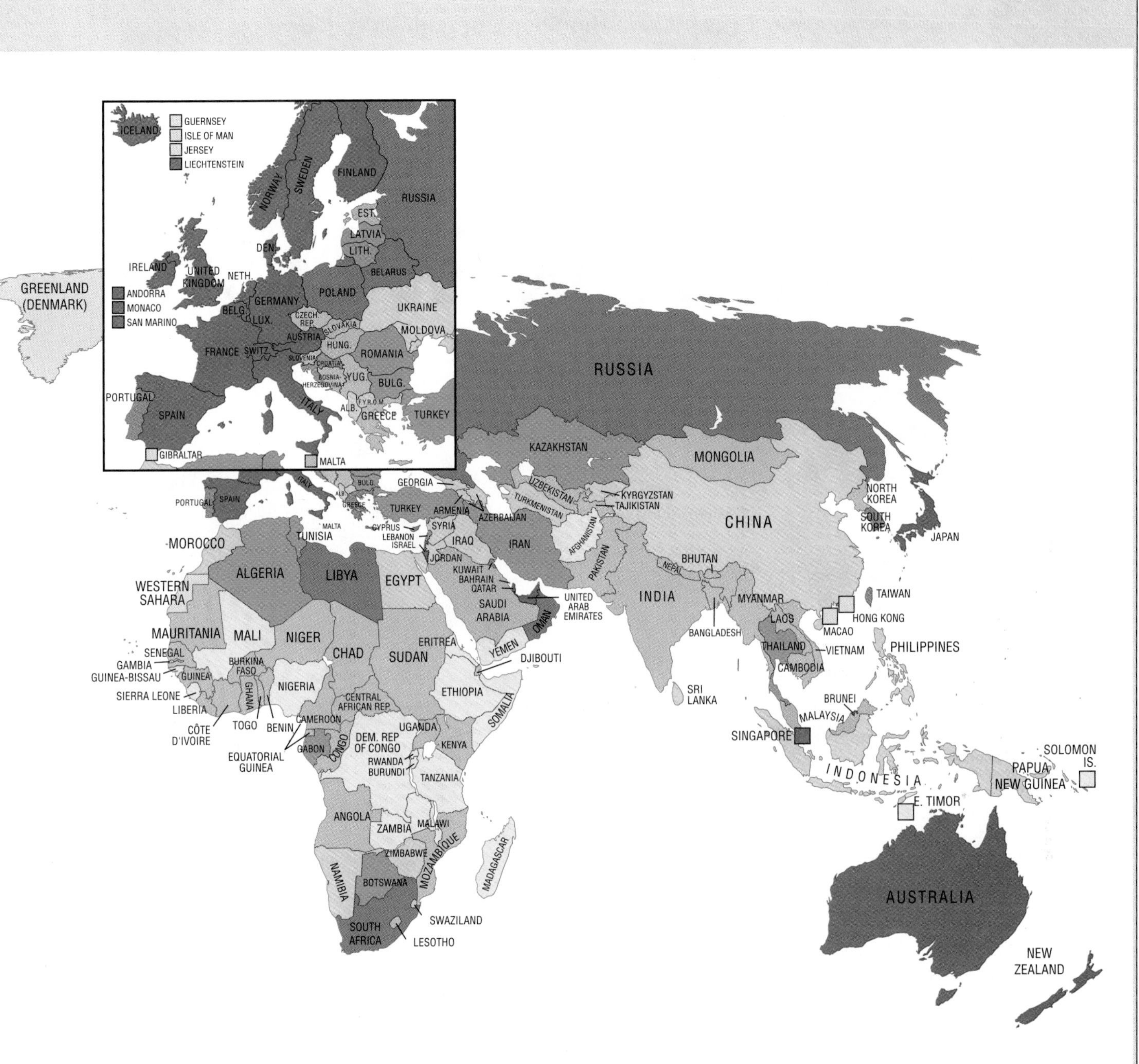

***http://www.bea.doc.gov** (accessed March 3, 2003).
Source: Based on *The World Almanac*, 2003.

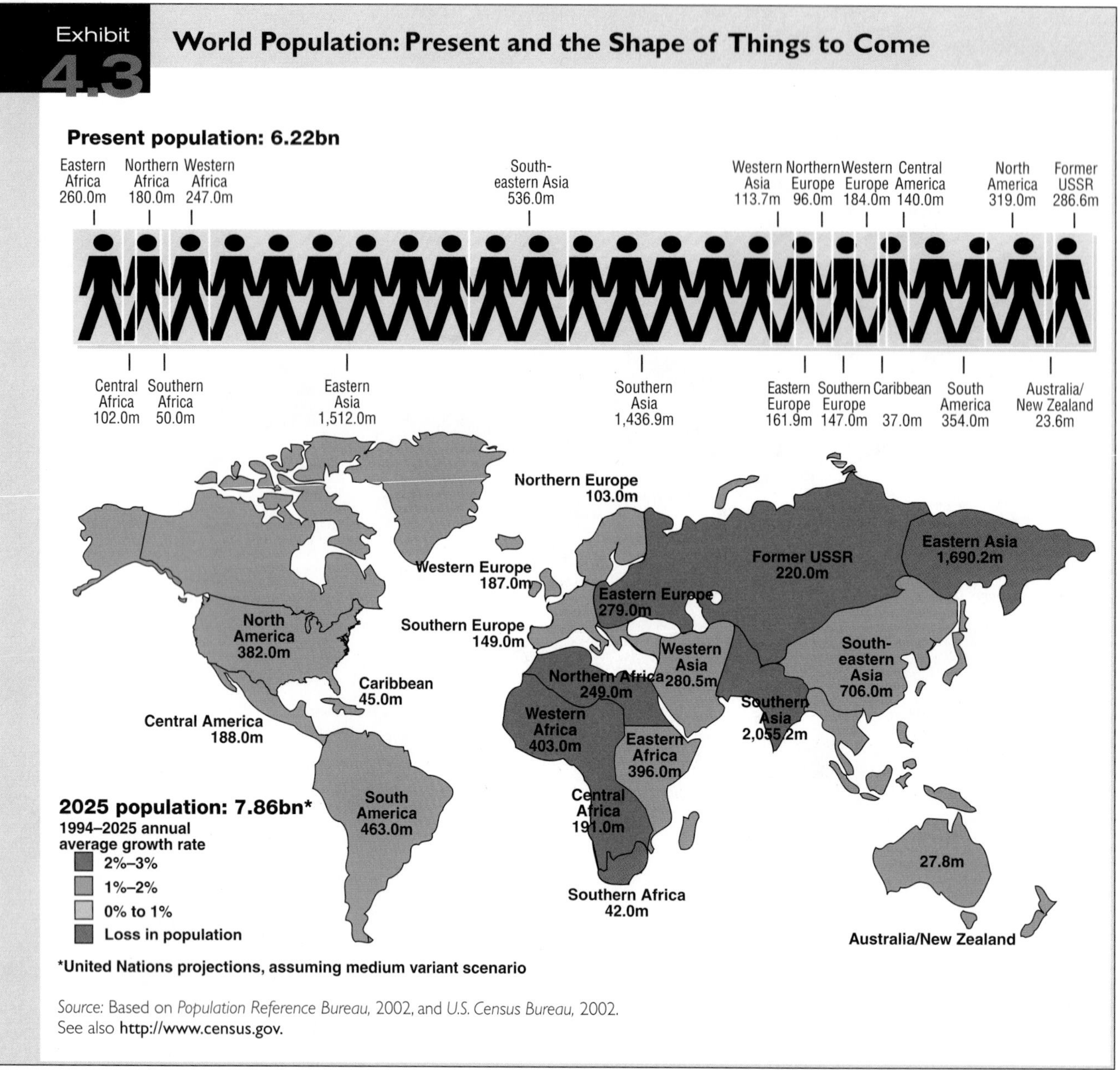

Exhibit 4.3 World Population: Present and the Shape of Things to Come

Source: Based on *Population Reference Bureau*, 2002, and *U.S. Census Bureau*, 2002. See also **http://www.census.gov.**

in the U.S. is similar to the EU at 2.5.[9] One factor behind the overall growth in the number of households, and the subsequent decline in the average size, has been the increase in the numbers of divorced and sole-survivor households. One-person households are most common in Norway and Germany. This compares strikingly with countries such as Colombia, where the average household size is six. With economic development usually bringing about more, but smaller-sized, households, global marketers of food products, appliances, and household goods have to adjust to patterns of demand; for example, they may offer smaller appliances and single-serving portions of frozen foods.

The increased urbanization of many markets has distinctly changed consumption patterns. Urban populations as a percentage of the total will vary from a low of 6 percent in Burundi to a high of 97 percent in Belgium. The degree of urbanization often dictates the nature of the marketing task the company faces, not only in terms of distribution but also in terms of market potential and buying habits. Urban areas provide larger groups of consumers who may be more receptive to marketing efforts because of their exposure to other consumers (the demonstration effect) and to communication media. In markets where urbanization is recent and taking place rapidly, the marketer faces additional responsibility as a change agent, especially when incomes may be low and the conditions for the proper use of the products may not be adequate. This is especially true in countries where rapid industrialization is taking place, such as Greece, Spain, and Portugal.

When using international data sources, the global marketer must recognize that definitions of a construct may vary among the many secondary sources. The concept of **urbanization**, for example, has different meanings depending on where one operates. In Canada, an urban area is defined as a place with a population of at least 1,000 and no fewer than 400 persons per square kilometre; in the U.S., it is a place of 2,500 or more inhabitants; in Sweden, it is a built-up area with at least 200 inhabitants and no more than 200 metres between houses; in Mauritius, it is a town with proclaimed legal limits. Comparability, therefore, is concerned with the ends and not the means (or the definition).

Income

Markets require not only people but also purchasing power, which is a function of income, prices, savings, and credit availability. Apart from basic staple items, for which population figures provide an estimate, income is most indicative of the market potential for most consumer and industrial products and services. For the marketer to make use of information on the gross national product of various nations, such as that summarized in Exhibit 4.4, further knowledge is needed on distribution of income. Per capita GNP is often used as a primary indicator for evaluating purchasing power. This figure shows great variation between countries, as indicated by Norway's $38,700 and Ethiopia's $99. The wide use of GNP figures can be explained by their easy availability, but they should nevertheless be used with caution. In industrialized countries, the richest 10 percent of the population consumes 20 percent of all goods and services, whereas the respective figure for developing countries may be as high as 50 percent.[10] In some markets, income distribution produces wide gaps between population groups. The more developed the economy, the more income distribution tends to converge toward the middle class.

The global marketer can use the following classifications as a planning guide:

1. *Very low family incomes.* Subsistence economies tend to be characterized by rural populations in which consumption relies on personal output or barter. Some urban centres may provide markets. Example: Cameroon.
2. *Very low, very high family incomes.* Some countries exhibit strongly bimodal income distributions. The majority of the population may live barely above the subsistence level, but there is a strong market in urban centres and a growing middle class. The affluent are truly affluent and will consume accordingly. Examples: India, Mexico.
3. *Low, medium, high family incomes.* Industrialization produces an emerging middle class with increasing disposable income. The very low and very high income classes tend to remain for traditional reasons of social class barriers. Example: Portugal.
4. *Mostly medium family incomes.* The advanced industrial nations tend to develop institutions and policies that reduce extremes in income distribution, resulting in a large and comfortable middle class able to purchase a wide array of both domestic and imported products and services. Example: Denmark.

Although the national income figures provide a general indication of a market's potential, they suffer from various distortions. Figures available from secondary sources are often in U.S. dollars. The per capita income figures may not be a true reflection of purchasing power if the currencies involved are distorted in some way. For example, fluctuations in the value of the U.S. dollar may distort real-income and standard-of-living figures. The goods and services in different countries have to be valued consistently if the differences are to reflect real differences in the volumes of goods produced. The use of **purchasing power parities (PPPs)** instead of exchange rates is intended to achieve this objective. PPPs show how many units of currency are needed in one country to buy the amount of goods and services that one unit of currency will buy in another country. Exhibit 4.5 provides an example of such data.

Exhibit 4.4 Gross Domestic Product per Capita for Selected Countries

Highest GDP per Head (in Dollars)

Rank	Country	GDP – per capita (PPP)	Rank	Country	GDP – per capita (PPP)
1	Bermuda	$69,900	21	Finland	$32,800
2	Luxembourg	$68,800	22	Belgium	$31,800
3	Equatorial Guinea	$50,200	23	Netherlands	$31,700
4	United Arab Emirates	$49,700	24	Sweden	$31,600
5	Norway	$47,800	25	Germany	$31,400
6	Guernsey	$44,600	26	United Kingdom	$31,400
7	Cayman Islands	$43,800	27	Faroe Islands	$31,000
8	Ireland	$43,600	28	Singapore	$30,900
9	United States	$43,500	29	France	$30,100
10	Jersey	$40,000	30	Italy	$29,700
11	British Virgin Islands	$38,500	31	Qatar	$29,400
12	Iceland	$38,100	32	European Union	$29,300
13	Denmark	$37,000	33	Taiwan	$29,000
14	Hong Kong	$36,500	34	Gibraltar	$27,900
15	Canada	$35,200	35	Isle of Man	$27,800
16	San Marino	$34,600	36	Monaco	$27,000
17	Austria	$34,100	37	Spain	$27,000
18	Switzerland	$33,600	38	Israel	$26,200
19	Japan	$33,100	39	New Zealand	$26,000
20	Australia	$32,900	40	Bahrain	$25,300

Lowest GDP per Head (in Dollars)

Rank	Country	GDP – per capita (PPP)	Rank	Country	GDP – per capita (PPP)
209	Djibouti	$1,000	219	Yemen	$900
210	Eritrea	$1,000	220	Afghanistan	$800
211	Ethiopia	$1,000	221	East Timor	$800
212	Liberia	$1,000	222	Tanzania	$800
213	Niger	$1,000	223	Burundi	$700
214	Tokelau	$1,000	224	Congo, Democratic Republic of the	$700
215	Zambia	$1,000	225	Comoros	$600
216	Guinea-Bissau	$900	226	Malawi	$600
217	Madagascar	$900	227	Solomon Islands	$600
218	Sierra Leone	$900	228	Somalia	$600

Source: Compiled from The World Factbook (2007), Field Listing- GDP per capita (PPP), **https://www.cia.gov.**

Second, using a monetary measure may not be a proper and all-inclusive measure of income. For example, in developing economies where most of the consumption is either self-produced or bartered, reliance on financial data alone would seriously understate the standard of living. Further, several of the service-related items (for example, protective services and travel), characteristic of the industrialized countries' national income figures, do not exist for markets at lower levels of development. Moreover, the marketer will have to take into consideration variations in market potential in individual markets. Major urban centres in developing countries may have income levels comparable to those in more developed markets, while rural areas may not have incomes needed to buy imported goods.

In general, income figures are useful in the initial screening of markets. However, in product-specific cases, income may not play a major role, and startling scenarios may emerge. Some products, such as motorcycles and television sets in China, are in demand

The Global MARKETPLACE 4.2

Income Disparity in Japan

As the Japanese economy emerges from its decade of economic recession, the problem of sharp income inequality is slowly being recognized. There is a widening gap between the haves and the have-nots in Japan—a country where conspicuous consumption is now fashionable and luxury condominiums priced at almost $900,000 change hands briskly. In Japan the number of millionaires has risen 10 percent from 2001 to 2004 and now stands at 1.4 million. At the same time, 23 percent of Japanese have no savings, and the percentage of the population living in poverty has increased from 8 percent in 1994 to 15 percent in 2000. The number of households receiving welfare has increased to 1 million—a level not seen since the country's safety net was established in the 1950s.

Economists point to a number of reasons for the growing income disparity in Japan. The country's aging population and the movement away from the notion of lifetime employment has led to layoffs and reduced household incomes. At the same time, the country's tax revenues have been reduced and the number of public works programs that traditionally supported unskilled Japanese has been cut back. As Japanese companies abandon traditional loyalties to employees, more and more—particularly younger—workers are being hired on a part-time or temporary basis at a fraction of the cost of retaining older workers.

Source: Adapted from Chisaki Watanabe, "Emergence of rich and poor rattles 'middle class' Japan," *Mainichi Daily News.* Used with permission of the Associated Press, © 2008, all rights reserved.

regardless of their high price in relation to wages because of their high prestige value. Some products are in demand because of their foreign origin. As an example, European luxury cars have lucrative markets in countries where per capita income figures may be low but there are wealthy consumers who are able and willing to buy them. For instance, Mercedes-Benz's target audience in India is families earning 1 million rupees (approximately $30,000).

Earnings at that level are enough for a lifestyle to rival that of a U.S. or European family with an income three times higher, due to a much higher level of disposable income.[11] Further, the lack of income in a market may preclude the marketing of a standardized product but, at the same time, provide an opportunity for an adjusted product. Microsoft, for example, markets a low-cost version of its popular Windows XP in Asia. Dubbed "XP Lite," the product offers fewer multitasking capabilities, fewer networking options, and lower resolution than the standard version. In Thailand, XP Lite retails for less than US$40. The security software maker Symantec has followed Microsoft's lead and also markets a low-cost version of its products in Asia with scaled-back capabilities. Whirlpool has also recognized that low income is not a constraint to global marketing; in India, China, and Brazil it sells inexpensive but stylish washing machines that cost half the price of those retailed in North America.[12]

Consumption Patterns

Depending on the sophistication of a country's data collection systems, economic data on consumption patterns can be obtained and analyzed. The share of income spent on necessities will provide an indication of the market's development level as well as an approximation of how much money the consumer has left for other purchases. Engel's laws provide some generalizations about consumers' spending patterns and are useful generalizations when precise data are not available. They state that, as a family's income increases, the percentage spent on food will decrease, the percentage spent on housing and household operations will be roughly constant, and the amount saved or spent on other purchases will increase. Private expenditure comparisons reveal that the percentage spent on food in 2005 varied from 10 percent in Canada to 7 percent in the United States and 54 percent in Indonesia (see Exhibit 4.6).

Gross Domestic Product/Purchasing Power Parities

	Gross Domestic Product (Billion U.S. dollars)				Gross Domestic Product per Capita (U.S. dollars)			
	2001	*2002*	*2003*	*2004*	*2001*	*2002*	*2003*	*2004*
United States	10,075.9	10,417.6	10,918.5	11,679.2	25,939	26,995	27,670	28,741
EU15	9,869.8	10,322.6	10,628.3	11,090.3	26,963	28,016	28,689	30,594
Japan	3,390.0	3,465.7	3,575.4	3,787.8	17,261	18,453	19,279	20,907
Germany	2,166.6	2,237.9	2,281.4	2,359.9	17,345	19,119	20,482	21,689
United Kingdom	1,598.7	1,718.5	1,790.3	1,881.0	35,309	36,142	37,510	39,732
France	1,664.7	1,720.5	1,749.1	1,837.6	26,313	27,132	27,647	28,605
Italy	1,488.9	1,528.2	1,549.0	1,610.2	26,632	27,196	28,016	29,664
Spain	907.0	981.4	1,052.3	1,090.8	27,322	28,152	28,987	30,361
Mexico	918.9	951.2	982.6	1,046.1	29,138	29,939	30,427	31,191
Korea	817.4	878.6	922.5	1,005.3	50,053	52,154	54,017	57,704
Canada	896.5	924.9	961.8	1,003.0	28,898	29,482	30,380	31,395
Australia	536.5	567.2	602.0	632.0	27,473	28,713	30,104	31,231
Turkey	420.9	453.9	492.9	551.9	27,045	28,969	30,061	31,436
Netherlands	467.5	483.4	493.7	507.6	21,365	22,270	23,230	24,498
Poland	411.7	427.9	441.9	482.8	18,104	18,820	18,793	19,388
Belgium	283.0	295.8	307.3	321.4	27,524	28,630	29,627	30,851
Sweden	243.1	251.3	259.7	273.1	30,580	32,492	32,719	33,678
Austria	234.8	242.0	249.9	261.1	29,195	29,943	30,786	31,944
Switzerland	222.8	238.6	242.3	252.0	6,135	6,520	6,971	7,687
Greece	189.9	210.1	225.8	239.8	13,244	14,365	15,091	15,946
Portugal	186.3	195.1	196.2	204.0	11,477	12,604	13,165	14,309
Czech Republic	158.6	169.2	176.8	188.6	15,516	16,585	17,329	18,467
Norway	167.5	166.2	169.4	178.0	10,762	11,193	11,569	12,647
Denmark	160.0	161.7	166.9	172.5	29,868	30,081	30,965	31,932
Hungary	134.9	145.9	152.9	161.2	29,265	28,907	29,358	32,590
Finland	139.9	145.7	149.6	159.9	27,271	28,009	28,303	29,554
Ireland	117.2	127.7	133.0	145.2	25,705	26,325	26,681	27,699
New Zealand	83.6	88.5	93.8	100.0	37,113	36,609	37,108	38,765
Slovak Republic	62.0	67.8	70.8	77.0	22,272	23,755	25,051	25,582
Luxembourg	22.1	23.3	24.3	26.1	9,184	9,381	9,567	10,059
Iceland	8.3	8.3	8.5	9.5	30,383	32,535	33,322	35,767

Source: Adapted from OECD Factbook 2006, Economic, Environmental and Social Statistics, ISBN 92-64-03561-3 © OECD 2006, http://stats.oecd.org.

In Western Europe, expenditures on clothing typically account for 5 to 9 percent of all spending, but in poorer countries the proportion may be lower. In some low-wage areas, a significant proportion of clothing is homemade or locally made at low cost, making comparisons not entirely accurate. Eastern European households spend an inordinate proportion of their incomes on foodstuffs but quite a low proportion on housing. The remaining, less absolutely central, areas of consumption (household goods, leisure, and transportation) are most vulnerable to short-term cancellation or postponement and thus serve as indicators of the strength of confidence in the market in general.

In large markets such as China and India, marketers need to exercise care in not assuming uniformity across regions. As seen in The Global Marketplace 4.3, regional differences may be marked. Similar gaps exist between urban and rural populations. In China, the average rural citizen spends \$4 on goods other than food and less than \$1 on entertainment, while the amount is \$10 for both in the cities.

Data on product saturation or diffusion—that is, information on the percentage of households in a market that owns a particular product—allow a further evaluation of

Exhibit 4.6 Consumer Spending by Category, as Percent of Total, 2005

	Food and Alcohol	Alcoholic Beverages and Tobacco	Clothing and Footwear	Housing	Household and Services	Health and Medical Services	Transport	Communications	Leisure and Recreation	Education	Hotels and Catering	Misc. Goods and Services
Argentina	25.5	1.7	7.2	16.3	6.3	7.6	9.9	2.8	6.6	3.5	6.7	6.0
Australia	10.2	4.4	3.9	20.6	5.9	5.3	11.5	2.9	12.0	2.3	7.5	13.6
Brazil	12.5	3.2	6.5	20.6	8.7	5.9	9.8	8.1	6.8	5.6	4.6	7.6
Canada	9.7	3.9	5.0	22.7	7.0	4.6	14.9	2.4	10.9	1.4	7.7	9.9
Chile	30.3	2.5	7.7	10.7	2.5	11.8	5.0	4.1	5.7	8.2	5.8	5.6
China	28.9	2.4	7.8	9.9	6.4	5.2	2.7	14.5	4.3	6.6	5.1	6.1
Colombia	26.7	4.6	5.5	16.2	6.2	4.7	10.4	2.9	5.3	6.1	5.5	6.0
Egypt	40.7	0.9	3.1	13.0	2.9	2.3	15.4	3.3	4.0	2.3	2.4	9.8
Hong Kong, China	12.5	0.7	12.6	19.8	11.7	4.6	9.2	1.9	5.7	2.7	10.8	7.8
India	43.4	3.1	4.7	10.8	2.9	7.9	12.7	1.0	1.4	2.3	1.4	8.3
Indonesia	53.6	4.7	6.0	13.5	4.7	2.0	2.6	1.2	1.6	4.4	4.0	1.7
Israel	20.1	1.8	3.3	29.1	7.1	1.0	2.9	1.6	6.8	4.0	3.1	19.0
Japan	14.5	3.4	4.8	25.6	4.4	4.0	10.6	2.7	10.0	2.2	7.4	10.4
Malaysia	22.4	2.6	3.6	21.1	5.3	2.3	16.1	3.0	4.1	1.9	13.1	4.5
Mexico	25.1	2.6	3.3	12.5	8.5	4.5	17.0	1.7	4.9	3.4	8.0	8.4
Morocco	33.0	2.2	8.2	16.6	6.0	6.0	14.8	3.4	2.5	1.3	2.0	4.2
New Zealand	12.8	4.6	4.7	21.0	8.2	3.5	15.0	2.7	7.0	5.6	8.2	6.6
Philippines	37.4	1.6	2.7	22.5	4.9	1.6	7.9	0.8	0.5	3.8	5.2	11.0
Saudi Arabia	23.9	1.3	10.0	17.3	7.2	2.8	9.1	3.2	7.5	3.1	3.6	10.9
Singapore	12.2	1.8	3.8	15.0	7.2	6.3	17.8	2.4	7.2	6.9	14.8	4.7
South Africa	18.8	8.8	4.9	12.0	9.6	7.9	16.9	1.9	4.6	2.5	2.6	9.5
South Korea	13.9	2.2	4.2	17.5	4.3	7.8	11.7	4.7	8.3	5.0	6.9	13.4
Taiwan	23.4	2.1	3.8	17.6	3.0	9.4	8.8	5.9	6.1	7.4	5.0	7.6
Thailand	27.2	7.3	12.1	9.9	9.1	7.7	9.7	1.4	3.1	1.4	9.0	2.1
USA	7.1	2.2	4.1	18.3	4.7	19.3	10.9	1.8	9.0	2.6	6.1	14.0
Venezuela	28.6	3.5	3.4	14.9	2.5	2.3	4.9	0.6	3.3	1.4	13.1	21.4
Vietnam	22.8	5.9	9.2	8.7	8.8	7.6	11.9	1.8	5.1	7.5	6.4	4.4

Source: Market intelligence firm Euromonitor International, **http://www.euromonitor.com.**

The Global MARKETPLACE 4.3

In Search of the New China

The complexity and vast changes of the Chinese market have always proved the biggest challenges for Western marketers. Geographically, regional difference is so distinct that China is regarded as a combination of many small markets. The consumption pattern varies significantly between coastal and central regions, and between the south and the north, mainly due to differences in cultural and economic backgrounds. The Gallup Organization conducted a broad range of surveys to better understand Chinese consumers from different regions. For example, there is much heavier consumption of beer in northern China than in other regions. In eastern China, people mostly read newspapers but do not listen to the radio. This has major implications for how marketers advertise their products.

On the other hand, the dynamics across different industries as well as within each industry also vary drastically. In China's personal computer market, for example, desktop PCs hold 90 percent of the market share, although the demand for laptop computers is growing quickly. In 2001, a total of 60 percent of PCs sold were sold in the economically developed east, north, and south. In the sub-market of PC servers, the share is even higher at

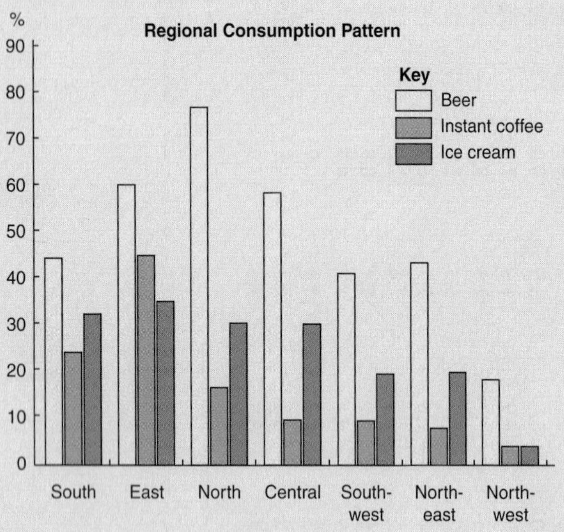

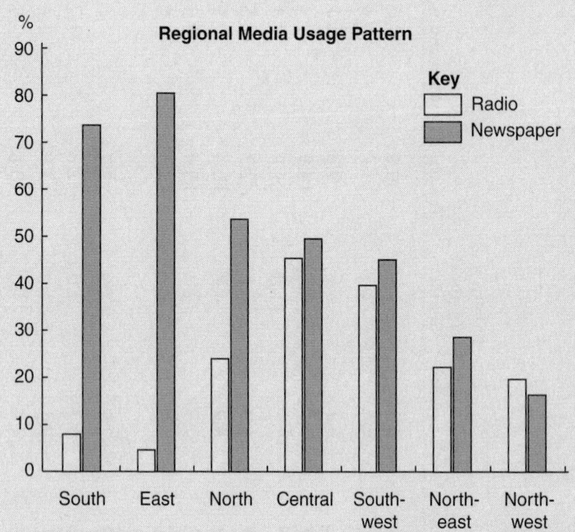

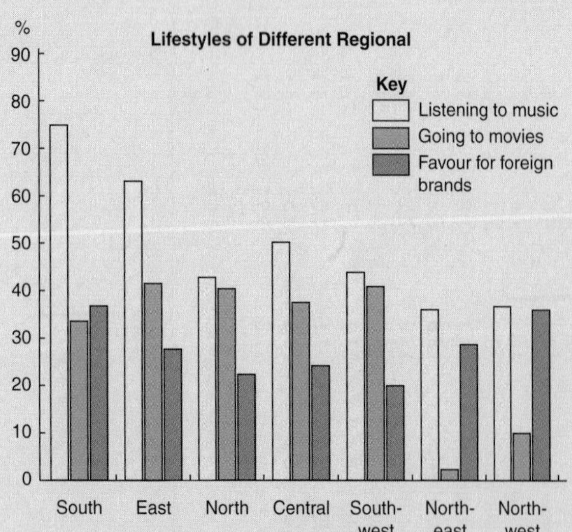

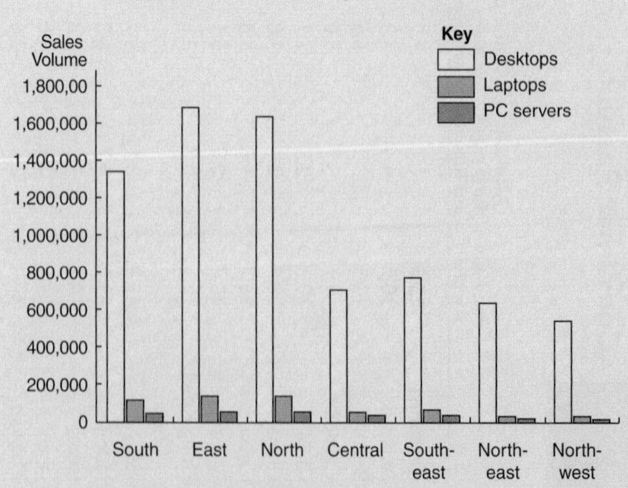

Source: Graphs *(top row and lower left)* © 1999 The Gallup Organization, "1999 Survey: Nationwide Study of Chinese Consumer Attitudes and Lifestyles." All rights reserved, used with permission. Graph *(lower right)* based on CCID, **http://www.doim.army.mil/ccid.**

65 percent. Among PC makers, local manufacturers have the majority of the market share. According to International Data Corporation, the domestic IT flagship Legend is the dominator in the PC market, with a market share around 31 percent in 2001. Founder is the second largest seller, with a market share ranging between 7 and 8 percent. Tsinghua Tongfang follows in third position. Among the overseas brands, Dell is the largest player, with a market share of 4.6 percent, the fourth largest among all the players.

Sources: "A Survey of China," *Economist*, April 8, 2000, 1–16; "In Search of the New China," *Fortune*, October 11, 1999, 230–32; "What the Chinese Want," *Fortune*, October 11, 1999, 233–37; "Sino-Foreign Consultancy Firms to Jointly Launch On-Line Survey," *Xinhua*, November 15, 2000.

market potential. Exhibit 4.7 presents the percentage of households that owns certain appliances and indicates that saturation levels in the markets for which the data exist are quite high. This does not necessarily indicate lack of market potential; replacement markets or the demand for auxiliary products may offer attractive opportunities to the global marketer. Low rates of diffusion should be approached cautiously because they can signal a market opportunity or lack thereof resulting from low income levels, use of a substitute product, or lack of acceptance. As an example of lack of acceptance, the time-saving characteristic of microwave ovens may not be as attractive in more tradition-bound societies as it is in Canada, the United States, or the EU.

General consumption figures are valuable, but they must be viewed with caution because they may conceal critical product-form differences; for example, appliances in European households tend to be smaller than their Canadian and U.S. counterparts. Information about existing product usage can nevertheless provide indirect help to global marketers. As an example, a large number of telephones, and their even distribution among the population or a target group, may allow market research via telephone interviewing.

A problem for marketers in general is **inflation**; varying inflation rates complicate this problem in international markets. Many of the industrialized countries, such as Canada, the United States, Germany, and Japan, have recently been able to keep inflation rates at single-digit levels, while some have suffered from chronic inflation (Exhibit 4.8). Inflation affects the ability of both industrial customers and consumers to buy; it also introduces uncertainty into both the marketer's planning process and consumers' buying habits. In high-inflation markets, the marketer may have to make changes in the product (more economical without compromising quality), promotion (more rational), and distribution (more customer involvement) to meet customer needs and maintain demand. In response to rapidly escalating prices, a government will often invoke price controls. The setting of maximum prices for products may cause the global marketer to face unacceptable profit situations in certain national markets, future investments may not be made, and production may even have to be stopped.[13]

Another challenge for global marketers is the **debt problem**. Many of the developing countries are saddled with a collective debt of $1.2 trillion (Exhibit 4.9). Debt crises crush nations' buying power and force imports down and exports up to meet interest payments. To continue growing, many companies are looking at developing nations because of the potential they see 10 to 15 years ahead. North American companies typically face competition in these regions from entities that are often assisted by their government's aid grants, as well as by Europeans who do business with the help of government export credits that have interest rates lower than those provided by North American entities. Access to these markets can be achieved by helping political leaders provide jobs and by increasing exports. To sell products in these markets, companies may have to engage in countertrade, either by accepting payment in goods or by supporting customers' efforts in their international marketing.[14] Many industrialized countries, such as Canada, Japan, France, and the United States, are seeking ways to ease the burden facing debtor nations.

Exhibit 4.7 Percentage of Households Owning Selected Appliances, 2005

	Passenger car	CD player	Dishwasher	Freezer	Microwave oven	Personal computer	Refrigerator	Telephone	Colour TV	Tumble dryer	Vacuum cleaner	Washing machine
Argentina	59.7	26.4	16.2	17.9	15.4	27.5	84.1	71.5	92.1	7.4	54.5	49.7
Australia	82.1	85.5	38.8	51.6	77.4	45.2	82.9	82.0	92.1	57.2	99.5	90.8
Brazil	49.6	16.9	6.8	7.6	6.1	29.0	84.5	47.8	87.9	2.2	36.6	24.7
Canada	86.7	81.5	55.5	58.9	91.1	60.5	99.5	88.7	98.8	86.5	98.6	86.4
Chile	50.2	12.1	2.4	16.8	10.1	25.0	65.3	83.0	63.4	8.4	53.7	47.9
China	3.1	2.4	1.5	0.5	0.5	15.8	6.8	28.4	46.8	1.8	2.0	2.7
Colombia	38.5	25.6	4.1	15.1	9.3	15.2	68.6	57.5	87.2	3.8	51.1	40.4
Egypt	11.4	4.9	0.4	3.3	2.8	3.1	72.1	18.6	52.4	2.2	3.9	5.3
Hong Kong, China	74.4	58.4	27.9	34.4	79.6	29.1	97.2	96.6	99.1	23.5	78.8	95.4
India	0.7	1.5	1.3	1.4	0.4	1.1	15.4	18.4	36.5	1.2	0.1	5.0
Indonesia	3.8	1.7	1.1	0.7	0.8	1.0	28.1	14.3	53.4	1.8	1.5	5.6
Israel	86.0	21.1	34.9	19.5	83.8	40.7	99.3	91.3	96.9	41.6	73.5	94.1
Japan	81.6	69.8	58.2	35.5	90.9	52.6	97.9	87.7	99.0	37.7	99.1	99.5
Malaysia	63.4	18.1	2.0	3.4	65.9	26.4	97.5	85.6	90.2	24.2	73.4	80.7
Mexico	23.3	10.2	8.4	6.0	24.9	9.8	69.2	31.8	90.9	5.0	11.5	41.4
Morocco	10.7	10.5	0.2	1.4	0.4	4.5	48.3	33.7	49.6	2.0	2.5	11.3
New Zealand	82.6	88.5	43.9	55.6	81.8	55.4	84.5	82.5	98.2	71.1	99.4	98.1
Philippines	7.7	3.9	0.7	1.5	0.5	3.3	45.1	12.8	68.5	1.7	1.6	8.1
Saudi Arabia	99.3	34.0	22.9	29.3	27.2	35.1	98.8	67.4	99.1	7.4	20.1	36.2
Singapore	44.5	56.0	32.7	21.5	55.6	65.6	99.5	96.7	98.7	23.6	85.4	95.6
South Africa	9.8	6.7	17.9	24.1	7.9	9.4	80.9	29.6	66.1	4.3	23.3	27.3
South Korea	43.5	22.6	3.0	3.1	46.9	32.5	96.5	98.2	93.8	36.1	65.5	67.6
Taiwan	51.3	70.6	4.8	15.9	46.8	40.7	99.5	98.5	99.3	25.3	56.3	94.9
Thailand	35.3	5.5	1.3	2.1	3.2	10.4	71.0	31.2	84.9	2.4	3.1	5.0
U.S.A.	93.3	61.3	60.2	37.8	86.0	74.2	99.4	86.0	99.7	69.2	99.2	83.3
Venezuela	47.6	10.0	3.4	21.9	13.6	13.8	83.8	43.0	96.3	5.6	42.6	40.0
Vietnam	1.9	1.4	0.8	0.1	0.5	0.7	19.5	8.4	42.2	0.9	0.1	2.6

Source: Market intelligence firm Euromonitor International, **http://www.euromonitor.com.**

Exhibit 4.8 Consumer Price Index

Prices - consumer and producer prices - consumer price indexes (CPI)
CPI: all items

Year 2000=100

	1997	1998	1999	2000	2001	2002	2003	2004
Australia	93.5	94.3	95.7	100.0	104.4	107.5	110.5	113.1
Austria	96.3	97.2	97.7	100.0	102.7	104.5	105.9	108.1
Belgium	95.5	96.4	97.5	100.0	102.5	104.2	105.8	108.0
Canada	94.7	95.7	97.3	100.0	102.5	104.8	107.7	109.7
Czech Republic	85.2	94.3	96.2	100.0	104.7	106.8	106.8	109.8
Denmark	93.1	94.8	97.2	100.0	102.4	104.8	107.0	108.3
Finland	94.6	95.9	97.0	100.0	102.6	104.2	105.1	105.3
France	97.2	97.8	98.3	100.0	101.6	103.6	105.8	108.0
Germany	97.1	98.0	98.6	100.0	102.0	103.4	104.5	106.2
Greece	90.2	94.5	96.9	100.0	103.4	107.1	110.9	114.1
Hungary	72.5	82.8	91.1	100.0	109.1	114.9	120.2	128.3
Iceland	90.6	92.1	95.1	100.0	106.4	111.9	114.2	117.8
Ireland	91.0	93.2	94.7	100.0	104.9	109.7	113.6	116.0
Italy	94.1	95.9	97.5	100.0	102.8	105.3	108.1	110.5
Japan	100.4	101.0	100.7	100.0	99.3	98.4	98.1	98.1
Korea	90.2	97.0	97.8	100.0	104.1	106.9	110.7	114.7
Luxembourg	95.1	96.0	96.9	100.0	102.7	104.8	106.9	109.3
Mexico	67.6	78.3	91.3	100.0	106.4	111.7	116.8	122.3
Netherlands	93.7	95.6	97.7	100.0	104.2	107.6	109.9	111.2
New Zealand	96.3	97.6	97.5	100.0	102.6	105.4	107.2	109.7
Norway	92.7	94.8	97.0	100.0	103.0	104.3	106.9	107.4
Poland	76.1	84.9	91.0	100.0	105.4	107.4	108.2	111.8
Portugal	92.4	95.0	97.2	100.0	104.4	108.1	111.6	114.2
Slovak Republic	75.7	80.7	89.3	100.0	107.3	110.7	120.2	129.2
Spain	92.8	94.5	96.7	100.0	103.6	106.8	110.0	113.4
Sweden[1]	98.0	98.4	98.7	100.0	102.6	105.1	107.3	107.8
Switzerland	97.7	97.7	98.5	100.0	101.0	101.6	102.3	103.1
Turkey	21.2	39.2	64.6	100.0	154.4	223.8	280.4	310.1
United Kingdom	92.5	95.7	97.2	100.0	101.8	103.5	106.5	109.7
United States	93.2	94.7	96.7	100.0	102.8	104.5	106.8	109.7
EU15	94.8	96.5	97.7	100.0	102.4	104.6	106.9	109.2
OECD total	89.5	93.0	96.2	100.0	103.5	106.2	108.9	111.5
Brazil	86.3	89.1	93.4	100.0	106.8	115.9	132.9	141.7
China	101.8	101.0	99.6	100.0	100.7	99.9	101.1	105.0
India	81.1	91.9	96.1	100.0	103.8	108.2	112.4	116.6
Russian Federation	34.9	44.6	82.8	100.0	121.5	140.7	159.9	177.3
South Africa	84.4	90.3	94.9	100.0	105.7	115.4	122.1	123.8

1. Figures are computed using the annual official Swedish inflation rate and differ from the annual official consumer price index.

Source: Adapted from OECD Factbook 2006: Economic, Environmental and Social Statistics, ISBN 92-64-03561-3 © OECD 2006, **http://stats.oecd.org.**

Exhibit 4.9

Nations in Debt: Debt Outstanding (Millions of Dollars) in 2000

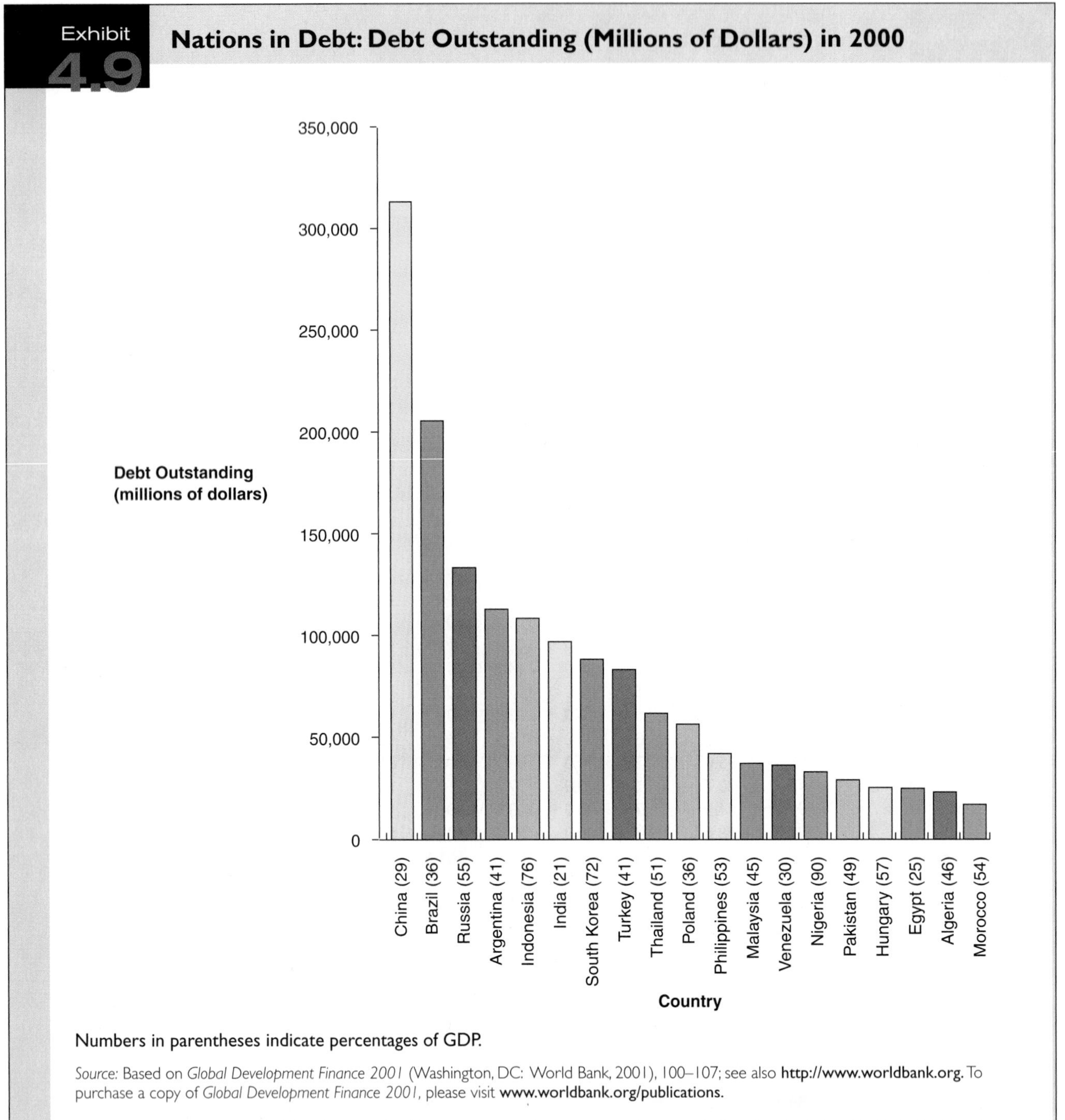

Numbers in parentheses indicate percentages of GDP.

Source: Based on *Global Development Finance 2001* (Washington, DC: World Bank, 2001), 100–107; see also **http://www.worldbank.org.** To purchase a copy of *Global Development Finance 2001*, please visit **www.worldbank.org/publications.**

Infrastructure

The availability and quality of infrastructure is critically important in evaluating marketing operations abroad. Each global marketer will rely heavily on services provided by the local market for transportation, communication, and energy as well as on organizations participating in the facilitating functions of marketing: marketing communications, distributing, information, and financing. Indicators such as steel consumption, cement production, and electricity production relate to the overall industrialization of the market and can be used effectively by suppliers of industrial products and services. As an example, energy consumption per capita may serve as an indicator of market potential for electrical markets, provided evenness of distribution exists over the market. Yet the marketer must make sure that the energy is affordable and compatible (in terms of current and voltage) with the products to be marketed.

The existence and expansion of basic infrastructure has contributed significantly to increased agricultural output in Asia and Latin America. The Philippines has allocated 5 percent of agricultural development funds to rural electrification programs. On a similar level, basic roads are essential to moving agricultural products. In many parts of Africa, farmers are more than a day's walk from the nearest road. As a result, measures to improve production without commensurate improvements in transportation and communications are of little use because the crops cannot reach the market. In addition, the lack of infrastructure cuts the farmers off from new technology, inputs, and ideas.

Transportation networks by land, rail, waterway, or air are essential for physical distribution. An analysis of rail traffic by freight tons per kilometre offers a possible way to begin an investigation of transportation capabilities; however, these figures may not always indicate the true state of the system. China's railway system carries five times as much freight as India's does, which is an amazing feat considering that only 20 percent of the network is double-tracked and that it is shared by an ever-growing amount of passenger traffic. In spite of the railway's greater use, the global marketer has to rely on other methods of distribution. The tremendous logistics challenge makes national distribution in China only a dream and slows down expansion from the major urban population centres of Guangzhou, Shanghai, and Beijing.[15] With the same type of caution, the number of passenger cars as well as buses and trucks can be used to analyze the state of road transportation and transportation networks.

Communication is as important as transportation. The ability of a firm to communicate with entities both outside and within the market can be estimated by using indicators of the communications infrastructure: telephones, computers, broadcast media, and print media in use. The countries of the former Eastern bloc possess some of the world's worst telephone systems. Western Europe has 49 main telephone lines per 100 people, while Russia has 12, Hungary has 9, and Poland has 8. Upgrading the telephone system will be expensive (estimated at $50 billion for Central Europe alone) but necessary for competing in the world market and attracting international investors. Official figures may not reveal the quality of the services provided and their possible reach. For example, the telephone system in Egypt, especially in Cairo, is notorious for its frequent breakdowns and lack of capacity. Wireless technology is poised to change the worldwide landscape as the number of cellular phones in use increases around the world. Canadian companies are at the forefront of the rollout of wireless technologies around the world. Using US$250 million in financing from Export Development Canada, Reliance Infocomm is undertaking a major wireless infrastructure project in India that will support the purchase of Ontario-based Nortel Network's equipment. SMARTS, the fourth largest mobile communications company in Russia, has also signed a multimillion-dollar contract to purchase Nortel equipment, while Hong Kong's Hutchison Telecommunications International Limited will also purchase Nortel technology for a major project in Vietnam. Nortel, a major Canadian telecommunications company, operates in over 150 countries and generates more than 90 percent of its sales outside of Canada.[16]

The diffusion of Internet technology into core business processes and into the lifestyles of consumers has been rapid, especially in industrialized countries. The number of Internet hosts (computers through which users connect to the network) has increased to 399 million by January 2006, up from 9.4 million in 1993 and 43.2 million in 1999.[17] While the United States still has the majority of these, Northern Europe is also very active (Exhibit 4.10). The total number of people using the Internet is difficult to estimate. One estimate in September 2002 placed the number at 605.6 million worldwide, with 182.67 million in North America, 190.91 million in Europe, 187.27 million in the Asia-Pacific region, 33.35 million in Latin America, 6.31 million in Africa, and 5.12 million in the Middle East.[18] Given the changes expected in the 21st century, all the estimates indicating explosive growth may be low. The number of users will start evening out around the globe, with new technologies assisting. Computers priced at less than $500 will boost global computer ownership and subsequent online activity. Developments in television, cable, phone, and wireless technologies not only will make the market broader but will also allow for more services to be delivered more efficiently. For example, with the advent of third-generation mobile communications technology, systems have a hundredfold increase in data transfer capability, allowing the viewing of videos on mobile phones. Television will also become a mainstream Internet access method of the future. While the interactive-TV market served only a few million viewers in Europe and North America in the 1990s, forecasts call for significant growth in the years ahead.

The careful assessment of infrastructure spells out important marketing opportunities. While 2 billion people in Asia are without electricity and only 16 in 1,000 have access to a telephone, the Asian market is the most keenly watched by marketers. China overtook the United States in pager use by late 1997 mainly because of the low cost of the needed infrastructure to support paging. The big winners will be companies like Motorola that are developing new products for this market, such as pagers that play back voice mail. The booming middle class in cities such as Bangkok will ensure that cellular phone sales continue at a record pace. With increasing affluence comes an increasing need for energy. General Electric estimates that China will place orders for 168,000 megawatts in additional power-generating capacity, and India more than 70,000 megawatts; the corresponding figure in the United States is 154,000.

Data on the availability of commercial (marketing-related) infrastructure are often not readily available. Data on which to base an assessment may be provided by government sources, such as Overseas Business Reports; by trade associations, such as the Business Equipment Manufacturers' Association; and by trade publications, such as *Advertising Age*. The more extensive the firm's international involvement, the more it can rely on its already existing support network of banks, advertising agencies, and distributors to assess new markets.

Exhibit 4.10 Network Effect (Internet Hosts per 1,000 Inhabitants in 2001)

Country	Internet Hosts per 10,000 Inhabitants in 2001
United States	3,714
Iceland	1,905
Finland	1,707
Netherlands	1,635
Australia	1,183
New Zealand	1,045
Denmark	1,045
Canada	932
Sweden	825
Switzerland	731
Norway	674
Hong Kong SAR	574
Japan	559
Singapore	479
Austria	401
Britain	371
Belgium	342
Ireland	334
France	313
Luxembourg	312
Germany	295
Israel	221
Hungary	168
Spain	133
Italy	117

Source: Reproduced with the kind permission of ITU.

Impact of the Economic Environment on Social Development

Economic success comes with a price tag. All the social traumas that were once believed endemic only to the West are now hitting other parts of the world as well. Many countries, including the nations of Southeast Asia, were able to achieve double-digit growth for decades while paying scant attention to problems that are now demanding treatment: infrastructure limits, labour shortages, demands for greater political freedom, environmental destruction, urban congestion, and even the spread of drug addiction.[19]

Because of the close relationship between economic and social development, many of the figures can be used as social indicators as well. Consider the following factors and their significance: share of urban population, life expectancy, number of physicians per capita, literacy rate, percentage of income received by the richest 5 percent of the population, and percentage of the population with access to electricity. In addition to these factors, several other variables can be used as cultural indicators: number of public libraries, registered borrowings, book titles published, and number of daily newspapers. The **Physical Quality of Life Index (PQLI)** is a composite measure of the level of welfare in a country. It has three components: life expectancy, infant mortality, and adult literacy rates.[20] The three components of the PQLI are among the few social indicators available to provide a comparison of progress through time in all of the countries of the world.

Differences in the degree of urbanization of target markets in lesser-developed countries influence global marketers' product strategies. If products are targeted only to urban areas, products need minimal adjustments, mainly to qualify them for market entry. However, when targeting national markets, firms may need to make extensive adaptations to match more closely the expectations and the more narrow consumption experiences of the rural population.[21]

In terms of infrastructure, improved access in rural areas brings with it an expansion of non-farm enterprises such as shops, repair services, and grain mills. It also changes customs, attitudes, and values. As an example, a World Bank study on the impact of rural roads in Yucatán, Mexico, found that roads offered an opportunity for expanding women's role by introducing new ideas, education, medical care, and economic alternatives to maize cultivation.[22] In particular, women married later, had fewer children, and pursued more non-domestic activities. The same impact has been observed with increased access to radio and television. These changes can, if properly understood and utilized, offer major new opportunities to the global marketer.

The presence of multinational corporations, which by their very nature are change agents, will accelerate social change. If government control is weak, the multinational corporation bears the social responsibility for its actions. In some cases, governments restrict the freedom of multinational corporations if their actions may affect the environment. As an example, the Indonesian government places construction restrictions (such as building height) on hotels in Bali to avoid the overcrowding and ecological problems caused in Hawaii when that state developed its tourism sector vigorously.

In More Detail 4.1

AN ALTERNATIVE MEASURE OF WELFARE

In addition to the Physical Quality of Life Index, global marketers may also wish to analyze the United Nations Human Development Index (HDI). The HDI was developed in 1990 by Pakistani economist Mahbub ul Haq and measures welfare on three dimensions of achievement: literacy rates, life expectancy, and Gross Domestic Product (GDP) at PPP. The HDI ranges from 0 to 1 and is often used to classify countries. An HDI of less than 0.5 is indicative of low development while a reading in excess of 0.8 is considered high development. Countries with an HDI greater than 0.8 include Canada, the U.S., Australia, Japan, France, the U.K., Hong Kong, and Germany. Countries at the bottom of the HDI ranking include most of the countries in Africa, as well as Haiti and Yemen.

Source: Human Development Index, in Wikipedia, **http://en.wikipedia.org/wiki/UN_Human_Development_Index** (accessed February 26, 2007).

Regional Economic Integration

Economic integration has been one of the main economic developments affecting world markets since World War II. Countries have wanted to engage in economic cooperation to use their respective resources more effectively and to provide larger markets for member-country producers. Some integration efforts have had quite ambitious goals, such as political integration; some have failed as the result of perceptions of unequal benefits from the arrangement or parting of ways politically. Exhibit 4.11, a summary of the major forms of economic cooperation in regional markets, shows the varying degrees of formality with which integration can take place. These economic integration efforts are dividing the world into trading blocs. Exhibit 4.12 presents basic data on the 17 active regional economic blocs in existence around the world.

The largest economic groupings based on population size are seen to be the EU with 496 million people, NAFTA at 430 million, ASEA with 554 million and SAARC with 1.4 billion. In terms of GDP per capita, the most significant groupings are EFTA at US$38,546 and NAFTA at US$35,491.

Levels of Economic Integration

Economic integration between countries can occur at various levels. Countries may opt for loose relationships involving the mere elimination of tariff barriers between members, or a more holistic economic or political union involving the harmonization of monetary and fiscal policies and political systems.

Free Trade Area

The **free trade area** is the least restrictive and loosest form of economic integration among nations. In a free trade area, all barriers to trade among member countries are removed. Goods and services are freely traded among member countries. No discriminatory taxes, quotas, tariffs, or other barriers are allowed. Sometimes a free trade area is

Exhibit 4.11 Forms of Economic Integration in Regional Markets

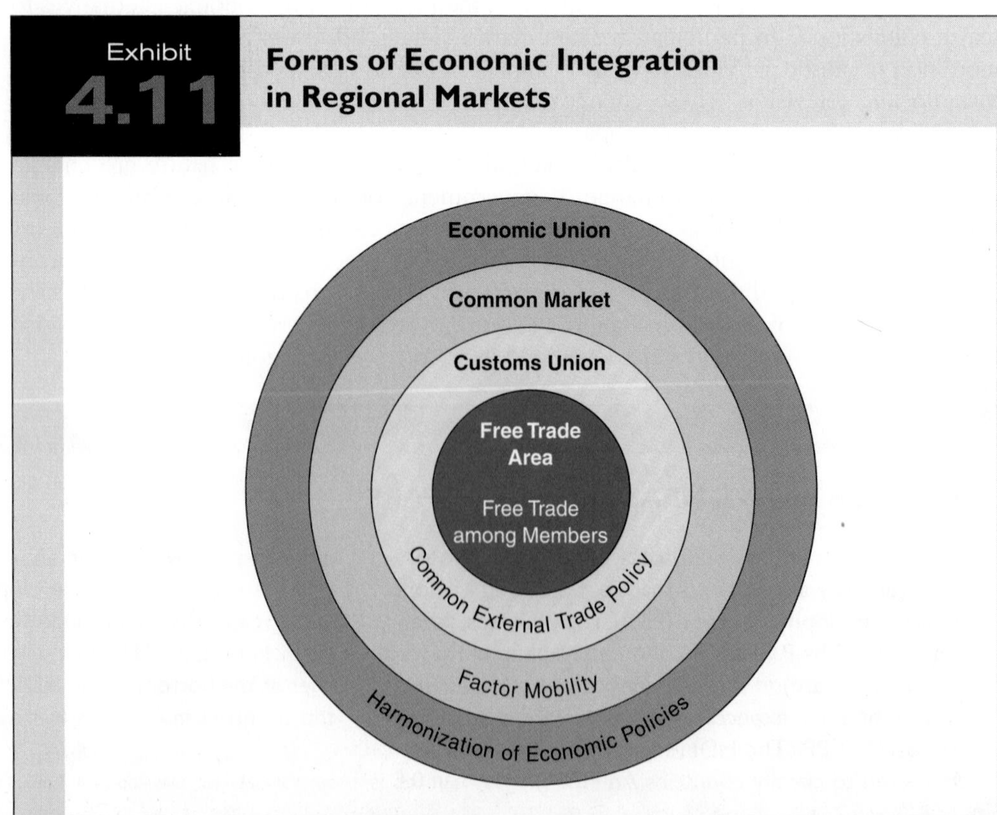

Exhibit 4.12

Active Regional Economic Blocs

Economic Grouping	Population	GDP (at PPP) US$ (millions)	Number of Member States
European Union (EU)	496,198,605	12,025,415	27
European Free Trade Association (EFTA)	12,233,467	471,547	4
Caribbean Community (CARICOM)	14,565,083	64,219	15
South American Community of Nations (CSN)	370,158,470	2,868,430	10
Economic Community of West African States (ECOWAS)	251,646,263	342,519	15
Economic and Monetary Community of Central Africa (CEMAC)	34,970,529	85,136	6
East African Community (EAC)	97,865,428	104,239	3
Southern African Customs Union (SACU)	51,055,878	541,433	5
Common Market for Eastern and Southern Africa (COMESA)	118,950,321	141,962	5
Agadir Agreement	126,066,286	513,674	4
Gulf Cooperation Council (GCC)	35,869,438	536,223	6
North American Free Trade Agreement (NAFTA)	430,495,039	15,279,000	3
Association of Southeast Asian Nations (ASEAN)	553,900,000	2,172,000	10
South Asian Association for Regional Cooperation (SAARC)	1,467,255,669	4,074,031	8
Eurasian Economic Community (EurAsEC)	208,067,618	1,689,137	6
Pacific Regional Trade Agreement (PARTA)	7,810,905	23,074	14
Central American Common Market (CACM)	37,816,598	159,536	5

Source: Trade Bloc, from wikipedia website, **http://en.wikipedia.org/wiki/Trade_bloc** (accessed February 26, 2007).

formed only for certain classes of goods and services. For example, before NAFTA, the United States and Canada already had sectoral free trade agreements, such as that for automobiles. A notable feature of free trade areas is that each member country continues to set its own policies in relation to non-members. This means that each member is free to set any tariffs or other restrictions that it chooses on trade with countries outside of the free trade area. Among such arrangements are the European Free Trade Association (EFTA) and the North American Free Trade Agreement (NAFTA). As an example of the freedom members have in terms of their policies toward non-members, Mexico has signed a number of bilateral free trade agreements with other blocs (the European Union) and nations (Chile) to both improve trade and to attract investment. Canada has also signed bilateral agreements with countries such as Chile.

Customs Union

The **customs union** is one step further along the spectrum of economic integration. As in the free trade area, members of the customs union dismantle barriers to trade in goods and services among members. In addition, however, the customs union establishes a common trade policy with respect to non-members. Typically, this takes the form of a common external tariff, whereby imports from non-members are subject to the same tariff when sold to any member country. The Southern African Customs Union is the oldest and most successful example of economic integration in Africa.

Common Market

The **common market** amounts to a customs union covering the exchange of goods and services, the prohibition of duties in exports and imports between members, and the adoption of a common external tariff in respect to non-members. In addition, factors of production (labour, capital, and technology) are mobile among members. Restrictions on immigration and cross-border investment are abolished. The importance of **factor mobility** for economic growth cannot be overstated. When factors of production are mobile, then capital, labour, and technology may be employed in their most productive uses. The Caribbean Single Market Economy (CSME), the proposed successor agreement to CARICOM, is an example of a common market.

Despite the obvious benefits, members of a common market must be prepared to cooperate closely in monetary, fiscal, and employment policies. Furthermore, although a common market will enhance the productivity of members in the aggregate, it is by no means clear that individual member countries will always benefit. Because of these difficulties, the goals of common markets have proved to be elusive in many areas of the world, notably Central and South America and Asia. In the mid 1980s, the European Community (EC) embarked on an ambitious effort to remove the barriers between the then 12 member countries to free the movement of goods, services, capital, and people. The process was ratified by the passing of the **Single European Act** in 1987 with the target date of December 31, 1992, to complete the internal market. In December 1991, the EC agreed in Maastricht that the so-called 1992 process would be a step toward cooperation beyond the economic dimension. While many of the directives aimed at opening borders and markets were completed on schedule, some sectors, such as automobiles, took longer to open up.

Economic Union

The creation of a true **economic union** requires integration of economic policies in addition to the free movement of goods, services, and factors of production across borders. Under an economic union, members will harmonize monetary policies, taxation, and government spending. In addition, a common currency is to be used by members. This could be accomplished, de facto, by a system of fixed exchange rates. Clearly, the formation of an economic union requires members to surrender a large measure of their national sovereignty to supranational authorities in community-wide institutions such as the European Parliament. The final step would be a **political union** calling for political unification. The ratification of the Maastricht Treaty in late 1993 by all of the 12 member countries of the EC created the European Union, effective January 1, 1994. The treaty (jointly with the Treaty of Amsterdam in 1997) set the foundation for economic and monetary union (EMU) with the establishment of the euro (€) as a common currency in January 2002. Thirteen EU countries are currently part of "Euroland," the set of EU member countries that have adopted the euro (Austria, Belgium, Finland, France, Germany, Greece, Holland, Ireland, Italy, Luxembourg, Portugal, Slovenia, and Spain). The European Central Bank, which was set up in 1998 under the Treaty on European Union, is responsible for the management of the single currency.[23] In addition, the EU is moving toward political union, with common foreign and security policy as well as judicial cooperation.

Economic Integration in Europe

The most important implication of the freedom of movement for products, services, people, and capital within the EU is the economic growth that is expected to result. Several specific sources of increased growth have been identified. First, there will be gains from eliminating the transaction costs associated with border patrols, customs procedures, and so forth. Second, economic growth will be spurred by the economies of scale that will be achieved when production facilities become more concentrated. Third, there will be gains from more intense competition among European companies. Firms that were monopolists in one country will now be subject to competition from firms in other member countries. The introduction of the euro has added to the efficiencies, especially in terms of consolidation of firms across industries and across countries. Furthermore, countries in Euroland enjoy lower transaction costs and reduced currency risks, and consumers and businesses will enjoy price transparency and increased price-based competition.

The enlargement of the EU has been a heavily debated issue. Issues surrounding the speed and cost of enlargement and disagreements over agriculture and the free movement of labour needed to be resolved. In 2004, 10 countries simultaneously joined the EU. By early 2007, the number of member countries had increased to 27: Austria, Belgium, Bulgaria, Cyprus, the Czech Republic, Denmark, Estonia, Finland, France, Germany, Greece,

Exhibit 4.13 **The Euro—Europe's Single Currency**

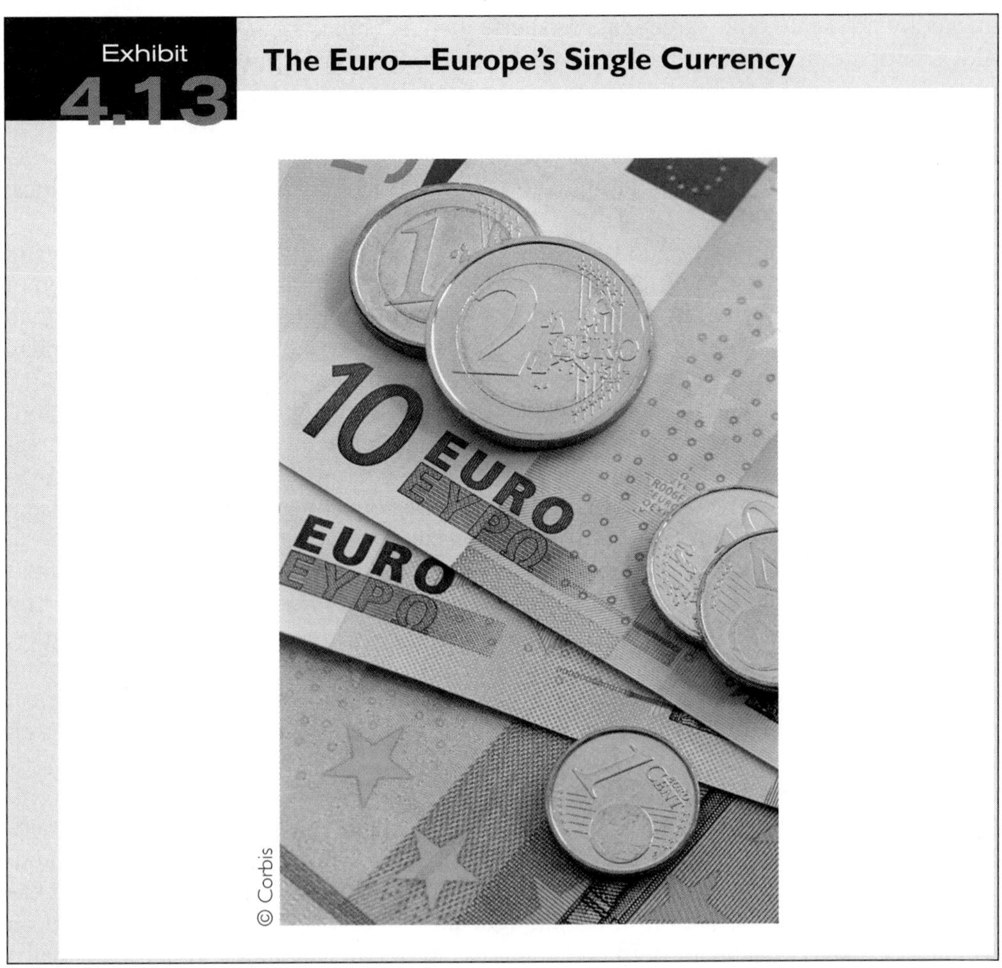

© Corbis

Hungary, Ireland, Italy, Latvia, Lithuania, Luxembourg, Malta, the Netherlands, Poland, Portugal, Romania, Slovakia, Slovenia, Spain, Sweden, and the United Kingdom. Other countries such as Croatia, Macedonia, Turkey, Albania, Bosnia and Herzegovina, Serbia, and Montenegro remain candidates for membership. The agreement on the European Economic Area (EEA) extends the single market of the EU to three of the four EFTA countries (Iceland, Liechtenstein, and Norway, with Switzerland opting to develop its relationship with the EU through bilateral agreements).[24]

The integration has important implications for firms within and outside Europe because it poses both threats and opportunities, benefits and costs. There will be substantial benefits for those firms already operating in Europe. These firms will gain because their operations in one country can now be freely expanded into others and their products may be freely sold across borders. In a borderless Europe, firms will have access to approximately 500 million consumers. Substantial economies of scale in production and marketing will also result. The extent of these economies of scale will depend on the ability of the marketers to find pan-regional segments or to homogenize tastes across borders through promotional activity.

For firms from non-member countries, there are various possibilities depending on the firm's position within the market. Exhibit 4.14 provides four different scenarios with proposed courses of action. Well-established global marketers will be able to take advantage of the new economies of scale. For example, 3M plants earlier turned out different versions of the company's products for various markets. Now, the 3M plant in Wales, for example, makes videotapes and videocassettes for all of Europe. Colgate-Palmolive has to watch out for competitors, like Germany's Henkel, in the brutally competitive detergent market. At the same time, large-scale retailers, such as France's Carrefour and Germany's Aldi group, are undertaking their own efforts to exploit the situation with hypermarkets supplied by central warehouses with computerized inventories. Their procurement policies have to be met by companies like Heinz. Many multinationals are developing pan-European strategies to exploit the emerging situation; that is, they are standardizing their products and processes to the greatest extent possible without compromising local input and implementation.

A company with a foothold in only one European market is faced with the danger of competitors who can use the strength of multiple markets. Furthermore, the elimination of barriers may do away with the company's competitive advantage. For example, more than half of the 45 major European food companies are in just 1 or 2 of the individual European markets and seriously lag behind broader-based North American and Swiss firms. Similarly, automakers PSA and Fiat are nowhere close to the cross-manufacturing presence of Ford and GM. The courses of action include expansion through acquisitions or mergers, formation of strategic alliances (for example, AT&T's joint venture with Spain's Telefonica to produce state-of-the-art microchips), rationalization by concentrating only on business segments in which the company can be a pan-European leader, and finally, divestment.

Exporters will need to worry about maintaining their competitive position and continued access to the market. Companies with a physical presence in Europe may be in a better position to assess and take advantage of the developments. In some industries, marketers do not see a reason either to be in Europe at all or to change from exporting to more involved modes of entry. Machinery and machine tools, for example, are in great demand in Europe, and marketers in these companies say they have little reason to manufacture there.

The term **Fortress Europe** has been used to describe the fears of many about a unified Europe. The concern is that while Europe dismantles internal barriers, it will raise external ones, making access to the European market difficult for Canadian and other non-EU firms. In a move designed to protect European farmers, for example, the EU has occasionally banned the import of certain agricultural goods. The EU has also called on members to limit the number of foreign television programs broadcast in Europe. Finally, many multinational firms are concerned about the relatively strict domestic content rules

Exhibit 4.14 Proposed Company Responses to European Integration

Company Status	Challenges	Response
Established multinational market/multiple markets	• Exploit opportunities from improved productivity • Meet challenge of competitors • Cater to customers/ intermediaries doing same	Pan-European strategy
Firm with one European subsidiary	• Competition • Loss of niche	Expansion Strategic alliances Rationalization Divestment
Exporter to Europe	• Competition • Access	European branch Selective acquisition Strategic alliance
No interest	• Competition at home • Lost opportunity	Entry

Source: Developed from John F. Magee, "1992: Moves Americans Must Make," *Harvard Business Review* 67 (May–June 1989): 78–84.

passed by the EU. These rules require certain products sold in Europe to be manufactured with European inputs. One effect of the perceived threat of Fortress Europe has been increased direct investment in Europe by foreign firms. Fears that the EU will erect barriers to exports and fears of the domestic content rules governing many goods have led many firms to initiate or expand European direct investment.

North American Integration

Although the EU is undoubtedly the most successful and best-known integrative effort, North American integration efforts have also gained momentum and attention. What started as a trading pact between two close and economically well-developed allies—Canada and the U.S.—has been expanded to include Mexico, and long-term plans call for further additions. However, North American integration is for purely economic reasons; there are no constituencies for political integration. Canadians have consistently rejected notions of closer political ties with the United States and has deviated from its ally to the south on key issues, such as participation in the Iraq war.

The ratification of NAFTA created the world's largest free market with 430 million consumers. The pact marked a bold departure: never before had industrialized countries created such a massive free trade area with a developing-country neighbour. The agreement gives firms in all three countries access to millions of additional consumers, and theoretically liberalized trade flows should result in higher economic growth in all three countries. Overall, the corporate view toward NAFTA is overwhelmingly positive. Trade between the three countries has increased significantly, and Mexico has witnessed a decrease in poverty levels and rising income as a result of the accord.

Canadian firms have benefited from the agreement. Transalta Corporation of Calgary, Alberta, now operates two electric power plants in Mexico—a 252 megawatt plant in the Yucatán Peninsula and a 259 megawatt facility in Chihuahua—that have contributed to the expansion of the power supply in that country. The contract for the operation of the two facilities is worth US$440 million. Quebec based Développement international Desjardins (DID) is also active in Mexico. This firm has won a contract with the State of Tabasco to open four credit unions in the municipalities of Macuspana, Tacotalpa, Nacajuca, and Cunduacan, where they will provide a range of savings products, as well as specialized credit products for women, production credit, and a group life insurance service. Even small companies have benefited; Montreal's Mad Science Group has been able to negotiate an exclusive franchise agreement with a Mexican firm to sell its line of children's educational science products.[25]

Opposition to NAFTA initially centred on issues relating to labour and the environment. Unions in particular worried about job loss to Mexico, given its lower wages and work standards. Distinctive features of NAFTA are the two side agreements that were worked out to correct perceived abuses in labour and the environment in Mexico. The North American Agreement for Environmental Cooperation (NAAEC) and the North American Agreement on Labour Cooperation (NAALC) were used by the Clinton administration to gain support for NAFTA, which had been signed by the Bush administration using the latter president's fast-track authority.

The NAALC was set up to hear complaints about worker abuse. This side agreement was also designed to foster cooperation among trade unions and social groups in all three countries in their demands for improved wages and working conditions. The NAAEC was established to address environmental issues that may arise as a result of implementation of the accord. This side agreement sought to ensure consistent environmental regulations across the three countries and preclude firms relocating to jurisdictions with more lax environmental restrictions. These side agreements have had little impact, however, mainly because the mechanisms have almost no enforcement power.[26]

After a remarkable start in increased trade and investment, NAFTA suffered a serious setback due to a significant devaluation of the Mexican peso in 1995 and its negative impact on trade. Critics argue that too much was expected too fast of a country whose political system and economy were not ready for open markets. In response, advocates argue that there was nothing wrong with the Mexican real economy and that the peso crisis was a political one that would be overcome with time.

NAFTA has provided both Mexico and Canada with greater access to the large U.S. export market. While not all analysts agree that the accord has been successful, proponents cite data that indicate that roughly 2.3 million jobs have been created in Canada since 1994 when the NAFTA agreement was executed. From 1993 to 2003, productivity gains in all three countries have been robust. Productivity increased by 28 percent in the U.S., 55 percent in Mexico, and 23 percent in Canada.[27] All member countries witnessed significant economic growth from 1993 to 2003—Canada at 31 percent, the U.S. at 38 percent, and Mexico at 30 percent. On the trade front, supporters of the agreement note that Mexico's share of the U.S. import market has almost doubled from 6.9 percent in 1993 to 11.6 percent in 2002.[28] Mexico's exports to Canada have increased from US$2.7 billion in 1993 to US$8.7 billion in 2003—a growth rate in excess of 200 percent. Canada's exports of goods and services to its NAFTA partners have increased over 100 percent, and the total volume of trade between all three signatories has increased from US$290 billion in 1993 to US$623 billion in 2003.[29]

In Mexico's growth toward a more advanced society, manufacturers of consumer goods have benefited. NAFTA has already had a major impact on the emergence of new retail chains, many of which were developed to handle new products from abroad.[30] Not only have U.S. retailers, such as Wal-Mart, expanded into and within Mexico, but Mexican retailers, such as Grupo Gigante, have entered the U.S. market.[31] Since its entry into Mexico in 1991, Wal-Mart has become that country's largest private-sector employer. Wal-Mart's use of lower tariffs, physical proximity, and buying power are changing the Mexican retail landscape, as shown in The Global Marketplace 4.4.

NAFTA was expected to result in a phasing out of the Mexican maquiladoras, plants that make goods and parts or process food for export to the United States. The supply of labour in the maquiladoras was plentiful, the pay and benefits low, and the work regulations lax by North American standards. In the last two decades, maquiladoras evolved from low-end garment or small-appliance assembly outfits to higher-end manufacturing of big-screen TVs, computers, and auto parts. The factories shipped almost half of Mexico's exports, most to the United States.

The maquiladora program is, however, in trouble. The NAFTA treaty required Mexico to strip maquiladoras of their duty-free status by 2001. Tariff breaks formerly given to all imported parts, supplies, equipment, and machinery used by foreign factories in Mexico now apply only to inputs from Canada, Mexico, and the United States. This effect has been felt most by Asian factories because they still import a large amount of components from across the Pacific (for example, 97 percent of components for TVs assembled in Tijuana are imported, most from Asia). There has been a lesser effect on Europeans because of Mexico's free trade agreement with the EU. Wages have also been rising, to $3.52 an hour (up from $2.29 in 1997), resulting in some low-end manufacturers of apparel and toys moving production to Asia.[32] While the Mexican government is eager to attract maquiladora investment, it is also keen to move away from using cheap labour as a central element of competitiveness. Since NAFTA has been enacted, some 528 maquiladoras have been closed and investment in the industry has significantly decreased—by just over 8 percent in 2002 alone.

NAFTA may be the first step toward a hemispheric bloc, although nobody expects it to happen anytime soon. It took more than three years of tough bargaining to reach an agreement between the United States and Canada—two countries with parallel economic, industrial, and social systems. The challenges of expanding free trade throughout Latin America will be significant. However, many of Latin America's groupings are making provisions to join in a hemispheric free trade area. Such a regime faces difficulties. As a first step, Chile was scheduled to join as a fourth member in 1997. However, the membership has not materialized due to U.S. political manoeuvring, and Chile has since entered into bilateral trade agreements with both Canada and Mexico and joined Mercosur as an associate member. This has meant that U.S. marketers are reporting trade deals lost to Canadian competitors, who are free of Chile's 11 percent tariffs.[33]

The Global MARKETPLACE 4.4

NAFTA and Wal-Mart: Re-shaping the Mexican Retail Market

Wal-Mart saw the promise of the Mexican market in 1991 when it stepped outside of the United States for the first time by launching Sam's Clubs in fifty-fifty partnership with Cifra, Mexico's largest retailer. The local partner was needed to provide operational expertise in a market significantly different in culture and income from Wal-Mart's domestic one. Within months, the first outlet—a bare-bones unit that sold bulk items at just above wholesale prices—was breaking all Wal-Mart records in sales. While tariffs still made imported goods pricey, "Made in the USA" merchandise also started appearing on the shelves.

After NAFTA took effect in 1994, tariffs tumbled, unleashing pent-up demand in Mexico for U.S.-made goods. The trade treaty also helped eliminate some of the transportation headaches and government red tape that had kept Wal-Mart from fully realizing its competitive advantage. NAFTA resulted in many European and Asian manufacturers setting up plants in Mexico, giving the retailer cheaper access to more foreign brands.

Wal-Mart's enormous buying power has kept it ahead of its Mexican competitors who are making similar moves. Because Wal-Mart consolidates its orders for all goods it sells outside of the United States, it can wring deeper discounts from suppliers than its local competitors. Wal-Mart Mexico has repeatedly exploited NAFTA and other economic forces to trigger price wars. For example, rather than pocket the windfall that resulted when tariffs on Lasko brand floor fans fell from 20 percent to 2 percent, price cuts took place equal to the tariff reductions.

Behind Wal-Mart's success are increasingly price-conscious consumers. The greater economic security of NAFTA has helped tame Mexico's once fierce inflation. The resulting price stability has made it easier for Mexican consumers to spot bargains. In addition, Wal-Mart's clean, brightly lit interiors, orderly and well-stocked aisles, and consistent pricing policies are a relief from the chaotic atmosphere that still prevails in many local stores.

Wal-Mart's aggressive tactics have resulted in complaints as well. In 2002, Mexico's Competition Commission was asked to probe into reports that Wal-Mart exerts undue pressure on suppliers to lower their prices. Local retailers, such as Comerci, Gigante, and Soriana, have seen their profits plummet but are forced to provide prices competitive to Wal-Mart's. In addition, they have engaged in aggressive overhauls of their operations. Soriana, for example, invested $250 million in new stores in 2002. It took out ads in local newspapers warning about "foreign supermarkets" when regulators fined a Wal-Mart in Monterrey because a shelf price did not match the price on the checkout receipt.

Wal-Mart's success continues as Mexico's number one retailer. The company now operates some 783 supermarkets, Supercenters, Sam's Club stores, restaurants, and department stores. Wal-Mart's sales in Mexico in 2005 were in excess of $15 billion—a 14 percent increase over the previous year. Same store sales in December 2005 rose 5 percent, more than double the rate in the U.S. for the same period. The Mexican subsidiary opened 93 new outlets in 2005, well ahead of projections.

Sources: "War of the Superstores," *Business Week*, September 23, 2002, 60; "How Well Does Wal-Mart Travel?" *Business Week*, September 3, 2001, 82–84; "How NAFTA Helped Wal-Mart Reshape the Mexican Market," *The Wall Street Journal*, August 31, 2001, A1–A2; and Vijay Govindarajan and Anil K. Gupta, "Taking Wal-Mart Global: Lessons from Retailing's Giant," *Strategy and Business*, 4th quarter, 1999, 45–56; Jane Bussey, "Wal-Mexico: Wal-Mart's biggest success," Knight Ridder, January 25, 2006.

Other Economic Alliances

Perhaps the world's developing countries have the most to gain from successful integrative efforts. Because many of these countries are also quite small, economic growth is difficult to generate internally. Many of these countries have adopted policies of **import substitution** to foster economic growth. An import substitution policy involves developing industries to produce goods that were formerly imported. Many of these industries, however, can be efficient producers only with a higher level of production than can be consumed by the domestic economy. Their success, therefore, depends on accessible export markets made possible by integrative efforts.

Integration in Latin America

Before the signing of the U.S.–Canada Free Trade Agreement, all the major trading bloc activity had taken place elsewhere in the Americas. However, none of the activity in Latin America has been hemispheric; that is, Central America had its structures, the Caribbean nations had theirs, and South America had its own different forms. However, for political and economic reasons, these attempts have never reached set objectives. In a dramatic transformation, these nations sought free trade as a salvation from stagnation, inflation, and debt. In response to these developments, Brazil, Argentina, Uruguay, and Paraguay set up a common market called Mercosur (Mercado Común del Sur).[34] Venezuela joined the group in 2006. Despite their own economic challenges and disagreements over trade policy, the Mercosur members and the five associate members (Bolivia, Ecuador, Columbia, Peru, and Chile) have agreed to economic-convergence targets similar to those the EU made as a precursor to the euro. These are in areas of inflation, public debt, and fiscal deficits. Many Latin nations are realizing that if they do not unite, they will become increasingly marginal in the global market. In approaching the EU with a free trade agreement, Mercosur members want to diversify their trade relationships and reduce their dependence on U.S. trade. Integration has, however, not been smooth. Bolivia, Chile, Colombia, Ecuador, and Peru formed the Andean Community of Nations (originally the Andean Pact) in 1969. Chile eventually withdrew in 1979. Venezuela joined in 1973 and withdrew in 2006 claiming that the trade agreements signed between Columbia, Peru, and the United States were not tolerable.

The ultimate goal is a free trade zone from Point Barrow, Alaska, to Patagonia under a framework called the **Free Trade Area of the Americas (FTAA)**.[35] The argument is that free trade throughout the Americas would channel investment and technology to Latin and Caribbean nations and spur economic growth. Ministerial meetings held since 1994 have established working groups to gather data and make recommendations in preparation for the FTAA negotiations and an agreement. The larger countries have agreed to consider giving smaller and lesser-developed countries more time to reduce tariffs, to open their economies to foreign investment, and to adopt effective laws in areas such as antitrust legislation, intellectual property rights, bank regulation, and prohibitions on corrupt business practices. At the same time, the less-developed countries have agreed to include labour and environmental standards in the negotiations.[36]

Free-market reforms and economic revival have had marketers ready to export and to invest in Latin America. Changes in corporate behaviour have followed attempts at integration. For example, Brazil's opening of its computer market has resulted in Hewlett-Packard establishing a joint venture to produce PCs. In the past, Kodak dealt with Latin America through 11 separate country organizations, but has since streamlined its operations to five "boundary-less" companies organized along product lines and taking advantage of trading openings, and has created centralized distribution, thereby making deliveries more efficient and decreasing inventory carrying costs.[37]

Integration in Asia

Development in Asia has been quite different from that in Europe and in the Americas. While European and North American arrangements have been driven by political will, market forces may force more formal integration on Asian politicians. The fact that regional integration is increasing around the world may drive Asian interest to it for pragmatic reasons. First, European and American markets are significant for the Asian producers, and some type of organization or bloc may be needed to maintain leverage and balance against the two other blocs. Second, given that much of the Asian trade growth is from intraregional trade, having common understandings and policies will become necessary. Future integration will most likely use the frame of the most established arrangement in the region, the Association of Southeast Asian Nations (ASEAN). Before late 1991, ASEAN had no real structures, and consensus was reached through informal consultations. In October 1991, ASEAN members announced the formation of a customs union called ASEAN Free Trade Area (AFTA). With 10 member countries, AFTA's goals are to increase ASEAN's competitive position as a manufacturing base serving global markets by the elimination of tariff and non-tariff barriers, and to attract foreign direct investment. ASEAN itself, it should be noted, is not a working arrangement as is the EU.

In 1990 Malaysia pushed for the formation of the East Asia Economic Caucus, which would have added China, Japan, and South Korea to the existing ASEAN membership list. This proposal did not gain support because of objections from Japan and the United States. Japan's reaction has been generally negative toward all types of regionalization efforts, mainly because it has the most to gain from free trade efforts. However, part of what has been driving regionalization has been Japan's reluctance to foster some of the elements that promote free trade, for example, reciprocity.[38] Should the other trading blocs turn against Japan, its only resort may be to work toward a more formal trade arrangement in the Asia-Pacific area.

In 1988, Australia proposed the Asia Pacific Economic Cooperation (APEC) as an annual forum to maintain a balance in negotiations. The proposal calls for ASEAN members to be joined by Australia, New Zealand, Japan, South Korea, Canada, Chile, Mexico, and the United States. Originally, the model for APEC was not the EU, with its Brussels bureaucracy, but the Organization for Economic Cooperation and Development (OECD), which is a centre for research and high-level discussion. However, APEC has now established an ultimate goal of achieving free trade in the area among its 21 members by 2010.[39]

Economic integration has also taken place on the Indian subcontinent. In 1985, seven nations of the region (India, Pakistan, Bangladesh, Sri Lanka, Nepal, Bhutan, and the Maldives) launched the South Asian Association for Regional Cooperation (SAARC). Cooperation has been limited to relatively non-controversial areas, such as agriculture and regional development, and is hampered by political disagreements.

Integration in Africa and the Middle East

Africa's economic groupings range from currency unions among European nations and their former colonies to customs unions between neighbouring states. In addition to wanting to liberalize trade among members, African countries want to gain better access to European and North American markets for farm and textile products. Given that most of the countries are too small to negotiate with the other blocs, alliances have been the solution. In 1975, sixteen West African nations attempted to create a megamarket large enough to interest investors from the industrialized world and reduce hardship through economic integration. The objective of the Economic Community of West African States (ECOWAS) was to form a customs union and eventually a common market. Although many of its objectives have not been reached, its combined population of 251 million represents the largest economic entity in sub-Saharan Africa. Other entities in Africa include the Common Market for Eastern and Southern Africa (COMESA), the Economic Community of Central African States (CEEAC), the Southern African Customs Union, the Southern African Development Community (SADC), and some smaller, less globally oriented blocs such as the Economic Community of the Great Lakes Countries, the Mano River Union, and the East African Community (EAC). Most member countries are part of more than one bloc (for example, Tanzania is a member in both the EAC and SADC). The blocs, for the most part, have not been successful due to small memberships and lack of economic infrastructure to produce goods to be traded within the blocs. Moreover, some of the blocs have been relatively inactive for substantial periods of time while their members endure internal political turmoil or even warfare among each other.[40] In 2002, African nations established the African Union (AU) for regional cooperation. Eventually, plans call for a pan-African parliament, a court of justice, a central bank, and a shared currency.[41]

Countries in the Arab world have made some progress in economic integration. The Arab Maghreb Union ties together Algeria, Libya, Mauritania, Morocco, and Tunisia in northern Africa. The Gulf Cooperation Council (GCC) is one of the most powerful of any trade groups. The GCC was formed in 1980 mainly as a defensive measure due to the perceived threat from the Iran-Iraq war. Its aim is to achieve free trade arrangements with the European nations.

Implications of Economic Integration for Global Marketing

Regional economic integration creates opportunities and potential problems for the global marketer. It may have an impact on a company's entry mode by favouring direct investment because one of the basic rationales of integration is to generate favourable conditions for local production and intraregional trade. By design, larger markets are created with potentially more opportunity. Because of harmonization efforts, regulations may be standardized, thus positively affecting the global marketer.

The global marketer must, however, make integration assessments and decisions from four points of view.[42] The first task is to envision the outcome of the change. Change in the competitive landscape can be dramatic if scale opportunities can be exploited in relatively homogeneous demand conditions. This could be the case, for example, for industrial goods, consumer durables such as cameras and watches, and professional services. The global marketer will have to take into consideration varying degrees of change readiness within the markets themselves; that is, governments and other stakeholders, such as labour unions, may oppose the liberalization of competition, especially where national champions such as airlines, automobiles, energy, and telecommunications are concerned. However, with deregulation, monopolies have had to transform into competitive industries. In Germany, for example, the price of long-distance calls has fallen 40 percent, forcing the former monopolist, Deutsche Telekom, to streamline its operations and seek new business abroad. By fostering a single market for capital, the euro is pushing Europe closer to a homogeneous market in goods and services, thereby exerting additional pressure on prices.[43]

The global marketer will then have to develop a strategic response to the new environment to maintain a sustainable long-term competitive advantage. Those companies already present in an integrated market should fill in gaps in European product/market portfolios through acquisitions or alliances to create a regional or global company. It is increasingly evident that even regional presence is not sufficient and companies need to set their sights on presence beyond that. In industries such as automobiles, mobile communications, and retailing, blocs in the 21st century may be dominated by two or three giants, leaving room only for niche players. Those with currently weak positions, or no presence at all, will have to create alliances for market entry and development with established firms. General Mills created Cereal Partners Worldwide with Nestlé to establish itself in Europe and to jointly develop new-market opportunities in Asia. An additional option for the global marketer is to leave the market altogether if it cannot remain competitive because of new competitive conditions or the level of investment needed. For example, Bank of America sold its operations in Italy to Deutsche Bank after it discovered the high cost of becoming a pan-European player.

Whatever changes are made, they will require company reorganization.[44] Structurally, authority will have to become more centralized to execute regional programs. In staffing, focus will have to be on individuals who understand the subtleties of consumer behaviour across markets and are therefore able to evaluate the similarities and differences between cultures and markets. In developing systems for the planning and implementation of regional programs, adjustments have to be made to incorporate views throughout the organization. If, for example, decisions on regional advertising campaigns are made at headquarters without consultation with country operations, resentment from the local marketing staff could lead to less-than-optimal execution. The introduction of the euro will mean increased coordination in pricing as compared to the relative autonomy in price setting enjoyed by country organizations in the past. Companies may even move corporate or divisional headquarters from the domestic market to be closer to the customer or centres of innovation. For example, after Procter & Gamble's reorganization, its fabric and home care business unit is headquartered in Brussels, Belgium.

Finally, economic integration will create its own powers and procedures similar to those of the EU commission and its directives. The global marketer is not powerless to influence both of them; as a matter of fact, a passive approach may result in competitors gaining an advantage or it may put the company at a disadvantage. Often, policymakers rely heavily on the knowledge and experience of the private sector to carry out its own work. Influencing change will therefore mean providing industry information, such as test results, to the policymakers. Many marketers consider lobbying a public relations activity and therefore go beyond the traditional approaches. Lobbying will usually have to take place at multiple levels simultaneously; within the EU, this means the European Commission in Brussels, the European Parliament in Strasbourg, or the national governments within the EU. Marketers with substantial resources have established their own lobbying offices in Brussels, while smaller companies get their voices heard through joint offices or their industry associations. At the same time, marketers operating in two or more major markets (such as the EU and North America) can work to produce more efficient trade through, for example, mutual recognition agreements (MRAs) on standards.[45]

Dealing with Financial Crises

A series of currency crises shook all emerging markets in the 1990s. The devaluation of the Mexican peso in 1994, the Asian crisis of July 1997, the Russian ruble collapse of August 1998, the fall of the Brazilian real in January 1999, and the Argentine default in 2001 have all provided a spectrum of emerging market economic failures, each with its own complex causes and unknown outlooks.

Causes of the Crises

Both the Mexican and Thai cases of currency devaluation led to regional effects in which international investors saw Mexico and Thailand as only the first domino in a long series of failures to come. For example, the historically stable Korean won fell from 900 to 1,100 won per U.S. dollar in one month. The reasons for the crises were largely in three areas allowing comparison: corporate socialism, corporate governance, and banking stability and management. In 1997, business liabilities exceeded the capacities of government to bail businesses out, and practices such as lifetime employment were no longer sustainable. Many firms in the Far East were often controlled by families or groups related to the governing party of the country. The interests of stockholders and creditors were secondary in an atmosphere of cronyism. With the speculative investments made by many banks failing, banks themselves had to close, severely hampering the ability of businesses to obtain the necessary capital financing needed for operations. The pivotal role of banking liquidity was the focus of the International Monetary Fund's bailout efforts.

The Asian crisis had a global impact. What started as a currency crisis quickly became a region-wide recession.[46] The slowed economies of the region caused major reductions in world demand for many products, especially commodities. World oil markets, copper markets, and agricultural products all saw severe price drops as demand kept falling. These changes were immediately noticeable in declined earnings and growth prospects for other emerging economies. The problems of Russia and Brazil were reflections of those declines. In Argentina, the government defaulted on its debt, blocked Argentines from paying obligations to foreigners, and stopped pegging the peso to the U.S. dollar.

Effects of the Crises

The collapse of the ruble in Russia and of Russia's access to international capital markets has brought into question the benefits of a free-market economy, long championed by the advocates of Western-style democracy. While Russia is the sixth most populous nation, a nuclear power, and the holder of a permanent seat in the Security Council of the United

Nations, its economic status is that of a developing country. There was a growing middle class, particularly in the largest cities. Some Russian businesses had revealed glimmerings of respect for shareholders, staff, and customers. Higher standards were encouraged by a growing international business presence. Many of these positive changes are now being lost or are in jeopardy.

In Brazil, similar effects are being felt. A total of 30 million consumers have left the middle class. Many of the free-trade experiments within Mercosur are being re-evaluated or endangered, especially by Brazilian moves in erecting tariff barriers. Many of the key sectors, such as automobiles, were hit by layoffs and suspended production.[47] In Argentina, the supply of most foreign-made goods was choked off.

Consumer and Marketer Responses

Changes in the economic environment affect both consumers and marketers. Consumer confidence is eroded and marketers have to weigh their marketing strategies carefully. Some of these adjustments are summarized in Exhibit 4.15.

Recessions have an impact on consumer spending. For example, the 30 million Brazilians who, as a result of the real crisis, were no longer able to consume in a middle-class

Exhibit 4.15 Consumer and Marketer Adjustment to Financial Crisis

Consumer Adjustment to Financial Hardship	Marketer Adjustment to Financial Hardship
• General reactions	• Marketing-mix strategies
Reduce consumption and wastefulness	Withdraw from weak markets
More careful decision making	Fortify in strong markets
More search for information	Acquire weak competitors
	Consider youth markets
	Resale market for durables
• Product adjustments	• Product strategies
Necessities rather than luxuries	Prune weak products
Switch to cheaper brands or generics	Avoid introducing new products in gaps
Local rather than foreign brands	Flanker brands
Smaller quantities/packages	Augment products with warranties
	Adaptive positioning
• Price adjustments	• Pricing strategies
Life-cycle costs—durability/value	Improve quality while maintaining price
Emphasis on economical prices	Reduce price while maintaining quality
	Consider product life-cycle pricing
• Promotion adjustments	• Promotion strategies
Rational approach	Maintain advertising budget
Reduced attraction to gifts	Focus on print media
Information rather than imagery	Assurances through rational appeals
	Expert endorsements
	Advisory tone
	Customer loyalty programs
	Train sales force to handle objections
• Shopping adjustments	• Distribution strategies
Increased window shopping	Location is critical
Preference for discount stores	Sell in discount and wholesale centres
Fewer end-of-aisle purchases	Prune marginal dealers
	Alternative channels

Source: Compiled from Swee Hoon Ang, Siew Meng Leong, and Philip Kotler, "The Asian Apocalypse: Crisis Marketing for Consumers and Businesses," *Long Range Planning* 33 (February 2000): 97–119, with permission from Elsevier.

tradition were also lost to many marketers. Rather than buying foreign products, they would consume more traditional and therefore less expensive items. Similarly, some consumption may turn not only toward local alternatives but even to generics. Especially hard hit may be big-ticket purchases—cars, furniture, appliances, and so on—that may be put on long-term hold.

Marketers' responses to these circumstances have varied from abandoning markets to substantially increasing their efforts. While Daihatsu pulled out of Thailand, GM has decided to stay, with a change in the car model to be produced and reduced production volume. Returning to a market having once abandoned it may prove to be difficult. For example, distribution channels may be blocked by competition, or suspicion about the long-term commitment of a returnee may surface among local partners. Deere & Co. would sell its farm equipment in Argentina only if payment was in U.S. dollars or to customers with bank accounts abroad.[48] Manipulating the marketing mix is also warranted. Imported products are going to be more expensive, sometimes many times what the local versions cost. Therefore, emphasizing the brand name, the country of origin, and other benefits may convince the consumer of a positive value-price relationship. Adaptive positioning means recasting the product in a new light rather than changing the product itself. For example, Michelin changed its positioning from "expensive, but worth it" to "surprisingly affordable" in Asian markets affected by the crisis.[49] If the perceived prices are too high, the product and/or its packaging may have to be changed by making the product smaller or the number of units in a pack fewer. For example, Unilever reduced the size of its ice-cream packs, making them cheaper, and offered premiums in conjunction with the purchase of soap products (for example, buy three, get one free).[50]

While marketers from North America and Europe may be faced by these challenges, local companies may have an advantage, not only at home but in foreign markets as well. Their lower prices give them an opportunity to expand outside their home markets or aggressively pursue expansion in new markets. Similarly, companies with sourcing in markets hit by currency crises may be able to benefit from lower procurement costs. The most interesting approach in the face of challenges is to increase efforts in building market share. This strategy is naturally based on the premise that the market will rebound in the foreseeable future, thus rewarding investments made earlier.

Summary

Economic variables relating to the various markets' characteristics—population, income, consumption patterns, infrastructure, geography, and attitudes toward foreign involvement in the economy—form a starting point for assessment of market potential for the international marketer. These data are readily available but should be used in conjunction with other, more interpretive data because the marketer's plans often require a long-term approach. Data on the economic environment produce a snapshot of the past; in some cases, old data are used to make decisions affecting operations two years in the future. Even if the data are recent, they cannot themselves indicate the growth and the intensity of development. Some economies remain stagnant, plagued by natural calamities, internal problems, and lack of export markets, whereas some witness booming economic development.

Economic data provide a baseline from which other more market- and/or product-specific and even experiential data can be collected. Understanding the composition and interrelationships between economic indicators is essential for the assessment of the other environments and their joint impact on market potential. The global marketer needs to understand the impact of the economic environment on social development.

The emergence of economic integration in the world economy poses unique opportunities and challenges to the international marketer. Eliminating barriers between member markets and erecting new ones vis-à-vis nonmembers will call for adjustments in past strategies to fully exploit the new situations. In the late 1980s and early 1990s, economic integration increased substantially. The signing of the North American Free Trade Agreement produced the largest trading bloc in the world, whereas the Europeans are moving in their cooperation beyond the pure trade dimension.

Economic crises have hit many of the world's markets in the last 10 years, especially countries that are emerging as the markets of the 21st century. In such a challenging environment, effective market planning and implementation take on additional significance. While withdrawal may be a feasible alternative, international marketers have found ways to grow market share even under adverse circumstances.

Key Terms

common market (p. 115)
customs union (p. 115)
debt problem (p. 107)
economic union (p. 116)
European Union (EU) (p. 96)
factor mobility (p. 115)
Fortress Europe (p. 118)
free trade area (p. 114)
Free Trade Area of the Americas (FTAA) (p. 122)
Group of Five (p. 95)
Group of Seven (p. 95)
Group of Ten (p. 95)
household (p. 97)
import substitution (p. 121)
inflation (p. 107)
Physical Quality of Life Index (PQLI) (p. 113)
political union (p. 116)
purchasing power parities (PPPs) (p. 101)
Single European Act (p. 116)
urbanization (p. 101)

Questions for Discussion

1. Place these markets in the framework that follows.

a. Indonesia
b. Mozambique
c. India
d. Bangladesh
e. Niger
f. Brazil
g. Turkey
h. Spain
i. Singapore
j. Nigeria
k. Algeria
l. Zambia
m. Peru
n. Jamaica
o. Poland
p. United Kingdom
q. Iraq
r. Saudi Arabia

	Income Level		
	Low	***Middle***	***High***
Trade Structure			
Industrial			
Developing			
• Semi-Industrial			
• Oil-Exporting			
• Primary Producing			
• Populous South Asia			
• Least Developed			

2. Using available data, assess the market potential for (a) power generators and (b) consumer appliances in (1) the Philippines, (2) Jordan, and (3) Portugal.

3. From the global marketers' point of view, what are the opportunities and problems caused by increased urbanization in developing countries?

4. Comment on this statement: "A low per capita income will render the market useless."

5. What can marketers do to advance regional economic integration?

6. Explain the difference between a free trade area and a common market. Speculate why negotiations were held for a North American Free Trade Agreement rather than for a North American Common Market.

Internet Exercises

1. Visit the website of the Economic Community of West African States (ECOWAS) at **http://www.ecowas.int/**. What is the mandate of this organization, and which countries are members? Why hasn't this economic bloc been very effective?

2. Why do Canadian companies such as Druide Laboratories Inc. (**http://www.druide.ca/**) engage in projects in developing countries? Outline both short-term and long-term benefits.

Recommended Readings

The Arthur Andersen North American Business Sourcebook. Chicago: Triumph Books, 1994.

Business Guide to Mercosur. London: Economist Intelligence Unit, 1998.

Clement, Norris C., ed. North American Economic Integration: Theory and Practice. London: Edward Elgar Publications, 2000.

Current issues of Country Monitor, Business Europe, Business East Europe, Business Asia, Business Latin America, Business China.

The European Union: A Guide for Americans. 2002 ed. Available at **http://www.eurunion.org/infores/euguide/Chapter1.htm**.

International Marketing Data and Statistics 2002. London: Euromonitor, 2002.

Marber, Peter. From Third World to World Class: The Future of Emerging Markets in the Global Economy. New York: Perseus Books, 1998.

Ohmae, Kenichi. The Borderless World: Power and Strategy in the Interlinked Economy. New York: Harper Business, 1999.

Ryans, John K., and Pradeep A. Rau. Marketing Strategies for the New Europe: A North American Perspective on 1992. Chicago: American Marketing Association, 1990.

Sueo, Sekiguchi, and Noda Makito, eds. Road to ASEAN-10: Japanese Perspectives on Economic Integration. Tokyo: Japan Center for International Exchange, 2000.

Venables, Anthony, Richard E. Baldwin, and Daniel Cohen, eds. Market Integration, Regionalism and the Global Economy. Cambridge: Cambridge University Press, 1999.

World Development Report 2002. New York: Oxford University Press, 2002.

The World in Figures. London: Economist Publications, 2002.

Yearbook of International Trade Statistics. New York: United Nations, 2002.

Notes

1. Global Business Policy Council, *Globalization Ledger* (Washington, DC: A.T. Kearney, 2000), 3.
2. OPEC website, **http://www.opec.org/aboutus/history/history.htm** (accessed July 29, 2006).
3. "African Debt, European Doubt," *Economist*, April 8, 2000, 46.
4. C.K. Prahalad and Stuart L. Hart, "The Fortune at the Bottom of the Pyramid," *Strategy and Business*, 1st quarter, 2002, 35–47.
5. For a current list of member countries and candidates, see the EU website at **http://europa.eu/abc/governments/index_en.htm** (accessed July 29, 2006).
6. Rahul Jacob, "The Big Rise," *Fortune*, May 30, 1994, 74–90.
7. Roger D. Blackwell, Paul W. Miniard, and James F. Engel, *Consumer Behavior* (Mason, OH: Thomson, 2001), 283.
8. *European Marketing Data and Statistics 2001* (London: Euromonitor, 2002), 380.
9. U.S. Census Bureau website, **http://www.census.gov/population/www/socdemo/hh-fam/cps2005.html** (accessed July 29, 2006).
10. The World Bank, *World Development Indicators* (Washington, DC: 2000), 85.
11. "In India, Luxury Is Within Reach of Many," *The Wall Street Journal*, October 17, 1995, A17.
12. Sachet marketing **http://www.trendwatching.com/trends/SACHET_MARKETING.htm** (accessed February 26, 2007).
13. Victor H. Frank, Jr., "Living with Price Control Abroad," *Harvard Business Review* 62 (March–April 1984): 137–42.
14. Bob Meyer, "The Original Meaning of Trade Meets the Future in Barter," *World Trade*, January 2000, 46–50.
15. Edward Tse, "The Right Way to Achieve Profitable Growth in the Chinese Market," *Strategy and Business*, 2nd quarter, 1998, 10–21.
16. EDC website, **http://www.edc.ca/english/publications_9219.htm** (accessed February 26, 2007).
17. Internet Systems Consortium (ISC) website, **http://www.isc.org/index.pl** (accessed July 30, 2006).
18. *How Many Online?*, available at **http://www.nua.ie/surveys/how_many_online/index.html.**
19. Global Business Policy Council, *Globalization Ledger* (Washington, DC: A.T. Kearney, April 2000).
20. Ben Crow and Alan Thomas, *Third World Atlas* (Milton Keynes, UK: Open University Press, 1984), 85.
21. John S. Hill and Richard R. Still, "Effects of Urbanization on Multinational Product Planning: Markets in Lesser-Developed Countries," *Columbia Journal of World Business* 19 (Summer 1984): 62–67.
22. The World Bank, *World Development Report 1982* (New York: Oxford University Press, 1982), 63.
23. Europa website, **http://europa.eu/institutions/financial/ecb/index_en.htm** (accessed July 30, 2006).
24. See **http://secretariat.efta.int.**
25. Foreign Affairs and International Trade Canada website, **http://www.dfait-maeci.gc.ca/tna-nac/stories107-en.asp** (accessed July 30, 2006).
26. John Cavanagh, Sarah Anderson, Jaime Serra, and J. Enrique Espinosa, "Happily Ever NAFTA," *Foreign Policy*, September/October 2002, 58–65.
27. NAFTA: A Decade of Success, **http://www.ustr.gov/Document_Library/Fact_Sheets/2004/NAFTA_A_Decade_of_Success.html** (accessed February 28, 2007).
28. See "NAFTA: A Foundation for Canada's Future Prosperity," Foreign Affairs and International Trade Canada website, **http://www.dfait-maeci.gc.ca/nafta-alena/over-en.asp** (accessed July 30, 2006).
29. NAFTA: A Decade of Success, **http://www.ustr.gov/Document_Library/Fact_Sheets/2004/NAFTA_A_Decade_of_Success.html** (accessed February 28, 2007).
30. Laura Heller, "The Latin Market Never Looked So Bueno," *DSN Retailing Today*, June 10, 2002, 125–26.
31. "Retail Oasis," *Business Mexico*, April 2001, 15.
32. "The Decline of the Maquiladora," *Business Week*, April 29, 2002, 59.
33. "Latin America Fears Stagnation in Trade Talks with the United States," *The New York Times*, April 19, 1998, D1.
34. "Latin Lesson," *Far Eastern Economic Review*, January 4, 2001, 109.
35. See the FTAA website, **http://www.ftaa-alca.org.**
36. "The Americas: A Cautious Yes to Pan-American Trade," *The Economist*, April 28, 2001, 35–36.
37. "Regional Commonalities Help Global Ad Campaigns Succeed in Latin America," *Business International*, February 17, 1992, 47–52; and "Ripping Down the Walls across the Americas," *Business Week*, December 26, 1994, 78–80.
38. Paul Krugman, "A Global Economy Is Not the Wave of the Future," *Financial Executive* 8 (March–April 1992): 10–13.
39. Robert Scollay, "The Changing Outlook for Asia-Pacific Regionalism," *The World Economy* 24 (September 2001): 1135–60.
40. "Afrabet Soup," *The Economist*, February 10, 2001, 77.
41. "Try, Try Again," *The Economist*, July 13, 2002, 41.
42. Eric Friberg, Risto Perttunen, Christian Caspar, and Dan Pittard, "The Challenges of Europe 1992," *The McKinsey Quarterly* 21, no. 2 (1988): 3–15.
43. "Lean, Mean, European," *The Economist*, April 29, 2000, 5–7.
44. Gianluigi Guido, "Implementing a Pan-European Marketing Strategy," *Long Range Planning* 24, no. 5 (1991): 23–33.

45. "TABD Uses Virtual Organization for Trade Lobbying," *Crossborder Monitor*, July 2, 1997, 1.

46. Pam Woodall, "Survey: East Asian Economies: Six Deadly Sins," *Economist*, March 7, 1998, S12–14.

47. "Latin America and the Market," *Economist*, November 21, 1998, 23–25.

48. "In Argentina, Going Without," *The Washington Post*, February 19, 2002, E1–E2.

49. Swee Hoon Ang, Siew Meng Leong, and Philip Kotler, "The Asian Apocalypse: Crisis Marketing for Consumers and Businesses," *Long Range Planning* 33 (February 2000): 97–119.

50. "Asia's Sinking Middle Class," *Far Eastern Economic Review*, April 9, 1998, 12–13.

Chapter 5

The Global Political and Legal Environments

The Global MARKETPLACE 5.1

Las Cristinas—Trouble for Crystallex

Las Cristinas is located in southeastern Venezuela and is the site of one of the world's largest gold deposits. Since 2002, Crystallex International Corporation, a Canadian mining company, has been involved a series of legal and political battles with the Venezuelan government over the ownership of the mine at Las Cristinas. The company signed a mining operation agreement with Corporacion Venezolana de Guayana (CVG) in 2002 that supposedly gave Crystallex the exclusive right to develop and exploit gold deposits at the site—estimated at some 18 million ounces. Crystallex has already completed the necessary environmental impact assessments and feasibility studies, but delays in issuing government permits have effectively stalled production. Disputes over the legal ownership of Las Cristinas date back to 1982 when Mrs. Culver-Lemon, the original holder of a 25-year concession, sued her business partner for breach of contract. A series of legal battles ensued that eventually saw Las Cristinas expropriated by the Venezuelan government in 1999 with the National Guard seizing the property. CVG was given the right to determine the fate of the property, and the president of CVG subsequently granted Crystallex the concession.

Since Crystallex gained control of the mine, however, the Hugo Chavez administration has stalled on its promises to grant Crystallex the permits it needs to operate the mine. However, while Crystallex waits for environmental approval, which is well overdue, the country's president has raised concerns about possible nationalization. Mr. Chavez is quoted as saying, "They [Crystallex] go around the world saying they have this much in gold reserves, but they are never going to exploit it."

Sources: Crystallex website, **http://www.crystallex.com/Projects/VenezuelaOperations/LasCristinas/default.aspx**; Venezuela: Crystallex Out, **http://www.vcrisis.com/index.php?content=letters/200509261713**; and The Saga That Is Las Cristinas, **http://www.worldpress.org/Americas/2268.cfm#down.**

As much as most managers would like to ignore them, political and legal factors often play a critical role in global marketing activities. In addition, the interpretation and application of regulations can sometimes lead to conflicting and even misleading results. As The Global Marketplace 5.1 illustrates, even the best business plans can go awry as a result of unexpected political or legal influences. The failure to anticipate these factors can be the undoing of an otherwise successful business venture.

Of course, a single international political and legal environment does not exist. The business executive must be aware of political and legal factors on a variety of levels. For example, although it is useful to understand the complexities of the host country legal system, such knowledge does not protect against a home-country-imposed **export embargo**.

The study of the global political and legal environments must therefore be broken down into several sub-segments. Many researchers do this by separating the legal from the political. This separation—although perhaps analytically useful—is somewhat artificial, because laws are generally the result of political decisions. Here no attempt will be made to separate legal and political factors, except when such a separation is essential. Instead, this chapter will examine the political-legal environment from the manager's point of view. In making decisions about his or her firm's global marketing activities, the manager will need to concentrate on three areas: the political and legal circumstances of the home country; those of the host country; and the bilateral and multilateral agreements, treaties, and laws governing the relations between host and home countries.

Home Country Political and Legal Environments

No manager can afford to ignore the policies and regulations of the country from which he or she conducts global marketing transactions. Wherever a firm is located, it will be affected by government policies and the legal system. Canadian businesses that do not have operations in the United States, for example, have been free to invest in Cuba and participate in that country's development while U.S.-owned corporations have been forced to adhere to their government's embargo on trade with that Caribbean island.

Many of these laws and regulations may not be designed specifically to address global marketing transactions, yet they can have a major impact on a firm's opportunities abroad. Minimum-wage legislation, for example, affects the international competitiveness of a firm using production processes that are highly labour intensive. The cost of domestic safety regulations may significantly affect the pricing policies of firms in their global marketing efforts. For example, Canada's minimum-wage legislation certainly drives up the cost of production for manufacturing firms in labour-intensive industries. Such legislation, while important to the protection of workers, may well put Canadian exporters at a competitive disadvantage in global markets.

Other legal and regulatory measures, however, are clearly aimed at global marketing activities. Some may be designed to help firms in their international efforts. The lack of enforcement of others may hurt the global marketer. For example, many firms are quite concerned about the lack of safeguards for **intellectual property rights** in China. Not only may counterfeiting result in inferior products and damage to the reputation of a company, but it also reduces the chances that an innovative firm can recoup its investment in research and development that spawns new products.

Violations of intellectual property rights can occur anywhere. As an example, in 1988, Anheuser-Busch agreed with Czechoslovak authorities to settle a trademark dispute with Budjovicky Budvar over the use of the name Budweiser. Anheuser-Busch agreed to give the Czech brewery a $15-million package—$10.3 million in brewing equipment and $4.7 million in cash—in return for which the two firms agreed to a division of the world into specified exclusive and shared markets. More recently, Research In Motion (RIM) agreed to pay $612 million to settle an intellectual property dispute with U.S.-based NTP over its Blackberry wireless technology.[1] The settlement, while significant, did allow the company to continue operating in the U.S.—its largest international market. Chapter 9 will provide further in-depth discussions of intellectual property rights problems and ways to protect a firm from infringement.

Another area in which governments may attempt to aid and protect the global marketing efforts of companies is grey-market activities. **Grey-market goods** are products that enter markets in ways not desired by their manufacturers. Companies may be hurt by their own products if they reach the consumer via uncontrolled distribution channels. Grey-market activities will be discussed in detail later in the book.

Apart from specific areas that result in government involvement, the political environment in most countries tends to provide general support for the global marketing efforts of the country's firms. For example, a government may work to reduce trade barriers or to increase trade opportunities through bilateral and multilateral negotiations. Such actions will affect individual firms to the extent that they affect the international climate for free trade.

Often, however, governments also have specific rules and regulations restricting global marketing. Such regulations are frequently political in nature and are based on the fact that governments believe commerce to be only one objective among others, such as foreign policy and national security. As shown in Exhibit 5.1, four main areas of governmental activities are of major concern to the global marketer here: embargoes or trade sanctions, export controls, import controls, and the regulation of international business behaviour.

Embargoes and Sanctions

The terms **trade sanctions** and **embargoes** as used here refer to governmental actions that distort the free flow of trade in goods, services, or ideas for decidedly adversarial and political, rather than strictly economic, purposes. To understand them better, we need to examine the auspices and legal justifications under which they are imposed.

Trade sanctions have been used quite frequently and successfully in times of war or to address specific grievances. For example, in 1284, the Hansa, an association of merchants in northern Germany, felt that its members were suffering from several injustices by Norway. On learning that one of its ships had been attacked and pillaged by the Norwegians, the Hansa called an assembly of its members and resolved on an economic blockade of Norway. The export of grain, flour, vegetables, and beer was prohibited on pain of fines and confiscation of the goods. The blockade was a complete success. Deprived of grain from Germany, the Norwegians were unable to obtain it from England or elsewhere. As a contemporary chronicler reports, "Then there broke out a famine so great that they were

Exhibit 5.1 **Government Control of Global Marketing**

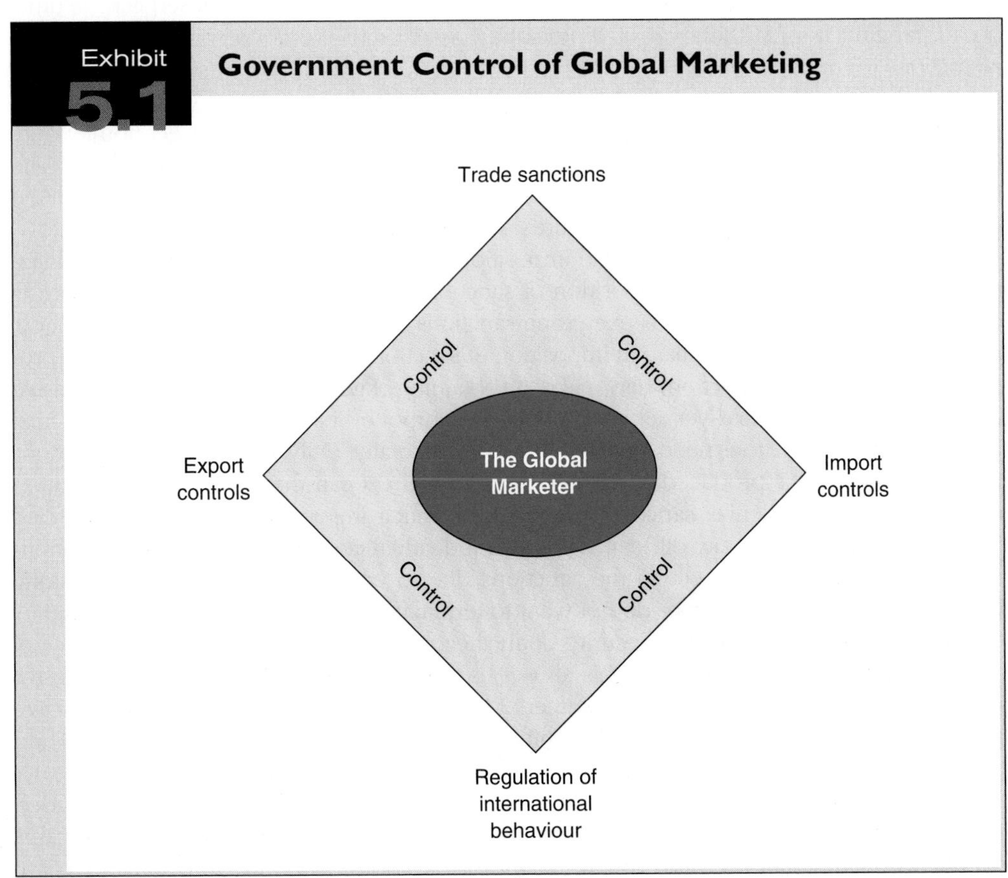

forced to make atonement." Norway was forced to pay indemnities for the financial losses that had been caused and to grant the Hansa extensive trade privileges.[2]

The League of Nations set a precedent for the international legal justification of economic sanctions by subscribing to a covenant that provided for penalties or sanctions for breaching its provisions. The members of the League of Nations did not intend to use military or economic measures separately, but the success of the blockades of World War I fostered the opinion that "the economic weapon, conceived not as an instrument of war but as a means of peaceful pressure, is the greatest discovery and most precious possession of the League."[3] The basic idea was that economic sanctions could force countries to behave peacefully in the international community.

The idea of the multilateral use of economic sanctions was again incorporated into international law under the charter of the United Nations, but greater emphasis was placed on the enforcement process. Once decided upon, sanctions are mandatory, even though each permanent member of the Security Council can veto efforts to impose sanctions. The charter also allows for sanctions as enforcement action by regional agencies such as the Organization of American States, the Arab League, and the Organization of African Unity, but only with the Security Council's authorization.

The apparent strength of the United Nations enforcement system was soon revealed to be flawed. Stalemates in the Security Council and vetoes by permanent members often led to a shift of emphasis to the General Assembly, where sanctions are not enforceable. Further, concepts such as "peace" and "breach of peace" are seldom perceived in the same way by all members, and thus no systematic sanctioning policy developed in the United Nations.[4]

Over the years, economic sanctions and embargoes have become an often-used foreign policy tool for many countries. Frequently, they have been imposed unilaterally in the hope of changing a country's government or at least changing its policies. At times the suggestion of economic sanctions has been used as a negotiation tool, as seen during the Canada-U.S. debate on softwood lumber. During those discussions, the prospect of Canada restricting energy supplies to the U.S. was being bandied about in political circles.[5] Reasons for the imposition of economic sanctions are varied, encompassing everything from human rights and nuclear nonproliferation to antiterrorism. The range of sanctions imposed can be quite broad, ranging from withdrawal of diplomatic contact with the country being ostracized, restrictions on trade and economic activity between Canada and the targeted country, and even the seizure of property and the freezing of assets held in Canada. Canadian foreign policy favours the multilateral, as opposed to the unilateral, imposition of economic sanctions wherever possible in order to maximize the effectiveness of the measures. The Canadian Parliament authorizes the application of economic sanctions through the United Nations Act, the Special Economic Measures Act, and the Export and Import Permits Act.

As noted above, Canada favours the imposition of economic sanctions within a multilateral framework. The unilateral imposition of sanctions tends to have major negative effects on the firms in the country that is exercising sanctions, mainly due to simple shifts in trade. Another key problem with unilateral imposition of sanctions is that they typically do not produce the desired result. Sanctions may make the obtaining of goods more difficult or expensive for the sanctioned country, yet achievement of the purported objective almost never occurs. In order to work, sanctions need to be imposed multilaterally. Only when virtually all nations in which a product is produced agree to deny it to a target can there be a true deprivation effect. Without such denial, sanctions do not have much impact. Yet to get all producing nations to agree can be quite difficult. Typically, individual countries have different relationships with the country subject to the sanctions due to economic, geographic, or historic reasons, and therefore cannot or do not want to terminate trade relations. China's reluctance to support the imposition of UN Security Council economic sanctions on the oil-rich Sudan, despite Sudan's record of human rights abuses, is a case in point. China is a major investor in Sudan's oil industry and a major consumer of its petroleum exports. China is also an active investor in other African countries with significant oil deposits (e.g., Nigeria and Angola) and as a result is not motivated to jeopardize its economic relationships in the region.[6]

Global cooperation can, however, be achieved. For example, when Iraq invaded Kuwait in August of 1990, virtually all members of the United Nations condemned this hostile action and joined a trade embargo against Iraq. Both major and minor Iraqi trading partners—including many Arab nations—honoured the United Nations trade embargo

In More Detail 5.1

THE LEGAL AUTHORITY FOR CANADIAN SANCTIONS

The United Nations Act This Act enables the Canadian government to give effect to resolutions passed by the United Nations Security Council. The Security Council may impose economic or trade sanctions against any member state if it determines that there is the potential for breach of the peace, that a breach of the peace has occurred, or that a country has engaged in an unwarranted act of aggression against another. The council determines what measures are appropriate, and Canada, as a member of the UN, must give effect to these measures in its domestic legislation; that is, Canada has a responsibility to enforce the Security Council's measures.

The Special Economic Measures Act In the absence of a Security Council resolution, this Act authorizes the governor in council to formulate regulations to impose sanctions on targeted states. The Special Economic Measures Act may be invoked to implement a resolution of an international organization of states or in circumstances where the governor in council believes a serious breach of the peace has occurred that could precipitate an international crisis. Under this Act, foreign property in Canada may be seized and Canadian firms and individuals may be prohibited from engaging in economic transactions with the targeted state.

The Export and Import Permits Act This Act allows the governor in council to require the issuance of permits for

- Canadian firms to export to certain countries on the Area Control List
- products on the Export Control List
- the importation into Canada of products on the Import Controls List

The Act allows the Canadian government to enforce trade sanctions, implement intergovernmental commitments, or introduce other measures such as restricting the export of military equipment to countries that may eventually pose a security risk to Canada.

Source: Department of Foreign Affairs and International Trade website, **http://www.dfait-maeci.gc.ca/trade/sanctions-eipa-en.asp** (accessed July 14, 2006).

and ceased trade with Iraq in the attempt to force it to withdraw its troops from Kuwait. Agreements were made to financially compensate those countries most adversely affected by the trade measures.

The terrorist attacks in the U.S., the U.K., Spain, and elsewhere have strengthened global resolve for the sanctioning mechanism of the United Nations. It may well be that sanctions will re-emerge as a powerful and effective international political tool in the world. When we consider that sanctions can be considered the middle ground between waging war and doing nothing, their effective functioning represents a powerful arrow in the quiver of international policy measures. Economic sanctions can be used to extend political control over foreign companies operating abroad, with or without the support of their local government.[7]

One key concern with sanctions is the fact that governments often consider them as being free of cost. However, even though they may not affect the budget of governments, sanctions imposed by governments can mean significant loss of business to firms. Due to these costs, the issue of compensating the domestic firms and industries affected by these sanctions needs to be raised. Yet, trying to impose sanctions slowly or making them less expensive to ease the burden on these firms undercuts their ultimate chance for success. The global marketing manager is often caught in this political web and loses business as a result. Frequently, firms try to anticipate sanctions based on their evaluations of the international political climate. Even when substantial precautions are taken, firms may still suffer significant losses due to contract cancellations. However, this can be seen as the cost of one's government's support for an open global trading and investing environment.

Export Controls

Many nations have **export control systems**, which are designed to deny or at least delay the acquisition of strategically important goods by adversaries. Most of these systems make controls the exception, rather than the rule, with exports considered to be independent of foreign policy. Other countries, however, differ substantially from this perspective, in that exports are considered to be a privilege rather than a right, and exporting is seen as an extension of foreign policy.

The legal basis for export controls varies across nations. In Canada, exports are regulated by the Export and Import Controls Bureau (EICB), which is responsible for the implementation of the Export and Import Permits Act.[8] Under this Act, the EICB is actively involved in regulating trade in military and dual-use products and preventing the supply of military goods to countries that may threaten Canada's security. The EICB is also actively involved in implementing UN sanctions that may prohibit exports to rogue non-compliant states. The Minister for International Trade is responsible for the regulation of products on the Export Control List (Exhibit 5.2).

As previously mentioned, export controls are implemented differently in countries around the world. For example, in Germany, armament exports are covered in the so-called War Weapons List, which is a part of the War Weapons Control Law. The exports of other goods are covered by the German Export List. **Dual-use items**, which are goods useful for both military and civilian purposes, are then controlled by the Joint List of the European Union.[9] In the U.S., the export control system is based on the Export Administration Act, administered by the Department of Commerce, and the Munitions Control Act, administered by the Department of State. The Commerce Department focuses on exports in general, while the State Department covers products designed or modified for military use, even if such products have commercial applicability. The determinants for controls are national security, foreign policy, short supply, and nuclear nonproliferation.

U.S. laws control all exports of goods, services, and ideas. It is important to note here that an export of goods occurs whenever goods are physically transferred from the United States. Services and ideas, however, are deemed exported whenever transferred to a foreign national, regardless of location. Permitting a foreign national from a controlled country to have access to a highly sensitive computer program in the United States is therefore deemed to be an export. The effect of such a perspective can be major, particularly on universities and for international students.

The global marketing repercussions of export controls are important. It is one thing to design an export control system that is effective and that restricts those international business activities subject to important national concerns. It is, however, quite another when controls lose their effectiveness and when one country's firms are placed at a competitive disadvantage vis à vis firms in other countries whose control systems are less extensive or even nonexistent.

Exhibit 5.2 **Canada's Export Control List**

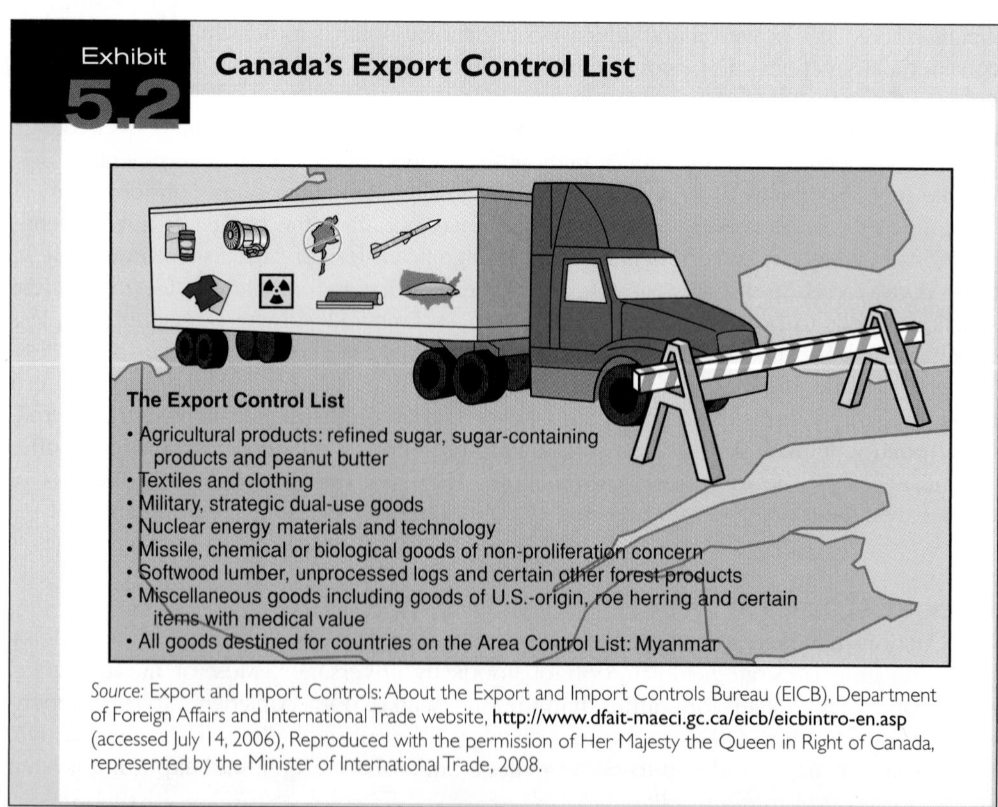

The Export Control List
• Agricultural products: refined sugar, sugar-containing products and peanut butter
• Textiles and clothing
• Military, strategic dual-use goods
• Nuclear energy materials and technology
• Missile, chemical or biological goods of non-proliferation concern
• Softwood lumber, unprocessed logs and certain other forest products
• Miscellaneous goods including goods of U.S.-origin, roe herring and certain items with medical value
• All goods destined for countries on the Area Control List: Myanmar

Source: Export and Import Controls: About the Export and Import Controls Bureau (EICB), Department of Foreign Affairs and International Trade website, **http://www.dfait-maeci.gc.ca/eicb/eicbintro-en.asp** (accessed July 14, 2006), Reproduced with the permission of Her Majesty the Queen in Right of Canada, represented by the Minister of International Trade, 2008.

A New Environment for Export Controls

The attacks of terrorists in the U.S., the U.K., and Spain, as well as planned attacks in Canada that were foiled in the summer of 2006, highlight the importance of export controls. Restricting the flow of materials can be crucial in avoiding the development of weapons of mass destruction; restricting technology can limit the ability to target missiles; restricting the flow of funds can inhibit funding of terrorist training. Exhibits 5.3 and 5.4 show the frequency of terrorist attacks and number of casualties by geographic region.

Exhibit 5.3 **Total International Attacks by Region, 1998–2003**

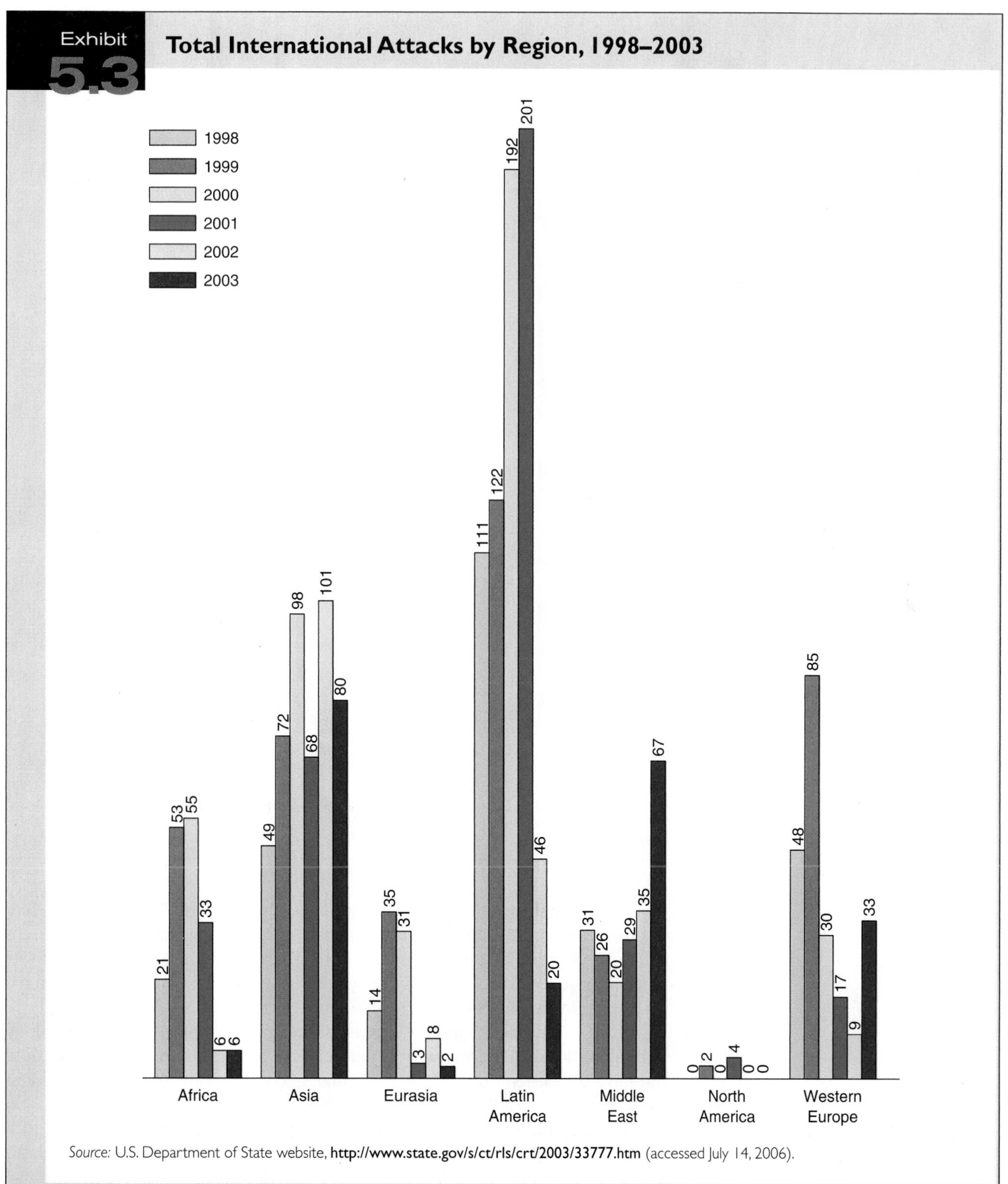

Source: U.S. Department of State website, **http://www.state.gov/s/ct/rls/crt/2003/33777.htm** (accessed July 14, 2006).

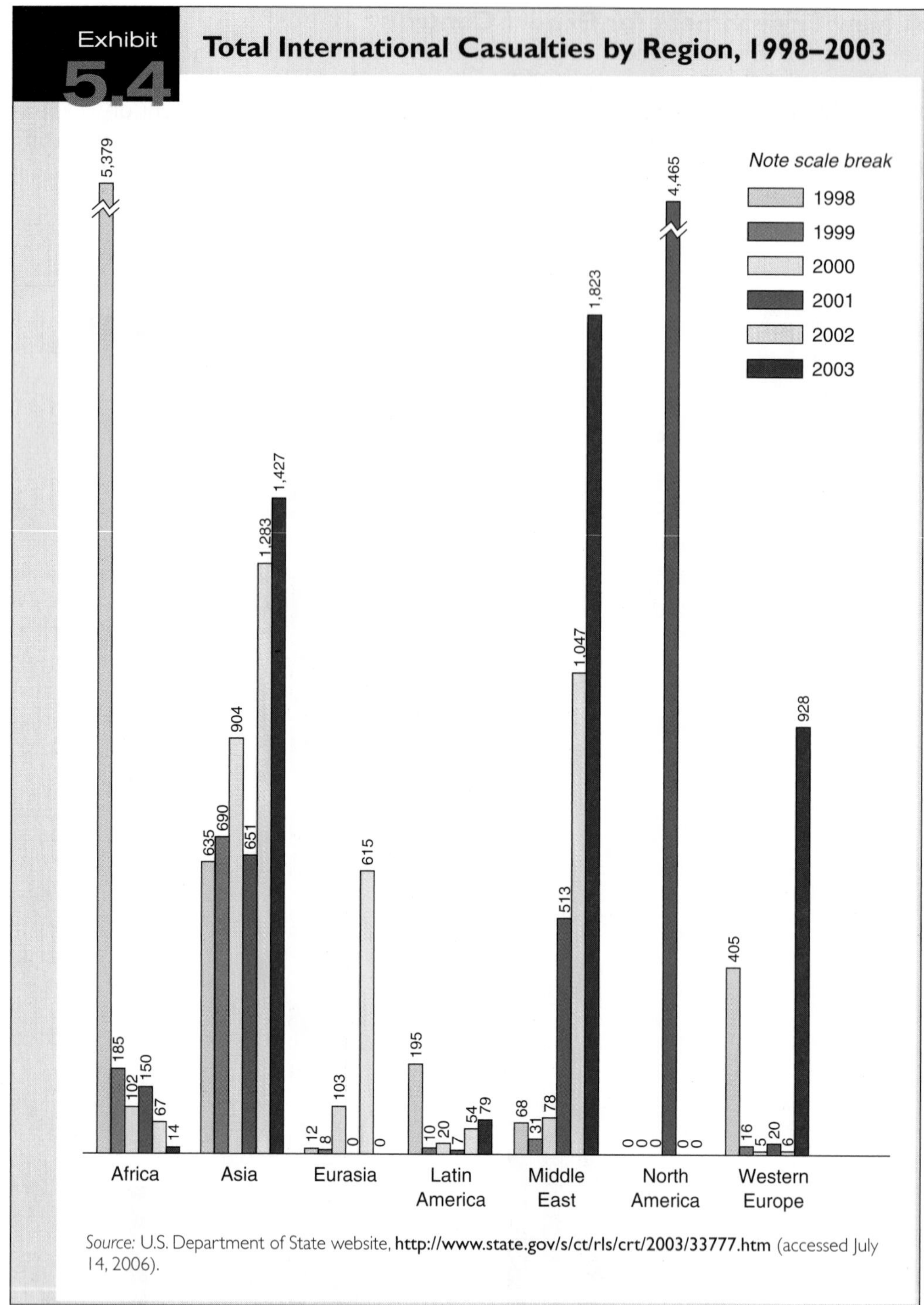

Exhibit 5.4 **Total International Casualties by Region, 1998–2003**

Source: U.S. Department of State website, **http://www.state.gov/s/ct/rls/crt/2003/33777.htm** (accessed July 14, 2006).

Nowadays, the principal focus of export controls must rest on the Third World. Quite a number of countries from this region want chemical and nuclear weapons and the technology to make use of them. For example, a country such as Libya can do little with its poison gas shells without a suitable delivery system. As a result, export controls have moved from a "strategic balance" to a "tactical balance" approach.

Major change has also resulted from the increased foreign availability of high-technology products. In the past decade, the number of participants in the international trade field has grown rapidly. In earlier decades, industrializing countries mainly participated in world trade due to wage-based competition. Today, they are increasingly focused on technology-based competition. As a result, high-technology products are available worldwide from many sources. The broad availability makes any denial of such products more difficult to enforce. If a nation does control the exports of widely available products, it imposes a major competitive burden on its firms.

The question arises as to how much of the latest technology is required for a country to engage in "dangerous" activity. For example, nuclear weapons and sophisticated delivery systems were developed by the United States and the Soviet Union long before supercomputers became available. Therefore, it is reasonable to assert that researchers in countries working with equipment that is less than state-of-the-art, or even obsolete, may well be able to achieve a threat capability that can result in major destruction and affect world safety.

From a control perspective, there is also the issue of equipment size. Due to their size, supercomputers and high-technology items used to be fairly difficult to hide, and any movement of such products was easily detectable. Nowadays, state-of-the-art technology has been miniaturized. Much leading-edge technological equipment is so small that it can fit into a briefcase, and most equipment is no larger than the luggage compartment of a car. Given these circumstances, it has become difficult to closely supervise the transfer of such equipment.

There is a continuing debate about what constitutes military-use products, civilian-use products, and dual-use products and whether multilateral agreement on such classifications can be achieved. Increasingly, goods are of a dual-use nature, meaning that they are commercial products which have potential military applications.[10] It is difficult enough to clearly define the term "weapons." It is even more problematic to achieve consensus among nations regarding dual-use goods.

Conflicts can result from the desire of nations to safeguard their own economic interests. Due to different industrial structures, these interests vary across nations. For example, Germany, with a strong world market position in machine tools, motors, and chemical raw materials, will think differently about controls than will a country, such as Canada, that sees information technology as an area of its competitive advantage.

The terrorist attacks on Washington, D.C., and New York have led to a renewal of international collaboration in the export control field. Policies are being scrutinized as to their sensibility in light of the dangers of proliferation and international terrorism. Such closer collaboration among countries has resulted in an easing of export control policies in the technology field.[11] The role of export controls and their sophistication can, however, be expected to increase.

Import Controls

Many nations exert substantial restraints on global marketers through import controls. This is particularly true of countries that suffer from major balance-of-trade deficits or major infrastructural problems. In these countries, either all imports or the imports of particular products are controlled through mechanisms such as tariffs, voluntary restraint agreements, or **quota systems** that result in quantitative import restraints. Canada's system of supply management is an example of the use of quotas to regulate the import of foreign products. On occasion, countries cut off imports of certain products entirely in order to stimulate the development of a domestic industry. For the global marketer, such restrictions may mean that the most efficient sources of supply are not available because government regulations restrict importation from those sources. The result is either second-best products or higher costs for restricted supplies. This in turn means that the customer receives inferior service and often has to pay significantly higher prices and that the firm is less competitive when trying to market its products internationally.

Policymakers are faced with several problems when trying to administer import controls. First, most of the time such controls exact a huge price from domestic consumers. Even though the wide distribution of the burden among many consumers may result in a less obvious burden, the social cost of these controls may be damaging to the economy and subject to severe attack by individuals. However, these attacks are counteracted by pressures from protected groups that benefit from import restrictions. For example, although Canadians and citizens of the European Union may be forced—because of import controls—to pay an elevated price for agricultural products they consume, agricultural producers in those countries benefit from higher levels of income. Achieving a proper tradeoff is often difficult, if not impossible, for the policymaker.

A second major problem resulting from import controls is the downstream change in import composition that results from these controls. For example, if the import of copper ore is restricted, either through voluntary restraints or through quotas, firms in copper-producing countries may opt to shift their production systems and produce copper wire instead, which they then export. As a result, initially narrowly defined protectionist measures may have to snowball in order to protect one downstream industry after another.

A final major problem that confronts the policymaker is that of efficiency. Import controls that are frequently designed to provide breathing room to a domestic industry in order that it may grow or recapture its competitive position often turn out not to work. Rather than improve the productivity of an industry, such controls provide it with a level of safety and a cushion of increased income yet let the drive for technological advancement fall behind. Alternatively, supply may respond to artificial stimulation and grow far beyond demand.

Regulation of International Business Behaviour

Home countries may implement special laws and regulations to ensure that the international business behaviour of their firms is conducted within the legal, moral, and ethical boundaries considered appropriate. The definition of appropriateness may vary from country to country and from government to government. Therefore, such regulations, their enforcement, and their impact on firms can differ substantially among nations.

Several major areas in which nations attempt to govern the global marketing activities of firms include **boycotts**, whereby firms refuse to do business with someone, often for political reasons; antitrust measures, wherein firms are seen as restricting competition; and corruption, which occurs when firms obtain contracts with bribes rather than through competitive bidding and performance. For example, Arab nations, following years of political tension and at times open hostility, have developed a list of companies that deal

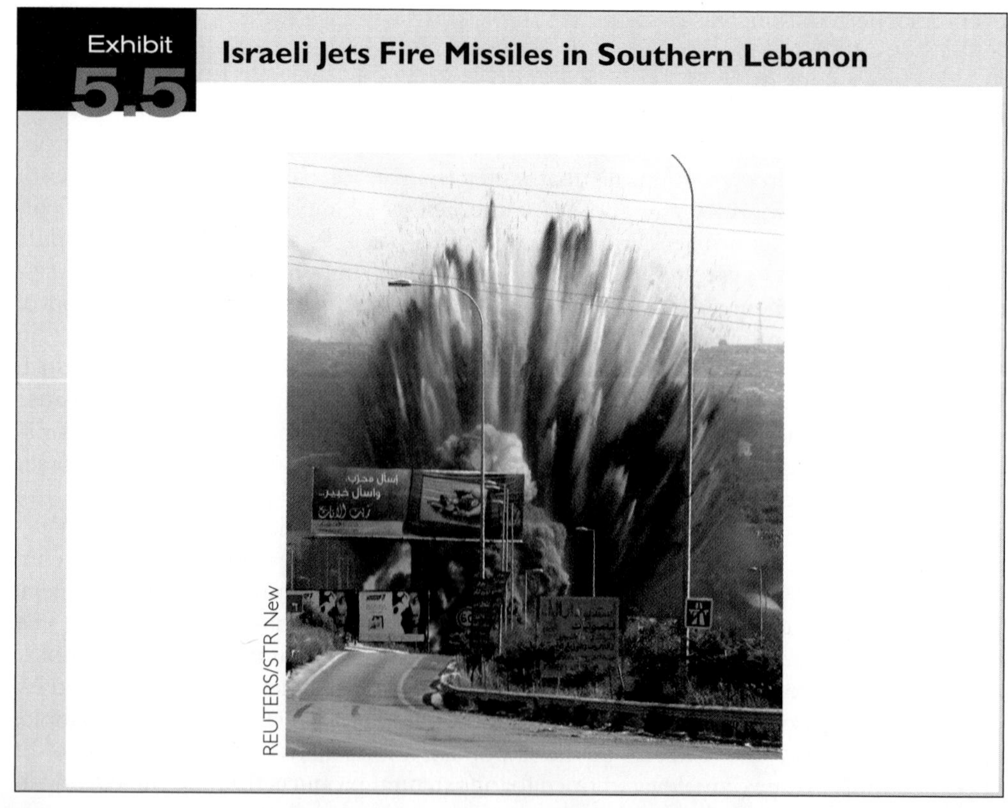

Exhibit 5.5 Israeli Jets Fire Missiles in Southern Lebanon

REUTERS/STR New

with Israel; Arab firms will not do business with firms on that list. Although these negative sentiments have decreased, some Arab customers still demand from their suppliers assurances that the source of the products purchased is not Israel and that the company does not do any business with Israel. The goal of these actions clearly is to impose a boycott on business with Israel. The U.S. government, in turn, because of U.S. political ties to Israel, has adopted a variety of laws to prevent U.S. firms from complying with the Arab boycott. These laws include a provision to deny foreign income-tax benefits to companies that comply with the boycott and also require notification of the U.S. government in case any boycott requests are received. U.S. firms that comply with the boycott are subject to heavy fines and denial of export privileges.

Boycott measures put firms in a difficult position. Caught in a web of governmental activity, they may be forced either to lose business or to pay fines. This is particularly the case if a firm's products are competitive yet not unique, so that the supplier can opt to purchase them elsewhere. Heightening of such conflict can sometimes force companies to withdraw operations entirely from a country.

The second area of regulatory activity affecting the global marketing efforts of firms is antitrust laws. These can apply to the international operations of firms as well as to domestic business. In the European Union, for example, the European Commission watches closely when any firm buys an overseas company, engages in a joint venture with a foreign firm, or makes an agreement with a competing firm. The commission evaluates the effect these activities will have on competition and has the right to disapprove such transactions. Microsoft came under the commission's scrutiny for the dominant position held by its Windows operating system and was fined for abuse of monopoly power.[12] However, given the increased globalization of national economies, some substantial rethinking is going on regarding the current approach to antitrust enforcement. One could question whether any country can still afford to define the competition only in a domestic sense or whether competition has to be seen on a worldwide scale. Similarly, one can wonder whether countries will accept the infringement on their sovereignty that results from the extraterritorial application of any nation's law abroad. There are precedents for making special allowances for global marketers with regard to antitrust laws. Due to ongoing globalization of production, competition, supply, and demand, it would appear that over time the application of antitrust laws to global marketing activities must be revised to reflect global rather than national dimensions.

A third area in which some governments regulate global marketing actions concerns bribery and corruption. In many countries, payments or favours are a way of life, and "a greasing of the wheels" is expected in return for government services. Canada has taken a leadership role in fighting bribery and corruption in international business transactions. Canada is a signatory to the Organization for Economic Cooperation and Development (OECD) convention on Combating Bribery of Foreign Public Officials in International Business Transactions, effective December 17, 1997. National implementing legislation to give effect to the convention, the Corruption of Foreign Public Officials Act, was enacted December 7, 1998. The OECD convention seeks to eliminate the flow of bribes to corrupt foreign government officials and remove corruption and bribery as non-tariff barriers to international trade.[13] Canada also adopted the Organization of American States' convention against corruption in June 2000 and is supportive of other international initiatives such as the United Nations Convention against Transnational Organized Crime and the United Nations Convention against Corruption.

The United States has also had to address the issue of bribery and corruption in international business. U.S. firms operating overseas are affected by U.S. laws against bribery and corruption. In the past, many U.S. companies doing business internationally routinely paid bribes or did favours for foreign officials in order to gain contracts. In the 1970s, major national debates erupted over these business practices, led by arguments that U.S. firms should provide ethical and moral leadership, and that contracts won through bribes do not reflect competitive market activity. As a result, the Foreign Corrupt Practices Act was passed in 1977, making it a crime for U.S. firms to bribe a foreign official for business purposes. A number of U.S. firms have complained about the Act, arguing that it hinders their efforts to compete internationally against companies from countries that have no such anti-bribery laws. In-depth research supports this claim by indicating that in the years after the anti-bribery legislation was enacted, U.S. business activity in those countries in which government officials routinely received bribes declined significantly.[14]

The problem for all global marketing managers is one of ethics versus practical needs and also, to some extent, the amounts involved. For example, it may be difficult to draw the line between providing a generous tip and paying a bribe in order to speed up a business transaction. Many business managers argue that Canada, the United States, and other countries that have taken a stand on bribery and corruption should not apply their moral principles to other societies and cultures in which bribery and corruption are endemic. If they are to compete internationally, these managers argue, they must be free to use the most common methods of competition in the host country. Particularly in industries that face limited or even shrinking markets, such stiff competition forces firms to find any edge possible to obtain a contract.

On the other hand, applying different standards to management and firms depending on whether they do business abroad or domestically is difficult to envision. Also, bribes may open the way for shoddy performance and loose moral standards among managers and employees and may result in a spreading of generally unethical business practices. Unrestricted bribery could result in a concentration on how best to bribe rather than on how best to produce and market products. The global marketing manager must carefully distinguish between reasonable ways of doing business internationally—including compliance with foreign expectations—and outright bribery and corruption. One researcher differentiates between **functional lubrication** and individual greed. As an example of functional lubrication, he points to the "express fee" charged in many countries, which has several characteristics: the amount is small, it is standardized, and it does not stay in the hands of the official who receives it but is passed on to others involved in the processing of the documents. Furthermore, the express service is available to anyone, with few exceptions. By contrast, in the process driven by individual greed, the amount depends on the individual official and is for the official's own personal use.[15] The facilitation of routine actions is not prohibited in many countries, and some degree of functional lubrication may be considered standard business practice. The global marketing manager needs to be aware, however, that in some parts of the world attempts to illegally influence government policy decisions through outright bribery and corruption can result in the imposition of severe fines and penalties for the firm and its executives.

The issue of corruption and bribery also has an effect on the host country. Research has shown that corruption does substantially reduce inward flows of foreign direct investment (FDI).[16] Companies clearly do not wish to do business in an environment in which the outcomes of their marketing actions are unduly influenced by the corrupt practices in the host nation. Reduced foreign investment will in turn negatively affect the country's economic growth and development and the wealth of its citizens. Empirical evidence also exists that corruption and bribery will also affect the form in which a foreign company would choose to invest in the country.[17] Research has shown that corruption is likely to encourage firms to pursue joint venture arrangements, where the foreign firm would collaborate with a host country firm, sharing risks and rewards.[18] Other research has shown, however, that developed country firms are more likely to invest in corrupt regimes using wholly owned subsidiaries, where the foreign firm making the investment has complete ownership and control of the operations.[19] The form of ownership used by the investing firm has implications for the host country in terms of taxation and the repatriation of profits.

The issue of global bribery has taken on new momentum as a result of the work of international organizations such as the OAS, the UN, and the OECD. The World Trade Organization has also been active on the issue. A good portion of this progress can be attributed to the public work done by Transparency International (TI). This nonprofit organization regularly publishes information about the perception of corruption in countries around the globe. Exhibit 5.6 shows the country ranking for 2005. The TI index defines corruption as the abuse of public office for private gain and is based on 16 surveys from 10 independent institutions that collected information from businesspeople and country analysts. Scores range from 10 for countries that are not perceived as being at all corrupt to 0 for those viewed as highly corrupt. Canada's score is 8.4.

Exhibit 5.6 The 2005 Transparency International Corruption Perceptions Index: Best and Worst Performing Countries

Country Rank	Country	2005 CPI Score
1	Iceland	9.7
2	Finland	9.6
	New Zealand	9.6
4	Denmark	9.5
5	Singapore	9.4
6	Sweden	9.2
7	Switzerland	9.1
8	Norway	8.9
9	Australia	8.8
10	Austria	8.7
11	Netherlands	8.6
	United Kingdom	8.6
13	Luxembourg	8.5
14	Canada	8.4
15	Hong Kong	8.3
16	Germany	8.2
17	United States	7.6
18	France	7.5
19	Belgium	7.4
137	Azerbaijan	2.2
	Cameroon	2.2
	Ethiopia	2.2
	Indonesia	2.2
	Iraq	2.2
	Liberia	2.2
	Uzbekistan	2.2
144	Congo, Democratic Republic of the	2.1
	Kenya	2.1
	Pakistan	2.1
	Paraguay	2.1
	Somalia	2.1
	Sudan	2.1
	Tajikistan	2.1
151	Angola	2.0
152	Côte d'Ivoire	1.9
	Equatorial Guinea	1.9
	Nigeria	1.9
155	Haiti	1.8
	Myanmar	1.8
	Turkmenistan	1.8
158	Bangladesh	1.7
	Chad	1.7

Source: Reprinted from Corruption Perceptions Index. Copyright 2005 Transparency International: The Global Coalition against Corruption. Used with permission. For more information, visit **http://www.transparency.org**.

A major issue that is critical for global marketers is that of general standards of behaviour and ethics. Increasingly, public concerns are raised about such issues as global warming, pollution, and moral behaviour. However, these issues are not of the same importance in every country. What may be frowned on or even illegal in one nation may be customary or at least acceptable in others. For example, cutting down the Brazilian rain forest may be acceptable to the government of Brazil, but scientists, concerned consumers, and environmentalists may object vehemently because of the effect of global warming and other climatic changes. The export of tobacco products by developed countries may be legal but also has resulted in accusations of exporting death to developing nations. China may use prison labour in producing products for export, but some countries' laws prohibit the importation of such products. Mexico may tolerate low safety standards for workers, but the buyers of Mexican products may object to the resulting dangers. In the area of moral behaviour, firms are increasingly not just subject to government rules but also held accountable by the public at large. For example, issues such as child labour, inappropriately low wages, or the running of sweatshops are raised by concerned individuals and communicated to customers. Firms can then be subject to public scorn, consumer boycotts, and investor scrutiny if their actions are seen as reprehensible, and they run the risk of losing much more money than they gained by engaging in such practices.

Global marketers are "selling" the world on two key issues: one is the benefit of market forces that result in the interplay of supply and demand. This interplay in turn uses price signals instead of government fiat to adjust activities, thrives on competition, and works within an environment of respect for profitability and private property. The second key proposition is that global marketers will do their best to identify market niches and bring their products and services to customers around the globe. Since these activities take up substantial financial resources, they provide individuals with the opportunity to invest their funds in the most productive and efficient manner.

Key underlying dimensions of both of these issues are managerial and corporate virtue, vision, and veracity. Unless the world can believe in what companies say they do, and trust the activities of global marketers, it will be hard, even impossible, to forge a global commitment between those doing the marketing and the ones being marketed to. It is

The Global MARKETPLACE 5.2

Marketing Opportunity in Post-War Iran?

The Supreme Leader Ayatollah Ali Khamenei has announced plans to privatize state companies in a number of industries. The Iranian government will sell off 80 percent of its stake in several key industries, including media, banking, transportation, and minerals. The privatization initiative does not apply to the oil and gas sector. Iran is the second largest oil producer in OPEC. Ayatollah Khamenei has promoted a strategy of privatization of state enterprises in the past, as has President Mahmoud Ahmadinejad's predecessor, Mohammad Khatami. President Ahmadinejad has, however, threatened to reverse sales of state enterprises made under Khatami's regime, arguing that public properties and factories have been sold off to special interest groups for a fraction of their value.

While Iran is a member of U.S. President George Bush's "axis of evil," it is still the largest market in the region, with a population of 69 million people. High oil prices have increased the country's revenues, and significant natural gas reserves may be tapped for major industrial projects. The country is growing at 5 percent per year, has hard currency reserves of $35 billion, and operates with a trade surplus. At the same time, economic restrictions have been imposed on Iran by Western nations since 1979 and these have created shortages of most basic goods. While improving economic conditions and supply-demand imbalances may spell opportunity for global marketers, an uncertain internal political situation and economic sanctions complicate efforts to do business in post-war Iran.

Sources: "Iran Unveils Major Privatisation Plan," Associated Press, July 4, 2006; and "Iran: The Mideast's Model Economy?" Business Week Online, May 24, 2004.

therefore of vital interest to marketers to ensure that corruption, bribery, lack of transparency, and the misleading of consumers, investors, and employees are systematically relegated to the history books where they belong. It will be the extent to which openness, responsiveness, long-term thinking, and truthfulness rule that will determine the degrees of freedom for global marketers.

Host Country Political and Legal Environment

The host country environment, both political and legal, affects the global marketing operations of firms in a variety of ways. A good manager will understand the country in which the firm operates so that he or she is able to work within the existing parameters and can anticipate and plan for changes that may occur.

Political Action and Risk

Firms usually prefer to conduct business in a country with a stable and friendly government, but such governments are not always easy to find. Managers must therefore continually monitor the government, its policies, and its stability to determine the potential for political change that could adversely affect corporate operations.

There is political risk in every nation, but the range of risks varies widely from country to country. **Political risk** is defined as the risk of loss, when investing in a given country, that is caused by changes in a country's political structure or policies, such as tax laws, tariffs, expropriation of assets, or restriction in repatriation of profits. For example, a company may suffer from such loss in the case of expropriation or tightened foreign exchange repatriation rules, or from increased credit risk if the government changes policies to make it difficult for the company to pay creditors. In general, political risk is lowest in countries that have a history of stability and consistency. Political risk tends to be highest in nations that do not have this sort of history. In a number of countries, however, consistency and stability that were apparent on the surface have been quickly swept away by major popular movements that drew on the bottled-up frustrations of the population. Three major types of political risk can be encountered: **ownership risk**, which exposes property and life; **operating risk**, which refers to interference with the ongoing operations of a firm; and **transfer risk**, which is mainly encountered when attempts are made to shift funds between countries. Political risk can be the result of government action, but it can also be outside the control of government. The types of actions and their effects are classified in Exhibit 5.7.

A major political risk in many countries involves conflict and violent change. A manager will want to think twice before conducting business in a country in which the likelihood of such change is high. To begin with, if conflict breaks out, violence directed toward the firm's property and employees is a strong possibility. Guerrilla warfare, civil disturbances, and terrorism often take an anti-industry bent, making companies and their employees potential targets. For example, in the spring of 1991, Detlev Rohwedder, chairman of the German Treuhand (the institution in charge of privatizing the state-owned firms of the former East Germany), was assassinated at his home in Germany by the Red Army Faction because of his "representation of capitalism."

International terrorists target U.S. facilities, operations, and personnel for attack in order to strike a blow against the United States and capitalism. Abroad, U.S. firms are prominent symbols of the United States' culture and government and by their nature they cannot have the elaborate security and restricted access of U.S. diplomatic offices and military bases. As a result, U.S. businesses are the primary target of terrorists worldwide and will likely remain the most vulnerable targets in the future.[20] These targets, however, may really be domestic rather than American in nature. For example, when we see pictures of a burning McDonald's establishment, it is typically the domestic franchisee and the local employees and investors who are suffering the most. But then, destruction and terrorism are not known for their thoughtfulness and logic. The methods used by terrorists against business facilities include bombing, arson, hijacking, and sabotage. To obtain

Exhibit 5.7 Exposure to Political Risk

Contingencies May Include:	Loss May Be the Result of: The actions of legitimate government authorities	Loss May Be the Result of: Events caused by factors outside the control of government
The involuntary loss of control over specific assets without adequate compensation	• Total or partial expropriation • Forced divestiture • Confiscation • Cancellation or unfair calling of performance bonds	• War • Revolution • Terrorism • Strikes • Extortion
A reduction in the value of a stream of benefits expected from the foreign-controlled affiliate	• Nonapplicability of "national treatment" • Restriction in access to financial, labor, or material markets • Controls on prices, outputs, or activities • Currency and remittance restrictions • Value-added and export performance requirements	• Nationalistic buyers or suppliers • Threats and disruption to operations by hostile groups • Externally induced financial constraints • Externally imposed limits on imports or exports

Source: José de la Torre and David H. Neckar, "Forecasting Political Risks for International Operations," in H. Vernon-Wortzel and L. Wortzel, *Global Strategic Management: The Essentials*, 2nd ed. (New York: John Wiley and Sons, 1990), 195.

funds, the terrorists resort to kidnapping, armed robbery, and extortion.[21] The frequency of such incidents around the world is shown in Exhibit 5.8. To reduce such international terrorism, recent experience has demonstrated that it is imperative to collaborate internationally in identifying and tracking terrorist groups and to systematically reduce their safe havens and financial support.

In many countries, particularly in the developing world, coups d'état can result in drastic changes in government. The new government may attack foreign multinational corporations as remnants of the Western-dominated colonial past, as has happened in Cuba, Nicaragua, and Iran. Even if such changes do not represent an immediate physical threat to firms and their employees, they can have drastic effects. The past few decades have seen such coups in the countries of Ghana, Ethiopia, and Venezuela, to name a few. These coups have seriously impeded the conduct of global marketing activities.

An important governmental action is **expropriation**, which is the seizure of foreign assets by a government with payment of compensation to the owners. Expropriation has appealed to some countries because it demonstrates nationalism and immediately transfers a certain amount of wealth and resources from foreign companies to the host country. It does have costs to the host country, however, to the extent that it makes other firms more hesitant to invest in the country. Expropriation does provide compensation to the former owners; however, compensation negotiations are often protracted and result in settlements that are frequently unsatisfactory to the owners. For example, governments may offer compensation in the form of local, non-transferable currency or may base the compensation on the book value of the firm. Even though firms that are expropriated may

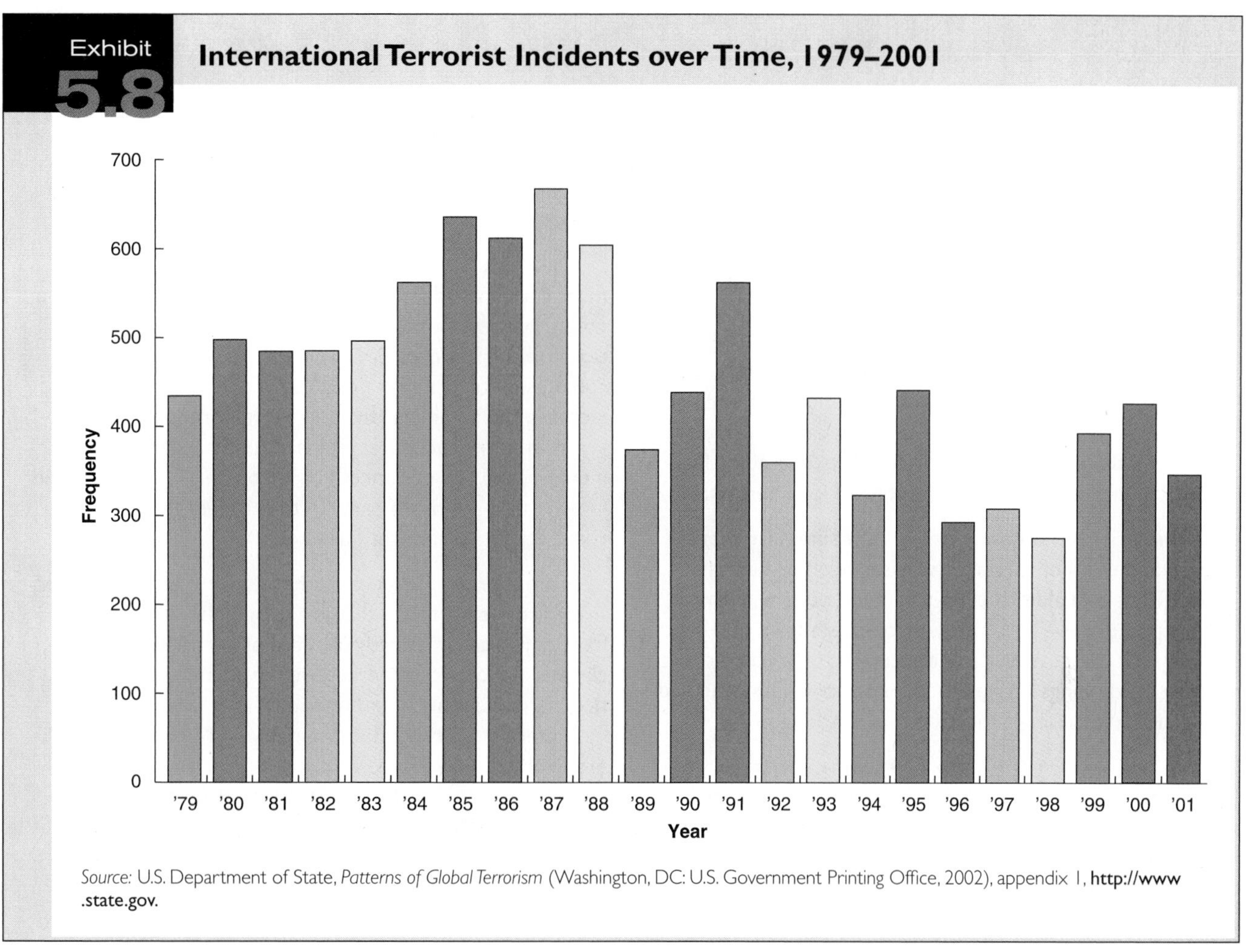

Exhibit 5.8 **International Terrorist Incidents over Time, 1979–2001**

Source: U.S. Department of State, *Patterns of Global Terrorism* (Washington, DC: U.S. Government Printing Office, 2002), appendix I, **http://www.state.gov.**

deplore the low levels of payment obtained, they frequently accept them in the absence of better alternatives.

The use of expropriation as a policy tool has sharply decreased over time. Apparently, governments have come to recognize that the damage inflicted on themselves through expropriation exceeds the benefits.[22]

Confiscation is similar to expropriation in that it results in a transfer of ownership from the foreign firm to the host country. However, its effects are even harsher in that it does not involve compensation for the firm. Some industries are more vulnerable than others to confiscation and expropriation because of their importance to the host country economy and their lack of ability to shift operations. For this reason, sectors such as mining, energy, public utilities, and banking have been targets of such government actions.

Confiscation and expropriation constitute major political risks for foreign investors. Other government actions, however, are nearly as damaging. Many countries are turning from confiscation and expropriation to more subtle forms of control, such as nationalization or **domestication**. The goal of domestication is the same—to gain control over foreign investment—but the method is different. Through domestication, the government demands partial transfer of ownership and management responsibility, and it imposes regulations to ensure that a large share of the product is locally produced and a larger share of the profit is retained in the country.

Domestication can have profound effects on the global marketer for a number of reasons. First, if a firm is forced to hire nationals as managers, poor cooperation and communication can result. If the domestication is imposed within a very short time span, corporate operations overseas may have to be headed by poorly trained and inexperienced local managers. Further, domestic content requirements may force a firm to purchase

In More Detail 5.2

TERRORISM AND GLOBAL MARKETING

Terrorism is the systematic use (or threat) of violence aimed at attaining a political goal and conveying a political message. International terrorism seeks to do this across national borders. While it has existed for centuries, terrorism's global impact has changed significantly in recent years: improved means of transportation lead to an omnipresence never previously experienced. The rise of terrorist incidents in Western nations, often carried out by foreign nationals, brings terrorism to countries once considered immune. Global mass media, meanwhile, have ensured the visibility of terrorist events, spreading fear and creating irrational expectations of localized attacks.

Terrorists direct their strikes at business far more than at any other target. Businesses need to be easily accessible and able to conduct transactions with many new persons every day; this introduces a level of vulnerability that is not typically encountered by government offices. Bombings are most common, followed by armed assaults, kidnapping, vandalism, and hijacking.

While always regrettable, terrorism nevertheless creates new opportunities for firms in a few industries like construction, security, and information technology. For most companies, however, terrorism results in reduced revenues or increased costs, and managers must prepare for this. Terrorists intend to affect supply and demand in order to shatter existing economic systems; this brings about both direct and indirect effects. The direct consequences to business are the immediate costs levied on individual firms. While harm is clear to individual firms, from a societal perspective, the direct effects tend to be less consequential than the indirect ones. The latter accumulate over time and are often not apparent immediately.

The indirect negative consequences of terrorism begin with macroeconomic phenomena such as the real or perceived decline in per capita income, purchasing power, and stock-market values. In the wake of a terror event, these trends cause a fall in the subjective (perceived) security of the nation. Buyers become uncertain about the state of their nation's economy, and a sharp reduction in demand for both consumer and industrial goods follows—a phenomenon we call "the chill effect."

A further effect on enterprises may be the failures in power, communication, transport, and other infrastructure due to actual physical damage incurred at the terrorists' hands. Indirectly, this leads to unpredictable shifts and interruption in the supply of inputs, resources, and services. Finally, international terrorism often causes tension between the countries whose property or citizens are involved; the deterioration of transnational relationships can affect foreign buyer and seller attitudes and thus the marketing activities of firms doing business abroad.

One key side effect of terrorism can be the government policies and laws it brings about. In order to make a country less vulnerable, politicians often enact restrictions on the business environment. New regulations in customs clearance may delay the supply of inputs, increase the administrative burden, and require firms to invest in new procedures. Transaction costs generally increase, and the commercial environment may be altered in ways that are more harmful to business than the terrorist attack itself might have been.

From a global perspective, these effects are present for many firms, even those that are geographically remote from any location directly affected by terrorism. Today's climate of global commerce involves countless interactions with customers and distributors; producers and marketers often rely on entire networks of diverse suppliers. Such exposure to a variety of actors leaves firms vulnerable to events that take place at a distance as well as nearby. Even firms perceived as having little international involvement may depend on the receipt of imported goods, and therefore they risk experiencing shortages or delays of input if economies abroad are disrupted.

Over time, terrorism will increasingly influence the evaluation and selection of markets, particularly those located abroad. Thus far, for instance, developing nations have proven to be most vulnerable to economic and consumption downturns following terrorism events. In a volatile world, marketing managers are the frontline response to business disruption. Although all corporate areas are likely to be affected by terrorist activity, the marketing field, which constitutes a key liaison with the world outside the firm, is likely to be under the most pressure. Marketers deal specifically with the activities of supply and demand that terrorists aim to destroy and are thus confronted with terrorism on a daily basis. Devising new distribution and logistics avenues in the case of attack, responding with pricing strategies to market dislocations, and communicating the firm's position to buyers and suppliers are all marketing activities.

Sources: Michael Czinkota, Gary Knight, and Peter Liesch, "Terrorism and International Business: Conceptual Foundations," in *Terrorism and the International Business Environment*, ed. G. Suder (Northampton, MA: Edward Elgar, 2004); U.S. Department of State, *Patterns of Global Terrorism 2003* (Washington, DC: 2004); and Michael Czinkota and Gary Knight, "On the Front Line: Marketers Combat Global Terrorism," *Marketing Management*, May/June 2005, 33–39.

Exhibit 5.9 **Bolivian Soldiers Guard the San Alberto Gas Plant**

REUTERS/Ho New

supplies and parts locally, which can result in increased costs, inefficiency, and lower-quality products, thus further damaging a firm's interest. Export requirements imposed on companies may also create havoc for the international distribution plan of a corporation and force it to change or even shut down operations in other countries. Finally, domestication will usually shield the industry within one country from foreign competition. As a result, inefficiencies will be allowed to grow due to a lack of market discipline. In the long run, this will affect the international competitiveness of an operation abroad and may become a major problem when, years later, the removal of domestication is considered by the government.

Most businesses operating abroad face a number of other risks that are less dangerous, but probably more common, than the drastic ones already described. Host governments that face a shortage of foreign currency sometimes will impose controls on the movement of capital in and out of the country. Such controls may make it difficult for a firm to remove its profits or investments from the host country. Sometimes, exchange controls are also levied selectively against certain products or companies in an effort to reduce the importation of goods that are considered to be a luxury or unnecessary. Such regulations are often difficult to deal with because they may affect the importation of parts, components, or supplies that are vital for production operations. Restrictions on such imports may force a firm to alter its production program or even shut down its entire plant. Prolonged negotiations with government officials may be necessary in order to reach a compromise agreement on what constitutes a "valid" expenditure of foreign currency resources. Because the goals of government officials and corporate managers may often be quite different, such compromises, even when they can be reached, may result in substantial damage to the global marketing operations of a firm.

Countries may also raise the tax rates applied to foreign investors in an effort to control firms and their capital. On occasion, different or stricter applications of the host country's tax codes are implemented for foreign investors. The rationale for such measures is often the seeming underpayment of taxes by such investors, when comparing their payments to those of long-established domestic competitors. Overlooked is the fact that new investors in foreign lands tend to "**over-invest**" by initially buying more land, space, and equipment than is needed immediately and by spending heavily so that facilities are state-of-the-art. This desire to accommodate future growth and to be highly competitive in the early investment stages will, in turn, produce lower profits and lower tax payments. Yet over time, these investment activities should be very successful, competitive, and job-creating. Selective tax increases for foreign investors may result in much-needed revenue for the coffers of the host country, but they can severely damage the operations of the foreign investors. This damage, in turn, may result in decreased income for the host country in the long run.

The global marketing manager must also worry about **price controls**. In many countries, domestic political pressures can force governments to control the prices of imported products or services, particularly in sectors that are considered to be highly sensitive from a political perspective, such as food or health care. If a foreign firm is involved in these areas, it is a vulnerable target of price controls because the government can play on its people's nationalistic tendencies to enforce the controls. Particularly in countries that suffer from high inflation and frequent devaluations, the global marketer may be forced to choose between shutting down the operation or continuing production at a loss in the hope of recouping that loss once the government chooses to loosen or remove its price restrictions. How a firm can adjust to price controls is discussed in greater detail later in the book.

Managers face political and economic risk whenever they conduct business overseas, but there may be ways to lessen the risk. Obviously, if a new government that is dedicated to the removal of all foreign influences comes into power, a firm can do little. In less extreme cases, however, managers can take actions to reduce the risk if they understand the root causes of the host country's policies. Most important is the accumulation and appreciation of factual information about a country's history, political background, and culture before making a long-term investment decision. Also, a high degree of sensitivity by a firm and its employees to country-specific approaches and concerns are important dimensions that help a firm to blend into the local landscape rather than stand out as a foreign object.

Adverse governmental actions are usually the result of a host country's nationalism, desire for independence, and opposition to colonialism. If a country's citizens feel exploited by foreign firms, government officials are more likely to take anti-foreign action. To reduce the risk of government intervention, a firm needs to demonstrate that it is concerned with the host country's society and that it considers itself an integral part of the host country rather than simply an exploitative foreign corporation. Ways to do this include intensive local hiring and training practices, good pay, more charity, and more societally useful investment. In addition, a company can form joint ventures with local partners to demonstrate a willingness to share its benefits with nationals. Although such actions will not guarantee freedom from risk, they will certainly lessen the exposure.

Corporations can also protect against political risk by closely monitoring political developments. Increasingly, private-sector firms offer assistance in such monitoring activities, permitting the overseas corporation to discover potential trouble spots as early as possible and react quickly to prevent major losses. Firms can also take out insurance to cover losses due to political risk. Most industrialized countries offer insurance programs for their firms doing business abroad. In Canada, the Export Development Corporation (EDC) provides exporters with insurance; in Germany, that function is provided by Hermes Kreditanstalt; in the U.S., the Overseas Private Investment Corporation (OPIC) provides a range of coverage options for the global marketing firm. Usually, insurance policies do not cover commercial risks and, in the event of a claim, cover only the actual loss—not lost profits. In the event of a major political upheaval, however, risk insurance can be critical to a firm's survival.

Some analysts have also observed that firms such as Canada's Bema Gold have operated successfully in high-risk countries by paying attention to their selection of a strategic partner. Bema operates successfully in Russia because it has partnered with a regional Russian government that holds 25 percent of the equity in the venture.[23] The idea is to appear to be more of a local as opposed to a foreign firm to observers in the host country. Other Canadian firms such as Crystallex Inc., profiled earlier in this chapter, have tried to mitigate political risk by "doing good" in the local community. Crystallex has been actively investing in the communities around its mine in the hope of winning the hearts and minds of local Venezuelans and influencing political opinion.

In More Detail 5.3

THE MEASUREMENT OF POLITICAL RISKS

Global marketers require factual information on the political risks they face in various countries. Several models are available that attempt to quantify the political risk inherent in a country. One such measure that is widely used is the Profit Opportunity Recommendation Index (POR) developed by Business Environment Risk Intelligence SA (BERI). The POR attempts to capture all facets of country risk and comprises three sub-measures and a composite score. The three sub-measures are

(a) the Political Risk Index (PRI), which focuses on socio-political conditions in the country. The PRI considers six internal causes of political risk, such as fractionalization of the political spectrum and fractionalization by language, ethnic, or religious groupings.

(b) the Operations Risk Index (ORI), which assesses the operations climate for foreign businesses. Included in this index are 15 variables that attempt to capture the degree to which national firms are given preference and the overall quality of the business climate in the country. Variables incorporated into the ORI include policy continuity, attitudes toward foreigners and profits, and the degree of privatization.

(c) the R Factor, which is focused on remittances and repatriation. Six criteria are used in this measure to assess the country's willingness and capacity for foreign firms to convert profits and capital to foreign exchange and transfer the proceeds. It also captures the extent to which firms have access to convertible currency to finance the importation of inputs.

The POR is an average of the three sub-measures discussed above. The scale ranges from 0 to 100 and is computed for 53 countries.

POR Scores, Selected Countries (2003)

Low Risk (POR 70–100)	
Switzerland	82
Singapore	77
Japan	72
Norway	71
Moderate Risk (POR 55–69)	
Canada	63
U.S.	66
U.K.	62
France	64
China	58
Sweden	65
Austria	69
High Risk (POR 40–54)	
Chile	52
India	45
Russia	43
Iran	43
Brazil	40
Mexico	41
Colombia	41
Prohibitive Risks (POR 0–39)	
Venezuela	36
Indonesia	39
Argentina	34

Global marketers also have access to alternative measures of political risks computed by organizations such as the Economic Intelligence Unit and Export Development Canada.

Sources: Business Risk Service (BRS) User Guide, BERI SA, 2001; and Alan Shapiro, *Multinational Financial Management*, 8th ed. (New York: John Wiley and Sons, 2006).

Clearly, the global marketer must consider the likelihood of negative political factors in making decisions on conducting business overseas. On the other hand, host country political and legal systems can have a positive impact on the conduct of international business. Many governments, for example, encourage foreign investments, especially if they believe that the investment will produce economic and political benefits domestically. Some governments have opened up their economy to foreign investors, placing only minimal constraints on them, in the hope that such policies will lead to rapid economic development. Others have provided for substantial subsidization of new investment activities in the hope that investments will generate additional employment. The global marketer, in his or her investment decision, can and should therefore also pay close attention to the extent and forms of incentives available from foreign governments. Although global marketing decisions should be driven by market forces, the basic economies of these decisions may change depending on incentives offered.

In this discussion of the political environment, laws have been mentioned only to the extent that they appear to be the direct result of political changes. However, each nation has laws regarding marketing, and the international manager must understand their effects on the firm's efforts.

Legal Differences and Restraints

Countries differ in their laws as well as in their use of these laws. Japan's legal tradition tends to minimize the role of the law and of lawyers, while the U.S. is viewed as being highly litigious. Some possible reasons include Japan's relatively small number of courts and attorneys; the delays, costs, and uncertainties associated with litigation; the limited doctrines of plaintiffs' standing and rights to bring class-action suits; the tendency of judges to encourage out-of-court settlements; and the easy availability of arbitration and mediation for dispute resolution.

Over the millennia of civilization, many different laws and legal systems emerged. King Hammurabi of Babylon codified a series of judges' decisions into a body of law. Hebrew law was considered to be the dictates of God. Legal issues in many African tribes were settled through the verdicts of clansmen. A key legal perspective that survives today is that of **theocracy**, which has faith and belief as its key focus and is a mix of societal, legal, and spiritual guidelines. Examples are Hebrew law and Islamic law (sharia), which are the result of scripture, prophetic utterances and practices, and scholarly interpretations.[24]

While these legal systems are important to society locally, from an international business perspective the two major legal systems worldwide can be categorized into common law and code law. **Common law** is based on tradition and depends less on written statutes and codes than on precedent and custom. Common law originated in England. On the other hand, **code law** is based on a comprehensive set of written statutes. Countries with code law try to spell out all possible legal rules explicitly. Code law is based on Roman law and is found in the majority of the nations of the world. In general, countries with the code-law system have much more rigid laws than those with the common-law system. In the latter, courts adopt precedents and customs to fit the cases, allowing the marketer a better idea of the basic judgment likely to be rendered in new situations. Although wide in theory, the differences between code law and common law and their impact on the global marketer are not always as broad in practice. For example, many common-law countries have adopted commercial codes to govern the conduct of business.

Host countries may adopt a number of laws that affect a company's ability to market. To begin with, there can be laws affecting the entry of goods, such as tariffs and quotas. Also in this category are **anti-dumping laws**, which prohibit below-cost sales of products, and laws that require export and import licensing. In addition, many countries have health and safety standards that may, by design or by accident, restrict the entry of foreign goods. Japan, for example, has particularly strict health standards that affect the import of pharmaceuticals. Rather than accepting test results from other nations, the Japanese government insists on conducting its own tests, which are time consuming and costly. It claims that these tests are necessary to take into account Japanese peculiarities. Yet some importers and their governments see these practices as thinly veiled protectionist barriers.

A growing global controversy surrounds the use of genetic technology. Governments are increasingly devising new rules that affect trade in genetically modified products. For example, Australia introduced a mandatory standard for foods produced using biotechnology that prohibits the sale of such products unless the food has been assessed by the Australia New Zealand Food Authority.

Other laws may be designed to protect domestic industries and reduce imports. For example, Russia charges a 20 percent value-added tax on most imported goods; assesses high excise taxes on goods such as cigarettes, automobiles, and alcoholic beverages; and provides a burdensome import licensing and quotas regime for alcohol and products containing alcohol to depress Russian demand for imports.[25]

Very specific legislation may also exist to regulate where a firm can advertise or what constitutes deceptive advertising. Many countries prohibit specific claims by marketers comparing their product to that of the competition and restrict the use of promotional devices. Some countries regulate the names of companies or the foreign-language content of a product's label. Even when no laws exist, the marketer may be hampered by regulations. For example, in many countries, governments require a firm to join the local chamber of commerce or become a member of the national trade association. These institutions in turn may have internal regulations that set standards for the conduct of business and may be seen as quite confining to the global marketer.

Finally, the enforcement of laws may have a different effect on national and on foreign marketers. For example, the simple requirement that an executive has to stay in a country until a business conflict is resolved may be a major burden for the global marketer.

Influencing Politics and Laws

To succeed in a market, the global marketer needs much more than business know-how. He or she must also deal with the intricacies of national politics and laws. Although a full understanding of another country's legal and political system will rarely be possible, the good manager will be aware of the importance of this system and will work with people who do understand how to operate within the system.

Many areas of politics and law are not immutable. Viewpoints can be modified or even reversed, and new laws can supersede old ones. Therefore, existing political and legal restraints do not always need to be accepted. To achieve change, however, there must be some impetus for it, such as the clamours of a constituency. Otherwise, systemic inertia is likely to allow the status quo to prevail.

The global marketer has various options. One approach may be to simply ignore prevailing rules and expect to get away with it. Pursuing this option is a high-risk strategy because of the possibility of objection and even prosecution. A second, traditional option is to provide input to trade negotiators and expect any problem areas to be resolved in multilateral negotiations. The drawback to this option is, of course, the quite time-consuming process involved.

A third option involves the development of coalitions or constituencies that can motivate legislators and politicians to consider and ultimately implement change. This option can be pursued in various ways. One direction can be the recasting or re-definition of issues. Often, specific terminology leads to conditioned though inappropriate responses. For example, before China's accession to the World Trade Organization (WTO) in 2001, the country's trade status with the United States was highly controversial for many years. The debate on this decision was always very contentious and acerbic and was often framed around the question of why China deserved to be treated in the "most favoured way." Lost in the debate was the fact that the term "most favoured" was simply taken from WTO terminology and indicated only that trade with China would be treated like that with any other country. Only in late 1999 was the terminology changed from "Most Favoured Nation" or MFN to NTR or "normal trade relations." Even though there was still considerable debate regarding China, the controversy about special treatment had been eliminated.[26]

Beyond terminology, marketers can also highlight the direct linkages and their cost and benefit to legislators and politicians. For example, the manager can explain the employment and economic effects of certain laws and regulations and demonstrate the benefits of change. The picture can be enlarged by including indirect linkages. For example, suppliers, customers, and distributors can be asked to participate in delineating to decision makers the benefit of change. Such groups can be quite influential.

Developing such coalitions is not an easy task. Companies often seek assistance in effectively influencing the government decision-making process. Such assistance usually is particularly beneficial when narrow economic objectives or single-issue campaigns are needed. Typical providers of this assistance are lobbyists. Usually, these are well-connected individuals and firms that can provide access to policymakers and legislators.

Although representation of the firm's interests to government decision makers and legislators is entirely appropriate, the global marketer must also consider any potential side effects. Major questions can be raised if such representation becomes very strong. In such instances, short-term gains may be far outweighed by long-term negative repercussions if the international marketer is perceived as exerting too much political influence.

The International Environment

In addition to the politics and laws of both the home and the host countries, the global marketer must consider the overall international political and legal environment. Relations between countries can have a profound impact on firms trying to do business internationally.

International Politics

The effect of politics on global marketing is determined by both the bilateral political relations between home and host countries and the multilateral agreements governing the relations among groups of countries.

The government-to-government relationship can have a profound effect, particularly if it becomes hostile. Numerous examples exist of the linkage between international politics and global marketing, such as the inability of U.S. firms to export to Cuba following the cooling of relations between the governments of the two countries. International political relations do not always have harmful effects on global marketers. If bilateral political relations between countries improve, business can benefit. A good example is the thawing of relations between the West and the countries of the former Soviet bloc. Political warming has opened up completely new frontiers for Western marketers in Hungary, Poland, and Russia, just to name a few countries. Activities such as selling computers, which would have been considered treasonous only a few years ago, are now routine.

The global marketer needs to be aware of political currents worldwide and must attempt to anticipate changes in the international political environment, good or bad, so that his or her firm can plan for them. Sometimes, however, management can only wait until the emotional fervour of conflict has subsided and hope that rational governmental negotiations will let cooler heads prevail.

International Law

International law plays an important role in the conduct of international business. Although no enforceable body of international law exists, certain treaties and agreements respected by a number of countries profoundly influence international business operations. As an example, the WTO defines internationally acceptable economic practices for its member nations. Although it does not directly affect individual firms, it does influence them indirectly by providing a more stable and predictable international market environment.

A number of efforts have been made to simplify the legal aspects of business procedures. For example, firms wanting to patent their products in the past had to register them separately in each country in order to have protection. In response to the chaos and expense of such procedures, several multilateral simplification efforts have been undertaken. European countries have been at the forefront of such efforts with the European Patent Convention and the Community Patent Convention.

Similar efforts have been undertaken with regard to trademarks so that firms can benefit from various multilateral agreements. The two major international conventions on trademarks are the International Convention for the Protection of Industrial Property and the Madrid Arrangement for International Registration of Trademarks. Several regional conventions include the Inter-American Convention for Trademark Protection and a similar agreement in French West Africa. In addition to multilateral agreements, firms are affected by bilateral treaties and conventions. It is important that the global marketer become familiar with the legislative framework that provides protection for intellectual property. Even large, well-established companies will find themselves embroiled in controversy from time to time. Starbucks, for example, has had to file an objection with India's Controller-General of Patents, Designs and Trademark over plans by an Indian entrepreneur to open a chain of retail coffee shops under the name "Starstrucks."[27] Starbucks claims that the name is deceptively similar to its own and infringes on its intellectual property rights.

The international legal environment also affects the marketer to the extent that firms must concern themselves with jurisdictional disputes. Because no single body of international law exists, firms usually are restricted by both home and host country laws. If a conflict occurs between contracting parties in two different countries, a question arises concerning which country's laws will be followed. Sometimes the contract will contain a jurisdictional clause, which settles the matter. If not, the parties to the dispute can follow either the laws of the country in which the agreement was made or those of the country in which the contract will have to be fulfilled. Deciding on the laws to be followed and the location to settle the dispute are two different decisions.

The parties to a business transaction can also choose either arbitration or litigation. Litigation is usually avoided for several reasons. It often involves extensive delays and is very costly. In addition, firms may fear discrimination in foreign countries. Companies therefore tend to prefer conciliation and arbitration because these processes result in much quicker decisions. Arbitration procedures are often spelled out in the original contract and usually provide for an intermediary who is judged to be impartial by both parties. Frequently, intermediaries will be representatives of chambers of commerce, trade associations, or third-country institutions. For example, the rules of the international chamber of commerce in Paris are frequently used for arbitration purposes.

Summary

The political and legal environment in the home country, the environment in the host country, and the laws and agreements governing relationships among nations are all important to the international marketer. Compliance with them is mandatory in order to do business abroad successfully. Such laws can control exports and imports both directly and indirectly and can also regulate the international business behaviour of firms, particularly in the areas of boycotts, antitrust, corruption, and ethics.

To avoid the problems that can result from changes in the political and legal environment, the global marketer must anticipate changes and develop strategies for coping with them. Whenever possible, the manager must avoid being taken by surprise and letting events control business decisions.

On occasion, the global marketer may be caught between clashing home and host country laws. In such instances, the firm needs to conduct a dialogue with the governments in order to seek a compromise solution. Alternatively, managers can encourage their government to engage in government-to-government negotiations to settle the dispute. By demonstrating the business volume at stake and the employment that may be lost through such governmental disputes, government negotiators can often be motivated to press hard for a settlement of such intergovernmental difficulties. Finally, the firm can seek redress in court. Such international legal action, however, may be quite slow and, even if resulting in a favourable judgment for the firm, may not be adhered to by the government against which the judgment is rendered.

In the final analysis, a firm conducting business internationally is subject to the vagaries of political and legal changes and may lose business as a result. The best the manager can do is be aware of political influences and laws and strive to adopt them as far as possible.

Key Terms

anti-dumping laws (p. 152)
boycotts (p. 140)
code law (p. 152)
common law (p. 152)
confiscation (p. 147)
domestication (p. 147)
dual-use items (p. 136)
embargoes (p. 133)
export control systems (p. 135)
export embargo (p. 132)
expropriation (p. 146)
functional lubrication (p. 142)
grey-market goods (p. 132)
intellectual property rights (p. 132)
operating risk (p. 145)
over-invest (p. 149)
ownership risk (p. 145)
political risk (p. 145)
price controls (p. 150)
quota systems (p. 139)
theocracy (p. 152)
trade sanctions (p. 133)
transfer risk (p. 145)

Questions for Discussion

1. Discuss this statement: "High political risk requires companies to seek a quick payback on their investments. Striving for such a quick payback, however, exposes firms to charges of exploitation and results in increased political risk."
2. How appropriate is it for governments to help drum up business for their companies abroad? Should commerce be completely separate from politics?
3. After you hand your passport to the immigration officer in country X, he misplaces it. A small "donation" would certainly help him find it again. Should you give him money? Is this a business expense to be charged to your company? Should it be tax deductible?
4. Discuss the advantages and disadvantages of common law versus code law for the global marketer.
5. What are your views on lobbying efforts by foreign firms?

Internet Exercises

1. Visit the website of the Export and Import Controls Bureau at **http://www.dfait-maeci.gc.ca/eicb/menu-en.asp.** Write a short summary on the role of this organization, the products it controls, its legislative mandate, and its method of operation.
2. Canada is a signatory to the Organization for Economic Cooperation and Development (OECD) convention on Combating Bribery of Foreign Public Officials in International Business Transactions. Visit the OECD website at **http://www.oecd.org/document/21/0,3343,en_2649_34859_2017813_1_1_1_1,00.html** and write a short paragraph outlining Canada's obligations under this convention.

Recommended Readings

Export Administration Annual Report 2002 Report on Foreign Policy Export Controls. Washington, DC: U.S. Department of Commerce, Bureau of Export Administration, 2002.

A Global Forum on Fighting Corruption. Washington, DC: Bureau for International Narcotics and Law Enforcement Affairs, U.S. Department of State, September 2001.

Haass, Richard, and Meghan L. O'Sullivan. *Honey and Vinegar: Incentives, Sanctions, and Foreign Policy.* Washington, DC: Brookings Institution, 2000.

Hirschhorn, Eric. *Export Controls Handbook.* New York: Oceana, 2000.

Hufbauer, Gary C., Jeffrey J. Schott, and Kimberly Ann Elliott. *Economic Sanctions Reconsidered: History and Current Policy.* 3rd ed. Washington, DC: Institute for International Economics, 2002.

The OECD Guidelines for Multinational Enterprises. Paris: Organization for Economic Cooperation and Development, 2001.

Notes

1. Canadian Business. RIM: Time to grow up, **http://www.canadianbusiness.com/innovation/article.jsp?content=20060313_75169_75169#adSkip.**
2. Quoted in Philippe Dollinger, *The German Hansa* (Stanford, CA: Stanford University Press, 1970), 49.
3. Robin Renwick, *Economic Sanctions* (Cambridge, MA: Harvard University Press, 1981), 11.
4. Margaret P. Doxey, *Economic Sanctions and International Enforcement* (New York: Oxford University Press, 1980), 10.
5. Beth Gorham, "Rice to Try Calming the Softwood Furor on Trip to Canada," Canadian Press, October 24, 2005, **http://www.smirkingchimp.com/comments.php?sid=23316&pid=253413&mode=&order=&thold=** (accessed July 14, 2006).
6. Fred Bridgland, "Enter the Dragon … in Africa's Darkest Nations," August 2005, **http://www.sundayherald.com/51455** (accessed July 14, 2006).
7. George E. Shambaugh, *States, Firms, and Power: Successful Sanctions in United States Foreign Policy* (Albany: State University of New York Press, 1999), 202.
8. See Department of Foreign Affairs and International Trade website, **http://www.dfait-maeci.gc.ca/eicb/menu-en.asp** (accessed July 14, 2006).
9. Michael R. Czinkota and Erwin Dichtl, "Export Controls and Global Changes," *Der Markt* 37, no. 5 (1996): 148–55.
10. The authors are grateful to David Danjczek of Manufacturer's Alliance for his helpful comments.
11. Michael R. Czinkota, "From Bowling Alone to Standing Together," *Marketing Management*, March/April 2002, 12–16.
12. "Microsoft hit by record EU fine," CNN website, **http://www.cnn.com/2004/BUSINESS/03/24/microsoft.eu/** (accessed August 1, 2006).

13. Department of Foreign Affairs website, **http://www.dfait-maeci.gc.ca/internationalcrime/6-report_parliament-en.asp** (accessed July 15, 2006).

14. James R. Hines, Jr., *Forbidden Payment: Foreign Bribery and American Business after 1977*, working paper 5266 (Cambridge, MA: National Bureau of Economic Research, September 1995), 1.

15. Magoroh Maruyama, "Bribing in Historical Context: The Case of Japan," *Human Systems Management* 15 (1996): 138–42.

16. Shang-Jin Wei and Andrei Shleifer, "Local Corruption and Global Capital Flows," Brookings Papers on Economic Activity (Washington, DC: 2000), iss. 2, p. 303, 52 pp. See also P. Egger and H. Winner, "Evidence on Corruption as an Incentive for Foreign Direct Investment," *European Journal of Political Economy* 21 (2005): 932–52.

17. Ayça Tekin-Koru, "Corruption and the Ownership Composition of the Multinational Firm at the Time of Entry: Evidence from Turkey," *Journal of Economics and Finance* 30, no. 2 (2006): 251–69.

18. B.K. Smarzynska and S. Wei, "Corruption and Composition of Foreign Direct Investment: Firm-Level Evidence," NBER working paper no: 7969 (2000).

19. Ayça Tekin-Koru, op. cit.

20. Michael G. Harvey, "A Survey of Corporate Programs for Managing Terrorist Threats," *Journal of International Business Studies*, 3rd quarter, 1993, 465–78.

21. Harvey J. Iglarsh, "Terrorism and Corporate Costs," *Terrorism* 10 (1987): 227–30.

22. Michael Minor, "LDCs, TNCs, and Expropriation in the 1980s," *CTC Reporter*, Spring 1988, 53.

23. Bema Gold victim of its own success, **http://www.canada.com/nationalpost/financialpost/story.html?id=5b7e1850-c047-48a5-8b78-41a6a0b7114b** (accessed March 15, 2007).

24. Surya Prakash Sinha, *What Is Law? The Differing Theories of Jurisprudence* (New York: Paragon House, 1989).

25. *National Trade Estimate Report on Foreign Trade Barriers* (Washington, DC: Office of the United States Trade Representative, 2002).

26. Michael R. Czinkota, "The Policy Gap in International Marketing," *Journal of International Marketing* 8, no. 1 (2000): 99–111.

27. See **http://news.moneycentral.msn.com/provider/providerarticle.aspx?feed=OBR&Date=20070304&ID=6565960** (accessed March 4, 2007).

Part
CASES
2

China's Beauty Industry: L'Oréal's Foray

"It's the beginning of the Chinese snowball. There have been three million Maybelline lipsticks sold. Our aim is to make sure every Chinese woman has a lipstick in her hand instead of the Little Red Book."[1]

—Lindsay Owen-Jones
CEO, L'Oréal

Introduction

L'Oréal, the world's largest cosmetics company, based in France, was keen on consolidating its position in Chinese markets. It entered China in 1996 and made its first profits in 2003. Twelve of its top fourteen brands like Lancome, Garnier, Vichy and Maybelline were sold in China in 2004. Since 1997, L'Oréal had invested US$120 million in China to develop markets for its brands. The acquisition of Mininurse, a popular local cosmetics brand, in December 2003 put L'Oréal in the second position, up from eleventh in China. In January 2004, it acquired another brand, Yue-Sai. Both the acquisitions were seen as a move to enter the two and three-tier towns of China, where L'Oréal was not strong. These acquisitions were also expected to help L'Oréal stave off competition from local companies and foreign brands like Avon, Mary Kay, and Shiseido. Another challenge L'Oréal faced was from counterfeit products that were interfering with its sales and tarnishing its brand image. But Lindsay Owen-Jones, CEO of L'Oréal was keen on achieving a greater share of the Chinese beauty care market.

Case Study Reference No. MES0021

This case was written by Kalyani Vemuri, under the direction of T Phani Madhav, ICFAI Business School Case Development Centre. It is intended to be used as the basis for class discussion rather than to illustrate either effective or ineffective handling of a management situation. This case was compiled from published sources.

Related Products Availability
Teaching Note
Structured Assignment

Phone : 91(40) 23435387 - 91
Fax : 91(40) 23435386
E-mail : info@ibscdc.org

Distributed and Printed by IBS-CDC, India
www.ibscdc.org

Learning to Lead

China's Beauty Industry

In 2004, China's beauty industry was booming. It was the fourth fastest-growing industry after real estate, automobiles, and tourism. There were an estimated 3,700 cosmetics companies producing more than 20,000 kinds of cosmetics products. Among them, 58% were private companies, 32% were foreign-invested businesses and state-owned firms made up the remaining 10%. Revenues from cosmetics were $6.27 billion in 2003. Total revenues generated by the beauty industry were $20.33 billion, accounting for 1.2% of the country's GDP. Analysts expected the total revenue from the industry to top $36.15 billion by 2010.[2] China is the eighth largest consumer of cosmetics in the world and the second largest market for beauty care products in Asia, next only to Japan (Exhibit 1).

Analysts attributed this boom to several factors. Firstly, China had a population of 1.3 billion out of which 480 million lived in urban areas. Better job opportunities were driving more rural Chinese into bigger towns and cities. Urban consumers were becoming very beauty-conscious. Since the early 1990s, rising income levels, better living standards and a growing awareness of foreign brands and products gave a fillip to the consumption of not just beauty-care products, but spas, beauty clinics, and other beauty-service providers. China had nearly 1.54 million beauty parlours in 2004.[3] Secondly, the number of white-collar women workers in

Exhibit 1

Annual Sales of China Cosmetic Industry (1990–2001)

Year	90	91	92	93	94	95	96	97	98	99	00	01
Annual sales (Billion RMB)	4	5	7	9	14	19	22	25.3	27.5	30	35	40
% change	—	25	40	29	56	36	16	15	8.5	7.1	16.7	14
Per capita consumption (RMB)	3.3	4.3	6.0	6.8	9.6	16	18	21	22	23	27	31

Note: The statistics contained in this table only cover retail sales of the following six product categories but do not include those sales to the beauty salons and barber shops:

1) Hair care (2-in-1, shampoos, conditioners, colorants, and styling agents)
2) Skin care (Facial, body, hand, and sun care)
3) Color cosmetics (Lipsticks, facial powder, eye shadow, nail polishes)
4) Personal care (Baby care, bath & shower, deodorants, shaving/grooming)
5) Oral hygiene (Toothpaste, toothbrushes, mouthwash, mouth fresher, dental floss)
6) Fragrance (Mass and premium)

Source: Li, Shuquan "China Cosmetic Market (A Report)", **http://strategis.ic.gc.ca,** June 5th 2003.

the cities had been steadily increasing. These women were willing to invest more time and money on cosmetics that would help them look professional and well groomed. Thirdly, China's one-child policy had resulted in youngsters being pampered by nearly six adults in the family and they had more spending power than the previous generation did.[4]

International brands accounted for almost 80% of revenues of cosmetics in China. According to Taylor Nelson Sofres, a market research firm, four out of the top five facial skin care brands in China were international brands. L'Oréal, Mary Kay, P&G, Avon, Kao, Henkel, Revlon, Estée Lauder, Nivea, Coty, and Shiseido were some of the foreign brands that were working on increasing their presence in the Chinese markets. During the 1990s, foreign cosmetic companies invested close to $300 million in the Chinese cosmetic industry. Almost 450 foreign-invested firms had been set up. Analysts said that foreign companies had an edge over local Chinese firms because they were financially stronger, had access to the latest market research and had strong product development facilities. But they faced a lot of challenges. The distribution system in China had a multi-tier structure that foreign firms found hard to penetrate. Moreover, reaching into far-flung rural areas was seen as a tough task. Local competitors were quick to adapt and were catching up with the major players like L'Oréal. Moreover, the cosmetics industry received a jolt in April 1998, when the Chinese government decided to ban direct marketing, the main form of marketing of companies like Mary Kay and Avon. Though the ban was lifted and the government formulated new rules under which direct marketing could be done, companies like Avon were forced to make changes in their business model, like opening "beauty boutiques" and selling at local department stores. In 2004, among foreign firms, L'Oréal through its two major acquisitions, Mininurse and Yue-Sai within a month of each other, was considered one of the most active players of the industry.

L'Oréal's International Expansion

When Lindsay Owen-Jones took over as L'Oréal's CEO in 1988, 95% of its sales were coming from European markets. Owen-Jones is credited with creating and executing L'Oréal's strategy of rapid expansion into foreign markets, acquiring national brands like Maybelline and Helena Rubenstein, giving them a marketing makeover and selling them to consumers across the world. Owen-Jones was a believer in multiculturalism, which means that consumers across the world would be interested in brands that epitomise different cultures and images. For example, Maybelline, an American brand that L'Oréal bought in 1996 was marketed in Japan as a brand that symbolises American attitude. It was a huge hit. Owen-Jones wanted L'Oréal to move away from being a quintessential French brand to a United Nations of beauty, where there were brands that suited the needs of different consumers from all cultures, age groups, and spending power levels. Under Owen-Jones' leadership, L'Oréal reported double-digit growth rates for 17 consecutive years. In 2004, only 52.7% of L'Oréal's sales (Euro 14 billion) were coming from Europe. Revenues from other parts of the world were increasing. For instance, sales in China rose by 70% in 2003 to reach Euro 159 million (Exhibits 2A and 2B).

Exhibit 2A Consolidated Sales of L'Oréal Group in 2003

Breakdown of consolidated sales by branch

	2001		2002		2003	
	€ millions	% of Total	€ millions	% of Total	€ millions	% of Total
Cosmetics	13,394.2	97.5	13,951.8	97.6	13,704.3	97.7
Dermatology	292.2	2.1	321.1	2.3	306.5	2.2
Other	54.0	0.4	15.1	0.1	18.3	0.1
Group	13,740.4	100.0	14,288.0	100.0	14,029.1	100.0

Source: www.loreal.com

Analysts felt that L'Oréal's strategy of expanding beyond France, especially into emerging markets like Russia, China, and Brazil had offset the sluggish growth in the developed markets of Europe. In Western Europe, sales of L'Oréal in 2003 increased by only 1.7%. Analysts cited weak economic growth and high levels of unemployment in the Euro nations as the reasons why consumers were turning to discount supermarkets for their purchases. These discount supermarkets either did not sell L'Oréal products or sold them at lower prices.[5] Supermarket operators had been negotiating with companies for lower prices. L'Oréal's competitors like Procter & Gamble had been giving deep price-cuts and increasing sales in Europe. Analysts felt that this constraint made it all the more important for L'Oréal to strengthen its position in developing markets like China and Russia.

L'Oréal's Foray into China

L'Oréal entered China in February 1996. Paolo Gasparrini (Gasparrini), who was serving as the President of L'Oréal Brazil, was asked to head the company's operations in China. At first, he operated from an office in Hong Kong with a staff of seven people, but quickly set up the company's offices in Mainland China, employing a staff of 40. L'Oréal was introduced to Chinese consumers as "Or Lai Ya", which means 'the beauty that comes from Europe.' The bestselling brands of L'Oréal like Maybelline were introduced in the bigger cities of China.

Meanwhile, Gasparrini studied the complex operating business environment of China, the existing competitive landscape, Chinese buying habits and aspects of China's work culture. He found that unlike Brazilians, who purchase on impulse, show low brand loyalty and are influenced by emotional triggers, Chinese consumers are meticulous in their research, are more rational and brand loyal. He found that the communist regime of the past five decades had suppressed sales of beauty and skin care products, but the opening up of the markets has given a boost to consumer spending on personal care. Chinese women, especially in the urban areas, were interested in purchasing medium to high-end foreign skin care and cosmetic brands. Increase in the number of female white-collar workers who wanted to present

Exhibit 2B Consolidated Sales of L'Oréal Group in 2003

Breakdown of consolidated sales by geographic zone

	2001		2002		2003	
	€ millions	% of Total	€ millions	% of Total	€ millions	% of Total
Western Europe	6,667.2	48.5	7,044.6	49.3	7,309.7	52.1
North America	4,450.5	32.4	4,438.7	31.1	3,981.4	28.4
Rest of the World	2,622.7	19.1	2,804.7	19.6	2,738.0	19.5
Group	13,740.4	100.0	14,288.0	100.0	14,029.1	100.0

Source: www.loreal.com

themselves as well-groomed professionals drove sales of skin-care products and lipsticks. Skin-whitening creams were especially popular, as urban women saw a pale complexion as a way to differentiate themselves from sunburnt rural women.

In 1997, L'Oréal's sales in China were $10 million, which rose to $20 million in 1998. In 1996, the company signed up Chinese actress Gong Li who acted in movies like *Raise the Red Lantern* for a fee of $1 million.[6] The company wanted her to become its face in China. Some analysts say, however, that the strategy was not very successful. Though the actress was very popular among western moviegoers, Chinese women couldn't relate to her. Analysts suggested that L'Oréal use celebrities with a girl-next-door image that Chinese women can identify with. L'Oréal then signed on other spokesmodels, one of them being actress Zhang Ziyi of the *Crouching Tiger, Hidden Dragon* fame. Also, L'Oréal found that Chinese do not appreciate very revealing or in-your-face type of advertising. "We don't do any daring advertising, but there is always some small sexy details but not too much, not bad taste,"[7] said Gasparrini. In April 2002, in order to reach Chinese consumers through the increasingly popular tool of the Internet, L'Oréal partnered with SINA, a leading Chinese media and Internet services company to create a website targeting Chinese women worldwide. "Women of China", the largest women's press group in China, provided the content.[8] The site was designed to provide a wide range of information and services to fulfill the daily personal and professional needs of Chinese women. Visitors who signed up received news about new product launches.

In 2002, after a study about Chinese men revealed that 70% of respondents used cleansing foam, and nearly 50% applied skin cream every day, L'Oréal introduced its Biotherm men's skin-care range. "It's time we suggest the idea of male beauty products in the domestic market and educate more consumers,"[9] said Jiang Qialong, brand manager of Biotherm. The line was targeted at men in the age group of 25–35 who earn more than 6000 Yuan a month. Jiang added, "Although most men interviewed held a positive attitude toward male beauty products, most use them passively by following girlfriends, or female family members. Few men buy the products themselves. Therefore, our promotional strategies will target women."[10] In the men's skin-care segment, Shiseido and Coty already had a presence by the time L'Oréal introduced Biotherm.

Gasparrini believed that L'Oréal's success was partly due to understanding the needs of its Chinese consumers. For example, L'Oréal adapted the formulae of its shampoos to suit the needs of Chinese, whose hair is stronger than that of Caucasians.[11] In 2004, L'Oréal announced that it would establish a research and development center in China, which would study Chinese skin and hair extensively. It would be on the same lines as its center in Chicago that specializes in studying the skin and hair properties of Afro-American consumers.

L'Oréal China .employed a workforce of 3000. Only eight of them were foreigners. "The average age in L'Oréal China is just 28 years old, exactly the same age as our consumer target," said Gasparrini. "This means that the Chinese work for Chinese inside the firm and out."[12] L'Oréal found it difficult to recruit people with significant work experience. So, the company had been going to China's top universities and recruiting promising graduates. They were put through a one-year training program where they learnt business management skills like budgeting and communication. They were also assigned a mentor each who would help them understand L'Oréal's culture.

Since the time it entered China, L'Oréal had invested US $120 million to develop markets for its products. It built production bases in the cities of Suzhou and Yichang and in the Pudong New District of Shanghai. Twelve out of the company's fourteen most successful brands were introduced in China by 2004. Some of them were already leaders in their categories, like Lancôme in the high-end market, Vichy in pharmacies, L'Oréal Professional in premium hair color, and Maybelline in mass makeup. In 2003, Maybelline brand lipstick had a 35% market share in lipsticks in China. Gasparrini declared that the company's China division began to earn profits in 2003. Sales in 2003 were $159 million, a 69.3% over 2002. Between 1997-2003, sales of the company in China rose 824%. In 2004, L'Oréal China was the fastest growing division of the company. Analysts believe that L'Oréal's acquisition of Mininurse and Yue-Sai, two major local brands was an important strategic move of the company to consolidate its position in the industry.

L'Oréal's Acquisitions

L'Oréal's research showed that there was a strong demand for local cosmetic brands as 15% of Chinese women between 15 and 35 years said that they preferred brands from their own country.[13] The preference for local brands was stronger in poorer rural provinces where women with limited disposable income were very price sensitive. L'Oréal wanted to enter the rural markets along with developing products for the urban consumers. "We are trying to have a brand for every need, and more and more in terms of purchasing power. We want to serve the rich consumer, and we want more and more to be close to people that have lower purchasing power," Gasparrini said and added, "L'Oréal will continue to enlarge the Chinese market shares through purchasing local brands and introducing international brands."[14]

In December 2003, L'Oréal acquired Mininurse, a Chinese brand, after four years of negotiations with Li Zhida, its owner. Launched in Chinese markets in 1992, Mininurse, one of China's most popular brands, enjoys a 5% share of the market with 2003 revenues of nearly $50 million. Mininurse products are sold through almost 280,000 outlets across China and L'Oréal is keen on using the outlets to sell its international brands like Maybelline and Garnier. L'Oréal hoped that Mininurse's wide reach would help it strengthen its hold in rural areas. According to A.C.Neilsen, Mininurse has 90% brand recognition among Chinese women and 96% among younger women.[15] This acquisition pushed up L'Oréal from the eleventh position to the second in the industry. Though the company didn't disclose the price it paid for Mininurse, analysts place it broadly between $48.6 million and $145.8 million. The deal also includes Mininurse's large factory in the Hubei province, which L'Oréal could use as a manufacturing base. "This acquisition is an outstanding opportunity to speed up our growth in the Chinese market. It is a major step forward in L'Oréal's development in a market which is strategically important for the company," said Lindsay Owen-Jones, L'Oréal's chairman and chief executive officer.[16]

After L'Oréal's acquisition of Mininurse, analysts expected P&G to bid for Yue-Sai, another prominent local cosmetics brand. P&G had been negotiating with Yue-Sai for a long time. But L'Oréal ultimately acquired it in January 2004, just one month after it bought Mininurse. According to Euromonitor International, a global business intelligence agency, Yue-Sai ranked third in a list of China's top 10 cosmetics brands in 2002. It had 11% share of the market and sales of €38 million in 2003. Set up by Yue-Sai Kan, a Chinese TV celebrity, the brand sells through 800 departmental stores across 240 cities. Urban consumers of the brand were avid followers of Yue-Sai Kan's beauty advice dispensed through TV shows. She was so famous in China, that the postal department issued stamps with her image. Though she sold her stake to Coty, her brand was considered to be China's most famous cosmetics brand. "After acquiring Mininurse at the end of last year, this new Chinese acquisition only serves to confirm our determination to step up the pace of growth in China,"[17] said Lindsay Owen-Jones. "The acquisition also obliges us to have an effort in developing more specific formula for Chinese customers with our world-class research capability. We will give the acquired brand a bright future and continue its development,"[18] said Gasparrini. Some analysts said that L'Oréal will try to give Yue-Sai the same makeover it gave to the brands it acquired in the past in other countries and sell its products as a distinctly Chinese line in International markets.

These acquisitions were seen as a step to win market share from competitors Mary Kay, Shiseido, Kanebo, and Avon. Also, Gasparrini hoped the acquisitions would help spread L'Oréal's consumer base from urban areas to two and three-tier towns in China.

Challenges

L'Oréal faced stiff competition from players like Mary Kay, which entered China in 1998 and enjoyed 8% share of the market in 2003. Estee Lauder, Amway, and Avon had all publicly announced that they intended to strengthen their positions in the Chinese markets. Japanese company Kanebo was planning to double the number of its distribution outlets to achieve sales of at least $20 million a year. Mary Kay and other companies were lobbying for ease on import restrictions that would enable them to import products into China without investing heavily into production facilities. Another challenge L'Oréal faced was from local firms that were nimble and were close to the market. Local firms have always enjoyed a better understanding of local consumers. After the success of foreign brands, some of the local firms were quickly copying new products and marketing them faster than foreign brands. They had also realised the importance of structured market research and were reported to be investing in it. Gasparrini said, "Local competitors are becoming stronger and stronger because they learn very fast."[19] He admitted that a local shampoo brand called Slek was eating into the share of L'Oréal's shampoos.

One more challenge was posed by counterfeits. Counterfeit products were a blessing in one way for L'Oréal as urban consumers were getting increasingly wary of fake products and were taking care to purchase only authentic foreign brands they trusted. But in rural areas, lesser-educated, price-conscious women were not being able to spot counterfeits and were purchasing them widely. China promised to protect copyrights when it joined the World Trade Organisation (WTO) in 2001, but according to researchers, it was the provincial authorities that were reluctant to put the central policies into practice. They did not want to lose the taxes paid by firms that produced counterfeits. Analysts opined that L'Oréal would be able to fight these challenges and increase its market share by building a strong brand identity in China and investing more in promotions than advertising.

Notes

1. Ozzard, Janet "L'Oréal's New Focus on Emerging Markets," WWD, October 1998
2. "Cosmetic Industry Embarks on Reshuffle," **www.chinadaily.com,** March 4th 2004
3. Ibid.
4. Hennock, Mary "Inside China's 'Me' Generation," **http://news.bbc.co.uk,** November 6th 2002
5. "L'Oréal Profit Rises 22% on Growth in China, Russia," **http://quote.bloomberg.com,** September 1st 2004
6. "8 Things You Didn't Know About Chinese Consumers," **http://www.asiaweek.com,** March 2000

7. "Inside China's 'Me' Generation," op. cit.
8. "L'Oréal Selected SINA as Host and Partner for Women Site Targeting Chinese Worldwide," **www.sina.com,** April 24th 2002
9. "Changing the Face of Men's Cosmetics," **http://www.iol.co.za,** July 15th 2002
10. Ibid.
11. Hennock, Mary "Changing the Face of China," **http://news.bbc.co.uk,** November 5th 2002
12. Ibid.
13. "Building Brand Equity a Tough Exercise for Chinese Companies," **http://en.ce.cn/Markets/Commodities/t20040525_922564.shtml,** May 25th 2004
14. "L'Oréal Posted CNY 1.5b Sales in China Last Year," *AsiaInfo Services*, March 15th 2004
15. "Beautiful Deal for Cosmetics Firm," **www.2.chinadaily.com,** December 12th 2003
16. Wen, Chen "Who Is the Fairest of All?" **http://www.bjreview.com.cn,** September 2004
17. "Chinese Expansion for L'Oréal," **www.cosmeticsdesign.com,** January 29th 2004
18. "L'Oréal to Use Yue-Sai Until 2013," **www.eastday.com,** January 31st 2004
19. "Changing the Face of Men's Cosmetics," op. cit.

Muslim Colas: Cola Wars or Cola Crusades?

During the prelude to the 2003 American-led invasion of Iraq, some consumers worldwide boycotted American products and brands. In the Philippines, 10 leading products were targeted, notably Coca-Cola, McDonald's, Citibank, and *Starbucks*. Among the reasons given by boycott leaders was "disgust and revulsion" at the invasion.[1] In some Russian and German cities, restaurant patrons were told that Coke was unavailable because of the current political situation.[2] Other countries with active boycotts discussed in the press included Argentina, Egypt, France, Greece, India, Indonesia, Italy, Malaysia, Pakistan, Saudi Arabia, Tunisia, and Yemen. Almost without exception, Coca-Cola figures prominently in the boycotted product lists. Coca-Cola has itself been targeted in a long-standing boycott over its bottling plant in occupied Palestine.[3] For years boycotts in support of the Palestinian Intifada have been in effect, as well as boycott threats in opposition to the Bush administration's international trade stance on biotech foods and other issues.[4]

Coca-Cola's prominence on boycott lists points to its paradigmatic status as an American brand. Variations on the *Coca-Cola* logo have been used as an image on anti-war posters, and in puns, as in 'COLA-teral Damage' by the Belgian group STOPUSA (www.stopusa.org).

Online Boycott Lists that Prominently Feature Coca-Cola

http://www.krysstal.com/democracy_whyusa_boycott.html (UK)

http://www.futureaustralia.net/get_active/boycott/global_boycott/ (Australia)

http://www.boycottbush.net/ (UK)

http://www.boycott.hpg.ig.com.br/index.html (Brazil)

http://www.loic-martin.net/boycot/ (France)

http://www.stopusa.be/ (Belgium)

Saskia Faulk and Jean-Claude Usunier prepared this case solely to provide material for class discussion. The authors do not intend to illustrate either effective or ineffective handling of a business situation. The authors may have disguised certain names and other identifying information to protect confidentiality.

Muslim Colas

Mecca Cola (www.mecca-cola.com) was launched by Tunisian-born entrepreneur Tawfik Mathlouthi in November, 2002. Its packaging is similar in color and style to that of Coca-Cola, however its philosophy is diametrically opposed to the drinks monolith: its logo is "No more drinking stupid – drink with commitment!", and "Don't shake me, shake your conscience!" The French company claimed that 10% of its net profits will be sent to Palestinian children's charities, plus another 10% to European charities favoring international peace and Palestinian causes. *Mecca* drinks (including Tonic, Classic, Mentha, and Vanilly) were distributed in Australia, Belgium, Canada, France, Germany, and Great Britain, according to the company.[5] In Great Britain, orders were brisk at over two million bottles per month[6] Mecca Cola "sponsored" the million-strong peace march in London in February, 2003, handing out 'Not in my name' t-shirts and Mecca Cola.

Across the Channel, Qibla Cola made its appearance in February, 2003. According to the Qibla Cola website (www.Qibla-cola.com), British entrepreneur Zahida Parveen founded the company to offer 'real alternatives to global consumer brands that support unjust policies'.[7] Like Mecca Cola, Qibla's offerings resemble those of Coca-Cola, and Qibla is the Arabic word for the direction to pray to Mecca, but the company is more than a nod at Mecca Cola. The company promotes Qibla Cola, Qibla Fantasy (orange and mango), Qibla 5 (lemon-lime) named for the five pillars of Islam, and spring water to 2.5 million Muslims in Britain, with an eye on Indonesia, Pakistan, and Bangladesh.[8] The company works with Islamic Aid, a registered charity that is to receive 10% of net profits. Qibla noted that it broke even after only two months, an exceptional performance for a start-up.[9] In an interview, Qibla CEO Zafer Iqbal proffered that the products' packaging and taste parallels with Coca-Cola were intended to "leverage" Coke's global image and make consumers aware of Islamic alternatives like Qibla.[10] Company spokesperson Abdul Hamid Ebrahim stated that the company's inspiration came from Iran's ZamZam Cola, a company that profited from a leading Iranian cleric's ruling that Coke and Pepsi were "un-Islamic".[11]

ZamZam Cola has a leading market share of 47% in its home country Iran, a net income of US$176 million last year and more than 7000 employees in 17 factories.[12] It is distributed throughout the Middle East, and some African and European countries, notably Denmark. The company was Coke's long-term partner in Iran, prior to the Islamic Revolution. In the autumn of 2002, ZamZam produced more than ten million bottles to meet rising demand in Saudi Arabia, spurred on by anger over American support for Israel.[13] As a consequence of boycotts and the advent of competitors like ZamZam, sales of Coca-Cola and Pepsi Cola fell from 20-40% in some Middle Eastern countries in 2002.[14]

There are other so-called Muslim colas dedicated to taking market share from Coca-Cola, including French brands Arab Cola (**http://www.arab-cola.com**), and MuslimUp (**www.muslim-up.com**), and Star Cola from the United Arab Emirates. All these cola companies face similar problems. They are up against the world's most valuable brand, Coca-Cola, valued at more than US$70 billion.[15] For all but ZamZam, securing capacity contracts with bottling plants has proven difficult. Distribution is often a problem, with supermarkets reluctant to take on a new 'niche' product with an unsure future although in France Arab Cola can proudly make the claim that it has the "trust" of its national super/hypermarket distributors Carrefour and E. Leclerc.* Distributors are also concerned about the capacity of cola suppliers to meet demand at a consistent quality level, which is often an issue in the Middle East where ambient temperatures may be excessive for many packaging and ingredient formulations. As a result, these alternative colas are often sold in small family-owned shops in areas populated by immigrants.[16] They may ride the wave of temporary consumer sentiment against U.S. brands, but people tend to revert to predictable quality brands over time.[17] It is unlikely that any of the Muslim colas poses a real and sustainable threat to the entrenched hegemony of Coke and Pepsi, however. As one consultant has put it, if the market for Muslim colas gets too big, Coke will simply buy them up, just as it did with upstart cola company Thums Up† in India.[18]

The issue may not be so much one of "Muslim" colas as one of identity. A number of regional colas have emerged over recent years, cashing in on patriotism and cultural identity. Examples of these include the following, with their websites:

Breizh Cola from Brittany, a region of France with a strong language and cultural identity: http://www.breizhcola.fr/

Inca Kola from Peru, a golden-colored and very sweet drink sold in a number of other countries; a history intertwined with *Coca-Cola:* http://www.incakola.com.pe

Cola Turka, Turkish cola company selling in Turkey and abroad; sponsor of Besiktas Basketball League Team and initiators of innovative advertising featuring American star Chevy Chase: http://www.colaturka.com.tr/

*Supermarket company sites *E. Leclerc*: **http://www.e-leclerc.com** and *Carrefour*: **http://www.carrefour.com/**

†Go to **http://www.coca-colaindia.com/thums-up/default.asp.**

Questions

1. Some analysts believe that companies like Qibla, Mecca, and Arab Cola are not capable of long-term market share, and that their initial success is due to publicity that will quickly fizzle out. Is this a likely scenario, given the competitive environment in which they operate?
2. Some Muslims object to the 'commercialization' of Islam, as represented by these cola companies' marketing strategies. Should these Muslim cola companies target a wider audience? If so, how? Give them some marketing ideas.
3. If you were the CEO of the leading company (Coca-Cola) how would you react to the emergence of Muslim colas? In non Muslim countries? In Muslim countries? Same question if you were the CEO of the longstanding challenger (Pepsi-Cola)?

Notes

1. BusinessWorld (2003) 'Anti-war, consumer groups launch boycott of 10 leading US products', *BusinessWorld (*Manila), March 27, 2003, p. 1.
2. O'Flynn, Kevin (2003) 'Americans and Dollars Not Welcome', *The Moscow Times* (online), March 26, 2003. Retrieved April 30, 2003 from **http://www.moscowtimes.ru.**
3. Anonymous (2003) 'Qibla Shows Its Bottle', *The Publican* (online), May 7, 2003. Retrieved May 7, 2003 from **http://www.thepublican.com/cgi-bin/item.cgi?id=9604&d=11&h=24&f=23&dateformat=%25o-%25B-%25Y.**
4. Cowen, Richard (2003) 'EU Official Sees Boycotts If US Files Biotech Suit' *Forbes* (online), May 6, 2003. Retrieved May 6, 2003 from **http://www.foodmarketexchange.com/wp/news_archive.php?p=394.**
5. Hundley, Tom (2003) 'New Colas Hope to Make Money off Muslim Rancor' *Chicago Tribune* (online), February 5, 2003. Retrieved April 30, 2003 from **http://pqasb.pqarchiver.com/chicagotribune/index.html?ts=1068678315.**
6. Jeffery, Simon (2003) 'Is It the Real Thing?' *The Guardian* (online), February 5, 2003. Retrieved April 30, 2003 from **http://shopping.guardian.co.uk/food/story/0,1587,889470,00.html.**
7. *Qibla* Cola (2003) '*Qibla* Cola Company Ltd. ... Liberate Your Taste' *Qibla* Cola website homepage (undated). Retrieved April 30, 2003 from **http://www.Qiblacola.co.uk.**

8. Hundley, Tom (2003) 'New Colas Hope to Make Money off Muslim Rancor' *Chicago Tribune* (online), February 5, 2003. Retrieved April 30, 2003 from **http://pqasb.pqarchiver.com/chicagotribune/index.html?ts=1068678315.**

9. Datson, Trevor (2003) 'Muslim Cola – Idealism or Marketing Froth?', *Reuters* (online), April 30, 2003. Retrieved April 30, 2003 from **http://www.reuters.co.uk.**

10. Datson, Trevor (2003) 'Muslim Cola – Idealism or Marketing Froth?', *Reuters* (online), April 30, 2003. Retrieved April 30, 2003 from **http://www.reuters.co.uk.**

11. Hundley, Tom (2003) 'New Colas Hope to Make Money off Muslim Rancor' *Chicago Tribune* (online), February 5, 2003. Retrieved April 30, 2003 from **http://pqasb.pqarchiver.com/chicagotribune/index.html?ts=1068678315.**

12. Fernandez-Fanjul, Eufrasio (2002) '*ZamZam* Cola crece con la ola Antiyanqui', *El Mundo* (online), September 8, 2002. Retrieved April 30, 2003 from **http://www.el-mundo.es/nuevaeconomia/2002/139/1031386792.html.**

13. Anonymous (2002) 'Iran Takes on Cola Giants', *Asia Times* online, October 17, 2002. Retrieved from **http://www.atimes.com/atimes/Middle_East/DJ17Ak06.html.**

14. Theodoulou, Michael, Charles Bremner, and Daniel McGrory (2002) 'Cola Wars as Islam Shuns the Real Thing', *The Times Online*, October 11, 2002. Retrieved April 30, 2003 from **http://www.timesonline.co.uk/article/0,,3821-443269,00.html.**

15. Ries, Al (2003) 'Coca Cola Gets It Right with 'Real', *Advertising Age* (online), January 20, 2003. Retrieved April 30, 2003 from **http://www.adage.com/paypoints/buyArticle.cms/login?newsId=36912&auth=.**

16. Majidi, Nassim, and Christina Passariello (2003) 'After Iraq, Cola Wars Heat up', *BusinessWeek Online*, April 17, 2003. Retrieved April 17, 2003 from **http://www.businessweek.com/bwdaily/dnflash/apr2003/nf20030417_5930_db039.htm.**

17. AME Info (2004). Coke and Pepsi battle it out, *AME Info*, April 8, 2004. Retrieved April 26, 2006 from **http://www.ameinfo.com/37492.html.**

18. Majidi, Nassim, and Christina Passariello (2003) 'After Iraq, Cola Wars Heat up', *BusinessWeek Online*, April 17, 2003. Retrieved April 17, 2003 from **http://www.businessweek.com/bwdaily/dnflash/apr2003/nf20030417_5930_db039.htm.**

Shrimp Farming in Ecuador

Xavier's Dilemma

Xavier was a shrimp farmer in Ecuador. He sold his shrimp to a packing plant which cleaned and froze the shrimp. The packing plant either exported the frozen shrimp directly, or else sold them to an exporter. Foreign processors, in turn, sold the final products to distributors and retailers.

Xavier attended an executive education course at the Instituto de Desarrollo Empresarial (IDE) in Guayaquil, where a Canadian professor led a discussion of the case "Fishery Products International" (FPI). One of the exporters participating in the course mentioned that he sold his shrimp to Victor Young at FPI in Newfoundland. Xavier realized that his shrimp were being cooked in Newfoundland and packaged in unique ways such as the FPI "shrimp roll." Some of his shrimp were even being cooked as part of frozen dinners that included a variety of vegetables. It was clear that the shrimp farmer received only a tiny portion of the revenue within the value chain. Xavier wondered whether he should try to expand into the value-added parts of the shrimp business.

IVEY

Richard Ivey School of Business
The University of Western Ontario

David Conklin prepared this case solely to provide material for class discussion. The author does not intend to illustrate either effective or ineffective handling of a managerial situation. The author may have disguised certain names and other identifying information to protect confidentiality.

The Family Business

One of Xavier's uncles, Jorge Kayser, had been the first shrimp farmer in Ecuador, and perhaps in the world. For centuries, fishermen had fished for shrimp in oceans and in the rivers that flowed into them. One day Xavier's uncle realized that he might be able to enclose a small portion of a river where shrimp naturally grew, and he might be able to increase the yield and facilitate the harvesting process by providing feed and by excluding other aquatic life that might eat the shrimp. The experiment was successful, and over the years the family shrimp business expanded.

A second uncle, Javier Hidalgo, used his profits from shrimp to expand into various businesses, including banana farms and the importation and sale of heavy equipment. A third uncle lived in Miami and operated businesses in the United States. Ecuador's projected rapid growth offered many business opportunities as alternatives to shrimp farming. The family expanded all its businesses only on the basis of retained earnings.

By March 1997, Xavier was farming 150 hectares of shrimp ponds. The ponds varied in size, from one hectare to 30 hectares. Each pond was about one-half metre deep. Xavier was an exceptionally talented businessperson, and he was happy to confront technological problems, which he was able to solve in a creative, entrepreneurial manner. In particular, Xavier had developed his own "hatchery"—a laboratory where he experimented with genetics and developed unique strains of shrimp. Most important, perhaps, was his ability to solve the problems plaguing the Asian shrimp farms—problems which resulted in the environmental destruction of the ponds and the death of the shrimp.

As a result of the rapid and substantial expansion of shrimp farming in Asia and Ecuador, the world price of shrimp fell by 50 per cent over the 1986–1996 decade. Still, revenue from shrimp farming ranged from US$1,500 to US$4,000 per hectare. Xavier worried that the global expansion of shrimp farming would depress shrimp prices in the future. On the other hand, health concerns were leading people throughout the world to shift towards the consumption of more fish. The depletion of fish in natural habitats throughout the world would likely lead to higher fish prices in the future. Japan was one country where fish consumption had reached very high levels, and the Japanese were eager to assist the Ecuador shrimp business.

The family was opposed to borrowing from the banking system in Ecuador. Real interest rates were extremely high. When inflation was running at 20 per cent, the nominal rate of interest they would have to pay was about 40 per cent. Faced with this situation, some Ecuadorian business people borrowed in other countries. Often the debt repayment was expressed in U.S. dollars. Some business people borrowed in Columbia and Uruguay, but there was always the fear that this might be drug money, and failure to repay one's debt might result in undesirable consequences. Perhaps the high real interest rate that the banks charged their customers was due to the lack of competition in the financial sector. Perhaps the entry of foreign banks into Ecuador might reduce this high real interest rate.

The Asian Shrimp Disaster

The Canadian professor in the IDE program told the class about an article in The Globe & Mail, July 13, 1996, that described the disastrous situation in Asian shrimp farms:

> A subsistence farmer who relied on one-fifth of a hectare of land, Mr. Aziz followed the advice of his government and some of the world's biggest foreign-aid donors when they suggested he convert his meagre rice field to a prawn farm. [Editor's note: In Asia, shrimp were referred to as "prawns."] He was told the small crustacean known as "pink gold" would end his days in poverty.
>
> Five years later, the Blue Revolution—the massive investment in aquaculture that was designed to help Asia's rice farmers develop new sources of income—is finished in Shyamnagar, and Mr. Aziz has lost almost everything. His animals, his vegetable garden, his bamboo trees and banana grove are all gone, ravaged like the barren landscape that now surrounds Shyamnagar.
>
> 'Before the prawn farms, this was beautiful paddy field,' Mr. Aziz said. 'People destroyed it for money.'
>
> Mr. Aziz's story increasingly is the story of coastal Asia, from southern India to the Mekong Delta, where massive investments in prawn farming and other forms of aquaculture have meant instant riches for some but ecological destruction and social uprooting for others.
>
> Promoted by governments, the World Bank and many large aid agencies, the Blue Revolution created huge export earnings for Asia, which accounts for 80 per cent of the world's $9-billion prawn trade. But in little more than a decade, prawn farms have destroyed an estimated 800,000 hectares of mangrove forests and created improbable saline deserts in some of the world's wettest countries.
>
> 'This could be only the tip of the iceberg of what is to come,' said Atiur Rahman, a senior research fellow at the Bangladesh Institute for Development Studies. 'Because of our greed for profit and foreign exchange, we are destroying the environment.'
>
> ... the emergence of a disease known as white-spot virus has jeopardized the industry's growth.
>
> ... for thousands of communities left in the industry's wake, the long-term cost of prawn farming already has been devastating.[1]

Environmentalists throughout the world, and particularly in the United States, were concerned about the impact of shrimp farming on the environment. They were also concerned about its impact on other species, such as turtles, and its impact on vegetation such as mangroves, the tree whose roots form a dense tangle that harbors marine life such as wild shrimp.

Xavier's Entrepreneurship

Xavier realized that shrimp ponds—whether in Asia or in Ecuador—had a lifetime limited to five to 10 years. Xavier built his ponds in order to make his farming environmentally sustainable. Each pond had a sophisticated system of intakes and outflows, so that fresh water would circulate through the pond without allowing any shrimp to escape. The process maintained the water level at a constant depth. After three to five years of farming, Xavier would completely drain the pond and remove any plants and algae that had accumulated. Only when the bottom of the pond was completely cleaned would he fill it again with water and baby shrimp.

A key to Xavier's success was the feed he provided to the baby shrimp after the eggs hatched. Xavier found that the baby shrimp thrived on feed obtained from Salt Lake City, Utah, where the very heavy concentration of salt in the water enabled the production of a uniquely high quality feed. After the baby shrimp were transferred to the shrimp farms, the traditional way of feeding, by casting food at random from a boat, resulted in the rapid growth of plants and algae which formed a natural habitat for disease. Xavier realized that he could create special equipment that would contain the feed, and the shrimp would learn to go to the feeders. About 10 feeders per hectare seemed to be the ideal. This greatly reduced the growth of plants and algae. It also enabled the farmer to measure precisely the amount of feed required. Each day, the equipment was raised to the surface of the water, and the amount of feed consumed was measured. This reduced the cost of feed as well as reducing the risk of disease.

Xavier was a leader in the creation of a public research institute for shrimp farmers. It was funded partially by the farmers, and also by the governments of Ecuador and Japan. From time to time, diseases suddenly attacked the shrimp. The institute had been able to analyze diseases as they appeared, and it had been able to prescribe antibiotics to be added to the ponds. However, in many countries there was a new social concern about the use of antibiotics in the food chain. Perhaps this concern

1. John Stackhouse, "Prawn Farming Holds Raise Promises of Instant Riches," *The Globe and Mail*, July 13, 1996.

might limit the market for shrimp. Furthermore, the drugs had to be imported from other countries where they were produced.

Xavier realized that the analysis of genetics could enable him to create better strains of shrimp that would be of uniformly large size, consistently high quality, and resistant to disease. Xavier was very proud of his hatchery where his specially selected female shrimp each gave birth to about one million eggs. However, he worried that competitors throughout the world would copy his entrepreneurial advances, and he wondered whether shrimp farming would inevitably become a commodity activity where profits would be competed away.

Xavier realized that there would always be new problems arising in shrimp farming. Just a year or two prior to this time, some shrimp farmers had become concerned that pesticides from the banana plantations were entering the rivers and poisoning the shrimp. This had led to a major public debate over bananas versus shrimp. In the end, the research institute had concluded that the shrimp had been attacked by a particular disease, for which they were able to provide appropriate antibiotics. However, one could be sure that more problems would arise in the future.

Investment Alternatives

Xavier believed that he would need ponds that covered 1,000 to 2,000 hectares in order to justify a packing plant where the shrimp would be cleaned, classified according to size, and frozen. In such a plant, the work was basically labor-intensive, with unsophisticated equipment for cleaning and freezing. Xavier felt that with retained earnings he could achieve this goal within three years. Nevertheless, Xavier realized that the volatile political situation could lead to the periodic shutdown of power supplies, and this might be a real threat.

Exporters purchased the shrimp from the packing plants and sold them to processors in other countries. These exporters faced significant foreign exchange risk. Xavier did not understand the concept of hedging, and he realized that this was a very different kind of business.

Xavier contemplated expanding his business to include a plant that would cook the shrimp. This would enable Xavier to sell packaged shrimp directly to distributors in other countries. Perhaps he could have his own unique brands. Perhaps he could even process the shrimp into frozen dinners, following the example of Victor Young at FPI.

These expansion possibilities would require substantial investments. Even the construction of a plant for cleaning, classifying, and freezing would probably cost a million dollars. A sophisticated plant to create frozen dinners, together with the staff to develop the distribution channels, would involve a commitment of tens of millions of dollars.

The Canadian professor had mentioned the view of his colleagues that a joint venture could solve many international business problems. If Xavier wished to become more than a shrimp farmer, perhaps he should consider a joint venture with a foreign company that could provide expertise in regard to further processing and marketing, as well as the required investment funds.

Any foreign investor would be worried about the environment of business in Ecuador. Would the problems of Ecuador prevent a joint venture with a foreign partner?

Part 3

Foreign Market Entry Analysis and Planning

Following the discussion of the macro-environment for global marketing in Part 2, the third part of the text focuses on issues related to strategic market planning and the formulation of foreign market entry strategies. Readers are introduced to the process of strategic market planning in a global environment, including the critical issues of country market selection and the segmentation of global markets. Part 3 also covers the process of internationalization and provides a discussion of the major entry mode options available to the global marketer. This part concludes with an examination of the process of conducting global marketing research—an essential prerequisite to the formulation and execution of global marketing strategy, activities discussed in Parts 4 and 5.

Chapter 6

Strategic Planning

The Global MARKETPLACE 6.1

Appliance Makers on a Global Quest

The $70-billion home-appliance market (expected to grow to $120 billion by 2010) is undergoing major consolidation and globalization. Many U.S.-based manufacturers are faced in their home markets with increased competition from foreign companies, such as the world's largest appliance maker, Electrolux, and newcomers such as China's Haier and Kelon. In addition, industry fundamentals in the United States are rather gloomy: stagnating sales, rising raw material prices, and price wars. On the other hand, markets abroad are full of opportunities. The European market, for example, is growing quite fast, and the expansion of the European Union has made establishing business there even more attractive. Market potential is significant as well: while 65 percent of U.S. homes have dryers, only 18 percent of Europeans have them. Markets in Latin America and Asia are showing similar trends as well; for example, only 15 percent of Brazil's households own microwave ovens compared with 91 percent in the United States. However, expansion was slowed down considerably by the financial crises of 1997–2002.

To take advantage of this growth, appliance makers have formed strategic alliances and made acquisitions. General Electric entered into a joint venture with Britain's General Electric PLC, and in its strategic shift to move the company's "centre of gravity" from the industrialized world to Asia and Latin America, joint ventures were established in India with Godrej and in Mexico with Mabe. A strictly North American manufacturer before 1989, Whirlpool purchased the appliance business of Dutch giant N.V. Phillips. Whirlpool's move gave it 10 plants on the European continent and some popular appliance lines, which is a major asset in a region characterized by loyalty to domestic brands. Today, Whirlpool is third in European market share after Electrolux and Bosch-Siemens. The company ranks first in the Americas, and while it only has a 1 percent market share in Asia, it is the region's largest Western appliance maker. Whirlpool's advantage in Brazil, for example, is the strong loyalty it has earned in 40 years of operations (which it lacks in some Asian markets). In the last 5 years, Whirlpool has expanded its operations in Eastern and Central Europe as well as South Africa, thus extending its total reach to 170 countries worldwide.

Product differences present global marketers with a considerable challenge. The British favour front-loading washing machines, while the French swear by top-loaders. The French prefer to cook their food at high temperatures, causing grease to splatter onto oven walls, which calls for self-cleaning ovens. This feature is in less demand in Germany, where lower temperatures are traditionally used. Manufacturers are hoping that European integration will bring about cost savings and product standardization. The danger to be avoided is the development of compromise products that in the end appeal to no one. Joint ventures present their share of challenges to the global marketers. For example, in Whirlpool's Shanghai facility, teams of American, Italian, and Chinese technicians must work through three interpreters to set up production.

Although opportunities do exist, competition is keen. Margins have suffered as manufacturers (more than 300 in Europe alone) fight for business. The major players have decided to compete in all the major markets of the world. "Becoming a global appliance player is clearly the best use of our management expertise and well-established brand lineup," Whirlpool executives have said. Whirlpool's long-term goal is to leverage its global manufacturing and brand assets strategically across the world.

The most recent entrants into the global home-appliance markets are China's Haier and Kelon, both mainly in refrigerators and air conditioners, industries in which China's technology is up to world standards. Haier's market share globally is still small (2.8 percent) compared to Whirlpool's (11.3 percent) and Electrolux's (8.2 percent), but the company is on an ambitious growth trajectory. While no foreign brand has made it big in the U.S. major-appliance market (mainly due to lack of brand recognition and distribution presence), Haier is currently selling 250 models of appliances through big retailers such as Wal-Mart and Costco and over 1,000 independent dealers. The company claims to have 50 percent of the U.S. market for small refrigerators (for offices and dorm rooms). The approach is to build brands with lower prices and dependable quality and move upscale with time. Haier is already the second largest maker of refrigerators in the world and ranks sixth in overall appliance sales.

Further consolidation in the industry occurred in late 2005, when Maytag was acquired by Whirlpool after a bidding war that included Haier from China. Apart from blocking a major global competitor, Whirlpool's $13 billion in annual sales will expand by Maytag's $4.7 billion.

Sources: "Maytag Corp.; Shareholders Approve Sale of Company to Whirlpool," *The Wall Street Journal,* December 25, 2005, p. Al; "China's Power Brands," *Business Week,* November 8, 2004, 77–84; "Haier's Purpose," *The Economist,* March 20, 2004, p. 72; Joshua Kurlantzick, "Making It in China," *U.S. News & World Report,* 7 October 2002, pp. 44–49; Jonathan Sprague, "Haier Reaches Higher," *Fortune,* 16 September 2002, pp. 43–46; "Chinese Multinationals Aim to Be Just That," *The Wall Street Journal,* 28 January 2002, p. A1; Russell Flannery, "China Goes Global," *Forbes,* 6 August 2001, pp. 35–38; "China's Brands," Business Week, 8 November 2004, pp. 77-84; **http://www.Whirlpool.com**; **http://www.GE.com**; and **http://www.HaierAmerica.com**.

© Sean Gallup/Getty Images

Global Marketing

Many marketing managers have to face the increasing globalization of markets and competition described in The Global Marketplace 6.1. The rules of survival have changed since the beginning of the 1980s when Theodore Levitt first coined the phrase *global marketing.*[1] Even the biggest companies in the biggest home markets cannot survive on domestic sales alone if they are in global industries such as cars, banking, consumer electronics, entertainment, pharmaceuticals, publishing, travel services, or home appliances.

They have to be in all major markets to survive the shakeouts expected to leave three to five players per industry at the beginning of the 21st century.[2]

Globalization reflects a business orientation based on the belief that the world is becoming more homogeneous and that distinctions between national markets are not only fading but, for some products, will eventually disappear. As a result, companies need to globalize their international strategy by formulating it across markets to take advantage of underlying market, cost, environmental, and competitive factors. This has meant, for example, that Chinese companies (in categories ranging from auto parts and appliances to telecommunications) have entered the main markets of the world such as Europe and North America to become global powerhouses.[3] Having a global presence ensures viability against other players in the home market as well.

As shown in Exhibit 6.1, global marketing can be seen as the culmination of a process of international market entry and expansion. Before globalization, marketers utilize a country-by-country multi-domestic strategy to a great extent, with each country organization operated as a profit centre. Each national entity markets a range of different products and services targeted to different customer segments, utilizing different marketing strategies with little or no coordination of operations between countries.

However, as national markets become increasingly similar and scale economies become increasingly important, the inefficiencies of duplicating product development and manufacture in each country become more apparent and the pressure to leverage resources and coordinate activities across borders gains urgency. Similarly, the increasing number of customers operating globally, as well as the same or similar competitors faced throughout the major markets, adds to the need for strategy integration.

It should be noted that global leverage means balancing three interests: global, regional, and local. In many cases, the exploitation of commonalities is best executed on a regional basis, given that some differences remain between groups of markets.[4] The same strategic principles apply to developing and implementing global and regional strategy. Naturally, the more a marketer can include the local dimension to efforts in each individual market, the more effective the strategy tends to be.[5] For example, consumers may prefer a global

Exhibit 6.1 Global Marketing Evolution

Phase I	Phase 2	Phase 3
Leverage of domestic capabilities: foreign market entry	Expansion of foreign market presence	Coordination of global operations
Objective: economies of scale	Objective: economies of scope	Objective: exploit synergies throughout network
	Corporate Actions	
Driven opportunistically, often by approach of distributor or customer Constrained by lack of funding (domestic growth still priority investment), so low-cost entry Risk minimized by entering close markets (geographically, culturally, economically) Entry based on core products with technical superiority	Slower domestic growth creates greater pressure for foreign sales growth New lines carried; sales mix broadens and reflects national market Search for new customer segments, requiring new management skills Countries develop own marketing programs New applications sought Decentralization of R & D, production Regional management reflects foreign experience	Product broadened, new emphasis on full-line service rather than proprietary technology Global account management Coordination mechanisms (global task forces) Learning transferred between countries Headquarters introduces global branding, packaging Requires common culture

Source: Adapted from Susan P. Douglas and C. Samuel Craig, "Evolution of Global Marketing Strategy: Scale, Scope, and Synergy," *Columbia Journal of World Business* 24 (Fall 1989): 47-58; and George S. Yip, *Total Global Strategy II* (Upper Saddle River, NJ: Pearson, 2002), chap. 2.

brand that has been adapted to the needs of local usage conditions. While the approach is localized, the global resources of a marketer provide the brand with a winning edge (e.g., in terms of quality or quality perceptions).

In this chapter, we commence by asking the fundamental question, why do firms internationalize? We then review key issues faced by firms in setting their internationalization strategies: When should we internationalize? What markets should we choose? How should we enter our chosen markets and with what competitive strategies? We elaborate on the issue of market segmentation, and point to the enduring importance of clear business definition. The chapter at this point moves from the strategic aspect to the question of program development, in which we consider, among other things, the product offering, the marketing approach, and the question of location of value-added activities. The chapter concludes with a review of some problems of implementing global marketing and considers the problems and opportunities of local companies in a globalization context.

Why Do Firms Internationalize?

A question fundamental to all global strategic planning is why do firms internationalize in the first place? A casual glance suggests that any number of motivating factors could be at work in individual cases. These objectives will determine the kind of strategic planning undertaken. For example, some firms will aim to increase market size, while others will want to spread risks, achieve large economies of scale, or reduce factor costs.

These issues, including the role of FDI (foreign direct investment) theory, will be dealt with in more detail in Chapter 8. At this point, however, it can be noted that no single agreed model exists to explain the internationalization process of firms.[6] Most recent research suggests that it may be best to consider this process in a "holistic" sense, that is, one that appreciates aspects of competing explanations.

This conclusion is supported on the basis of a comparison of Canadian and U.K. high-tech small and medium-sized enterprises (SMEs). One survey highlights three significant factors that influence the decision to pursue (and maintain) an international strategy.[7] The first is the existence and utilization of existing contacts. This supports the "networking view," that is, that firms are stimulated to pursue overseas ventures because they already enjoy favourable connections or liaisons. The second factor is the utilization of resources, defined in a general sense to include financial and managerial resources (experience), which enables firms to become prepared for international development—for example, by targeting growth markets. The third factor is reaction to environmental events, including "serendipitous" (i.e., unforeseen but fortunate) ones. This survey also concluded that the relative importance of these factors depended on circumstances, both internal and external, facing entrepreneurs and management teams at particular points in time.

Therefore, the internationalization processes adopted by individual firms varied in light of these specific circumstances, and in some cases could include part-rational and part-intuitive elements. However, in pragmatic terms, the implications of this study are a warning not to view internationalization as flowing from any one of these three influencing factors in isolation. In other words, a combination of issues affected both the initial and subsequent decisions of both the Canadian and British firms. It can be noted here that the subsequent internationalization decisions facing companies do not neatly become more manageable as knowledge and experience are gained in the foreign market. As one source notes, expansion into transition economies such as China, Eastern Europe, and the former Soviet republics, which are characterized by great environmental turbulence, demands considerable organizational learning to overcome the liability of "foreignness."[8] *Within* each of these countries, fragmented markets, unfamiliar organizational forms, and inconsistent regulations have often forced even multinational enterprises (MNEs) to learn how to operate in local markets.[9]

Another important point is that, in the case of high-tech SMEs, which are typical of Canadian experience, these frequently operate in fast-moving environments characterized by conditions of market turbulence. In consequence, emergent strategies may be utilized by taking advantage of "windows of opportunity" that may not stay open for long periods of time. In such an environment, opportunistic strategies may bring more value than systematic ones.[10] It is also worth noting here that because of their narrow product scope, the fast obsolescence of their products, and a limited domestic demand, some firms need to have an international or even a global focus from inception. Such businesses—sometimes referred to as "born globals" or "international new ventures"—can be thought of as organizations that, from the outset, seek to derive significant competitive advantages from the use of resources and sale of outputs in multiple countries.

Aspects of internationalization strategy in fact are not always planned in a way that much of strategy literature suggests.[11] Instead, chance encounters and random events can have a role to play in explaining some firms' strategies. But it has long been noted[12] that in addition to a *random* process, there is also a *sequential* process at work. In this case, firms go through different stages in sequential order—evaluation of markets, weighting of alternatives, selection of market, and so on—whereas in the random process, firms bypass or leap over certain stages. This in turn gives a mistaken impression that there is a right way and a wrong way to pursue internationalization. In reality, the mode of foreign market entry and evaluation of global strategy must always be contingent upon the specific situation of the target market, including projections of market potential and the resources the company is willing and able to devote to that market, given a certain level of risk and assumed payback period. This gives considerable scope for the exercise of managerial judgment, which in turn may suggest that some stages can and should be skipped.

In other words, the normative rational/economic models of strategic planning, including step-by-step procedures, will have to recognize an intuitive or idiosyncratic component in the case of internationalization decisions. In some circumstances and for some firms, this component may be decisive. This does not mean, of course, that companies are generally lurching into totally unplanned overseas ventures. Many if not most companies will attempt some kind of formal planning, a process that has been summarized as a sequence of steps in Exhibit 6.2, although as noted, many of the stages can occur simultaneously, and feedback as a result of evaluation and control may restart the process at any stage.

Exhibit 6.2 **Global Strategy Formulation**

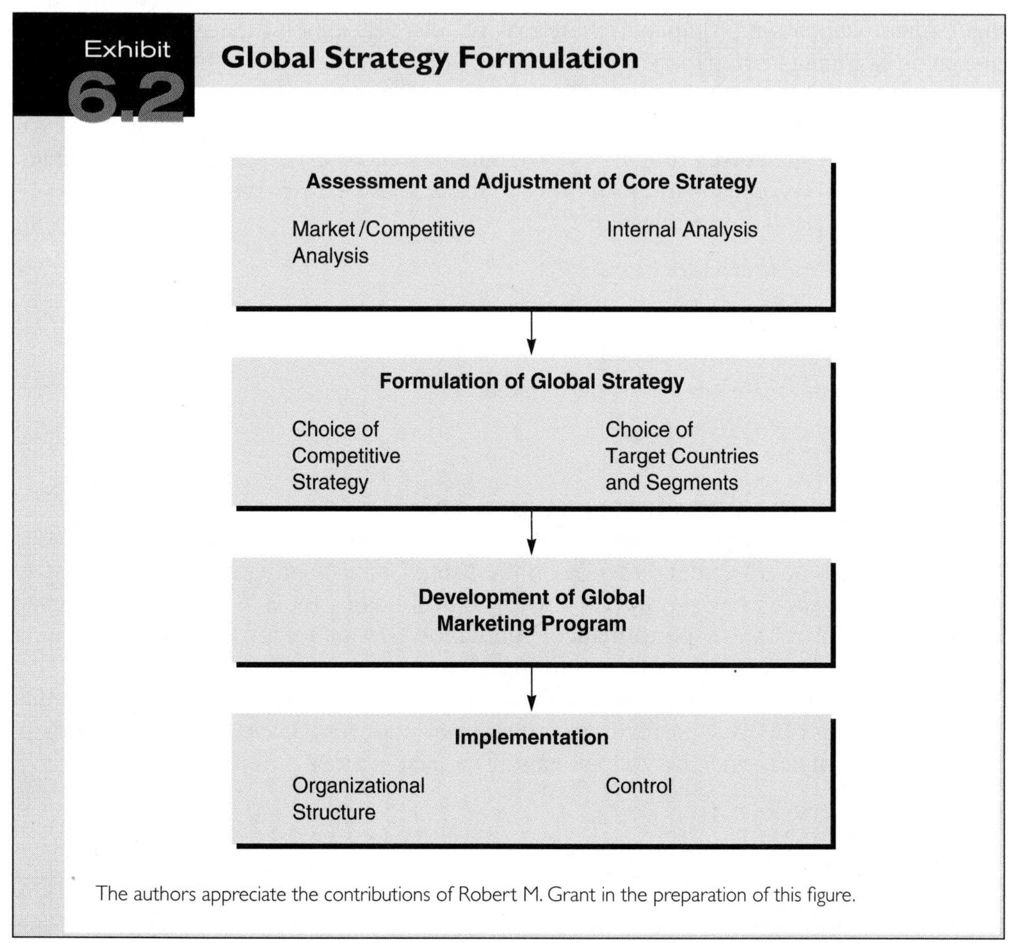

The authors appreciate the contributions of Robert M. Grant in the preparation of this figure.

In some cases, the management teams' previous international experience will influence the expansion of firms through established international networks. Building on experience is a clear counterweight to over-dependence on a less systematic approach.[13] Indeed, for globally committed marketers, the contribution of formal strategic planning to both financial performance and non-financial objectives cannot be understated.[14] These benefits include raising the efficacy of new product launches, cost reduction efforts, and improving product quality and market-share performance. Internally, these efforts increase cohesion and improve understanding among different units. But while not denying the importance of "formal" strategic planning, serendipitous events must also be recognized as a powerful force in explaining the nature and direction of the firm's internationalization strategy.

Issues in Internationalization Strategy

Against the background of the above section, we can now look at some specific challenges facing Canadian firms when formulating their internationalization strategies or when contemplating such a course.

In general, internationalization can be looked on as part of the ongoing strategy process of most business firms.[15] The main differences between internationalization and other types of processes are twofold: the necessity for the firm to choose the country with whom transactions will take place, and the need to select a foreign market entry strategy.[16] Internationalization strategy, in common with other forms of strategy, must be guided by the fundamental need to identify and maintain profitable competitive advantages, including early recognition of any sources of competitive disadvantage.

The firm faces a miscellany of strategic decisions: for example, when and where to internationalize, how to overcome entry barriers, and whether emerging markets should be targeted. Issues such as whether to globalize or regionalize the business and determining the location and linkages of activities across countries are also pertinent and are dealt with later in this chapter. Trade barriers are also a key issue and are dealt with in Chapter 2. Barriers facing international service marketers are discussed in Chapter 10. Here we will note that for internationalizing companies these may be relatively minor, such as increased documentation or routine testing to demonstrate compliance with standards. The impact can also be dramatic, such as when import tariffs make importation prohibitive. Non-tariff barriers (e.g., labelling requirements or poor access to distribution) remain a challenge in particular markets and may be difficult to quantify. The internationalizing company needs the fullest information on all potential barriers in order to make sensible market selection decisions.

Here we will ask five key questions:

1. When should the firm internationalize?
2. What markets should be chosen to enter?
3. Should developing country markets be targeted?
4. What competitive strategy should be adopted?
5. How should the firm enter the market?

When Should the Firm Internationalize?

Canadian companies are frequently urged to explore international markets more. Often they are advised to reduce dependence on the United States market and find newer avenues elsewhere, such as in the BRIC countries (Brazil, Russia, India, China). References to Canada's "lacklustre" trade performance[17] underline the importance to firms of understanding their state of readiness for venturing abroad.

One way to approach the internationalization timing issue is in managerial terms; that is, a company can be thought ready to embark on internationalization when a series of interlocking, company-wide conditions exist. The factors are as follows:[18]

- management commitment
- in-depth experience with the product or service
- adequate cash flow
- capacity and capability to produce international products

Management Commitment

Organizational resources have to be used as a reality check for any strategic choice, because they determine a company's capacity to establish a sustainable competitive advantage in global markets. Resource commitment depends in turn on strong managerial commitment. Thinly capitalized companies will have to proceed prudently. One resource problem is in the area of human resources: good marketing managers, technicians, and production managers may be difficult to find. This difficulty will be compounded if the search is for managers with substantial cross-cultural experience to run future regional or global operations. Such problems will not be overcome with a lukewarm commitment to internationalization by senior management.

In-Depth Experience with the Product or Service

A company is ill-advised to embark on international expansion without clearly understanding how the product or service yields a comparative advantage in the marketplace. This knowledge can be acquired through practical experience of the domestic market, which will in turn help in identifying which foreign markets will be suitable for the product. In many cases, assessing a product's readiness to face the competitive environment may mean making painful decisions to focus on some products and abandon others. For example, Nokia, the world's largest manufacturer of mobile phones, started its rise in the industry when a decision was made at the company in 1992 to focus on digital cellular phones and sell off dozens of other product lines (such as personal computers, automotive tires, and toilet tissue). By focusing its efforts on this line, the company was able to bring new products to market quickly, build scale economies into its manufacturing, and concentrate on its customers, thereby communicating a commitment to their needs. Nokia's current 33 percent market share allows it the best global visibility of and by the market.[19]

Adequate Cash Flow

The internationalization strategy chosen by the firm must fit its financial resources. How much funding is needed depends on the nature of the strategy and opportunities it identifies. For example, direct entry to a market will demand more cash than indirect entry. Failure to integrate the financial component into overall strategy will lead to poor performance, lost sales, and the likelihood of failure.

Capacity and Capability to Produce International Products

It is perhaps self-evident that firms should not commit themselves to foreign activities if they are unprepared to fulfill orders. This in turn leads to channel frustration and loss of customers. This stricture will apply even if the firm is producing under licence abroad or is in partnership. Such concerns also influence services. Necessary staff and support services need to be in place to accommodate customer demand, and expertise must be available to adapt the service offering to international differences in how the service is used, for example, in the case of international accounting standards.

But bearing in mind our earlier comments about serendipitous events, "readiness" may translate into a foray into a "low psychic distance" market, or no action at all. Managerial inclination and discretion, as well as unforeseen external events, will frequently play a decisive role, especially where the complexities facing internationalizing SMEs are concerned. Stage models do not capture these complexities, especially in the high-tech sector. Again, critical incidents—for example, a change in management or ownership of the firm, a fresh infusion of capital, or a change in the scope of a domestic customer—may strongly influence the internationalization strategy. The timing of market entry is not therefore something that will necessarily be resolved easily.

What Markets Should Be Chosen to Enter?

In formulating strategy, the firm needs to be as clear as possible on the attractiveness of particular foreign markets, including assessment of how the markets might change in the future, taking into account such factors as technological changes, substitute products, and government policy. However, as we saw earlier, many firms do not necessarily go about things systematically, and they may not pursue the detailed market, industry, and environmental research implied by a systematic approach to market selection. Many firms prefer instead to start their internationalization by moving into those markets with the lowest "psychic distance,"[20] that is, those they can most easily understand. Only later will some firms enter more distant markets, thus following an incremental pattern in their choice of foreign markets. In this it is easy to recognize the behaviour of many Canadian firms attracted by the huge U.S. market as the obvious initial target for their internationalization strategy.

Aspects of Market Analysis

For global marketers, planning on a country-by-country basis can result in spotty worldwide market performance. The starting point for global strategic planning is to understand that the underlying forces that determine business success are common to the different countries in which the firm competes. Planning processes that focus simultaneously across a broad range of markets provide global marketers with tools to help balance risks, resource requirements, competitive economies of scale, and profitability to gain stronger long-term positions.[21] On the demand side this requires an understanding of the common features of customer requirements and choice factors. In terms of competition, the key is to understand the structure of the global industry in order to identify the forces that will drive competition and determine profitability.[22]

Smaller companies seeking to establish an international marketing strategy might start more simply, by trying to be clear on market definition. This is illustrated by a Canadian consumer goods company seeking to expand sales in the United States—Magick Woods, a Toronto-based manufacturer of bath and kitchen cabinets. Although the company's products were to be found on the shelves of many specialty boutique stores and some home centres in Canada, future Canadian growth was thought to be limited, and the firm increasingly looked toward the U.S. for new markets. A need was felt to adopt a more methodical and statistical approach to defining markets than in the past; therefore, a specialist with expertise in demographics and business management was hired. A key finding of the new research was a demographic one: people with incomes between $80,000 and $150,000 who live in homes of 2,000 to 2,800 square feet and who renovate their bathrooms themselves were found to be the firm's core market.

Basic though this finding might appear, Magick Woods was able to use it to persuade a major U.S. home-centre retailer that the company's products were compatible with the centre's target market, thus achieving a significant breakthrough into the American market. In 2001, 75 percent of the firm's sales were in Canada and 25 percent in the United States. In 2002, the proportion of U.S. sales increased to 45 percent, and future U.S. sales of 60–65 percent are projected. This company can potentially conduct further, more in-depth studies of the American market and perhaps other foreign markets in future. But the case suggests that smaller companies should not shirk from asking the most basic questions about their markets, because it is from these underpinnings that global strategic planning will develop.

In More Detail 6.1

THE CASE OF AUTOMOBILES

For any automobile company, for example, strategy begins not with individual national markets, but with understanding trends and sources of profit in the global automobile market. What are the trends in world demand? What are the underlying trends in lifestyles and transportation patterns that will shape customer expectations and preferences with respect to safety, economy, design, and performance? What is the emerging structure of the industry, especially with regard to consolidation among both automakers and their suppliers? What will determine the intensity of competition between the different automakers? The level of excess capacity (currently about 40 percent in the worldwide auto industry) is likely to be a key influence.[23] If competition is likely to intensify, which companies will emerge as winners? An understanding of scale economies, the state of technology, and the other factors that determine cost efficiency is likely to be critically important.

Country-Market Choice

A global strategy does not imply that a company should serve the entire globe. Critical choices relate to the allocation of a company's resources between different countries and segments. A general approach to foreign market selection, if we consider a systematic step-by-step approach, views the evaluation process as composed of stages such as preliminary screening, identification/in-depth screening, and final selection. Preliminary assessment or screening identifies potential markets as candidates for subsequent in-depth analysis. Macro-level indicators are used to eliminate countries that do not meet the firm's objectives. Market size, growth rate, fit between customer preferences and the product, and competitive rivalry make up proposed screening criteria. The identification stage involves assessment of industry attractiveness (see below) and forecasts of costs and revenues for the short-listed countries. The final stage determines the country market that best matches the company's objectives and available resource leverages. Grouping approaches cluster countries on the similarities of social, economic, and political indicators.

The usual approach is first to start with regions and further split the analysis by country. Many marketers use multiple levels of regional groupings to follow the organizational structure of the company, such as splitting Europe into northern, central, and southern regions that display similarities in demographic and behavioural traits. An important consideration is that data may be more readily available if existing structures and frameworks are used.[24]

Portfolio Analysis

Various portfolio models have been proposed as tools for this analysis. They typically involve two measures—internal strength and external attractiveness.[25] As indicators of internal strength, the following variables have been used: relative market share, product fit, contribution margin, and market presence, which would incorporate the level of support by constituents as well as resources allocated by the company itself. Country attractiveness has been measured using market size, market growth rate, number and type of competitors, and governmental regulation, as well as economic and political stability.

An example of such a matrix is provided in Exhibit 6.3. The 3-3-3 matrix on country attractiveness and company strength is applied to the European markets. Markets in the invest/grow position will require continued commitment by management to research and development, investment in facilities, and the training of personnel at the country level. In cases of relative weakness in growing markets, the company's position may have to be strengthened (through acquisitions or strategic alliances) or a decision to divest may be necessary. For example, General Mills signed a complementary marketing arrangement with Nestlé to enter the European market dominated by its main global rival, Kellogg. This arrangement allowed General Mills effective market entry and Nestlé more efficient utilization of its distribution channels in Europe, as well as entry to a new product market. The alliance has since resulted in the formation of Cereal Partners Worldwide, which has a combined worldwide market share of 21 percent and sells its products in 130 countries.[26]

In choosing country markets, a company must make decisions beyond those relating to market attractiveness and company position. A market expansion policy will determine the allocation of resources among various markets. The basic alternatives are **concentration** on a small number of markets and **diversification**, which is characterized by growth in a relatively large number of markets. Expansion strategy is determined by market-, mix-, and company-related factors, listed in Exhibit 6.4. Market-related factors determine the attractiveness of the market in the first place. With high and stable growth rates only in certain markets, the firm will likely opt for a concentration strategy, which is often the case for innovative products early in their life cycle. If demand is strong worldwide, as the case may be for consumer goods, diversification may be attractive. If markets respond to marketing efforts at increasing rates, concentration will occur; however, when the cost of market-share points in any one market becomes too high, marketers tend to begin looking for diversification opportunities.

The uniqueness of the product offering with respect to competition is also a factor in expansion strategy. If lead-time over competition is considerable, the decision to diversify may not seem urgent. Very few products, however, afford such a luxury. In many product

Exhibit 6.3

Example of a Market-Portfolio Matrix

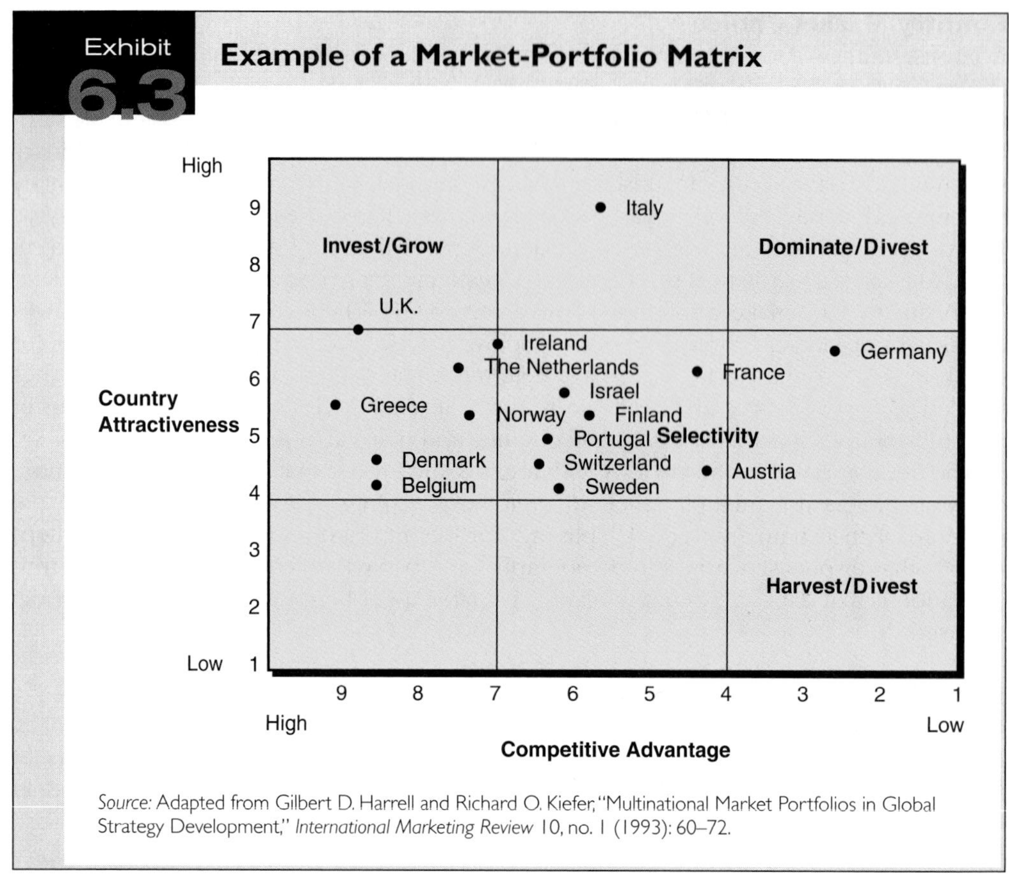

Source: Adapted from Gilbert D. Harrell and Richard O. Kiefer, "Multinational Market Portfolios in Global Strategy Development," *International Marketing Review* 10, no. 1 (1993): 60–72.

Exhibit 6.4

Factors Affecting the Choice between Concentration and Diversification Strategies

Factor	Diversification	Concentration
MARKET		
Market growth rate	Low	High
Sales stability	Low	High
Sales response function	Decreasing	Increasing
Extent of constraints	Low	High
MARKETING		
Competitive lead time	Short	Long
Spillover effects	High	Low
Need for product adaptation	Low	High
Need for communication adaptation	Low	High
Economies of scale in distribution	Low	High
Program control requirements	Low	High

Source: Adapted from Igal Ayal and Jehiel Zif, "Marketing Expansion Strategies in Multinational Marketing," *Journal of Marketing* 43 (Spring 1979): 89. Adapted with permission from the American Marketing Association.

categories, marketers will be affected by spillover effects. Consider, for example, the impact of satellite channels on advertising in Europe or in Asia, where ads for a product now reach most of the market. The greater the degree to which marketing-mix elements can be standardized, the more diversification is probable. Overall savings through economies of scale can then be utilized in marketing efforts. Finally, the objectives and policies of the company itself will guide the decision making on expansion. If extensive interaction with intermediaries and clients is called for, efforts are most likely to be concentrated because of resource constraints.

The conventional wisdom of globalization requires a presence in all of the major markets of the world (but note the cautionary points below). In some cases, markets may not be attractive in their own right but may have some other significance, such as being the home market of the most demanding customers, thereby aiding in product development, or being the home market of a significant competitor (a preemptive rationale). For example, Procter & Gamble rolled its Charmin toilet paper into European markets in 2000 to counter an upsurge in European paper products sales by its global rival, Kimberly-Clark.[27] European PC makers, such as Germany's Maxdata, are taking aim at the U.S. market based on the premise that if they can compete with the big multinationals (Dell, Hewlett-Packard, and Gateway) at home, there is no reason why they cannot be competitive in North America as well.[28]

In this context, it is well to remember that the vast majority of the world's largest firms have most of their sales in their home region of the triad.[29] (As we saw in Chapter 1, by "triad" is meant the European Union [EU], the North American Free Trade [NAFTA] area, and the Asia-Pacific region). To speak of companies penetrating all major world markets is unrealistic, even simplistic. While each region has three truly global firms, Europe has 86 home-region-oriented firms, North America has 167, and Asia has 66. Canada has 14. Realistically, therefore, the majority of firms are likely to be pursuing concentration strategies, relatively few firms diversification strategies.

Bearing these strictures in mind, for global marketers three factors should determine country selection: (1) the stand-alone attractiveness of a market (e.g., China in consumer products due to its size), (2) global strategic importance (e.g., Finland in shipbuilding due to its lead in technological development in vessel design), and (3) possible synergies (e.g., entry into Latvia and Lithuania after success in the Estonian market, given the market similarities).

Should Developing Country Markets Be Targeted?

Canadian companies are urged to consider emerging markets for possible opportunities on the commonsense ground that business should be done where their most growth can be derived.[30] The rapid growth of the BRIC countries and their overpopulated urban centres have created an increasing demand for raw and specialized products. Important potential market segments include infrastructure (roads, rails, ports), transportation, telecommunications, health-related products, agribusiness, and environmental technology. Clear opportunities exist for Canadian companies, and as we have seen from case studies, Canadian firms are already taking advantage of these opportunities.

But it ought to be recognized that, contrary to conventional wisdom, the intensity of competition in leading emerging markets is certainly no less, if not greater, than that observed in advanced countries. While the firm may approach the entry decision by a formal analysis of attractiveness and risks, full recognition must be given to the fact that one is dealing with countries at different levels of development and governance capacities. It may not be immediately clear what entry or competition strategy to follow. Indeed, many different competitive strategies to seek attractive business opportunities in fast-changing competitive environments will be found in use.[31]

One study reveals seven strategic types explaining how new ventures in different competitive markets set strategies to develop organizational capabilities and get higher performance.[32] Different characteristics among new venture strategies are summarized in Exhibit 6.5. Some of these strategies refer to the behaviour of local companies but still remain very relevant to the Canadian company because they contribute to the competitive environment. Canadian companies will be familiar with global niche strategies but may be less familiar with some of the others, for example "Creative Imitation." In this case, new ventures have technological capabilities in the emerging industries in the local market and base their approach on a "follower" strategy.

Canadian firms seriously considering the potential of developing country markets need to move beyond a basic understanding of what products and services are likely to be in demand to a sophisticated appreciation of the competitive environment and the various

Exhibit 6.5 Major Characteristics of New Venture Strategies

Strategy	Description
Reactive Imitation	Local followers in the local existing market
Import Substitution	Local pioneers in the local existing market
Proactive Localization	Local followers in the local emerging market
Creative Imitation	Local pioneers/global followers in the local emerging/global existing market
Global Niche	Global pioneers in the global existing market
Early Market Entry	Global followers in the global emerging market
Global Innovator	Global pioneers in the global emerging market

Source: Sangmoon Park and Zong-Tae Bae, "New Venture Strategies in a Developing Country: Identifying a Typology and Examining Growth Patterns through Case Studies," *Journal of Business Venturing* 19, no. 1 (2004): 81–105. Reprinted with permission from Elsevier.

entry methods possible. Developing a conscious recognition of the possible difficulties involved, and the complex competitive scene, is a desirable objective in its own right and should precede any strategy determination.

What Competitive Strategy Should Be Adopted?

In dealing with global markets, Porter told us some time ago that the marketing manager has three general choices of strategies, as shown in Exhibit 6.6: (1) cost leadership, (2) differentiation, or (3) focus. While factors such as costs and product differentiation will never "go out of fashion," it is as well to move on and ask what newer developments in competitive strategy should be considered.

Beyond Porter

According to one source,[33] there have been two key developments—one in the strategy literature and one in the business environment—that have collectively stimulated a re-conceptualization of the Porter-based perspective.

Firstly, note that Porter's view is expressed as a "typology"; that is, it is based on a group of strategy "types." However, according to this source, much of the prominent work in business strategy literature has shifted from a typology orientation to a more enhanced role for organization-specific factors as characterized by the resource-based perspective.

Exhibit 6.6 Competitive Strategies

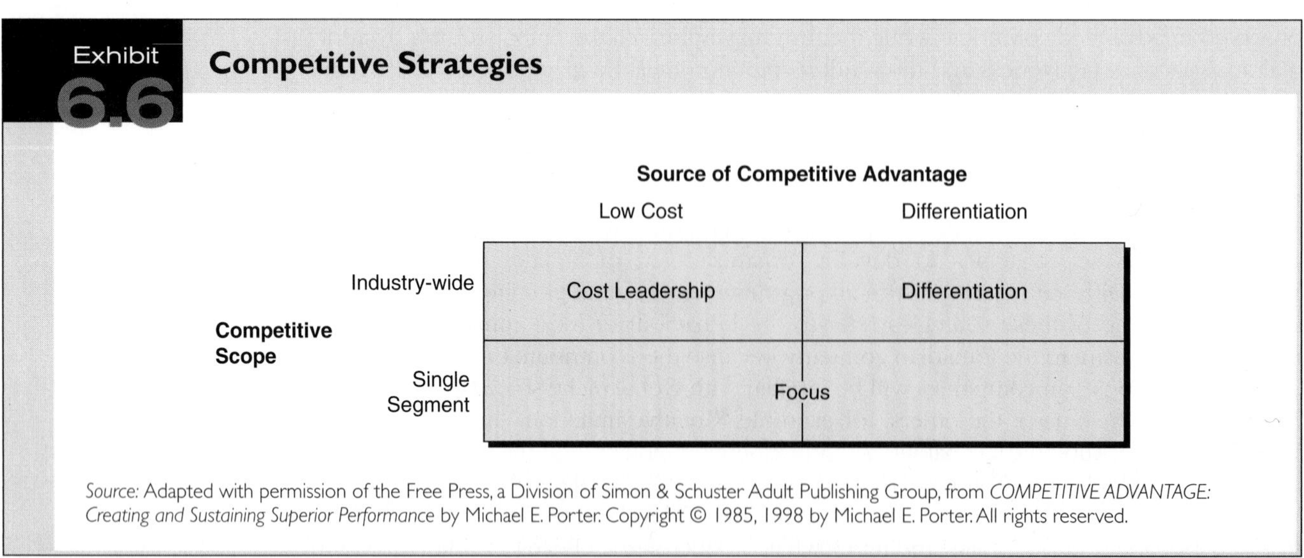

Source: Adapted with permission of the Free Press, a Division of Simon & Schuster Adult Publishing Group, from *COMPETITIVE ADVANTAGE: Creating and Sustaining Superior Performance* by Michael E. Porter. Copyright © 1985, 1998 by Michael E. Porter. All rights reserved.

For example, rather than trying to understand strategy in terms of a cost-differentiation-focus framework, one might equally ask how company resources (production capacity, R & D resources, sales force) influence strategy. The point is that the emphasis on resources combined with an accompanying decline in typology development suggests a growing view that the Porter framework is incomplete and may not be completely compatible with the resource-based view of the firm. (But note that strategic typologies can still be useful, including that of Porter, and integration of competing perspectives remains possible).[34]

Secondly, because the pace and intensity of change in the global business environment is now so much more intense, rapid response to customer needs has become more valuable as a competitive weapon, as the Dahl Brothers case shows (see end of this section). Also, the Internet has minimized the importance of physical boundaries and distance, enabling firms to serve larger markets more efficiently. In this context the relevance of simple, static strategy models is increasingly questioned. However, this is not to say that Porter-style frameworks can no longer be developed, only that they face greater challenges if they are to reflect the realities of modern global markets.

One new strategy framework uses Porter's approach as a foundation, integrates recent research, and proposes a new strategy typology based on market control and value.[35] The justification for using these two elements is as follows: With regard to value, the key to successful competitive strategy is seen not in terms of low costs, differentiation, or focus as such, but in terms of how the various components of the firm's strategy are integrated into an effective overall value proposition. Organizations with more attractive value propositions will be more competitive than those with less attractive ones. With regard to market control, this refers to the application of organizational resources to configure the market in ways beneficial to the firm, such as by excluding competitors (entry barriers) or by controlling suppliers. The shortcomings of this approach are clear, however—barriers may eventually fall, and firms relying on a control emphasis will eventually fall prey to more value-oriented rivals. However some firms may be able to maintain their market control positions over a period of time.

Using this approach, five conceptual "anchors" are derived; these describe how a business would be characterized in relation to its competitors. It is claimed that this approach incorporates Porter's original framework, and that it represents a balance between generalizable strategy group models and the key tenets of the resource-based perspective. Two key questions for practitioners are prompted: How do environmental and other factors influence the degree of market control a firm can exercise? And what resources available to the firm confer an ability to secure a superior value proposition? Answers to these questions will guide the type of strategy ultimately adopted.

The conceptual anchors are

1. emphasis on value
2. emphasis on market control
3. moderate market control and value emphasis
4. strong market control and value emphasis
5. lack of emphasis on either value or market control

The researchers discuss the relevance of each for the firm's competitive strategy. For example, a firm implementing a strategy emphasizing value recognizes that competitors and customers can exercise choice freely; therefore a value strategy is most likely to result in repeat patronage. The grocery industry, where market control by any one supplier is difficult to assert, is an example. In the case of emphasis on market control, the business may not offer the market a strong value proposition but is able to exert considerable control over its market by restricting the entry of new competitors. A network television station operating in a small city is suggested as an example of this strategy.

Global Competition in Practice

It is a truism that global markets are becoming increasingly competitive. One example is China, which, it is widely believed, will before long supplant Canada as America's leading source of imported goods. Global competitors are challenging Canadian firms not only in large international markets such as the U.S. but also in more limited, specialized, and regional markets, segments that small firms, including many Canadian niche players, once thought relative free from competition.

Rival firms will seek to challenge the Canadian supplier on *any* aspect of its activity on which comparative advantages are being built, including the product (its design, quality, performance, aesthetic appeal, and other factors) and services offered (e.g., after-sales services, operator training, installation services, and others). In order to compete effectively, Canadian firms need to appreciate a fundamental change in the competitive landscape, as many do. Historically, competing firms usually occupied niches along the "price-benefits continuum": cheaper but lower quality goods, faster delivery but less customization, and so on. However, in the present global environment, it is common to find competitors setting new standards in two or more dimensions simultaneously, dimensions previously thought mutually unattainable—for example, higher quality (or more customized) products, but with *lower* prices and *faster* delivery times. Thus rather than viewing these dimensions as necessary tradeoffs, new global competitors increasingly see them as syngeristic, with improved performance in one dimension enhancing performance in one or more of the others. This is the nature of the competition that Canadian firms will increasingly encounter.

A number of the traditional customer-choice criteria that firms formerly competed on are now, in effect, assumed. These might be called "order qualifiers": being at a competitive level in these factors (for example, meeting price or delivery requirements) merely qualifies the vendor to participate in the competition. On the other hand, winning international products or brands are successful because of their performance on another "higher level" set of factors—quality, response time, customization, and price—high performance in each of which can be achieved simultaneously. Such combinations of factors have been called "order winners"[36] and are fundamentally influenced by the enlightened use of an array of manufacturing technologies such as flexible manufacturing systems.[37]

Can Canadian companies become order winners in this environment? A positive response to this question can be derived from considering different case examples, two of which are provided below.

Example 1: Dahl Brothers Canada Ltd., Ontario

The president of an Ontario-based manufacturer of ball valves, Dahl Brothers Canada Ltd., remarked that "where we compete is on design, quality, response time, and customer choice."[38] In a state-of-the art plant, this company manufactures more than 1,000 different mini-ball valves and is thus able to meet the diverse needs of its North American customers. Automation of the production line facilitates sustained product quality and low prices. However, the company does more. When their customers feel the "competitive pinch" in their (the customers') end markets, which they frequently do, they approach the ball manufacturer for cost relief. Dahl Brothers then responds by searching comprehensively throughout the company for any possible avenue for cost-cutting to facilitate lowering price even further. This further illustrates the point that, today, global customers expect exceptional performance on a variety of dimensions simultaneously: competitive prices with high quality, rapid response time, and customization.

Example 2: Minaean International Corporation, Vancouver

This company specializes in the manufacture of quick-build modular structures, such as service stations, using light-gauge steel technology. Customers value the speed of installation of units, various design aspects (visual appeal, environmental friendliness), the quality and durability of the units, and their cost effectiveness. As a result of these and other combined factors, the company has achieved substantial contracts overseas, for example with Shell India.[39]

In determining competitive strategy, Canadian firms need to move from a broad view of their strengths and weaknesses to a fundamental and precise concern with actual competitive advantages and disadvantages. It is only on this basis that "order-winning" strategies will be possible.

How Should the Firm Enter the Market?

Elsewhere in the text (Chapter 8) we review different modes of foreign market entry. Even if the firm successfully identifies potentially viable markets, it still faces the problem that strategies needed to meet these markets will vary depending on a variety of geographical and cultural factors. For example, Bulgaria has a population of around 7 million and an ethnic Turkish minority of around 1 million. This does not necessarily mean that the Turkish community can be isolated as a segment, that is, not unless the firm can provide a product that will appeal to the community at large irrespective of individual characteristics such as age, socioeconomic class, and personal disposable earnings.

Distribution is one obvious example of variance. Different country markets with apparently similar market requirements may well have different distribution systems, necessitating strategic flexibility. There is no one correct mode of foreign market entry; instead, Canadian firms are well advised to adopt a contingency approach to international markets and be prepared to accept a portfolio of market entry methods best suited to the particular market in question. Moreover, it may be advisable to adopt what has been called a "sow and reap" or trial-and-error approach to distributor selection. As one study shows, it may take years to screen and develop successful distributor relationships.[40] There are other modes of international entry, of course. But the internationalizing Canadian company needs to recognize that clear-cut decisions on entry modes may be uncertain, difficult though this may be to accept.

Market Segmentation

We have mentioned various market selection issues at different points in this chapter. Market knowledge is clearly a key input to internationalization decisions. It may be useful at this stage to say something more about market segmentation, a knowledge of which is important in choosing and dividing markets. Basic approaches to market segmentation are well known, but here we will illustrate the concept with international examples. Effective use of segmentation—that is, the recognition that groups within markets differ enough to warrant individual marketing mixes—allows global marketers to take advantage of the benefits of standardization (e.g., economies of scale and consistency in positioning) while addressing the unique needs and expectations of a specific target group. This approach means looking at markets on a global or regional basis, thereby ignoring the political boundaries that otherwise define markets in many cases. The identification and cultivation of such inter-market segments is necessary for any standardization of marketing programs to work.[41]

The emergence of segments that spans markets is already evident in the world marketplace. Global marketers have successfully targeted the teenage segment, which is converging as a result of common tastes in sports and music fuelled by teens' computer literacy, travels abroad, and, in many countries, financial independence.[42] Furthermore, a media revolution is creating a common fabric of attitudes and tastes among teenagers. Today, satellite TV and global network concepts such as MTV are both helping to create this segment and providing global marketers access to the teen audience around the world. For example, Reebok used a global ad campaign to launch its Insta Pump line of running shoes in the United States, Germany, Japan, and 137 other countries. Given that teenagers around the world are concerned with social issues, particularly environmentalism, Reebok has introduced a new ecological climbing shoe made from recycled and environmentally sensitive materials. Similarly, two other distinct segments have been detected to be ready for a pan-regional approach. One includes wealthier, better-educated trendsetters who tend to value independence, refuse consumer stereotypes, and appreciate exclusive products. The second one includes well-to-do European businesspeople who travel abroad regularly and have a taste for luxury goods.

Despite convergence, global marketers still have to make adjustments in some of the marketing-mix elements for maximum impact. For example, while Levi's jeans are globally accepted by the teenage segment, European teens reacted negatively to the urban realism of Levi's U.S. ads. Levi's converted its ads in Europe, drawing on images of a mythical America.[43] Similarly, segment sizes vary from one market to another even in cohesive regions such as Europe. The value-oriented segment in Germany accounts for 32 percent of the grocery sales, but only 9 percent in the United Kingdom and 8 percent in France.[44]

The greatest challenge for the global marketer is the choice of an appropriate base for the segmentation effort. The objective is to arrive at a grouping or groupings that are substantial enough to merit the segmentation effort (for example, there are nearly 230 million teenagers in the Americas, Europe, and the Asia-Pacific, with the teenagers of the Americas spending nearly $60 billion of their own money yearly) and are reachable as well by the marketing effort (for example, the majority of MTV's audience consists of teenagers).

The possible bases for segmentation are summarized in Exhibit 6.7. Marketers have traditionally used environmental bases for segmentation. However, using geographic proximity, political system characteristics, economic standing, or cultural traits on a stand-alone basis may not provide relevant data for decision making. Using a combination of them, however, may produce more meaningful results. One of the segments pursued by global marketers around the world is the middle-class family. Defining the composition of this global middle class is tricky, given the varying levels of development among nations in Latin America and Asia. However, some experts estimate that 25 percent of the world population enjoys a middle-class standard of living—some 300 million people in India alone.[45] Using only household income may be quite a poor gauge of class. Income figures ignore vast differences in international purchasing power. Chinese consumers, for example, spend less than 5 percent of their total outlay on rent, transportation, and health, while a typical U.S. household spends 45 to 50 percent. Additionally, income distinctions do not reflect education or values—two increasingly important barometers of middle-class status. A global segmentation effort using cultural values is provided in The Global Marketplace 6.2.

Exhibit 6.7 **Bases for Global Market Segmentation**

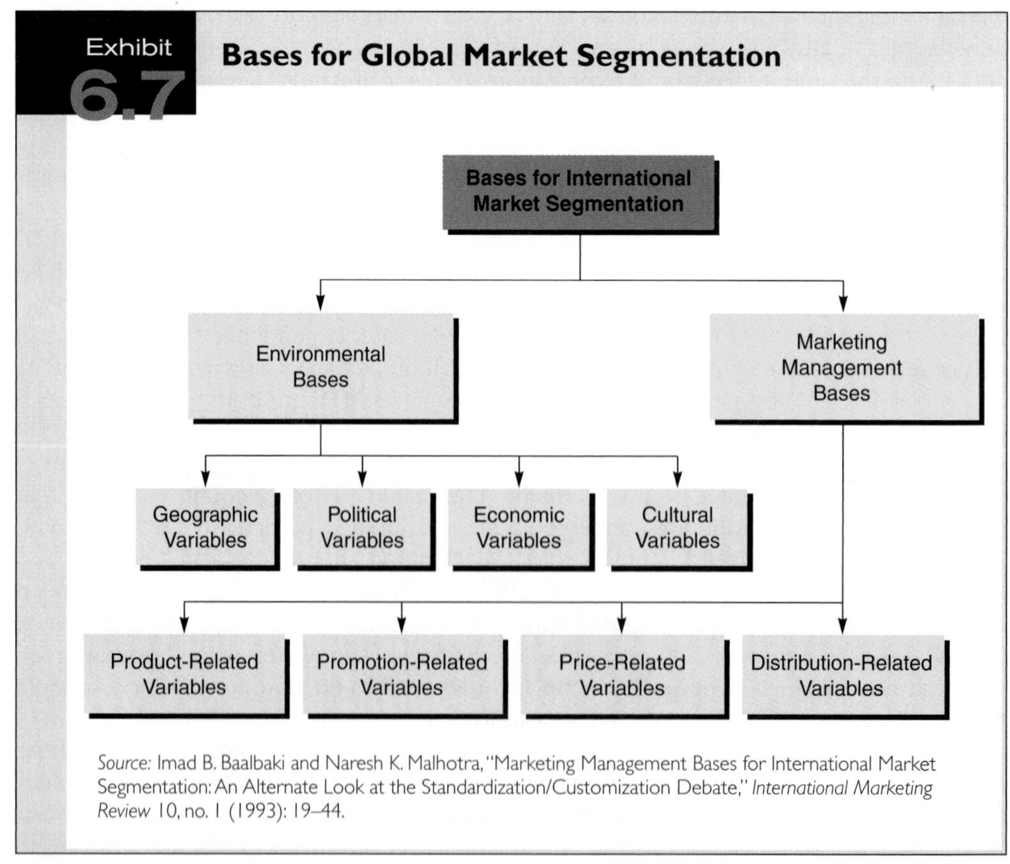

Source: Imad B. Baalbaki and Naresh K. Malhotra, "Marketing Management Bases for International Market Segmentation: An Alternate Look at the Standardization/Customization Debate," *International Marketing Review* 10, no. 1 (1993): 19–44.

The Global MARKETPLACE 6.2

Segmenting Global Markets by Cultural Values

Three critical factors—nationality, demographics, and values—play major roles in determining the nature and evolution of global consumer markets, but their importance relative to one another depends on the product or service category with which marketers are dealing. Core values go much deeper than behaviour or attitude, and they determine, at a basic level, people's choices and desires over the long term. Behaviour changes quickly in response to outside forces of all kinds, including whether a person got a good night's sleep or how long the line was at the grocery store. Although slower to change, attitudes also are prone to external influences. Core values, on the other hand, are intrinsic to a person's identity and inherent beliefs. By appealing to people's inner selves, it's possible to influence their outer selves—their purchase behaviour.

As part of a Roper Reports Worldwide Global Consumer Survey, 1,000 people were interviewed in their homes in each of 35 countries. As part of their responses, they ranked 56 values by the importance they hold as guiding principles in their lives. Among adults, six global values segments emerged, residing in all 35 countries, but to varying degrees in each. Interestingly, the largest values segment across the globe focuses on the material world, while the second-largest centres on the soul.

Although most people fall into a particular category, some values cut across many categories and countries. For example, "protecting the family" ranks in the top 10 for all 6 groups. All 35 countries rank family in their top 5 guiding principles, except for Indonesia, which ranks respecting ancestors as number 1. All the Asian countries surveyed place family in their top 2. Protecting the family was given top value in 22 countries, including the United States. A country-by-country analysis reveals that Great Britain leads the world in wanting to protect the family, Brazil has the most fun seekers, Saudi Arabia ranks first in faith, the Netherlands has the highest percentage worldwide in esteeming honesty, and Korea is the global front-runner in valuing health and fitness.

The research shows that people in different segments generally pursue different activities, buy different products, and use different media. Knowing which segments dominate in a country helps with marketing efforts and enables advertisers to tailor their message to those parts of the population most likely to buy. Profiles of the values segments around the world give marketers the tools to refine their strategies, identify potential consumers, reinforce loyal customer bases, and buffer them again competitive moves.

Segment	Characteristics	Geographics
Strivers	More likely to be men; place more emphasis on material and professional goals	One-third of people in developing Asia; one-quarter in Russia and developed Asia
Devouts	22 percent of adults; women more than men; tradition and duty are paramount	Africa, Asia, Middle East; least common in Europe
Altruists	18 percent of adults; larger portion of females; interested in social issues and welfare of society; older	Latin America and Russia
Intimates	15 percent of population; personal relationships and family take precedence	Europeans and North Americans
Fun Seekers	12 percent of population; youngest group	Disproportionately more in developed Asia
Creatives	10 percent worldwide; strong interest in education, knowledge, and technology	Europe and Latin America

Source: Tom Miller, "Global Segments from 'Strivers' to 'Creatives,'" *Marketing News*, July 20, 1998, 11. See also **http://www.gfkamerica.com/products/roper_reports_worldwide.htm.**

It has also been proposed that markets that reflect a high degree of homogeneity with respect to marketing-mix variables could be grouped into segments and thereby targeted with a largely standardized marketing strategy. Whether bases related to product, promotion, pricing, or distribution are used, their influence should be related to environmentally based variables. Product-related bases include the degree to which products are culture-based, which stage of the life cycle they occupy, consumption patterns, and attitudes toward product attributes (such as country of origin), as well as consumption infrastructure (for example, telephone lines for modems). The growth of microwave sales, for example, has been surprising in low-income countries; however, microwaves have become status symbols and buying them more of an emotional issue. Many consumers in these markets also want to make sure they get the same product as available in developed markets, thereby eliminating the need in many cases to develop market-specific products. Adjustments will have to made, however. Noticing that, for reasons of status and space, many Asian consumers put their refrigerators in their living rooms, Whirlpool makes refrigerators available in striking colours such as red and blue.

With promotion, customers' values and norms set the baseline for global versus regional versus local solutions. The significant emphasis on family relationships among many Europeans and North Americans creates a multi-regional segment that can be exploited by consumer-goods and consumer-services marketers (such as car marketers or telecommunications service providers). On the pricing side, dimensions such as customers' price sensitivity may lead the marketer to go after segments that insist on high quality despite high price in markets where overall purchasing power may be low, to ensure global or regional uniformity in the marketing approach. Affordability is a major issue for customers whose buying power may fall short at least for the time being. Offering only one option may exclude potential customers of the future who are not yet part of a targeted segment; companies like Procter & Gamble and Unilever offer an array of products at different price points to attract them and to keep them as they move up the income scale.[46] As distribution systems converge, for example, with the increase of global chains, markets can also be segmented by outlet types that reach environmentally defined groups. For example, toy manufacturers may look at markets not only in terms of numbers of children but by how effectively and efficiently they can be reached by global chains such as Toys R Us, as opposed to purely local outlets.

For a case example of one Canadian company's approach to market segmentation, see The Global Marketplace 6.3.

***The Global* MARKETPLACE 6.3**

How to Segment the Robotic Equipment Market

To illustrate segmentation in practice, take the example of a medium-sized Canadian company manufacturing mobile robotic equipment with built-in surveillance systems. The firm's closed-circuit television pipeline inspection cameras and crawler systems find deployment in three broad areas: confined spaces (e.g., oil pipeline inspection), hazardous areas (e.g., nuclear energy sites), and under water (e.g., inspection of tanks).

The company finds market segments in key application areas such as potable water, hydroelectricity, oil and gas, nuclear energy, the military, security, and search and rescue. There are substantial competitors to be contended with in these areas, yet the company has been able to carve out its own niches by offering exceptional customer service allied with advanced technology solutions (the firm has developed a crawler system capable of travelling more than six times further than competing systems).

The company continues to find imaginative applications for its products; in effect, these are the forerunners of new market segments, for example, search-and-rescue missions (in the U.S., searching for survivors in the deep rubble of the World Trade Center towers after September 11, 2001), weld seam inspection in radioactive waste fuel storage areas (in Japan), and seeking out smuggled contraband in pipes near seaports (in Taiwan). Initially it may seem that these applications are too specialized to be considered market segments, but researching potential clients on a global scale in each case suggests otherwise. As this company's experience shows, developing a specialized product and service and focusing on specific niches can create differential advantages for Canadian firms, who can then create a strong reputation within the niche or market segment.

Sources: Inuktun Services Ltd., **http://www.inuktun.com** (accessed February 19, 2006). See also Jane Daly, "Inuktun Finds a Space in Tight Spaces," *Exportwise*, Summer 2005.

Why Segmentation Is Important to Canadian Companies

In addition to the reasons outlined above, segmentation is especially important to Canadian companies because of the huge size of this country's primary export market, the United States. The sheer volume of product required to penetrate some American markets often causes disbelief in Canadian product-based businesses and manufacturers. The Canadian exporter simply cannot compete on the basis of quantity, regardless of the quality of the product. For example, a distributor of food products in New York may be interested in a Canadian supplier's product; however, the distributor will conceivably have more customers in New York City than the Canadian firm currently supplies in the whole of Canada, and typically a business cannot double its production overnight.

Similar circumstances are encountered in the industrial market, such as in the case of construction services (including architectural and engineering services, project management, and materials procurement).[47] Because these services are relatively portable, they have given numerous Canadian construction companies a natural entry point into the global market, enabling them to become service exporters despite the fact that Canada, from an international perspective, is a relatively small player in this market.

In fact, Canadian construction service companies, although large by Canadian standards, are dwarfed by some of the U.S., European, and Asian firms that can provide the on-the-ground labour force required for major overseas projects. However, Canadian companies are internationally known for supplying their customers with specialized, high-quality construction project services and systems. Moreover, while many competitors in the export market can build run-of-the-mill shopping malls, apartments, and office buildings, Canada is particularly strong in specialized construction projects, such as airports, hospitals, and laboratories. Finding specialized segments of the market can therefore be seen to be vital for Canadian exporters in both the industrial- and consumer-goods fields, as the case described in The Global Marketplace 6.3 illustrates.

The reality is, therefore, that size considerations will dictate that many Canadian companies will pursue highly focused marketing strategies, concentrating on defining appropriate market segments. This will apply worldwide, but also closer to home. There is no doubt that globalization is Canada's future, including the huge emerging markets of China and India. But the near-term opportunities for many firms are in the Americas, specifically the U.S. itself. Yet saying "I plan to sell my products in the U.S." downplays the tremendous diversity of the country and the importance of understanding the differences in its markets. Even viewing the U.S. as 50 markets—1 for each state—is misleading. What is needed is a willingness to study the intricacies and differences of the country, because this can open up opportunities for gaining a foothold in whole new segments of the market.

For example, despite our many similarities, Canadian and American cultures are clearly different, as becomes apparent when one looks at regional areas within the U.S. Within major metropolitan areas can be found city-sized populations of people from Italy, Vietnam, the U.K., China, and many other countries (although Canadian cities are no strangers to such strong ethnically based groupings). Also, culturally diverse cities in one part of the U.S. are distinctly different from those in others. Metropolitan centres in the west are different from those in the Midwest or on the east coast. Even Los Angeles and San Francisco differ substantially though they are both in the same state. Rural differences are also apparent—rural Mississippi and rural Montana, for example, have very little in common.

These demographic differences are clues that can help Canadian exporters decide on the most important market segments. Thinking in geographical terms also provides clues. Examining the country state by state or city by city has limitations. Considering larger regional divisions such as New England, the mid-Atlantic states, the South, or the Pacific northwest is likely to be more fruitful because of commonalities within the regions.

Other Aspects of Global Strategy: The Business Definition Issue

Our focus to this point has naturally been on the firm's internationalization strategies. However, other aspects of strategy should not be ignored. Any planning process needs to begin with a clear definition of the business for which strategy, including internationalization strategy, is to be developed.

Generally, the strategic business unit (SBU) is the unit around which decisions are based. In practice, SBUs represent groupings based on product-market similarities centred around (1) needs or wants to be met, (2) end-user customers to be targeted, or (3) the product or service used to meet the needs of specific customers. For a global marketer such as Black & Decker, the options may be to define the business to be analyzed as the home improvement business, the do-it-yourself business, or the power-tool business. Ideally, these SBUs should have primary responsibility and authority in managing their basic business functions. Of course, smaller companies, perhaps embarking on exporting for the first time, will not have the resources to justify an SBU setup. For them, the company itself will be the SBU. However, a discussion of the workings of SBUs clarifies the key decisions that all internationally-oriented companies are obliged to make. For case examples of business definitions adopted by Canadian exporting companies, see The Global Marketplace 6.4.

The Global MARKETPLACE 6.4

Canadian Practice in Business Definition

Canadian firms marketing abroad do not hesitate to think creatively about the basic purpose of their organizations and the most appropriate markets to serve. For example, one Canadian international manufacturer of automation devices sees its key mission as "feeding the world's appetite for productivity," an excellent example of "the business we are in" thinking. Another firm, a manufacturer of fabrics for high-performance applications, with strong international sales, sees itself as "creating fabrics to protect your most valuable asset: your people." Such definitions show a sensitivity to the long-term needs met by the companies' products rather than a narrow focus on today's technology and capabilities.

At the same time, Canadian companies are conscious that the market will value world-class products, quality, service, and close attention to customer needs, derived from investment in appropriate plant facilities and technology. One major Canadian tool manufacturer, for example, sees itself as "a leader in the development and production of service tools and engine components" and its mission as being "to supply our customers with world-class products and services." This claim is backed up by a company-wide preoccupation with improving production operations, which results in short lead-times and low-cost tooling and end products. The result, says the company, is that "we provide our customers with exactly what they want, when they want it," a result clearly appreciated in the firm's foreign markets. To give an example from the consumer-goods field, a Canadian manufacturer of nondairy frozen foods selling internationally sees the key elements of its mission as "a spirit of innovation; a commitment to exceeding customer needs through quality products and exemplary service; and an adherence to continuously improving processes."

These examples suggest that international Canadian firms are not only conscious of the overall market need underlying demand for their products, they are also willing to take the necessary steps, in terms of resources and capabilities, to meet and exceed the key success factors in the international marketplace. Mission statements or business definitions that link customer need and production operations can obviously be very powerful in setting benchmarks or guidelines for implementing international marketing strategy, because they connect two aspects of mission: *customer mission* (the customer needs we are going to meet), and *key value mission* (what we will *do*—our commitment to world-class quality and service).

Sources: Automation Devices, Inc., **http://www.autodev.com** (accessed January 21, 2006); Lincoln Fabrics Ltd., **http://www.lincolnfabrics.com** (accessed January 21, 2006); K-Line International (Canada) Ltd., **http://www.k-line.ca.** (accessed January 22, 2006); and Rich Products Corp., **http://www.richs.com** (accessed January 21, 2006).

This phase of the planning process requires the participation of executives from different functions, especially marketing, production, finance, distribution, and procurement. Geographic representation should be from the major markets or regions as well as from the smaller, yet emerging, markets. With appropriate members, the committee can focus on product and markets as well as competitors whom they face in different markets, whether they are global, regional, or purely local. Heading this effort should be an executive with highest-level experience in regional or global markets; for example, one global firm called on the president of its European operations to come back to headquarters to head the global planning effort. This effort calls for commitment by the company itself, both in calling on the best talent to participate in the planning effort and later in implementing their proposals. In the case of SMEs, the luxury of a committee may have to be forgone, and decisions instead taken by the owner-manager and perhaps one or two senior executives. Complex formal planning may have to give way to something more intuitive, at least in part.

It should be noted that this assessment against environmental realities may mean a dramatic change in direction and approach. For example, the once-separate sectors of computing and mobile telephony are colliding, and the direction of future products is still uncertain. The computer industry believes in miniaturizing the general-purpose computer, while the mobile-phone industry believes in adding new features (such as photo-messaging, gaming, and location-based information) to its existing products.[48] The joint venture between Ericsson and Sony aims at taking advantage of this trend, something that neither party could have done on its own.

Issues in the Development of Global Marketing Strategy

Decisions need to be made regarding how best to utilize the conditions set by globalization drivers within the framework of competitive challenges and the resources of the firm. (As we saw in Chapter 1, globalization drivers are the various factors that create favourable conditions for expanding the firm globally: for example, increased sales opportunities, unit cost reductions derived from scale economies, and the reduction of trade barriers worldwide.) Marketing-related decisions will have to be made in four areas: (1) the degree of standardization in the product offering, (2) the marketing program beyond the product variable, (3) location and extent of value-adding activities, and (4) competitive moves to be made.

Product Offering

Globalization is not equal to standardization except in the case of the core product or the technology used to produce the product. The need to localize varies by product. Fashion or fashion products depend for their appeal on sameness. Information technology products are susceptible to power requirements, keyboard configurations (e.g., Europe alone may require 20 different keyboards), instruction-manual language, and warning labels compliant with local regulations.[49] Product standardization may result in significant cost savings upstream. For example, as a compromise between the French preference for handsaws with plastic handles and "soft teeth" and the British preference for wooden handles and "hard teeth," Stanley Works produced a plastic-handled saw with "hard teeth," thereby allowing consolidation for production and resulting in substantial economies of scale. Most automakers have reduced the number of platforms they offer worldwide to achieve greater economies of scale. For example, Toyota has reduced the number of its platforms from 11 to 6. This is not to reduce variety but to deliver it more cost-effectively.[50] Shania Twain's double CD *Up!* is an example of catering to multiple segments at the same time: both discs contain the same 19 tracks, but one has the effects pop fans appreciate while the other has a more country-music sound. A third disc with "an Asian, Indian vibe" replaces the country disc in Europe.[51]

Marketing Approach

Nowhere is the need for the local touch as critical as in the execution of the marketing program. Uniformity is sought especially in elements that are strategic in nature (e.g., positioning), whereas care is taken to localize necessary tactical elements (e.g., distribution). This approach has been called "**glocalization**," as we saw in Chapter 1. For example, Unilever achieved great success with a fabric softener that used a common positioning, advertising theme, and symbol (a teddy bear) but differing brand names (Snuggle, Cajoline, Kuschelweich, Mimosin, and Yumos) and bottle sizes. Gillette Co. scored a huge success with its Sensor shaver when it was rolled out in the United States, Europe, and Japan with a common approach based on the premise that men everywhere want the same thing in a shave. Although the language of its TV commercials varied, the theme ("the best a man can get") and most of the footage were the same. A comparison of the marketing-mix elements of two global marketers is given in Exhibit 6.8. Notice that adaptation is present even at Coca-Cola, which is acknowledged to be one of the world's most global marketers.

Location of Value-Adding Activities

Globalization strives to reduce costs by pooling production or other activities or exploiting factor costs or capabilities within a system. Rather than duplicating activities in multiple, or even all, country organizations, a firm concentrates its activities. Nokia's over 20,000 research and development people work in centres in 12 different countries, including China, Finland, Germany, Hungary, and China. The company has also entered into development agreements with operators (such as France Telecom and Vodafone) to bring innovations to market more efficiently.[52] Many global marketers have established R & D centres next to key production facilities so that concurrent engineering can take place every day on the factory floor. To enhance the global exchange of ideas, the centres have joint projects and are in real-time contact with each other.

The quest for cost savings and improved transportation and transfer methods has allowed some marketers to concentrate customer service activities rather than having them present in all country markets. For example, Sony used to have repair centres in all the Scandinavian countries and Finland; today, all service and maintenance activities are performed in a regional centre in Stockholm, Sweden. Similarly, MasterCard has teamed up with Mascon Global in Chennai, India, where MasterCard's core processing functions—authorization, clearing, and settlement—for worldwide operations are handled.[53]

Exhibit 6.8 Globalization of the Marketing Mix

	Adaptation		Standardization	
Marketing Mix Elements	Full	Partial	Full	Partial
Product design			C	N
Brand name			C	N
Product positioning		N	C	
Packaging				C/N
Advertising theme		N	C	
Pricing		N		C
Advertising copy	N		C	C
Distribution	N	C		
Sales promotion	N	C		
Customer service	N	C		

Key: C = Coca-Cola; N = Nestlé

Source: Adapted from John A. Quelch and Edward J. Hoff, "Customizing Global Marketing," *Harvard Business Review,* May–June 1986 (Boston: Harvard Business School Publishing Division), 61.

To show commitment to a given market, both economically and politically, centres may be established in these markets. Philips Electronics, for example, has chosen China as their Asian centre for global product research and development.[54]

Competitive Moves

A company with a regional or global presence will not have to respond to competitive moves only in the market where it is being attacked. A competitor may be attacked in its profit sanctuary to drain its resources, or its position in its home market may be challenged.[55] When Fuji began cutting into Kodak's market share in the United States, Kodak responded by drastically increasing its advertising in Japan and creating a new subsidiary to deal strictly with that market.

Cross-subsidization, or the use of resources accumulated in one part of the world to fight a competitive battle in another, may be the competitive advantage needed for the long term.[56] One major market lost may mean losses in others, resulting in a domino effect. Jockeying for overall global leadership may result in competitive action in any part of the world. This has manifested itself in the form of "wars" between major global players in industries such as soft drinks, automotive tires, computers, and cellular phones. The opening of new markets often signals a new battle, as happened in Russia in the 1990s, in Mexico after the signing of the North American Free Trade Agreement, and in Vietnam after the normalization of relations with the United States. Given their multiple bases of operation, global marketers may defend against a competitive attack in one country by countering in another country or, if the competitors operate in multiple businesses, countering in a different product category altogether. In the mobile-phone category, the winners in the future will be those who can better attack developing and emerging markets with cheaper phones while providing Internet-based devices elsewhere.[57] In a study of how automakers develop strategies that balance the conflicting pressures of local responsiveness and regional integration in Europe, Japanese marketers were found to practice standardization in model offerings but selectively respond to differences in market conditions by manipulating prices and advertising levels.[58]

Implementing Global Marketing Strategy

The successful global marketers of the future will be those who can achieve a balance between local and regional/global concerns. Marketers who have tried the global concept have often run into problems with local differences. Especially early on, global marketing was seen as a standardized marketing effort dictated to the country organizations by headquarters. For example, when Coca-Cola reentered the Indian market in 1993, it invested most heavily in its Coke brand, using its typical global positioning, and saw its market leadership slip to Pepsi. Recognizing the mistake, Coke re-emphasized a popular local cola brand (Thums Up) and refocused the Coke brand advertising to be more relevant to the local Indian consumer.[59] In the past 10 years, Coca-Cola has been acquiring local soft-drink brands (such as Inca Cola in Peru), which now account for 10 percent of company sales.[60]

Challenges of Global Marketing

Pitfalls that handicap global marketing programs and contribute to their sub-optimal performance include market-related reasons, such as insufficient research and a tendency to over-standardize, as well as internal reasons, such as inflexibility in planning and implementation.

If a product is to be launched on a broader scale without formal research as to regional or local differences, the result may be failure. An example of this is Lego A/S, the Danish toy manufacturer, which decided to transfer sales-promotional tactics successful in the U.S. market unaltered to other markets, such as Japan. This promotion included approaches such as "bonus packs" and gift promotions. However, Japanese consumers considered these promotions wasteful, expensive, and not very appealing.[61] Going too local has its drawbacks as well. With too much customization or with local production, the marketer may lose its import positioning. For example, when Miller Brewing Company started brewing Löwenbräu under license in the United States, the brand lost its prestigious import image. Often, the necessary research is conducted only after a product or a program has failed.

Globalization by design requires a balance between sensitivity to local needs and deployment of technologies and concepts globally. This means that neither headquarters nor independent country managers can alone call the shots. If country organizations are not part of the planning process, or if adoption is forced on them by headquarters, local resistance in the form of the **not-invented-here (NIH) syndrome** may lead to the demise of the global program or, worse still, to an overall decline in morale. Subsidiary resistance may stem from resistance to any idea originating from the outside or from valid concerns about the applicability of a concept to that particular market. Without local commitment, no global program will survive.

Localizing Global Marketing

In Chapter 1 we noted that companies have come to realize the importance of balancing global marketing (with its focus on standardization) and local marketing (with its focus on adaptation to country differences). This concept has a number of ramifications that are explored below. In terms of the locus of management decisions, the successful global marketers of the new century will be those who can achieve a balance between country managers and global product managers at headquarters. This balance may be achieved by a series of actions to improve a company's ability to develop and implement global strategy. These actions relate to management processes, organization structures, and overall corporate culture, all of which should ensure cross-fertilization within the firm.[62]

Management Processes

In the multi-domestic approach (see Chapter 1), country organizations had very little need to exchange ideas. Globalization, however, requires transfer of information not only between headquarters and country organizations but also among the country organizations themselves. By facilitating the flow of information, ideas are exchanged and organizational values strengthened. Information exchange can be achieved through periodic meetings of marketing managers or through worldwide conferences to allow employees to discuss their issues and local approaches to solving them. IBM, for example, has a Worldwide Opportunity Council, which sponsors fellowships for employees to listen to business cases from around the world and develop global platforms or solutions. IBM has found that some country organizations find it easier to accept input of other country organizations than that coming directly from headquarters. The approach used at Levi Strauss & Co. is described in The Global Marketplace 6.5.

Part of the preparation for becoming global has to be personnel interchange. Many companies encourage (or even require) mid-level managers to gain experience abroad during the early or middle stages of their careers. The more experience people have in working with others from different nationalities—getting to know other markets and surroundings—the better a company's global philosophy, strategy, and actions will be integrated locally.

The role of headquarters staff should be that of coordinating and leveraging the resources of the corporation. For example, this may mean activities focused on combining good ideas that come from different parts of the company to be fed into global planning. Many global companies also employ world-class advertising and market research staff, whose role should include helping personnel in subsidiary companies upgrade their skills and raise their sights beyond purely local concerns to include an appreciation of the impact of larger global issues.

Globalization calls for the centralization of decision-making authority far beyond that of the multi-domestic approach. Once a strategy has been jointly developed, headquarters may want to permit local managers to develop their own programs—within specified parameters and subject to approval—rather than forcing them to adhere strictly to the formulated strategy. For example, Colgate-Palmolive allows local units to use their own ads,

The Global MARKETPLACE 6.5

Finding the Fit Overseas

Twice a year, Levi Strauss & Co. calls together managers from its worldwide operations for a meeting of the minds. In sessions that could be described as a cross between the United Nations General Assembly and MTV, the participants brainstorm and exchange ideas on what seems to work in their respective markets, regionally or globally. If a marketing manager finds an advertising campaign appealing, he or she is encouraged to take it back home to sell more Levi's blue jeans.

All told, Levi's marketing approach epitomizes a slogan that is becoming popular among companies around the world: "Think globally, act locally." Levi's has deftly capitalized on the Levi's name abroad by marketing it as an enshrined piece of Americana, and foreign consumers have responded by paying top dollar for the product. An Indonesian commercial shows Levi's-clad teenagers cruising around Dubuque, Iowa, in 1960s convertibles. In Japan, James Dean serves as a centrepiece in virtually all Levi's advertising. Overseas, Levi's products have been positioned as an upscale product, which has meant highly satisfactory profit margins. To protect the image, Levi's has avoided the use of mass merchants and discounters in its distribution efforts.

Levi's success turns on its ability to fashion a global strategy that does not stifle local initiative. It is a delicate balancing act, one that often means giving foreign managers the freedom needed to adjust their tactics to meet the changing tastes of their home markets. In Brazil, Levi's prospers by letting local managers call the shots on distribution. For instance, Levi's penetrated the huge, fragmented Brazilian market by launching a chain of 400 Levi's Only stores, some of them in tiny rural towns. Levi's is also sensitive to local tastes in Brazil, where it developed the Feminina line of jeans exclusively for women who prefer ultra-tight jeans. What Levi's learns in one market can often be adopted in another. The Dockers line of chino pants and casual wear originated in the company's Argentine unit and was applied to loosely cut pants by Levi's Japanese subsidiary. The company's U.S. operation adopted both in 1986, and the line now generates significant North American as well as European revenues. In 2002, Dockers unveiled its Go Khaki with Stain Defender line in the United States, followed by a quick rollout in other major markets. In 2003, the company launched the Levi Strauss Signature brand, aimed at giving value-conscious consumers high-quality and fashionable clothing from a company they trust.

Headquarters managers exercise control where necessary. To protect Levi's cherished brand identity and image of quality, the company has organized its foreign operations as subsidiaries rather than relying on a patchwork of licensees. It is important for a brand to have a single face; it cannot be controlled if there are 20 to 25 licensees around the world interpreting it in different ways. The company also keeps ahead of its competition by exporting its pioneering use of computers to track sales and manufacturing.

The company has also launched a reorganization to focus more on consumer needs. The Levi's website has been redesigned to feature a virtual dressing room, an option to order custom-tailored jeans, and virtual salespeople who offer tips on matching outfits.

Levi's continues to focus on global sales with its three divisions—the Americas (NAFTA plus Latin America); Europe, Middle East, and Africa; and Asia-Pacific—employing 8,850 people worldwide. In 2004, the Americas contributed 59 percent of its sales; Europe, the Middle East, and Africa, 24 percent; and Asia-Pacific, 17 percent of $4.1 billion total sales.

Sources: "How Levi Strauss Rekindled the Allure of Brand America," *World Trade*, March 2005, 28; Michele Orecklin, "Look, Ma, No Stains," *Time*, December 9, 2002, 64–65; "Levi Strauss & Co. Fiscal 2001 Financial Results," **http://www.levistrauss.com**; Alice Z. Cuneo, "Levi Strauss Begins 1st Online Sales Effort," *Advertising Age*, November 23, 1998, 18; and "For Levi's, a Flattering Fit Overseas," *Business Week*, November 5, 1990, 76–77.

but only if they can prove they beat the global "benchmark" version. With a properly managed approval process, effective control can be exerted without unduly dampening a country manager's creativity.

Overall, the best defence against the emergence of the NIH syndrome uses various motivational policies, such as (1) ensuring that local managers participate in the development of marketing strategies and programs for global brands, (2) encouraging local managers to generate ideas for possible regional or global use, (3) maintaining a product portfolio that includes local as well as regional and global brands, and (4) allowing local managers control over their marketing budgets so that they can respond to local customer needs and counter global competition (rather than depleting budgets by forcing them to participate only in uniform campaigns). Acknowledging this local potential, global marketers can pick up successful brands in one country and make them cross-border stars. Since Nestlé acquired British candy maker Rowntree Mackintosh, it has increased its exports by 60 percent and made formerly local brands, such as After Eight dinner mints, into pan-European hits. When global marketers get their hands on an innovation or a product with global potential, rolling it out in other regions or worldwide is important.

Organization Structures

Various organization structures have emerged to support the globalization effort. Some companies have established global or regional product managers and their support groups at headquarters. Their tasks are to develop long-term strategies for product categories on a worldwide basis and to act as the support system for the country organizations. This matrix structure that is focused on customers, which has replaced the traditional country-by-country approach, is considered more effective in today's global marketplace by companies that have adopted it.

Whenever a product group has global potential, firms such as Procter & Gamble, 3M, and Henkel create strategic-planning units to work on the programs. These units, such as 3M's EMATs (European Marketing Action Teams), consist of members from the country organizations that market the products, managers from both global and regional headquarters, and technical specialists.

To deal with the globalization of customers, marketers are extending national account management programs across countries, typically for the most important customers.[63] In a study of 165 multinational companies, 13 percent of their revenues came from global customers (revenues from all international customers were 46 percent). While relatively small, this 13 percent comes from the most important customers who cannot be ignored.[64] AT&T, for example, distinguishes between international and global customers and provides the global customers with special services, including a single point of contact for domestic and international operations and consistent worldwide service. Executing **global account management** programs not only builds relationships with important customers but also allows for the development of internal systems and interaction. It will require, however, a new organizational overlay, and will demand new ways of working for anyone involved in marketing to global customers. One of the main challenges is in evaluating and rewarding sales efforts. If Nokia sells equipment to Telefonica in Brazil, should the sale be credited to the sales manager in Brazil or to the global account manager for Telefonica? The answer in most cases is to double-count the credit.[65]

Corporate Culture

Corporate culture affects and is affected by two dimensions: the overall way in which the company holds its operations together and makes them a single entity, and the commitment to the global marketplace.

An example of a manifestation of the global commitment is a global identity that favours no specific country (especially the "home country" of the company). The management features several nationalities, and whenever teams are assembled, people from various country's organizations get represented. The management development system has to be transparent, allowing non-national executives an equal chance for the fast track to top management.[66]

Whirlpool's corporate profile states the following: "Beyond selling products around the world, being a global home-appliance company means identifying and respecting genuine national and regional differences in customer expectations, but also recognizing and responding to similarities in product development, engineering, purchasing, manufacturing, marketing and sales, distribution, and other areas." Companies that exploit the efficiencies from these similarities will outperform others in terms of market share, cost, quality, productivity, innovation, and return to shareholders. In truly global companies, very little decision making occurs that does not support the goal of treating the world as a single market. Programs are planned for and executed on a worldwide basis.

In More Detail 6.2

HOW TOYOTA DOES THINGS

"The Toyota Way," which embodies the Japanese automaker's culture, has five distinct elements:

1. *Kaizen,* the well-known Japanese process of continuous improvement, is more a frame of mind than a business process. Toyota employees come to work each day determined and committed to become a little better at whatever it is they are doing than they were the day before.
2. *Genchi genbutsu* (GG), roughly translated, means "go to the source." Western companies are criticized for spending too little time defining what business problem they are facing and too much time coming up with solutions. GG puts the emphasis the other way around, with the view that only by going to the source of the problem can the true solution be discovered.
3. Toyota employees are encouraged to see problems in a positive way—that is, not as something undesirable, but as something that can help them improve their performance further. Authority of leaders derives not from hierarchy but from their proficiency as practitioners.
4. Teamwork plays a pivotal role at Toyota. Much of this does not come naturally, and Toyota devotes a lot of time and money to on-the-job training.
5. Workers are encouraged to respect other people, not just as people, but also for their skills and the special knowledge that derives from their particular position in the company. Toyota believes that if two people always agree, one of them is superfluous. Different opinions must be expressed, but in a respectful way.

Once these values are inculcated into a worker, they guide decision making throughout the day. There is no need to refer matters up the silo to ask what to do. Everyone knows what solution should be adopted, so decision making is dramatically accelerated. Japanese colleagues who know the culture well reach a point of "emotional fortitude" where their behaviour is entirely consistent with the organization's culture and beliefs. In the West, where individual interests tend to be put before those of any group, it is more difficult for employees to reach this state (i.e., high versus low individualism).[67]

The Local Company in the Global Environment

The global marketplace presents significant challenges, but also opportunities, for local firms.[68] As global marketers such as Boeing, Honda, McDonald's, and Volkswagen expand their presence, there are local companies that must defend their positions or lose out. They can no longer rely on the government to protect or support them. If selling out or becoming a part of a bigger global entity is not an acceptable option, the local marketer will have to build on an existing competitive advantage or adopt a creative growth strategy globally. To counter the significant resources of global marketers (such as powerful brands and sizable promotional budgets), the local company can compete successfully in the local market by emphasizing the perceived advantages of its product and marketing.[69] More proactively, the local company can pursue its own globalization strategy through segments that have similar features to the local marketer's home market or segments that global marketers have not catered to.

Strategies available to the local company depend on both external and internal realities. The degree and strength of globalization in an industry will determine the pressure that the local marketer will be under. Internally, the extent to which the company's assets are transferable (as opposed to having only local relevance) will determine the opportunity dimension. Exhibit 6.9 provides a summary of the options to be considered.

In markets where a local company has enjoyed government protection, the liberalization of markets as a result of economic integration or WTO membership may mean hardship for the local company. A **dodger** may have to rethink its entire strategy. With the collapse of Communism and introduction of free-market reforms, the Czech automaker Škoda found its models to be outdated and with little appeal in comparison to Western makes that became available for consumers. The company became part of the largest privatization deal in Eastern Europe in its sale to Volkswagen in 1991. Rather than being merged with VW's operations, Škoda has followed VW's formula for success:

Exhibit 6.9 **Competitive Strategies for Local Companies**

		Competitive assets	
		Customized to home market	Transferable abroad
Pressures to globalize in the industry	High	**Dodger** Sells out to a global player or becomes part of an alliance	**Contender** Upgrades capabilities to match globals in niches
	Low	**Defender** Leverages local assets in segments where globals are weak	**Extender** Expands into markets similar to home base

Source: Adapted from Niraj Dawar and Tony Frost, "Competing with the Giants: Survival Strategies for Local Companies in Emerging Markets," *Harvard Business Review* 77 (March–April 1999): 119–29.

performance-oriented management, cooperative labour relations, utilitarian marketing, and an emphasis on design. It has benefited from wholesale implementation of the latest technologies and working practices and has been able to leapfrog into leaner and more intelligent supply and distribution networks. With sales in 85 countries, Škoda is a leading emerging global brand in one of the most competitive industries.[70]

A **defender** is a local company that has assets that give it a competitive advantage only in its home market. Ideally, this asset is something that an entering global marketer cannot easily replicate; for example, channel penetration, or a product line that has a strong local-customer franchise. Many believed that small local retailers in Latin America would be swept away with the sector's consolidation and the entry of global players such as Carrefour. This has been the case in developed markets, where small retailers have retained only 10 to 20 percent of the consumer packaged-goods market as large retailers have expanded. In Latin America, however, their share has remained at 45–61 percent, because they not only are meeting the needs of emerging consumers, but in many ways are serving them better. For emerging-market consumers, price is not the determining factor of retailer choice; it is the total cost of purchases (including cost of transportation, time, the burden of carrying purchases, and ability to store purchased items).[71] Similarly, while U.S. chocolate companies Mars and Hershey have established only a marginal presence in Latin America with their larger chocolate bars, Arcor and Nacional de Chocolates have maintained their businesses selling bite-sized chocolates that are affordable to low-income consumers, cater to their tastes, and can be bought in remote rural stores.[72]

If a local company's assets are transferable, the company may be able to compete head-on with the established global players worldwide. While Airbus and Boeing have been competing by developing and launching ever-bigger aircraft, the niche for jets that carry 70 to 110 passengers has been left open for others. In the last 10 years, the number of regional jet routes has grown 1,000 percent in Europe and 1,400 percent in North America. Much of that increase has come from commuter airlines that the majors own or contract with to connect smaller markets with their hubs. The **contender** that has taken advantage of the increased demand is Brazil's Embraer, which has challenged the market leader, Canada's Bombardier. When demand took off faster than expected, Bombardier could not meet demand, thus opening the door for Embraer. Currently, Brazil's lower labour costs allow Embraer to undercut its competitor on prices.[73]

An **extender** is able to exploit its success at home as a platform for expansion elsewhere. This calls for markets or segments that are similar in terms of customer preferences;

for example, sizable expatriate communities. The number of Indians in the United States has doubled in the last 10 years to 2.5 million, making them the largest and fastest-growing Asian minority group.[74] This will provide an opportunity for Bollywood to extend its marketing beyond India. Televisa from Mexico, Venevision from Venezuela, and Globo TV in Brazil have emerged as leading producers and marketers of telenovelas, especially to culturally close markets in Europe.[75] Some local marketers have been seasoned in competing against global players and subsequently extended their market presence to new markets abroad. In its home market of the Philippines, Jollibee Foods Corporation challenged McDonald's with its products and services customized to local tastes; it subsequently expanded its presence to other markets with sizable Filipino communities, such as Hong Kong and California. Jollibee now has 24 restaurants operating in seven countries and continues to grow.[76]

Multiple strategies are available to the local marketers when global markets and marketers challenge them. The key is to innovate, rather than imitate, and exploit the inherent competitive advantages over global players.

Summary

Globalization has become one of the most important strategy issues for marketing managers in the last 10 years. Many forces, both external and internal, are driving companies to globalize by expanding and coordinating their participation in foreign markets. A globalized world demands that strategic planning should be formulated not simply with individual countries in mind, but more broadly across markets and national boundaries. Firms that are able to exploit commonalities across borders and do so with competent marketing managers in country organizations are able to see the benefits in their overall performance.[77]

The firm's first decision is whether to internationalize or not. There is no neat formula to provide an answer. Numerous factors will influence the decision, varying by individual company. Rigorous, step-by-step procedures may not always be thought appropriate. Chance encounters and random events will influence the outcome. Also, managements may want to act quickly to exploit opportunities in foreign markets, ahead of objective "proof" that their actions are warranted. Various challenges facing internationalizing Canadian companies include when to internationalize, what markets to enter, whether developing markets should be targeted, what competitive strategies to use, and how to enter the foreign market.

Entering any market, whether domestic or foreign, demands a knowledge of what segments of the market will be most attractive to the firm. The chapter dwells on global aspects, and emphasizes why a knowledge of segmentation is particularly important to Canadian firms seeking international expansion. Also, internationalizing firms still need a clear definition of their business, and this is illustrated by a number of Canadian examples.

Once a decision to internationalize has been taken, four key marketing-related decisions have to be made: (1) the degree of product standardization, (2) the marketing program in addition to the product element, (3) the location and extent of value-adding activities, and (4) the competitive moves to be made. Successful implementation will be enjoyed by those firms who can achieve a balance between local and regional/global concerns. The task of balancing these extremes has various ramifications, notably in the areas of management processes (e.g., personnel exchange between different organizational levels), organizational structure, and organizational culture, as suggested by the phrase, "Think globally, act locally."

Globalization will have considerable impacts on local companies; some of these will benefit, while others will suffer. A "dodger" may have to rethink its entire strategy, and perhaps sell out to an entering global player; a "contender" may exploit its local assets in segments where global companies are weak or in which they have no strategic interest. These local impacts are discussed in the chapter.

Key Terms

concentration (p. 181)
contender (p. 200)
cross-subsidization (p. 195)
defender (p. 200)
diversification (p. 181)
dodger (p. 199)
extender (p. 200)
global account management (p. 198)
glocalization (p. 194)
not-invented-here (NIH) syndrome (p. 196)

Questions for Discussion

1. What is the danger in oversimplifying the globalization approach? Would you agree with the statement that "if something is working in a big way in one market, you'd better assume it will work in all markets"?
2. In addition to teenagers as a global segment, are there possibly other such groups with similar traits and behaviours that have emerged worldwide?
3. Suggest ways in which a global marketer is better equipped to initiate and respond to competitive moves.
4. Why is the assessment of internal resources as early as possible critical in developing a global strategic plan?
5. What are the critical ways in which the multidomestic and global approaches differ in country-market selection?
6. Outline the basic reasons why a company does not necessarily have to be large and have years of experience to succeed in the global marketplace.

Internet Exercises

1. Using the material available at Unilever's website (**http://www.unilever.com**), suggest ways in which Unilever's business groups can take advantage of global and regional strategies due to interconnections in production and marketing.
2. Whirlpool's goal is "a Whirlpool product in every home, everywhere." Using its website at **http://www.whirlpoolcorp.com/about/vision_and_strategy/default.asp,** describe what needs to take place for this vision to become a reality.

Recommended Readings

Arnold, David. Mirage of Global Markets: How Globalizing Companies Can Succeed as Markets Localize. Englewood Cliffs, NJ: Prentice-Hall, 2003.

Birkinshaw, Julian. Entrepreneurship in the Global Firm. Thousand Oaks, CA: Sage Publications, 2000.

The Economist Intelligence Unit. 151 Checklists for Global Management. New York: The Economist Intelligence Unit, 1993.

Feist, William R., James A. Heely, Min H. Lau, and Roy L. Nersesian. Managing a Global Enterprise. Westport, CT: Quorum, 1999.

Grant, Robert M. Contemporary Strategy Analysis: Concepts, Techniques, Applications. Oxford: Blackwell, 2005.

Grant, Robert M., and Kent E. Neupert. Cases in Contemporary Strategy Analysis. Oxford: Blackwell, 1999.

Grosse, Robert E., ed. Thunderbird on Global Business Strategy. New York: Wiley Investment, 2000.

Inkpen, Andrew, and Kannan Ramaswamy. Global Strategy: Creating and Sustaining Advantage across Borders. Oxford: Oxford University Press, 2005.

Irwin, Douglas A. Free Trade under Fire. Princeton, NJ: Princeton University Press, 2002.

Kanter, Rosabeth Moss. World Class. New York: Simon & Schuster, 1995.

Lindsey, Brink. Against the Dead Hand: The Uncertain Struggle for Global Capitalism. New York: John Wiley and Sons, 2001.

Prahalad, C.K., and Yves L. Doz. The Multinational Mission: Balancing Local and Global Vision. New York: Free Press, 1987.

Rosensweig, Jeffrey. Winning the Global Game: A Strategy for Linking People and Profits. New York: Free Press, 1998.

Schwab, Klaus, Michael Porter, and Jeffrey Sachs. The Global Competitiveness Report 2001–2002. Oxford: Oxford University Press, 2002.

Scott, Allen J. Regions and the World Economy: The Coming Shape of Global Production, Competition, and Political Order. Oxford: Oxford University Press, 2000.

Soros, George. George Soros on Globalization. New York: Public Affairs, 2002.

Stiglitz, Joseph E. Globalization and Its Discontents. New York: W.W. Norton & Co., 2002.

Notes

1. Theodore Levitt, *The Marketing Imagination* (New York: Free Press, 1983), 20–49.
2. Michael R. Czinkota and Ilkka A. Ronkainen, "A Forecast of Globalization, International Business and Trade: Report from a Delphi Study," *Journal of World Business* 40 (Winter 2005): 111–23.
3. Jonathan Sprague, "China's Manufacturing Beachhead," *Fortune*, October 28, 2002, I192A–J.
4. Pankaj Ghemawat, "Regional Strategies for Global Leadership," *Harvard Business Review* 83 (December 2005): 98–108.
5. Bruce Greenwald and Judd Kahn, "All Strategy is Local," *Harvard Business Review* 83 (September 2005): 94–107.
6. Martine Spence and Dave Crick, "A Comparative Investigation into the Internationalization of Canadian and UK High-Tech SMEs," *International Marketing Review* 23, no. 5 (2006): 524–48.
7. Spence and Crick, op. cit.
8. Yadong Luo and Mike W Peng, "Learning to Compete in a Transition Economy: Experience, Environment and Performance," *Journal of International Business Studies* 30, no. 2 (1999): 269–95.
9. Luo and Peng, op. cit.
10. J. Bell, D. Crick, and S. Young, "Small firm Internationalization and Business Strategy: An Exploratory Study of 'Knowledge-Intensive" and 'Traditional' Manufacturing Firms in the UK," *International Small Business Journal* 22, no. 1 (2004): 23–56.
11. S. Andersson, "The Internationalization of the Firm from an Entrepreneurial Perspective," *International Studies of Management and Organization* 30, no. 1 (2000): 63–92.
12. S.T. Cavusgil, "On the Internationalization Process of Firms," *European Research* 8 (1980): 273–81.
13. M.V. Jones, "The Internationalization of Small High Technology firms," *Journal of International Marketing* 7, no. 4 (1999): 15–41.
14. Myung-Su Chae and John S. Hill, "Determinants and Benefits of Global Strategic Planning Formality," *International Marketing Review* 17, no. 6 (2000): 538–62.
15. L. Melin, "Internationalization as a Strategy Process," *Strategic Management Journal* 13 (1992): 99–118.
16. O. Anderson, "Internationalization and Market Entry Mode," *Management International Review* 37, no. 2 (1997): 27–42.
17. Stephen S. Poloz, "Export Sectors Showing Massive Growth Divergence," *Exportwise*, (Summer 2007): 31.
18. James F. Foley, *The Global Entrepreneur: Taking Your Business International* (Chicago: Dearborn Publishing, 1999), 11–21.
19. "Nokia Up in 2005," *Telecommworldwide*, November 22, 2005, 1.
20. J. Johanson and J.-E. Vahlne, "The Mechanism of Internationalization," *International Marketing Review* 7, no. 4 (1990): 11–24.
21. C. Samuel Craig and Susan P. Douglas, "Configural Advantage in Global Markets," *Journal of International Marketing* 8, no. 1 (2000): 6–26.
22. Michael E. Porter, *Competitive Strategy: Techniques for Analyzing Industries and Competitors* (New York: Free Press, 1998), chap. 1.
23. "Europe's Car Makers Expect Tidy Profits," *The Wall Street Journal*, January 27, 2000, A16.
24. George S. Yip, *Total Global Strategy II* (Upper Saddle River, NJ: Prentice Hall, 2002), chap. 10.
25. The models referred to are GE/McKinsey, Shell International, and A.D. Little portfolio models.
26. "Company CV: Cereal Partners Worldwide," *Marketing*, November 29, 2001, 50. See also **http://www.generalmills.com/corporate/company/joint_ventures.aspx.**
27. "Tissue Titans Target Globally with Key Brands," *Advertising Age*, December 20, 1999, 4.
28. Richard Tomlinson, "Europe's New Computer Game," *Fortune*, February 21, 2000, 219–24.
29. Alan M. Rugman and Simon Collinson, "Multinational Enterprises in the New Europe: Are They Really Global?" *Organizational Dynamics* 34, no. 3 (2005): 258–72.
30. The Business Development Bank of Canada, "Doing Business in Emerging Markets," **http://www.bdc.ca/en/my_projects** (accessed August 8, 2007).
31. Sangmoon Park and Zong-Tae Bae, "New Venture Strategies in a Developing Country: Identifying a Typology and Examining Growth Patterns through Case Studies," *Journal of Business Venturing* 19, no. 1 (2004): 81–105.
32. The Business Development Bank of Canada, "Doing Business in Emerging Markets," **http://www.bdc.ca/en/my_projects** (accessed August 8, 2007).
33. John A. Parnell, "Generic Strategies after Two Decades: A Reconceptualization of Competitive Strategy," *Management Decision* 44, no. 8 (2006): 1139–54.
34. M.J. Leiblein, "The Choice of Organizational Governance Form and Performance: Predictions from Transaction Cost, Resource-Based, and Real Options," *Journal of Management* 29 (2003): 937–61.
35. Parnell, op. cit.
36. Terry Hill, *Manufacturing Strategy: Text and Cases*, 3rd ed. (Boston: McGraw-Hill Irwin, 1999).
37. Hill, op. cit.
38. "Entrepreneur Profiles—Dahl Brothers Canada Ltd.," *National Post*, June 18, 2006.
39. Toby Herscovitch, "Exporting Success Stories: Minaean International Corporation," *Exportwise*, Summer, 2007, 4.
40. Sylvie Chetty and Colin Campbell-Hunt, "Explosive International Growth and Problems of Success amongst Small to Medium-sized Firms," *International Small Business Journal* 21, no. 1 (2003): 5–27.
41. Saeed Samiee and Kendall Roth, "The Influence of Global Marketing Standardization on Performance," *Journal of Marketing* 56 (April 1992): 1–17.
42. "Euroteen Market Grabs U.S. Attention," *Marketing News*, October 22, 2001, 15.
43. "The American Connection," *The Washington Post*, May 25, 2002, E1–E2.
44. Peter N. Child, Suzanne Heywood, and Michael Kliger, "Do Retail Brands Travel?" *The McKinsey Quarterly* 38, no. 1 (2002): 73–77.
45. Aruna Chandra and John K. Ryans, "Why India Now?" *Marketing Management*, March/April 2002, 43–45.
46. C.K. Prahalad and Stuart L. Hart, "The Fortune at the Bottom of the Pyramid," *Strategy and Business* 7 (1st quarter, 2002): 35–47.
47. Dennis Jones and Sandi Jones, "Construction Services: Building Bridges ... and Everything Else," *Exportwise*, Summer, 2005.
48. "Computing's New Shape," *The Economist*, November 23, 2002, 11–12.
49. Pascal Cagni, "Think Global, Act European," *Developments in Strategy and Business*, August 30, 2004, **http://www.strategy-business.com/export/export.php? article_id=4510703.**
50. Pankaj Ghemawat, "Regional Strategies for Global Leadership," *Harvard Business Review* 83 (December 2005): 98–108.
51. "Shania Reigns," *Time*, December 9, 2002, 80–85.
52. See http://www.nokia.com/A402785.
53. Larry Greenemeier, "Offshore Outsourcing Grows to Global Proportions," *Information Week*, February 2002, 56–58.
54. "Philips Electronics to Make China One of Three Big Research Centers," *The Wall Street Journal*, December 20, 2002, B4.

55. W. Chan Kim and R. A. Mauborgne, "Becoming an Effective Global Competitor," *Journal of Business Strategy* 8 (January–February 1988): 33–37.

56. Gary Hamel and C. K. Prahalad, "Do You Really Have a Global Strategy?" *Harvard Business Review* 63 (July–August 1985): 75–82.

57. "Nokia Widens Lead in Wireless Market While Motorola, Ericsson Fall Back," *The Wall Street Journal*, February 8, 2000, B8.

58. Andreas F. Grein, C. Samuel Craig, and Hirokazu Takada, "Integration and Responsiveness: Marketing Strategies of Japanese and European Automobile Manufacturers," *Journal of International Marketing* 9, no. 2 (2001): 19–50.

59. James A. Gingrich, "Five Rules for Winning Emerging Market Consumers," *Strategy and Business* 4 (2nd quarter, 1999): 19–33.

60. "Does Globalization Have Staying Power?" *Marketing Management*, March/April 2002, 18–23.

61. Kamran Kashani, "Beware the Pitfalls of Global Marketing," *Harvard Business Review* 67 (September–October 1989): 91–98.

62. George S. Yip, Pierre M. Loewe, and Michael Y. Yoshino, "How to Take Your Company to the Global Market," *Columbia Journal of World Business* 23 (Winter 1988): 28–40.

63. George S. Yip and Tammy L. Madsen, "Global Account Management: The New Frontier in Relationship Marketing," *International Marketing Review* 13, no. 3 (1996): 24–42.

64. David B. Montgomery and George S. Yip, "The Challenge of Global Customer Management," *Marketing Management*, Winter 2000, 22–29.

65. Julian Birkinshaw, "Global Account Management: New Structures, New Tasks," *FT Mastering Management*, 2001, available at **http://www.ftmastering.com/mmo/mmo05_2.htm.**

66. John A. Quelch and Helen Bloom, "Ten Steps to Global Human Resources Strategy," *Strategy and Business* 4 (1st quarter, 1999): 18–29.

67. "Teaming with Bright Ideas," *The Economist*, January 19, 2006, 5–6; "Inculcating Culture," *The Economist*, January 19, 2006, 6; Philip Evans and Bob Wolf, "Collaboration Rules," *Harvard Business* Review 83 (July–August 2005): 96–104; and Gerard Fairtlough, *The Three Ways of Getting Things Done* (London: Triarchy Press, 2005), chap. 3, sec. 3.

68. This section draws from Niraj Dawar and Tony Frost, "Competing with the Giants: Survival Strategies for Local Companies in Emerging Markets," *Harvard Business Review* 77 (March–April 1999): 119–29; and Güliz Ger, "Localizing in the Global Village: Local Firms Competing in Global Markets," *California Management Review* 41 (Summer 1999): 64–83.

69. John H. Roberts, "Defensive Marketing: How a Strong Incumbent Can Protect Its Position," *Harvard Business Review* 83 (November 2005): 150–63.

70. Jonathan Ledgard, "Škoda Leaps to Market," *Strategy and Business* 10 (Fall 2005): 1–12.

71. Guillermo D'Andrea, E. Alejandro Stengel, and Anne Goebel-Krstelj, "6 Truths About Emerging-Market Consumers," *Strategy and Business* 10 (Spring 2004): 59–69.

72. Alonso Martinez, Ivan De Souza, and Francis Liu, "Multinationals vs. Multilatinas," *Strategy and Business* 9 (Fall 2003): 56–67.

73. "The Little Aircraft Company That Could," *Fortune*, November 14, 2005, 201–8.

74. "Chasing Desi Dollars," *Time Inside Business*, August 2005, A22–A24.

75. Ibsen Martínez, "Romancing the Globe," *Foreign Policy*, November/December 2005, 48–56.

76. See **http://www.jollibee.com.ph/corporate/international.htm.**

77. Sharon O'Donnell and Insik Jeong, "Marketing Standardization within Global Industries," *International Marketing Review* 17, no. 1 (2000): 19–33.

Chapter 7

Global Marketing Research

The Global MARKETPLACE 7.1

The Toasted Deli Sandwich

McDonald's has been operating in Canada since 1967. In that year the company opened its first restaurant outside of the U.S. with the launch of its Richmond, British Columbia, outlet. McDonald's restaurants now number in excess of 1,300 in Canada, and it has evolved into a national chain of corporate and franchise restaurants employing more than 77,000 Canadians. The company's restaurants are visited by millions of consumers every day. McDonald's is constantly striving to introduce new and innovative products and maintain a close connection with its customers. To achieve this, the firm relies on its marketing research department.

Senior executives at McDonald's were interested in introducing a new product to the Canadian market to capitalize on the deli-sandwich category, which had been identified as a $2-billion market segment and one with considerable growth potential. The toasted deli sandwich had been tested in the U.S. market for four years but had not yet been launched nationwide. In order to have some assurance that the product would be well received in the Canadian market, it was necessary to undertake market research. The task fell to Ailene MacDougall, Senior Director, Strategic Planning and Consumer/Business Insights for McDonald's Restaurants of Canada. She explained that the Canadian marketing research group made use of both secondary and primary data to analyze the potential of the product in the Canadian market.

Ailene and her staff followed a systematic process in evaluating the potential for this product. The process involved, first, market opportunity identification and validation of the product format to ensure that the new product would meet the quality standards and the taste and flavour preferences of Canadian consumers. The marketing research team next conducted a price-sensitivity analysis and an operations test to ensure that the product would actually work in the company's restaurants. An advertising and sales test was undertaken as the next step, and this included in-restaurant consumer research to ensure that the product would be successful in Canada.

The Canadian marketing research team in conducting its evaluation of this new product was able to utilize existing protocols and methodologies developed by the company's global market research team. These are fairly standardized across national markets. In addition, the toasted deli sandwich had been previously launched in two other major markets—Australia and the U.K.—and the research from these national markets was also made available to the Canadian team in their market evaluation work. Ailene also points out that with the successful launch of the toasted deli sandwich in Canada, her team's research findings are now being disseminated to teams in other parts of the world—including the U.S. marketing research at McDonald's emphasizes the synthesis of market knowledge from around the world and the sharing and exchange of that knowledge between research teams working in various national markets.

Source: Personal interview with Ailene MacDougall, Senior Director, Strategic Planning and Consumer/Business Insights for McDonald's Restaurants of Canada, conducted March 16, 2007.

Even though most managers recognize the need for domestic marketing research, the single most important cause of failure in the global marketplace is insufficient preparation and information. Major mistakes often occur because the firm and its managers do not have an adequate understanding of the business environment. Hindsight, however, does not lead to an automatic increase in global marketing research. Many firms either do not believe that global market research is worthwhile or they face labour and resource bottlenecks that impede such research. The latter is particularly true of small and medium-sized enterprises in Canada. The increase in global marketing practice is also not reflected in the orientation of the articles published in key research journals.[1] Yet building a good knowledge base is a key condition for subsequent marketing success abroad. To do so, one needs to accumulate data and information through research. Two basic forms of research are available to the firm: **primary research**, where data are collected for specific research purposes, and **secondary research**, where data that have already been collected are used. This chapter will first present a definition of global marketing research and then discuss how it differs from purely domestic research activities. The process of conducting global marketing research is then discussed in some detail. A step-by-step approach is presented, one which elaborates on key issues such as definition of the research problem, assessment of information needs, data collection, and analysis. Issues related to the management of global research projects are also discussed in this chapter. The chapter concludes with an appendix that introduces several of the more common data analysis techniques used in global marketing research.

Marketing Research Defined

The American Marketing Association (AMA) defines marketing research as "the function that links the consumer, customer, and public to the marketer through information—information used to identify and define marketing opportunities and problems; generate, refine, and evaluate marketing actions; monitor marketing performance; and improve understanding of marketing as a process. Marketing research specifies the information required to address these issues, designs the method for collecting information, manages and implements the data collection process, analyzes the results, and communicates the findings and their implications."[2] This very broad statement highlights the fact that research is the link between marketer and market, without which marketing cannot function. It also emphasizes the fact that marketing actions need to be monitored and outlines the key steps of the research process.

A more recent definition states that marketing research is the "systematic and objective identification, collection, analysis, and dissemination of information for the purpose of improving decision making related to the identification and solution of problems and opportunities in marketing."[3] This statement is more specific to research activities for several reasons: It highlights the need for systematic work, indicating that research should be the result of planned and organized activity rather than coincidence. It stresses the need for objectivity and information, reducing the roles of bias, emotion, and subjective judgment. Finally, it addresses the need for the information to relate to specific problems. Marketing research cannot take place in a void; rather, it must have a business purpose.

Global Marketing Research

Global marketing research may be defined as research that spans geographic borders and involves respondents and researchers from different countries and cultures. Global marketing research will generally fall into one of the following categories:

- research that involves collecting data and making inferences in two or more countries within the context of the same project
- research on a single country conducted by a researcher from another country with a view to understanding similarities and differences vis-à-vis the researcher's home market
- research that involves work on immigrant populations to better understand attitudes and behaviours when people from one culture move to another culture[4]

The tools and techniques of global marketing research are said by some to be exactly the same as those of domestic marketing research, and only the environment differs. However, the environment is precisely what determines how well the tools, techniques, and concepts apply to the international market. Although the objectives of marketing research may be the same, the execution of global marketing research may differ substantially from the process of domestic research. As a result, entirely new tools and techniques may need to be developed. Four factors serve to differentiate global marketing research from purely domestic marketing research (Exhibit 7.1). Global marketing research must take into consideration new parameters, new environments, an increase in the number of factors involved in the analysis, and a broader definition of competition.

New Parameters

In crossing national borders, a firm encounters parameters not found in domestic marketing. Examples include duties, foreign currencies and changes in their value, global logistics, international documentation, and port facilities. A firm that has done business only domestically will have had little or no prior experience with these requirements and conditions. Information about each of them must be obtained in order for management to make appropriate business decisions. New parameters also emerge because of differing modes of operating internationally. For example, a firm can export, it can license its products, it can engage in a joint venture, or it can carry out foreign direct investment.

New Environments

When deciding to go international in its marketing activities, a firm exposes itself to an unfamiliar environment. Many of the assumptions on which the firm was founded and on which its domestic activities were based may not hold true in foreign markets. A company

Exhibit 7.1 **Factors Unique to Global Marketing Research**

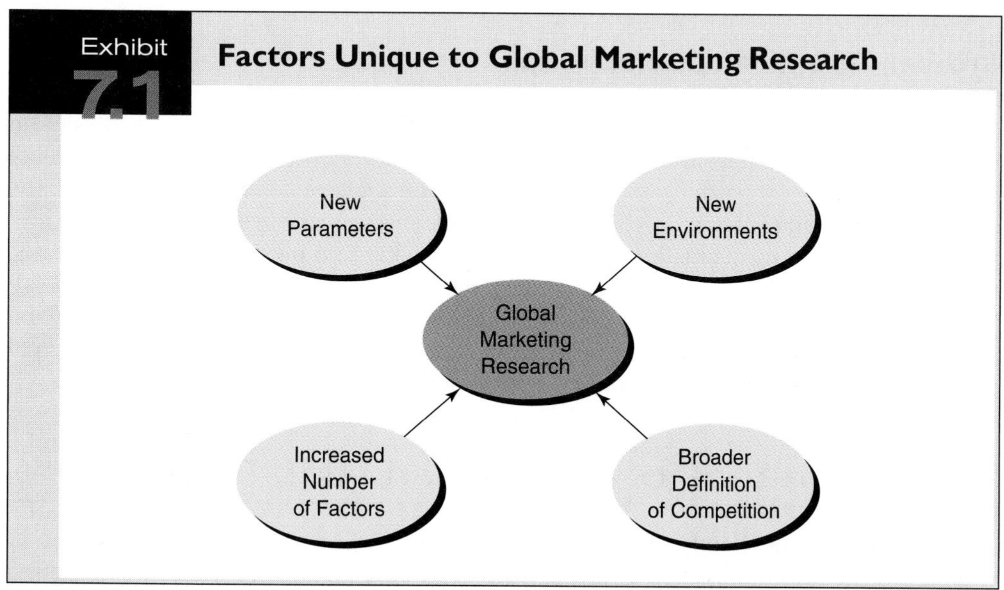

such as Tim Hortons, for example, that has achieved phenomenal success in the Canadian market by leveraging the company's association with a legendary Canadian hockey player may have some difficulty translating this success into foreign markets such as the U.S. Firms need to learn about the culture of the host country, understand its political system, determine its stability, and appreciate the differences in societal structures and language. In addition, they must fully comprehend pertinent legal and regulatory issues in the host country to avoid operating contrary to local legislation. For example, Edmonton-based CV Technologies, the marketer of COLD-fX, has had to modify its promotional message when doing business in the U.S. Health Canada has allowed the manufacturer of cold remedies to make promotional statements to the effect that COLD-fX "helps reduce the frequency, severity, and duration of cold and flu symptoms by boosting the immune system." The U.S. Food and Drug Administration, however, has not allowed the company to make therapeutic claims, forcing the company to adjust its promotional strategy. In the U.S., the company's promotional material states—*This product is not intended to diagnose, treat, cure, or prevent disease.... In accordance with U.S. regulations, this product is not intended to treat, cure, or prevent upper respiratory infections due to cold or influenza-like viruses.*[5] Developing an understanding of the differences in the regulatory environments between Canada and the U.S. has been critical to the launch of COLD-fX in the United States.

Firms should also incorporate the technological level of the society in the marketing plan and understand the economic environment. In short, all the assumptions formulated over the years in the domestic market must be re-evaluated. This crucial point has often been neglected because most managers were born into the environment of their domestic operations and have subconsciously learned to understand the constraints and opportunities of their business activities. The process is analogous to learning one's native language. Being born to a language makes speaking it seem easy. Only in attempting to learn a foreign language do we begin to appreciate the complex structure of languages, the need for rules, and the existence of different patterns. Such errors can be costly for the firm, as KFC discovered when it entered the Japanese markets using its drive-through concept. Although the concept was well established in the U.S., at the time of the launch most Japanese consumers did not own cars, and the drive-through restaurants failed. Failure to research the level of economic development of the host country may well prove problematic for the global marketer.

Number of Factors Involved

Marketing globally means entering into more than one market. As a result, the number of changing dimensions increases exponentially. Even if every dimension is understood, management must also appreciate the interaction between them. Because of the sheer number of factors, coordination of the interaction becomes increasingly difficult. The marketing research process can help management with this undertaking.

Broader Definition of Competition

By entering the global market, the firm exposes itself to a much greater variety of competition than existed in the domestic market. For example, when expanding the analysis of an island's food production from a local to an international level, fishery products compete not only with other fishery products but also with meat or even vegetarian substitutes. Similarly, firms that offer labour-saving devices in the domestic marketplace may suddenly face competition from cheap manual labour abroad. Therefore, the firm must, on an ongoing basis, determine the breadth of the competition, track the competitive activities, and, finally, evaluate the actual and potential impact on its own operations. Environmental scanning may be used by the firm to monitor the competitive landscape as well as other changes in external conditions that may affect the company's operation (see In More Detail 7.1).

The Importance of Global Marketing Research

To serve a market efficiently, firms must learn what customers want, why they want it, and how to go about filling their needs. To enter a foreign market without conducting marketing research places firms, their assets, and their entire operation at risk. Even

In More Detail 7.1

ENVIRONMENTAL SCANNING

Any changes in the business environment, whether domestic or foreign, may have serious repercussions on the marketing activities of the firm. Corporations therefore should understand the necessity for tracking new developments and obtaining continuous updates. To carry out this task, some large multinational organizations have formed environmental scanning groups. Environmental scanning activities are useful to continuously receive information on political, social, and economic affairs internationally; on changes of attitudes held by public institutions and private citizens; and on possible upcoming alterations in international markets.

The precision required for environmental scanning varies with its purpose. Whether the information is to be used for mind stretching or for budgeting, for example, must be taken into account when constructing the framework and variables that will enter the scanning process. The more immediate and precise the exercise is to be in its application within the corporation, the greater the need for detailed information. At the same time, such heightened precision may lessen the utility of environmental scanning for the strategic corporate purpose, which is more long-term in its orientation.

Environmental scanning can be performed in various ways. One method consists of obtaining factual input regarding many variables. For example, international organizations such as the World Bank, the OECD, and the United Nations collect, evaluate, and adjust data on a wide variety of demographic, social, and economic characteristics of foreign countries. Estimates for all countries of the world are developed, particularly on economic variables such as labour force statistics, GDP, and income statistics, but also on health and nutrition variables.

Frequently, corporations believe that such factual data alone are insufficient for their information needs. Particularly for forecasting future developments, other methods are used to capture underlying dimensions of social change. One significant method is **content analysis**. This technique investigates the content of communication in a society and entails literally counting the number of times preselected words, themes, symbols, or pictures appear in a given medium. It can be used productively in global marketing to monitor the social, economic, cultural, and technological environment in which the marketing organization is operating. Corporations can use content analysis to pinpoint upcoming changes in their line of business, as well as new opportunities, by attempting to identify trendsetting events. For example, the Alaska oil spill by the tanker *Exxon Valdez* resulted in entirely new international concern about environmental protection and safety, reaching far beyond the incident itself.

Environmental scanning is conducted by a variety of groups within and outside the corporation. Frequently, a small corporate staff at headquarters coordinates the information flow. In addition, subsidiary staff can be used to provide occasional intelligence reports. Groups of volunteers are also assembled to gather and analyze information worldwide and feed individual analyses back to corporate headquarters, where they can be used to form the "big picture."

though most firms recognize the need for domestic marketing research, this need is not fully understood for global marketing activities. Often, decisions concerning entry and expansion in overseas markets and the selection and appointment of distributors are made after a cursory subjective assessment of the situation. The research done is less rigorous, less formal, and less quantitative than for domestic marketing activities. Many business executives appear to view foreign market research as relatively unimportant.

As illustrated in Exhibit 7.2, global marketing research is important to firms for several reasons:[6]

1. *Provides sensitivity to geographic differences.* Firms that take the time to conduct global marketing research reduce the potential for costly errors due to geographic insensitivity. When Microsoft launched Windows 95 in India, for example, it did not show the disputed Jammu-Kashmir region as part of India in its colour-coded map of the area. This map was used in the company's promotional materials. India and Pakistan have fought several wars over the Jammu-Kashmir region, including the Indo-Pakistan wars of 1965 and 1971 and the Kargil war of 1999.

   The Indian government banned the sale of Windows 95 across India in retaliation for what they viewed as Microsoft's insult. The company's sales in India declined significantly as a result. When Office 97 was launched, however, Microsoft eliminated the colour coding and the company sold 100,000 copies of the product.

The Global MARKETPLACE 7.2

Welcoming China to Global Marketing Research

China's entry into the World Trade Organization was a major step in the transition from a planned economy to a free market system. However, China did not drop its planned approach to the economy overnight—rather, it has been moving steadily toward a free market system for over a decade. During this period, an indigenous marketing research industry also developed in response to industries' need to understand consumers.

Marketing research firms have proliferated all over China, with the epicentre of research activity in Guangzhou. In 1985, Guangzhou Soft Science Co. set up a marketing department with the help of the Chinese government. From this department, Guangzhou Market Research Co. (GMR), China's first marketing research firm, emerged in 1988.

GMR served as the starting point and model for future marketing research firms. Ex-employees of GMR started new firms, such as South China Marketing Research Co. Ltd., Far-East Marketing Research Co., East Marketing Research Co. Ltd., Guangdong General Marketing Research Ltd., and Market Insight. The birth of GMR and its offspring would not have been possible without the aid of U.S. firm Procter & Gamble (P&G). Support from P&G came in several forms: technology (both software and hardware), professional training, and revenue (P&G was the source of more than 90 percent of GMR's revenues in the early 1990s).

Today, the Chinese marketing research industry has grown to include about 400 firms. While the industry has expanded immensely, most of the firms are small, with almost half of them bringing in annual revenues between $10,000 and $50,000. Total research revenue for 2000 was $181 million, with the majority of projects coming from state-sponsored (government or university) firms.

With the growing sophistication of the Chinese consumer, companies must increasingly rely on marketing research in order to obtain up-to-date information. International firms, eager to appeal to China's massive consumer population, will look to its marketing research sector for insight into local traditions and trends. This will provide an opportunity for rapid growth of China's competitive marketing research industry. The presence of international marketing research firms, such as Gallup and ACNielsen, brings capital and new research techniques to the region. Today, the Chinese marketing research industry may be considered small by world standards. Yet, given sufficiently trained and supported local talent combined with low wages, Chinese marketing research has the potential to grow into a global competitor.

Source: Adapted from Barton Lee, Soumya Saklani, and David Tatterson, "Growing in Guangzhou," *Marketing News*, American Marketing Association, June 10, 2002, 12. Adapted with permission from the American Marketing Association.

2. *Provides an understanding of cultural change.* Global marketing research can assist the firm in identifying and better understanding trends in the structure of consumption, brand choices, lifestyle, and media influences. Particularly in large emerging markets such as India and China, inter-country comparisons can alert the global marketer to significant trends. For example, the speed with which Chinese consumers are abandoning their traditional bicycles in favour of cars has caught many Western auto executives off guard.
3. *Identifies appropriate advertising appeals.* Global marketing research can assist the company in identifying advertising appeals that would best position its products in foreign markets. Coke's research in Brazil, for example, helped that company to identify the female kangaroo as the most effective advertising device to reach Brazilian women. The company's research project found that although there are no kangaroos in Brazil, the animals tested well with women—representing freedom yet responsibility and caring for children. Coke's "Mom knows everything" ad campaign featured a female kangaroo wearing sunglasses and carrying cans of Coke instead of a baby. The research project cost Coke $800,000. Women in Brazil now represent 80 percent of the company's $3.5 billion in sales in that country.
4. *Assesses translation errors.* Global marketing research can assist the company in avoiding translation errors. Proctor and Gamble (P&G) uncovered an unusual twist to the problem of poor translation when it entered the Eastern European market. The company translated its detergent product labels into Polish and Czech in order to adapt to the local market.

Exhibit 7.2 **Importance of Global Marketing Research**

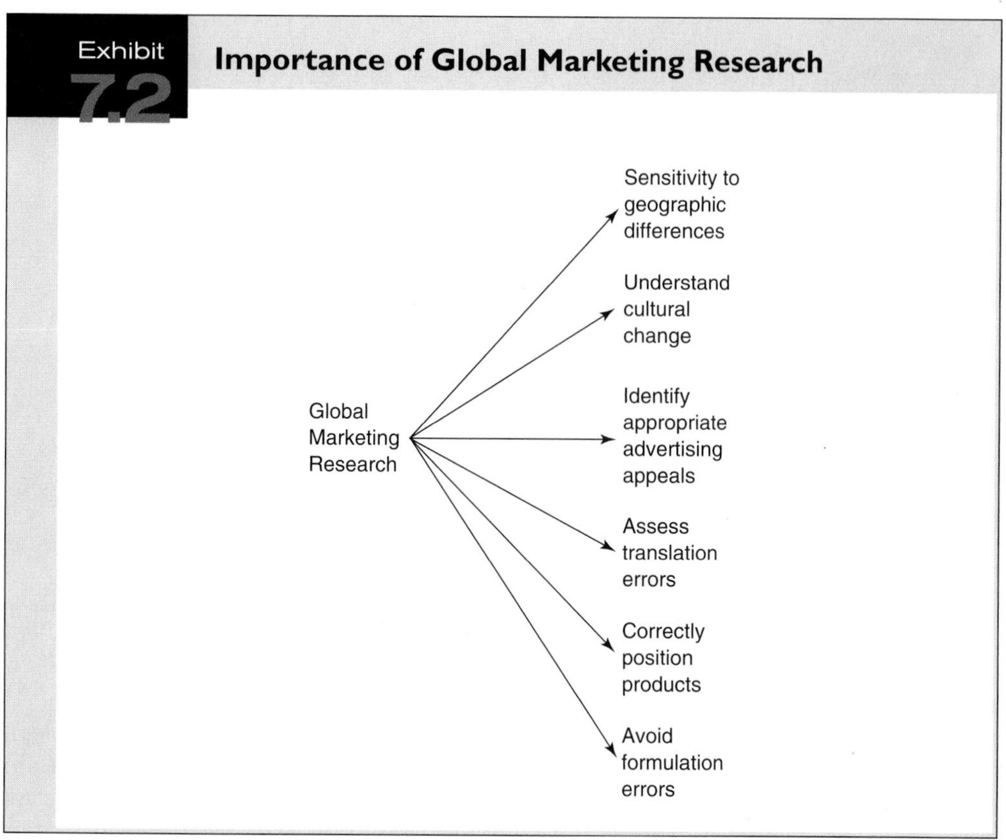

Consumer reaction was, however, negative as the company's translation efforts were viewed as a ploy to pass P&G off as an Eastern European company. Subsequent research revealed that consumers would react more favourably to labels written in imperfect Polish, as it would demonstrate that the company was trying to fit in. P&G's translation was viewed as too perfect! Without systematic research, P&G, a U.S. company, would perhaps never have discovered the reason for its poor performance in Eastern Europe.

5. *Correctly positions new products.* Companies can use global marketing research to correctly position new products in foreign markets. PepsiCo launched its Frito-Lay potato chips in China. The company soon discovered, however, that consumer reaction to the product was less than enthusiastic. Sales were well below expectation, and the summer months were found to be particularly bad. The company's research subsequently found that in China, fried foods are associated with *yang,* which is believed to generate body heat. PepsiCo decided, based on the research results, to re-position the product. It introduced a cool lemon variety and used pastel-coloured packaging to reflect *yin,* a cool feeling. Sales of the product subsequently recovered.
6. *Avoids formulation errors.* In adapting products to international markets, research can assist the company in avoiding formulation errors. H.J. Heinz Company, for example, discovered this when it was planning the introduction of its oat-based baby food in China. The company's internal research found that Chinese people were not familiar with oats and therefore a product formulated with this ingredient would not likely be successful. Acting on the research findings, Heinz re-formulated the product using whitebait (a small fish that is a staple of the Chinese diet) and oats. The product was highly successful in the Chinese market because Heinz took the time to assess the need for re-formulation.

The Process of Global Marketing Research

The process of conducting global marketing research may be divided into six major steps, as illustrated in Exhibit 7.3. The steps are discussed in detail below.

Exhibit 7.3
The Process of Global Marketing Research
Step1: Define the Research Problem
Step 2: Determine Information Needs
Step 3: Develop Research Design
Step 4: Data Collection
Step 5: Data Analysis
Step 6: Presentation of Research Findings

Define the Research Problem

Global marketing research is driven by the company's need to solve a business problem. Such business problems may include the observation that the company's sales in Latin America have been declining consistently over the last year, or that despite significant advertising expenditures in Eastern Europe the firm's market share has not increased as forecasted. The company's senior managers are often keenly aware of the business problems and generally have no difficulty articulating them and discussing their impact on the company's bottom line. The job of the global marketing researcher is to translate the firm's business problems into research questions that are amenable to analysis. Specific research questions must be formulated to determine precisely the information that is sought. The following are examples of such research questions:

- What is the market potential for our furniture in Indonesia?
- How much does the typical Nigerian consumer spend on soft drinks?
- What will happen to demand in Brazil if we raise our product price along monthly inflation levels?
- What effect will a new type of packaging have on our "green" consumers in Germany, France, and England?

Only when information requirements are determined as precisely as possible will the researcher be able to develop a research program that will deliver a useful product. In essence, global marketing research must be seen as an aid to the firm's decision-making process as it seeks to satisfy customer needs in its markets around the world.

Determine the Information Needs

Precisely defined research questions will facilitate the second step in the process of global marketing research, which is the determination of information needs. Information will be required to support any decision the firm makes to solve its problems in global markets. These decisions may be classified as being either strategic or tactical. Strategic decisions are high-level corporate decisions that affect the long-term direction of the firm. In global marketing, strategic decisions would include the following:

- which countries to enter
- how those countries should be entered (that is, what institutional methods should be used)
- what product market opportunities should be pursued in the foreign countries targeted

The global marketer may also need information to support the firm's tactical decisions. Tactical decisions are more operational and short-term in nature and would relate to areas such as changes in advertising copy, product adaptation to meet the needs of specific geographic market segments, or the use of specific sales promotion techniques to stimulate sales in a particular market.

Develop the Research Design

The development of the research design for the global marketing research project involves a consideration of several factors.

Unit of Analysis

In designing the research project, the global market researcher must take into consideration the unit of analysis. The geographic scope of the project is an important consideration here, as depending on the nature of the project it may be focused at the level of an individual country, at the level of a region such as the EU or NAFTA, or at the worldwide level. Increased geographic scope implies increased complexity, time, and cost for the firm. At this stage of the process, the researcher also has to consider whether the project will attempt to generate data on all customers or business organizations existing in the target geographic unit, or whether it will focus more tightly on a subgroup of these. The researcher also has the option to define these subgroups in a number of ways, such as consumption patterns, income levels, and so on, depending on the relevance to the research project and the business problem being addressed.

Information Sources

As part of the research design, the global marketing researcher must also consider the sources of information that may be tapped to answer the research questions that are to be addressed. The firm may make use of its own prior research or that generated by academic institutions and consultants, whether secondary data or primary data.

Prior Research

Prior research published by academics may be useful to the firm in developing a conceptual framework to tackle its own real world problem. Such research may well serve to highlight and identify key variables that need to be considered in the firm's analysis. In the case of large multinational corporations, the firm may have already undertaken or sponsored research on another country market or product line that may be relevant to the research problem currently at hand. The company may in fact have already developed a decision support system that may contain useful information and analyses (see In More Detail 7.2).

Secondary Data

The global marketing researcher should also consider the need for secondary data, that is, data that have already been collected for some other purpose but are relevant to addressing the firm's current research problem. The firm may obtain secondary data from a number of sources:

a) *Governments.* Of all data sources, governments typically have the greatest variety of data available. The information provided by governments addresses either macro or micro issues or offers specific data services. Macro information includes population trends, general trade flows between countries, and world agricultural production. Micro information includes materials on specific industries in a country, their growth prospects, and their foreign trade activities. Specific data services might provide custom-tailored information responding to the detailed needs of a firm. Alternatively, some data services may concentrate on a specific geographic region.

   Most countries have a wide array of national and international trade data available. Increasingly these data are available on the Internet, which makes them much more current than ever before. Closer collaboration between governmental statistical agencies also

In More Detail 7.2

DECISION SUPPORT SYSTEMS

Many organizations have data needs going beyond specific global marketing research projects. Most of the time, daily decisions must be made, and there is neither time nor money for special research. An information system already in place is needed to provide the decision maker with basic data for most ongoing decisions. Corporations have responded by developing marketing decision support systems. Defined as "an integrated system of data, statistical analysis, modeling, and display formats using computer hardware and software technology," such a system serves as a mechanism to coordinate the flow of information to corporate managers for decision-making purposes.[7]

To be useful to the decision maker, the system needs various attributes. First, the information must be *relevant*. The data gathered must have meaning for the manager's decision-making process. Only rarely can corporations afford to spend large amounts of money on information that is simply "nice to know." Second, the information must be *timely*. It is of little benefit to the manager if decision information help that is needed today does not become available until a month from now. To be of use to the international decision maker, the system must therefore feed from a variety of international sources and be updated frequently. For multinational corporations, this means a real-time linkage between international subsidiaries and a broad-based ongoing data input operation.

Third, information must be *flexible*—that is, it must be available in the forms needed by management. A marketing decision support system must therefore permit manipulation of the format and combining of the data. Consequently, great effort must be expended to make diverse international data compatible with and comparable to each other. Fourth, information contained in the system must be *accurate*. This attribute is particularly relevant in the international field because information quickly becomes outdated as a result of major changes. Obviously, a system is of no value if it provides incorrect information that leads to poor decisions. Fifth, the system's information bank must be reasonably *exhaustive*. Because of the interrelationship between variables, factors that may influence a particular decision must be appropriately represented in the information system. This means that the marketing decision support system must be based on a broad variety of factors. Finally, to be useful to managers, the system must be *convenient*, both to use and to access. Systems that are cumbersome and time-consuming to reach and to use will not be used enough to justify corporate expenditures to build and maintain them.

makes the data more accurate and reliable, since it is now much easier to compare data such as bilateral exports and imports to each other. These information sources are often available at embassies and consulates, whose mission includes the enhancement of trade activities. The commercial counsellor or commercial attaché can provide the information available from these sources. Statistics Canada is the government department primarily responsible for the collection and dissemination of data on the Canadian economy, including information on international trade. Departments such as Industry Canada, the Department of Foreign Affairs and International Trade, as well as Agriculture and Agri-Food Canada provide data and analysis of specific foreign markets and sectors. The Canadian Trade Commissioner Service (CTCS), part of International Trade Canada, maintains offices in over 140 cities around the world. These offices are staffed with trade professionals who can provide Canadian firms with a range of market intelligence services, including assistance in assessing foreign market potential and a range of sector-specific marketing research reports. The CTCS will also facilitate foreign market visits to allow Canadian firms to collect primary data and cultivate contacts. Canadian firms will also find the CTCS's online portal, *Virtual Commissioner*, to be particularly useful for requesting services and reports.[8] As The Global Marketplace 7.3 illustrates, small, resource-constrained Canadian companies should not hesitate to tap into Government sources of foreign market information.

b) *International Organizations.* International organizations often provide useful data for the researcher. The *Statistical Yearbook* produced by the United Nations (UN) contains international trade data on products and provides information on exports and imports by country. Because of the time needed for worldwide data collection, the information is often dated. Additional information is compiled and made available by specialized substruc-

Exhibit 7.4 The Virtual Commissioner

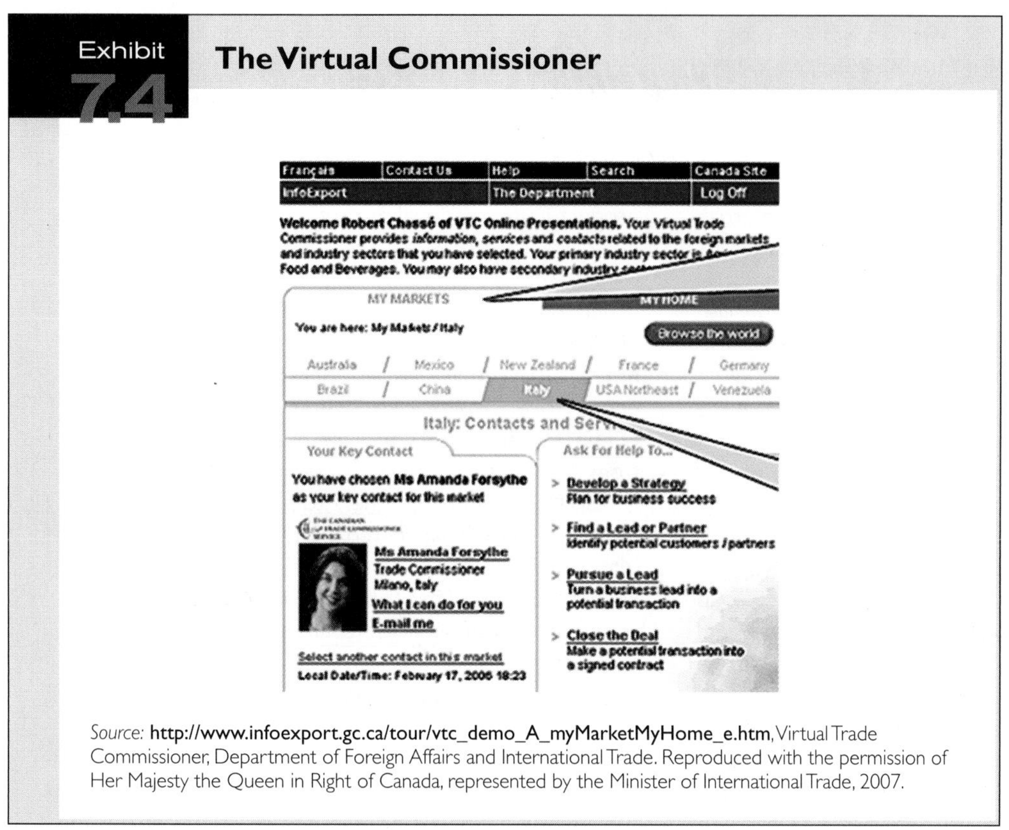

Source: **http://www.infoexport.gc.ca/tour/vtc_demo_A_myMarketMyHome_e.htm**, Virtual Trade Commissioner, Department of Foreign Affairs and International Trade. Reproduced with the permission of Her Majesty the Queen in Right of Canada, represented by the Minister of International Trade, 2007.

tures of the UN. Some of these are the UN Conference on Trade and Development (which concentrates primarily on international issues surrounding developing nations, such as debt and market access), the UN Center on Transnational Corporations, and the International Trade Center. The *World Atlas* published by the World Bank provides useful general data on population, growth trends, and GNP figures. The World Trade Organization (WTO) and the Organization for Economic Cooperation and Development (OECD) also publish quarterly and annual trade data on their member countries. Organizations such as the International Monetary Fund (IMF) and the World Bank publish summary economic data and occasional staff papers that evaluate region- or country-specific issues in depth.

c) *Service Organizations*. A wide variety of service organizations that may provide information include banks, accounting firms, freight forwarders, airlines, and international trade consultants. Frequently, they are able to provide data on business practices, legislative or regulatory requirements, and political stability, as well as basic trade data. Although some of this information is available without charge, its basic intent is to serve as an "appetizer." Much of the initial information is quite general in nature; more detailed answers often require an appropriate fee.

d) *Trade Associations*. Associations such as world trade clubs and domestic and international chambers of commerce can provide valuable information about local markets. Often, files are maintained on international trade issues and trends affecting global marketers. Useful information can also be obtained from industry associations. These groups, formed to represent entire industry segments, often collect from their members a wide variety of data that is then published in an aggregate form. The information provided is often quite general in nature because of the wide variety of clientele served. It can provide valuable initial insights into international markets, since it permits a benchmarking effort through which the global marketer can establish how it is faring when compared to its competition. For example, an industry summary that indicates firm average exports to be 10 percent of sales, and export sales growth to take place mainly in Asia, allows a better evaluation of a specific firm's performance by the global marketer.

e) *Directories and Newsletters*. Many industry directories are available on local, national, and international levels. These directories primarily serve to identify firms and to provide very

The Global MARKETPLACE 7.3

Domaine Pinnacle

Government agencies can be critically important in providing data on overseas market opportunities. Charles and Susan Crawford, founders of Domaine Pinnacle—an orchard and cidery located on the slopes of the Pinnacle Mountain in Frelighsburg, Eastern Quebec, Canada, attest to the importance. The company manufactures ice cider produced from a hand-picked blend of six varieties of apples harvested after frost and extracted over the course of the winter months. The extract is fermented at low temperatures for up to eight months. The company's product portfolio includes *Domaine Pinnacle Ice Cider, Domaine Pinnacle Sparkling Ice Cider,* and *Signature Special Reserve.* The company's orchard boasts almost ideal growing conditions located on the 49th parallel on a south facing slope that benefits from intensely cold winter weather. This unique set of growing conditions makes production of the company's ice cider possible. Domaine Pinnacle began operations in 2000 and occupies some 430 acres, including the cidery and a retail boutique. The company started off as the family's part-time project in Montreal, Quebec, and is now the world's leading manufacturer of ice cider, or ice apple wine as it is known internationally.

Crawford always believed that ice apple wine had tremendous potential outside of the local market and was committed to tapping this potential. The company, to its credit, used a methodical and systematic approach to exploring their product's international potential. This entailed doing the groundwork first before attempting to launch the product in international markets. Crawford, as part of his due diligence, met with officials from the Department of Foreign Affairs and International Trade Canada (DFAIT) in order to tap into their foreign market knowledge and benefit from their international business expertise. Crawford notes: "Doing your homework first and finding the right people to work with is key," He recalls meeting with DFAIT representatives at conferences and benefitting from their individual advice. Crawford also spent time researching potential partners to great success. In 2003, Domaine Pinnacle partnered with Camus La Grande Marque, the world's largest family-owned maker of fine cognacs. Camus added Domaine Pinnacle Ice Apple Wine to the list of products that it sells around the world. Camus products are marketed in 150 countries, and the company's cognacs have won four gold medals at international competitions. It's clear that Crawford's hard work has paid off. Since partnering with Camus, Domaine Pinnacle's international business has grown fivefold and the Pinnacle brand has become something of a household name. In 2005, Korean Air began selling Domaine Pinnacle Ice Apple Wine through its Sky Shopping Channel. Domaine now does business in over 20 countries around the world.

Sources: Quebec Company Reaches The Pinnacle of Success: **http://www.international.gc.ca/commerce/success/pinnacle-en.asp** (accessed March 8, 2007); Domaine Pinnacle website: **http://www.domainepinnacle.com/en/about.html** (accessed February 2, 2008); Wine and alcohol website: **http://www.wineandalcohol.com/alcohol/camus-cognac** (accessed February 2, 2008).

general background information such as the name of the chief executive officer, the address and telephone number, and some information about a firm's products. The quality of a directory depends, of course, on the quality of input and the frequency of updates. Some of the directories are becoming increasingly sophisticated and can provide quite detailed information to the researcher.

Many newsletters are devoted to specific international issues such as international trade finance, international contracting, bartering, countertrade, international payment flows, and customs news. Published by banks or accounting firms in order to keep their clientele current on international developments, newsletters usually cater to narrow audiences but can provide important information to the firm interested in a specific area.

f) *Electronic Information Services.* When information is needed, managers often cannot spend a lot of time, energy, or money finding, sifting through, and categorizing existing materials. Consider labouring through every copy of a trade publication to find out the latest news on how environmental concerns are affecting marketing decisions in Mexico. With electronic information services, search results can be obtained almost immediately. International online computer database services, numbering in the thousands, can be purchased to supply information external to the firm, such as exchange rates, international news, and import restrictions. Most database hosts do not charge any sign-up fee and request payment only for actual use. The selection of initial database hosts depends on the choice of relevant databases, taking into account their product and market limitations, language used, and geographical location.

A large number of databases and search engines provide information about products and markets. Many of the main news agencies through online databases provide information about events that affect certain markets. Some databases cover extensive lists of companies in given countries and the products they buy and sell. A large number of databases exist that cover various categories of trade statistics. The main economic indicators of the UN, IMF, OECD, and EU are available online. Standards institutes in most of the G8 nations provide online access to their databases of technical standards and trade regulations on specific products.

Before obtaining secondary data, the researcher needs to evaluate their appropriateness for the task at hand. As the first step of such an evaluation, the quality of the data source needs to be considered, with a primary focus on the purpose and method of the original data collection. Next, the quality of the actual data needs to be assessed, which should include a determination of data accuracy, reliability, and recency. Obviously, outdated data may mislead rather than improve the decision-making process. In addition, the compatibility and comparability of the data need to be considered. Since they were collected with another purpose in mind, we need to determine whether the data can help with the issue of concern to the firm. In international research, it is also important to ensure that data categories are comparable to each other, in order to avoid misleading conclusions. For example, the term *middle class* is likely to have very different implications for income and consumption patterns in different parts of the world. Complying with the data privacy laws in the countries in which the firm is collecting data is also important, as illustrated in In More Detail 7.3.

In More Detail 7.3

DATA PRIVACY

In conducting global marketing research, the attitude of society toward obtaining and using both secondary and primary data must be taken into account. Many societies are increasingly sensitive to the issue of data privacy, and the concern has grown exponentially as a result of e-business. Readily accessible databases may contain information valuable to marketers, but they may also be considered privileged by individuals who have provided the data.

In 2002, the European Union (EU) passed a directive on privacy and electronic communications. Extending earlier legislation, it maintains high standards of data privacy to ensure the free flow of data throughout the member states. The new directive requires member states to block transmission of data to non-EU countries if these countries do not have domestic legislation that provides for a level of protection judged as adequate by the European Union. The EU has a strict interpretation of its citizens' rights to privacy. There is an opt-in approach for unsolicited e-mails: online marketing firms and other Internet operators can send commercial e-mails only after the customer has specifically asked them to do so. The placement of invisible data-tracking devices such as "cookies" on a computer is prohibited until after a user has been provided with adequate information about their purpose.

The directive also reflects an EU compromise in light of the September 11, 2001, attacks and the growing frequency of cybercrime. Due to requests by key e-commerce partners, revisions were made to EU policy to accommodate criminal investigation. Under the new directive, companies in the EU will still have to erase information immediately after the one- to two-month period needed for billing purposes. However, governments can now require operators to store data for longer periods of time, if deemed necessary for security reasons.[9]

In order to settle conflicts between divergent government policies, companies are increasingly likely to adapt global privacy rules for managing information online and to get certified by watchdog groups, which tell users when a site adheres to specific privacy guidelines.[10] Overall, the global marketer must pay careful attention to the privacy laws and expectations in different nations and to possible consumer reactions to the use of data in the marketing effort.

Primary Data

The global marketing researcher may not be able to address the firm's business problems with the use of prior research or secondary data only. In these cases, primary data will need to be collected. The collection of primary data in foreign markets will necessarily involve a cost to the firm and will prove more challenging for the researcher, as it would most likely involve overseas travel, translation problems, availability of trained field staff, and a great deal of cultural literacy.

Primary research, that is, research undertaken with primary data, is conducted to fill specific information needs. Despite the cost and difficulty involved in conducting international primary research, it remains indispensable in addressing many research problems. Primary research is essential for the formulation of strategic marketing plans. One particular area of research interest is international market segmentation. Historically, firms segmented international markets based on macro variables such as income per capita or consumer spending on certain product categories. Increasingly, however, firms recognize that segmentation variables, such as lifestyles, attitudes, or personality, can play a major role in identifying similar consumer groups in different countries, which can then be targeted across borders. These groups, in other words, form global segments. One such group could consist, for example, of educationally elite readers who read *Scientific American, Time, Newsweek, Maclean's, Canadian Business, The Financial Times,* and *The Economist.* Members of this group, regardless of the country in which they reside, are likely to have more in common with one another than with their fellow citizens.[11] Alternatively, in marketing to women, it is important to understand the degree to which they have entered the work force in a country and how women in different economic segments make or influence purchase decisions. In order to identify these groups and to devise ways of meeting their needs, primary international market data are indispensable.

Variable Definitions

Variables of interest to the global researcher may be defined differently in different parts of the world. These differences in variable definitions need to be carefully considered in the design of the research project in order for the analysis to generate meaningful and consistent results. Depending on culture and the level of socioeconomic development in the country, consumers in one country may see a washing machine as a luxury item while those in another country may see it as a necessity. Unless the researcher conducting an assessment of the household-appliance market is careful in defining terms such as "luxury" and "necessity," the data collected may well lead to misleading results. In conducting research that crosses national borders, the equivalence of the variables must be carefully considered.

Research Techniques

An important research design consideration is the choice of research technique to be employed. The technique selected must be appropriate to the research problem to be solved.

Selection of the research technique depends on a variety of factors. First, the objectivity of the data sought must be determined. Standardized techniques are more useful in the collection of objective data than of subjective data. *Unstructured data* will require more open-ended questions and more time to collect and analyze than will structured data. Since the willingness and ability of respondents to spend the time and provide a freeform response are heavily influenced by factors such as culture and education, the prevailing conditions in the country and segments to be studied need to be understood in making these decisions. Whether the data are to be collected in the real world or in a controlled environment also must be decided. Finally, a decision needs to be made as to whether the research is to collect historical facts or gather information about future developments. This is particularly important for consumer research, because firms frequently desire to determine consumers' future intentions to purchase a certain product.

Cultural and individual preferences, which vary significantly among nations, play a major role in determining research techniques. North American managers frequently prefer to gather large quantities of hard data through surveys, which provide numbers that can be statistically manipulated and directly compared to other sets of data. In some other countries, managers appear to prefer the "soft" approach. For example, much of Japanese-style market research relies heavily on two kinds of information: soft data obtained from visits to dealers and other channel members and hard data about shipments, inventory levels, and retail sales.

Once the structure of the type of data sought has been determined, a choice must be made among the types of research techniques available. Each provides a different depth of information and has its unique strengths and weaknesses.

Interviews

Interviews with knowledgeable persons can be of great value to a corporation desiring foreign market information. Because bias from the individual may be part of the findings, the intent should be to obtain in-depth information rather than a wide variety of data. Particularly when specific answers are sought to very narrow questions, interviews can be most useful. Canada's Department of Foreign Affairs and International Trade provides some useful tips for conducting interviews in foreign countries (see In More Detail 7.4).

Focus Groups

Focus groups are a useful research tool. A group of knowledgeable persons is gathered for a limited period of time (two to four hours). Usually, the ideal size for a focus group is 7 to 10 participants. A specific topic is introduced and thoroughly discussed by all group members. Because of the interaction, hidden issues are sometimes raised that would not have been addressed in an individual interview. The skill of the group leader in stimulating discussion is crucial to the success of a focus group. Discussions are often recorded and subsequently analyzed in detail. Focus groups, like in-depth interviews, do not provide statistically significant information; however, they can be helpful in providing information about perceptions, emotions, and other less-tangible factors. In addition, once individuals are gathered, focus groups are highly efficient in terms of rapidly accumulating a substantial amount of information. With the advances occurring in the

In More Detail 7.4

TIPS FOR CONDUCTING INTERVIEWS IN FOREIGN MARKETS

Interviews can be an essential element of primary market research. They are used to gather valuable information directly from potential customers, clients, and other sources. Understanding the challenges of interviewing people of different cultures will improve your chances of getting the information you require. Just remember to follow these important tips:

- Prepare in advance. Learn the proper pronunciation of names, countries, cities, or other places you will be mentioning. In this way, you are less likely to confuse or insult the person you are interviewing.
- Communicate your objectives clearly. Establish your company's objectives prior to initiating the interview and present your questions in a clear and concise manner. Avoid slang, regional, or industry jargon. It may not be understood by other cultures; even worse, it may have a different meaning altogether.
- Avoid getting too personal too quickly. Let the other person take the lead in this regard. You may be asked personal questions, but do not initiate such a discussion.
- If you are communicating in person, discreetly observe the individual's body language for clues regarding his or her feelings to your questions. Body language is also considered more significant in some cultures (Greece and Italy, for example) than others.
- Pace your speech. This will assist the person with whom you are speaking if his or her first language is different from that in which you are conducting the interview.
- Respect age, rank, and titles. In many nations, age and hierarchical position in an organization are the gauges for respect. You may need to present yourself as a peer or equal in order to obtain an audience.

Source: Adapted from "Conducting Interviews in Foreign Markets," Curtis and Michelle Cook, **http://exportsource.ca/gol/exportsource/site.nsf/en/es02793.html** (accessed March 7, 2007).

communications field, cross-border focus groups can also be conducted, with interaction between groups.

When conducting international research via focus groups, the researcher must be aware of the importance of culture in the discussion process. Not all societies encourage frank and open exchange and disagreement among individuals. Status consciousness may result in situations in which the opinion of one is reflected by all other participants. Disagreement may be seen as impolite, or certain topics may be taboo.

The Global Marketplace 7.4 explains in more detail how research processes need to adjust to cultural constraints.

Observation

Observation techniques require the researcher to play the role of a non-participating observer of activity and behaviour. Observation can be personal or impersonal (for example, mechanical). Observation can be obtrusive or unobtrusive, depending on whether the subject is aware or unaware of being observed. In global marketing research, observation can be extremely useful in shedding light on practices not previously encountered or understood. This aspect is particularly valuable for the researcher who is totally unfamiliar with a market or market situation, and can be quickly achieved through, for example, participation in a trade mission. Observation can also help in understanding phenomena that would have been difficult to assess with other techniques. For example, Toyota sent a group of its engineers and designers to southern California to unobtrusively observe

The Global MARKETPLACE 7.4

Adapting Research Procedures to Local Conditions

Globalization has brought marketing research to new regions of the world. A key challenge is to adapt research procedures to the local environment. Just as understanding culture is important to the development of marketing strategy, it is equally important to keep local traditions and constraints in mind when initiating marketing research efforts.

The distinct cultural environment of Middle Eastern countries requires changes in traditional Western-style approaches to marketing research. One such change concerns gender roles. For example, focus groups are typically a popular way for researchers to obtain information about local consumers. By gathering a random group of people together, the researcher hopes to obtain ideas about which products are popular and which marketing tactics are successful. However, traditional Muslim culture favours male dominance, and strict interpretation of Islam demands segregation of the sexes. As a result, mixed-gender focus groups are difficult, if not illegal, to congregate. Even when permissible in the most Westernized countries, such as Egypt, mixed focus groups tend to suffer from male dominance, which makes their insights unbalanced: women will often defer to men and allow them to speak on their behalf. Also, female marketing researchers will encounter difficulties in countries where women are barred from assuming professional roles.

The growing need to use technology in foreign marketing research also proves problematic in some countries. For one, the postal system is often unreliable and Internet access is limited. In countries where governments restrict access to Western ideas via the Internet, web-based surveys also have to be ruled out as a widely used method of information collection. The small percentage of the population that does have access to the Internet is primarily composed of the upper class; thus Internet surveys would yield skewed results and fail to represent the population as a whole.

As a result of barriers to communication, research efforts in many Muslim countries tend to take much longer than those in Western countries. Researchers must rely on word-of-mouth in order to recruit participants, which in itself can be difficult due to the unfamiliarity of the general public with the concept of marketing research. Furthermore, word-of-mouth contacts can lead to collection of information from a small range of participants: if each person is recruited by someone they know, chances are that variety in opinion and experiences is not great.

Source: Adapted from Steve Jarvis, "Western-Style Research in the Middle East," *Marketing News*, April 29, 2002, 37. Adapted with permission from the American Marketing Association.

how women get into and operate their cars. They found that women with long fingernails had trouble opening the door and operating various knobs on the dashboard. Through their observations, Toyota engineers and designers became aware of the women's plight and re-drew some of the automobile exterior and interior designs.[12]

Conducting observations can also have its pitfalls. For example, people may react differently to the discovery that their behaviour has been observed. The degree to which the observer has to be familiarized or introduced to other participants may vary. The complexity of the task may differ due to the use of multiple languages. To conduct in-store research in Europe, for example, store checks, photo audits of shelves, and store interviews must be scheduled well in advance and need to be preceded by a full round of introductions of the researchers to store management and personnel. In some countries, such as Belgium, a researcher must remember that four different languages are spoken and their use may change from store to store.

The research techniques discussed so far—interviews, focus groups, and observation—are useful primarily for gathering **qualitative data**. The intent is not to amass data or to search for statistical significance, but rather to obtain a better understanding of given situations, behavioural patterns, or underlying dimensions. When **quantitative data** are desired, surveys are an appropriate research technique.

Surveys

Survey research is useful in providing the opportunity to quantify concepts. In the social sciences, the cross-cultural survey is generally accepted as a powerful method of hypothesis testing. Surveys are usually conducted via questionnaires that are administered personally, by mail, or by telephone. Use of the survey technique presupposes that the population under study is able to comprehend and respond to the questions posed. Also, particularly in the case of mail and telephone surveys, a major precondition is the feasibility of using the postal system or the widespread availability of telephones. In many countries, only limited records are available about dwellings, their location, and their occupants. In Venezuela, for example, most houses are not numbered but rather are given individual names like "Casa Rosa" or "El Retiro." In some countries, street maps are not available. As a result, it becomes virtually impossible to reach respondents by mail. In other countries, obtaining a correct address may be easy, but the postal system may not function well. The Italian postal service, for example, repeatedly has suffered from scandals that exposed such practices as selling undelivered mail to paper mills for recycling.

Telephone surveys may also be inappropriate if telephone ownership is rare. In such instances, any information obtained would be highly biased even if the researcher randomizes the calls. In some instances, telephone networks and systems may also prevent the researcher from conducting surveys. Frequent line congestion and a lack of telephone directories are examples. There are also great variations between countries or regions of countries in terms of unlisted telephone numbers; the percentage of households with unlisted telephone numbers varies widely by country and even by city. Because of its global reach and ease of customization, the Internet is also an important tool for conducting international surveys, as illustrated in In More Detail 7.5.

Surveys can be hampered by social and cultural constraints. Recipients of letters may be illiterate or may be reluctant to respond in writing. In some nations, entire population segments—for example, women—may be totally inaccessible to interviewers. One must also assess the purpose of the survey in the context of the population surveyed. It has been argued, for example, that one should not rely on consumer surveys for new product development information. Key reasons are the absence of responsibility—the consumer is sincere when spending but not when talking; conservative attitudes—ordinary consumers are conservative and tend to react negatively to a new product; vanity—it is human nature to exaggerate and put on a good appearance; and insufficient information—the research results depend on the product characteristics information that is given to survey participants and that may be incomplete or unabsorbed.[13] In spite of all these difficulties, however, the survey technique remains a useful one because it allows the researcher to rapidly accumulate a large quantity of data amenable to statistical analysis.

In More Detail 7.5

ONLINE SURVEYS

The growing use of technology has given rise to new marketing research approaches that allow consumers to be heard more often and permit firms to work much harder at their listening skills. Two primary research approaches are rapidly growing in their use: web-based research and e-mail-based surveys.

The increasing degree to which the World Wide Web truly lives up to its name is making it possible for global marketers to use this medium in their research efforts. The technology allows them to reach out in a low-cost fashion and provides innovative ways to present stimuli and collect data. For example, on a website, product details, pictures of products, brands, and the shopping environment can be portrayed with integrated graphics and sound—thus bringing the issues to be researched much closer to the respondent. In addition, the behaviour of visitors to a site can be traced and interpreted with regard to their interest in products, services, or information.[14]

Surveys can be administered either through a website or through e-mail. If they are posted on a site, surveys can be of the pop-up nature, where visitors can be targeted specifically. An e-mail survey format eliminates the need for postage and printing. As a result, larger and geographically much more diverse audiences can be the focus of an inquiry. Research indicates that there is a higher and faster response rate to such electronic inquiries. In addition, the process of data entry can be automated so that responses are automatically fed into data analysis software.[15]

However, it would be too simplistic to assume that the digitalization of survey content is all that it takes to go global on the Web. There are cultural differences that must be taken into account by the researcher. Global visitors to a site should encounter research that is embedded in their own cultural values, rituals, and, symbols, and testimonials or encouragement should be delivered by culture-specific heroes. For example, a website might first offer a visitor from Korea the opportunity to become part of a product user community. A low-context visitor from Canada or the United States may in turn be exposed to product features immediately.[16]

Such electronic research suffers from a lack of confidentiality of the participants because e-mails disclose the identity of the sender. This issue, in turn, triggers concerns and rules of data privacy that may limit the use of these tools in some nations or regions. Nonetheless, the new technology offers global marketers an entire array of new opportunities that will grow rather than diminish. As stated by a leading marketing research expert, web-based survey research will become the norm, not the exception, in the not-too-distant future.[17]

Even though quite difficult, **international comparative research** has been carried out very successfully between nations, particularly if the environments studied are sufficiently similar so that the impact of uncontrollable macro variables is limited. However, even in environments that are quite dissimilar, in-depth comparative research can be carried out.[18] Doing so may require a country-by-country adjustment of details while preserving the similarity of research thrust. For example, researchers have reported good results in mail surveys conducted simultaneously in Japan and the United States after adjusting the size of the return envelope, outgoing envelope, address style, signature, and cover letter to meet specific societal expectations.[19] With constantly expanding technological capabilities, international marketers will be able to use the survey technique more frequently in the future.

Measurement Instruments

A key consideration in the design of the global research exercise is the development of measurement instruments. Measurement instruments such as questionnaires and observation forms may be used to guide data collection in qualitative research projects, but they play an even more important role in quantitative data collection exercises. In global marketing research, it is imperative that the measurement instrument be adapted to the specific cultural context in which it is to be used. It is also important that the instrument not be biased in favour of any one country or cultural group, particularly when cross-country comparisons are to be attempted. In some global projects the researcher may also use multi-item scales to measure constructs of interest, such as the degree of consumer ethno-

In More Detail 7.6

VALIDITY VERSUS RELIABILITY

A key consideration in conducting global marketing research is providing the firm with robust results. To achieve this, the measurement instruments used must be both valid and reliable. These concepts are not the same, but both are important to the measurement of variables of interest. A measurement instrument that works satisfactorily in Western cultures may not perform as well when applied in Asia. Multi-item scales developed to measure particular constructs should be evaluated for **reliability** and validity in the cultural context in which they are to be used.

The measurement instrument used must be reliable, which means that if the instrument were to be used repeatedly under the same conditions to measure the same phenomenon (e.g., the degree of consumer ethnocentricity in the society), similar results would be obtained on each occasion. Such an instrument would be said to be reliable.

It is not, however, sufficient that the measurement instrument be reliable. Validity is also important. There are various types of validity. **Construct validity** means that the phenomenon that the researcher sets out to measure has in fact been measured by the instrument used. Construct validity may be established in three ways. **Convergent validity** refers to whether the same results are obtained when the construct is measured in two different ways. For the global marketer, this means measuring the construct in two different ways in each of the countries under consideration and testing the strength of the correlations between them. For the instrument to be considered valid, the correlations should be strong. **Discriminant validity** refers to whether or not the construct is different from other concepts. Discriminant validity is established only if the correlations between the concepts across countries is weak. **Nomological validity** refers to whether the construct is related to some other external criterion. In global marketing research the external criterion used, such as ownership of foreign products, must be available in the countries under consideration.[20]

A measurement instrument can be reliable but not valid. Under no circumstances, however, can an unreliable measurement instrument be valid. The global marketing researcher must also recognize that a measurement instrument that is shown to be reliable and valid in one culture may be unreliable and invalid in another culture.[21]

centrism in the population or the degree of perceived globalness of the firm's brand. In such situations, the researcher must also be concerned with the reliability and validity of the measures used (see In More Detail 7.6).

Foreign market surveys are usually conducted with questionnaires. These questionnaires should contain questions that are clear and easy to comprehend by the respondents, as well as easy for the data collector to administer. Much attention must therefore be paid to question format, content, and wording.

Question Format

Questions can be structured or unstructured. Unstructured or open-ended questions permit the capture of more in-depth information, but they also increase the potential for interviewer bias. Even at the cost of potential bias, however, "the use of open-ended questions appears quite useful in cross-cultural surveys, because they may help identify the frame of reference of the respondents, or may even be designed to permit the respondent to set his or her own frame of reference."[22]

Another question format decision is the choice between direct and indirect questions. Societies have different degrees of sensitivity to certain questions. Questions related to the income or age of a respondent may be accepted differently in different countries. Also, the social desirability of answers may vary. In some cultures, questions about employees, performance, standards, and financing may be asked directly of a respondent, while in others, particularly in Asia or the Middle East, these questions are thought to be rude and insulting.[23] As a result, the researcher must be sure that the questions are culturally acceptable. This may mean that questions that can be asked directly in some cultures will have to be asked indirectly in others. For example, rather than ask, "How old are you?" one could ask, "In what year were you born?"

The researcher must also be sure to adapt the complexity of the question to the level of understanding of the respondent. For example, a multi-point scaling method, which may be effectively used in a developed country to discover the attitudes and attributes of company executives, may be a very poor instrument if used among rural entrepreneurs. It has been found that demonstration aids are useful in surveys among poorly educated respondents.[24]

The question format should also ensure data equivalence in global marketing research. This requires categories used in questionnaires to be comparatively structured. In a developed country, for example, a white-collar worker may be part of the middle class, whereas in a less-developed country, the same person would be part of the upper class. Before using categories in a questionnaire, the researcher must therefore determine their appropriateness in different environments. This is particularly important for questions that attempt to collect attitudinal, psychographic, or lifestyle data, since cultural variations are most pronounced in these areas. As pointed out earlier in this chapter, it is important to precisely define the variables used in the research exercise.

Question Content

Major consideration must be given to the ability and willingness of respondents to supply the answers. The knowledge and information available to respondents may vary substantially because of different educational levels and may affect their ability to answer questions. Further, societal demands and restrictions may influence the willingness of respondents to answer certain questions. For various reasons, respondents may also be motivated to supply incorrect answers. For example, in countries where the tax collection system is consistently eluded by taxpayers, questions regarding level of income may deliberately be answered inaccurately. Distrust in the researcher, and the fear that research results may be passed on to the government, may also lead individuals to consistently understate their assets. Because of government restrictions in Brazil, for example, individuals will rarely admit to owning an imported car. Nevertheless, when we observe the streets of Rio de Janeiro, a substantial number of foreign cars are seen. The global market researcher is unlikely to change the societal context of a country. The objective of the content planning process should therefore be to adapt the questions to societal constraints.

Question Wording

The impact of language and culture is of particular importance when wording questions. The goal for the global marketing researcher should be to ensure that the potential for misunderstandings and misinterpretations of spoken or written words is minimized. Both language and cultural differences make this issue an extremely sensitive one in the global marketing research process. As a result, attention must be paid to the translation equivalence of verbal and nonverbal questions that can change in the course of translation. One of this book's authors, for example, used the term *group discussion* in a questionnaire for Russian executives, only to learn that the translated meaning of the term was "political indoctrination session."

The key is to keep questions clear by using simple rather than complex words, by avoiding ambiguous words and questions, by omitting leading questions, and by asking questions in specific terms, thus avoiding generalizations and estimates.[25] To reduce problems of question wording, it is helpful to use a **translation–back-translation** approach. The researcher formulates the questions, has them translated into the language of the country under investigation, and subsequently has a second translator return the foreign text to the researcher's native language. Through the use of this method, the researcher can hope to detect possible blunders. An additional safeguard is the use of alternative wording. Here the researcher uses questions that address the same issue but are worded differently and resurface at various points in the questionnaire, in order to check for consistency in question interpretation by the respondents.

In spite of superb research planning, a poorly designed instrument will yield poor results. No matter how comfortable and experienced the researcher is in international research activities, an instrument should always be pretested. Ideally, such a **pretest** is carried out with a subset of the population under study. At the least, a pretest with knowledgeable experts and individuals should be conducted. Even though a pretest may mean time delays and additional cost, the risks of poor research are simply too great for this process to be omitted.

Sampling and Survey Methodology

Integral to the process of designing the global research project is consideration of sampling and survey methodology. In most cases, such as global consumer research, it may be impossible to contact all potential respondents. The sheer number of consumers and their geographic dispersion will make any such attempt prohibitively costly and time consuming. The selection of a sample of the population of potential respondents becomes important. Issues of method of contact and the training of field enumerators also need to be considered.

The Sampling Frame

To obtain representative results, the researcher must reach representative members of the population under study. Many methods that have been developed in industrialized countries for this purpose are useless abroad. For example, address directories may simply not be available. Multiple families may live in one dwelling. Differences between population groups living, for example, in highlands and lowlands may make it imperative to differentiate these segments. Lack of basic demographic information may prevent the design of a sampling frame. In instances in which comparative research addresses very different countries (e.g., China and Canada), it may be virtually impossible to match samples.[26]

Sampling Technique

The global marketing researcher must keep in mind the complexities of the market under study and prepare his or her sampling plan accordingly. Often, samples need to be stratified to reflect different population groups, and innovative sampling methods need to be devised in order to assure representative and relevant responses. For example, a survey concerning grocery-shopping habits might require data from homemakers in one country, but from maids in another.[27]

In terms of sampling technique, the global researcher has the option of using either probability-based sampling or non-probability-based sampling. With the former it is possible to determine in advance an individual's chance of being included in the sample. Random sampling is a probability-based sampling technique in which each individual in the population has an equal chance of being included in the sample. With non-probability-based sampling, it is not possible to determine a priori the likelihood of a given individual's inclusion in the sample selected. With non-probability-based samples, it is usually inappropriate to generalize the findings to the total population.

Sample Size

The global marketing researcher must also consider the size of the sample to be selected for the specific exercise. As a general rule, the larger the sample size, the smaller will be the sampling error. With large sample sizes, the results generated will more closely reflect the situation in the population as a whole. The downside is that increasing the size of the sample also increases the cost of the research project. The global marketing researcher may determine an appropriate sample size using the following:

1. Budgetary constraints, that is, the amount of money available for data collection and the cost per individual of collecting the data.
2. A standard statistical approach based on a knowledge of the population variance. In most cases, however, little is known of the underlying population; therefore, this approach is likely to be of little practical value to the global marketing researcher.
3. Rules of thumb. If management has undertaken a number of prior research projects in their industry, executives may "have a feel for" what constitutes an adequate sample size.

Selection of Data Analysis Technique

The global marketing researcher should, during the research design stage, develop a clear understanding of what data analysis techniques will be used in the research project. The selection of a specific technique of data analysis will be driven by the nature of the business/research problem that is to be addressed and the type and quality of data that is to be collected.

The choice of data analysis method will also be driven by the level of aggregation at which the research is to be conducted.[28] Global marketing research that involves several countries may require that data analysis be intra-country, inter-country or pan-country in scope. With intra-country analysis, data are analyzed within the country and inferences made about relationship between variables within the country. This is essentially equivalent to domestic research. With inter-country analysis, the focus is on comparing relationships across countries, while with pan-country analysis, data from all countries are grouped and analyzed without regard to their geographic location. A number of data analysis techniques are discussed in Appendix A.

Collect the Data

Having finalized the research design, the global marketer would necessarily move to the next step in the process, which is the actual collection of the data required. The global marketing researcher must check the quality of the data collection process. In some cultures, questionnaire administration is seen as useless by the local population. Instruments are administered primarily to humour the researcher. In such cases, interviewers may cheat quite frequently. Spot checks on the administration procedures are vital to ensure reasonable data quality. A **realism check** of data should also be used. For example, if marketing research in Italy reports that very little pasta is consumed, the researcher should perhaps consider whether individuals responded to their use of purchased pasta rather than homemade pasta. The collected data should therefore be compared with secondary information and with analogous information from a similar market in order to obtain a preliminary understanding of data quality.

Analyze and Interpret the Data

Interpretation and analysis of accumulated information are required to answer the research questions that were posed initially. The researcher should, of course, use the best tools available and appropriate for analysis. The fact that a market may be in a less-developed country does not preclude the collection of good data and the use of good analytical methods. On the other hand, international researchers should be cautioned against using overly sophisticated tools for unsophisticated data. Even the best of tools will not improve data quality. The quality of data must be matched with the quality of the research tools to achieve appropriately sophisticated analysis and yet not overstate the value of the data.

Forecasting Techniques

In global marketing research, the researcher must often use the available data to project the future course of events. In deciding to enter a specific country market, for example, the firm may be interested in obtaining an estimate of its future market potential. The researcher may use **lead-lag analysis** to project the size of the potential market. With lead-lag analysis, the researcher uses time series data from one country to project sales in other countries. The approach makes the assumption that the fundamental drivers of demand are the same in both countries and that only time separates them. Exhibit 7.5 shows a hypothetical example of lead-lag analysis for the flat-screen-TV markets in Canada and Jamaica. According to the graph, in 2006 30 percent of Canadian households owned a flat-screen TV, whereas only 10 percent of Jamaican households owned one. If it is known that there is a five-year time lag between the countries, then market potential

Exhibit 7.5 **Lead-Lag Analysis**

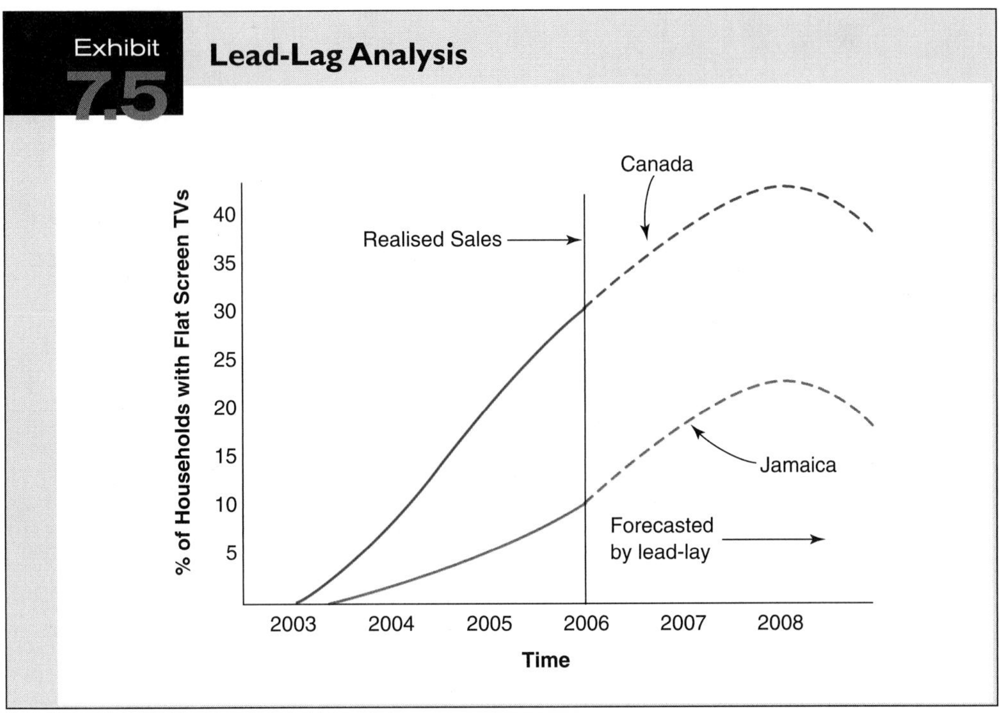

in Jamaica could easily be estimated via parallel displacement of the Canadian S-shaped adoption curve. While the approach has considerable intuitive appeal, the precise determination of the time lag may be problematic.

In attempting to forecast foreign market potential, researchers may also use **estimation by analogy**. Here again data collected during the research process are used to develop a projection of future demand. In this technique, the researcher must first establish a relationship between the foreign market demand to be estimated and a factor, such as population size, that is to be used in the estimation. Once the correlation between the demand and population has been established, then the foreign market demand in question is estimated from the known situation. For example, the demand for ice wine in the U.K. may be estimated based on knowledge of ice wine consumption in Canada, population in Canada, and population in the U.K.:

Population of Canada = 32 million

Population of the U.K. = 61 million

Consumption in Canada = 2 million bottles

Consumption in the U.K. = (61/32) × 2 million bottles = 3.8 million bottles

The approach produces an estimate of potential market demand in the U.K. that may be reasonably accurate if the factors that affect demand (other than population) are the same in both countries. Consumption, tastes, taxes, and so on should be similar if the global marketing researcher is to have confidence in the forecast.

Potential foreign market demand may also be estimated by the use of proxy information. A **proxy variable** is a substitute for a variable that one cannot directly measure. For example, the market penetration of television sets may be used as a proxy variable for the potential market demand for DVD players. Similarly, in an industrial setting, information about plans for new port facilities may be useful in determining future containerization requirements. Also, the level of computerization of a society may indicate the future need for software.

To forecast broader, more macro developments in the global marketing environment, the firm may employ techniques such as **Delphi forecasting**, which is described in In More Detail 7.7.

In More Detail 7.7

DELPHI FORECASTING

The global marketing researcher may also be interested in forecasting broad macro trends in foreign markets. Before committing resources to the Chinese market, for example, the firm may wish to have some sense of whether democracy and economic liberalization is likely to continue or be reversed by risk factors that may just be coming to the surface. Delphi studies are one method that may be used for such situations. These studies are particularly useful in the global marketing environment because they are "a means for aggregating the judgments of a number of ... experts ... who cannot come together physically."[29] This type of research approach clearly aims at qualitative rather than quantitative measures by aggregating the information of a group of experts. It seeks to obtain answers from those who know instead of seeking the average responses of many with only limited knowledge.

Typically, Delphi studies are carried out with groups of about 30 well-chosen participants who possess particular in-depth expertise in an area of concern, such as future developments in the international trade environment. These participants are asked via mail to identify the major issues in the area of concern. They are also requested to rank their statements according to importance and explain the rationale behind the order. Next, the aggregated information is returned to all participants, who are encouraged to state clearly their agreements or disagreements with the various rank orders and comments. Statements can be challenged, and in another round, participants can respond to the challenges. After several rounds of challenge and response, a reasonably coherent consensus is developed.

The Delphi technique is particularly valuable because it uses mail or fax communication to bridge large distances and therefore makes individuals quite accessible at a reasonable cost. It does not suffer from the drawback of ordinary mail investigations: lack of interaction among the participants. One drawback of the technique is that it requires several steps, and therefore months may elapse before the information is obtained. Even though the increasing availability of electronic mail may hasten the process, the researcher must be cautious to factor in the different penetration and acceptance levels of such technology. One should not let the research process be driven by technology to the exclusion of valuable key informants who utilize less sophisticated methods of communication.

Also, substantial effort must be expended in selecting the appropriate participants and in motivating them to participate in this exercise with enthusiasm and continuity. When obtained on a regular basis, Delphi information can provide crucial augmentation to the factual data available for the marketing information system.

Present the Research Findings

The primary focus in the presentation of research results must be communication. In global marketing research, communication must take place not only with management at headquarters but also with managers in the local operations. Otherwise, little or no transference of research results will occur, and the synergistic benefits of a global operation will be lost. To minimize time devoted to reading reports, the researcher must present results clearly and concisely. In the worldwide operations of a firm, particularly in communication efforts, lengthy data and analytical demonstrations should be avoided. The availability of data and the techniques used should be mentioned, however, so that subsidiary operations can receive the information on request.

The researcher should also demonstrate in the presentation how research results relate to the original research objective and fit with overall corporate strategy. At least schematically, possibilities for analogous application should be highlighted. These possibilities should then also be communicated to local subsidiaries, perhaps through a short monthly newsletter. A newsletter format, ideally distributed through an intranet, may be a very effective means of disseminating the research results. It is important to maintain such communication in order for the entire organization to learn and to improve its global marketing research capabilities.

Follow-Up and Review

Although the research process may be considered to be at an end at the presentation stage, from a managerial perspective, one more stage is important. Now that the research has been carried out, appropriate managerial decisions must be made based on the research, and the organization must absorb the research. For example, if it has been found that a product needs to have certain attributes to sell well in Latin America, the manager must determine whether the product development area is aware of this finding and the degree to which the knowledge is now incorporated into new product projects. Without such follow-up, the role of research tends to become a mere "staff" function, increasingly isolated from corporate "line" activity and lacking major impact on corporate activity. If that is the case, research will diminish and even be disregarded—resulting in an organization at risk.

Research Administration

The research process described above is generally the same for all projects the firm would undertake. The firm does, however, have a number of options in deciding on an organizational approach for conducting the project, that is, deciding who will undertake the work. The firm may use a centralized, coordinated, or decentralized approach to the assignment or may engage an outside research service. The level of control that corporate headquarters exercises over global marketing research activities is a function of the overall organizational structure of the firm and the nature and importance of the decision to be made.

Approaches to Research Administration

The *centralized approach* clearly affords the most control to headquarters. All **research specifications** such as focus, thrust, and design are directed by the home office and are forwarded to the local country operations for implementation. The subsequent analysis of gathered information again takes place at headquarters. Such an approach can be quite valuable when foreign market research is intended to influence corporate policies and strategy. It also ensures that all foreign market studies remain comparable to one another. On the other hand, some risks exist. For example, headquarters management may not be sufficiently familiar with the local market situation to be able to adapt the research appropriately. Also, cultural bias at headquarters may influence the research activities. Finally, headquarters staff may be too small or insufficiently skilled to provide proper guidance for multiple foreign market research studies.

A *coordinated research approach* uses an intermediary such as an outside research agency to bring headquarters and country operations together. This approach provides for more interaction and review of the global marketing research plan by both headquarters and the local operations and ensures more responsiveness to both strategic and local concerns. If the intermediary used is of high quality, the research capabilities of a corporation can be greatly enhanced through a coordinated approach.

The *decentralized approach* requires corporate headquarters to establish the broad thrust of research activities and to then delegate the further design and implementation to the local countries. The entire research is then carried out locally under the supervision of the local country operation, and only a final report is provided to headquarters. This approach has particular value when international markets differ significantly, because it permits detailed adaptation to local circumstances. However, implementing research activities on a country-by-country basis may cause unnecessary duplication, lack of knowledge transference, and lack of comparable results.

Local country operations may not be aware of research carried out by corporate units in other countries and may reinvent the wheel. This problem can be avoided if a proper intracorporate flow of information exists so that local units can check whether similar information has already been collected elsewhere within the firm. Corporate units that operate in markets similar to one another can then benefit from the exchange of research findings.

Local units may also develop their own research thrusts, tools, and analyses. A researcher in one country may, for example, develop a creative way of dealing with a non-response problem. This new technique could be valuable to company researchers who face similar difficulties in other countries. However, for the technique to become widely known, systems must be in place to circulate information to the firm as a whole.

Finally, if left to their own devices, researchers will develop different ways of collecting and tabulating data. As a result, findings in different markets may not be comparable, and potentially valuable information about major changes and trends may be lost to the corporation.

Global market research activities will always be carried out subject to the organizational structure of a firm. Ideally, a middle ground between centralization and decentralization will be found, one that permits local flexibility together with an ongoing exchange of information within the corporation. As the extent of a firm's international activities grows, the exchange of information becomes particularly important, because global rather than local optimization is the major goal of the multinational corporation.

Outside Research Services

One major factor in deciding whether or not to use outside research services is, of course, the size of the international operations of a firm. No matter how large a firm is, however, it is unlikely to possess specialized expertise in foreign market research for every single market it currently serves or is planning to serve in the future. Rather than overstretch the capabilities of its staff or assert a degree of expertise that does not exist, a corporation may wish to delegate the research task to outside groups. This is particularly the case when corporate headquarters has little or no familiarity with the local research environment. Exhibit 7.6 provides an example of such a situation. The use of outside research agencies may be especially appropriate for large-scale foreign market research projects or when highly specialized research skills are required. Increasingly, marketing research agencies operate worldwide, in order to accommodate the research needs of their clients.

Exhibit 7.6 Research Agencies Understand the Importance of Cultural Adaptation

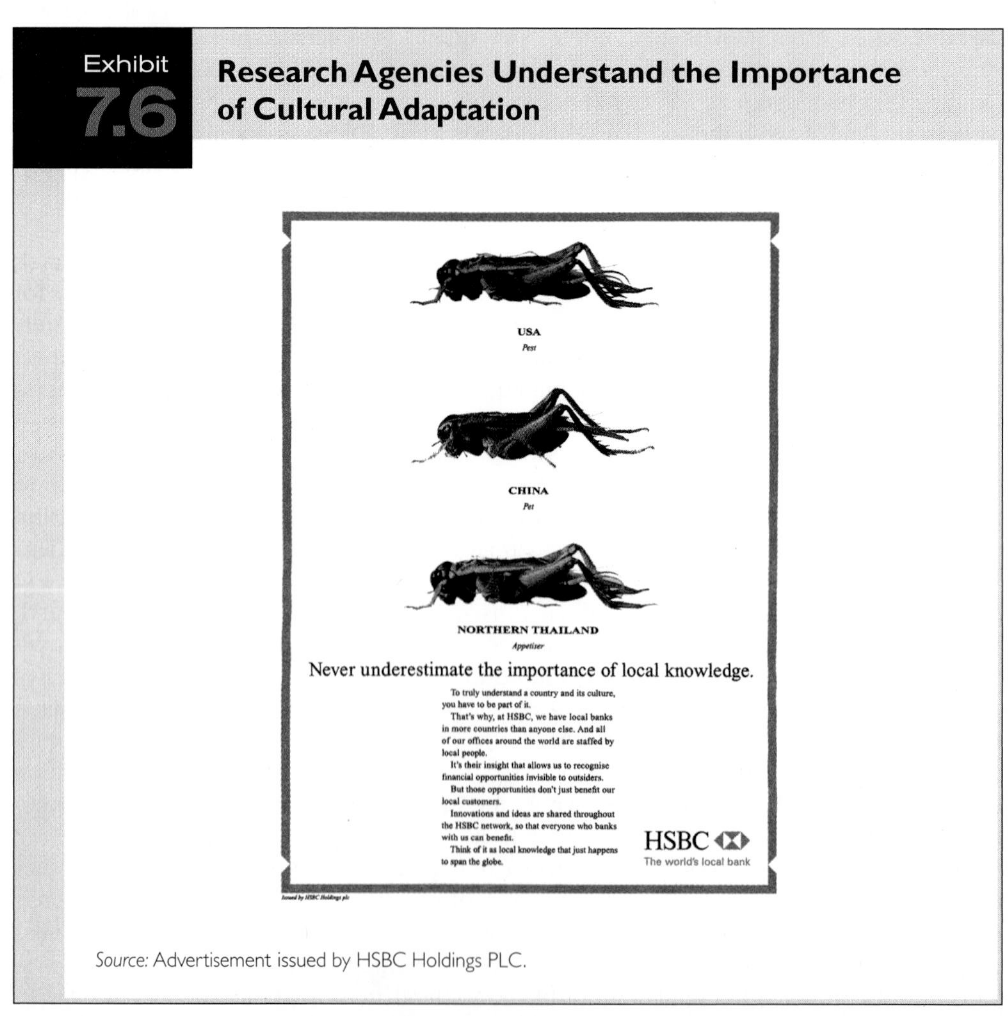

Source: Advertisement issued by HSBC Holdings PLC.

The selection process for outside research providers should emphasize the quality of information rather than the cost. Low price is no substitute for data pertinence or accuracy. Before a decision is made, the capabilities of an outside organization should be carefully evaluated and compared with the capabilities available in-house and from competing firms. Although general technical capabilities are important, the prime selection criterion should be previous research experience in a particular country and a particular industry. Some experience is transferable from one industry or country to another; however, the more the corporation's research needs overlap an agency's past research accomplishments, the more likely it is that the research task will be carried out satisfactorily. Although the research may be more difficult to administer, multinational corporations should consider subcontracting each major global marketing research task to specialists, even if research within one country is carried out by various international marketing research agencies as a result. To have experts working on a problem is usually more efficient than to conserve corporate resources by centralizing all research activities with one service provider who is only marginally familiar with key aspects of the research. However, if different firms carry out the research, it becomes very important to ensure that the data are comparable. Otherwise, the international firm will not be able to transfer lessons learned from one market to another.

Summary

Constraints of time, resources, and expertise are the major inhibitors of global marketing research. Nevertheless, firms need to carry out planned and organized research in order to explore international market alternatives successfully. Such research needs to be closely linked to the decision-making process.

Global market research differs from domestic research in that the environment, which determines how well tools, techniques, and concepts apply, is different abroad. In addition, the manager needs to deal with new parameters such as duties, exchange rates, and international documentation; a greater number of interacting factors; and a much broader definition of the concept of competition.

Given the scarcity of resources, companies beginning their international effort often need to use data that have already been collected, that is, secondary data. Such data are available from governments, international organizations, directories, trade associations, or online databases.

To respond to specific information requirements, firms frequently need primary research. The researcher needs to select an appropriate research technique to collect the information needed. Sensitivity to different international environments and cultures will guide the researcher in deciding whether to use interviews, focus groups, observation, surveys, or experimentation as data collection techniques. The same sensitivity applies to the design of the research instrument, where issues such as question format, content, and wording are decided. Also, the sampling plan needs to be appropriate for the local environment in order to ensure representative and useful responses.

Once the data have been collected, care must be taken to use analytical tools appropriate for the quality of data collected so that management is not misled about the sophistication of the research. Finally, the research results must be presented in a concise and useful form so that management can benefit in its decision making, and implementation of the research needs to be tracked.

To provide ongoing information to management, an international decision support system is useful. Such a system will provide for the systematic and continuous gathering, analysis, and reporting of data for decision-making purposes.

Key Terms

construct validity (p. 223)
content analysis (p. 209)
convergent validity (p. 223)
Delphi forecasting (p. 227)
discriminant validity (p. 223)
estimation by analogy (p. 227)
international comparative research (p. 222)
lead-lag analysis (p. 226)
nomological validity (p. 223)
pretest (p. 224)
primary research (p. 206)
proxy variable (p. 227)
qualitative data (p. 221)
quantitative data (p. 221)
realism check (p. 226)
reliability (p. 223)
research specifications (p. 229)
secondary research (p. 206)
translation–back-translation (p. 224)

Questions for Discussion

1. Discuss the possible shortcomings of secondary data.
2. Why would a firm collect primary data in its global marketing research?
3. Discuss the tradeoffs between centralized and decentralized global marketing research.
4. How is global marketing research affected by differences in language?
5. What are some of the crucial variables you would track in an international information system?

Internet Exercises

1. Take a tour of the Virtual Trade Commissioner website at **http://www.infoexport.gc.ca/registration/CCRegistrationBenefits.jsp?lang=en.** How useful do you believe this site will be to executives who are new to global marketing? Justify your answer.
2. Using the Google search engine at **http://www.google.ca/,** identify three companies with offices in Canada that are capable of undertaking global marketing research. How similar/different are the services they offer?

Recommended Readings

Brookes, Richard. *Marketing Research in a .com Environment.* Amsterdam: ESOMAR, 2002.

Churchill, Gilbert A., and Dawn Iacobucci. *Marketing Research: Methodological Foundations.* 8th ed. Mason, OH: South-Western, 2002.

Coyle, James. *Internet Resources and Services for International Marketing.* Westport, CT: Oryx, 2002.

Craig, Samuel C., and Susan P. Douglas. *International Marketing Research.* 3rd ed. Chichester: John Wiley and Sons, 2005.

Directory of Online Databases. Santa Monica, CA: Cuadra Associates, published annually.

Export Programs Guide. Trade Information Center, U.S. Department of Commerce, Washington, DC: 2002. **http://www.usatrade.gov.**

Forrest, Edward. *Internet Marketing Intelligence.* New York: McGraw-Hill, 2003.

International Trade Center. *Selected Bibliography of Published Market Research.* Geneva: ITC, 2002.

Predicasts Services. Cleveland, OH, published monthly.

Notes

1. Naresh K. Malhotra, Mark Peterson, and Susan Bardi Kleiser, "Marketing Research: A State-of-the-Art Review and Directions for the Twenty-First Century," *Journal of the Academy of Marketing Science* 27, no. 2 (1999): 160–83.
2. Marketing Definitions, **http://MarketingPower.com,** website of the American Marketing Association (accessed October 8, 2002).
3. Naresh K. Malhotra, *Marketing Research: An Applied Orientation,* 4th ed. (Upper Saddle River, NJ: Prentice-Hall, 2003).
4. Adapted from C.S. Craig and S.P. Douglas, *International Marketing Research,* 3rd ed. (Chichester, UK: John Wiley and Sons, 2005).
5. CV Technologies to bolster marketing of Cold-fX in U.S., **http://money.canoe.ca/News/TopPhoto/2007/02/22/3653554-cp.html** (accessed February 22, 2007).
6. Adapted from Craig and Douglas, op. cit.
7. Thomas C. Kinnear and James R. Taylor, *Marketing Research: An Applied Approach,* 5th ed. (New York: McGraw-Hill, 1996).
8. See **http://www.international.gc.ca/index.aspx** (accessed March 8, 2007).
9. "EU Vote Relaxes E-Privacy Rules," Reuters, May 31, 2002, **http://zdnet.com.com/2102-1105-929605.html** (accessed October 10, 2002).
10. Elizabeth De Bony, "EU, U.S. Plug Away at Data Privacy Accord," *Industry Standard,* December 10, 1998, 45–46.
11. Salah S. Hassan and A. Coskun Samli, "The New Frontiers of Intermarket Segmentation," in *Global Marketing: Perspectives and Cases,* ed. Salah S. Hassan and Roger D. Blackwell (Fort Worth, TX: The Dryden Press, 1994): 76–100.
12. Michael R. Czinkota and Masaaki Kotabe, "Product Development the Japanese Way," in *Trends in International Business: Critical Perspectives,* eds. M. Czinkota and M. Kotabe (Oxford: Blackwell Publishers, 1998), 153–58.
13. C. Samuel Craig and Susan P. Douglas, "Conducting International Marketing Research in the Twenty-First Century," *International Marketing Review* 18, no. 1 (2001): 80–90.

14. Janet Ilieva, Steve Baron, and Nigel M. Healey, "On-line Surveys in Marketing Research: Pros and Cons," *International Journal of Marketing Research* 44, no. 3 (2002): 361–76.

15. David Luna, Laura A. Peracchio, and Maria D. de Juan, "Cross-Cultural and Cognitive Aspects of Web Site Navigation," *Journal of the Academy of Marketing Science* 30, no. 4 (2002): 397–410.

16. William D. Neal, "Still Got It: Shortcomings Plague the Industry," *Marketing News*, September 16, 2002, 37.

17. R. Nishikawa, "New Product Planning at Hitachi," *Long Range Planning* 22 (1989): 20–24.

18. For an excellent example, see Alan Dubinsky, Marvin Jolson, Masaaki Kotabe, and Chae Lim, "A Cross-National Investigation of Industrial Salespeople's Ethical Perceptions," *Journal of International Business Studies* 22 (1991): 651–70.

19. Raymond A. Jussaume Jr. and Yoshiharu Yamada, "A Comparison of the Viability of Mail Surveys in Japan and the United States, *The Public Opinion Quarterly* 54, no. 2 (Summer 1990): 222.

20. Craig and Douglas, op. cit.

21. S. Hollensen, *Global Marketing: A Decision-Oriented Approach*, 3rd ed. (Harlow, UK: Prentice Hall, 2004).

22. Sydney Verba, "Cross-National Survey Research: The Problem of Credibility," in *Comparative Methods in Sociology: Essays on Trends and Applications,* ed. I. Vallier (Berkeley: University of California Press, 1971), 322–23.

23. Camille P. Schuster and Michael J. Copeland, "Global Business Exchanges: Similarities and Differences around the World," *Journal of International Marketing* 7, no. 2 (1999): 63–80.

24. Kavil Ramachandran, "Data Collection for Management Research in Developing Countries," in *The Management Research Handbook*, ed. N. Craig Smith and Paul Dainty (London: Routledge, 1991), 304.

25. Gilbert A. Churchill Jr. and Dawn Iacobucci, *Marketing Research: Methodological Foundations*, 8th ed. (Mason, OH: South-Western, 2002).

26. Kathleen Brewer Doran, "Lessons Learned in Cross-Cultural Research of Chinese and North American Consumers," *Journal of Business Research* 55 (2002): 823–29.

27. Craig and Douglas, op. cit.

28. Craig and Douglas, op. cit.

29. Andre L. Delbecq, Andrew H. Van de Ven, and David H. Gustafson, *Group Techniques for Program Planning* (Glenview, IL: Scott Foresman, 1975), 83.

Appendix A

Data Analysis Techniques

This chapter has discussed a number of approaches to the collection of data in global marketing research. Data may have been collected within a single country or across a number of countries. Whether the data have been collected for one country or a group of countries, they have to be analyzed to provide meaningful insights for management. Multi-country analysis is more complex, as it must shed light on the problems that exist *within* a given national market and must also allow for comparisons *across* national markets. Several techniques are available to the global marketing researcher. These are described briefly below.

Cross-Tabulation

Cross-tabulation is used to determine whether there is a significant difference between two categorical variables. A researcher may, for example, be interested in the relationship between age and product consumption in two national markets—say Canada and Mexico. Based on survey data, consumers in the two countries may be classified by age grouping (teenagers versus adults) and product usage (heavy users versus light users). The variables may then be cross-tabulated to determine whether there is a statistically significant relationship between age and product usage in the two markets. A chi-square statistic can be computed to determine whether there are statistically significant differences between the groups in each national market. The analysis may reveal, for example, that there is a statistically significant relationship between age and usage level in Mexico but that the relationship does not hold in the Canadian market. It should be noted that while cross-tabulation will identify statistically significant relationships, it will not provide the global market researcher with an explanation. The technique does not shed any light on why age is related to usage level in Mexico but not in Canada.

t-Tests

Researchers may use t-tests to determine whether the mean of a variable in one country is significantly different from its mean in another country. In developing a market entry strategy for Africa, a Canadian exporter may well wish to determine whether there is a significant difference in the purchase intentions between consumers in South Africa and Nigeria. Surveys conducted in both countries will provide data on purchase intentions in the two countries from which national means may be easily computed. The Canadian exporter must next determine whether a difference in the mean values of the number of consumers expressing a willingness to purchase the company's product is statistically significant and points to a real difference in relative attractiveness of the two markets. As with cross-tabulation, the t-test does not shed light on the reasons for differences that the global marketing researcher may observe.

Multiple Regression

Multiple regression is a well-known statistical technique that uses a number of independent variables to explain the underlying variance in a dependent variable. The global marketing researcher may, for example, construct a regression model to explain differences in the levels of consumption in two or more foreign countries. The researcher may hypothesize that consumption levels are dependent on factors such as income, price, and the degree of consumer ethnocentrism. Data collected on each dependent and independent variable may be analyzed using multiple regression, which will allow the researcher to determine the extent to which each independent variable contributes to the underlying variance in the consumption variable, as well as the model's overall fit. The model is run separately for each country of interest to the researcher and the results compared from one country to the others for which data have been collected. The researcher may find, for example, that the greater the degree of consumer ethnocentrism, the lower is the consumption of the company's products and that this independent variable is more important than price and income in explaining consumption levels in some countries. The researcher may also find that in countries with low levels of consumer ethnocentrism, price is the dominant factor driving consumption. Such analysis is extremely useful to the global marketer in the development of foreign market entry strategies or for expanding the firm's market presence in a country or region of interest. Regression analysis, unlike cross-tabulation and t-tests, does provide an explanation of the relationship between variables.

Cluster Analysis

The global marketing researcher is often interested in grouping objects based on their degree of similarity. In market entry analysis, for example, the researcher may be interested in isolating countries based on income, level of economic development, religion, or some other variable important to the company's entry strategy. Cluster analysis is a useful tool that allows the researcher to group countries based on some variable of interest. The technique maybe also be used to identify subgroups within individual countries. If population growth is critical to the success of the company's product over time, then this variable may be used as the basis for clustering countries. Using appropriate secondary data, the researcher will be able to produce a visual representation that groups all countries with high population growth rates, with low population growth rate countries falling into a separate cluster. Once relevant clusters have been formed and the universe of countries has been effectively narrowed, the researcher may subject the cluster of interest to more in-depth research.

Factor Analysis

Factor analysis is a data reduction technique. With the technique, data on a large number of variables are reduced to a small number of factors consisting of variables that are highly correlated. In essence, each factor is formed by variables that load most strongly on that particular factor. Several highly correlated variables are reduced to a single factor that may be used by the researcher in subsequent analysis. The global marketing researcher may compare the results of factor analysis for data from two or more countries in order to determine whether the underlying data structure is similar. Factor analysis may, for example, be used by the global researcher in understanding the structure of consumer demand in different countries. In one country some variables may load strongly on one factor but prove to be relatively unimportant to the structure of demand in another country. Variables such as ethnicity, number of siblings in the household, and individual career aspirations may be found to constitute a latent factor that is important to consumer demand. Factor analysis as described above is more precisely identified as exploratory factor analysis and has been criticized for not being theory-based. The technique does not begin with established theoretical relationships between variables but seeks to uncover relationships in the data. This is a serious limitation of exploratory factor analysis.

Additional Reading

Craig, C.S., and S.P. Douglas. *International Marketing Research*, 3rd ed. Chichester, UK: John Wiley and Sons, 2005.

Stevens, J. *Applied Multivariate Statistics for the Social Sciences.* 4th ed. Malwah, NJ: Lawrence Erlbaum Associates Publishers, 2002.

Chapter 8

Foreign Market Entry Strategies

The Global MARKETPLACE 8.1

Gen-u-Wine Storage

Gen-u-Wine Storage is a small company based in Winnipeg Canada. The firm builds custom-made wine cellars that it markets to clients across Canada, Europe, and the U.S. The company started as an "experiment" in 1995 and now has showrooms and representatives in all major Canadian cities, in several U.S. centres, and in Europe. "Today," says Robb Denomme, the company's Director of Operations, "Gen-u-Wine is a familiar, trusted, and highly respected name among wine lovers and aficionados everywhere." Wine needs to be protected from excessive humidity, rapid temperature fluctuations, vibrations, and light. To safeguard their investments, private wine collectors and institutions such as restaurants are turning to custom wine cellar manufacturers such as Gen-u-Wine Storage. In fact, temperature-controlled wine storage is becoming as standard in new home developments as home theatre systems.

Over the past decade Gen-u-Wine's two employees have become more than 20, and an 800-square-foot garage with the machinery placed on wheels to save space is now a 20,000 square foot (1,858 m^2) state-of-the-art manufacturing plant. The company's product portfolio has also expanded significantly from modest add-ons for existing homes to custom-built cellars costing well into the six figures. Gen-u-wine turned its attention to the potentially lucrative U.S. market in the early 2000s. By that time the company had already developed a reputation in the Canadian market and had sales approaching $500,000. The company received support from the Canadian federal and provincial governments for its ambitious expansion program and the firm now generates some 65% of its gross sales from U.S. clients. Gen-u-wine Storage is now a multimillion-dollar company. Although more than 90 percent of the cellars it builds are for private homes, Gen-u-Wine cellars can be found at quality locations such as the CN Tower, the Banff Springs Hotel, and the Air Canada Centre.

Sources: "Uncorking Success in Foreign Markets," Department of Foreign Affairs and International Trade (DFAIT) website: **http://www.international.gc.ca/commerce/success/genuwine-en.asp** (accessed March 10, 2007); The Basics—How Do I establish My Own Wine Cellar, Liquor Control Board of Ontario (LCBO) website: **http://www.lcbo.com/learn/establishcellar.shtml** (accessed February 2, 2008); "Wine cellars come of age—Home storage options range from simple to elaborate." Winnipeg Free Press, December 30, 2007. Available at: **http://www.winnipegfreepress.com/subscriber/homes/renohomes/v-arkiv/story/4099945p-4698214c.html.** (accessed February 2, 2008).

As The Global Marketplace 8.1 shows, participation in international markets is increasingly within the grasp of small firms. A company does not have to be large to be engaged in the global marketplace. Participation in international markets can be very rewarding and may turn out to be the key to prosperity for corporations, employees, and national governments. Research has found that firms that participate in global markets grow faster, are more productive, and, equally important, have employees who tend to earn more.[1] But most firms cannot simply jump into global marketing and expect to be successful. New activities in an unfamiliar environment also increase a firm's risk and may lead to significant financial losses. Failed attempts to enter international markets may also result in the erosion of the firm's brand equity and reputation in the eyes of foreign consumers. Therefore, companies must prepare their entry strategies and adjust to the needs and opportunities of international markets in order to become long-term participants.

Companies have a number of strategic options when deciding how foreign markets should be entered. These are termed **modes of entry** and represent institutional arrangements that firms may use to penetrate foreign markets. These modes of entry include exporting, licensing, franchising, foreign sales subsidiaries, strategic alliances, and foreign direct investment (FDI). The selection of an appropriate mode of entry is critical to long-term success in international markets. Each option has its strengths and weaknesses. A mode of entry that may be well suited to penetrating the U.K. market may be totally ineffective when entering the Chinese or Japanese markets. The company's experience operating globally also has a bearing on the selection of an entry mode. Some modes of entry, such as exporting, require little specialized expertise or foreign market insight. Others, such as foreign direct investment, necessitate a substantial understanding of legal, regulatory, and market conditions in the foreign country targeted, and considerably more managerial sophistication. The various modes of entry are also associated with varying levels of risk for the firm. As companies become more engaged globally, they may well migrate from simpler and less risky entry modes to those requiring the acceptance of higher risk and necessitating greater levels of managerial expertise.

This chapter explores the various modes of entry open to the global marketing manager. The factors that motivate firms to seek entry into international markets are first explored before the discussion focuses on specific entry modes. Key questions addressed in this chapter include the following: Why should firms wish to become engaged globally? What are some of the factors, both external and internal, that make entry into international markets a strategic priority for the firm? What factors should the company consider in selecting a specific mode of entry? The pros and cons of the various entry-mode choices are also presented. The discussion in this chapter will assist students in understanding the complexity of the decisions involved in entry-mode selection.

Motivations to Enter Foreign Markets

Why do firms go global? Many researchers have worked on determining the reasons. A key factor is apparently the type and quality of management. Dynamic management is important when firms take their first international steps. Over the long term, management commitment and management's perceptions and attitudes are also good predictors of global market success.[2] To a large extent, this conclusion has been formulated by reverse deduction: the managers of firms that are unsuccessful or inactive in the international marketplace usually exhibit a lack of determination to pursue, or a lack of preparation for, global marketing. International markets cannot be penetrated overnight—to succeed in them requires substantial market development activity, market research, and the identification of and response to foreign market factors. For example, it can take as long as two years for a novice firm to successfully complete its first export order.[3] That firm may require several more years before it is sufficiently comfortable with foreign markets to consider establishing a foreign subsidiary or embarking on an international joint venture. Therefore, a high level of commitment to global markets is crucial. This commitment must be able to endure stagnation, and sometimes even setbacks and failure. To obtain such a commitment, it is important to involve all levels of management early on in planning the foreign market entry process and to impress on all players that the effort will only succeed with a commitment that is company-wide. Planning and execution of an international venture must be incorporated into the firm's strategic management process. A firm that sets no strategic goals for its global initiative is less likely to make the venture a long-term success.[4]

In addition to broad commitment, it is also important to establish a specific organizational structure in which someone has the responsibility for global operations. Without some specified responsibility centre, the focus that is necessary for success is lost. Just one person assigned part-time to global marketing activities can begin exploring and entering international markets, but it is crucial to assign the global responsibility to a specific person.

In most business activities, one factor alone rarely accounts for any given action. Usually a mixture of factors results in firms taking steps in a given direction. This is true of the process of foreign market entry; there are a variety of motivations both pushing and pulling firms to enter foreign markets. Exhibit 8.1 provides an overview of the major motivations to go international. They are differentiated into proactive and reactive motivations. Proactive motivations represent stimuli to attempt strategic change. Reactive motivations influence firms that are responsive to environmental changes and that adjust to them by changing their activities over time. In other words, proactive firms go international because they want to, while reactive ones go international because they have to.

Proactive Motivations

The most stimulating proactive motivation to become involved in global marketing is the profit advantage. Management may perceive international sales as a potential source of higher profit margins or of additional profits. Of course, the perceived profitability when planning to enter international markets is often quite different from the profitability actually attained. The actual initial profitability of international start-up operations may be quite low,[5] mainly due to relatively high start-up costs. The gap between perception and reality may be particularly large when the firm has not previously engaged in international market activities. Despite thorough planning, imponderable influences often shift the profit picture substantially. For example, a sudden shift in exchange rates may drastically alter profit forecasts even though they were based on careful market evaluation.

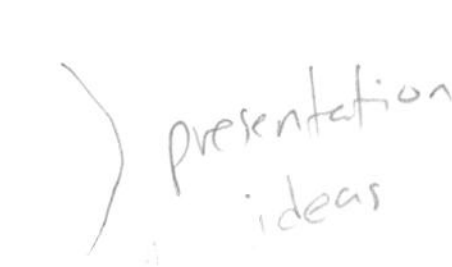

A second major stimulus results either from unique products or from a technological advantage. A firm may produce goods or services that are not widely available from international competitors or may have made technological advances in a specialized field. Again, real and perceived advantages should be differentiated. Many firms believe that theirs are unique products or services, even though this may not be the case in the global market. If products or technology are unique, however, it can certainly provide a competitive edge and result in major business success abroad. The intensity of marketing's

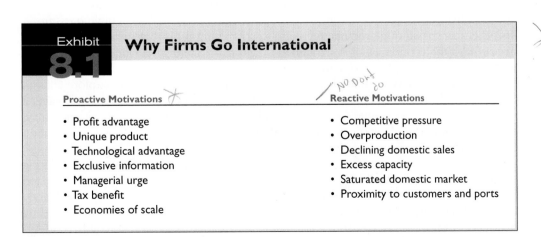

Exhibit 8.1 Why Firms Go International

Proactive Motivations	Reactive Motivations
• Profit advantage	• Competitive pressure
• Unique product	• Overproduction
• Technological advantage	• Declining domestic sales
• Exclusive information	• Excess capacity
• Managerial urge	• Saturated domestic market
• Tax benefit	• Proximity to customers and ports
• Economies of scale	

interaction with the research and development function, as well as the level of R & D investment, can have a major effect on foreign market success.

One issue to consider is how long such a technological or product advantage will continue. Historically, a firm with a competitive edge could count on being the sole supplier to international markets for years to come. This type of advantage, however, has shrunk dramatically because of competing technologies and a frequent lack of intellectual property rights protection in some key markets.

Exclusive market information is another proactive stimulus. This includes knowledge about foreign customers, marketplaces, or market situations that is not widely shared by other firms. Such special knowledge may result from particular insights based on a firm's international research, special contacts a firm may have, or simply being in the right place at the right time (for example, recognizing a good business situation during a vacation trip). Although exclusivity can serve well as an initial stimulus for global marketing activities, it will rarely provide prolonged motivation because competitors—at least in the medium term—can be expected to catch up with the information advantage of the firm, particularly in light of the growing ease of global information access.

Managerial urge is a motivation that reflects the desire, drive, and enthusiasm of management toward global marketing activities. This enthusiasm can exist simply because managers like to be part of a firm that operates internationally. It sounds impressive. Further, it can often provide a good reason for international travel—for example, to call on a major customer in the Bahamas during a cold winter month. Often, however, the managerial urge to enter foreign markets is simply the reflection of general entrepreneurial motivation—of a desire for continuous growth and market expansion.[6]

Tax benefits have historically also played a major motivating role. Many countries offer tax concessions to their firms in order to encourage export activities. However, the rules of the World Trade Organization prohibit the subsidization of exports by all but the poorest countries.

A final major proactive motivation is economies of scale. Becoming a participant in international markets may enable the firm to increase its output and therefore slide down more rapidly on the experience curve. Ever since the Boston Consulting Group showed that a doubling of output can reduce production costs up to 30 percent, this effect has been very much sought. Increased production for the international market can therefore also help in reducing the cost of production for domestic sales and make the firm more competitive domestically as well.[7] This effect often results in seeking market share as a primary objective. Initially, this may mean an increased search for export markets; later on, it can result in the opening of foreign subsidiaries and foreign production facilities.

Reactive Motivations

A second type of motivation, primarily characterized as reactive, influences firms to respond to changes and pressures in the business environment rather than attempt to blaze trails. As illustrated in The Global Marketplace 8.2, changes in the home market may essentially push firms "over the edge," forcing them to explore foreign market opportunities. A primary reactive motivation to develop foreign markets is competitive pressure. A firm may fear losing domestic market share to competing firms that have benefited from the effect of the economies of scale gained by global marketing activities. Further, it may fear losing foreign markets permanently to domestic competitors that decide to focus on these markets. Observing that domestic competitors are beginning to explore foreign markets, and knowing that market share is most easily retained by the firm that obtains it initially, firms frequently enter the international market head over heels. Quick entry may, however, result in similarly quick withdrawal once the firm recognizes that its preparation has been insufficient.

Similarly, overproduction can serve as a major reactive motivation. Historically, during downturns in the domestic business cycle, markets abroad were initially unaffected because of time lags. They provided an ideal outlet for inventories that were significantly above desired levels. Frequently, however, international market expansion motivated by overproduction did not represent full commitment by management, but rather **safety-**

The Global MARKETPLACE 8.2

Russian Vodka Manufacturers Go Global

Russian vodka manufacturers are facing declining home country sales and increased competition from major international and regional players such as Diageo, Nemiroff, and Ukraine's Soyuz-Victan. The Russian vodka market is huge. In 2005, Russians consumed 1.8 billion litres of vodka. While significant, this level of consumption is down sharply from previous years when over 2 billion litres were being consumed. The trend in consumption is decidedly negative with sales expected to fall an additional 25 percent by 2010. Faced with challenges at home, Russian vodka producers have set their sights on North America and Western Europe.

Building market share in international markets outside the Commonwealth of Independent States (CIS) and Israel—traditionally strong markets for Russian producers—will be difficult. The North American and Western European markets, while large and growing, are also hotly contested at every price point. Russian manufacturers will have to rely on their heritage and reputation for producing a quality product. For example, Parliament Vodka touts its 18th-century production process that uses milk to remove unwanted particles and is followed by a multistage purification procedure. The process improves product quality but is costly and complicated; consequently, it is not used by many other companies. Other Russian brands rely more heavily on cultural associations. Legend of Kremlin is presented in a hand-decorated bottle and is available only in small quantities via an offshoot of President Putin's administration. Russia is viewed as the spiritual home of vodka, and manufacturers will have to capitalize on this perception if they are to be successful in competitive Western markets.

Source: Market intelligence firm Euromonitor International, **http://www.euromonitor.com**.

valve activity designed for short-term activities only. Instead of developing a global marketing perspective by adjusting the marketing mix to needs abroad, firms using this strategy typically stimulate international sales with short-term price cuts.[8] As soon as the domestic market demand returns to previous levels, foreign market activities are curtailed or even terminated. Firms that have used such a strategy once may encounter difficulties when trying to employ it again, because many foreign customers are not interested in temporary or sporadic business relationships. This reaction from abroad, together with the lessons learned about the danger of large inventories and the fact that the major industrial economies appear to be increasingly synchronized, may well lead to a decrease in the importance of this motivation over time.

Stable or declining domestic sales, whether measured in sales volume or market share, have a similar motivating effect. Products marketed by the firm domestically may be at the declining stage of the product life cycle. Instead of attempting a push-back of the life cycle process at home, or in addition to such an effort, firms may opt to prolong the product life cycle by expanding the market. In the past, such efforts often met with success because customers in many countries only gradually reached a level of need and sophistication already attained by customers in industrialized nations. Increasingly, however, if lag times exist at all in foreign markets, they are quite short. Nevertheless, this motivation is still a valid one, particularly in the context of developing nations, which often still have very good use for products for which the demand in the industrialized world is already on the decline. This holds particularly true for high-technology products that are outdated by the latest innovations. Such "just-dated" technology can be highly useful to economic development and offers vast progress in the manufacturing or services sectors.

Excess capacity can also be a powerful motivation. If equipment for production is not fully utilized, firms may see expansion into the international market as an ideal possibility for achieving broader distribution of fixed costs. Alternatively, if all fixed costs are assigned to domestic production, the firm can penetrate foreign markets with a pricing scheme that focuses mainly on variable costs. Although such a strategy may be useful in the short term, it may result in the offering of products abroad at a cost lower than at home, which in turn may trigger dumping charges. In the long run, fixed costs have to be recovered to ensure replacement of production equipment that growing international market activities may overtax. Market penetration strategy based on variable cost alone is, therefore, not feasible over the long term.

The reactive motivation of a saturated domestic market is similar in results to that of declining domestic sales. Again, firms in this situation can use the international market to prolong the life cycle of their product and of their organization. As shown in Exhibit 8.2, the firm may prolong global sales of its product by sequential introductions in foreign markets. The approach allows the firm to counter declining home country prospects by capitalizing on growth opportunities abroad.

A final major reactive motivation is proximity to customers and ports. Physical closeness to the international market can often play a major role in the export activities of a firm. For example, Canadian firms established near the U.S. border may not even perceive of their integrated market activities in the United States as global marketing. Rather, they are simply an extension of domestic activities, without any particular attention paid to the fact that some of the products go abroad. Similarly, most European firms automatically become global marketers simply because their neighbours are so close. As an example, a European company operating in the heart of Belgium needs to go only 80 kilometres to be in multiple foreign markets.

In this context, the concept of psychic or **psychological distance** needs to be understood. Geographic closeness to foreign markets may not necessarily translate into real or perceived closeness to the foreign customer. Sometimes cultural variables, legal factors, and other societal norms make a foreign market that is geographically close seem psychologically distant. For example, research has shown that U.S. firms perceive Canada to be much closer psychologically than Mexico. Even England, mainly because of the similarity in language, is perceived by many U.S. firms to be much closer than Mexico or other Latin American countries, despite the geographic distances. However, in light of the reduction of trade barriers as a result of the North American Free Trade Agreement (NAFTA), and a growing proportion of the U.S. population with Hispanic background, this long-standing perception may be changing rapidly.

It is important to remember two major issues in the context of psychological distance. First, some of the distance seen by firms is based on perception rather than reality. For

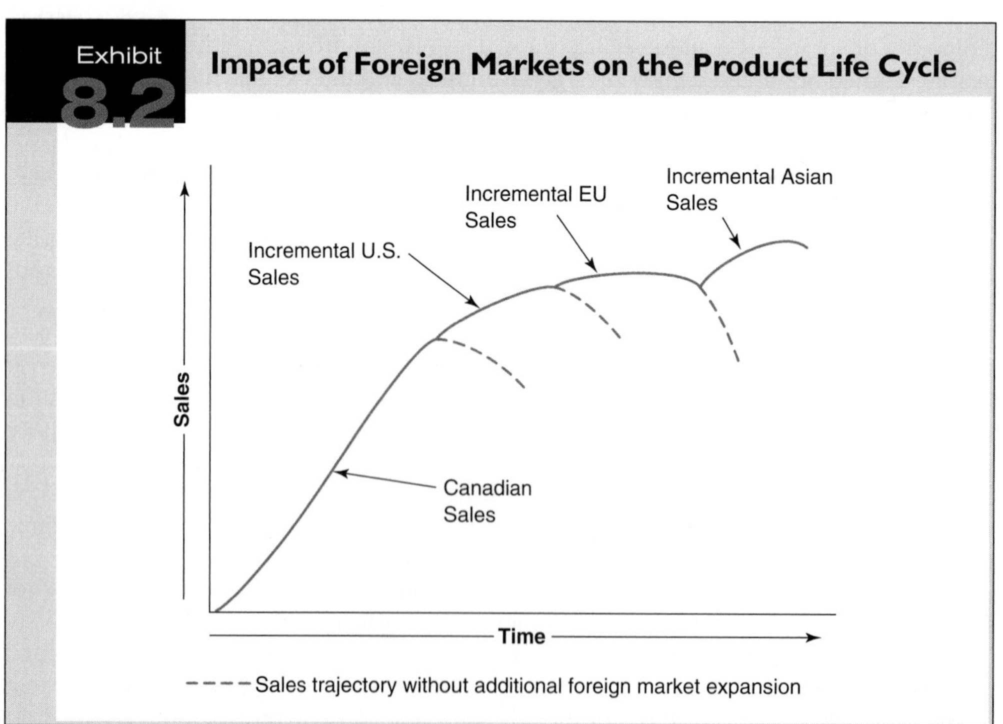

In More Detail 8.1

WATERFALL VS. SPRINKLER: FOREIGN MARKET EXPANSION STRATEGIES

A company's expansion into foreign markets will generally follow one of two patterns. The firm may pursue a waterfall or a sprinkler approach to foreign market expansion. With a **waterfall strategy**, the company gradually moves its products and services into overseas markets. Given success in the home market, the firm gradually begins marketing activities in psychologically close markets, then moves into other mature but high-growth markets, and finally into more risky developing-country markets. With this strategy, foreign market expansion takes place in an orderly sequence, giving the firm's managers time to learn the culture of each new market and adjust to their nuances. Marketing skills developed in one market can be applied more readily to subsequent markets.

In contrast, the firm may opt to pursue a **sprinkler strategy** in foreign market expansion. Here a number of unrelated markets are entered simultaneously or within a short time period. Selection of country markets for entry is based on the size of the potential growth opportunity, with little attention paid to psychic distance. The approach allows the firm to rapidly develop a global presence and may be a workable strategy in highly competitive markets. A sprinkler strategy by its very nature will be more taxing on the managerial capabilities of the firm.

Source: Reproduced by permission of SAGE publications, London, from Baron Weitz and Robin Wensley, (eds), "Global Marketing: Research on Foreign Entry; Local Marketing, Global Management" from *Handbook of Marketing,* Copyright © Johansson J., 2003: 459–460.

example, German firms may view the Austrian market simply as an extension of their home market because of so many superficial similarities, just as many firms in, say, Ontario, Canada, may see the United Kingdom as psychologically very close due to the similarity in language. However, the attitudes and values of managers and customers may vary substantially between markets. Too much of a focus on the similarities may let the firm lose sight of the differences. Many Canadian firms have incurred high costs in learning this lesson when entering the United States.[9] At the same time, closer psychological proximity does make it easier for firms to enter markets. Therefore, for firms new to global marketing, it may be advantageous to begin this new activity by entering the psychologically closer markets first in order to gather experience before venturing into markets that are farther away.[10] Alternative strategies for global market expansion are described in In More Detail 8.1.

An overall contemplation of these motivations should also consider the following factors. First, firms that are most successful globally are motivated by proactive—that is, firm-internal—factors. Second, the motivations of firms do not seem to shift dramatically over the short term but are rather stable. For the student who seeks involvement in international markets and is searching for firms most likely to provide good opportunities, an important consideration should be whether a firm is proactive or reactive.

Proactive firms are also more likely to be service-oriented than are reactive firms. Further, it is frequently more marketing- and strategy-oriented than reactive firms, which have operational issues as their major concern. The clearest differentiation between the two types of firms can probably be made after the fact by determining how they initially entered international markets. Proactive firms are also more likely to solicit their first international market order, whereas reactive firms frequently begin foreign market activities after receiving an unsolicited order from abroad.

The Internationalization Process

The term **internationalization** is used to describe the process by which firms become gradually more engaged in global markets. Companies may, for example, start off as exporters and gradually increase their commitment to foreign markets to the point where they have established manufacturing operations overseas. Researchers have found that companies gradually move through five stages as they become more engaged and committed to markets overseas. Companies may begin as **indirect exporters**, marketing their products to home country intermediaries that in turn export the products to foreign mar-

Exhibit 8.3 Stages in the Process of Internationalization

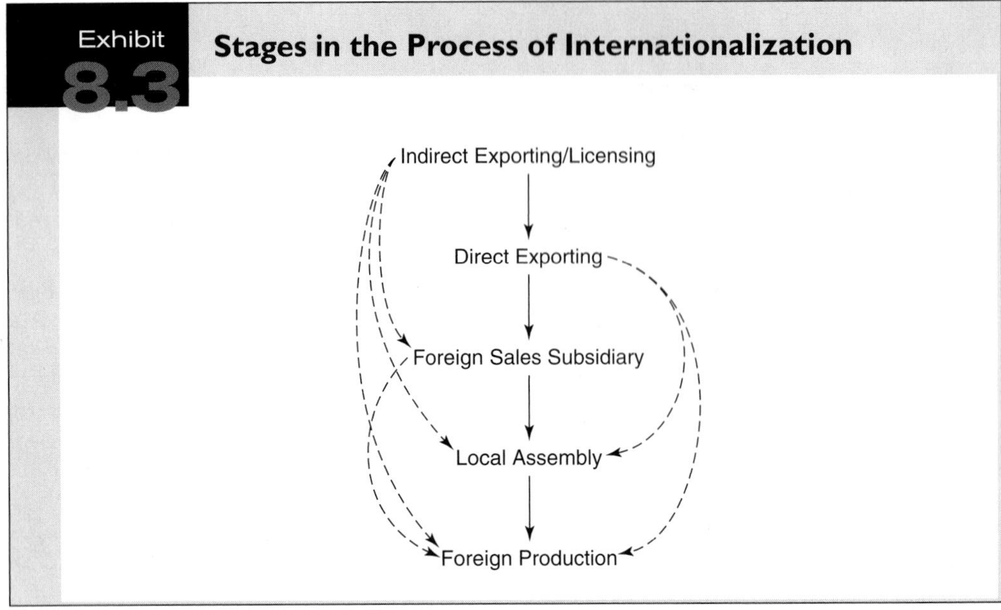

kets, or via a **licensing** agreement, where their technology or business system is provided to a foreign entity in exchange for royalty payments. This initial stage may be followed by the companies themselves becoming **direct exporters**, in which case they transact directly with an intermediary in the foreign country. The direct exporting stage may be followed by firms establishing their own **foreign sales subsidiary** and hiring dedicated sales professionals to handle marketing operations in the foreign country. The fourth stage in the process of internationalization is **local assembly**. Companies at this level of global engagement may source components from the home country and assemble and market the final product in a foreign country. The fifth and final stage in the process of internationalization is **foreign production**, where companies establish full-fledged manufacturing operations in the foreign country, investing in plant and equipment and maintaining a complement of production and management staff. It should be noted that not all companies follow the sequence of stages as outlined above. There is empirical support for leapfrogging, in which one or more stages are completely skipped (see Exhibit 8.3). As a result of this evidence, some researchers have taken issue with the standard model of the internationalization process presented above.[11]

Modes of Entry

Given the motivation to enter international markets, firms are faced with a number of choices with respect to the institutional arrangements they may use. Termed modes of entry, these institutional arrangements to enter foreign markets range from relatively arms-length exporting arrangements to more involved foreign direct investment. These modes of entry carry varying levels of financial risk for the firm, vary in their demands on management, and are associated with varying levels of potential return for the company. The selection of an entry mode will be driven by a number of factors, such as firm size, international experience, and financial resources. In More Detail 8.2 outlines a number of approaches to entry-mode selection.

Exporting

With exporting, products manufactured in the firm's home country are shipped to and marketed in one or more foreign countries. Firms may engage in direct exporting or indirect exporting, depending on whether a home country marketing intermediary is involved. With direct exporting, the firm transacts directly with a market intermediary located in a

The Global MARKETPLACE 8.3

GV Snowshoes

A walk through the forest on a cold January morning, unimpeded by deep snow and buried trails, is an exhilarating experience. The freedom to move through nature, gliding over the fluffy white stuff instead of sinking into it, covering terrain that would otherwise be inaccessible in mere boots—that is the snowshoe experience. And that is the experience that GV Snowshoes wants to share with the world. At least the snowy part of the world!

Founded in 1959, GV Snowshoes is the world's only manufacturer specializing in traditional, aluminum-framed, and composite snowshoes. This Aboriginal company makes an extensive line of both traditionally crafted snowshoes and high-tech designs to suit all skill levels and tastes. According to Eric Beaulieu, director of sales and marketing for GV Snowshoes, exporting was a natural extension for the company when it consolidated the local snowshoe manufacturing industry through a number of acquisitions in 1982. As a result of this strategy, GV Snowshoes, based in Wendake, Quebec, has been exporting its quality products to winter lovers in the United States for 20 years. The company has since developed markets in Finland, Switzerland, Germany, France, and Chile.

With a staff of 50 employees producing one of the largest product lines in the world, Eric Beaulieu's explanation for the firm's export strategy is simple logic. "We are a manufacturer, so the more we sell, the more we produce. We try to broaden our market so that we can manufacture snowshoes year-round even though our products are designed for winter activities."

Mr. Beaulieu clearly understands the advantages of exporting as a business growth strategy, yet he is quick to mention the additional benefits in his advice to Canadian exporters and potential exporters. "Never give up. The rewards and experience you gain dealing with other countries are so great. Not only do you increase your volume of sales, the image and reputation of your company improves as well. But the most important reward is the personal knowledge and experience that you receive from each different country. It helps you understand different points of view that make you stronger to approach any other challenge."

Source: Adapted from "GV Snowshoes: Exporting Winter Fun," **http://www.exportsource.ca/gol/exportsource/site.nsf/en/es02792.html** (accessed November 11, 2006).

foreign country. Such intermediaries may be distributors, wholesalers, or retailers based in the foreign market. In the case of indirect exporting, the firm transacts with an intermediary based in its own home country. This intermediary in turn takes responsibility for exporting the product to one or more foreign countries.

Most Canadian exporters, such as GV Snowshoes profiled in The Global Marketplace 8.3, are small and medium-sized firms. Some firms may very well be *born global*— founded for the explicit purpose of marketing abroad because of the recognized importance of global marketing and because the domestic economy may be too small to support their activities. A company such as Waterloo-based Research In Motion (RIM) may well fit this

In More Detail 8.2

ENTRY-MODE SELECTION

Research has shown that firms follow one of three approaches to entry-mode selection. As they expand globally, firms may simply use the same entry mode irrespective of the foreign market to be penetrated. This has been termed the **naive rule**, because it does not reflect the need to recognize country and firm differences. Some firms, however, may opt to follow the **pragmatic rule,** where the focus is on always selecting the mode of entry that minimizes the firm's exposure to risk in the particular transaction. A third rule that may guide the entry-mode selection decision is termed the **strategy rule**. Here the firm systematically analyzes each entry mode and applies a common evaluative metric, such as the potential to maximize net profit contribution; the entry mode that will result in the highest net contribution is selected. Under this rule, the firm will apply this principle on each prospective transaction in a foreign market.

profile. It appears that in some countries more than a third of exporting firms commenced their export activities within two years of establishment.[12] Such **innate exporters** (or "start-up" exporters) may have a distinct role to play in an economy's international trade involvement.

In most instances today, firms begin their operations in the domestic market. From their home location, they gradually expand, and, over time, some of them become interested in the international market. The development of this interest typically appears to proceed in several stages. In each one of these stages, firms are measurably different in their capabilities, problems, and needs.[13] Initially, the vast majority of firms are not at all interested in the international marketplace. Frequently, management will not even fill an unsolicited export order if one is received. Should unsolicited orders or other international market stimuli continue over time, however, a firm may gradually become a **partially interested exporter**. Management will then fill unsolicited export orders.

Prime candidates among firms to make this transition from uninterested to partially interested are those companies that have a track record of domestic market expansion.[14] In the next stage, the firm gradually begins to explore international markets, and management is willing to consider the feasibility of exporting. After this **exploratory stage**, the firm becomes an **experimental exporter**, usually to psychologically close countries. However, management is still far from being committed to global marketing activities.

At the next stage, the firm evaluates the impact that exporting has had on its general activities. Here, of course, the possibility exists that a firm will be disappointed with its international market performance and will withdraw from these activities. On the other hand, frequently, it will continue to exist as an experienced small exporter. The final stage of this process is that of **export adaptation**. Here a firm is an experienced exporter to a particular country and adjusts its activities to changing exchange rates, tariffs, and other variables. Management is ready to explore the feasibility of exporting to additional countries that are psychologically farther away. Frequently, this level of adaptation is reached once export transactions comprise 15 percent of sales volume. Just as parking-ticket income, originally seen as unexpected revenue, gradually became incorporated into city budgets, the income from export marketing may become incorporated into the budget and plans of the firm. In these instances, the firm can be considered a strategic participant in the global marketplace. The population of exporting firms within these stages does not remain stable.

As can be expected, firms in different stages are faced with different problems. Firms at an export awareness stage—partially interested in the international market—are primarily concerned with operational matters such as information flow and the mechanics of carrying out international business transactions. They understand that a totally new body of knowledge and expertise is needed and try to acquire it. Companies that have already had some exposure to international markets begin to think about tactical marketing issues such as communication and sales effort. Finally, firms that have reached the export adaptation phase are mainly strategy- and service-oriented, which is to say that they worry about longer-range issues such as service delivery and regulatory changes. Utilizing the traditional marketing concept, one can therefore recognize that increased sophistication in international markets translates into increased application of marketing knowledge on the part of firms. The more they become active in international markets, the more firms recognize that a marketing orientation internationally is just as essential as it is in the domestic market.

Export Intermediaries

As The Global Marketplace 8.4 illustrates, foreign market intermediaries are often critical to a firm's success in international markets. However, firms that do not care to export directly can still participate in foreign markets by making use of market intermediaries in their own home country. For example, many products are sold to multinational corporations that use them as input for their foreign sales. Alternatively, an exporter may buy products domestically to round out an international product line, or a buyer from abroad may purchase goods during a visit.

The Global MARKETPLACE 8.4

Jamaica Pepper Exports

Gray's Pepper Products is a small Jamaican company that is committed to the export market. With only 24 full-time employees, the firm exports its line of condiments—Gray's Hot Pepper Sauce, Gray's Spicy Sauce, and Gray's Extra Hot Habanero Pepper Sauce—to Canada and the United States. The company was established 30 years ago as a home-based business. In those days the founder of the company manually processed and bottled by hand. Today the company operates a modern, fully automated processing plant capable of processing one million peppers annually.

The company works with exclusive distributors in New Jersey and Toronto to service its customers in North America. The company has recorded consistently increasing export sales to North America through its distributor relationships but notes that hotels and resorts in Jamaica are another channel. North American and European visitors to the island who are exposed to the company's products often contact the company on their return home to inquire where in their own country they can purchase the company's fiery products.

Source: Adapted from "Gray's Pepper Products Ltd – A Pioneer in Export – Bringing Spice to Taste Buds across the Globe," May 12, 2006, *Jamaica Gleaner*, **http://www.jamaica-gleaner.com/gleaner/20060512/business/business4.html** (accessed May 12, 2006). Adapted with permission from the Jamaica Exporters' Association.

Frequently, firms enter the international market with the help of market intermediaries who specialize in bringing firms or their goods and services to the global market. These intermediaries often have detailed information about the competitive conditions in certain markets or have personal contacts with potential buyers abroad. They can also evaluate credit risk, call on customers abroad, and manage the physical delivery of the product. Two key intermediaries are export management companies and trading companies.

Export Management Companies

Export management companies (EMCs) are domestic firms that specialize in performing global marketing services as commission representatives or as distributors for several other firms. Most EMCs are quite small. They are frequently formed by one or two principals who have experience in global marketing or in a particular geographic area. Their expertise enables them to offer specialized services to domestic corporations.

EMCs have two primary forms of operation. They either take title to goods and operate internationally on their own account, or they perform services as agents. In the first instance, the EMC offers a conventional export channel in that it does not have any form of geographic exclusivity and tends to negotiate price with suppliers on every transaction. As an agent, an EMC is likely to have either an informal or a formal contractual relationship, which specifies exclusivity agreements and, often, sales quotas. In addition, price arrangements and promotional support payments are agreed on, which simplifies ongoing transactions.[15] Because EMCs often serve a variety of clients, their mode of operation may vary from client to client and from transaction to transaction—that is, an EMC may act as an agent for one client, whereas for another client, or even for the same one on a different occasion, it may operate as a distributor.

When serving as an agent, the EMC is primarily in charge of developing foreign marketing and sales strategies and establishing contacts abroad. Because the EMC does not share in the profits from a sale, it depends heavily on a high sales volume, on which it charges commission. It may therefore be tempted to take on as many products and as many clients as possible in order to obtain a high turnover. The risk in this is that the EMC will spread itself too thinly and will not be able to adequately represent all the clients and products it carries. This risk is particularly great for small EMCs.

When operating as a distributor, the EMC purchases products from the domestic firm, takes title, and assumes the trading risk. Selling in its own name offers the EMC an opportunity to reap greater profits than does acting as an agent. The potential for greater profitability is appropriate because the EMC has drastically reduced the risk for the domestic firm while increasing its own risk. The burden of the merchandise acquired provides a major motivation to complete an international sale successfully. The domestic firm selling to the EMC is in the comfortable position of having sold its merchandise and received its money without having to deal with the complexities of the international market. On the other hand, the firm is unlikely to gather much foreign market expertise and therefore relegates itself to some extent to remaining a purely domestic firm.

For the concept of an export management company to work, both parties must fully recognize the delegation of responsibilities; the costs associated with these activities; and the need for information sharing, cooperation, and mutual reliance. On the manufacturer's side, use of an EMC should be viewed as a major channel commitment. This requires a thorough investigation of the intermediary and the advisability of relying on its efforts, a willingness to cooperate on a prolonged basis, and a willingness to reward it properly for these efforts. The EMC in turn must adopt a flexible approach to managing the export relationship. As access to the Internet is making customers increasingly sophisticated, export management companies must ensure that they continue to deliver true added value. They must acquire, develop, and deploy resources, such as new knowledge about foreign markets or about export processes, in order to lower their client firm's export-related transaction costs and therefore remain useful intermediaries.[16] By doing so, the EMC can clearly let the client know that the cost is worth the service.

Trading Companies

Another major intermediary is the trading company. The concept was originated centuries ago by the European trading houses such as the Fuggers and was soon formalized by the monarchs. Hoping to expand their imperial powers and wealth, kings chartered traders to form corporate bodies that enjoyed exclusive trading rights and protection by the naval forces in exchange for tax payments. Today, the most famous trading companies are the **sogoshosha** of Japan. Names like Sumitomo, Mitsubishi, Mitsui, and C. Itoh have become household words around the world. These general trading companies play a unique role in world commerce by importing, exporting, countertrading, investing, and manufacturing. Because of their vast size, they can benefit from economies of scale and perform their operations at very low profit margins.

Licensing and Franchising

In addition to exporting, licensing and franchising are alternatives open to and used by all types of firms, large and small. They offer flexibility in the international market approach, reflecting the needs of the firm and the circumstances in the market. A small firm, for example, may choose to use licensing to benefit from a foreign business concept or to expand without much capital investment. A multinational corporation may use the same strategy to rapidly enter foreign markets in order to take advantage of new conditions and foreclose some opportunities to its competition. It is important to recognize licensing and franchising as additional opportunities for market entry. These options can be used in lieu of or in addition to the export strategy discussed previously.

Licensing

Under a licensing agreement, one firm, the licensor, permits another to use its intellectual property in exchange for compensation designated as a royalty. The recipient firm is the licensee. The property might include patents, trademarks, copyrights, technology, technical know-how, or specific marketing skills. For example, a firm that has developed new packaging for liquids can permit other firms abroad to use the same process. Licensing therefore amounts to exporting and importing intangibles. As The Global Marketplace 8.5 shows, licensing has great potential that may increase for a long time to come.

Licensing has intuitive appeal to many potential global marketers. As an entry strategy, it may not require capital investment in, knowledge of, or marketing strength in foreign markets. By earning royalty income, it provides an opportunity to obtain an additional return on research and development investments already incurred. After initial costs, the licensor can reap benefits until the end of the contract period. Licensing reduces risk of exposure to government intervention in that the licensee is typically a local company that can provide leverage against government action. Licensing will help to avoid host-country regulations that are focused on equity ventures. It may also serve as a stage in the internationalization of the firm by providing a means by which foreign markets can be tested without major involvement of capital or management time. Similarly, licensing can be used as a strategy to preempt a market before the entry of competition, especially if the licensor's resources permit full-scale involvement only in selected markets. A final reason that licensing activities are increasing is the growing global protection of intellectual property rights. In many countries, pirated technology, processes, and products are still abundant. However, progress by the World Trade Organization has improved the protection of intellectual property and the enforcement of such protection by governments. With greater protection of their proprietary knowledge, companies are more willing to transfer

The Global MARKETPLACE 8.5

International Franchising That Will Melt in Your Mouth

The United Arab Emirates (UAE) is a federation of seven independent states located in the southeastern corner of the Arabian Peninsula. It is bordered by the Persian Gulf to the north, Saudi Arabia to the south and west, and Oman and the Gulf of Oman to the east. Rich in oil, the region has enjoyed rapid growth and modernization. An estimated 86 percent of the country's population is urban. The city of Abu Dhabi—the federal capital and largest city of the UAE—serves as the financial, transportation, and communications centre of this major petroleum-producing area. The city embodies the unique blend of traditional and modern life that marks the region.

Those who have visited the growing metropolis of Abu Dhabi will not associate the city's name with huge billboards advertising a Colorado-based, women-owned chocolate factory. But that is exactly what a visitor would find ever since a master franchise licensing agreement was signed between Rocky Mountain Chocolate Factory, Inc., and the family-owned Al Muhairy Group, which operates franchises in the UAE, Saudi Arabia, Oman, Kuwait, Bahrain, and Qatar.

Rocky Mountain Chocolate Factory, Inc., is a confectionary manufacturer that produces an extensive line of chocolate and other confectionary candies in old-fashioned Victorian candy kitchens using traditional American candy-making methods. The company touts its reputation for its "entertaining fudge-making demonstrations, old-fashioned caramel apples, and larger-than-life handmade chocolates." In addition, it is also an international franchiser with 228 retail locations in the United States and Canada. Most recently, Rocky Mountain has added the Middle East to its repertoire, thanks to a franchising agreement with the Al Muhairy Group.

Greg Pope, Rocky Mountain's vice president of franchise development, states: "We are learning that Europeans and Middle Eastern cultures are keen on our theme of in-store candy preparation.... Chocolate has a universal appeal and is considered a gourmet luxury. Rocky Mountain's dark chocolates, Butter English Toffee, and Rocky Pop are particular favourites of the UAE consumers."

So how did the market entry come about? Rocky Mountain's owners decided to enlist the aid of the Commercial Service—a global network of international trade experts from the U.S. Commerce Department who help small and mid-sized U.S. companies succeed in global markets. The firm sent marketing packets to Commercial Service offices around the world and attended a franchising trade show in Milan, Italy. An advertisement in the American Business Information Center in Abu Dhabi caught the eye of Sanjay Duggal, a local entrepreneur, who came for a visit to Rocky Mountain's headquarters in Durango, Colorado.

In May 2000, the Al Muhairy Group, which had become the master franchise license holder for the Gulf Region, opened a Rocky Mountain Chocolate Factory franchise in Al Muhairy Centre, an upscale shopping centre in Abu Dhabi. Within a few months, the venture was a success and Rocky Mountain hosted a Chocoholics Evening for 120 locals and expatriates in its new Middle Eastern hometown.

Sources: Rocky Mountain Chocolate Factory website, **http://www.rmcf.com** (accessed September 3, 2002); and Sandra Necessary and Nancy Charles-Parker, "Chocolate-Covered Exports: Colorado Firm Finds Sweet Tooth in Mideast," *Export America—Success Stories* 2 (January 2001).

such knowledge internationally.[17] In instances of high levels of piracy, a licensing agreement with a strong foreign partner may also add value, because now the partner becomes a local force with a distinct interest in rooting out unlicensed activities.

Licensing offers a foreign entity the opportunity for immediate market entry with a proven concept. It therefore reduces the risk of R & D failures, the cost of designing around the licensor's patents, or the fear of patent infringement litigation. Furthermore, most licensing agreements provide for ongoing cooperation and support, thus enabling the licensee to benefit from new developments. Licensing may also enable the global marketer to enter a foreign market that is closed to either imports or direct foreign investments.

Licensing is not without disadvantages. To a large degree, it may leave foreign market activities to the licensee. As a result, the licensor may not gain sufficient foreign country marketing expertise to ready itself for subsequent world market penetration. Moreover, the initial toehold in the foreign market may not be a foot in the door. Indeed, depending on the licensing arrangement, quite the opposite may take place. In exchange for the royalty, the licensor may create its own competitor, not only in the markets for which the agreement was made but also in third markets.

Principal Issues in Negotiating Licensing Agreements

The key issues in negotiating licensing agreements include the scope of the rights conveyed, compensation, licensee compliance, dispute resolution, and the term and termination of the agreement.[18] The more clearly these are spelled out, the more trouble-free the association between the two parties can be.

The rights conveyed are product and/or patent rights. Defining their scope involves specifying the technology, know-how, or show-how to be included; the format; and guarantees. An example of format specification is an agreement on whether manuals will be translated into the licensee's language.

Compensation issues may be heavily disputed and argued. The costs the licensor wants to cover are (1) **transfer costs**, which are all variable costs incurred in transferring technology to a licensee and all ongoing costs of maintaining the agreement, (2) **R & D costs** incurred in researching and developing the licensed technology, and (3) **opportunity costs** incurred in the foreclosure of other sources of profit, such as exports or direct investment. To cover these costs, the licensor wants a share of the profits generated from the use of the license.

Licensees usually do not want to include allowances for opportunity costs, and they often argue that R & D costs have already been covered by the licensor through the profit from previous sales. In theory, royalties can be seen as profit sharing; in practice, royalties are a function of both the licensor's minimum necessary return and the cost of the licensee's next-best alternative.

The methods of compensating the licensor can take the form of running royalties, such as 5 percent of the licensee sales, and/or up-front payments, service fees, and disclosure fees (for proprietary data). Sometimes, government regulations pose an obstacle to the collection of royalty payments. In such instances, the know-how transferred can be capitalized as part of a cooperative venture, where a specific value is attributed to the information. Payments are then received as profits or dividends.

Licensee compliance on a number of dimensions must be stipulated in the agreement: (1) export control regulations, (2) confidentiality of the intellectual property and technology provided, and (3) record keeping and provisions for licensor audits, which are done periodically, usually a minimum of once a year.

Finally, the term, termination, and survival of rights must be specified. Government regulations in the licensee's market will have to be studied, and if the conditions are not favourable (for example, in terms of the maximum allowable duration), a waiver should be applied for.

Trademark Licensing

For companies that can trade on their names and characters, **trademark licensing** has become a substantial source of worldwide revenue. The names or logos of designers, literary characters, sports teams, and movie stars appear on merchandise such as clothing, games, foods and beverages, gifts and novelties, toys, and home furnishings. British designer Laura Ashley started the first major furniture program, licensing her name to Henredon Furniture Industries. Coca-Cola licensed its name to Murjani to be used on blue jeans, sweatshirts, and windbreakers, and Canadian designer Brian Gluckstein has recently partnered with The Bay to create Glucksteinhome, a line of designer-driven products for the home.[19] The licensors are likely to make millions of dollars with little effort, whereas the licensees can produce a branded product that consumers will recognize immediately. Fees can range between 7 and 12 percent of net sales for merchandising license agreements.[20]

Both licensor and licensee may run into difficulty if the trademark is used for a product too far removed from the original success or if the licensed product casts a shadow on the reputation of the licensor. In licensing a trademark, consumer perceptions have to be researched to make sure the brand's positioning will not change. As an example, when Löwenbräu was exported to the United States, it was the number-one imported beer sold in the market. However, when the product name was licensed to Miller Brewing Company for domestic production, the beer's positioning (and subsequently its target audience) changed drastically in the minds of the consumers, resulting in a major decline in sales.

Franchising

In franchising, a parent company (the franchiser) grants another independent entity (the franchisee) the right to do business in a specified manner. This right can take the form of selling the franchiser's products or using its name, its production, preparation, and marketing techniques, or its business approach. Usually, franchising involves a combination of these elements. The major forms of franchising are manufacturer–retailer systems (such as car dealerships), manufacturer–wholesaler systems (such as soft-drink companies), and service firm–retailer systems (such as lodging services and fast-food outlets). Tim Hortons, the Canadian coffee and doughnut chain, for example, has used the franchise concept to expand into the U.S. market. This fast-food chain operates several hundred outlets in the U.S., primarily in the border states.

One can differentiate between product/trade franchising, in which the major emphasis rests on the product or commodity to be sold, and business format franchising, in which the focus is on ways of doing business. Even though many franchising firms are large, franchising can be a useful international market expansion method for any business operation with international appeal.

The origins of the concept of franchising lie in Bavaria, but it has been adopted by various types of businesses in many countries. Franchisers are penetrating international markets and are doing so quite aggressively. For example, 24 percent of British franchisers and 30 percent of French franchisers are active outside their home countries.[21] In the Vietnamese market, one can encounter several Asian-owned franchises such as the South Korean–based Burger Khan, Thailand's Five Star Chicken, and Japan's Lotto Burger.[22]

The typical reasons for the international expansion of franchise systems are market potential, financial gain, and saturated domestic markets. From a franchisee's perspective, the franchise is beneficial because it reduces risk by implementing a proven concept. In Malaysia, for example, the success rate in the franchise business is 90 percent, compared to the 80 percent failure rate of all new businesses.[23] Franchising agreements are usually also beneficial from a governmental perspective. From a source-country view, franchising does not replace exports or export jobs. From a recipient-country view, franchising requires little outflow of foreign exchange, and the bulk of the profit generated remains within the country.[24]

With all its benefits, franchising also presents some problems. One key issue is that companies first need to find out what their special capabilities are. This requires that there be an identification and codification of knowledge assets in firms—that "they know what they have."[25] After such an investigation, companies can then launch an aggressive program to share knowledge.

A second concern is the need for a great degree of standardization. Without such standardization, many of the benefits of the transferred know-how are lost. Typically, such standardization will include the use of a common business name, similar layout, and similar production or service processes. Apart from leading to efficient operations, all of these factors will also contribute to a high degree of international recognition. At the same time, however, standardization does not mean 100 percent uniformity. Adjustments may be necessary in the final end product so that local market conditions can be taken into account. For example, fast-food outlets in Europe often need to serve beer and wine to be attractive to the local clientele. In order to enter the Indian market, where cows are considered sacred, McDonald's has developed non-beef burgers. Key to success is the development of a franchising program that maintains a high degree of recognition and efficiency benefits while being responsive to local cultural preferences.

Another key issue is the protection of the total business system that a franchise offers. Once a business concept catches on, local competition may emerge quite quickly with an imitation of the product and the general style of operation, and even with a similar name.

Government intervention can also represent major problems. For example, government restrictions on the type of services to be offered or on royalty remissions can prevent franchising arrangements or lead to a separation between a company and its franchisees.

Another key concern is the selection and training of franchisees. Many franchise systems have run into difficulty by expanding too quickly and granting franchises to unqualified entities. Although the local franchisee knows the market best, the franchiser still needs to understand the market for product adaptation purposes and operational details. The franchiser should be the conductor of a coordinated effort by the individual franchisees—for example, in terms of sharing ideas and engaging in joint marketing efforts, such as cooperative advertising. However, even here difficulties can emerge consisting mostly of complications in selecting appropriate advertising media, effective copy testing, effective translation of the franchiser's message, and the use of appropriate sales promotion tools. Exhibit 8.4 summarizes research findings regarding the challenges faced in international franchising.

To encourage better-organized and more successful growth, many companies turn to the **master franchising system**, wherein foreign partners are selected and awarded the rights to a large territory in which they are permitted to sub-franchise. As a result, the franchiser gains market expertise and an effective screening mechanism for new franchises, without incurring costly mistakes.[26]

Exhibit 8.4 Key Impediments to International Franchising

- Meeting and training of qualified and reliable franchisees overseas
- Security and protection of industrial property and trademarks in foreign countries
- Keeping current with market prospects overseas
- Familiarity with business practices overseas
- Foreign government regulations on business operations
- Foreign regulations or limitations on royalty fees
- Negotiation with foreign franchisees
- Foreign regulations or limitations on entry of franchise business
- Collection and transfer of franchise fee
- Control of quality or quantity of product or service
- Provision of technical support overseas
- Pricing of franchise for a foreign market
- Promotion and advertising opportunities for franchise overseas
- Sourcing and availability of raw materials, equipment, and other products
- Shipping and distribution of raw materials required to operate a foreign franchise
- Financing of franchise operations overseas
- Shipping and handling of equipment needed to operate a foreign franchise

Source: Adapted from Ben L. Kedia, David J. Ackerman, and Robert T. Justis, "Changing Barriers to the Internationalization of Franchising Operations: Perceptions of Domestic and International Franchisors," *The International Executive* 37 (July/August 1995): 329–48.

The Global MARKETPLACE 8.6

Saputo Inc.—Growth by Acquisition

Saputo is the largest dairy processor in Canada. The company is a major supplier of mozzarella, cheddar, and specialty cheese as well as dairy products to retail, food-service, and industrial markets in Canada and internationally. The company founded in 1954 as a small mozzarella cheese producer has grown by acquisition. The firm's major cheese brands include *Amstrong, Frigo,* and *Stella* and its product line includes a portfolio of snack-cakes, cookies and tarts marketed under such brand names as *Vachon, Rondeau,* and *Granny's.*

In early 2007, the company announced the acquisition of the industrial cheese activities of Land O'Lakes in California. The purchase price of US$216 million gave Saputo two additional industrial plants in the U.S. which in 2006 generated annual sales of approximately US$415 million and earnings before interest, taxes and amortization of US$20 million. Saputo is committed to its growth by acquisition strategy and plans to build on its earlier direct foreign investments in Latin America and Europe. In the words of the company's president:

> There are two objectives to our international expansion strategy. First, we are looking primarily for manufacturing platforms that show great potential for growth. We are currently examining such opportunities in the global marketplace. Second, we seek out international growth from a sales perspective. As we gain access to raw material, the world becomes our market. Therefore, we are always identifying opportunities to penetrate new markets and increase our export possibilities. In this regard, Argentina is proving to be an excellent base. Through this platform, our products are exported in more than 30 countries and we are still on the lookout for new avenues that might arise in different parts of the world. Indeed, we recently entered the European dairy industry with the acquisition of the cheese manufacturing activities of Spezialitäten-Käserei De Lucia GmbH in Germany. This acquisition will complement our current activities and provide us with a local presence in Europe and additional knowledge to pursue our global expansion. The German operation also represents a platform from which we will be able to increase our exporting capabilities. This first foray outside of the Americas underscores our commitment to be a world-class dairy processor.

Sources: A Word from the President, June 6, 2006, **http://www.saputo.com/corpo/client/en/Corpo/Investisseurs/President.asp** (2006 Annual Report; retrieved March 13, 2007); Saputo Acquires American Facilities, Le Devoir, February 22, 2007, **http://www.mri.gouv.qc.ca/usa/_scripts/Actualites/ViewNewQcNews.asp?ID=466&lang=en** (retrieved March 13, 2007); and Saputo Inc. Hoovers, **http://www.answers.com/topic/saputo-inc.**

Foreign Direct Investment

Foreign direct investment represents one component of the international investment flow. The other component is portfolio investment, which is the purchase of stocks and bonds internationally. Portfolio investment is a primary concern to the international financial community. As illustrated in The Global Marketplace 8.6, the global marketer makes foreign direct investments to create or expand a permanent interest in an enterprise. They imply a degree of control over the enterprise.

Foreign direct investments have grown tremendously. The total global value of such investment, which in 1967 was estimated to be $105 billion, had climbed to $9 trillion by 2004.[27] This stock of investment is attributable to the activities of some 70,000 transnational corporations and their almost 700,000 foreign affiliates. Foreign direct investment has clearly become a major avenue for foreign market entry and expansion. Exhibit 8.5, which shows how confident businesspeople are about making foreign direct investments around the world, suggests that foreign direct investment is likely to continue to expand in the future, with China and India as the major beneficiaries.

Major Foreign Investors

Multinational corporations are defined by the United Nations as "enterprises which own or control production or service facilities outside the country in which they are based."[28] As a result of this definition, all foreign direct investors are multinational corporations. Yet large corporations are the key players. Exhibit 8.6 lists the 40 largest corporations around

Exhibit 8.5 **The Foreign Direct Investment Confidence Index**

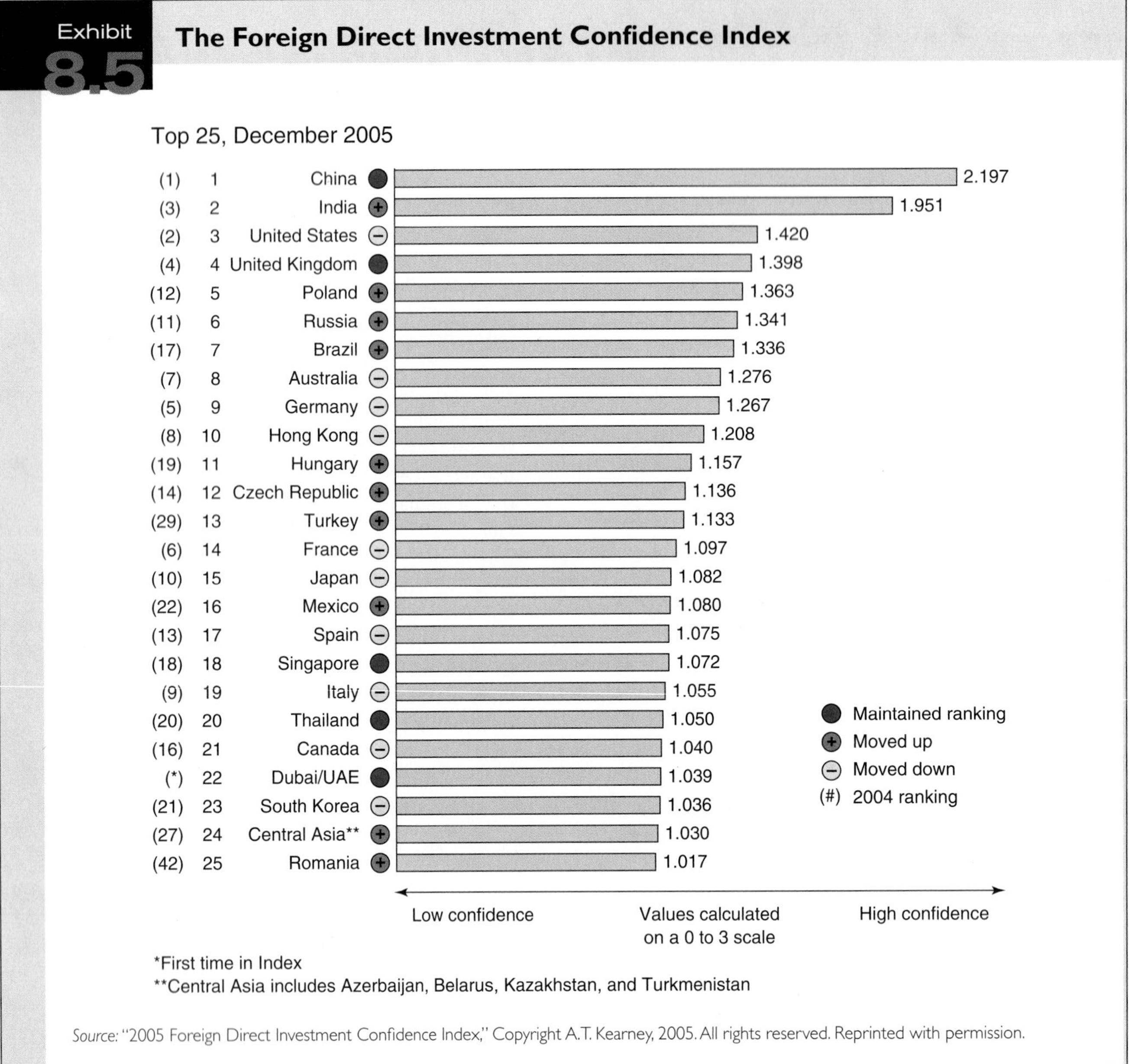

Source: "2005 Foreign Direct Investment Confidence Index," Copyright A.T. Kearney, 2005. All rights reserved. Reprinted with permission.

the world. They come from a wide variety of countries, depend heavily on their international sales, and, in terms of sales, are larger than many countries. As these firms keep growing, they appear to benefit from greater abilities to cope with new, unfamiliar situations.[29] Yet it also appears that there is an optimal size that, when exceeded, increases the costs of operations.[30] Exhibit 8.7 lists the top 14 Canadian companies by global revenues. It is observed that Manulife Financial, the largest Canadian firm by revenue, does not make it into the global top-40 ranking, which is dominated by U.S. and European conglomerates.

Many of the large multinationals operate in well over 100 countries. In some firms, even the terms *domestic* and *foreign* have fallen into disuse. Others are working to consider issues only from a global perspective. For example, in management meetings of ABB (Asea Brown Boveri), individuals get fined $100 every time the words *foreign* and *domestic* are used. Most multinationals, however, generate the majority of their sales from their own regional markets and are not in fact truly global.[31] These firms are best described as regional multinationals.

Top 40 Global Corporations Ranked by Revenue

Rank	Company	Revenues ($ millions)	Profits ($ millions)
1	Exxon Mobil	339,938.0	36,130.0
2	Wal-Mart Stores	315,654.0	11,231.0
3	Royal Dutch Shell	306,731.0	25,311.0
4	BP	267,600.0	22,341.0
5	General Motors	192,604.0	−10,567.0
6	Chevron	189,481.0	14,099.0
7	DaimlerChrysler	186,106.3	3,536.3
8	Toyota Motor	185,805.0	12,119.6
9	Ford Motor	177,210.0	2,024.0
10	ConocoPhillips	166,683.0	13,529.0
11	General Electric	157,153.0	16,353.0
12	Total	152,360.7	15,250.0
13	ING Group	138,235.3	8,958.9
14	Citigroup	131,045.0	24,589.0
15	AXA	129,839.2	5,186.5
16	Allianz	121,406.0	5,442.4
17	Volkswagen	118,376.6	1,391.7
18	Fortis	112,351.4	4,896.3
19	Crédit Agricole	110,764.6	7,434.3
20	American Intl. Group	108,905.0	10,477.0
21	Assicurazioni Generali	101,403.8	2,384.0
22	Siemens	100,098.7	2,854.9
23	Sinopec	98,784.9	2,668.4
24	Nippon Telegraph & Telephone	94,869.3	4,404.6
25	Carrefour	94,454.5	1,784.3
26	HSBC Holdings	93,494.0	15,873.0
27	ENI	92,603.3	10,919.7
28	Aviva	92,579.4	3,211.4
29	Intl. Business Machines	91,134.0	7,934.0
30	McKesson	88,050.0	751.0
31	Honda Motor	87,510.7	5,273.2
32	State Grid	86,984.3	1,073.5
33	Hewlett-Packard	86,696.0	2,398.0
34	BNP Paribas	85,687.2	7,271.5
35	PDVSA	85,618.0	4,661.0
36	UBS	84,707.6	11,257.5
37	Bank of America Corp.	83,980.0	16,465.0
38	Hitachi	83,596.3	329.6
39	China National Petroleum	83,556.5	12,950.0
40	Pemex	83,381.7	−7,001.7

Source: Fortune Global 500, © 2007 Time Inc. All rights reserved.

Through their investment, multinational corporations bring economic vitality and jobs to their host countries and often pay higher wages than the average domestically oriented firms.[32] At the same time, however, trade follows investment. This means that foreign direct investors often bring with them imports on an ongoing basis. The flow of imports in turn may contribute to the weakening of a nation's international trade position.

Exhibit 8.7

Top Canadian Firms by Revenue

Country Rank	Company	Rank	Revenues ($ millions)	City
1	Manulife Financial	227	26,446.5	Toronto
2	George Weston	232	25,947.2	Toronto
3	Royal Bank of Canada	250	24,145.6	Toronto
4	Magna International	273	22,811.0	Aurora
5	Power Corp. of Canada	290	21,962.1	Montreal
6	Alcan	313	20,659.0	Montreal
7	Sun Life Financial Services	356	18,087.6	Toronto
8	EnCana	396	16,801.0	Calgary
9	BCE	405	16,506.4	Montreal
10	Canadian Imperial Bank of Commerce	436	15,431.9	Toronto
11	Toronto-Dominion Bank	440	15,327.6	Toronto
12	Bank of Nova Scotia	446	15,054.2	Toronto
13	Bombardier	453	14,903.0	Montreal
14	Onex	474	14,395.5	Toronto

Source: Fortune Global 500,

Reasons for Foreign Direct Investment

Firms expand internationally for a wide variety of reasons. Exhibit 8.8 provides an overview of the major determinants of foreign direct investment.

Marketing Factors

Marketing considerations and the corporate desire for growth are major causes for the increase in foreign direct investment. This is understandable since growth typically means greater responsibilities and more pay for those who contribute to it. Even large domestic markets present limitations to growth. Today's competitive demands require firms to operate simultaneously in the "triad" of the United States, Western Europe, and Japan, and most other markets of the world as well. Corporations, therefore, need to seek wider market access in order to maintain and increase their sales. This objective can be achieved most quickly through the acquisition of foreign firms. Through such expansion, the corporation also gains ownership advantages consisting of political know-how and influence.

Another incentive is that foreign direct investment permits corporations to circumvent current barriers to trade and operate abroad as a domestic firm, unaffected by duties, tariffs, or other import restrictions. For example, research on Japanese foreign direct investment in Europe found that a substantial number of firms have invested there in order to counteract future trade friction.[33]

In addition to government-erected barriers, restrictions may be imposed by customers through their insistence on domestic goods and services, either as a result of nationalistic tendencies or as a function of cultural differences. Having the origin of a product associated with a specific country may also bring positive effects with it, particularly if the country is known for the particular product category. An investment in a Swiss dairy firm by a cheese producer, for example, should generate positive benefits. Further, local buyers may wish to buy from sources that they perceive to be reliable in their supply, which means buying from local producers.

Still another incentive is the cost factor, with corporations attempting to obtain low-cost resources and ensure their sources of supply. Finally, once the decision is made to invest internationally, the investment climate plays a major role. Corporations will seek to invest in those geographic areas where their investment is most protected and has the best chance to flourish.

Exhibit 8.8 Major Determinants of Direct Foreign Investment

A. Marketing Factors
   1. Size of market
   2. Market growth
   3. Desire to maintain share of market
   4. Desire to advance exports of parent company
   5. Need to maintain close customer contact
   6. Dissatisfaction with existing market arrangements
   7. Export base

B. Trade Restrictions
   1. Barriers to trade
   2. Preference of local customers for local products

C. Cost Factors
   1. Desire to be near source of supply
   2. Availability of labour
   3. Availability of raw materials
   4. Availability of capital/technology
   5. Lower labour costs
   6. Lower production costs other than labour
   7. Lower transport costs
   8. Financial (and other) inducements by government
   9. More favourable cost levels

D. Investment Climate
   1. General attitude toward foreign investment
   2. Political stability
   3. Limitation on ownership
   4. Currency exchange regulations
   5. Stability of foreign exchange
   6. Tax structure
   7. Familiarity with country

E. General
   1. Expected higher profits

Source: International Investment and Multinational Enterprises (Paris: Organization for Economic Cooperation and Development, 1983), 41; and **http://www.oecd.org.**

These determinants will have varying impacts on the foreign direct investment decision, depending on the characteristics of the firm and its management, on its objectives, and on external conditions. Firms have been categorized as resource seekers, market seekers, and efficiency seekers.[34] **Resource seekers** search for either natural resources or human resources. Natural resources typically are based on mineral, agricultural, or oceanographic advantages and result in firms locating in areas where these resources are available. The alternatives open to firms therefore depend on the availability of the natural resources sought. Chinese companies, for example, have been extremely active in this area, making strategic investments in the resource sectors of numerous countries in Africa, Latin America, and other parts of the developing world.[35] With the creation of a new fund to invest China's $1 trillion in foreign reserves, one may expect the pace of investment to accelerate as it goes forward.[36]

Companies seeking human resources are likely to base their location decision on the availability of low-cost labour that matches their needs in terms of output quality. Alternatively, companies may select an area because of the availability of highly skilled labour. If natural resources are not involved, the location decision can be altered over time if the labour advantage changes. When the differential between labour costs in different locales becomes substantial, a corporation, in continuing to improve its human resource access, may relocate to take advantage of the "better" resources. A good example of such shifts was observed in Europe. In the 1980s, many non-European firms decided to gain their foothold in Europe by investing in the low-wage countries of Portugal, Spain, and Greece. In light of the major political changes of the 1990s, however, the investment interest shifted and began to focus on Hungary, the former East Germany, and the Czech Republic.

Corporations primarily in search of better opportunities to enter and expand within markets are **market seekers**. Particularly when markets are closed or access is restricted, corporations have a major incentive to locate in them. **Efficiency seekers** attempt to obtain the most economic sources of production. They frequently have affiliates in multiple markets with highly specialized product lines or components and exchange their production in order to maximize the benefits to the corporation. The reasons why firms engage in foreign investment can change over time. For example, firms entering China may have done so originally as market seekers, but many of them have been converted into resource seekers over time.

Following Customers

A second major cause for the increase in foreign direct investment is the need for suppliers to follow established customers that have moved abroad. As large multinational firms move abroad, they are quite interested in maintaining their established business relationships with other firms. Therefore, they frequently encourage their suppliers to follow them and continue to supply them from a foreign location. As a result, a few direct investments can gradually form an important investment preference for subsequent investment flows and even lead to centres of excellence. The same phenomenon holds true for service firms. Advertising agencies often move abroad to service foreign affiliates of their domestic clients. Similarly, engineering firms, insurance companies, and law firms are often invited to provide their services abroad. Yet not all of these developments are the result of encouragement by client firms. Often, suppliers invest abroad out of fear that their clients might find good sources abroad and therefore begin to import the products of services they currently supply. Many firms therefore invest abroad in order to forestall such a potentially dangerous development.

Government Incentives

A third major cause for the increase in foreign direct investment is government incentives. Governments are increasingly under pressure to provide jobs for their citizens. Over time, many have come to recognize that foreign direct investment can serve as a major means to increase employment and income. Countries such as Canada have been promoting government incentive schemes for foreign direct investment for decades. Increasingly, provincial governments are also participating in investment promotion activities, as seen with Ontario's $500 million Automotive Investment Strategy, which the provincial government claims has the potential to generate up to $5 billion in automotive investments. Honda, for example, has been manufacturing vehicles in Ontario since the 1980s with output exported to the U.S., Japan, and several other countries.

Government incentives are mainly of three types: fiscal, financial, and non-financial. **Fiscal incentives** are specific tax measures designed to serve as an attraction to the foreign investor. They typically consist of special depreciation allowances, tax credits or rebates, special deductions for capital expenditures, tax holidays, and other reductions of the tax burden on the investor. **Financial incentives** offer special funding for the investor by providing land or buildings, loans, loan guarantees, or wage subsidies. Finally, **non-financial incentives** can consist of guaranteed government purchases; special protection from competition through tariffs, import quotas, and local content requirements; and investments in infrastructure facilities.

Incentives are designed primarily to attract industry and create more jobs. They may slightly alter the advantage of a region and therefore make it more palatable for the investor to choose to invest in that region. By themselves, they are unlikely to spur an investment decision if proper market conditions do not exist. Consequently, when individual provinces or regions within a country offer special incentives to foreign direct investors, they may be competing against each other for a limited pie rather than increasing the size of the pie. Furthermore, a question exists about the extent to which new jobs are actually created by foreign direct investment. Because many foreign investors import equipment, parts, and even personnel, the expected benefits in terms of job creation may often be either less than initially envisioned or only temporary. One additional concern arises from the competitive position of domestic firms already in existence. Since their "old" investment typically does not benefit from incentives designed to attract new investment, established firms may encounter problems when competing against the newcomer.

A Perspective on Foreign Direct Investors

All foreign direct investors, and particularly multinational corporations, are viewed with a mixture of awe and dismay. Governments and individuals praise them for bringing capital, economic activity, and employment, and investors are seen as key transferers of technology and managerial skills. Through these transfers, competition, market choice, and competitiveness are enhanced.

At the same time, many have negative views of dependence on multinational corporations. Just as the establishment of a corporation can create all sorts of benefits, its disappearance can also take them away again. Very often, international direct investors are accused of actually draining resources from their host countries. By employing the best and the brightest, they are said to deprive domestic firms of talent, thus causing a **brain drain**. Once they have hired locals, multinational firms are often accused of not promoting them high enough, and of imposing many new rules on their employees abroad.

By raising money locally, multinationals are seen to starve smaller capital markets. By bringing in foreign technology, they are viewed either as discouraging local technology development or as perhaps transferring only outmoded knowledge. By increasing competition, they are declared the enemy of domestic firms. There are concerns about foreign investors' economic and political loyalty toward their host government and a fear that such investors will always protect only their own interests and those of their home governments. And, of course, their sheer size, which sometimes exceeds the financial assets that the government controls, makes foreign investors suspect.

Clearly, a love-hate relationship frequently exists between governments and the foreign direct investor. As the firm's size and investment volume grow, the benefits it brings to the economy increase. At the same time, the dependence of the economy on the firm increases as well. Given the many highly specialized activities of firms, their experts are often more knowledgeable than government employees and are therefore able to circumvent government rules. Particularly in developing countries, the knowledge advantage of foreign investors may offer opportunities for exploitation. There seems to be a distinct "liability of foreignness" to which multinational firms are exposed. Such disadvantages can result from governmental resentment of greater opportunities by multinational firms. But they can also be the consequences of corporate actions, such as the decision to have many expatriates rotate in top management positions, which may weaken the standing of the subsidiary and its local employees.[37]

In light of the desire for foreign investment and the accompanying fear of it, a substantial array of guidelines for corporate behaviour abroad has been publicized by organizations such as the United Nations, the Organization for Economic Cooperation and Development, and the International Labor Organization. Typically, these recommendations address the behaviour of foreign investors in areas such as employment practices, consumer and environmental protection, political activity, and human rights. Corporations may not be legally bound by the guidelines, but they should consider their implications for corporate activities. While the social acceptability of certain practices may vary among nations, the foreign investor should transfer the best business practices across nations. The multinational firm can and should be a leader in improving economic and business practices and standards of living around the world. It will be managerial virtue, vision, and veracity combined with corporate openness, responsiveness, long-term thinking, and truthfulness that will determine the degrees of freedom and success of global business in the future.[38]

Types of Ownership

In carrying out its foreign direct investment, a corporation has a wide variety of ownership choices, ranging from 100 percent ownership to a minority interest. The different levels of ownership will result in varying degrees of flexibility for the corporation, a changing ability to control business plans and strategy, and differences in the level of risk assumed. In some instances, firms appear to select specific foreign ownership structures based on their experience with similar structures in the past.[39] In other words, these firms tend to keep using the same ownership model. However, it may be better to have the ownership decision be either a strategic response to corporate capabilities and needs or a necessary consequence of government regulation.

Full Ownership

For many firms, the foreign direct investment decision is, at least initially, considered in the context of 100 percent ownership. Sometimes, this is the result of ethnocentric considerations, based on the belief that no outside entity should have an impact on corporation management. At other times, the issue is one of principle.

To make a rational decision about the extent of ownership, management must evaluate the extent to which total control is important for the success of its global marketing activities. Often, full ownership may be a desirable, but not a necessary, prerequisite for international success. At other times, it may be necessary, particularly when strong linkages exist within the corporation. Interdependencies between and among local operations and headquarters may be so strong that anything short of total coordination will result in a less-than-acceptable benefit to the firm as a whole. This may be the case if central product design, pricing, or advertising is needed. Corporations sometimes insist on full ownership for major strategic reasons. Even in such instances, however, it is important to determine whether these reasons are important enough to warrant such a policy or whether the needs of the firm can be accommodated with other ownership arrangements. In many countries, the international environment is quite hostile to full ownership by multinational firms.

Many governments exert political pressure to obtain national control of foreign operations. Commercial activities under the control of foreigners are frequently believed to reflect the wishes, desires, and needs of headquarters abroad much more than those of the domestic economy. Governments fear that domestic economic policies may be counteracted by such firms, and employees are afraid that little local responsibility and empathy exists at headquarters. A major concern is the "fairness" of **profit repatriation**, or transfer of profits, and the extent to which firms operating abroad need to reinvest in their foreign operations. Governments often believe that transfer-pricing mechanisms are used to amass profits in a place most advantageous for the firm and that, as a consequence, local operations often show very low levels of performance. By reducing the foreign control of firms, they hope to put an end to such practices.

Ownership options can be limited either through outright legal restrictions or through measures designed to make foreign ownership less attractive—such as limitations on profit repatriation. The global marketer is therefore frequently faced with the choice either of abiding by existing restraints and accepting a reduction in control or of losing the opportunity to operate in the country.

In addition to the pressure from host governments, general market instability can also serve as a major deterrent to full ownership of foreign direct investment. Instability may result from political upheavals or changes in regimes. More often, it results from threats of political action, complex and drawn-out bureaucratic procedures, and the prospect of arbitrary and unpredictable alterations in regulations after the investment decision has been made.[40]

Joint Ventures

Joint ventures are a collaboration of two or more organizations for more than a transitory period.[41] In this collaboration, the participating partners share assets, risks, and profits. Equality of partners is not necessary. In some joint ventures, each partner holds an equal share; in others, one partner has the majority of shares. The partners' contributions to the joint venture can also vary widely. Contributions may consist of funds, technology, know-how, sales organizations, or plant and equipment.

Advantages of Joint Ventures

The two major reasons for carrying out foreign direct investments in the form of joint ventures are governmental and commercial. Governments often pressure firms either to form or accept joint ventures or to forgo participation in the local market. Such restrictions are designed to reduce the extent of control that foreign firms can exercise over local operations. As a basis for defining control, most countries have employed percentage levels of ownership. Over time, countries have shown an increasing tendency to reduce the thresholds of ownerships that define control. This tendency developed as it became apparent that even small, organized groups of stockholders may influence control of an enterprise, particularly if overall ownership is widely distributed. At the same time, however, many countries are also recognizing the beneficial effects of foreign direct investment in terms of technological progress and international competitiveness and are permitting more control of local firms by foreign entities. Another reason may be the economic orientation of governments and a resulting requirement for joint venture collaboration. Joint ventures can help overcome existing market access restrictions and open up or maintain market opportunities that otherwise would not be available.

Equally important to the formation of joint ventures are commercial considerations. If a corporation can identify a partner with a common goal, and if the international activities do not infringe on the autonomy of the individual partner, joint ventures may represent the most viable vehicle for international expansion. Joint ventures are valuable when the pooling of resources results in a better outcome for each partner than if each attempted to carry out its activities individually. This is particularly the case when each partner has a specialized advantage in areas that benefit the joint venture. For example, a firm may have new technology available, yet lack sufficient capital to carry out foreign direct investment on its own. By joining forces with a partner, the technology can be used more quickly and market penetration is easier. Similarly, one of the partners may have a distribution system already established or have better access to local suppliers, either of which permits a greater volume of sales in a shorter period of time.

Joint ventures also permit better relationships with local organizations—governments, local authorities, or labour unions. Government-related reasons are the major rationale for joint ventures in developing countries. If the local partner can bring political influence to the undertaking, the new venture may be eligible for tax incentives, grants, and government support and may be less vulnerable to political risk. Negotiations for certifications or licences may be easier because authorities may not perceive themselves as dealing with a foreign firm. Relationships between the local partner and the local financial establishment may enable the joint venture to tap local capital markets. The greater experience—and therefore greater familiarity—with the culture and environment of the local partner may enable the joint venture to be more aware of cultural sensitivities and to benefit from greater insights into changing market conditions and needs.

Disadvantages of Joint Ventures

Problem areas in joint ventures, as in all partnerships, involve implementing the concept and maintaining the relationship. Many governments that require a joint venture formation are inexperienced in foreign direct investment. Therefore, joint venture legislation and the ensuing regulations are often subject to substantial interpretation and arbitrariness. Frequently, different levels of control are permitted depending on the type of product and the shipment destination. In some instances, only portions of joint venture legislation are made public. Other internal regulations are communicated only when necessary. Such situations create uncertainty, which increases the risk for the joint venture participants.

Major problems can also arise in assuring the maintenance of the joint venture relationship. Many joint ventures are found to fall short of expectations and are disbanded. The reasons typically relate to conflicts of interest, problems with disclosure of sensitive information, and disagreement over how profits are to be shared; these are typically the result of a lack of communication before, during, and after the formation of the venture. In some cases, managers are interested in launching the venture but are too little concerned with actually running the enterprise. In other instances, managers dispatched to the joint venture by the partners may feel differing degrees of loyalty to the venture and its partners. Reconciling such conflicts of loyalty is one of the greatest human resource challenges for joint ventures.[42] Many of the problems encountered by joint ventures stem from a lack of careful, advance consideration of how to manage the new endeavour. A partnership works on the basis of trust and commitment, or not at all.

Areas of possible disagreement include the whole range of business decisions covering strategic vision, management style, accounting and control, marketing policies and practices, production, research and development, and personnel.[43] The joint venture may, for example, identify a particular market as a profitable target, yet the headquarters of one of the partners may already have plans for serving this market, plans that would require competing against its own joint venture.

Similarly, the issue of profit accumulation and distribution may cause discontent. If one partner supplies the joint venture with a product, that partner will prefer that any profits accumulate at headquarters and accrue 100 percent to one firm rather than at the joint venture, where profits are partitioned according to equity participation. Such a decision may not be greeted with enthusiasm by the other partner. Further, once profits are accumulated, their distribution may lead to dispute. For example, one partner may insist on a high payout of dividends because of financial needs, whereas the other may prefer the reinvestment of profits into a growing operation.

Strategic Alliances

One special form of joint venture consists of strategic alliances, or partnerships. The result of growing global competition, rapid increases in the investment required for technological progress, and growing risk of failure, strategic alliances are informal or formal arrangements between two or more companies with a common business objective. They are more than the traditional customer–vendor relationship, but less than an outright acquisition. The great advantage of such alliances is their ongoing flexibility, since they can be formed, adjusted, and dissolved rapidly in response to changing conditions. In essence, strategic alliances are networks of companies that collaborate in the achievement of a given project or objective. However, partners for one project may well be fierce competitors for another.

Alliances can take forms ranging from information cooperation in the market development area to joint ownership of worldwide operations. There are many reasons for the growth in such alliances. Market development is one common focus. Penetrating foreign markets is a primary objective of many companies. In Japan, Motorola is sharing chip designs and manufacturing facilities with Toshiba to gain greater access to the Japanese market. Some alliances are aimed at defending home markets. Another focus is spreading the cost and risk inherent in production and development efforts. Some alliances are also formed to block or co-opt competitors.[44] For example, Caterpillar formed a heavy-equipment joint venture with Mitsubishi in Japan to strike back at its main global rival, Komatsu, in Komatsu's home market.

Of course, companies must carefully evaluate the effects of entering such a coalition. Depending on the objectives of the other partners, companies may wind up having their strategy partially driven by their competitors. Partners may also gain strength through coalitions and transfers of technology. As a result, they might become unexpected competitors. The most successful alliances are those that match the complementary strengths of partners to satisfy a joint objective. Often the partners have different product, geographic, or functional strengths, which the alliance can build on in order to achieve success with a new strategy or in a new market. In light of growing international competition and the rising cost of innovation in technology, strategic alliances are likely to continue their growth in the future.

Recommendations

The first requirement when forming a joint venture is to find the right partner. Partners should have a commonality of orientation and goals, possess relatively similar organizational cultures,[45] and bring complementary and relevant benefits to the joint venture. The venture makes little sense if the expertise of both partners is in the same area—for example, if both have production experience but neither has distribution know-how. Similarly, bringing a good distribution system to the joint venture may be of little use if the established system is in the field of consumer products and the joint venture will produce industrial products.

Second, great care needs to be taken in negotiating the joint venture agreement. In these negotiations, extensive provisions must be made for contingencies. Questions such as profit accumulation and distribution and market orientation must be addressed in the initial agreement; otherwise, they may surface as points of contention over time. A joint venture agreement, although comparable to a marriage contract, should contain the elements of a divorce contract. Changing business conditions and priorities may make dissolution necessary. Agreements should therefore cover issues such as conditions of termination, disposition of assets and liabilities, protection of proprietary information and property, rights over sales territories, and obligations to customers. In addition, it is important to plan for the continued employment or termination of the people working in a dissolved joint venture.[46]

Finally, joint ventures operate in dynamic business environments and therefore must be able to adjust to changing market conditions. The agreement should provide for changes in the original concept so that the venture can grow and flourish.

Government Consortia

One form of cooperation takes place at the industry level and is typically characterized by government support or even subsidization. Usually, it is the reflection of escalating cost and a governmental goal of developing or maintaining global leadership in a particular sector. A new drug can cost hundreds of millions of dollars to develop and bring to market; a new mainframe computer or a telecommunications switch can require $1 billion. To combat the high costs and risks of research and development, **research consortia** have emerged in several countries. These consortia pool their resources for research into technologies ranging from artificial intelligence and electric car batteries to semiconductor manufacturing. The Europeans have several mega-projects to develop new technologies registered under the names BRITE, COMET, ESPRIT, EUREKA, RACE, and SOKRATES. Japanese consortia have worked on producing the world's highest-capacity memory chip and advanced computer technologies. On the manufacturing side, the formation of Airbus Industries secured European production of commercial jets. This consortium emerged from the linkup of DaimlerChrysler Aerospace AG of Germany, Aerospatiale Matra of France, and CASA of Spain. It has become a prime global competitor and is now backed by the European Aeronautic Defence and Space Company (EADS).

Contractual Arrangements

One final major form of international market participation is contractual arrangements. Firms have found this method to be a useful alternative or complement to other international options, since it permits the international use of corporate resources and can also be an acceptable response to government ownership restrictions. Such an arrangement may focus on cross-marketing, where the contracting parties carry out complementary activities. For example, Nestlé and General Mills had an agreement whereby Honey Nut Cheerios and Golden Grahams were made in General Mills's U.S. plants and shipped in bulk to Europe for packaging at a Nestlé plant.[47] This alliance evolved into a joint venture, Cereal Partners Worldwide, which markets both companies' products in Europe and Asia. Firms also can have a reciprocal arrangement whereby each partner provides the other access to its market. International airlines have started to share hubs, coordinate schedules, and simplify ticketing. Alliances such as Star (joining airlines such as Air Canada, United, and Lufthansa) provide worldwide coverage for their customers both in the travel and shipping communities. As corporations look for ways to grow simultaneously and focus on their competitive advantage, outsourcing has become a powerful new tool for achieving these goals. Firms increasingly also develop arrangements for contract manufacturing, which allows the corporation to separate the physical production of goods from the research, development, and marketing stages, especially if the latter are the core competencies of the firm. Such contracting has become particularly popular in the footwear and garment industries.

In a **management contract**, the supplier brings together a package of skills that will provide an integrated service to the client without incurring the risk and benefit of ownership. The activity is quite different from other contractual arrangements because people actually move and directly implement the relevant skills and knowledge in the client organization.[48] Management contracts can be used by the global marketer in various ways. When equity participation, in the form of either full ownership or a joint venture, is not possible or must be relinquished, a management contract can serve to maintain participation in a venture. Depending on the extensiveness of the contract, it may even permit some measure of control. As an example, the manufacturing process might have to be relinquished to foreign firms, yet international distribution is needed for the product. A management contract could serve to maintain a strong hold on the operation by ensuring that all the distribution channels remain firmly controlled.

Management contracts should not, however, be seen as a last line of defence. Whenever lack of expertise exists in a particular venture, management contracts can be a most useful tool to help overcome barriers to global marketing activities. This is particularly useful if an outside party has specialized knowledge that is crucial to international marketing success, whether in the area of distribution technology, marketing know-how, or worldwide contacts. Some companies in the service sector have independent entities that specialize in delivering management services. For example, the German airline Lufthansa manages the operations of many airlines by handling the accounting system, setting salary and customer-service levels, and providing training programs.

A management contract can also be the critical element in the success of a project. Such a contract and a lender's faith in the contractor may be crucial in obtaining financial support for a project, particularly in the early planning stages.

One specialized form of management contract is the **turnkey operation**. Here, the arrangement permits a client to acquire a complete operational system together with the skills investment sufficient to allow unassisted maintenance and operation of the system following its completion.[49] The client need not search for individual contractors and subcontractors or deal with scheduling conflicts and difficulties in assigning responsibilities and blame. Instead, a package arrangement permits the accumulation of responsibility in one hand and greatly eases the negotiation and supervision requirements and subsequent accountability issues for the client.

Management contracts have clear benefits for the client. They can provide organizational skills that are not available locally, expertise that is immediately available rather than built up, and management assistance in the form of support services that would be difficult and costly to replicate locally. In addition, the outside involvement is clearly limited. When a turnkey project is online, the system will be totally owned, controlled, and operated by the customer. As a result, management contracts are seen by many governments as a useful alternative to foreign direct investment and the resulting control by non-domestic entities.

Similar advantages exist for the supplier. The risk of participating in an international venture is substantially lowered because no equity capital is at stake. At the same time, a significant amount of operational control can be exercised. Clearly, being on the inside represents a strategic advantage in influencing decisions. In addition, existing know-how that has been built up with significant investment can be commercialized. Frequently, the impact of fluctuations in business volume can be reduced by making use of experienced personnel who otherwise would have to be laid off. In industrialized countries like Canada, with economies that are increasingly service based, accumulated service knowledge and comparative advantage should be used internationally. Management contracts permit a firm to do so.

From the client's perspective, the main drawbacks to consider are the risks of overdependence and loss of control. For example, if the management contractor maintains all international relationships, little if any expertise may be passed on to the local operation.

Instead of a gradual transfer of skills leading to increasing independence, the client may have to rely more and more on the performance of the contractor.

On the contractor's side, the major risks to consider are: (1) the effects of the loss or termination of a contract and the resulting personnel problems, and (2) a bid made without fully detailed insight into actual expenses. Winning a management contract could result in Pyrrhic victories, with the income not worth the expense.

Summary

Firms do not become experienced globalists overnight; rather, they progress gradually through an international development process. The motivations to become engaged in global marketing activities can be either proactive or reactive. Proactive motivations are initiated by the firm's management and can consist of a perceived profit advantage, technological advantage, product advantage, exclusive market information, or managerial urge. Reactive motivations are the responses of management to environmental changes and pressures. Typical are competitive pressures, overproduction, declining domestic sales, or excess capacity. Firms that are primarily stimulated by proactive motivations are more likely to enter international markets aggressively and successfully.

Over time, firms will progress through stages of international expertise and activity. In each one of these stages—exporting, licensing, foreign sales subsidiaries, local assembly and foreign production—firms are likely to have a distinct level of interest in the international market and require different types of information and help. Their outlook toward international markets is likely to progress gradually from purely operational concerns to a strategic international orientation.

Firms may expand internationally via licensing and franchising. The basic advantage of licensing is that it requires relatively less capital investment or knowledge of foreign markets than most other forms of international involvement. The major disadvantage is that licensing agreements typically have time limits, often prescribed by foreign governments, and may even result in creating a competitor. The reasons for global franchising expansion are typically market potential, financial gain, and saturated domestic markets. Franchisers must strike a balance between the need to adapt to local environments and the need to standardize to maintain international recognition.

In spite of temporary unfavourable conditions for risk and profit, management must understand that export activities only develop gradually through the internationalization stages, and that satisfactory international performance consists of the three dimensions of growing sales and market share, higher profitability, and an improved competitive position.

Foreign direct investment represents a major market-expansion alternative. Although such investment can be carried out by any type of firm, large or small, it typically occurs after some experience has been gathered with alternative forms of internationalization, such as exporting. The most visible and powerful players in the foreign direct investment field are larger-sized firms and multinational corporations. Market factors, barriers to trade, cost factors, and investment climate are the major causes of foreign direct investment, with market factors usually playing the major role.

Different ownership levels of foreign investments are possible, ranging from wholly owned subsidiaries to joint ventures. Although many firms prefer full ownership in order to retain full control, such a posture is often not possible because of governmental regulations. It may not even be desirable. Depending on the global organization and strategic needs of the firm, joint ventures with only partial ownership may be a profitable alternative.

In a joint venture, the partners can complement each other by contributing the strengths and resources that each is best equipped to supply. Joint ventures offer significant benefits in terms of closeness to markets, better acceptance by the foreign environment, and a lessening of the risks involved, but they also pose new problems due to potential clashes of corporate cultures, business orientations, and marketing policies. It is therefore important to select the appropriate joint venture partner and to design an agreement that ensures the long-term approval of all participants.

Strategic alliances, or partnerships, are a special form of joint venture in which the participants, at either the industry or the corporate level, join forces in order to make major strategic progress toward technology development and competitiveness. Given the complexities and cost of technological progress, the number of these alliances, sometimes encouraged through government-sponsored consortia, is rapidly growing.

As countries increasingly develop a service-based economy, the usefulness of contractual arrangements grows. Such contracts can enable the involvement of the global marketer in a project when equity participation is not possible or desirable. They also permit a client to acquire operational skills and turnkey systems without relinquishing ownership of a project. Because management assistance, service delivery, and project planning are increasingly important, international marketers can use management contracting to carve out a profitable market niche.

Key Terms

brain drain (p. 259)
direct exporters (p. 244)
efficiency seekers (p. 258)
experimental exporter (p. 246)
exploratory stage (p. 246)
export adaptation (p. 246)
financial incentives (p. 258)
fiscal incentives (p. 258)
foreign production (p. 244)
foreign sales subsidiary (p. 244)
indirect exporters (p. 243)
innate exporters (p. 246)
internationalization (p. 243)
licensing (p. 244)
local assembly (p. 244)
management contract (p. 264)
market seekers (p. 258)
master franchising system (p. 252)
modes of entry (p. 238)
naive rule (p. 245)
non-financial incentives (p. 258)
opportunity costs (p. 250)
partially interested exporter (p. 246)
pragmatic rule (p. 245)
profit repatriation (p. 260)
psychological distance (p. 242)
R & D costs (p. 250)
research consortia (p. 263)
resource seekers (p. 257)
safety-valve activity (p. 240)
sogoshosha (p. 248)
sprinkler strategy (p. 243)
strategy rule (p. 245)
trademark licensing (p. 250)
transfer costs (p. 250)
turnkey operation (p. 264)
waterfall strategy (p. 243)

Questions for Discussion

1. How might advances in information technology encourage a potential exporter to pursue international sales?
2. Discuss the difference between a proactive and a reactive firm, focusing your discussion on the international market.
3. Explain the benefits that international sales can have for domestic market activities.
4. Discuss the benefits and the drawbacks of treating international market activities as a safety-valve mechanism.
5. What is meant by the concept of psychological distance?
6. How can an export intermediary avoid circumvention by a client or customer?
7. Comment on this statement: "Licensing is really not a form of international involvement, because it requires no substantial additional effort on the part of the licensor."
8. Suggest reasons for the explosive international expansion of franchise systems.
9. As a government official, would you prefer the foreign direct investment of a resource seeker, efficiency seeker, or market seeker?
10. Give some reasons why a multinational corporation might insist on 100 percent ownership abroad.
11. At what level of ownership would you consider a firm to be foreign controlled?
12. Discuss the benefits and drawbacks of strategic partnering at the corporate level.

Internet Exercises

1. Use the United Nations Conference on Trade and Development FDI database available at **http://www.unctad.org/Templates/StartPage.asp?intItemID=2068** to research the foreign direct investment profile of a country of your choice.
2. What are the key objectives of Ontario's Automotive Investment Strategy (**http://www.2ontario.com/software/brochures/autoInvestment.asp**). Do you believe that this is an effective way of attracting FDI to this Canadian province? Why or why not?

Recommended Readings

Alon, Ilan. *The Internationalization of U.S. Franchising Systems.* New York: Garland Publishing, 2000.

Bamford, James, Benjamin Gomes-Casseres, and Michael Robinson. *Mastering Alliance Strategy: A Comprehensive Guide to Design, Management, and Organization.* San Francisco: Jossey-Bass, 2002.

Buckley, Peter J., and Pervez N. Ghauri. *The Global Challenge for Multinational Enterprises.* New York: Pergamon Press, 2000.

Culpan, Refik. *Global Business Alliances: Theory and Practice.* New York: Quorum, 2002.

Goldman, Steven M., and Richard M. Asbill. *Fundamentals of International Franchising.* Chicago: American Bar Association, 2001.

Gutterman, Alan. *International Joint Ventures: Negotiating, Forming, and Operating the International Joint Venture.* Novato, CA: World Trade Press, 2001.

Hood, Neil, and Stephen Young. *The Globalization of Multinational Enterprise Activity and Economic Development.* New York: Macmillan, 2000.

International Trade Center. *Export Quality Management: An Answer Book for Small and Medium-Sized Exporters.* Geneva: ITC, 2001.

International Trade Center. *World Directory of Importer's Associations.* Geneva: ITC, 2002.

Johnson, Thomas E. *Export/Import Procedures.* New York: AMACOM, 2002.

Joyner, Nelson T. *How to Build an Export Business.* 2nd ed. Reston, VA: Federation of International Trade Associations, 2000.

McCue, Sarah. *Trade Secrets: The Export Answer Book.* Geneva: ITC, 2001.

Mendelsohn, Martin. *The Guide to Franchising.* 6th ed. New York: Cassell Academic, 2000.

Noonan, Chris. *Cim Handbook of Export Marketing.* Boston: Butterworth-Heinemann, 2000.

Rosenbloom, Arthur H. *Due Diligence for Global Deal Making: The Definitive Guide to Cross-Border Mergers and Acquisitions, Joint Ventures, Financings, and Strategic Alliances.* New York: Bloomberg Press, 2002.

Spekman, Robert E., Lynn A. Isabella, and Thomas C. MacAvoy. *Alliance Competence: Maximizing the Value of Your Partnerships.* New York: Wiley, 2000.

Woznick, Alexandra, and Edward G. Hinkelman. *A Basic Guide to Exporting.* 3rd ed. Novato, CA: World Trade Press, 2000.

Notes

1. Howard Lewis III and J. David Richardson, *Why Global Commitment Really Matters!* (Washington, DC: Institute for International Economics, 2001).
2. Michael R. Czinkota, "U.S. Exporters in the Global Marketplace: An Analysis of the Strengths and Vulnerabilities of Small and Medium-Sized Manufacturers," testimony before the 107th Congress of the United States, House of Representatives, Committee on Small Business, Washington, DC, April 24, 2002.
3. *The 2002 National Export Strategy*, Trade Promotion Coordination Committee (Washington, DC, 2002), 24.
4. S. Tamer Cavusgil and Shaoming Zou, "Marketing Strategy–Performance Relationship: An Investigation of the Empirical Link in Export Marketing Ventures," *Journal of Marketing* 58 (no. 1, 1994): 1–21.
5. Masaaki Kotabe and Michael R. Czinkota, "State Government Promotion of Manufacturing Exports: A Gap Analysis," *Trends in International Business* (Malden: Blackwell, 1998), 78–96.
6. Yoo S. Yang, Robert P. Leone, and Dana L. Alden, "A Market Expansion Ability Approach to Identify Potential Exporters," *Journal of Marketing* 56 (January 1992): 84–96.
7. Michael L. Ursic and Michael R. Czinkota, "An Experience Curve Explanation of Export Expansion," in *International Marketing Strategy: Environmental Assessment and Entry Strategies* (Fort Worth, TX: The Dryden Press, 1994), 133–41.
8. C. P. Rao, M. Krishna Erramilli, and Gopala K. Ganesh, "Impact of Domestic Recession on Export Marketing Behaviour," *International Marketing Review* 7 (1990): 54–65.
9. Aviv Shoham and Gerald S. Albaum, "Reducing the Impact of Barriers to Exporting: A Managerial Perspective," *Journal of International Marketing* 3, no. 4 (1995): 85–105.
10. P. Pauwels and P. Matthyssens, "Strategic Flexibility and the Internationalization Process Model: An Exploratory Study," paper presented at the AIB conference, Sydney, 2001.
11. Shawna O'Grady and Henry W. Lane, "The Psychic Distance Paradox," *Journal of International Business Studies* 27, no. 2 (1996): 309–33.
12. Oystein Moen and Per Servais, "Born Global or Gradual Global? Examining the Export Behavior of Small and Medium-Sized Enterprises," *Journal of International Marketing* 10, no. 3 (2002): 49–72.
13. Farok J. Contractor and Sumit K. Kundu, "Franchising versus Company-Run Operations: Modal Choice in the Global Hotel Sector," *Journal of International Marketing* 6, no. 2 (1998): 28–53.
14. Masaaki Kotabe and Michael R. Czinkota, "State Government Promotion of Manufacturing Exports: A Gap Analysis," *Journal of International Business Studies* 23 (Winter 1992): 637–58.
15. Yoo S. Yang, Robert P. Leone, and Dana L. Alden, "A Market Expansion Ability Approach to Identify Potential Exporters," *Journal of Marketing* 56 (January 1992): 84–96.
16. Daniel C. Bello and Nicholas C. Williamson, "Contractual Arrangement and Marketing Practices in the Indirect Export Channel," *Journal of International Business Studies* 16 (Summer 1985): 65–82.
17. Mike W. Peng and Anne Y. Ilinitch, "Export Intermediary Firms: A Note on Export Development Research," *Journal of International Business Studies* 3 (1998): 609–20.
18. Martin F. Connor, "International Technology Licensing," Seminars in International Trade, National Center for Export-Import Studies, Washington, DC.
19. Canadian Interior Designer Brian Gluckstein's Collection, GlucksteinHome, Coming to the Bay, **http://www.hbc.com/hbc/mediacentre/press/bay/press.asp?prId=78** (accessed July 20, 2006).
20. Pamela M. Deese and Sean Wooden, "Managing Intellectual Property in Licensing Agreements," *Franchising World* 33 (September 2001): 66–67.
21. Josh Martin, "Profitable Supply Chain Supporting Franchises," *Journal of Commerce*, Global Commerce Section (March 11, 1998): 1C.
22. George W. Russell, "Into the Frying Pan," *Asian Business* 37 (October 2001): 28–29.

23. Leonard N. Swartz, *International Trends in Retailing*, December 1999.

24. Farok J. Contractor, "Economic and Environmental Reasons for the Continuing Growth in Alliances and Interfirm Cooperation," in *Emerging Issues in International Business Research*, ed. M. Kotabe and P. Aulakh (Northampton, MA: Elgar Publishing, 2002).

25. Farok J. Contractor, ibid.

26. Marko Grünhagen and Carl L. Witte, "Franchising as an Export Product and Its Role as an Economic Development Tool for Emerging Economies," in *Enhancing Knowledge Development in Marketing*, vol. 13, ed. W. Kehoe and J. Lindgren Jr. (Chicago: American Marketing Association, 2002), 414–15.

27. United Nations, World Investment Report, 2005.

28. United Nations, Department of Economic and Social Affairs, *Multinational Corporations in World Development* (New York: United Nations, 1973), 23.

29. Bernard L. Simonin, "Transfer of Marketing Know-How in International Strategic Alliances: An Empirical Investigation of the Role and Antecedents of Knowledge Ambiguity," *Journal of International Business Studies* 30, no. 3 (1999): 463–90.

30. Lenn Gomes and Kannan Ramaswamy, "An Empirical Examination of the Form of the Relationship between Multinationality and Performance," *Journal of International Business Studies* 30, no. 1 (1999): 173–88.

31. A. Rugman and A. Verbeke, "A Perspective on Regional and Global Strategies of Multinational Enterprises," *Journal of International Business Studies* 35, no. 1 (January 2004): 3.

32. Howard Lewis III and David Richardson, *Why Global Commitment Really Matters!* (Washington, DC: Institute for International Economics, 2001).

33. Detlev Nitsch, Paul Beamish, and Shige Makino, "Characteristics and Performance of Japanese Foreign Direct Investment in Europe," *European Management Journal* 13, no. 3 (1995): 276–85.

34. Jack N. Behrman, "Transnational Corporations in the New International Economic Order," *Journal of International Business Studies* 12 (Spring–Summer 1981): 29–42.

35. Overseas investment: Hunt for resources in the developing world, **http://www.uofaweb.ualberta.ca/chinainstitute/nav03.cfm?nav03=54212&nav02=43884&nav01=43092** (accessed March 12, 2007).

36. New Chinese fund will invest currency reserves, **http://www.globeinvestor.com/servlet/story/RTGAM.20070309.wchinainvest0309/GIStory/** (accessed March 12, 2007).

37. John M. Mezias, "How to Identify Liabilities of Foreignness and Assess Their Effects on Multinational Corporations," *Journal of International Management* 8, no. 3 (2002): 265–82.

38. Michael R. Czinkota, "Success of Globalization Rests on Good Business Reputations," *The Japan Times*, October 12, 2002, 19.

39. Prasad Padmanabhan and Kang Rae Cho, "Decision Specific Experience in Foreign Ownership and Establishment Strategies: Evidence from Japanese Firms," *Journal of International Business Studies* 30, no. 1 (1999): 25–44.

40. Isaiah Frank, *Foreign Enterprise in Developing Countries* (Baltimore: Johns Hopkins University, 1980).

41. W.G. Friedman and G. Kalmanoff, *Joint International Business Ventures* (New York: Columbia University Press, 1961).

42. Oded Shenkar and Shmuel Ellis, "Death of the 'Organization Man': Temporal Relations in Strategic Alliances," *The International Executive* 37, no. 6 (November/December 1995): 537–53.

43. R.H. Holton, "Making International Joint Ventures Work," in *The Management of Headquarters: Subsidiary Relationships in Multinational Corporations*, ed. L. Otterbeck (New York: St. Martin's Press, 1981), 7.

44. Jordan D. Lewis, *Partnerships for Profit: Structuring and Managing Strategic Alliances* (New York: Free Press, 1990), 85–87.

45. Vijay Pothukuchi, Fariborz Damanpour, Jaepil Choi, Chao C. Chen, and Seung Ho Park, "National and Organizational Culture Differences and International Joint Venture Performance," *Journal of International Business Studies* 33 (2nd quarter, 2002): 243–65.

46. Manuel G. Serapio, Jr., and Wayne F. Cascio, "End-Games in International Alliances," *Academy of Management Executive* 10, no. 1 (1996): 62–73.

47. Richard Gibson, "Cereal Venture Is Planning Honey of a Battle in Europe," *The Wall Street Journal*, November 14, 1990, B1, B8.

48. Lawrence S. Welch and Anubis Pacifico, "Management Contracts: A Role in Internationalization?" *International Marketing Review* 7 (1990): 64–74.

49. Richard W. Wright and Colin Russel, "Joint Ventures in Developing Countries: Realities and Responses," *Columbia Journal of World Business* 10 (Spring 1975): 74–80.

Exporting Chopsticks to Japan

Company Background

Ian J. Ward was an export merchant in trouble. His company, Ward, Bedas Canadian Ltd., had successfully sold Canadian lumber and salmon to countries in the Persian Gulf. Over time, the company had opened four offices worldwide. However, when the Iran–Iraq war erupted, most of Ward's long-term trading relationships disappeared within a matter of months. In addition, the international lumber market began to collapse. As a result, Ward, Bedas Canadian Ltd. went into a survivalist mode and sent employees all over the world to look for new markets and business opportunities. Late that year, the company received an interesting order. A firm in Korea urgently needed to purchase lumber for the production of chopsticks.

Learning About the Chopstick Market

In discussing the wood deal with the Koreans, Ward learned that in the production of good chopsticks, more than 60 percent of the wood fiber is wasted. Given the high transportation cost involved, the large degree of wasted materials, and his need for new business, Ward decided to explore the Korean and Japanese chopstick industry in more detail.

He quickly determined that chopstick making in the Far East is a fragmented industry, working with old technology and suffering from a lack of natural resources. In Asia, chopsticks are produced in very small quantities, often by family organizations. Even the largest of the 450 chopstick factories in Japan turns out only 5 million chopsticks a month. This compares with an overall market size of 130 million pairs of disposable chopsticks a day. In addition, chopsticks represent a growing market. With increased wealth in Asia, people eat out more often and therefore have a greater demand for disposable chopsticks. The fear of communicable diseases has greatly reduced the utilization of reusable chopsticks. Renewable plastic chopsticks have been attacked by many groups as too newfangled and as causing future ecological problems.

From his research, Ward concluded that a competitive niche existed in the world chopstick market. He believed that if he could use low-cost raw materials and ensure that the labour-cost component would remain small, he could successfully compete in the world market.

The Founding of Lakewood Forest Products

In exploring opportunities afforded by the newly identified international marketing niche for chopsticks, Ward set four criteria for plant location:

1. Access to suitable raw materials
2. Proximity of other wood product users who could make use of the 60 percent waste for their production purposes
3. Proximity to a port that would facilitate shipment to the Far East
4. Availability of labour

In addition, Ward was aware of the importance of product quality. Because people use chopsticks on a daily basis and are accustomed to products that are visually inspected one by one, he would have to live up to high quality expectations in order to compete successfully. Chopsticks could not be bowed or misshapen, have blemishes in the wood, or splinter.

To implement his plan, Ward needed financing. Private lenders were skeptical and slow to provide funds. This skepticism resulted from the unusual direction of Ward's proposal. Far Eastern companies have generally held the cost advantage in a variety of industries, espe-

Sources: This case was written by Michael R. Czinkota based on the following sources: Mark Clayton, "Minnesota Chopstick Maker Finds Japanese Eager to Import His Quality Waribashi," *Christian Science Monitor*, October 16, 1987, 11; Roger Worthington, "Improbable Chopstick Capitol of the World," *Chicago Tribune*, June 5, 1988, 39; Mark Gill, "The Great American Chopstick Master," *American Way*, August 1, 1987, 34, 78–79; "Perpich of Croatia," *The Economist*, April 20, 1991, 27; and personal interview with Ian J. Ward, president, Lakewood Forest Products.

cially those as labour-intensive as chopstick manufacturing. U.S. companies rarely have an advantage in producing low-cost items. Furthermore, only a very small domestic market exists for chopsticks.

Yet Ward found that the state of Minnesota was willing to participate in this new venture. Since the decline of the mining industry, regional unemployment had been rising rapidly in the state. In 1983, unemployment in Minnesota's Iron Range peaked at 22 percent. Therefore, state and local officials were eager to attract new industries that would be independent of mining activities. Of particular help was the enthusiasm of Governor Rudy Perpich. The governor had been boosting Minnesota business on the international scene by traveling abroad and receiving many foreign visitors. He was excited about Ward's plans, which called for the creation of over 100 new jobs within a year.

Hibbing, Minnesota, turned out to be an ideal location for Ward's project. The area had an abundance of aspen wood, which, because it grows in clay soil, tends to be unmarred. The fact that Hibbing was the hometown of the governor also did not hurt. In addition, Hibbing boasted an excellent labour pool, and both the city and the state were willing to make loans totaling $500,000. The Iron Range Resources Rehabilitation Board was willing to sell $3.4 million in industrial revenue bonds for the project. Together with jobs and training wage subsidies, enterprise zone credits, and tax increment financing benefits, the initial public support of the project added up to about 30 percent of its start-up costs. The potential benefit of the new venture to the region was quite clear. When Lakewood Forest Products advertised its first 30 jobs, more than 3,000 people showed up to apply.

The Production and Sale of Chopsticks

Ward insisted that in order to truly penetrate the international market, he would need to keep his labour cost low. As a result, he decided to automate as much of the production as possible. However, no equipment was readily available to produce chopsticks because no one had automated the process before.

After much searching, Ward identified a European equipment manufacturer that produced machinery for making popsicle sticks. He purchased equipment from this Danish firm in order to better carry out the sorting and finishing processes. Since aspen wood is quite different from the wood the machine was designed for, as was the final product, substantial design adjustments had to be made. Sophisticated equipment was also purchased to strip the bark from the wood and peel it into long, thin sheets. Finally, a computer vision system was acquired to detect defects in the chopsticks. This system rejected over 20 percent of the chopsticks and yet some of the chopsticks that passed inspection were splintering. However, Ward firmly believed that further fine-tuning of the equipment and training of the new workforce would gradually take care of the problem.

Given this fully automated process, Lakewood Forest Products was able to develop a capacity for up to 7 million pairs of chopsticks a day. With a unit manufacturing cost of $0.03 per pair and an anticipated unit selling price of $0.057, Ward expected to earn a pretax profit of $4.7 million in the first year of operations.

Due to intense marketing efforts in Japan and the fact that Japanese customers were struggling to obtain sufficient supplies of disposable chopsticks, Ward was able to presell the first five years of production quite quickly. Lakewood Forest Products was ready to enter the international market. With an ample supply of raw materials and an almost totally automated plant, Lakewood was positioned as the world's largest and least labor-intensive manufacturer of chopsticks. The first shipment of six containers with a load of 12 million pairs of chopsticks was sent to Japan.

Questions for Discussion

1. Is Lakewood Forest Products ready for exports? Using the export-readiness framework developed by the U.S. Department of Commerce and available through various sites such as **http://www.tradeport.org** (from "Export Tutorial" go to "Getting Started" and finally to "Assessing Export Readiness"), determine whether Lakewood's commitment, resources, and product warrant the action they have undertaken.
2. What are the environmental factors that are working for and against Lakewood Forest Products both at home in the United States and in the target market, Japan?
3. New-product success is a function of trial and repurchase. How do Lakewood's chances look along these two dimensions?

Global Market Opportunity in the Olive Oil Industry: The Case of Baser Food

Altay Ayhan gazed out of his Istanbul office window in early January 2002, where the snow was falling slowly onto the streets below. As sales and marketing director for Baser Food, a wholly-owned subsidiary of Baser Holding, a major Turkish industrial group, Ayhan was responsible for determining the future strategic direction of the company's olive oil business. He had a meeting in 2 weeks with his boss, Mehmet Baser, and was expected to present his recommendations regarding growth strategies for packaged olive oil.

There were several options that occurred to Ayhan, each offering prospects for growth but with varying levels of risk. A fundamental question was whether Baser Food should focus on its domestic market or seek to expand its operations in its existing export markets. Since 1998, the company had embarked on an ambitious global effort, exporting its branded olive oils to the United States, Russia, and several other countries. This was due both to Ayhan's own efforts and the commitment of Mehmet Baser, who saw enormous potential in global markets. Alternatively, Ayhan could recommend a strategy of identifying potential new markets. Countries such as China and India with their large populations were attractive, although their unfamiliarity with the product meant that an expensive marketing campaign would have to be developed in order to change deeply-held food habits. He could also focus on the major olive oil producing and consuming countries such as Italy, Spain, and Greece with whose brands Baser already competed in several markets. Ayhan anticipated that if he pursued the latter strategy, he would face an uphill struggle, because the local producers would fight hard to protect their home turf. Another factor he had to consider was the prolonged economic crisis that Turkey had been mired in since 2000. With a high annual inflation rate, and the resulting drop in real incomes, many Turkish consumers were switching to cheaper edible oils such as sunflower and corn oil. Ayhan realized that he was in for a difficult 2 weeks while he weighed his options and made his decision.

Laurier Business & Economics

This case was written by Ven Siram, University of Baltimore, and Zeynep Bilgin, Marmara University.

We gratefully acknowledge the help and support of Mr. Mehmet Baser and Mr. Altay Ayhan in writing this case. This case was written when the first author was visiting professor at the School of Economics and Administrative Sciences at Marmara University, Istanbul, Turkey. He was at Marmara University as a Fulbright Scholar.

Background

Edible Oils

Edible oils, also called *pourable oils*, were liquid oils and formed a part of most diets around the world. Taste preferences varied regionally depending on the climate and availability of suitable seeds and vegetables. For instance, coconut oil was used in many parts of Southeast Asia, whereas in some African countries, cottonseed, peanut, and palm seed oil were used. Similarly mustard, sesame, sunflowers, corn, and soybeans were also processed into edible oils in different areas. In the Mediterranean region, olive oil was an integral part of the cuisine, although its use was spreading to other parts of the world as well. Olive oil was the only edible oil produced from a fresh fruit and was therefore considered a vegetable oil.

Olive Oil

Olive trees grew best in warm climates with the right soil conditions. Each tree yielded on average about 15 to 20 kilograms (kg.) of olives—about 3 to 4 litres of olive oil annually.[1] The major olive-growing countries in the world—Spain, France, Italy, Greece, and Turkey in Europe; Syria, Lebanon, and Israel in the Middle East; Morocco, Tunisia, and Algeria in Africa; Cyprus in the Mediterranean Sea; California in the United States—possessed these climatic and soil conditions. In Turkey, olive oil trees grew primarily along the southern coast of the Marmara Sea and along the Aegean coast.

Environmental and other conditions had a significant impact on olive yield, thus affecting the production of olive oil. Olive flies harmed the trees and decreased olive growth rates. In years when the climatic conditions were mild, output was high. In high productivity seasons and years, European buyers tried to cut the price.[2]

Olive output was also affected by harvesting practices. This was especially so in countries such as Turkey, where olives were not picked mechanically. Instead, branches were hit with sticks in order to dislodge the fruit. It took at least a year for the damaged branches to regenerate and become productive again. Therefore, years with low volumes of production often followed high productivity years. In Turkey, climatic conditions had improved over the last 5 years, and new olive trees had been planted. Growers had been encouraged to increase olive production and had also been trained in the care and watering of trees. As a result, production volumes had increased.[3]

Production Process

Unlike other vegetable and seed-based oils however, olive oils were not commonly seen as a commodity for two major reasons. First, much like wine, the weather, soil, and other conditions determined the taste and flavor of the fruit and, as a result, the oil. Therefore, customers, particularly in the Mediterranean, have developed preferences for olives from specific regions. In fact, in countries such as Turkey, producers of packaged olives and olive oil frequently stated the place of origin on their labels. Second, olive oils were categorized based on taste, aroma, and colour. The best quality olives were crushed and pressed to yield oil, which, after filtration, was then ready for consumption. Extra virgin (called "sizma" in Turkey) and virgin (called "naturel" in Turkey) olive oils were processed mechanically or manually and did not involve any chemical processing. Extra virgin oil had an acidity level of less than 1.0 percent and was the premium product that commanded the highest prices and margins; virgin had an acidity level of 1 to 2 percent. In the case of light, or refined, olive oil (called "rafine" or "kizartmalik" in Turkey), the product was refined, because the olives used would not be appropriate for consumption by merely crushing and pressing. A mixture of 84 to 90 percent refined olive oil and 10 to 15 percent extra virgin oil was called pure ("riviera" in Turkey).[4] Pomace ('pirina" in Turkey), the lowest quality olive oil with a natural acidity level of over 2 percent, was refined, deodorized, and bleached to reduce its acidity level. In most markets, it was not usually used for cooking but for other purposes such as in the manufacture of soaps and as animal feed.

Olive Oil and Health

Olive oil consumption has been increasing even in countries where it was not traditionally used. A major reason for its popularity was its health benefits. In countries such as the United States, where there was a growing health-consciousness among some segments of the society, the industry had done a good job promoting the product's benefits: its effectiveness in lowering LDL cholesterol, raising HDL cholesterol, the fact that it was natural and rich in vitamins, and so forth. It was used both for cooking as well as a salad dressing.[5]

Olive oil provided the basic fatty acids necessary for the body and also had a high caloric value; besides, some basic vitamins such A, D, E, and K could only be dissolved in oil. It was the only natural fruit oil that could directly be consumed like fruit juice based on its natural odor, taste, and colour. Besides its health benefits, olive oil was believed to contribute to a soft, healthy, and young-looking skin.[6]

Industry in Turkey

Market Conditions

Since November 2000, Turkey had been going through the worst recession in its history. The economic crises of November 2000 and February 2001 had shown the weaknesses of the economy, and budget deficits had continued in a highly inflationary environment. For 2000, the wholesale price index rose by 51.4 percent and the consumer price index by 54.9 percent. For 2001, inflation rates were 88.6 percent for wholesale goods and 68.5 percent for consumer goods.[7]

The economy was highly unstable even after a year of attempts to stabilize it. Energy costs were increasing as a result of high government taxes, negatively affecting the structure of production costs. The overall domestic market shrunk by almost 10 percent in 2001.

Edible Oil Sector

For the olive oil sector, huge export opportunities existed in the Middle East and Turkic Republics. Lack of governmental support for the sector was a setback for Turkish olive oil exports in the year 2000.[8]

Ayhan estimated the annual volume of domestic consumption of vegetable oils (e.g., sunflower, corn, cottonseed,

Exhibit 1

Turkey's Olive Oil Exports by Type (tons and U.S. $ million)

	1997		1998		1999		2000	
Types	**Tons**	**U.S. $**	**Tons**	**U.S. $**	**Tons**	**U.S. $**	**Tons**	**U.S. $**
Extra Virgin	4,684	10,523	9,660	15,977	22,630	41,528	5,081	9,627
Virgin	4,362	8,797	3,755	5,966	11,819	16,243	1,453	2,587
Refined	23,980	47,592	14,751	22,420	26,144	44,143	1,844	3,747
Pure	6,636	14,775	18,096	27,845	36,291	64,066	6,250	13,077
Other	8,639	5,654	2,018	1,463	6,209	4,070	1,786	1,369
Total	48,328	87,413	49,016	75,386	103,093	170,050	16,414	30,407

Source: Foreign Trade Department, **www.igeme.org.tr.**

and soybean) to be around 1 to 1.2 million tons. (Tons here and elsewhere in the case refers to metric tons, i.e., 1,000 kg.) The annual vegetable oil consumption was 17 kg. per capita, whereas around 1 kg. of olive per person was consumed annually in Turkey. This contrasted with an annual per capita consumption in the European Union of almost 4 kg. However, the EU figures masked the fact that per capita consumption in Mediterranean member countries such as Greece, Italy, and Spain was well over 10 kg. annually. A comparison of the consumption of corn oil to sunflower oil revealed that the market share of corn oil had increased while the market share of sunflower oil was decreasing. This was partly due to the price difference resulting from the different rates of customs duties—38 percent for sunflower oil and 12 percent for corn oil.[9] Ayhan's data showed that by volume, sunflower oil accounted for 81 percent of all edible oil consumption in Turkey in 2000, followed by olive oil with 10 percent and corn oil with 9 percent. By value, sunflower oil's share was 66 percent, followed by olive oil with 25 percent and corn oil with 8 percent. These differences in volume and value shares indicated that olive oil was more expensive than the other edible oils in Turkey.

In the period 1990/1991 to 1994/1995 an average of 81,000 tons of olive oil were produced annually, and in the period 1995/1996 to 1999/2000, the average annual olive oil production was 100,000 tons.[10]

Turkey's Foreign Trade/Exports

Turkey's olive oil exports (Exhibit 1) reflected some dramatic fluctuations from year to year. The reasons behind this were agricultural problems with olive growth and, as a result, olive oil production. Other important factors influencing Turkish olive oil exports were problems with marketing policy development and fluctuations in the supply of olive oil from other producing countries.

As a result of the increase in consumption and demand for olive oil in the world, new export market opportunities for Turkey had emerged. In total, Turkey exported olive oil to about 70 countries. The major importers of Turkish olive oil can be seen from Exhibit 2.

Spain and Italy, which were also producers and exporters of olive oil, received a major share of Turkish olive oil exports between 1996 and 2000. Turkey's exports to these countries were dependent on their own production levels and demand structures. Turkish olive oil exports to these countries were mostly unbranded and in bulk form, and therefore demand was high in periods when these countries were faced with agricultural problems and their own processing volumes were low. Bulk olive oil imported from Turkey was then processed and sold in these markets or re-exported to other markets under Spanish or Italian brand names. This meant that Turkish firms then were faced with competition from Turkish olive oil packaged and branded by re-exporters from other countries.

Turkey's Foreign Trade/Imports

Although Turkey was self-sufficient in terms of olive oil to meet the domestic demand, there was also a small amount (1,088 tons, U.S. $2.06 million in 2000) of olive oil imports. Imports took place in seasons when the domestic produc-

Exhibit 2

Turkish Olive Oil Exports by Country (%)

Country	1996–2000	2000
United States	23.0	36.0
Italy	31.0	6.0
Spain	24.0	14.0
Saudi Arabia	3.0	9.0
Switzerland	2.0	—
Argentina	—	8.0
United Arab Emirates	—	4.0
Other	17.0	23.0
Total	100.0	100.0

Source: Foreign Trade Department, **www.igeme.org.tr.**

tion was insufficient. The major exporters to Turkey were Tunisia, Italy, Saudi Arabia, and Egypt.

Competition

Although Turkey was a major olive oil producer, olive oil only accounted for a small share of the total liquid oil market. Although there were unbranded and unpackaged products, almost all branded sales went through supermarkets. The major brands were Komili (a Unilever Turkey brand), Taris (manufactured by a government cooperative), and others such as Kristal, Bizim, and Luna. Ayhan estimated that Komili and Taris together accounted for about 60 percent of the market by value. Komili positioned their brand as healthy and as part of a modern lifestyle; Taris was positioned as being more economical. Both had ongoing media campaigns and, as a result, some brand loyalty.

However, partly as a result of Turkey's economic crisis, some olive oil consumers had been switching to cheaper brands (Taris' market share had been increasing while Komili's had been declining); while others were switching to less expensive cooking oils such as sunflower and corn. The high inflation rate was also a factor in making consumers more price sensitive and less brand loyal.

The World of Olive Oil

Production

Although olives could be grown in many parts of the world with the right temperature, soil, and climatic conditions, the bulk of world olive oil production was still concentrated in the traditional olive-growing region, the Mediterranean rim. The European Union and six other countries (Turkey, Syria, Morocco, the United States, Argentina, and Egypt) accounted for almost 90 percent of world table olive production and almost all of world exports, according to provisional 2000–2001 data.[11] In the European Union, the major producing countries were Spain, Italy, and Greece.

Not surprisingly, the countries that were the largest olive growers were also the largest producers of olive oil (Exhibit 3). The average global annual olive oil production between 1990–1991 and 1997–1998 was 1.992 million tons.[12] Of the EU total, Spain, Italy, and Greece accounted for almost the entire production. The other olive oil producers included Israel, Lebanon, Cyprus, Iran, and Egypt.

Consumption

As can be seen from Exhibit 4, world consumption of olive oil had been increasing steadily. Interestingly, however, the major producing countries were also the major consuming ones, and this made Ayhan wonder whether cooking and eating habits could be changed so that consumers in nonproducing countries would also switch to using olive oil, as they appeared to be doing in the United States.

Based on some internal company data from the mid-1990s, Ayhan could see that per capita consumption figures (Exhibit 5) from selected countries showed that olive oil consumption was very small relative to vegetable oils both globally and in many of the major markets. However, given the increase in global olive oil consumption, Ayhan was sure that olive oil now accounted for a higher percentage of vegetable oil consumption, particularly in countries where segments of the population were health-conscious.

Exhibit 3 World Olive Oil Production ('000 tons)

	1995–1996	1996–1997	1997–1998	1998–1999	1999–2000	2000–2001
Algeria	51.5	50.5	15.0	54.5	33.5	50.0
Argentina	11.0	11.5	8.0	6.5	11.0	3.0
European Union	1403.5	1754.5	2116.5	1707.0	1878.5	1919.5
Jordan	14.0	23.0	14.0	21.5	6.5	27.0
Morocco	35.0	110.0	70.0	65.0	40.0	35.0
Palestine	12.0	12.0	9.0	5.5	2.0	20.0
Syria	76.0	125.0	70.0	115.0	81.0	165.0
Tunisia	60.0	270.0	93.0	215.0	210.0	130.0
Turkey	40.0	200.0	40.0	170.0	70.0	200.0
Other	32.5	38.5	30.0	40.5	41.5	41.0
Total	1735.5	2595.0	2465.5	2400.5	2374.0	2590.5

Note: 2000–2001 data are provisional.

Source: www.internationaloliveoil.org/eng/Eco-OliveOilProduction.html.

Exhibit 4 World Olive Oil Consumption ('000 tons)

	1995–1996	1996–1997	1997–1998	1998–1999	1999–2000	2000–2001
Algeria	36.0	50.0	31.5	44.0	42.0	45.0
European Union	1387.0	1566.5	1705.5	1709.0	1731.0	1776.5
Israel	7.5	7.5	6.5	9.5	12.5	13.0
Jordan	16.0	22.0	19.0	19.0	9.0	23.0
Morocco	25.0	50.0	55.0	55.0	55.0	47.0
Syria	78.0	85.0	95.0	88.0	90.0	110.0
Tunisia	34.5	70.0	52.0	49.0	60.0	60.0
Turkey	63.0	75.0	85.0	85.0	60.0	75.0
Australia	16.5	21.5	17.5	24.0	25.5	31.0
Brazil	23.0	21.5	27.5	23.5	32.0	35.0
Libya	5.0	10.0	7.0	16.0	11.0	12.0
United States	101.0	130.5	142.5	151.0	169.0	190.5
Canada	14.0	19.0	17.5	18.5	23.0	25.0
Japan	16.5	26.0	34.0	28.5	27.0	29.0
Other	24.5	84.0	84.5	93.0	75.0	108.5
Total	1892.5	2238.5	2380.0	2413.0	2422.0	2580.5

Note: 2000–2001 data are provisional.

Source: www.internationaloliveoil.org/eng/Eco-OliveOilConsumption.html.

Exhibit 5 Per Capita Annual Edible Oil Consumption

	Olive Oil (kg.)	Vegetable Oil (kg.)	% Olive Oil Share
Argentina	0.1	15.8	0.4
Australia	0.9	11.9	7.3
Brazil	0.1	13.0	1.1
Canada	0.5	17.4	2.9
Japan	0.1	12.5	1.1
United States	0.4	24.0	1.6
European Union	3.9	19.5	19.8
World	0.3	9.5	3.6

Source: Internal company data, 1995.

World Exports and Imports

As has been stated earlier, the Mediterranean countries accounted for the majority of global exports of olive oil (Exhibit 6). Given the importance of olive exports to the economies of these countries, they, particularly the EU members, had been engaged in promotional programs in order to increase global olive oil import and consumption. In the 1998–1999 season, Spain exported 275,000 tons, and Italy and Greece 180,000 tons each. These numbers add up to more than the EU's export volume stated in Exhibit 6 because all the EU figures in the case refer only to EU trade with non-EU countries, whereas figures for individual countries reflect their total trade.

As can be seen from Exhibit 7, there had been steady increases in world imports, due in part to the increased awareness of the health and other benefits of olive oil.

Company

History

Baser Food was a wholly-owned subsidiary of Baser Holding, one of the leading industrial, commercial, and financial groups in Turkey. Baser began in 1973 in chemicals and extended its operations into plastics, packaging, textiles, food, foreign trade, and finance. The group's companies, such as Baser Chemicals, which operated a joint venture with Colgate Palmolive, have been successful in different sectors. Baser Food was a 100 percent family-owned company. Both Mehmet Baser and Altay Ayhan worked for several years for Colgate Palmolive in Turkey and were experienced brand managers in the fast-moving consumer goods sector.

Corporate Vision and Mission

Baser Food's vision was to produce the highest quality olive oil for customers all over the world. Therefore, Ayhan's major focus was on sales and marketing activities for Baser's olive oil in both the domestic and international

Exhibit 6

World Olive Oil Exports ('000 tons)

	1995–1996	1996–1997	1997–1998	1998–1999	1999–2000	2000–2001
Argentina	4.5	6.0	7.5	6.0	6.0	4.0
European Union	165.0	220.0	227.0	208.5	298.5	305.0
Morocco	11.5	35.0	7.5	15.5	0.0	0.0
Syria	11.0	6.0	3.0	4.0	2.5	10.0
Tunisia	26.5	115.0	117.0	175.0	112.0	108.0
Turkey	19.0	40.5	35.0	86.0	16.6	85.0
United States	9.0	8.0	4.5	6.0	5.5	6.0
Other	10.0	7.5	5.5	5.0	3.4	5.0
Total	256.5	438.0	407.0	506.0	444.5	523.0

Note: 2000–2001 data is provisional.

Source: www.internationaloliveoil.org/eng/Eco-OliveOilExports.html.

Exhibit 7

World Olive Oil Imports ('000 tons)

	1995–1996	1996–1997	1997–1998	1998–1999	1999–2000	2000–2001
Argentina	0.5	6.5	7.0	3.5	2.0	7.5
European Union	73.5	145.5	118.0	225.5	116.5	107.5
Australia	16.0	21.5	17.5	23.5	25.0	30.0
Brazil	23.0	21.5	27.5	23.5	32.0	35.0
United States	105.0	140.0	144.0	155.0	175.0	198.0
Canada	14.0	19.0	17.5	18.5	23.0	25.5
Japan	16.5	26.0	34.0	28.5	27.0	29.0
Switzerland	3.5	5.0	5.5	6.0	8.0	8.0
Other	40.5	49.5	50.0	67.0	59.5	77.0
Total	292.5	434.5	421.0	551.0	486.0	517.5

Note: 2000–2001 data is provisional.

Source: www.internationaloliveoil.org/eng/Eco-OliveOilImports.html.

markets, and to assure a global brand presence. Both Mehmet Baser and Ayhan were committed to making the company's flagship olive oil brand (Cavallo d'Oro) a global one. However, given the high cost of global expansion, they were very careful in selecting export markets. Initially, they intended to focus on countries with per capita incomes over US$2,000 and on certain low-income countries with large populations. In developing countries, it was felt that the higher socioeconomic classes might be more willing to change cooking and eating habits and could also afford olive oil.

Product Lines and the Production

Baser Food specialized in the production of olive oil and was among the major olive oil producers in Turkey. Olive oil production, filling, and packaging activities took place in the factory located in Mugla/Yatagan, on Turkey's Aegean coast. The factory employed the most recent technologies for the production of olive oil in accordance with the standards set by the International Olive Oil Council (IOOC) and regulations of the U.S. Food and Drug Administration. The processing, filling, and packaging capacity of the plant in Mugla was around 3,000 tons per month.[13] The company was the only major Turkish olive oil producer that did not manufacture any products other than olive oil. In high-yield years, the plant operated at approximately 80 percent of capacity, and this fell to 40 percent during the alternate years, when olive oil production declined.

At the end of 2001, the company had an annual sales turnover of about US$25 million and employed approximately 50 people. Of its volume, $20 million was exported and the remainder was sold in Turkey both as a private label ($4 million) and under the company's brand, Cavallo d'Oro ($1 million). Private label brands included department store brands such as Migros and Metro in Turkey, and Quality, Tip, and Aro in other European

Exhibit 8 Cavallo d'Oro Strategy Statement

Brand:	Cavallo d'Oro
Primary positioning:	Cavallo d'Oro branded olive oil contains only the best selected olives from the Ayvalik region of Western Turkey to give a delightfully aromatic taste to healthy meals; "the finest olive oil"
Objectives:	Brand awareness and trial in the short run; to be a strong brand in the long run
Types:	Extra virgin olive oil; pure olive oil; refined olive oil (light)
Competitors:	Spanish, Italian, and Greek brands
Source of business:	Sunflower oil, corn oil, soybean oil, and margarine users; other olive oil brands in the market
Target market:	Health and taste conscious people
Physical benefits:	Nutritional, good health, controlling cholesterol level, cell renovations, delays aging and heart disease; improves muscles in children; improves calcium in bones in older people
Emotional benefits:	Feeling of health and confidence
Reason to buy:	Top quality olive oil from best selected olives of Western Turkey with right acidity and offering an enriched life
Brand character:	Natural, pure, tasty, authentic
Pricing strategy:	85 to 90 percent of market leader
Promotions:	Taste approval through sampling by taste panels, sachets, and on-pack promotions
Sizes:	250ml–500ml–1lt glass; 250ml–500ml–1lt–2lt plastic; 3lt and 5lt tins

countries. Distributor brands such as Sclafani, Aurora, and Roland were used in the United States and Canada. Of the export volume, $12 million was unbranded, bulk exports, primarily to importers in Italy and Spain, where it was then repackaged and sold under the importers' brands. In many countries, these exports were labeled as Italian or Spanish olive oil even though the contents were Turkish. U.S. regulations required that such products had to be labeled as being imported from Turkey and state the source country of the olive oil, although the label could indicate that the contents had been packed in Italy or Spain. Exports under the Cavallo d'Oro and other company brand names (MedOlive) accounted for $3 million of export volume, and the balance was private label export such as the distributor brands mentioned earlier. Domestic sales growth had averaged a steady 10 to 15 percent over the last few years, whereas exports had doubled over the past year. Margins varied from country to country and were approximately 15 percent for the company as a whole.

Brands

The key brand of the firm was Cavallo d'Oro. This brand was highly regarded in the many world markets where it had been introduced, due to favourable consumer perceptions about the quality of the oil, its attractive packaging, and its strong image. The brand had been launched in the Turkish domestic market as well in retail chains such as Carrefour. Exhibit 8 shows the brand positioning statement.

In certain foreign markets, such as Hungary and Israel, the company also used other brands such as MedOlive because the company used multiple distributors and each asked for a separate brand. Whereas Cavallo d'Oro was the main brand as part of Baser's policy, the secondary brands were seen as well on store shelves in these markets. Baser felt that because many consumers in the United States and elsewhere had strong favourable perceptions about Italian olive oil, it was to the company's advantage to use Italian rather than Turkish-sounding brand names.

International Operations

Baser Food was a member of the North American Olive Oil Association (NAOOA). The firm started to export Cavallo d'Oro at the end of 1999 and became the largest Turkish branded olive oil exporter in 2000. Thinking back over the past year's operations, Ayhan leaned back in his chair and felt very proud of the accomplishments of Baser Food. For the period November 1999 to September 2000, Ayhan estimated that his company had realized 37 percent of the total packaged olive oil exports of Turkey. Now in 2002, the company operated in about 20 international markets.[14] The main export market for Cavallo d'Oro was the United States, where the product was offered for sale in major chain stores in 15 states. In addition, Baser Food also operated in other countries including Spain, Italy, Germany, Taiwan, Venezuela, Russia, Poland, Bulgaria, Georgia, Azerbaijan, South Korea, Malaysia, Canada, Romania, Saudi Arabia, and Ukraine.

In most foreign markets, Baser employed exclusive distributors who were not permitted to represent other companies' products. However, one of the two U.S. distributors also distributed Spanish olive oil as well as other canned food products such as fruits, tuna, and tomato paste. Two managers (one who majored in international trade and the other with a degree in economics/business administration) and two support staff assisted Ayhan at the Istanbul headquarters of Baser Food. Most market visits and distributor contacts overseas were handled directly by Ayhan. The assistants monitored and followed up the company's plans and represented Baser Food at the many international food shows in which the company participated.

Because both Mehmet Baser and Ayhan traveled regularly to foreign markets and developed global strategic plans, they understood the need for patience when it came to international markets. Their experience with Colgate Palmolive, Polgat of Israel, and with the sister company of Baser Chemicals' operations in Ukraine had created an atmosphere in Baser Food that was strong in its international focus. The liaison offices in Russia and Kazakhstan were signs of the company's commitment to global business. Because Baser was an exporter, it faced little asset risk overseas but there were risks involved in the collection of accounts receivables. The use of a factoring payment system (i.e., selling receivables to a third party) and export credit insurance reduced these risks, but Ayhan recognized that some risk was unavoidable.

Future Objectives

Recently, the firm had begun to enter markets in the Far East and the Pacific Rim, including Japan, Australia, Taiwan, and Malaysia; Mehmet Baser and Ayhan were very optimistic about the market opportunities in this part of the world. However, China with its 1.3 billion people only imported 2,000 tons of olive oil annually (pure and extra virgin accounted for 40 percent each and pomace, because of its low price, the other 20 percent). This small volume of imports highlighted the task that lay ahead if a strategy of growth from nontraditional markets was to be pursued. At this point, the focus in these new markets was to gain distribution access and shelf space, particularly in supermarkets that stocked and sold international foods.

Potential Markets

There were several foreign markets that Baser Food had entered and others where olive oil consumption was expected to increase due to the promotional efforts of the IOOC.[15] Although the domestic market was important, Ayhan had to weigh the risks and opportunities of focusing on Turkey versus attempting to expand in the markets Baser had already entered, or even enter new ones. He could certainly pursue multiple markets, but his resource constraints were forcing him to prioritize. He had gathered the following data on his key export markets.

United States

Ayhan attended the 2001 midyear meeting of the NAOOA in San Diego, California. At this meeting, the association's chairman presented the following key data on the U.S. retail market (based on Nielsen and U.S. Department of Commerce data):

- Nearly 50 new brands of olive oil had appeared in the U.S. market in 2000.
- Import volume for 2000 grew by 15 percent with extra virgin accounting for 45 percent of imports, up from 28 percent in 1991. At the retail level, extra virgin accounted for 37 percent of sales volume, up from 26 percent in 1996 and 47 percent by value, up from 35 percent in 1996.
- Olive oil accounted for 10 percent of all pourable oil retail sales by volume, and the category grew by over 16 percent in 2000. In terms of dollar sales, olive oil represented 32 percent of the value, making it the largest category by value. Annual sales were estimated at US$370 million.
- Household penetration was almost 30 percent.
- Most olive oil purchases were made in households with annual family incomes greater than $70,000, with a concentration on the East Coast. The New York metropolitan area accounted for over 33 percent of U.S. olive oil sales.

The growing trend in U.S. olive oil consumption can be seen from Exhibits 9 and 10. Household consumption had increased, partly due to the health benefits of the product, the growing interest in Mediterranean food

Exhibit 9 U.S. Pourable Oils: Percent Volume Sales by Type

Type	1995	1996	1997	1998	1999	2000
Canola	22.9	23.2	23.0	26.1	25.7	25.4
Corn	20.4	20.7	19.6	18.5	18.2	17.5
Vegetable	47.0	46.9	47.0	44.5	45.2	44.4
Olive	7.7	7.0	8.0	8.4	8.3	9.6
Others	2.0	2.2	2.4	2.5	2.6	3.1
Total (pounds MM)	1,157	1,184	1,192	1,182	1,200	1,211

Source: AC Nielsen, quoted in NAOOA chairman's report, midyear meeting, January 2001.

Exhibit 10 U.S. Pourable Oils: Percent Value Sales by Type

Type	1995	1996	1997	1998	1999	2000
Canola	20.4	18.8	18.1	20.9	20.5	19.3
Corn	17.0	15.7	14.9	14.6	14.4	13.0
Vegetable	36.4	34.6	33.7	33.0	33.1	31.0
Olive	22.7	27.1	29.1	27.5	27.8	32.0
Others	3.6	3.8	4.0	4.0	4.2	4.6
Total ($ MM)	1,037	1,236	1,221	1,179	1,158	1,158

Source: AC Nielsen, quoted in NAOOA chairman's report, midyear meeting, January 2001.

Exhibit 11 U.S. Olive Oil Imports by Country and Type ($ '000)

	1995	1996	1997	1998
Italy	248,929 (39)	341,937 (39)	313,140 (45)	243,350 (48)
Spain	46,265 (59)	63,996 (65)	53,782 (65)	53,349 (66)
Turkey	28,611 (23)	23,944 (23)	26,871 (40)	16,679 (31)
Portugal	2,076 (4)	2,936 (2)	2,805 (6)	3,320 (22)
Greece	9,500 (48)	12,584 (69)	13,098 (74)	9,981 (77)
Morocco	1,416 (28)	8,873 (65)	5,939 (52)	4,551 (84)
Tunisia	4,920 (81)	n.a.	2,876 (99)	3,511 (88)
Other	4,255	14,042	6,403	4,595
Total	345,972 (41)	468,312 (44)	424,914 (49)	339,336 (52)

Source: Compiled from Goksu, Caglar (2000). Olive Oil Export Market Research, IGEME.

(particularly Italian and Greek), and the incorporation of this cuisine into a healthy lifestyle. The success of Italian food chains meant that olive oil sales had been increasing in the food service sector as well; many of these restaurants used olive oil in their cooking and often served it as an accompaniment to bread. ConAgra hoped to tap into this trend by launching Fleischmann's Premium Blend spread made with olive oil.[16] Also, the efforts of industry associations such as the NAOOA (www.naooa.org) and the California Olive Oil Council (COOC) (www.cooc.com) helped increase the awareness and usage of olive oil in the United States, although the efforts of the COOC to promote U.S.-produced olive oils could hurt non-U.S. producers such as Baser.

Although the U.S. market undoubtedly represented huge potential for Baser Food, the high costs and low margins concerned Ayhan. Because of the fierce competition and relative lack of brand loyalty, chain store retailers were able to negotiate aggressively with manufacturers both in terms of prices and access to shelf space. Ayhan estimated margins for Baser to be 10 to 15 percent and slotting fees to be between $25,000 and $50,000 for each SKU (stock keeping units) for the chain stores. Almost all of Baser Food's $500,000 annual marketing budget was spent on store-level promotion in order to gain retail support. Ayhan also estimated that $2 million would be required to implement a TV and radio campaign to build the brand. In 2000, Hormel Foods launched the Italian olive oil brand Carapelli in the U.S. market with a $13 million TV and print campaign (compared with $8.5 million in total media expenditure for the entire category in 1999). Carapelli became the third largest brand in the United States, with annual sales of $31 million; Unilever's Bertolli brand led the market with $128 million in sales.[17]

The growth trend was also supported by AC Nielsen household panel data that showed a penetration of 29.8 percent for olive oil, up from 26.2 percent in 1997. At the retail level, olive oil sales had increased from $259 million in 1995 to $370 million in 2000. Canola oil continued to be popular because it was two to three times less expensive than olive oil. Also, some U.S. companies imported canola oil and extra virgin olive oil that they then blended and packaged in the United States. This blend retailed for a price lower than olive oil.

One trend in U.S. imports (Exhibit 11) was that virgin olive oil consumption, and therefore imports, was increasing, possibly due to its perceived health benefits and the industry's promotion efforts. (The figures in parentheses in Exhibit 11 represent the percentage share of virgin olive oil of total imports. For instance, 39 percent of imports from Italy in 1995 were of virgin olive oil.)

Australia

Australia was another country Ayhan was seriously considering as part of his expansion plans. There were several factors that made Australia an attractive potential market. These included:

- Its relatively high per capita income
- Political and economic stability
- Familiarity with Mediterranean cuisine as a result of immigrants from Italy, Greece, and other countries in the region
- Australians' general concern with health and their diets; olive oil imports had grown at an average of 15 percent per year over the past several years
- Although there was some domestic production, over 95 percent of olive oil consumed was imported, valued at close to US$100 million annually
- Among the nontraditional olive oil consuming countries, its per capita consumption was high

As can be seen from Exhibit 12, with the exception of a dip in 1997–1998, there had been a steady increase in import volume. This suggested a growing acceptance of the product among Australian consumers. The olive oil market was less price competitive than in the United States, and this enabled Baser Food to enjoy margins of 25 to 30 percent. Also, Ayhan believed that an initial investment of $100,000, in which local distributors would be willing to participate, would be sufficient to enter the market. Based on IOOC and Australian customs statistics for 1999–2000, Ayhan estimated 25 percent of these imports to be virgin/extra virgin, 74 percent pure, and the remainder, pomace.

Others

In addition to the United States and Australia, the IOOC had identified several other countries that they felt represented potentially viable markets. These were Brazil, Canada, China, Japan, Mexico, Taiwan, and Thailand. As a result of the IOOC's promotional efforts and the increasing popularity of the Mediterranean diet emphasized by the EU promotional campaigns, olive oil consumption had begun to spread into these nontraditional markets.[18] However, there was some instability because for the majority of the consumers in these markets, olive oil was still a nonessential product, and the demand was therefore both more price- and income-elastic than in the traditional consuming countries such as Spain, Italy, or Greece. One way of approaching these new markets would be for the major Turkish producers to create a joint fund, with some support from the Turkish government perhaps, to stimulate primary demand. However, Mehmet Baser felt that this was not likely in the near future, and any demand stimulation would have to be done by Baser Food alone. This could prove to be very expensive.

Another opportunity for growth came from Turkey's membership in the Black Sea Economic Cooperation (BSEC) agreement and its customs union arrangement with the EU. As a result, Turkish exports enjoyed tariff-free movement within the BSEC and EU. Ayhan was considering the possibility of taking advantage of this by focusing on some of the member countries of these trading blocs (e.g., Russia, Bulgaria, and Greece) as a way to increase Baser Food's global sales.

Ahyan had very limited information about these markets but knew that some behavioral change would be necessary in consumers' dietary habits in order for olive oil sales to increase significantly. This would clearly require heavy promotion to create awareness of the product and its health and other benefits before consumer acceptance could be achieved. For China, Ayhan estimated that it would cost US$1 million to properly launch Cavallo d'Oro in the Shanghai region alone. In

Exhibit 12 **Australia's Olive Oil Imports by Country (tons)**

	1996/1997	1997/1998	1998/1999	1999/2000	2000/2001
Spain	14,276	9,937	13,978	14,460	15,501
Italy	5,301	5,954	7,368	8,118	10,781
Greece	1,430	1,574	1,157	1,764	1,882
Turkey	143	156	671	87	540
Other	272	183	208	362	1,195
Total	21,422	17,804	23,382	24,791	29,899

Source: www.internationaloliveoil.org/tm/australia/STATS06.html.

many ways it was easier to grow from markets where the product was accepted and the category was already represented on supermarket shelves rather than to develop the entire category single-handedly. In other potential markets such as Eastern Europe, Baser played the role of the follower, allowing large companies from Italy and elsewhere to bear the high costs of gaining product acceptance and distribution. As a result, Baser spent just $200,000, shared with the distributor, to gain entry into Poland, for example.

On the other hand, some first-mover advantages were possible, despite the high initial entry costs, if Baser entered these countries before the competition did. Mehmet Baser was also of the view that some of the emerging markets would be easier to penetrate because they had very few established competitors and the resource requirements needed to gain brand awareness and retail presence would be lower than in the more established olive oil consuming countries. Ayhan believed that the choice of market was critical for a small, emerging market multinational like Baser Food, particularly when the competition included companies such as Unilever Bestfoods and its powerful Bertolli brand.

Endnotes

1. Kirmanli, Nilay (2000). Zeytin-Zeytinyagi Sektor Arastirmasi. (Olive—Olive Oil Sector Study). ITO. Yayinlari 22/12/00.
2. Sektor Dosyasi—Kati ve Sivi Yaglar (Sector Report—Fat and Oil). *GIDA Magazine*, Year: 6, November 2000; No. 2000-11. Dunya Publications: Istanbul.
3. **www.igeme.org.tr.**
4. Kirmanli, Nilay (2000); Akcay Tuna, Sabahat (1997). Zeytin Agaci, Zeytin, Zeytinyagi (Olive Tree, Olive, Olive Oil); Interview with Altay Ayhan, April 15, 2002.
5. Akcay Tuna, Sabahat (1997).
6. Viola, Publio (1997). Olive Oil and Health—International Olive Oil Council: Spain. State Institute of Statistics—National Accounts.
7. **www.die.gov.tr/seed/nation/page12.html.**
8. Tuglular, Taskin (2000). Bitkisel Yag Sektoru. *GIDA Magazine*, Year 6, November 2000, No. 2000-11. Dunya Publications: Istanbul, p. 42.
9. Ibid.
10. Kirmanli, Nilay (2000).
11. **www.internationaloliveoil.org.**
12. Goksu, Caglar (2000). Olive Oil Export Market Research, IGEME: Aegean Olive and Olive Oil Exporters Union, Working Report 2000–01.
13. **www.Baserfood.com.**
14. Interview with Altay Ayhan, December 2001 and January 2002.
15. **www.internationaloliveoil.org.**
16. Thompson, Stephanie (2001). Spreading Out Into Olive Oil. *Advertising Age 72*, Issue 34 (August 20), p. 39.
17. Ibid.
18. Quaranta, G., and V. Rotundo (2002). Economic and Commercial Prospects for Olive Oil in View of the Changes in the Common Market Organization (CMO)—Part One, OLIVÆ, No. 91 (April), pp. 20–24.

Dr. Eris: Cosmetics from Poland

Dr. Irena Eris is famous in Poland. In 1999 the Business Centre Club honored her with the title Business Woman of the Decade, in 2003 she was recognized for the creation of an internationally competitive Polish brand, and in 2004 she was placed on the list of influential women in Polish history that had turned the course of events, overcome stereotypes, and initiated new thinking. In 2005 she received the Economic Award of the President of Poland.

It all started in 1982 when Dr. Eris, a Ph.D. from the Faculty of Pharmacology at Berlin's Humboldt University, inherited the equivalent of six small Fiat cars. With this inheritance she and her husband opened a cottage workshop producing nourishing facial cream in 1983. The first cosmetic products were mixed in a makeshift machine made by a local locksmith friend.

The Polish Cosmetics Market

With its population of 40 million people, Poland is the eighth largest country in Europe. Its per-capita consumption is only one-fifth of the average of the pre-2004 European Union (EU) member countries. The key competitive factors are price, quality, and brand recognition. Packaging and advertising have become increasingly important. Poles tend to be risk averse when choosing everyday cosmetics. They prefer to buy a known brand from a known store. Purchasing decisions are determined by company reputation and brand recognition.

Poland has long traditions in the production of cosmetics. Max Faktor—born in Łódź, Poland, during the 1870s—became the founder of modern make-up, creating the global Max Factor brand. Helena Rubinstein, a Polish immigrant to the United States, is one of the biggest names in facial care. In the Communist Era, Poland was by far the largest cosmetics producer in the former socialist countries. The cosmetics of Pollena and Nivea were cherished by women and men of all ages. Poland was also a large market for cosmetics. Most of the cosmetics products were affordably priced. Only 5 percent represented luxury products, most of them imported. The collapse of the CMEA (Council for Mutual Economic Assistance) market at the beginning of the 1990s caused the market for Polish cosmetics to stagnate. Existing procurement and distribution networks in the domestic and foreign Soviet Bloc markets were dismantled. Market positions in the big Russian market and in the other markets of Central and Eastern Europe were lost.

Today, the cosmetics industry in Poland employs approximately 19,000 people. It has remained a key employer in a volatile labour market, but the transition process to a market-led economy has caused enormous job losses. The "shock therapy" approach to the privatization of state-owned enterprises led to the mushrooming of small domestic cosmetics companies; by the end of 2005 there were more than 470. Less than 15 percent of these employed more than 50 people. International cosmetics manufacturers were quick to enter the Polish cosmetics industry via acquisition of former state-owned companies or greenfield investment. They have big production capacity, premier facilities, established retail clout, and high brand recognition.

In the last 10 years the production of cosmetics in Poland has experienced steady annual growth (see Exhibit 1). In 2002 the market was valued at 1.85 billion Polish Zloty (PLN), the equivalent of US$450 million at the current exchange rate. The value of Polish cosmetics exports in 2002 was US$291 million, representing almost 10 percent growth over 2001. More than two-thirds of all exports went to former CMEA markets and about 30 percent to the European Union member countries. The major importers were Russia (18 percent of the total value of Polish exports), Hungary (14 percent), Lithuania (12 percent), Ukraine (11 percent), Germany (8 percent), and the United Kingdom (7 percent). Avon Cosmetics, Miraculum, Cussons Group, Kolastyna, Ziaja, Dr. Irena Eris, Polena Ewa, and L'Oréal are the biggest exporters.

This case was developed by Svetla T. Marinova and Marin A. Marinov. It is intended to be used as a basis for classroom discussion rather than to illustrate either effective or ineffective handling of a business situation. The authors acknowledge the assistance of Dr. Irena Eris and her personal assistant Ms. Aleksandra Trzcinska in developing the case.

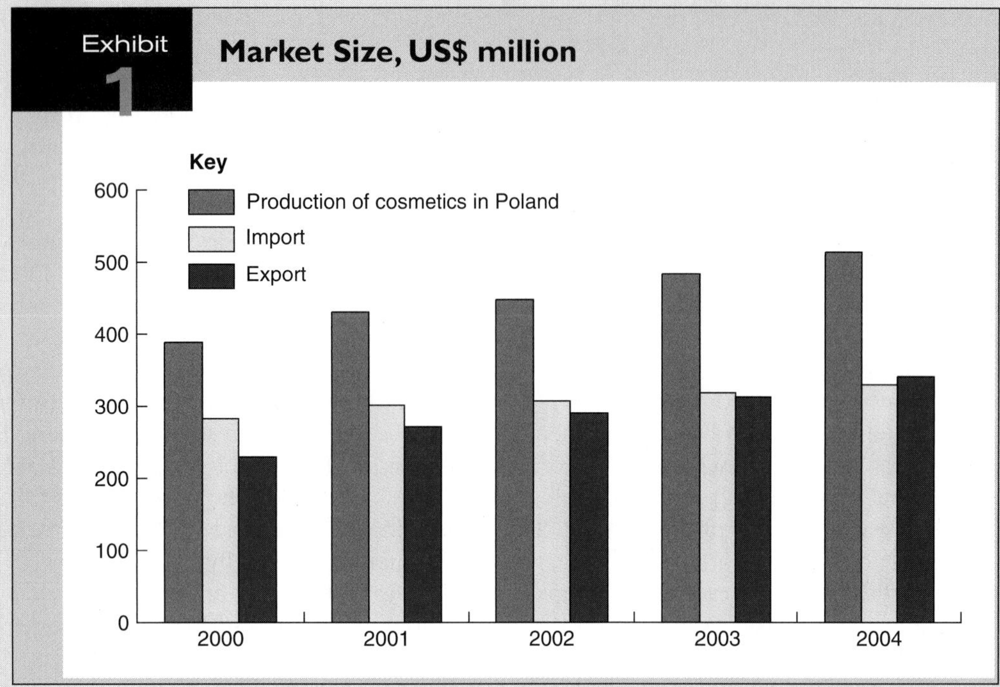

Cosmetics imports come from Germany (23 percent), France (21 percent), the United Kingdom (17 percent), and Italy and Spain (6 percent each). Imported cosmetics sell at a price premium and enjoy high brand recognition.

Cosmetics manufacturers in Poland can be divided into four groups:

1. Producers owned by the Pollena conglomerate, owned by foreign investors (Beiersdorf, Cussons Group, and Unilever). They develop and introduce new products in the Polish market and upgrade the acquired cosmetic products.
2. Formerly state-owned cosmetics manufacturers, privatized and functioning independently (Pollena Ewa and Miraculum)
3. A large group of Polish private cosmetics firms established in the 1980s and 1990s (Inter-Fragrances, Dr. Irena Eris Cosmetics Laboratories, Kolastyna, Soraya, Dax Cosmetics, Dermika, and Ziaja)
4. New factories built by global cosmetics companies (Johnson & Johnson, L'Oréal, Avon, and Oriflame)

The strong domestic producers have established positions in the skin and body care product market segment and control about two-thirds of this market. The market leader is Beiersdorf-Lechia with almost a 30 percent share, followed by Johnson & Johnson (8 percent), Unilever (7 percent), Kolastyna (6.5 percent), and Dr. Irena Eris (5 percent).

The facial care cosmetics market segment is dominated by Dr. Irena Eris (16 percent), followed by Ziaja (10 percent), Oceanic (9 percent), and Cussons (8 percent). All foreign facial care brands have positioned themselves in the middle or premium sector of the market. For example, the U.S. firm Johnson & Johnson dominates the mid-market with 45 percent market share, while the French Garnier with its brand L'Oréal leads in the premium sector with more than 50 percent market share. The market pressure from foreign brands has pushed most of the Polish facial care brands into the low-price mass markets. The self-tanning cosmetics segment is dominated by L'Oréal with 27.5 percent, Beiersdorf with 25.3 percent, and Dr. Irena Eris with 12.2 percent market share.

Premium cosmetics brands are sold via specialized networks of stores such as Empik, Galeria Centrum, Ina Center, and French Sephora. The medium- and low-priced cosmetics are distributed via hypermarket and supermarket chains, drug stores, and specialty stores. Companies such as Avon, Oriflame, and Amway use direct selling. The largest distributor of cosmetics is Polbita, a privately owned company established in 1990. Polbita owns 20 percent of the cosmetics distribution system in Poland. Its store chain Drogeria Natura has more than 330 retail outlets.

Since 1988 almost all global and international cosmetics brands have entered the Polish market. They seek new market development and expansion. The best recognized foreign brands are: Christian Dior, Guerlain, Yves Saint Laurent, Yves Rocher, Yves Saint Rocher, L'Oréal, Laboratories Paris, Lancôme, Paloma Picasso, Guy Laroche, Giorgio Armani, Cacharel, Coty, Elizabeth Arden, Pierre Robert, Colgate Palmolive, Nivea, Jean Pierresand, Vichy Laboratories, Jade, Max Factor, Revlon, Maybelline, Biotherm, Givenchy, Nino Cerruti, Margaret Astor, and Rimmel. They have all set up their own exclusive stores and beauty salons. Aggressive advertising, new product development, and simultaneous product introduction in Paris and Warsaw reinforce their premium market position.

The ongoing process of market liberalization and EU enlargement has been favourable for the growing market presence of foreign cosmetics brands in Poland. The variety of products and services has led to a much greater consumer choice. This has increased the competitive pressure on Polish brands that are mostly too small to compete against global multinationals. One manager of a Polish medium-sized cosmetics company stated: "Small and medium-sized cosmetics companies do not have enough market power. I cannot see how they can compete successfully against the multinationals after the EU enlargement. It is unlikely that the Polish Government will protect us. It will not provide financial help for consolidation. Foreign giants will have no problem pushing us out of business. There will be more products, but Polish brands will gradually disappear."

Nevertheless, domestically owned cosmetics companies in Poland have been increasingly trying to gain market presence in the EU markets. Some managers believe that the EU enlargement can provide more opportunities for export and participation in partnerships with other cosmetics firms from the wider Europe.

The Company

Dr. Irena Eris Cosmetic Laboratories was set up in socialist Poland in 1982 with a monthly production output of 3,000 packages. Demand for Eris cosmetics constantly increased and the company expanded its operations rapidly.

The transition period with its diverse economic and political reforms created new opportunities for business growth. The increased productivity and profitability of the company in the early 1990s led to the launch of a new plant. Dr. Eris reinvested most of the company profits in product innovation and new technologies.

Presently, the company employs 350 employees and produces 300 types of products grouped into several product lines. The monthly output is approximately 1,000,000 units. All company cosmetics products meet the quality standards of the European Union and the U.S. Food and Drug Administration. Dr. Irena Eris holds ISO 9001 (since 1996) and Environment Management ISO 14001 (since 2001). Those certificates guarantee that its cosmetics are of global quality and their production is environmentally friendly.

Dr. Eris's focus is on innovation and research and development (R&D). Its R&D investment in 2004 was 3.4 percent of company turnover, growing to 4.6 percent in 2005. A large team of dermatologists, allergy specialists, biologists, and molecular biologists works on various projects at the company's Centre for Science and Research set up in 2001 (see Exhibit 2). R&D is the core of the company's strategy to develop scientifically advanced products.[1] Consumers who are interested in scientifically created cosmetics are the main targets.

Scientific research and innovative solutions are key to the brand positioning strategy of Dr. Irena Eris. All products are original and based on in-company research. This

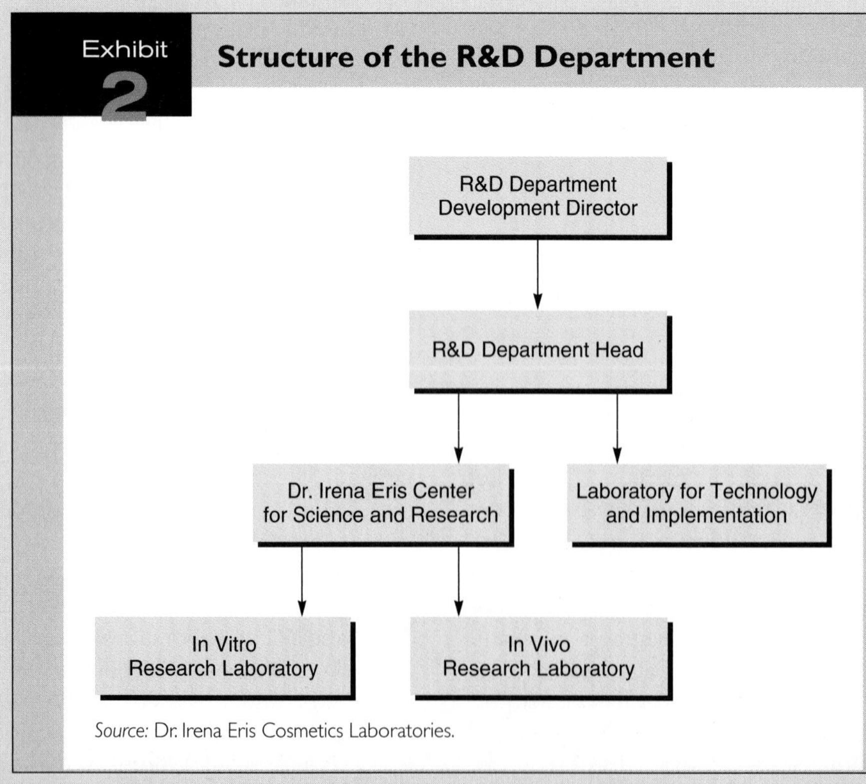

Source: Dr. Irena Eris Cosmetics Laboratories.

Exhibit 3 **Market Segments and Company Brands**

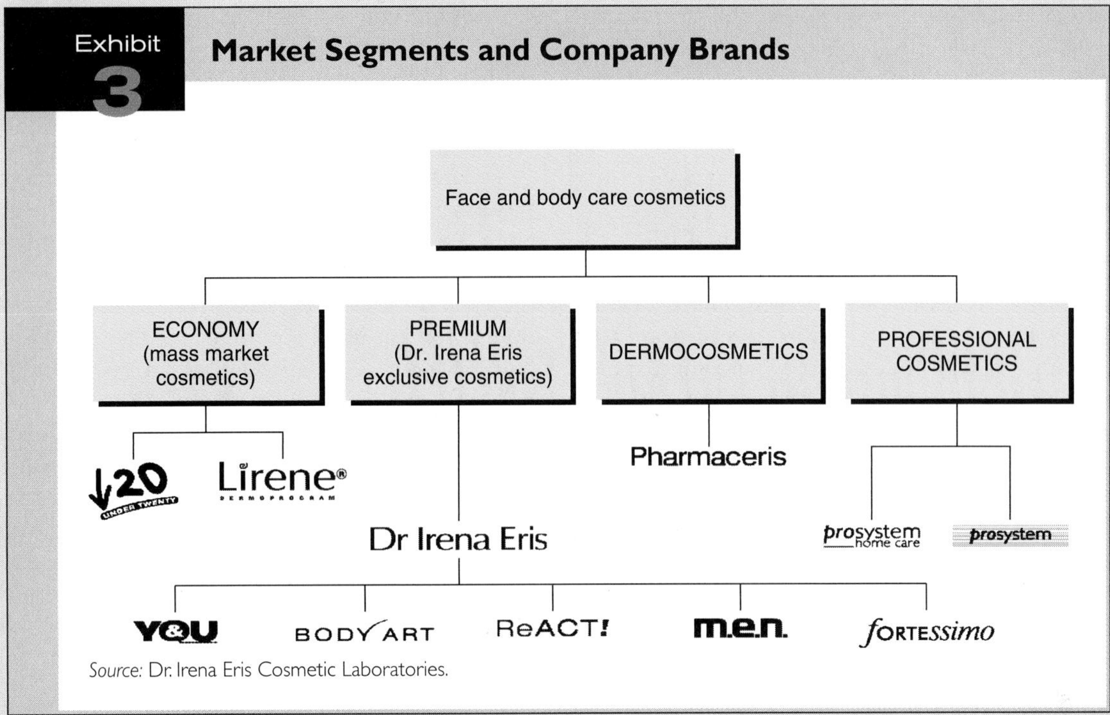

Source: Dr. Irena Eris Cosmetic Laboratories.

makes them distinctive and more difficult for competitors to copy. In the mid-1990s, Dr. Eris was the first in Europe to propose the use of vitamin K in cosmetics. More recently, it was the first company in the world to test and use the innovative complex FitoDHEA 1 folacin in its products.

Brand Image

The brand image of Dr. Irena Eris is built on respect for people, stressing their individual nature and the importance of cooperation. The brand development strategy reflects the value of interpersonal relationships within the company and with its clients. The brand value of Dr. Irena Eris is based on its holistic approach to the individual specific needs and preferences of customers. It offers an individual skin care program for home use and for use in specialised professional salons and spa hotels.

The brand has also gained international recognition. In 2005 it was nominated to the 2005 Beauty Awards for the best cosmetics introduced in the U.K. market. It was also awarded the Gold Glamour award by the British edition of Glamour.

The target segments of Dr. Irena Eris span all age groups. Users are women who prioritize cosmetic efficiency based on research. They wish to use high-quality products that are modern and pleasant to use. There are four segments (see Exhibit 3).

The company targets the economy segment with mass products. The premium segment is reached with innovative products. The dermocosmetics segment is served with health and hygienic products. Specialised products are designed for the professional segment. These segments are reached via 20,000 retail points of sale for widely distributed products and 1,000 points of sale for products destined for limited distribution via pharmacies, beauty salons, and centers.

Diversification

The company has diversified in related activities. Following the success of a four-star Spa Hotel, Dr. Irena Eris, in Krynica Zdrój in Poland, it has invested in a second Spa Hotel, Dr. Irena Eris Wzgórza Dylewskie, in Wysoka Wieś near Ostróda, which is to be completed in the first half of 2006. The Spa Hotels offer a comprehensive, tailor made skin treatment and revitalizing program. Skin treatment is complemented by a range of health improvement packages including exercises, massage, spa therapy and physical activities. The spa hotel concept promotes Dr. Eris as a modern lifestyle brand.

Moreover, the brand Dr. Irena Eris has been extended to the franchise chain Dr. Irena Eris Cosmetics Institutes. There are 22 of them established in the largest Polish cities. Such institutes were also opened in Moscow, Russia, and Bogota, Colombia. It is projected that ten new Institutes will serve clients in Poland and abroad by 2007. The Institutes offer several basic company treatments based on the Dr. Irena Eris Professional Program. The treatments are carried out using preparations from the company's own specialised line of cosmetics. They are exclusively used in beauty salons (Prosystem). The therapy is complemented by a line of products for subsequent home care (Prosystem home care). The treatments are selected individually and preceded by obligatory skin diagnosis by dermatologists partnering with Dr. Irena Eris Cosmetic Institutes. The personnel of the Institutes consists of beauty therapists trained at the company's own center.

Marketing Communications

The marketing communications strategy of Dr. Irena Eris is consistent with its strategic focus on innovation. It is the Polish company with the highest advertising expenditure. In Poland the company advertises on national and regional state-owned and private TV channels, on billboards, and in fashion and women's magazines. Advertising and public relations activities in the key international markets are generally standardized but adapted to the local language. Private TV channels are mostly used for the firm's international advertising campaigns. Next come advertisements in fashion magazines and in-store promotions. The company has strengthened its position in the professional segment by developing close relationships with leading business customers and participating in international fairs.

Dr. Irena Eris Cosmetic Laboratories donates PLN500,000 worth of products and money for charitable causes. It is a key contributor to the Always Healthy and Active Club programs set up to meet the needs of seven million adult Polish women. The program aims to increase the knowledge of mature women about health- related issues, and improve their general health and quality of life. In 2001, Dr. Eris was awarded the Summa Bonitas award from the foundation Zdąży ć z pomocą for its corporate social responsibility.[2]

The 2004 sales of Dr. Irena Eris Cosmetics Laboratories were PLN97.6 million (€24 million) from domestic and export sales. This was 15 percent growth compared with the results in 2003. In 2004 after-tax profit was PLN7 million.

Internationalization

Most of the initial attempts to go international were driven by opportunities based on personal contacts. In 1989 the company started exporting its products. The debut was made in the vast U.S. market. The large Polish community in the U.S. formed a formidable basis for foreign market expansion. Personal relationships and contacts were of foremost importance. Currently, Dr. Eris cosmetics are available in over 1,000 specialised U.S. salons.

After tapping into the U.S. market, Dr. Eris turned her sights on the neighbouring German and the former CMEA markets. Geographic proximity, low psychic distance, and previously strong positions of Polish cosmetics in these markets proved to help market entry and penetration.

Dr. Irena Eris developed its international presence systematically since the mid-1990s. Direct exporting has been the preferred mode of foreign market entry. Management has recognized the benefits of economies of scope and uses various sources of information in support of foreign market expansion. The firm works with a range of exclusive distributors. In 2004, Dr. Irena Eris products were introduced to the British market via the retailer Boots. The growth of exports has been substantial and in 2004 the company recorded an increase of international sales by 40 percent. By 2006, the products of Dr. Irena Eris were available in 24 countries around the globe. They are sold in beauty shops, pharmacies, supermarkets and beauty salons. Major markets are the United States, Lithuania, Russia, the Czech Republic, Hungary, the Slovak Republic, the Ukraine, Germany, Tasmania, Taiwan, and Singapore.

Franchising has been used for the company's international growth in the form of cosmetics institutes. Apart from the two franchise operations in Moscow and Bogota, an expansion of franchise operations is planned across Europe.

Questions for Discussion

1. What does the future hold for Polish small- and medium-sized cosmetics manufacturers? Do you agree with the statement of the Polish manager?
2. What should Dr. Irena Eris Cosmetics Laboratories do to secure its future as market leader in the facial cosmetics segment in the Polish market?
3. Explain the internationalization of Dr. Irena Eris Cosmetics Laboratories in the United States.

Notes

1. More details about the research program can be obtained from: **http://www.drirenaeris.pl/badania/en/badania.php** and **http://www.drirenaeris.pl/en/kosmetyki_skladniki.php.**
2. For more information, see **http://www.businessweek.com/magazine/content/04_19/b3882011.htm.**

Ruth's Chris: The High Stakes of International Expansion

"Well, I was so lucky that I fell into something that I really, really love. And I think that if you ever go into business, you better find something you really love, because you spend so many hours with it ... it almost becomes your life."

Ruth Fertel, 1927–2002
Founder of Ruth's Chris Steak House

In 2006, Ruth's Chris Steak House (Ruth's Chris) was fresh off a sizzling initial public offering (IPO). Dan Hannah, vice-president for business development since June 2004, was responsible for the development of a new business strategy focused on continued growth of franchise and company-operated restaurants. He also oversaw franchisee relations. Now a public company, Ruth's Chris had to meet Wall Street's expectations for revenue growth. Current stores were seeing consistent incremental revenue growth, but new restaurants were critical and Hannah knew that the international opportunities offered a tremendous upside.

With restaurants in just five countries including the United States, the challenge for Hannah was to decide where to go to next. Ruth's Chris regularly received inquiries from would-be franchisees all over the world, but strict criteria—liquid net worth of at least US$1 million, verifiable experience within the hospitality industry, and an ability and desire to develop multiple locations—eliminated many of the prospects. And the cost of a franchise—a US$100,000 per restaurant franchise fee, a five percent of gross sales royalty fee, and a two percent of gross sales fee as a contribution to the national advertising campaign—eliminated some qualified prospects. All this was coupled with a debate within Ruth's Chris senior management team about the need and desire to grow its international business. So where was Hannah to look for new international franchisees and what countries would be best suited for the fine dining that made Ruth's Chris famous?

The House That Ruth Built

Ruth Fertel, the founder of Ruth's Chris, was born in New Orleans in 1927. She skipped several grades in grammar school, and later entered Louisiana State University in Baton Rouge at the age of 15 to pursue degrees in chemistry and physics. After graduation, Fertel landed a job teaching at McNeese State University. The majority of her students were football players who not only towered over her, but were actually older than she was. Fertel taught for two semesters. In 1948, the former Ruth Ann Adstad married Rodney Fertel who lived in Baton Rouge and shared her love of horses. They had two sons, Jerry and Randy. They opened a racing stable in Baton Rouge. Ruth Fertel earned a thoroughbred trainer's license, making her the first female horse trainer in Louisiana. Ruth and Rodney Fertel divorced in 1958.

In 1965, Ruth Fertel spotted an ad in the *New Orleans Times-Picayune* selling a steak house. She mortgaged her home for US$22,000 to purchase Chris Steak House, a 60-seat restaurant on the corner of Broad and Ursuline in New Orleans, near the fairgrounds racetrack. In September of 1965, the city of New Orleans was ravaged by Hurricane Betsy just a few months after Fertel purchased Chris Steak House. The restaurant was left without power, so she

IVEY

Richard Ivey School of Business
The University of Western Ontario

Allen H. Kupetz and Professor Ilan Alon wrote this case solely to provide material for class discussion. The authors do not intend to illustrate either effective or ineffective handling of a managerial situation. The authors may have disguised certain names and other identifying information to protect confidentiality.

Exhibit 1

Fine Dining Steak Houses by Brand in the United States (2005)

Company Name	Number of Restaurants
Ruth's Chris	92
Morton's	66
Fleming's	32
Palm	28
Capital Grille	22
Shula's	16
Sullivan's	15
Smith & Wollensky	11
Del Frisco	6

Source: Ruth's Chris Steak House files.

cooked everything she had and brought it to her brother in devastated Plaquemines Parish to aid in the relief effort.

In 1976, the thriving restaurant was destroyed in a kitchen fire. Fertel bought a new property a few blocks away on Broad Street and soon opened under a new name, "Ruth's Chris Steak House," since her original contract with former owner, Chris Matulich, precluded her from using the name Chris Steak House in a different location. After years of failed attempts, Tom Moran, a regular customer and business owner from Baton Rouge, convinced a hesitant Fertel to let him open the first Ruth's Chris franchise in 1976. It opened on Airline Highway in Baton Rouge. Fertel reluctantly began awarding more and more franchises. In the 1980s, the little corner steak house grew into a global phenomenon with restaurants opening every year in cities around the nation and the world. Fertel became something of an icon herself and was dubbed by her peers *The First Lady of American Restaurants.*

Ruth's Chris grew to become the largest fine dining steak house in the United States (see Exhibit 1) with its focus on an unwavering commitment to customer satisfaction and its broad selection of USDA Prime grade steaks (USDA Prime is a meat grade label that refers to evenly distributed marbling that enhances the flavour of the steak). The menu also included premium quality lamb chops, veal chops, fish, chicken and lobster. Steak and seafood combinations and a vegetable platter were also available at selected restaurants. Dinner entrees were generally priced between US$18 to US$38. Three company-owned restaurants were open for lunch and offered entrees generally ranging in price from US$11 to US$24. The Ruth's Chris core menu was similar at all of its restaurants. The company occasionally introduced new items as specials that allowed the restaurant to offer its guests additional choices, such as items inspired by Ruth's Chris New Orleans heritage.[1]

In 2005, Ruth's Chris enjoyed a significant milestone, completing a successful IPO that raised more than US$154 million in new equity capital. In their 2005 Annual Report, the company said it had plans "to embark on an accelerated development plan and expand our footprint through both company-owned and franchised locations." 2005 restaurant sales grew to a record US$415.8 million from 82 locations in the United States and 10 international locations including Canada (1995, 2003), Hong Kong (1997, 2001), Mexico (1993, 1996, 2001) and Taiwan (1993, 1996, 2001). As of December 2005, 41 of the 92 Ruth's Chris restaurants were company-owned and 51 were franchisee-owned, including all 10 of the international restaurants (see Exhibit 2).

Ruth's Chris's 51 franchisee-owned restaurants were owned by just 17 franchisees, with five new franchisees having the rights to develop a new restaurant, and the three largest-franchisees owning eight, six and five restaurants respectively. Prior to 2004, each franchisee entered into a 10-year franchise agreement with three 10-year renewal options for each restaurant. Each agreement granted the franchisee territorial protection, with the option to develop a certain number of restaurants in their territory. Ruth's Chris's franchisee agreements generally included termination clauses in the event of nonperformance by the franchisee.[2]

A World of Opportunities

As part of the international market selection process, Hannah considered four standard models (see Figure 2):

1. Product development—new kinds of restaurants in existing markets
2. Diversification—new kinds of restaurants in new markets
3. Penetration—more of the same restaurants in the same market
4. Market development—more of the same restaurants in new markets

The product development model (new kinds of restaurants in existing markets) was never seriously considered by Ruth's Chris. It had built a brand based on fine dining steak houses and, with only 92 stores, the company saw little need and no value in diversifying with new kinds of restaurants.

The diversification model (new kinds of restaurants in new markets) was also never considered by Ruth's Chris. In only four international markets, Hannah knew that the current fine dining steak house model would work in new markets without the risk of brand dilution or brand confusion.

The penetration model (more of the same restaurants in the same market) was already underway in a small way with new restaurants opening up in Canada. The limiting factor was simply that fine dining establishments would never be as ubiquitous as quick service restaurants (i.e. fast food) like McDonald's. Even the largest cities in the world would be unlikely to host more than five to six Ruth's Chris steak houses.

Exhibit 2

Ruth's Chris Locations in the United States (2005)

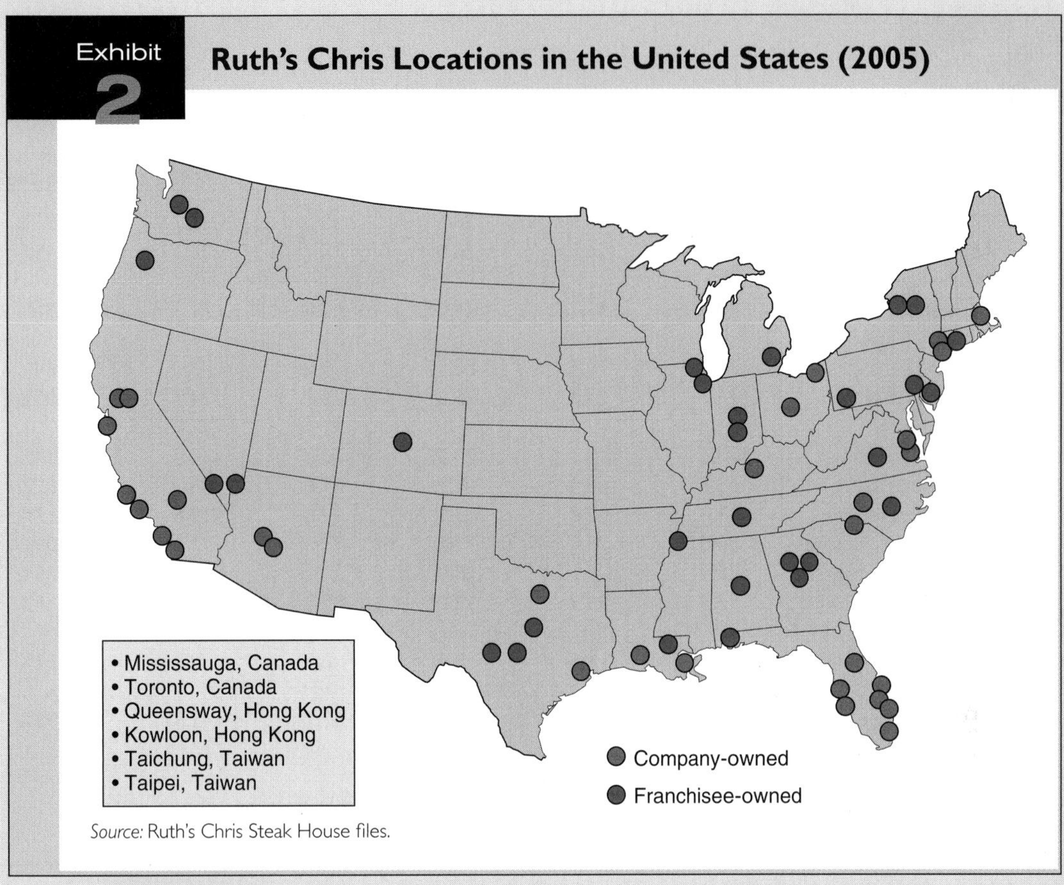

Source: Ruth's Chris Steak House files.

Figure 1

Ruth's Chris Restaurant Growth by Decade

Decade	New Restaurants (total)	New Restaurants (company-owned)	New Restaurants (franchises)
1965–1969	1	1	0
1970–1979	4	2	2
1980–1989	19	8	11
1990–1999	44	19	25
2000–2005	25	12	13
	93[3]	42	51

Source: Ruth's Chris Steak House files.

Figure 2

Restaurant Growth Paths[4]

		Restaurant Brands: Existing	Restaurant Brands: New
Market	Existing	**Penetration** (more restaurants) *Same market, same product*	**Product development** (new brands) *Same market, new product*
Market	New	**Market development** (new markets) *New market, same product*	**Diversification** (new brands for new market) *New product, new market*

Exhibit 3 Meat Consumption per Capita* (in kilograms)

Region/Classification	2002	2001	2000	1999	1998	Growth Rate 1998–2002
World	39.7	38.8	38.6	38.0	37.7	5.31%
Asia (excluding Middle East)	27.8	26.9	26.6	25.7	25.4	9.45%
Central America/Caribbean	46.9	45.7	44.8	42.9	41.3	13.56%
Europe	74.3	72.5	70.5	70.6	73.1	1.64%
Middle East/North Africa	25.7	25.7	26.0	25.1	24.7	4.05%
North America	123.2	119.1	120.5	122.2	118.3	4.14%
South America	69.7	68.4	69.1	67.6	64.2	8.57%
Sub-Saharan Africa	13.0	12.9	13.1	12.8	12.6	3.17%
Developed Countries	80.0	78.0	77.2	77.3	77.6	3.09%
Developing Countries	28.9	28.1	28.0	27.1	26.6	8.65%
High-Income Countries	93.5	91.9	92.0	92.2	90.9	2.86%
Low-Income Countries	8.8	8.6	8.4	8.3	8.2	7.32%
Middle-Income Countries	46.1	44.6	43.9	42.7	42.3	8.98%

* World Resources Institute, "Meat Consumption: Per Capita (1984–2002)," retrieved on June 7, 2006 from **http://earthtrends.wri.org/text/agriculture-food/variable-193.html.**

The market development model (more of the same restaurants in new markets) appeared the most obvious path to increased revenue. Franchisees in the four international markets—Canada, Hong Kong, Mexico and Taiwan—were profitable and could offer testimony to would-be franchisees of the value of a Ruth's Chris franchise.

With the management team agreed on a model, the challenge shifted to market selection criteria. The key success factors were well-defined:

- Beef-eaters: Ruth's Chris was a steak house (though there were several fish items on the menu) and, thus, its primary customers were people who enjoy beef. According to the World Resources Institute, in 2002 there were 17 countries above the mean per capita of annual beef consumption for high-income countries (93.5 kilograms—see Exhibit 3).[5]
- Legal to import U.S. beef: The current Ruth's Chris model used only USDA Prime beef, thus it had to be exportable to the target country. In some cases, Australian beef was able to meet the same high U.S. standard.
- Population/high urbanization rates: With the target customer being a well-to-do beef-eater, restaurants needed to be in densely populated areas to have a large enough pool. Most large centres probably met this requirement.
- High disposable income: Ruth's Chris is a fine dining experience and the average cost of a meal for a customer ordering an entrée was over US$70 at a Ruth's Chris in the United States. While this might seem to eliminate many countries quickly, there are countries (e.g. China) that have such large populations that even a very small percentage of high disposable income people could create an appropriate pool of potential customers.
- Do people go out to eat? This was a critical factor. If well-to-do beef-eaters did not go out to eat, these countries had to be removed from the target list.
- Affinity for U.S. brands: The name "Ruth's Chris" was uniquely American as was the Ruth Fertel story. Countries that were overtly anti-United States would be eliminated from—or at least pushed down—the target list. One measure of affinity could be the presence of existing U.S. restaurants and successful franchises.

What Should Ruth's Chris Do Next?

Hannah had many years of experience in the restaurant franchising business, and thus had both personal preferences and good instincts about where Ruth's Chris should be looking for new markets. "Which markets should we enter first?" he thought to himself. Market entry was critical, but there were other issues too. Should franchising continue to be Ruth's Chris exclusive international mode of entry? Were there opportunities for joint ventures or company-owned stores in certain markets? How could he identify and evaluate new potential franchisees? Was there an opportunity to find a global partner/brand with which to partner?

Hannah gathered information from several reliable U.S. government and related websites and created the

Exhibit 4 **Data Table**

Country	Per Capita Beef Consumption (kg)	Population (1,000s)	Urbanization Rate (%)	Per Capita GDP (PPP in US$)
Argentina	97.6	39,921	90%	$13,100
Bahamas	123.6	303	89%	$20,200
Belgium	86.1	10,379	97%	$31,400
Brazil	82.4	188,078	83%	$8,400
Chile	66.4	16,134	87%	$11,300
China	52.4	1,313,973	39%	$6,800
Costa Rica	40.4	4,075	61%	$11,100
Czech Rep	77.3	10,235	74%	$19,500
France	101.1	60,876	76%	$29,900
Germany	82.1	82,422	88%	$30,400
Greece	78.7	10,688	61%	$22,200
Hungary	100.7	9,981	65%	$16,300
Ireland	106.3	4,062	60%	$41,000
Israel	97.1	6,352	92%	$24,600
Italy	90.4	58,133	67%	$29,200
Japan	43.9	127,463	65%	$31,500
Kuwait	60.2	2,418	96%	$19,200
Malaysia	50.9	24,385	64%	$12,100
Netherlands	89.3	16,491	66%	$30,500
Panama	54.5	3,191	57%	$7,200
Poland	78.1	38,536	62%	$13,300
Portugal	91.1	10,605	55%	$19,300
Russia	51	142,893	73%	$11,100
Singapore	71.1	4,492	100%	$28,100
South Africa	39	44,187	57%	$12,000
South Korea	48	48,846	80%	$20,400
Spain	118.6	40,397	77%	$25,500
Switzerland	72.9	7,523	68%	$32,300
Turkey	19.3	70,413	66%	$8,200
UAE/Dubai	74.4	2,602	85%	$43,400
U.K.	79.6	60,609	89%	$30,300
United States	124.8	298,444	80%	$41,800
Vietnam	28.6	84,402	26%	$2,800

Source: World Resources Institute, "Meat Consumption: Per Capita (1984–2002)," retrieved on June 7, 2006 from **http://earthtrends.wri.org/text/agriculture-food/variable-193.html** and World Bank Key Development Data & Statistics, **http://web.worldbank.org/WBSITE/EXTERNAL/DATASTATISTICS/0,,contentMDK:20535285~menuPK:232599~pagePK:64133150~piPK:64133175~theSitePK:239419,00.html,** retrieved on June 7, 2006.

table in Exhibit 4. He noted that many of his top prospects currently did not allow the importation of U.S. beef, but he felt that this was a political (rather than a cultural) variable and thus could change quickly under the right circumstances and with what he felt was the trend toward ever more free trade. He could not find any data on how often people went out to eat or a measure of their affinity toward U.S. brands. Maybe the success of U.S. casual dining restaurants in a country might be a good indicator of how its citizens felt toward U.S. restaurants. With his spreadsheet open, he went to work on the numbers and began contemplating the future global expansion of the company.

"If you've ever had a filet this good, welcome back."

Ruth Fertel, 1927–2002

Founder of Ruth's Chris Steak House

Notes

1. Ruth's Chris Steak House 2005 Annual Report, p. 7.
2. Due to damage caused by Hurricane Katrina, Ruth's Chris was forced to temporarily close its restaurant in New Orleans, Louisiana.
3. Ruth's Chris Steak House 2005 Annual Report p. 10.
4. This diagram is based on Ansoff's Product/Market Matrix, first published in "Strategies for Diversification," *Harvard Business Review,* 1957.
5. World Resources Institute, "Meat Consumption: Per Capita (1984–2002)," retrieved on June 7, 2006 from **http://earthtrends.wri.org/text/agriculture-food/variable-193.html.**

Tri Star International

Tri Star International (TSI), a public limited company, was established in 1975 as a strategic business unit of Star Group at Kota. Most of Tri Star executives had either worked abroad or had experience in the exports industry. Kota was an ideal location for a leather plant since Rajasthan boasts of the highest cattle population in the country. Along with this, the Rajasthan government had offered several incentives like land at concessional rates and tax rebates to industries located in this industrial belt. Tri Star International soon became a well established firm and was used as a benchmark by others for norms in the area. Initially, TSI predominantly exported finished leather. It was exporting seventy percent of its leather directly, and the remaining indirectly. In 1976, TSI decided to enter into leather garment exports as this forward integration would result in value addition and higher margins.

In 1978, TSI decided to explore the opportunities in shoe exports. Since full shoes were reserved for a small scale sector, it had to restrict its export to shoe uppers. Shoe uppers fetched a better margin and provided an opportunity for value addition. The company hoped to move from finished leather exports to finished products. This move to shoe uppers was a step in that direction. They expected to export sixty five percent of their shoe uppers. Their European clientele consisted of branded shoe manufacturers to whom they supplied finished leather and shoe uppers. Soon the company started exporting to Germany, U.K., Italy, and Belgium.

The competitive advantage enjoyed by the company was the availability of good quality leather, in-house skilled and trained manpower and niche products like stitched on last, which only TSI could offer. Although the company could achieve a high volume export, it continued as a job worker for the established brands. Since it was exporting uppers, which were an intermediate product, they could not be directly used by end users. Most of the shoe uppers exported by TSI were manufactured in-house. Though Indian products did not enjoy good brand equity, TSI through its concerted efforts had built a good customer base in the European market. Thus, though the products of TSI enjoyed a good image with manufacturers, they did not have brand identity.

Changing Face of Shoe Industry (1988)

- Manufacturing base in European countries was shrinking due to the labour intensive nature of the product.
- Environmental concerns in the developed countries saw the shoe manufacturing industry shift from developed countries to developing countries.
- The Indian Government dereserved shoe manufacturing allowing big and organized players to enter the market.

TSI saw a readymade opportunity as it could convert its buyers of shoe uppers to full shoes. However, to be successful in full shoes required a separate set of strategies such as superior product design, established brand name and ability to offer variety. Sourabh Sharma, General Marketing Manager in charge of footwear, started planning for the new venture.

Product Design

In the full shoes, design was important. To come up with unique designs, TSI established an in-house design department as well as appointed freelance designers abroad who would design products for them. Along with this, the foreign agents provided the company with information about latest style, trends, and designs regularly. This ensured that TSI had sufficient information about the design expectations of its customers. They also attended trade fairs and participated in fashion accessories shows.

This case was written by Mala Srivastava, Richa Agrawal, Sapna Parashar, SL Kale, and Yashwant Thakur, Prestige Institute of Management and Research. It is intended to be used as the basis for class discussion rather than to illustrate either effective or ineffective handling of a management situation. The case was made possible by the co-operation of an organization which wishes to remain anonymous.

Brand

It was increasingly felt that to gain success in the international market, TSI needed to sell its products under its own brand name. Building its brand internationally was an expensive proposition, as TSI did not have a history in shoe making as compared to the other branded manufacturers. Secondly, Indian products did not enjoy good brand equity in the international market. The company was thinking of acquiring an established international brand, which would provide an easy and quick access to the branded market. They were also contemplating how selling under their own brand would affect their relationship with the existing buyers of the shoe uppers and full shoes. To gain a foothold in export market, TSI entered into a manufacturing as well as marketing joint venture with a major Italian brand at Bangalore. Italy is the hub of fashion and is a trendsetter. It was felt that this association with the Italians would provide TSI with some additional leverage and they would be able to fetch a premium price.

Large volumes (facilitating economies of scale) were a necessary prerequisite for success in the shoe industry. As TSI had limited capacity, it hoped to achieve large volumes through its supply chain. It would be outsourcing eighty percent of its exported volume through supply chain expansion. To ensure that quality was not compromised the company laid down strict quality norms. TSI created a SSMG (Star Strategic Management Group), which was entrusted with the job of formulating guidelines for sourcing of the products. They would maintain control over the raw material, design, and finished products through regular quality inspections. They now needed to walk on the tight rope, balancing orders for full shoes and ensuring purchase of raw materials to fulfill the same.

Competitive Advantage

Designing: they had come up with the latest innovative designs, which matched the changing trends.
Customer loyalty: TSI supplied seventy five percent of its products to the end users and had been able to retain most of its customers since its establishment.
Technology and Product Quality: TSI used the latest technology, and although it pushed up the cost of production TSI was able to provide premium quality products.
Marketing: the company had several years of experience and an extensive marketing network which included overseas offices and warehouses which added value to TSI products.
Finance: the company enjoyed a sound financial position.

In the European market, TSI predominantly sold ladies shoes since it was found that women owned six pairs of shoes as compared to one pair per man. In the European market their shoes were generally sold to brands which were positioned as commercial brands and value for money was the deciding factor. Soon TSI became the largest exporter of shoes from India. Though TSI's exports to Europe rose dramatically and they were also able to develop an effective marketing strategy, promoting a brand in Europe remained a dream. The full shoe market was extremely competitive. TSI was facing competition from the large Indian manufacturers as well as from the Indian unorganized sector. In the European market, it faced competition from the low priced exports coming from the Far East, Spain, Portugal, Italy, Brazil, and China. Availability of low price and comparable products made the customer price sensitive.

In 2000, TSI did business worth Rs. 2400 crore, of which the leather division contribution was Rs. 300 crore. The company had a vision of becoming a billion dollar company by 2004. This required rapid growth in the garment and footwear division, which would provide them higher margins. TSI was able to establish itself in the European market, which had always been quality, design, and style conscious. But after the unification of Germany (major market), it was observed that customers were becoming price sensitive. Sourabh Sharma realized that to achieve this target TSI would have to tap markets other than Europe. The U.S. footwear market was the largest in the world and seventy percent of the U.S. market needs were met by exports from China. There was an opportunity to enter the U.S. market because seventy percent of TSI's leather was exported from Hong Kong warehouse to China, where it was processed and converted to full shoes before being exported to the United States.

China's Competitive Advantages

- Most Favoured Nation (MFN) status with the U.S., thus Chinese products entered the U.S. at concessional rates
- Chinese plants with high manufacturing capacity were able to manufacture 10,000–15,000 shoes per day unlike Indian plants having a capacity of 1,000–1,200 shoes per day
- The component industry was well developed; providing standardized heels, soles, uppers in large volumes
- A well developed infrastructure was available in China, which facilitated exports
- Most Chinese manufacturers followed strict quality norms enforced by U.S. quality inspections

Sourabh Sharma knew that to be successful in the U.S. market it needed to develop similar skills and competitive advantages as enjoyed by the Chinese firms. So after a lot of brain storming he thought that the best strategy for TSI to enter the U.S. market would be shifting of production facilities to the Chinese mainland, where labour cost was low as compared to India. Leasing a Chinese facility could be a good strategy, also outsourcing the shoes from the supply chain could be an alternative strategy.

Questions

1. How far do you think that Sourabh Sharma's formulation of strategies would work in the existing scenario?
2. What other strategies could be adopted by TSI to enter the U.S. market?

Part 4

Global Marketing Strategy

In light of the environmental influences discussed in Part 2 and the problems of foreign market entry highlighted in Part 3, Part 4 deals with the global strategies and programs that the firm needs in order to begin competing in the international marketplace. This part focuses on six key elements of the global marketing mix, emphasizing the nature and characteristics of goods and services, distribution channels and logistics, pricing policies, promotional practices, and international sales management. In each case, attention is given to the key problems encountered and the actions needed by firms to compete successfully in global markets.

Chapter

9

Product Strategies and Global Brand Management

The Global MARKETPLACE 9.1

Using Canadian Product Innovation to Meet Global Energy Needs

In the early years of the new millennium, geopolitical tensions and supply-demand imbalances in the world's energy markets resulted in a sharp spike in crude oil prices. This translated into higher prices at the pumps for North American consumers and financial hardship for many families. At the same time, environmentally conscious consumers railed against the over-reliance on fossil fuels and their deleterious impact on the environment. Iogen, a relatively small Ottawa-based company, has risen to the challenge and is attempting to meet the needs of consumers with an innovative new product. The company's EcoEthanol offers the advantages of a biofuel without the risk of reducing the food supply. Traditional ethanol is produced from grains such as wheat and corn. While ethanol reduces greenhouse gas emissions and reduces reliance on fossil fuels, it diverts important carbohydrate sources from the food supply. Iogen's product innovation uses byproduct fibre such as cornstalks, grass, and straw to produce bioethanol, which generates 90 percent lower greenhouse gas emissions than gasoline. Iogen's patented enzyme technology, which is used in the production of its bioethanol, has also found applications in other industries such as pulp and paper, textiles, and alcoholic beverages.

Iogen employs 140 people and generates revenues of $10–12 million per year. Its partnerships with Petro Canada, Royal Dutch/Shell, and Goldman Sachs have provided the company with significant capital injections. Iogen is aggressively pursuing the licensing of its technology through turnkey plant construction projects around the world.

Sources: Government of Canada, *The Practice of Innovation*, **http://www.innovation.gc.ca** (accessed November 10, 2006); Iogen website, **http://www.iogen.ca/partners/overview/index.html** (accessed November 10, 2006).

As The Global Marketplace 9.1 illustrates, identifying and satisfying customer needs and expectations is the key to successful marketing. With a focus on satisfying the needs of global consumers, research findings on market needs and potential should be used to determine the optimal degree of customization needed in products and product lines. The degree of customization undertaken is also, however, driven by the incremental cost of the effort. Companies operating in the global marketplace need to make decisions with respect to how their brands will be managed across national markets. Government regulations and consumer behaviour differences across countries and regions necessitate that the firm develop and implement a comprehensive product and brand management strategy. Adapting to new markets should be seen not only in the context of one market but also in terms of how these changes can contribute to operations elsewhere. A new feature for a product or a new line item may have applicability on a broader scale, including the market that originated the product in the first place.[1]

This chapter is concerned with how the global marketer should adjust the firm's product offering to the marketplace, and it discusses the influence of an array of both external and internal variables. The global marketing of services is discussed in Chapter 10. A delicate balance has to be achieved between the advantages of product standardization and those of adaptation in order to maximize performance in global markets. The challenge of intellectual property violation will be focused on as a specialty topic. Global marketers must be ready to defend themselves against theft of their ideas and innovations.

Product Variables

The core of a firm's international operations is a product or service. The firm's product or service can be defined as the complex combination of tangible and intangible elements that distinguishes it from the other entities in the marketplace. Products can be differentiated by their composition, by their country of origin, by their tangible features such as packaging or quality, or by their augmented features such as their warranty. To the potential buyer, a product is a complete cluster of value satisfactions. A customer attaches value to a product in proportion to its perceived ability to help solve problems or meet needs. This will go beyond the technical capabilities of the product to include intangible benefits sought. In some cases, customer behaviour has to be understood from a broader perspective. For example, while Chinese customers may view Japanese products quite positively regarding their quality, historic animosity toward Japan may prevent them from buying Japanese goods or cause them to prefer goods from other sources.[2] Given such dramatic variation from market to market, careful assessment of product dimensions is called for.

Standardization versus Adaptation

Adaptation

The first question, after the internationalization decision has been made, concerns the product modifications that are needed or warranted. As shown in Exhibit 9.1, a firm has four basic alternatives in approaching international markets: (1) selling the product as is in the international marketplace, (2) modifying products for different countries and/or regions, (3) designing new products for foreign markets, and (4) incorporating all the differences into one product design and introducing a global product. Different approaches for implementing these alternatives exist. For example, a firm may identify only target markets where products can be marketed with little or no modification. In its product line for any given market, a large consumer products marketer may have global products, regional products, and purely local products. Some of these products developed for one market may later be introduced elsewhere, including the global marketer's "home" market. Occasionally, the international marketplace may want something that the domestic market discards. For example, Canadian exports of chicken to countries such as Russia and the Philippines have increased significantly over the last 10 years. The increase in exports to these countries is driven by their demand for dark meat such as chicken legs—a product that is in oversupply in Canada. Canadian consumers have a preference for white meat. Exports of dark meat that would normally have been discarded instead result in Russia and the Philippines ranking among the top five importers of Canadian chicken.[3]

The overall advantages and drawbacks of standardization versus adaptation are summarized in Exhibit 9.2. The benefits of standardization—that is, selling the same product worldwide—are cost savings in production and marketing. In addition to these economies

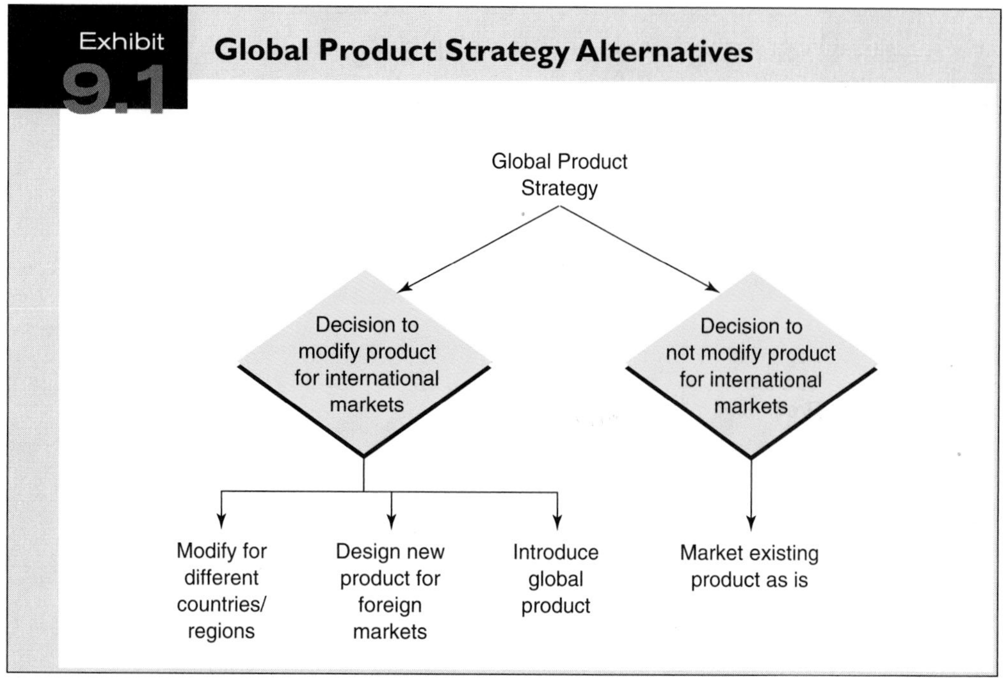

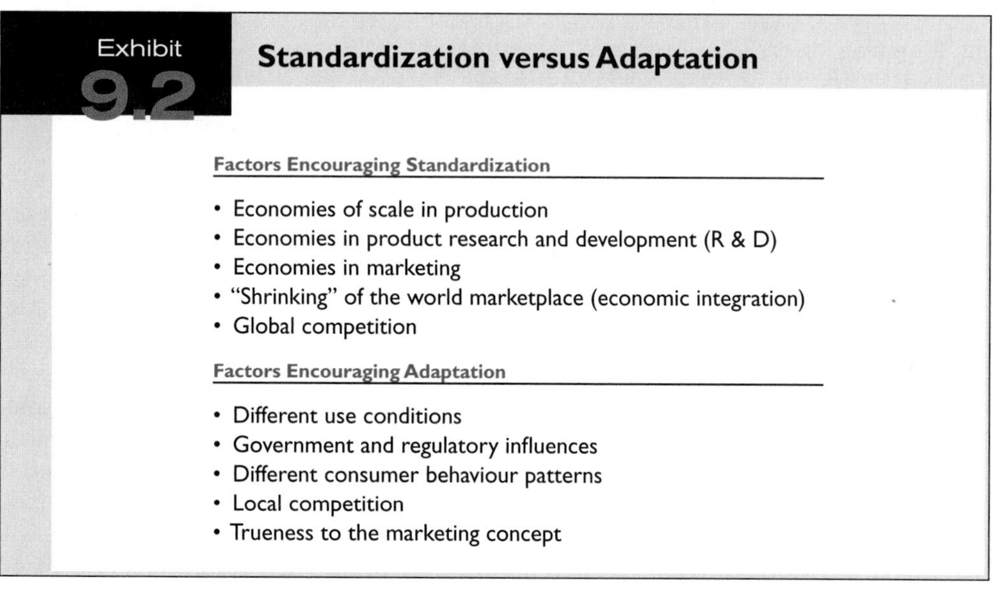

of scale, many point to economic integration as a driving force in making markets more unified. As a response to integration efforts around the world, especially in Europe, many global marketers are indeed standardizing many of their marketing approaches, such as branding and packaging, across markets. Similarly, having to face the same competitors in the major markets of the world will increase the pressure to develop a global approach to marketing. However, in most cases, demand and usage conditions vary sufficiently to require some changes in the product or service itself.

Exhibit 9.2
Standardization versus Adaptation
Factors Encouraging Standardization
• Economies of scale in production
• Economies in product research and development (R & D)
• Economies in marketing
• "Shrinking" of the world marketplace (economic integration)
• Global competition
Factors Encouraging Adaptation
• Different use conditions
• Government and regulatory influences
• Different consumer behaviour patterns
• Local competition
• Trueness to the marketing concept

Coca-Cola, Levi's jeans, and Colgate toothpaste have been cited as evidence that universal product and marketing strategy can work. Yet the argument that the world is becoming more homogenized may actually be true for only a limited number of products that have universal brand recognition and minimal product knowledge requirements for use.[4] Although product standardization is generally increasing, there are still substantial differences in company practices, depending on the products marketed and where they are marketed. As shown in Exhibit 9.3, industrial products such as steel, chemicals, and

Exhibit 9.3 **Strategic Adaptation to Foreign Markets**

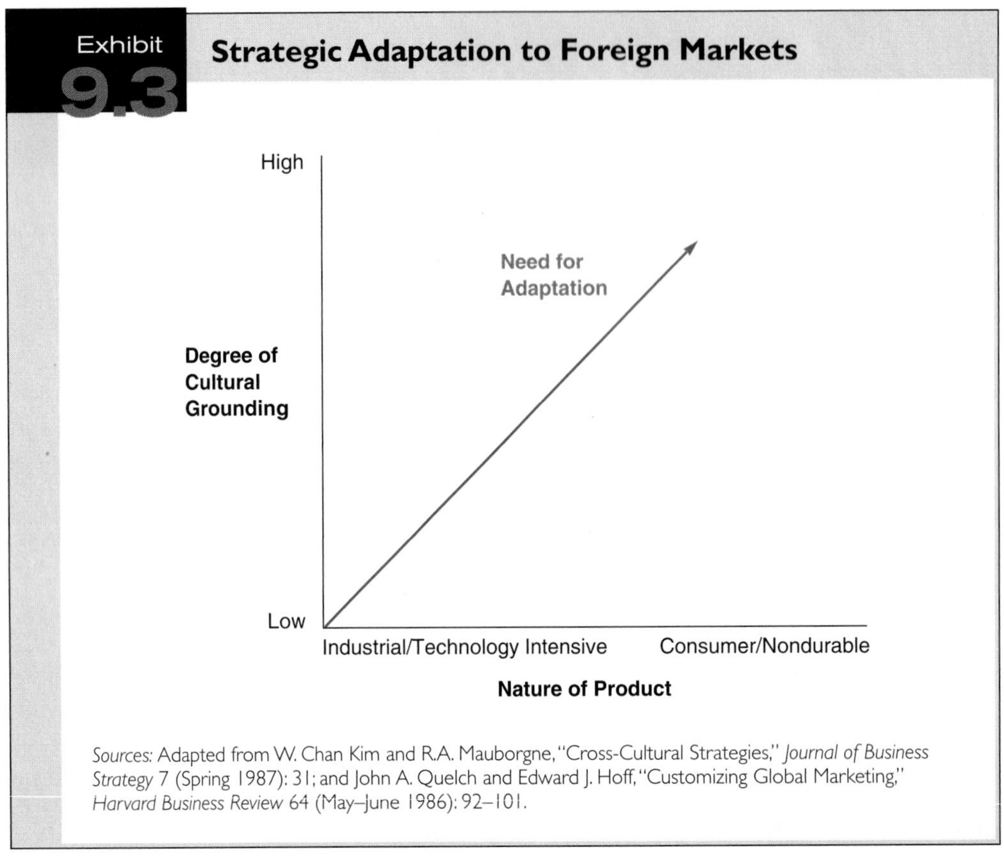

Sources: Adapted from W. Chan Kim and R.A. Mauborgne, "Cross-Cultural Strategies," *Journal of Business Strategy* 7 (Spring 1987): 31; and John A. Quelch and Edward J. Hoff, "Customizing Global Marketing," *Harvard Business Review* 64 (May–June 1986): 92–101.

agricultural equipment tend to be less culturally grounded and warrant less adjustment than consumer goods. Similarly, marketers in technology-intensive industries such as scientific instruments or medical equipment find universal acceptability for their products.[5] Within consumer products, luxury goods and personal-care products tend to have high levels of standardization while food products do not.

Adaptation needs in the industrial sector may exist even though they may not be overt. As an example, capacity performance is seen from different perspectives in different countries. Typically, the performance specifications of a German product are quite precise. For example, if a German product is said to have a lifting capacity of 1,000 kilograms, it will perform precisely up to that level. The North American counterpart, however, is likely to maintain a safety factor of 1.5 or even 2.0, resulting in a substantially higher payload capacity. Buyers of Japanese machine tools have also found that these tools will perform at the specified level, not beyond them, as would their North American–made counterparts.

Consumer goods generally require product adaptation because of their higher degree of cultural grounding. The amount of change introduced in consumer goods depends not only on cultural differences but also on economic conditions in the target market. Low incomes may cause pressure to simplify the product to make it affordable in the market.

Beyond the dichotomy of standardization and adaptation, there exist other approaches. The global marketer may design and introduce new products for foreign markets in addition to the firm's relatively standardized "flagship" products and brands. Some of these products, developed specifically for foreign clients, may later be introduced elsewhere, including in the domestic market. Even companies that are noted for following the same methods worldwide have made numerous changes in their product offerings. Some products, like Coca-Cola's Hi-C Soy Milk in Hong Kong, may be restricted to markets for which they were specifically developed. Although Colgate toothpaste is available worldwide, the company also markets some products locally, such as a spicy toothpaste formulated especially for the Middle East. McDonald's serves abroad the same menu of hamburgers, soft drinks, and other foods that it does in North America, and the restaurants look the same. But McDonald's has also tried to tailor its product to local styles; for example, in Japan, the chain's trademark character, known as Ronald McDonald in North America, is called Donald McDonald because it is easier to pronounce that way. Menu adjustments include beer in Germany and wine in France, mutton burgers in India, and rye-bread burgers in Finland.

Increasingly, companies are attempting to develop global products by incorporating differences regionally or worldwide into one basic design. This is not pure standardization, however. To develop a standard in Canada, for example, and use it as a model for other markets is dramatically different from obtaining input from the intended markets and using the data to create a standard. What is important is that adaptability is built into the product around a standardized core. For example, IBM makes more than 20 different keyboards for its relatively standardized personal computers in order to adjust to language differences in Europe alone. The global marketer attempts to exploit the common denominators, but local needs are considered from product development to the eventual marketing of the product. Car manufacturers like Ford and Nissan may develop basic models for regional, or even global, use, but they allow for substantial discretion in adjusting the models to local preferences.

Factors Affecting Adaptation

In deciding the form in which the product is to be marketed abroad, the firm should consider three sets of factors: (1) the market(s) that have been targeted, (2) the product and its characteristics, and (3) company characteristics such as resources and policy (see Exhibit 9.4). For most firms, the key question linked to adaptation is whether the effort is worth the cost involved. Additional costs include adjusting production runs, stock control, servicing, and the investigative research involved in determining, for example, features that would be most appealing. For most firms, the expense of modifying products should be moderate. In practice, however, this may mean that the expense is moderate when modifications are considered and acted upon. Modifications are considered but rejected when the projected cost is substantial.

Studies on product adaptation show that the majority of products have to be modified for the international marketplace one way or another. Changes typically affect packaging, measurement units, labelling, product constituents and features, usage instructions, and, to a lesser extent, logos and brand names.[6] Woodman's Sea Products of Trinity Bay, Newfoundland, for example, has been making tremendous strides in the Japanese market for snow crab. The company boils the crabs and freezes them—a process that results in a less salty-tasting product that is more acceptable to the Japanese palate. The crabs shipped to Japan are also selected for their bright red colour, which is more in keeping with the preferences of Japanese consumers.[7]

There is no panacea for resolving questions of adaptation. Many firms are formulating decision-support systems to aid in product adaptation, and some consider every situation

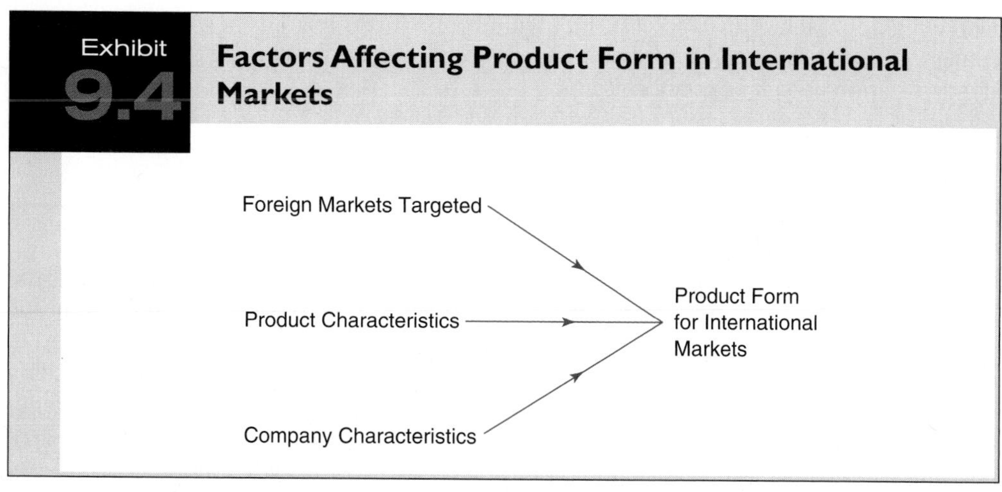

Exhibit 9.5 **Snow Crabs for Export**

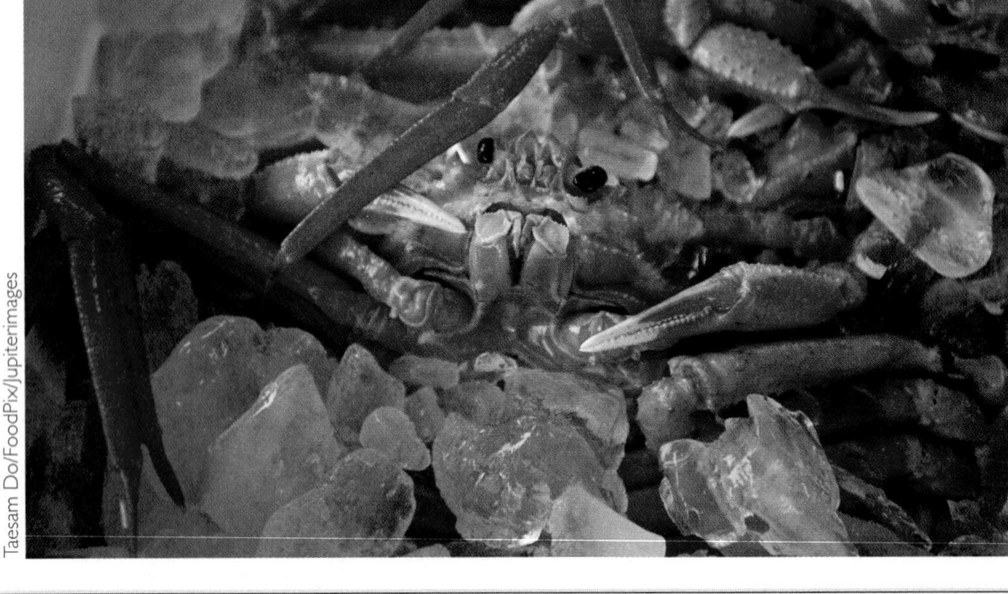

Taesam Do/FoodPix/Jupiterimages

independently. Exhibit 9.6 provides a summary of the factors that determine the need for either **mandatory** or **discretionary product adaptation**. All products have to conform to the prevailing environmental conditions over which the global marketer has no control. These relate to legal and economic conditions in the market and the country's climatic conditions. Further adaptation decisions are made to enhance the firm's competitiveness in the marketplace. This is achieved by matching competitive offers, catering to customer preferences, and meeting demands of local distribution systems.

The adaptation decision will also have to be assessed as a function of time and market involvement. The more firms learn about local market characteristics in individual markets, the more they are able to establish similarities and, as a result, standardize their marketing approach. This market insight will give the firms legitimacy with the local consumers and representatives in developing a common understanding of the extent of standardization versus adaptation.[8]

The Market Environment

Government Regulations

Government regulations often present the most stringent requirements. Some of the requirements may serve no purpose other than political (such as protection of domestic industry or response to political pressures). Some regulations, however, may be related to health and safety considerations such as Canada's bilingual (English and French) labelling requirement for imported food products. Violations of a country's health and safety regulations, it should be noted, may result in unwanted negative publicity and a loss of consumer confidence. Chinese exporters of toys discovered this when news of the use of

Exhibit 9.6 **Factors Affecting Product-Adaptation Decisions**

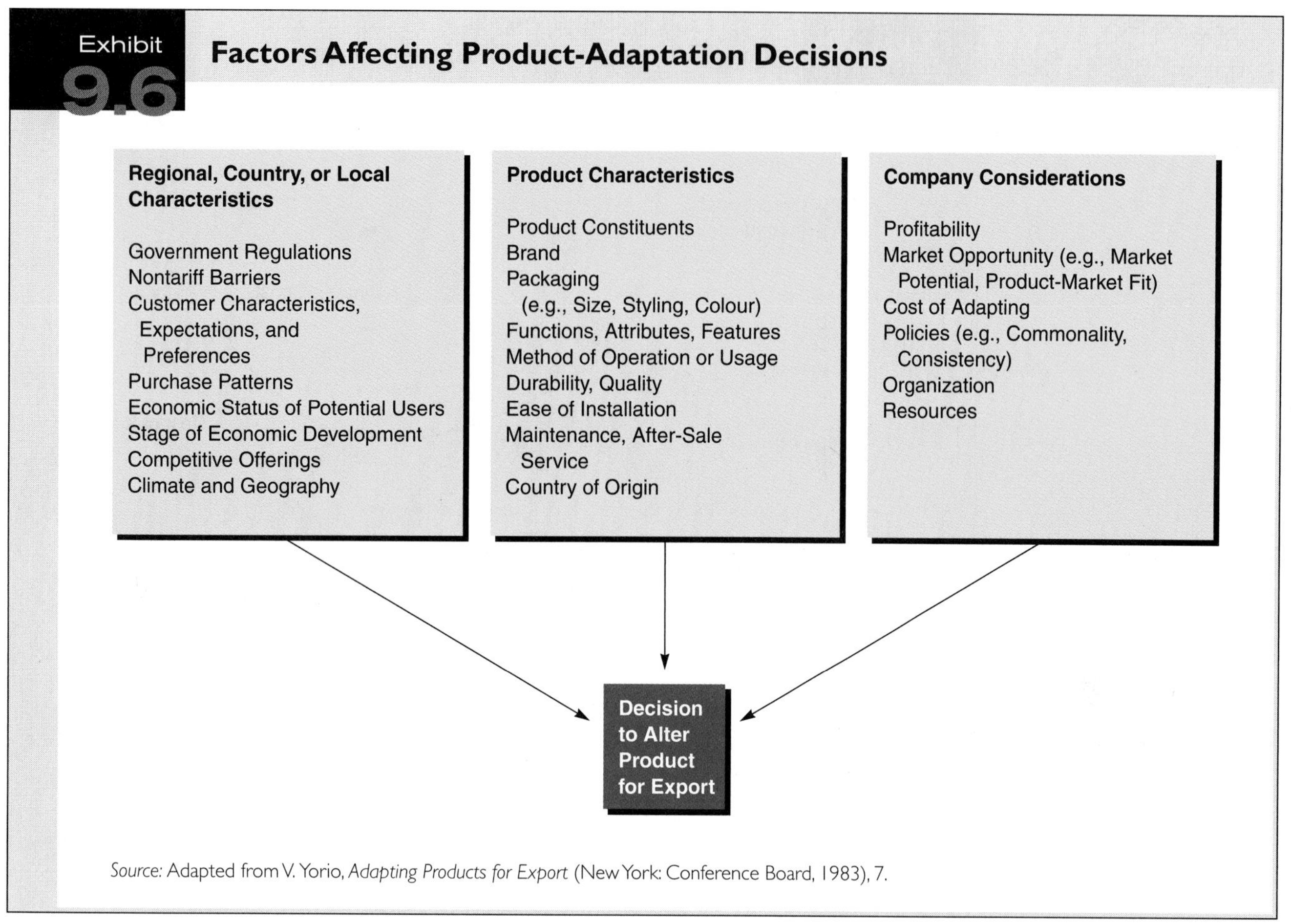

Source: Adapted from V. Yorio, *Adapting Products for Export* (New York: Conference Board, 1983), 7.

lead paint on their products came to the attention of the public in late 2007. Lead-based paints are toxic and known to impair children's development. Because of the sovereignty of nations, individual firms need to comply with government regulations but can influence the situation by lobbying, directly or through their industry associations, for the issue to be raised during trade negotiations. Government regulations may be spelled out, but firms need to be ever vigilant in terms of changes and exceptions.

Sweden was the first country in the world to enact legislation against most aerosol sprays on the grounds that they may harm the environment. The ban, which went into effect January 1, 1979, covers thousands of hair sprays, deodorants, air fresheners, insecticides, paints, waxes, and assorted sprays that use Freon gases as propellants. It does not

In More Detail 9.1

THE ECONOMICS OF PRODUCT ADAPTATION

The extent of adaptation the firm should undertake may be addressed within a cost economics framework. As shown in Exhibit 9.7, the firm's incremental manufacturing costs will decrease steadily as it moves from producing a fully adapted or customized product to one that is fully standardized. Increased standardization, however, also results in lost sales as the product will be mistargeted in a number of country markets. A standardized product will not precisely meet the needs of customers in each country in which it is sold, resulting in lost sales in those markets. The cost of lost sales and the cost of manufacturing may be combined to determine the extent of adaptation a firm should undertake. The optimal point of product adaptation is represented by the point at which these combined costs are minimized.

Exhibit 9.7 **The Economics of Product Adaptation**

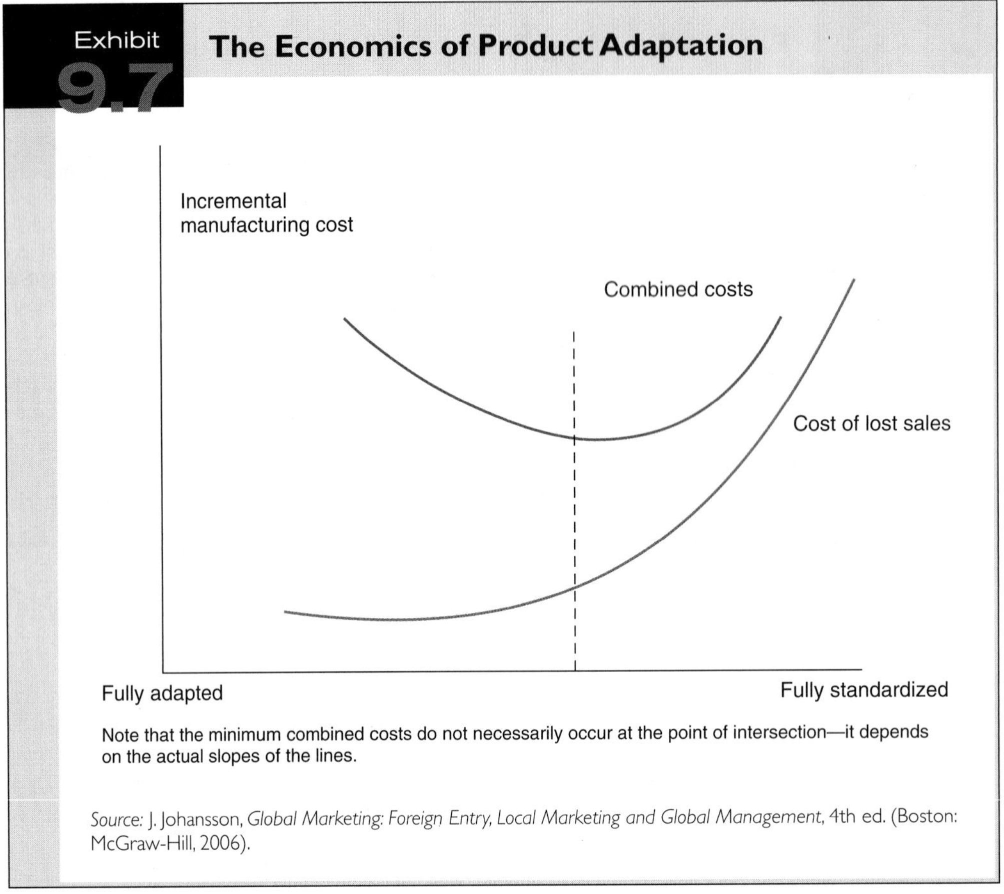

Note that the minimum combined costs do not necessarily occur at the point of intersection—it depends on the actual slopes of the lines.

Source: J. Johansson, *Global Marketing: Foreign Entry, Local Marketing and Global Management*, 4th ed. (Boston: McGraw-Hill, 2006).

apply to certain medical sprays, especially those used by people who suffer from asthma. The Swedish government, which has one of the world's most active environmental protection departments, was the first to take seriously warnings by scientists that continued release of these chemicals could eventually degrade the earth's ozone layer. As a matter of fact, certain markets, such as Sweden, often serve as precursors of changes to come in broader markets and should, therefore, be monitored by marketers.

Government regulations are probably the single most important factor contributing to product adaptation and, because of bureaucratic red tape, often the most cumbersome and frustrating factor to deal with. In some cases, government regulations have been passed and are enforced to protect local industry from competition from abroad.

Non-Tariff Barriers

Non-tariff barriers include product standards, testing or approval procedures, subsidies for local products, and bureaucratic red tape. The non-tariff barriers affecting product adjustments usually concern elements outside the core product. For example, France requires the use of the French language in any offer, presentation, or advertisement, whether written or spoken, in instructions for use, in specifications or guarantee terms for goods or services, and in invoices and receipts. Because non-tariff barriers are usually in place to keep foreign products out and/or to protect domestic producers, getting around them may be the toughest single problem for the global marketer. The cost of compliance with government regulations may be high.

Small companies with limited resources may simply give up in the face of seemingly arbitrary harassment. For example, product testing and certification requirements have made the entry of many foreign companies into Japanese markets quite difficult, if not impossible.[9] Japan requires testing of all pharmaceutical products in Japanese laboratories, maintaining that these tests are needed because the Japanese may be physiologically different from other peoples. Similarly, foreign ski products are kept out of the country because Japanese snow is somehow considered unique. Many foreign firms, rather than try to move mountains of red tape, have found ways to accommodate Japanese regulations, such as by creating separate product batches for that market.

With a substantial decrease in tariff barriers, non-tariff forms of protectionism have increased. On volume alone, agriculture dominates the list. For example, the United States, Canada, and the European Union (EU) have fought over beef produced with the aid of hormones. Although it was declared safe for consumption by UN health authorities, the Europeans have banned the importation of such beef and now demand appropriate labelling as a precondition for market entry. In a similar debate, an international trade agreement was reached in 2000 that requires the labelling of genetically modified food in the world market. This will mean that U.S. and Canadian farmers have to separate the increasingly controversial foods from the overall supply.[10]

One way to keep a particular product or producer out of a market is to insist on particular standards. Since the EU chose ISO 9000 as a basis to harmonize varying technical norms of its member states, some of its trading partners have accused it of erecting a new trade barrier against outsiders.[11] ISO 9000 and ISO 14000 are a family of management system standards created by the International Organization for Standardization (ISO). The system represents a set of technical standards designed to offer a uniform way of determining whether manufacturing plants and service organizations implement and document sound quality procedures. The ISO itself does not administer or regulate these standards; that job is left to the 157 countries that have voluntarily adopted them. The feeling that ISO registration is a trade barrier comes from the Europeans' earlier start and subsequent control of the program. There is no legal requirement to adopt the standards. However, many agree that these guidelines are already determining what may be sold to and within the EU and, increasingly, around the world. This is especially true for products for which there are safety or liability issues, such as food products, or ones that require exact measurements or calibration, such as medical or exercise equipment. Agropur, Canada's largest dairy cooperative, headquartered in Granby, Quebec, has been ISO certified since 1994. The company recognized early on that certification would open the doors to foreign markets and that in countries such as the U.K., the firm would not be taken seriously without ISO certification.[12]

The International Organization for Standardization also issued the first standards on environmental management, the ISO 14000 series in 1996. The standards, which basically require that a firm design an environmental management system, do provide benefits for the adopters, such as substantial efficiencies in pollution control (e.g., packaging) and a better public image.[13] However, these standards can also serve as a non-tariff barrier if advanced nations impose their own requirements and systems on developing countries that often lack the knowledge and resources to meet such conditions. Canada, Europe, Japan, and the U.S. account for 75 percent of ISO 14000 registrations and absorb two-thirds of world exports.[14]

Customer Characteristics, Expectations, and Preferences

The characteristics and behaviour of intended customer groups are as important as governmental influences on the product adaptation decision. Even when the benefits sought are quite similar, the physical characteristics of customers may dictate product adaptation. Quaker Oats' extension of the Snapple soft-drink product to Japan suffered from lack of fit on three dimensions: the glass bottles the drink comes in are almost twice the size that Japanese customers are used to, the product itself was too sweet for the Japanese palate, and the Japanese did not feel comfortable with the sediment that characteristically collects at the bottom of the bottle.[15] Similarly, Tefal, the world leader in cookware, makes available pans with detachable handles in Japan, enabling storage in the traditionally tighter spaces of Japanese kitchens. The general expectation is that products should be economical in purchase, use, and maintenance.[16] Product decisions of consumer-product marketers are especially affected by local behaviour, tastes, attitudes, and traditions—all reflecting the marketer's need to gain customers' approval. This group of variables is critical in that it is the most difficult to quantify but is nevertheless essential in making a go/no-go decision.

Three groups of factors determine cultural and psychological specificity in relation to products and services: consumption patterns, psychosocial characteristics, and general cultural criteria. The types of questions asked in Exhibit 9.8 should be answered and systematically recorded for every product under consideration. Use of the list of questions

Exhibit 9.8 **Cultural and Psychological Factors Affecting Product Adaptation**

I. Consumption Patterns

A. Pattern of Purchase

1. Is the product or service purchased by relatively the same consumer income group from one country to another?
2. Do the same family members motivate the purchase in all target countries?
3. Do the same family members dictate brand choice in all target countries?
4. Do most consumers expect a product to have the same appearance?
5. Is the purchase rate the same regardless of the country?
6. Are most of the purchases made at the same kind of retail outlet?
7. Do most consumers spend the same amount of time making the purchase?

B. Pattern of Usage

1. Do most consumers use the product or service for the same purpose or purposes?
2. Is the product or service used in different amounts from one target area or country to another?
3. Is the method of preparation the same in all target countries?
4. Is the product or service used along with other products or services?

II. Psychosocial Characteristics

A. Attitudes toward the Product or Service

1. Are the basic psychological, social, and economic factors motivating the purchase and use of the product the same for all target countries?
2. Are the advantages and disadvantages of the product or service in the minds of consumers basically the same from one country to another?
3. Does the symbolic content of the product or service differ from one country to another?
4. Is the psychic cost of purchasing or using the product or service the same, whatever the country?
5. Does the appeal of the product or service for a cosmopolitan market differ from one market to another?

B. Attitudes toward the Brand

1. Is the brand name equally known and accepted in all target countries?
2. Are customer attitudes toward the package basically the same?
3. Are customer attitudes toward pricing basically the same?
4. Is brand loyalty the same throughout target countries for the product or service under consideration?

III. Cultural Criteria

1. Does society restrict the purchase and/or use of the product or service to a particular group?
2. Is there a stigma attached to the product or service?
3. Does the usage of the product or service interfere with tradition in one or more of the targeted markets?

Source: Adapted from Steuart Henderson Britt, "Standardizing Marketing for the International Market," *Journal of World Business* 9 (Winter 1974): 32–40.

The Global MARKETPLACE 9.2

Jeans for Muslims

Al Quds, a small company in Northern Italy, markets jeans targeted at the Muslim community. The innovative product targets a segment of the market that is not well served by other manufacturers. Al Quds jeans for Muslims fit high around the waist and are loose around the legs to facilitate repeated bending during prayers. The emphasis is on comfort. The jeans are also manufactured with ample pockets for storing items that must be taken off while praying and are produced with green seams because green is the sacred colour of Islam. The idea for the jeans originated when the man who is now president of Al Quds saw a newspaper photograph of a sea of jeans-clad Muslims bent over during prayers. His subsequent research revealed that there were no jeans on the market targeted to this segment of the population.

The company markets the jeans to the over 1 million Muslims living in Italy and plans to expand its target market to the over 25 million Muslims across Europe. Al Quds manufactures its jeans in a plant in Karachi, Pakistan, that employs some 15,000 people.

Source: Maria Sanminiatelli, "Italian Company Designs Jeans for Muslims," **http://money.canoe.ca/News/TopPhoto/2006/03/21/1498649.html** (accessed October 7, 2006). Used with permission of the Associated Press.

will guide the global marketer through the analysis, ensuring that all the necessary points are dealt with before a decision is made. The benefits to adaptation on cultural grounds may be significant, as illustrated in The Global Marketplace 9.2.

Because Brazilians are rarely breakfast eaters, Dunkin' Donuts is marketing doughnuts in Brazil as snacks, desserts, and party food. To further appeal to Brazilians, the company makes doughnuts with local fruit fillings like papaya and guava. Campbell Soup Company failed in Brazil with its offerings of vegetable and beef combinations, mainly because Brazilians prefer the dehydrated products of competitors such as Knorr and Maggi; Brazilians could use these products as soup starters but still add their own ingredients and flair. The only way of solving this problem is through proper customer testing, which can be formidably expensive for the company.

Often, no concrete product changes are needed, only a change in the product's **positioning**. Positioning refers to consumers' perception of a brand as compared with that of competitors' brands—that is, the mental image that a brand, or the company as a whole, evokes. For example, Gillette has a consistent image worldwide as a masculine, sports-oriented company. A brand's positioning, however, may have to change to reflect the differing lifestyles of the targeted market. The Coca-Cola Company took a risk in marketing Diet Coke in Japan, because trying to sell a diet drink is difficult in a nation where "diet" is a dirty word and the population is not overweight by Western standards. The problem was addressed by changing the name of the drink to Coke Light and subtly shifting the promotion theme from "weight loss" to "figure maintenance." Japanese women do not like to admit that they are dieting by drinking something clearly labelled "diet." Coca-Cola positioned its product as a soft drink that would help people feel and look their best rather than one solely centred around weight loss. The company hoped that consumers would perceive these characteristics just by looking at the product's graphics, regardless of the name it bore.

Health and beauty-care products often rely on careful positioning to attain a competitive advantage. Timotei shampoo, which is Unilever's brand leader in that category, has a natural-looking image with a focus on mildness and purity. Because people around the world have different hair, Timotei's formula varies, but it always has the same image. The selling of "lifestyle" brands is common for consumer goods for which differentiation may be more difficult. Lifestyles may be more difficult for competitors to copy, but they are also more susceptible to changes in fashion.[17]

The influence of culture is especially of concern where society may restrict the purchase of the product, or when the product or one of its features may be subject to a stigma. A symbol in packaging may seem fully appropriate in one culture yet be an insult elsewhere. In parts of North Africa, for example, dogs are considered unclean and a sign of bad luck. A U.S. cologne manufacturer discovered this after launching a product featuring a man and his dog in a rural setting.

Even the export of TV culture, which is considered by many as a local product, can succeed abroad if concepts are adjusted to reflect local values. The Russian version of *Sesame Street* is 70 percent locally produced and features Aunt Dasha, a quintessential Russian character who lives in a traditional cottage and spouts folklore and homespun wisdom. In China, new characters such as Xiao Mei ("Little Berry") were added for local colour. The creators of the joint Israeli-Palestinian production, called *Sesame Stories*, hope that the exploits of Dafi, a purple Israeli Muppet, and Haneen, an orange Palestinian one, will help teach mutual respect and understanding by exposing children to each other's culture and breaking down stereotypes.

Economic Development

Management must take into account the present stage of economic development of the overseas market. As a country's economy advances, buyers are in a better position to buy and to demand more sophisticated products and product versions. With broad country considerations in mind, the firm can determine potential for selling certain kinds of products and services. This means managing affordability in a way that makes the marketer's products accessible. For example, C&A, an apparel retailer from the Netherlands, has been able to build a successful business in Latin American countries because it offers reasonable-quality goods at various price points—the best $10, $20, and $30 dresses on the market. In Brazil, two-thirds of its sales are to families with incomes below $8,000 per year.[18] In some cases, the situation in a developing market may require **backward innovation**; that is, the market may require a drastically simplified version of the firm's product due to lack of purchasing power or usage conditions.

Economic conditions will affect packaging in terms of size and units sold in a package. In developing markets, products such as cigarettes and razor blades are often sold by the piece so that consumers with limited incomes can afford them. Soft-drink companies have introduced four-can packs in Europe, where cans are sold singly even in large stores. On the other hand, products oriented to families, such as food products, appear in larger sizes in developing markets. Pillsbury packages its products in six- and eight-serving sizes for developing countries, whereas the most popular size in the North American market is for two.

Economic conditions may change rapidly, thus warranting change in the product or the product line. During the Asian currency crisis, McDonald's replaced French fries with rice in its Indonesian restaurants due to cost considerations. With the collapse of the local rupiah, potatoes, the only ingredient McDonald's imports into Indonesia, quintupled in price. In addition, a new rice-and-egg dish was introduced in order to maintain as many customers as possible despite the economic hardship.[19]

Competitive Offerings

Monitoring competitors' product features, as well as determining what has to be done to meet and beat them, is critical. Competitive offerings may provide a baseline against which the firm's resources can be measured—for example, what it takes to reach a critical market share in a given competitive situation. An analysis of competitors' offerings may reveal holes in the market or suggest avoiding certain market segments.

In many markets, the global marketer is competing with other global players and local manufacturers and must overcome traditional purchasing relationships and the certainty they provide. What is needed is a niche-breaking product that is adjusted to local needs. TeleGea has had success in Japan because its technology (which has been adjusted to support Asian languages) automates the service-fulfillment process for telecom companies, cutting their delivery costs by more than 30 percent.[20]

Climate and Geography

Climate and geography will usually have an effect on the total product offering: the core product, tangible elements (mainly packaging), and the augmented features. Some products, by design, are vulnerable to the elements. Marketing of chocolate products is challenging in hot climates, which may restrict companies' options. Cadbury Schweppes has its own display cases in shops, while Toblerone has confined its distribution to air-conditioned outlets. Nestlé's solution was to produce a slightly different Kit Kat chocolate wafer for Asia with reduced fat content to raise the candy's melting point. The global marketer must consider two sometimes contradictory aspects of packaging for the international market. On the one hand, the product itself has to be protected against longer transit times and possibly for longer shelf life; on the other hand, care has to be taken that no prohibited preservatives are used. If a product is exposed to a lot of sunshine and heat as a result of being sold on street corners, as may be the case in developing countries, marketers are advised to use special varnishing or to gloss the product wrappers. Without this, the package colouring may fade and make the product unattractive to the customer.

Product Characteristics

Product characteristics (whether actual or perceived) are the inherent features of the product offering. The inherent characteristics of products and the benefits they provide to consumers in the various markets make certain products good candidates for standardization, others not. Nondurable consumer goods, such as food products, generally show the highest amount of sensitivity toward differences in national tastes and habits. Consumer durables, such as cameras and home electronics, are subject to far more homogeneous demand and more predictable adjustment (for example, adjustment to a different technical system in television sets and videotape recorders). Industrial products tend to be more shielded from cultural influences. However, substantial modifications may sometimes be required—in the telecommunications industry, for example—as a result of government regulations and restraints.

Product Constituents

The global marketer must make sure products do not contain ingredients that might be in violation of legal requirements or religious or social customs. When religion or custom determines consumption, ingredients may have to be replaced in order for the product to be acceptable. In Islamic countries, for example, vegetable shortening should be used instead of lard (a pork product). In India, in deference to Hindu beliefs, McDonald's "Maharaja Mac" is made with mutton or chicken rather than beef.

Branding

Brand names convey the image of the product or service. The term **brand** refers to a name, term, symbol, sign, or design used by a firm to differentiate its offerings from those of its competitors. Brands are one of the most easily standardized items in the product offering, and they may allow further standardization of other marketing elements such as promotional items. The brand name is the part of the brand that can be vocalized, while the brand mark is the part of the brand that cannot be vocalized (for example, Royal Bank Group's lion). The brand mark may become invaluable when the product itself cannot be promoted but the symbol can be used. As an example, Marlboro cannot be advertised in most European countries because of legal restrictions on cigarette advertising; however, Philip Morris features advertisements showing only the Marlboro cowboy, who is known throughout the world. Unfortunately, most brands do not have such recognition. The term *trademark* refers to the legally protected part of the brand, indicated by the symbol ®. Increasingly, global marketers have found their trademarks violated by counterfeiters who are illegally using or abusing the marketers' brand names.

The global marketer has a number of options in choosing a branding strategy. The marketer may choose to be a contract manufacturer to a distributor (the generics approach) or to establish national, regional, or worldwide brands. The use of standardization in branding is strongest in culturally similar markets; for example, for Canadian marketers this means the United States and the United Kingdom. Standardization of product and brand do not necessarily move hand in hand; a regional brand may well have local features, or a highly standardized product may have local brand names.[21]

The establishment of worldwide brands is difficult. How can a consumer marketer establish world brands when it sells 800 products in more than 200 countries, most of them under different names? This is Gillette's situation. A typical example is Silkience hair conditioner, which is sold as Soyance in France, Sientel in Italy, and Silkience in Germany. But many companies do have massive standardization programs of brand names, packaging, and advertising.[22] Standardizing names to reap promotional benefits can be difficult, because a particular name may already be established in each market and the action may raise objections from local constituents. Despite the opposition, however, globalizing brands presents huge opportunities to cut costs and achieve new economies of scale.[23]

The psychological power of brands is enormous. Brands are not usually listed on balance sheets, but by allowing the marketer to demand premium prices, they can go further in determining success than technological breakthroughs.[24] Brand loyalty translates into profits despite the fact that favoured brands may not be superior by any tangible measure. New brands may be very difficult and expensive to build, and as a result, the company may seek a tie-in with something that the customer feels positively toward.

Brand names often do not travel well. Semantic variations can hinder a firm's product overseas. Even the company name or the trade name should be checked out. For instance, Mirabell, the manufacturer of the genuine Mozart Kugel (a chocolate ball of marzipan and nougat), initially translated the name of its products as "Mozart balls" but has since changed the name to the "Mozart round."[25] Most problems associated with brands are not as severe but require attention nevertheless. Brands are powerful marketing tools; for example, the chemicals and natural ingredients in any popular perfume retailing for $140 an ounce may be worth less than $3.

In some markets, brand-name changes are required by the government. In Korea, unnecessary foreign words are barred from use; for example, Sprite has been re-named Kin. The same situation has emerged in Mexico, where local branding is primarily required to control foreign companies in terms of the marketing leverage they would have with a universal brand.

Packaging

Packaging serves three major functions: protection, promotion, and user convenience. The major consideration for the global marketer is making sure the product reaches the ultimate user in the form intended. Packaging will vary as a function of transportation mode, transit conditions, and length of time in transit. Because of the longer time that products spend in channels of distribution, firms in the international marketplace, especially those exporting food products, have had to use more expensive packaging materials and/or more expensive transportation modes. The solution of food processors has been to utilize airtight, re-sealable containers that reject moisture and other contaminants.

Pilferage is a problem in a number of markets and has forced companies to use only shipping codes on outside packaging.[26] With larger shipments, containerization has helped alleviate the theft problem. The global marketer should anticipate inadequate, careless, or primitive loading methods. The labels and loading instructions should be not only in English but also in the market's language, as well as in symbols.

The promotional aspect of packaging relates mostly to labelling. The major adjustments concern bilingual legal requirements, as in the case of Canada (French and English), Belgium (French and Flemish), and Finland (Finnish and Swedish). Even when the same language is spoken across markets, nuances will exist, requiring labelling adaptation. Ace Hardware's Paint Division had to be careful in translating the world "plaster" into Spanish.

In Venezuela, *friso* is used, while Mexicans use *yeso*. In the end, *yeso* was used for the paint labels, because the word was understood in all of Latin America.[27] Governmental requirements include more informative labelling on products. Inadequate identification, failure to use the needed languages, or inadequate or incorrect descriptions printed on the labels may cause problems. If in doubt, a company should study foreign competitors' labels.

Package aesthetics must be a consideration in terms of the promotional role of packaging. This mainly involves the prudent choice of colours and package shapes. African nations, for example, often prefer bold colours, but flag colours may be alternately preferred or disallowed. Red is associated with death or witchcraft in some countries. Colour in packaging may be faddish. White is losing popularity in industrialized countries because name brands do not want to be confused with generic products, usually packaged in white. Black, on the other hand, is increasingly popular and is now used to suggest quality, excellence, and "class." Package shapes may serve an important promotional role as well. When Grey Goose, a French brand of vodka, researched its international market entry, the development of the bottle took centre stage. The company finally settled on a tall (taller than the competition) bottle that was a mélange of clear glass, frosted glass, a cutaway of geese in flight, and the French flag.[28]

Package size varies according to purchasing patterns and market conditions. For instance, a six-pack format for soft drinks may not be feasible in certain markets because of the lack of refrigeration capacity in households. Quite often, overseas consumers with modest or low discretionary purchasing power buy smaller sizes or even single units in order to stretch a limited budget. The marketer also has to take into consideration perceptions concerning product multiples. In the West, the number 7 is considered lucky, whereas 13 is its opposite. In Japan, the word for the number 4 sounds the same as the word for death. Therefore, consumer products in multiples of 4 have experienced limited sales. On the other hand, 3 and 5 are considered lucky numbers there.

Finally, the consumer mandate for marketers to make products more environmentally friendly also affects the packaging dimension, especially in terms of the four Rs: redesign, reduce, recycle, and reuse. The EU has strict policies on the amounts of packaging waste that are generated and the levels of recycling of such materials.[29] Depending on the packaging materials (20 percent for plastics and 60 percent for glass), producers, importers, distributors, wholesalers, and retailers are held responsible for generating the waste. In Germany, which has the toughest requirements, all packaging must be reusable or recyclable, and packaging must be kept to the minimum needed for proper protection and marketing of the product. Marketers doing business in the EU must find distributors who can fulfill such requirements and agree how to split the costs of such compliance.

Appearance

Product adaptation strictly refers to changes made to the product to better suit the tastes and preferences of the target market. Adaptations in product styling, colour, size, and other appearance features are more common in consumer marketing than in industrial marketing. Colour plays an important role in the way consumers perceive a product, and marketers must be aware of the signal being sent by the product's colour.[30] Colour can be used for brand identification—for example, the orange of ING Direct Canada, the blue of the Royal Bank, or the red of Tim Hortons. It can be used for feature reinforcement; for example, Honda adopted the colour black to give its motorcycles a "Darth Vader" look, whereas Rolls Royce uses a dazzling silver paint that connotes luxury. Colours communicate in a subtle way in developed societies; they have direct meaning in more traditional societies. For instance, in the late 1950s, when Pepsi-Cola changed the colour of its coolers and vending machines from deep, regal blue to light ice blue, the result was catastrophic in Southeast Asia. Pepsi's dominant market share was lost to Coca-Cola, because light blue is associated with death and mourning in that part of the world.

Method of Operation or Usage

The product as it is offered in the domestic market may not be operable in the foreign market. Products may have to be **localized**, that is, modified to function, in order to be saleable in some foreign markets. One of the major differences faced by appliance manufacturers is electrical power systems. Variations may exist even within a country, as is the case in Brazil. The global marketer can learn about these differences through local government representatives or various trade publications. However, marketers should determine for themselves the adjustments that are required by observing competitive products or having their product tested by a local entity.

Many complicating factors may be eliminated in the future through standardization efforts by international organizations and by the conversion of most countries to the metric system. Some companies have adjusted their products to operate in different systems; for example, VCRs that will record and play back on different colour systems.

Different operating systems and environments can also provide new opportunities. When Canada adopted the metric system in 1977–78, many U.S. companies were affected. The Perfect Measuring Tape Company in Toledo, for example, had to convert to metric if it wanted to continue selling disposable paper measuring tapes to textile firms in Canada. Once the conversion was made, the company found an entire world of untapped markets. It was soon shipping nearly 30 percent of its tapes to overseas markets as disparate as Australia and Zimbabwe.

Success in global markets may also require adaptation of the product to different languages. Calgary-based Smart Technologies Inc. is an innovator in the manufacture and marketing of interactive whiteboards. The company generates over 90 percent of its sales outside of Canada and is active in established markets such as the U.S. and the U.K., but also increasingly in emerging markets such as China and Mexico. The company launched its sixth version of its product—SMARTBoard Interactive—with a range of product improvements, including making the software available in 27 languages.[31]

A global marketer may also have to adapt the product to different uses. MicroTouch Systems, which produces touch-activated computer screens for video-poker machines and ATMs, makes a series of adjustments in this regard. Ticket-vending machines for the French subway need to be waterproof, since they are hosed down. Similarly, for the Australian market, video-poker screens are built to take a beating, because gamblers there take losing more personally than anywhere else.[32]

The global marketer should be open to ideas for new uses for the product being offered. New uses may substantially expand the market potential of the product. For example, Turbo Tek, Inc., which produces a hose attachment for washing cars, has found that foreign customers have expanded the product's functions. In Japan, Turbo-Wash is used for cleaning bamboo, and the Dutch use it to wash windows, plants, and the siding of their houses.[33] To capture these phenomena, observational research, rather than asking direct questions, may be the most appropriate approach. This is especially true in emerging and developing markets in order to understand how consumers relate to products in general and to the marketer's offer in particular.[34]

Quality

Many Western companies must emphasize quality in their strategies because they cannot compete on price alone. Many new exporters compete on value in the particular segments in which they have chosen to compete. In some cases, producers of cheaper Asian products have forced global marketers to reexamine their strategies, allowing them to win contracts on the basis of technical advantage. To maintain a position of product superiority, global firms must invest in research and development for new products as well as manufacturing methods. For example, Sargent and Burton, a small Australian producer of high-technology racing boats, invested in CAD/CAM technology to develop state-of-the-art racing boats that have proven successful in international competition against sophisticated overseas entries.[35] Interstar, a Canadian company that manufactures pigments, admixtures, and fibre for the concrete industry, has also achieved success in international markets by focusing on technology and quality manufacturing to stay ahead of international competitors. The firm adheres to the principles of "Lean Six Sigma" and utilizes multidisciplinary teams of specialists to continuously innovate for the markets it serves around the world. The firm is active in markets such as the U.S., Mexico, and Brazil and generates over 50 percent of its sales outside of Canada.[36]

Marketers themselves may seek endorsement of their efforts from governmental or consumer organizations. Many car exporters have become popular in the global marketplace by doing well in J.D. Power and other car rankings, a fact that may then be used in promotional efforts.

Service

When a product sold overseas requires repairs, parts, or service, the problem of obtaining, training, and retaining a sophisticated engineering or repair staff is not easy. If the product breaks down, and the repair arrangements are not up to standard, the image of the product will suffer. In some cases, products abroad may not even be used for their intended purpose and may thus require modifications not only in product configuration but also in service frequency. Closely related to servicing is the issue of product warranties. Warranties not only are instructions to customers about what to do if the product fails within a specified period of time but also are effective promotional tools.

Country-of-Origin Effects

The country of origin of a product, typically communicated by the phrase "made in (name of country)," has a considerable influence on the quality perceptions of a product. The manufacture of products in certain countries is affected by a built-in positive or negative stereotype of product quality. These stereotypes become critical when important dimensions of a product category are also associated with a country's image.[37] For example, if a firm has a positive match of quality and performance for its car exports, the country of origin should be a prominent feature in promotional campaigns. If there is a mismatch, the country of origin may have to be hidden or the product sold with the help of prestigious partners whose image overshadows concerns about negative country-of-origin perceptions. This issue may be especially important for developing countries that need to increase exports and for importers that source products from countries different from those where they are sold.[38] In some markets, however, there may be a tendency to reject domestic goods and embrace imports of all kinds.

Some products have fared well in the international marketplace despite negative country-of-origin perceptions. For example, Belarus tractors (manufactured both in Belarus and Russia) have fared well in Europe and North America not only because of their reasonable price tag but also because of their ruggedness. Only the lack of an effective network has hindered the company's ability to penetrate Western markets to a greater degree.[39]

Country-of-origin effects lessen as customers become more informed. Also, as more countries develop the necessary bases to manufacture products, the origin of the products becomes less important. The argument has been made that with the advent of more economic integration, national borders become less important.[40] However, many countries have started strategic campaigns to improve their images to promote exports; some are even participating in joint promotional efforts. In some cases, this means the development of new positive associations rather than trying to refute past negative ones.[41]

Company Considerations

Before launching a product in the international marketplace, the marketer needs to consider organizational capabilities as well as the nature of the product and the level of adaptation needed to accommodate various market-related differences between domestic and international markets.

The issue of product adaptation most often climaxes in the question "Is it worth it?" The answer depends on the firm's ability to control costs, to correctly estimate market potential, and finally, to secure profitability, especially in the long term. While new markets, such as those in central Europe, may at present require product adaptation, some marketers may feel that the markets are too small to warrant such adjustments, believing that the markets may quite soon converge with western European ones. While sales of a standard product may be smaller in the short term, long-term benefits will warrant the adoption of this approach.[42] The question that used to be posed as "Can we afford to do it?" should now be "Can we afford not to do it?"

The decision to adapt should be preceded by a thorough analysis of the market. Formal market research with primary data collection and/or testing is warranted. From the financial standpoint, some firms have specific return-on-investment levels to be satisfied before adaptation (for instance, 25 percent), whereas some let the requirement vary as a function of the market considered and also the time in the market—that is, profitability may be initially compromised for proper market entry.

Most companies aim for consistency in their marketing efforts. This translates into the requirement that all products fit in terms of quality, price, and user perceptions. An example of where consistency may be difficult to control is in the area of warranties. Warranties can be uniform only if the use conditions do not vary drastically and if the company is able to deliver equally on its promise anywhere it has a presence.

A critical element of the adaptation decision has to be human resources, that is, individuals who will make the appropriate decisions, who are willing to take risks, and who know about existing market conditions. Many companies benefit from having managers from different countries, giving them the experience and the expertise to make decisions between standardization and adaptation.

Product Counterfeiting

Counterfeit goods are any goods bearing an unauthorized representation of a trademark, patented invention, or copyrighted work that is legally protected in the country where it is marketed. Hardest hit are the most innovative, fastest-growing industries, such as computer software, pharmaceuticals, and entertainment.

The practice of product counterfeiting has spread to high-technology products and services from the traditionally counterfeited products, high-visibility consumer goods with strong brand names. In addition, while previously the only concern was whether a company's product was being counterfeited, now companies have to worry about whether the raw materials and components purchased for production are themselves real.[43] The International Chamber of Commerce estimates that the global counterfeit trade is worth as much as US$350 billion. Other groups put the estimate much higher, at US$600 billion.[44] Counterfeit products cost Canadian firms an estimated $20–30 billion per year.[45] In general, countries with lower per capita incomes, higher levels of corruption in government, and lower levels of involvement in the international trade community tend to have higher levels of intellectual property violation.[46] Roughly 66 percent of the counterfeit products coming into the U.S. and the EU originate in China. Canada, while not a major source of counterfeit products, is a major transshipment point for fakes destined for other markets such as the U.S.[47]

Counterfeiting problems occur in three ways and, depending on the origin of the products and where they are marketed, require different courses of action. Counterfeit products that originate overseas and that are marketed in North America should be stopped by the customs barrier. Enforcement has been problematic because of the lack of adequate personnel and the increasingly high-tech character of the products. When an infringement occurs overseas, action can be brought under the laws of the country in which it occurs. The sources of the largest number of counterfeit goods are China, Brazil, Taiwan, Korea, and India, which are a problem to the legitimate owners of intellectual property on two accounts: the size of these countries' own markets and their capability to export. For example, Nintendo estimates its annual losses to video-game piracy at $700 million, with

The Global MARKETPLACE 9.3

The Phantom Pirates

Video pirates moved faster than a speeding pod racer to release the first *Star Wars* prequel, *The Phantom Menace: Episode One,* in Southeast Asia. The first copies appeared in Malaysia only two days after the U.S. opening, with videodisc copies also reaching other parts of Asia, Europe, South Africa, and Latin America. "This shows how amazingly efficient this industry has become," said Michael Ellis, the Asia anti-piracy chief of the Motion Picture Association. "They have gotten it down to a sophisticated science."

With advances in technology and continued demand for U.S. films abroad, pirate-video making has become big business. The Motion Picture Association of America estimates that worldwide piracy costs Hollywood $3 billion annually. Asia remains by far the biggest producer and consumer of pirate versions.

The three main types of copies of *The Phantom Menace* in Asia each have their own distinctive marks and character, depending on how and when they were filmed. The "Z" Species, named for the computer-generated letter that dances across the screen's edge, was filmed in a crowded theater and is marked by a loud scream of "Yeah, wooo!" throughout the opening sequence, and frequent applause for Yoda. "The Shakes" features shaky camera work, with a number of audience members getting up to go to the washrooms during the important Darth Maul scene. The "Flying Horse" version is also called "AB" for the blinking letters on the screen and a flying horse on the package cover. It features audience noise and frequent flashes of light from viewers taking flashbulb pictures.

It is unclear how the smugglers got the videodiscs (VCDs) to market so quickly. Most of the copies sold in Asia appear to have come from the three master versions, which had been shipped via air courier to Malaysia and Hong Kong, where they were transferred to VCD production lines in Malaysia. New technologies have facilitated the process as well. Whereas a pirated VCR tape has to be recorded in real time, taking up to two hours for each copy, a videodisc can be stamped out in three seconds and quite inexpensively. Consumers can buy a VCD player for under $100, and movies are typically less than $5.

Officials suspect that most of the copies were produced in Malaysia. With its lax law enforcement, low labour costs, and central location in Asia, Malaysia has become the new hub of the pirate CD industry. Whereas Hong Kong and Macau used to be the capital for this activity, crackdowns have chased the industry away. Malaysian officials have been repeatedly told of the violations, but little action has been taken. Experts say most of the factories producing the films are legitimate CD makers that produce pirate products on the side.

Moviemaking is a risky proposition in that only 1 in 10 movies ever retrieves its investment from domestic exhibition. In 2000, the average movie cost $55 million to produce and an additional $27 million to market. The protection of the intellectual property in such endeavours is therefore critical to the industry. As the movie industry becomes digitalized, the challenges of infringement become manifold.

DOUG KANTER/AFP/Getty Images

Source: "Video Pirates Rush Out *Phantom Menace,*" *The Wall Street Journal,* May 28, 1999, B1, B4; and **http://www.mpaa.org.**

the origin of the counterfeits being mainly China and Taiwan.[48] Countries in Central America and the Middle East are typically not sources of but rather markets for counterfeit goods. Counterfeiting is a pervasive problem not only in terms of geographic reach but also in terms of the ability of the counterfeiters to deliver products, and the market's willingness to buy them.

The first task in fighting intellectual property violation is to use patent application or registration of trademarks or mask works (for semiconductors). The rights granted by a patent, trademark, copyright, or mask work registration in Canada or the United States confer no protection in a foreign country. There is no such thing as an international patent, trademark, or copyright. Although there is no shortcut to worldwide protection, some advantages exist under treaties or other international agreements. These treaties, under the World Intellectual Property Organization (WIPO), include the Paris Convention for the Protection of Industrial Property, the Patent Cooperation Treaty, the Berne Convention for the Protection of Literary and Artistic Works, and the Universal Copyright Convention, as well as regional patent and trademark offices such as the European Patent Office. Applicants are typically granted international protection throughout the member countries of these organizations.

After securing valuable intellectual property rights, the global marketer must act to enforce, and have enforced, these rights. Several types of action against counterfeiting may be used, including joint private-sector action and measures taken by individual companies.

A number of private-sector joint efforts have emerged in the battle against counterfeit goods. The Canadian Anti-Counterfeiting Network (CACN), for example, is a coalition of individuals, firms, and associations involved in the fight against product counterfeiting and copyright piracy in Canada. CACN members include the Canadian Association of Importers and Exporters, the Canadian Standards Association, and the Canadian Motion Picture Distributors Association. The coalition works to increase awareness of the counterfeiting problem and lobbies the Canadian federal and provincial governments for legislative changes and additional resources to combat counterfeiting.[49] Other organizations are also active in this area. In 1978, the International AntiCounterfeiting Coalition (IACC) was founded to lobby for stronger legal sanctions worldwide. The coalition consists of 375 members. The International Chamber of Commerce (ICC) established the Counterfeiting Intelligence Bureau in London, England, which acts as a clearinghouse capable of synthesizing global data on counterfeiting.

In today's environment, companies are taking more aggressive steps to protect themselves. The victimized companies are losing not only sales but also goodwill in the longer term if customers believe they have the real product rather than a copy of inferior quality. In addition to the normal measures of registering trademarks and copyrights, companies are taking steps in product development to prevent knockoffs of trademarked goods. For example, new authentication materials in labelling are extremely difficult to duplicate. Pfizer, for instance, has begun to ship its products containing radio frequency identification (RFID) tags that allow pharmacies and wholesalers to verify the unique electronic product code on Viagra packaging. The use of RFID is a deterrent to counterfeiting, as the tags affixed to every bottle, case, and pallet are difficult and expensive to duplicate. Pharmacists and wholesalers are able to use special scanners to communicate the product code to a secure Pfizer website.[50]

Pfizer has also sent communications bulletins to pharmacists with information on how to identify counterfeit Viagra (see Exhibit 9.9). Other companies, such as Disney, have tried to legitimize offenders by converting them into authorized licenses. These local companies would then be a part of the fight against counterfeiters, because their profits would be the most affected by fakes.

Many companies maintain close contact with the government and the various agencies charged with helping them. Computer makers, for example, lend testing equipment to customs officers at all major ports, and company attorneys regularly conduct seminars on how to detect pirated software and hardware. Other companies retain outside investigators to monitor the market and stage raids with the help of law enforcement officers. For

Exhibit 9.9 **Identifying Counterfeit Viagra**

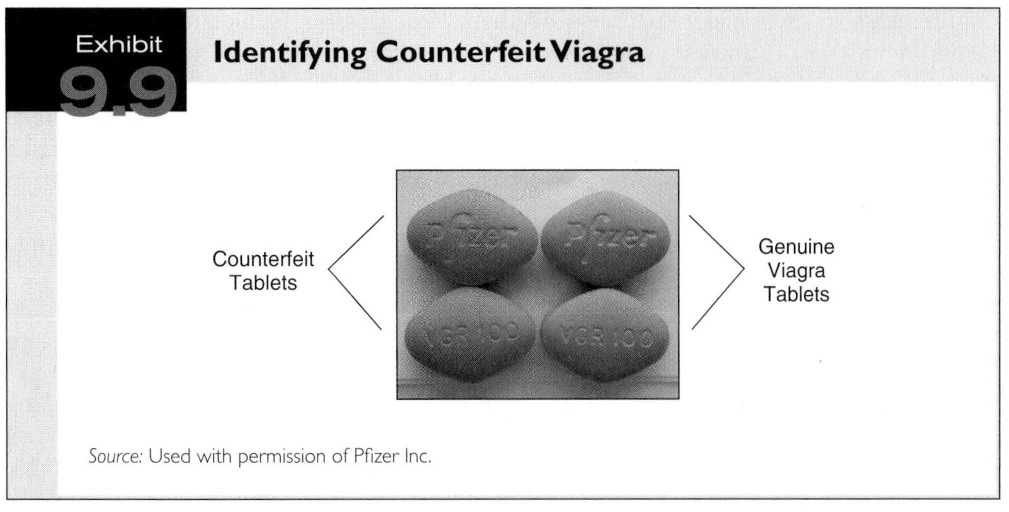

Source: Used with permission of Pfizer Inc.

example, Art In Motion, based in British Columbia, Canada, is a publisher of fine art reproductions. The company's executives make regular trips to China to monitor the counterfeiting situation in that country. The company along with several others in the publishing business recently initiated legal action against Chinese counterfeiters. The evidence-gathering process took two years to complete and cost the group several thousand dollars. At the end of the process, the Chinese authorities seized and destroyed the counterfeiters' products. Unfortunately in this case no action was taken against the perpetrators.[51] Other companies have had similar experiences. When executives at WD-40 Co., the maker of an all-purpose lubricant, realized a counterfeit version of their product was being sold in China, they launched an investigation and then approached local authorities about the problem. Offending retailers were promptly raided and, in turn, led police to the counterfeiter.[52]

The issue of intellectual property protection will become more important for Western countries in future years. It is a different problem from what it was a decade ago, when the principal victims were manufacturers of designer items. Today, the protection of intellectual property is crucial in high technology, one of the strongest areas of Canadian competitiveness in the world marketplace. The ease with which technology can be transferred and the lack of adequate protection of the developers' rights in certain markets make this a serious problem.[53]

Global Product Development and Brand Management

Global Product Development

Product development is at the heart of the global marketing process. New products should be developed, or old ones modified, to cater to new or changing customer needs on a global or regional basis. At the same time, corporate objectives of technical feasibility and financial profitability must be satisfied. With competition increasingly able to react quickly when new products are introduced, worldwide planning at the product level provides a number of tangible benefits. A firm that adopts a worldwide approach is better able to develop products with specifications compatible on a worldwide scale. A firm that leaves product development to independent units will incur greater difficulties in transferring its experience and technology.

In many multinational corporations, each product is developed for potential worldwide usage, and unique multinational market requirements are incorporated whenever technically feasible. Some design their products to meet the regulations and other key requirements in their major markets and then, if necessary, smaller markets' requirements are met on a country-by-country basis. For example, Nissan develops lead-country models that can, with minor changes, be made suitable for local sales in the majority of markets. For the remaining situations, the company also provides a range of additional models that can be adapted to the needs of local segments. Using this approach, Nissan has been able to reduce their number of basic models from 48 to 28.[54] This approach also means that the new product can be introduced concurrently into all the firm's markets. Companies such as 3M and Xerox develop most of their products with this objective in mind.

Some markets may require unique approaches to developing global products. At Gillette, timing is the only concession to local taste. Developing markets, such as Eastern Europe and China, are first weaned on older, cheaper products before they are sold up-to-date versions.[55] In a world economy where most of the growth is occurring in developing markets, the traditional approach of introducing a global product may keep new products out of the hands of consumers due to their premium price. As a result, Procter & Gamble figures out what consumers in various countries can afford and then develops products they can pay for. For example, in Brazil, the company introduced a diaper called Pampers Uni, a less-expensive version of its mainstream product. The strategy is to create price tiers, hooking customers early and then encouraging them to trade up as their incomes and desire for better products grow.[56]

The main goal of the product development process, therefore, is not to develop a standard product or product line but to build adaptability into products and product lines that are being developed to achieve worldwide appeal. To accomplish the right balance, marketers need to develop a basic capability for capturing consumer information within their country organizations. If consumers are willing to talk about their preferences, traditional approaches such as focus groups and interviews work well. Procter & Gamble, for example, generates Chinese consumer information using a 30-person market research team.[57]

The Product Development Process

The product development process begins with idea generation (see Exhibit 9.10). Ideas may come from within the company—from the research and development staff, sales personnel, or almost anyone who becomes involved in the company's efforts. Intermediaries may suggest ideas because they are closer to the changing, and often different, needs of international customers. In franchising operations, franchisees are a source of many new products. For example, the McFlurry, McDonald's ice-cream dessert, was the brainchild of a Canadian operator.[58] Competitors are a major outside source of ideas. A competitive idea from abroad may be modified and improved to suit another market's characteristics.

For a number of companies, especially those producing industrial goods, customers provide the best source of ideas for new products.[59] Many new commercially important products are initially thought of and even prototyped by users rather than manufacturers. They tend to be developed by **lead users**—companies, organizations, or individuals who are ahead of trends or have needs that go beyond what is available at present. For example, a car company in need of a new braking system may look to racing teams for ideas—or even to the aerospace industry, which has a strong incentive to stop its vehicles before they run out of runway.[60] With the increased diffusion of the Internet, chat rooms about products and features are becoming an important source of information pertinent to product development and adjustment. For example, Sony set up a website to support hackers who are interested in exploring and developing new types of games that could be played on the Sony PlayStation. In the field of industrial products, users are invited to use toolkits to design products and services that fit their own needs precisely.[61]

Most companies develop hundreds of ideas every year; for example, 3M may have 1,000 new product ideas competing for scarce development funds annually. Idea screening is the second step in the process of developing a new product. Product ideas must be

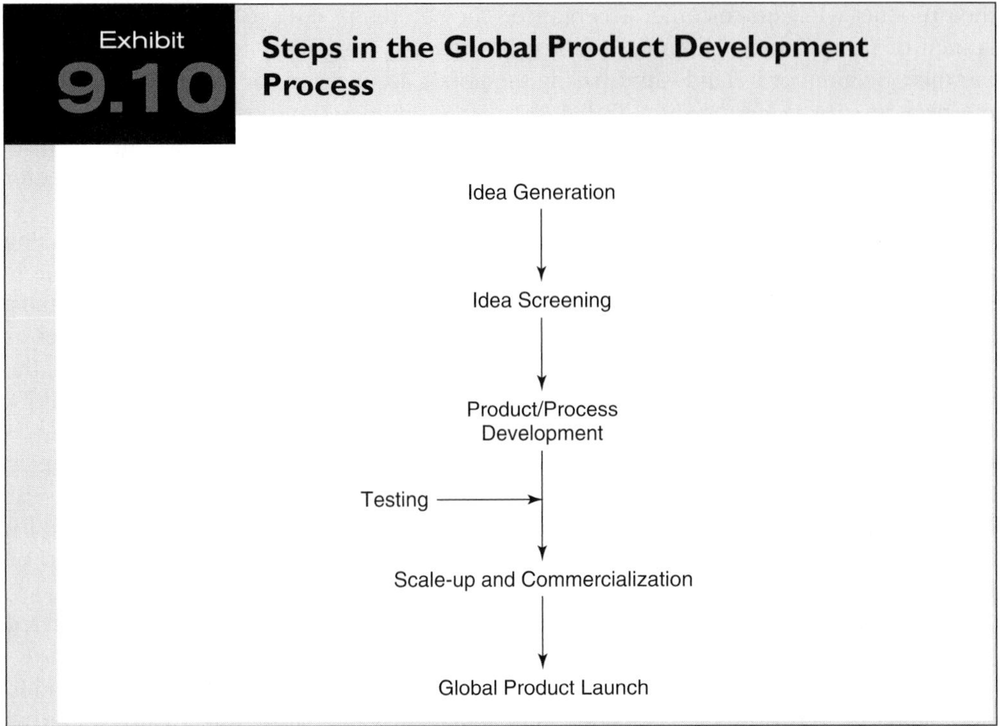

screened on market, technical, and financial criteria: Is the market substantial and penetrable? Can the product be mass produced? And if the answer to both of these questions is affirmative, can the company produce and market it profitably? Too often, companies focus on understanding only the current demand of the consumer. A re-positioning of the concept may overcome an initial negative assessment; for example, in countries with no significant breakfast habit, cereal marketers present their products as snacks. Procter & Gamble created the perception that dandruff—traditionally a nonissue for the Chinese—is a social stigma and offered a product (Head & Shoulders anti-dandruff shampoo) to solve the problem. Today, P&G controls more than half the shampoo market in China.[62]

A product idea that at some stage fails to earn a go-ahead is not necessarily scrapped. Most progressive companies maintain data banks of "miscellaneous opportunities." Often, data from these banks are used in the development of other products. One of the most famous examples concerns 3M. After developing a new woven fabric some 50 years ago, 3M's commercial office supply division did not know what to do with the technology. Among the applications rejected were seamless brassiere cups and disposable diapers. The fabric was finally used to make surgical and industrial masks.

Ideas that have been screened move to the next stage of product and process development. At this stage, working prototypes are designed and tested. This step has been greatly facilitated through the use of **computer-aided design (CAD)**. Some companies are able to design their products so that they meet most standards and requirements around the world, with minor modifications on a country-by-country basis. Successful product and process development allows the firm to proceed to the next step of scale-up and commercialization.

The final stages of the product development process will involve testing the product in terms of both its performance and its projected market acceptance. Depending on the product, testing procedures range from reliability tests in the pilot plant to mini-launches from which the product's performance in world markets will be estimated. Any testing will delay full-scale commercialization and increase the possibility of competitive reaction. Further, the cost of test marketing is substantial—on average, $1–1.5 million per market.

Because of the high rate of new product failure (estimated at 67–95 per cent[63] and usually attributed to market or marketing reasons), most companies want to be assured that their product will gain customer acceptance. They therefore engage in testing or a limited launch of the product. This may involve introducing the product in one country—for instance, Belgium or Ireland—and basing the go-ahead decision for the rest of Europe on the performance of the product in that test market. Some countries are emerging as test markets for global products. Brazil is a test market used by Procter & Gamble and Colgate before rollout into the Latin American market. Unilever uses Thailand for a test market for the Asian market.

In many cases, companies rely too much on instinct and hunch in their marketing abroad, although in domestic markets they make extensive use of testing and research. Lack of testing has led to a number of major product disasters over the years. The most serious blunder is to assume that other markets have the same priorities and lifestyles as the domestic market. After a failure in introducing canned soups in Italy in the 1960s, the Campbell Soup Company repeated the experience by introducing them in Brazil in 1979. Research conducted in Brazil after the failure revealed that women fulfill their roles as homemakers in part by performing such tasks as making soups from scratch. A similar finding had emerged in Italy more than 20 years earlier. However, when Campbell was ready to enter the Eastern and Central European markets in the 1990s, it was prepared for this and was careful to position the product initially as a soup starter or a product to be kept for emergencies.

Other reasons for product failure are a lack of product distinctiveness, unexpected technical problems, and mismatches between functions.[64] Mismatches between functions may occur not only between, for example, engineering and marketing, but within the marketing function as well. Engineering may design features in the product that established distribution channels or selling approaches cannot exploit. Advertising may promise the customer something that the other functions within marketing cannot deliver.

The trend is toward a complete testing of the marketing mix. All the components of the brand are tested, including formulation, packaging, advertising, and pricing. Test marketing is indispensable because prelaunch testing is an artificial situation; it tells the researcher what people say they will do, not what they will actually do. Test marketing carries major financial risks, which can be limited only if the testing can be conducted in a limited area. Ideally, this would utilize localized advertising media—that is, broadcast and print media to which only a limited region would be exposed. However, localized media are lacking even in developed markets such as Western Europe.

Because test marketing in Europe and elsewhere is risky or even impossible, researchers have developed three research methods to cope with the difficulty. **Laboratory test markets** are the least realistic in terms of consumer behaviour over time, but this method allows the participants to be exposed to television advertisements, and their reactions can be measured in a controlled environment. **Microtest marketing** involves a continuous panel of consumers serviced by a retail grocery operated by the research agency. The panelists are exposed to new products through high-quality colour print ads, coupons, and free samples. Initial willingness to buy and repeat buying are monitored. **Forced distribution tests** are based on a continuously reporting panel of consumers that encounters new products in normal retail outlets. This is realistic, but competitors are immediately aware of the new product. An important criterion for successful testing is to gain the cooperation of key retailing organizations in the market. Mars Confectionery, which was testing a new chocolate malted-milk drink in England, could not get distribution in major supermarkets for test products. As a result, Mars changed its approach and focused its marketing on the home-delivery market.[65]

The Global Product Launch

The impact of an effective global product launch can be great, but so can the cost of one that is poorly executed.[66] High development costs as well as competitive pressures are forcing companies to rush products into as many markets as possible. But at the same time, a company can ill afford new products that are not effectively introduced, marketed, and supported in each market the company competes in.

A global product launch means introducing a product into countries in three or more regions within a narrow time frame. To achieve this, a company must undertake a number of measures. The country managers should be involved in the first stage of product strategy formulation to ensure that local and regional considerations are part of the overall corporate and product messages. More important, inter-country coordination of the roll-out preparations will ultimately determine the level of success in the introduction. A product launch team (consisting of product, marketing, manufacturing, sales, service, engineering, and communications representatives) can also approach problems from an industry standpoint, as opposed to a home-country perspective, enhancing product competitiveness in all markets.

Adequate consideration should be given to localization and translation requirements before the launch. This means that right messages are formulated and transmitted to key internal and external audiences. Support materials have to take into account both cultural and technical differences. The advantage of a simultaneous launch is that it boosts the overall momentum and attractiveness of the product by making it immediately available in key geographic markets. Global product launches typically require more education and support of the sales channel than do domestic efforts. This is due to the diversity of the distribution channels in terms of the support and education they may require before the launch.

A successfully executed global launch offers several benefits. First, it permits the company to showcase its technology in all major markets at the same time. Setting a single date for the launch functions as a strict discipline to force the entire organization to gear up quickly for a successful worldwide effort. A simultaneous worldwide introduction also solves the "lame duck" dilemma of having old models available in some markets while customers know of the existence of the new product. If margins are most lucrative at the early stages of the new product's life cycle, they should be exploited by getting the product to as many markets as possible from the outset. With product development costs increasing and product life cycles shortening, marketers have to consider this approach seriously. An additional benefit of a worldwide launch may be added publicity to benefit the marketer's efforts, as happened with the introductions worldwide of Microsoft's Windows 95, 98, 2000, and XP versions.

The Location of R & D Activities

Most multinational corporations have located most of their product development operations within the parent corporation. Recently, however, a number of experts have called for companies to start using foreign-based resources to improve their ability to compete internationally. At Asea Brown Boveri, for example, 90 percent of R & D is done in worldwide business units rather than in an isolated business laboratory.[67] Dutch electronics giant Philips once funded its entire R & D program centrally, but now 70 percent of its funding comes from business units.[68] The benefits are accrued from acquiring international contacts and having R & D investments abroad as ways to add new items to the company's existing product line, thus increasing chances for global success.[69] Although the costs are high and recruitment difficult, W.R. Grace opened an $8 million R & D centre in Japan. Japan provides the company heightened awareness of and access to technological developments that can be used to be more responsive not only to local markets but to global markets as well. The R & D centre is part of Grace's triad approach involving the three leading areas for diffusion of technology: the United States, Europe, and Japan. Similarly Campbell's R & D centre in Hong Kong was initially set up to adjust the company's product offering to the Chinese market. It has since acquired a new role of transferring product concepts developed for the Asian market to the Americas and Europe, due to an increasing interest in ethnic foods. Savi Technology, a provider of real-time solutions for managing supply chains, established its R & D Center for IT Logistics Excellence in Singapore because the city-state is a major starting point for many supply chains and Savi's major customers operate from there.[70]

Investments for R & D abroad are made for four general reasons: (1) to aid technology transfer from parent to subsidiary, (2) to develop new and improved products expressly for foreign markets, (3) to develop new products and processes for simultaneous application in world markets of the firm, and (4) to generate new technology of a long-term exploratory nature. The commitment of the firm to international operations increases from the first type of investment to the third and fourth, in which there is no or little bias toward headquarters performing the job.[71]

In truly global companies, the location of R & D is determined by the existence of specific skills. At Ford Motor Company, development of a specific car or component will be allotted to whichever technical centre has the greatest expertise. Placing R & D operations abroad may also ensure access to foreign scientific and technical personnel and information, either in industry or at leading universities. The location decision may also be driven by the unique features of the market. For example, most of the major automakers have design centres in California to allow for the monitoring of the technical, social, and aesthetic values of the fifth-largest car market in the world. Furthermore, the many technological innovations and design trends that have originated there give it a trendsetting image. Working with the most demanding customers (on issues such as quality) will give companies assurance of success in broader markets.[72]

The Organization of Global Product Development

It should be noted that the product development process can be initiated by any unit of the organization, in the parent country or abroad. If the initiating entity is a subsidiary that lacks technical and financial resources for implementation, another entity of the firm is assigned the responsibility. Most often this is the parent and its central R & D department. Larger multinational corporations naturally have development laboratories in multiple locations that can assume the task. In these cases, coordination and information flow between the units are especially critical.

For larger global firms, the product development activity may take place in the parent country with all the affected units actively participating in development and market planning for a new product. For example, a subsidiary would communicate directly with the product division at the headquarters level and also with the international staff, who could support the subsidiary on the scene of the actual development activity. This often also involves the transfer of people from one location to another for such projects. For example, when Fiat wanted to build a car specifically for emerging markets, the task to develop the Palio was given to a 300-strong team which assembled in Turin, Italy. Among them were 120 Brazilians, ranging from engineers to shop-floor workers, as well as Argentines, Turks, and Poles.[73]

The ability to leverage global corporate resources to facilitate product development is not, however, the reality for most Canadian firms. Small and medium-sized Canadian firms often have to rely on government resources to aid the product development process. In Canada, the Industrial Research Assistance Program (IRAP) of National Research Council Canada (NRC) provides a range of technical services and business advisory services to growth-oriented small and medium-sized Canadian firms.[74] Through this support, smaller firms are better equipped to perform basic R & D, to commercialize new products and processes, and to access new markets.

The success of the federal government's IRAP is measured by the large number of small and medium-sized Canadian firms—over 12,000 annually—which take advantage of customized solutions to their new-product problems.[75] As a result of participation in IRAP, a Canadian firm has successfully developed cholesterol-lowering food ingredients and has obtained approval from European regulatory authorities to market them in a variety of food groups, including milk-based products, soy drinks, spicy sausages, and salad dressings. For this firm, sales opportunities in the European Union have increased significantly as a result, and licensing agreements have been signed for the use of the product in the United Kingdom and Finland. Another IRAP client has successfully developed an over-the-counter health product clinically proven to combat the common cold. The firm successfully completed clinical trials regulated by the United States Food and Drug Administration. Developed at the University of Alberta, the product is currently being marketed in the United States and Australia. A third IRAP participant has successfully pioneered underground communications products to improve safety and productivity for mine and tunnel operators by enabling two-way voice and data communications underground, regardless of tunnel size or length. Innovative features of the products include voice, data, video, and diagnostic capability that results in immediate payback for mine and tunnel operators. Sixty to 70 percent of the firm's revenues are now derived from exports to the world's mining community, including customers in the United States, Latin America, and Eastern Europe.

Product development activity is undertaken by specific teams whose task it is to subject new products to tough scrutiny at specified points in the development cycle in order to eliminate weak products before too much is invested in them and to guide promising prototypes from labs to the market.[76] Representatives of all the affected functional areas serve on each team to ensure the integrity of the project. A marketing team member is needed to assess the customer base for the new product, engineering to make sure that the product can be produced in the intended format, and finance to keep costs under control. An international team member should be assigned a permanent role in the product development process and not simply called in when a need arises. Organizational relationships have to be such that the firm's knowledge-based assets are easily transferable and transferred.[77]

In addition to having international representation on each product development team, some multinational corporations hold periodic meetings of purely international teams. A typical international team may consist of five members, each of whom also has a product responsibility (such as cable accessories) as well as a geographical responsibility (such as the Middle East). Others may be from central R & D and domestic marketing planning. The function of international teams is to provide both support to subsidiaries and international input to overall planning efforts. A critical part of this effort is customer input before a new product design is finalized. This is achieved by requiring team members to visit key customers throughout the process. A key input of international team members is the potential for universal features that can be used worldwide as well as unique features that may be required for individual markets.

Such multidisciplinary teams maximize the payoff from R & D by streamlining decision making; that is, they reduce the need for elaborate reporting mechanisms and layers of committee approvals. With the need to slash development time, these teams can be especially useful in a highly competitive environment.

Challenges to using teams or approaches that require cooperation between R & D centres are often language and cultural barriers. For example, pragmatic engineers in North America may distrust their more theoretically thinking European counterparts. National rivalries may also inhibit the acceptance by others of solutions developed by one entity of the organization. Many companies have solved these problems with increased communication and exchange of personnel.

With the costs of basic research rising and product life cycles shortening, many companies have joined forces in **R & D consortia**. These can provide the benefits and face the challenges of any strategic alliance. Countering the benefits of sharing costs and risks are management woes from mixing corporate cultures as well as varying levels of enthusiasm by the participants. As long as participants work on core technologies that each can then apply in their own way in their own fields, these consortia can work very effectively.

Management of the Product and Brand Portfolio

Most marketers have a considerable number of individual items in their product portfolios, consisting of different product lines, that is, groupings of products managed and marketed as a unit. The options for a particular portfolio (or multiple portfolios) are to expand geographically to new markets or new segments and to add to existing market operations through new product lines or new product business. The marketer will need to have a balanced product and market portfolio—a proper mix of new, growing, and mature products to provide a sustainable competitive advantage.[78]

The assessment of the product portfolio will have to take into account various interlinkages, both external and internal to the firm. Geographic interlinkages call attention to market similarities, especially to possibilities of extending operations across borders. Product-market interlinkages are manifested in common customers and competitors. Finally, the similarities in present-day operations should be assessed in terms of product lines, brands, and brand positioning. As a result of such an analysis, Mars has stayed out of the U.S. chocolate-milk market, despite a product-company fit, because the market is dominated by Hershey and Nestlé. However, it has entered this particular market in other regions, such as Europe.

Analyzing the Product Portfolio

The specific approach chosen and the variables included will vary by company according to corporate objectives and characteristics as well as the nature of the product market. A product portfolio approach based on growth rates and market-share positions allows the analysis of business entities, product lines, or individual products. Exhibit 9.11 represents the product-market portfolio of Company A, which markets the same product line in several countries. The company is a leader in most of the markets in which it has operations, as indicated by its relative market shares. It has two "cash cows" (United States and Canada), four "stars" (Germany, Great Britain, France, and Spain), and one "problem child" (Brazil). In the mature U.S. market, Company A has its largest volume but only a small market-share advantage compared with competition. Company A's dominance is more pronounced in Canada and in the EU countries.

At the same time, Company B, its main competitor, although not a threat in Company A's major markets, has a commanding lead in two fast-growing markets: Japan and Brazil. As this illustration indicates, an analysis should be conducted not only of the firm's own portfolio but also of competitors' portfolios, along with a projection of the firm's and the competitors' future international products—market portfolios. Building future scenarios based on industry estimates will allow Company A to take remedial long-term action to counter Company B's advances. In this case, Company A should direct resources to build market share in fast-growing markets such as Japan and Brazil.

Portfolios should also be used to assess market, product, and business interlinkages.[79] This effort will allow the exploitation of increasing market similarities through corporate adjustments in setting up appropriate strategic business units (SBUs) and the standardization of product lines, products, and marketing programs.

Advantages of the Product Portfolio Approach

The major advantages provided by the product portfolio approach are as follows:

1. A global view of the competitive structure, especially when longer-term considerations are included
2. A guide for the formulation of a global marketing strategy based on the suggested allocation of scarce resources between product lines
3. A guide for the formulation of marketing objectives for specific markets based on an outline of the role of each product line in each of the markets served—for example, to generate cash or to block the expansion of competition
4. A convenient visual communication goal, achieved by integrating a substantial amount of information in an appealingly simple format including assessment of interlinkages between units and products

Before making strategic choices based on such a portfolio, the global marketer should consider the risks related to variables such as entry mode and exchange rates; management preferences for idiosyncratic objectives, such as concentrating on countries with similar market characteristics; and marketing costs. For example, the cost of entry into one market may be less because the company already has a presence there in another product category and the possibility exists that distribution networks may be shared. Similarly, ideas for new products and marketing programs can be leveraged across

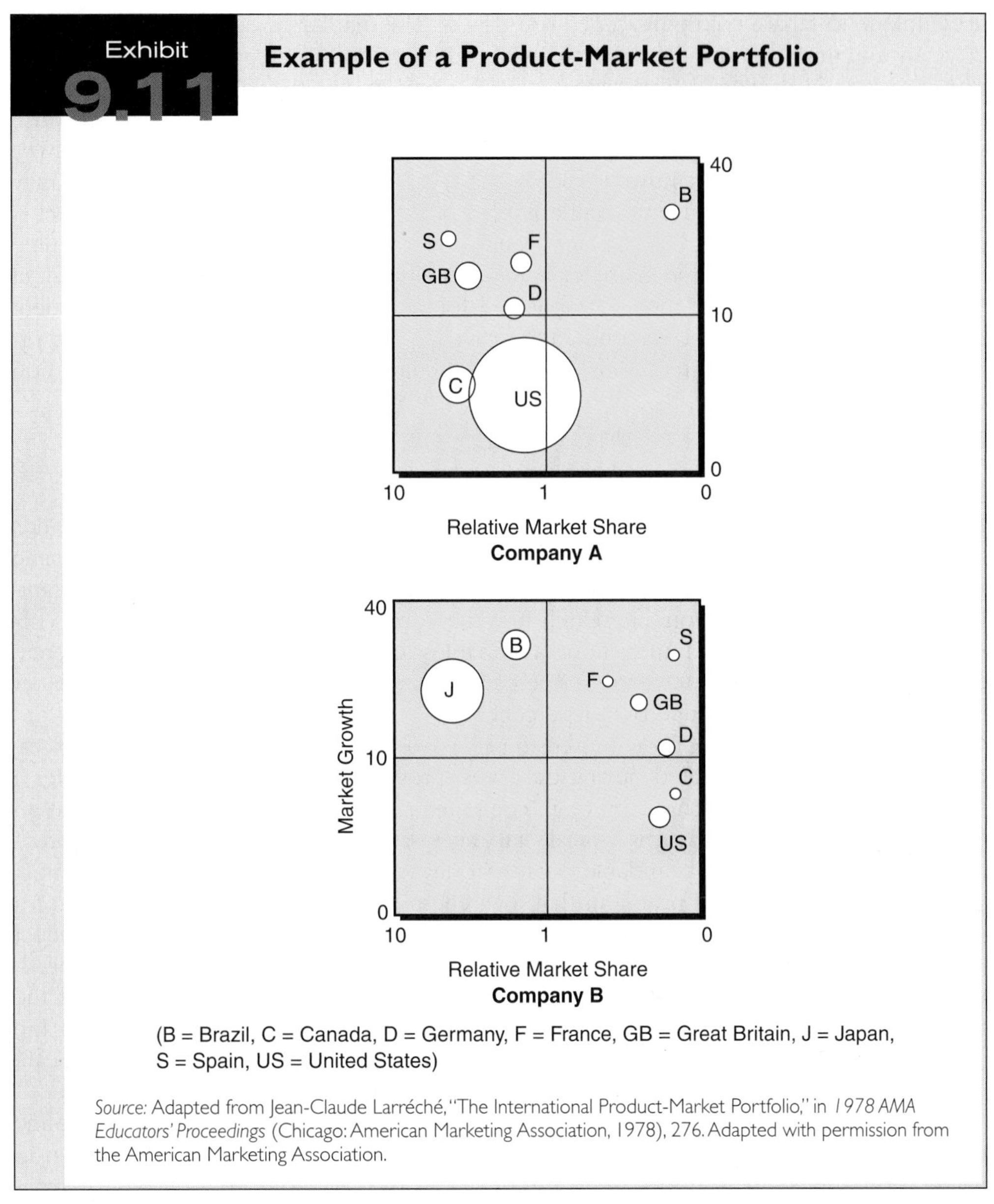

Exhibit 9.11 **Example of a Product-Market Portfolio**

(B = Brazil, C = Canada, D = Germany, F = France, GB = Great Britain, J = Japan, S = Spain, US = United States)

Source: Adapted from Jean-Claude Larréché, "The International Product-Market Portfolio," in *1978 AMA Educators' Proceedings* (Chicago: American Marketing Association, 1978), 276. Adapted with permission from the American Marketing Association.

geographies based on both market characteristics and company position in those markets.[80]

Disadvantages of the Product Portfolio Approach

The application of the product portfolio approach has a number of limitations. International competitive behaviour does not always follow the same rules as in the firm's domestic market; for example, the major local competitor may be a government-owned firm whose main objective is to maintain employment. The relationship between market share and profitability may also be blurred by a number of factors in the marketing environment. Government regulations in every market will have an impact on the products a company can market.

Product lines offered will also be affected by various local content laws—those stipulating that a prescribed percentage of the value of the final product must be manufactured locally. Market tastes have an important impact on product lines. These may not only alter the content of a product but may also require an addition in a given market that is not available elsewhere. The Coca-Cola Company has market leadership in a product category unique to Japan: coffee-flavoured soft drinks. The market came into existence some 20 years ago and grew rapidly, eventually accounting for 10 percent of soft-drink sales. The beverage is packaged like any other soft drink and is available through vending machines, which dispense hot cans in the winter and cold servings during warm weather.

The fact that multinational firms produce the same products in different locations may have an impact on consumer perceptions of product risk and quality. If the product is produced in a developing country, for example, the global marketer has to determine whether a well-known brand name can compensate for the concern a customer might feel. The situation may be more complicated for retailers importing from independent producers in developing nations under the retailer's private labels. In general, country-of-origin effects on product perceptions are more difficult to determine since the introduction of hybrid products.

Managing the Brand Portfolio

Branding is one of the major beneficiaries of a well-conducted portfolio analysis. Brands are important because they shape customer decisions and, ultimately, create economic value. Brand is a key factor behind the decision to purchase in both consumer and business-to-business situations. Research into the connection of brand strength and corporate performance at 130 multinational companies revealed that strong brands generate total returns to shareholders that are 1.9 percent above the industry average, while weaker brands lag behind the average by 3.1 percent.[81]

Brands are a major benefit to the customer as well. They simplify everyday choices, reduce the risk of complicated buying decisions, provide emotional benefits, and offer a sense of community. In technology (e.g., computer chips), where products change at an ever-increasing pace, branding is critical—far more so than in packaged goods, where a product may be more understandable because it stays the same or very similar over time.

In addition to the price premium that awareness and loyalty allow, the benefit of a strong brand name is the ability to exploit the brand in a new market or a new product category. In a global marketplace, customers are aware of brands even though the products themselves may not be available. This was the case, for example, in many of the former Soviet republics before their markets opened up. Starbucks has relied on the strength of its brand in breaking into new markets, including Vienna, Europe's café capital.[82]

Market power is usually in the hands of brand-name companies that have to determine the most effective use of this asset across markets. The value of brands can be seen in recent acquisitions where prices have been many times over the book value of the company purchased. Nestlé, for example, paid five times the book value for the British Rowntree, the owner of such brands as Kit Kat and After Eight. Many of the world's leading brands command high brand-equity values—in other words, the price premium the brand commands multiplied by the extra volume it moves divided by the price of an average brand.[83] It should be noted that the measurement of brand value is complex. Some industry analysts may utilize the relief-from-royalty method, which attempts to determine how much the company would need to pay a third party to rent the assets that constitute its brand. Other analysts may simply rely on the goodwill number reported on the company's balance sheet.[84] A ranking of the top Canadian brands is provided in Exhibit 9.12.

Brand Strategy Decisions

Global marketers have three choices of branding within the global, regional, and local dimensions: they can have brands that feature the corporate name, they can have family brands for a wide range of products or product variations, or they can have individual brands for each item in the product line. With the increase in strategic alliances, co-branding, in which two or more well-known brands are combined in an offer, has also become popular. Examples of these approaches include Heinz, which has a policy of

Exhibit 9.12

Canada's Most Valuable Brands

Company	Brand Value 2005 ($m)
Royal Bank	4,527
Loblaw	3,332
Bell Canada	3,130
CIBC	2,805
Toronto Dominion	2,761
Bank of Nova Scotia	2,210
Bank of Montreal	1,795
Canadian Tire	1,668

Source: John Gray, "What's in a Brand," *Canadian Business*, (December 28–January 15, 2004), 73–74.

using its corporate name in all its products, Procter & Gamble, which has a policy of stand-alone products or product lines, and Nestlé, which uses a mixture of Nestlé and Nes-designated brands and stand-alones. In the case of marketing alliances, the brand portfolio may be a combination of both partners' brands. General Mills' alliance with Nestlé in cereals, Cereal Partners Worldwide, features General Mills brands such as Trix and Nestlé brands such as Chocapic.

Branding is an integral part of the overall identity management of the firm.[85] Therefore, it is typically a centralized function to exploit to the fullest the brand's assets as well as to protect the asset from dilution by, for example, extending the brand to inappropriate new lines. The role of headquarters, strategic business unit management, global teams, or global managers charged with a product is to provide guidelines for the effort without hampering local initiative at the same time.[86] In addition to the use of a global brand name from the very beginning, many marketers are consolidating their previously different brand names (often for the same or similar products) with global or regional brand names. For example, Mars replaced its Treets and Bonitas names with M&M's worldwide and renamed its British bestseller, Marathon, with the Snickers name it uses in North and South America. The benefits in global branding are in marketing economies and higher acceptance of products by consumers and intermediaries. The drawbacks are in the loss of local flavour, especially when a local brand is replaced by a regional or global brand name. At these times, internal marketing becomes critical to instill ownership of the global brands in the personnel of the country organizations.[87]

The mechanics of brand changeover present a few options for the global marketer. For the introduction of global brands in national markets in which local brands are well established, the firm may pursue a **fade-in/fade-out strategy** in which the global brand is associated with the local brand for a specified period of time, after which the local brand is dropped. This approach involves a transition phase that allows consumers to adjust to the global brand. The linking or association of the global and local brands may take place in a number of ways. One brand may be used to introduce the other or both brands may be presented side by side during the transition period. A second option for the firm is **summary axing**, in which the local brand is simply dropped and the global brand simultaneously introduced. This latter approach may anger loyal customers and cause sales to decline. A third option for the firm is to **forewarn**, that is, to inform consumers in advance that their local brand will soon be known by its global name.[88]

The brand portfolio needs to be periodically and regularly assessed. A number of global marketers are focusing their attention on A brands with the greatest growth potential. By continuing to dispose of non-core brands, the marketer can concentrate on the global ones and reduce production, marketing, storage, and distribution costs. It is increasingly difficult for the global company to manage purely local brands. The surge of private-label products has also put additional pressure on B brands.[89]

However before disposing of a brand, managers need to assess it in terms of current sales, loyalty, potential, and trends. For example, eliminating a local brand that has a strong and loyal following, has been created by local management, and shows potential to be extended to nearby markets is not necessarily in the best interests of the company. Three approaches for purely local brands may work: a penetration price approach, a cultural approach that positions the product as a true defender of local culture, and a "chameleon" approach, in which the brand tries not to look local.[90] The number one chewing-gum brand in France for the past 25 years has been Hollywood.

Private-Brand Policies

The emergence of strong intermediaries has led to the significant increase in private-brand goods, that is, the intermediaries' own branded products or "store brands." Two general approaches have been used: umbrella branding, where a number of products are covered using the same brand (often the intermediary's name), and separate brand names for individual products or product lines.

While private-brand success can be shown to be affected strongly by economic conditions and the self-interest of retailers who want to improve their bottom lines through the contribution of private-label goods, new factors have emerged to make the phenomenon more long-lived and significant in changing the product choices worldwide. The level of private-brand share will vary by country and by product category, reflecting variations in customer perceptions, intermediary strength, and behaviour of leading branders.[91]

Summary

Marketers may routinely exaggerate the attractiveness of international markets, especially in terms of their similarity. Despite the dramatic impact of globalization as far as market convergence is concerned, distances, especially cultural and economic, challenge the marketer to be vigilant.[92] The global marketer must pay careful attention to variables that may call for an adaptation in the product offering. The target market will influence the adaptation decision through factors such as government regulation and customer preferences and expectations. The product itself may not be in a form ready for international market entry in terms of its brand name, its packaging, or its appearance. Some marketers make a conscious decision to offer only standardized products; some adjust their offerings by market.

Like the soft-drink and packaged-goods marketers that have led the way, the newest marketers of world brands are producing not necessarily identical products but recognizable products. As an example, the success of McDonald's in the world marketplace has been based on variation, not on offering the same product worldwide. Had it not been for the variations, McDonald's would have limited its appeal unnecessarily and would have been far more subject to local competitors' challenges.

Firms entering or participating in the global marketplace will certainly find it difficult to cope with the conflicting needs of the domestic and international markets. They will be certain to ask whether adjustments in their product offerings, if the marketplace requires them, are worthwhile. There are, unfortunately, no magic formulas for addressing the problem of product adaptation. The answer seems to lie in adopting formal procedures to assess products in terms of the markets' and the company's own needs.

The theft of intellectual property—ideas and innovations protected by copyrights, patents, and trademarks—is a critical problem for many industries and countries, accelerating with the pace of market globalization. Governments have long argued about intellectual property protection, but the lack of results in some parts of the world has forced companies themselves to take action on this front.

The global marketer must also be concerned with the coordination and implementation of product development and brand management strategies across country markets. The global product planning effort must determine two critical decisions: (1) how and where the company's products should be developed, and (2) how and where the present and future product lines should be marketed.

In product development, multinational corporations are increasingly striving toward finding common denominators to rationalize worldwide production. This is achieved through careful coordination of the product development process by worldwide or regional development teams. No longer is the parent company the only source of new products. New product ideas emerge throughout the system and are developed by the entity most qualified to do so.

The global marketer's product line is not the same worldwide. The standard line items are augmented by local items or localized variations of products to better cater to the unique needs of individual markets. External variables such as competition and regulations often determine the final composition of the line and how broadly it is marketed.

Global marketers will also have to determine the extent to which they will use one of their greatest assets—brands—across national markets. Marketers will have to choose among global brands, regional brands, and purely local approaches, and decide whether to forgo their own branding in favour of becoming a supplier for private-brand efforts of retailers. Efficiencies of standardization must be balanced with customer preferences and internal issues of motivation at the country-market level.

Key Terms

backward innovation (p. 308)
brand (p. 309)
computer-aided design (CAD) (p. 319)
discretionary product adaptation (p. 302)
fade-in/fade-out strategy (p. 327)
forced distribution tests (p. 320)
forewarn (p. 327)
laboratory test markets (p. 320)
lead users (p. 318)
localized (p. 312)
mandatory product adaptation (p. 302)
microtest marketing (p. 320)
positioning (p. 307)
R & D consortia (p. 323)
summary axing (p. 327)

Questions for Discussion

1. How can a company's product line reflect the maxim "think globally, act locally"?
2. Will a globally oriented company have an advantage over a multi-domestic, or even a domestic, company in the next generation of new product ideas?
3. What factors should be considered when deciding on the location of research and development facilities?
4. What factors make product testing more complicated in the international marketplace?
5. What are the benefits of a coordinated global product launch? What factors will have to be taken into consideration before the actual launch?
6. Argue for and against the use of the corporate name in global branding.
7. Comment on the statement "It is our policy not to adapt products for export."
8. What are the major problems facing companies, especially smaller ones, in resolving product adaptation issues?
9. How do governments affect product adaptation decisions of firms?
10. Is any product ever the same everywhere it is sold?
11. Propose ways in which intellectual property piracy could be stopped permanently.

Internet Exercises

1. Visit the website of the Canadian Anti-Counterfeiting Network (CACN) at **http://www.cacn.ca.** What is the mandate of this organization? What services does it provide? How similar is the CACN to the International AntiCounterfeiting Coalition (**http://www.iacc.org/**) in scope and method of operation?
2. Visit the Interbrand website (**http://www.interbrand.com/surveys.asp**) and review its rankings of the top Canadian brands. Why do you believe some brands are ranked higher than others?

Recommended Readings

Aaker, David A. *Building Strong Brands.* New York: The Free Press, 1996.

Aaker, David, and Erich Joachimsthaler. *Brand Leadership: The Next Level of Brand Revolution.* New York: The Free Press, 2000.

Bedbury, Scott. *A Brand New World: Eight Principles for Achieving Brand Leadership in the 21st Century.* New York: Viking Press, 2002.

Cooper, Robert G. *Product Leadership: Creating and Launching Superior New Products.* New York: Perseus Books, 2000.

Cooper, Robert G. *Winning at New Products: Accelerating the Process from Idea to Launch.* New York: Perseus Books, 2001.

Deschamps, Jean-Philippe, and P. Raganath Nayak. *Product Juggernauts: How Companies Mobilize to Generate a Stream of Market Winners.* Boston: Harvard Business School Press, 1995.

Gregory, James R., and Jack G. Wiechman. *Branding across Borders: A Guide to Global Brand Marketing.* New York: McGraw-Hill, 2001.

Kapferer, Jean-Noël. *Strategic Brand Management.* New York: The Free Press, 1992.

Keller, Kevin L. *Strategic Brand Management: Building, Measuring, and Managing Brand Equity.* Upper Saddle River, NJ: Prentice Hall, 2002.

Kitcho, Catherine. *High Tech Product Launch.* Mountain View, CA: Pele Publications, 1999.

Kotabe, Masaaki. *Global Sourcing Strategy: R&D, Manufacturing, and Marketing Interfaces.* Greenwich, CT: Greenwood Publishing Group, 1992.

Lasalle, Diane, and Terry A. Britton. *Priceless: Turning Ordinary Products into Extraordinary Experiences.* Boston, MA: Harvard Business School Press, 2002.

Levitt, Theodore. *The Marketing Imagination.* New York: Free Press, 1986.

Lorenz, C. *The Design Dimension: Product Strategy and the Challenge of Global Markets.* New York: Basil Blackwell, 1996.

Macrae, Chris. *The Brand Chartering Handbook.* Harlow, UK: Addison-Wesley, 1996.

Nelson, Carl A. *Exporting: A Manager's Guide to the Export Market.* Mason, OH: International Thomson Business Press, 1999.

Papadopoulos, Nicolas, and Louise A. Heslop. *Product-Country Images.* Binghamton, NY: International Business Press, 1993.

Renner, Sandra L., and W. Gary Winget. *Fast-Track Exporting.* New York: AMACOM, 1991.

Ries, Laura, and Al Ries. *The 22 Immutable Laws of Branding: How to Build a Product or Service into a World-Class Brand.* New York: HarperCollins, 1998.

Rodkin, Henry. *The Ultimate Overseas Business Guide for Growing Companies.* Homewood, IL: Dow Jones-Irwin, 1990.

Schmitt, Bernd, and Alexander Simonson. *Marketing Aesthetics: The Strategic Management of Brands, Identity and Image.* New York: The Free Press, 1997.

Tuller, Lawrence W. *Exporting, Importing, and Beyond: How to "Go Global" with Your Small Business.* Avon, MA: Adams Media Corporation, 1997.

Notes

1. Jeffrey E. Garten, "Globalization without Tears: A New Social Compact for CEOs," *Strategy and Business*, 4th quarter, 2002, 36–45.
2. Jill G. Klein, Richard Ettenson, and Marlene Morris, "The Animosity Model of Foreign Product Purchase: An Empirical Test in the People's Republic of China," *Journal of Marketing* 62 (January 1998): 89–100.
3. Agriculture Canada, **http://www.agr.gc.ca/poultry/prindc6_e.htm.**
4. Thomas L. Friedman, *The Lexus and the Olive Tree: Understanding Globalization* (New York: Anchor Books, 2000), chaps. 3 and 15.
5. S. Tamer Cavusgil and Shaoming Zou, "Marketing Strategy-Performance Relationship: An Investigation of the Empirical Link in Export Market Ventures," *Journal of Marketing* 58 (January 1994): 1–21.
6. Jean-Noël Kapferer, *Survey among 210 European Brand Managers* (Paris: Euro-RSCG, 1998).
7. Foreign Affairs and International Trade Canada website, **http://geo.international.gc.ca/asia/main/newsletter/ciap-2006-09-en.asp** (accessed November 10, 2006).
8. Carl A. Sohlberg, "The Perennial Issue of Adaptation or Standardization of International Marketing Communication: Organizational Contingencies and Performance," *Journal of International Marketing* 10, no. 3 (2002): 1–21.
9. James D. Southwick, "Addressing Market Access Barriers in Japan through the WTO: A Survey of Typical Japan Market Access Issues and the Possibility to Address Them through WTP Dispute Resolution Procedures," *Law and Policy in International Business* 31 (Spring 2000): 923–76.
10. "EU Nears Stricter GMO Food Labels," *The Wall Street Journal*, July 5, 2002, A8.
11. Davis Goodman, "Thinking Export? Think ISO 9000," *World Trade*, August 1998, 48–49.
12. "ISOing your Operation," **http://www.findarticles.com/p/articles/mi_m3301/is_n2_v97/ai_18542042/print** (accessed November 10, 2006).
13. Enrique Sierra, "The New ISO 14000 Series: What Exporters Should Know," *Trade Forum* no. 3 (1996): 16–31.
14. A. Prakash and M. Patoski, "Globalization and ISO 14001," **http://faculty.washington.edu/aseem/isonews.pdf.**
15. Kirk Loncar, "Look Before You Leap," *World Trade*, June 1997, 92–93.
16. Drew Martin and Paul Herbig, "Marketing Implications of Japan's Social-Cultural Underpinnings," *Journal of Brand Management* 9 (January 2002): 171–79.
17. Jennifer Aaker, "Dimensions of Measuring Brand Personality," *Journal of Marketing Research* 34 (August 1997): 347–56.
18. James A. Gingrich, "Five Rules for Winning Emerging Market Consumers," *Strategy and Business*, 2nd quarter, 1999, 35–42.
19. "Holding the Fries—At the Border," *Business Week*, December 14, 1998, 8.
20. "Exporting to Survive," *Time Global Business*, September 2002, A20–A22.

21. Robert Gray, "Local on a Global Scale," *Marketing*, September 27, 2001, 22–23.
22. Jean-Noël Kapferer, "Is There Really No Hope for Local Brands?" *Journal of Brand Management* 9 (January 2002): 163–70.
23. Alan Mitchell, "Few Brands Can Achieve a Truly Global Presence," *Marketing Week*, February 7, 2002, 32–33.
24. "The Best Global Brands," *Business Week*, August 5, 2002, 92–108.
25. "Mozart's Genius Extends to Selling Lederhosen in Japan," *The Wall Street Journal Europe*, January 6, 1992, sec. 1.1.
26. Barry M. Tarnef, "How to Protect Your Goods in Transit without Going Along for a Ride," *Export Today* 9 (May 1993): 55–57.
27. Jesse Wilson, "Are Your Spanish Translations Culturally Correct?" *Export Today* 10 (May 1994): 68–69.
28. Dan McGinn, "Vodka with Punch," **http://mbajungle.com,** September/October 2002, 34–36.
29. "Waste Not," *Business Europe*, February 20, 2002, 4.
30. Thomas J. Madden, Kelly Hewett, and Martin S. Roth, "Managing Images in Different Cultures: A Cross-National Study of Color Meanings and Preferences," *Journal of International Marketing* 8, no. 4 (2000): 90–107.
31. Foreign Affairs and International Trade Canada website, **http://www.infoexport.gc.ca/awards-prix/awards/2005/smart_e.htm.**
32. Carla Kruytbosch, "The Minds behind the Winners," *International Business*, January 1994, 56–70.
33. "Awash in Export Sales," *Export Today* 5 (February 1989): 11.
34. Dana James, "B2-4B Spells Profits," *Marketing News*, November 5, 2001, 1, 11–12.
35. Ian Wilkinson and Nigel Barrett, "In Search of Excellence in Exports: An Analysis of the 1986 Australian Export Award Winners," paper given at the Australian Export Award presentations, Sydney, November 28, 1986.
36. Foreign Affairs and International Trade website, **http://www.infoexport.gc.ca/awards-prix/awards/2005/interstar_e.htm.**
37. Martin S. Roth and Jean B. Romeo, "Matching Product Category and Country Image Perceptions: A Framework for Managing Country-of-Origin Effects," *Journal of International Business Studies* 23 (3rd quarter, 1992): 477–97.
38. Warren J. Bilkey and Erik Nes, "Country-of-Origin Effects on Product Evaluations," *Journal of International Business Studies* 13 (Spring–Summer 1982): 88–99.
39. Johny K. Johansson, Ilkka A. Ronkainen, and Michael R. Czinkota, "Negative Country-of-Origin Effects: The Case of the New Russia," *Journal of International Business Studies* 25 (1st quarter, 1994): 1–21.
40. Johny K. Johansson, "Determinants and Effects of the Use of 'Made in' Labels," *International Marketing Review* 6 (1989): 47–58.
41. Philip Kotler and David Gertner, "Country as Brand, Product, and Beyond: A Place Marketing and Brand Management Perspective," *Journal of Brand Management* 9 (April 2002): 249–61.
42. Arnold Schuh, "Global Standardization as a Success Formula for Marketing in Central Eastern Europe," *Journal of World Business* 35 (Summer 2000): 133–48.
43. Ilkka A. Ronkainen, "Imitation as the Worst Kind of Flattery: Product Counterfeiting," *Trade Analyst* 2 (July–August 1986): 2.
44. Katherine Macklem, "Not what they seem: Knock-offs of brand-name goods aren't just cheap and popular. They're illegal," **http://www.macleans.ca/** (accessed November 8, 2006).
45. Wendy Leung, "Global trade in counterfeits includes B.C.," *The Vancouver Sun*, May 8, 2006, **http://www.canada.com/vancouversun/news/business/story.html?id=dc63e42f-13ab-4ae1-af87-3d5a859b6987&rfp=dta** (accessed November 8, 2006).
46. Ilkka A. Ronkainen and Jose-Luis Guerrero-Cusumano, "Correlates of Intellectual Property Violation," *Multinational Business Review* 9, no. 1 (2001): 59–65.
47. See **http://www.macleans.ca/topstories/business/article.jsp?content=20050620_107695_107695#** (accessed November 8, 2006).
48. "In Pursuit of Pokémon Pirates," *The Wall Street Journal*, November 8, 1999, B1, B4.
49. Canadian Anti-Counterfeiting Network website, **http://www.cacn.ca/.**
50. "Pfizer Introduces Radio Frequency Identification Technology to Combat Counterfeiting, Protect Patient Health," **http://www.pfizer.com/pfizer/are/investors_releases/2006pr/mn_2006_0106.jsp.**
51. Wendy Leung, "Global trade in counterfeits includes B.C." *The Vancouver Sun*, May 8, 2006, **http://www.canada.com/vancouversun/news/business/story.html?id=dc63e42f-13ab-4ae1-af87-3d5a859b6987&rfp=dta** (accessed November 8, 2006).
52. "Lubricating a Crackdown," *Export Today*, June 1999, 29.
53. Michael G. Harvey and Ilkka A. Ronkainen, "International Counterfeiters: Marketing Success without the Cost and the Risk," *Columbia Journal of World Business* 20 (Fall 1985): 37–45.
54. "The Zen of Nissan," *Business Week*, July 22, 2002, 18–20.
55. "Blade-runner," *The Economist*, April 10, 1993, 68.
56. Bill Saporito, "Behind the Tumult at P&G," *Fortune*, March 7, 1994, 74–82.
57. Edward Tse, "Competing in China: An Integrated Approach," *Strategy and Business* 3 (4th quarter, 1998): 45–52.
58. Ben Van Houten, "Foreign Interpreter," *Restaurant Business*, November 1, 1999, 32.
59. Eric von Hippel, *The Sources of Innovation* (Oxford: Oxford University Press, 1997), chap. 1.
60. Eric von Hippel, Stefan Thomke, and Mary Sonnack, "Creating Breakthroughs at 3M," *Harvard Business Review* 77 (September–October 1999): 47–57.
61. Eric von Hippel and Ralph Katz, "Shifting Innovation to Users via Toolkits," *Management Science* 48 (July 2002): 821–33.
62. Edward Tse, "The Right Way to Achieve Profitable Growth in the Chinese Market," *Strategy & Business* 3 (2nd quarter, 1998): 10–21.
63. A.C. Nielsen, "New-Product Introduction—Successful Innovation/Failure: Fragile Boundary," *A.C. Nielsen BASES*, June 24, 1999, 1; Robert G. Cooper and Elko J. Kleinschmidt, "New Product Processes at Leading Industrial Firms," *Industrial Marketing Management* 14 (May 1991): 137–47; and David S. Hopkins, "Survey Finds 67% of New Products Fail," *Marketing News*, February 8, 1986, 1.
64. Eric Berggren and Thomas Nacher, "Introducing New Products Can Be Hazardous to Your Company," *The Academy of Management Executive* 15 (August 2001): 92–101.
65. Laurel Wentz, "Mars Widens Its Line in U.K.," *Advertising Age*, May 16, 1988, 37.
66. Sources for this section include Veronica Wong, "Antecedents of International New Product Rollout Timeliness," *International Marketing Review* 19, no. 2 (2002): 120–32; Robert Michelet and Laura Elmore, "Launching Your Product Globally," *Export Today* 6 (September 1990): 13–15; and Laura Elmore and Robert Michelet, "The Global Product Launch," *Export Today* 6 (November–December 1990): 49–52.
67. "In the Labs, the Fight to Spend Less, Get More," *Business Week*, June 28, 1993, 102–4.
68. "For Best Results, Decentralize R&D," *Business Week*, June 28, 1993, 134.
69. Alphonso O. Ogbuehi and Ralph A. Bellas, Jr., "Decentralized R&D for Global Product Development: Strategic Implications for

the Multinational Corporation," *International Marketing Review* 9, no. 5 (1992): 60–70.

70. "Savi Launches Global R&D Center in Singapore," *Transportation & Distribution*, July 2002, 16.

71. Robert Ronstadt, "International R&D: The Establishment and Evolution of Research and Development Abroad by U.S. Multinationals," *Journal of International Business Studies* 9 (Spring–Summer 1978): 7–24.

72. Michelle Fellman, "Auto Researchers' Focus on Customers Can Help Drive Sales in Other Industries," *Marketing News*, January 4, 1999, 12.

73. "A Car Is Born," *Economist*, September 13, 1997, 68–69.

74. National Research Council Canada, *Innovation at Work for Canada* (January 2005).

75. National Research Council Canada, *NRC-IRAP Clients* (June 2002).

76. Rajesh Sethi, Daniel Smith, and C. Whan Park, "Cross-Functional Product Development Teams, Creativity, and the Innovativeness of New Consumer Products," *Journal of Marketing Research* 38 (February 2001): 73–85.

77. Julian Birkinshaw, "Managing Internal R&D Networks in Global Firms—What Sort of Knowledge Is Involved?" *Long Range Planning* 35 (June 2002): 245–67.

78. George S. Day, "Diagnosing the Product Portfolio," *Journal of Marketing* 41 (April 1977): 9–19.

79. Susan P. Douglas and C. Samuel Craig, "Global Portfolio Planning and Market Interconnectedness," *Journal of International Marketing* 4, no. 1 (1996): 93–110.

80. C. Samuel Craig and Susan P. Douglas, "Configural Advantage in Global Markets," *Journal of International Marketing* 8, no. 1 (2000): 6–26.

81. David C. Court, Mark G. Leiter, and Mark A. Loch, "Brand Leverage," *The McKinsey Quarterly* 35, no. 2 (1999): 100–110.

82. "Starbucks: Keeping the Brew Hot," *Business Week Online*, August 6, 2001.

83. David A. Aaker, Managing Brand Equity: Capitalizing on the Value of a Brand Name (New York: Free Press, 1995), 21–33.

84. John Gray, "What's in a Brand," *Canadian Business*, December 28–January 15, 2004, 73–74.

85. Bernd Schmitt and Alexander Simonson, *Marketing Aesthetics: The Strategic Management of Brands, Identity, and Image* (New York: Free Press, 1997), chap. 1.

86. David Aaker and Erich Joachimsthaler, "The Lure of Global Branding," *Harvard Business Review* 77 (November/December 1999): 137–44.

87. Colin Mitchell, "Selling the Brand Inside," *Harvard Business Review* 80 (January 2002): 99–105.

88. This section draws heavily on J. Johansson, *Global Marketing: Foreign Entry, Local Marketing and Global Management*, 3rd ed. (New York: McGraw-Hill Irwin, 2003).

89. "Unilever's Goal: Power Brands," *Advertising Age*, January 3, 2000, 1, 12; and "Why Unilever B-Brands Must Be Cast Aside," *Marketing*, June 10, 1999, 13.

90. Jean-Noël Kapferer, "Is There Really No Hope for Local Brands?" *Journal of Brand Management* 9 (January 2002): 163–70.

91. David Dunne and Chakravarthi Narasimhan, "The New Appeal of Private Labels," *Harvard Business Review* 77 (May–June 1999): 41–52; and John A. Quelch and David Harding, "Brands versus Private Labels," *Harvard Business Review* 74 (January–February 1996): 99–109.

92. Pankaj Ghemawat, "Distance Still Matters: The Hard Reality of Global Expansion," *Harvard Business Review* 79 (September 2001): 137–47.

Chapter

10

International Services Marketing

The Global MARKETPLACE 10.1

Cell Phones in Africa

The new frontiers in telecommunications are the wireless opportunities of sub-Saharan African countries such as Niger, Kenya, Zambia, and Botswana. The technological divide between this region and the industrialized world has long been a roadblock to development. However, the region is now the world's fastest-growing market for mobile phone services.

Wireless services are succeeding here in part due to the dismal lack of fixed-line telephone connections. The latter are more expensive and cumbersome to set up, and they are usually tied to governmental laws and bureaucratic restrictions. Meanwhile, small communities can share a cellular phone if they cannot afford more than one per village, gaining the same advantage in

AP Photo/Sayyid Azim

communication as with a fixed line, but with the added benefits of mobility.

The increased possibility of sharing has, in fact, expanded mobile subscribers from just the elite to a much wider public. Villages previously ignored by publicly owned fixed-line phone service companies are now participating in the communication boom. They are discovering that cellular phones—thought of as a rich man's toy when the towers were first built—are well suited to their needs.

The possession of wireless communication has become a tool of economic empowerment. The World Bank forecasts that up to one-quarter of sub-Saharan Africa's overall GDP growth can be attributed to growing telecommunications. Farmers have begun using mobile phones to increase their own economic efficiency. A reliable connection to faraway villages, available in sub-Saharan Africa for the first time, allows for a wider selection of potential buyers. Producers and consumers situated far from traditional trade routes can now find each other and carry out more lucrative transactions.

Being able to communicate with fellow countrymen far and wide has benefited the unemployed. The ability to enter the job market rises significantly with the ability to transmit information outside of one's usual social circle. Also, a comparison of worker qualifications and employer offers is made more easily over a mobile phone than by long-distance travel of employer and employee. A wider selection of people and places with whom to connect is, therefore, the greatest appeal of wireless communication in this vast and often scarcely populated area.

Sources: Andy Reinhardt, "Africa: The Next Wide-Open Wireless Frontier," *Business Week Online*, February 2, 2004; Federal Information & News Dispatch, "Wireless Technology Helping Shrink Digital Divide," Voice of America Press Releases and Documents, May 6, 2005.

International services marketing is a major component of world business. As The Global Marketplace 10.1 shows, services themselves can be crucial globally. This chapter will highlight marketing dimensions that are specific to services, with particular attention given to their international features. A discussion of the differences between the marketing of services and of goods will be offered at the outset. Although some readers will be familiar with this material, it is felt that a review might be helpful. This is followed by insights into the role of services in the Canadian and world economy. International trade in services has not been problem-free, and the chapter looks at some regulatory and strategic problems that suppliers have had to face and are still facing. Countering this trend has been the impact of the Internet on international services marketing, which is opening new horizons, although as noted in the chapter, a degree of caution is still needed. Finally, the chapter outlines some problems facing companies developing services marketing programs, then reviews international strategic marketing issues from the viewpoint of marketing mix optimization.

Differences between Services and Goods

We rarely contemplate or analyze the precise role of services in our lives. Services often accompany goods, but they are also, by themselves, an increasingly important part of our economy, domestically and internationally. One writer has contrasted services and products by stating that "a good is an object, a device, a thing; a service is a deed, a performance, an effort."[1] This definition, although quite general, captures the essence of the difference between goods and services. Services tend to be more intangible, personalized, and custom-made than goods. Services are also often marketed differently from goods. While goods are typically distributed to the customer, services can be transferred across borders or originated abroad, and the service provider can be transferred to the customer or the customer can be transferred to the service territory. Services also typically use a different approach to customer satisfaction. It has been stated that "service firms do not have products in the form of preproduced solutions to customers' problems; they have processes as solutions to such problems."[2]

Services are the fastest-growing sector of world trade, far outpacing the growth in the trade of goods (see Exhibit 10.1). These major differences add dimensions to services that are not present in goods and thus call for a major differentiation.

Exhibit 10.1 Services as a Portion of Gross Domestic Product

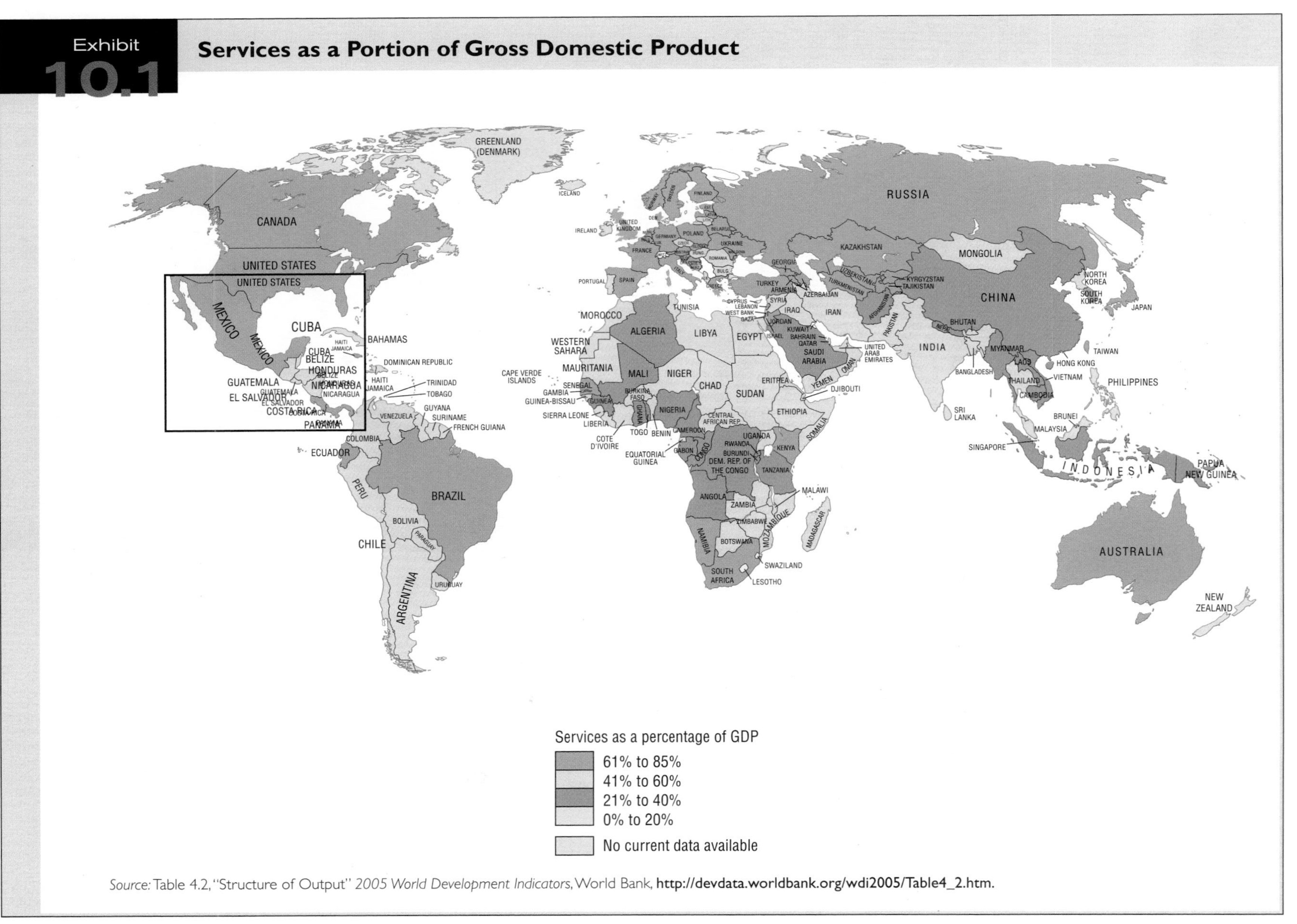

Source: Table 4.2, "Structure of Output" *2005 World Development Indicators*, World Bank, **http://devdata.worldbank.org/wdi2005/Table4_2.htm.**

Linkage between Services and Goods

Services may complement goods; at other times, goods may complement services. Offering goods that are in need of substantial technological support and maintenance may be useless if no proper assurance for service can be provided. For this reason, the initial contract of sale often includes important service dimensions.

This linkage between goods and services can make international marketing efforts quite difficult. A foreign buyer, for example, may wish to purchase helicopters and contract for service support over a period of 10 years. If the sale involves a Canadian firm, both the helicopter and the service sale will require an export license. Such licenses, however, are issued only for an immediate sale. Therefore, over the 10 years, the seller will have to apply for an export license each time service is to be provided. Because the issuance of a license is often dependent on the political climate, the buyer and seller are haunted by uncertainty. As a result, sales may be lost to firms in countries that can unconditionally guarantee the long-term supply of support services.

Services can be just as dependent on goods. For example, an airline that prides itself on providing an efficient reservation system and excellent linkups with rental cars and hotel reservations could not survive without its airplanes. As a result, many offerings in the marketplace consist of a combination of goods and services. A graphic illustration of the tangible and intangible elements in the market offering of an airline is provided in Exhibit 10.2.

The simple knowledge that services and goods interact, however, is not enough. Successful managers must recognize that different customer groups will frequently view the service/goods combination differently. The type of use and usage conditions will also affect evaluations of the market offering. For example, the intangible dimension of "on-time arrival" by airlines may be valued differently by college students than by business

Exhibit 10.2 **Tangible and Intangible Offerings of Airlines**

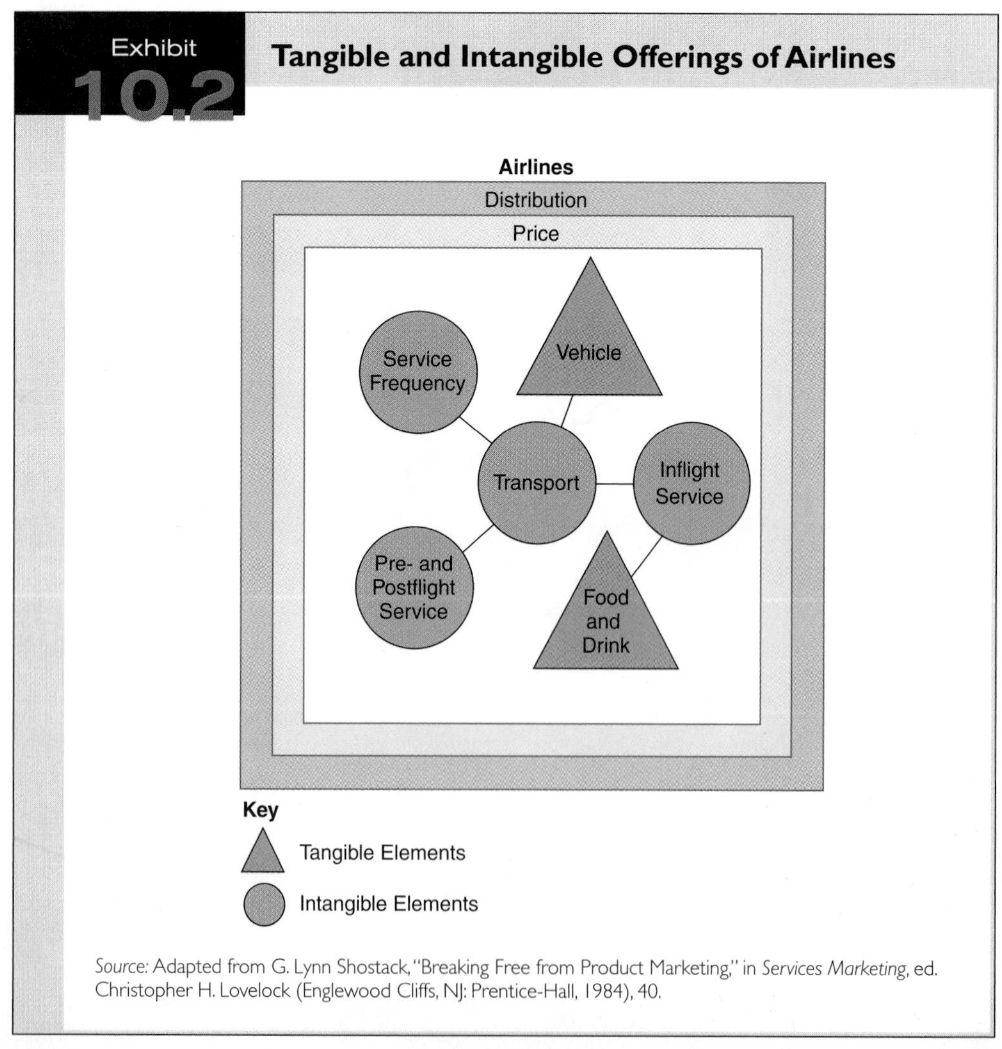

Source: Adapted from G. Lynn Shostack, "Breaking Free from Product Marketing," in *Services Marketing*, ed. Christopher H. Lovelock (Englewood Cliffs, NJ: Prentice-Hall, 1984), 40.

executives. Similarly, a 20-minute delay will be judged differently by a passenger arriving at her final destination than by one who has just missed an overseas connection. As a result, adjustment possibilities in both the service and the goods area can be used as strategic tools to stimulate demand and increase profitability. For different offerings, service and goods elements may vary substantially. The marketer must identify the role of each and adjust all of them to meet the desires of the target customer group.

Stand-Alone Services

Services do not always come in unison with goods. Increasingly, they compete against goods and become an alternative offering. For example, rather than buy an in-house computer, the business executive can contract computing work to a local or foreign service firm. Similarly, the purchase of a car (a good) can be converted into the purchase of a service by leasing the car from an agency.

Services may also compete against each other. As an example, a store may have the option of offering full service to consumers who purchase there or of converting to the self-service format. With automated checkout services, consumers may self-serve all activities such as selection, transportation, packaging, and pricing.

Services differ from goods most strongly in their **intangibility**: they are frequently consumed rather than possessed. Even though the intangibility of services is a primary differentiating criterion, it is not always present. Another major difference concerns the storing of services. Because of their nature, services are difficult to inventory. If they are not used, the "brown around the edges" syndrome tends to result in high services **perishability**. Unused capacity in the form of an empty seat on an airplane, for example, becomes non-saleable quickly. Similarly, the difficulty of keeping services in inventory makes it troublesome to provide service backup for peak demand. To maintain **service capacity** constantly at levels necessary to satisfy peak demand would be very expensive. The marketer must therefore attempt to smooth out demand levels through price or promotion activities in order to optimize the use of capacity.

For many service offerings, the time of production is very close to or even simultaneous with the time of consumption. This fact points toward close **customer involvement** in the production of services. Customers frequently either perform their own service or cooperate in the delivery of services. As a result, the service provider often needs to be physically present when the service is delivered. For example, close interaction with the customer requires a much greater understanding of and emphasis on the cultural dimension. A good service delivered in a culturally unacceptable fashion is doomed to failure. Sensitivity to culture, beliefs, and preferences is imperative in the services industry. In some instances, the need to be sensitive to diverse customer groups in domestic markets can assist a company greatly in preparing for international market expansion. A common pattern of internationalization for service businesses is therefore to develop stand-alone business systems in each country.

The close interaction with customers also points toward the fact that services often are custom-made. This raises an associated problem in that, in order to fulfill customer expectations, **service consistency** is required. In the case of services offered online, however, consistency is difficult to maintain over the long run. The human element in the service offering therefore takes on a much greater role than in the offering of goods, and errors can enter the system. However, efforts to increase quality control through uniformity may sometimes be seen by customers as a reduction in service choices.

Buyers have more problems in observing and evaluating services than goods. Even when sellers of services are willing and able to provide more **market transparency**, where the details of the service are clear, comparable, and available to all interested parties, the buyer's problem is complicated: customers receiving the same service may use it differently, and service quality may vary for each delivery. Since production lines cannot be established to deliver an identical service each time, and the quality of a service cannot be tightly controlled, the problem of service heterogeneity emerges,[3] meaning that services may never be the same from one delivery to another.

Services often require entirely new forms of distribution. Traditional channels are often multi-tiered and long—and therefore slow. They often cannot be used because of the perishability of services. As a result, direct delivery and short distribution channels are

Exhibit 10.3 Some Possible Differences between Services and Goods

Service Attributes	Goods Attributes
• tend to be intangible	• tend to be tangible
• re-selling is unusual	• can be re-sold
• most cannot be stored	• can be stored and inventoried
• quality usually hard to measure	• most aspects of quality measurable
• high consumer interaction	• sold at distance from production
• difficult to transport	• can be transported
• site important for customer contact	• site of production less important to user
• difficult to automate	• production can be automated
• customer is part of process	• customer not part of production process
• response time is shorter; markets often local	• longer response time due to separation of production and sales

often required. When they do not exist, which is often the case internationally, service providers need to be distribution innovators in order to reach their market.

All these aspects of services exist in both international and domestic settings. Their impact, however, takes on greater importance for the international marketer. For example, because of the longer distances involved, service perishability that may be an obstacle in domestic business becomes a barrier internationally. Similarly, the issue of quality control for global services may be much more difficult to deal with due to different service uses, changing expectations, and varying national regulations. For a summary of some key differences between goods and services, see Exhibit 10.3.

Because they are delivered directly to the user, services are frequently much more sensitive to cultural factors than are products. National leaders who place strong emphasis on national cultural identity frequently denounce foreign services and attempt to hinder their market penetration. Even some dimensions that appear to be highly standardized around the globe may need to be adapted. For an example, see Exhibit 10.4. As can be seen, many nations have developed their own unique interpretations of the well-known symbol "@." Similarly, services are subject to many political vagaries occurring almost daily. Yet coping with these changes can become the service provider's competitive advantage.

The Role of Services in the Canadian Economy

The past decades have seen a broad structural shift toward services in the Canadian economy. Services have increased from just over half of Canada's gross domestic product in 1961 to approximately two-thirds today.[4] The percentage of Canadian workers employed in services is also increasing, employing about three out of four (compared with just over half in 1961), and between 1992 and 2002, services created about 80 percent of all new jobs. It is clear that it is less and less realistic to characterize Canada's economy as mainly a resource-based or a goods-producing one.

Canada's trade in services continues to grow more rapidly than its goods trade and significantly faster than the rate of growth of the economy.[5] As Exhibit 10.5 shows, the service sector has consistently represented more than 45 percent of the economy's GDP. Refer now to Exhibit 10.6, which shows recent statistics. This indicates that in a context of increasing GDP growth for all sectors of the economy between 2000 and 2005, the service sector (apart from construction) had the highest average annual growth rate (3.04 percent) in GDP terms. This is slightly larger than the growth rate for the whole economy. In terms of employment, the service sector had a growth rate higher than the industrial average and representing 78 percent of total employment in 2005.

Canada's experience is not unique: the growth of service industries is a worldwide phenomenon.[6] As Exhibit 10.7 shows, total world trade amounted to US$6.6 trillion in 1998, of

Exhibit 10.4 Symbolism

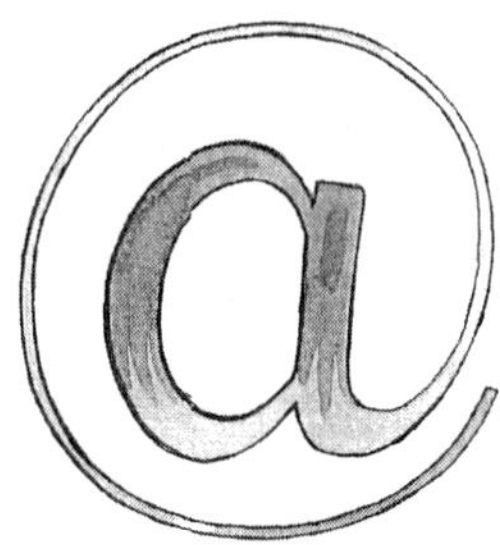

What do people around the world call the "@" symbol, so prevalent in e-mail addresses? While in the United States most people say "at," in other countries it's referred to by different, and often humorous, names associated with what the @ reminds speakers of.

DOG

In Russia, the most common word for @ is *sobaka* or *sobachka,* meaning "dog" and "little doggie," respectively.

MONKEY

In countries such as Bulgaria, Poland, and Serbia, the @ symbol seems to remind speakers of a monkey with a long tail. They refer to it as *alpa* (Polish), *majmunkso* (Bulgarian), and *majmun* (Serbian). Another variation is "ape's tail," said as *aapstert* in Afrikaans, *apestaart* in Dutch, and *apsvans* in Swedish.

SNAIL

While traditional stamp and envelope mail is often referred to as "snail mail," many speakers insert a snail into their e-mail addresses. In Korea, @ is known as *dalphaengi* and in Italian it's *chiocciola* (both literally meaning "snail").

CAT

When Poles aren't referring to @ as a monkey, they know it as a curled up kitten *(kotek).* Similarly, Finns use the phrase *miuku mauku.*

FISH

A quite creative name for the @ is *zavinac,* or "rolled-up pickled herring," in Slovakia and the Czech Republic.

ELEPHANT

In Denmark, you would refer to @ as *snabel,* or elephant's trunk.

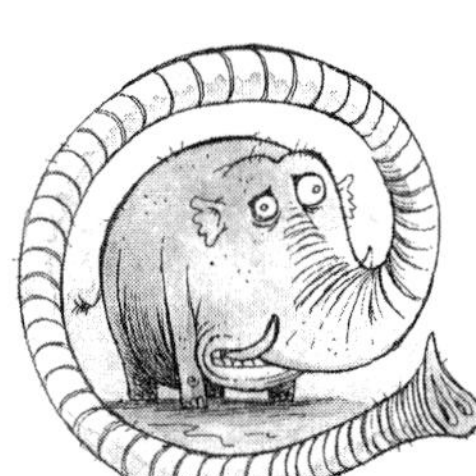

MOUSE

In China, the word "mouse" used in reference to a computer means more than that object you click and point with. *Xiao lao shu* ("little mouse") is also used for the symbol @.

WORM

In Hungary, the mental image of a *kukac* (literally "worm") is associated with @.

Source: Adapted from Szokan, Nancy, "Where It's At—and Where It's Not," *The Washington Post,* October 2, 2005, p. B2. © 2005, The Washington Post, reprinted with permission. *IMAGE SOURCE: © David Clark.*

Exhibit 10.5 GDP Trend for All Sectors of the Economy, 1985–2005

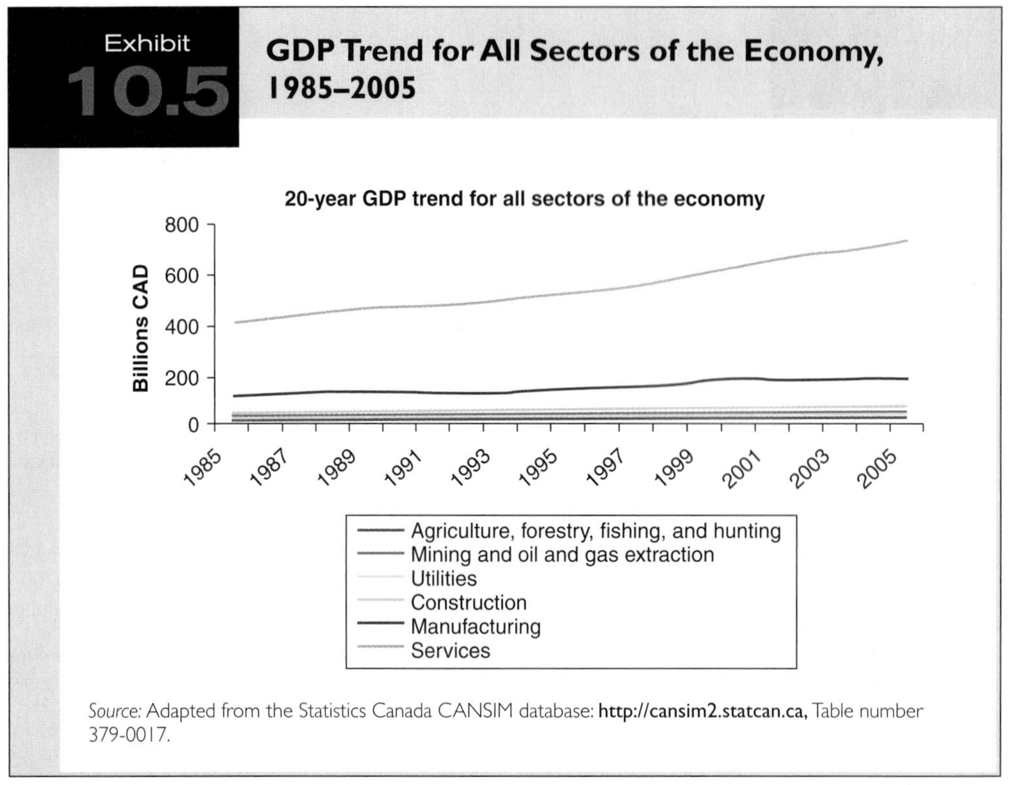

Source: Adapted from the Statistics Canada CANSIM database: **http://cansim2.statcan.ca,** Table number 379-0017.

Exhibit 10.6 GDP Trend for All Sectors of the Economy, 2000–2005

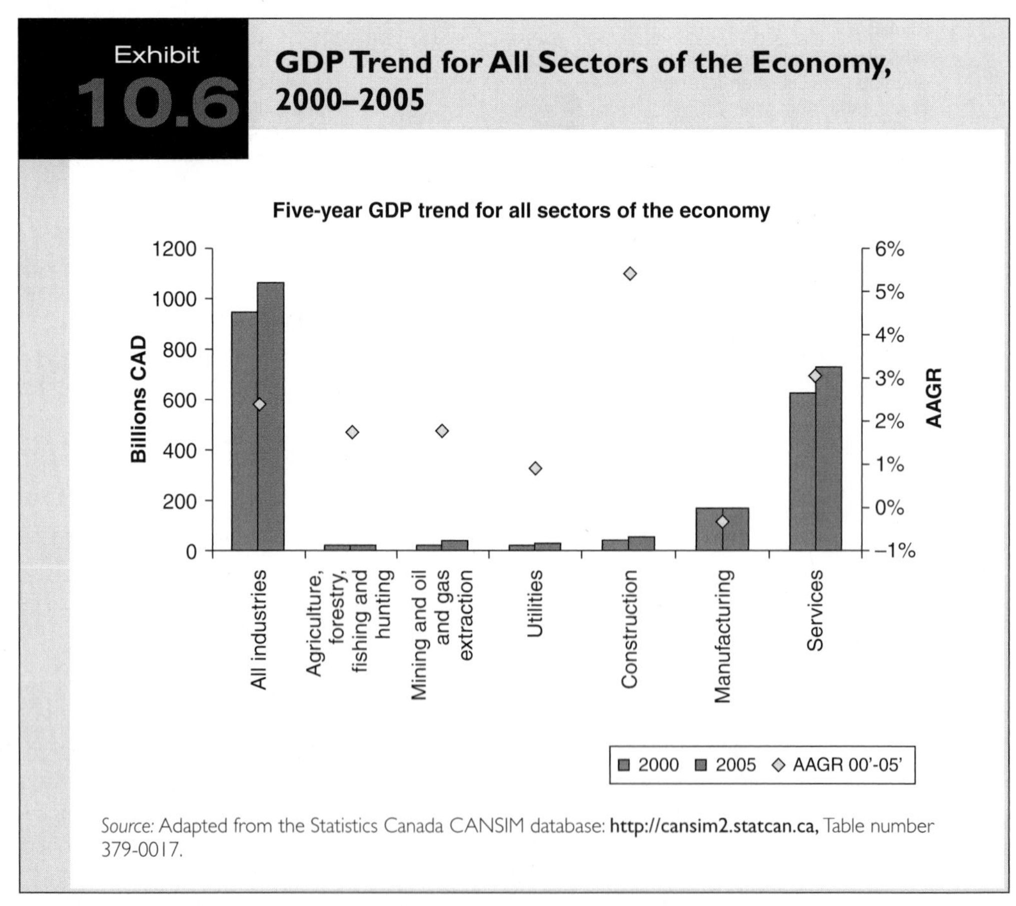

Source: Adapted from the Statistics Canada CANSIM database: **http://cansim2.statcan.ca,** Table number 379-0017.

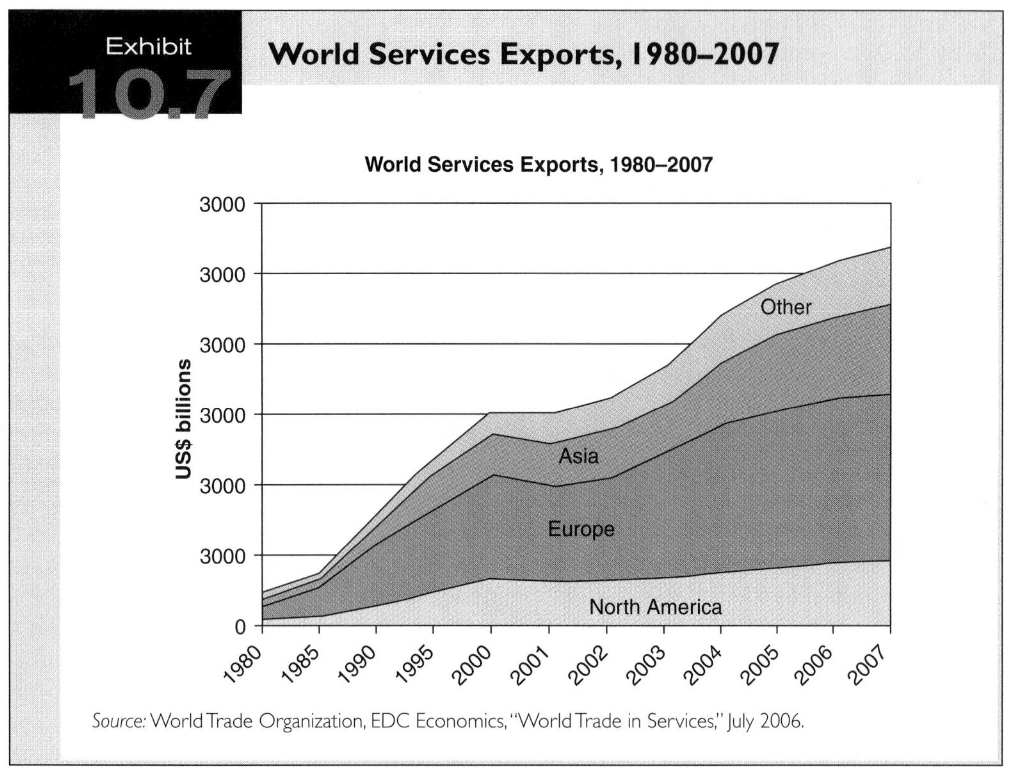

Exhibit 10.7 World Services Exports, 1980–2007

Source: World Trade Organization, EDC Economics, "World Trade in Services," July 2006.

which services accounted for US$1.3 trillion (19 percent of total trade). Between 1990 and 1997, world services exports grew at an annual rate of 8 percent while goods exports grew at 7 percent. This growth continued through 2007, with the percentage shares of North America, Europe, and Asia also expanding. The service sector, especially knowledge-based industries connected with information technology and telecommunications, is the fastest growing segment of the Canadian economy. Moreover, this country, together with its WTO partners, is negotiating the further liberalization of trade in services. This fact, together with continuing advances in IT technologies, means that the prospects for even more rapid growth in services trade by Canada are extremely positive.

The U.S. remains Canada's principal trading partner in services, accounting for 59.2 of this country's total services exports in 2001, compared with 85 percent of goods exports.[7] However, Canada's service exports are less dependent on the U.S. market than in the case of goods, and this country's fastest-growing markets are elsewhere. Between 1992 and 2000, for example, commercial services exports to Brazil grew by 38.3 percent annually; to Chile by 17.6 percent; to China by 14 percent, and to the U.S. by 13 percent.

Statistics Canada recognizes four broad categories of services:[8]

1. Commercial services, including management services, research and development, communications, architectural and engineering services, and miscellaneous business and communications services
2. Travel, including business and personal travel
3. Transportation, including transportation of persons and goods (freight)
4. Government services of various kinds

Of the above, commercial services exports are the most important and fastest-growing sector, creating high-paying jobs in knowledge-intensive industries such as R & D and financial services. In 2001, commercial services accounted for 49.4 percent of service exports and 49.2 percent of imports—the largest share of Canada's service trade. Exports of commercial services have grown by 8.9 percent since 1995 to total $35.1 billion in 2005. For a detailed breakdown of the elements of Canada's trade in commercial services, see Exhibit 10.8.

Note that, historically, Canada has operated a deficit in service trade. This is accounted for by foreign-controlled firms, notably U.S. ones, importing commercial services from affiliates or parent companies. A deficit trend was apparent from 1980 to 1993, but since that time the trade balance has been steadily improving.

The productivity and competitiveness of the Canadian service sector is being enhanced by investments in capital equipment.[9] In 1999, services accounted for 53 percent of investments in fixed capital (construction accounted for only 2 percent). There has been a notable increase in recent years as service firms have substantially increased their use of IT and communications technology. Most of this service investment is in machinery and equipment related to computers, communications, and office equipment.

These developments have resulted in numerous international service "success stories" that have been compiled and reported by Foreign Affairs and International Trade Canada.[10] For example, EVS Environment Consultants (North Vancouver, British Columbia) has been involved in more than 2,500 projects through North America, Australia, South America, and Asia, providing a wide-range of field sampling and data collection support activities. Another example is Matrikan Inc. (Edmonton, Alberta), an engineering and consulting firm that has developed a wide range of Web-based products and services that help clients turn massive volumes of data into usable information and knowledge. Matrikan's clients can be found in a variety of industries (oil and gas, cement, pharmaceuticals, and various others) and regions around the world (the U.S., Japan, the U.K., the Middle East, and Costa Rica, for example). Many successful Canadian companies also benefit from the extensive support of organizations such as Export Development Canada (EDC), which provide a wide range of financial services. (See Exhibit 10.9 for a recent EDC advertisement.)

Exhibit 10.8

Canada's Trade in Commercial Services, 1990–2005

	Exports ($million)			Imports ($million)		
	1990	2005	Annual Growth (%)	1990	2005	Annual Growth (%)
Commercial services total	9,061	35,115	9.5	12,554	37,946	7.7
Communications	1,220	2,655	5.3	1,210	2,062	3.6
Construction	52	167	8.1	35	134	9.4
Insurance	1,957	3,716	4.4	2,238	5,759	6.5
Other financial	490	2,131	10.3	733	2,724	9.1
Computer and information	546	4,141	14.5	344	2,542	14.3
Royalty and license fees	173	4,206	23.7	1,941	8,046	9.9
Non-financial commissions	306	906	7.5	341	651	4.4
Equipment rentals	197	282	2.4	308	788	6.5
Management	849	4,855	12.3	1,419	4,692	8.3
Advertising	124	449	9.0	211	666	8.0
Research and development	700	2,910	10.0	483	1,105	5.7
Architectural, etc.	549	4,077	14.3	439	2,531	12.4
Miscellaneous business	1,392	2,614	4.3	2,018	3,887	4.5
Audio-visual	348	1,768	11.4	709	2,146	7.7
Personal, etc.	157	240	2.9	123	211	3.7

Source: Adapted from the Statistics Canada publication "Canada's International Trade in Services", Catalogue 67-203-XWE Released March 24, 2006 **http://www.statcan.ca/english/freepub/67-203-XIE/0000467-203-XIE.htm.**

Exhibit 10.9

Canada's EDC Promotes Its Wide Range of Insurance and Financial Services to Help Exporters

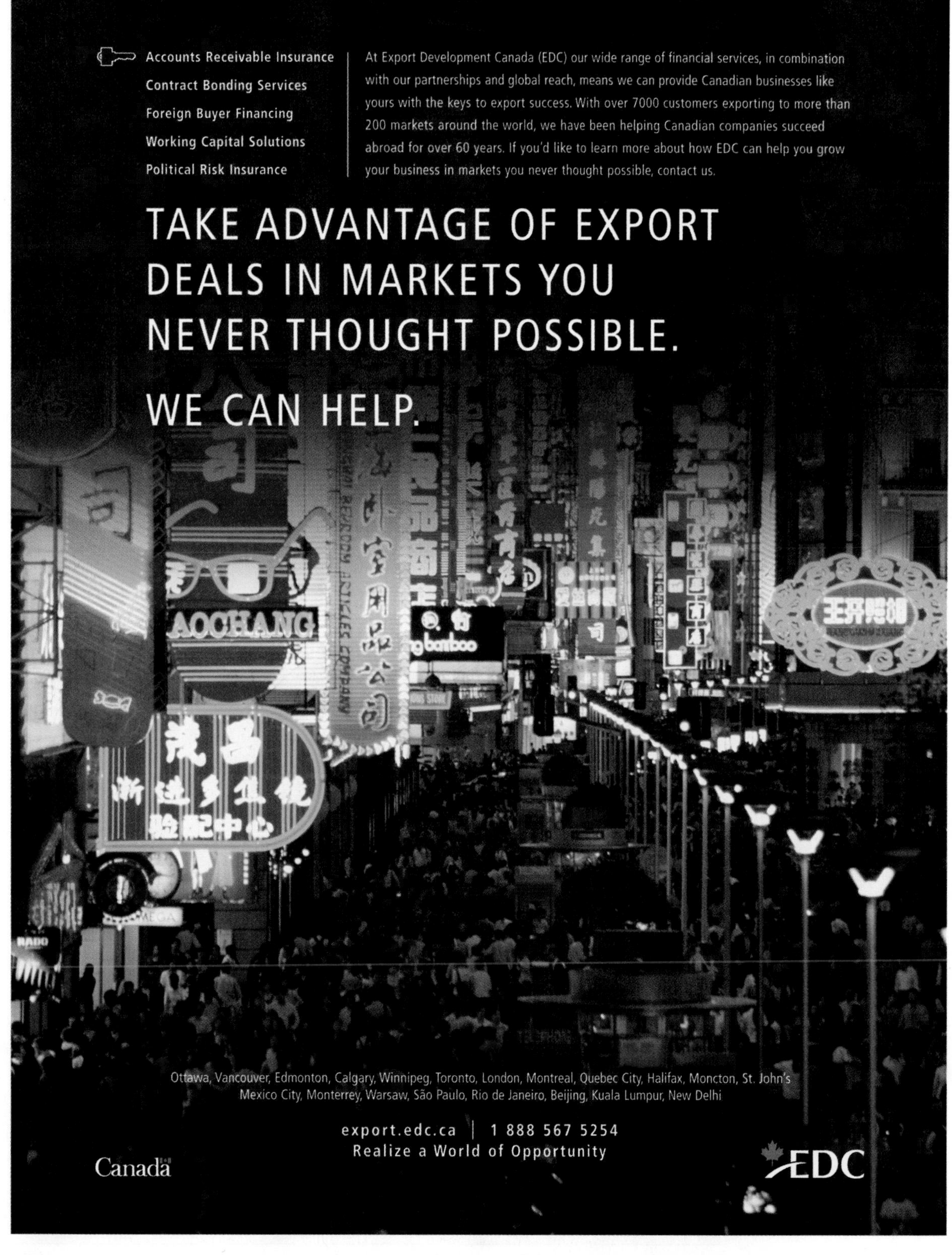

Source: © 2006 Export Development Canada: **www.edc.ca.**

This review of the Canadian service sector has been deliberately upbeat. There can be no gainsaying that companies are thoroughly competitive internationally and have made the necessary investments and technological advancements to stay at the forefront of world developments. Yet it is entirely possible that Canadian trade in services is actually being underestimated.[11] This is partly because of complexity in measurement and the growing problems of tracking this trade in the context of rapid technological advances, but it is also partly because the current product classification system for service industries is lacking. Statistics Canada points out that it continues to make progress in developing appropriate statistics, but difficult challenges still have to be faced.[12]

The Role of Services in the Global Economy

The rise of the service sector, as we noted above, is a global phenomenon. Services contribute an average of more than 60 percent to the gross national product of industrial nations. Services are also rapidly moving to the forefront in many other nations as well, accounting for 66 percent of GDP in Argentina, 69 percent in Mexico, 66 percent in South Africa, and about 50 percent in Thailand.[13] Even in the least developed countries, services typically contribute at least 45 percent of GDP. With growth rates higher than other sectors such as agriculture and manufacturing, services are instrumental in job creation in these countries.[14] Exhibit 10.10 shows the importance of the service sector across the world. Within these countries, the names of such firms as American

Exhibit 10.10 Services across the World

Country	Services as Percentage of GDP	Percentage of Workforce in Services
United States	78.3%	83%
Canada	68.7	74
Brazil	50.6	66
Australia	69.6	70
Japan	73.5	70
Kenya	65.1	n/a
European Union	70.1	66.9
Austria	66.3	67
Belgium	74	74.2
Denmark	73.8	79
Finland	66.5	70
France	76.1	71.5
Germany	70.3	63.8
Greece	71.7	68
Ireland	49	63
Italy	69.1	63
Luxembourg	83.1	86
The Netherlands	73.5	73
Portugal	65.9	60
Spain	67.9	64.4
Sweden	69.7	74
United Kingdom	72.9	79.5

Source: The World Factbook 2005, **https://www.cia.gov** (accessed January 26, 2006).

Express, McDonald's, Club Med, Thomas Cook, Mitsubishi, and Hilton have become widely familiar.

Global Trade Problems in Services

We discussed the role of trade barriers in Chapter 2, so the reader will already be familiar with the broad nature of such obstacles. The service sector must also cope with these barriers. Together with the increasing importance of service marketing, trade impediments present new problems for the service sector. Even though many of these problems have been characterized as affecting mainly the negotiations between nations, they are of sufficient importance to the firm in its global activities to merit a brief additional review.

Regulation of Services Trade

Typical obstacles to services trade can be categorized into two major types: barriers to entry and problems in performing services. Governments often justify **barriers to entry** by referring to **national security** and economic security. For example, the impact of banking on domestic economic activity is given as a reason why banking should be carried out only by nationals or indeed be operated entirely under government control. Sometimes, the protection of service users is cited, particularly that of bank depositors and insurance policyholders. Some countries claim that competition in societally important services is unnecessary, wasteful, and should be avoided. Another justification for barriers is the frequently used **infant industry** argument: "With sufficient time to develop on our own, we can compete in world markets." Often, however, this argument is used simply to prolong the ample licensing profits generated by restricted entry. Impediments to services consist of either tariff or non-tariff barriers. Tariff barriers typically restrict or inhibit market entry for the service provider or consumer, while non-tariff barriers tend to impede service performance. Yet, defining a barrier to service marketing is not always easy. For example, Germany gives an extensive written examination to prospective accountants (as do most countries) to ensure that licensed accountants are qualified to practice. Naturally, the examination is given in German. The fact that few Canadian accountants read and write German does not necessarily constitute a barrier to trade in accountancy services.

Even if barriers to entry are nonexistent or can be overcome, service companies often have difficulty in performing effectively abroad once they have achieved access to the local market. One reason is that rules and regulations based on tradition may inhibit innovation. A more important reason is that governments aim to pursue social or cultural objectives through national regulations. Of primary importance here is the distinction between **discriminatory regulations** and **non-discriminatory regulations**. Regulations that impose larger operating costs on foreign service providers than on the local competitors, that provide subsidies to local firms only, or that deny competitive opportunities to foreign suppliers are a proper cause for international concern. The discrimination problem becomes even more acute when foreign firms face competition from government-owned or government-controlled enterprises, examples of which can still be found in various countries despite privatization and trends toward free trade. On the other hand, non-discriminatory regulations may be inconvenient and may hamper business operations, but they offer less opportunity for international criticism.

Regulations make it difficult for the international service marketer to penetrate world markets. At the governmental level, services frequently are not recognized as a major facet of world trade or are viewed with suspicion because of a lack of understanding, and barriers to entry often result. To make progress in tearing them down, much educational work needs to be done. However, advances are visible. The Council for Trade in Services met in early 2000 to start negotiations on services. In November 2001, the Doha Ministerial Conference set January 1, 2005, as the deadline for the conclusion of the negotiations. However, since this date, the Doha round has run into difficulties, and hope for resolutions have had to be put on hold.

Global Strategic Challenges in Services

Strategic challenges for international service providers also arise from ongoing changes in the global economy and various peculiarities associated with international services marketing. The latter includes peculiarities in the nature of the service product, peculiarities in the demand for these services, and the intense competitive environment. These are discussed below.

Country of Origin Effects

One such consideration is the impact of country-of-origin influences, discussed in the last chapter. Much has been said about these effects on consumers' perceptions of goods from different countries, and a positive influence on product evaluation has been noted in different studies.[15] But the question is, does the country of origin (COO) have an impact on the consumption of international services? One authority answers in the affirmative and offers evidence from the point of view of, inter alia, core services (e.g., travel services) and supplementary services (e.g., warranties).[16]

Regarding core services, which are the main outputs of the service firm that buyers look for, "consumers tend to prefer core services from their own country, from countries with a similar culture to their own, and from economically progressive countries."[17] Therefore there appears to be little difference in search criteria between consumers of tangible goods and consumers of core services as far as COO is concerned.

Regarding supplementary services, that is, services offered along with the sale of products, these can be extremely important to the firm in establishing a competitive advantage. Core services are usually provided with a range of supplementary items that add value, provide a differentiation niche, and offer opportunities to devise international strategies.[18] Examples from the industrial products field include assistance with product installation, provision of operator training, pre- and post-sales services, spare parts, and troubleshooting services. There are grounds for believing that many consumers hold negative images of products from countries that are economically less progressive; therefore, supplementary services play a key role in reassuring buyers.[19] Also, supplementary services take on greater significance when products are perceived to be more complex and technologically sophisticated.

Consumer Ethnocentric Tendencies

Apart from the COO effects, there is growing recognition that evaluations of goods and services can be influenced by what has been described as **consumer ethnocentrism** or **consumer patriotism**, that is, when consumers prefer domestic goods because of strong nationalistic feelings.[20] For example, one researcher examined Canadian national loyalty and the country of air carrier in the selection process and found that Canadian consumers displayed high national loyalty, preferring a national carrier for an international flight where other foreign carriers are in direct competition with the national carriers.[21]

Unfortunately, studies of this sort are thin on the ground, though two more may be cited briefly, supporting the view that consumer ethnocentric tendencies affect consumer evaluation of foreign services. In one investigation of professional services providers in the health care industry, the perceived nationality of the health care provider emerged as being more important to consumers than the extra services offered by the provider.[22] Another study of various services found a correlation between Dutch consumer ethnocentric tendencies toward services and patriotism.[23] However, as globalization proceeds, it is likely that countries will become increasingly open to foreign cultures and will probably be less ethnocentric toward services. As Canadian service providers extend their global reach, care must be taken to assess the balance of influences at work, from whatever direction.

Cross-Cultural Incongruence

Different cultures have varying impacts on the marketing of services internationally. Cultural elements such as religious beliefs, language, and education have a significant impact on the acceptability and adoption patterns of services. Since any relationship between the service provider and the customer typically involves a degree of social interaction, Hofstede's dimensions (see Chapter 3) appear relevant to any study of relationships in service settings across cultures.[24] A growing challenge for international service firms is the development of trusting relationships with customers, especially for those firms whose offerings directly involve customer contact. A lack of knowledge of even the simplest and most obvious gestures or body language (e.g., eye contact) may produce undesirable results. As one authority states, "difficulties in marketing services internationally are due largely to close cultural relationships between a society and the services offered in that society."[25] This raises the question of the need for competence in cross-cultural business interactions, a topic that is taken up in more detail in Chapter 16.

International Delivery of Information Content

A country different in cultural, technological, governmental, and other dimensions may call for the use of different services for the delivery of information content. Field research work shows a strong association between information content and social/cultural values.[26] For example, in high-context cultures such as India and China, consumers prefer image-based or symbolic appeals that express the positive consequences of a particular purchase. On the other hand, people in individualistic cultures such as Canada tend to depend on specific facts to assist them in their decision-making. Whatever the nature and strength of a country's cultural and other differences, a good-quality service that is delivered, perhaps electronically, without attention to culturally sensitive issues will fail. (Exhibit 10.11 portrays Visa as promoting cultural harmony through its electronic communications.)

The Competitive Context

We have already noted the growth of service industries on a global scale. It is worth emphasizing that worldwide trade in services grew faster than trade in merchandise during the 1990s. Total world trade in services is forecast to reach $2.7 trillion in 2007.[27] Competition is intensified in part because service growth is not restricted to Canada and other industrialized nations. In fact, international trade in services is relatively more important to some other nations (e.g., The Netherlands and Austria), and emerging Asian economies such as those of South Korea and Hong Kong have in the last decade experienced faster growth in service exports than in goods.[28] In short, service-sector growth can be clearly witnessed in all developed and developing economies. Services are the fastest-growing segment of world trade and investment, including developing countries, a situation that is creating unprecedented opportunities for providers but also a severely competitive landscape.

Drivers of Global Services Growth

In what has now become a virtually borderless world, the following areas can be cited as the key driving forces underlying the importance and growth of global services:[29]

- The establishment of the World Trade Organization (WTO) and its focus on internationalizing services have created more opportunities to deploy a broad range of services across the globe.
- Several protective measures in such areas as intellectual property rights, copyrights, patents, trademarks, and so on have boosted the confidence of marketers in taking their product service offerings international.
- Governments' changing attitudes toward trade and foreign direct investment have facilitated the growth and significance of the service sector in both developed and developing/transition economies.
- Regional economic blocs such as NAFTA and the EU are creating bigger markets and thus more opportunities for goods and services.
- Advancements in computer and information technologies and transportation are making it easier, faster, and more economical to move data, people, service products, and so on across national borders.

Exhibit 10.11 Visa's Card Is Presented as Forging Cultural Harmony

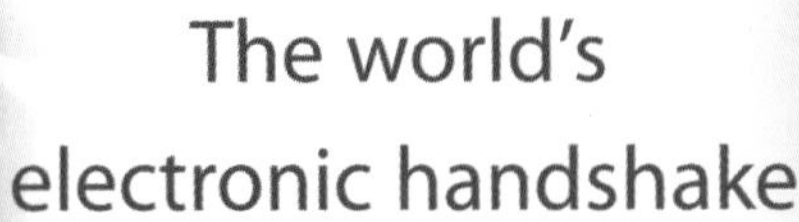

A visitor from Shanghai planning a trip to the Olympic Winter Games can deal with a hotel owner in Vancouver with confidence through Visa.
There's more to Visa than just a piece of plastic. We help tourism flourish, which plays an important role in strengthening Canada's economy.
Everyday in all kinds of situations, Visa creates trust between 100 million strangers.
VISA
visa.ca
Trademark of Visa International; Visa Canada is a licensed user.

Source: This advertisement has been reprinted with the permission of Visa Canada ("Visa"). Any other use of this material is expressly prohibited without prior permission from Visa. Visa® is a registered trademark of Visa International; Visa Canada is a licensed user.

- Changing consumer lifestyle demographics (increasing affluence, more leisure time, better education, more women in the workforce) across national economies are creating more demand for services, ranging from the most complex (e.g., technology intensive) to the most basic (e.g., cleaning).

However, some of these influences will also have an impact on global trade in physical goods. It is therefore instructive to ask what special features of services in general will tend to accentuate their competitive difficulties. There are several reasons for these particular problems, and these cannot be expected to diminish in the international environment:[30]

- *Low entry barriers.* Service inventions cannot be patented; innovations are easily copied. In addition, for a competitor to enter the market the capital intensity and investment necessary may be relatively low. However, some barriers do exist, such as the use of specialized equipment by suppliers (e.g., to place an order, a customer might use a specialized computer terminal that is provided by the supplier) or the existence of strong customer loyalty to local providers.
- *Opportunities for economies of scale.* Because most services are produced and consumed simultaneously and either the service or the customer must travel to consumption points, economies of scale are often low. The opportunities for large batches or runs of services that can be stored as inventory are minimal. In addition, the necessity for physical travel will often limit the outlet size of the service provider.
- *Erratic demand levels.* Service levels are often a function of the time of day or day of the week—although there are also random and seasonal elements.
- *Size and power disadvantages.* Many service suppliers are small-scale operations (though one must recognize large-scale players such as large financial institutions and hotel chains). The SME service supplier, however, is often at a disadvantage when dealing with supply-system partners (customers or suppliers) that are much larger in size and more dominant in the market.
- *Product and service combination substitution.* Those offerings that tend to emphasize a higher service content can often be quickly and easily substituted using new innovations and creative developments. For example, many similar service providers often exist, and a visit to a particular banking outlet with long lines and waiting times can easily be substituted by accessing another outlet. In the case of medical equipment, some medical checks can now be performed at home using self-diagnostic techniques that were once only available at the medical practitioner.
- *Exit barriers.* SME service providers will often have the flexibility and agility to move into similar markets or different ones altogether because of low capital investment (and financial exposure) and the drive and enthusiasm of the owners or managers of the firms concerned. This will work toward increasing the overall level of competitiveness in a given market.

For any service industry, the trade problems and strategic challenges we have discussed have to be considered when formulating a marketing strategy. As a backgrounder, we can note at this point that Canadian global service providers can expect to face more competition to provide high-quality services while keeping costs to a minimum. This also involves building and sustaining a competitive advantage in a given country or region, and each country's economic development and technological advancement will combine to change the competitive landscape of how services are marketed there. Advanced countries such as Canada can expect to enjoy competitive advantages, at least in the short term, because of an abundance of human capital and technological innovations. The many published examples of Canadian service companies "success stories" are testimony to this. But in light of the challenges posed by new competitors, one is bound to ask, for how long?

The Internet and the Global Marketing of Services

Electronic commerce has opened up new horizons for global services' reach and has drastically reduced the meaning of distance. For example, when geographic obstacles make the establishment of retail outlets cumbersome and expensive, firms can approach their customers via the World Wide Web. Government regulations that might be prohibitive to a transfer of goods may not have any effect on the international marketing of services. Also, regardless of size, companies are finding it increasingly easy to appeal to a global marketplace. The Internet can help service firms develop and transitional economies overcome two of the biggest challenges they face: gaining credibility in global markets and saving on travel costs. Little-known firms can become instantly "visible" on the Internet. Even a small firm can develop a polished and sophisticated Web presence and promotional strategy. Customers are less concerned about geographic location if they feel the firm is electronically accessible. An increasing number of service providers have never met their foreign customers except "virtually," online.[31]

Nonetheless, several notes of caution must be kept in mind. First, the penetration of the Internet has occurred at different rates in different countries. There are still many businesses and consumers who do not have access to electronic business media. Unless they are to be excluded from a company's focus, more traditional ways of reaching them must be considered. Also, firms need to prepare their Internet presence for global visitors. For example, the language of the Internet is English—at least as far as large corporations are concerned. Yet, many of the visitors coming to websites either may not have English as their first language or may not speak English at all. A study by International Data Corporation (IDC) showed that while 85 percent of all Web pages are in English, only 45 percent of current online users speak the language.[32]

Many companies do not permit any interaction on their websites, thus missing out on feedback or even order placement from visitors. Some websites are so culture-bound that they often leave their visitors bewildered and disappointed. Yet over time, increasing understanding about doing business in the global marketplace will enable companies to be more refined in their approach to their customers.

Typical International Services

Although many firms are already active in the global service arena, others often do not perceive their existing competitive advantage. Numerous services have great potential for globalization.

Financial institutions can offer some functions very competitively in the international field of banking services. Increased mergers and acquisitions on a global basis have led to the emergence of financial giants in Europe, Japan, and the United States. With the increased reach made possible by electronic commerce, they can develop direct linkages to clients around the world, offering tailor-made financial services and reductions in intermediation costs. A Canadian example is Scotiabank. With more than 2,000 branches and offices in 50 countries, Scotiabank is the most international of the Canadian banks and has been doing business internationally for over 100 years. For example, it has the largest presence in mainland China of all Canadian banks, having been established there for more than 20 years, and it is one of a small number of foreign banks with an investment in a domestic Chinese bank, Xi'an City Commercial Bank.

Another area with great global potential is construction, design, and engineering services. Economies of scale work not only for machinery and material but also for areas such as human resources management and the overall management of projects. Particularly for international projects that are large scale and long term, the experience advantage could weigh heavily in favour of seasoned firms. The economic significance of these services far exceeds their direct turnover because they encourage subsequent demand for capital goods. For example, having an engineering consultant of a certain nationality increases the chances that contracts for the supply of equipment, technology, and know-how will be won by an enterprise of the same nationality, given the advantages enjoyed in terms of information, language, and technical specification.[33]

Firms in the fields of legal and accounting services can aid their domestic clients abroad through support activities; they can also aid foreign firms and countries in improving business and governmental operations. In computer and data services, global potential is growing rapidly. Knowledge of computer operations, data manipulations, data transmission, and data analysis are insufficiently exploited internationally by many small and medium-sized firms. For example, India is increasingly participating in the provision of international data services. Although some aspects of the data field are high-technology intensive, many operations still require skilled human service input. The coding and entering of data often has to be performed manually because appropriate machine-readable forms may not be available or usable. Because of lower wages, Indian companies can offer data-entry services at a rate much lower than in more industrialized countries. As a result, data are transmitted in raw form to India, where they are encoded on a proper medium and returned to the ultimate user. To some extent, this transformation can be equated to the value-added steps that take place in the transformation of a raw commodity into a finished product. Obviously, using its comparative advantage for this labour-intensive task, India can compete in the field of international services. In 2001, India's software industry exports reached $7.65 billion. Sixty-four percent of exports went to Canada and the United States, with another 23 percent exported to the European Union.[34]

Many opportunities exist in the field of teaching services. Both the academic and the corporate education sectors have concentrated their work in the domestic market, yet the teaching of knowledge is in high global demand and offers new opportunities for growth. Technology allows teachers to go global via video conferences, e-mail office hours, and Internet-relayed teaching materials. Removing the confinement of the classroom may well trigger a very large surge in learning.

Management consulting services can be provided by firms to institutions and corporations around the globe. Of particular value is management expertise in areas where firms possess global leadership, be it in manufacturing or process activities. For example, companies with highly refined transportation or logistics activities can sell their management experience abroad, yet consulting services are particularly sensitive to the cultural environment, and their use varies significantly by country and field of expertise.

All domestic service expenditures funded from abroad by foreign citizens also represent a service export. This makes tourism an increasingly important area of services trade. For example, every foreign visitor who spends foreign currency in a country contributes to an improvement in that nation's current account. The natural resources and beauty offered by so many countries have already made tourism one of the most important services trade components. Exhibit 10.12 shows the top 10 rankings for tourism destinations, earning, and spending around the world.

A proper mix in international services might also be achieved by pairing the strengths of different partners. For example, information technology expertise from one country could be combined with financial resources from another. The strengths of both partners can then be used to obtain maximum benefits.

Exhibit 10.12

World Tourism: The Top 10

Rank	Tourism Destination	Tourism Earners	Tourism Spenders
1	France	United States	United States
2	Spain	Spain	Japan
3	United States	France	Germany
4	Italy	Italy	United Kingdom
5	China	Germany	France
6	United Kingdom	United Kingdom	Italy
7	Austria	China	Spain
8	Mexico	Austria	China
9	Germany	Turkey	Canada
10	Canada	Greece	Mexico

Sources: World Travel & Tourism Council, Executive Summary; *The 2005 Travel & Tourism Economic Research I: Travel & Tourism: Sowing the Seeds of Growth,* **http://www.wttc.org,** 2003 data (accessed January 26, 2006).

Combining international advantages in services may ultimately result in the development of an even newer and more dramatic comparative lead. For example, if a firm has an international head start in such areas as high technology, information gathering, information processing, and information analysis, the major thrust of its international service might not rely on providing these service components individually but rather on enabling clients, based on all resources, to make better decisions. If better decision making is transferable to a wide variety of international situations, that in itself might become the overriding future competitive advantage of the firm in the international market.

Starting to Market Services Internationally

For many firms, participation on the Internet will offer the most attractive starting point in marketing services internationally. By setting up a website, a firm can allow visitors from any place on the globe to come and see its offering. Of course, the most important problem will be communicating the existence of the site and enticing visitors to it. For that, very traditional advertising and communication approaches often need to be used. In some countries, for example, rolling billboards announce websites and their benefits. Overall, however, we need to keep in mind that not everywhere do firms and individuals have access to or make use of the new e-commerce opportunities.

For services that are delivered mainly in the support of or in conjunction with goods, the most sensible approach for the international novice is to follow the path of the good. For years, many large accounting and banking firms have done so by determining where their major multinational clients have set up new operations and then following them. Smaller service marketers who cooperate closely with manufacturing firms can determine where the manufacturing firms are operating internationally. Ideally, of course, it would be possible to follow clusters of manufacturers in order to obtain economies of scale internationally while, at the same time, looking for entirely new client groups abroad.

For service providers whose activities are independent from goods, a different strategy is needed. These individuals and firms must search for market situations abroad that are similar to the domestic market. Such a search should concentrate in their area of expertise. For example, a design firm learning about construction projects abroad can investigate the possibility of rendering its design services. Similarly, a management consultant learning about the plans of a foreign country or firm to computerize operations can explore the possibility of overseeing a smooth transition from manual to computerized activities. What is required is the understanding that similar problems are likely to occur in similar situations.

Another opportunity consists in identifying and understanding points of transition abroad. Just as Canadian society has undergone change, foreign societies are subject to a changing domestic environment. If, for example, new transportation services are introduced, an expert in containerization may wish to consider whether to offer services to improve the efficiency of the new system.

Leads for international service opportunities can also be gained by staying informed about international projects sponsored by domestic organizations such as the Canadian International Development Agency (CIDA) as well as international organizations such as the United Nations, the International Finance Corporation, or the World Bank. Very frequently, such projects are in need of support through services. Overall, the international service marketer needs to search for familiar situations or similar problems requiring similar solutions in order to formulate an effective international expansion strategy.

Strategic Implications of International Services Marketing

To be successful, the international service marketer must first determine the nature and the aim of the service offering—that is, whether the service will be aimed at people or at things, and whether the service act in itself will result in tangible or intangible actions. Exhibit 10.13 provides examples of such a classification that will help the marketer to better determine the position of the services effort.

Exhibit 10.13 **Understanding the Service Act**

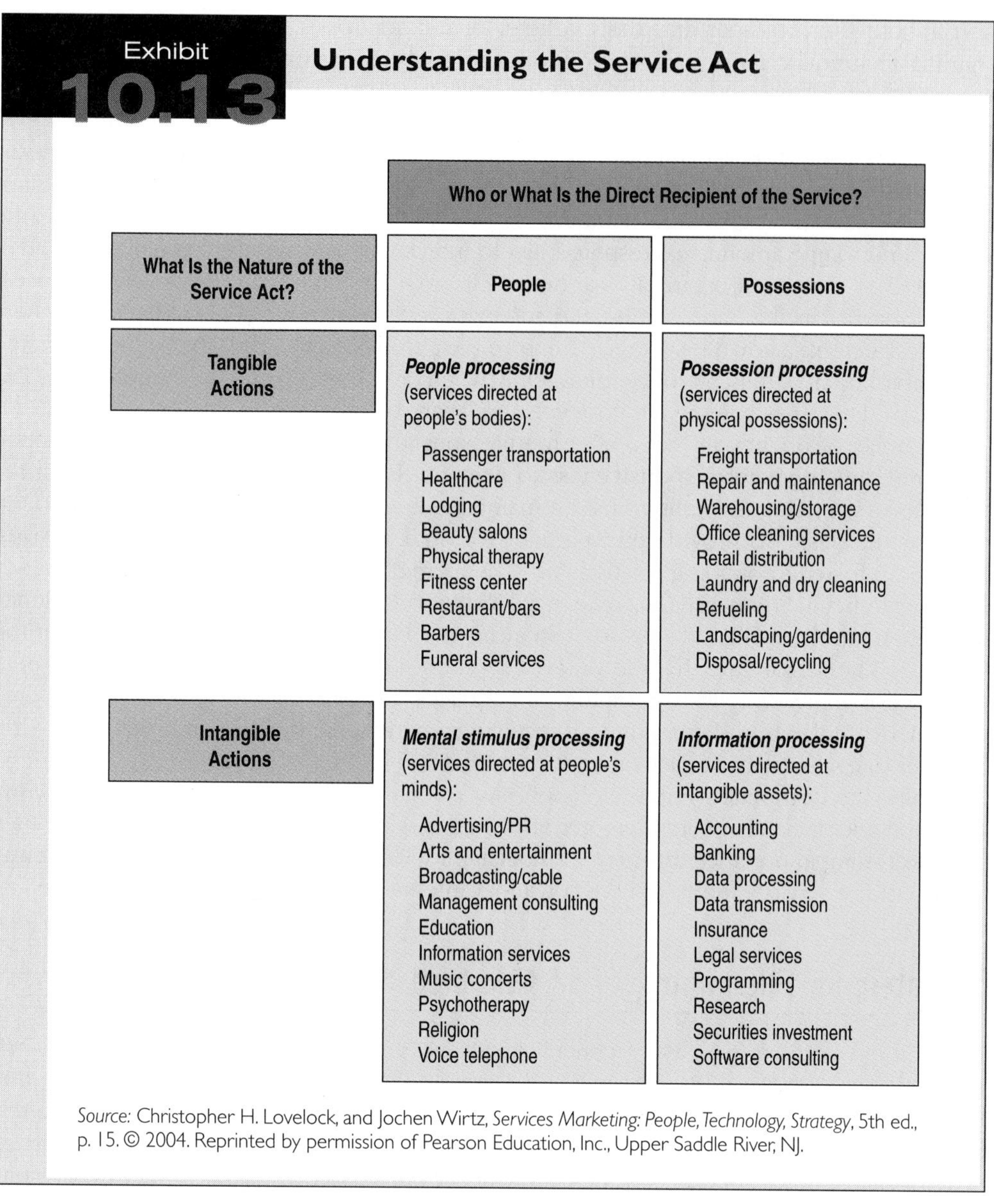

What Is the Nature of the Service Act?	Who or What Is the Direct Recipient of the Service? — People	Who or What Is the Direct Recipient of the Service? — Possessions
Tangible Actions	***People processing*** (services directed at people's bodies): Passenger transportation Healthcare Lodging Beauty salons Physical therapy Fitness center Restaurant/bars Barbers Funeral services	***Possession processing*** (services directed at physical possessions): Freight transportation Repair and maintenance Warehousing/storage Office cleaning services Retail distribution Laundry and dry cleaning Refueling Landscaping/gardening Disposal/recycling
Intangible Actions	***Mental stimulus processing*** (services directed at people's minds): Advertising/PR Arts and entertainment Broadcasting/cable Management consulting Education Information services Music concerts Psychotherapy Religion Voice telephone	***Information processing*** (services directed at intangible assets): Accounting Banking Data processing Data transmission Insurance Legal services Programming Research Securities investment Software consulting

Source: Christopher H. Lovelock, and Jochen Wirtz, *Services Marketing: People, Technology, Strategy*, 5th ed., p. 15. © 2004. Reprinted by permission of Pearson Education, Inc., Upper Saddle River, NJ.

During this determination, the marketer must consider other tactical variables that have an impact on the preparation of the service offering. The measurement of services capacity and delivery efficiency often remains highly qualitative rather than quantitative. In the field of communications, the intangibility of the service reduces the marketer's ability to provide samples. This makes communicating the service offer much more difficult than communicating an offer for a good. Brochures or catalogues explaining services often must show a "proxy" for the service in order to provide the prospective customer with tangible clues. A cleaning service, for instance, can show a picture of an individual removing trash or cleaning a window. Yet the picture will not fully communicate the performance of the service. Because of the different needs and requirements of individual consumers, the marketer must pay very close attention to the two-way flow of communication. Mass communication must often be supported by intimate one-on-one follow-up.

The role of personnel deserves special consideration in the global marketing of services. Because the customer interface is intense, proper provisions need to be made for training personnel both domestically and internationally. Major emphasis must be placed on appearance. The person delivering the service—rather than the service itself—will communicate the spirit, value, and attitudes of the service corporation. The service person is both the producer and the marketer of the service. Therefore, recruitment and training techniques must focus on dimensions such as customer relationship management and image projection as well as competence in the design and delivery of the service.[35]

This close interaction with the consumer will also have organizational implications. Whereas tight control over personnel may be desired, the individual interaction that is required points toward the need for a global decentralization of service delivery. This, in turn, requires both delegation of large amounts of responsibility to individuals and service "subsidiaries" and a great deal of trust in all organizational units. This trust, of course, can be greatly enhanced through proper methods of training and supervision. Sole ownership also helps strengthen trust. Research has shown that service firms, in their global expansion, tend to greatly prefer the establishment of full-control ventures. Only when costs escalate and the company-specific advantage diminishes will service firms seek out shared-control ventures.[36]

The areas of pricing and financing require special attention. Because services cannot be stored, much greater responsiveness to demand fluctuation must exist, and therefore, much greater pricing flexibility must be maintained. At the same time, flexibility is countered by the desire to provide transparency for both the seller and the buyer of services in order to foster an ongoing relationship. The intangibility of services also makes financing more difficult. Frequently, even financial institutions with large amounts of international experience are less willing to provide financial support for international services than for products. The reasons are that the value of services is more difficult to assess, service performance is more difficult to monitor, and services are difficult to repossess. Therefore, customer complaints and difficulties in receiving payment are much more troublesome for a lender to evaluate for services than for products.

Finally, the distribution implications of international services must be considered. Usually, short and direct channels are required. Within these channels, closeness to the customer is of overriding importance in order to understand what the customer really wants, to trace the use of the service, and to aid the consumer in obtaining a truly tailor-made service.

Strategic Planning for Global Services Marketing

In the above sections we gave a general overview of the problems of marketing services internationally, against a background of the peculiar problems to be encountered. In this section we will discuss systematically and in more detail the problems of establishing the services marketing mix, with particular reference, where possible, to Canadian experience.

As we have noted, because of the characteristics of services—notably, intangibility and the unusually severe competitive environment that providers face—development of a total international marketing program in a service industry will often be uniquely challenging. This situation is not helped by what one writer has called "the paucity of research on international services marketing," which he goes on to describe as "alarming" when one considers "the importance of services in the global environment."[37] The intricacies of international services marketing will be better understood the more research is focused on it in order to explain, predict, and provide practical guidance to companies. In the meantime, service providers simply "get on with the job" of global marketing, which, as in the marketing of goods, involves defining marketing goals and selecting target markets. Thereafter, management needs to design and implement marketing mix strategies to reach its markets and fulfill its marketing goals.

Selecting Target Markets

As we mentioned in Chapter 6, the selection of target markets calls first of all for an understanding of the key indicators associated with likely success. For example, a supplier of educational consulting services will be guided by knowledge of such factors as illiteracy rates in the country, unemployment rates among youth, and new social policies on lifelong learning. A supplier of information technology or computer services will want to know about any increase in expenditures on IT in a given industry, pressure for increased productivity (and therefore use of IT), increased public use of online service delivery (e.g., Internet, e-mail, e-commerce), and pressures to reduce costs (and therefore use of IT).

Five indicators are of particular interest to service suppliers:

- demographic factors
- macroeconomic factors
- government policies
- environmental factors
- industry-specific factors

To illustrate how these indicators might be used in practice, let us examine the case of architectural services, a sector that is growing in Canada at the strong rate of more than 14 percent annually (see Exhibit 10.6). Below are examples of indicators that are of importance to architectural services providers.

Demographic factors:	• increased leisure activities • increased independent living (seniors)
Macroeconomic factors:	• GDP growth leading to increased housing demand
Government policies:	• new environmental regulations for buildings
Environmental factors:	• natural disasters creating the need to rebuild • indications that existing infrastructure is wearing out
Industry-specific factors	• increased level of construction and/or renovation • increased activity of foreign contractors and building suppliers

Once the individual company is satisfied that sufficient information has been gathered for individual countries on these and similar factors, one approach is to give weighted scores to the indicators to develop an idea as to which markets should be given a high or low priority. Obviously this is only a beginning—a decision actually to enter a given market raises a whole host of additional considerations, such as the competitive environment, the ability to gain comparative advantages, the existence of adequate financing, and so on.

In practice, whether as a result of formal planning or not, in the 1990s Canadian service exports found their way to a variety of countries including Brazil, Sweden, Taiwan, Mexico, the Middle East, and Malaysia, in addition to the United States. Today Canadian providers are increasingly exporting their services to emerging markets such as China and India, as well as several countries in Eastern Europe as they prepare to join the European Union.

The Role of Marketing Research

In Chapter 7 we discussed a variety of marketing research issues and dwelt on different techniques and approaches. A good deal of this material also has relevance to the international services area. In pursuing the architectural services sector, for example, a variety of research methods will obviously be desirable, especially ones that will yield needed information about foreign markets and provide insights that may not be available through more formal means. But are international services "different" as far as the use of marketing research is concerned?

Data are essential to understanding trade in services. However, for various reasons the development of useful international services data has been very slow.[38] Recent developments promise to change this. Most notable among these new additions is the North American Industry Classification System (NAICS), which has been designed to replace the 60-year-old Standard Industrial Classification (SIC) system and promises meaningful international services data collection.

Despite these developments, the unique aspects of services, such as intangibility and perishability, make the task of gathering data more difficult and, as a result, require sophisticated tools and experienced personnel.

In More Detail 10.1

DEVELOPMENTS IN NAICS

NAICS identifies 358 new industries, of which 250 are services. Developed in cooperation with Statistics Canada and Mexico's Instituto Nacional de Estadistíca, Geografia e Informatica (INEGI), NAICS includes new and advanced technologies and service industries and provides comparable statistics among the NAFTA countries previously unavailable under the SIC. This new approach covers nine service sectors, including communications services (e.g., software publishing and online services), professional services (e.g., computer systems design and marketing consulting), educational services, accommodation and food services, and waste management/remediation services. The NAICS also promised new data as far as the United States is concerned, but problems still remain for many countries outside NAFTA.

Planning the Product Offering

From the discussion of product policy and strategy issues in Chapter 9, it will be clear that many problems in the physical product field will also be found in services. But complications do set in when we consider the marketing of services internationally. This section will discuss some of these.

Defining and Classifying International Service Products

An obvious problem when conceptualizing the service product is its convergence or interconnectedness with goods, as commonly seen with the sale of industrial products accompanied by services of various kinds. However, regardless of these connections, many classes of services will always be distinguished from goods because the customer receives value but no tangible object. Every tangible product necessarily contains some services because without them exchange would be impossible. Thus even though such activities as quoting prices, taking orders, billing, and making payments are intangible (i.e., are services), they merely facilitate sales, and without them there would be no revenue. However, in realistic terms, only services that can be targeted as profit centres and marketed accordingly qualify as true services. As legal, technological, economic, and competitive environments change over time, it is probable that certain cost-centre-type services can be converted into profit centres. A familiar example would be ATMs, which were initially conceived to support banking services, but whose increasing popularity led banks to view them as profit centres for which fees could be charged.

Issues such as these call attention to the need for a generally accepted method of classifying services. However, the emergence of such a categorization still remains elusive, with the result that the formulation of appropriate generic international marketing strategies is handicapped.[39] Given that services are frequently embedded in tangible goods, this absence also complicates the problem of developing effective global product strategies. In practice, the range of services offered internationally by Canada, let alone global providers, is quite wide and involves different industries that have developed highly specialized skills, capabilities, and knowledge over a period of time, enabling them to compete internationally. Although numerous classifications for service trades have been offered,[40] industry-based classifications have been commonly used internationally. This is quite understandable and practical in light of so many unrelated service sectors, but the existence of a widely accepted system of categorization would help to clarify product/service marketing decisions.

As far as international classification systems are concerned, the position we have reached is one in which particular systems are proposed and discussed but not necessarily widely accepted or adopted right away. This should not be thought of as detracting from the effort and thought needed to develop new schemes, only perhaps as pointing to an implementation gap between concept development and actual practice. For illustration, here is an outline of two proposed classification systems.

One authority proposes the classification of international services into three groups depending on the nature of the process (whether it is primarily tangible or intangible) and the extent to which customers need to be present during service "production."[41] (This classification was subsequently extended to include **mental stimulus processing**—services directed at people's minds—for example, music concerts and psychotherapy services. See Exhibit 10.13 for additional detail).

People-processing services involve tangible actions to customers in person. Customers need to enter the "service factory" supplied by, for example, Air Canada to air passengers; one can see the same principle at work in food, health care, and lodging services.

Possession-processing services involve tangible actions to physical products to improve their value to customers. Here the product needs to be involved in the production process (e.g., a business computer) but the customer does not, although the customer may enjoy, say, electronic troubleshooting services later from a distance, perhaps even from another country. Canadian providers of logistics, warehousing, and freight transportation services illustrate this category, as do suppliers of different types of capital equipment whose value may be improved by providing services such as operator training or customer service centres.

Information-based services are those that provide value to the customer as a result of the collection, analysis, manipulation, and transmission of data. This is an area of considerable familiarity to Canadian companies, examples being accounting, banking, management consulting, educational, insurance, and legal services. (See Exhibit 10.6.) As Canadian experience shows, this category presents many opportunities for international marketing development.

The persuasive logic of this categorization will appeal to many observers, but as already noted, this does not necessarily mean that it will be quickly adopted by international service providers as an aid to strategy formulation. Also, the categories may not be mutually exclusive and exhaustive for all services. For comparison, consider another classification that also offers interesting insights.[42] This approach is based on two levels of "tangibility" of the service and two levels of "face-to-face" contact with the client in service delivery, the resulting cells thus being labelled as follows:

1. Low face-to-face and low tangibility – location-free professional services
2. High face-to-face and low tangibility – location-bound customized projects
3. Low face-to-face and high tangibility – standardized services packages
4. High face-to-face and high tangibility – value-added customized services

Cell 4 is of particular relevance to Canadian commercial services companies. These are mostly medium-sized firms that engage in a good deal of customization of their services; thus they need significant provider-client contact for successful service "manufacture." However, Cell 2 is also of relevance; in this case, continuous close contact with the client is required as the companies concerned pursue major engineering, management consultancy, and project management contracts worldwide. This often calls for some form of more permanent local presence (e.g., a branch office) in the foreign country. However, as might be expected, Cell 2 has a concentration of very large firms, which will be the exception rather than the rule for Canadian companies.

As far as Cells 1 and 3 are concerned, there is no doubt that these will also apply to some Canadian international companies. In the case of Cell 1, these are low-contact services of a short duration with limited client involvement, for example, a marketing research assignment where most time is spent "in the field." Transportation services, insurance, and some banking services would also fall into this category. In the case of Cell 3, these tend to be service packages bundled with goods such as software development, standardized distance education courses, or the technical service component of a hardware installation (e.g., on computer or telecommunications equipment). In both quadrants 1 and 3, companies are usually smaller than other firms and offer more standardized off-the-shelf services, whether they are stand-alone or embodied in physical goods.

Although these classification schemes are still in their infancy, they already show some usefulness in propelling us beyond traditional frameworks based on industry classifications toward something more appropriate to deal with the increasingly complex global environment.

Marketing Strategy for Supplementary Services

Use of phrases such "augmented product," "extended product," and "product package" point to the well-known fact that the core service product is usually accompanied by a variety of supplementary elements, of which there are numerous possibilities and combinations. Many of these elements are based on informational processes that can be located in one part of the world and delivered electronically to another. It is also well established that companies can move along a spectrum from pure-product to pure-service providers, as might a manufacturer seeking to incorporate progressively more product-related services in its end product. Such companies are usually urged to seek maximum integration of services into their core product offerings. However, what has probably received less attention is the question of how the firm should formulate international marketing strategies for these supplementary services.

When an equipment manufacturer ascertains that its foreign market and potential customers rate uninterrupted satisfaction highly, then the service component responsible for delivering such continuity must receive attention equal to the customer rating. In this case, the motivation of buyers is that they expect to acquire a long period of trouble-free satisfaction from their purchase. However, such customers are bound to consider the possibility of breakdown, and when this does occur, the mental approach of the customer is completely dominated by the speed with which the defect, whatever its nature, is rectified. A major factor in marketing strategy should therefore be to minimize this fear by setting up the necessary services as part of the marketing mix. Also, this service must be seen to be available before any purchase is made. As we can see from the Canadian manufacturer of heavy-duty metal cutting equipment described in The Global Marketplace 10.2, various service elements have come to be important to customers, such as the savings generated by reduced downtime, as well as customer service benefits such as start-up assistance, on-going technical support, and on-site training. Customers also increasingly demand highly competitive payment conditions, which puts a premium on being able to offer very attractive financial service packages. These have obviously been brought to the forefront of this company's marketing strategy, even if the equipment is highly technical. The company also has a notable global reach that encompasses the Russian Federation, China, North and South Korea, and elsewhere.

Another example of the importance of formulating support service strategy is evident in the area of new product development. In light of shortening product life cycles and growing international competitive pressures, companies need to exercise much care in establishing the strength of the physical product component as a source of market advantage. They must perform a careful and objective assessment of the likelihood that the strength of the advantage will be sustained over time. Also, there is a need for realism as to the possibility of competitive inroads. If the period of physical product advantage is judged to be short in any foreign market, as might pertain in the rapidly evolving IT sector, every effort must be made to consolidate the temporary product advantage through the best possible support service so that customers will remain loyal to the firm after the entry of competitively similar products. In Olympia Engineering's case, competitors may find it much easier to duplicate the company's use of polymer castings than to emulate their dedication to customer service and customer problem solving.

In short, it would be foolish for companies to allocate ample resources to new product development, important though this is, and shortchange the supporting services. This failure to achieve an appropriate balance between the two will only facilitate the entry of competitors. Let us stress that support services (e.g., delivery services, quality assurance, after-sales service) are less visible, usually contain a high human element, and are much more difficult for competitors to imitate. They are therefore potentially more powerful as a source of sustainable comparative advantage if allied with sound product evolution policy. The firm's international product policy thus needs to be seen as an amalgam of product and service elements aimed at achieving the most profitable, long-term differential advantage.

A fundamental point to be made here is that supplementary services are probably misnamed, the title belying their strategic marketing importance. This can be seen in terms of how services affect and are affected by other elements in the marketing mix. For example, quick rectification of a technical fault—or, more broadly, a growing international reputation for service excellence—will enhance the firm's brand standing to the foreign customer. However, in the absence of investment in services, advertising may be unproductive because of an obvious defect in marketing strategy, and repeat sales based on customer satisfaction will be difficult. The standard of service offered will also be influenced by the firm's product range policy. A reduction or simplification of the range helps to promote familiarity with each type of product and should result in a higher or more consistent level of service. Moreover, a simplified range, by reducing the

The Global MARKETPLACE 10.2

How Technical and Financial Services Help Heavy-Equipment Marketing

Relying on innovation and a strong focus on customer service, one Canadian company based in Concord, Ontario, is competing successfully against substantial international competition. This is Phillips Olympia, formerly Olympia Engineering, a builder of medium- to large-sized machine tools. Olympia's customer list contains many substantial, immediately recognizable names—GE, Pratt and Whitney, Caterpillar, Sikorsky, Goodyear, Siemens Westinghouse, Halliburton Energy. These, and many SMEs, have adopted Olympia's technological solutions. The firm designs and custom builds heavy-duty metal-cutting equipment for such customers, and through a quality dealer network throughout North America and overseas, also offers installation, start-up assistance, on-site training, ongoing technical support, and 24-hour service available from Toronto or through one of the many dealers. Proximity to Pearson Airport also facilitates delivery services.

According to Lev Kishlyansky, president of Phillips Olympia, the company has spent the last 20 years developing machine tool technologies for more efficient and accurate cutting. Now the firm is ready to use this accumulated knowledge and experience to offer total manufacturing for increased productivity. This is reflected in the firm's mission, which is to form permanent partnerships with customers and to work on sustaining these relationships. In short, the company does a great deal more than simply sell machines. Installing machinery is only the first stage in a relationship-building process, and all customers are offered comprehensive parts and labour warranties, as well as lifetime free training. After-sales support covers every facet of the proper operation and implementation of the machine tool purchased.

In a highly competitive industry with many well-entrenched rivals, Olympia can be regarded as a major supplier of highly productive equipment, continually proving their ability to offer product and service innovations that solve long-standing customer problems. The use of polymer castings for heavy-duty metal is one such innovation. Olympia machines can reach higher speeds because their polymer castings reduce vibrations, which results in customer benefits such as better performance, greater cutting accuracy, and longer tool life. The company has also pioneered the use of total intelligent tool management systems, a service innovation greatly valued by several customers.

Not only is Olympia able to offer product and technical service advantages, they also provide financial advantages to those choosing to deal with them. This results from working closely with EDC and using a variety of their products such as contract bonding, note purchase programs, and loan agreements. When the company took an order for three new machines without the usual 30 percent up-front down payment, EDC was able to provide the necessary working capital solution needed by Olympia to fulfill the required contracts, thereby also providing an excellent financial package for the customer. One of the most difficult challenges for smaller Canadian exporters competing for bigger contracts occurs when buyers demand competitive payment conditions such as small or no up-front and progress payments. Working with EDC and the Canadian banks can help to alleviate this problem.

Source: Phillips Olympia, Concord, Ontario, *Techspex: Specifiers Technical Data*, **http://www.techspex.com** (accessed October 24, 2007); Canadian Company Capabilities: Phillips Olympia, **http://www.strategis.gc.ca** (accessed October 24, 2007); Bonita Williams, "Exporter Showcase: Olympia: On the Cutting Edge," *Exportwise* (Winter 2003); "Large Parts Machining: Think Process Not Just Machine," *Metalworking*, May (2005); and Phillips Olympia website, **http://www.phillipset.com** (accessed October 27, 2007).

knowledge needed by foreign distributors, enables intermediaries to be used more effectively and reduces the fear of undesirable consequences from allowing advice and service functions to pass into dealer control. A positioning strategy of adding benefits to obtain a competitive edge will thus have numerous ramifications across the spectrum of marketing activities.

Despite the importance of integrating services into the core product offering, manufacturers do not necessarily always move boldly to achieve this. Indeed, the transition into service by manufacturers has been described as "relatively slow and cautious."[43] In part, this is a result of skepticism by firms as to the economic benefit of the service component for their end products. As one company executive remarks, "It is difficult for an engineer who has designed a multimillion-dollar piece of equipment to get excited about a contract worth $10,000 for cleaning it."[44] Of course firms might also decide that providing services is beyond their core capabilities, or they might doubt their ability to deploy a service strategy successfully. The case for integrating services into overall marketing strategy may appear clear, certainly to marketers, but may be extraordinarily difficult for some firms to accomplish, not least because the emphasis of the business model needs to be shifted from transactions to relationships, not the easiest task.

Standardization versus Local Adaptation

An important issue in marketing services internationally is the extent to which each service might be standardized. It is not difficult to see how problems could arise. Because services are "performances" (i.e., they inherently involve some level of the human element), they cannot be standardized in the same way that goods can, as in the cases of consumer electronic devices, soft drinks, and computer hardware. These product categories provide many examples of successful global standardization because common customer needs provide a globalizing impetus. But it should be noted, as one authority emphasizes, that the simultaneous presence of successful *local* strategies in these and other categories in no way undermines the global prospect for pursuing opportunities of global standardizing in the appropriate industry.[45]

Although at times hobbled by standardization difficulties, the nature of service delivery—at the point of consumption in many instances—provides an element of flexibility not available in the case of tangible goods. With regard to goods manufacturing, balancing standardization and customization calls for major tradeoffs. However, in the case of services, local elements (e.g., indigenous bank tellers) can easily be added to a global formula (international consumer banking) and thereby overcome the foreignness of a largely standardized service. Thus in many instances a globally standardized core service can be augmented and differentiated by nationally customized supplementary service elements, and this tends to more feasible for services than for manufacturing businesses. For example, McDonald's well-known products and services are sold throughout the world, but local menus are frequently subject to strong local adaptation, including the product element. Canadian locations have a Value Picks menu, Australia has the McOz (similar to a Quarter Pounder but with beet), and Morocco has the *Recette Moutarde* ("mustard burger"), released in late 2006.

Service providers sometimes confront conflicting pressures when seeking to determine which, if any, supplementary services should be consistent across all markets and which should be tailored to meet local needs, expectations, and competitive dynamics. A major pressure toward customization comes from the numerous host government regulations in various service sectors. Accounting and financial service markets, for example, are governed by very different rules around the world, and although efforts by regional markets such as the European Union are helping to reduce regulatory problems, many difficulties remain. Even if regulations were entirely removed, differences in cultural influences would still make standardization difficult. However, as large corporate customers become global, they will often seek to standardize and simplify the array of services they consume. For example, firms may seek to minimize the number of auditors they use around the world, using major accounting firms that can apply a consistent worldwide approach. In any event, national rules within each country of operation need to be observed by small and large providers alike. Common procedures and standards are also obligatory in other instances; for example, airlines depend critically on their aircraft being maintained in the same way everywhere in the world, and it can be expected that consumers of factory and machinery maintenance services will increasingly seek consistency in standards.

However, the need to customize services to local needs remains a necessity for many managers. In the case of Canadian professional service firms, many of these will vary in their ability to provide a globally standardized service. To the extent that such firms are SMEs, the pressure toward seeking out niche markets abroad will already be evident; hence, a company's choice of local customization may be a matter of marketing strategy. In general, the level of product and marketing standardization noticed in the international market for goods is not likely to be matched consistently over all service sectors, and the global marketing of some services may not be a realistic goal. It is likely that a multi-domestic or multi-local pattern of internationalization might be the most appropriate in some sectors.[46]

The variety of viewpoints expressed in this section underlines a point made earlier—the need for better classification systems to introduce greater clarity into service marketing decisions. Indeed, improved classification methods would be of value if they merely clarified the areas of uncertainty. Thus using the categorization mentioned above (i.e., that based on possession-processing, people-processing, and information-based services), we can see that possession-processing businesses can be thought of as providing the most globally standardized offerings, because the customer is not involved in the "production" process, with consumption of the output tending to follow production. On the other hand, in the case of people-processing services, the customer needs to enter the "service factory," hence local adaptability by the provider is obligatory.

A Note on Service Quality

Regardless of whether the service is standardized globally or not, companies need to establish and maintain a consistent quality standard. This should be based on the commercial viability of the chosen standard in light of the current state of the foreign market and the competitive suppliers of that market. In some industries and in some countries there will be legally enforced standards governing quality (as with pharmaceutical products, in the case of goods), or there will be a widely accepted standard, such as those of the American Petroleum Institute and the British Standards Institution. In the case of international services, as an example, all publicly traded companies in the European Union must, from 2005, adopt the International Financial Reporting Standards (IFRS) issued by the International Accounting Standards Board. Many other countries have also adopted these standards. Obviously accepting such limits on quality standards is completely obligatory from the standpoint of the intending provider.

As in the case of goods, attaining superior quality ("delighting the customer") can lead to important strategic benefits, including greater customer loyalty, greater productivity, responsiveness to demand, market share improvements, and building a competitive advantage.[47] Service quality dimensions will vary across segments, but attempts have been made to identify general dimensions of service quality. One authority's framework embraces such quality dimensions as reliability, accessibility, responsiveness, competence, courtesy, communications, credibility, and understanding of the customer.[48] The global services provider faces the task of either offering a standardized global services "mix" or modifying the mix to suit individual foreign markets. For example, there are grounds for believing that different emphases will be needed in developed countries compared with developing ones.[49] Service quality dimensions of reliability, access, and understanding the customer may be relatively more important to consumers in developed countries.

Consider the problems of professional services firms, a service sector very important to Canada. A strong reputation for quality and strong relationships is critical to their success. Thus the competitive advantage of these firms is highly perishable and depends as much on consistent quality and interpersonal relations as on legal protection and patents. Also, quality is exceedingly difficult to control in a foreign environment, making the export of professional services very risky and costly, and an endeavour that requires significant know-how and contacts. For example, even though engineering is a service that is very much needed in overseas markets and is a sector where Canadian and other country companies can provide world-class service, the American Consulting Engineering Council reports that only 10 percent of its members are marketing services internationally.[50]

Sales Promotion and Pricing

In Chapter 13 we will explore various issues in connection with global advertising and sales promotion. Much of this material will have application to the services area because global advertising works equally well for goods-based and service-based businesses. Predictably, we would be naive to assume the likelihood of any uniformity of approach across service industries generally. Indeed, services advertising may be used in quite glaringly controversial ways, as is shown in The Global Marketplace 10.3. For the purposes of this section, it might be useful to provide illustrations of two extreme cases: in the first, where global branding and advertising can be justified; and in the second, where more individualistic sales promotion is most likely to be effective. A wide number of variants between these extremes will be possible, of course.

It is well known that travel-related service, as an example, can benefit from global advertising, although the communications task may vary by country. The factors that encourage large-scale advertising are numerous, but key among them are common global needs and the importance of global customers or channels. Some providers may favour a dual campaign, one for global themes and one for more local messages. For example, British Airways for many years had a succession of dramatic global advertising campaigns to establish its position as "the world's favourite airline." At the same time, BA provided a smaller budget for local campaigns focusing on schedules, prices, and promotion of special tour packages. (See Exhibit 10.14 for an example of British Airways advertising.)

With regard to branding, the uncertainty created by intangibility requires strong branding to offset it. Thus the primary task of the brand name or trademark for a service is to offer recognition and reassurance. McDonald's, for example, has to be the same name throughout the world so that both local customers and travellers can be confident they will obtain the authentic McDonald's experience. Global branding should be supported by global advertising and globally consistent corporate design featuring recognizable colour schemes (for example, bright blue and yellow for IKEA stores), an easily identified logo and trademark, and even consistency in retail office design in different parts of the world (as favoured by Citibank). A key challenge when creating global campaigns is to create visual themes that will travel well across different cultures.

In contrast to the above, consider the case of companies selling capital goods (with supplementary services), and/or individual business services such as environmental services, interior design consulting, or commercial education and training. In these instances, the market may be far from populous and may indeed be highly fragmented and specialized. A key problem facing companies is that while the professional staff will be highly trained technically, they may have little training in international business or marketing necessary for them to effectively establish contact and credibility, and win critical first orders. In the case of industrial product/service service packages, individual buyers will have a strong notion of what they want and need within perhaps quite narrow tolerances on physical specifications, quality, price, support services, and any other detail which might affect the well-being of their enterprise. This almost predetermined approach to product/service needs does not preclude the use of large-scale advertising and sales promotion techniques, but it does throw the balance in favour of strong quality and relational reputation for market success.

As is shown in The Global Marketplace 10.4, actually winning a critical order overseas (in this case a new airport project in Ecuador) may take many years of planning and collaboration with a variety of partners, lenders, and agencies. Note that in this case a variety

The Global MARKETPLACE 10.3

Royal Bank of Canada Faces Combative Advertising in the U.S.

Financial Post/John Godbey

Royal Bank of Canada's retail banking strategy in the United States is under attack at the corner of Alabama Highway 67 and Cedar Street. A couple of weeks ago, a competitor, local bank Superior Bancorp, put up a billboard at the intersection on the edge of Decatur, Alabama—population 53,929—where the giant Canadian intruder has just opened a branch. The billboard reads "Sweet Home Canada," but the word "Canada" is crossed out, and replaced by "Alabama." And then the kicker: "It didn't sound right to us either."

Tom Jung, an executive with Superior Bancorp, which has 26 branches in Alabama and parts of Florida, remarked, "Whenever you have a new entrant to the market, you always think of how to combat it." He goes on to say that the billboard has been "very well received" by local people who have a strong affiliation to their state and who react negatively to being told that the new bank is Canadian-owned.

"A lot of times, people don't really appreciate bigger banks coming in," is the view of Jim Schultz, a bank analyst at Sterne Agee and Leach Inc. in Birmingham, Alabama. According to Mr. Schultz, many people in Alabama probably do not know RBC is Canadian, so Superior Bancorp's billboard strategy is smart because it points that out and plays to local sentiments that are opposed to big businesses from outside the state.

RBC's two Canadian rivals, Bank of Montreal and the Toronto-Dominion Bank, both of whom have a retail presence in the United States, have also recognized the importance of playing to local affiliations. For example, Bank of Montreal's 202 branches in and around Chicago and Northwest Indiana operate under the banner of a subsidiary of Harris Bank, retaining a link to a brand with 125 years of history in the United States. The Royal Bank of Canada operates in the U.S. under the name RBC Centura Bank. Its entry into Alabama was facilitated through the acquisition of 39 local AmSouth Bank branches in cities such as Huntsville, Decatur, and Montgomery. RBC Centura is now this state's seventh largest bank.

Sources: Duncan Mavin, "Alabama Town Not So Sweet for Royal Bank Subsidiary: Anti-Canada Campaign," *Financial Post* (Friday, April 20, 2007). Available at **http://www.financialpost.com/story.html?id=2774e466-1f43-4903-b976-599800e6d207&k=23128**; RBC Centura, "RBC Centura completes acquisition of 39 Am South branches in Alabama," *In the News*, **http://www.rbccentura.com/about/news/030907_Amsouth.html** (accessed February 6, 2007).

of services will accompany the construction proposal, including those needed to operate the airport. Commitment and patience are the keys to success. In this extended process, there is obviously a continuous need to persuade the potential customer or client that the proposer is capable of achieving the desired end in a manner superior to all competitors. Therefore a strong role for selling exists, even if in practice multiple relationships have to be developed with the customer and others, and the factual assessment of the proposer's capability is the dominant consideration.

Exhibit 10.14 British Airways Shows How Their Flat Beds Help to Give Passengers the Best Service

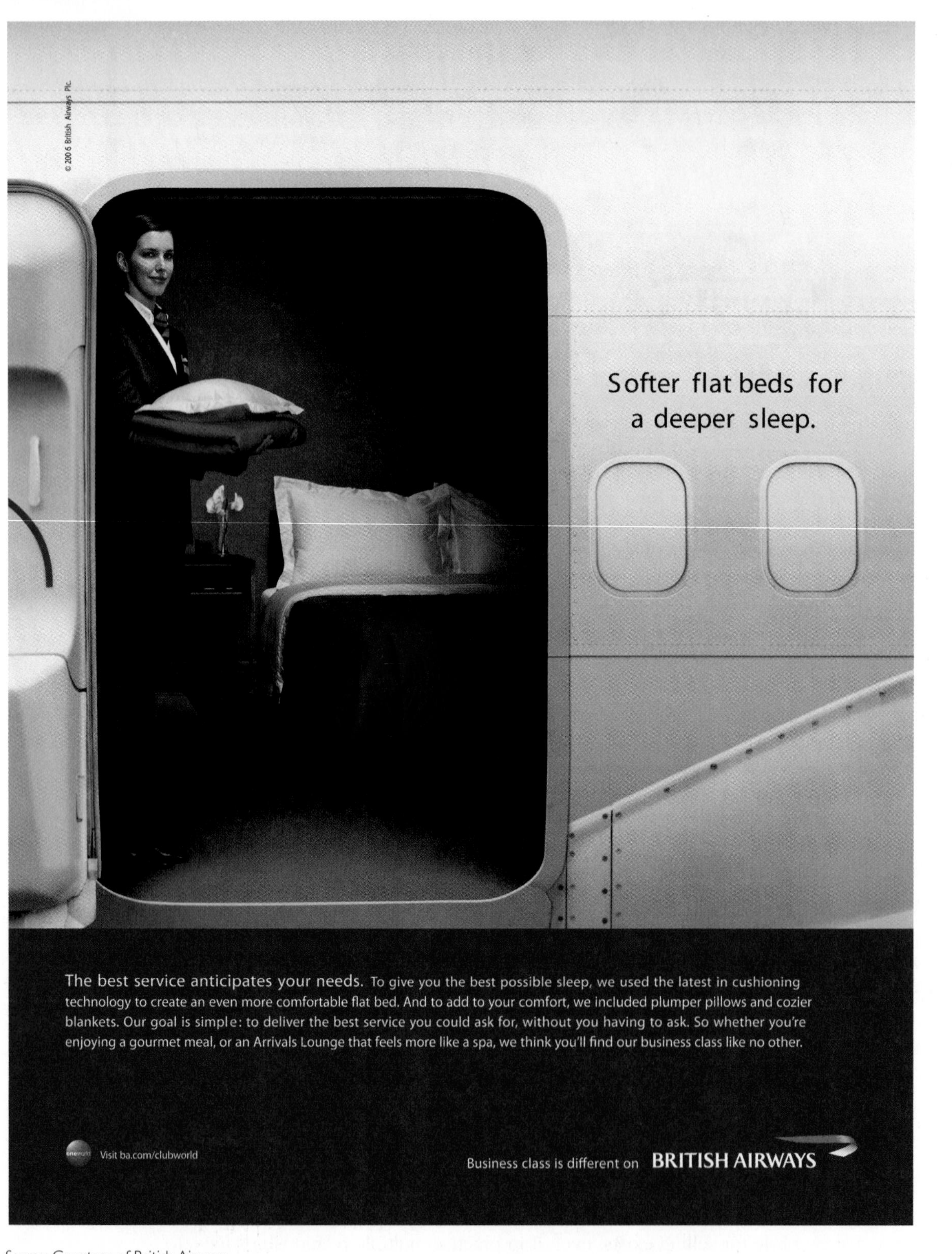

Source: Courtesy of British Airways

These extremes underline the need to avoid talking in broad-brush terms about the service sector and service industries as though all organizations faced more or less the same global promotional or strategic marketing problem. However, given the predominance of SMEs in Canada's international services marketing, and given the niche marketing approach of many of these firms, issues of global branding and advertising will often give way to more concentrated direct selling activities.

The Pricing Issue

Pursuing the theme of the above section, it can be demonstrated that price determination will not follow a neat formula across international service sectors. Charging uniform prices will be possible in some instances, such as in the case of "possession-processing" services mentioned earlier (e.g., aircraft maintenance or package delivery). In these cases, because multinational customers will be present, it will be necessary to pursue a coordinated global marketing strategy and offer uniform terms of service. On the other hand, in the case of "people-processing" services (e.g., lodging services or passenger transportation), uniform pricing will be much more difficult given the wide international variations in both costs and per capita incomes. (But companies in this sector stand to gain from unified branding campaigns to build recognition, showing that the extent of the globalization that can be achieved varies by the marketing mix element under consideration).

When considering the variety of price approaches to be found in international services marketing, bear in mind that in order to win business contracts many organizations face the challenge of formal competitive bidding, as is illustrated in The Global Marketplace 10.4. A key point of interest here is the **Swiss Challenge Process** by which the company, the Aecon Group, was obliged to submit a comprehensive proposal; this information was then used by the government to open up bidding, in effect allowing third parties to make better offers (challenges). In more conventional sealed-bid pricing situations, all bidders must submit quotations simultaneously. But in both cases, pricing will reflect expectations of how it is thought competitors will bid, not necessarily a rigid estimation of costs and demand. A key feature of the Swiss Challenge Process is using the bid of one competitor as a benchmark against which to measure rival bids. Though the original bidder has the opportunity to counter any superior offers that subsequently emerge, the process is obviously risky and costly. Yet for many Canadian firms in the important commercial services field, developing an ability to prepare effective price bids, and being willing to develop effective competitive intelligence systems, will be of major importance to market success.

International Channels of Distribution for Services

Delivery of services across national borders is dictated by the inherent nature of the service, the customer preferences, the attitudes of the host government, and the degree of control of operations.[51] Globalization has brought changes in that service providers are confronted with a variety of entry-mode choices. We have discussed market entry choices elsewhere in the book, but in the case of international services, possible modes will include direct exporting, licensing, franchising, management contracts, turnkey operations, joint ventures, and wholly owned subsidiaries. (Note, however, that some of these will work well for manufactured goods as well). We should also add to this list the ubiquitous option of electronic marketing.

Basically, a Canadian service firm that plans to start to market its services internationally needs to find a way of making its services accessible in the chosen foreign market. The World Trade Organization lists four modes of delivery; these are outlined below.[52] In practice, firms may well employ a mix of these methods.

Mode 1: Cross-Border—The Service Itself Crosses the Border

Cross-border trade takes place when the service itself crosses the border from one country to another, without the movement of persons. The service is being transported either via electronic means or by infrastructure such as transportation services (air, rail, land, sea) or

The Global MARKETPLACE 10.4

Winning Service Contracts is Long, Hard Work

Perseverance is well known to be important in many areas of human endeavour. This is especially true in the case of some international projects, for example, a new airport in Ecuador. In August 2005, the Toronto-based firm Aecon Group announced the signing of financing documents by Aecon, its concession partners, and the project lenders for the new Quito International Airport project. According to Bill Pearson, executive vice president of the company, "Today is the result of over four years of hard work, not just by Aecon but also by our partners in the project." Mr. Pearson goes on to thank a variety of collaborators including four public-sector lenders, three private-sector partners, and the Canadian government, which, through the Canadian Commercial Corporation, the Export Development Corporation, and the Canadian International Development Agency, "did so much to make the project a reality." Mayor Paco Moncayo of Quito is also praised for his foresight and creativity in serving his city, and is credited as being "the real driving force behind the project."

Demand for airport services in Quito has been growing steadily over the years, overtaxing the existing facilities. A decision therefore had to be made to close down the airport, which is located in the downtown core of the capital city of Quito, and build a new one on a site where future expansion would be possible. A location some 18 kilometres east of the city was chosen. A major concern of Mayor Moncayo is to attract manufacturing and create jobs. This will be greatly facilitated by having a larger international airport with a free trade zone. Air traffic is expected to grow 4.5 to 5.5 percent per year for the foreseeable future, and the planned 3.6 km runway will be expanded to 4.1 km before a second runway is added.

Historically, the original airport was built some 70 years ago but eventually the city's economic growth began to put excessive strain on it. (This has also happened elsewhere; for example, in Hong Kong, where the one-runway Kai Tak Airport, first built in 1925, was replaced by the new airport at Chek Lap Kok in 1998).

On this occasion the government used the Swiss Challenge Process. Aecon found this risky because their proposal was used to open up bidding, a process with similarities to an auction. Also, the company did not at the time have the necessary funding in place to undertake all the needed work upfront. But in the end, financing was obtained and the contract secured. In September 2002, Aecon and its new partners, operating under the name Quiport, were awarded a 35-year concession contract to design, build, finance, and operate the new airport and the concession rights to continue operating the existing airport, with numerous accompanying services, until construction is complete, which is expected to be in 2010.

Dominique Bergevin, a political risk analyst with EDC, is quoted as saying that political instability in Ecuador and the revolving-door bureaucracy have created a challenging environment for foreign investment. "Anti-government protests and strikes are common and can influence the government's course of action," she says. "Foreign investors operating in Ecuador have been engaged in contractual disputes with the government over fiscal matters."

Moreover, according to Leslie Smith, second vice president of the Ecuadorian-Canadian Chamber of Commerce, companies themselves often have to sort out problems such as invasions of mining concessions by local prospectors and the setting up of roadblocks. Because the police may be reluctant to intervene, Canadian companies have to learn how to deal with the locals directly, and they are becoming increasingly efficient at doing this, in Mr. Smith's view.

Following from this, Bill Pearson believes that you cannot go into a country like Ecuador without a strong, legally knowledgeable partner able to help with the intricacies and idiosyncrasies of doing business in such a country. Mr. Smith echoes this: "It is important to get an Ecuadorian partner that can basically provide you with political insurance so that when you have contractual difficulties with the government—and there almost always are those—there are people who can go and sort it out."

Mr. Pearson adds that it is important to settle in for the long haul by picking a few key markets that you want to pursue. "It takes time to make the right contacts and establish the trust that's needed to operate in any country outside of Canada. You can't expect to get in and out quickly and make a few bucks. You need to be committed and patient—then, and only then, will you start to see the payoff." Again, Mr. Smith's views are similar. He encourages Canadians who plan business projects in Ecuador to learn Spanish, to have a fluent staff, and to become as familiar as possible with the country. "The successful projects that have been completed by Canadians are the ones where the Canadians come down and learn to live the project, live the life here, and become totally immersed in the culture."

Sources: Celeste Mackenzie, "How to Do Business in Ecuador: Successful Canadian Companies Absorb the Local Culture," *Canadian Business* (February 28–March 13, 2005), **http://www.canadianbusiness.com/managing/strategy/article.jsp?content=20060109_1650;** Aecon Group, news release, "Quito Airport Financing Documents Signed," August 25, 2005, **http://www.aecon.com/News_Releases/news08250501.aspx;** Brenda Brown, "Aecon Group: Building Ecuador's International Airport," *Exportwise* (Spring 2006): 4-5; Patricia Williams, "Quito Airport Project Ready to Fly," *Daily Commercial News* (June 23, 2006), **http://www.dailycommercialnews.com/article/20060623300;** and "Aecon Flying High with Quito Airport Project," *Daily Commercial News* (June 26, 2007), **http://www.dcnonl.com/article/id23280.**

telecommunications (telephone, radio). Examples include management consulting, marketing research, consulting engineering, and education and training. The Internet is prompting many service firms to rethink their global strategy as they realize that when only the service needs to cross the border, there can be considerable savings in time and money, and it may be relatively straightforward to enter new markets.

Mode 2: Consumption Abroad—The Consumer Travels across the Border

This mode relates to services the firm might provide to nationals of another country, which requires them to travel to the company's location for those services. If the organization providing the services is paid in foreign currency, technically the services are being exported without leaving the country. One example of this mode is tourism services and its various subsets (e.g., business tourism, ecotourism, edu-tourism). Another is legal services where the client seeks legal advice in the local market and will travel within the market to obtain it.

Mode 3: Commercial Presence—Establishment of an Office or Entity

Commercial presence refers to instances where a company from one country sets up subsidiaries or branches to provide services in another country. Examples include financial services (a bank sets up local branches), construction engineering (a company sets up project offices to manage local infrastructure projects), information technology (a firm sets up local service facilities), distribution (a shipping or logistics company sets up local warehousing). The importance of having knowledgeable staff "on the ground" to cater to local needs will be of prime importance to firms setting up abroad.

Mode 4: Movement of Natural Persons—The Services Supplier Travels across the Border

Movement of natural persons refers to individuals travelling from their own country in order to supply services in another. Examples include construction (architects travelling abroad to sites), education and training (trainers and professional speakers working abroad), and recreation and sport (coaches, trainers, and promoters working in a foreign country). Such individuals will do well to acquire some knowledge of the culture of the countries they are visiting before starting the trip.

Summary

Services are taking on an increasing importance in global marketing. They need to be considered separately from the marketing of goods because they no longer simply complement goods. Increasingly, goods complement services or are in competition with them. Because of service attributes such as intangibility, perishability, customization, and cultural sensitivity, the global marketing of services is frequently more complex than that of goods.

Services play an increasingly important role not just in the Canadian economy but also in the global one. As a result, international growth and competition in the sector outstrips that of merchandise trade and is likely to intensify in the future. Even though services are unlikely to replace production, the sector will account for the shaping of new comparative advantages internationally, particularly in light of new facilitating technologies that encourage electronic commerce. However, in a similar fashion to goods, services face significant problems in the global arena, for example, regulations imposed on service trade by individual countries.

Many Canadian firms now operating domestically need to investigate the possibility of going global. It will be beneficial for them to adopt a strategic planning approach to global services marketing. This calls for an understanding of the key indicators that will determine success in the market, along with the development of appropriate products. Planning the market offering involves various problems, for example, determining the degree of standardization versus local adaptation. Global marketing strategy also encompasses sales promotion, pricing, and distribution. As shown in the chapter, setting down hard and fast rules for these decisions can be complex.

The historical patterns in which service providers followed manufacturers abroad have become obsolete as stand-alone services have become more important to world trade. Management must therefore assess its vulnerability to international service competition and explore opportunities to provide its services around the world.

Key Terms

barriers to entry (p. 345)
consumer ethnocentrism (p. 346)
consumer patriotism (p. 346)
cross-cultural incongruence (p. 346)
customer involvement (p. 337)
discriminatory regulations (p. 345)
infant industry (p. 345)
intangibility (p. 337)
market transparency (p. 337)
mental stimulus processing (p. 357)
national security (p. 345)
non-discriminatory regulations (p. 345)
people-processing services (p. 357)
perishability (p. 337)
service capacity (p. 337)
service consistency (p. 337)
Swiss Challenge Process (p. 365)

Questions for Discussion

1. How has the Internet affected your service purchases?
2. Discuss the major reasons for the growth of international services.
3. How does the international sale of services differ from the sale of goods?
4. What are some of the international marketing implications of service intangibility?
5. Discuss the effects of cultural sensitivity on international services.
6. Explain the country-of-origin effect. How will this influence the choice of a service provider?
7. Is it useful to try to classify services? Why? Why not?
8. What are the special problems of marketing supplementary services internationally?
9. What are some ways for a firm to expand its services internationally?
10. How can a firm in a developing country participate in the international services boom?
11. Which services would be expected to migrate globally in the next decade? Why?

Internet Exercises

1. Find the most current data on the five leading export and import countries for commercial services. The information is available on the World Trade Organization website (**http://www.wto.org**). Click on "Statistics."
2. What are the key Canadian services exports and imports? What are the key trends in the last 10 years? Go to the Statistics Canada website (**http://www.statscan.ca**) and look under "Statistics by Subject."

Recommended Readings

Business Guide to the World Trading System. Geneva: International Trade Centre UNCTAD/WTO and London, Commonwealth Secretariat, 1999.

Cuadrado-Roura, Juan R., Luis Rubalcaba-Bermejo, John R. Bryson, and Witold J. Henisz, eds. *Trading Services in the Global Economy.* Northampton, MA: Edward Elgar, 2002.

Hoffman, Douglas K., and John E.G. Bateson. *Essentials of Services Marketing*. Mason, OH: South-Western, 2002.

Lovelock, Christopher H. *Services Marketing: People, Technology, Strategy*. 5th ed. Upper Saddle River, NJ: Prentice-Hall, 2005.

Meyer, Anton, and Frank Dornach. *The German Customer Barometer*. Annual. Munich: FMG-Verlag, 2006.

Stern, Robert M., ed. *Services in the International Economy*. Ann Arbor: University of Michigan Press, 2001.

U.S. Coalition of Service Industries. Policy Issues and Links to Industries. **http://uscsi.org.**

U.S. Department of Commerce, International Trade Administration, Office of Service Industries. *Results of Services 2002*. Washington, DC: 2002.

Zeithaml, Valerie, and Mary Jo Bitner. *Services Marketing*. 3rd ed. New York: McGraw-Hill, 2003.

Notes

1. Leonard L. Berry, "Services Marketing Is Different," in *Services Marketing*, ed. Christopher H. Lovelock (Englewood Cliffs, NJ: Prentice-Hall, 1984), 30.
2. Christian Grönroos, "Marketing Services: The Case of a Missing Product," *Journal of Business & Industrial Marketing* 13, no. 4/5 (1998): 322–38.
3. Pierre Berthon, Leyland Pitt, Constantine S. Katsikeas, and Jean Paul Berthon, "Virtual Services Go International: International Services in the Marketspace," *Journal of International Marketing* 7, no. 3 (1999): 84–106.
4. Foreign Affairs and International Trade Canada, "Trade in Services: Canada and Trade in Services," **http://www.international.gc.ca** (accessed October 12, 2006).
5. Industry Canada, "Service Industries: Overview of Canada's Trade in Services: Canada in a Global Context," **http://strategis.ic.gc.ca** (accessed October 13, 2006).
6. Export Development Canada, "World Trade in Services," (July 2006).
7. Foreign Affairs and International Trade Canada, "Trade in Services: Canada and Trade in Services," **http://www.international.gc.ca** (accessed October 12, 2006).
8. Export Development Canada, "World Trade in Services," (July 2006).
9. Industry Canada, "Services Industries: Introduction: Canada in a Global Context," **http://www.strategis.ic.gc.ca** (accessed October 13, 2006).
10. Foreign Affairs and International Trade Canada, "Trade and the Canadian Economy: Stories of the Week," July 8, 2002, **http://www.international.gc.ca** (accessed October 13, 2006).
11. Industry Canada, "Services Industries: Introduction: Canada in a Global Context," **http://www.strategis.ic.gc.ca** (accessed October 13, 2006).
12. Foreign Affairs and International Trade Canada, "Trade in Services: Canada and Trade in Services," **http://www.international.gc.ca** (accessed October 12, 2006).
13. *The World Factbook* 2002, **https://www.cia.gov** (accessed October 30, 2002).
14. International Trade Centre, Geneva, **http://www.intracen.org/servicexport,** September 1999.
15. K.I. Al-Sulaiti and M.J. Baker, "Country of Origin Effects: A Literature Review," *Marketing Intelligence and Planning* 16, no. 3 (1998): 150–99.
16. R.G. Javalgi, B. Cutler, and W.A. Winans, "At Your Service! Does Country of Origin Research Apply?" *Journal of Services Marketing* 15, no. 6/7 (2001): 565–82.
17. Al-Sulaiti and Baker, op. cit.
18. C.H. Lovelock, "Developing Marketing Strategies for Transnational Service Operations," *Journal of Services Marketing* 13, no. 4/5 (1999): 278–89.
19. Javalgi, Cutler, and Winans, op. cit.
20. C.M. Han, "The Role of Consumer Patriotism in the Choice of Domestic vs. Foreign Products," *Journal of Advertising Research* (June/July 1988): 25–32.
21. E.R. Bruning, "Country of Origin, National Loyalty and Product Choice: the Case of International Air Travel," *International Marketing Review* 14, no. 1 (1997): 59–74.
22. L.J. Harrison-Walker, "The Relative Effects of National Stereotype and Advertising Information on the Selection of a Service Provider," *Journal of Services Marketing* 9, no. 1 (1995): 47–59.
23. M. Wetzels, M. Birgelen, and K. Ruyter, "Ain't It Much, If It Ain't Dutch? An Application of the Consumer Ethnocentrism Concept to International Services in The Netherlands," in *European Marketing Academy, Proceedings* 2, ed. J.K. Beracs, A. Bauer, and J. Simon (Budapest: Budapest University of Economic Sciences, 1996): 1255–69.
24. P.G. Patterson and T. Smith, "Relationship Benefits in Service Industries: A Replication in a Southeast Asian Context," *Journal of Services Marketing* 15, no. 6 (2001): 425–43.
25. L.D. Dahringer, "Marketing Services Internationally: Barriers and Management Strategies," *Journal of Services Marketing* 5, no. 3 (1991): 5–17.
26. H.C.S. Tai and Y.K.R. Chan, "Cross-Cultural Studies on Information Content of Service Advertising," *Journal of Services Marketing* 15, no. 7 (2001): 547–64.
27. "EDC Report on World Trade in Services," **http://www.edc.ca/english/print/mediaroom_11409.htm.**
28. Samiee Saeed, "The Internationalization of Services: Trends, Obstacles and Issues," *Journal of Services Marketing* 13, no. 4/5 (1999): 319–28.
29. Kavalgi, op. cit.
30. J.A. Fitzsimmons and M.J. Fitzsimmons, *Service Management, Service Development and Process Design,* 3rd ed. (New York: McGraw-Hill, 2001).
31. Dorothy Riddle, "Using the Internet for Service Exporting: Tips for Service Firms," *International Trade Forum* 1 (1999): 19–23.
32. Alex Garden, "Why Multilingual Makes Sense," Netinsites, **http://www.netinsites.com/article3.cfm?ArticleID=90** (accessed December 10, 2007).
33. "Engineering, Technical, and Other Services to Industry," *Synthesis Report* (Paris: Organization for Economic Cooperation and Development, 1988).
34. Business Line, "Software exports to US up 32 pc," July 23, 2002, **http://www.blonnet.com/2002/07/04/stories/2002070401220600.htm** (accessed October 30, 2002).
35. Paul G. Patterson and Muris Cicic, "A Typology of Service Firms in International Markets: An Empirical Investigation," *Journal of International Marketing* 3, no. 4 (1995): 57–83.

36. M. Krishna Erramilli and C. P. Rao, "Service Firms' International Entry-Mode Choice: A Modified Transaction–Cost Analysis Approach," *Journal of Marketing* 57 (July 1993): 19–38.

37. R.G. Javalgi and D. Steven White, "Strategic Challenges for the Marketing of Services Internationally," *International Marketing Review* 19, no. 6 (2002): 563–81.

38. C.C. Wolfe, "US Services Trade Data," *Business America* 119, no. 4 (1998): 44.

39. Saeed, op. cit.

40. T. Clark, D. Rajaratnam, and T. Smith, "Toward a Theory of International Services: Marketing Intangibles in a World of Nations," *Journal of International Marketing* 4, no. 2 (1996): 9–28.

41. C.H. Lovelock and G.S. Yip, "Developing Global Strategies for Service Businesses," *California Management Review* 38, no. 2 (1996): 64–86.

42. P.G. Patterson and M. Cicic, "A Typology of Service Firms in International Markets: An Empirical Investigation," *Journal of International Marketing* 3, no. 4 (1995): 57–84.

43. Rogelio Oliva and Robert Kallenberg, "Managing the Transition from Products to Services," *International Journal of Service Industry Management* 14, no. 2 (2003): 160–72.

44. Oliva and Kallenberg, op. cit.

45. Lovelock and Yip, op. cit.

46. C. McLaughlin and J. Fitzsimmons, "Strategies for Globalization of Service Operations," *International Journal of Service Industry Management* 7, no. 4 (1996): 43–57.

47. J.E. Ross and D.A. Georgoff, "A Survey of Productivity and Quality Issues in Manufacturing: The State of the Industry," *Industrial Management* 33, no. 1 (1991): 3–9.

48. A. Parasuraman, V.A. Zeithaml, and L.L. Berry, "A Conceptual Model of Service Quality and its Implications for Future Research," *Journal of Marketing* 49, no. 4 (1985): 41–50.

49. N.K. Malhotra, F.M. Ulgadi, J. Agarwal, and I.B. Baalbaki, "International Services Marketing: A Comparative Evaluation of the Dimensions of Service Quality between Developed Countries and Developing Countries," *International Marketing Review* 11, no. 2 (1994): 5–15.

50. Kathryn F. Winsted and Paul G. Patterson, "Internationalization of Services: The Service Exporting Decision," *Journal of Services Marketing* 12, no. 4 (1998): 294–311.

51. A. Zimmerman, "Impacts of Service Trade Barriers: A Study of Insurance Industry," *Journal of Services Marketing* 14, no. 3 (1999): 211–28.

52. "Company Competencies: Four Modes of Delivery," Exportsource.ca, **http://www.exportsource.ca/gol/exportsource/site.nsf/en-print/es02491.html** (accessed April 12, 2007).

Chapter 11

Global Pricing Strategies

The Global MARKETPLACE 11.1

Price Fixing in the Cargo Services Industry

The Canadian Competition Bureau has launched an investigation into allegations of price fixing in the international air cargo services industry. Air Canada, Canada's largest airline, has been asked to provide information on the pricing of its cargo services into and out of Canada. At the same time that the bureau made its request, U.S. and European authorities raided airlines on both sides of the Atlantic in their search for evidence to support their allegations of global price fixing in the air cargo industry. The European Union's executive arm and the U.S. Justice Department were involved in the raids, which included searches at KLM, American Airlines, United Airlines, Lufthansa, and freight airline Cargolux. In most countries, it is against the law for companies to set prices or divide market territories. It is alleged that more than a dozen cargo carriers entered into tacit agreements to impose certain surcharges on their customers to offset the rising cost of fuel and the additional security measures enacted after the terrorist attacks of September 11, 2001. The cargo service providers are also alleged to have agreed among themselves to impose surcharges on their customers to cover war risk insurance premiums with the outbreak of war in Iraq in 2003.

Air Canada operates cargo services into Europe and Asia. As with other airlines, Air Canada has suffered from declining passenger loads as the industry has faced a host of structural problems since the 2001 terrorist attacks. Most airlines are increasingly focusing on cargo transportation as a means of offsetting declining revenues from passenger traffic. While cargo operations have historically been notoriously inefficient, there is now increased pressure to raise prices in that segment of the market.

Sources: "Air Canada in Inquiry over Cargo Price-fixing," *Financial Post*, February 15, 2006; "Cargo Carriers," *Financial Post*, February 16, 2006.

This chapter will focus on pricing decisions in global marketing. A firm's pricing decisions in international markets have a major impact on sales and profitability. The chapter provides a discussion of the factors firms need to consider in the development and execution of their pricing strategy. Corporate objectives, cost considerations, the nature of the demand for the product, and a range of environmental factors are discussed. As The Global Marketplace 11.1 illustrates, the impact of government regulations cannot be ignored. The discussion in this chapter highlights the complexity of international pricing decisions. In a global market environment, firms also need to decide on their approach for the coordination of prices across multiple country markets. The degree of head-office control—or, conversely, subsidiary autonomy—needs to be decided. Alternative approaches to coordination are explored in this chapter. Of course, in the case of multinational corporations, decisions must also be made as to how prices should be set, not only for products sold to external customers, but also for inputs, intermediate, and final products sold to divisions and subsidiaries within the same firm. Such internal transactions take us into the area of transfer pricing, a subject of increasing significance to Canadian firms as they bulk up to take on global competitors. Given the importance of exports to the Canadian economy, this chapter also provides a comprehensive discussion of export pricing. The setting of export prices is complicated by factors such as increased distance from the markets, currency fluctuations, governmental policies (e.g., duties), and typically longer and different types of channels of distribution. In spite of the factors influencing the pricing decision, the objective remains the same: to create demand for the marketer's offerings and to do so profitably over the long term. In achieving this, financing arrangements for export transactions are critical. Two reasons may be advanced: (1) to secure sales, and (2) to combat various types of risk. A special consideration in export pricing, dumping, is also discussed in this chapter.

Price Dynamics

Price is the only element of the marketing mix that is revenue generating; all the others are costs. Price should therefore be used as an active instrument of strategy in the major areas of marketing decision making. Price serves as a means of communication with the buyer by providing a basis for judging the attractiveness of the offer. It is a major competitive tool in meeting and beating close rivals and substitutes. Competition will often force prices down, whereas intra-company financial considerations have an opposite effect. Prices, along with costs, will determine the long-term viability of the enterprise.

Price should not be determined in isolation from the other marketing mix elements. It may be used effectively in positioning the product in the marketplace. The feasibility range for price setting established by demand, competition, costs, and legal considerations may be narrow or wide in a given situation (for example, the pricing of a commodity versus an innovation). Regardless of how narrow the gap allowed by these factors, however, pricing should never be considered a static element. The marketer's ultimate goal is to make the customer's demand as inelastic as possible; i.e., the customer should prefer the marketer's offer even at a price premium.

Similarly, pricing decisions cannot be made in isolation from the other functions of the firm. Effective financial arrangements can significantly support the marketing program if they are carefully formulated between the finance and marketing areas. Sales are often won or lost on the basis of favourable credit terms to the buyer. With large numbers of competent firms active in international markets, financing packages—often put together with the help of governmental support—have become more important. Customers abroad may be prepared to accept higher prices if they can obtain attractive credit terms.

A summary of international pricing situations is provided as a matrix in Exhibit 11.1. Pricing challenges—such as pricing for a new market entry, changing price either as an attack strategy or in response to competitive changes, and multiple-product coordination in cases of related demand—are technically the same as problems encountered in domestic markets. The scope of these pricing situations will vary according to the degree of foreign involvement and the type of market encountered.

In first-time pricing, the general alternatives are (1) skimming, (2) following the market price, and (3) penetration pricing. The objective of **skimming** is to achieve the highest possible contribution in a short time period. For a global marketer to use this approach, the product has to be unique, and some segments of the market must be willing to pay the high price. As more segments are targeted and more of the product is made available,

Exhibit 11.1 **International Pricing Situations**

Pricing Situation	International Involvement		
	Exporting	Foreign-Market Pricing	Intracompany Pricing
First-Time Pricing			
Changing Pricing			
Multiple-Product Pricing			

Sources: Elements of the model adapted from Howard Forman and Richard A. Lancioni, "International Industrial Pricing Strategic Decisions and the Pricing Manager: Some Key Issues," *Professional Pricing Society,* October 9, 1999, at **http://www.pricing-advisor.com/jour_article2.htm;** and Helmut Becker, "Pricing: An International Marketing Challenge," in *International Marketing Strategy,* ed. Hans Thorelli and Helmut Becker (New York: Pergamon Press, 1980): 203–15.

the price is gradually lowered. The success of skimming depends on the ability and speed of competitive reaction.

If similar products already exist in the target market, **market pricing** can be used. The final customer price is determined based on competitive prices, and then both production and marketing must be adjusted to the price. This approach requires the company to have a thorough knowledge of product costs, as well as confidence that the product life cycle is long enough to warrant entry into the market. It is a reactive approach and may lead to problems if sales volumes never rise to sufficient levels to produce a satisfactory return. Although firms typically use pricing as a differentiation tool, the global marketing manager may have no choice but to accept the prevailing world market price.

When **penetration pricing** is used, the product is offered at a low price intended to generate volume sales and achieve high market share, which would compensate for a lower per-unit return. One company found, for example, that a 20 percent reduction in average pricing roughly doubled the demand for its product.[1] This approach typically requires mass markets, price-sensitive customers, and decreasing production and marketing costs as sales volumes increase. Clearly, firms which are able to achieve economies of scale in production will be in a better position, because of lower per-unit costs, to price more aggressively in the marketplace. The basic assumption of penetration pricing is that the lower price will increase sales, which may not always be the case. This approach can also be used to discourage other marketers from entering the market.

Price changes are called for when a new product is launched, when a change occurs in overall market conditions (such as a change in the value of the billing currency), or when there is a change in the company's internal situation, such as costs of production. A company may elect not to change price even though the result may be lower profitability. However, if a decision is made to change prices, related changes must also be considered. For example, if an increase in price is required, it may at least initially be accompanied by increased promotional efforts. Price changes usually follow changes in the product's stage in the life cycle. As the product matures, more pressure will be put on the price to keep the product competitive despite increased competition and less possibility of differentiation.

With multiple-product pricing, the various items in the line may be differentiated by pricing them appropriately to indicate, for example, an economy version, a standard version, and a top-of-the-line version. One of the products in the line may be priced to protect against competitors or to gain market share from existing competitors. The other items in the line are then expected to make up for the lost contribution of such a "fighting brand."

Pricing in Foreign Markets

Pricing within individual foreign markets in which the company operates is determined by (1) corporate objectives, (2) costs, (3) customer behaviour and market conditions, (4) market structure, and (5) environmental constraints.[2] Because all these factors vary among the countries in which the firm might have a presence, the pricing policy is under pressure to vary as well. With price holding a position of importance with customers, a market-driven firm must be informed and sensitive to customer views and realities.[3] This is especially critical for those marketers wanting to position their products as premium alternatives.

Although many global marketers emphasize non-price methods of competition, they rank pricing high as a marketing tool overseas, even though the non-domestic pricing decisions are made at the middle management level in a majority of firms.[4] Pricing decisions also tend to be made more at the local level, with coordination from headquarters in more strategic decision situations.[5] With increased trade liberalization and advanced economic integration, this coordination is becoming more important.

Corporate Objectives

Global marketers must set and adjust their objectives, both financial (such as return on investment) and marketing-related (such as maintaining or increasing market share), based on the prevailing conditions in each of their markets. Pricing may well influence the overall strategic moves of the company as a whole. This is well illustrated by the decision of many foreign-based companies, automakers for example, to begin production in North America rather than to continue exporting. Apart from trade barriers, many have had their market shares erode because of higher wages in their home markets, increasing shipping costs, and unfavourable exchange rates. Market share very often plays a major role in pricing decisions in that marketers may be willing to sacrifice immediate earnings for market share gain or maintenance. This is especially true in highly competitive situations; for example, during a period of extremely high competitive activity in Japan in the computer sector, the local Fujitsu's one-year net income was only 5 percent of sales, compared with IBM's 12.7 percent worldwide and 7.6 percent in Japan.

Pricing decisions will also vary depending on the pricing situation. The basics of first-time pricing, price adjustment, and product-line pricing apply to pricing within non-domestic situations as well. Companies that introduce all of their new products worldwide within a very short time period have an option of either skimming or penetration pricing. If the product is an innovation, the marketer may decide to charge a premium for the product. If, however, competition is keen or expected to increase in the near future, lower prices may be used to make the product more attractive to the buyers and the market less attractive to the competition. The Korean conglomerates (such as Daewoo, Goldstar, Hyundai, and Samsung) were able to penetrate and capture the low end of many consumer goods markets in Canada, the United States, and Europe based on price competitiveness over the past 10 years.

Price changes may be frequent if the company's objective is to undersell a major competitor. A marketer may, for example, decide to maintain a price level 10 to 20 percent below that of a major competitor; price changes would be necessary whenever the competitor made significant changes in its prices. Price changes may also be required because of changes in foreign exchange rates. To remain competitive, marketers may have to reduce their international prices, for example, if the host country's currency weakens, making imported products more expensive. With longer-term unfavourable currency changes, marketers have to improve their efficiency and/or shift production bases. These ideas are borne out by a recent survey of Canadian firms by the Bank of Canada. In a survey of 170 Canadian businesses, the bank found that the most important motivators for price changes were the price changes of competing firms, changes in domestic input costs, and changes in product demand. Interestingly, the bank's research found that firms with a significant export sales base tended to change prices more often, suggesting that exposure to international customers demands more pricing flexibility from globally oriented firms.[6]

Product-line pricing typically occurs in conjunction with positioning decisions. The global marketer may have a premium line as well as a standard line and, in some cases, may sell directly to retailers for their private-label sales. Products facing mass markets have keener competition and smaller profit margins than premium products, which may well be priced more liberally because there is less competition.

Costs

Costs are frequently used as a basis for price determination largely because they are easily measured and provide a floor under which prices cannot go in the long term. These include procurement, manufacturing, logistics, and marketing costs, as well as overhead. Quality at an affordable price drives most procurement systems. The decision to turn to offshore suppliers may often be influenced by their lower prices, which enable the marketer to remain competitive.[7] Locating manufacturing facilities in different parts of the world may lower various costs, such as labour or distribution costs, although this may create new challenges. While a market may be attractive as far as labour costs are concerned, issues such as productivity, additional costs (such as logistics), and political risk will have to be factored in. Furthermore, a country may lose its attraction due to increasing costs (for example, the average industrial wage rose 110 percent in Korea in the 1990s), and the marketer may have to start the cycle anew by going to new markets (such as Indonesia or Vietnam).

Varying inflation rates will have a major impact on the administration of prices, especially because they are usually accompanied by government controls. The task of the parent company is to aid subsidiaries in their planning to ensure that they reach margin targets despite unfavourable market conditions. Most experienced companies in emerging markets generally have strong country managers who create significant value through their understanding of the local environment. Their ability to be more agile in a turbulent environment is a significant competitive advantage. Inflationary environments call for constant price adjustments; in markets with hyperinflation, pricing may be in a stable currency such as the Canadian dollar, the U.S. dollar, or the euro with daily translation into the local currency. In such volatile environments, the marketer may want to shift supply arrangements to cost-effective alternatives, pursue rapid inventory turnovers, shorten credit terms, and make sure contracts have appropriate safety mechanisms against inflation (e.g., choice of currency or escalator clause).

The opposite scenario may also be encountered; that is, prices cannot be increased due to economic conditions. Inflation has been kept in check in developed economies for a number of reasons. Globalization has increased the number of competitors, and the Internet has made it easy for customers to shop for the lowest prices. Big intermediaries, such as Wal-Mart, are demanding prices at near cost from their suppliers. In Europe, the advent of the euro has made prices even more transparent.[8] Strategies for thriving in disinflationary times may include (1) target pricing, in which efficiencies are sought in production and marketing to meet price-driven costing; (2) value pricing, to move away from coupons, discounts, and promotions to everyday low prices; (3) stripping down products, to offer quality without all the frills; (4) adding value by introducing innovative products sold at a modest premium (accompanied by strong merchandising and promotion) but perceived by customers to be worth it; and (5) getting close to customers by using new technologies such as Electronic Data Interchange (EDI) and the Internet to track their needs and the firm's costs more closely.[9] An example of Nike's adjustment to the new realities in Asia appears in The Global Marketplace 11.2.

Internally, controversy may arise in determining which manufacturing and marketing costs to include. For example, controversy may arise over the amounts of research and development to charge to subsidiaries or over how to divide the costs of a pan-regional advertising campaign when costs are incurred primarily on satellite channels and viewership varies dramatically from one market to the next.

The Global MARKETPLACE 11.2

Just Do It in a Recession!

Nike's international revenues have grown gradually and now compare well with sales in its home country, the United States. When the Asian recession sapped purchasing power in Southeast Asia, Nike targeted teens living in the region's rural and suburban areas with a range of "entry-level" footwear. The Nike Play Series line, launched in September 1999 in India, Indonesia, Singapore, and Thailand, retails for about $25, roughly half the price of most Nike shoes and far less than the $150 charged for its top-range products.

Asian kids in rural areas might be playing sports with no shoes at all, so they cannot relate to Nike's high-end products. Nike Play Series was created to introduce them to the concept of different shoes for different sports. Even among those who purchase luxury products, sales have fallen 30 percent in the Asian markets hardest hit by the 1997–98 Asian currency crisis.

Ads for the new product line use the slogan "It's My Turn" and depict young Asian athletes (such as Singaporean soccer sensation Aliff Shafaein and Philippine basketball star Alvin Patrimonio) alongside images of major sports stars. Nike also built branded Play Zones in new or refurbished urban centres such as Singapore, Kuala Lumpur, Bangkok, Manila, and Johor Bahru. Each includes a multi-court facility where kids play everything from badminton to basketball, highlighted by "event days" with tournaments. In rural areas, Nike donated equipment such as basketball hoops and football goal posts to raise the profile of the Nike Play Series.

Sources: "How Nike Got Its Game Back," *Business Week*, November 4, 2002, 129; Normandy Madden, "Nike Sells $25 Shoe Line in Recession-Hit Region," *Advertising Age*, November 1999, 17; and **http://nikebiz.com/community/gcastry.shtml.**

Demand and Market Factors

Demand will set a price ceiling in a given market. Despite the difficulties in obtaining data on foreign markets and forecasting potential demand, the global marketer must make judgments concerning the quantities that can be sold at different prices in each foreign market. The global marketer must understand the **price elasticity of consumer demand** to determine appropriate price levels, especially if cost structures change. A status-conscious market that insists on products with established reputations will be inelastic, allowing for far more pricing freedom than a market where price-consciousness drives demand. With the increased information and travel that globalization has brought about, status-consciousness is being replaced by a more practical consumerist sensibility: top quality at competitive prices.

The marketer's freedom in making pricing decisions is closely tied to customer perceptions of the product offering and the marketing communication tied to it. Toyota is able to outsell Chevrolet on identical models which are both produced by NUMMI Inc., a joint venture between Toyota and GM, even though its version (the Corolla) is priced $2,000 higher on the average. Similarly, Korean automakers have had a challenging time in shedding their image as a risky purchase. For example, consumers who liked the Hyundai Santa Fe said they would pay $10,000 less because it was a Hyundai.[10]

Prices have to be set keeping in mind not only the ultimate consumers but also the intermediaries involved. The success of a particular pricing strategy will depend on the willingness of both the manufacturer and the intermediary to cooperate. For example, if the marketer wants to undercut its competition, it has to make sure that retailers' margins remain adequate and competitive to ensure appropriate implementation. At the same time, there is enormous pressure on manufacturers' margins from the side of intermediaries who are growing in both size and global presence. These intermediaries, such as the French Carrefour and the British Marks & Spencer, demand low-cost, direct-supply contracts, which many manufacturers may not be willing or able to furnish.[11] The only other option may be to resort to alternate distribution modes, which may be impossible.

Market Structure and Competition

Competition helps set the price within the parameters of cost and demand. Depending on the marketer's objectives and competitive position, it may choose to compete directly on price or elect for non-price measures. If a pricing response is sought, the marketer can offer bundled prices (i.e., value deals on a combination of products) or loyalty programs to insulate the firm from a price war. Price cuts can also be executed selectively rather than across the board. New products can be introduced to counter price challenges. For example, when Japanese Kao introduced a low-priced diskette to compete against 3M, rather than drop its prices 3M introduced a new brand, Highland, that effectively outflanked Kao's competitive incursion. Simply dropping the price on the 3M brand could have badly diluted its image. On the non-price front, the company can opt to fight back on quality by adding and promoting value-adding features.[12]

If a company's position is being eroded by competitors who focus on price, the marketer may have no choice but to respond. For example, IBM's operation in Japan lost market share in mainframes largely because competitors undersold the company. A Japanese mainframe was typically listed at 10 percent less than its IBM counterpart, and it frequently carried an additional 10 to 20 percent discount beyond that. This created an extremely competitive market. IBM's reaction was to respond in kind with aggressive promotion of its own, with the result that it began regaining its lost share. Motorola and Nokia, the leading mobile phone makers, are facing tough conditions in the Korean market. In addition to being competitive in price and quality, local companies such as Samsung and Goldstar are quick to come up with new models to satisfy the fast-changing needs of consumers while providing better after-sales service, free of charge or at a marginal price, than the two global players.[13]

In some cases, strategic realignment may be needed. To hold on to its eroding worldwide market share, Caterpillar has striven to shrink costs and move away from its old practice of competing only by building advanced, enduring machines and selling them at premium prices. Instead, the company has cut prices and has used strategic alliances overseas to produce competitive equipment to better suit local and regional needs.

Some global marketers can fend off price competition by emphasizing other elements of the marketing mix, even if they are at an absolute disadvantage in price. Singer Sewing Machine Co., which gains nearly half its $500 million in sales from developing countries, emphasizes its established reputation, product quality, and liberal credit terms, as well as other services (such as sewing classes), rather than competing head-on with lower-cost producers.[14]

Environmental Constraints

Governments influence prices as well as the firm's pricing strategy. In addition to the policy measures, such as tariffs and taxes, governments may also elect to directly control price levels. Once under **price controls**, the global marketer has to operate as it would in a regulated industry. Setting maximum prices has been defended primarily on political grounds: it stops inflation and an accelerating wage-price spiral, and consumers want it. Supporters also maintain that price controls raise the income of the poor. Operating in such circumstances is difficult. Achieving change in prices can be frustrating; for example, a company may wait 30 to 45 days for an acknowledgment of a price-increase petition. In Canada, for example, the Patented Medicine Prices Review Board (PMPRB) monitors prescription drug prices with a view to ensuring that they are not excessive. In addition, individual provinces maintain a list of prescription medicines that are eligible for reimbursement under provincial health care programs. Multinational drug companies have a pecuniary interest in ensuring that their prices are competitive lest their brands are dropped from the approved list.[15]

To fight price controls, multinational corporations can demonstrate that they are getting an unacceptable return on investment and that, without an acceptable profit opportunity, future investments will not be made and production perhaps will be stopped. These have been the arguments of U.S. and European pharmaceutical marketers in China.[16] Cadbury Schweppes sold its plant in Kenya because price controls made its operation unprofitable. At one time, Coca-Cola and PepsiCo withdrew their products from the shelves in Mexico until they received a price increase. Pakistani milk producers terminated their business when they could not raise prices, and Glaxo Wellcome, a pharmaceutical manufacturer, cancelled its expansion plans in Pakistan because of price controls.

Pricing Strategies in Global Markets

The issue of standard worldwide pricing is mostly a theoretical one because of the influence of the factors already discussed. However, coordination of the pricing function is necessary, especially in larger, regional markets such as the European Union, following the introduction of the euro, and NAFTA countries. With the increasing level of integration efforts around the world, and even discussion of further common currency agreements, control and coordination of global and regional pricing takes on a new meaning.

With more global and regional brands in the global marketer's offering, control of pricing is increasingly important. Of course, this has to be balanced against the need to allow subsidiaries latitude in pricing so that they may make effective use of their country knowledge and quickly react to specific market conditions. Some multinational corporations allow their subsidiaries considerable latitude to set prices in their geographic location, while others insist on more head-office involvement.

Studies have shown that foreign-based multinational corporations allow their U.S. subsidiaries considerable freedom in pricing. This has been explained by the size and unique features of the market. These subsidiaries often control the North American market so that a Canadian customer cannot get a better deal in the United States, and vice versa. Geographic distances in North America create a natural barrier against arbitrage practices that would be more likely to emerge in Europe. Even with the common currency, different rules and standards, economic disparities, and information differences may make deal-hunting difficult for European consumers.[17] However, recent experience has shown that pricing coordination has to be worldwide because parallel imports will surface in any markets in which price discrepancies exist, regardless of distances.

Companies may use one of three approaches to price coordination in global markets.[18] With a **polycentric** pricing strategy, the firm sets prices in each country market independent of head-office involvement. Subsidiaries are completely free to make pricing decisions based on the unique market and competitive conditions in their country. This approach allows for maximum flexibility in responding to changes in the marketplace and increases the speed with which adjustments can be made. The downside of this approach is that it may present an arbitrage opportunity as prices are likely to vary significantly across the world and even within a defined geographic region. In other words, a polycentric pricing strategy will allow firms or individuals to purchase the product at a low price in one country and re-sell it at a higher price in some other country. This may well be a profitable endeavour if transaction costs are low. The firm also has the option of utilizing a **geocentric** pricing strategy. With such a strategy, the firm establishes a minimum floor price below which the product cannot be sold by its subsidiaries in any country. Managers are, however, allowed to add a country markup to better reflect demand and competitive conditions in their national markets. Geocentric pricing does not allow the firm to get around the potential problem of price arbitrage, but it does allow subsidiaries some autonomy in responding to local market conditions. The firm also has the option of pursuing an **ethnocentric** pricing strategy, in which a single worldwide price is set and country managers have no latitude to tailor these set prices to local conditions. Ethnocentric prices are usually derived from a full-cost formula to ensure coverage of the firm's fixed and variable costs. This approach is simple but is not responsive to differences that may exist in the various national markets. As noted earlier, the notion of a single worldwide price is largely theoretical.

Transfer Pricing

Transfer pricing, or intra-corporate pricing, is the pricing of sales to members of the extended corporate family. With rapid globalization and consolidation across borders, estimates have up to two-thirds of world trade taking place between related parties, including shipments and transfers from parent companies to affiliates as well as trade between alliance partners.[19] This means that transfer pricing has to be managed in a world characterized by different tax rates, different foreign exchange rates, varying governmental regulations, and other economic and social challenges. Allocation of resources among the various units of the multinational corporation requires the central management of the corporation to establish the appropriate transfer price to achieve these objectives:[20]

- competitiveness in the international marketplace
- reduction of taxes and tariffs
- management of cash flows
- minimization of foreign exchange risks
- avoidance of conflicts with home and host governments
- internal concerns such as goal congruence and motivation of subsidiary managers

Intra-corporate sales can so easily change the consolidated global results that they represent one of the most important ongoing decision areas in the company. This is quite a change from the past when many executives dismissed internal pricing as the sole responsibility of the accounting department and as a compliance matter. Transfer pricing, when viewed from a company-wide perspective, enhances operational performance (including marketing), minimizes the overall tax burden, and reduces legal exposure both at home and abroad.[21] According to an annual survey, 87 percent of Canadian multinationals identified transfer pricing as one of the three most important tax issues they face, with 39 percent ranking it as the most important issue.[22]

Transfer prices can be based on costs or on market prices.[23] The cost approach uses an internally calculated cost with a percentage markup added. The market price approach is based on an established market selling price, and the products are usually sold at that price minus a discount to allow some margin of profit for the buying division. In general, cost-based prices are easier to manipulate because the cost base itself may be any one of these three: full cost, variable cost, or marginal cost.

Factors that have a major influence on intra-company prices are listed in Exhibit 11.2. Market conditions in general, and those relating to the competitive situation in particular, are typically mentioned as key variables in balancing operational goals and tax considerations. In some markets, especially in the Far East, competition may prevent the global marketer from pricing at will. Prices may have to be adjusted to meet local competition with lower labour costs. This practice may provide entry to the market and a reasonable profit to the affiliate. However, in the long term, it may also become a subsidy to an inefficient business. Further, tax and customs authorities may object because underpricing means that the seller is earning less income than it would otherwise receive in the country of origin and is paying duties on a lower base price on entry to the destination country.

Economic conditions in a market, especially the imposition of controls on movements of funds, may require the use of transfer pricing to allow the company to repatriate revenues. As an example, a multinational corporation with central procurement facilities required its subsidiaries to buy all raw materials from the parent. It began charging a standard 7 percent for its services, which included guaranteeing on-time delivery and appropriate quality. The company estimates that its revenue remittances from a single Latin American country, which had placed restrictions on remittances from subsidiaries to parent companies, increased by $900,000 after the surcharge was put into effect.[24]

A new dimension is emerging with the increase in e-commerce activity. Given a lack of clear understanding and agreement of tax authorities on taxation of electronic transfer pricing activities, companies have to be particularly explicit on how pricing decisions are made to avoid transfer-price audits.[25] The issue of transfer-price audits is a major concern

Exhibit 11.2 Influences on Transfer Pricing Decisions

1. Market conditions in target countries
2. Competition in target countries
3. Corporate taxes at home and in target countries
4. Economic conditions in target countries
5. Import restrictions
6. Customs duties
7. Price controls
8. Exchange controls
9. Reasonable profit for foreign affiliates

Source: Compiled from Robert Feinschreiber, "Business Facets of Transfer Pricing," in *Transfer Pricing Handbook* (New York: John Wiley & Sons, 2002), chap. 1; and Jane O. Burns, "Transfer Pricing Decisions in U.S. Multinational Corporations," *Journal of International Business Studies* 11 (Fall 1980): 23–39.

to multinational corporations. In Canada, for example, 28 percent of parent companies in 2005 reported being audited, with 81 percent of these audits resulting in a tax adjustment. It should be noted that in 2004 Canada formed a transfer pricing review committee and has imposed penalties on over half the cases it has reviewed.[26]

International transfer pricing objectives may lead to conflicting objectives, especially if the influencing factors vary dramatically from one market to another. For example, it may be quite difficult to perfectly match subsidiary goals with the global goals of the multinational corporation. Specific policies should therefore exist that would motivate subsidiary managers to avoid making decisions that would be in conflict with overall corporate goals. If transfer pricing policies lead to an inaccurate financial measure of the subsidiary's performance, this should be taken into account when a performance evaluation is made.

Transfer Prices and Corporate Objectives

Three philosophies of transfer pricing have emerged over time: (1) cost-based (direct cost or cost-plus), (2) market-based (discounted "dealer" price derived from end-market prices), and (3) **arm's-length price**, or the price that unrelated parties would have reached on the same transaction. The rationale for transferring at cost is that it increases the profits of affiliates, and their profitability will eventually benefit the entire corporation. In most cases, cost-plus is used, requiring every affiliate to be a profit centre. Deriving transfer prices from the market is the most marketing-oriented method because it takes local conditions into account. Arm's-length pricing is favoured by many constituents, such as governments, to ensure proper intra-company pricing. However, the method becomes difficult when sales to outside parties do not occur in a product category. Additionally, it is often difficult to convince external authorities that true negotiation occurred between two entities controlled by the same parent. Generally tax authorities will honour agreements among companies provided those agreements are commercially reasonable and the companies abide by the agreements consistently.[27]

The effect of environmental influences in overseas markets can be alleviated by manipulating transfer prices, at least in principle. High transfer prices on goods shipped to a subsidiary and low ones on goods imported from it result in minimizing the tax liability of a subsidiary operating in a country with a high income tax. On the other hand, a higher transfer price may have an effect on the import duty, especially if it is assessed on an ad valorem basis. Exceeding a certain threshold may boost the duty substantially when the product is considered a luxury and will have a negative impact on the subsidiary's competitive posture. Adjusting transfer prices for the opposite effects of taxes and duties is, therefore, a delicate balancing act.

Transfer prices may be adjusted to balance the effects of fluctuating currencies when one partner is operating in a low-inflation environment and the other in one of rampant inflation. Economic restrictions such as controls on dividend remittances and allowable deductions for expenses incurred can also be blunted. For example, if certain services performed by corporate headquarters (such as product development or strategic planning assistance) cannot be charged to the subsidiaries, costs for these services can be recouped through increases in the transfer prices of other product components. A subsidiary's financial and competitive position can be manipulated by the use of lower transfer prices. Start-up costs can be lowered, a market niche carved more quickly, and long-term survival guaranteed. Ultimately, the entire transfer price and taxation question is best dealt with at a time when the company is considering a major expansion or restructuring of operations. For example, if it fits the overall plan, a portion of a unit's R & D and marketing activities could be funded in a relatively low tax jurisdiction.

Transfer pricing problems grow geometrically as all of the subsidiaries with differing environmental concerns are added to the planning exercise, calling for more detailed intra-company data for decision making. Further, fluctuating exchange rates make the planning even more challenging. However, to prevent double taxation and meet arm's-length requirements, it is essential that the corporation's pricing practices be uniform. Many have adopted a philosophy of maintaining a good-citizen fiscal approach (that is, one that recognizes the obligation to pay taxes and duties in every country of operation and to avoid artificial tax-avoidance schemes) and a belief that the primary goal of transfer pricing is to support and develop commercial activities.[28] Some companies make explicit mention of this obligation of good citizenship in their corporate codes of conduct.

Transfer Pricing Challenges

Transfer pricing policies face two general types of challenges. The first is internal to the multinational corporation and concerns the motivation of those affected by the pricing policies of the corporation. The second, an external one, deals with relations between the corporation and tax authorities in both the home country and the host countries.

Performance Measurement

Manipulating intra-corporate prices complicates internal control measures and, without proper documentation, will cause major problems. If the firm operates on a profit centre basis, some consideration must be given to the effect of transfer pricing on the subsidiary's apparent profit performance and its actual performance. To judge a subsidiary's profit performance as not satisfactory when it was targeted to be a net source of funds can easily create morale problems. The situation may be further complicated by cultural differences in the subsidiary's management, especially if the need to subsidize less-efficient members of the corporate family is not made clear. An adjustment in the control mechanism is called for to give appropriate credit to divisions for their actual contributions. The method may range from dual bookkeeping to compensation in budgets and profit plans. Regardless of the method, proper organizational communication is necessary to avoid conflict between subsidiaries and headquarters.

Taxation

Transfer prices will by definition involve the tax and regulatory jurisdictions of the countries in which the company does business. Sales and transfers of tangible properties and transfers of intangibles such as patent rights and manufacturing know-how are subject to close review and to determinations about the adequacy of compensation received. This quite often puts the multinational corporation in a difficult position.

The starting point for testing the appropriateness of transfer prices is a comparison with *comparable uncontrolled* transactions, involving unrelated parties. Uncontrolled prices exist when (1) sales are made by members of the multinational corporation to unrelated parties, (2) purchases are made by members of the multinational corporation from unrelated parties, and (3) sales are made between two unrelated parties, neither of which is a member of the multinational corporation. In some cases, marketers have created third-party trading where none existed before. Instead of selling 100 percent of the product in a market to a related party, the seller can arrange a small number of direct transactions with unrelated parties to create a benchmark against which to measure related-party transactions.

If this method does not apply, the *resale* method can be used. This usually applies best to transfers made to sales subsidiaries for ultimate distribution. The arm's-length approximation is arrived at by subtracting the subsidiary's profit from an uncontrolled selling price. The appropriateness of the amount is determined by comparison with a similar product being marketed by the multinational corporation.

The *cost-plus* approach is most applicable for transfers of components or unfinished goods to overseas subsidiaries. The arm's-length approximation is achieved by adding an appropriate markup for profit to the seller's total cost of the product.[29] The key is to apply such markups consistently over time and across markets.

Such comparisons, however, are not always possible even under the most favourable circumstances and may remain burdened with arbitrariness.[30] Comparisons are impossible for products that are unique or when goods are traded only with related parties. Adjusting price comparisons for differences in the product mix, or for the inherently different facts and circumstances surrounding specific transactions between unrelated parties, undermines the reliance that can be placed on any such comparisons. The most accepted of the other reasonable methods is the *functional analysis approach*. The functional analysis measures the profits of each of the related companies and compares them with the proportionate contribution to total income of the corporate group. It addresses the question of what profit would have been reported if the intra-corporate transactions had involved unrelated parties. Understanding the functional interrelationships of the various parties (that is, which entity does what) is basic to determining each entity's economic contribution via-à-vis total income of the corporate group.

Export Pricing

The Process of Setting Export Prices

In setting the export price, a company can use a process such as the one summarized in Exhibit 11.3. The setting of the export price is influenced by both internal and external factors, as well as their interaction.[31] Internal factors include the company's philosophy, goals, and objectives; the costs of developing, producing, and marketing the export product; and the nature of the exporter's product and industry. External factors relate to international markets in general or to a specific target market in particular and include such factors as customer, regulatory, competitive, and financial (mainly foreign exchange) characteristics. The interaction of these elements causes pricing opportunities and constraints in different markets. For example, company management may have decided to challenge its main foreign competitor in the competitor's home market. Regulation in that market requires expensive product adaptation, the cost of which has to be absorbed now for the product to remain competitive.

As in all marketing decisions, the intended target market will establish the basic premise for pricing. Factors to be considered include the importance of price in customer decision making (in particular, the ability to pay), the strength of perceived price-quality relationships, and potential reactions to marketing-mix manipulations by marketers. For example, an exporter extending a first-world product to an emerging market may find its potential unnecessarily limited and thus opt for a new version of a product that costs a fraction of the original version. Customers' demands will also have to be considered in terms of support required by the intermediary. The marketing mix must be planned to match the characteristics of the target market. Pricing will be a major factor in determining the desired brand image as well as the distribution channels to be used and the level of promotional support required. Conversely, mix elements affect the degrees of freedom in pricing. If the use of specialty channels is needed to maintain product positioning, price will be affected.

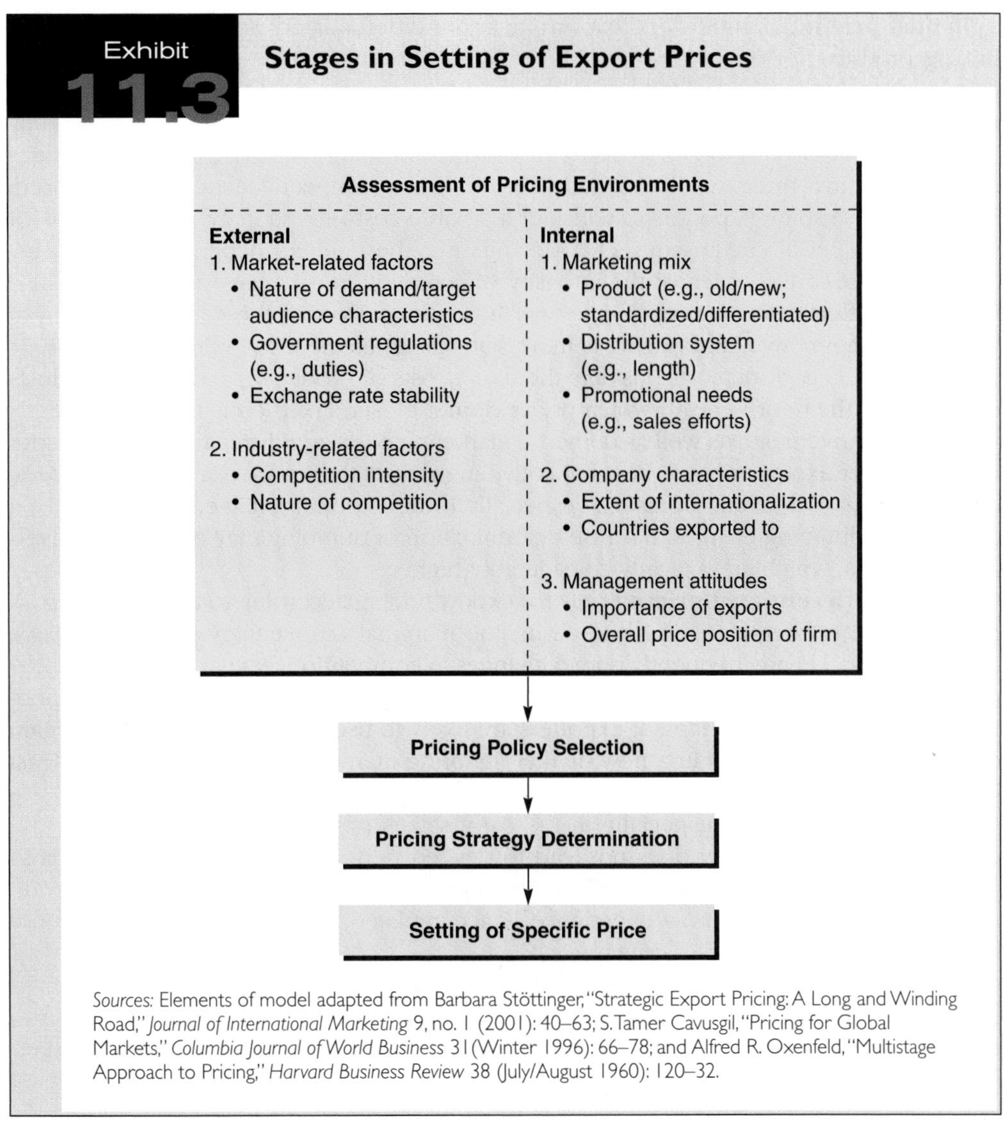

Exhibit 11.3
Stages in Setting of Export Prices
Assessment of Pricing Environments
External
1. Market-related factors
• Nature of demand/target audience characteristics
• Government regulations (e.g., duties)
• Exchange rate stability
2. Industry-related factors
• Competition intensity
• Nature of competition
Internal
1. Marketing mix
• Product (e.g., old/new; standardized/differentiated)
• Distribution system (e.g., length)
• Promotional needs (e.g., sales efforts)
2. Company characteristics
• Extent of internationalization
• Countries exported to
3. Management attitudes
• Importance of exports
• Overall price position of firm
Pricing Policy Selection
Pricing Strategy Determination
Setting of Specific Price

Sources: Elements of model adapted from Barbara Stöttinger, "Strategic Export Pricing: A Long and Winding Road," *Journal of International Marketing* 9, no. 1 (2001): 40–63; S. Tamer Cavusgil, "Pricing for Global Markets," *Columbia Journal of World Business* 31 (Winter 1996): 66–78; and Alfred R. Oxenfeld, "Multistage Approach to Pricing," *Harvard Business Review* 38 (July/August 1960): 120–32.

Pricing policies follow from the overall objectives of the firm for a particular target market and involve general principles or rules that a firm follows in making pricing decisions.[32] Policies include profit maximization, market share, survival, percentage return on investment, and various competitive policies such as copying competitors' prices, following a particular competitor's prices, or pricing so as to discourage competitors from entering the market. For example, an exporter entering a new market may allow wholesalers and retailers above-normal profit margins to encourage maximum sales volume, geographic distribution, and loyalty.

Strategies for Setting Export Prices

Three general price-setting strategies in global marketing are a standard worldwide price; dual pricing, which differentiates between domestic and export prices; and market-differentiated pricing. The first two methods are cost-oriented pricing methods that are relatively simple to establish and easy to understand. The third strategy is based on demand orientation and may thus be more consistent with the marketing concept. However, even the third approach has to acknowledge costs in the long term.

The **standard worldwide price** may be the same price regardless of the buyer (if foreign product or foreign marketing costs are negligible) or may be based on average fixed, variable, and export-related costs per unit.

In **dual pricing**, domestic and export prices are differentiated, and two approaches to pricing products for export are available: cost-driven and market-driven methods. If a cost-based approach is decided upon, the marketer can choose between the **cost-plus method** and the **marginal cost method**. The cost-plus strategy is the true cost, fully allocating domestic and foreign costs to the product. Although this type of pricing ensures margins, the final price may be so high that the firm's competitiveness is compromised. This may cause some exporters to consider a flexible cost-plus strategy, which allows for variations in special circumstances.[33] Discounts may be granted, depending on the customer, the size of the order, or the intensity of competition. Changes in prices may also be put into effect to counter exchange rate fluctuations. Despite these allowances, profit is still a driving motive, and pricing is more static as an element of the marketing mix.

The marginal cost method considers the direct costs of producing and selling products for export as the floor beneath which prices cannot be set. Fixed costs for plants, R & D, and domestic overhead, as well as domestic marketing costs, are disregarded. An exporter can thus lower export prices to be competitive in markets that otherwise might have been beyond access. On certain occasions, especially if the exporter is large, this may open a company to dumping charges, because determination of dumping may be based on average total costs, which are typically considerably higher.

Market-differentiated pricing calls for export pricing according to the dynamic conditions of the marketplace. For these firms, the marginal cost strategy provides a basis, and prices may change frequently due to changes in competition, exchange rates, or other environmental factors. The need for information and controls becomes crucial if this pricing alternative is to be attempted. Exporters are likely to use market-based pricing to gain entry or better penetration in a new market, ignoring many of the cost elements, at least in the short term.

While most exporters, especially in the early stages of their internationalization, use cost-plus pricing, it usually does not lead to desired performance.[34] It typically leads to pricing too high in weak markets and too low in strong markets by not reflecting prevailing market conditions. But as experience is accumulated, the process allows for more flexibility and is more market-driven.

Overall, exporters see the pricing decision as a critical one, which means that it is typically taken centrally under the supervision of top-level management. In addition to product quality, correct pricing is seen as the major determinant of international marketing success.[35]

Export-Related Costs

In preparing a quotation, the exporter must be careful to take into account and, if possible, include unique export-related costs. These are in addition to the normal costs shared with the domestic side of the transaction. They include the following:

- the cost of modifying the product for foreign markets
- operational costs of the export operation: personnel, market research, additional shipping and insurance costs, communications costs with foreign customers, and overseas promotional costs
- costs incurred in entering the foreign markets: tariffs and taxes; risks associated with a buyer in a different market (mainly commercial credit risks and political risks); and risks from dealing in other than the exporter's domestic currency—that is, foreign exchange risk

The combined effect of both clear-cut and hidden costs results in export prices that far exceed domestic prices. The cause is termed **price escalation**. Four different export scenarios are compared with a typical domestic situation in Exhibit 11.4. The first case is relatively simple, adding only the CIF (cost, insurance, freight) and tariff charges. The second adds a foreign importer and thus lengthens the foreign part of the distribution channel. In the third case, a **value-added tax (VAT)**, such as the Goods and Services Tax (GST) in Canada or the value added taxes used within the European Union, is included in the calculations. This is imposed on the full export selling price, which represents the "value added" to or introduced into the country from abroad. In Italy, for example, where most

Exhibit 11.4 Export Price Escalation

International Marketing Channel Elements and Cost Factors	Domestic Wholesale-Retail Channel	Export Market Cases: Case 1 Same as Domestic with Direct Wholesale Import CIF/Tariff	Case 2 Same as 1 with Foreign Importer Added to Channel	Case 3 Same as 2 with VAT Added	Case 4 Same as 3 with Local Foreign Jobber Added to Channel
Manufacturer's net price	6.00	6.00	6.00	6.00	6.00
+ Insurance and shipping cost (CIF)	—	2.50	2.50	2.50	2.50
= Landed cost (CIF value)	—	8.50	8.50	8.50	8.50
+ Tariff (20% on CIF value)	—	1.70	1.70	1.70	1.70
= Importer's cost (CIF value + tariff)	—	10.20	10.20	10.20	10.20
+ Importer's margin (25% on cost)	—	—	2.55	2.55	2.55
+ VAT (16% on full cost plus margin)	—	—	—	2.04	2.04
= Wholesaler's cost (= importer's price)	6.00	10.20	12.75	14.79	14.79
+ Wholesaler's margin (33 1/3% on cost)	2.00	3.40	4.25	4.93	4.93
+ VAT (16% on margin)	—	—	—	.79	.79
= Local foreign jobber's cost (= wholesale price)	—	—	—	—	20.51
+ Jobber's margin (33 1/3% on cost)	—	—	—	—	6.84
+ VAT (16% on margin)	—	—	—	—	1.09
= Retailer's cost (= wholesale or jobber price)	8.00	13.60	17.00	20.51	28.44
+ Retailer's margin (50% on cost)	4.00	6.80	8.50	10.26	14.22
+ VAT (16% on margin)	—	—	—	1.64	2.28
= Retail price (what consumer pays)	12.00	20.40	25.50	32.41	44.94
Percentage price escalation over domestic		70%	113%	170%	275%
Percentage price escalation over Case 1			25%	59%	120%
Percentage price escalation over Case 2				27%	76%
Percentage price escalation over Case 3					39%

Source: Helmut Becker, "Pricing: An International Marketing Challenge," in *International Marketing Strategy*, ed. Hans Thorelli and Helmut Becker (New York: Pergamon Press, 1980), 215.

food items are taxed at 2 percent, processed meat is taxed at 18 percent because the government wants to use the VAT to help reduce its trade deficit. The fourth case simulates a situation typically found in less-developed countries where distribution channels are longer. Lengthy channels can easily double the landed (CIF) price.

Complicating price escalation in today's environment may be the fact that price increases are of different sizes across markets. If customers are willing to shop around before purchasing, the problem of price differentials will make distributors unhappy and could result in a particular market being abandoned altogether.

Price escalation can be overcome through creative strategies, depending on the price elasticity of demand in the particular market. Typical methods, such as the following, focus on cost cutting:

1. Reorganize the channel of distribution. The example in Exhibit 11.5, based on import channels for spaghetti and macaroni in Japan, shows how the flow of merchandise through the various wholesaling levels has been reduced to only an internal wholesale distribution cen-

tre, resulting in savings of 25 percent and increasing the overall potential for imports. Shortening of channels may, however, bring about other costs such as demands for better discounts if a new intermediary takes the role of multiple previous ones.

2. Adapt the product. The product itself can be re-formulated by including less expensive ingredients or unbundling costly features, which can be made optional. Remaining features, such as packaging, can also be made less expensive. If price escalation causes price differentials between markets, the product can be altered to avoid cross-border price shopping by customers.
3. Use new or more economical tariff or tax classifications. In many cases, products may qualify for entry under different categories that have different charges levied against them. The marketer may have to engage in a lobbying effort to get changes made in existing systems, but the results may be considerable savings. For example, when the U.S. Customs Service ruled that multi-purpose vehicles were light trucks and, therefore, subject to 25 percent tariffs (and not the 2.5 percent levied on passenger cars), Britain's Land Rover had to argue that its $56,000 luxury vehicle, the Range Rover, was not a truck. When the United States introduced a luxury tax (10 percent of the portion of a car's price that exceeded $33,000), Land Rover worked closely with the U.S. Internal Revenue Service to establish that its vehicles were trucks (since trucks were free of such tax). Before Land Rover got its way, however, it had to make slight adjustments to the vehicle, since the IRS defines a minimum weight for trucks at 6,000 lbs. Land Rover's model the following year weighed in at 6,019 lbs.[36]
4. Assemble or produce overseas. In the longer term, the exporter may resort to overseas sourcing or eventually production. Through foreign sourcing, the exporter may accrue an additional benefit to lower cost: **duty drawbacks.** In the United States, an exporter may be refunded up to 99 percent of duties paid on imported goods when they are exported or incorporated in articles that are subsequently exported within five years of the importation.[37] Levi Strauss, for example, imports zippers from China that are sewn into the company's jackets and jeans in the United States. The amount that Levi's re-claims can be

Exhibit 11.5 **Distribution Adjustment to Decrease Price Escalation**

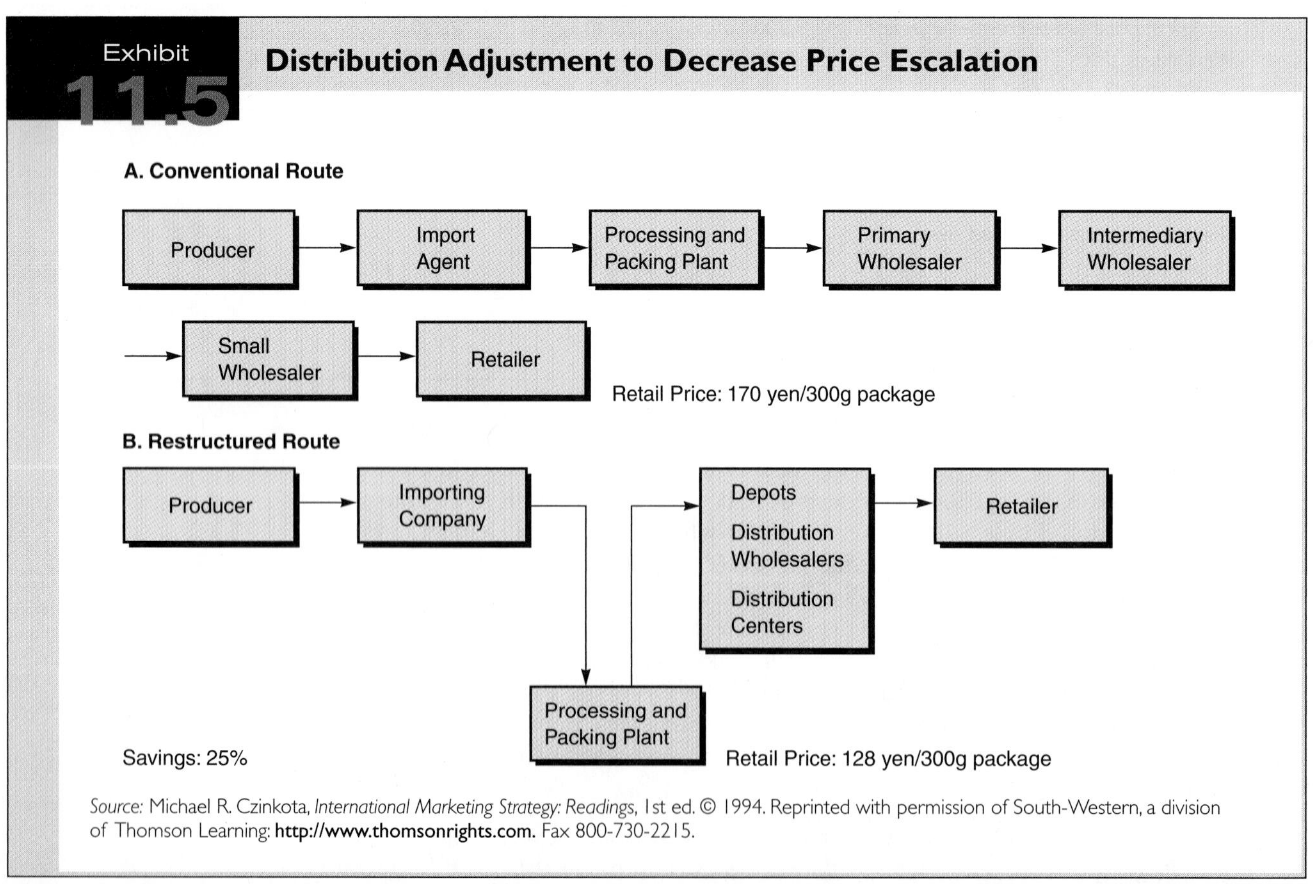

Source: Michael R. Czinkota, *International Marketing Strategy: Readings*, 1st ed. © 1994. Reprinted with permission of South-Western, a division of Thomson Learning: **http://www.thomsonrights.com.** Fax 800-730-2215.

significant, because the duty on zippers can climb to 30 percent of the product's value.[38] The same holds true in Canada. Importers may apply for a drawback of duties paid on imported goods that were subsequently exported. Customs duties, excise taxes, and any anti-dumping and countervailing duties paid at the time of importation may be returned. If the products imported are not used in Canada and are exported within 30 days, the GST paid may also be reimbursed.[39]

If the marketer is able to convey a premium image, it may then be able to pass the increased amounts to the final price.

Appropriate export pricing requires the establishment of accounting procedures to assess export performance. Without such a process, hidden costs may bring surprises. For example, negotiations in Middle Eastern countries or Russia may last three times longer than the average domestic negotiation, dramatically increasing the costs of doing business abroad. Furthermore, without accurate information, a company cannot combat phenomena such as price escalation.

Terms of Sale

The responsibilities of the buyer and the seller should be spelled out as they relate to what is and what is not included in the price quotation and when ownership of goods passes from seller to buyer. **Incoterms** are the internationally accepted standard definitions for terms of sale set by the International Chamber of Commerce (ICC) since 1936. The Incoterms 2000 went into effect on January 1, 2000, with significant revisions to better reflect changing transportation technologies and the increased use of electronic communications.[40] Although the same terms may be used in domestic transactions, they gain new meaning in the international arena. The terms are grouped into four categories, starting with the term whereby the seller makes the goods available to the buyer only at the seller's own premises (the "E"-terms), followed by the group whereby the seller is called upon to deliver the goods to a carrier appointed by the buyer (the "F"-terms). Next are the "C"-terms, whereby the seller has to contract for carriage but without assuming the risk of loss or damage to the goods or additional costs after the dispatch, and finally the "D"-terms, whereby the seller has to bear all costs and risks to bring the goods to the destination determined by the buyer. The most common of the Incoterms used in international marketing are summarized in Exhibit 11.6. Incoterms are available in 31 languages.

Prices quoted *ex-works (EXW)* apply only at the point of origin, and the seller agrees to place the goods at the disposal of the buyer at the specified place on the date or within a fixed period. All other charges are the responsibility of the buyer.

One of the new Incoterms is *free carrier (FCA),* which replaced a variety of FOB terms for all modes of transportation except vessel. FCA (named inland point) applies only at a designated inland shipping point. The seller is responsible for loading goods into the means of transportation; the buyer is responsible for all subsequent expenses. If a port of exportation is named, the costs of transporting the goods to the named port are included in the price.

Free alongside ship (FAS) at a named Canadian port of export means that the exporter quotes a price for the goods that includes charges for delivery of the goods alongside a vessel at the port. The seller handles the cost of unloading and wharfage; loading, ocean transportation, and insurance are left to the buyer.

Free on board (FOB) applies only to vessel shipments. The seller quotes a price covering all expenses up to and including delivery of goods on an overseas vessel provided by or for the buyer.

Under *cost and freight (CFR)* to a named overseas port of import, the seller quotes a price for the goods that includes the cost of transportation to the named port of debarkation. The cost of insurance and the choice of insurer are left to the buyer.

With cost, insurance, and freight (*CIF*) to a named overseas port of import, the seller quotes a price including insurance, all transportation, and miscellaneous charges to the point of debarkation from the vessel. If other than waterway transport is used, the terms are *CPT* (carriage paid to) or *CIP* (carriage and insurance paid to).

Exhibit 11.6

Selected Trade Terms (Incoterms)

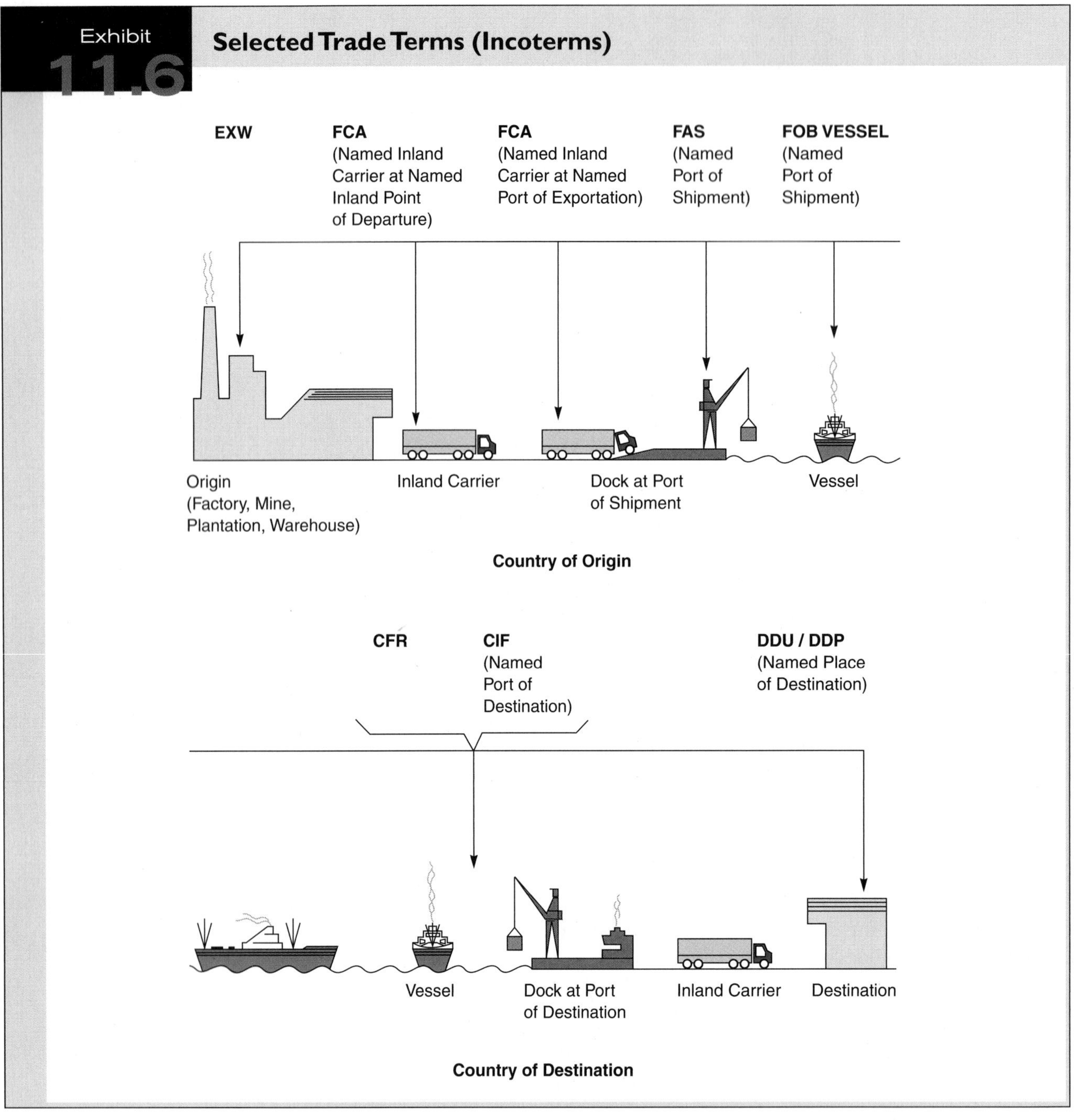

With *delivered duty paid (DDP),* the seller delivers the goods, with import duties paid, including inland transportation from import point to the buyer's premises. With *delivered duty unpaid (DDU),* only the destination customs duty and taxes are paid by the consignee. Ex-works signifies the maximum obligation for the buyer; delivered duty paid puts the maximum burden on the seller.

Careful determination and clear understanding of terms used, and their acceptance by the parties involved, are vital if subsequent misunderstandings and disputes are to be avoided, not only between the parties but also within the marketer's own organization.[41]

These terms are also powerful competitive tools. The exporter should therefore learn what importers usually prefer in the particular market and what the specific transaction may require. An inexperienced Finnish importer may be discouraged from further action by a quote such as ex-plant Halifax, whereas CIF Helsinki will enable the importer to handle the remaining costs because they are incurred in a familiar environment.

The Global MARKETPLACE 11.3

Penetrating Foreign Markets by Controlling Export Transport

Companies that once sought short-term customers to smooth out recessions are searching for every means to get an edge over rivals in foreign markets. To achieve that, they are increasingly concerned about controlling quality and costs at every step, including the transportation process.

International transport costs are far higher than domestic shipping expenses. International ocean transport typically accounts for 4 to 20 percent of the product's delivered cost but can reach as high as 50 percent for commodity items. That makes transport a factor in situations in which a single price disadvantage can cause a sale to be lost to a competitor.

Still, most North American companies continue to abdicate responsibility for export shipping—either because they lack sophistication or simply because they do not want to be bothered. Increasingly, however, companies such as Deere & Co. are paying for, controlling, and often insuring transport from their factories either to foreign ports or to the purchasing companies' doorsteps. This means that they are shipping on a DDP basis.

Deere exports premium-quality farm and lawn equipment worldwide. For years, it has insisted on overseeing transportation because it boosts sales, cuts costs, and ensures quality. "We have a long-term relationship with our dealers. It is in our best interest to do the transport job," says Ann Salaber, an order control manager in the export order department.

One goal of Deere's approach to transportation is to ensure that equipment is delivered to customers in good condition—a factor that Deere considers central to its image as a quality producer. The goal is to avoid cases like the one in which an inexperienced customer insisted on shipping a tractor himself. The tractor was unwittingly put on a ship's deck during a long, stormy sea voyage and arrived in terrible shape.

The process also helps when Deere tractor windows are inadvertently broken during transport. Because Deere closely monitors the tractors, it can quickly install new windows at the port and avoid the huge cost of flying replacements to a customer as far away as Argentina.

Cost is an important consideration as well. Depending on where a $150,000 combine is shipped, transport costs can range between $7,500 and $30,000, or between 5 and 20 percent of delivered cost. Deere's ability to buy steamship space in volume enables it to reduce transport costs by 10 percent. That in turn enables it to cut the combine's delivered cost by between $750 and $3,000. "That adds up," says Salaber. Because of those savings, "you do not have to discount so much, and Deere gets more profit."

Sources: Toby B. Gooley, "Incoterms 2000: What the Changes Mean to You," *Logistics Management and Distribution Report* 39 (January 2000): 49–51; "How Badly Will the Dollar Whack the U.S.?" *Business Week*, May 5, 1997; Gregory L. Miles, "Exporter's New Bully Stick," *International Business*, December 1993, 46–49; **http://www.iccwbo.org**; and **http://www.deere.com**.

Increasingly, exporters are quoting more inclusive terms. The benefits of taking charge of the transportation on either a CIF or DDP basis include the following: (1) exporters can offer foreign buyers an easy-to-understand "delivered cost" for the deal; (2) by getting discounts on volume purchases for transportation services, exporters cut shipping costs and can offer lower overall prices to prospective buyers; (3) control of product quality and service is extended to transport, enabling the exporter to ensure that goods arrive in good condition; and (4) administrative procedures are cut for both the exporter and the buyer.[42] These benefits are highlighted in The Global Marketplace 11.3.

When taking control of transportation costs, however, the exporter must know well in advance what impact the additional costs will have on the bottom line. If the approach is implemented incorrectly, exporters can be faced with volatile shipping rates, unexpected import duties, and restive customers. Most exporters do not want to go beyond the CIF quotation because of uncontrollable or unknown factors in the destination country. Whatever terms are chosen, the program should be agreed to by the exporter and the buyer(s) rather than imposed solely by the exporter.

Freight forwarders are useful in determining costs, preparing quotations, and making sure that unexpected changes do not cause the exporter to lose money. Freight forwarders are useful to the exporter not only as facilitators and advisors but also in keeping down some of the export-related costs. Rates for freight and insurance provided to freight forwarders may be far more economical than those provided to an individual exporter because of large-volume purchases, especially if export sales are infrequent. Some freight forwarders can also provide additional value-added services, such as taking care of the marketer's duty-drawback receivables.

Terms of Payment

Export credit and terms add another dimension to the profitability of an export transaction. The exporter has in all likelihood already formulated a credit policy that determines the degree of risk the firm is willing to assume and the preferred selling terms. The main objective is to meet the importer's requirements without jeopardizing the firm's financial goals. The exporter will be concerned over being paid for the goods shipped and will therefore consider the following factors in negotiating terms of payment: (1) the amount of payment and the need for protection, (2) terms offered by competitors, (3) practices in the industry, (4) capacity for financing international transactions, and (5) relative strength of the parties involved.[43] If the exporter is well established in the market with a unique product and accompanying service, price and terms of trade can be set to fit the exporter's desires. If, on the other hand, the exporter is breaking into a new market or if competitive pressures call for action, pricing and selling terms should be used as major competitive tools. Both parties have their own concerns and sensitivities; therefore, this very basic issue should be put on the negotiating table at the beginning of the relationship.

The basic methods of payment for exports vary in terms of their attractiveness to the buyer and the seller, from cash in advance to open-account or consignment selling. Neither of the extremes will be feasible for longer-term relationships, but they do have their use in certain situations. For example, in the 1999–2000 period, very few companies were exporting into Russia except on a cash-in-advance basis, due to the country's financial turmoil. A marketer may use multiple methods of payment with the same buyer. For example, in a distributor relationship, the distributor may purchase samples on open account, but orders have to be paid for with a letter of credit. These methods are depicted in the risk triangle presented in Exhibit 11.7.

Exhibit 11.7 **Methods of Payment for Exports**

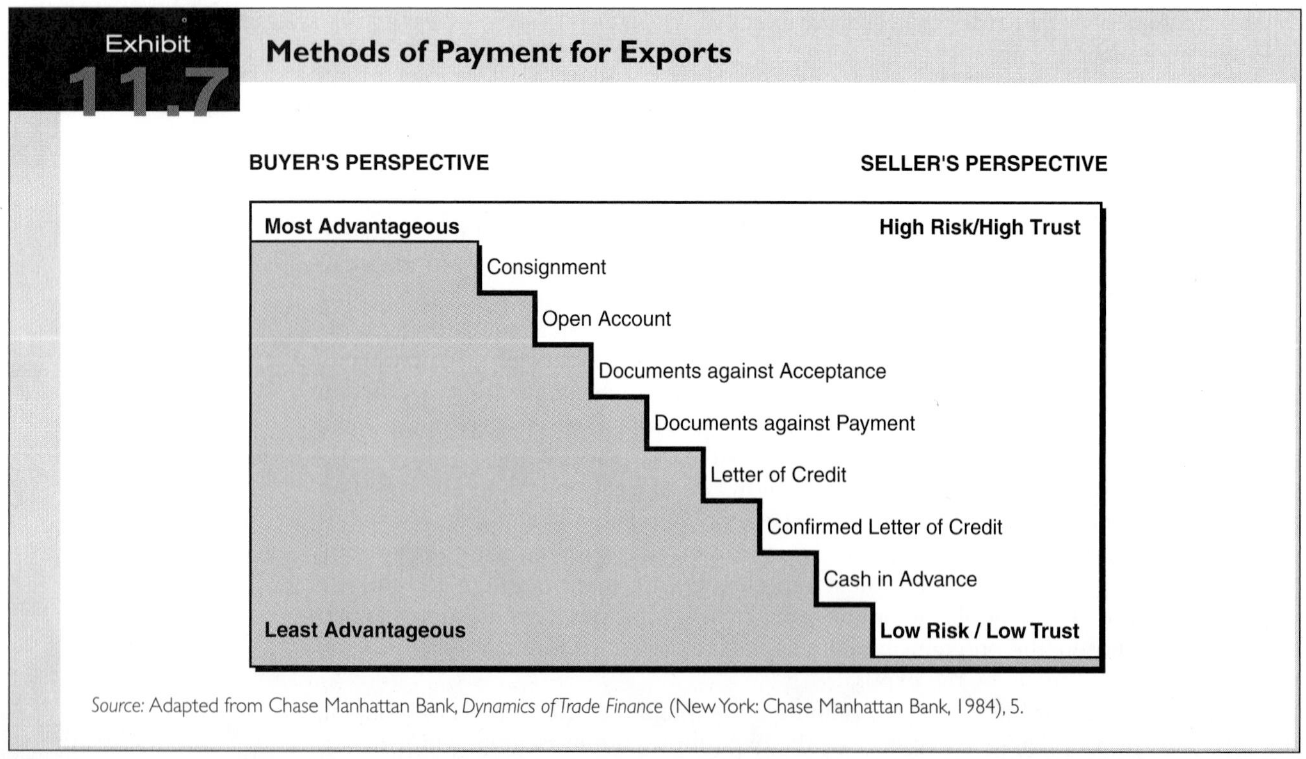

Source: Adapted from Chase Manhattan Bank, *Dynamics of Trade Finance* (New York: Chase Manhattan Bank, 1984), 5.

The most favourable term to the exporter is **cash in advance** because it relieves the exporter of all risk and allows for immediate use of the money. It is not widely used, however, except for smaller, first-time transactions or situations in which the exporter has reason to doubt the importer's ability to pay. Cash-in-advance terms are also found when orders are for custom-made products, because the risk to the exporter is beyond that of a normal transaction. In some instances, the importer may not be able to buy on a cash-in-advance basis because of insufficient funds or government restrictions.

A **letter of credit** is an instrument issued by a bank at the request of a buyer. The bank promises to pay a specified amount of money on presentation of documents stipulated in the letter of credit, usually the bill of lading, consular invoice, and a description of the goods.[44] Letters of credit are one of the most frequently used methods of payment in international transactions. They can be classified based on three dimensions:

1. *Irrevocable versus revocable.* An irrevocable letter of credit can neither be cancelled nor modified without the consent of the beneficiary (exporter), thus guaranteeing payment. According to the new rules drawn by the International Chamber of Commerce, all letters of credit are considered irrevocable unless otherwise stated.[45]
2. *Confirmed versus unconfirmed.* In the case of a Canadian exporter, a Canadian bank might confirm the letter of credit and thus assume the risk, including the transaction (exchange) risk. The single best method of payment for the exporter in most cases is a confirmed, irrevocable letter of credit. Banks may also assume an advisory role but not assume the risk; the underlying assumption is that the bank and its correspondent(s) are better able to judge the credibility of the bank issuing the letter of credit than is the exporter.
3. *Revolving versus non-revolving.* Most letters of credit are non-revolving; that is, they are valid for the one transaction only. In case of established relationships, a revolving letter of credit may be issued.

Exhibit 11.8 provides an example of a letter of credit issued by a Canadian bank.

The letter of credit provides advantages to both the exporter and the importer, which explains its wide use. The approach substitutes the credit of the bank for the credit of the buyer and is as good as the issuing bank's access to dollars. The exporter is therefore protected from the risk of non-payment by the foreign buyer. In custom-made orders, an irrevocable letter of credit may help the exporter secure pre-export financing. The importer will not need to pay until the documents have arrived and been accepted by the bank, thus giving an additional float. The major caveat is that the exporter has to comply with all the terms of the letter of credit.[46] For example, if the documents state that shipment is made in crates measuring $4 \times 4 \times 4$ and the goods are shipped in crates measuring $4 \times 3 \times 4$, the bank will not honour the letter of credit. This offers some protection to the importer who has a vested interest in having the products shipped in accordance with the specifications agreed to with the exporter. If there are changes, the letter of credit can be amended to ensure payment. Importers have occasionally been accused of creating discrepancies to slow down the payment process or to drive down the agreed-upon price.[47] In some cases, the exporter must watch out for fraudulent letters of credit. In these cases, exporters are advised to ship only on the basis of an irrevocable letter of credit, confirmed by their bank, even after the credentials of the foreign contact have been established.

The letter of credit is a promise to pay but not a means of payment. Actual payment is accomplished by means of a **draft**, which is similar to a personal cheque. Like a cheque, it is an order by one party to pay another. Most drafts are documentary, which means that the buyer must obtain possession of various shipping documents before obtaining possession of the goods involved in the transaction. Clean drafts—orders to pay without any other documents—are mainly used by multinational corporations in their dealings with their own subsidiaries and in well-established business relationships.

In **documentary collection** situations, the seller ships the goods, and the shipping documents and the draft demanding payment are presented to the importer through banks acting as the seller's agent. The draft, also known as the bill of exchange, may be either a sight draft or a time draft (Exhibit 11.9). A sight draft documents against payment and is payable on presentation to the drawee, that is, the party to whom the draft is

Exhibit 11.8

Letter of Credit

E-FORM 1003 (04/2007)

APPLICATION AND AGREEMENT FOR STANDBY LETTER OF CREDIT OR GUARANTEE

Date:

1. ROYAL BANK OF CANADA

Transit

Branch Address

2. PLEASE ISSUE:

☐ Standby Letter of credit according to: ☐ ICC PUB 500 ☐ ICC PUB 590
☐ Demand Guarantee
☐ As per attached sample

3. FROM APPLICANT (Full Name and Address)

4. COMPANY CONTACT

Name:

Tel: Fax:

5. IN FAVOUR OF: (BENEFICIARY) (Full Name and Address)

6. FOR (a) CURRENCY **(b) AMOUNT**

7. PURPOSE:

a. ☐ As per attached details b. ☐ Details as below
Details:

8. EXPIRY DATE: (Select One)

☐ One year from date of issue ☐ On ____ (State date)

* Where standby L/C or guarantee automatically renews, complete section 12.a*

9. DELIVERY INSTRUCTIONS - BENEFICIARY IN CANADA
(Complete section 13. for beneficiary outside Canada) (Select One)

☐ Applicant ☐ Beneficiary ☐ Royal Bank Branch in 1 above
☐ Other Instructions (Specify):

10. DRAWINGS: (Select One)

Beneficiary can make ☐ One ☐ Multiple demands for payment (drawings)

11. DOCUMENTS REQUIRED FOR DRAWINGS (Optional)

☐ Demand in writing ☐ Sight Draft
☐ Signed Beneficiary Certificate stating a default
☐ Copy of Transport Document (Specify)
☐ Copy of Invoice ☐ Document as per format attached
☐ Other (Specify):

12. SPECIAL INSTRUCTIONS (Optional)

a. ☐ Automatically renew this standby L/C or Guarantee: (Specify)
Every:
Notification time re: non-renewal ____ Days

b. ☐ Drawings not permitted prior to ____

c. ☐ This standby L/C or Guarantee will automatically reduce by ____ (Amount)
____ (Frequency) Commencing ____ (Date)

d. ☐ Other (Specify):

13. DELIVERY INSTRUCTIONS - BENEFICIARY OUTSIDE CANADA
(Complete Section 9. for beneficiary in Canada)

a. Method of Advice (Select One)

☐ Telex to Foreign Bank only ☐ Airmail to ☐ Foreign Bank ☐ Beneficiary

☐ Original to Royal Bank branch in 1. above

b. Instruct your correspondent bank in country of beneficiary to (Select One)

☐ Advise to beneficiary
☐ Issue on your behalf and deliver to: (Select One)
☐ Our Agent (Name, address, phone no.) ☐ Beneficiary

14. BY SIGNING THIS FORM, THE CUSTOMER HEREBY ACKNOWLEDGES, AGREES AND RATIFIES THE TERMS AND CONDITIONS ATTACHED THEREOF. IN CASE OF INCORPORATED COMPANIES AND OTHER ORGANIZATIONS THIS FORM MUST BE SIGNED BY PROPERLY AUTHORIZED OFFICIALS. LIABILITY WILL BE RECORDED IN NAME OF COMPANY, ORGANIZATION OR INDIVIDUAL INDICATED BELOW.COMPANY NAME (WHERE) APPLICABLE.

Per: Per:

FOR BANK USE ONLY

SRF NO. (Applicant)	TRANSIT RE LIABILITY	BRR (Refer L3-10-3) / Rate EFFECTIVE DATE	FACILITY ACCOUNT NO.	SPECIAL RATE (Where Applicable) EFFECTIVE DATE
LIABILITY PARTY (if other than applicant)		LIABILITY PARTY SRF NO.	GUARANTEE NO. ☐ Financial ☐ Non-Financial Trade ☐ Non-Financial Other	
DEBIT A/C AT TRANSIT: SRF No. (if different to Liability Party)		☐ CAD A/C NO. ☐ USD A/C NO.	CONTACT AT BRANCH / BSG TEL:	
COMMISSION FREQUENCY: (Select One) ☐ Annually ☐ Semi-annually ☐ Quarterly ☐ Monthly ☐ In Full		TIME OF COLLECTION ☐ In advance ☐ At end of period	☐ On Anniversary ☐ On Calendar Basis	☐ AUTOMATIC RENEWAL AND/OR EXCEEDING YEAR - DISTRICT APPROVAL HELD
ACCOUNT MANAGER No. Tel.		WE CERTIFY THAT THE INSTRUCTIONS IN CIRCULAR S3-25-05 AND WHERE APPLICABLE FOLIO TR-4-1-2- HAVE BEEN OBSERVED AUTHORIZED SIGNATURE	SIGNATURE STAMP	

ORIGINAL - FORWARD TO YOUR BRANCH/BUSINESS SERVICE CENTRE

Source: Royal Bank of Canada.

Exhibit 11.9 Documentary Collection

CANADIAN IMPERIAL
BANK OF COMMERCE
TRADE FINANCE CENTRE
THE ATRIUM ON BAY 7TH FL
595 BAY STREET
TORONTO ONT M5G 2M8

SWIFT ADDRESS "CIBCCATT"
TELEX : 065 24116
FAX : (416) 217-8608
TEL : (416) 217-8816

ALWAYS QUOTE OUR REFERENCE NO.
OUDT

DATE:

MAIL TO:

DRAWEE:

DETAILS OF DRAFT(S)

TENOR	CURRENCY	AMOUNT

DRAWER:

REF/INVOICE NO:

WE ENCLOSE FOR COLLECTION

DOCUMENTS ATTACHED	DRAFTS	BILL OF LADING	INSURANCE CERTIFICATE	COMMERCIAL	INVOICES CUSTOMS	CONSULAR	PACKING LIST	CERTIFICATE ORIGIN			
FIRST MAIL											
SECOND MAIL											

FOLLOW INSTRUCTIONS MARKED "X"

DOCUMENTS	☐ DELIVERY AGAINST PAYMENT	☐ DELIVERY AGAINST ACCEPTANCE	☐ HOLD FOR ARRIVAL OF GOODS
PROTEST	☐ PROTEST NON-PAYMENT	☐ PROTEST NON-ACCEPTANCE	☐ DO NOT PROTEST
ALL YOUR CHARGES (INCLUDING STAMPS, EXCHANGE, TAXES, ETC)	☐ ACCOUNT DRAWER ☐ INCUR NO SWIFT/TELEX EXPENSE	☐ ACCOUNT DRAWEE ☐ COLLECT OUR CHARGES $	☐ DO NOT WAIVE CHARGES. IF CHARGES REFUSED, DO NOT RELEASE DOCUMENTS.
COLLECT INTEREST	☐ COLLECT IN ACCORDANCE WITH CLAUSE ENFACED ON DRAFT ☐ IN THE EVENT OF DELAY IN PAYMENT COLLECT ADDITIONAL INTEREST @ % P.A. FROM DUE DATE UNTIL APPROXIMATE ARRIVAL OF FUNDS AT DESTINATION.	☐ ALLOW A DISCOUNT OF $	IF PAID ON OR BEFORE ☐ DO NOT WAIVE INTEREST
ADVICES AIRMAIL	☐ ACCEPTANCE	☐ NON-ACCEPTANCE	☐ NON-PAYMENT
ADVICES SWIFT/TELEX	☐ ACCEPTANCE	☐ NON-ACCEPTANCE	☐ NON-PAYMENT
REMIT PROCEEDS	☐ BY MAIL ☐ BY SWIFT/TELEX	☐ BY DRAFT ON ☐ DRAWER'S EXPENSE	☐ DRAWEE'S EXPENSE
LOCAL CURRENCY	☐ IN EVENT FOREIGN EXCHANGE IS NOT IMMEDIATELY AVAILABLE A PROVISIONAL DEPOSIT OF LOCAL CURRENCY MAY BE ACCEPTED UNDER DRAWEE'S WRITTEN UNDERTAKING TO ASSUME ALL EXCHANGE RISKS. DO NOT SURRENDER DRAFT UNTIL FINAL SETTLEMENT FOR FACE AMOUNT IS AVAILABLE FOR REMITTANCE.		

GOODS: **B/L No.:** **DATED:** **CARRIER;**	**IN CASE OF NEED, REFER TO:**	☐ WHO WILL ENDEAVOUR IN HAVING DRAFT HONOURED AS DRAWN ☐ WHOSE INSTRUCTIONS MAY BE FOLLOWED IN EVERY RESPECT

PAYMENT INSTRUCTIONS FOR CAD & CURRENCY OTHER THAN USD: REMIT VIA SWIFT MT202 OR TESTED TELEX DIRECT TO CIBC TORONTO, ONT. (CIBCCATT) FOR FURTHER CREDIT TO /000012345 CIBC TRADE FINANCE CENTRE, TOR, ONT. ATTN DOC. COLLECTION QUOTING OUR REFERENCE.

PAYMENT INSTRUCTIONS FOR USD: REMIT VIA SWIFT MT202 OR TESTED TELEX TO BANK OF AMERICA NT AND SA, NEW YORK FOR CREDIT TO CIBC TORONTO, ONT. (CIBCCATT) ACCT #1234-5-67890 FOR FURTHER CREDIT TO /000012345 CIBC TRADE FINANCE CENTRES, TOR, ONT. ATTN DOC. COLLECTION QUOTING OUR REFERENCE.

THIS COLLECTION IS SUBJECT TO THE 1995 REVISION OF UNIFORM RULES FOR COLLECTIONS, PUBLICATION 522 OF THE INTERNATIONAL CHAMBER OF COMMERCE OR CURRENT REVISION.	PLEASE HANDLE FOR THE ACCOUNT OF THE ABOVE NAMED OFFICE OF **CANADIAN IMPERIAL BANK OF COMMERCE** TO WHOM YOUR ACKNOWLEDGEMENT AND FURTHER COMMUNICATION SHOULD BE ADDRESSED AND TO WHOM PAYMENT SHOULD BE REMITTED. Signature

Source: Courtesy of CIBC Global Banking & Trade Solutions.

addressed. A time draft documents against acceptance and allows for a delay of 30, 60, 90, 120, or 180 days. When a time draft is drawn on and accepted by a bank, it becomes a **banker's acceptance**, which is sold in the short-term money market. Time drafts drawn on and accepted by a business firm become trader's acceptances, which are normally not marketable. A draft is presented to the drawee, who accepts it by writing or stamping a notice of acceptance on it. With both sight and time drafts, the buyer can effectively extend the period of credit by avoiding receipt of the goods. A date draft requires payment on a specified date, regardless of the date on which the goods and the draft are accepted by the buyer.

To illustrate, an exporter may have a time draft accepted by the CIBC for $1 million to be paid in 90 days. Like many exporters who extend credit for competitive reasons, the firm may have immediate need for the funds. It could contact an acceptance dealer and sell the acceptance at a discount, with the rate depending on the market rate of interest. If the annual interest rate was 6 percent, for example, the acceptance could be sold for $985,222 ($1 million divided by 1.015).

Even if the draft is not sold in the secondary market, the exporter may convert it into cash by **discounting**. To discount the draft simply means that the draft is sold to a bank at a discount from face value. If the discounting is with recourse, the exporter is liable for the payment to the bank if the importer defaults. If the discounting is without recourse, the exporter will not be liable even if the importer does not pay the bank. Discounting without recourse is known as factoring or, in the case of higher credit risk and longer-term receivables, forfaiting.

The normal manner of doing business in the domestic market is **open account** (open terms). The exporter selling on open account removes both real and psychological barriers to importing. However, no written evidence of the debt exists, and the exporter has to put full faith in the references contacted. Worst of all, there is no guarantee of payment. If the debt turns bad, the problems of overseas litigation are considerable. Bad debts are normally easier to avoid than to rectify. In less-developed countries, importers will usually need proof of debt in the application to the central bank for hard currency, which will not allow them to deal on an open-account basis. Again, open account is used by multinationals in their internal transactions and when there is implicit trust among the partners.

The most favourable term to the importer is **consignment selling**, which allows the importer to defer payment until the goods are actually sold. This approach places all the burden on the exporter, and its use should be carefully weighed against the objectives of the transaction. If the exporter wants entry into a specific market through specific intermediaries, consignment selling may be the only method of gaining acceptance by intermediaries. The arrangement will require clear understanding as to the parties' responsibilities—for example, which party is responsible for insurance until the goods have actually been sold. If the goods are not sold, returning them will be costly and time-consuming; for example, there is getting through customs or paying, avoiding paying, or trying to get refunds on duties. Due to its burdensome characteristics, consignment is not widely used.

Getting Paid for Exports

The exporter needs to minimize the risk of not being paid if a transaction occurs. The term **commercial risk** refers primarily to the insolvency of, or protracted payment default by, an overseas buyer. Commercial defaults, in turn, usually result from deterioration of conditions in the buyer's market, fluctuations in demand, unanticipated competition, or technological changes. These naturally emerge domestically as well, but the geographic and cultural distances in international markets make them more severe and more difficult to anticipate. In addition, non-commercial or **political risk** is completely beyond the control of either the buyer or the seller. For example, the foreign buyer may be willing to pay but the local government may use every trick in the book to delay payment as far into the future as possible.

These challenges must be addressed through actions by either the company itself or support systems. The decision must be an informed one, based on detailed and up-to-date information in international credit and country conditions. In many respects, the assessment of a buyer's creditworthiness requires the same attention to credit checking and financial analysis as for domestic buyers; however, the assessment of a foreign private buyer is complicated by some of the following factors:

- Credit reports may not be reliable.
- Audited reports may not be available.
- Financial reports may have been prepared according to different accounting rules.
- Many governments require that assets be re-evaluated upward annually, which can distort results.
- Statements are in local currency.
- The buyer may have the financial resources in local currency but may be precluded from converting to dollars because of exchange controls and other government actions.

Canadian companies may wish to work with the Export Development Corporation (EDC) and their commercial bank in assessing the creditworthiness of prospective foreign customers. Team Canada, a network of Canadian government departments, also recommends that a clause be included in the contract dealing with the potential of the client's bankruptcy and the insurance of receivables.[48]

Managing Foreign Exchange Risk

Unless the exporter and the importer share the same currency (as is the case in the countries of Euroland), exchange rate movements may harm one or the other of the parties. If the price is quoted in the exporter's currency, the exporter will get exactly the price it wants but may lose some sales due to lack of customer orientation. If the exporter needs the sale, the invoice may be in the importer's currency, and the exchange risk will be the burden of the exporter. Some exporters, if they are unable to secure payment in their own currency, try to minimize the risk by negotiating shorter terms of payment, such as 10 or 15 days. Exchange risks may be a result of an appreciating or depreciating currency or result from a revaluation or devaluation of a currency by a central bank.

Two types of approaches to protect against currency-related risk are proposed: (1) risk shifting, such as foreign currency contractual hedging, and/or (2) risk modifying, such as manipulating prices and other elements of a marketing strategy.

When invoicing in foreign currencies, an exporter cannot insulate itself from the problems of currency movements, but it can at least know how much it will eventually receive by using the mechanism of the **forward exchange market**. In essence, the exporter gets a bank to agree to a rate at which it will buy the foreign currency the exporter will receive when the importer makes payment. The rate is expressed as either a premium or a discount on the current spot rate. The risk still remains if the exchange rate does not move as anticipated, and the exporter may be worse off than if it had not bought forward. Although forward contracts are the most common foreign currency contractual hedge, other financial instruments and derivatives, such as currency options and futures, are available. An **option** gives the holder the right to buy or sell foreign currency at a pre-specified price on or up to a pre-specified date. The difference between the currency options market and the forward market is that the transaction in the former gives the global marketer the right to buy or sell, whereas a transaction in the forward market entails a contractual obligation to buy or sell. This means that if an exporter does not have any or the appropriate amount of currency when the contract comes due, it would have to go into the foreign exchange markets to buy the currency, potentially exposing itself to major losses if the currency has appreciated in the meantime. The greater flexibility in the options contract makes it more expensive, however. The currency **futures** market is conceptually similar to the forward market; that is, to buy futures on the British pound sterling implies an obligation to buy in the future at a pre-specified price. However, the minimum transaction sizes are considerably smaller on the futures market. Forward quotes apply to transactions of $1 million or more, whereas on the futures market transactions will typically be well below $100,000. The market, therefore, allows relatively small firms engaged in international trade to lock in exchange rates and lower their risk. Forward contracts, options, and futures are available from banks, the Chicago Mercantile Exchange, and the Philadelphia Stock Exchange. Export Development Canada releases periodic market assessment reports to allow exporters to gauge the foreign exchange risks inherent in a number of countries.

Canadian exporters have faced both high and low values of the Canadian dollar with respect to U.S. and other currencies. When commodity prices are high, currency traders tend to bid up the price of the Canadian dollar. When commodity prices are depressed, however, the value of the Canadian dollar has tended to fall. When the exporter's domestic currency is weak, strategies should include stressing the price advantage to customers and expanding the scale and scope of the export operation. Sourcing can be shifted to domestic markets and the export price can be subjected to full-costing. However, under the opposite scenario, the exporter needs to engage in non-price competition, minimizing the price dimension as much as possible. Costs should be reduced by every means, including enhancing productivity. At this time, the exporter should prioritize efforts to markets that show the greatest returns. Global marketers may also attempt to protect themselves by manipulating leads and lags in export and import payments or receivables in anticipation of either currency revaluations or devaluations. This, however, will require thorough market knowledge and leverage over overseas partners.

Sources of Export Financing

Except in the case of larger companies that may have their own financing entities, most global marketers assist their customers abroad in securing appropriate financing. Export financing terms can significantly affect the final price paid by buyers. Consider, for example, two competitors for a $1-million sale. Exporter A offers an 8 percent interest rate over a 10-year payment period, while B offers 9 percent for the same term. Over the 10 years, the difference in interest is $55,000. In some cases, buyers will award a contract to the provider of cheaper credit and overlook differences in quality and price.

Financing assistance is available from both the private and the public sectors. The global marketer should assess not only domestic programs but also those in other countries. For example, Japan and Taiwan have import financing programs that provide exporters added potential in penetrating these significant markets. In Canada, the Business Development Bank of Canada and Export Development Canada are sources of domestic export financing.

Commercial Banks

Commercial banks the world over provide trade financing depending on their relationship with the exporter, the nature of the transaction, the country of the borrower, and the availability of export insurance. This usually means that financing assistance is provided only to first-rate credit risks, leaving many Canadian exporters to report major problems in enlisting assistance from commercial banks. Furthermore, some Canadian banks do not see international trade finance as part of their core competence. Although the situation has improved, exporters still continue to complain about lack of export financing as it pertains to developing countries, financing high technology, or lending against foreign receivables. Many exporters complain that banks will not deal with them without rock-solid collateral, such as property and/or equipment.

However, as the share of international sales and reach of companies increases, banking relationships become all the more important, a fact that is also noted by banks themselves. Many banks offer enhanced services, such as electronic services, that help exporters monitor and expedite their international transactions to customers who do a certain amount of business with them. As with all suppliers, the more business done with a bank, the higher the level of service, usually at a better price. As the relationship builds, bankers feel more comfortable about the exporter's business and are more likely to go out of their way to help, particularly with difficult transactions. It is clear that the development of an effective credit policy requires teamwork between the company's marketing and finance staffs and its bankers.

In addition to using the types of services a bank can provide as a criterion of choice, an exporter should assess the bank's overseas reach.[49] This is a combination of the bank's own network of facilities (Scotiabank, for example, has a strong retail presence and deep expertise in Latin American and Caribbean markets) and correspondent relationships. While money-centre banks can provide the greatest amount of coverage through their own offices and staff, they still use correspondents in regions outside the main banking or political centres of foreign markets. For example, Citibank has a worldwide correspondent network of 5,000 institutions in addition to its facilities in more than 100 countries.

Some banks have formed alliances to extend their reach to markets that their customers are entering. Foreign banks can provide a competitive advantage to exporters because of their home country connections and their strong global networks. For example, Commerzbank, Germany's third largest bank, has branches in the Far East, Latin America, South America, and Eastern Europe to support its international trade financing activities in the NAFTA area.[50] Regardless of the arrangement, the bank's own branches or correspondents play an important role at all stages of the international transaction, from gathering market intelligence about potential new customers to actually processing payments. Additional services include reference checks on customers in their home markets and suggestions for possible candidates to serve as intermediaries.

Forfaiting and Factoring

Forfaiting provides the exporter with cash at the time of the shipment. In a typical forfait deal, the importer pays the exporter with bills of exchange or promissory notes guaranteed by a leading bank in the importer's country. The exporter can sell them to a third party (for example, Scotiabank) at a discount from their face value for immediate cash. The sale is without recourse to the exporter, and the buyer of the notes assumes all the risks. The discount rate takes into account the buyer's creditworthiness and country, the quality of the guaranteeing bank, and the interest cost over the term of the credit.

The benefits to the exporter are the reduction of risk, simplicity of documentation (because the documents used are well known in the market), and 100 percent coverage, which official sources such as export-import banks do not provide. In addition, forfaiting does not involve either content or country restrictions, which many of the official trade financing sources may have.[51] The major complaints about forfaiting centre on availability and cost. Forfaiting is not available where exporters need it most, that is, the high-risk countries. Furthermore, it is usually a little more expensive than public sources of trade insurance.

Certain companies, known as **factoring** houses, may purchase an exporter's receivables for a discounted price (2 to 4 percent less than face value). Factors not only buy receivables but also provide the exporter with a complete financial package that combines credit protection, accounts-receivable bookkeeping, and collection services to take away many of the challenges that come with doing business overseas.[52] Arrangements are typically with recourse, leaving the exporter ultimately liable for repaying the factor in case of a default. Some factors accept export receivables without recourse but require a large discount.

Although the forfaiting and factoring methods appear similar, they differ in three significant ways: (1) factors usually want a large percentage of the exporter's business, while most forfaiters work on a one-shot basis; (2) forfaiters work with medium-term receivables (over 180 days to 5 years), while factors work with short-term receivables; and (3) factors usually do not have strong capabilities in the developing countries, but since forfaiters usually require a bank guarantee, most are willing to deal with receivables from these countries. Furthermore, forfaiters work with capital goods, factors typically with consumer goods.[53]

Official Trade Finance

Official financing can take the form of either a loan or a guarantee, including credit insurance. In a loan, the government provides funds to finance the sale and charges interest on those funds at a stated fixed rate. The government lender accepts the risk of a possible default. In a guarantee, a private-sector lender provides the funds and sets the interest rate, with the government assuring that it will reimburse the lender if the loan is unpaid. The government is providing not funds but rather risk protection. The programs provide assurance that the governmental agency will pay for a major portion of the loss should the foreign buyer default on payment. The advantages are significant: (1) protection in the riskiest part of an exporter's business (foreign sales receivables), (2) protection against political and commercial risks over which the exporter does not have control, (3) encouragement to exporters to make competitive offers by extending

In More Detail 11.1

EDC EXPORT FINANCING

The EDC is a Canadian Crown Corporation that provides financing and risk management services to Canadian exporters. In 2005 the EDC facilitated some $58 billion in transactions and worked with almost 7,000 Canadian companies—90 percent of which are small and medium-sized firms. The EDC has been involved in financing transactions in as many as 200 countries around the world and has worked on deals involving numerous emerging markets. The EDC is self-financing and operates on commercial principles. The EDC provides a range of financing services for Canadian exporters, including pre-shipment financing, facilitating factoring arrangements with commercial banks, equity financing to facilitate growth of an export business, financing solutions for foreign buyers of Canadian products, and foreign direct investment to allow Canadian firms to expand globally. For foreign firms, the EDC offers lines of credit for repeated purchases of Canadian goods, structures and arranges loan syndications for Canadian and foreign firms, and provides a bank guarantee program to cover Canadian and foreign banks involved in financing the export of Canadian products to customers in developing countries.

An awkward fact has to be faced, however. A 2004 survey of almost 10,000 Canadian SMEs by the Canadian Federation of Independent Business found that a surprising 83 percent did not use the services of Export Development Canada.[55] Another perplexing survey finding, this time by Statistics Canada covering 3,850 companies, shows that exporting SMEs in 2002 mainly relied on personal sources of finance during start-up, 78 percent using personal savings, a smaller percentage using credit cards, personal lines of credit, and money borrowed from friends or relatives.[56] Only 16 percent of exporting SME respondents used commercial loans and lines of credit, despite the availability of comprehensive public- and private-sector financing available.

It is difficult to explain this apparent anomaly. Because exporting is such a desirable activity for Canada, it attracts a great deal of government support, as we have seen. However, and perhaps paradoxically, this support may be undervalued by some firms precisely because it is free or subsidized. Other explanations can be put forward, of course, including the need for more creative promotion of official services, but one optimistic view is worth stressing: there is probably considerable unrealized potential for further export development in the country if substantially more SMEs could be persuaded to take advantage of available help. Here the challenge is not just for companies themselves to take action, but also for official agencies to explore why their services are so often neglected, and if necessary, to adapt their product and marketing strategies.

Source: EDC website, **http://www.edc.ca/english/index.htm** (accessed November 11, 2006); "Report on Trade," *Canadian Federation of Independent Business* (Oct. 2004); "Survey on Financing of Small and Medium Enterprises," *Statistics Canada* (2002).

terms of payment, (4) broadening of potential markets by minimizing exporter risks, (5) the possibility of leveraging exporter accounts receivable, and (6) through the government guarantee, the opportunity for commercial banks to remain active in the international finance arena.[54]

Because credit has emerged as an increasingly important component in export selling, governments of most industrialized countries have established entities that insure credit risks for exports. Officially supported export credit agencies (ECAs), such as the Export Development Bank, the French Coface, or the German Hermes, are organizations whose central purpose is to promote national trade objectives by providing financial support for national exports. ECAs benefit from varying degrees of explicit or implicit support from national governments. Some ECAs are divisions of government trade missions. Other ECAs operate as autonomous or even private institutions, but most require a degree of recourse to national government support.

The ability to offer financing or credit terms is often critical in competing for, and winning, export contracts. Increasingly, foreign buyers expect suppliers to offer open-account or unsecured credit terms rather than requiring letters of credit, which may be expensive. Yet for small exporters, extending credit terms to foreign customers may represent an unacceptable risk, especially when the exporter's bank is unwilling to accept foreign receivables as collateral for working lines of credit. The solution is export credit insurance, wherein, for a reasonable premium, an institution (e.g., an insurance company or an ECA) guarantees payment to the seller if the buyer defaults.

It should be noted that the EDC is not the only source of government-sponsored export financing for Canadian firms. The Business Development Bank of Canada (BDC) and Canadian Commercial Corporation (CCC) are also active in this area. BDC is wholly owned by the government of Canada and provides various financial products and services to support SME exporting. Among these are working capital finance, political risk insurance, credit checks, and letters of credit. BDC also provides consulting services and venture capital. Canadian Commercial Corporation is more specialized in its mandate. Like EDC, it is a Crown corporation reporting to Parliament. While its main objective is to foster international trade, its primary focus is in the public procurement sector in other countries, assisting Canadian exporters to access overseas markets. As mainly a contracting agency specializing in public contracts, CCC supports not only main contractors but in some cases large numbers of SMEs supporting a single large exporter, as in the case of, say, a construction project.

Dumping

Inexpensive imports often trigger accusations of dumping—that is, selling goods overseas for less than in the exporter's home market or at a price below the cost of production, or both. Charges of dumping range from those of Florida tomato growers, who said that Mexican vegetables were being dumped across the border, to those of the Canadian Anti-Dumping Tribunal, which ruled that U.S. firms were dumping radioactive diagnostic reagents in Canada. Such disputes have become quite common, especially in highly competitive industries such as computer chips, ball bearings, and steel. Also, the European Union was asked to investigate dumping of fibres by Asian producers, whose share grew 56 percent in 1998 alone to account for 12 percent of the market. The concern by the European fibre industry was that Asian producers were selling their product in the European market below cost of production, simply to generate cash flow for their beleaguered domestic operations.[57]

Dumping ranges from predatory dumping to unintentional dumping. **Predatory dumping** refers to a tactic whereby a foreign firm intentionally sells at a loss in another country in order to increase its market share at the expense of domestic producers, which amounts to an international price war. **Unintentional dumping** is the result of time lags between the dates of sales transaction, shipment, and arrival. Prices, including exchange rates, can change in such a way that the final sales price turns out to be below the cost of production or below the price prevailing in the exporter's home market. It has been argued that current dumping laws do not adequately take into account such developments as floating exchange rates, which make dumping appear to be more widespread.[58]

Domestic producers may petition the government to impose anti-dumping duties on imports alleged to be dumped. Duties may be imposed if it is found that the domestic industry is being, or is threatened with being, materially injured by the imports. The remedy is an **anti-dumping duty** equal to the dumping margin. International agreements and Canadian law provide for **countervailing duties**, which may be imposed on imports that are found to be subsidized by foreign governments and which are designed to offset the advantages imports would otherwise receive from the subsidy. The prevalence of anti-dumping actions has increased sharply. The WTO reports an increase in anti-dumping measures taken by member countries over the period 1995 to 2005. A total of 119 measures were taken in 1995, while the total for 2005 stood at 131. Of the 131 anti-dumping measures taken in 2005, 18 were taken by the U.S., 17 by India, 21 by the European Commission, 18 by China, and 4 by Canada.[59] As more developing and emerging markets are reducing tariffs to comply with WTO agreements, they may be switching to anti-dumping penalties to protect domestic firms. However, governmental action against dumping and subsidized exports violating WTO agreements may result in hurting the very industries seeking relief as they result in retaliatory actions.

In some cases, dumping suits have strong competitive motivations, for example, to discourage an aggressive competitor by accusing it of selling at unfair prices. Anti-dumping and unfair subsidy suits have led in some cases to formal agreements on voluntary restraints, whereby foreign producers agree that they will supply only a certain percentage of the foreign market.

To minimize the risk of being accused of dumping (as well to be protected from dumping), the marketer can focus on value-added products and increase differentiation by including services in the product offering. If the company operates in areas made sensitive by virtue of the industry (such as electronics) or by the fact that local competition is economically vulnerable yet powerful with respect to the government, it may seek to collaborate with local companies in gaining market access, for example.[60]

Non-Price Options

Countertrade

General Motors exchanged automobiles for a trainload of strawberries. The government of India has swapped palm oil from Sudan for the construction of a railroad link. These are examples of countertrade activities carried out around the world.

Countertrade is a sale that encompasses more than an exchange of goods, services, or ideas for money. In the international market, countertrade transactions "are those transactions which have as a basic characteristic a linkage, legal or otherwise, between exports and imports of goods or services in addition to, or in place of, financial settlements."[61] Historically, countertrade was mainly conducted in the form of barter, which is a direct exchange of goods of approximately equal value, with no money involved. These transactions were the very essence of business at times when no money—that is, a common medium of exchange—existed or was available. Over time, money emerged to unlink transactions from individual parties and permit greater flexibility in trading activities. Repeatedly, however, we can see returns to the barter system as a result of economic circumstances. During periods of high inflation in Europe in the 1920s, goods such as bread, meat, and gold were seen as much more useful and secure than paper money, which decreased in real value every hour.

Countertrade transactions have therefore always arisen when economic circumstances have encouraged a direct exchange of goods rather than the use of money as an intermediary. Conditions that encourage such business activities are lack of money, lack of value of money, lack of acceptability of money as an exchange medium, or greater ease of transaction by using goods. However, the shrinking of established markets and the existence of a substantial product surplus are also conditions that foster countertrade.

These same reasons prevail in today's resurgence of countertrade activities. Throughout the past decades, the use of countertrade has steadily increased. In 1972, countertrade was used by only 15 countries. By 1983, the countries conducting countertrade transactions numbered 88, and by the late 1990s the number was more than 100. Estimates of the total global countertrade volume vary widely. The British government estimates that countertrade transactions make up between 10 percent and 15 percent of world trade.[62]

Why Countertrade?

Many countries are deciding that countertrade transactions are more beneficial to them than transactions based on financial exchange alone. A primary reason is that world debt crises and exchange rate volatility have made ordinary trade financing very risky. Many countries in the developing world cannot obtain the trade credit or financial assistance necessary to afford desired imports. Heavily indebted nations, faced with the possibility of not being able to afford imports at all, resort to countertrade to maintain product inflow.

The use of countertrade permits the covert reduction of prices and therefore allows firms and governments to circumvent price and exchange controls. Particularly in commodity markets with operative cartel arrangements, such as oil or agriculture, this benefit may be very useful to a producer. For example, by using oil as a countertraded product for industrial equipment, a surreptitious discount (by using a higher price for the acquired products) may expand market share. In a similar fashion, the countertrading of products at higher prices than their economic value has the potential to mask dumping activities.[63]

Countertrade is also often viewed by firms and nations alike as an excellent mechanism to gain entry into new markets. When a producer believes that marketing is not its strong suit, particularly in product areas that face strong international competition, it often sees countertrade as useful. The producer often hopes that the party receiving the goods will serve as a new distributor, opening up new international marketing channels and ultimately expanding the original market. Conversely, markets with high demand and little cash can provide major opportunities for firms if they are willing to accept countertrade. A firm that welcomes countertrade welcomes new buyers and sets itself apart from the competition.

Countertrade also can provide stability for long-term sales. For example, if a firm is tied to a countertrade agreement, it will need to source the product from a particular supplier, whether or not it wants to do so. This stability is often valued very highly because it eliminates, or at least reduces, vast swings in demand and thus allows for better planning.

Under certain conditions, countertrade can ensure the quality of an international transaction. In instances where the seller of technology is paid in output produced by the technology delivered, the seller's revenue depends on the success of the technology transfer and maintenance services in production. Therefore, the seller is more likely to be dedicated in the provision of services, maintenance, and general technology transfer.[64] In such instances, the second part of the transaction serves as a "hostage" that induces both trading partners to fulfill their contractual obligations. Particularly under conditions of limited legal and social protection, countertrade can be equated to an exchange of hostages that ensures that all parties involved live up to their agreement.[65]

In spite of all these apparent benefits of countertrade, there are strong economic arguments against this activity. These arguments are based mainly on efficiency grounds. As economist Paul Samuelson stated, "Instead of there being a double coincidence of wants, there is likely to be a want of coincidence; so that, unless a hungry tailor happens to find an undraped farmer, who has both food and a desire for a pair of pants, neither can make a trade."[66] Instead of trade balances being settled on a multilateral basis, with surpluses from one country being balanced by deficits with another, countertrade requires that accounts must now be settled on a country-by-country or even transaction-by-transaction basis. Trade then results only from the ability of two parties or countries to purchase specified goods from one another rather than from competition. As a result, uncompetitive goods may be marketed. In consequence, the ability of countries and their industries to adjust structurally to more efficient production may be restricted. Countertrade can therefore be seen as eroding the quality and efficiency of production and as lowering world consumption. These economic arguments notwithstanding, however, countries and companies increasingly see countertrade as an alternative that may be flawed but worthwhile to undertake. As far as the unilateral focus is concerned, it may well be that this restriction can be removed through electronic commerce. With growing ease of reach, it may well become possible to create an online global barter economy that addresses itself to those transactions that cannot be conducted on regular financial terms.

Types of Countertrade

Under the traditional types of **barter** arrangements, goods are exchanged directly for other goods of approximately equal value. However, simple barter transactions are less often used today.

Increasingly, participants in countertrade have resorted to more sophisticated versions of exchanging goods that often also include some use of money. Exhibit 11.10 provides an overview of the different forms of countertrade that are in use today. One refinement of simple barter is the **counterpurchase**, or parallel barter, agreement. The participating parties sign two separate contracts that specify the goods and services to be exchanged. Frequently, the exchange is not of precisely equal value; therefore, some amount of cash will be involved. However, because an exchange of goods for goods does take place, the transaction can rightfully be called barter.

Another common form of countertrade is the **buyback**, or compensation, arrangement. One party agrees to supply technology or equipment that enables the other party to produce goods with which the price of the supplied products or technology is repaid. One example of such a buyback arrangement is an agreement entered into by Levi Strauss and Hungary. The company transferred the know-how and the Levi's trademark to Hungary. A Hungarian firm began producing Levi's products. Some of the output is sold domestically, and the rest is marketed in Western Europe by Levi Strauss, in compensation for the know-how.

A more refined form of barter, aimed at reducing the effect of the immediacy of the transaction, is called **clearing arrangements**. Here, clearing accounts are established, into which firms can deposit (and from which they can withdraw) the results of their countertrade activities. These currencies merely represent purchasing power, however, and cannot be directly withdrawn in cash. As a result, each party can agree in a single contract to purchase goods or services of a specified value. Although the account may be out of balance on a transaction-by-transaction basis, the agreement stipulates that over the long term, a balance in the account will be restored. Frequently, the goods available for purchase with clearing account funds are tightly stipulated. In fact, funds have on occasion been labelled "apple clearing dollars" or "horseradish clearing funds." Sometimes, additional flexibility is given to the clearing account by permitting **switch-trading**, in which credits in the account can be sold or transferred to a third party. Doing so can provide creative intermediaries with opportunities for deal making by identifying clearing account relationships with major imbalances and structuring business transactions to reduce them.

Another key form of barter arrangement is called **offset**, which is the industrial compensation mandated by governments when purchasing defence-related goods and services in order to offset the effect of this purchase on the balance of payments. Offsets can include co-production, licences production, subcontractor production, technology transfer, or overseas investment. Typically, in order to secure the sale of military equipment,

Exhibit 11.10

Classification of Forms of Countertrade

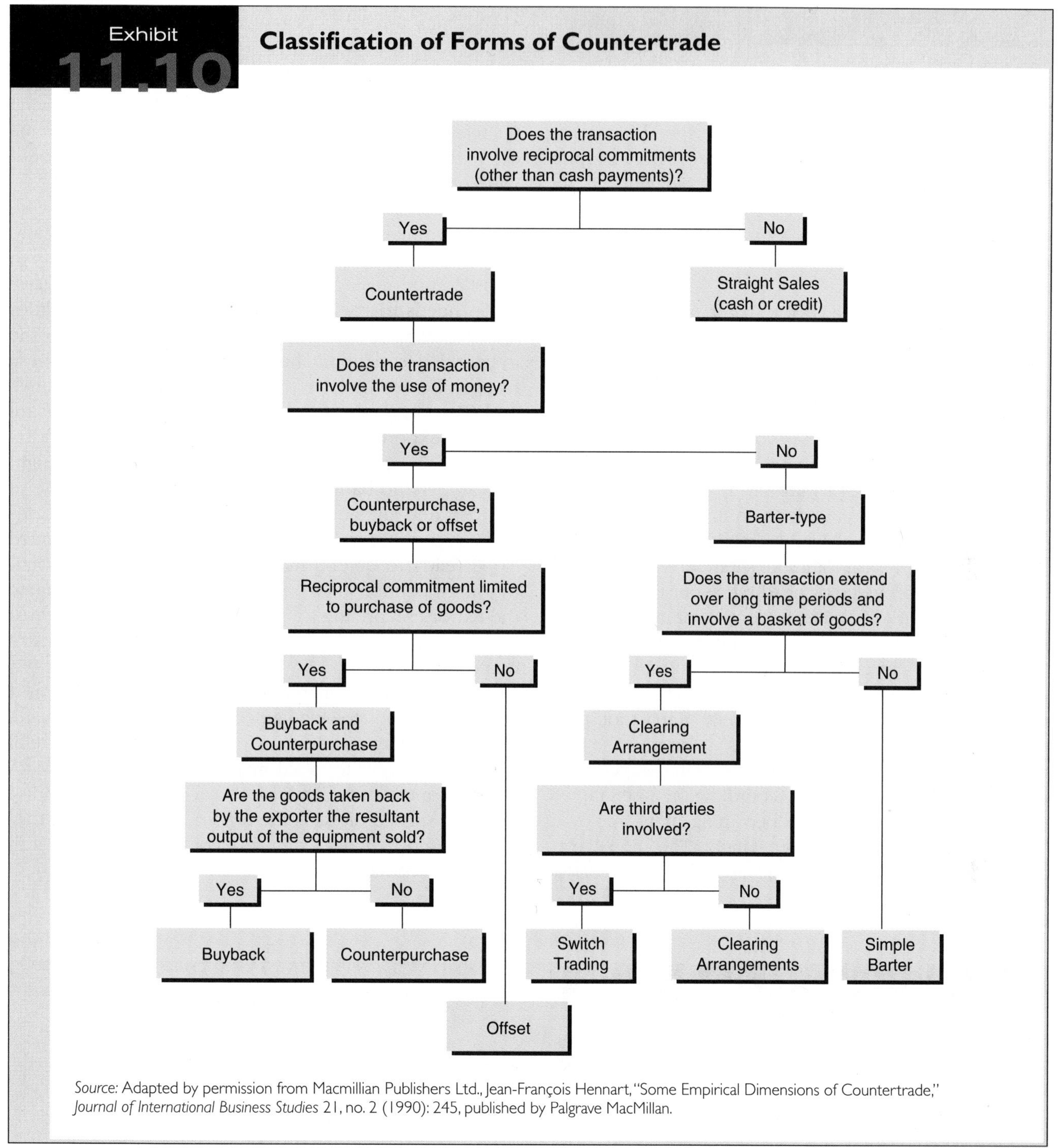

Source: Adapted by permission from Macmillian Publishers Ltd., Jean-François Hennart, "Some Empirical Dimensions of Countertrade," *Journal of International Business Studies* 21, no. 2 (1990): 245, published by Palgrave MacMillan.

the selling companies have to offset the cost of the arms through investment in non-related industries. The offsets frequently reach or exceed the price of the defence equipment, to the delight of the buyer but often to the chagrin of the home country government of the selling firms.

With the increasing sophistication of countertrade, the original form of straight barter is used less today. The most frequently completed forms of countertrade are counterpurchase, buyback agreements and, due to continued major military expenditures around the world, offsets.

Summary

In a world of increasing competition, government regulation, accelerating inflation, and widely fluctuating exchange rates, global marketers must spend increasing amounts of time planning pricing strategy. Because pricing is the only revenue-generating element of the marketing mix, its role in meeting corporate objectives is enhanced. However, it comes under increasing governmental scrutiny as well, as evidenced by intra-company transfer pricing.

The three philosophies of transfer pricing that have emerged over time are cost-based, market-based, and arm's-length. Transfer pricing concerns are both internal and external to the company. Internally, manipulating transfer prices may complicate control procedures and documentation. Externally, problems arise from the tax and regulatory entities of the countries involved.

Multinational firms vary in the degree of head-office involvement in the pricing decision. In some firms country managers have considerable latitude in setting prices, while in other firms this latitude is tempered by the planning assistance provided by head-office personnel. Pricing in individual markets comes under the influence of environmental variables, each market with its own unique set. This set consists of corporate objectives, costs, customer behaviour, market conditions, market structure, and environmental constraints. The individual impact of these variables and the result of their interaction must be thoroughly understood by the global marketer, especially if regional, or even worldwide, coordination is attempted. Control and coordination are becoming more important with increasing economic integration. The global marketer has to consider how pricing decisions are to be coordinated and controlled across various country markets. The firm may opt for strategies that give varying degrees of autonomy to its local subsidiaries. In extreme cases, the firm may elect to use a single invariant worldwide price across all its markets.

The process of setting an export price must start with the determination of an appropriate cost baseline and should include variables such as export-related costs to avoid compromising the desired profit margin. The quotation needs to spell out the respective responsibilities of the buyer and the seller in getting the goods to the intended destination. The terms of sale indicate these responsibilities but may also be used as a competitive tool. The terms of payment have to be clarified to ensure that the exporter will indeed get paid for the products and services rendered. Facilitating agents such as freight forwarders and banks are often used to absorb some of the risk and uncertainty in preparing price quotations and establishing terms of payment. Exporters also need to be ready to defend their pricing practices. Competitors may petition their own government to investigate the exporter's pricing to determine the degree to which it reflects costs and prices prevailing in the exporter's domestic market.

Corporations are increasingly using countertrade as a competitive tool to maintain or increase market share. The complexity of these transactions requires careful planning in order to avoid major corporate losses. Management must consider how the acquired merchandise will be disposed of, what the potential for market disruptions is, and to what extent the countertraded goods fit with the corporate mission.

Key Terms

anti-dumping duty (p. 400)
arm's-length price (p. 380)
banker's acceptance (p. 394)
barter (p. 402)
buyback (p. 402)
cash in advance (p. 391)
clearing arrangements (p. 402)
commercial risk (p. 394)
consignment selling (p. 394)
cost-plus method (p. 384)
counterpurchase (p. 402)
countertrade (p. 400)
countervailing duties (p. 400)
discounting (p. 394)
documentary collection (p. 391)
draft (p. 391)
dual pricing (p. 384)
duty drawbacks (p. 386)
ethnocentric (p. 378)
factoring (p. 397)
forfaiting (p. 397)
forward exchange market (p. 395)
futures (p. 395)
geocentric (p. 378)
Incoterms (p. 387)
letter of credit (p. 391)
marginal cost method (p. 384)
market-differentiated pricing (p. 384)
market pricing (p. 373)
offset (p. 402)
open account (p. 394)
option (p. 395)
penetration pricing (p. 373)
political risk (p. 394)
polycentric (p. 378)
predatory dumping (p. 399)
price controls (p. 377)
price elasticity of consumer demand (p. 376)
price escalation (p. 384)
skimming (p. 372)
standard worldwide price (p. 383)
switch-trading (p. 402)
unintentional dumping (p. 399)
value-added tax (VAT) (p. 384)

Questions for Discussion

1. Comment on the pricing philosophy "Sometimes price should be wrong by design."
2. The standard worldwide base price is most likely looked on by management as full-cost pricing, including an allowance for manufacturing overhead, general overhead, and selling expenses. What factors are overlooked?
3. In combating price controls, multinational corporations will deal with agency administrators rather than policymakers. How can they convince administrators that price relief is fair to the company and also in the best interest of the host country?
4. Which elements of pricing can be standardized?
5. Discuss the advantages and drawbacks of countertrade.
6. Propose scenarios in which export prices are higher/lower than domestic prices.
7. What are the implications of price escalation?
8. Discuss the use of the currency of quotation as a competitive tool.
9. Argue for the use of more inclusive shipping terms from the marketing point of view.
10. Suggest different importer reactions to a price offer and how you, as an exporter, could respond to them.
11. Who is harmed, and who is helped, by dumping?

Internet Exercises

1. Compare and contrast the role of Canada's Export Development Corporation (**http://www.edc.ca/english/index.htm**) and Canadian Commercial Corporation (**http://www.ccc.ca/eng/home.cfm**) and the services they provide to Canadian exporters. Which organization do you believe is most effective in promoting Canadian exports? Why?
2. Visit the Team Canada website at **http://www.teamcanada.gc.ca/menu-en.asp.** What is the purpose of Team Canada missions? Who participates in these missions? How effective do you believe they are in promoting trade and investment for Canada?

Recommended Readings

Calderón Carrero, José Manuel. *Advance Pricing Agreements: A Global Analysis.* Cambridge, MA: Kluwer Law International, 1999.

Chabot, Christian N. *Understanding the Euro: The Clear and Concise Guide to the New Trans-European Currency.* New York: McGraw-Hill, 1998.

Contino, Richard M., and Tony Valmis, eds. *Handbook of Equipment Leasing: A Deal Maker's Guide.* New York: AMACOM, 1996.

Dolan, Robert J., and Hermann Simon. *Power Pricing: How Managing Price Transforms the Bottom Line.* New York: Free Press, 1997.

Engelson, Morris. *Pricing Strategy: An Interdisciplinary Approach.* New York: Joint Management Strategy, 1995.

Feinschreiber, Robert. *Transfer Pricing Handbook.* New York: John Wiley & Sons, 2002.

Hinkelman, Edward G., and Molly Thurmond. *A Short Course in International Payments.* New York: World Trade Press, 1998.

Jackson, John H., and Edwin A. Vermulst, eds. *Antidumping Law and Practice.* Ann Arbor: University of Michigan Press, 1989.

Jagoe, John R., and Agnes Brown. *Pricing Your Products for Export & Budgeting for Export.* Minneapolis, MN: The Export Institute, 1998.

Johnson, Thomas E. *Export/Import Procedures and Documentation.* New York: AMACOM, 1997.

Lowell, Julia, and Loren Yager. *Pricing and Markets: U.S. and Japanese Responses to Currency Fluctuations.* Santa Monica, CA: Rand Corporation, 1994.

Monroe, Kent B. *Pricing: Making Profitable Decisions.* New York: McGraw-Hill, 2003.

Nagle, Thomas T., and Reed K. Holden. *The Strategy and Tactics of Pricing: A Guide to Profitable Decision Making.* Englewood Cliffs, NJ: Prentice-Hall, 2002.

Palmer, Howard. *International Trade Finance and Pre-Export Finance.* London: Euromoney Publications, 1999.

Ramberg, Jan. *ICC Guide to Incoterms.* Paris: ICC Publishing, 2000.

Tang, Y.W. *Current Trends and Corporate Cases in Transfer Pricing.* Westport, CT: Quorum Books, 2002.

U.S. Department of Treasury. *A Basic Guide to Importing.* Lincolnwood, IL: NTC Business Books, 1995.

Venedikian, Harry M., and Gerald A. Warfield. *Export-Import Financing.* New York: John Wiley & Co., 1996.

Woznick, Alexandra, and Edward G. Hinkelman. *A Basic Guide to Exporting.* New York: World Trade Press, 2000.

Zurawicki, Leon. *International Countertrade.* New York: Pergamon Press, 2003.

Notes

1. James A. Gingrich, "Five Rules for Winning Emerging Market Consumers," *Strategy and Business,* 2nd quarter, 1999, 35–46.
2. Kent B. Monroe, *Pricing: Making Profitable Decisions* (New York: McGraw-Hill, 2003), 12.
3. Douglas W. Vorhies, Michael Harker, and C.P. Rao, "The Capabilities and Performance Advantages of Market-Driven Firms," *European Journal of Marketing* 33, no. 11/12 (1999): 1171–1202.
4. J.J. Boddewyn, Robin Soehl, and Jacques Picard, "Standardization in International Marketing: Is Ted Levitt in Fact Right?" *Business Horizons* 29 (November–December 1986): 69–75; Saeed Samiee, "Pricing in Marketing Strategies of U.S.- and Foreign-Based Companies," *Journal of Business Research* 15 (March 1987): 17–30.
5. John U. Farley, James M. Hulbert, and David Weinstein, "Price Setting and Volume Planning by Two European Industrial Companies: A Study and Comparison of Decision Processes," *Journal of Marketing* 44 (Winter 1980): 46–54.
6. Bank of Canada, "Survey of Price Setting Behaviour of Canadian Firms," (working paper 2006-35, September, 2006).
7. Janet Purdy Levaux, "Now It Is Time to Think about Expanding Overseas Sourcing," *World Trade,* June 2000, 52–56.
8. "The Price Is Wrong," *The Economist,* May 25, 2002, 59.
9. "Stuck!" *Business Week,* November 15, 1993, 146–55.
10. "Hyundai Gets Hot," *Business Week,* December 17, 2001, 84–86.
11. Richard Tomlinson, "Who's Afraid of Wal-Mart?" *Fortune,* June 26, 2000, 58–62.
12. Akshay R. Rao, Mark E. Bergen, and Scott Davis, "How to Fight a Price War," *Harvard Business Review* 78 (March–April 2000): 107–16.
13. "Domestic Electronic Products Overtaking Foreign Goods," *Korea Times,* May 12, 1996, 8.
14. Louis Kraar, "How to Sell to Cashless Buyers," *Fortune,* November 7, 1988, 147–54.
15. C. Farrell and G. Fearon, "Prescription Drug Exports to the United States: An Analysis of the Online Communication Strategies of Canadian e-Pharmacies," *Journal of Medical Marketing* 5, no. 4 (2005).
16. Wang Yuguan and Jiang Song, "China: A Future Star for Foreign Pharma Companies," *Pharmaceutical Executive,* August 1999, 78–87.
17. "Borders and Barriers: A Survey of European Business and the Euro," *The Economist* December 1, 2001, 10–11.
18. J. Johansson, *Global Marketing, Foreign Entry, Local Marketing and Global Management,* 3rd ed. (New York: McGraw-Hill Irwin, 2003).
19. Victor H. Miesel, Harlow H. Higinbotham, and Chun W. Yi, "International Transfer Pricing: Practical Solutions for Intercompany Pricing," *International Tax Journal* 28 (Fall 2002): 1–22.
20. Wagdy M. Abdallah, "How to Motivate and Evaluate Managers with International Transfer Pricing Systems," *Management International Review* 29 (1989): 65–71.
21. Sherif Assef and Surjya Mitra, "Making the Most of Transfer Pricing," *Insurance Executive,* Summer 1999, 2–4.
22. Ernst & Young, *2005–2006 Global Transfer Pricing Survey* (New York: Ernst & Young, November 2005.
23. Robert Feinschreiber, "Practical Aspects of Transfer Pricing" in *Transfer Pricing Handbook* (New York: John Wiley & Sons, 2002), chap. 2.
24. "How to Free Blocked Funds via Supplier Surcharges," *Business International,* December 7, 1984, 387.
25. Wagdy Abdallah, "Global Transfer Pricing of Multinationals and e-Commerce in the 21st Century," *Multinational Business Review* 10 (Fall 2002): 62–71.
26. Ernst and Young, *2005–2006 Global Transfer Pricing Survey* (New York: Ernst & Young, November 2005).
27. Erika Morphy, "Spend and Tax Politics," *Export Today* 15 (April 1999): 50–56.
28. Michael P. Casey, "International Transfer Pricing," *Management Accounting* 66 (October 1985): 31–35.
29. Robert B. Stack, Maria de Castello, and Natan J. Leyva, "Transfer Pricing in the United States and Latin America," *Tax Management International Journal* 31, no. 1 (2002): 24–43.
30. Victor H. Miesel, Harlow H. Higinbotham, and Chun W. Yi, "International Transfer Pricing: Practical Solutions for Intercompany Pricing: Part II," *International Tax Journal* 29 (Winter 2003): 1–23.
31. Matthew B. Myers and S. Tamer Cavusgil, "Export Pricing Strategy-Performance Relationship: A Conceptual Framework," *Advances in International Marketing* 8 (1996): 159–78.
32. Howard Forman and Richard A. Lancioni, "International Industrial Pricing Strategic Decisions and the Pricing Manager: Some Key Issues," Professional Pricing Society, October 9, 1999.
33. S. Tamer Cavusgil, "Unraveling the Mystique of Export Pricing," *Business Horizons* 31 (May–June 1988): 54–63.
34. Thomas T. Nagle and Reed K. Holden, *The Strategy and Tactics of Pricing: A Guide to Profitable Decision Making* (Englewood Cliffs, NJ: Prentice-Hall, 2002), chap. 3.
35. Barbara Stöttinger, "Strategic Export Pricing: A Long and Winding Road," *Journal of International Marketing* 9, no. 1 (2001): 40–63.
36. "What's in a Name," *Economist,* February 2, 1991, 60.
37. Al D'Amico, "Duty Drawback: An Overlooked Customs Refund Program," *Export Today* 9 (May 1993): 46–48. See also **http://www.customs.treas.gov.**
38. Michael D. White, "Money-Back Guarantees," *World Trade,* September 1999, 74–77.
39. See the Canada Border Services Agency for more details, **http://www.cbsa-asfc.gc.ca/E/pub/cm/d7-4-2/d7-4-2-e.pdf.**
40. International Chambers of Commerce, *Incoterms 2000* (Paris: ICC Publishing, 2000). See also **http://www.iccwbo.org.**
41. Kevin Maloney, "Incoterms: Clarity at the Profit Margin," *Export Today* 6 (November–December 1990): 45–46.
42. Alexandra Woznik and Edward G. Hinkelman, *A Basic Guide to Exporting* (Novate, CA: World Trade Press, 2000), chap. 10.

43. "Getting Paid: Or What's a Transaction For?" *World Trade*, September 1999, 42–52; and Chase Manhattan Bank, *Dynamics of Trade Finance* (New York: Chase Manhattan Bank, 1984): 10–11.

44. David K. Eiteman, Arthur I. Stonehill, and Michael H. Moffett, *Multinational Business Finance* (Reading, MA: Addison-Wesley, 2001), 460–88.

45. International Chamber of Commerce, *Uniform Customs and Practice for Documentary Credits* (New York: ICC Publishing Corp., 2002).

46. Vincent M. Maulella, "Payment Pitfalls for the Unwary," *World Trade*, April 1999, 76–79.

47. Erika Morphy, "Form vs. Format," *Export Today* 15 (August 1999): 47–52.

48. Team Canada website, **http://www.exportsource.ca/gol/exportsource/site.nsf/en/es02759.html** (accessed November 11, 2006).

49. Miles Maguire, "Reading Your Bank's Correspondence," *Export Today* 11 (November/December 1995): 27–31.

50. Miles Maguire, "Mergers and Money," *Export Today* 11 (September 1995): 24–30.

51. Lawrence W. Tuller, "Beyond the LC," *Export Today* 12 (August 1996): 70–74.

52. Daniel S. Levine, "Factoring Pays Off," *World Trade*, September 1998, 79–80.

53. Mary Ann Ring, "Innovative Export Financing," *Business America*, January 11, 1993, 12–14.

54. "EXIM-Bank Program Summary," in *Export-Import Bank of the United States* (Washington, DC: EXIM Bank, 1985), 1; updated for 2002.

55. "Report on Trade," Canadian Federation of Independent Business (October 2004).

56. Survey on Financing of Small and Medium Enterprises," Statistics Canada (2002).

57. "EU Charges Asian Fiber Dumping," *Textile World*, May 1999, 134.

58. Paul Magnusson, "Bring Anti-Dumping Laws Up to Date," *Business Week*, July 19, 1999, 45.

59. See WTO website at **http://www.wto.org/english/tratop_e/adp_e/adp_e.htm#statistics.**

60. Delener Nejdet, "An Ethical and Legal Synthesis of Dumping: Growing Concerns in International Marketing," *Journal of Business Ethics* 17 (November 1998): 1747–53.

61. "Current Activities of International Organizations in the Field of Barter and Barter-like Transactions," *Report of the Secretary General*, United Nations, General Assembly, 1984, 4.

62. Trade Partners UK, **https://www.uktradeinvest.gov.uk/.**

63. Dorothy A. Paun, Larry D. Compeau, and Dhruv Grewal, "A Model of the Influence of Marketing Objectives on Pricing Strategies in International Countertrade," *Journal of Public Policy and Marketing* 16, no. 1 (1997): 69–82.

64. Rolf Mirus and Bernard Yeung, "Why Countertrade? An Economic Perspective," *The International Trade Journal* 7, no. 4 (1993): 409–33.

65. Chong Ju Choi, Soo Hee Lee, and Jai Boem Kim, "A Note on Countertrade: Contractual Uncertainty and Transaction Governance in Emerging Economies," *Journal of International Business Studies* 30, no. 1 (1999): 189–202.

66. Paul Samuelson, *Economics*, 11th ed. (New York: McGraw-Hill, 1980), 260.

Chapter 12

Global Distribution and Logistics

The Global MARKETPLACE 12.1

"Just Chill'n"

Perishable food manufacturers are increasingly outsourcing their refrigerated logistics needs to third party providers. Quite apart from the typical problems involved in moving goods in a supply chain, perishable food manufacturers have to deal with the issue of limited shelf life of their products, which demand special handling both in-transit as well as in storage. Problems in either or both of these areas may well translate into a shortened selling window, poor product quality, and ultimately unsatisfied consumers. With globalization, these problems are magnified as companies source food products from diverse offshore locations. These pressures have forced food manufacturers to consider decentralized distribution systems, low inventory strategies, and solutions that put the product closer to the final consumer. The refrigerated and temperature-controlled logistics industry is growing and innovating to meet these challenges. Companies in this sector now offer food manufacturers a range of outsourced services, from freeze-blasting and variable temperature storage to integrated rail movement and LTL consolidation. Major food manufacturers such as Canada's McCain Foods are making extensive use of these solutions.

McCain Foods is a $1.6 billion potato-product and snack-food manufacturer with headquarters in Florenceville, New Brunswick, and with significant operations in the United States. McCain Foods has partnered with AmeriCold Logistics to outsource cold storage and distribution at 12 of the logistics provider's facilities across the U.S. Third-party logistics (3PL) providers such as AmeriCold own and operate refrigerated and temperature-controlled warehouses and offer a value proposition similar to public refrigerated warehouses but with more flexibility and scalability. McCain Foods manufactures a third of the world's French fries and services major customers such as Wendy's and McDonald's. The company operates four manufacturing facilities for potato production and six for snack foods. AmeriCold handles product from all four potato plants and from five of the company's six snack-food plants. The logistics provider is responsible for some 1.7 billion pounds of inbound receipts and accounts for 60 percent of McCain's outsourced logistics spend. The outsourcing of refrigerated logistics is an important part of McCain's global marketing strategy. Some of McCain's customer contracts are short-term, and this makes construction of dedicated cold-storage facilities risky and uneconomic. Partnership with AmeriCold gives McCain flexibility in responding to consumer demand and the opportunity to leverage the logistics provider's expertise and resources to streamline its supply chain.

Source: Joseph O'Reilly, "Cold Comfort," **Inboundlogistics.com**, August 2006, **http://www.inboundlogistics.com/articles/features/0806_feature02.shtml** (accessed November 12, 2006).

Channels of distribution provide the essential linkages that connect producers and customers. The links are intra-company and extra-company entities that perform a number of functions. Optimal distribution systems are flexible and are able to adjust to market conditions. In general, companies use one or more of the following distribution systems: (1) the firm sells directly to customers through its own field sales force or through electronic commerce; (2) the company operates through independent intermediaries, usually at the local level; or (3) the business depends on an outside distribution system that may have regional or global coverage. Canadian firms depend on the services of companies such as TNT Logistics North America and CAT Inc. to provide them with a range of distribution services in foreign markets around the world.

A channel of distribution should be seen as more than a sequence of marketing institutions connecting producers and consumers; it should be a team working toward a common goal.[1] Too often, intermediaries are mistakenly perceived as temporary market-entry vehicles and not the partners with whom marketing efforts are planned and implemented. In today's marketing environment, being close to customers, be they the final consumer or intermediary, and solving their problems are vital to bringing about success.

Since most marketers cannot or do not want to control the distribution function completely, structuring channel relationships becomes a crucial task. The importance of this task is further compounded by the fact that the channel decision is the most long-term of the marketing mix decisions in that, once established, it cannot easily be changed. The decisions involved in the structuring and management of the export channel of distribution are discussed in this chapter.

The firm must also be concerned with coordination within the distribution channel and across country markets. For the global firm, customer locations and sourcing opportunities are widely dispersed. As The Global Marketplace 12.1 illustrates, the physical distribution and logistics aspects of global marketing therefore have great importance. To obtain and maintain favourable results from the complex international environment, the international logistics manager must coordinate activities globally, both within and outside the firm. Neglect of logistics issues brings not only higher costs but also the risk of eventual non-competitiveness due to diminished market share, more expensive supplies, or lower profits. In an era of new trade opportunities in regions that may be suffering from major shortcomings in logistical infrastructure, competent logistics management is more important than ever before. International logistics and outsourcing are therefore discussed in this chapter.

The Structure of Global Distribution Channels

A generalization of channel configurations for consumer and industrial products as well as services is provided in Exhibit 12.1. Channels can vary from direct, producer-to-consumer types to elaborate, multi-level channels employing many types of intermediaries, each serving a particular purpose. Channel configurations for the same product will vary within industries, even within the same firm, because national markets quite often have unique features. This may mean dramatic departures from accepted policy for a company. For example, to reach the British market, which is dominated by a few retailers such as J. Sainsbury, Tesco, and ASDA, global marketers such as Heinz may have to become suppliers to these retailers' private-label programs in addition to making their own efforts.[2] A firm's international market experience will also cause variation in distribution patterns. AMPAK, a manufacturer of packaging machinery, uses locally based distributors in markets where it is well established. Others are entered indirectly by using domestically based intermediaries, either by using the services of trading companies or through selling to larger companies, which then market the products alongside their own.

The connections made by marketing institutions are not solely for the physical movement of goods. They also serve as transactional title flows and informational communications flows. Rather than unidirectional, downward from the producer, the flows are usually

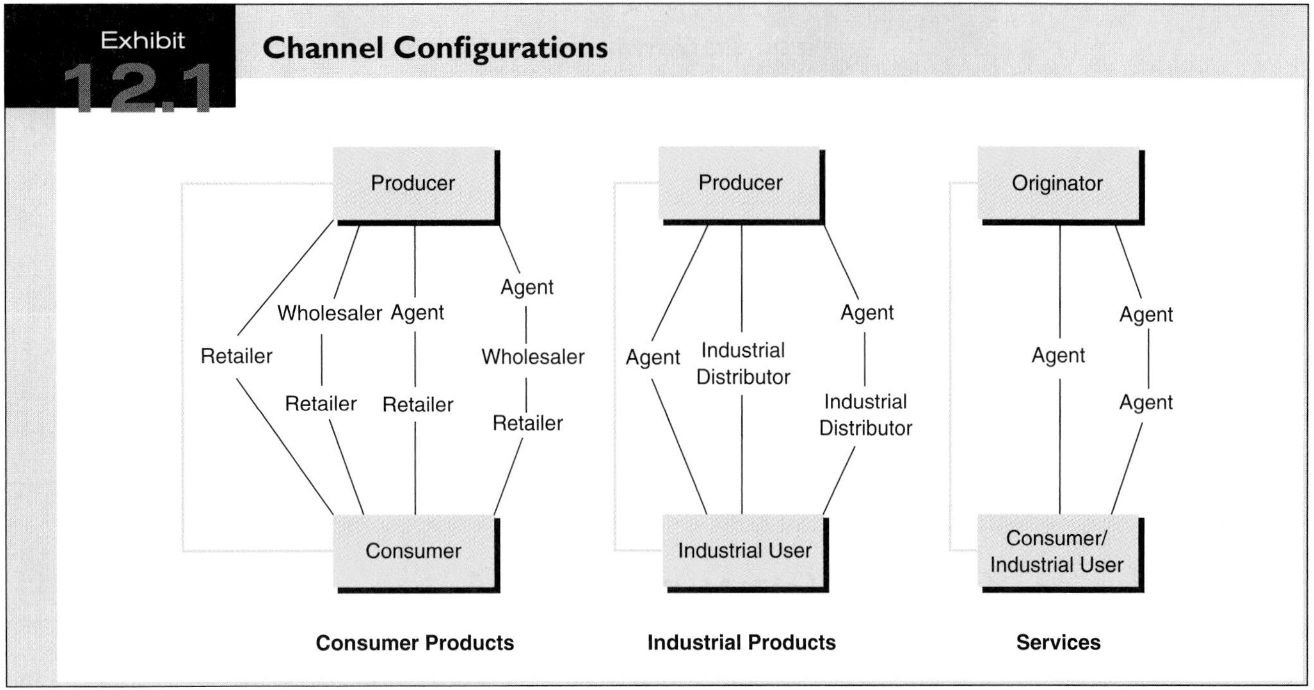

multidirectional, both vertical and horizontal. As an example, the manufacturer relies heavily on the retailer population for data on possible changes in demand. Communications from retailers may be needed to coordinate a cooperative advertising campaign instituted by a manufacturer. The three flows—physical, transactional, and informational—do not necessarily take place simultaneously or occur at every level of the channel. Agent intermediaries, for example, act only to facilitate the information flow; they do not take title and often do not physically handle the goods. Because only a few products are sold directly to ultimate users, a global marketer has to decide on alternative ways to move products to chosen markets. The basic marketing functions of exchange, physical movement, and various facilitating activities must be performed, but the marketer may not be equipped to handle them. Intermediaries can therefore be used to gain quick, easy, and relatively low-cost entry to a targeted market.

Design of Global Distribution Channels

The term **channel design** refers to the length and the width of the channel employed.[3] Length is determined by the number of levels, or different types, of intermediaries. In the case of consumer products, the most traditional is the producer-wholesaler-retailer-customer configuration. Channel width is determined by the number of institutions of each type in the channel. An industrial goods marketer may grant exclusive distribution rights to a foreign entity, whereas a consumer goods marketer may want to use as many intermediaries as possible to ensure intensive distribution.

Channel design is determined by factors that can be summarized as the 11 Cs, listed in Exhibit 12.2. These factors are integral to both the development of new marketing channels and the modification and management of existing ones. Their individual influences will vary from one market to another, and seldom, if ever, can one factor be considered without the interactive effects of the others. The marketer should use the 11 Cs checklist to determine the proper approach to reach intended target audiences before selecting channel members to fill the roles. The first three factors are givens, since the firm must adjust to the existing structures. The other eight are controllable to a certain extent by the global marketer.

Exhibit 12.2 **Determinants of Channel Structure and Relationships**

EXTERNAL	INTERNAL
Customer characteristics	Company objectives
Culture	Character
Competition	Capital
	Cost
	Coverage
	Control
	Continuity
	Communication

Customer Characteristics

The demographic and psychographic characteristics of targeted customers will form the basis for channel design decisions. Answers to questions such as what customers need—as well as why, when, and how they buy—are used to determine ways in which the products should be made available to generate a competitive advantage. As an example, Anheuser-Busch entered Japan when Suntory, one of the country's largest liquor distillers, acquired the importing rights. Suntory's marketing plan stressed distribution of Budweiser in discos, pubs, and other nightspots where Japan's affluent, well-travelled youth gather. Young people in Japan are influenced by U.S. culture and adapt themselves more readily to new products than do older Japanese. Taking advantage of this fact, Suntory concentrated its efforts on one generation, and on-premise sales led to major off-premise (retail outlet) sales as well.

In the early stages of product introduction, the global marketer may concentrate efforts on only the most attractive markets and later, having attained a foothold, expand distribution. When Kronenbourg, the best-selling beer in Europe, entered the U.S. market, distribution was initiated in New York City and then extended to the metropolitan area. The reason was the area's prominence in both domestic and imported beer consumption. The national rollout took place five years later. In the industrial sector, certain industries cluster geographically, allowing the global marketer to take a more direct approach.

Customer characteristics may cause the same product to be distributed through two different types of channels. Many industrial goods marketers' sales, such as those of Caterpillar, are handled by individual dealers, except when the customer might be the central government or one of its entities, in which case sales are direct from the company itself. Furthermore, primary target audiences may change from one market to another. For example, in Japan, McDonald's did not follow the North American pattern of locating restaurants in the suburbs. The masses of young pedestrians that flood Japanese cities were more promising than affluent but tradition-minded car owners in the suburbs.

In business-to-business marketing, the adoption of e-commerce provides new opportunities for global marketers. New international markets can be accessed by expanding network and customer bases. The explosive growth of the Internet, however, poses a direct threat and challenge to traditional intermediaries, leading possibly to elimination or disintermediation.[4]

Culture

In planning a distribution system, the marketer must analyze existing channel structures, or what might be called **distribution culture**. As an example, the manner in which Japanese channels of distribution are structured and managed presents one of the major reasons for the apparent failure of foreign firms to establish major market penetration in

Japan.[5] In any case, and in every country, global marketers must study distribution systems in general and the types of linkages between channel members for their specific type of product. Usually, the global marketer has to adjust to existing structures to gain distribution. For example, in Finland, 95 percent of all distribution of nondurable consumer goods is through four wholesale chains. Without their support, no significant penetration of the market is possible.

In addition to structure, functions performed by the various types of intermediaries have to be outlined. Retailers in Japan demand more from manufacturers and wholesalers than do North American retailers; for example, they expect returns of merchandise to be fully accepted even if there is no reason other than lack of sales. Retailers also expect significant amounts of financing and frequent delivery of products. Retailers, for their part, offer substantial services to their clientele and take great pains to build close relationships with their customers. As can be seen in Exhibit 12.3, which lists channel members in the Japanese cosmetics industry, functions are—and should be—clearly delineated. Manufacturers concentrate mainly on production and promotional activities; intermediaries work on logistics activities, financing, and communication with manufacturers and retailers; retailers focus on sales and promotional activities.

Changing existing distribution systems may be quite difficult. Porsche tried to change the way it sold automobiles in the United States from traditional independent franchised dealers to a "dealerless system." Whereas dealers buy cars for resale, Porsche would have instituted agents who would order cars as they sold them and work on an 8 percent commission rather than the normal 16 to 18 percent margin. After a dealer uproar, Porsche abandoned the plan. Toys 'R' Us, which opened its first outlet in Japan in the 1990s, initially had a difficult time getting Japanese toy manufacturers to sell to it directly (as happens in North America) rather than through multiple layers of distributors. Wal-Mart, for its part, has caused significant changes in supplier operating procedures with its demand that vendors forgo all other amenities and quote the lowest price. This has been traumatic in markets such as the United Kingdom where suppliers and competitors have used government regulation to operate in a less-competitive environment.[6]

Additionally, an analysis is needed of the relationships between channel members—for example, the extent of vertical integration. The linkage can be based on ownership, contract, or the use of expert or referent power by one of the channel members. The Japanese distribution system often financially links producers, importers, distributors, and retailers, either directly or through a bank or a trading company. Interdependence in a number of

Exhibit 12.3 Examples of Function Performance in the Channel System for the Japanese Cosmetics Industry

Channel Member		
Manufacturer	**Intermediary**	**Retail**
Production	Order taking	Selling
Advertising	Inventory maintenance	Organizing consumers
National sales promotion	Space control at the retail level	In-store promotion
Dealer aids	Product assortment	
Education of dealers	Dispatching of sales support personnel	
Financing	Area marketing	
	Financing	

Source: Michael R. Czinkota, *International Marketing Strategy: Readings*, 1st ed. © 1994 Reprinted with permission of South-Western, a division of Thomson Learning: **http://www.thomsonrights.com.** Fax 800-730-2215.

southern European markets is forged through family relationships or is understood as an obligation.

Foreign legislation affecting distributors and agents is an essential part of the distribution culture of a market. For example, legislation may require that foreign firms be represented only by firms that are 100 percent locally owned. Before China's entry into the WTO in late 2001, foreign companies were barred from importing their own products, distributing them, or providing after-sales service. These functions were to be performed by Chinese companies or Sino–foreign joint ventures. These restrictions have been phased out.

While distribution decisions have been mostly tactical and made on a market-by-market basis, marketing managers have to be cognizant of globalization in the distribution function as well. This is taking place in two significant ways.[7] Distribution formats are crossing borders, especially to newly emerging markets. While supermarkets accounted only for 8 percent of consumer nondurable sales in urban areas in Thailand in 1990, the figure today is over 50 percent. Other such formats include department stores, mini-marts, and supercentres. The second globalization trend is the globalization of intermediaries themselves, either independently or through strategic alliances. Entities such as Toys 'R' Us from the United States, Galeries Lafayette from France, Marks & Spencer from the United Kingdom, and Takashimaya and Isetan from Japan have expanded to both well-developed and newly emerging markets. Within the European Union (EU), a growing number of EU-based retailers are merging and establishing a presence in other EU markets. For example, the merger of France's Carrefour and Promodes in 1999 created the world's second-largest retailer after Wal-Mart. The merger was partly in response to Wal-Mart's European expansion.[8] Some intermediaries are entering foreign markets by acquiring local entities (e.g., Germany's Tengelmann and Holland's Ahold acquiring the U.S. chains A&P and Giant, respectively) or forming alliances. For example, in Mexico, joint ventures between Wal-Mart and Cifra, Fleming Cos. and Gigante, and Price/Costco and Comercial Mexicana are changing the distribution landscape by concentrating retail power. Beyond opportunity for marketers for more and broader-based sales, these entities are applying the same type of margin pressure marketers find in more developed markets. In many cases, marketers are providing new technologies to these intermediaries and helping to train them with the hope of establishing solid relationships that will withstand competition, especially from local entities that typically start beefing up their own operations.[9] However, not all cross-border retail expansions are successful. Canadian pharmacy giant Jean Coutu Group Inc. abandoned its U.S. expansion plans and sold its Eckerd and Brooks drugstore chain to Rite Aid Corp. for $3.4 billion. In 2004 Jean Coutu implemented its national U.S. distribution strategy by purchasing 1,500 Eckerd drugstores, which made it the fourth-largest drugstore chain in the U.S.[10]

Competition

Channels used by competitors may be the only product distribution system that is accepted by both the trade and consumers. In this case, the global marketer's task is to use the structure effectively and efficiently, or even innovatively. This may mean, for example, that the exporter chooses a partner capable of developing markets rather than one who has existing contacts. The most obvious distributors may be content with the status quo in the market and be ready to push products that are the most profitable for them regardless of who made them. Two approaches may be applicable if those serving major customer prospects with similar product lines are not satisfactory. First, an exporter may form jointly owned sales companies with distributors (or with other exporters) to exercise more control. Second, the approach may be to seek a good company fit in terms of goals and objectives. Should a new approach be chosen, it must be carefully analyzed and tested against the cultural, political, and legal environments in which it is to be introduced.

In some cases, the global marketer cannot manipulate the distribution variable. For example, in Sweden and Finland, all alcoholic beverages must be distributed through state monopoly–owned outlets, while in the Canadian province of Ontario the Liquor Control Board of Ontario (LCBO) holds a monopoly for distribution of spirits. In Japan, the Japan Tobacco & Salt Public Corporation is a state monopoly that controls all tobacco imports and charges a 20 percent fee for distribution. In other cases, all feasible channels may be blocked by domestic competitors either through contractual agreements or through other means. Foreign suppliers of soda ash, which is used in glass, steel, and chemical products, have not been able to penetrate the Japanese market even though they may offer a price advantage. The reason is the cartel-like condition developed by the Japan Soda Industry Association, which allegedly sets import levels, specifies which local trading company is to deal with each supplier, and buys the imports at lower prices for resale by its members at higher Japanese prices. Efforts by foreign producers to distribute directly or through smaller, unaffiliated traders have faced strong resistance. The end users and traders fear alienating the domestic producers, on whom their business depends.

Company Objectives

A set of management considerations will have an effect on channel design. No channel of distribution can be properly selected unless it meets the requirements set by overall company objectives for market share and profitability. A food company, for example, that has positioned itself as a market-share leader may well wish to emphasize channel width in its design—ensuring that its products are in the hands of a large number of intermediaries that can provide the necessary coverage. In distribution, concern for company objectives often calls for a compromise between cost and control objectives. While integrated channels (company owned and operated) may be preferred because they facilitate the protection of knowledge-based assets and provide needed high levels of customer service, the cost may be 15 to 35 percent of sales, whereas using distributors may drop the expense to 10 to 15 percent.

Often the use of multiple channels arises with the need to increase sales volume.[11] For example, in France, Xerox set up a chain of retail outlets in large cities to support its copier sales. To cover rural areas and smaller towns, Xerox withdrew its direct sales force and replaced it with independent distributors, *concessionaires,* who work on an exclusive basis. Rapid expansion can also be achieved through partnerships, as shown by the Starbucks example in Exhibit 12.4. Partnerships can provide the firm with several key success factors, such as the ability to expand while minimizing capital outlays and a sharing of business risks. If appropriate controls are in place, partnerships can be a sound basis for expansion. However, if expansion is too rapid and the adjustments made to local market conditions too extensive, a major asset—standardization and economies of scale and scope—can be lost.

Character

The nature of the product, its character, will have an impact on the design of the channel. Generally, the more specialized, expensive, bulky, or perishable the product and the more after-sale service it may require, the more likely the channel is to be relatively short. Staple items, such as soap, tend to have longer channels.

The type of channel chosen must match the overall positioning of the product in the market. Changes in overall market conditions, such as currency fluctuations, may require changes in distribution as well. An increase in the value of the billing currency may cause a re-positioning of the marketed product as a luxury item, necessitating an appropriate channel (such as an upper-grade department store) for its distribution.

Capital

The term *capital* is used to describe the financial requirements in setting up a channel system. The global marketer's financial strength will determine the type of channel and the basis on which channel relationships will be built. The stronger the marketer's finances, the more able the firm is to establish channels it either owns or controls. Intermediaries' requirements for beginning inventories, selling on a consignment basis, preferential loans, and need for training all will have an impact on the type of approach chosen by the global

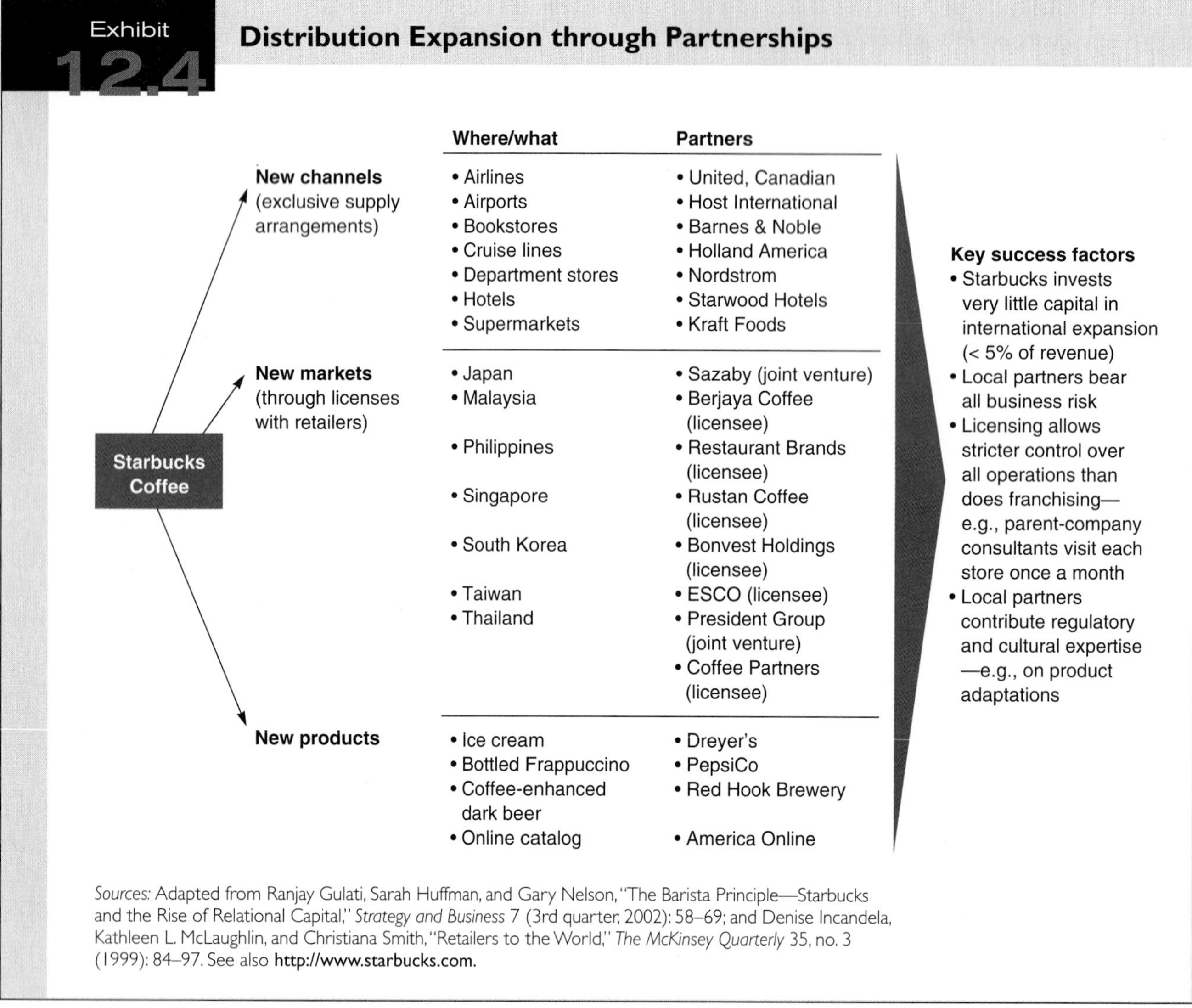

Exhibit 12.4
Distribution Expansion through Partnerships
Starbucks Coffee
Where/what
Partners
New channels (exclusive supply arrangements)
• Airlines
• Airports
• Bookstores
• Cruise lines
• Department stores
• Hotels
• Supermarkets
• United, Canadian
• Host International
• Barnes & Noble
• Holland America
• Nordstrom
• Starwood Hotels
• Kraft Foods
New markets (through licenses with retailers)
• Japan
• Malaysia
• Philippines
• Singapore
• South Korea
• Taiwan
• Thailand
• Sazaby (joint venture)
• Berjaya Coffee (licensee)
• Restaurant Brands (licensee)
• Rustan Coffee (licensee)
• Bonvest Holdings (licensee)
• ESCO (licensee)
• President Group (joint venture)
• Coffee Partners (licensee)
New products
• Ice cream
• Bottled Frappuccino
• Coffee-enhanced dark beer
• Online catalog
• Dreyer's
• PepsiCo
• Red Hook Brewery
• America Online
Key success factors
• Starbucks invests very little capital in international expansion (< 5% of revenue)
• Local partners bear all business risk
• Licensing allows stricter control over all operations than does franchising—e.g., parent-company consultants visit each store once a month
• Local partners contribute regulatory and cultural expertise—e.g., on product adaptations

Sources: Adapted from Ranjay Gulati, Sarah Huffman, and Gary Nelson, "The Barista Principle—Starbucks and the Rise of Relational Capital," *Strategy and Business* 7 (3rd quarter, 2002): 58–69; and Denise Incandela, Kathleen L. McLaughlin, and Christiana Smith, "Retailers to the World," *The McKinsey Quarterly* 35, no. 3 (1999): 84–97. See also **http://www.starbucks.com.**

marketer. For example, an industrial goods manufacturer may find that potential distributors in a particular country lack the capability of servicing the product. The marketer then has two options: (1) set up an elaborate training program at headquarters or regionally or (2) institute company-owned service centres to help distributors. Either approach will require a significant investment but is necessary to ensure customer trust through superior execution of marketing programs.

Cost

Closely related to the capital dimension is cost—that is, the expenditure incurred in maintaining a channel once it is established. Costs will naturally vary over the life cycle of a relationship with a particular channel member as well as over the life cycle of the products marketed. An example of the costs involved is promotional money spent by a distributor for the marketer's product. A cooperative advertising deal between the global marketer and the intermediary would typically split the costs of the promotional campaign executed in the local market.

Costs will vary in terms of the relative power of the manufacturer vis-à-vis its intermediaries. There has been considerable consolidation in retail in North America and Europe. This consolidation includes not only large retailers but also smaller retailers that have joined forces to form buying groups. One of the most significant is Expert Global, which has a total of 7,400 participating retailers in Europe, Canada, the U.S., and Latin America. The concentrated distribution systems being developed by such groups are eroding the marketing strength of manufacturers, which lay in their networks of distribution depots that delivered direct to stores. Now, retailers want delivery to their central distribution centres. In addition, they are pushing stockholding costs to manufacturers by demanding more frequent deliveries, in smaller, mixed loads, with shorter delivery time.[12]

Coverage

The term *coverage* is used to describe both the number of areas in which the marketer's products are represented and the quality of that representation. Coverage is therefore two-dimensional in that horizontal coverage and vertical coverage need to be considered in channel design. The number of areas to be covered depends on the dispersion of demand in the market and also on the time elapsed since the product's introduction to the market. Three different approaches are available:

1. Intensive coverage, which calls for distributing the product through the largest number of different types of intermediaries and the largest number of individual intermediaries of each type
2. Selective coverage, which entails choosing a number of intermediaries for each area to be penetrated
3. Exclusive coverage, which involves only one entity in a market

Generally, intensive and selective coverage call for longer channels using different types of intermediaries, usually wholesalers and agents. Exclusive distribution is conducive to more direct sales. For some products, such as ethnic or industrial products, customers are concentrated geographically and allow for more intensive distribution with a more direct channel. A company typically enters a market with one local distributor, but as volume expands, the distribution base often has to be adjusted.

Control

The use of intermediaries will automatically lead to loss of some control over the marketing of the firm's products.[13] The looser the relationship is between the marketer and intermediaries, the less control the marketer can exert. The longer the channel, the more difficult it becomes for the marketer to have a final say in pricing, promotion, and the types of outlets in which the product will be made available.

In the initial stages of internationalization or specific market entry, an intermediary's specialized knowledge and working relationships are needed, but as the global marketer's experience base and sales in the market increase, many opt to establish their own sales offices. Use of intermediaries provides quick entry using an existing system in which complementary products provide synergistic benefits. Furthermore, payments are received from one entity rather than from multiple customers.

The issue of control correlates heavily with the type of product or service being marketed. In the case of industrial and high-technology products, control will be easier to institute because intermediaries are dependent on the marketer for new products and service. Where the firm's marketing strategy calls for a high level of service, integrated channels are used to ensure that the service does get performed.[14] Later on, a global marketer may want to coordinate programs across markets on a regional basis, which is much easier if the channel is controlled.

The global marketer's ability and willingness to exercise any type of power—whether reward, coercive, legitimate, referent, or expert—determines the extent of control. The exercise of control causes more incidents of conflict in channels of distribution than any other activity in the relationship. This points to the need for careful communication with foreign intermediaries about the marketer's intentions and also the need for certain control measures. These might include the marketer's need to be the sole source of advertising copy or to be in charge of all product-modification activities. Generally, the more control the marketer wishes to have, the more cost is involved in securing that control.

Continuity

Channel design decisions are the most long-term of the marketing mix decisions. Utmost care must therefore be taken in choosing the right type of channel, given the types of intermediaries available and any environmental threats that may affect the channel design. Occasionally, however, unpredictable events may occur. As an example, Cockspur, the largest distiller of rum in Barbados, negotiated an arrangement with one of the largest distributors in the United States. Almost immediately, the distributor was acquired by a company that thought liquor distribution did not fit its mission and thus eliminated the products and reassigned the salespeople. Years later, Cockspur was still without substantial distribution in the United States.[15]

Nurturing continuity rests heavily on the marketer because foreign distributors may have a more short-term view of the relationship. For example, Japanese wholesalers believe that it is important for manufacturers to follow up initial success with continuous improvement of the product. If such improvements are not forthcoming, competitors are likely to enter the market with similar, lower-priced products, and the wholesalers of the imported product will turn to the Japanese suppliers.

Continuity is also expressed through visible market commitment. Industries abroad may be quite conservative; distributors will not generally support an outsider until they are sure it is in the market to stay. Such commitments include sending in technical or sales personnel or offering training, and setting up wholly owned sales subsidiaries from the start—and staffing them with locals to help communicate that the company is there for the long term.[16] Investment in distributors may be literal (resulting in co-ownership in the future) or abstract (resulting in more solid commitment in the relationship).

Communication

Communication provides the exchange of information that is essential to the functioning of the channel. Communication is an important consideration in channel design, and it gains more emphasis in international distribution because of various types of distances that may cause problems. In the buyer–seller relationships in international markets, the distance that is perceived to exist between a buyer and a seller has five aspects, all of which are amplified in the international setting:[17]

1. Social distance: the extent to which each of the two entities in a relationship is familiar with the other's ways of operating
2. Cultural distance: the degree to which the norms, values, or working methods between the two entities differ because of their separate national characteristics
3. Technological distance: the differences between the product or process technologies of the two entities
4. Time distance: the time that must elapse between establishing contact or placing an order and the actual transfer of the product or service involved
5. Geographical distance: the physical distance between the locations of the two entities

All these dimensions must be considered when determining whether to use intermediaries and, if they are to be used, what types to use.

Communication, if properly utilized, will assist the global marketer in conveying the firm's goals to the distributors, in solving conflict situations, and in marketing the product overall. Communication is a two-way process that does not permit the marketer to dictate to intermediaries. Cases are well known in which the marketer is not able to make the firm's marketing program functional. Prices may not be competitive; promotional materials may be obsolete or inaccurate and badly received overall. This may be compounded if the global marketer tries to transplant abroad procedures and programs used domestically.[18] Solving these types of problems is important to the welfare of both parties.

Channels of distribution, because of their sequential positioning of the entities involved, are not conducive to noiseless communication. The marketer must design a channel and choose intermediaries that guarantee good information flow. Proper communication involves not only the passage of information between channel members but also a better understanding of each party's needs and goals. This can be achieved through personal visits, exchange of personnel, or distribution advisory councils. Consisting of members from all channel participants, advisory councils meet regularly to discuss opportunities and problems that may have arisen.

Selection of Intermediaries

Once the basic design of the channel has been determined, the global marketer must begin a search to fill the defined roles with the best available candidates and must secure their cooperation.

Types of Intermediaries

Two basic decisions are involved in choosing the type of intermediary to serve a particular market. First, the marketer must determine the type of relationship to have with intermediaries. The alternatives are a distributorship or an agency relationship. **Distributors** will purchase the product and will therefore exercise more independence than agencies. Distributors are typically organized along product lines and provide the global marketer with complete marketing services. **Agents** have less freedom of movement than distributors because they operate on a commission basis and do not usually physically handle the goods. This, in turn, allows the marketer control to make sure, for example, that the customer gets the most recent and appropriate product version. In addition to the business implications, the choice of type will have legal implications in terms of what the intermediary can commit its principal to and the ease of termination of the agreement.

Second, the global marketer must decide whether to utilize indirect exporting, direct exporting, or integrated distribution in penetrating a foreign market. **Indirect exporting** requires dealing with another domestic firm that acts as a sales intermediary for the marketer, often taking over the international side of the marketer's operations. The benefits, especially in the short term, are that the exporter can use someone else's international channels without having to pay to set them up. But there may be long-term concerns in using this strategy if the marketer wants to actively and aggressively get into the markets itself. Indirect exporting is only practised by firms very early on in their internationalization process. With **direct exporting**, the marketer takes direct responsibility for its products abroad by either selling directly to the foreign customer or finding a representative in the foreign country to sell its products in the market. The third category of export marketing strategy, **integrated distribution**, requires the marketer to make an investment in the foreign market for the purpose of selling its products in that market or more broadly. This investment could be the opening, for example, of a German or EU sales office, a distribution hub, or even an assembly operation or manufacturing facility. Although the last set of strategies indicates longer-term commitment to a market, it is riskier than the first two because the marketer is making a major financial investment. For example, if the firm moves from an agency agreement to a sales office, its costs for that market are now fixed costs (i.e., the costs will be incurred even if no sales are made) instead of the previous variable costs. Setting up even a modest office may be expensive.[19] Operating expenses may approach half a million dollars per year, and real estate costs can be substantial if the office is in a main business district.

Sources for Finding Intermediaries

As illustrated in The Global Marketplace 12.2, firms that have successful international distribution attest to the importance of finding top representatives.[20] This undertaking should be held in the same regard as recruiting and hiring within the company, because an inef-

The Global MARKETPLACE 12.2

Clinotech Diagnostics

Started in 1997 in Richmond, British Columbia, Clinotech Diagnostics and Pharmaceuticals Inc. was established to meet the need, as seen by its founder, Dr. Harrison Ofiyai, for one-stop medical diagnostic devices, especially in developing countries. Dr. Ofiyai's previous experience in numerous countries as a physician for Doctors Without Borders led him to become a maker of tools and products for the early detection of human diseases. Prominent among these are diagnostic kits containing chemicals and indicator strips for diagnosing diseases such as hepatitis, tropical illnesses, and tuberculosis.

Dr. Ofiyai enjoyed a wide network of medical colleagues and friends located in the markets he proposed to target. A key strategic decision at the outset was to capitalize on these contacts to find suitable distributors. His first venture was in Turkey. As he was aware, Turkish hospital directors generally have relations with local medical distributors and are reluctant to deal with a foreign supplier. His former medical colleagues assisted Dr. Ofiyai in identifying a number of possible distributors. Out of these, one was eventually selected and engaged.

Building on this experience, the company, using the same approach, went on to hire further distributors in Turkey, ending with three: one in Ankara, one in Izmir, and one in the biggest Turkish market, Istanbul. The distributors were selected partly on the basis of their networks of sub-distributors throughout the country. This enabled kits to be adopted quickly in various state and private hospitals.

Beyond Turkey, the company began to develop other markets. Distributors were successfully found in Jordan and then Iran as a basis for developing the Middle Eastern market. Attention was then directed to Greece, Cyprus, Bulgaria, Azerbaijan, and Syria, using the same modus operandi. Later followed distributor appointments in Latin American markets (Bolivia, Paraguay, Uruguay, Chile, and Guatemala) and, most recently, the Pacific Rim (Vietnam, Cambodia, Indonesia, and Sri Lanka).

The company's approach to distributor selection can be summarized as follow:

1. Use network of physician contacts and friends in the target country to identify medical suppliers and distributors to local hospitals.
2. Obtain company profile of potential distributors. This is done partly using the company's website. Distributors are given an information sheet to tell Clinotech about themselves. Clinotech uses the data, together with hospital recommendations, to evaluate the suitability of the distributor and identify any weaknesses.
3. If distributor prospects look promising, provide the organizations with a list of Clinotech products and ask for a business plan showing how they would deal with different aspects of distribution (how they would set prices, what support they would need, how they would deal with competition).
4. Send sample kits to promising distributors for hospital trial in the distributor's geographical area.
5. If trials are favourable and other elements (profile, business plan, contract) satisfactory, hire a distributor.

The company's initial strategy was to avoid awarding exclusive rights. This was, in the company's view, in order to maintain flexibility and to avoid being tied to any one middleman in any market. With time, however, this has changed. Now, if the distributor can do "all that is needed" and can produce a three-year business plan showing acceptable sales projections, exclusivity will be granted.

Not all target markets have been successful in terms of hiring distributors. Africa was found to have inadequate communications—cellular phones, Internet use—to justify going ahead. Medical distributors in Mexico were found to be too close to their U.S. suppliers and not sufficiently interested in finding new ones. In Brazil, the time to get product approval—6 to 12 months—was thought unacceptably long. However, these drawbacks have been more than compensated by developments elsewhere, and as expansion has gone on, the company finds itself increasingly approached directly by distributors seeking to represent Clinotech.

In addition to evolving a successful approach to finding and choosing distributors, the company has found that this must be supplemented by constant personal attention to the needs of partners and customers in individual markets. The company strongly emphasizes the following:

1. Visit markets regularly to give after-market support. Clinotech trains distributor sales staff and shows them how to answer the technical questions the medical staff will have.
2. Nurture trust in distributors so that they know Clinotech is always behind them when they sell to hospitals and doctors. This is particularly important when faced with many competing firms from the Far East. In his visits, Dr. Ofiyai emphasizes that he believes in the company's products and so can distributors: he will provide "the best kits at cost-effective prices."

3. Emphasize to distributors that they will always have Clinotech's after-sales support as well as technical and clinical support. Other companies may dump their kits on middlemen and leave them to their own devices. Not so Clinotech.
4. Visit medical trade shows regularly. This enables one-on-one personal contact with distributors, purchasing agents, doctors, and opinion leaders, whose technical questions can be answered directly, and boosts the confidence of distributors that Clinotech service will always be there. Invariably these visits result in new contacts.
5. Use constant-reminder advertising and the latest company information to keep emphasizing Clinotech quality and service. The company sees this as vital in a highly competitive market.

In two years, using this strategy, Clinotech has established more than 30 distributors in 30 different countries, from the Middle East to Latin America. As the founder remarks: "I owe a lot to my doctor friends in this part of the world. Without that network, building my business would be much more difficult, if not impossible." Sales have now reached the point where the company has been able to establish its own plant. "Now we have a real factory I can walk around in, and we have customers all over the world," says Dr. Ofiyai. As he states, success has been built on a quality product, consistently reliable service with excellent after-sales support, a solid, scientific background—and loyal distributors.

Source: Excerpted from Dennis Jones and Sandi Jones, "Diary of an Exporter: Clinotech," Parts 1–4, *Exportwise*, Winter 2004, Summer and Fall 2005.

fective foreign distributor can set the global marketer back years; it is almost better to have no distributor than a bad one in a major market.

The approach can be either passive or active. Foreign operations for a number of smaller firms start through an unsolicited order; the same can happen with foreign distribution. Distributors, wherever they are, are always on the lookout for product representation that can be profitable and status enhancing. The initial contact may result from an advertisement or from a trade show in which the marketer has participated. For example, Timberland has traditionally expanded to new markets by responding to intermediaries who have approached it.[21]

The global marketer's best interest lies in taking an active role. The marketer should not simply use the first intermediary to show an interest in the firm. The choice should be a result of a careful planning process. The firm should start by gaining an understanding of market conditions in order to define what is expected of an intermediary and what the marketer can offer in the relationship. At the same time, procedures need to be set for intermediary identification and evaluation.[22] The exporter does not have to do all of this independently; both governmental and private agencies can assist the marketer in locating intermediary candidates. The Canadian Trade Commissioner Service in the target country is often able to provide Canadian firms with a list of distributors in their jurisdiction and an assessment of their capabilities.

Screening Intermediaries

In most firms, the evaluation of candidates involves both what to look for and where to go for the information. At this stage, the global marketer knows the type of distributor that is needed. The potential candidates must now be compared and contrasted against established criteria. Although the criteria to be used vary by industry and by product, factors normally considered include reputation, financial strength, physical facilities, relationship with local governments, territorial coverage, and previous sales performance.

The Distributor Agreement

When the global marketer has found a suitable intermediary, a foreign sales agreement is drawn up.[23] The agreement can be relatively simple, but given the numerous differences in the market environments, certain elements such as territorial coverage, product coverage, payment methods, method of communication, distributor duties, manufacturer's rights, and procedures for dealing with disputes are essential. Contract duration is also important, especially when an agreement is signed with a new distributor. In general, distribution agreements should be for a specified, relatively short period (one or two years). The initial contract with a new distributor should stipulate a trial period of either three or six months, possibly with minimum purchase requirements. Duration should be determined with an eye on the local laws and their stipulations on distributor agreements. These will be discussed later in conjunction with distributor termination.

Geographic boundaries for the distributor should be determined with care, especially by smaller firms. Future expansion of the product market might be complicated if a distributor claims rights to certain territories. The marketer should retain the right to distribute products independently, reserving the right to certain customers. For example, many marketers maintain a dual distribution system, dealing directly with certain large accounts. This type of arrangement should be explicitly stated in the agreement. Transshipments, or sales to customers outside the agreed-upon territory or customer type, have to be explicitly prohibited to prevent the occurrence of parallel importation.

The payment section of the contract should stipulate the methods of payment as well as how the distributor or agent is to draw compensation. Distributors derive compensation from various discounts (such as the functional discount), whereas agents earn a specific commission percentage of net sales (such as 15 percent). Given the volatility of currency markets, the agreement should also state the currency to be used. The global marketer also needs to make sure that none of the compensation forwarded to the distributor is a violation of OECD bribery guidelines.

Product and conditions of sale need to be agreed on. The products or product lines included should be stipulated, as well as the functions and responsibilities of the intermediary in terms of carrying the goods in inventory, providing service in conjunction with them, and promoting them. Conditions of sale determine which party is to be responsible for some of the expenses involved, which will in turn have an effect on the price to the distributor. These conditions include credit and shipment terms.

Effective means of communication between the parties must be stipulated in the agreement if a marketer–distributor relationship is to succeed. The global marketer should have access to all information concerning the marketing of his or her products in the distributor's territory, including past records, present situation assessments, and marketing research concerning the future. Communication channels should be formal for the distributor to voice formal grievances. The contract should state the confidentiality of the information provided by either party and protect the intellectual property rights (such as patents) involved.

Channel Management

A channel relationship can be likened to a marriage in that it brings together two independent entities that have shared goals. For the relationship to work, each party must be open about its expectations and communicate changes perceived in the other's behaviour that might be contrary to the agreement. The closer the relationship is to a distribution partnership, the more likely marketing success will materialize. Conflict will arise, ranging from small grievances (such as billing errors) to major ones (rivalry over channel duties), but it can be managed to enhance the overall channel relationship. In some cases, conflict may be caused by an outside entity, such as grey markets, in which unauthorized intermediaries compete for market share with legitimate importers and exclusive distributors. Nevertheless, the global marketer must be prepared to solve these problems.

The relationship has to be managed for the long term. A global marketer, for example, may in some countries have a seller's market situation that allows it to exert pressure on its intermediaries for concessions. However, if environmental conditions change, the firm may find that the channel support it needs to succeed is not there because of the manner in which it managed channel relationships in the past.[24] Firms with harmonious relationships are typically those with more experience abroad and those that are proactive in managing the channel relationship. Harmonious relationships are also characterized by more trust, communication, and cooperation between the entities and, as a result, by less conflict and perceived uncertainty.[25]

As the global marketer's operations expand, the need for coordination across markets will grow. Therefore, the firm may want to establish distributor advisory councils to help in reactive measures (e.g., how to combat parallel importation) or proactive measures (e.g., how to transfer best practice from one distributor to another). Naturally, such councils are instrumental in building esprit de corps for the long-term success of the distribution system.

Factors in Channel Management

An excellent framework for managing channel relationships is shown in Exhibit 12.5. The complicating factors that separate the two parties fall into three categories: ownership; geographic, cultural, and economic distance; and different rules of law. Rather than lament their existence, both parties need to take strong action to remedy them. Often, the major step is acknowledgment that differences do indeed exist.

In global marketing, manufacturers and distributors are usually independent entities. Distributors typically carry the products of more than one manufacturer and judge products by their ability to generate revenue without added expense. The global marketer, in order to receive disproportionate attention for its concerns, may offer both monetary and psychological rewards.

Distance, whether it is geographic, psychological, economic, or a combination, can be bridged through effective two-way communication. This should go beyond normal routine business communication to include innovative ways of sharing pertinent information. The global marketer may place one person in charge of distributor-related communications or put into effect an interpenetration strategy—that is, an exchange of personnel so that both organizations gain further insight into the workings of the other.[26] The existence

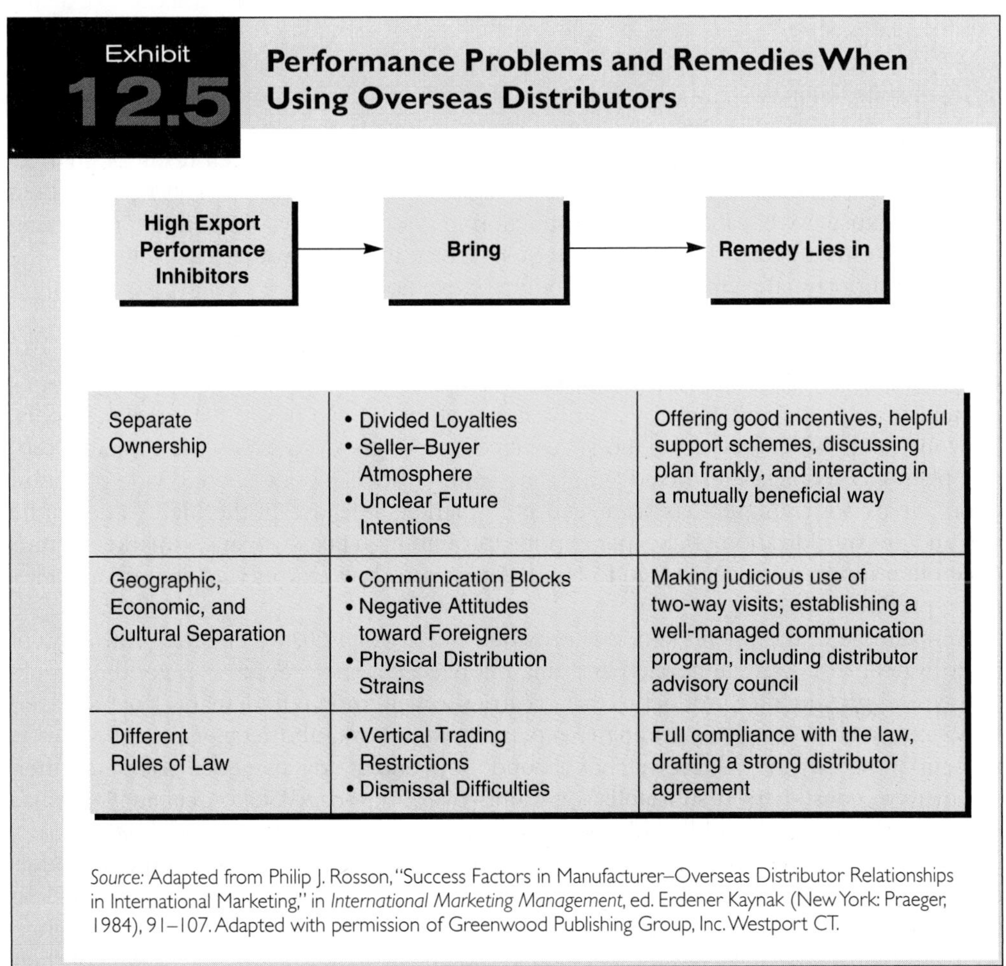

Exhibit 12.5 Performance Problems and Remedies When Using Overseas Distributors

High Export Performance Inhibitors →	Bring →	Remedy Lies in
Separate Ownership	• Divided Loyalties • Seller–Buyer Atmosphere • Unclear Future Intentions	Offering good incentives, helpful support schemes, discussing plan frankly, and interacting in a mutually beneficial way
Geographic, Economic, and Cultural Separation	• Communication Blocks • Negative Attitudes toward Foreigners • Physical Distribution Strains	Making judicious use of two-way visits; establishing a well-managed communication program, including distributor advisory council
Different Rules of Law	• Vertical Trading Restrictions • Dismissal Difficulties	Full compliance with the law, drafting a strong distributor agreement

Source: Adapted from Philip J. Rosson, "Success Factors in Manufacturer–Overseas Distributor Relationships in International Marketing," in *International Marketing Management*, ed. Erdener Kaynak (New York: Praeger, 1984), 91–107. Adapted with permission of Greenwood Publishing Group, Inc. Westport CT.

of cross-cultural differences in people's belief systems and behaviour patterns has to be acknowledged and acted on for effective channel management. For example, in markets where individualism is stressed, local channel partners may seek arrangements that foster their own self-interest and may expect their counterparts to watch out for themselves. Conflict is seen as a natural phenomenon. In societies of low individualism, however, a common purpose is fostered between the partners.[27]

Economic distance manifests itself in exchange rates, for example. Instability of exchange rates can create serious difficulties for distributors in their trading activities, not only with their suppliers but also with their domestic customers. Manufacturers and distributors should develop and deploy mutually acceptable mechanisms that allow for some flexibility in interactions when unforeseen rate fluctuations occur.[28]

Laws and regulations in many markets may restrict the manufacturer in terms of control. For example, in the EU, the marketer cannot prevent a distributor from re-exporting products to customers in another member country, even though the marketer has another distributor in that market. EU law insists on a single market where goods and services can be sold throughout the area without restriction. In 1998, VW was fined €90 million and in 2000, GM was fined €43 million for taking steps to limit intra-EU imports. Even monitoring parallel imports (see below) may be considered to be in restraint of trade.

Most of the criteria used in selecting intermediaries can be used to evaluate existing intermediaries as well. If not conducted properly and fairly, however, evaluation can be a source of conflict. In addition to being given the evaluation results in order to take appropriate action, the distributor should be informed of the evaluative criteria and should be a part of the overall assessment process. Again, the approach should be focused on serving mutual benefits. For example, it is important that the exporter receive detailed market and financial performance data from the distributor. Most distributors identify these data as the key sources of power in distribution and may, therefore, be inherently reluctant to provide them in full detail. The exchange of such data is often the best indicator of a successful relationship.[29]

A part of the management process is channel adjustment. This can take the form of channel shift (eliminating a particular type of channel), channel modification (changing individual members while leaving channel structure intact), or role or relationship modification (changing the functions performed or the reward structure) as a result of channel evaluation. The need for channel change should be well established and not executed hastily, because it will cause a major distraction in the operations of the firm. Some companies have instituted procedures that require executives to consider carefully all of the aspects and potential results of change before execution.

Grey Markets

Grey markets, or **parallel importation**, refer to the sale of authentic and legitimately manufactured trademark items by intermediaries other than authorized channel members. Grey-market products vary from inexpensive consumer goods to expensive capital goods. The phenomenon is not restricted to any one country but is indeed a worldwide phenomenon. Japan, for example, has witnessed grey markets because of the high value of the yen and the subsidization of cheaper exports through high taxes. Japanese marketers thus have often found it cheaper to go to North America to buy export versions of Japanese-made products.

An example of the phenomenon is provided in Exhibit 12.6, which shows the flow of Seiko watches through authorized and unauthorized channels. Seiko is a good example of a typical grey-market product in that it carries a well-known trademark. Unauthorized importers, such as Progress Trading Company in New York, and retailers, such as Kmart or Gem of the Day, buy Seiko watches around the world at advantageous prices and then sell them to consumers at substantial discounts over authorized Seiko dealers. Seiko has fought back, for example, by advertising warnings to consumers against buying grey-market watches on the grounds that these products may be obsolete or worn-out models and that consumers might have problems with their warranties. Many grey marketers, however, provide their own warranty-related service and guarantee watches sold through them. Since watches have strong commercial potential online due to the power of their

Exhibit 12.6 **Seiko's Authorized and Unauthorized Channels of Distribution**

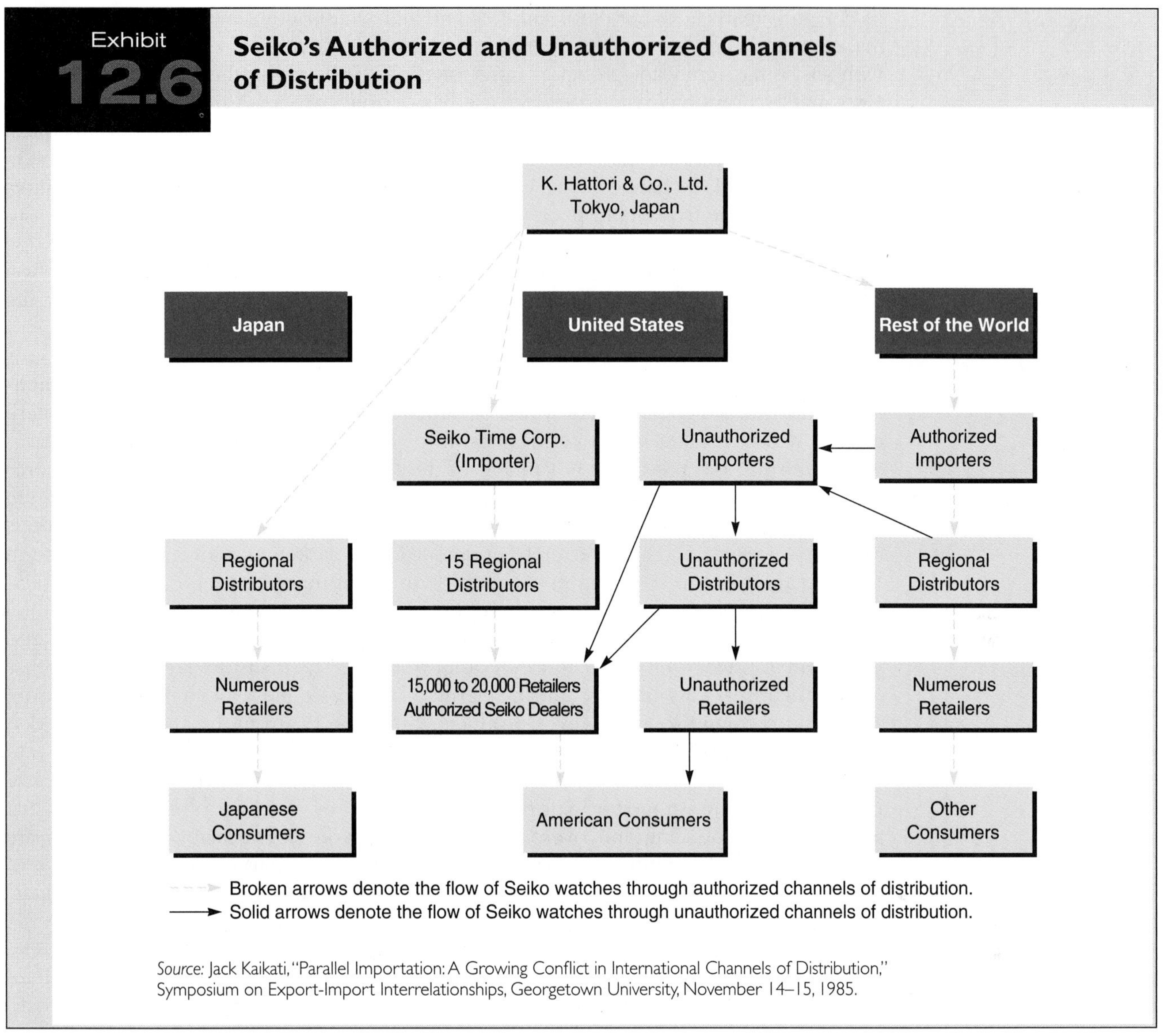

Source: Jack Kaikati, "Parallel Importation: A Growing Conflict in International Channels of Distribution," Symposium on Export-Import Interrelationships, Georgetown University, November 14–15, 1985.

brand identities, grey-market watch websites are having the most impact on higher-priced watch lines selling for over $1,000 retail. Authorized retailers are being forced to take bigger discounts to keep from losing sales.[30]

Various conditions allow unauthorized re-sellers to exist. The most important are wide price differences between markets. Competitive conditions may require the global marketer to sell essentially the same product at different prices in different markets or to different customers.[31] Because many products are priced higher in, for example, Canada, a grey marketer can purchase them in Europe or the Far East and offer discounts between 10 and 40 percent below list price when re-selling them in the Canadian market. Exchange rate fluctuations can cause price differentials and thus opportunities for grey marketers. For example, during the Asian financial crisis, grey marketers imported Caterpillar, Deere, and Komatsu construction and earth-moving equipment no longer needed for halted projects in markets such as Thailand and Indonesia—and usually never used—for as little as 60 percent of what North American dealers paid wholesale.[32] In some cases, grey markets emerge as a result of product shortages. However, in these cases, the grey market goods typically cost more than those usually available through authorized suppliers. In other cases, if there are multiple production sites for the same product, grey markets can emerge due to negative perceptions about the country of origin.

For grey markets to develop, logistics and transaction costs must be low. The grey marketer must be able to ship the product from the low-price to the high-price market without losing significant profits to transportation, tariffs, and other transactional costs. Grey market flows have therefore increased as current barriers to trade have been eliminated. The EU has significant parallel importation due to wide price differentials in ethical drugs, which are in turn the result of differences in regulation, insurance coverage, medical practice, and exchange rates. Of the 15 member countries, only Denmark grants manufacturers the freedom to price their ethical drugs. The share of parallel trade is estimated at 15 percent and is expected to grow since the European Commission is supporting the practice.[33] A similar controversy has emerged in the United States, where prescription drugs are priced at 34 percent higher than in Canada and where some are advocating the re-importation of these drugs from Canada to the United States.

Opponents and supporters of the practice disagree on whether the central issue is price or trade rights. Detractors typically cite the following arguments: (1) the grey market unduly hurts the legitimate owners of trademarks; (2) without protection, trademark owners will have little incentive to invest in product development; (3) grey marketers will "free-ride" or take unfair advantage of the trademark owners' marketing and promotional activities; and (4) parallel imports can deceive consumers by not meeting product standards or their normal expectations of after-sale service. The bottom line is that grey-market goods can severely undercut local marketing plans, erode long-term brand images, eat up costly promotion funds, and sour manufacturer–intermediary relations. The opponents scored a major victory when the European Court of Justice ruled in 2001 against Tesco, which imported cheap Levi's jeans from the United States and sold them at prices well below those of other retailers. The decision backed Levi Strauss & Co.'s claim that its image could be harmed if it lost control of import distribution. Tesco can continue sourcing Levi's products within the EU from the cheapest provider, but not from outside it.[34]

Proponents of parallel importation approach the issue from an altogether different point of view. They argue for their right to "free trade" by pointing to manufacturers that are both overproducing and overpricing in some markets. The main beneficiaries are consumers, who benefit from lower prices and discount distributors, with whom some of the manufacturers do not want to deal and who have now, because of grey markets, found a profitable market niche.

In response to the challenge, manufacturers have chosen various approaches. The solution for the most part lies with the contractual relationships that tie businesses together. In almost all cases of grey marketing, someone in the authorized channel commits a diversion, thus violating the agreements signed. One of the standard responses is therefore disenfranchisement of such violators. This approach is a clear response to complaints from the authorized dealers who are being hurt by transshipments. Tracking down offenders is quite expensive and time consuming, however. It may be more prudent for the global marketer to use **supply interference**, an approach in which attempts are made to build a better relationship with distributors, with efforts made to screen orders more effectively and revisit their procedures for dealing with surplus inventory.

The global marketer may also consider a **dealer interference** strategy, in which grey products are tracked down in the importing country and the offending dealer is asked to destroy the products. Once located, some grey marketers may even be added to the authorized dealer network if mutually acceptable terms can be reached, thereby increasing control of the channel of distribution.[35]

Some companies have used a **strategic attack** strategy, in which they create stronger reasons for consumers to patronize authorized dealers, such as price incentives. The Swedish camera manufacturer Hasselblad offers rebates to purchasers of legally imported, serial-numbered camera bodies, lenses, and roll-fill magazines. Many manufacturers use **demand interference**, in which advertisements are rolled out that educate consumers on the benefits of dealing with authorized dealers (and, thereby, the dangers of dealing with grey-market dealers).[35a] For example, Rolex's message states that authorized dealers are the only ones who are capable of providing genuine accessories and who can ensure that the customer gets an authentic product and the appropriate warranty. Another example is provided by Nikon Canada, which posted the following notice on its website (**http://www.nikon.ca/about/greymarket.asp**):

> **Important Notice To All Consumers—Beware of Purchasing Grey Market Nikon Products**
> It has come to our attention that certain Nikon branded photographic and digital imaging product is being imported and sold by unauthorized retailers, both over the Internet and in retail locations. Please note that Nikon Canada is the only official authorized Canadian source for all Nikon branded photographic and digital imaging products. Nikon Canada distributes these products through a network of Authorized Nikon Canada Dealers. Always confirm that your camera retailer (whether electronic or 'bricks & mortar') is an Authorized Nikon Canada Dealer. Please consult the Dealer Locator for a list of Authorized Nikon Canada Dealers.
>
> If you purchase Nikon branded photographic or digital imaging product from anyone other than an authorized Nikon Canada dealer, beware that Nikon Canada does not, and will not, provide parts, repair services, warranty service or technical support for any such product.
>
> Nikon Canada only offers repair services or parts (including warranty service and technical support) for products purchased from one of its Authorized Nikon Dealers.
>
> *Source:* Nikon Canada

Termination of the Channel Relationship

Many reasons exist for the termination of a channel relationship, but the most typical are changes in the global marketer's distribution approach (for example, establishing a sales office) or a (perceived) lack of performance by the intermediary. On occasion, termination may result from either party not honouring agreements, for example, by selling outside assigned territories and initiating price wars.[36]

Channel relationships go through a life cycle. The concept of an international distribution life cycle is presented in Exhibit 12.7. Over time, the manufacturer's marketing capabilities increase while a distributor's ability and willingness to grow the manufacturer's business in that market decreases. When a producer expands its market presence, it may expect more of a distributor's effort than the distributor is willing to make available. Furthermore, with expansion, the manufacturer may want to expand its product line to items that the distributor is neither interested in nor able to support. In some cases, intermediaries may not be interested in growing the business beyond a certain point (e.g., due to progressive taxation in the country) or as aggressively as the principal may expect (i.e., being more of an order-taker than an order-getter). As a marketer's operations expand, it may want to start to coordinate operations across markets for efficiency and customer-service reasons or to cater

Exhibit 12.7 **International Distribution Life Cycle**

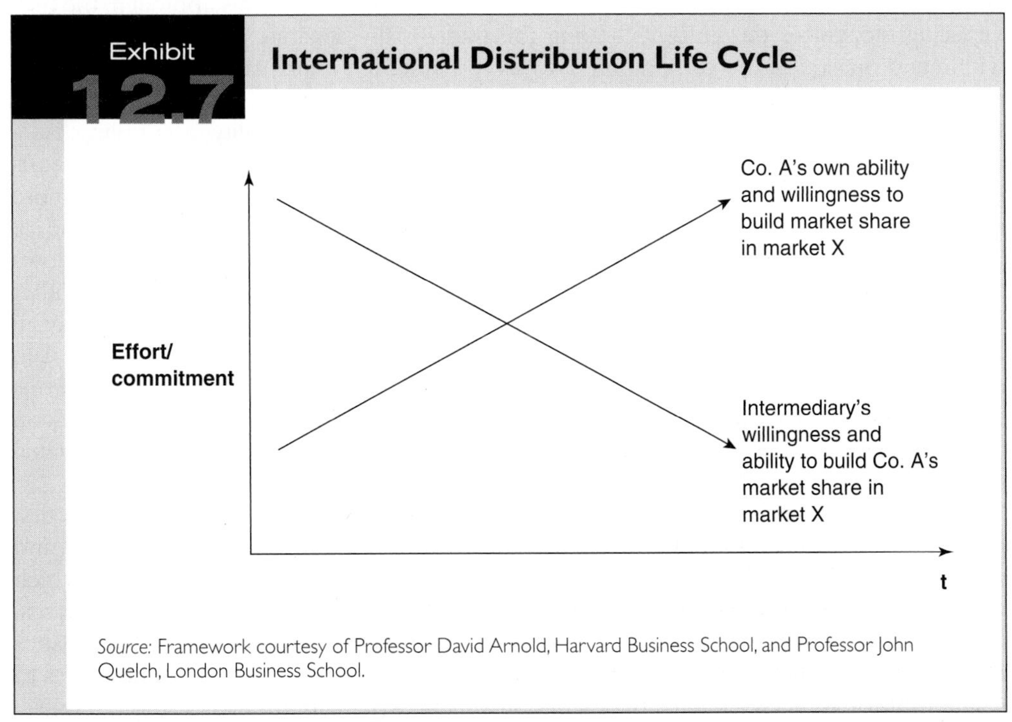

Source: Framework courtesy of Professor David Arnold, Harvard Business School, and Professor John Quelch, London Business School.

to global accounts—thereby needing to control distribution to a degree that independent intermediaries are not willing to accept, or requiring a level of service that they may not be able to deliver. If termination is a result of such a structural change, the situation has to be handled carefully. The effect of termination on the intermediary has to be understood, and open communication is needed to make the transition smooth. For example, the intermediary can be compensated for investments made, and major customers can be visited jointly to assure them that service will be uninterrupted.

Termination conditions are one of the most important considerations in the distributor agreement, because the just causes for termination vary and the penalties for the global marketer may be substantial. Just causes include fraud or deceit, damage to the other party's interest, or failure to comply with contract obligations concerning minimum inventory requirements or minimum sales levels. These must be spelled out carefully, because local courts are often favourably disposed toward local businesses. In some countries, termination may not even be possible. In the EU and Latin America, terminating an ineffective intermediary is time-consuming and expensive. One year's average commissions are typical for termination without justification. A notice of termination has to be given three to six months in advance. In Austria, termination without just cause and/or failure to give notice of termination may result in damages amounting to average commissions for between 1 and 15 years.

The time to think about such issues is before the overseas distribution agreement is signed. It is especially prudent to find out what local laws say about termination and to check what type of experience other firms have had in the particular country. Careful preparation can allow the global marketer to negotiate a termination without litigation. If the distributor's performance is unsatisfactory, careful documentation and clearly defined performance measures may help show that the distributor has more to gain by going quietly than by fighting.

Global Logistics

A Definition of Global Logistics

Global logistics is the design and management of a system that controls the flow of materials into, through, and out of the global corporation. It encompasses the total movement concept by covering the entire range of operations concerned with goods movement, including both exports and imports simultaneously. By taking a systems approach, the firm explicitly recognizes the linkages among the traditionally separate logistics components within and outside of the corporation. By incorporating the interaction with outside organizations and individuals such as suppliers and customers, the firm is enabled to build on synergy of purpose by all partners in the areas of performance, quality, and timing. As a result of implementing these systems considerations successfully, the firm can develop just-in-time (JIT) delivery for lower inventory cost, electronic data interchange (EDI) for more efficient order processing, and early supplier involvement (ESI) for better planning of goods development and movement. In addition, the use of such a systems approach allows a firm to concentrate on its core competencies and to form outsourcing alliances with other companies. For example, a firm can choose to focus on manufacturing and leave all aspects of order filling and delivery to an outside provider. Outsourcing is discussed in more detail later in this chapter. By working closely with customers such as retailers, firms can also develop efficient customer response (ECR) systems that can track sales activity on the retail level. As a result, manufacturers can precisely coordinate production in response to actual shelf replenishment needs, rather than based on forecasts.

Two major phases in the movement of materials are of logistical importance. The first phase is **materials management**, or the timely movement of raw materials, parts, and supplies into and through the firm. The second phase is **physical distribution**, which involves the movement of the firm's finished product to its customers. In both phases, movement is seen within the context of the entire process. The basic goal of logistics management is the effective coordination of both phases and their various components to result in maximum cost-effectiveness while maintaining service goals and requirements.

The growth of logistics as a field has brought to the forefront three major concepts: the systems concept, the total cost concept, and the tradeoff concept. The **systems concept** is based on the notion that materials-flow activities within and outside of the firm are so extensive and complex that they can be considered only in the context of their interaction. Instead of each corporate function, supplier, and customer operating with the goal of individual optimization, the systems concept stipulates that some components may have to work sub-optimally to maximize the benefits of the system as a whole. The systems concept intends to provide the firm, its suppliers, and its customers, both domestic and foreign, with the benefits of synergism expected from the coordinated application of size.

In order for the systems concept to work, information flows and partnership trust are instrumental. Logistics capability is highly information dependent, since information availability is key to planning and to process implementation. Long-term partnership and trust are required in order to forge closer links between firms and managers.

A logical outgrowth of the systems concept is the development of the **total cost concept**. To evaluate and optimize logistical activities, cost is used as a basis for measurement. The purpose of the total cost concept is to minimize the firm's overall logistics cost by implementing the systems concept appropriately. Implementation of the total cost concept requires that the members of the system understand the sources of costs. To develop such understanding, a system of activity-based costing has been developed, which is a technique designed to more accurately assign the indirect and direct resources of an organization to the activities performed based on consumption.[37] In the international arena, the total cost concept must also incorporate the consideration of total after-tax profit by taking the impact of national tax policies on the logistics function into account. The objective is to maximize after-tax profits rather than minimizing total cost.

The **tradeoff concept**, finally, recognizes the linkages within logistics systems that result from the interaction of their components. For example, locating a warehouse near the customer may reduce the cost of transportation. However, the new warehouse will lead to increased storage costs. Similarly, a reduction of inventories will save money but may increase the need for costly emergency shipments. Managers can maximize performance of logistics systems only by formulating decisions based on the recognition and analysis of such tradeoffs. A tradeoff of costs may go against one's immediate interests.

Although transportation management and other logistical functions are universal, they are influenced differently by the tradition, culture, economy, infrastructure, laws, and topography, among others, in each country or region. In countries such as the United States, the border states may be reached with relatively low cost and efficiency by Canadian marketers. But because America is very large geographically, serving customers elsewhere within its borders, for example in the southwest, demands that products must be moved over much longer distances. Canadian firms, therefore, have to face higher transport and inventory costs.

In geographically more concentrated countries such as Japan and the United Kingdom, the costs of transportation to destination ports must be met, of course, but in addition, in such geographically compact countries, firms tend to incur relatively more warehousing, customer service, and general administrative costs. This is because a wide selection of products with varied features have to be stored to meet the multiple needs of customers in compressed areas. To take another case, that of emerging markets such as India and China, it is not difficult to see how costs might rise when setting up local logistical systems. Problems can arise in terms of, for example, infrastructure (e.g., special customs processes and laws, state of roads and highways), intellectual expertise (e.g., educational level of available labour, including local supervisory and management personnel), and cultural sensitivity (e.g., adaptation to linguistic and work culture).

Described as we have done above, the array of logistical activities and the problems of global logistics will appear challenging, even daunting, to smaller firms entering the international arena. Yet many Canadian firms have for decades demonstrated their ability to operate international logistics "pipelines," notably across the Canada–U.S. border. However, extending logistics networks across oceans substantially increases the challenges. Should companies confront these challenges? Many small and medium-sized firms think so. One benefit of global logistics is low-cost sourcing for components, labour, or expertise. Another is to increase revenue streams beyond what is available in the Canadian market alone. A final opportunity, which is being sought by many Canadian companies, is that of achieving increased economies of scale, particularly in production by spreading substantial capital costs across a global marketplace. While these benefits are attractive and are being sought by many firms, some of the challenges are probably being understated.

The New Dimensions of Global Logistics

In domestic operations, logistics decisions are guided by the experience of the manager, possible industry comparison, an intimate knowledge of trends, and the development of heuristics—or rules of thumb. The logistics manager in the international firm, on the other hand, frequently has to depend on educated guesses to determine the steps required to obtain a desired service level. Variations in locale mean variations in environment. Lack of familiarity with these variations leads to uncertainty in the decision-making process. By applying decision rules developed at home, the firm will be unable to adapt well to the new environment, and the result will be inadequate profit performance. The long-term survival of international activities depends on an understanding of the differences inherent in the international logistics field.

Basic Differences

Basic differences in global logistics emerge because the corporation is active in more than one country. One example of a basic difference is distance. Global marketing activities frequently require goods to be shipped farther to reach final customers. These distances in turn result in longer lead times, more opportunities for things to go wrong, more inventories—in short, greater complexity. **Currency variation** is a second basic difference in global logistics. The corporation must adjust its planning to incorporate different currencies and changes in exchange rates. The border-crossing process brings with it the need for conformance with national regulations, an inspection at customs, and proper documentation. As a result, additional intermediaries participate in the international logistics process. They include freight forwarders, customs agents, customs brokers, banks, and other financial intermediaries. Finally, the **transportation modes** may also be different. Most domestic transportation is either by truck or by rail, whereas the multinational corporation quite frequently ships its products by air or by sea. Airfreight and ocean freight have their own stipulations and rules that require new knowledge and skills.

Country-Specific Differences

Within each country, the firm faces specific logistical attributes that may be quite different from those experienced at home. Transportation systems and intermediaries may vary. The reliability of carriers may be different. The computation of freight rates may be unfamiliar. Packaging and labelling requirements differ from country to country. Management must consider all of these factors in order to develop an efficient international logistics operation.

International Transportation Issues

International transportation is of major concern to the international firm because transportation determines how and when goods will be received. The transportation issue can be divided into three components: infrastructure, the availability of modes, and the choice of modes.

Transportation Infrastructure

In industrialized nations such as Canada, firms can count on an established transportation network. Internationally, however, major infrastructural variations may be encountered. Some countries may have excellent inbound and outbound transportation systems but weak transportation links within the country. This is particularly true in former colonies,

In More Detail 12.1

THE ROLE OF FREIGHT FORWARDERS

Canadian exporters stand to benefit from third-party help in refining their international logistical operations. Referring to the array of documents needed when delivering products to foreign markets, Team Canada states, "You don't normally do it all yourself," and points to the range of advisory, administrative, and physical services of freight forwarders and customs brokers in facilitating the international movement of goods.

In essence, freight forwarders are multi-modal transportation specialists with expertise in selecting the lowest cost and most appropriate method of transportation for particular product types. Freight forwarders distribute approximately 15 percent of Canada's international shipments. In carrying out their functions, these organizations can, among other things, do the following: recommend the optimal (economical/timely/safe) routing for the product and book space with a carrier; advise on or arrange the appropriate packaging, marking, and labelling; arrange transportation insurance; arrange storage of the product and give advice on warehousing facilities, rates, and procedures; and find alternative ways of moving the goods in the event of emergency.

Because of the economics of scale, freight forwarders can also offer transportation consolidation services that can be less costly than those the exporter could arrange directly with the transportation company. The freight forwarder can consolidate the shipment with other small shipments from several clients into a larger, more economical load if the exporter has insufficient volumes to fill an ocean container or highway truck. At the destination, the freight forwarder or agent will unload and deliver the "de-consolidated" shipment to the destination in the target country.

In light of these benefits, it is easy to see why SMEs might be better off using the services of an experienced freight forwarder rather than developing an in-house transportation management unit. Also, selecting an efficient freight forwarder will not present a major obstacle in light of official help, and the fact that many belong to the Canadian International Freight Forwarders Association (CIFFA), which lists more than 150 members.

Source: Team Canada, *Step-by-Step Guide to Exporting*, 3rd ed. (Minister of Public Works and Government Services Canada, 2005).

where the original transportation systems were designed to maximize the extractive potential of the countries. In such instances, shipping to the market may be easy, but distribution within the market may represent a very difficult and time-consuming task.

The global marketer must therefore learn about existing and planned infrastructures abroad. In some countries, for example, railroads may be an excellent transportation mode, far surpassing the performance of trucking, whereas in others, the use of railroads for freight distribution may be a gamble at best. The future routing of pipelines must be determined before any major commitments are made to a particular location if the product is amenable to pipeline transportation. The transportation methods used to carry cargo to seaports or airports must also be investigated. Mistakes in the evaluation of transportation options can prove to be very costly. One researcher reported the case of a food-processing firm that built a pineapple cannery at the delta of a river in Mexico. Since the pineapple plantation was located upstream, the company planned to float the ripe fruit down to the cannery on barges. To its dismay, the firm discovered that at harvest time the river current was far too strong for barge traffic. Since no other feasible alternative method of transportation existed, the plant was closed, and the new equipment was sold for a fraction of its original cost.[38]

Extreme variations also exist in the frequency of transportation services. For example, a particular port may not be visited by a ship for weeks or even months. Sometimes, only carriers with particular characteristics, such as small size, will serve a given location. All of these infrastructural concerns must be taken into account in the initial planning of the firm's transportation service.

Availability of Modes

Even though goods are shipped abroad by rail or truck, international transportation frequently requires ocean or airfreight modes, which many corporations only rarely use domestically. In addition, combinations such as land bridges or sea bridges frequently permit the transfer of freight among various modes of transportation, resulting in inter-modal movements. The global marketer must understand the specific properties of the different modes in order to use them intelligently.

Ocean Shipping

Water transportation is a key mode for international freight movements. An interruption of ocean-based transportation can have quite serious consequences for an economy. Three types of vessels operating in ocean shipping can be distinguished by their service: liner service, bulk service, and tramp (or charter) service. **Liner service** offers regularly scheduled passage on established routes. **Bulk service** mainly provides contractual services for individual voyages or for prolonged periods of time. **Tramp service** is available for irregular routes and is scheduled only on demand.

In addition to the services offered by ocean carriers, the type of cargo a vessel can carry is also important. Most common are conventional (break bulk) cargo vessels, container ships, and roll-on-roll-off (RORO) vessels. Conventional cargo vessels are useful for oversized and unusual cargoes but may be less efficient in their port operations. The premium assigned to speed and ease of handling has caused a decline in the use of general cargo vessels and a sharp increase in the growth of **container ships**, which carry standardized containers that greatly facilitate the loading and unloading of cargo and inter-modal transfers. As a result, the time the ship has to spend in port is reduced. RORO vessels are essentially oceangoing ferries. Trucks can drive onto built-in ramps and roll off at the destination. Another vessel similar to the RORO vessel is the LASH (lighter aboard ship) vessel. LASH vessels consist of barges stored on the ship and lowered at the point of destination. These individual barges can then operate on inland waterways, a feature that is particularly useful in shallow water.

The availability of a certain type of vessel, however, does not automatically mean that it can be used. The greatest constraint in international ocean shipping is the lack of ports and port services. For example, modern container ships cannot serve some ports because the local equipment is unable to handle the resulting traffic. This problem is often found in developing countries, where local authorities lack the funds to develop facilities. In some instances, governments purposely limit the development of ports to impede the inflow of imports. Increasingly, however, nations recognize the importance of appropriate port structures and are developing such facilities in spite of the heavy investments necessary. If such investments are accompanied by concurrent changes in the overall infrastructure, transportation efficiency should, in the long run, more than recoup the original investment. The issue of industrial action at port facilities can also have a significant impact on business, as illustrated in The Global Marketplace 12.3.

Large investments in infrastructure are usually necessary to produce results. Selective allocation of funds to transportation tends to only shift bottlenecks to some other point in the infrastructure. If these bottlenecks are not removed, the consequences may be felt in the overall economic performance of the nation. A good example is provided by the Caribbean. Even though geographically close to North America, many Caribbean nations are served poorly by ocean carriers. As a result, products that could be exported from the region to Canada and the U.S. are at a disadvantage because they take a long time to reach these markets. For many products, quick delivery is essential because of required high levels of industry responsiveness to orders. From a regional perspective, maintaining adequate facilities is therefore imperative in order to remain on the list of areas and ports served by international carriers. Investment in leading-edge port technology can also provide an instrumental competitive edge and cause entire distribution systems to be re-configured to take advantage of possible savings.

Air Shipping

Airfreight is available to and from most countries. This includes the developing world, where it is often a matter of national prestige to operate a national airline. The total volume of airfreight in relation to the total volume of shipping in international business remains quite small. Roughly 40 percent of the world's manufactured exports by value travel by air.[39] Clearly, high-value items are more likely to be shipped by air, particularly if they have a high **density**, that is, a high weight-to-volume ratio.

The Global MARKETPLACE 12.3

Vancouver Port Strike

Sears Canada, along with a number of other major companies, is re-evaluating the port of Vancouver. Industrial action at the port in 2005 resulted in significant losses for companies shipping products into and out of Canada through this gateway. The strike virtually stopped all short-haul container movement and caused a redirection of traffic to U.S. port facilities. Estimates put losses at $30 million per week as containers sat idle on the docks. The Vancouver Port Authority (VPA) owns three terminals, which are leased to private operators: Centerm, operated by P&O Ports; Vanterm; and Deltaport, operated by TSI terminals. The Vancouver Container Truckers Association noted that rates paid by transport companies are extremely low, and the problem was exacerbated by increasing fuel costs. This, the association claims, was the rationale for the industrial action. Most association members own their own tractors and were finding it increasingly difficult to operate. Roughly 30–40 percent of the shipments into and out of the port travelled via truck and were affected by the industrial action.

Word of the strike caused suppliers in Europe to hold back goods destined for Vancouver in order to minimize the impact on their operations. Throughout the country railways refused to load marine containers destined for Vancouver. One company, Intercon Enterprises, had a container-load of machine oil drums shipped in from Germany unloaded in Montreal because CN Rail issued an embargo on shipments into Vancouver. Small firms such as Vancouver-based W.H. Puddifoot Ltd., which supplies glasses, plates, and other supplies to restaurants and hotels, were hit with exorbitant storage charges.

Sources: "Vancouver Port Strike's Ripple Effect," **http://72.14.205.104/search?q=cache:zamDCo1gEdkJ:www.ghyoung.ca/news-2005-7-14.html+vancouver+port+strike&hl=en&gl+ca&ct+cink&cd=9** (accessed November 12, 2006). "Vancouver Port Strike Has Wide-Ranging Consequences," **http://www.logisticstoday.com/sNO/7322/LT/displayStory.asp** (accessed November 12, 2006); "Small Firms Left to Mop Up after Port Strike," **http://www.businessedge.ca/printArticle.cfm/newsID/10315.cfm** (accessed November 12, 2006).

Exhibit 12.8 **Containers at the Vancouver Port**

A.G.E. Foto Stock/First Light

Over the years, airlines have made major efforts to increase the volume of airfreight. Many of these activities have concentrated on developing better, more efficient ground facilities, introducing airfreight containers, and providing and marketing a wide variety of special services to shippers. In addition, some airfreight companies have specialized and become partners in the global logistics effort.

Changes have also taken place within the aircraft. Forty years ago, the holds of large propeller aircraft could take only about 10 tons of cargo. Today's jumbo jets can load up to 105 metric tons of cargo with an available space of 636 cubic metres and can therefore transport bulky products, as Exhibit 12.9 shows.[40] In addition, aircraft manufacturers have responded to industry demands by developing both jumbo cargo planes and combination passenger and cargo aircraft. The latter carry passengers in one section of the main deck and freight in another. These hybrids can be used by carriers on routes that would be uneconomical for passengers or freight alone.

From the shipper's perspective, the products involved must be amenable to air shipment in terms of their size. In addition, the market situation for any given product must be evaluated. For example, airfreight may be needed if a product is perishable or if, for other reasons, it requires a short transit time. The level of customer service needs and expectations can also play a decisive role. For example, the shipment of an industrial product that is vital to the ongoing operations of a customer may be much more urgent than the shipment of packaged consumer products.

Choice of Modes

The global marketer must make the appropriate selection from the available modes of transportation. This decision, of course, will be heavily influenced by the needs of the firm and its customers. The manager must consider the performance of each mode on four dimensions: transit time, predictability, cost, and non-economic factors.

Exhibit 12.9 **Loading Bulky Cargo on a Plane**

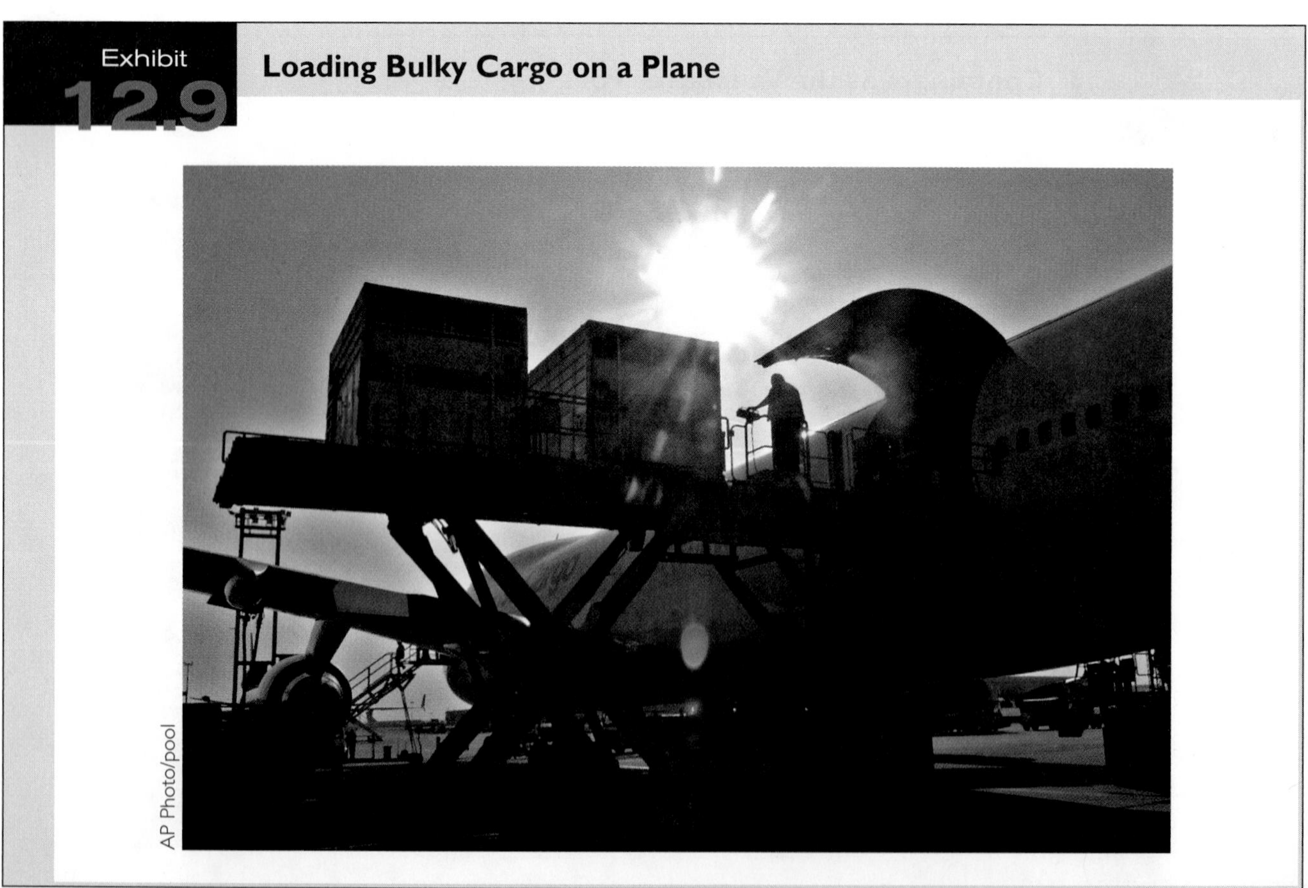

AP Photo/pool

Transit Time

The period between departure and arrival of the carrier varies significantly between ocean freight and airfreight. For example, the 45-day transit time of an ocean shipment can be reduced to 24 hours if the firm chooses airfreight. The length of transit time will have a major impact on the overall operations of the firm. As an example, a short transit time may reduce or even eliminate the need for an overseas depot. Also, inventories can be significantly reduced if they are replenished frequently. As a result, capital can be freed up and used to finance other corporate opportunities. Transit time can also play a major role in emergency situations. For example, if the shipper is about to miss an important delivery date because of production delays, a shipment normally made by ocean freight can be made by air.

Perishable products such as winter vegetables require shorter transit times. Rapid transportation prolongs the shelf life in the foreign market. For products with a short life span, air delivery may be the only way to enter foreign markets successfully. For example, international sales of cut flowers have reached their current volume only as a result of airfreight. At all times, the global marketing manager must understand the interactions between different components of the logistics process and their effect on transit times. Unless a smooth flow can be assured throughout the entire supply chain, bottlenecks will deny any timing benefits from specific improvements. For example, Levi Strauss, the blue jeans manufacturer, offered customers in some of its stores the chance to be measured by a body scanner to get custom-made jeans. Less than an hour after such measurement, a Levi's factory began to cut the jeans of the customer's choice. Unfortunately, it then took 10 days to get the finished product to the customer.[41]

Predictability

Providers of both ocean freight and airfreight service wrestle with the issue of **reliability**. Both modes are subject to the vagaries of nature, which may impose delays. Yet because reliability is a relative measure, the delay of one day for airfreight tends to be seen as much more severe and "unreliable" than the same delay for ocean freight. But delays tend to be shorter in absolute time for air shipments. As a result, arrival time via air is more predictable. This attribute has a major influence on corporate strategy. For example, because of the higher predictability of airfreight, inventory safety stock can be kept at lower levels. Greater predictability can also serve as a useful sales tool for foreign distributors, who are able to make more precise delivery promises to their customers. If inadequate port facilities exist, airfreight may again be the better alternative. Unloading operations from oceangoing vessels are more cumbersome and time-consuming than for planes. Finally, merchandise shipped via air is likely to suffer less loss and damage from exposure of the cargo to movement. Therefore, once the merchandise arrives, it is more likely to be ready for immediate delivery—a facet that also enhances predictability.

Cost

A major consideration in choosing international transportation modes is the cost factor. International transportation services are usually priced on the basis of both cost of the service provided and value of the service to the shipper. Because of the high value of the products shipped by air, airfreight is often priced according to the value of the service. In this instance, of course, price becomes a function of market demand and the monopolistic power of the carrier.

The global marketer must decide whether the clearly higher cost of airfreight can be justified. In part, this will depend on the cargo's properties. For example, the physical density and the value of the cargo will affect the decision. Bulky products may be too expensive to ship by air, whereas very compact products may be more amenable to airfreight transportation. High-priced items can absorb transportation cost more easily than low-priced goods because the cost of transportation as a percentage of total product cost will be lower. As a result, sending diamonds by airfreight is easier to justify than sending coal by air. To keep cost down, a shipper can join groups such as shippers' associations, which give the shipper more leverage in negotiations. Alternatively, a shipper can decide to mix modes of transportation in order to reduce overall cost and time delays. For example, part of the shipment route can be covered by air, while another portion can be covered by truck or ship.

Exhibit 12.10

Evaluating Transportation Choices

	Mode of Transportation				
Characteristics of Mode	**Air**	**Pipeline**	**Highway**	**Rail**	**Water**
Speed (1 = fastest)	1	4	2	3	5
Cost (1 = highest)	1	4	2	3	5
Loss and Damage (1 = least)	3	1	4	5	2
Frequency* (1 = best)	3	1	2	4	5
Dependability (1 = best)	5	1	2	3	4
Capacity† (1 = best)	4	5	3	2	1
Availability (1 = best)	3	5	1	2	4

*Frequency: number of times mode is available during a given time period

†Capacity: ability of mode to handle large or heavy goods

Source: Ronald H. Ballou, *Business Logistics Management*, 4th ed. © 1998, 146. Reprinted by permission of Pearson Education, Inc., Upper Saddle River, NJ.

Most important, however, are the overall logistical considerations of the firm. The manager must determine how important it is for merchandise to arrive on time, which will be different for regular garments than for high-fashion dresses. The effect of transportation cost on price and the need for product availability abroad must also be considered. For example, some firms may wish to use airfreight as a new tool for aggressive market expansion. Airfreight may also be considered a good way to begin operations in new markets without making sizable investments for warehouses and distribution centres.

Although costs are the major consideration in modal choice, an overall perspective must be employed. Simply comparing transportation modes on the basis of price alone is insufficient. The manager must factor in all corporate activities that are affected by modal choice and explore the total cost effects of each alternative. The final selection of a mode will depend on the importance of different modal dimensions to the markets under consideration. A useful overall comparison between different modes of transportation is provided in Exhibit 12.10.

Non-Economic Factors

Often, non-economic dimensions will enter into the selection process for a proper form of transportation. The transportation sector, nationally and internationally, both benefits and suffers from heavy government involvement. Carriers may be owned or heavily subsidized by governments. As a result, governmental pressure is exerted on shippers to use national carriers, even if more economical alternatives exist. Such preferential policies are most often enforced when government cargo is being transported. Restrictions are not limited to developing countries. For example, in Canada, all government cargo and all official government travellers must use national flag carriers when available.

The International Shipment

International shipments usually involve not just one carrier but multiple types of carriers. The shipment must be routed to the port of export, where it is transferred to another mode of transportation—for example, from truck or rail to vessel. Documentation for international shipments is universally perceived as so complicated, especially by smaller firms, that it can be a trade barrier. Recognizing the impact both in terms of time and money that documentation can have, the European Union has greatly simplified its required documentation for shipments. Whereas drivers earlier needed two pounds of documents on a route, for example, from Amsterdam to Lisbon, they now need only a single piece of paper. The savings on the elimination of this red tape are significant.

Documentation

In the simplest form of exporting, the only documents needed are a bill of lading and an export declaration. In most countries, these documents are available either from the government or from transportation firms. For example, a bill of lading can be obtained in Canada from a shipper (e.g., Manitoulin Transport, **http://www.manitoulintransport.com**). Most exports fit under a general licence, which is a generalized authorization consisting simply of a number to be shown on the documents. Certain goods and data require a special validated licence for export. For importation, the basic documents are a bill of lading and an invoice.

The **bill of lading** is the document most important to the shipper, the carrier, and the buyer. It acknowledges receipt of the goods, represents the basic contract between the shipper and the carrier, and serves as evidence of title to the goods for collection by the purchaser. Various types of bills of lading exist. The inland bill of lading is a contract between the inland carrier and the shipper. Bills of lading may be negotiable instruments in that they may be endorsed to other parties (order bill) or may be non-negotiable (straight). The **shipper's export declaration** states proper authorization for export and serves as a means for governmental data collection efforts.

The packing list, if used, lists in some detail the contents, the gross and net weights, and the dimensions of each package. Some shipments, such as corrosives, flammables, and poisons, require a **shipper's declaration for dangerous goods**. When the marketer is responsible for moving the goods to the port of export, a dock receipt (for ocean freight) or a warehouse receipt (if the goods are stored) is issued before the issuance of the bill of lading. Collection documents must also be produced and always include a commercial invoice (a detailed description of the transaction), often a **consular invoice** (required by certain countries for data collection purposes), and a **certificate of origin** (required by certain countries to ensure correct tariffs). Insurance documents are produced when stipulated by the transaction. In certain countries, especially in Latin America, two additional documents are needed. An **import licence** may be required for certain types or amounts of particular goods, while a **foreign exchange licence** allows the importer to secure the needed hard currency to pay for the shipment. The exporter has to provide the importer with the data needed to obtain these licences from governmental authorities and should make sure, before the actual shipment, that the importer has indeed secured the documents.

Two guidelines are critical in dealing with customs anywhere in the world: sufficient knowledge or experience in dealing with the customs service in question and sufficient preparation for the process. Whatever the required documents, their proper preparation and timing are of crucial importance, particularly since the terrorist attacks of 2001. Many governments expect detailed information about cargo well in advance of its arrival in port. Improper or missing documents can easily lead to difficulties that will delay payment or even prevent it. Furthermore, improper documentation may cause problems with customs. If a customs service seizes the merchandise, delays can be measured in weeks and may end up in a total financial loss for the particular shipment.

Assistance with International Shipments

Several intermediaries provide services in the physical movement of goods. One very important distribution decision a global marketer makes is the selection of an international freight forwarder. As described earlier in this chapter, such an **international freight forwarder** acts as an agent for the marketer in moving cargo to the overseas destination. The forwarder advises the marketer on shipping documentation and packing costs and will prepare and review the documents to ensure that they are in order. Forwarders will also book the necessary space aboard a carrier. They will make necessary arrangements to clear outbound goods with customs and, after clearance, forward the documents either to the customer or to the paying bank. A **customs broker** serves as an agent for an importer, with authority to clear inbound goods through customs and ship them on to their destination. These functions are performed for a fee.

Management of Global Logistics

Because the very purpose of a multinational firm is to benefit from system synergism, a persuasive argument can be made for the coordination of global logistics at corporate headquarters. Without coordination, subsidiaries will tend to optimize their individual efficiency but jeopardize the overall performance of the firm.

Centralized Logistics Management

A significant characteristic of the centralized approach to global logistics is the existence of headquarters staff that retains decision-making power over logistics activities affecting international subsidiaries. Such an approach is particularly valuable in instances where corporations have become international by rapid growth and have lost the benefit of a cohesive strategy.

If headquarters exerts control, it must also take the primary responsibility for its decisions. Clearly, ill will may arise if local managers are appraised and rewarded on the basis of performance they do not control. This may be particularly problematic if headquarters staff suffers from a lack of information or expertise.

To avoid internal problems, both headquarters staff and local logistics management should report to one person. This person, whether the vice president for global logistics or the president of the firm, can then become the final arbiter to decide the firm's priorities. Of course, this individual should also be in charge of determining appropriate rewards for managers, both at headquarters and abroad, so that corporate decisions that alter a manager's performance level will not affect the manager's appraisal and evaluation. Further, this individual can contribute an objective view when inevitable conflicts arise in logistics coordination. The internationally centralized decision-making process leads to an overall logistics management perspective that can dramatically improve profitability.

Decentralized Logistics Management

When a firm serves many international markets that are diverse in nature, total centralization would leave the firm unresponsive to local adaptation needs. If each subsidiary is made a profit centre in itself, each one carries the full responsibility for its performance, which can lead to greater local management satisfaction and to better adaptation to local market conditions. Yet often such decentralization deprives the logistics function of the benefits of coordination. For example, whereas headquarters, referring to its large volume of total international shipments, may be able to extract bottom rates from transportation firms, individual subsidiaries by themselves may not have similar bargaining power. The same argument applies also to the sourcing situation, where the coordination of shipments by the purchasing firm may be much more cost-effective than individual shipments from many small suppliers around the world.

Once products are within a specific market, however, increased input from local logistics operations should be expected and encouraged. At the very least, local managers should be able to provide input into the logistics decisions generated by headquarters. Ideally, within a frequent planning cycle, local managers can identify the logistics benefits and constraints existing in their particular market and communicate them to headquarters. Headquarters can then either adjust its international logistics strategy accordingly or can explain to the manager why system optimization requires actions different from the ones recommended. Such a justification process will greatly help in reducing the potential for animosity between local and headquarters operations.

Contract Logistics

While the choice is open to maintain either centralized or decentralized in-house logistical management, a growing preference among international firms is to outsource, which means to employ outside logistical expertise. Often referred to as contract, or "third-party," logistics, it is a rapidly expanding industry. An Ontario based 3PL, for example, offers transportation, logistics, warehousing, and customs brokering services for its customers, whether directly or by outsourcing some of these services. In More Detail 12.2 provides additional information on the outsourcing of services. Using information management tools, the company takes the enterprise resources planning (ERP) data of the customer, from open order to purchase orders, and "populates" its own shipping system. This not only enables the company to track the client's goods, it also enables customers to be advised on their profitability, even in terms of each stock keeping unit (SKU) of the client. By investing significantly in software development to facilitate these activities, the company achieves considerable flexibility, enabling it to respond to the needs of both large and small clients. A measure of the customer satisfaction achieved is that in five years the company's business revenues have doubled as it acquired it own fleet, warehousing, and logistics divisions.[42]

More than 70 percent of Fortune 500 companies have outsourced at least one major logistics function such as transportation management, freight payment, warehouse management, shipment tracking, or other transportation-related functions.[43] The main thrust behind the idea is that individual firms are experts in their industry and should therefore concentrate only on their operations. Third-party logistics providers, on the other hand, are experts solely at logistics, with the knowledge and means to perform efficient and innovative services for those companies in need. The goal is improved service at equal or lower cost.

In More Detail 12.2

GLOBAL OUTSOURCING

Outsourcing, the practice of contracting business functions to third parties outside the firm, has long been a common practice around the world. It is a strong contributor to the growth of international services trading and to the growth of service exports by particular countries and regions (for example, Asia). Businesses across industries use outsourcing as a means to reduce costs, improve employee productivity, and focus on core business functions. For example, manufacturers have long outsourced aspects of parts manufacture to smaller firms, and in the public sector, institutions such as hospitals outsource laundry or meal services.

While the practice of outsourcing is not new, information, communications, and technology (ICT) has both facilitated and increased the demand for outsourcing. Specifically, ICT enables services to be provided outside the country, or "offshore," often in lower-cost destinations such as China or India that are perceived publicly to have lower labour standards and exploitative human rights and labour practices. As a result of these factors, the practice of outsourcing has at times taken place against virulent public opposition, leading some commentators to predict the demise of such arrangements.

In reality these predictions have proved wrong. Instead, the outsourcing industry, the international aggregation of firms providing services in information technology, finance, human resource management, engineering, procurement, among others, that replace corresponding in-house functions, is becoming ever more widespread and sophisticated. In fact, outsourcing of numerous business processing services might be described as a boom with no signs of slowing, one that is attracting the attention of Canadian firms. One research firm estimates that outsourcing within North America is growing at an average of 10–15 percent annually. Such growth demonstrates that outsourcing will continue to develop as a significant component of international commerce. Moreover, many less-developed countries are finding their niches in the outsourcing market, which is in turn bringing sometimes dramatic economic growth and prosperity to them.

Leading Canadian companies say that their initial decision to outsource tended to be tactical and project-based; for example, they would outsource because there was a shortage of local resources, and moving particular segments of their operations offshore was much more cost effective. However, companies also say that cost is rarely the only factor involved, and services are typically outsourced to the location where the "cost versus quality of service" mix is best.

Sources: Vinay Couto and Ashok Divakaran, "How to be an Outsourcing Virtuoso," *Strategy and Business* 44 (Autumn 2006): 42–53; TMCnet, "Outsourcing Boom Entices Canadian Firm to Set Up Shop," November 22, 2005; Robert Scott, David Ticoll, and Thomas Garner, *A Fine Balance: The Impact of Offshore IT Services on Canada's IT Landscape* (PricewaterhouseCoopers, 2004); and Public Policy Forum, "IT Offshore Outsourcing Practices in Canada," Ottawa, Ontario, May 20, 2004.

Logistics providers' services vary in scope. For instance, some may use their own assets in physical transportation, while others subcontract out portions of the job. Certain other providers are not involved as much with the actual transportation as they are with developing systems and databases or consulting on administrative management services. In many instances, the partnership consists of working closely with established transport providers such as Federal Express or UPS. The concept of improving service, cutting costs, and unloading the daily management onto willing experts is driving the momentum of contract logistics.

One of the greatest benefits of contracting out the logistics function in a foreign market is the ability to take advantage of an existing network complete with resources and experience. The local expertise and image are crucial when a business is just starting up. The prospect of newly entering a region such as Europe with different regions, business formats, and languages can be frightening without access to a seasoned and familiar logistics provider.

One of the main arguments levelled against contract logistics is the loss of the firm's control. Yet contract logistics does not and should not require the handing over of control. Rather, it offers concentration on one's specialization—a division of labour. The control and responsibility toward the customer remain with the firm, even though operations may move to a highly trained outside organization.

Summary

Channels of distribution consist of the marketing efforts and intermediaries that facilitate the movement of goods and services. Decisions that must be made to establish an international channel of distribution focus on channel design and the selection of intermediaries for the roles that the international marketer will not perform. The channel must be designed to meet the requirements of the intended customer base, coverage, long-term continuity of the channel once it is established, and the quality of coverage to be achieved. Having determined the basic design of the channel, the international marketer will then decide on the number of different types of intermediaries to use and how many of each type, or whether to use intermediaries at all, which would be the case in direct distribution using, for example, sales offices or e-commerce. The process is important because the majority of international sales involve distributors and because channel decisions are the most long-term of all marketing decisions. The more the channel operation resembles a team, rather than a collection of independent businesses, the more effective the overall marketing effort will be.

International logistics is concerned with the flow of materials into, through, and out of the international corporation and therefore includes materials management as well as physical distribution. The logistician must recognize the total systems demands of the firm in order to develop tradeoffs between various logistics components. Global logistics differs from domestic activities in that it deals with greater distances, new variables, and greater complexity because of country-specific differences. One major factor to consider is transportation. The global marketer needs to understand transportation infrastructures in other countries and modes of transportation such as ocean shipping and airfreight. The choice among these modes will depend on the customer's demands and the firm's transit time, predictability, and cost requirements. In addition, non-economic factors such as government regulations weigh heavily in this decision.

Key Terms

agents (p. 419)
bill of lading (p. 437)
bulk service (p. 432)
certificate of origin (p. 437)
channel design (p. 411)
consular invoice (p. 437)
container ships (p. 432)
currency variation (p. 430)
customs broker (p. 437)
dealer interference (p. 426)
demand interference (p. 426)
density (p. 432)
direct exporting (p. 419)
distribution culture (p. 412)
distributors (p. 419)
foreign exchange licence (p. 437)
import licence (p. 437)
indirect exporting (p. 419)
integrated distribution (p. 419)
international freight forwarder (p. 437)
liner service (p. 432)
materials management (p. 428)
parallel importation (p. 424)
physical distribution (p. 428)
reliability (p. 435)
shipper's declaration for dangerous goods (p. 437)
shipper's export declaration (p. 437)
strategic attack (p. 426)
supply interference (p. 426)
systems concept (p. 429)
total cost concept (p. 429)
tradeoff concept (p. 429)
tramp service (p. 432)
transportation modes (p. 430)

Questions for Discussion

1. Relate the following statements: "A channel of distribution can be compared to a marriage" and "The number one reason given for divorce is lack of communication."
2. Channels of distribution tend to vary according to the level of economic development of a market: the more developed the economy, the shorter the channels tend to be. Why?
3. If a small exporter lacks the resources for an on-site inspection, what measures would you propose for screening potential distributors?
4. The international marketer and the distributor will have different expectations concerning the relationship. Why should these expectations be spelled out and clarified in the contract?
5. One method of screening candidates is to ask distributors for a simple marketing plan. What items would you want included in this plan?
6. Is grey marketing a trademark issue, a pricing issue, or a distribution issue?
7. Contrast the use of ocean shipping to airfreight.
8. Explain the meaning of "supply chain management."
9. What is the impact of transit time on international logistics and how can a firm improve its performance?
10. Why should customer service levels differ internationally? Is it, for example, ethical to offer a lower customer service level in developing countries than in industrialized countries?
11. How can an improved logistics infrastructure contribute to the economic development of Eastern Europe?

Internet Exercises

1. Visit the website of the Canadian International Freight Forwarders Association (**http://www.ciffa.com/**). What is the role of this organization and how is it structured?
2. The Alliance for Gray Market and Counterfeit Abatement (**http://www.agmaglobal.org/**) is "committed to addressing the global impact of the gray market and counterfeiting of goods on the technology industry." Is it appropriate to equate the two? Should Canadian technology companies find this coalition's arguments convincing?

Recommended Readings

Anderson, David. *Mass Customization: The Ultimate Supply Chain Management and Lean Manufacturing Strategy.* London: CIM, 2002.

Burt, David, Donald Dobler, and Stephen Starling. *World Class Management: The Key to Supply Chain Management.* Boston: McGraw-Hill, 2003.

Hutt, Michael D., and Thomas W. Speh. *Business Marketing Management.* 8th ed. Mason, OH: South-Western, 2004.

International Chamber of Commerce. *The ICC Agency Model Contract.* New York: ICC Publishing Corp., 1999.

International Chamber of Commerce. *Incoterms 2000.* New York: ICC Publishing Corp., 2000.

Monczka, Robert, Robert B. Handfield, and Robert J. Trent. *Purchasing and Supply Chain Management.* Mason, OH: South-Western, 2001.

Rosenbloom, Bert. *Marketing Channels: A Management View.* 6th ed. Mason, OH: South-Western, 1999.

Schechter, Damon, and Gordon F. Sander. *Delivering the Goods: The Art of Managing Your Supply Chain.* New York: John Wiley & Sons, 2002.

Simchi-Levi, David, Philip Kaminsky, and Edith Simchi-Levi. *Designing and Managing the Supply Chain: Concepts, Strategies, and Case Studies.* Boston: McGraw-Hill, 2003.

Stock, James R., and Douglas M. Lambert. *Strategic Logistics Management.* 4th ed. Burr Ridge, IL: McGraw-Hill, 2001.

Stroh, Michael. *A Practical Guide to Transportation and Logistics.* Dumont, NJ: Logistics Network, 2001.

Notes

1. Donald V. Fites, "Make Your Dealers Your Partners," *Harvard Business Review* 74 (March–April 1996): 84–95.
2. Rajiv Vaidyanathan and Praveen Aggarwal, "Strategic Brand Alliance: Implications of Ingredient Branding for National and Private Label Brands," *The Journal of Product and Brand Management* 9, no. 4 (2000): 214–28.
3. Erin Anderson, George S. Day, and V. Kasturi Rangan, "Strategic Channel Design," *Sloan Management Review* 39 (Summer 1997): 59–69.
4. Rajshkhtar Javalgi and Rosemary Ramsey, "Strategic Issues of e-Commerce as an Alternative Global Distribution System," *International Marketing Review* 18, no. 4 (2001): 376–91.
5. Michael R. Czinkota and Jon Woronoff, *Unlocking Japan's Market* (Rutland, VT: Tuttle, 1993).
6. Stephen J. Arnold and John Fernie, "Wal-Mart in Europe: Prospects for the UK," *International Marketing Review* 17, nos. 4 and 5 (2000): 416–32.
7. Nicholas Alexander and Hayley Myers, "The Retail Internationalization Process," *International Marketing Review* 17, nos. 4 and 5 (2000): 334–53.
8. "European Retailing: French Fusion," *The Economist*, September 4, 1999, 68–69.
9. Vijay Govindarajan and Anil K. Gupta, "Taking Wal-Mart Global: Lessons from Retailing's Giant," *Strategy and Business* 4 (4th quarter, 1999): 14–25.
10. "Coutu Bails Out of U.S.," *National Post*, August 25, 2006, FP1.
11. Rod B. McNaughton, "The Use of Multiple Channels by Small Knowledge-Intensive Firms," *International Marketing Review* 19, no. 2 (2002): 190–203.
12. See **http://www.expert.org.**
13. Erin Anderson and Hubert Gatignon, "Modes of Foreign Entry: A Transaction Cost Analysis and Propositions," *Journal of International Business Studies* 17 (Fall 1986): 1–26.
14. Erin Anderson and Anne T. Coughlan, "International Market Entry and Expansion via Independent or Integrated Channels of Distribution," *Journal of Marketing* 51 (January 1987): 71–82.
15. The authors are indebted to Dr. James H. Sood of the American University for this example.
16. Andrea Knox, "The European Minefield," *World Trade*, November 1999, 36–40.
17. Soumava Bandyopadhyay and Robert H. Robicheaux, "Dealer Satisfaction through Relationship Marketing across Cultures," *Journal of Marketing Channels* 6, no. 2 (1997): 35–55.
18. Daniel C. Bello and David I. Gilliland, "The Effect of Output Controls, Process Controls, and Flexibility on Export Channel Performance," *Journal of Marketing* 61 (January 1997): 22–38.
19. "It Could Be Worse," *International Business*, April 1996, 8.
20. S. Tamer Cavusgil, Poh-Lin Yeoh, and Michel Mitri, "Selecting Foreign Distributors: An Export Systems Approach," *Industrial Marketing Management* 24 (Winter 1995): 297–304.
21. Sherrie E. Zhan, "Booting Up in Santiago," *World Trade*, July 1999, 30–34.
22. "Five Steps to Finding the Right Business Partners Abroad," *World Trade*, March 1999, 86–87.
23. For a detailed discussion, see International Chambers of Commerce, *The ICC Model Distributorship Contract* (Paris: ICC Publishing, 2002), chaps. 1–3; and **http://www.iccwbo.org.**
24. Gary L. Frazier, James D. Gill, and Sudhir H. Kale, "Dealer Dependence Levels and Reciprocal Actions in a Channel of Distribution in a Developing Country," *Journal of Marketing* 53 (January 1989): 50–69.
25. Leonidas C. Leonidou, Constantine S. Katsikeas, and John Hadjimarcou, "Building Successful Export Business Relationships: A Behavioral Perspective," *Journal of International Marketing* 10, no. 3 (2002): 96–115.
26. Bert Rosenbloom, *Marketing Channels: A Management View*, 6th ed. (Mason, OH: South-Western, 1999), chap. 9.
27. Sudhir H. Kale and Roger P. McIntyre, "Distribution Channel Relationships in Diverse Cultures," *International Marketing Review* 8 (1991): 31–45.
28. Constantine S. Katsikeas and Tevfik Dalgic, "Importing Problems Experienced by Distributors: The Importance of Level-of-Import Development," *Journal of International Marketing* 3, no. 2 (1995): 51–70.
29. David Arnold, "Seven Rules of International Distribution," *Harvard Business Review* 78 (November–December 2000): 131–37.
30. Jeff Prine, "Time On-Line, the New Global Grey Market," *Modern Jeweler*, November 1998, 45–48.
31. Frank V. Cespedes, E. Raymond Corey, and V. Kasturi Rangan, "Gray Markets: Causes and Cures," *Harvard Business Review* 66 (July–August 1988): 75–82.
32. "The Earth Is Shifting under Heavy Equipment," *Business Week*, April 6, 1998, 44.
33. Peggy E. Chaudry and Michael G. Walsh, "Managing the Gray Market in the European Union: The Case of the Pharmaceutical Industry," *Journal of International Marketing* 3, no. 3 (1995): 11–33; and "Parallel Trade and Comparative Pricing of Medicines: Poor Choice for Patients," *Pfizer Forum*, 1996.
34. "European Court Supports Levi Strauss in Tesco Case," *The Wall Street Journal*, November 21, 2001, A11.
35. For a comprehensive discussion on remedies, see Robert E. Weigand, "Parallel Import Channel—Options for Preserving Territorial Integrity," *Columbia Journal of World Business* 26 (Spring 1991): 53–60; and S. Tamer Cavusgil and Ed Sikora, "How Multinationals Can Counter Gray Market Imports," *Columbia Journal of World Business* 23 (Winter 1988): 75–85.

35a. J. Johansson, *Global Marketing: Foreign Entry, Local marketing and Global Management*, 3rd ed., McGraw-Hill Irwin, 2005.

36. Hong Liu and Yen Po Wang, "Co-ordination of International Channel Relationships," *Journal of Business and Industrial Marketing* 14, no. 2 (1999): 130–50.
37. Bernard LaLonde and James Ginter, "Activity-Based Costing: Best Practices," research paper 606, The Supply Chain Management Research Group, Ohio State University, September 1996.
38. David A. Ricks, *Blunders in International Business*, 3rd ed. (Oxford: Blackwell, 2000), 20.
39. See **http://www.iata.org** (accessed October 15, 2002).
40. Ian Putzger, "Pricing: Based on Volume or Weight?" *Journal of Commerce*, February 15, 2000, 10.
41. Survey: E-Management," *The Economist*, November 11, 2000, 36.
42. Herscovitch, Toby, "Wide Range: Cutting the Cost of Crossing Borders," *Exportwise*, Winter 2006.
43. Tim Wilson, "Outsourcing Cuts Logistics Complexity," *Internet Week*, November 2001, **http://www.internetweek.com** (accessed November 18, 2002).

Chapter 13

Global Advertising and Sales Promotion

The Global MARKETPLACE 13.1

Canwest Global Communications: Growth of an International Media Conglomerate

Canwest Global is one of Canada's leading international media companies. The firm owns a range of television, radio, and print assets in Canada and around the world. The company started operations in Winnipeg in 1974 when it received a licence from the Canadian Radio and Television Commission (CRTC) for the operation of a single television station, CKND-TV. The company later moved to acquire the assets of Toronto-based Global Television, which was in financial difficulty, and, in the 1980s, expanded its national reach to acquire broadcasting assets in Saskatchewan and Vancouver. The 1980s and 1990s also saw the company acquire television stations in Halifax and Quebec in an attempt to consolidate its position in the Canadian market. The company entered the newspaper business in 2000 with the acquisition of the newspaper assets of Hollinger Inc. The company now owns 11 major metro daily newspapers across Canada (including the *National Post*) as well as 20 paid or free weekly newspapers in smaller communities.

Following an initial public offering in 1991, the company began execution of its global expansion strategy. In 1991 the company acquired a stake in TV3 New Zealand and in 1992 purchased a stake in Australia's Network Ten. These investments were followed by the purchase of the remaining shares of New Zealand's TV3 and the launch of TV4 in that country. Expansion into Europe followed. In 1998, Canwest Global launched TV3 in the Republic of Ireland and Ulster Television in Northern Ireland.

Canwest entered the global radio business in 1997 with the purchase of More FM in New Zealand, which operates stations in all of that country's major urban markets. Although the company would divest itself of its New Zealand operations a decade later, it did deepen its commitment to radio advertising in other geographic regions. For example, Canwest acquired RadioWorks NZ in 2001, purchased four Turkish radio stations in 2005, and launched Original 106 FM in the U.K. in 2006, Original 106 FM Bristol also in 2006, and Original 106 FM Aberdeen (the company's third UK radio licence) in 2007. In 2000 the company also entered the out-of-home advertising market when Australia's Network Ten acquired a majority stake in Eye Corporation, one of that country's largest players in outdoor signage, airport advertising, visual advertising, and shopping mall advertising. This investment also extended Canwest's reach into southeast Asia, including Indonesia and Malaysia. In 2007 Canwest assumed a controlling interest in Ten Network Holdings Limited, the parent company of Australia's Network Ten television stations.

Global print media is also an area of strategic focus for the company. In 2007 Canwest, through a wholly owned subsidiary, acquired a 100 percent interest in The New Republic—a 93-year-old U.S.-based political magazine. The company also expanded its network of domestic and international newspaper operations with the opening of a number of news bureaus, both in Canada and abroad. News bureaus are carded to be opened in Washington, New York, Paris, Jerusalem, and Shanghai by the end of 2007.

Canwest Global takes a unified approach to delivering content to global consumers and provides the opportunity for advertisers to leverage the firm's international assets.

Source: "History and Milestones of an International Media Conglomerate," Canwest Mediaworks website: **http://www.canwestmediaworks.com/thecompany/history.asp**. Retrieved November 19, 2006.

Effective communication is particularly important in global marketing because of the geographic and psychic distances that separate a firm from its intermediaries and customers. By definition, communication is a process of establishing a "commonness" of thought between a sender and a receiver.[1] This process extends beyond the conveying of ideas to include persuasion and thus enables the marketing process to function more effectively and efficiently. Ideally, marketing communication is a dialogue that allows organizations and consumers to achieve mutually satisfying exchange agreements. This definition emphasizes the two-way nature of the process, with listening and responsiveness as integral parts. A relationship has to be established from the beginning and deepened over time. The majority of communication is verbal, but nonverbal communication and the concept of silent languages must also be considered, because they often create challenges for global marketers.

The chapter will focus on the management of the international communications mix from the marketer's point of view. Because the firm's alternatives may be limited by the entry mode and by resources available, a range of promotional alternatives that may be used by firms of any size are explored. The Global Marketplace 13.1 presents a profile of one company that offers the global marketer a range of promotional options in overseas markets.

Given that the firm may be operative in several overseas markets simultaneously, the issue of coordination of the promotional effort is also discussed. Increasingly, marketers opt for varying degrees of pan-regional and integrative approaches to take advantage of similarities in markets they serve. The technology is in place for global communication efforts, but difficult challenges still remain in the form of cultural, economic, ethnic, regulatory, and demographic differences in the various countries and regions. Standardization of any magnitude requires sound management systems and excellent communication to ensure uniform strategic and tactical thinking of all the professionals in the overseas marketing chain.[2] One marketer has suggested the development of a worldwide visual language that would be understandable and that would not offend cultural sensitivities.

This chapter will also analyze the elements to be managed in promotional efforts in terms of environmental opportunities and constraints. A framework is provided for the planning of promotional campaigns. Although the discussion focuses mostly on advertising, other elements of the promotion mix, especially sales promotion and publicity, fit integrally into the planning model.

Formulation of Global Marketing Communications Strategy

The global marketing manager has the responsibility of formulating a communications strategy for the promotion of the company and its products and services. The basic steps of such a strategy are outlined in Exhibit 13.1 and discussed below.

Few, if any, firms can afford expenditures for promotion that is done as "art for art's sake" or only because major competitors do it. The first step in developing a communica-

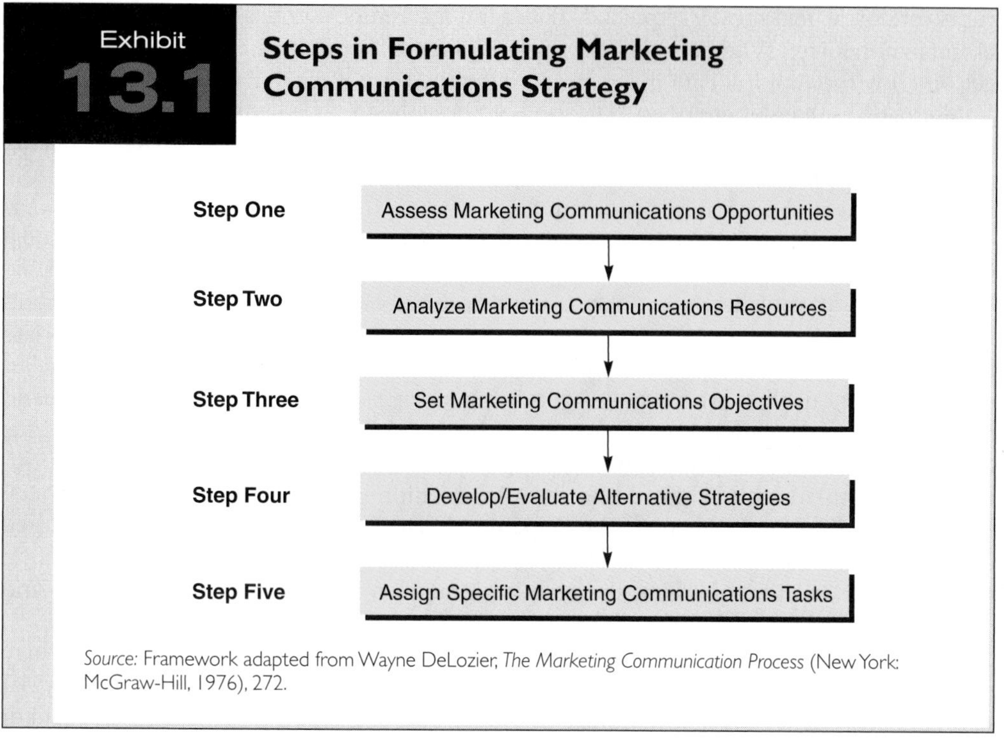

Source: Framework adapted from Wayne DeLozier, *The Marketing Communication Process* (New York: McGraw-Hill, 1976), 272.

tions strategy is therefore assessing what company or product characteristics and benefits should be communicated to the international market. This requires constant monitoring of the various environments and target audience characteristics. For example, Volvo has used safety and quality as its primary themes in its worldwide promotional campaigns since the 1950s. This approach has provided continuity, repetition, and uniformity in positioning Volvo in relation to its primary competitors: Mercedes-Benz (prestige) and BMW (sportiness).

Certain rules of thumb can be followed in evaluating resources to be allocated for global marketing communications efforts (Exhibit 13.1, step 2). A sufficient commitment is necessary, which may mean a relatively large amount of money. The marketer has to operate in foreign markets according to the rules of the marketplace, which in North America, for example, means high promotional costs—perhaps 30 percent of sales or even more during the early stage of entry. With heavily contested markets, the level of spending may have to increase even more. For example, the Swedish vodka manufacturer Absolut posted promotional expenditures in 2001 of $31 million in measured media.[3] From a very small advertising base, Absolut has grown to number 10 in volume and number 3 in revenue in the U.S. spirits category. In addition to a strong marketing effort, Absolut has also benefited from changing U.S. drinking habits.[4] Vodka is now the largest category in the distilled spirits business, with Absolut ruling the high-class vodka crowd.

The third step in the process is the establishment of marketing communications objectives. Because of monetary constraints that all firms face, promotional efforts should be concentrated on key markets. For example, European liquor marketers traditionally concentrate their promotional efforts on North America, where volume consumption is greatest, and Great Britain, which is considered the world capital of the liquor trade. A specific objective might be to spend more than the closest competitors do in this market. In the United States, for example, this would require a new import brand, aimed at the lower-price segment, to spend a minimum of $10 million during the rollout year.[5] In some cases, a global marketer will have to limit this to one country, even one area, at a time to achieve set goals with the available budget. International campaigns require patient investment; the market has to progress through awareness, knowledge, liking, preference, and favourable purchase intentions before payback begins. Payback periods of one or two years cannot be realistically expected. For many marketers, a critical factor is the support of the intermediary. Whether a distributor is willing to contribute a $3-million media budget or a few thousand dollars makes a big difference.

Alternative strategies are needed to spell out how the firm's resources can be combined and adapted to market opportunities. This is the fourth step in the process of formulating the firm's marketing communications strategy. The tools the global marketer has available to form a total communications program for use in the targeted markets are referred to as the **promotional mix**: advertising, publicity, sales promotion, sponsorship, and personal selling.

The choice of tools leads to either a push or a pull emphasis in marketing communications. **Push strategies** focus on the use of personal selling and may be appropriate for industrial goods, which typically have shorter channels of distribution and smaller target populations than do consumer goods. On the other hand, **pull strategies** depend on mass communications tools, mainly advertising. Advertising is appropriate for consumer-oriented products with large target audiences and long channels of distribution. No promotional tool should be used in isolation or without regard to the others; hence, we see a trend toward **integrated marketing communications**. Promotional tools should be coordinated according to target market and product characteristics, the size of the promotional budget, the type and length of international involvement, and control considerations.

Finally, specific marketing communications tasks must be assigned, which may require deciding on a division of labour with foreign intermediaries or with other global marketers for cooperative communications efforts. For example, Ernie Ball, the maker of Gauge, Slinky, and Earthwood guitar strings, cooperates closely with its distributors in the marketing of its products. Local distributors have adapted North American programs to their markets, such as Battle of Bands for Europe, which is the largest live-music promotion in the industry. The company also uses the Internet for contest promotions such as the best guitarist and the best bassist.[6] Cooperative programs allow the global marketer control of the promotional effort while getting distribution partners to contribute to the effort financially.

In cases in which the locally based intermediaries are small and may not have the resources to engage in promotional efforts, the marketer may suggest dealer-participatory programs. In exchange for including the intermediaries' names in promotional material without any expense to them—for example, in announcing a sweepstakes—the global marketer may request increased volume purchases from the intermediaries.

Planning Global Promotional Campaigns

Having established an overarching global marketing communication strategy, the firm must next plan and execute its promotional campaigns. Planning a global promotional campaign involves seven steps. These steps usually overlap or take place concurrently, especially after the basics of the campaign have been agreed on. The steps are as follows:

1. Determine the target audience
2. Determine specific campaign objectives
3. Determine the budget
4. Determine media strategy
5. Determine the message
6. Determine the campaign approach
7. Determine campaign effectiveness[7]

The actual content of these stages will change by type of campaign situation. If one compares a local campaign for which headquarters provides support versus a global corporate image campaign, there will be differences in terms of, for example, audience, budget, objectives, and campaign approach.

The Target Audience

Global marketers face multiple audiences beyond customers. The expectations of these audiences have to be researched to ensure the appropriateness of campaign decision making. Consider the following publics with whom communication is necessary: suppliers, intermediaries, government, the local community, bankers and creditors, media organizations, shareholders, and employees. Each can be reached with an appropriate mix of tools. A multinational corporation that wants to boost its image with the government and the local community may sponsor events. One of the approaches available is **cause-related marketing**, in which the company, or one of its brands, is linked with a cause such as environmental protection or children's health. For example, in 2002, Tupperware, a global direct seller of home, kitchen, and personal-care products ran a fundraising program for Mothers Against Drunk Driving (MADD) Canada under which Tupperware donated a dollar to MADD Canada for every item sold. MADD Canada has also partnered with MBNA to create the MADD Canada MasterCard. A percentage of the value of merchandise charged to this card is donated to MADD Canada.[8] Unilever's Funfit Program for its Persil brand laundry detergent in Europe creates resource packs for teachers to help boost children's fitness through physical education lessons. Microsoft launched a website in Singapore to further the use of information technology. For every page hit within the site, Microsoft donated one cent to three local charities. This type of activity can benefit a brand but must be backed by a genuine effort within the company to behave responsibly.[9]

Some campaigns may be targeted at multiple audiences. For example, British Airways' "Manhattan Landing" campaign (in which Manhattan Island takes to the air and lands in London) was directed not only at international business travellers but also at employees, the travel industry, and potential stockholders (the campaign coincided with the privatization of the airline). Once the re-positioning was achieved, the airline focused on establishing its global stature with the "Face" campaign and switched later to service enhancements with "Sweet Dreams."[10] As companies such as airlines become more internationally involved, target audience characteristics change. American Airlines, which enjoys a huge domestic market, had foreign routes generate 28 percent of passenger miles in 2001 compared with virtually none in 1980.[11]

An important aspect of research is to determine multi-market target audience similarities. If such exist, pan-regional or global campaigns can be attempted. Grey Advertising checks for commonalities in variables such as economic expectations, demographics, income, and education. Consumer needs and wants are assessed for common features. An increasing number of companies are engaging in **corporate image advertising** in support of their more traditional tactical product-specific and local advertising efforts.[12] Especially for multi-divisional companies, an umbrella campaign may help either to boost the image of lesser-known product lines or to make the company itself be understood correctly or perceived more positively. ABB, the global engineering and technology company, wants to be better known among its constituents and launched a major global campaign to ensure that (an example of which is provided in Exhibit 13.2). Costs may also be saved in engaging in global image campaigning, especially if the same campaign or core concepts can be used across borders.

Often, however, problems may emerge. For example, Tang was marketed in the United States as an orange juice substitute, which did not succeed in testing abroad. In France, for example, Tang was re-positioned as a refreshment, because the French rarely drink orange juice at breakfast. In countries such as the Philippines, Tang could be marketed as a premium drink, whereas in Brazil, it was a low-priced item.[13] Audience similarities are more easily found in business markets.[14]

Campaign Objectives

Nothing is more essential to the planning of global communication campaigns than the establishment of clearly defined, measurable objectives. These objectives can be divided into overall global and regional objectives as well as local objectives. The objectives that are set at the local level are more specific and establish measurable targets for individual

Exhibit 13.2 **An Example of a Corporate Image Campaign**

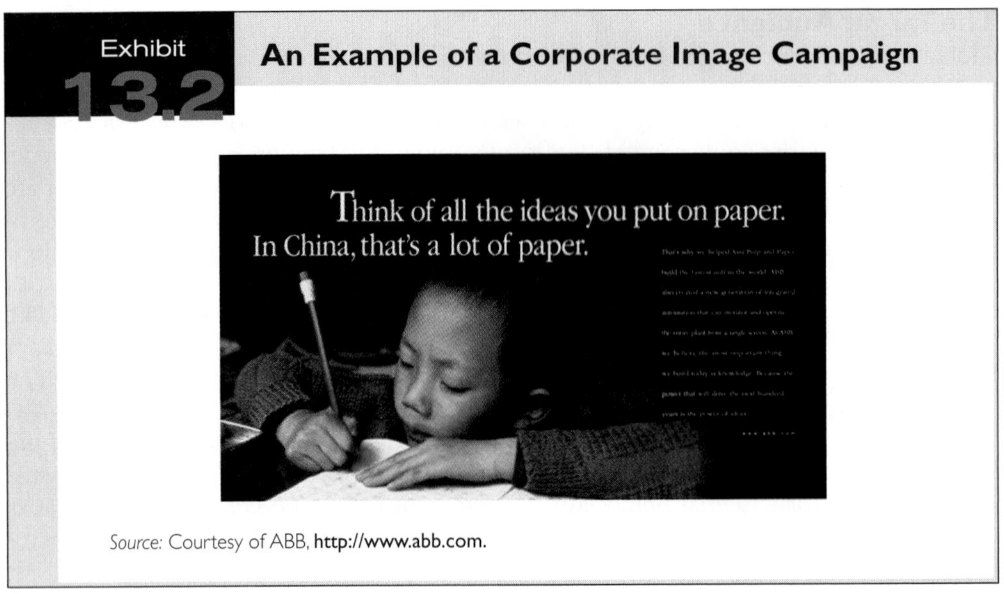

Think of all the ideas you put on paper.
In China, that's a lot of paper.

Source: Courtesy of ABB, **http://www.abb.com.**

markets. These objectives may be product- or service-related or related to the entity itself. Typical goals are to increase awareness, enhance image, and improve market share in a particular market. Whatever the objective, it has to be measurable for control purposes.

While FedEx is one of the top three transportation companies in Latin America, it is not the household name there that it is in Canada and the United States. The company wanted to increase brand awareness among its target audience of small and medium-sized international shippers. Among large corporate clients, FedEx has no concerns and marketing to them is usually done through personal visits by the FedEx sales force. To reach the intended target, FedEx created a 30-second television spot featuring a soccer team manager's distress over the fate of missing uniforms he had shipped to Madrid for a big match. Using soccer in the region is an effective way to cut through languages and cultures.[15]

There is a move by many governments to influence how their countries are perceived to gain commercial or political advantage.[16] For example, after September 11, 2001, the United States recognized that it needed to build a new level of understanding of the country and its values and policies, especially in countries where resentment of its power and influence may be high. Part of this effort is a $10-million advertising campaign from McCann Erickson featuring stories of Muslim life in the United States. It ran on TV and radio from Indonesia through the Middle East. The campaign was based on the premise that Arab and U.S. cultures share family as a common core value. This campaign is also very much in the interests of U.S. marketers who have found that their brands are on the firing line as symbols of the United States.[17] So far Canadian marketers have not had to deal with such a backlash.

Local objectives are typically developed as a combination of headquarters (global or regional) and country organization involvement. Basic guidelines are initiated by headquarters, whereas local organizations set the actual country-specific goals. These goals are subject to headquarters approval, mainly to ensure consistency. Although some campaigns, especially global ones may have more headquarters involvement than usual, local input is still quite important, especially to ensure appropriate implementation of the subsequent programs at the local level.

The Budget

The promotional budget links established objectives with media, message, and control decisions. Ideally, the budget would be set as a response to the objectives to be met, but resource constraints often preclude this approach. Many marketers use an objective and task method, as a survey of 484 advertising managers for consumer goods in 15 countries indicates (see Exhibit 13.3). This approach requires that the global marketing manager determine and cost the specific tasks that must be performed in order to reach the corpo-

Exhibit 13.3

Budgeting Methods for Promotional Programs

Budgeting Method	Percentage of Respondents Using this Method*	Lowest Percentages	Highest Percentages
Objective and task	64%	Sweden (36%) Argentina (44%)	Canada (87%) Singapore (86%)
Percentage of sales	48	Germany (31%)	Brazil (73%) Hong Kong (70%)
Executive judgment	33	Finland (8%) Germany (8%)	USA (64%) Denmark (51%) Brazil (46%) Great Britain (46%)
All-you-can-afford	12	Argentina (0%) Israel (0%)	Sweden (30%) Germany (25%) Great Britain (24%)
Matched competitors	12	Denmark (0%) Israel (0%)	Germany (33%) Sweden (33%) Great Britain (22%)
Same as last year plus a little more	9	Israel (0%)	
Same as last year	3		
Other	10	Finland (0%) Germany (0%) Israel (0%)	Canada (24%) Mexico (21%)

*Total exceeds 100 percent because respondents checked all budgeting methods that they used.

Source: Nicolaos E. Synodinos, Charles F. Keown, and Laurence W. Jacobs, "Transnational Advertising Practices," *Journal of Advertising Research* 29 (April–May 1989): 43–50. © 1989, by the Advertising Research Foundation. Reprinted by permission.

rate objectives specified. Realities may, however, force compromises between ideal choices and resources available.[18] As a matter of fact, available funds may dictate the basis from which the objective and task method can start. Furthermore, advertising budgets should be set on a market-by-market basis because of competitive differences across markets. When it comes to global image campaigns, for example, headquarters should provide country organizations extra funds for their implementation.

Budgets can also be used as a control mechanism if headquarters retains final budget approval. In these cases, headquarters decision makers must have a clear understanding of cost and market differences to be able to make rational decisions.

Nielsen Media Research compiles a list of the top 100 global advertising spenders. In 2005, the top 10 advertisers were Procter & Gamble ($8.2 billion), Unilever ($4.3 billion), General Motors ($2.42 billion), L'Oreal ($2.77 billion), Toyota ($2.8 billion), Ford ($2.6 billion), Time Warner ($2.5 billion), DaimlerChrysler ($2.1 billion), Nestlé ($2 billion), and Johnson and Johnson ($1.96 billion). Canadian firms are notably absent from the top 100 list. The Molson Coors Brewing Company is the only firm on the list with Canadian roots, and it comes in at number 94 with global ad spending of $262 million.[19] Within the North American market, Procter & Gamble is again the leader in advertising expenditure, with the major telecommunications companies BCE, Rogers Communications, and Telus also being major players (see Exhibit 13.4).

Media Strategy

Target audience characteristics, campaign objectives, and the budget form the basis for the choice between media vehicles and the development of a media schedule. The major factors determining the choice of media vehicles to be used are (1) the availability of the

Exhibit 13.4 Advertising Expenditures in North America, 2005

Company	Expenditure (US$ millions)
Proctor & Gamble	172
Rogers	106.5
GM	98.6
Telus	70.9
BCE	67.1
Wendy's	61.1
L'Oréal	58.9
Sony	56.9
Toyota	56.4
Hyundai	54.4

Source: Reprinted with permission from the Advertising Age 20th Annual Global Marketers issue. Copyright, Crain Communications Inc.

media in a given local market, (2) the product or service itself, (3) media habits of the intended audience, and (4) the availability of global media.

Media Availability

Media spending, which totalled $312 billion in 2002, varies dramatically around the world, as seen in Exhibit 13.5. In absolute terms, the United States spends more money on advertising than most of the other major advertising nations combined. Other major spenders are Japan, the United Kingdom, Germany, Canada, and France. The mature U.S. market anticipates continued growth in the future, but European integration and the development of the Pacific Rim's consumer markets are likely to fuel major growth after a two-year (2001–02) advertising recession.[20]

Naturally, this spending varies by market. Countries devoting the highest percentage to television were Peru (84 percent), Mexico (73 percent), and Venezuela (67 percent). In some countries, the percentage devoted to print is still high: Kuwait (91 percent), Norway (77 percent), and Sweden (77 percent). Radio accounts for more than 20 percent of total measured media in only a few countries, such as Trinidad and Tobago, Nepal, and Hon-

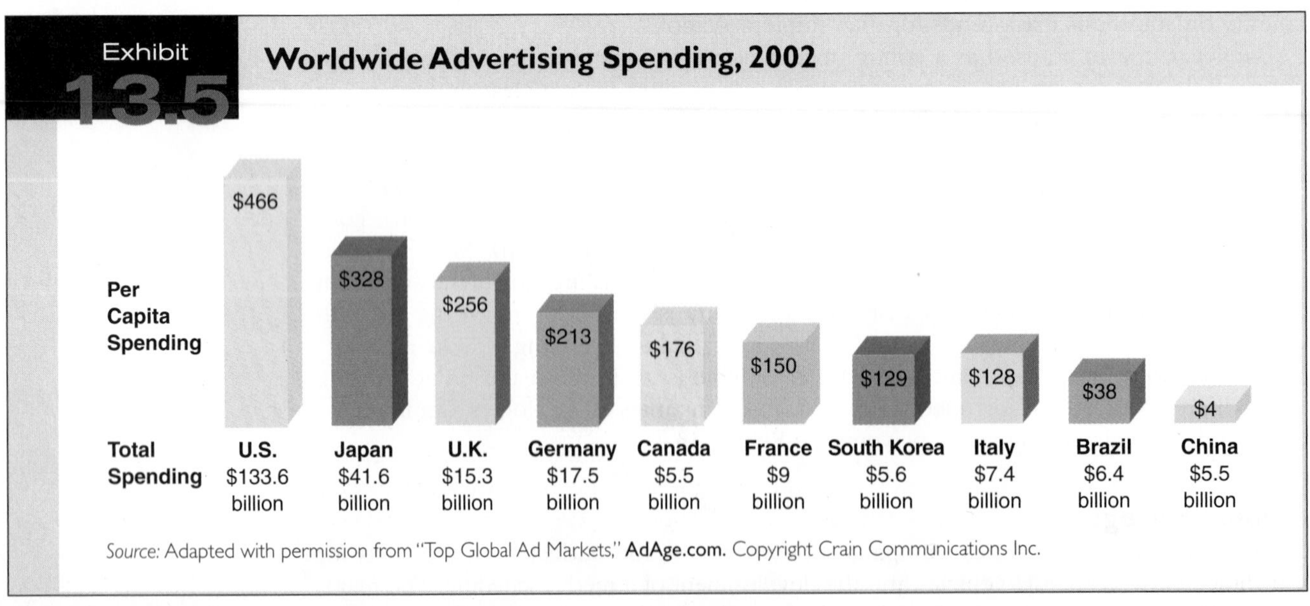

Source: Adapted with permission from "Top Global Ad Markets," **AdAge.com.** Copyright Crain Communications Inc.

Exhibit 13.6

Forecast of the Internet's Contribution to Global Advertising by Region

Region	Percentage of Spending (2008)
Asia-Pacific	
Japan	11.7
Australia	12.5
South Korea	10.4
Taiwan	13
New Zealand	5
Europe	
U.K.	12.9
Sweden	10.5
North America	**8.9**

Source: http://asia.advertising.msn.com.

duras. Outdoor/transit advertising accounted for 48 percent of Bolivia's media spending but only 3 percent in Germany.[21] Cinema advertising is important in countries such as India and Nigeria. Until a few years ago, the prevailing advertising technique used by the Chinese consisted of outdoor boards and posters found outside factories; today, more new TV and radio stations are coming on-air. The Internet is well on the way to establishing itself as a complementary advertising medium in Europe, Asia, and the Americas. In Japan, the Internet is expected to account for 11.7 percent of advertising spending by 2008, while the medium's contribution is expected to be 12.5 percent in Australia, 12.9 percent in the U.K., and almost 9 percent in North America, as shown in Exhibit 13.6. In addition to PCs, mobile phones and interactive TV will become delivery mechanisms.

The media available to the global marketer in major ad markets are summarized in Exhibit 13.7. The breakdown by media points to the enormous diversity in how media are used in a given market. These figures do not tell the whole story, however, which emphasizes the need for careful homework on the part of the global marketing manager charged with media strategy. As an example, Brazil has five television networks, but one of them—Globo TV—corners 50 percent of all television advertising spending. Throughout Latin America, the tendency is to allocate half or more of total advertising budgets to television, with the most coveted spots on prime-time soap operas that attract viewers from Mexico to Brazil. In general, advertising in Latin America requires flexibility and creativity. Inflation rates have caused advertising rates to increase dramatically in countries such as Argentina. In Mexico, advertisers can use the "French Plan," which protects participating advertisers from price increases during the year and additionally gives the advertiser two spots for the price of one. For these concessions, the advertiser must pay for the year's entire advertising schedule by October of the year before.

The major problems affecting global promotional efforts involve conflicting national regulations. Even within the European Union (EU), there is no uniform legal standard. Conditions do vary from country to country, and ads must comply with national regulation. Most European countries either observe the Code of Advertising Practice of the International Chamber of Commerce or have their guidelines based on it.[22] Some of the regulations include limits on the amount of time available for advertisements; for example, in Italy, the state channels allow a maximum of 12 percent advertising per hour and 4 percent per week, and commercial stations allow 18 percent per hour and 15 percent per week. Furthermore, the leading Italian stations do not guarantee audience delivery when spots are bought. Strict separation between programs and commercials is almost a universal requirement, preventing North American-style sponsored programs. Restrictions on items such as comparative claims and gender stereotypes are prevalent; for example, Germany prohibits the use of superlatives such as "best."

Exhibit 13.7

Global Media Breakdown

Market/Media Fact	United States	Japan	Germany	United Kingdom	France	Italy	Brazil	South Korea	Canada	China
Ad Spending, 2002 ($ billions)	$133.6	$41.6	$17.5	$15.3	$9	$7.4	$6.4	$6.1	$5.5	$5.5
Media Percentage										
Newspaper	32.9%	27.3%	43.5%	40.3%	43.5%	22%	35.4%	47%	39%	23%*
TV	38.0%	46.1%	24.3%	29.8%	24.3%	52%	48.4%	28%	39%	67%
Magazine	11.2%	9.6%	23.5%	17.5%	23.5%	16%	11.4%	4%	5%	—
Radio	14.2%	4.6%	3.8%	4.6%	3.8%	5%	3.1%	2%	13%	1%
Outdoor	3.7%	12.4%	3.9%	6.3%	3.9%	5%	1.7%	—	4%	9%
Cinema	—	—	1%	1.5%	1%	—	—	—	—	—
Top Advertiser ($ millions)	GM $2,188	Toyota $716	Ferrero $218	COI $216	France Telecom $310	Fiat $182	Imovel $85.3	SK Telecom $88.9	N/A	Taita $113
Top Ad Category ($ millions)	Auto $14,400	Food $2,730	Media $1,586	Finance $1,800	Retail $1,400	Food $976	Retail $1,976	Computer $629	Retail $653	Pharma $3,300
Online Ad Spending ($ millions)	$5,600	$600	$197	$254	$81	$93	$88	$94	$72	N/A
Technology Percentage										
Internet	58.7%	34%	42%	31%	20%	24%	8%	53%	69%	22%
PC	66.7%	46%	48.2%	48%	34%	37%	9%	54%	63%	27%
Mobile	45.4%	69%	65%	58%	62%	83%	16%	57%	49%	30%

*Includes all print media.

Source: Reprinted with permission from "Top 10 Global Ad Markets," *Advertising Age Global*, April 2002, 18–23. Copyright, Crain Communications Inc.

Product Influences

Global marketers and advertising agencies are currently frustrated by wildly differing restrictions on how products can be advertised in different countries around the world. Agencies often have to produce several separate versions to comply with various national regulations. Consumer protection in general has dominated the regulatory scene in the EU and the United States.[23] The same applies in Canada. For example, in Canada prior to 1988 there were no restrictions on tobacco advertising. Restrictions were imposed post-1988 by the Tobacco Products Control Act, which stipulated that all tobacco products show attributed warnings about their dangers. A series of legal challenges led to confirmation of the legality of the Tobacco Products Control Act but struck down the provisions that warnings be attributed.[24] The EU Directive on Tobacco Advertising, which was enacted in 2003, bans all tobacco advertising that crosses national borders. The directive covers press, radio, and Internet advertising, as well as sponsorship of sport events. Indirect advertising programs such as brand sharing and national advertising campaigns within member countries are not covered by the directive.[25] Television advertising is banned under separate legislation, the Television without Frontiers Directive. Tobacco products, alcoholic beverages, and pharmaceuticals are the most heavily regulated products in terms of promotion. In Canada, tobacco advertising is heavily regulated. There are currently prohibitions on radio and television advertisements, event sponsorship, promotional giveaways, and any form of brand advertising. In-store displays are also banned.

However, the manufacturers of these heavily regulated products have not abandoned their promotional efforts. Altria Group (formerly Philip Morris) engages in corporate image advertising using its cowboy spokesperson. Some European cigarette manufacturers have diversified into the entertainment business, acquiring restaurants, lounges, and movie theatres and naming them after their cigarette brands. AstraZeneca, a leading global pharmaceutical, funded a TV campaign run by the French Migraine Association, which discussed medical advances but made no mention of the company. Novo Nordisk has set up an Internet page on diabetes separate from its home page and established the World Diabetes Foundation awareness group.[26]

Certain products are subject to special rules. In the United Kingdom, for example, advertisers cannot show a real person applying an underarm deodorant; the way around this problem is to show an animated person applying the product. What is and is not allowable is very much a reflection of the country imposing the rules. Explicit advertisements of contraceptives are commonplace in Sweden, for example, but far less frequent in other parts of the world. A number of countries have varying restrictions on advertisements of toys; Greece bans them altogether, and Belgium restricts their use before and after children's programming.

Beyond the traditional media, the global marketer may also consider **product placement** in movies, TV shows, games, or websites. Although there is disagreement about the effectiveness of the method beyond creating brand awareness,[27] products from makers such as BMW, Omega, Nokia, and Heineken have been placed in movies to help both parties to the deal: to create a brand definition for the product and a dimension of reality for the film.[28] In some markets, product placement may be an effective method of attracting attention due to constraints on traditional media. In China, for example, most commercials on Chinese state-run television are played back-to-back in 10-minute segments, making it difficult for any 30-second ad to be singled out. Placing products in soap operas such as "Love Talks" has been found to be an effective way to get to the burgeoning middle class in the world's most populous country.[29] Some marketers have started to create stand-alone entertainment vehicles around a brand, such as the BMW film series on the Internet.[30]

Audience Characteristics

A major objective of media strategy is to reach the intended target audience with a minimum of waste. As an example, Amoco Oil Company wanted to launch a corporate image campaign in China in the hope of receiving drilling contracts. Identifying the appropriate decision makers was not difficult because they all work for the government. The selection of appropriate media proved to be equally simple because most of the decision makers overseeing petroleum exploration were found to read the vertical trade publications: *International Industrial Review*, *Petroleum Production*, and *Offshore Petroleum*.

If conditions are ideal, and they seldom are in international markets, the media strategist would need data on (1) media distribution, that is, the number of copies of the print medium or the number of sets for broadcast; (2) media audiences; and (3) advertising exposure. For instance, an advertiser interested in using television in Brazil would like to know that the top adult TV program is "O Clone," a soap opera. In markets where more sophisticated market research services are available, data on advertising perception and consumer response may be available. In many cases, advertisers have found circulation figures to be unreliable or even fabricated.

An issue related to audience characteristics is the move by some governments to protect their own national media from foreign ones. In Canada, for example, the government prevents foreign publishers from selling space to Canadian advertisers in so-called split-run editions that, in effect, have no local content. If U.S. publications such as *Sports Illustrated* were allowed to do it, Canadian publications would be threatened with insufficient amounts of advertising.[31]

Global Media

Media vehicles that have target audiences on at least three continents and for which the media buying takes place through a centralized office are considered to be **global media**.[32] Global media have traditionally been publications that, in addition to the worldwide edition, have provided advertisers the option of using regional editions. For example, *Time* provides 133 editions, enabling advertisers to reach a particular country, continent, or the world. In print media, global vehicles include dailies such as *International Herald Tribune*, weeklies such as *The Economist*, and monthlies such as *National Geographic*. Included on the broadcast side are BBC Worldwide TV, CNN, the Discovery Channel, and MTV. The Discovery Channel reaches more than 700 million subscribers in 155 countries in 33 languages through Discovery Channel–Europe, Discovery Channel–Latin America/Iberia, Discovery Channel–Asia, Discovery Canada, Discovery New Zealand, and several other language-tailored networks. The argument that global media drown out local content is not borne out in fact.[33] MTV as a global medium is profiled in The Global Marketplace 13.2.

The Global MARKETPLACE 13.2

The World Wants Its MTV!

MTV has emerged as a significant global medium, with more than 375 million households in 164 countries subscribing to its services. The reason for its success is simple—MTV offers consistent, high-quality programming that reflects the tastes and lifestyle of young people.

Its balance of fashion, film, news, competitions, and comedy wrapped in the best music and strong visual identity has made it "the best bet to succeed as a pan-European thematic channel, with its aim to be in every household in Europe," according to *Music Week*, Britain's leading music trade paper. Given that 79 percent of the channel's viewers are in the elusive 16–34 age group, MTV is a force as an advertising medium for those who want to closely target their campaigns. MTV has proven to be the ultimate youth marketing vehicle for companies such as Wrangler, Wrigley, Braun, Britvic, Levi Strauss, PepsiCo, Pentax, and many others. Although many knockoffs have been started around the world, the enormous cost of building a worldwide music video channel will most likely protect MTV.

MTV's best response to threats from competition has been to make programming as local as possible. Its policy of 70 percent local content has resulted in some of the network's more creative shows, such as Brazil's month-long Rockgol, which pitted musicians against record industry executives, and Russia's Twelve Angry Viewers, a talk show focused on the latest videos.

Digital compression allows the number of services offered on a satellite feed to be multiplied. The network will use the new capacity to complement pan-regional programming and playlists, customizing them to local tastes in key areas. For example, MTV Asia has launched MTV India to have 5 hours of India-specific programming during the 24-hour satellite feed to the subcontinent.

Owned by Viacom, MTV's global network consists of the following entities:

- **MTV USA** is seen 24 hours a day on cable television in over 85 million U.S. television homes. Presented in stereo, MTV's overall on-air environment is unpredictable and irreverent, reflecting the cutting-edge spirit of rock 'n' roll that is the heart of its programming. Through its graphic look, VJs, music news, promotions, interviews, concert tour information, specials, and documentaries, as well as its original strip programming, MTV has become an international institution of pop culture and the leading authority on rock music since it launched on August 1, 1981.
- **MTV Europe** reaches 43 territories (124 million households) 24 hours a day in stereo, via satellite, cable, and terrestrial distribution. The station acquires its own video clips, drawing from the domestic markets in individual European countries to discover bands making an international sound. It has its own team of VJs presenting shows specially tailored for the European market. The channel's programming mix reflects its diverse audience, with coverage of music, style, news, movie information, comedy, and more. MTV Europe has five local programming feeds and five local advertising windows—U.K./Ireland; MTV Central (Austria, Germany, and Switzerland); MTV European (76 territories, including France and Israel); MTV Southern (Italy); and MTV Nordic (Sweden, Norway, and others). It was launched August 1, 1987.
- **MTV Asia** was launched September 15, 1991, and reaches over 138 million households in 21 territories. Programming is tailored to the musical tastes, lifestyles, and sensibilities of Asian audiences in three regions: MTV Mandarin, MTV Southeast Asia, and MTV India.
- Although **MTV Japan** was originally launched in October 1984 under a licensing agreement, it was re-introduced in 2001 as a wholly-owned entity of MTV Networks International. The 24-hour music television channel and website feature original Japanese-language programming and reach 2.8 million households.
- **MTV Latin America** reaches 28 million households in 21 countries and territories. The network features a mix of U.S. and Latin music, regional production, music and entertainment news, artist interviews, concert coverage, and specials.

- **MTV Internacional** is a 1-hour weekly Spanish-language program. MTV Internacional is a mix of Spanish- and English-language videos, interviews, entertainment news, and on-location specials. The program is broadcast in the United States on the Telemundo Network and in various Latin American countries. It is distributed by MTV Syndication Sales.
- **MTV Brazil** was launched in 1990 and is a joint venture of MTVNetworks and Abril S.A., Brazil's leading magazine publisher. The Portuguese-language network, viewed in 16 million households, is broadcast via UHF in São Paulo and via VHF in Rio de Janeiro.
- **MTV Russia**, launched in September 1998, is a free over-the-air service reaching more than 20 million homes in major cities. The entity was established with BIZ Enterprises in a multi-year licensing agreement. In 2000, MTV Networks International gained an equity position in MTV Russia. Programming includes music videos from Russian and international artists, as well as coverage of social issues relevant to Russian youth.

Sources: Claudia Penteado, "MTV Breaks New Ground," *Advertising Age Global*, March 2002, 8; "MTV's World," *Business Week*, February 18, 2002, 81–84; "MTV Asia's Hit Man," *Advertising Age Global*, December 2001, 10; "Focus: Trends in TV," *Advertising Age International*, January 11, 1999, 33; "MTV Fights Back from Nadir to Hit High Notes in India," *Advertising Age International*, March 30, 1998, 10; "High Tech Helps MTV Evolve," *World Trade*, June 1996, 10; "Will MTV Have to Share the Stage?" *Business Week*, February 21, 1994, 38; and **http://www.mtv.com.**

Advertising in global media is dominated by major consumer ad categories, particularly airlines, financial services, telecommunications, automobiles, and tobacco. The aircraft industry represents business market advertisers.[34] Companies spending in global media include AT&T, IBM, and General Motors. In choosing global media, media buyers consider the three most important media characteristics: targetability, client-compatible editorial, and editorial quality.[35] Some global publications have found that some parts of the globe are more appealing to advertisers than others; for example, some publications have eliminated editions in Africa (due to lack of advertising) and in Asia and Latin America (due to financial crises).

The Internet provides the marketer with a global medium. North American firms have been slow to adopt their websites to service international markets. One simple way of getting started is to choose a few key languages for the website. For example, Gillette decided to add German and Japanese to its Mach3 website after studying the number of Internet users in those countries.[36] If the marketer elects to have a global site and region-specific sites (e.g., organized by country), they all should have a similar look, especially in terms of the level of sophistication. Another method is to join forces with Internet service providers. For example, Unilever has expanded its sponsorship of the Microsoft online network in the United States to France, Germany, and the United Kingdom.[37] Under the agreement, Unilever will provide banner ads, links, and sponsorship to MSN sites, particularly MSN Women. Premier sponsorship on the MSN sites will include logo placement at the top right corner of the webpages.

The Promotional Message

The creative people must have a clear idea of the characteristics of the audience expected to be exposed to the message. In this sense, the principles of creating effective advertising are the same as in the domestic marketplace. The marketer must determine what the consumer is really buying—that is, the customer's motivations. These will vary, depending on the following:

1. The diffusion of the product or service into the market. For example, it is difficult to penetrate Third World markets with business computers when potential customers in some countries may not know how to type or with Internet advertising when the infrastructure is lacking.
2. The criteria on which the customer will evaluate the product. For example, in traditional societies, advertising the time-saving qualities of a product may not be the best approach, as Campbell Soup Company learned in Italy, Brazil, and Poland, where women felt inadequate as homemakers if they did not make soups from scratch.

3. The product's positioning. For example, Parker Pen's upscale market image around the world may not be profitable enough in a market that is more or less a commodity business. The solution is to create an image for a commodity product and make the public pay for it—for example, the positioning of Perrier in Canada as a premium mineral water.

The ideal situation in developing message strategy is to have a world brand—a product that is manufactured, packaged, and positioned the same around the world. Companies that have been successful with the global approach have shown flexibility in the execution of the campaigns. The idea may be global, but overseas subsidiaries then tailor the message to suit local market conditions and regulations. Executing an advertising campaign in multiple markets requires a balance between conveying the message and allowing for local nuances. The localization of global ideas can be achieved by various tactics, such as adopting a modular approach, localizing international symbols, and using international advertising agencies.[38]

Marketers may develop multiple broadcast and print ads from which country organizations can choose the most appropriate for their operations. This can provide local operations with cost savings and allow them to use their budgets on tactical campaigns (which may also be developed around the global idea). For example, the "Membership Has Its Privileges" campaign of American Express, which has run in 24 countries on TV and 3 more in print, was adjusted in some markets to make sure that "privileges" did not have a snob or elitist appeal, especially in countries with a strong caste or class system. An example of local adjustment in a global campaign for Marriott International is provided in Exhibit 13.8. While the ads share common graphic elements, two distinct approaches are evident. The top set of advertisements from the United States and Saudi Arabia is an example of a relatively standard approach, given the similarity in target audiences (i.e., the business traveller) and in the competitive conditions in the markets. The second set features ads for Latin America and German-speaking Europe. While the Latin American advertisement stresses comfort, the German version focuses on results. While most of Marriott's ads translate the theme ("When you're comfortable you can do anything"), the German version keeps the original English-language theme. McDonald's launched its first global advertising campaign in Germany on September 2, 2003, with the English version on September 29, 2003. The "i'm lovin' it" campaign was targeted at 15–24 year olds across the globe. Exhibit 13.9 shows the translation of the tag line in various countries and in French Canada.

Product-related regulations will affect advertising messages as well. When General Mills Toy Group's European subsidiary launched a product line related to G.I. Joe–type war toys and soldiers, it had to develop two television commercials, a general version for most European countries and another for countries that bar advertisements for products with military or violent themes. As a result, in the version running in Germany, Holland, and Belgium, Jeeps replaced the toy tanks, and guns were removed from the hands of the toy soldiers. Other countries, such as the United Kingdom, do not allow children to appear in advertisements.

Global marketers may also want to localize their international symbols. Some of the most effective global advertising campaigns have capitalized on the popularity of pop music worldwide and have used well-known artists in the commercials, such as Pepsi's use of Tina Turner. In some versions, local stars have been included with the international stars to localize the campaign. Aesthetics play a role in localizing campaigns. The global marketer does not want to risk the censoring of the company's ads or offending customers. For example, even though importers of perfumes into Saudi Arabia want to use the same campaigns as are used in Europe, they occasionally have to make adjustments dictated by moral standards. In one case, the European version shows a man's hand clutching a perfume bottle and a woman's hand seizing his bare forearm. In the Saudi Arabian version, the man's arm is clothed in a dark suit sleeve, and the woman's hand is merely brushing his hand.

The environmental influences that call for these modifications, or in some cases totally unique approaches, are culture, economic development, and lifestyle. It is quite evident

Exhibit 13.8 Local Adjustments in a Global Campaign

Source:

Exhibit 13.9 McDonald's Global Advertising Campaign

Title	Language	Literal Meaning	Used in
i'm lovin' it	English	"I am loving it."	Australia, Austria, Belarus, Belgium, Bulgaria, Canada, Czech Republic, Denmark, Estonia, Finland, Greece, Guatemala, Hong Kong, India, Indonesia, Republic of Ireland, Israel, Italy, Japan, South Korea, Macau, Malaysia, Malta, the Netherlands, New Zealand, Norway, Poland, Portugal, Romania, Singapore, Slovakia, Slovenia, South Africa, Spain, Suriname, Sweden, Switzerland, Taiwan, United Kingdom, and United States
أنا أحبه *(ana uhibbuhu)* as well as اكيد بحبه *(akid behibuhu)*	Arabic	"I love it."	Arabic-speaking countries in the Middle East
我就喜(Pinyin: *Wǒ jiù xǐhuān*)	Chinese	"I just like (it)."	Mainland China
c'est tout ce que j'aime	French	"It is all (that) I love."	France, French-speaking countries in West Africa
c'est ça que j'm	French	"That's what I love." *(j'm = j'aime)*	Canada
ich liebe es	German	"I love it."	Germany
love ko 'to	Filipino	"I love this."	Philippines
amo muito tudo isso	Portuguese	"I really love all that."	Brazil
me encanta	Spanish	"I love it."	Most Spanish-speaking countries in Latin America and United States
me encanta todo eso	Spanish	"I love all that."	Argentina, Chile
işte bunu seviyorum	Turkish	"I love this."	Turkey
вот что я люблю	Russian	"Here's what I love."	Russia
я це люблю	Ukrainian	"I love it."	Ukraine
man tas patīk	Latvian	"I like it."	Latvia (though the English-language version is still common)
kocham to	Polish	"I love it."	Poland
Ja' tyck' om ä'	Swedish	"I like it."	Sweden (Norrland)

Source: Used with permission from McDonald's Corporation.

that customers prefer localized to foreign-sourced advertising.[39] Of the cultural variables, language is most apparent in its influence on promotional campaigns. Advertisers in the Arab world have sometimes found that the voices in a TV commercial speak in the wrong Arabic dialect. The challenge of language is often most pronounced in translating themes. For example, Coca-Cola's worldwide theme "Can't Beat the Feeling" is the equivalent of "I Feel Coke" in Japan, "Unique Sensation" in Italy, and "The Feeling of Life" in Chile. In Germany, where no translation really worked, the original English language theme was used. One way of getting around this is to have no copy or very little copy and to use innovative approaches, such as pantomime. Using any type of symbolism will naturally require adequate copy testing to determine how the target market perceives the message. In More Detail 13.1 more fully discusses culture's influence on advertising style.

The stage of economic development—and therefore the potential demand for and degree of awareness of the product—may vary and differentiate the message from one market to another. Whereas developed markets may require persuasive messages (to combat other alternatives), a developing market may require a purely informative campaign. Campaigns may also have to be dramatically adjusted to cater to lifestyle differences in regions that are demographically quite similar. For example, N.W. Ayer's Bahamas tourism campaign for the European market emphasized clean water, beaches, and air. The exceptions are in Germany, where it focuses on sports activities, and in the United Kingdom, where it features humour.

In More Detail 13.1

CULTURE AND ADVERTISING STYLE

In domestic communication, sender and receiver share an understanding of conventions. The sender and receiver share a common cultural context within which messages may be interpreted. In global communication, where advertising messages cross national borders, no such shared conventions exist. The firm's advertising style will have to be adjusted to take cultural differences into account. Advertising style may be thought of in terms of the communication appeal used, the communication approach (that is, whether the message is explicit or implicit, direct or indirect), advertising form (that is, whether testimonial, entertainment, or drama is used), and the approach to execution. As shown in Exhibit 13.10, culture and advertising style may be mapped in order to better understand the role of culture in communication. In cultures that exhibit strong levels of uncertainty avoidance (e.g., Germany), advertising is likely to be highly structured with an emphasis on how products work and a serious approach to execution of the visual elements of the advertising campaign. In societies with weak levels of uncertainty avoidance, where ambiguity is not a problem for viewers, a more lighthearted approach may be employed. In masculine cultures such as the U.S. and the U.K., celebrities will tend to be used; that is, advertising style will emphasize personal characteristics. In more feminine societies such as Scandinavia, personalities will be downplayed (see two left quadrants of Exhibit 13.10).

In countries with high individualism, high power distance, and high uncertainty avoidance (e.g., France), advertising style would favour a more implicit and subdued approach. The emphasis here is on building an emotional bond with the consumer through proper use of aesthetic elements and entertainment. Emphasis on the functional aspects of the product is less important. In collectivist societies with medium/large power distance and weak/moderate uncertainty avoidance (e.g., China, India, and Singapore), advertising should make use of symbolism, drama, and metaphor.

Unique market conditions may require localized approaches. Although IBM has utilized global campaigns (the Little Tramp campaign, for example), it has also used major local campaigns in Japan and Europe for specific purposes. In Japan, it used a popular television star in poster and door-board ads to tell viewers, "Friends, the time is ripe" (for buying an IBM personal computer). The campaign was designed to bolster the idea that the machine represents a class act from America. At the same time, IBM was trying to overcome a problem in Europe of being perceived as "too American." Stressing that IBM is actually a "European company," an advertising campaign told of IBM's large factories, research facilities, and tax-paying subsidiaries within the EU.

The Campaign Approach

Many multinational corporations are staffed and equipped to perform the full range of promotional activities. In most cases, however, they will rely on the outside expertise of advertising agencies and other promotions-related companies such as media-buying companies and specialty marketing firms. In the organization of promotional efforts, a company has two basic decisions to make: (1) what type of outside services to use and (2) how to establish decision-making authority for promotional efforts.

Outside Services

Of all the outside promotion-related services, advertising agencies are by far the most significant. A list of the world's top 50 agencies and agency groups is given in Exhibit 13.11. Of the top 50 agencies, 26 are based in the United States, 9 in Japan, and the rest in the United Kingdom, France, Australia, South Korea, Italy, Canada, and Germany. Whereas the Japanese agencies tend to have few operations outside their home country, U.S. and European agencies are engaged in worldwide expansion. Size is measured in terms of gross income and billings. Billings are the cost of advertising time and space placed by the agency plus fees for certain extra services, which are converted by formula to correspond to media billings in terms of value of services performed. Agencies do not receive billings as income; in general, agency income is approximately 15 percent of billing.

Exhibit 13.10 **The Impact of Culture on Advertising Style**

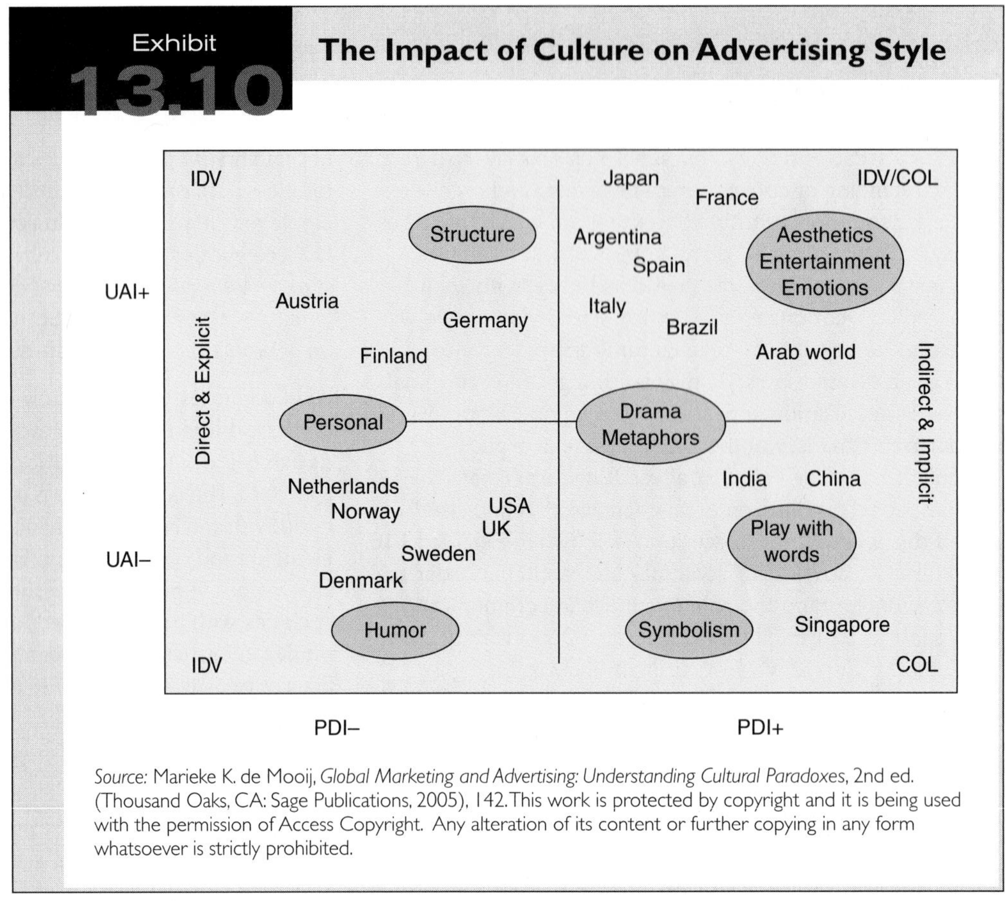

Source: Marieke K. de Mooij, *Global Marketing and Advertising: Understanding Cultural Paradoxes*, 2nd ed. (Thousand Oaks, CA: Sage Publications, 2005), 142. This work is protected by copyright and it is being used with the permission of Access Copyright. Any alteration of its content or further copying in any form whatsoever is strictly prohibited.

Agencies form world groups for better coverage. One of the largest world holding groups, WPP Group, includes such entities as Ogilvy & Mather, J. Walter Thompson, Young & Rubicam, and Red Cell. Smaller advertising agencies have affiliated local agencies in foreign markets.

The choice of an agency will largely depend on the quality of coverage the agency will be able to give the multinational company. Global marketing requires global advertising, according to proponents of the globalization trend. The reason is not that significant cost savings can be realized through a single worldwide ad campaign but that such a global campaign is inseparable from the idea of global marketing. Some predict that the whole industry will be concentrated into a few huge multinational agencies. Agencies with networks too small to compete have become prime takeover targets in the creation of worldwide mega-agencies. Many believe that local, midsize agencies can compete in the face of globalization by developing local solutions and/or joining international networks.[40]

The main concern arising from the use of mega-agencies is conflict. With only a few giant agencies to choose from, the global marketer may end up with the same agency as its main competitor. The mega-agencies believe they can meet any objections by structuring their companies as rigidly separate, watertight agency networks (such as the Interpublic Group) under the umbrella of a holding group. Following that logic, Procter & Gamble, a client of Saatchi & Saatchi Advertising Worldwide, and Colgate-Palmolive, a client of Ted Bates, should not worry about falling into the same network's client base. However, when the Saatchi & Saatchi network purchased Ted Bates, Colgate-Palmolive left the agency.

Despite the globalization trend, local agencies will survive as a result of governmental regulations. In Peru, for example, a law mandates that any commercial aired on Peruvian television must be 100 percent nationally produced. Local agencies also tend to forge ties with foreign agencies for better coverage and customer service and thus

Exhibit 13.11

Top 50 Advertising Organizations Worldwide

2001	2000	Advertising Organization	Headquarters	Worldwide Gross Income ($m) 2001	Worldwide Billings ($m) 2001
1	2	WPP Group	London	$8,165.0	$75,711.0
2	1	Interpublic Group of Cos.	New York	7,981.4	66,689.1
3	3	Omnicom Group	New York	7,404.2	58,080.1
4	4	Publicis Groupe (includes Bcom3 Group)	Paris	4,769.9	52,892.2
5	5	Dentsu	Tokyo	2,795.5	20,847.8
6	6	Havas Advertising	Levallois-Perret, France	2,733.1	26,268.5
7	7	Grey Global Group	New York	1,863.6	12,105.7
8	8	Cordiant Communications Group	London	1,174.5	13,388.0
9	9	Hakuhodo	Tokyo	874.3	6,862.2
10	10	Asatsu-DK	Tokyo	394.6	3,500.6
11	11	TMP Worldwide	New York	358.5	1,705.6
12	12	Carlson Marketing Group	Minneapolis	356.1	2,611.1
13	17	Incepta Group	London	248.4	695.0
14	13	DigitasA	Boston	235.5	N/A
15	15	Tokyu Agency	Tokyo	203.9	1,782.6
16	16	Daiko Advertising	Tokyo	203.0	1,585.0
17	14	Aspen Marketing Group	Los Angeles	189.2	1,262.2
18	18	Maxxcom	Toronto	177.1	386.7
19	20	Cheil Communications	Seoul	142.0	796.0
20	23	Doner	Southfield, MI	114.2	1,070.8
21	19	Ha-Lo Industries	Niles, IL	105.0	N/A
22	22	Yomiko Advertising	Tokyo	102.2	1,022.2
23	21	SPAR Group	Tarrytown, NY	101.8	678.8
24	30	Cossette Communication Group	Quebec City	95.2	488.2
25	28	DVC Worldwide	Morristown, NJ	92.6	680.9
26	25	Clemenger Group	Melbourne, Australia	91.0	606.9
27	29	Rubin Postaer & Associates	Santa Monica, CA	90.3	851.4
28	27	Hawkeye Communications	New York	87.8	585.4
29	24	Panoramic Communications	New York	86.2	1,194.1
30	31	Richard Group	Dallas	84.5	570.5
31	26	Asahi Advertising	Tokyo	84.3	572.0
32	45	inChord Communications (Gerbig Snell/Weishemer)	Westerville, OH	76.1	630.1
33	35	Bartle Bogle Hegarty	London	73.9	581.3
34	32	Wieden & Kennedy	Portland, OR	73.8	777.2
35	38	Cramer-Krasselt	Chicago	72.7	478.2
36	37	M&C Saatchi Worldwide	London	71.7	577.1
37	34	LG Ad	Seoul	67.6	492.4
38	33	Nikkeisha	Tokyo	66.5	440.1
39	36	AKQA	San Francisco	66.0	264.0
40	40	Armando Testa Group	Turin, Italy	62.9	698.4
41	43	Sogei	Tokyo	61.3	437.2
42	48	Springer & Jacoby	Hamburg, Germany	60.6	404.4
43	47	ChoicePoint Direct	Peoria, IL	59.4	396.3
44	44	Gage	Minneapolis	58.6	391.1
45	39	Harte-Hanks Direct & Interactive	Langhome, PA	57.0	353.8
46	59	360 Youth	Cranberry, NJ	56.7	407.2
47	51	Ryan Partnership	Westport, CT	56.3	319.9
48	46	Envoy Communications Group	Toronto	54.8	N/A
49	54	MARC	Pittsburgh	53.2	586.0
50	64	Data Marketing	Santa Clara, CA	52.8	N/A

Source: Reprinted with permission from the April 22, 2002, issue of *Advertising Age*. Copyright, Crain Communications Inc., 2002.

become part of the general globalization effort. A basic fear in the advertising industry is that accounts will be taken away from agencies that cannot handle world brands. An additional factor is contributing to the fear of losing accounts. In the past, many multinational corporations allowed local subsidiaries to make advertising decisions entirely on their own. Others gave subsidiaries an approved list of agencies and some guidance. Still others allowed local decisions subject only to headquarters' approval. Now the trend is toward centralization of all advertising decisions, including those concerning the creative product.

Decision-Making Authority

The alternatives for allocating decision-making authority range from complete centralization to decentralization. With complete centralization, the headquarters level is perceived to have all the right answers and has adequate power to impose its suggestions on all of its operating units. Decentralization involves relaxing most of the controls over foreign affiliates and allowing them to pursue their own promotional approaches.

Of 40 multinational marketers, 26 percent have centralized their advertising strategies, citing as their rationale the search for economies of scale, synergies, and brand consistency. Xerox's reason is that its technology is universal and opportunities abound for global messages. Centralization is also occurring at the regional level. GM's Opel division in Europe is seeking to unify its brand-building efforts with central direction. A total of 34 percent of the companies favour decentralization with regional input. This approach benefits from proximity to market, flexibility, cultural sensitivity, and faster response time. FedEx allows local teams to make advertising decisions as needed. The majority of marketers use central coordination with local input. While Ford Motor Company conceives brand strategy on a global level, ad execution is done at the regional level, and retail work is local.[41] However, multinational corporations are at various stages in their quest for centralization. Procter & Gamble and Gillette generally have an approved list of agencies, whereas Quaker (a division of PepsiCo) and Johnson & Johnson give autonomy to their local subsidiaries but will veto those decisions occasionally.

The important question is not who should make decisions but how advertising quality can be improved at the local level. Gaining approval in multinational corporations is an interactive approach using coordinated decentralization. This nine-step program, which is summarized in Exhibit 13.12, strives for development of common strategy but flexible execution. The approach maintains strong central control but at the same time capitalizes on the greatest asset of the individual markets: market knowledge. Interaction between the central authority and the local levels takes place at every single stage of the planning process. The central authority is charged with finding the commonalities in the data provided by the individual market areas. This procedure will avoid one of the most common problems associated with acceptance of plans—the NIH syndrome (not invented here)—by allowing for local participation by the eventual implementers.

A good example of this approach was Eastman Kodak's launch of its Ektaprint copier-duplicator line in 11 separate markets in Europe. For economic and organizational reasons, Kodak did not want to deal with different campaigns or parameters. It wanted the same ad graphics in each country, accompanied by the theme "first name in photography, last word in copying." Translations varied slightly from country to country, but the campaign was identifiable from one country to another. A single agency directed the campaign, which was more economical than campaigns in each country would have been and was more unified and identifiable through Europe. The psychological benefit of association of the Kodak name with photography was not lost in the campaign.

Agencies are adjusting their operations to centrally run client operations. Many accounts are now handled by a lead agency, usually in the country where the client is based. More and more agencies are moving to a strong international supervisor for global accounts. This supervisor can overrule local agencies and make personnel changes. Specialty units have emerged as well. For example, Ogilvy & Mather established the Worldwide Client Service organization at headquarters in New York specializing in developing global campaigns for its clients.[42]

Exhibit 13.12

Coordinated Approach to Pan-Regional Campaign Development

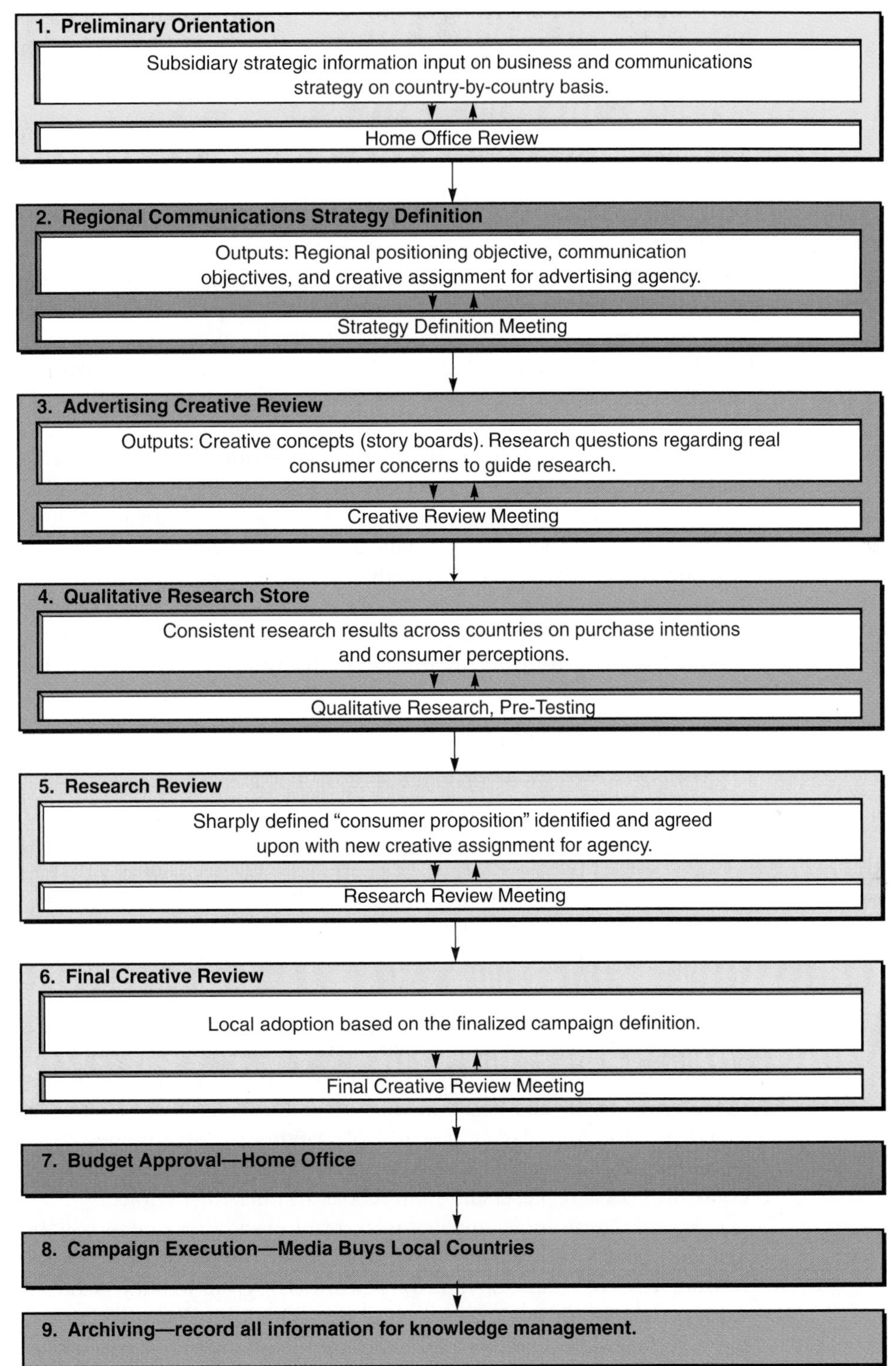

1. Preliminary Orientation
Subsidiary strategic information input on business and communications strategy on country-by-country basis.
Home Office Review
2. Regional Communications Strategy Definition
Outputs: Regional positioning objective, communication objectives, and creative assignment for advertising agency.
Strategy Definition Meeting
3. Advertising Creative Review
Outputs: Creative concepts (story boards). Research questions regarding real consumer concerns to guide research.
Creative Review Meeting
4. Qualitative Research Store
Consistent research results across countries on purchase intentions and consumer perceptions.
Qualitative Research, Pre-Testing
5. Research Review
Sharply defined "consumer proposition" identified and agreed upon with new creative assignment for agency.
Research Review Meeting
6. Final Creative Review
Local adoption based on the finalized campaign definition.
Final Creative Review Meeting
7. Budget Approval—Home Office
8. Campaign Execution—Media Buys Local Countries
9. Archiving—record all information for knowledge management.

Sources: Jae H. Pae, Saeed Samiee, and Susan Tai, "Global Advertising Strategy: The Moderating Role of Brand Familiarity and Execution Style," *International Marketing Review* 19, no. 2 (2002): 176–89; Clive Nancarrow and Chris Woolston, "Pre-Testing International Press Advertising," *Qualitative Market Research: An International Journal* (1998): 25–38; and David A. Hanni, John K. Ryans, Jr., and Ivan R. Vernon, "Coordinating International Advertising: The Goodyear Case Revisited for Latin America," *Journal of International Marketing* 3, no. 2 (1995): 83–98.

Measurement of Advertising Effectiveness

John Wanamaker reportedly said, "I know half the money I spend on advertising is wasted. Now, if I only knew which half." Whether or not advertising effectiveness can be measured, most companies engage in the attempt. Measures of advertising effectiveness should range from pretesting of copy appeal and recognition, to post-testing of recognition, all the way to sales effects. The measures most used are sales, awareness, recall, executive judgment, intention to buy, profitability, and coupon return, regardless of the medium used.[43]

The technical side of these measurement efforts does not differ from that in the domestic market, but the conditions are different. Very often, syndicated services, such as AC Nielsen, are not available to the global marketer. If available, their quality may not be at an acceptable level. Testing is also quite expensive and may not be undertaken for the smaller markets. Compared with costs in North American markets, the costs of research in the international market are higher in relation to the overall expenditure on advertising.[44] The biggest challenge to advertising research will come from the increase of global and regional campaigns. Comprehensive and reliable measures of campaigns for a mass European market, for example, are difficult because audience measurement techniques and analysis differ for each country. Advertisers are pushing for universally accepted parameters to compare audiences in one country to those in another.

It should be noted that there is empirical evidence that supports the effectiveness of global advertising. Based on a survey of U.S. and Japanese subsidiaries operating in the U.K., researchers have found that the global advertising campaigns of these firms were effective in improving their financial and strategic performance.[45] In this study, the researchers view advertising effectiveness as the degree to which the company's advertising campaign causes the consumer to like the company's brand, develop a positive image of the brand, and/or purchase the brand. A seven-point, four-item, semantic differential scale is used to quantify advertising effectiveness. The following items were included:

- Our advertising is generally well liked in the markets in which it is run.
- Consumers react positively to our advertising.
- Our advertising improves the consumers' image of our brand.
- Our advertising makes it more likely that consumers will purchase our brand.

This study provides empirical support for the proposition that global advertising is effective in improving firms' financial and strategic performance.

Communications Tools

The main tools used by global marketers to communicate with the foreign marketplace from their domestic base are business and trade journals, directories, direct advertising, the Internet, trade fairs, and trade missions. If the marketer's strategy calls for a major promotional effort in a market, it is advisable either to use a domestic agency with extensive operations in the intended market or to use a local agency and work closely with the company's local representatives in media and message choices.

Because the promoter–agency relationship is a close one, it may be helpful if the marketer's domestic agency has an affiliate in the target foreign market. The management function and coordination can be performed by the agency at home, while the affiliate can execute the program as it seems appropriate in that market. A global marketer, if it has a sufficient budget, may ask its domestic agency to set up a branch overseas. Some marketers, especially those that have a more significant presence overseas, leave the choice of the agency to local managers. If a local agency is to be chosen, the exporter must make sure that coordination and cooperation between the agency and the marketer's domestic agency can be achieved. Whatever the approach used, the key criterion must be the competence of the people who will be in charge of the creation and implementation of the promotional programs.

Business/Trade Journals and Directories

Many varied business and trade publications, as well as directories, are available to the marketer. Some, such as *Canadian Business*, *Business Week*, *Fortune*, *The Economist*, *The Wall Street Journal*, and *Financial Times*, are standard information sources worldwide. Extensions of these are their regional editions; for example, *The Asian Wall Street Journal* or *Business Week–Europe*. Trade publications can be classified as (1) horizontal, which cater to a particular job function cutting across industry lines (e.g., *Purchasing World* or *Industrial Distribution*) and (2) vertical, which deal with a specific industry (e.g., *Chemical Engineering* or *International Hospital Supplies*). These journals are global, regional, or country-specific in their approaches.

The global marketer should also be aware of the potential of government-sponsored publications. The Government of Canada's export portal (**http://www.export.ca/default.asp**) contains an online directory that lists Canadian exporters and their product interest. The site also features a marketplace that lists inquiries to buy and offers to sell a range of products from around the world. Export Development Canada publishes its quarterly newsletter, *ExportWise*, and a monthly publication, *Export Trends and Tips*. Canadian firms are routinely profiled in these publications, providing them with low-cost and wide-ranging exposure.

The two main concerns when selecting media are effectiveness in reaching the appropriate target audience(s) and efficiency in minimizing the cost of doing so, measured in terms of cost per thousand. If the global marketer is in a position to define the target audience clearly (for example, in terms of demographics or product-related variables), the choice of media will be easier. In addition, consideration should be given to how well a given medium will work with the other tools the marketer wishes to employ. For example, advertisements in publications and directories may have the function of driving customers and prospects to the marketer's website.[46]

Direct Marketing

The purpose of direct marketing is to establish a relationship with a customer in order to initiate immediate and measurable responses.[47] This is accomplished through direct-response advertising, telemarketing, and direct selling.

Direct mail is by far the dominant direct-response medium, but some advertising is also placed in mass media, such as television, magazines, and newspapers. Direct mail can be a highly personalized tool of communication if the target audience can be identified and defined narrowly. Ranging from notices to actual samples, it allows for flexibility in the amount of information conveyed and in its format. Direct mail is related in its effectiveness to the availability and quality of the mailing lists. Mailing lists may not be available around the world in the same degree that they are in, say, Canada and the United States. However, more and better lists are surfacing in Asia, Latin America, and the Middle East. In addition, reliable, economical, global postal service has become available.[48] Magnavox CATV, which markets cable television equipment, has boosted its international mailings to support its broad schedule of trade shows, many of which are in developing regions.

Even when mailing lists are available, they may not be as up-to-date or as precise as the global marketer would desire. In China, for example, lists are available to send literature directly to factories, ministries, professional societies, research institutes, and universities. However, such mailings can be extremely costly and produce few results. An effective and efficient direct-mail campaign requires extensive market-by-market planning of materials, format, and mode of mailing.

Catalogues are typically distributed to overseas customers through direct mail, although many catalogues have online versions as well. Their function is to make the marketer's name known, generate requests for further information, stimulate orders, and serve as a reminder between transactions. Catalogues are particularly useful if a firm's products are in a highly specialized field of technology and if only the most highly qualified specialists are to be contacted. In many markets, especially the developing ones, people may be starving for technology information and will share any mailings they receive. Due to this unsatisfied demand, a very small investment can reach many potential end users.

The growing mail-order segment is attracting an increasing number of foreign entrants to markets previously dominated by local firms. However, because consumers are wary of sending orders and money to an unknown company overseas, the key to market penetration is a local address. In Japan, the U.S. outdoor-clothing merchandiser L.L. Bean works through McCann Direct, the specialized direct-marketing division of McCann-Erickson Hakuhodo Inc., Japan's largest foreign advertising agency. L.L. Bean places ads for its catalogues in Japanese media, orders for catalogues are sent to McCann Direct, and McCann Direct then forwards the addresses to L.L. Bean's headquarters in Maine, where all the orders for catalogues or goods are filled.[49] Despite the economic promise of emerging markets such as China, India, and Russia, the development of direct marketing is constrained by negative attitudes toward Western business practices and problems with distribution networks and marketing support systems, as well as bureaucratic obstacles.[50]

In the past, global marketers thought that country-specific offices were almost essential to bringing their companies closer to overseas customers. Now, with functioning telecommunication systems and deregulation in the industry, **telemarketing** (including sales, customer service, and help-desk-related support) is flourishing throughout the world. A growing number of countries in Latin America, Asia, and Europe are experiencing growth in this area as consumers are becoming more accustomed to calling toll-free numbers and more willing to receive calls from marketers.

In Europe, companies using this service publicize their assigned local phone numbers on television or print ads, direct mailings, catalogues, or websites, and then the calls are routed to a call centre. The number and location of such call centres will depend on a variety of issues, such as what the distribution area of the product is, what the fulfillment logistics are, how important local presence is, and how important certain capabilities are, such as language and the ability to handle calls from various time zones.[51] Costa Rica is the choice for Central and Latin American call-centre operations, Australia for the Asia-Pacific, and Singapore for Asia itself, while Belgium, Holland, Ireland, and Portugal are leading locations in Europe (see Exhibit 13.13).[52] If only one centre is used in Europe, for example, access to a multilingual work force is a major factor in selecting the location. When a call comes in, the name of the country in which the call originates is displayed above the switchboard so that it can be taken by an operator who speaks the language(s) native to that country.[53]

Call-centre activity has developed more slowly in Asia than it has in North America and Europe, mostly because of infrastructural reasons and cultural resistance to the new form of communicating with business. However, new technologies are helping to overcome such resistance. **Database marketing** allows the creation of an individual relationship with each customer or prospect. For example, a call-centre operator will know a customer's background with the company or overall purchasing habits.[54] The development of the needed databases through direct mail or the Internet will advance the use of telemarketing. Some global marketers see the use of call centres as a preliminary step to entering an international market with a deeper presence such as a sales office.

Internet

Having a website is seen as necessary if for no other reason than image; lack of a Web presence may convey a negative image to the various constituents of the marketer.[55] The website should be linked to the overall marketing strategy and not just be there for appearance's sake.[56] This means having a well-designed and well-marketed site.[57] Quality is especially critical if customers use the website to find more information or clarification, as triggered by the marketer's other communications efforts, such as advertisements or telemarketing efforts.

Having a Web presence will support the global marketer's marketing communications effort in a number of ways. First, it allows the company to increase its presence in

Exhibit 13.13 An Example of an International Call Centre

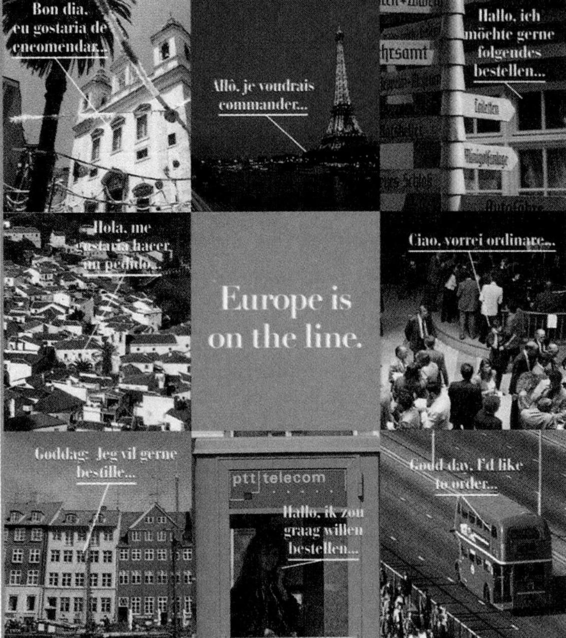

Bon dia. eu gostaria de encomendar...
Allô, je voudrais commander...
Hallo, ich möchte gerne folgendes bestellen...
Hola, me gustaría hacer un pedido...
Europe is on the line.
Ciao, vorrei ordinare...
Goddag: Jeg vil gerne bestille...
ptt telecom
Hallo, ik zou graag willen bestellen...
Good day. I'd like to order...
FOR PAN-EUROPEAN CALL CENTERS, PTT TELECOM HAS THE ANSWER.
Whether you're looking to establish, expand, or enhance your European presence, look to PTT Telecom Netherlands to provide the seamless telecommunications services your company can depend on. Only PTT Telecom Netherlands provides a 99.9% call completion rate, fastest call set-up times, and the lowest call failure rate in all of Europe. We also offer distinct advantages unique to the Netherlands: a highly trained workforce (over 75% of our Call Center agents speak 3 or more languages), and a sophisticated distribution infrastructure (49% of the Fortune 500 companies have European distribution centers located here). In fact, working with our sister KPN companies, we can provide you with cost-effective, seamless solutions for your entire European enterprise. From turnkey call center solutions to invoice and collection services, warehousing, distribution and fulfillment, call 800.777.6842. Find out how PTT Telecom Netherlands can bring Europe together for you.
kpn telecom
A KPN COMPANY
Visit us on the internet. http://www.dutch-tele.com/us/

Source: © Courtesy of KPN.

the marketplace and to communicate its overall mission and information about its marketing mix. Second, the Internet will allow 24-hour access to customers and prospects. Providing important information during decision making can help the customer clarify the search. The potential interactivity of the website (e.g., in providing tailor-made solutions to the customer's concerns) may provide a competitive advantage as the customer compares alternative sites. For example, the website for apparel marketer Lands' End allows consumers to identify their body type and then mix and match clothing items that suit them. Interactivity is also critical when the site is designed, in determining what features to include (e.g., whether sites should adjust to different dialects of a language in a region).

Third, the Internet can improve customer service by allowing customers to serve themselves when and where they choose. This is an area where an exporter's Web presence can reduce overall communications costs in the most significant way. Naturally, the marketer must have the necessary capacity to serve all interested customers through the website, especially if there is an increase in interest and demand. An important dimension of customer service is after-sales service to solve consumer problems and to facilitate the formation of consumer groups. A Web forum where customers can exchange news and views on product use will not only facilitate product research, it also will build loyalty among consumers.

The fourth advantage is the ability of the marketer to gather information, which has its uses not only in research but also in database development for subsequent marketing efforts. While the data collected may be biased, they are also very inexpensive to collect. If the data are used to better cater to existing customers, then data collected through Internet interaction are the best possible.

The fifth advantage of the Internet is the opportunity to actually close sales. This function is within the realm of e-commerce. It will require a significant commitment on the part of the global marketer in terms of investment in infrastructure to deliver not only information but also the product to the customer.

In addition to communications with customers, the Internet provides the possibility to communicate with internal constituents. Marketers may have part of their websites set up with detailed product and price information that only their agents, representatives, or distributors have access to. Especially when changes are called for, this is an efficient way of communicating about them without having to mail or fax each and every overseas party.[58] Websites can also be used in the recruitment of intermediaries and partners. P&D Creative, a manufacturer of environmentally safe cleaning products, uses its site (**http://www.pdcreativeinc.com**) to attract intermediaries. The company promotes its site in search engines and internationally oriented newsgroups and provides information of special interest to intermediaries.

The challenges faced by global marketers in Internet-based communications are related to the newness of the medium and the degree to which adjustments need to be made for each market served. A very large portion of the world population has yet to adopt the Internet, and its users have a distinct profile. In some cases this might match the marketer's intended target market (such as for online music); however, in many cases Internet diffusion has yet to reach the targeted customer.

While English-only websites can deliver information and support to some international customers, having local-language sites and registering with local search engines demonstrate appropriate market and cultural sensitivity. The choice of languages will depend on the target audience. The most popular languages are French, Spanish, German, Japanese, and Chinese. For some, a dialect must be specified; for example, Spanish has three main variants: European, Mexican, and South American. The exporter needs also to determine which pages have to be modified. Pages that emphasize marketing, sales, and corporate identity are normally the ones chosen.[59]

While the exporter's local websites may (and for global product or service offerings, should) be quite similar in terms of aesthetics, adjustments should also be made for such dimensions as depth of product line and level of market presence. Customers who are familiar with the Internet may access information about products and services before purchasing them and may visit sites in several countries. Second-generation technology is increasing the interactivity of advertising on the Web. Given that individuals around the world have different information needs, varying levels of company and product familiarity, and different user capabilities, exporters can adjust their websites' content and develop paths tailored to each group of customers or even to an individual customer. Overall, the incorporation of the Internet into the firm's marketing strategy will enhance market orientation, marketing competence, and eventually marketing performance.[60]

Marketers using the Web as an advertising medium will have to be concerned about market-by-market differences in regulations. For example, Germany sued Benetton for "exploiting feelings of pity" with one of its "United Colors of Benetton" campaigns.[61] Finally, online communications strategy should also include provisions for technological development. For example, a full-colour site with lots of text will not be legible or attractive on the monochrome screens of smart phones using WAP (wireless application protocol) technology, already in use in Northern Europe.

Trade Shows and Missions

Marketing goods and services through trade shows is a European tradition that dates back to A.D. 1240. After sales-force costs, trade shows are one of the most significant cost items in marketing budgets. Although they are usually associated with industrial firms, some consumer-products firms are represented as well. Typically, a trade show is an event at which manufacturers, distributors, and other vendors display their products or describe their services to current and prospective customers, suppliers, other business associates, and the press.[62] The International Automotive Services Industries Show and the International Coal Show, for example, run 8 hours for 3 days, plus 1 or 2 preview days, and register 25,000 attendees. In the consumer-goods area, expositions are the most common type of show. Tickets are usually sold; typical expositions include home/garden, boat, auto, stereo, and antiques.

Whether a marketer should participate in a trade show depends largely on the type of business relationship it wants to develop with a particular country. More than 16,000 trade shows create an annual $50 billion in business worldwide.[63] A company looking only for one-time or short-term sales might find the expense prohibitive, but a firm looking for long-term involvement may find the investment worthwhile. Canadian firms are advised to focus on niche opportunities where they can make a bigger impression rather than focusing on the larger shows where they may not have the visibility.[64] Arguments in favour of participation in trade shows generally include the following:

1. Some products, by their very nature, are difficult to market without providing the potential customer a chance to examine them or see them in action. Trade fairs provide an excellent opportunity to introduce, promote, and demonstrate new products. Auto shows, such as the ones in Detroit, Geneva, and Tokyo, feature "concept" cars to gauge industry and public opinion. Recently, many of these new models have been environmentally friendly, such as being 90 percent recyclable.
2. An appearance at a show produces goodwill and allows for periodic cultivation of contacts. Beyond the impact of displaying specific products, many firms place strong emphasis on "waving the company flag" against competition. This facet also includes morale boosting of the firm's sales personnel and distributors.
3. The opportunity to find an intermediary may be one of the best reasons to attend a trade show. A show is a cost-effective way to solicit and screen candidates to represent the firm, especially in a new market. Copylite Products of Fort Lauderdale used the CeBIT computer-and-automation show in Hannover, Germany, to establish itself in Europe. The result was a distribution centre in Rotterdam and six distributors covering eight countries. Its $40,000 investment in the trade show has reaped millions in new business.[65]
4. Attendance is one of the best ways to contact government officials and decision makers, especially in China. For example, participation in the Chinese Export Commodities Fair, which is held twice a year in Guangzhou, China, is "expected" by the host government.
5. Trade fairs provide an excellent chance for market research and collecting competitive intelligence. The exporter is able to view most rivals at the same time and to test comparative buyer reactions. Trade fairs provide one of the most inexpensive ways of obtaining evaluative data on the effectiveness of a promotional campaign.
6. Marketers are able to reach a sizable number of sales prospects in a brief time period at a reasonable cost per contact. According to research by Hannover Messe, more than 86 percent of all attendees represent buying influences (managers with direct responsibility for purchasing products and services). Of equal significance is the fact that trade show visitors are there because they have a specific interest in the exhibits.[66] Similarly, suppliers can be identified.

On the other hand, the following are among the reasons cited for non-participation in trade fairs:

1. High costs. A marketer can, however, lower the costs by sharing expenses with distributors or representatives. Further, the costs of closing a sale through trade shows are estimated to be much lower than for a sale closed through personal representation.

2. Difficulty in choosing the appropriate trade fairs for participation. This is a critical decision. Because of scarce resources, many firms rely on suggestions from their foreign distributors on which fairs to attend and what specifically to exhibit. Caterpillar, for example, usually allows its foreign dealers to make the selections for themselves. In markets where conditions are more restricted for exporters, such as China, Caterpillar in effect serves as the dealer and thus participates itself.
3. For larger marketing firms with multiple divisions, the problem of coordination. Several divisions may be required to participate in the same fair under the company banner. Similarly, coordination is required with distributors and agents if joint participation is desired, which requires joint planning.

Trade show participation is too expensive to be limited to the exhibit alone. A clear set of promotional objectives would include targeting accounts and attracting them to the show with pre-show promotion using mailings, advertisements in trade journals, or website information. Contests and giveaways are effective in attracting participants to the company's exhibition area. Major customers and attractive prospects often attend, and they should be acknowledged, for example, by arranging for a hospitality suite.[67] Finally, a system is needed to evaluate post-show performance and to track qualified leads.

Global marketers may participate in general or specialized trade shows. General trade fairs are held in Hannover, Germany (see The Global Marketplace 13.3), and Milan, Italy. An example of a specialized one is Retail Solutions, a four-day trade show on store automation held in London. Participants planning to exhibit at large trade shows may elect to do so independently or as part of a national pavilion. For small and medium-sized companies, the benefit of a group pavilion is in both cost and ease of the arrangements. These pavilions are often part of governmental export-promotion programs. Even foreign government assistance may be available; for example, the Japanese External Trade Organization (JETRO) helps non-Japanese companies participate in the country's two largest trade shows.

Other promotional events that the exporter can use are trade missions, seminar missions, solo exhibitions, video/catalogue exhibitions, and virtual trade shows. **Trade missions** can be Canadian specialized trade missions or industry-organized, government-approved (IOGA) trade missions, both of which aim at expanding the sales of Canadian goods and services and the establishment of agencies and representation abroad. The Department of Foreign Affairs and International Trade is actively involved in assistance of both types. **Seminar missions** are events in which 8 to 10 firms are invited to participate in a 1- to 4-day forum, during which the team members conduct generic discussions on technological issues—that is, follow a soft-sell approach. This is followed up by individual meetings with end users, government agencies, research institutions, and other potentially useful contacts. Individual firms may introduce themselves to certain markets by proposing a technical seminar there. Synopses of several alternative proposed lectures, together with company details and the qualifications of the speakers, must be forwarded to the proper body, which will circulate the proposals to interested prospects and coordinate all the arrangements. The major drawback is the time required to arrange such a seminar, which may be as much as a year. **Solo exhibitions** are generally limited to one, or at the most, a few product themes and are held only when market conditions warrant them. **Video/catalogue exhibitions** allow marketers to publicize their products at low cost. They consist of 20 to 35 product presentations on videotapes, each lasting 5 to 10 minutes. They provide the advantage of actually showing the product in use to potential customers. **Virtual trade shows** enable marketers to promote their products and services over the Internet and to have an electronic presence without actually attending a trade show. Trade leads and international sales interests are collected and forwarded by the sponsor to the companies for follow-up. The information stays online for 365 days for a flat fee. The virtual trade zone is promoted heavily at the trade shows, giving buyers at the show a chance to review company information for possible contact.

The Global MARKETPLACE 13.3

At the Fair

CeBIT is the Olympic Games of industrial exposition. With more than 4,000,000 square feet (370,000 square metres) of indoor exhibition space and 7,000 exhibitors, the Hannover-based event is 10 times as large as most trade shows anywhere in the world. It is superbly organized, with its own train station, post office, over 30 restaurants, and 600 permanent staff. While the range of exhibits covers everything available in information technology and communications, the 2003 fair focused particularly on the convergence of technologies. This included, for example, the entire spectrum of digital products for home automation.

© Courtesy of Deutsche Messe AG

The sheer magnitude of the fair and the technology displayed there are impressive but are not necessarily the most significant aspects of the event. Rather, it is the opportunity it presents for people from everywhere in the world to view the latest developments and learn an incredible amount about their potential. Most important, it provides the opportunity to meet hundreds of people who can become invaluable future resources, if not necessarily direct sources of future business. More than 670,000 visitors attended in 2002, including 137,000 from abroad (26,800 from Asia; 9,000 from the Americas; 4,200 from Africa; and 1,800 from the Asia-Pacific region). Over 11,000 journalists from 70 countries cover the event annually.

A total of 7,074 exhibitors from 65 countries booked space for 2003, of which 2,767 (39 percent) were from outside Germany. Asia and Australia constituted 42 percent of the foreign exhibitor contingent. The worldwide participation numbers are significant, especially considering that, in addition to Hannover, regional CeBIT fairs are also available for exhibitors in Istanbul, Long Beach, New York, Shanghai, and Sydney.

For the first time in 2003, the fair was preceded by a summit meeting of the industry's key decision makers and influencers. ICT World Forum @ CeBIT 2003 brought together many of the world's leading players in the information technology and telecommunications industries to discuss new trends and formulate new strategies.

Sources: Press releases available at **http://presse.messe.de**; "Hannover Fair 2002 Delivers as Expected," *Control Engineering* 49 (May 2002): 17; "Hannover's Trade Fair: The Week of the Widget," *The Washington Post*, April 29, 1996, A13; Valerio Giannini, "The Hannover Messe," *Export Today* 9 (July–August 1993): 29–32; **http://www.cebit.de**; and **http://www.ictwf.com**.

Other Promotional Techniques

Sales Promotion

Sales promotion directed at consumers involves such activities as couponing, sampling, premiums, consumer education and demonstration activities, cents-off packs, point-of-purchase materials, and direct mail. The use of sales promotions as alternatives and as support for advertising is increasing worldwide. The appeal is related to several factors: cost and clutter of media advertising, simpler targeting of customers compared with advertising, and easier tracking of promotional effectiveness (for example, coupon returns provide a clear measure of effectiveness).

The success in Latin America of Tang, General Foods' pre-sweetened powdered juice substitute, is for the most part traceable to successful sales promotion efforts. One promotion involved trading Tang pouches for free popsicles from Kibon, General Foods' Brazilian subsidiary. Kibon also placed coupons for free groceries in Tang pouches. In Puerto Rico,

General Foods ran Tang sweepstakes. In Argentina, in-store sampling featured Tang pitchers and girls in orange Tang dresses. Decorative Tang pitchers were a hit throughout Latin America. Sales promotion directed at intermediaries, also known as trade promotion, includes activities such as trade shows and exhibits, trade discounts, and cooperative advertising.

For sales promotion to be effective, the campaign planned by manufacturers, or their agencies, must gain the support of the local retailer population. Coupons from consumers, for example, have to be redeemed and sent to the manufacturer or to the company handling the promotion. AC Nielsen tried to introduce cents-off coupons in Chile and ran into trouble with the nation's supermarket union, which notified its members that it opposed the project and recommended that coupons not be accepted. The main complaint was that an intermediary, like Nielsen, would unnecessarily raise costs and thus the prices to be charged to consumers. Also, some critics felt that coupons would limit individual negotiations because Chileans often bargain for their purchases.

Global marketers are well advised to take advantage of local or regional opportunities. In Brazil, gas delivery people are used to distribute product samples to households by companies such as Nestlé, Johnson & Johnson, and Unilever. The delivery people are usually assigned to the same district for years and have, therefore, earned their clientele's trust. For the marketers, distributing samples this way is not only effective, it is very economical: they are charged five cents for each unit distributed. The gas companies benefit as well in that their relationship with customers is enhanced through these "presents."[68]

Sales promotion tools fall under varying regulations, as can be seen from Exhibit 13.14. A particular level of incentive may be permissible in one market but illegal in another. The Northern European countries present the greatest difficulties in this respect because every promotion has to be approved by a government body. In France, a gift cannot be worth more than 4 percent of the retail value of the product being promoted, making certain promotions virtually impossible. Although competitions are allowed in most of Europe, to insist on receiving proofs of purchase as a condition of entry is not permitted in Germany.

Regulations such as these make truly global sales promotions rare and difficult to launch. Although only a few multinational brands have been promoted on a multi-territory basis, the approach can work. In general, such multi-country promotions may be suitable for products such as soft drinks, liquor, airlines, credit cards, and jeans, which span cultural divides. Naturally, local laws and cultural differences have to be taken into account at the planning stage. Although many of the promotions may be funded centrally, they will be implemented differently in each market so that they can be tied with the local company's other promotional activities. For example, Johnson & Johnson Vision Care offered trials of its one-day Acuvue contact lenses throughout Europe, Africa, and the Middle East. The aim was to deliver the brand message of "Enhancing Everyday Experiences" and encourage consumers to book a sight test. The venue was a road-show event that adapted well to local market conditions. Professional lens fitters offered on-the-spot trials at gyms, sports clubs, and leisure centres. The program was devised and tested in Germany and has since been executed in 18 different countries. The creative materials were translated into 14 languages, and a virtual network using intranets ensured that all offices shared information and best practice.[69]

In Canada, in the province of Quebec advertisers must pay a tax on the value of the prizes they offer in a contest, whether the prize is a trip, money, or a car. The amount of the tax depends on the geographical extent of the contest. If it is open only to residents of Quebec, the tax is 10 percent; if open to all of Canada, 3 percent; if worldwide, 1 percent. Subtle distinctions are drawn in the regulations between a premium and a prize. As an example, the Manic soccer team was involved with both McDonald's and Provigo Food stores. The team offered a dollar off the price of four tickets, and the stubs could be cashed for a special at McDonald's. Provigo was involved in a contest offering a year's supply of groceries. The Manic–McDonald's offer was a premium that involved no special tax; Provigo, however, was taxed because it was involved in a contest. According to the regulation, a premium is available to everyone, whereas a prize is available to a certain number of people among those who participate. In some cases, industries may self-regulate the use of promotional items.

Exhibit 13.14

Regulations Regarding Premiums, Gifts, and Competitions in Selected Countries

Country	Category	No Restrictions or Minor Ones	Authorized with Major Restrictions	General Ban with Important Exceptions	Almost Total Prohibition
Australia	Premiums	X			
	Gifts	X			
	Competitions		X		
Austria	Premiums				X
	Gifts		X		
	Competitions		X		
Canada	Premiums	X			
	Gifts	X			
	Competitions		X		
Denmark	Premiums			X	
	Gifts		X		
	Competitions			X	
France	Premiums	X			
	Gifts	X			
	Competitions	X			
Germany	Premiums				X
	Gifts		X		
	Competitions		X		
Hong Kong	Premiums	X			
	Gifts	X			
	Competitions	X			
Japan	Premiums		X		
	Gifts		X		
	Competitions		X		
Korea	Premiums		X		
	Gifts		X		
	Competitions		X		
United Kingdom	Premiums	X			
	Gifts	X			
	Competitions		X		
United States	Premiums	X			
	Gifts	X			
	Competitions	X			
Venezuela	Premiums		X		
	Gifts		X		
	Competitions		X		

Source: Jean J. Boddewyn, *Premiums, Gifts, and Competitions*, 1988, published by International Advertising Association, 342 Madison Avenue, Suite 2000, NYC, NY 10017. Reprinted with permission.

Public Relations

Image—the way a multinational corporation relates to and is perceived by its key constituents—is a bottom-line issue for management. Public relations is the marketing communications function charged with executing programs to earn public understanding and acceptance, which means both internal and external communication. The function can further be divided into proactive and reactive forms.

Internal Public Relations

Especially in multinational corporations, internal communication is important to create an appropriate corporate culture.[70] The Japanese have perfected this in achieving a *wa* ("we") spirit. Everyone in an organization is, in one way or another, in marketing and will require additional targeted information on issues not necessarily related to his or her day-to-day functions. A basic part of most internal programs is the employee publication produced and edited typically by the company's public relations or advertising department and usually provided in both hard-copy and electronic formats. Some have foreign-language versions. More often, as at ExxonMobil, each affiliate publishes its own employee publication. The better this vehicle can satisfy the information needs of employees, the less they will have to rely on others, especially informal sources such as the grapevine. Audio-visual media in the form of e-mails, films, videotapes, slides, and videoconferencing are being used, especially for training and indoctrination purposes. Some of the materials that are used internally can be provided to other publics as well; for example, booklets, manuals, and handbooks are provided to employees, distributors, and visitors to the company.

External Public Relations

External public relations (also known as marketing public relations) is focused on interactions with customers. In the *proactive* context, marketers are concerned about establishing global identities to increase sales, differentiate products and services, and attract employees. These activities have been seen as necessary to compete against companies with strong local identities. External campaigns can be achieved through the use of corporate symbols, corporate advertising, customer relations programs, and publicity. For example, Black & Decker's corporate logo, which is in the shape and colour of an orange hexagon, is used for all B&D products. Specific brand books are developed to guide marketing personnel worldwide on the proper use of these symbols to ensure a consistent global image.

Unanticipated developments in the marketplace can place the company in a position that requires *reactive* public relations, including anticipating and countering criticism. The criticisms range from general ones against all multinational corporations to more specific ones. They may be based, for example, on a market doing business with prison factories in China. Or they may concern a product: for example, Nestlé's practice of advertising and promoting infant formula in developing countries where infant mortality is unacceptably high. They may centre on conduct in a given situation, such as Union Carbide's perceived lack of response in the Bhopal disaster. The key concern is that, if not addressed, these criticisms can lead to more significant problems, such as the internationally orchestrated boycott of Nestlé's products. The 6-year boycott did not so much harm earnings as it harmed image and employee morale.

Crisis management is becoming more formalized in companies, with specially assigned task forces ready to step in if problems arise. In general, companies must adopt policies that will allow them to effectively respond to pressure and criticism, which will continue to surface. Crisis management policies should have the following traits: (1) openness about corporate activities, with a focus on how these activities enhance social and economic performance; (2) preparedness to utilize the tremendous power of the multinational corporation in a responsible manner and, in the case of pressure, to counter criticisms swiftly; (3) integrity, which often means that the marketer must avoid not only actual wrongdoing but the mere appearance of it; and (4) clarity, which will help ameliorate hostility if a common language is used with those pressuring the corporation.[71] The marketer's role is one of enlightened self-interest; reasonable critics understand that the marketer cannot compromise the bottom line.

Complicating the situation often is the fact that groups in one market criticize what the marketer is doing in another market. For example, Levi Strauss decided to withdraw from $40-million worth of production contracts in China after consultations with a variety of sources, including human rights organizations, experts on China, and representatives of the U.S. government, led it to conclude that there was pervasive abuse of human rights.[72]

The public relations function can be handled in-house or with the assistance of an agency. The use and extent of public relations activity will vary by company and the type of activity needed. Product-marketing PR may work best with a strong component of control at the local level and a local PR firm, while crisis management—given the potential for worldwide adverse impact—will probably be controlled principally from a global centre.[73] This has meant that global marketers funnel short-term projects to single offices for their local expertise while maintaining contact with the global agencies for their worldwide reach when a universal message is needed. Some multinational corporations maintain public relations staffs in their main offices around the world, while others use the services of firms such as Burson-Marsteller, Hill and Knowlton, and Porter Novelli on specific projects.

Publicity

Publicity, in particular, is of interest to the multinational corporation. Publicity is the securing of editorial space (as opposed to paid advertising) to further marketing objectives. Because it is editorial in content, the consuming public perceives it as more trustworthy than advertising. A good example of how publicity can be used to aid in advertising efforts was the introduction by Princess Lines of a new liner, the *Royal Princess.* Because of its innovative design and size, the *Royal Princess* was granted substantial press coverage, which was especially beneficial in the travel and leisure magazines. Such coverage does not come automatically but has to be coordinated and initiated by the public relations staff of the company.

Sponsorship Marketing

Sponsorship involves the marketer's investment in events or causes. Sponsorship funds worldwide are directed for the most part at sports events (both individual and team sports) and cultural events (both in the popular and high-culture categories). Sponsorship spending is relatively even around the world: of the nearly $25 billion spent in 2002, North America contributed $9.6, Europe $7.1, Asia-Pacific $4.3, and Latin America $2.1 billion.[74] Bombardier, for example, has sponsored numerous sporting events since 1997. In 2002, the company became a sponsor of the Indianapolis Motor Speedway, signing a 5-year agreement that gave it the naming rights to the landmark Pagoda control tower at the speedway. Since 2005, the company has also sponsored the Canadian Alpine ski team, launching an eye-catching ad campaign to showcase its involvement (Exhibit 13.15).

Other examples include Coca-Cola's sponsorship of the 2004 Olympic Games in Athens and MasterCard's sponsorship of World Cup Soccer in 2002 in Japan and South Korea, as well as Visa's sponsorship of Eric Clapton's tour and Ford's sponsorship of the Montreux Detroit Jazz Festival. Sponsorship of events such as the Olympics is driven by the desire to be associated with a worldwide event that has a positive image, global reach, and a proven strategic positioning of excellence.

The challenge is that an event may become embroiled in controversy, thus hurting the sponsors' images as well. Furthermore, in light of the high expense of sponsorship, marketers worry about **ambush marketing** by competitors. Ambush marketing is the unauthorized use of an event without the permission of the event owner. For example, an advertising campaign could suggest a presumed sponsorship relationship. During the Atlanta Olympic Games in 1996, some of the sponsors' competitors garnered a higher profile than the sponsors themselves. For example, Pepsi erected stands outside venues and plastered the town with signs. Nike secured substantial amounts of airtime on radio and TV stations. Fuji bought billboards on the route from the airport into downtown Atlanta. None of the three contributed anything to the International Olympic Committee during this time.[75]

Cause-related marketing, as discussed earlier, is a combination of public relations, sales promotion, and corporate philanthropy. This activity should not be developed merely as a response to a crisis, nor should it be a fuzzy, piecemeal effort to generate publicity; instead, marketers should have a social vision and a planned long-term social policy. For example, in Casanare, Colombia, where it is developing oil interests, British Petroleum invests in activities that support its business plan and contribute to the region's development. This has meant an investment of $10 million in setting up a loan fund for entrepreneurs, giving students technical training, supporting a centre for pregnant women and nursing mothers, working on reforestation, building aqueducts, and helping to create jobs outside the oil industry.[76]

Exhibit 13.15

Canadian Alpine Ski Team

"That's a Bombardier."
Bombardier is a sponsor of the Canadian alpine ski team. And we're proud of it.
BOMBARDIER

Source: Reprinted with permission from Bombardier, Inc.

Summary

Effective and efficient communication is needed for the dual purpose of (1) informing prospective customers about the availability of products or services and (2) persuading customers to opt for the marketer's offering over those of competitors. Within the framework of the company's opportunities, resources, and objectives, decisions must be made about whether to direct communications to present customers, potential customers, the general public, or intermediaries. Decisions must be made on how to reach each of the intended target audiences without wasting valuable resources. A decision also has to be made about who will control the communications effort: the global marketer, an agency, or local representatives.

The global marketer must also choose tools to use in the communications effort. Usually mass selling through business and trade journals, direct mail, the Internet, trade shows, and trade missions are used to bring the global marketer face to face with the targeted customer. As multinational corporations manage the various elements of the promotions mix in differing environmental conditions, decisions must be made about channels to be used in communication, the message, who is to execute or help execute the program, and how the success of the endeavour is to be measured. The trend is toward more harmonization of strategy, at the same time allowing for flexibility at the local level and early incorporation of local needs into the promotional plans.

The effective implementation of the promotional program is a key ingredient in the marketing success of the firm. The promotional tools must be used within the opportunities and constraints posed by the communications channels as well as by the laws and regulations governing marketing communications. Advertising agencies are key facilitators in communicating with the firm's constituent groups. Many multinational corporations are realigning their accounts worldwide in an attempt to streamline their promotional efforts and achieve a global approach.

The use of other promotional tools tends to be more localized to fit the conditions of the individual markets. An area of increasing challenge to multinational corporations is public relations. Multinationals, by their very design, draw attention to their activities. The best interest of the marketer lies in anticipating problems with both internal and external constituencies and managing them, through communications, to the satisfaction of all parties.

Key Terms

ambush marketing (p. 475)
cause-related marketing (p. 447)
corporate image advertising (p. 447)
database marketing (p. 466)
global media (p. 453)
integrated marketing communications (p. 446)
product placement (p. 453)
promotional mix (p. 446)
pull strategies (p. 446)
push strategies (p. 446)
seminar missions (p. 470)
solo exhibitions (p. 470)
telemarketing (p. 466)
trade missions (p. 470)
video/catalogue exhibitions (p. 470)
virtual trade shows (p. 470)

Questions for Discussion

1. What is potentially harmful in going out of one's way to make clients feel comfortable by playing down status distinctions such as titles?
2. Compare and contrast the usefulness of elements of the promotional mix to a novice exporter.
3. Some exporters report that they value above all the broad exposure afforded through exhibiting at a trade show, regardless of whether they are able to sell directly at the event. Comment on this philosophy.
4. MasterCard sponsors the World Cup and Visa the Olympics. Who gets the "better deal," since the expense of sponsorship is about the same for both?
5. Comment on the opinion that "practically speaking, neither an entirely standardized nor an entirely localized advertising approach is necessarily best."
6. What type of adjustments must advertising agencies make as more companies want "one sight, one sound, one sell" campaigns?
7. Assess the programmed management approach for coordinating international advertising efforts.
8. Discuss problems associated with measuring advertising effectiveness in foreign markets.
9. Is international personal selling a reality? Or is all personal selling national, regardless of who performs it?

Internet Exercises

1. The FIFA World Cup is a marketing platform from which Canadian companies can create awareness, enhance their image, and foster goodwill. FIFA offers sponsors a multitude of ways to promote themselves and their products in conjunction with the FIFA World Cup as well as other FIFA events. Using FIFA's website (**http://www.fifa.com**), assess the different ways a sponsor can benefit from this association. Also assess FIFA's efforts to curb ambush marketing.

2. A company wishing to pursue global markets using the Internet should ensure that its regional and local websites are consistent with its home country website and of the same calibre. Visit the Bombardier corporate website (**http://corp.brp.com/**) and determine if its various international sites satisfy those criteria.

Recommended Readings

Anholt, Simon. *Another One Bites the Grass: Making Sense of International Advertising.* New York: John Wiley & Sons, 2000.

Bly, Robert W. *Advertising Manager's Handbook.* New York: Aspen Publishers, 2002.

Burnett, Leo. *Worldwide Advertising and Media Fact Book.* Chicago, IL: Triumph Books, 1994.

De Mooij, Marieke K. *Global Marketing and Advertising: Understanding Cultural Paradoxes.* San Francisco: Sage Publications, 1997.

Grey, Anne-Marie, and Kim Skildum-Reid. *The Sponsorship Seeker's Toolkit.* New York: McGraw-Hill, 1999.

Handbook of International Direct and E-Marketing. London: Kogan Page Ltd., 2001.

Hendon, Donald W., Rebecca A. Hendon, and Paul Herbig. *Cross-Cultural Business Negotiations.* New York: Praeger, 1999.

Hodge, Sheida. *Global Smarts: The Art of Communicating and Deal Making Anywhere in the World.* New York: John Wiley and Sons, 2000.

Jagoe, John R., and Agnes Brown. *Export Sales and Marketing Manual.* Washington, DC: Export Institute, 2001.

Jones, John Philip. *International Advertising: Realities and Myths.* San Francisco: Sage Publications, 1999.

Monye, Sylvester O. *The Handbook of International Marketing Communications.* Malden, MA: Blackwell Publishers, 2000.

Moses, Elissa. *The $100 Billion Allowance: How to Get Your Share of the Global Teen Market.* New York: John Wiley and Sons, 2000.

Niefeld, Jaye S. *The Making of an Advertising Campaign: The Silk of China.* Englewood Cliffs, NJ: Prentice Hall, 1989.

Peebles, Dean M., and John K. Ryans. *Management of International Advertising: A Marketing Approach.* Boston: Allyn & Bacon, 1984.

Reedy, Joel, Shauna Schullo, and Kenneth Zimmerman. *Electronic Marketing.* Mason, OH: South-Western, 2003.

Roberts, Mary-Lou, and Robert D. Berger. *Direct Marketing Management.* Englewood Cliffs, NJ: Prentice Hall, 1999.

Schultz, Don E., and Philip J. Kitchen. *Communicating Globally: An Integrated Marketing Approach.* New York: McGraw-Hill, 2000.

Schuster, Camille P., and Michael J. Copeland. *Global Business: Planning for Sales and Negotiations.* Mason, OH: International Thomson Publishing, 1997.

Shimp, Terence A. *Advertising, Promotion, and Supplemental Aspects of Integrated Marketing Communications.* Mason, OH: South-Western, 2003.

Tussie, Diane, ed. *The Environment and International Trade Negotiations.* London: St. Martin's Press, 1999.

Zeff, Robbin Lee, and Brad Aronson. *Advertising on the Internet.* New York: John Wiley and Sons, 1999.

Zenith Media. *Advertising Expenditure Forecasts.* London: Zenith Media, December 2002.

Zimmerman, Jan, and Hoon Meng Ong. *Marketing on the Internet.* New York: Maximum Press, 2002.

Notes

1. Wilbur Schramm and Donald F. Roberts, *The Process and Effects of Mass Communications* (Urbana: University of Illinois Press, 1971), 12–17.
2. Carl Arthur Sohlberg, "The Perennial Issue of Adaptation or Standardization of International Marketing Communication: Organizational Contingencies and Performance," *Journal of International Marketing* 10, no. 3 (2002): 1–21.
3. "TBWA/Chiat/Day to Serve Competing Spirits Giants," *Advertising Age*, April 8, 2002, 45.

4. "2002 State of the Industry Report," *Beverage Industry*, June 2002, 38–40.

5. Gary Levin, "Russian Vodka Plans U.S. Rollout," *Advertising Age*, November 11, 1991, 4.

6. Lara Sowinski, "Breaking All the Rules," *World Trade*, May 2002, 16–19. See also **http://www.ernieball.com.**

7. Framework adapted from Dean M. Peebles and John K. Ryans, *Management of International Advertising: A Marketing Approach* (Boston: Allyn & Bacon, 1984), 72–73.

8. MADD Canada, **http://www.madd.ca/english/donating/causerelated.html.**

9. "Why P&G Is Linking Brands to Good Causes," *Marketing*, August 26, 1999, 11; and "Microsoft's Singapore Site Ties Page Views to Charity," *Advertising Age International*, October 1999, 4.

10. "The Material Years 1982–1992," *Marketing*, July 4, 2002, 22–23.

11. See **http://www.amrcorp.com.**

12. "Corporate Campaigns Attract Bigger Slices of Advertising Pie," *Advertising Age International*, March 8, 1999, 2.

13. Robert E. Hite and Cynthia Fraser, "International Advertising Strategies of Multinational Corporations," *Journal of Advertising Research* 28 (August–September 1988): 9–17.

14. William J. Holstein, "Canon Takes Aim at Xerox," *Fortune*, October 14, 2002, 215–20.

15. Paula Andruss, "FedEx Kicks Up Brand through Humor," *Marketing News*, July 30, 2001, 4–5.

16. Chris Powell, "Are Countries Brands?" *Advertising Age Global*, December 2001, 5.

17. Ira Tenowitz, "Beers Draws Mixed Reviews after One Year," *Advertising Age*, September 23, 2002, 3, 57.

18. J. Enrique Bigne, "Advertising Budget Practices: A Review," *Journal of Current Issues and Research in Advertising* 17 (Fall 1995): 17–32.

19. Advertising Age's 20th Annual Global Marketers, **http://adage.com/datacenter/article?article_id=114009.**

20. "Signs of Recovery," *Zenith Optimedia*, December 9, 2002, **http://www.zenithmedia.com.**

21. Compiled from Leo Burnett, *Worldwide Advertising and Media Fact Book* (Chicago: Triumph Books, 1994).

22. See **http://www.iccwbo.org/home/statements_rules/rules/1997/advercod.asp.**

23. Ross D. Petty, "Advertising Law in the United States and European Union," *Journal of Public Policy and Marketing* 16 (Spring 1997): 2–13.

24. See **http://en.wikipedia.org/wiki/Tobacco_advertising** (accessed November 20, 2006).

25. See **http://www.newash.org.uk/.**

26. "Pushing Pills: In Europe, Prescription-Drug Ads Are Banned," *The Wall Street Journal*, March 15, 2002, B1.

27. Pola B. Gupta and Kenneth R. Lord, "Product Placement in Movies: The Effect of Prominence and Mode on Audience Recall," *Journal of Current Issues and Research in Advertising* 20 (Spring 1998): 47–60.

28. Allyson Stewart-Allen, "Product Placement Helps Sell Brand," *Marketing News*, February 15, 1999, 8.

29. "Chinese TV Discovers Product Placement," *The Wall Street Journal*, January 26, 2000, B12.

30. Hank Kim, "Madison Avenue Melds Pitches and Content," *Advertising Age*, October 7, 2002, 1, 14–16.

31. "Canada Moves toward New Laws on Magazines," *Advertising Age International*, January 11, 1999, 29.

32. "Global Media," *Advertising Age International*, February 8, 1999, 23.

33. Benjamin Compaine, "Global Media," *Foreign Policy*, November–December 2002, 20–28.

34. "Marketers Take New Look at Trying Panregional TV," *Advertising Age International*, March 30, 1999, 2.

35. David W. Stewart and Kevin J. McAuliffe, "Determinants of International Media Buying," *Journal of Advertising* 17 (Fall 1988): 22–26.

36. "The Internet," *Advertising Age International*, June 1999, 42.

37. "Unilever, Microsoft in European Net Deal," *The Wall Street Journal*, February 2, 2000, B8.

38. "Global Marketing Campaigns with a Local Touch," *Business International*, July 4, 1988, 205–10.

39. Jae H. Pae, Saeed Samiee, and Susan Tai, "Global Advertising Strategy: The Moderating Role of Brand Familiarity and Execution Style," *International Marketing Review* 19, no. 2 (2002): 176–89.

40. "So What Was the Fuss About?" *The Economist*, June 22, 1996, 59–60.

41. "Centralization," *Advertising Age International*, June 1999, 40.

42. *Global Vision* (New York: Ogilvy & Mather, 1994), 8; see also **http://www.ogilvy.com.**

43. Debra A. Williamson, "ARF to Spearhead Study on Measuring Web Ads," *Advertising Age*, February 10, 1997, 8; and Gerard J. Tellis and Doyle L. Weiss, "Does TV Advertising Really Affect Sales? The Role of Measures, Models, and Data Aggregation," *Journal of Advertising* 24 (Fall 1995): 1–12.

44. Joseph T. Plummer, "The Role of Copy Research in Multinational Advertising," *Journal of Advertising Research* 26 (October–November 1986): 11–15.

45. S. Okazaki, C. Taylor, and S. Zou, "Advertising Standardization's Positive Impact on the Bottom Line," *Journal of Advertising* 35, no. 3 (Fall 2006): 17–33.

46. Sean Callahan, "McCann-Erickson Offers B-to-B Clients the World," *Business Marketing*, January 2000, 35.

47. *The Handbook of International Direct and E-Marketing* (London: Kogan Page, 2001), chap. 1.

48. Hope Katz Gibbs, "Mediums for the Message," *Export Today* 15 (June 1999): 22–27.

49. Deborah Begum, "U.S. Retailers Find Mail-Order Happiness in Japan," *World Trade* 13 (May 1996): 22–25.

50. William McDonald, "International Direct Marketing in a Rapidly Changing World," *Direct Marketing* 61 (March 1999): 44–47.

51. Hope Katz Gibbs, "It's Your Call," *Export Today* 13 (May 1997): 46–51. For examples, see Brendan Reid, "Call Center Showcase," *Call Center Magazine* 15 (March 2002): 40–41.

52. Sam Bloomfield, "Reach Out and Touch Someone Far, Far Away," *World Trade*, April 1999, 80–84.

53. Roger Hickey, "Toll-Free Europe: Continental Call Centers," *Export Today* 11 (January 1995): 20–21.

54. Rolf Rykken, "Call Waiting?" *Export Today* 14 (November 1998): 55–57.

55. For a discussion on marketing on the Internet, see K. Douglas Hoffman, Michael R. Czinkota, Peter R. Dickson, Patrick Dunne, Abbie Griffith, Michael D. Hutt, John H. Lindgren, Robert F. Lusch, Ilkka A. Ronkainen, Bert Rosenbloom, Jagdish N. Sheth, Terence A. Shimp, Judy A. Siguaw, Penny M. Simpson, Thomas W. Speh, and Joel E. Urbany, *Marketing: Best Practices* (Mason, OH: South-Western, 2003), chap. 15.

56. C. Farrell and M. Han, "Incorporating the Internet into International Marketing Strategy," Proceedings International Business Division, ASAC 2004.

57. P. Rajan Varadarajan and Manjit Yadav, "Marketing Strategy and the Internet," *Academy of Marketing Science* 30 (Fall 2002): 296–312.

58. Carl R. Jacobsen, "How Connecticut Companies Use the Internet for Exporting," *Business America*, January 1998, 17.

59. Gerry Dempsey, "A Hands-On Guide for Multilingual Web Sites," *World Trade*, September 1999, 68–70.

60. V. Kanti Prasad, K. Ramamurthy, and G.M. Naidu, "The Influence of Internet-Marketing Integration on Marketing Competencies and Export Performance," *Journal of International Marketing* 9, no. 4 (2001): 82–110.

61. Lewis Rose, "Before You Advertise on the Net—Check the International Marketing Laws," *Bank Marketing*, May 1996, 40–42.

62. Thomas V. Bonoma, "Get More Out of Your Trade Shows," *Harvard Business Review* 61 (January–February 1983): 137–45.

63. Kathleen V. Schmidt, "Trading Plätze," *Marketing News*, July 19, 1999, 11.

64. ExportSource, "Trade Shows for Exporters" **http://www.exportsource.ca/gol/exportsource/site.nsf/en/es02431.html.**

65. Richard B. Golik, "The Lure of Foreign Trade Shows," *International Business*, March 1996, 16–20.

66. See **http://www.messe.de/** for "Trade Shows as a B2B Communication Tool."

67. Bob Lamons, "Involve Your Staff in Trade Shows for Better Results," *Marketing News*, March 1, 1999, 9–10.

68. "Fuel and Freebies," *The Wall Street Journal*, June 10, 2002, B1, B6.

69. Robert McLuhan, "Face to Face with Global Consumers," *Marketing*, August 22, 2002, 34.

70. Tim R. V. Davis, "Integrating Internal Marketing with Participative Management," *Management Decision* 39, no. 2 (2001): 121–38.

71. Oliver Williams, "Who Cast the First Stone?" *Harvard Business Review* 62 (September–October 1984): 151–60.

72. C. Miller, "Levi's to Sever Link with China; Critics Contend It's Just a PR Move," *Marketing News*, June 7, 1993, 10.

73. Michael Carberry, "Global Public Relations," keynote speech at Public Relations Association of Puerto Rico's Annual Convention, San Juan, September 17, 1993.

74. Data by IEG made available in "Event/Sponsorships," *Marketing News*, July 8, 2002, 23.

75. "Olympic Torch Burns Sponsors' Fingers," *Financial Times*, December 13, 1999, 6.

76. Bradley K. Googins, "Why Community Relations Is a Strategic Imperative," *Strategy and Business* 2 (3rd quarter, 1997): 64–67.

Chapter 14

Management of the Global Sales Force

The Global MARKETPLACE 14.1

Why Personal Selling Matters to Canadian Companies

The Canadian business press frequently publishes accounts of exporting success stories, telling how Canadian companies have succeeded in penetrating world markets. Often, and quite rightly, these stories make much of the technological advances the companies have achieved, advances which lie at the heart of market success. In addition, much is often made, and again quite rightly, of the contribution of government agencies such as Export Development Canada (EDC) in providing the companies with often quite strikingly imaginative financial solutions. These can be critical in closing particular deals.

But global business does not just "happen." Potential customers have to be located; those responsible for influencing and deciding on the purchase must be identified and contacted; the benefits of the product or service—though probably obvious to the Canadian supplier—must be demonstrated to a perhaps skeptical and culturally-unfamiliar audience; questions and objections need to be listened to and answered so that a perception of competitive superiority is established; and ultimately the deal needs to be closed and order papers signed.

Whether conducted by someone called a "salesperson" or by members of higher management, these activities inevitably demand a high proportion of selling functions calling for the exercise of a whole gamut of research and face-to-face interactions. In many foreign markets, they may take place over a prolonged period of time. For example, RVA Aerospace Systems, located in Orangeville, Ontario, which produces and markets advanced flight inspection systems for global markets, found that it took 8 years to secure its largest contract, worth more than $5 million, with the government of China. This is expected to lead to future sales in the region, but it was also RVA's "biggest challenge to date" involving prolonged negotiation, persistence, and patience.

In light of such cases, it is all the more surprising that the importance of personal selling to Canadian companies is not more widely acknowledged and publicized. But in at least one instance, this importance is fully recognized. This relates, probably unexpectedly, to the geophysics industry and will be of much interest to a Canadian audience, given the importance of the energy industry to the country. In this case, a publication of the Society of Exploration Geophysicists notes that over the past 20 years it has "covered pioneers, wild-catters, innovators, etc. who played key roles in transforming the energy business through the development and employment of advanced geophysical technologies. *However, one group of professions that gets little respect are the salespeople* [authors' italics]. They provide an important link between the developers and end-users. Service companies have always had to stay ahead of the technology curve to remain in business. Thus, these companies relied on their sales staff to be on the front line to sell technical services to the independents and major oil companies."

Today, a growing percentage of the sales staff working for these service companies are former geophysicists, trained by exploration and production (E and P) companies, who have struggled to make the transition from their former technical roles to sales positions. They face a daunting task. The global energy business employs high-calibre professionals with advanced education and training. It is very challenging to develop the most appropriate selling strategies for each independent or major oil company, because their needs reflect different exploration and production goals. Appropriate strategies demand that the salesperson fully understand their needs and what solutions can be offered. Once a sale is made, however, and the salesperson continues to deliver consistently superior results, he or she may eventually participate in the customer's E and P program, a gratifying result for the seller.

The E and P business is high risk. To address this issue, E and P companies have formed multidisciplinary teams to maximize employees' productivity. Geophysical service companies have responded by utilizing a team effort in sales. This has become necessary because it has become apparent that the decision-making process will typically involve a committee, composed of geophysicists, geologists, and even petroleum engineers, that will make the final recommendation. The service company's sales team needs to win the support of everyone to stand a chance of being awarded the project. In addition, the geophysical technology has become technically complex. As a result, sales teams need to be complemented by expert technologists to assist in analyzing the customer's challenges, provide appropriate solutions, and thoroughly answer their technical questions.

Canada takes pride in the global success of its high-tech and services companies. These companies cover a variety of products and technologies and are therefore not mirror images of geophysics services companies. Nevertheless, many Canadian global managers will easily recognize and relate to the sales challenges of their counterparts in the oil business. Being on the cutting edge of technological advances is fundamental to penetrating new foreign markets. Success stories testify to Canadians' ability to meet technological challenges worldwide in different fields. However, the role of the sales force is critical, too, but is often unheralded and unsung. It should not be, as the geophysics case demonstrates.

Sources: Toby Herscovitch, "Export Success Stories," *Exportwise*, Winter 2007, 4–5; Lawrence M. Gochioco, "Sales and Salesmanship in Geophysics," *The Learning Edge* 22, no. 5 (May 2003): 442–46.

Personal selling, unlike advertising or sales promotion, involves direct relations between the seller and the prospective buyer or customer. Its important role in the firm's marketing is underlined in The Global Marketplace 14.1. Personal selling can be defined as a two-way flow of communication between a potential buyer and a salesperson that is designed to accomplish at least three tasks: (1) identify the buyer's needs; (2) match these needs to one or more of the firm's products; and (3), on the basis of this match, convince the buyer to purchase the product. The personal selling element of the promotion mix can encompass a variety of interactions between a salesperson and a potential buyer, including face-to-face, telephone, and written contacts, but also includes interactions facilitated by electronic communications, and newer means such as videoconferencing.

For many firms, the success of their marketing efforts, both at home and overseas, depends on the ability of the sales force to contact customers and secure orders. However, the development of a stable, productive, and motivated sales force does not happen automatically. Selling is not a single, homogeneous activity; one kind of sales work (e.g., door-to-door canvassing) calls for a radically different type of person from another (e.g., sale of advanced information technology). Also, salespeople must be trained, coached, and managed in different ways if they are to be effective in helping the company to meet its goals.

A firm's salespeople are employed to persuade others to purchase, for themselves or on behalf of their organizations, the products, services, or ideas that it sells. For most salespeople, this task is carried out in an unsupervised, socially lonely environment in diverse foreign cultures, with reliance on carefully crafted sales techniques that may often fail. Frequent customer resistance or outright refusal to buy erodes both faith in the techniques and the salesperson's morale. Therefore most sales forces and individual salespeople need ongoing sales training, motivation, and firm leadership. It is the task of sales management to orchestrate these management techniques in order to multiply sales through individual and collective effort.

The role of personal selling is greatest when the company sells directly to the end user or to governmental agencies, such as foreign trade organizations. Firms selling products with high price tags (e.g., Bombardier's jet aircraft) or companies selling to monopsonies (e.g., Seagram selling liquor to certain Northern European countries, where all liquor sales are through state-controlled outlets) must rely heavily on person-to-person communication, oral presentations, and direct-marketing efforts. Many of these firms can expand their business only if their markets are knowledgeable about what they do. This may require corporate advertising and publicity generation through extensive public relations efforts.

This chapter examines the process of personal selling in the international context; it also explores the role of sales management in planning, implementing, and controlling the sales force. As a precursor to these discussions, the chapter examines the implications of viewing the sales force from a company-resource or transaction-cost point of view. It then shows how the sales process is influenced by the degree of internationalization of the firm. It examines the critical issues of sales-force size, geographical dispersion, and the question of own versus contract sales force. In addition, the chapter reviews a variety of implementation issues including sales-force recruitment, selection, training, motivation, and compensation. The chapter also considers problems of sales-force control, including the role of automation, and concludes by looking at the role of expatriates in global sales forces.

The Sales Force as a Company Resource

Among the various resources that can be owned by firms, marketing resources have been recognized as a crucial subset.[1] Therefore, for some firms, acquisition of other companies may be regarded as a means of capturing new marketing resources, such as a sales force, that have been difficult to develop internally.[2] Sales forces contribute significantly to the development and maintenance of marketing relationships. The strategic value of these relationships is widely recognized.[3]

Conceptualizing the sales force as an actual or potential company resource depends heavily on what has come to be called the "resource-based" view of the firm. This view has found considerable support in strategy literature, in which it was first introduced.[4] Proponents of this view see the successful firm as a "bundle" of somewhat unique resources and capabilities. If the company's core capabilities are scarce, durable, defensible, or hard to imitate, and if they can be closely aligned with the key success factors of target markets, they can form the basis of sustainable competitive advantage and profit. The central focus of the approach is on developing those capabilities, including the sales force, that will be effective in various possible market segments and in several different possible futures. Notice the contrast in this view with that of the "marketing concept," which has traditionally seen the market as the starting point for guiding resource-development decisions.

The interest of marketing specialists in the resource-based view is more recent.[5] Marketers, however, have long been interested in specific resources and organizational capabilities, as seen in the long-standing debate on the influence of so-called market orientation on performance differences between competing firms.[6] However, there is a strong connection between this particular debate and resource-based approaches, in that "orientation" of the firm will be managerially or internally driven, not driven by external market forces. Marketers are also increasingly recognizing the value of developing and maintaining marketing relationships, in part through sales-force contributions.

However, using the sales force as a resource to create long-lasting competitive advantages is far from easy, because the maintenance of complex buyer-seller connections needs team-selling approaches and an ability to span functional and divisional boundaries.[7] Not all companies possess this capability. It is not difficult to see how these problems will be compounded when dealing with customers on a global scale. As firms pursue the strengthening of their customer relationships, the social complexity of the team selling function is bound to increase.[8] This in turn confers a uniqueness on the individual firm's sales organization that competitors will find difficult to copy or emulate.[9]

The Resource-Based View and Company Resources

As we noted above, the **resource-based view** of the firm is concerned with the efficient utilization of a company's resources and capabilities. In addition, the development of capabilities is also a concern, because competing successfully in the global marketplace calls for a complex set of skills, including selling and inter-company relational capabilities. A robust and sustainable advantage may require a firm to operate in different markets in order to develop various different though associated capabilities and thus benefit from the idiosyncratic skills rooted in the particular country. For example, a Canadian firm's presence in a country such as the U.S. or Germany may be partially explained by a desire to remain at the forefront of technological development in pharmaceuticals or advanced manufacturing. Of course this process will also work in reverse, with some firms choosing to set up in Canada in order to benefit from Canadian expertise in, for example, transportation.[10]

In contrast to the resource-based view is the **transaction-cost approach** (see Chapter 2) based on the notion that, because markets (not resources) preexist or are a natural starting point, transactions should be the basic unit of analysis. With regard to exporting, for example, the most appropriate forms of entry can be considered in light of their transaction costs.[11] Following this argument, firms involved with **direct exports** can either contract exporting arrangements to third parties or conduct these themselves. As we have seen, transaction-cost analysis suggests that the most appropriate governance structure for exporting (direct or indirect) will depend on the transactions costs involved in carrying out these tasks.

This approach has its critics, who maintain, for example, that it downplays the production side and production costs. Also, it raises dilemmas for international marketers: a decision to beef up the sales force may, from one point of view, be welcomed as resource-enhancing, but from another, be seen as an undesirable increase in transaction costs. In the future, attempts to integrate the resource-based and transaction-cost approaches can be expected.[12] It is also pertinent to add that any decision to enter foreign markets or to expand within them will run into the question of how to treat any increments in transaction costs. Taking a cost-minimizing view will at the least lead to a rigorous questioning of any proposed addition to sales resources, as well as pleas for cost control (not to be despised in general, of course), which will in turn influence the level of international involvement the firm chooses.

It is worth bearing in mind that even a minor incursion into the international market, such as responding to an unsolicited overseas order, can bring with it surprising and unexpected costs, not all of which, of course, can be neatly categorized as transaction costs. Incremental costs will include consultations with financial service providers (to arrange finance); research costs (to determine the extent of export and import regulations, for example, for packaging and labelling); due diligence costs; preparation of export documentation; and transportation, insurance, and customs costs.[13] The company faces the decision of whether incurring the costs is "worth it" in terms of profitability and future potential for growth.

Personal Selling and the Degree of Internationalization of the Firm

Personal selling is the most effective of the promotional tools available to the marketer; however, its costs per contact are high. The average cost of sales calls may vary from \$200 to \$1,100, depending on the industry and the product or service. Personal selling allows for immediate feedback on customer reaction as well as information on markets.

The sales force forms part of any company's global marketing mix. As such, it will be found in operation in a wide range of circumstances, from the large multi-national organization to the smallest, beginning exporter. It will play a vital role in helping the firm to enter new foreign markets, either directly or through partnership with other companies at home or abroad. Also, strategic alliances, one of the simplest ways to penetrate new markets, will likely involve using the other company's marketing expertise, including personal selling. Established MNEs, with locally based sales forces around the world, face the problem of implementing effective marketing and sales programs in several diverse country markets, a problem not likely to be solved by the easy assumption that what works in Canada will work well somewhere else. Personal selling approaches need to be modified so that business can be successfully transacted in the culturally varied global marketplace.

The company's sales approach is determined by the degree of internationalization in its efforts, as shown in Exhibit 14.1. This in turn will be influenced by managerial attitudes toward the use of company resources and transaction costs, as discussed in the previous section. Note that the point of view taken in Exhibit 14.1 is that of the exporter. This is pertinent to the Canadian situation, given Canada's dependence on the U.S. and the fact that many forays into this market begin as export ventures, perhaps via distributors or agents. However, as pointed out above, personal selling is a pervasive activity in global marketing; therefore, although exporting is vitally important, it is only one area in which personal selling will be found. Nevertheless the analysis should be useful in clarifying the different stages of internationalization. Bearing this stricture in mind, it can be expected that as the degree of internationalization advances, so will the exporter's own role in carrying out or controlling the sales function. This raises the question of the degree of internationalization of Canadian exporters. Clearly the less developed this process is, the less dependent on the sales force the firm will be.

Indirect Exports

When the exporter uses **indirect exports** to reach international markets, the export process is externalized; in other words, the intermediary, such as an export management company (EMC), will assume responsibility for the international sales effort. While there

Exhibit 14.1 **Levels of Exporter Involvement in International Sales**

Level	Type of Involvement	Target of Sales Effort	Level of Exporter Involvement	Advantage/Disadvantage
1	Indirect exports	Home-country-based intermediary	Low	+ No major investment
2	Direct exports	Locally based market	Medium	+ International sales
3	Integrated exports	Customer	High	– Minor learning from/ control of effort + Direct contact with local intermediary – Possibly gate keeping by intermediary + Generation of market-specific assets – Cost/risk

Source: Framework adapted from Reijo Luostarinen and Lawrence Welch, *International Operations of the Firm* (Helsinki, FI: Helsinki School of Economics, 1990), chap. 1.

is no investment in international sales by the marketer, there is also no, or very little, learning about sales in the markets that buy the product. The sales effort is basically a domestic one directed at the local intermediary. This may change somewhat if the marketer becomes party to an export trading company (ETC) with other similar producers. Even in that case, the ETC will have its own sales force, and exposure to the effort may be limited. Any learning that takes place is indirect; for example, the intermediary may advise the marketer of product adaptation requirements to enhance sales.

Direct Exports

At some stage, the exporter may find it necessary to establish direct contact with the target market(s), although the ultimate customer contact is still handled by locally based intermediaries, such as agents or distributors. Communication with intermediaries must ensure both that they are satisfied with the arrangement and that they are equipped to market and promote the exporter's product appropriately. Whatever the distribution arrangement, the exporter must provide basic selling-aid communications, such as product specification and data literature, catalogues, the results of product testing, and demonstrated performance information—everything needed to present products to potential customers. In some cases, the exporter has to provide the intermediaries with incentives to engage in local advertising efforts. These may include special discounts, push money, or cooperative advertising. Cooperative advertising will give the exporter's product local flavour and increase the overall promotional budget for the product. However, the exporter needs to be concerned that the advertising is of sufficient quality and that the funds are spent as agreed.

For the marketer–intermediary interaction to work, four general guidelines have to be satisfied.[14]

1. *Know the sales scene.* Often what works in the exporter's home market will not work somewhere else. This is true especially in terms of compensation schemes. In Canadian firms, incentives and commission play a significant role, while in most other markets salaries are the major share of compensation. The best way to approach this is to study the salary structures and incentive plans in other competitive organizations in the market in question.
2. *Research the customer.* Customer behaviour will vary across markets, meaning the sales effort must adjust as well. ECA International, a global organization that sells marketing information worldwide based on a membership concept (companies purchase memberships to both participate in information gathering and receive appropriate data), found that its partners' sales forces could not sell the concept in Asia. Customers wanted instead to purchase information piece by piece. Only after research and modification of the sales effort was ECA able to sell the membership idea to customers.
3. *Work with the culture.* Realistic objectives have to be set for the salespeople based on their cultural expectations. This is especially true in setting goals and establishing measures such as quotas. If either of these is set unrealistically, the result will be frustration for both parties. Cultural sensitivity also is required in situations where the exporter has to interact with the intermediary's sales force—in training situations, for example. In some cultures, such as those in Asia, the exporter is expected to act as a teacher and more or less dictate how things are done, while in some others, such as in Northern Europe, training sessions may be conducted in a seminar-like atmosphere of give and take.
4. *Learn from your local representatives.* If the sales force perceives a lack of fit between the marketer's product and the market, as well as inability to do anything about it, the result will be sub-optimal. A local sales force is an asset to the exporter, given its close contact with customers. Beyond daily feedback, the exporter is wise to undertake two additional approaches to exploit the experience of local salespeople. First, the exporter should have a program by which local salespeople can visit the exporter's operations and interact with the staff. If the exporter is active in multiple markets of the same region, it is advisable to develop ways to put salespeople in charge of the exporter's products in different markets to exchange ideas and best practice. Naturally, it is in the best interest of the exporter also to make regular periodic visits to markets entered.

An approach that requires more commitment from the exporter is that of employing its own sales representatives, whose main functions are to represent the firm abroad to existing and potential customers and to seek new leads. It is also important to sell with intermediaries, by supporting and augmenting their efforts. This type of presence becomes increasingly important as the firm increases its international involvement. Other promotional tools can facilitate foreign market entry, but eventually some personal selling must take place. A cooperative effort with the intermediaries is important at this stage, in that some of them may be concerned about the motives of the exporter in the long term. For example, an intermediary may worry that once the exporter has learned enough about the market, it will no longer need the services of the intermediary. If these suspicions become prevalent, sales information may no longer flow to the exporter in the quantity and quality needed.

Integrated Exports

In the final stage of export-based internationalization, that of **integrated exports**, the exporter internalizes the effort through either a sales office in the target market or a direct contact with the buyer from home base. This is part of the exporter's perceived need for increased **customer relationship management**, where the sales effort is linked to call-centre technologies, customer-service departments, and the company's website. This may also include automating the sales force (see The Global Marketplace 14.4 later in this chapter). The establishment of a sales office does not have to mean an end to the use of intermediaries; the exporter's salespeople may be dedicated to supporting intermediaries' sales efforts. At this stage, expatriate sales personnel, especially those needed to manage the effort locally or regionally, may be used. (The role of expatriates in the management of a global sales force is examined in the final section of this chapter.)

The Canadian Case

In Canada, some 85 percent of exporters are small businesses (defined as enterprises with fewer than 100 employees).[15] Moreover, while Canada is normally regarded as a leader in economic globalization, 14 out of 16 of Canada's largest multinationals have more than 50 percent of their sales in their home region of North America, and it can be argued that none are "global," in the sense of deriving important percentages of their revenues from all major regions of the world, especially the three triad regions.[16]

It is true that Canada can boast a high position in world rankings of large multinational companies, with 16 Canadian-owned MNEs in 2001 making the world's top 500.[17] However, this should be compared with other countries, notably the United States, which has 169 organizations in that category. Also, in terms of taking advantage of the size and rapid growth of such countries as China, Canada's presence has been described as "weak" when compared with successful companies from Germany, Australia, and America.[18] The latter have benefited from investing in a significant presence in the country, with high-quality manufacturing facilities integrated into their supply chains. Larger firms are better able to marshal the resources needed to make these commitments, although there are many examples of smaller Canadian companies achieving remarkable successes abroad.

The point to be made here is that, while not doubting the existence of many successful medium and large Canadian exporters, including MNEs, the predominance of small companies in the country's overall export effort is not to be denied. This means that the level of Canadian involvement in exporting should properly be categorized as level 2 in Exhibit 14.1—that is, direct exports. This needs to be borne in mind when we discuss the personal-selling and sales-management behaviours of Canadian firms, activities that are most likely to be characteristic of firms categorized as level 3—integrated marketing.

Personal Selling Effectiveness

Personal selling is based on the idea of a battery of (to a large extent) teachable principles, yet the process is as much an art as a science, and depends for its success on various unfathomable aspects of human personality and creativity. Also, as noted earlier, the sales process involves increasing emphasis on team selling and relationship building, which increases the social complexity of the activity, and hence the problems of prescribing sets of "rules" for its efficient conduct.

These difficulties have not prevented researchers from attempting to understand the causative factors underlying success and failure. For example, two widely accepted concepts in the sales literature are that (1) influence tactics are the mechanism through which salespeople persuade buyers in interactions[19] and (2) adapting sales tactics to different buyers is important for superior performance.[20] However, because research at the intersection of these two propositions is limited, "little guidance is provided to salespeople regarding what influence tactics they should use with different types of buyers."[21] Therefore marketers must depend on their field experience to determine what approaches work best, a problem that can only be accentuated in the international context.

A similar conclusion applies to another research stream, that of attribution theory. Here the focus is on how salespeople's attribution processes influence their expectancies for success and failure. Take for example the case of failure to close a sale, a matter of much concern in both domestic and international selling. A salesperson who attributes his or her failure wrongly (for example, by blaming buyer intransigence more than presentation ineptitude) is likely to go off on the wrong track when adjusting future behaviour. Attributional research—asking why something occurred—helps salespeople to adapt to different buying situations, thereby propelling them toward better understanding and new behaviour and helping them reach their sales goals.[22] However, work on developing full sets of attributional and behavioural scales has been limited despite the potential value of these to sales managers.[23] Because the primary role of sales management is to direct and improve sales-force performance, recognizing how salespeople make attributions as to success and failure is clearly important. More help and guidance in this area would be beneficial in the international context.

The Sales Process and Relationship Selling

The sales process is typically described as a series of steps—**prospecting** (gathering sales leads), the **pre-approach** (selecting which leads to pursue), the **approach** itself, **overcoming buyer objections, closing,** and **follow-up** (maintaining relationships). These stages, which are fully relevant to international selling, have been much discussed. Their basic features can be reviewed in various introductory marketing texts.[24] At first blush, the process appears "old hat," yet it has proved to be remarkably durable because what it seeks to achieve—finding prospective customers, arguing the case for adopting the firm's products, closing sales, maintaining customer contact—is as old as trade itself. Also when these tasks are carried out in connection with highly complex products and services (e.g., advanced IT applications), the mixture of technological and sales ability demanded of the salesperson is of a very high order.

Familiar though the basic process may be, the dynamics of its application in changing market and company circumstances needs to be emphasized. An important case in point is the key tasks of building and maintaining customer and other relationships. The Global Marketplace 14.2 describes the efforts of one Canadian company to develop business and establish relationships in Nigeria. The company stresses the importance of devoting senior management time to achieve these purposes. Note also the references to the need for patience and to the importance of spending time in the country to "smell the air, meet the people, and develop relationships."

However, if relationships are to rise beyond the purely social, important thought that is, to a point where real sales are achieved and business development goals are met, a sales orientation must at some point be built into and become part and parcel of the relationship. Such a sales orientation must of course be compatible with the social and relational aspects of the customer interchange. Much more will be needed than the use of (some would say dubious) persuasion techniques to obtain short-term orders, an unfortunate view of selling that still persists. As the case shows, developing business abroad—which is bound to entail a variety of skills usually associated with personal selling—will increasingly become part of the purview of senior management teams seeking business development objectives. This is not to deny that separate sales forces will be built up to achieve particular objectives, only

The Global MARKETPLACE 14.2

Relationship Building in Developing Markets: The Case of Nigeria

Twenty years ago it was rare to find an African country seriously considering privatizing its railroads, ports, or power systems, but today most of these countries are engaging in infrastructure renewal. Critical infrastructure is frequently technologically outdated, increasingly fragile, and inadequate to meet even the most basic needs.

One Canadian company is playing an active role in helping this revitalization process. Canadian Pacific Consulting Services Ltd. (CPCS), located in Ottawa, specializes in assisting governments to commercialize and privatize their transportation organizations, especially roads, railways, and ports. In December 2006 the company won a contract valued at almost $6 million to help the Nigerian government privatize its national power system. This recent project was one of many undertaken by CPCS in Africa; the company previously won contracts in Cameroon, Tanzania, Kenya, Sierra Leone, and South Africa. These contracts included assisting in the privatization of nine railways in Africa.

In propelling itself to a position of world leadership in the field of infrastructure restructuring and privatization, the firm has relied on a fundamental capability: dealing successfully with international financial institutions (IFIs), exemplified by the World Bank and its associated organizations. Over the last 5 years CPCS has had contracts with 48 countries, with IFI-funded work accounting for approximately 60 to 70 percent of company business. Over time, the organization has had to perfect its ability to navigate through the pre-qualifying, bidding, and other procedural demands of these financial bodies, involving a deep understanding of the roles of key individuals. It has also had to face the major challenge of the emphasis by IFIs on corporate experience, in the absence of which firms cannot get beyond the pre-qualifying stage in order to bid. Thus companies with established track records, including the painstaking building of key relationships, have the edge.

Referring to Nigeria, Mr. Jeff Murphy, senior consultant of CPCS, remarks: "To do business effectively in the country, you must spend time there; smell the air, meet the people, and develop relationships. You can't expect to be successful by relying on meetings in airport lounges or communicating solely by phone or e-mail." Mr. Murphy adds that the government of Nigeria has undertaken massive reforms to encourage private-sector participation in the transportation sector, but exploiting this trend demands an investment of time by companies to establish themselves in the country and accept the risks of doing business in a developing market.

The World Bank itself advocates visits to its headquarters if a firm is interested in consulting business opportunities funded by the bank, another example of the contact-making, relationship-building activity needed to operate successfully in the IFI market. Three categories of bank officer are of particular importance: *task managers* (assigned to each World Bank project in a managerial/supervisory role), *country officers* (charged with strategic oversight of the bank's lending portfolio in a specific country), and *sectoral technical specialists* (responsible for supporting the task managers by providing them with advice on technical elements of their projects). If a company feels that a contact needs to be made with one or more of these individuals, establishing good relationships is a clear requirement.

Nigeria is a country of contrasts, with many different tribes, religions, and languages. Canadian firms need to become familiar with, at times, substantial cultural differences. Moreover, reports of appalling urban conditions are still heard despite progress in many infrastructural areas. For example, as one group of writers notes, it can take hours to travel even a couple of miles by car in the metropolitan area of Lagos, the former capital city, a "messy but familiar problem." However, there is a danger of exaggeration, as in the case of reports of kidnappings and government corruption. Events taking place in one region may not be repeated elsewhere, giving an unbalanced view of the country.

Despite these considerations, CPCS has a very positive view of the country. "In our experience, it is a good place to do business," says Mr. Kieran. As in any developing country, being aware of the current political climate is as important as partnering with trusted and competent local firms who understand local economic and social conditions. Being willing to develop relationships at different levels and in different contexts is also of prime importance.

"You must be prepared to devote financial resources and ongoing senior management time to business development and relationship management," Mr. Kieran states. "I would also recommend patience—relationships are important in Nigeria and it takes time to develop them."

Sources: Huixia Sun, "Exporting Expertise to Africa," *Embassy*, January 17, 2007, **http://www.embassymag.ca/html/index.php?display=story&full_path=/2007/january/17/e/**; Marc-Andre Roy and Peter Kieran, "Rail Privatisation Rolls Across the Continent," *International Railway Journal*, March 2006, **http://www.cpcstran.com**; Peggy O'Neil, "CPCS Transcom Makes Inroads in Nigeria," *Exportwise*, Summer 2006, **http://www.edc.ca/english/publications_11596.htm**; "Ottawa Consulting Firm Expands Niche through Asian Development Bank," *Foreign Affairs and International Trade Canada* (IFInet), **http://www.infoexport.gc.ca/ifinet/success/CPCS-e.htm**; "World Bank," *FAITC* (IFInet), **http://www.infoexport.gc.ca/ifinet/ifi/worldbank-e.htm**; and Viren Doshi, Gary Schulman, and Daniel Gabaldon, "Lights! Water! Motion!" *Strategy and Business*, special issue, Autumn 2007, 103–19.

to say that, where relationship teams are involved, the fundamental concepts of selling will increasingly have to inform the activities of all or most of the participants.

It would be helpful to international marketers if research could be found that provided guidance on how to optimize buyer–seller relationships over time. Unfortunately, such a convenient store of information is lacking, despite much initial enthusiasm for the potentiality of relationship marketing. As one writer puts it, "There is little empirical research in business marketing that informs academics and practitioners of the process through which industrial buyer-seller relationships evolve over time."[25] This gap has prompted calls for more field-based research on the multiple exchange episodes, including sales interactions, that make up relationships and offer insights into the process of how relationships are initiated and maintained.[26]

We might summarize the points made here by emphasizing the importance of a flexible outlook when thinking about personal selling, and avoiding any dogmatizing of the activity, that is, interpreting it into ever-narrower and more inflexible rules. An early marketing writer, Theodore Levitt, has sounded this warning for marketing as a whole, cautioning against any rigid and lasting interpretation of what the marketing concept means for the specific ways in which a company should operate.[27] The world is volatile, he emphasizes. The marketing concept remains broadly "in charge," but it has to be adapted to meet the changing circumstances of the firm.

This same argument can also be put forward forcibly in the case of personal selling. Fundamental sales activities will always be present but need to be modified in their application, as in the case of relationship marketing. A case in point, as instanced by Levitt, is IBM, whose early growth depended on a large educational element to market effectively. While this element was important in the 1950s, it gave way to a "harder" approach in the '60s and '70s because buyers became progressively more informed. Today, IBM's "Signature" sales-training method, used throughout the world, is adapted to suit highly knowledgeable buyers and relationship building, but it is still built around a step-by-step process.[28] In light of limited research help, as discussed above, companies such as IBM will depend on lengthy field experience to determine the scope and nature of the sales approaches they will adopt and the adaptations they will make to familiar procedural steps. A basic knowledge of the key selling steps can only be an introduction to the problems of their implementation in various practical settings. (Exhibit 14.2 shows one company advertising its sales process software.)

Personal Selling in Practice

At this point let us illustrate some of the problems arising throughout the sales process in international selling. In this the intent is highly pragmatic—to give some practical flavour of the "real world" dilemmas encountered in foreign markets. This is intended to flesh out the familiar basic selling steps.

Prospecting

In the case of cold calling, refusal rates can be high; cold calling is frowned upon in most Asian and Latin American societies. In the United States, cold canvassing is now regulated, as is telemarketing, because of consumer complaints about intrusion into privacy.

In the industrial market, marketing analysis can aid in the search for new international prospects by predetermining those industrial firms most likely to use a particular product. This can be done by employing a combination of the NAICS industrial classification system (which classifies the various segments of industry, e.g., agricultural machinery, pumps, structural steel products) and appropriate industrial directories and published surveys, to determine the most promising targets for sales calls. (See Chapter 7 for further information on marketing research methods.) It should be noted that the NAICS classification system is standard throughout many parts of the world, as are international directories (e.g., Kompass) that provide data on various countries. In addition, secondary information sources are frequently modern and sophisticated in other countries such as the U.S. and the U.K. and rival those enjoyed in Canada. But difficulties can be expected in proportion as one moves away from the English language or attempts desk research in less well-endowed locales abroad.

Using Software to Enhance Selling Stages—a Company Example

Landslide™

SALES WORKSTYLE MANAGEMENT

Put that coffee down. Coffee is for closers!

Created by salespeople for salespeople, Landslide™ is unique sales software that raises the performance of everyone of your sales team to a new level. It lets you implement a **consistent sales process** based on your own best practices, and gives your salespeople clear, effective guidance when they need it most - during the actual sales engagement. So they can **develop high-impact conversations** and penetrate further up the customer sales hierarchy. **While differentiating your company through a one-of-a-kind buying experience.**

FREE TRIAL

Give us a try and we'll give your sales team the jolt of Landslide.
www.landslide.com

contact | 412-489-1700 | inquiries@landslide.com

www.landslide.com

Source: Reprinted with permission from Landslide Technologies Inc., **www.landslide.com.**

Pre-Approach

The firm that is new to foreign markets faces the difficult challenge of establishing reputation and credibility where it is unknown and mitigating any fear of the unproven supplier. The pre-approach may well yield plenty of promising prospects, but much remains to be done to establish the bona fides of the selling company and its general trustworthiness in the market. This can only be achieved if it is based on respect for the expectations of the society's business culture. In cultures such as Latin America and Asia, for example, third-party testimonials are especially important to enhance the firm's perceived credibility and standing. This cannot be achieved overnight, but companies targeting new foreign markets should waste no time in starting.

In regard to developing contacts in the foreign market, Canada's multicultural environment provides companies with excellent opportunities. Canada is rich in business people who have immigrated from other countries and who maintain foreign connections. However, finding the right person, that is, one who will facilitate the right links and introductions in a particular country, means casting a wide net—only a small percentage of those contacted will eventually be of value. A useful starting point is to review all possible potential prospects from a wide range of sources. In other words, it makes sense to start with a large list, then to narrow it down.

In light of the Canadian government's comprehensive support programs for exporters, some companies will want to start here. An example is the Canadian Virtual Trade Commissioner Service.[29] This provides free access to hundreds of sector market studies and country-specific reports. Registrants to this service receive a personalized Web service that includes business leads matching the firm's international business interests. By participating in the database, companies can obtain introductions to potential clients, foreign buyers, distributors, and other contacts. Other official or semiofficial sources include Canadian embassy staff in the target market, the consul for the target market, Canadian international trade or business services, and trade and industry publications. In addition, leads can be sought from a miscellany of other sources including current and former employees, customers or suppliers from the firm's market, business colleagues currently working in the target market, university alumni, and even friends and acquaintances.

It may seem impossible to establish connections and cultivate relationships among the list of prospects generated, even after winnowing out the least promising ones, but with experience headway can be made. National and international trade organizations and conferences can provide a networking opportunity to find the right contacts.

Approach

Approach effectiveness in foreign markets depends critically upon sensitivity to cultural realities. It is during face-to-face interactions that the greatest problems can occur. Meeting protocol must be understood and adapted to. Gestures and even words may seem familiar on the surface but may convey very different messages across cultures. Outside Canada, considerable time is often devoted to non-business discussion to establish a rapport

In More Detail 14.1

TARGETING THE CHILEAN MARKET

One Montreal web-design firm wanted to target the Chilean market, in which it had no connections. The firm's owner joined a local (Quebec) Chamber of Commerce with Chilean-Canadian members and connections to the Canadian-Chile Chamber of Commerce in Santiago, the latter regularly hosting various Latin-American trade events. By seeking out the Chilean-Canadian members in Montreal, and sharing her business interests with them, the owner became known to the local Chamber membership and established credibility for her company. Not only did this lead to a contract with a Chilean-Canadian firm, who were willing to provide a referral, but the client was willing to provide letters of introduction that, after follow-up, yielded several promising leads.[30]

between buyer and seller, a potential source of frustration for the salesperson who is anxious to move things along and perhaps is selling on a commission basis. This may occur in a highly informal, unstructured way. In Saudi Arabia, for example, interruptions of the discussion may be frequent, and concurrent conversations are a normal part of interaction. Elsewhere in the Middle East, and in South Africa and Asia, it is common for two or three meetings to occur before business matters are addressed. This adds to the exasperation of the Canadian sales team accustomed to meetings proceeding in a linear fashion, but such cultural idiosyncrasies need to be borne with good grace if favourable relations are to be established and maintained, and business won.

Other factors, though seemingly minor, can turn out to be important. Attempting to shake hands with a woman in the Middle East may not be well received, and may even be politely declined, but a firm handshake is expected in the U.S., where prospective customers will also expect the salesperson to get quickly to the point. Effective face-to-face interactions require absolute familiarity with embedded protocols and a willingness to overcome assumptions, stereotypes, and language barriers.

Presentation

In general, the key to effective presentation in foreign countries is to know the essential message to deliver and the local learning styles and preferences. Presentations, proposals, and promotion materials are all used internationally, but a standard approach—that is, one not adequately adapted to the peculiarities of the particular audience—is likely to fail. Different cultures assimilate information differently and respond differently to different presentation styles, colours, and cues. For example, Germans, who are influenced by facts and data and prefer detailed information, are likely to appreciate a rigorous, logically developed presentation. Such an approach may have less appeal in countries where language problems are a real issue and where managers, who should not in any way be talked down to, might appreciate a visually striking approach, or even a storytelling one, with ample use of illustrations and photographs.

There will be differences, too, in the receptivity of audiences to the presenter himself or herself. Physical appearance creates image credibility. Being female may create problems in some cultures, while being older may create greater respect in others. In developing the presentation, various specific points should be borne in mind. For example, attempts at humour may fall flat in any culture unless the presenter knows exactly what he or she is doing. It may be necessary to acknowledge VIPs or senior status figures, and perhaps be introduced by one. In trying to establish a good personal rapport with the audience it may be necessary to invite their viewpoints, and comment favourably, as a visitor, on the country, even saying a few words in the local language in the introduction. Using proper colours and symbols should be given careful thought; as an example, in Asia, the colour white is a symbol of death, whereas in Canada it represents cleanliness and purity.

Overcoming Objections

In other cultures, objections may not mean "no" but indicate confusion or a need for more information. In these circumstances, it may be necessary to ask clarifying questions to ensure that the prospective customer understands the proposal. The salesperson must also be prepared for tactics that are unfamiliar or may seem unfair. In Japan, agreement may not be possible immediately, as decisions often require consensus by a larger group. Here, patience in overcoming objections and putting the proposal in its best light is a strong strategy. In China, objections may come surprisingly late in a negotiation even after the main terms have been agreed. Moreover, the objections may never be voiced in a forthright, overt manner that would enable counteraction.

For example, a delegation of Canadian health care consultants and their Chinese counterparts finalized an agreement to provide technology and management assistance to the Chinese, only for the Canadians to discover that the Chinese had altered the agreed list in their favour without prior consultation. The leader of the Canadian team became angry and wanted to call off the negotiations, challenging the trustworthiness of the Chinese, who, for their part, were upset and puzzled by the Canadian anger, feeling they would lose face by agreeing to a deal that could have been improved on. The Chinese believed the Canadians would have argued more strenuously over the initial terms if they were not willing to improve upon them.

Closing

The Canadian team in the above example had actually closed the sale successfully—they had obtained agreement. But something went wrong. What salespersons need are closing methods that will stick, or are final, even in the trickiest, most culturally sensitive environments.

Of course great caution in the approach adopted is needed. In countries such as the United Kingdom, the United States, and Australia, there is an expectation that the salesperson will "ask for the order early and often" (a quotation from one company's sales-training manual). English-speaking countries with broadly similar cultures share similar business practices, at least up to a point. But in some countries the salesperson may have to deal with unusual circumstances, for example, being given misleading or false information. Stalling for time, or continually delaying or haggling may be a normal experience in other countries, forestalling any effort to close the sale. Canadians might assume that others perceive, judge, think, and reason in the same way they do. However, cultures like that of the U.S. focus on making the deal and so are comfortable with early closing; on the other hand, the Japanese are more interested in long-term relationships. In other words, different cultures have different perceptions of the negotiating process and its outcomes, so it is essential to be familiar with local bargaining strategies and motivations and to be able to adjust the selling approach accordingly.

An important point to be made here is that selling techniques, including closing methods that are taught and applied in Canada, may in fact often work quite well in other cultures. It is too extreme to believe that domestic practices can never be transplanted. Sensitivity to the needs of prospective buyers is paramount, of course, and this is as important elsewhere as it is at home. So-called **adaptive selling,** including "indirect" or **low-pressure selling**, common when big ticket items are being sold and buyers are rationally motivated, is based upon achieving such sensitivity.[31]

Adaptive salespersons using low pressure will tailor their sales presentations, probing techniques, closure skills, and so on based on the culture, customer type, or selling environment. For example, an adaptive seller may choose a concise, cost-driven presentation when calling on a hurried, economic buyer such as a purchasing agent in the U.S., and the seller may even come close to high pressure. The same salesperson could select a socially driven approach that emphasizes the features, advantages, and benefits of the product when calling on a product operator in, say, Indonesia, where business people are usually slow and deliberate in decision making and a low-key, thoughtful appeal is appreciated. Selling in such circumstances becomes the process of "arraying logical forces" (i.e., stressing the rational-economic case for buying) before the purchaser so that, through the purchaser's own thought processes, he or she is drawn to think favourably about the product.

In reality, there are numerous ways in which the salesperson can ask for the order, either directly or indirectly, but the key, as in all stages of the sales process, is to adapt to the cultural and other expectations of the prospective buyer. The importance of adaptive selling (that is, a sales approach that is altered during a sales interaction, or across customer interactions, based on information provided or obtained through questioning) is now widely acknowledged.[32] Moreover, research suggests that job performance is strongly related to adoption of this approach.[33] However, returning to the problem of closing, it is clear that all previous stages of the sales process are worthless if an order is not obtained, hence the reason this final stage is so critical. Important though adaptive selling is, it must be accompanied by **order-mindedness**, an extremely difficult combination to achieve. This is why we have emphasized the idea of adaptive selling, which many companies find appropriate in achieving this balance, and in practice will apply in individualistic ways in particular country settings.

Follow-Up

This final, post-sales stage marks the beginning of the relationship between seller and buyer. Keeping in touch presents special problems if this has to be done at a distance. If sales agents or independent distributors are used in a foreign country, it may be necessary to depend on them, and their performance may, of course, be perfectly satisfactory. But sometimes more direct contact may be needed. Many cultures in Asia, the Middle East, South America, and parts of Europe will judge foreign companies by their perceived level of commitment to the market. Companies should explore all possible avenues for developing and maintaining contact with key individuals, for example, by sending new product information and articles or by adding the customer's name to the house journal mailing list. But returning to the market in person as often as possible will do most to show commitment, even if arranged as a side trip to an adjacent country or market.

Internally, the company should reap benefits from an efficient system for capturing global expertise within the firm, for example, by informal presentations or debriefings from individuals recently returned from abroad, or by circulating relevant articles about the firm's markets or international publications. Any demonstration of interest and commitment to the market will be noticed and appreciated by customers.

Management of the Global Sales Force

Selling must be managed if it is going to contribute to the firm's international marketing objectives. This presents problems if strongly independent agents and distributors with their own sales forces are used, although collaborative arrangements can be set up. Canadian firms have the option of hiring their own company sales forces, and this will be increasingly likely as more companies set up abroad.

International sales managers face, on a much expanded basis, similar duties to those dealt with domestically. However, adopting international strategies increases the complexity of the sales management process. Although firms differ in the specifics of how salespeople and the selling effort are managed, the sales management process is broadly similar across firms. An important characteristic needs to be emphasized. While, as we saw in Chapter 13, it is quite legitimate to speak of a global advertising campaign or global media, the notion of global personal selling, implying a uniformity of approach across diverse countries, is much more problematic. This is because personal selling is largely concerned with interpersonal relations and is much more culture-bound than impersonal advertising. The sales approach employed, the organizational structure used, the type of training required, and so on, will all have to reflect the local conditions in which selling has to be conducted. In other words, global personal selling will still be carried out mainly on a national basis, with associated problems of coordination.

Growing globalization and the need to sustain competitive advantages internationally provide strong imperatives for managements to understand the factors underlying sales performance in an international context.[34] Surprisingly, very limited research attention has

In More Detail 14.2

GEARING UP FOR SALES IN INDIA

Major Canadian companies such as SNC Lavalin, Bombardier, Sun Life Insurance, and Bell Helicopters have been operating in this country for a considerable time and have been joined by Magna, the second largest auto-parts manufacturer in the world, which has a permanent representative there. Other Canadian companies (including many SMEs) looking to India are from sectors such as telecommunications, agro-processing, environmental technology, and health services. Much expansion of bilateral trade seems in prospect between Canada and India, and of course with other countries as well, and with expansion will come increasing need for sales management skills.

been given to sales management control outside the United States,[35] despite recognition of the critical role of the sales manager in international selling.[36] In particular, an area that has received scant research attention in the international marketing field concerns the personal selling and sales management activities that firms adopt to enter, penetrate, and expand in export markets.[37]

As Canadian companies expand internationally, they may wish to homogenize their client management practices to provide a consistent sales approach and support level across large market areas such as the United States or the European Union. For example, when Siebel, a customer relations management software provider, first moved into Europe in 1996, the compensation systems and sales objectives were identical for Portuguese, French, and German salespeople.

Yet such a standardized approach takes no account of the way in which salespeople in different countries perceive their management. Substantial country differences need to be allowed for. At the sales management level, developing the European example, Spanish, French, and Italian sales managers appear to earn far less than their German or British counterparts.[38] These discrepancies indicate that standardized sales-force governance systems are likely to have significantly different effects on salespeople of various nationalities. Sales managers need more information on the nature of these differences in order to optimize the way they monitor, direct, evaluate, and compensate salespeople in areas such as Europe and, of course, elsewhere.

The three major functions making up the sales management process are (1) formulating sales plans, including organizing the sales force; (2) implementing successful marketing strategies, including the selection and motivation of salespeople, in distinct parts of the world; and (3) providing control mechanisms that improve the performance of personnel with different cultural expectations and objectives. A general overview of these areas is provided below, but the need for more research to inform sales management decisions should be borne in mind.

Formulating the Sales Plan

Formulation of the sales plan is the most fundamental of the three sales management functions. The company needs first of all to set its core strategic plan. Goals and strategies connected with the sales function are a subset of this larger view; therefore, for each foreign market to be targeted, they must be coordinated to reflect the purpose of the overall long-range plan. In other words, it is inadvisable for a firm to have all its sales managers carry out strategic planning independently. A sales plan will set out detailed objectives and where and how the selling effort of salespeople is to be deployed. Formulating the sales plan involves two key activities: setting objectives and organizing the sales force.

Setting Objectives

As suggested above, setting sales-force objectives depends on predetermining the larger strategic objectives. For example, the firm may want to enter the foreign market at the "bottom end" as a low-cost provider. Or it may decide that building strong customer relationships is the vital concern. Once these objectives are determined, the company can evaluate what roles the sales force will play to reach them. These roles become, in effect, the objectives of the sales force. They set out what the sales force will be expected to do, whether **"missionary" selling** to carry promotional messages and introduce new products, or **relationship selling**—building ties to customers over time, based on attention and commitment to customer needs.

The entire sales management process, from selecting appropriate salespeople to assessing sales effectiveness, will be influenced by the objectives adopted. If the objective is aggressive penetration of a new foreign market, this will guide the types of salespeople sought and how they are to be motivated and trained. Sales-force objectives will determine the emphasis placed on cold calling versus account maintenance, local agent support versus company sales calls, selling existing versus new products, and so on.

The kind of sales objective adopted is also a function of what competitors do. Intense global competition influences the sales organization created to meet it. Sales management strategy needs to be aligned closely with the firm's overall competitive strategy if corporate performance is to be maximized. As one source states:

> Personal selling and the sales management process are about more than simply closing sales and meeting quotas. Personal selling is—or at least should be—a critical component in the long-term competitive strategy for most, if not all firms. The sales force plays a pivotal role in implementing business and marketing strategies. Sales management policy should be developed with an eye toward enhancing the likelihood of the company meeting its market and financial goals.[39]

Objectives might involve more (or less) concentration on a foreign market in order to extract as many sales as possible (or to allow these to be generated over a longer period of time). A given potential in a market could be exploited quickly or slowly, much depending on the likelihood and strength of competition. The size of an order for, say, expensive capital equipment or major project engineering consultancy could well depend on the frequency of sales calls, which, in turn, may be influenced by fear of losing the account to an aggressive competitor. Clearly, the greater the number of calls to be made, or the more intensive the selling, the greater the sales force needed.

Inevitably, the setting of international **sales management objectives** will be influenced by the culture and business practices of the target country. Some customization of approach will be obligatory in some countries but less so in others (although knowing exactly what to do may be problematic unless detailed country information is available). Given the cultural similarities between Canada and its largest trading partner, the United States, the least customization is likely to be needed in this case. In other cases, substantial adjustment may be needed—for example, where there is a marked preference for local distributors, as in the case of some categories of industrial goods sold to Turkey and elsewhere—with the result that the Canadian company has little option but to negotiate partnership arrangements as the initial entry strategy.[40]

Organizing the Sales Force

The organizational structure decided for the sales force will determine the physical positioning and responsibilities of each salesperson. Simply to copy the home market sales organization, in effect showing a lack of sensitivity to local markets, increases the proba-

In More Detail 14.3

WHY STRONG INTERNATIONAL SALES MANAGEMENT IS IMPORTANT

In any global sales operation strong sales management is vital because of the separation of the firm's head office from the field sales organization. Sales personnel must have effective communications with the local sales manager, and the latter must have effective communications with centrally based sales executives.

The local sales manager should provide various kinds of support. He or she should:

- Provide information on the firm's products and policies, the needs of foreign customers, and their methods of conducting business. Such information is vital to "indirect" selling based on solving customer problems.
- Develop the skills and work habits of salespersons under his or her control.
- Carry out sales calls personally, thereby conditioning customers to subsequent calls by salespersons.
- Contribute to the emotional needs of salespersons. The latter operate alone often with infrequent contact with colleagues, find themselves in an unfamiliar and very competitive environment, and cannot seek sales management help at critical points in face-to-face interaction such as closing.

Because of these job peculiarities and the foreign environment, salespersons are susceptible to fluctuating emotions. They therefore welcome strong local supervision because of the opportunity to discuss problems and difficulties. The field sales manager thus plays a crucial role in maintaining the morale of the sales force and in helping them to maintain a positive outlook. In particular, the sales manager must ensure that the lessons learned in sales training are not forgotten, but are sustained and nurtured through good supervision and follow-on training activities.

bility of poor sales results. Designing an appropriate structure for foreign markets demands that at least the following factors be considered: (1) geographical size of market, (2) sales potential, (3) ease of access to customers, (4) customer expectations ("sell the way the buyer wants to buy"), (5) current selling practices, and (6) languages spoken.

A geographically based structure will be suggested by underdeveloped markets, small sales volumes, similar language or culture, and a single product line. Small markets cannot economically justify sales specialists by product or customer. Where the market is more established, a product-based organizational structure may be more appropriate. Broader product lines may argue a customer-based structure. Where sales volumes are large, the market is substantial and well developed, and the firm is dealing with a distinct market or culture, a combined approach may be used.

In practice, in international markets, firms will often organize their sales forces similarly to domestic structures, regardless of differences.[41] Also, a number of multinational corporations organize their sales forces along simple geographical lines, despite the potential drawbacks, especially in developing countries.[42] Bearing in mind the preponderance of SMEs in Canada, simple overseas sales management structures are likely to be the norm. However, there is a strong case for arguing that companies, whether large or small, should try to establish the "ideal" sales-force size. This might be more rationally determined by estimating the number of sales calls needed in the market and the number of salespersons required to make the required number of visits, though more sophisticated methods of calculating size are available.[43] A simple geographical structure might distort the optimum number of needed salespeople by failing to take account of geographical disparities such as high sales potential in the city and less in the hinterland. Also, salespeople must allow for the special requirements of particular cultures; for example, buyers in some countries may have to be "nursed" more and given time to accustom themselves to the Canadian seller. Such factors affect sales-force size and argue the importance of a thorough review of all determining factors as the best way forward.

As far as exporting is concerned, sales territories will likely be designed to simplify export sales operations. This can be achieved by assigning a number of present and potential export customers within a given region (e.g., countries in the Middle East) to a specific export manager. A number of benefits flow from right-sized foreign sales territories for the export unit, including deeper coverage of the international marketplace, reduction of overseas selling expenses, better customer identification, and improvement of export customer relations.[44] Importantly, territory design is a major determinant of salespeople's opportunity to perform well and of their ability to earn incentive pay where incentives are linked directly to territory-level individual performance.[45] Faulty territory-design decisions prevent optimal utilization of expensive selling efforts and may negatively affect salespeople's attitudes and behaviour.

Implementing the Sales Plan

The implementation phase of the sales plan is concerned with linking objectives to practical, day-to-day realization in the foreign marketplace. Implementation involves carrying out the various component tasks of the plan, in particular (1) global recruitment and selection of salespeople, (2) training a global sales force, and (3) motivating and compensating an international sales team.

Global Recruitment and Selection

Salespeople working in Canada principally need to have the attributes that will make them successful in carrying out sales tasks. To this must be added the complications of working internationally. Sales managers need to know what they expect of those they recruit. These expectations can be incorporated in a job description, which will ideally include special criteria relevant to the country of interest. This procedure also helps to identify early in the process whether expatriates or foreign nationals are best for the position.

Canadian companies face a kind of "league table" or hierarchy of cultural situations to which their salespeople must adapt. At one end of the scale is the hugely important American market. Many Canadian firms will feel comfortable conducting sales business in the U.S., and many have done so for substantial periods of time. But as one ventures further afield, problems crowd in. A year's sales assignment in New York or San Francisco is one thing. A lengthy stay in Shanghai, Bangkok, or São Paulo is something else, with the reality of diverse languages, dissimilar cultural heritages, and remote geographical locations having to be faced. In some locations, pressures can multiply from a variety of such sources with potentially drastic impacts on the salesperson. This results in a great need for adaptability. For example, the salesperson must be open to other, perhaps unusual opinions, be able to handle criticism, perhaps be willing to learn the basics of another language, and even be able to withstand extremes of climate, such as the heat of the Middle East or Africa. Emotional stability is also needed if the salesperson is to be successful in making independent decisions in an unfamiliar environment, without head office support immediately available, and if he or she is to continue to show cultural sensitivity even when local customs or practices are difficult to comprehend.

In addition to such qualities, sales recruiters need to take some highly practical matters into account, such as the individual's health, language ability, and family situation. How does one deal with a salesperson who has young children, for example, or children settled in a Canadian high school? All the factors deemed pertinent to the final selection decision can be listed, and interviewing conducted on the basis of the candidate's ability to meet the requirements. But above all, recruiters will want to hire candidates they believe will be effective salespeople. A great deal has been said about the qualities of the ideal salesperson, and it would be rash to lay down mechanistic rules. The path to success is a varied one and can be achieved by different individuals of varying educational backgrounds, personalities, or temperaments. It is the difficult task of the recruiter to determine if the particular combination offered by any one candidate will be best for the overseas position.

Sales Training

Most sales training takes place in the home country of the salesperson, but what the training objectives should be will be viewed differently in each culture.[46] Caution is therefore needed when transplanting particular methods. As we saw in the previous section, the sales process consists of a series of stages. At each of these, salespeople can be taught what the company believes are appropriate approaches and methods; however, each stage (approaching, presenting, closing) raises peculiar problems in individual cultures. A counsel of perfection would be to adapt or customize the sales training program to fit the requirements of each major target market—not the easiest of tasks, in that salespeople would need to possess, or be sympathetic to, the values, thought patterns, and communication style of specific cultures.[47]

Other important aspects of selling, apart from the cultural, interactive aspects, can be more standardized, for example, clarifying company policies, product training, and providing up-to-date information on local market conditions, in particular the existing customer base and the competitive situation. As The Global Marketplace 14.3 suggests, according to one industry source, global sales training increasingly needs to be related closely with the achievement of corporate goals and with the provision of more detailed product information to the sales force. Also, training in the basic nature of the client's culture and how sales are accomplished in the country can be presented in uniform blocks. Hofstede's classification (see Chapter 3) can be used to highlight training differences in terms of formal aspects (e.g., product training) and "softer" aspects (e.g., customer sensitivity training). Thus sales activities in low context cultures such as the Netherlands and Finland can be expected to place more emphasis on the formal aspects of transactions (e.g., product features, prices, transportation, and financing), and sales training will most likely stress product knowledge as well as company policies and procedures.[48] In contrast, sales transactions in high context cultures such as Spain and Portugal are based on trust; salespeople need to develop a friendly relationship with their customers and understand not only their business needs but also their personal ones.[49] In this case, sales training may emphasize customer knowledge so that salespeople are in a better position to develop a long-term relationship with their customers based on trust and respect.

Other training issues can be mentioned briefly. The method of instruction may have to be varied to suit the local culture; for example, on-the-job training may be preferred in

The Global MARKETPLACE 14.3

The Information Needs of Global Salespeople

Forward-thinking companies are making the jobs of their training professionals a little more difficult—but a lot more rewarding. Training has moved up the corporate ladder into a role integral to bottom-line success, bridging the marketing and selling gap and ensuring that the right information gets to the right salesperson at the right time.

Most training efforts are traditionally far removed from the point at which sales actually take place. Salespeople are frequently taken out of the field to receive training at head office. But in a globalized world, they are no longer the consumer's only source of information. Today's instant access to information is demanding changes in customary training approaches. In many cases, the Internet provides consumers with access to as much information as sellers, creating a problem for salespeople who may find themselves at a disadvantage. While advertising and marketing might get consumers in the door, salespeople are the key to converting interest into sales. If sellers lack key information, company sales will be lost.

Therefore companies need to empower their sales force with a greater depth and breadth of product information about the brands they represent. This becomes even more important for businesses that distribute and sell their products via secondary channels. These companies must take extraordinary measures to ensure that these channels are properly representing their brand promise and that every ultimate consumer receives a consistent experience. However, as companies pursue their sales objectives among increasingly sophisticated and informed consumers, the question increasingly asked is, are our sales performance goals adequately linked with the kind of sales training we are providing?

At the present time, when it comes to measuring their learning initiatives, most companies do not link their product training initiatives with key performance indicators such as sales. This is all the more surprising since modern technology, notably new Internet-based tools, facilitates the achievement of this end result. Effective training technologies are now available that generate new benefits and efficiencies that can be tangibly linked to business impact. Some companies, such as Whirlpool, have advanced from the traditional high-cost annual off-site sales meeting to one where only sales representatives who have demonstrated a high level of competence are invited to leave the field and attend an in-person event. This not only reduces cost, but also increases the success of expensive events such annual sales meetings.

"Going global" demands more than simply having an address in a foreign country. It requires the external-facing end of a company's operations, the sales force, to be prepared for an increasingly knowledgeable and demanding consumer. By creating a comprehensive knowledge infrastructure that keeps all salespeople informed on the brands and products they represent, e-learning software and forward-thinking learning management systems can help global companies circumvent knowledge obstacles that globalization can cause. No longer just an administrative or human resources concern, measurable training solutions unencumbered by language or cultural differences must be the focal point for worldwide sales and the cornerstone of corporate expansion.

Global success hinges not on being in a new country, but on truly becoming a part of it. And, as any traveller knows, you need your passport to get in. A complete, comprehensive system for transferring knowledge from the boardroom to the point of sales transaction provides each customer-facing employee with his or her very own passport.

Source: Adapted from Ara A. Ohanian, "Smarter Sales," *Training Magazine*, June 07, 2007, http://www.salesandmarketing.com/msg/search/article_display.jsp?vnu_content_id=1003592536.

some Asian countries so that constructive criticism does not cause the instructor to lose face.[50] Similarly, it can be expected that flexible training methods such as open and distance learning, which call for active trainee participation, may be more popular in low uncertainty-avoidance and low power-distance cultures (e.g., the United Kingdom and Finland), where rules and procedures are less necessary and salespeople may prefer the discretion that goes with such training methods. They may therefore be more comfortable with self-directed activities.[51] On-the-job training, as another example, has strong advantages in general; for example, new recruits en route for overseas assignments can work with experienced expatriates. Another issue is the depth of cultural understanding the salesperson should have. No one doubts the need for this knowledge in principle, but the value of lengthy immersion in, say, local religions or cultural history, will be questioned. (Exhibit 14.3 shows one company advertising its sales training services.)

Customized Sales Training to Aid Selling Strategy—a Company Example

this little piggy
sells on price

this little piggy Sells on Value

Grow Your Sales: Compete on Value not Price

Successful sales organizations know that there's more to the sales cycle than simply competing on price to win an order. Instead, they know how to break the bank by selling on value. Master the proven methods of driving up sales one conversation at a time, and you'll see your sales performance grow, too.

ValueSelling Framework™ is a practical, sustainable methodology that uncovers a prospect's critical business issues and enables the salesperson to link the unique value of your solution to those issues.

Through personalized classroom instruction, we arm sales executives with strategies to:

- **Sell to senior levels**
- **Generate leads**
- **Understand your product or service**
- **Differentiate from competitive alternatives**
- **Increase their business and financial acumen**
- **Forecast accurately**
- **Win more deals**

Get a free white paper on how to better qualify prospects at www.valueselling.com/whitepaper or call 800-559-6419.

The proven formula for accelerating sales results

Source: Reproduced with permission from ValueSelling Associates, **www.valueselling.com.**

Motivation and Compensation

The motivation and compensation of sales personnel are closely related. In fact, good compensation packages are in themselves major motivators for some salespeople and inducements for those considering a sales career. Such is the case in Canada and the U.S., but not necessarily in other countries. Each culture has its own motivations and expectations; therefore, the notion of a simple adaptation of home-based compensation programs is an oversimplification.

Basically, the company needs to design compensation packages that meet local needs and are compatible with cultural expectations. In a country where selling has a low perceived status, the company may experiment with non-monetary incentives such as titles, perquisites, and foreign travel (perhaps to the home office). Finding the right mix between monetary and non-monetary incentives is a major challenge. Commission-based arrangements are frequently rejected in some countries (e.g., in Japan and the Middle East) because it is felt they reinforce a negative image of salespeople. However such packages will often be welcomed in North America because of the opportunity for the sales force to earn substantial sums. Selling a high-priced big-ticket item at even a relatively low commission rate can yield an impressive monetary return for the salesperson.

There are dangers, however, in over-reliance on sales management control approaches that depend mainly on incentive pay to achieve results. This view is supported in multi-country studies. In a study of sales behaviour in Greece, India, and Malaysia, a key implication was that the traditional assumptions about managing international sales operations may be misleading. As the authors state:

> The danger is that beyond a certain point higher levels of incentive pay may, in fact, negatively impact salesperson behaviour performance, as salespeople divert efforts into the activities that create higher short-term sales results and thus higher income.[52]

A danger is that, at a time when managements are emphasizing strong customer relations and customer retention, this may produce immediate sales results acquired at the expense of good relationships and long-term market position. A particular problem is faced by expatriates who receive enhanced remuneration to go abroad, then find a downward adjustment of salary on return. Also, the expatriate may work alongside lower-paid local salespeople who resent the differential.

Sales Force Control and Evaluation

Sales management control is concerned with how the sales manager fulfills his or her responsibilities in the direct supervision of salespeople. Typically the field sales manager has responsibility for 10 or fewer salespeople, who make up the sales unit. In all managerial processes, control and evaluation play a critical role. It is not only a way to endorse what has been done, but a way to re-orient the global sales force if need be. One way to think about sales-force evaluation is in terms of **activity objectives** and **results objectives**. Activity objectives apply when the salesperson is being judged on factors such as the number of sales calls made per period of time, or the extent to which his or her portfolio of accounts is expanding. The salesperson is being judged on results when the focus shifts to the profitability of the portfolio.

Another way to describe this, using different terminology, is to speak in terms of *behaviour* (activity) control and *outcome* (results) control. Assessing behaviour performance is relevant to management because salespeople exercise more control over their activities than over the outcome of these actions. Sales managers are understandably concerned with sales results; however, behaviour performance is receiving increasing attention because of growing preoccupation with team and customer-relations issues, as previously noted, as well as sales results. In other words, outcomes are important, but the behaviour (input) that leads to sales results must also be emphasized. As far as outcomes are concerned, the challenge for management is to identify those that are directly attributable to the salesperson—for example, sales volume, sales of high-margin products, or sales of new products.

However, the key question is what control and evaluative criteria should be used in each country. Canadian and U.S. companies, for example, try to maximize profits, which results in a preference for numbers or a bottom-line orientation. Most Asian countries, on the other hand, tend to de-emphasize numbers for control purposes and use fewer quantitative measures.[53] The essential rule is to use control mechanisms that are sensitive to local needs and conditions. Moreover, these also need to take into account the type of salespeople employed; are they expatriates, host-country nationals, or third-country nationals? Expatriates may be comfortable with the use of controls because they are accustomed to them in Canada. Foreign nationals may not, and their frustration will be accentuated if they have been delegated substantial negotiating and decision authority to act in the local environment. However, knowledge of the impact of sales control systems on salespeople's attitudes and behaviour *in a cross-national setting* is still limited as far as theoretical and empirical research is concerned.[54] More research work in this direction can be expected in the future to guide decisions in this area.

Sales-Force Automation

Interest in applying **sales-force automation (SFA)**, that is, using technology to improve selling efficiency and reduce costs, goes back at least to the 1980s, when laptop computers first emerged. The early 1990s seemed to suggest that an era of full-blown SFA had been born, with one often-quoted survey finding 64 percent of the 124 responding companies believing that SFA had paid off and 80 percent of these also believing that productivity had increased because of these systems.[55] By 1996 it was estimated that, in the United States alone, 2.2 million salespeople were using SFA systems, with a yearly growth rate of 40 percent.[56] The Global Marketplace 14.4 offers background on some SFA implementation problems.

Today, in order for salespeople to meet the rapidly changing expectations of customers, they need to know more—and more speedily. In broad terms, technology enables salespeople to store, retrieve, and analyze customer data and make specific recommendations that are customized for long-term business solutions. Technology also assists with the management of key information during sales cycles, and allows salespeople to communicate in real time with their companies and other sales team members, an ever-increasing need. Although technology advances the practice of selling and the maintenance of inter-organizational relations in many ways, it also creates substantial additional burdens on salespeople. For example, it increases demands for more customer information in real time and requires salespeople to incorporate new technology into already busy work schedules without let-up from their primary selling responsibilities.

In practice, SFA tools are frequently implemented on a global scale to facilitate customer relationship management (CRM) processes as part of a relationship marketing philosophy.[57] This should not be thought of as a narrow application of technology. In fact this automation subsumes a variety of applications including contact and lead management, account analysis, order processing and follow-up, document management, sales presentations, and product and sales training. As a result, the way in which traditional selling is performed and salespeople are managed is changing. Managers are understandably attracted by the prospects of increased productivity, decreased selling costs, better sales control, and improved customer relations management, both domestically and internationally, that is promised by the technology. In short, by improving the speed and quality of information flow among the salesperson, the customer, and the organization, SFA tools support the sales process.

In addition, many SFA vendors offer tools that are intended to make repetitive (usually administrative) tasks more efficient. These vendors stress that salespeople who complete routine tasks more quickly or efficiently become more productive overall by re-allocating time gains to more "face time" with buyers. For example, contact management software helps salespeople manage leads, track all communications with customers, schedule follow-ups, and handle time-management and planning tasks. In reality, salespeople use an even broader range of technologies for managing relationships than those offered by sales-based CRM or SFA vendors, including general-purpose hardware and software tools.

The Global MARKETPLACE 14.4

Automating the Sales Force

Dataram Corp. saw its sales shrivelling and its distributor-based sales struggling to meet the needs of a rapidly changing market. To survive, Dataram executives decided the company had to go directly to its worldwide customers. However, with only a few in-house sales representatives and inadequate mechanisms to track leads and service customers, the New Jersey–based supplier of storage and memory products for high-end computers faced an uphill battle against formidable odds.

The most critical decision in Dataram's change of approach was to automate its sales force. The company's sales representatives and managers worldwide are now equipped with Dell notebook computers listing vital information about their clients and the company's products and services. The system is used to manage database marketing activity such as lead generation and tracking, trade shows, telemarketing, advertising tracking, product support, and customer service. Management can also spot emerging trends, avert impending disasters, and forecast sales with the help of the system. "When a sales rep can answer a question in 15 minutes instead of 3 days, the company is perceived as a consultant as much as a vendor," say company officials. Recruiting salespeople may be easier when a company can offer state-of-the-art support. Furthermore, if turnover takes place, important customer information is not lost but preserved in the database.

Sales-force automation (SFA), like anything else in marketing, is subject to the realities of the international environment: borders, time zones, languages, and cultures. Sales professionals may see their customer accounts as proprietary and may not be willing to share information for fear of losing their leverage. Furthermore, in markets in which personal relationships drive sales practices, such as in Latin America, technological wizardry may be frowned upon. Representatives in every country may want to do things slightly differently, which means that a system that can be localized is needed. This localization may be as comprehensive as complete language translations or as minor as changing address fields in the database. Another issue to be considered is cost—hardware costs are higher in Europe, and telecommunications costs have to be factored in. Finally, with transoceanic support needs, the company may want to look for local support or invest in keeping desk personnel on board at off-hours.

A significant concern is the cost. A Latin American company may face a price tag of $2 million for a large company or $700,000 for a midsize or small firm. However, according to a recent study, automated companies have realized sales increases of 10 to 30 percent, and in some cases as much as 100 percent.

Complaints are also heard. While initial reactions to the use of technology are normally high, six months after implementation some companies report negative job-related perceptions by salespeople, some even going so far as to reject the technology. Poor results are especially likely when salespeople feel that their jobs or roles are being threatened. These facts need to be incorporated into the implementation plan of any SFA program.

Sources: "How Sales Teams Should Use CRM," *Customer Relationship Management* 10 (February 2006): 30–35; Cheri Speier and Viswanath Venkatesh, "The Hidden Minefields in the Adoption of Sales Force Automation Techniques," *Journal of Marketing* 66 (July 2002): 98–111; "Increasing Sales Force Performance," *Industrial Distribution*, July 2002, 30; Kathleen V. Schmidt, "Why SFA Is a Tough Sell in Latin America," *Marketing News*, January 3, 2000; Steven Barth, "Building a Global Infrastructure," *World Trade*, April 1999, S8–S10; Eric J. Adams, "Sales Force Automation: The Second Time Around," *World Trade*, March 1996, 72–74; "Risky Business," *World Trade*, December 1995, 50–51; and "Power Tool," *World Trade*, November 1993, 42–44. See also **http://www.dataram.com**.

For example, salespeople use cell phones (for communications) and spreadsheets (for analysis), two technology tools that sales managers will frequently consider essential to manage customer relations, yet these will typically not be regarded as CRM or SFA technologies. However, it can be stressed that gains in efficiency will have a net positive effect only if they free salespeople from time spent on non-selling activities and if the salesperson redirects that incremental time to tasks that improve relationship-building performance with customers. As firms begin to shift more "efficient" administrative work (e.g., record keeping) on to the shoulders of salespeople, the latter may find that this work still takes time and detracts from the hoped-for increase in customer-related activity.

Beyond SFA and CRM, we need to recognize that salespeople use a broad range of information technologies (IT) to facilitate or enable their performance. These might be called *sales technology tools* and will include, for example, graphics software, relational

In More Detail 14.4

EUROPEAN EXPERIENCE OF SFA

The SFA systems in use in all three countries were very similar in design and capability, even though three entirely different software systems (custom-developed by three different vendors) were in use. All were laptop computer–based systems that connected via modem to a central server, allowing for communications between all parties throughout the particular country. The systems allowed the salesperson to do such things as access customer databases, keep track of customers seen, record results of sales calls (call reports), send and receive sales data, and complete basic sales analyses via spreadsheet software. All systems allowed sales management and headquarters to analyze sales-call activity and effectiveness; all included word-processing software, e-mail capability, and the ability to receive and/or use various training programs from head office. The systems were developed with teams consisting of salespeople, field sales managers, and internal management, along with the system developers and consultants; an SFA need survey was conducted in each country prior to final development. While improvements were continually being sought, reasonable satisfaction with the working of the systems was reported.

database programs, sales forecasting tools, computer-based presentations, and so on. In other words, sales technology tools span the entire gamut of ITs that salespeople use to perform their roles, not simply the subset designated as sales CRM or SFA tools.

International Aspects of Sales-Force Automation

Focusing specifically on SFA, we find that, in practice, sales-force automation systems are increasingly designed to support multiple markets. In addition, the software is normally fully customizable; for example, if the company wishes to add a field for "time zone" to keep track of where its people are internationally, they can do so. This is not to say that implementation problems are absent;[58] however, significant sales increases have been attributable to automation in different countries.[59] According to industry sources, most Canadian companies with internationally based sales forces use a Web-based system, such as Salesforce.com,[60] because it is easier to keep accurate real-time data.

A measure of the international scope of sales-force automation is given by the fact that many vendors are themselves global companies, for example, organizations such as SAP, Baan, and Seibel. Their customers include both global companies that want a single, proven platform worldwide that can be locally customized and local companies that seek to leverage world-class technology. A Canadian-based vendor, Salesboom, illustrates this trend, and also its recency.[61] A world leader in on-demand customer relations management solutions, the company was founded in 2002 in Halifax. It has over 23,000 subscribers and 3,000 customers in over 148 countries around the world. Appropriately for Canada, Salesboom sees itself as a provider dedicated to small business. The company's software supports multiple languages so that SMEs can receive data in virtually any language required, thereby obtaining a fully global view of their organization's customer relations management data. Traditionally, many firms built costly IT systems independently. Today the advent of automated sales-force technologies enables businesses to subscribe to already-built, on-demand, customizable services that rival conventional approaches.

International Case Study

Research on the use of SFA in different countries is sparse, but we can cite one study that examined the experiences of the sales forces of a large pharmaceutical company, all using first-generation SFA systems and having used them for several years at the time of the enquiry.[62] The sales forces were operating in Germany, England, and the United States.

Problems of SFA Implementation

The fact that SFA has been adopted successfully in an international context should not blind us to the implementation difficulties that have been encountered and that continue to be faced. Salesperson discomfort with and skepticism toward new technology should not cause overmuch surprise, but as one authority states, the result of these reactions is that "technology adoption by the sales force is lagging, and firms lament the financial losses occurring as a result of huge technology investments that produce lackluster returns on investment."[63]

Moreover, existing research on technology use in the SFA area indicates that high SFA resistance brings unintended negative consequences, such as unfavourable job attitudes and turnover intentions as a result of adopting technology. Clearly, SFA adoption depends upon the extent of salesperson buy-in, yet salespeople may not be able to forecast accurately their assessment of relative advantages ahead of a period of trial operation. In other words, perceptions of relative advantage may be high initially, yet the benefits provided by SFA may not be wanted when the technology is put to practical use.[64] It would be useful to have some kind of early warning of possible problems prior to implementation, but salespeople will find it difficult to articulate these without hands-on experience.

One way of overcoming SFA resistance is to involve salespeople in the implementation process and then appropriately train them.[65] Recall that, in the case study above, salespeople and others were involved in the development of the SFA systems that were eventually successfully installed. We might also note that in this case, all countries carried out pilot projects prior to the rollouts and conducted comprehensive training programs, including follow-up sessions throughout the first year, following the implementation and periodically thereafter. In this way, negative feelings, such as the perception of being displaced by SFA tools, were identified and dealt with early.

Where SFA tools might truly replace the functionality provided by the salesperson, the organization could choose not to proceed to implementation because of the fear of alienating successful salespeople and the higher potential of the SFA technologies to be rejected. For example, for some customer interactions, a website providing design recommendations may be preferred by the company, potentially undermining experienced sales engineers. However, a decision not to proceed with SFA may create long-term competitive disadvantages with either higher selling costs or comparative inefficiencies in the sales process. At the very least, firms need a careful assessment of how SFA tools change the salesperson's role, along with an appreciation of the sales behaviours that should remain "unautomated."

At worst, salespersons may feel that, where the firm proposes to employ "competence-destroying" technologies, their role as intermediary between company and customer is being dislocated. In addition, management can utilize technology to increase control over the sales force through, for example, easy access to data on the salesperson's sales-call frequency. This increases the perceived power distance between salesperson and sales manager in the latter's favour, a development not likely to be welcomed by most salespeople. Companies need to be sensitive to such perceptions if they are to make effective technology adoption decisions.

Future Prospects for Sales-Force Automation

Although we have emphasized implementation difficulties, the fact is that firms invest billions of dollars worldwide in sales-force technologies in order to improve sales-force effectiveness and efficiency. Areas of gain include better customer targeting, good time management, better call planning, improved communications with field sales, better information flow to and from salespeople, and administrative savings and efficiencies. But despite the expectations of productivity improvements, the gains have been realized very slowly.[66] Taking a more macro view of this dilemma, it may be that what we are seeing is basically an illustration of the well-known tendency for productivity in service industry sectors and service functions to lag significantly behind increases in manufacturing technology.

For companies, measurement of the advantages of SFA in cost-benefit terms may give initially disappointing results. The technology may contribute to improved sales performance, but the costs of the technology, in terms of initial investment and upgrading costs, can exceed the profit contribution from the increased sales. The problem facing firms is clear: invest in SFA and risk a potential reduction in profitability, or postpone the investment and run another kind of risk—loss of business to competitors who have made the investment and are therefore employing superior sales technology.

A compromise appears to be in order: make the investment (because global markets will increasingly expect technology to support their purchases or relationships) and work to find solutions to problems of implementation. As to implementation, salespeople with greater technology orientation are better able to leverage information (i.e., make the available information more effective), which should, in turn, facilitate adaptive behaviours that are positively related to effecting selling.[67] In other words, SFA influences key aspects of sales performance, and this is important as far as sale managers are concerned when evaluating the relationship-building efforts of the sales force. The fact that younger salespeople often are more "technology literate" may create something of a gender gap in some companies, and it has been argued that highly experienced salespeople will gain the least performance benefits from SFA system use.[68]

While it is important to understand sales-force perception of new technology and to encourage its use, it may be important to get beyond the adoption issue as such by taking a broader perspective. For example, companies might think in terms of aligning the CRM program properly with employees, processes, and technology—that is, pursuing the most appropriate balance between the demands of relationship management and the capabilities of the firm's employees. Consideration of SFA would then be seen as a subset within this larger framework.[69] As far as marketing and sales strategists are concerned, consideration of SFA might be positioned in the wider context of the interplay between modern relational selling and an information-intensive environment, which drives the importance of sales technology.[70] (Exhibit 14.4 shows a company advertisement for customer relations management software.)

In the process of reviewing CRM and technology adoption issues, recent research suggests that companies will have to consider some very fundamental re-conceptualizations of the salesperson's role. This will involve seeing the salesperson not only as part of the promotion but also as an important part of the firm's *product.* When a product is viewed as the "need-satisfying offering of a firm," customers evaluate the offering on the basis of the total satisfaction it provides.[71] Therefore, salespeople represent an important means for achieving total satisfaction by differentiating the firm's offering. IBM and several other firms rely on this sales-service differentiation and consultative selling to provide superior value to their customers. An important precursor to delivering high-quality consultative sales services is the salesperson's relationship-building capability with customers. It is within this context that SFA investments should ideally be evaluated.

Selling Through Distributor Partners

The Canadian SME's initial foray into international markets is typically achieved through an agent or distributor with whom relationships will have to be built up and toward whom sales activities are directed. The problems of selling to distributors are therefore worthy of some further attention. (See also the discussion in Chapter 12 regarding distributors in global marketing.) However, let us emphasize that distributors are not the only type of partner through whom the company might operate. Joint ventures, licensing, or local subsidiary arrangements can also involve partnering.

Looking specifically at distributors, the wise exporter will regard these as a group or segment of customers. As such, they should be the focal point of the exporter's marketing planning and therefore deserving of as much selling attention as any other customer group. Sales to them and by them will be encouraged or discouraged by the nature and scale of the selling effort directed at them, including building good relationships.

An important factor influencing the type and level of selling by the exporter is the sorts of distributors actually chosen. Granting exclusive selling rights to a small number of agents will lead to a relatively close relationship with the principal. In contrast, selling to a wide range of distributors (e.g., for minor products in the building industry) with no exclusivity arrangements will be less binding on both parties.

Exhibit 14.4 An Example of CRM Software for Enhancing Customer Relations

{the ugly truth}

THE LIFE OF A SALESPERSON IS HARD

The right solutions take the pain away.
Whatever you can do to improve the effectiveness of your team's prospecting, account planning and sales-call preparation makes them happier and more productive.

Factiva SalesWorks™ from Dow Jones offers the highest-powered customer intelligence and tools that give salespeople a competitive edge.

Learn what you can do to make it easier for your people to sell more. Download Factiva's free white paper "Why Is It So Tough to Sell Today and What to Do About It."
www.factiva.com/toughtosell

Better decisions. Faster.®

Source: Factiva Sales Works, by Dow Jones. Ad used with permission of Factiva, Inc. 2007.

In some instances, selling to an exclusive agent will involve various activities, such as assisting with the selection of the agent's sales force, advising on sales methods found appropriate by the exporter, and generally providing sales management help. By reducing the agent's burden of sales planning in this way, the principal is better placed to get acceptance of selling restrictions associated with the award of exclusive rights. On the other hand, small companies with little or no sales experience in the foreign market may be a good deal more dependent on the agent's skills and resources, at least initially.

Through visits to the overseas market, a variety of tasks can be performed by the exporter's sales representative. He or she can ensure the distributors do stock the product and that the stocks are adequately maintained. Also, if needed, the sales representative can give on-the-spot support to ensure that everything is being done to move the product out—for example, by checking the local impact of exporter advertising, or by checking on the attitude of final consumers to the product's functioning, packaging, and presentation.

Obviously, much depends on the length of stay of the visiting salesperson. If time permits he or she might join the distributor in joint selling and promotional work or arrange training courses covering product aspects or sales techniques. In the absence of a presence abroad, the exporter must depend on the local operatives, supported by communications through e-mail and conference calls. The latter are clearly not a complete substitute for one-on-one communications; they also suffer if there are language difficulties among the parties involved or substantial time differences between the two countries.

Problems of Selling Through Distributors

The beginning stage of exporting is particularly difficult if a strong selling effort is needed to break into desired accounts. This should be taken as normal in the fiercely competitive U.S. market, an obvious first destination of the intending exporter. If the final customer is satisfied with his existing supplier, the task becomes doubly challenging. In this case, the customer must be persuaded that it is economically beneficial to change and that no risk is involved. Achieving this aim is problematic enough in the home market, but headaches are added when a distant, unknown culture, and a new (to the exporter) distributor team is responsible for sales.

A specific problem is that sales techniques employed successfully in the domestic market may not be fully applicable abroad. This hampers the well-intentioned support efforts of the exporter's sales staff. For example, the Japanese sales process is known to be far more people- and time-oriented than in the West, reflecting that culture's emphasis on personal service and personal relationships. There are typically more preliminary visits with the customer, and it may take months to establish a relationship. Shortcutting the process is not considered an option. In Korea, "friendship selling" is widespread, favouring the local representative with contacts. The exporter must adapt to these conditions. Although no stranger to relationship selling, the Canadian firm needs to accept a different interpretation of this in some markets if success is to be achieved.

This problem is not confined to far-distant markets, however. In the case of the United States, which is frequently thought of as a uniform, monolithic entity, there are actually several geographic divisions with very different values, lifestyles, and buying behaviours. For example, the New England states still reflect traditional British culture in many ways, whereas the large urban centres (Chicago, New York, Detroit) are more cosmopolitan. Differences are less dramatic, of course, than in more far-flung locations, and the language is common, but exporters still need to choose distributors who understand the values of consumers in each region and who have developed appropriate selling approaches. A selling approach working well in one setting may not transfer well to another, unless great adaptability is possible.

Regardless of cultural gaps, the company needs to give distributors all necessary product and service support, especially if the distributor's sales force faces strong competition from similar products. There is a clear possibility that in some markets sales performance will be maintained largely by the personal qualities and acceptability of the sales force, rather than by the perceived benefits and competitive advantages of the firm's products.

The exporter may find this a potentially unstable—even volatile—situation, and therefore the more that can be learned about the underlying reasons for any relationship advantage in the foreign market, the better. Such knowledge may not be available immediately, but it is likely to increase with time as the market develops and relationships are solidified.

As a company gains experience working with distributors in a particular foreign market, it may become evident that even more success might be achieved by gaining more control of and feedback from the foreign market. Such a need may only become apparent over time, but companies may eventually find themselves under increasing pressure to become more involved in the foreign market. This may initially take the form of a foreign sales and marketing office, but could eventually lead to a distribution centre, customer support/repair centre, and foreign manufacturing.

With regard to setting up a foreign sales office, this might initially be quite modest, involving, say, the hiring of a local salesperson, but expansion can take place as required, perhaps triggered by a move from exclusive to non-exclusive distribution. Once the distributor loses his exclusive protection, it will naturally decrease his local marketing activities. The foreign sales office would then take on these responsibilities. A decision to locate a sales force in the foreign market is in effect a foreign direct investment (FDI) decision. The long-term benefits of such a strategy must be assessed and weighed against the potential risks. Benefits include increase in control, feedback, access to local resources, and lower export barriers. Against this must be weighed increased money, time, and resource commitments by the firm. Each company will make its individual decision based on the peculiar circumstances it faces.

The Role of Expatriates in Global Sales-Force Management

It has been a recurring if not a dominant theme of this book that international marketing presents numerous specialized problems arising from cross-cultural differences. It will therefore not be surprising if expatriate Canadians working abroad encounter difficulties. As the pace of globalization quickens, the likelihood is that an increasing number of Canadian companies will choose to locate abroad and will decide to use Canadian nationals in sales and sales management roles in foreign countries. Expatriates are favoured by, for example, technical companies because of their high product knowledge and ability to give follow-up service.[72] Many big-ticket products are sold directly from the head office with automatic involvement of expatriates. Also, overseas duty gives companies opportunities to train managers and prepare junior executives for promotion. Moreover, expatriates enable a global firm to maintain a physical presence and degree of control over international marketing and sales activities. However, international relocation is risky and problematic, both from the company's and the expatriate's point of view. Some of these problems are discussed below.

High Cost

Fifty percent of expatriate benefit packages cost between 3 and 3.9 times the expatriate's salary.[73] Also, expatriates are more expensive than local equivalents.[74] The result is that companies send as few people abroad as possible. Therefore, expatriates carry more responsibility than if they stayed at home. Because of this responsibility element, companies tend to send their best people, who find that their success or failure has a major impact on their careers. It is thus very important to ensure the level of commitment of expatriates before they are sent overseas and to ensure they are given enough incentive to stay with the company once they return to Canada. Ironically, as globalization breaks down barriers and as the expatriate builds intercultural communications skills, he or she becomes an increasingly valuable commodity in the employment market as a whole. It becomes more difficult to retain an expatriate who enjoys a growing potential for a range of future career possibilities and is able to command higher salary and benefits.

Uncertain Outcomes

Success in international assignments is by no means guaranteed. Although the lure of overseas travel attracts many, the likelihood is high—between 20 and 30 percent—that expatriates will fail to complete the tour.[75] In the early 1990s, Sun Microsystems experienced failure rates of up to 62 percent.[76] Up to 50 percent of those sent overseas and who remain in their positions until the end of their assignments are either ineffective or only marginally effective.[77] This may in part be due to poor selection procedures.[78] International assignments are therefore a financial risk for the company, but also a potential source of other problems—poor sales and deterioration of customer relations in the foreign market, for example. The career risk for the non-performing individual is also clear.

These international failures result more from inability to adjust to a new environment than from poor innate capabilities or business-related issues.[79] Therefore the probability of success is most likely to flow from sound preparation of both expatriates and their families for the adjustments they will have to make. Expatriates, for their part, must appreciate the dramatic effect on their professional and personal lives that can occur.

Training

Expatriates must be carefully trained and sensitized to the culture of the overseas market, including a basic knowledge of the area's language and cultural beliefs. No matter how loyal to the company or how knowledgeable the expatriate salesperson may be, cultural alienation can make him or her ineffectual. In Singapore, for example, people strive for the yin-yang balance in a harmonization of traditional customs and beliefs with the creation of an economically advanced society. Modern high-rise buildings contain every high-tech facility imaginable, but in the stairwell one might find an offering of joss sticks and oranges stacked in even numbers. This seemingly incongruous juxtaposition of modern and traditional ways of life can be a great mystery to Canadian and other expatriates. If ignored, it can lead to a subtle resisting of the expatriate's instructions and the creation of an invisible obstacle.[80]

Initially, salespeople and their families need to examine their lifestyles and values and take into account differences in beliefs, interpersonal communications, and behaviour in the new environment. The entire gamut of sales activities—conducting meetings, dealing with sales calls, making presentations, negotiating, and closing—can be handled differently abroad, as we have seen in previous sections of the chapter. Spouses and children present particular problems. The spouse may resent having to give up his or her job in Canada, or may find it difficult to obtain work abroad because of cultural or language barriers. Children may have to be taken out of school at an awkward time, and the curriculum followed in the overseas school may be different from the Canadian one. Other issues include security, housing, health care, and transportation.

Despite numerous problems, the expatriate stands to benefit in different ways. For example, there should be career enhancement flowing from useful new experience, and promotion often accompanies the assignment. Salary and benefits will probably be attractive, including the prospect of lower taxes (as in the Middle East) and lower living costs. At the personal level, the exposure to new ways of thinking leads to a broadening of perspective, and the expatriate's skill base should be widened. Travelling abroad also helps to build the expatriate's contact network, which can be useful in any number of ways once he or she returns home.

Other Options

With proper cross-cultural training and preparation, companies can get better value for money and better results from expatriate assignments. However, there are other options.

Hiring Host-Country Nationals

Hiring a salesperson who already lives in the target country brings the benefit of local market and cultural knowledge, language skills, and familiarity with local business conditions.[81] Also, the company can "get going" more quickly by eliminating the adjustment period. However, locals may need extensive product training, and loyalty to the company cannot be automatically assumed. The increased use of English in the last one or two decades has reduced the importance of local language skills except for locally oriented industries.

Hiring Third-Country Nationals

These salespersons can offer the same cultural sensitivity and language skills as host-country nationals and may be less costly to hire. But they share some of the disadvantages of host-country nationals, and they have additional problems, such as identity; third-country salespeople have no strong connection with where they work or for whom.[82] Also, they face adaptation problems similar to those encountered by expatriates. However, in many cases, and particularly for regionally focused companies, third-country nationals can be an effective compromise between expatriates and host-country nationals.[83]

Staying at Home

This may seem an unusual option, but the question remains: why pull up stakes at all? Thanks to technological developments, from e-mail to computer networking, it is increasingly possible to maintain one's job at home while assuming responsibilities abroad, a trend that is becoming increasingly common as Canadian business expands internationally.[84] This option will not be appropriate in all circumstances, but consider two examples. Royal Bank of Canada investment advisers in RBC's global private banking group deal with clients all over the world including Asia, Europe, South America, and the Middle East. Clients wish to deal with bank representatives located in Canada. Visits abroad are still necessary—face-to-face contact is difficult to eliminate entirely—but because of available technology, the pressure to relocate abroad is greatly reduced. This is encouraged by companies because of lower costs, and welcomed by advisers, who do not have to contemplate a disruption in their lives.

Another example is Amec Inc., an international project management and service company with Canadian operational headquarters in Oakville, Ontario. The company uses electronic data sharing and teleconferencing to create working links between home-based employees to projects throughout the world. The organization has become attractive to employees, because they like the ability to gain world experience without having to commit to a move.

"Staying at home" will be more adaptable to some aspects of the selling process and sales management than to others. When a one-on-one contact is vital and the company is not well-known, dealing from a distance has obvious disadvantages. But once relationships are established, international executives may be able to maintain a home base and rely on regular visits abroad.

Summary

This chapter reviews issues in international selling and sales management. The implications for the firm's international strategy of adopting a resource-based or transaction-cost view of the firm are discussed at the outset. The extent of company involvement in personal selling is then noted to be a function of the degree of internationalization of the firm, and Canada is shown to be at an intermediate stage. The various stages of personal selling are discussed, and the importance of cross-cultural sensitivity at each stage is emphasized. Issues in sales management are reviewed, including sales planning, plan implementation, and sales-force evaluation, with reference to international implications. Issues of hiring, motivating, training, and compensating international salespeople are discussed. Attention is drawn to the international impact of sales-force automation, and to the special problems faced by exporters selling to and through intermediaries. This is important given the preponderance of small Canadian companies involved in exporting. The chapter concludes by discussing the problems experienced by companies and employees who are faced with working overseas.

Key Terms

activity objectives (p. 502)
adaptive selling (p. 494)
approach (p. 488)
closing (p. 488)
customer relationship management (p. 487)
direct exports (p. 484)
follow-up (p. 488)
indirect exports (p. 485)
integrated exports (p. 487)
low-pressure selling (p. 494)
missionary selling (p. 496)
order-mindedness (p. 494)
overcoming buyer objections (p. 488)
pre-approach (p. 488)
prospecting (p. 488)
relationship selling (p. 496)
resource-based view (p. 484)
results objectives (p. 502)
sales-force automation (SFA) (p. 503)
sales management objectives (p. 497)
transaction-cost approach (p. 484)

Questions for Discussion

1. Many countries are engaged in international marketing. Some are more heavily involved in selling and sales management activities than others. Discuss reasons for this.
2. Is adaptive selling appropriate to international selling? Why or why not?
3. International salespeople should be "sales-minded," but they should also be culturally sensitive. Discuss how sales managers should accommodate these orientations in hiring, training, motivating, and compensating the sales force.
4. What are the advantages and disadvantages of sales-force automation from the point of view of a small exporter?
5. After graduation, you accept a sales position with a small company making educational software. The company plans to send you to China for 6 months to "explore the market." What preparations would you make for the trip? What help would you expect from the company?
6. Compare and contrast the problems of selling through foreign agents and distributors with selling directly to end users abroad.

Internet Exercises

1. A resource for the latest developments in personal selling and sales management is the Sales Marketing Network (SMN) at **http://www.info-now.com**. It includes reports on various topics, including many discussed in this chapter (e.g., sales training and sales management). Visit the SMN site. Select a topic covered in the chapter (e.g., sales-force automation) and summarize the critical issues identified for this practice.
2. SolutionInc is a small Canadian telecommunications company facing competition from far larger companies and operating in a world where innovation is a matter of survival. Visit its website at **http://www.solutioninc.com**. Familiarize yourself with the company's products. Also visit **http://www.edc.ca/exportwise** and read the article "SolutionInc: Nothing Succeeds Like Access." What role do you think personal selling as discussed in the chapter has played in the company's success?

Recommended Readings

Bauer, Gerald J., Mark S. Baunchalk, Thomas N. Ingram, and Raymond W. LaForge. *Emerging Thoughts in Sales Thought and Practice.* Westport CT: Quorum Books, 1998.

Daly, John L., ed. *Training in Developing Nations: A Handbook for Expatriates.* Armonk, NY: M.E. Sharpe, 2005.

Griffin, John P. *International Sales and the Middleman.* 2nd rev. ed. Cirencester, UK: Management Books 2000, 1998.

Hess, Melissa Brayer, and Patricia Linderman. *The Expert Expatriate: Your Guide to Successful Relocation Abroad.* Yarmouth, ME: Intercultural Press, 2002.

Hodge, Sheida. *Global Smarts: The Art of Communicating and Deal Making Anywhere in the World.* New York: John Wiley and Sons, 2000.

Holliday, Adrian, John Kullman, and Martin Hyde. *Intercultural Communication: An Advanced Resource Book.* London: Routledge, 2004.

Honeycutt, Earl D., John B. Ford, and Antonis C. Simintiras. *Sales Management: A Global Perspective.* New York: Routledge, 2003.

Honeycutt, Earl D., and Lew Kurtzman. *Selling Outside Your Culture Zone: A Guide for Sales Success in Today's Cross-Cultural Marketplace.* Dallas, TX: Behavioural Sciences Research Press, 2006.

Rugman, Alan M. *The Regional Multinationals: MNEs and Global Strategic Management.* Cambridge: Cambridge University Press, 2005.

Schuster, Camille P., and Michael J. Copeland. *Global Business: Planning for Sales and Negotiations.* Mason, OH: International Thomson Publishing, 1997.

Notes

1. George S. Day, "The Capabilities of Market-Driven Organizations," *Journal of Marketing* 58 (October 1994): 37–52.
2. Laurence Capron and John Hulland, "Redeployment of Brands, Sales Forces, and General Marketing Management Expertise Following Horizontal Acquisitions: A Resource-Based View," *Journal of Marketing* 63 (April 1999): 41–54.
3. Frederick E. Webster, Jr., "The Changing Role of Marketing in the Corporation," *Journal of Marketing* 56 (October 1992): 1–17.
4. Birger Wernerfelt, "A Resource-Based View of the Firm," *Strategic Management Journal* 5, no. 2 (1984): 171–80.
5. Capron and Hulland, op. cit.
6. Bernard J. Jaworski and Ajay K. Kohli, "Marketing Orientation: Antecedents and Consequences," *Journal of Marketing* 57 (July 1993): 53–70.
7. J. Brock Smith and Donald W. Barclay, "The Effects of Organizational Differences and Trust on the Effectiveness of Selling Partner Relationships," *Journal of Marketing* 61 (January 1997): 3–21.
8. J. Brock Smith and Donald W. Barclay, "Team Selling Effectiveness: A Small Group Perspective," *Journal of Business-to-Business Marketing* 1, no. 2 (1993): 3–32.
9. Smith and Barclay, 1993, op. cit.
10. Ronald Coase, "The Nature of the Firm," in *The Nature of the Firm,* ed. O.E. Williamson and G. Winter (Oxford: Oxford University Press, 1991); and O.E. Williamson, "Transaction Cost Economics: The Governance of Contractual Relations," *Journal of Law and Economics* 22 (1979): 233–61.
11. E. Anderson and H. Gatignon, "Modes of Foreign Entry: A Transaction Cost Analysis and Propositions," *Journal of International Business Studies* 11 (Fall 1986): 1–26.
12. Anoop Madhok, "Reassessing the Fundamentals and Beyond: Ronald Coase, the Transaction Cost and Resource-Based Theories of the Firm and the Institutional Structure of Production," *Strategic Management Journal* 23, no. 6 (April 2002): 535–50.
13. "Responding to Unsolicited International Orders," http://www.exportsource.ca/gol/exportsource/site.nsf/en/es03268.html.
14. Charlene Solomon, "Managing an Overseas Sales Force," *World Trade,* April 1999, S4–S6.
15. Statistics Canada, *A Profile of Canadian Exporters, 1993–2002,* Catalogue No. 65-506-XIE, November 2004.
16. Karl Moore and Alan Rugman, "Canadian Multinationals Are Regional, Not Global," *Options Politiques,* August 2003, 44–46.
17. Moore and Rugman, op. cit.
18. Rob Wright, "Getting a Grip on China," *Exportwise,* Winter 2006, 2.
19. Steven P. Brown, "Use of Closed Influence Tactics by Salespeople: Incidence and Buyer Attributions," *Journal of Personal Selling and Sales Management* 10 (Fall 1990), 17–29.
20. Rosann L. Spiro and Barton A. Weitz, "Adaptive Selling: Conceptualization, Measurement, and Nomological Validity," *Journal of Marketing Research* 27 (February 1990).
21. Richard G. McFarland, Goutam N. Challagalla, and Tasadduq A. Shervani, "Influence Tactics for Effective Adaptive Selling," *Journal of Marketing* 70 (October 2006), 103–17.
22. Bernard Weiner, *An Attributional Theory of Motivation and Emotion* (New York: Springer-Verlag, 1986).
23. Andrea Dixon, Rosann L. Spiro, and Maqbul Jamil, "Successful and Unsuccessful Sales Calls: Measuring Salesperson Attributions and Behavioural Intentions," *Journal of Marketing* 65 (July 2001): 64–78.
24. Roger A. Kerin, Steven W. Hartley, Eric N. Berkowitz, and William Rudelius, *Marketing,* 8th ed. (New York: McGraw-Hill Irwin, 2006), 533–39.
25. Das Narayandas and V. Kasturi Rangan, "Building and Sustaining Buyer-Seller Relationships in Mature Industrial Markets," *Journal of Marketing* 65, no. 3 (July 2004): 63–77.
26. Narayandas and Rangan, op. cit.
27. Theodore Levitt, *Industrial Purchasing Behaviour* (Cambridge, MA.: Harvard Business School, 1965).
28. IBM International Technical Support Organization, *Selling IBM's Innovative Solutions,* (January 2007), **http://www.redbooks.ibm.com/redbooks/pdfs/sg246330.pdf**.
29. The Virtual Trade Commissioners Service, **http://www.infoexport.gc.ca/ie-en/MarketReportsAndServices.jsp**.
30. Industry Canada, *Service Industries: The Cross-Cultural Marketing Edge,* **http://strategis.ic.gc.ca** (accessed October 20, 2006).
31. E.C. Bursk, *Text and Cases in Marketing: A Scientific Approach* (Englewood Cliffs, N.J.: Prentice-Hall, 1962).
32. Michael Levy and Arun Sharma, "Adaptive Selling: The Role of Gender, Age, Sales Experience, and Education," *Journal of Business Research* 31 (1994): 39–47; Barton Weitz, "Sales Effectiveness through Adaptation to Situational Demands," in *Personal Selling,* ed. J. Jacoby and C.S. Craig (Toronto: Lexington Books, 1984).
33. Mark C Johlke, "Sales Presentation Skills and Salesperson Job Performance," *Journal of Business and Industrial Marketing* 21, no. 5 (2006): 311–19.
34. A.J. Magrath, "From the Practitioner's Desk: A Comment on 'Personal Selling and Sales Management in the New Millenium,'" *Journal of Personal Selling and Sales Management* 17, no. 1 (1997): 45–47.
35. R.B. Money and J.L. Graham, "Salesperson Performance, Pay, and Job Satisfaction: Tests of a Model Using Data Collected in the United States and Japan," *Journal of International Business Studies* 30, no. 1 (1999): 149–72.
36. T.E. DeCarlo, R.C. Rody, and J.E. DeCarlo, "A Cross National Example of Supervisory Management Practices in the Sales Force," *Journal of Personal Selling and Sales Management* 19 (Winter 1999): 1–14.
37. O.C. Ferrell, T.N. Ingram, and R.W. LaForge, "Initiating Structure for Legal and Ethical Decisions in a Global Sales Organization," *Industrial Marketing Management* 29, no. 6 (2000): 555–64.
38. Hewitt Associates–Maesina International Search, "Dernier de Cordee" (Last in Line), *Action Commerciale* 170 (January 1998): 77.
39. Eric M. Olson, David W. Cravens, and Stanley F. Slater, "Competitiveness and Sales Management: A Marriage of Strategies," *Business Horizons* (March–April 2001): 25–37.

40. Dennis Jones and Sandi Jones, "Diary of an Exporter: Clinotech," Parts 1–4, *Exportwise,* Winter 2004, Summer 2005, Fall 2005.

41. John S. Hill and Richard R. Still, "Organizing the Overseas Sales Force: How Multinationals Do It," *Journal of Personal Selling and Sales Management* 10, no. 2 (Spring 1990): 57–66.

42. Mark W. Johnston, Neil M. Ford, Greg W. Marshall, Gilbert A. Churchill, Orville C. Walker, *Sales Force Management,* 7th ed. (Boston: McGraw-Hill Irwin, 2003).

43. Gregory A. Rich, William H. Bommer, Scott B. McKenzie, Philip M. Podaskoff, and Jonathan L. Johnson, "Apples and Apples or Apples and Oranges? A Meta-Analysis of Objectives and Subjective Measures of Salesperson Performance," *Journal of Personal Selling and Sales Management* (Fall 1999): 41–52.

44. B. Donaldson, *Sales Management: Theory and Practice* (London: Macmillan, 1990).

45. K. Grant, D.W. Cravens, G.S. Low, and W.C. Moncrief, "The Role of Satisfaction with Territory Design on the Modification, Attitudes, and Work Outcomes of Salespeople," *Journal of the Academy of Marketing Science* (Spring 2001): 165–78.

46. Sergio Roman and Salvador Ruiz, "A Comparative Analysis of Sales Training in Europe: Implications for International Sales Negotiations," *International Marketing Review* 28, no. 3 (2003): 304–27.

47. V.D. Bush, G.M. Rose, F. Gilbert, and T.N. Ingram, "Managing Culturally Diverse Buyer-Seller Relationships: The Role of Intercultural Dispositions and Adaptive Selling in Developing Intercultural Communication Competence," *Journal of the Academy of Marketing Science* 29, no. 4 (2001): 391–404.

48. Roman and Ruiz, op. cit.

49. J. Kennedy and A. Everest, "Put Diversity in Context," *Secured Lender* 52, no. 4 (1996): 54–56.

50. E.D. Honeycutt Jr, R.A. Lupton, and T.B. Flaherty, "Selecting and Training the International Sales Force: Comparison of China and Slovakia," *Industrial Marketing Management,* November 1999, 627–36.

51. J.D. Dalrymple, W.L. Cron, and T.E. DeCarlo, *Sales Management,* 7th ed. (New York: John Wiley and Sons, 2001).

52. Nigel F. Piercy, George S. Low, and David W. Cravens, "Examining the Effectiveness of Sales Management Control Practices in Developing Countries," *Journal of World Business* 39 (2004): 255–67.

53. Y.H. Wong and Thomas K. Leung, *Guanxi: Relationship Marketing in a Chinese Context* (Binghampton, NY: Haworth Press, 2001), chap. 3.

54. Dominique Rouzies and Anne Macquin, "An Exploratory Investigation of the Impact of Culture on Sales Force Management Control Systems in Europe," *Journal of Personal Selling and Sales Management* 23, no. 1 (Winter 2002–3), 61–72.

55. T.C. Taylor, "Computers Bring Quick Return," *Sales and Marketing Management,* September 1993, 22–5.

56. S. DeGarmo, "Becoming a Sales Leader," *Selling Success,* May 1996, 4.

57. Cheri Speier and Viswanath Venkatesh, "The Hidden Minefields in the Adoption of Sales Force Automation Technologies, *Journal of Marketing* 66, no. 3 (2002): 98–111.

58. Amy J. Morgan and Scott Inks, "Technology and the Sales Force: Increasing Acceptance of Sales Force Automation," *Industrial Marketing Management* 30, no. 5 (July 2001): 463–72.

59. Robert L. Engle, Michael C. Barnes, "Sales Force Automation Usage, Effectiveness, and Cost-Benefit in Germany, England and the United States," *Journal of Business and Industrial Marketing* 15, no. 4 (July 2000): 216–41.

60. See *http://www.salesforce.com* (accessed September 10, 2006).

61. "Salesboom Multilingual Web Based CRM Software for Small Business," *http://www.salesboom.com/products/tools-multilanguage.html* (accessed November 2, 2006).

62. Engle and Barnes, op. cit.

63. Eli Jones, Steven P. Brown, Andris A. Zoltners, and Barton A. Weitz, "The Changing Environment of Selling and Sales Management," *Journal of Personal Selling and Sales Management* 25, no. 2 (Spring 2005): 105–11.

64. Speier and Venkatesh, op. cit.

65. Speier and Venkatesh, op. cit.

66. Erika Rasmusson, "The Five Steps to Successful Sales Force Automation," *Sales and Marketing Management* 151, no. 3 (1999): 34–40.

67. Engle and Barnes, op. cit.

68. Spiro and Weitz, op. cit.

69. Speier and Venkatesh, op. cit.

70. Alex R. Zablah, Danny L. Bellenger, and Wesley J. Johnston, "Customer Relationship Management Implementation Gaps," *Journal of Personal Selling and Sales Management* 24, no. 4 (Fall 2004): 279–95.

71. Gary K. Hunter and William D. Perreault Jr, "Sales Technology Orientation, Information Effectiveness, and Sales Performance," *Journal of Personal Selling and Sales Management* 26, no. 2 (Spring 2006): 95–113.

72. Nakiye Boyacigiller, "The Role of Expatriates in the Management of Interdependence, Complexity, and Risk in Multinational Corporations, *Journal of International Business Studies* 21, no. 3 (1990): 357–81.

73. Lionel Laroche, "Relocating Abroad," *Engineering Dimensions,* January–February 1999, 33–35.

74. Michael G. Harvey, "The Multinational Corporation's Expatriate Problem: An Application of Murphy's Law," *Business Horizons,* January–February 1983, 71–78.

75. Rosalie L. Tung, "Selection and Training Procedures of U.S., European, and Japanese Multinationals, *Californian Management Review* 25, no. 1 (1982): 57–71.

76. P.M. Carey, "Coming Home: Employers Are Scrambling to Combat the Loss of Returning Expatriates," *CFO Magazine,* June 1988.

77. J.S. Black and M. Mendenhall, "Cross-Cultural Training Effectiveness: A Review and a Theoretical Framework for Future Research," *Academy of Management Review* 15, no. 1 (1990): 113–36.

78. L. Copeland and L. Griggs, *Going International* (New York: Random House, 1985).

79. I. Dolins, "Global Relocation Trends: Surveying the State of International Relocation," *International HR Journal,* Winter 1997.

80. "Intercultural Systems," *http://www.intercultural-systems.com/articles_2.html* (accessed November 8, 2006).

81. Subhash C. Jain, *International Marketing Management* (Cincinnati, OH: South-Western Publishing, 2001); and Sak Onkvisit and John J. Shaw, *International Marketing: Analysis and Strategy* (Upper Saddle River, NJ: Prentice-Hall, 1997).

82. Philip R. Cateora, *International Marketing,* 11th ed. (New York: McGraw-Hill Irwin, 2002).

83. Earl D. Honeycutt Jr and John B. Ford, "Guidelines for Managing an International Sales Force," *Industrial Marketing Management* 24 (1995): 135–44.

84. Jean-Marc Hachey, *The Canadian Guide to Living and Working Abroad* (Ottawa: International Systems, 2004).

Polar-adidas

Introduction

On Sunday, April 3, 2005, in a downtown hotel in Erlangen, Germany, Mr. Jorma Kallio, managing Director of Polar Electro Oy, a Finnish family-owned manufacturer of heart rate monitors, was preparing his opening speech to a group of some 100 Polar Electro employees and partners. He was in central Germany for an internal launch of a partnership between Polar Electro and adidas, the second largest sporting goods manufacturer in the world. The next day, on the premises of the expansive headquarters complex of adidas in Herzogenaurach, the partnership and "Project Fusion," the world's first completely integrated training system, would be introduced to marketing and sales personnel. The project had been under development for the last year and a half and kept confidential—only some 40 people within Polar Electro knew about it. Project Fusion was a new, complete solution for runners to be launched in 2006, consisting of adidas shoes with built-in electronics, running textiles that had built-in sensors, and watch-type sports computers that would display such information as heart rate data, speed, and distance to the runner (see Exhibit 1). The electronics technology is provided by Polar, but the textiles and shoes will be sold as premium adidas-branded goods.

Mr. Kallio was convinced that the partnership with adidas would be very beneficial for his company. First of all, becoming a trusted partner of adidas, an icon in sporting goods, was like a top-grade seal of approval for Polar. Polar would certainly benefit from the great brand equity that adidas owned. The majority of consumers around the world have heard of adidas, but selected few were aware of Polar. The adidas partnership would certainly raise consumer awareness of the Polar brand, something that Polar needed if it was to achieve its ambitious goals of both growing its sports-related business and extending from the core of serious sports into lifestyle applications. Second, the partnership could give a boost to the distribution of Polar goods. While Polar was represented through some 35,000 retailers in 50 countries, the channel power of adidas could not be ignored by wholesalers or retailers. Third, there was certainly a lot to learn from a successful company like adidas, be it in concept development or marketing processes.

There were some concerns, however. First of all, the sheer difference in size between the two companies: Polar's sales in 2004 had been 170 million euros, whereas adidas sales exceeded 5 billion euros, making it 30 times the size of Polar. The track record of alliances in general is not great and significant size differences between partners can cause difficulties in the relationship sooner or later. As an example, when adidas could appoint 5 people to a certain part of the project, Polar could afford two at most. Executives who were to implement the partnership, such as Christian Franke, Director of Brand Marketing at Polar, would have a lot on their plates. Another concern was the ability of Polar to perform in the relationship. Even though Kallio had full confidence in the capabilities of his managers, the fact that Polar was engaged in the development of very demanding high-tech electronics, whereas adidas would be responsible for shoes and textiles, was a factor that might bring surprises. His concern was that if there were unexpected difficulties in the development of electronics, the schedule of introducing new, jointly developed products with adidas might turn out to be frighteningly tight. A large company could hire an additional twenty R&D engineers if there were unexpected challenges in the development work, but for a company of Polar's size that would be financially an extreme solution. In terms of the classic risk of enabling and creating a future competitor, Kallio did not see it very relevant in this very case. He had full confidence in the partner, largely thanks to the solid personal relationship that existed between Kallio and key executives at adidas. Referring to the key executives in both of the companies, Kallio said: "We all understand and in fact love sports, so we talk the same language—that is a great starting point for the relationship."

About Partnership Agreements

The agreement with adidas comprised, first of all, joint development of technology for endeavors such as "Project Fusion." Polar is responsible for providing the

This case was authored by Hannu Seristö of the Helsinki School of Economics and Ilkka A. Ronkainen. For further information on the companies and their strategies, see **http://www.adidas-polar.com; http://www.polar.fi/ polar/channels/eng/; http://www.adidas-group.com/en/home/welcome.asp;** and **http://www.nokia.com.**

Exhibit 1 Press Release on the Launch of Project Fusion

Helsinki/Herzogenaurach—August 4, 2005

adidas and Polar introduce the world's first completely integrated training system

Polar Electro, the innovative leader in heart rate monitoring, and adidas, one of the world's leading sports brands, have formed a partnership that will introduce the world's first completely integrated training system. Called "Project Fusion," it seamlessly integrates Polar heart rate and speed and distance monitoring equipment into adidas apparel and footwear.

The integration simplifies use and increases comfort, allowing the products to become part of the athlete. Included in the project are the adidas adiStar Fusion range of apparel (t-shirts, long sleeve shirts, bras, women's tops), the adidas adiStar Fusion shoe, Polar's s3™ Stride Sensor, The Polar WearLink™ transmitter, and The Polar RS800™ Running Computer.

How does it work? Special fibers bonded onto adidas tops work in conjunction with Polar's Wear Link™ technology to eliminate the need for a separate chest strap to monitor heart rate. Just snap the tiny Polar WearLink connector onto the front of the shirt and go. The data are sent to the Polar RS 800™ wrist-mounted running computer, which easily displays and records all information in real time. Simply put, your shirt talks to your running computer.

The adiStar Fusion shoe has a strategically placed cavity in the midsole which can house the very light Polar s3™ Stride Sensor, making it easier to use, more comfortable and more consistently accurate than top-of-shoe systems. And you won't even know it's there when your shoe is talking to your running computer.

Information like speed and distance, chronograph functions, along with heart rate, are also shown on the RS800™ in real time. And when the workout is over, all data can be downloaded onto a computer so workouts can be easily managed and analyzed, meaning the whole system talks to you.

"The great thing about the system is that it's so easy to use," says Michael Birke, adidas Running Business Unit Manager. "By putting all the best equipment into one package, it's made training simpler, more comfortable and more precise. The system is greater than the sum of its parts."

"An athlete can train more effectively with the right objective information," says Marco Suvilaakso, Running Segment Manager for Polar Electro. "This system caters to the individual, with precise and personalized feedback."

Purchasing the entire system—Polar RS 800™, Polar s3™ Stride Sensor, adiStar Fusion top, and adiStar Fusion shoe—will be around 640 Euros/680 dollars. The products are available as separate pieces as well, and available in Spring of 2006.

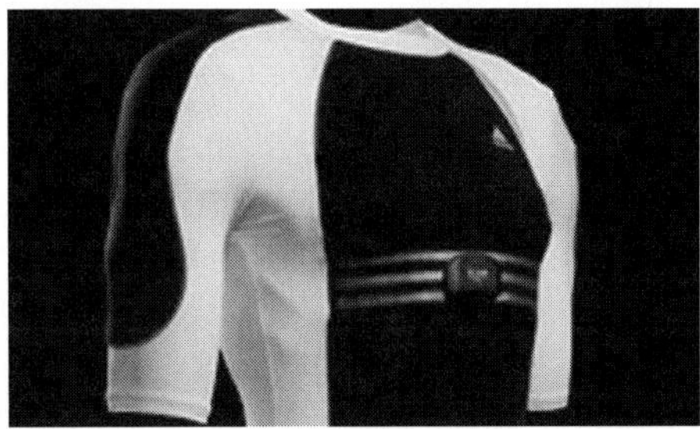

sensor, but joint work is needed particularly in fusing the textiles and sensor technology, which inevitably means shared engineering and industrial design. In shared engineering, a challenging issue typically is to decide which partner owns the jointly-create intellectual property. Also, as "Project Fusion" is a complete package, or solution, the industrial design has to be coordinated in terms of form and appearance. Rights concerning the design issues should normally be covered in partnership agreements.

Partnership agreements need to address the issues of exclusivity; that is, can certain technologies or solutions be offered to other companies beyond the main partners. Normally it is not recommended to lock oneself into one partner only, since it would compromise one's flexibility or stand-alone capability. On the other hand, exclusivity given to a partner is bound to enhance commitment and trust in the relationship.

The second part of the agreement deals with joint marketing efforts. Channels where there is joint presence and sales efforts have to be specified, including complementary marketing efforts (i.e., whereby Polar uses the adidas distribution system to get its products to the world marketplace). A considerable benefit for Polar is that adidas controls globally 145 flagship stores, such as adidas Originals Georgetown in Washington, D.C., Performance Store Abasto in Buenos Aires, adidas Concept Store Nevski in St. Petersburg, and adidas Originals Sydney. As for promotion, the choice of media for shared appearance and, for instance, joint web sites (such as **http://www.adidas-polar.com**) are important issues to address in the agreement.

In implementation, the management of the partnership should be clarified in the agreement. Whether there is, for example, a steering board composed of members from both partners, and who will serve as its chairperson, are some of the questions to settle. Also, determination of areas of responsibilities between the partners and the sharing of costs and revenues is normally a standard clause in an agreement of this sort. Finally, the agreements normally should address issues like the term and termination procedures of the partnership, and the settlement of disputes.

The Growth of Polar Electro Oy

The origins of the Finnish sports instruments producer Polar Electro can be traced back to the need of cross-country skiing coaches for a device to measure an athlete's heart rate during training sessions in the field, as opposed to this being possible only in a laboratory environment. There were no light, portable devices available, only large expensive laboratory equipment. Promoted by this need, Professor Säynäjäkangas of the technology faculty at Oulu University started development work on technology that would make such measurements possible. Work was done partly with colleagues at the Oulu University, and eventually a company called Polar Electro was founded in Oulu in 1977, with Säynäjäkangas as the owner. The first heart rate monitor (HRM) was a battery-powered device that measured the heart rate from a fingertip. By the year 1982, the technology had advanced to the point that the first wireless heart rate monitor was ready. The first computer interface was introduced in 1984. The zone feature was launched in 1987, which was a predecessor to the so-called OwnZone feature of today. The principle is that the suitable intensity levels of training may vary daily due to factors such as fatigue, illness, or jetlag, and the athlete should check the right intensity levels before each training session.

In the 1980s, Polar Electro sought cooperation with top-level competitive athletes and world-class trainers and coaches. Relationships with leading universities and research institutes in the area of sports medicine were established. The target customers for Polar technology were competitive national and Olympic level athletes. From the very beginning the company was compelled to take a global look at the markets, because the chosen niche was narrow. Domestic market sales would have been in hundreds of units during the early years.

During this era, Polar Electro was first and foremost a technology company that conducted research, developed new technological solutions and started to build manufacturing capacity for the large-scale production of heart rate monitors. Early on, the company benefited from financial support for promising high-technology start-ups in developing regions by Finnish government agencies. Products were sold mostly under other brands, through private label arrangements, particularly in the U.S. market, which was then the key market for Polar Electro. Marketing to the masses existed only in long-term plans. By the end of the 1980s, Polar Electro had grown to a company of one hundred employees with annual sales of almost 20 million dollars.

At this point, the target market was broadened from the original devices aimed at competitive top-level athletes. The first steps to the so-called fitness market were taken in 1987. New models were developed for ordinary people who wanted to monitor the intensity of training through heart rate measurement while they were exercising. The Polar brand became a focus of development in 1989. Polar's target was defined as being "anyone with a heart." Indeed, the company provided an HRM for race horses, which they continue to provide to this day.

Throughout the 1990s, Polar started to put more emphasis on marketing, partly driven by increasing competitive pressures. The heart rate monitor business had caught the attention of some big firms and entrepreneurs, all hoping to challenge Polar in this potentially sizeable business area. Large players like the U.S. watchmaker Timex and the Japanese electronics company Casio started to work on HRM products, and in Europe such companies as Sigma from Germany and Cardiosport from the U.K. introduced comparable HRMs. However, in terms of features, technology, quality, and even production costs, Polar was able to maintain its lead of a couple of years in this race. The building of an extensive international dealer network became the key focus of marketing efforts.

The key products by Polar in the 1990s comprised specific models for runners, bicyclists, and fitness users. Two special product groups were developed: Team Systems, to be used in the training of football or ice-hockey teams; and Educational Systems that were used in the physical education classes of school children, mostly in the United States, where the Federal Government provided support for schools that adopted innovative equipment to improve the quality of physical education. The largest product category for Polar was Fitness, because the products appealed to many different kinds of users. Several trailblazing technologies were introduced at this time, including the first integrated one-piece transmitter of heart rate measures in 1992; coded transmission of heart rate measures (from the chest transmitter unit to the wristwatch unit) in 1995; the first HRM combined with a bicycle computer, which had speed, cadence, and altitude measurement in 1996; personalized OwnZone training intensity zone and OwnCal energy consumption solutions in 1997; and the Polar fitness test, which provided a very accurate estimate of physical condition, even when measured while the person is not exercising but simply lying down for about 5 minutes, in 1999.

Polar Electro has used aggressive patenting policy to protect its inventions and intellectual property. In 2000, the company introduced a soft and very user-friendly textile transmitter belt to replace the traditional rather hard plastic model. The launch of a speed and distance measurement device in 2004 brought a new dimension to running computers: a pod attached to the running shoe measures acceleration and sends the information to the wrist unit with an accuracy of 99 percent. Now runners can see on their wrist units not only their heart rate and training intensity information, but also their real-time pace or speed and the distance covered. Competitors to this speed-and-distance technology include GPS-based running computers by the U.S. company Garmin and by Nike, developed with the Dutch electronics firm Philips. Outdoor computers were also launched in 2004. These wristwatch type devices have an electronic compass, barometer, altimeter, thermometer, and various watch and diary functions in addition to the advanced heart rate measurement features.

Polar spends some 10 percent of its sales on research and development, which takes place mostly in Oulu. The company benefits from the supply of high-quality engineers from the University of Oulu. Oulu is a city with a concentration of high-tech companies, particularly in the area of electronics (Nokia, the world's largest mobile-phone manufacturer, has a significant R&D and manufacturing presence in the city). The company also maintains collaborative ties with well-known institutes, such as Cooper Institute in Dallas, Texas, and leading universities in the areas of cardiology and sports medicine.

After-sales service is an essential component of the HRM business. The devices are rather complicated pieces of technology, and consumers often need support in installing software updates or setting up data transfer between the devices and the PC. These computers are also very personal objects, literally close to heart, and consumers typically want support immediately if they have a problem in the use of the equipment. The objective is to provide an answer to consumers' or retailers' questions within 24 hours, anywhere in the world. Competitors have not been able to match Polar's level in after-sales service, making Polar users very loyal customers.

Industrial design has been a focus in the last two years. The design and looks of the products were somewhat soulless until a new generation of more fashionable and colorful models was launched in 2004. In particular, female consumers were targeted with specific light and colorful fitness computers. Polar received international recognition for its improved design in 2004, when its new outdoor computer AXN 500 received an award in the German IF design competition.

Today, Polar Electro sees its mission as being to provide people the best solution to achieve their personal well-being, sports, and performance goals. The company exists to improve people's quality of life by generating innovative, high-quality, and user-friendly products. The Polar brand's essence is captured in the statement that "Polar is the leading brand and the true partner in improving human health and well-being through its understanding of personal physiology and the environment." Physiology refers to the monitoring of heart, and the environment refers to the measurement of altitude, direction, speed, distance, and temperature.

Most of Polar's €170 million in sales come from Western Europe and the United States, while the Asian market represents a very small share of business. Volume production is in the Far East, while the R&D and the manufacturing of the most advanced premium models remain in Oulu. Some 1,700 people work in Finland and in the 15 wholly-owned foreign marketing subsidiaries in the key world markets.

Polar may be a household name for competitive athletes and the most active exercisers, but the average consumer does not really know the brand. Potential markets include millions of people that could need and want a heart rate monitor. Driving this potential is an increasing realization by individuals, societies, and national economies that if people exercise more and are in better physical condition, the result is fewer health problems and lower consequent costs to the society. Populations particularly in Western Europe and Japan are aging, and the elderly want to stay active and healthy to lead rewarding lives after retirement. Obesity is increasingly a problem, particularly in North America, but also in Western Europe, and possibly soon in many Asian countries as well. Competition in the future is more in the area of marketing rather than in the pure development of technology. Design, trends, and fashion are becoming an essential part of this business, making HRMs a lifestyle product.

Polar Marketing

The heart rate monitor consists of two parts: the transmitter and the receiver. The transmitter is worn around one's chest, as close to the heart as possible to ensure accurate sensing of the heartbeat. Modern generation transmitters, provided only by Polar, are soft fabric belts where the sensors, or electrodes, are woven into the fabric, and the signal is sent to the receiver through a separate little unit that is snapped onto the belt. The fabric transmitters are much more comfortable to use than the old versions. The retail cost of a transmitter is in the region of 40 euros.

The receiver is like a sports wristwatch that functions mainly as the display for measured information. The receiver typically has heart rate measurement functions, watch and chronometer functions, and a variety of other features. The simplest models display only time and the current heart rate, whereas the most advanced models have several test features; a training diary and training program features; measure air pressure, altitude, and temperature; have compass functions; and display speed and distance information. The case of the receiver is typically made of different grades of plastics, but some expensive models are made of steel or titanium.

The basic heart rate monitors by Polar cost about 60 euros in retail, whereas the most advanced models with a titanium case can cost close to 500 euros. The cheapest heart rate monitors in the market, often by Asian manufacturers, can be bought for as little as 20 euros, but these are typically of poor quality, poor usability, and with no product support nor real warranty.

Polar heart rate monitors are distributed through sporting goods stores, specialty stores, department stores, and in some cases catalog sellers and online stores. The products are so rich in features that the expertise and professionalism of the sales personnel is a key factor in the sales process. As a result, Polar has committed significant resources to the training of sales people throughout the channel.

Polar provides extensive online support for its products. Software can be downloaded from the Polar website, and consumers can create their own training programs and diaries on the global web site (**http://www.polar.fi**).

Other Partnerships

In early 2004, a technology and marketing partnership between Nokia and Polar was made public. Polar offers a few heart rate monitor models that have the capability to communicate with a certain Nokia mobile phone, model 5140. This compatibility allows the user to transmit training data from the wrist computer to the mobile phone, and again send it via mobile phone network, for instance, to the PC of one's coach. So, for instance, a distance-runner who is training in the warm conditions of South Africa in January can easily send his daily training session information for analysis by his trainer in Northern Europe in order to get instructions for the following day's training. Nokia and Polar were very visible in a joint marketing campaign, with the theme "Training Mates," during the 2004 Tour de France.

A key product that had the Nokia compatibility is the running computer model S625X. It was launched in the summer of 2004 and was a great success from the very beginning. The S625X has a speed-and-distance feature that is based on acceleration technology. Acceleration data are turned into information on distance covered and speed or pace of the runner, and then displayed on the wrist receiver. The accuracy is very high, with error rates of less than 1 percent (i.e., when running 10 kilometers, the error in the distance information is expected to be less than 100 meters). Runners love it and media have praised it. Even though the product is relatively expensive (€400), it appears that S625X is becoming one of the most successful running computers Polar has ever made.

Growth Prospects of Polar

Polar Electro has many of the ingredients to grow and become a truly significant global company. It has a solid technological basis, processes in place, and very capable personnel. In its own niche market, it is the world market leader. However, it has to acknowledge its limited resources: there are numerous potential new business areas and an abundance of ideas, but the development of completely new products takes millions of euros. Brand marketing is obviously very important in the future, but doing that with a real impact can easily consume tens of millions of euros per year. Asia is undoubtedly the market for the future, as in almost every business, but the question is how to go there, since it appears to be quite different from Europe and North America: what products (adapted or not), which features, which markets (alone or with partners, or through which channels), are some of the key questions. Moreover, the human resources might turn out to be a challenge—there are limitless opportunities, but the current managers may not be able to handle all the new issues simultaneously. Both the owners and the management see the numerous avenues for growth, but there are a multitude of factors to assess when choosing the right path to follow.

In terms of financial benefits, it is perhaps too early to assess the value of these partnerships. For one thing, the measurement of inputs and outputs is not that simple. For instance, how do you measure accurately the management effort that has been put into the partnerships, and whether that effort could have been used more effectively somewhere else?

Mr. Kallio was convinced that the adidas partnership was very valuable for Polar especially in the long term. Some questions remained, however. How can a relatively small company make sure that it can perform in a relationship with a significantly larger partner like adidas, and not let the partner down? How can Polar make sure that it gets most of the possible value out of the partnerships—for instance, through learning from a more experienced company? How about assessing the inputs and outputs—how should Polar measure whether the relationship is producing value to the company?

Questions for Discussion

1. How does the alliance with adidas fit with Polar's growth objectives?
2. What are the pros and cons of having a company like adidas as an alliance partner?
3. By 2010, what is the likely outcome of this alliance (e.g., will Polar become part of adidas)?

Nova Scotia

The U.S. Market for Canadian Travel Services

The more than 15 million Americans who travel to Canada annually constitute 28 percent of all departures from the United States. The U.S. market is of crucial importance to the Canadian tourism industry because 79 percent of all non-Canadian tourists are Americans, who spend approximately $13.5 billion a year on these trips.

Campaigns to lure tourists to a particular state or foreign country have increased dramatically. The Canadian Tourism Commission, the government tourist organization, has launched umbrella campaigns with themes such as "Come to the world next door" and "Keep exploring" for Canada as a whole. The provinces conduct their own independent campaigns to segments they deem most attractive and profitable. For example, ads for Manitoba are mostly written for the outdoor vacationer.

Overall, U.S. visitors to Canada rate their stays higher in satisfaction and value than their vacations in the United States. The aided and unaided awareness of Canada declines gradually with greater distance from Canada. Therefore, it is not surprising to find the top seven states for Canada-bound travel to be New York, Michigan, Washington, California, Ohio, Massachusetts, and Pennsylvania. While Canada earns high marks on dimensions such as exploration and safety, the main reasons to reject Canada include bad weather, other more interesting and exotic places, unfavorable exchange rates, price of gasoline, and lack of interest ("been there, done that"). Canada gained more share of the U.S. market post 9-11, but has since been losing it again. For example, since 2002, Canada has lost 9 percent of leisure person-stays, representing $1.2 billion in foregone revenues.[1] The bottom line for Canada as a whole is that it needs a unique emotive element to separate it from competition.

This case was written by Arch G. Woodside and Ilkka A. Ronkainen for discussion purposes and not to exemplify correct or incorrect decision-making. The case is largely based on Arch G. Woodside, "Positioning a Province Using Travel Research," *Journal of Travel Research* 20 (Winter 1982): 2–6. For additional information, please see **http://www.gov.ns.ca** and **http://www.canadatourism.com.**

The Commission sponsored a large-scale benefit-segmentation study of the American market for pleasure travel to Canada, the results of which are summarized in Exhibit 1. Segmenting the market by benefits provides many advantages over other methods. Segmenting by attitude toward Canada or by geographic area would be feasible if substantial variation occurred. This is not the case, however. Segmenting by benefits reveals what consumers were and are seeking in their vacations. Knowing this is central to planning effective marketing programs.

A Benefit-Matching Model

Exhibit 2 summarizes a strategic view for understanding tourism behavior and developing a marketing campaign. The model emphasizes the dominant need to define markets by benefits sought and the fact that separate markets seek unique benefits or activity packages. Membership in the segments will fluctuate from year to year; the same individuals may seek rest and relaxation one year and foreign adventure the next.

Identifying benefits is not enough, however. Competition (that is, other countries or areas) may present the same type of benefits to the consumers. Because travelers seriously consider only a few destinations, a sharp focus is needed for promoting a destination. This also means that a destination should avoid trying to be "everything to everybody" by promoting too many benefits. Combining all of these concerns calls for positioning, that is, generating a unique, differentiated image in the mind of the consumer.

Three destinations are shown in Exhibit 2. Each destination provides unique as well as similar benefits for travelers. Marketers have the opportunity to select one or two specific benefits from a set of benefits when developing a marketing program to attract visitors. The benefits selected for promotion can match or mismatch the benefits sought by specific market segments. The letters S, M, and N in the table express the degree of fit between the benefits provided and those sought. For example, a mismatch is promoting the wrong benefit to the wrong market, such as promoting the scenic mountain beauty of North Carolina to Tennessee residents.

Exhibit 1 Benefit Segments of U.S. Travelers to Canada

Segment	Segment Contents	Size	Segment Objective
I	Friends and relatives—nonactive visitor	29%	Seek familiar surroundings where they can visit friends.
II	Friends and relatives—active city visitor	12%	Seek familiar surroundings where they can visit friends and relatives but are more inclined to participate in activities (i.e., sightseeing, shopping, cultural, entertainment).
III	Family sightseers	6%	Look for new vacation place that would be a treat for the children and an enriching experience.
IV	Outdoor vacationer	19%	Seek clean air, rest, quiet, and beautiful scenery. Many are campers, and availability of recreation facilities is important. Children are also an important factor.
V	Resort vacationer	19%	Most interested in water sports (for example, swimming) and good weather. Prefer a popular place with a big-city atmosphere.
VI	Foreign vacationer	26%	Look for a place they have never been before with a foreign atmosphere and beautiful scenery. Money is not of major concern but good accommodation and service are. They want an exciting, enriching experience.

Source: Shirley Young, Leland Ott, and Barbara Feigin, "Some Practical Considerations in Market Segmentation," *Journal of Marketing Research* 15 (August 1978): 405–412. Reprinted with permission.

Exhibit 2 Benefit-Matching Model

Markets		Benefits Sought		Benefit Match		Benefits Provided		Destinations
A	→	A_s, B_s	→	S	→	A_p, B_p	→	X
B	→	B_s, C_s	→	M	→	C_p, D_p	→	Y
C	→	C_s, D_s	→	N	→	E_p, F_p	→	Z

S = supermatch; M = match; N = no match

Source: Arch G. Woodside, "Positioning a Province Using Travel Research," *Journal of Travel Research* 20 (Winter 1982): 3.

The Case of Nova Scotia

Nova Scotia is one of ten provinces and two territories that make up Canada. Given its location, it is known as Canada's Ocean Playground (see Exhibit 3). For many Nova Scotians the sea is their main source of livelihood and leisure. For 200 years the sea has played an integral role in the history and economy of the province (see Exhibit 4). It was the abundant fisheries that drew settlers into the area. Today, many of their descendants work in a variety of professions related to the water, including tourism. The importance of tourism has increased with both the mining and fishing sectors having difficulties from their resources drying up. Total tourism receipts exceed $1.22 billion and over 33,500 workers are employed directly and in spin-off jobs. More than a million people visit the province every year, with almost a quarter of these coming from outside of Canada, mainly the United States. Halifax was tenth among Canadian cities visited by tourists from the United States, with 264,000 overnight visits in 2004 (with Toronto as number 1 with 2,335,000 visits).

Canada as a whole has a rather vague and diffused image among Americans. This is particularly true of the Atlantic provinces. The majority of Nova Scotia's nonresident travelers reside in New England and the mid-Atlantic states of New York, Pennsylvania, and New Jersey. Most of these travelers include households with married couples having incomes substantially above the U.S. national average, that is, $50,000 and above. Such households

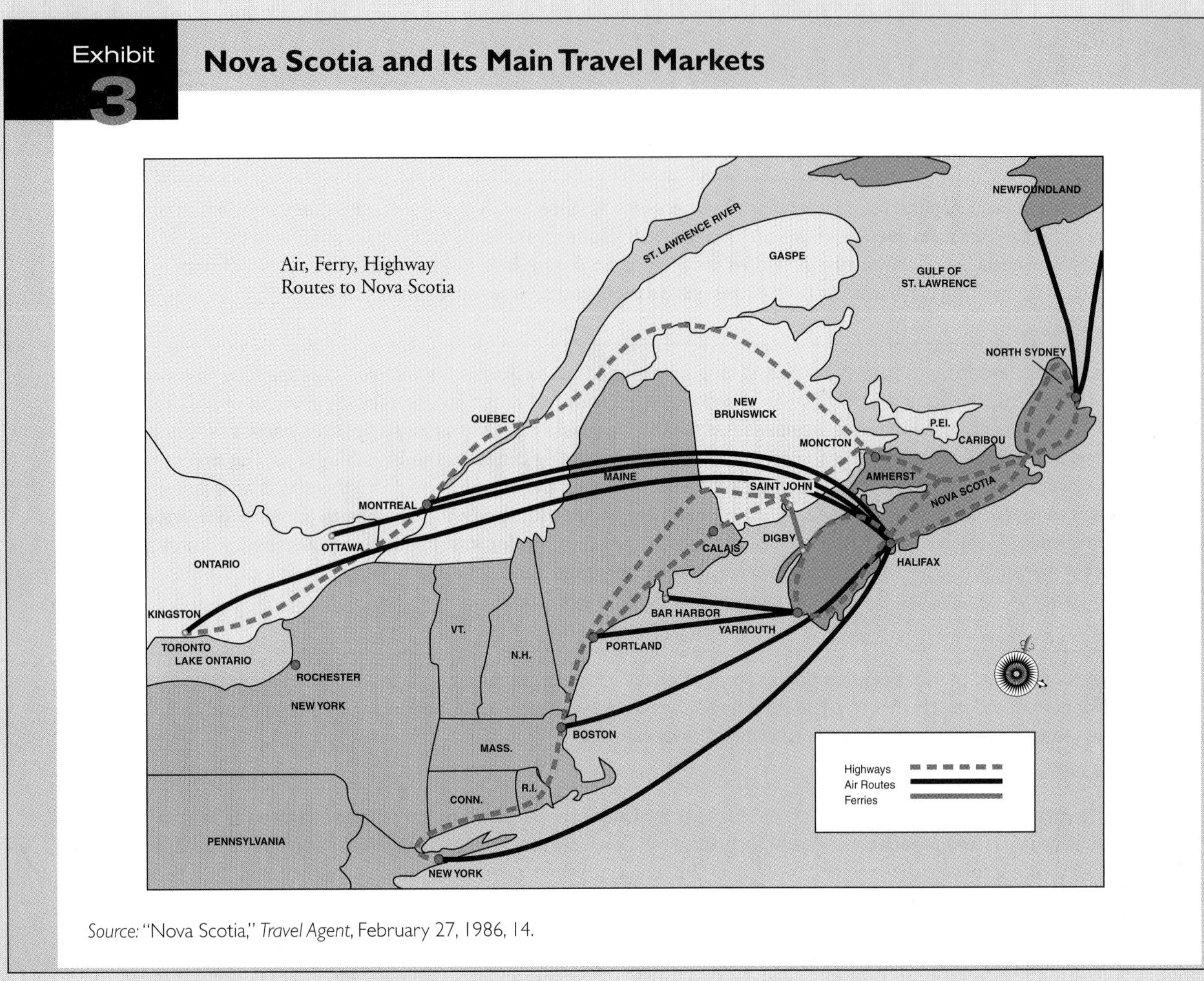

Exhibit 3 **Nova Scotia and Its Main Travel Markets**

Source: "Nova Scotia," *Travel Agent*, February 27, 1986, 14.

represent a huge, accessible market—10 million households that are one to two and a half days' drive from Halifax, the capital. Most households in this market have not visited the Atlantic provinces and have no plans to do so. Thus, the market exhibits three of the four requirements necessary to be a very profitable customer base for the province: size, accessibility, and purchasing power. The market lacks the intention to visit for most of the households described. Nova Scotia is not one of the destinations considered when the next vacation or pleasure trip is being planned. Worse still, Nova Scotia does not exist in the minds of its largest potential market.

In the past, Nova Scotia had a number of diverse marketing themes, such as "Good times are here," "International gathering of the clans," "The 375th anniversary of Acadia," "Seaside spectacular," and the most recent, "There's so much to sea." These almost annual changes in marketing strategy contributed to the present situation both by confusing the consumer as to what Nova Scotia is all about and by failing to create a focused image based on the relative strengths of the province. Some critics argue that Nova Scotia is not being promoted on its unique features but on benefits that other locations can provide as well or better.

Examples of Successful Positioning

Most North Atlantic passengers flying to Europe used to have a vague impression of Belgium. This presented a problem to the tourism authorities, who wanted travelers to stay for longer periods. Part of the problem was a former "Gateway to Europe" campaign that had positioned Belgium as a country to pass through on the way to somewhere else.

The idea for new positioning was found in the *Michelin Guides*, which rate cities as they do restaurants. The Benelux countries have six three-star cities (the highest ranking), of which five are in Belgium and only one (Amsterdam) is in the Netherlands. The theme generated was "In Belgium, there are five Amsterdams." This strategy was correct in three different ways: (1) it related Belgium to a destination that was known to the traveler, Amsterdam; (2) the *Michelin Guides*, another entity already known to the traveler, gave the concept credibility; and (3) the "five cities to visit" made Belgium a bona fide destination.[2]

The state of Florida attracts far more eastern North American beach seekers than does South Carolina. Tour-

Exhibit 4 Nova Scotia Facts

The Land

Nova Scotia is surrounded by four bodies of water—the Atlantic, the Bay of Fundy, the Northumberland Strait, and the Gulf of St. Lawrence. Its average width of 70 miles (128 kilometers) means that no part of the province is far from the sea. Nova Scotia lies in the northern temperate zone and although it is surrounded by water, the climate is continental rather than maritime. The temperature extremes are moderated, however, by the ocean.

The History

The Micmac Indians inhabited Nova Scotia long before the first explorers arrived from Europe. The first visitors were Norsemen (in 1000), and, in 1497, Italian explorer John Cabot had noted the rich fishing grounds in the area. In the seventeenth century, all of Nova Scotia was settled by the French and formed a larger area known as Acadia. Feuds between the British and the French resulted in all of Acadia being ceded to the British in 1713. The British perceived the Acadians as a security threat and expelled them to Virginia and Louisiana. In 1783 there was an influx of loyalists from the newly independent New England states. Nova Scotia and three other provinces joined a federation called the Dominion of Canada in 1867. At the time, the province was known for international shipbuilding and trade in fish and lumber. The First and Second World Wars emphasized the importance of Halifax, Nova Scotia's capital, as a staging point for convoys and confirmed it as one of the world's major ports.

The People

Over 80 percent of Nova Scotia's population of 937,800 trace their ancestry to the British Isles, while 18 percent of residents are of French ancestry. The next largest groups by ancestry are German and Dutch. Almost 22,000 residents have Indian roots, primarily belonging to the Micmac nation.

The Economy

Nova Scotia's economy is highly diversified, having evolved from resource-based employment to manufacturing as well as business and personal services. The breakdown is as follows: (1) manufacturing/fish, 62 percent; (2) tourism, 12 percent; (3) forestry, 10 percent; (4) mining, 7 percent; (5) fishing, 5 percent; and (6) agriculture, 3 percent.

Source: "Canadian Provinces and Territories," **http://www.canada.gc.ca.**

ism officials in South Carolina had to find a way in which the state could be positioned against Florida.

The positioning theme generated was "You get two more days in the sun by coming to Myrtle Beach, South Carolina, instead of Florida." Florida's major beaches are a one-day drive beyond the Grand Strand of South Carolina—and one additional day back. Most travelers to Florida go in the May-to-October season when the weather is similar to that in South Carolina. Thus, more beach time and less driving time became the central benefit provided by the state.

Positioning Nova Scotia

The benefits of Nova Scotia as a Canadian travel destination cover segments III to VI of U.S. travelers (see Exhibit 1). Those providing input to the planning process point out water activities, sea-side activities, camping, or scenic activities. The segment interested in foreign adventure could be lured by festivals and other related activities.

The planners' argument centers not so much on which benefits to promote but on which should be emphasized if differentiation is desired. The decision is important because of (1) the importance of the industry to the province and (2) the overall rise in competition for the travelers in Nova Scotia's market, especially competition by U.S. states.

Questions for Discussion

1. How would you position Nova Scotia to potential American travelers? Use the benefit-matching model to achieve your supermatch.
2. Constructively criticize past positioning attempts, such as "There's so much to sea."
3. What other variables, apart from positioning, will determine whether Americans will choose Nova Scotia as a destination?

Notes

1. Canadian Tourism Commission *Changing U.S. Travel Trends to Canada*, February 3, 2006, available at **http://www.canadatourism.com.**
2. Al Ries and Jack Trout, *Positioning: The Battle for Your Mind* (New York: McGraw-Hill, 2000), 171–178.

Starwood Hotels & Resorts Worldwide Inc.: Cross-Marketing Strategies

Starwood Hotels and Resorts Worldwide Inc. (Starwood), is a large hotel chain based in the U.S. with a global presence. The company has six hotel brands, each having a distinct name, price and image. Known for creating 'experiences' for its guests that is unique to each hotel, Starwood has constantly tried to differentiate itself with innovative ideas and services. However, with fierce competition in the global hotel industry, Starwood observed lack of brand loyalty among its customers. To strengthen the brand image of each of its hotel brands and increase customer loyalty, Starwood initiated cross-branding partnerships with various apparel and media companies. As per the terms of those deals, products of different consumer brands would be made available inside guests' rooms, which Starwood felt would enhance the overall hotel experience for its guests. However some felt that such partnerships with consumer brands would create brand clutter. While some analysts argued that it might lead to annoying guests with too many products and promotions, others feared that a misconstrued partnership might dilute and even harm the hotel's image.

This case was written by Priti Krishnan, under the direction of Sumit Kumar Chaudhuri, ICFAI Business School Case Development Centre. It is intended to be used as the basis for class discussion rather than to illustrate either effective or ineffective handling of a management situation. This case was compiled from published sources.

Phone : 91(40) 23435387 - 91
Fax : 91(40) 23435386
E-mail : info@ibscdc.org

Distributed and Printed by IBS-CDC, India
www.ibscdc.org

Starwood Hotels and Resorts: A Business Profile

Founded in 1991 by Barry Sternlicht (Barry), former chairman and CEO of Starwood, Starwood Hotels and Resorts is one of the world's largest hotel and leisure companies, having more than 730 hotels with 231,000 rooms across 83 countries[1] (Exhibit 1). Operating through owned, leased, managed and franchised properties, the company's business is grouped into two segments—hotels and vacation ownership operations. In 2002, hotels accounted for 91% of Starwood's revenues (Exhibit 2A). While its owned hotels accounted for 74% of Starwood's revenues, managed and franchised hotels contributed 18% to the same (Exhibit 2B).

Since its inception, Starwood has established a strong presence in the global hospitality industry through its first-class offerings. Its strength lies in the combination of its strong brands. Starwood has six brands, which include Four Points by Sheraton, Sheraton, St. Regis, Westin, W hotels, and the Luxury Collection. Sheraton hotels & Resorts and Westin hotels & Resorts are the largest brands of Starwood Vacation Ownership,[2] accounting for a large part of its revenues (Exhibit 3). Being one of the largest of Starwood's brands, Sheraton hotels & Resorts caters to both business and leisure travelers through its full-service hotels and luxurious resorts across the major cities of the world. In 1995, Sheraton introduced a new, mid-scale hotel brand called Four Points by Sheraton, which offers full-service hotel experience at reasonable prices. Although Four Points is the sister brand of Sheraton, it has maintained a distinct brand image for itself.

The Luxury Collection is a group of hotels and resorts that delivers extraordinary service to the elite clientele. The hotel was acquired by Starwood in 1998. The same year, Starwood also acquired St. Regis from Colonel John Jacob Astor IV, whose objective in establishing the hotel

Source: Wolchuk, Sally and Scoviak, Mary "HOTELS' 325", **www.hotelsmag.com,** July 2004.

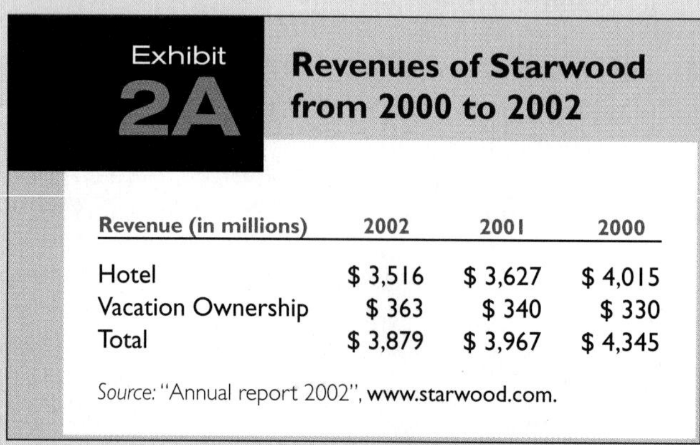

Exhibit 2A

Revenues of Starwood from 2000 to 2002

Revenue (in millions)	2002	2001	2000
Hotel	$ 3,516	$ 3,627	$ 4,015
Vacation Ownership	$ 363	$ 340	$ 330
Total	$ 3,879	$ 3,967	$ 4,345

Source: "Annual report 2002", **www.starwood.com.**

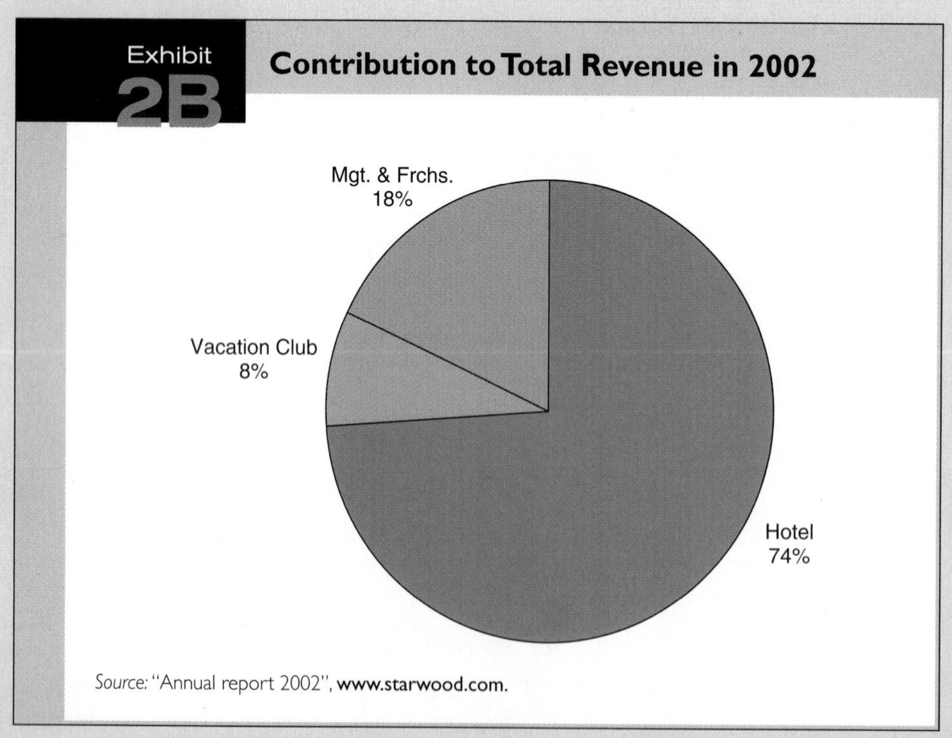

Source: "Annual report 2002", **www.starwood.com.**

was to bring the warmth, service, and hospitality of the early 20th century into the 21st century. After acquiring St. Regis, Starwood followed the same objective and positioned the brand as its luxury offering.

The upscale hotel experience was redefined by Starwood when it introduced the W hotel brand in 1998. The brand, which was started with the realization that there are customers who look for a balance between style and substance, features modern properties with hip designs, contemporary facilities and a young staff. By combining the personality and style of an independent hotel along with the reliability and consistency of big hotels, the W hotels proved to be one of most successful hotel brands of Starwood. Barry said, "The launch of W Hotels represented an important evolution in the hotel industry—the first style hotel for the business traveler. Each property has its own personality and a strong sense of style—something which really did not exist in the business-travel market. While sharing a common style and standard of service, each W has its own distinct personality, bringing together the best of what each city has to offer. Breaking the traditional hotel mould, W is more theatre and definitely more fun."[3]

Another hotel brand acquired by Starwood in 1998 was the Westin hotel. The brand caters to the upscale market with 121 hotels across 30 countries. Providing a 'relaxing personal and renewing experience' to its guests, the Westin hotel has been positioned as a haven of serenity. Known for anticipating customer needs and satisfying them efficiently, the Westin hotel created many innovative services and products like 'the Heavenly Bed.' The bed was introduced in 1999 at the behest of Barry, who felt that hotel beds were very uncomfortable. Research proved that customers also shared the same feeling. In order to fulfill customer satisfaction, Starwood spent millions of dollars to make its hotel beds the best in the hotel business and introduced the Heavenly Bed. The beds became so popular that Starwood even developed a catalog for visitors who wanted to order the beds or its accoutrements for their homes. On an average, the company sells $4 million Heavenly Bed and associated products per year directly to its customers. Steven J. Heyer (Steven), Chief Executive Officer for Starwood Hotels & Resorts Worldwide Inc. said, "We have worked hard to redefine our brands and develop innovative signature services that communicate each brand's unique positioning."[4] With amenities like the Heavenly Bed and the Heavenly Bath (Annexure I), the Westin hotel created a distinct image for itself. Sue Brush, Senior Vice President, Westin Hotels & Resorts, said, "This is a story of a little hotel chain that grew from 17 properties in the Northwest to become a world leader. Today, we have over 120 hotels in 24 countries, including some of the world's most prestigious properties. And all the while, we've maintained our commitment to quality, people, consistency, and innovation. Today we're obsessed with creating unforgettable guest experiences and infusing a spirit of renewal into every aspect of the Westin experience."[5]

The six brands of Starwood have constantly evolved and enhanced the company's presence in affluent markets. Starwood has received various awards for its strong hotel brands. In the 'Annual Top U.S. Hotel Chain Survey', conducted in 2002 by *Business Travel News,* the W Hotels and Westin Hotels & Resorts swept the number one and number two positions respectively in the upper-upscale category. Barry said, "We are extremely proud of how well our brands performed in this year's *BTN* Survey,

Exhibit 3 Revenues of Selective Brands of Starwood

	Sheraton	Westin	St. Regis
% Of total 2005 revenues	26%	68%	6%
Target customer: Household income Age Net worth	 >$50 K 35–54 $75 K–750 K	 >$75 K 35–64 $150 K–1 M	 >$150 K 35–74 $1 M+

Source: "Starwood vacation ownership-Susquehanna Financial Group", **www.starwoodhotels.com,** March 2nd 2006

which we take very seriously at Starwood, because it represents feedback from travel pros and our most valued customers. The W and Westin brands are the industry's innovators in every aspect of the guest experience; from the chic personality and style found at each W hotel to Westin's acclaimed Heavenly Bed. We have spent a lot of money renovating our Sheratons and improving service standards and this survey validates that investment and backs up the dramatic increases reported by our own Guest Satisfaction Indexes. Four Points earned top honors in the midscale category which is terrific, and I'm glad to see Luxury Collection and St. Regis earning acclaim among some very tough competitors."[6]

It is observed that competition amongst hotel owners in the upscale market is fierce. Starwood has four major competitors—Marriott, which made the highest revenues in 2005 (Exhibit 4), Hyatt, Hilton and Intercontinental. While the primary focus of all Starwood hotels and resorts has been in the luxury and upscale market, each of its brands has a distinct name and price point (Exhibit 5) that caters to a different sub market (Exhibit 6). Sue Brush said, "When you have that many brands together, you see the importance of differentiation."[7] Starwood set a clear strategy of creating 'different,' 'better,' and 'special' experiences that impact the senses of every guest. Steven said, "We are not just in the business of selling beds or guestrooms, but rather experiences and memories."[8] In doing so, Starwood created a sustainable competitive advantage over its competitors, dominating the various markets in the hospitality business.

The differentiation strategy of Starwood enabled it to generate strong operating income. Commenting on its performance in 2005, Steven said, "Our results this quarter were outstanding and we are pleased to be raising our guidance for the remainder of the year. For the eleventh quarter in a row we've gained market share. I am thrilled with the progress we are making on our brand-building efforts and service innovation, which I believe

Exhibit 4 Sales and Revenues (Net Income) of Main Players in the Lodging Industry—Year 2005 & 2002

	2005		2002	
Company	Sales in millions	Net income in millions	Sales in millions	Net income in millions
Starwood Hotel & Resorts Worldwide Inc.	$ 5,977	$ 422	$ 4,659	$ 355
Marriott International	$ 11,550	$ 669	$ 8,441	$ 277
Hilton Hotel Corp.	$ 3,831	$ 460	$ 2,540	$ 198

Compiled by the author.

Exhibit 5 Target Segment and Room Rates of the Main Players in the Hotel Industry

		Rate per Day		
Company Name	Type of Market	Lowest	Highest	Average
Starwood	Mid-scale	$ 301.00	$ 378.50	$ 339.75
	Upscale	$ 330.00	$ 475.00	$ 402.50
	Upper-Upscale and luxury	$ 324.25	$ 861.75	$ 593.00
Marriott	Mid-scale	$ 130.39	$ 204.39	$ 167.39
	Original	$ 382.00	$ 499.00	$ 440.50
	Upper-Upscale and luxury	$ 394.50	$ 1022.50	$ 708.50
Intercontinental	Mid-scale	$ 163.88	$ 223.88	$ 193.88
	Original	$ 285.94	$ 385.00	$ 335.47
	Upper-Upscale and luxury	$ 208.00	$ 599.00	$ 403.50

Compiled by the author.

Exhibit 6 Segmentation and the Portfolio of Hotels

Target Market		
Mid-scale	**Upscale**	**Upper-Upscale and luxury**
Four points by Sheraton	Westin Sheraton	St. Regis W hotels Luxury Collection

Compiled by the author.

will continue to keep us ahead of our competition and will accelerate our market share growth. The marketing and service programs we have and are developing will help us secure an emotional connection with our guests and cement our position as brand leader in the upper upscale and luxury segments."[9]

However, it is opined that although Starwood has established a distinctive brand image for each of its brands, consumers rarely show any brand loyalty as every transaction for a hotel customer is a new decision. To change that, Starwood aims to strike cross-marketing deals with various consumer brands. Steven said, "We need to be bigger. I don't want to be bigger for the sake of it though. I want to be bigger with different brands and to have a broader reach. We want to be a one-stop shop and take the [customer] relationship at the Starwood level, as opposed to the brand level, and strengthen it."[10]

Cross-Marketing Strategies

To reinforce the image of each brand, Starwood is seeking partnerships with consumer brands that would match with the character of each hotel. Steven said, "As we sell experiences, we can partner with brands that reflect that experience."[11] To strengthen the 'flirty escape for hip insiders' image of W hotel brand, Starwood has entered into a deal with Victoria's Secret chain. According to the agreement, the W hotel guests would receive discounts on Victoria's Secret merchandise as well as tickets for the brand's fashion shows. Victoria's Secret products would also feature in guest rooms.

Starwood is also negotiating with media companies, telecommunications firms, and other businesses that would help each of Starwood's brands to differentiate itself from its competitors. Apart from strengthening the image of each brand, it would also generate additional revenues for the hotel. In a previous attempt, Starwood partnered with Yahoo! when the Yahoo! link service was made available at selected Sheraton Hotels. Under this service, guests were provided with an all-in-one Internet center, which included free Wi-fi[12] and a one month free trial of several of Yahoo!'s most popular services. The company believes that through this strategic partnership, Yahoo! and Sheraton Hotels help visitors to stay connected by offering them access to the same resources that they would have in the comfort of their home or office, at any point of time. Javier Benito, executive vice president and chief marketing officer for Starwood Hotels & Resorts, Inc. said, "At Sheraton Hotels we provide our guests with a sense of community, helping them connect to what is important to them. In the Yahoo! Link @ Sheraton guests will find a warm, comfortable environment where they can catch up on work, email their family and friends, or just sit back and relax."[13]

Starwood spends $50 million on advertising per year.[14] To make the most of that, Steven said that the company would increase its advertising spend in return for which media company Time Warner Inc. would offer certain assets for use in Starwood hotels. Under the terms of the partnership (yet to be finalized), the W hotel, for example, would serve as a center for celebrity interviews and events. The video clips would be later streamed online by America Online which can be accessed by members of Starwood's loyalty program. In addition to this, Time Warner magazines would also be made available inside guests' room. Much like a mini-bar item, the guests would be able to read the magazine by breaking open the seal, for which a fee would be charged.

Although Starwood's cross-brand deals are an attempt by the company to build brand loyalty, some feel that providing merchandise in rooms would not enhance the hotel experience. Neither would it make customers prefer one hotel over another. With 231,000 hotel rooms, it was also opined that Starwood's partnership with consumer brands might lead to brand clutter, bombarding guests with numerous products and promotions. While it is observed that the key is to match the right consumer brands with the right hotel, Allen Adamsson, managing director at Landor Associates,[15] a global-branding consultancy in New York, said, "no one wants to be in a room where everything is for sale."[16]

Notes

1. "Starwood Hotels & Resorts Worldwide Inc", **www.hoovers.com.**
2. Starwood Vacation Ownership is a developer and operator of high quality vacation resorts that can be owned temporarily.
3. Shellum, Steve "Preview of the Wonderful and Wacky World of the W Seoul; Aiming to Break the Mould of Asia's Traditional Hotels", **www.hotel-online.com,** October 2003.
4. "Westin Stresses Emotion Over Appearances", **www.brandweek.com**, March 13th 2006.
5. "A History of Success", **www.starwood.com.**

6. "Travel Pros Give Starwood Brands Top Honors in Business Travel News' US Hotel Chain Survey", **www.starwood.com,** February 11th 2002.
7. Carey, Jeanine "Westin launches 'R.S.V.P' Ad Campaign", **www.supplierinteractive.com,** September 19th 2000.
8. "Westin Stresses Emotion Over Appearances", op.cit.
9. "Starwood Reports Record Second Quarter 2005 Results", **www.highbeam.com,** July 26th 2005.
10. Richter, Allan "Son of W", **www.hotelinteractive.com,** June 6th 2005.
11. Sanders, Peter "Starwood's Secret: Cross-Marketing", The Wall Street Journal, February 15th 2006, p 28.
12. WiFi is the wireless way to handle networking.
13. "Yahoo! Link @ Sheraton", **www.promotionworld.com,** January 9th 2006.
14. "Starwood's Secret: Cross-Marketing", op.cit.
15. Founded in 1941 by Walter Landor, Landor Associates is the world's leading strategic brand and creative design consultancy.
16. "Starwood's Secret: Cross-Marketing", op.cit.

Annexure I Special Amenities Designed by Westin for its Guests

The Heavenly Bed®

Unlike any other bed in the industry, the Heavenly Bed is our signature innovation, winning glowing reviews and loyal fans since its introduction in 1999. Sumptuous and stylish, the all-white Heavenly Bed is made up of a custom designed pillow-top mattress set, a cozy down blanket, three crisp sheets ranging in thread count from 180 to 250, a comforter, duvet, and five plush pillows.

The Heavenly Bath®

The Heavenly Bath® is an industry first, offering guests a fully customizable shower experience via their exclusive dual showerhead configuration and a revolutionary curved shower rod affording eight additional inches of elbowroom. Indulgent signature spa amenities, Brazilian combed cotton bath sheets and custom-designed velour bathrobes complete this lavish picture and add even more incentive to get out of bed.

The Heavenly Crib®

Designed to exceed current U.S. safety standards, the Heavenly Crib® offers parents peace of mind and babies the luxury of sweet dreams in a cloud of comfort. Safer and more restful for tiny travelers, the Heavenly Crib® is equipped with a cushioned 4-inch thick mattress (2 inches thicker than most portable hotel cribs) a special deep-pocketed fitted sheet and padded bumpers—all crafted from fire-safe fabrics and non-toxic materials.

Westin Kids Club®

Traveling with kids can be daunting, which is why Westin created a kids' program designed to make the experience more enjoyable, safer and easier for families on the go. Beyond the basic babysitting services and children's menus, Westin Kids Club® delivers services, furnishings, and amenities geared for kids of all ages, including infants.

Westin workout ® Powered by Reebok Gym

Staying fit on the road has never been easier or more convenient with a variety of choices to peak your interest and cardio levels. Check out our state-of-the-art fitness facilities or enjoy an in-room workout. If you prefer to pound the pavement, look for RUNWestin, a program dedicated to runners at all levels that offers scenic and safe morning runs with a specially trained Running Concierge.

Source: "Innovative by Design", www.starwoodhotels.com.

Medi-Cult: Pricing a Radical Innovation

"This is the biggest revolution ever to hit reproductive therapy!" exclaimed Henrik Krogen, president of Medi-Cult. Krogen was referring to In Vitro Maturation (IVM), a procedure and medium that his biotech company had developed for infertile couples, which significantly reduced the time needed to mature an egg from 30 days to just 2 days. The most important advantage of IVM was that it was a hormone-free treatment; it spared women the physical and psychological side effects caused by the 30 days of hormone stimulation required under the current In Vitro Fertilization (IVF) method.

In August 1998, the first baby using the IVM method was born, and the early success of IVM caught Medi-Cult by surprise. Initially, Krogen had thought the product would hit the market in the year 2001 or 2002. "Success rates with IVM were pathetic everywhere else in the world," Krogen explained. "We were caught somewhat by surprise. IVM hadn't really been included companywide as something of strategic value."

Although Krogen was confident that IVM would revolutionize the way infertile couples have babies, he was uncertain of what price to charge for the new technology. If he priced it too low, he could suboptimize potential profitability and risk having the credibility of his product questioned. If he priced it too high, he might attract only a limited number of the infertile couples who seek treatment each year, while perhaps making the industry more attractive for potential competitors.

As Krogen pondered what price to charge for a single dosage of IVM, he began to ask himself the following questions: (1) How would patients, governments, insurance companies, and health care providers receive IVM? (2) What price would the market bear? (3) What percentage of the market would IVM attract?

This case was prepared by Research Associate Brian Rogers under the supervision of Professor Nirmalya Kumar as a basis for class discussion rather than to illustrate either effective or ineffective handling of a business situation.

This case won the 2005 European Case Award in the Marketing category, granted by the ECCH in association with *Business Week*.

Company Background

Medi-Cult, a Danish biotechnology company, developed and manufactured cell culture media. Cell culture media allowed cells to exist and propagate outside their natural environment (the human body). In 1986, Professor Kjell Bertheussen developed and patented Synthetic Serum Replacement (SSR), a protein-free culture medium that could be substituted in the place of animal and human sera. SSR, unlike animal and human sera, effectively minimized the risk of transferring diseases to the embryo. This was considered a breakthrough in the field of Assisted Reproductive Technologies (ART), and a comfort to couples who wished to conceive through IVF.

In 1987, Bertheussen and a number of partners established Medi-Cult to exploit this proprietary cell culture technology in two major application markets. The first was a *clinical* application of cell culture in the field of ART. The second was an *industrial* application, where cells were used in the production of active pharmaceutical substances and marketed to the biopharmaceutical industry.

Three fully owned subsidiaries in France, Great Britain, and the United States were responsible for sales of Medi-Cult products in those countries. A fourth subsidiary, Amdex A/S, with headquarters in Copenhagen, had been created to supply highly innovative technologies to the international diagnostic industry. Medi-Cult serviced clients all over the world through its extensive network of 35 independent distributors, who had been awarded exclusive territories by the company. In August 1998, Medi-Cult hoped to strengthen its position in the U.S. market by signing a letter of intent to acquire Unisyn, Inc., a Boston-based biopharmaceutical contract producer.

In 1997, Medi-Cult had total sales of DKK (Danish krone) 20,560,000 or roughly US$3 million. (*Refer to Exhibit 1 for more data.*) Practically all the sales revenues in 1997 came from IVF products. Forecasted growth was

Exhibit 1 Medi-Cult Financial Information 1996–1997

Statement of Income

Thousand DKK *1 US $ = 6.4 DKK (01.01.99)*	1996	1997
Net turnover	15,600	20,560
Production costs	5,786	8,053
Gross result	9,814	12,507
Sales and marketing costs	5,656	10,039
General and administrative costs	6,111	7,378
Research and development costs	2,011	4,981
Result before financial items	–3,954	–9,891
Financial items net	839	2,553
Result before extraordinary costs and tax	–3,115	–7,338
Extraordinary expenses	223	148
Result before tax	–3,338	–7,486

Balance Sheet

Thousand DKK		
Fixed assets	2,034	3,385
Current assets	63,535	42,146
Assets in total	65,569	45,531
Equity	60,911	39,513
Long-term debt	776	0
Short-term debt	3,882	6,018
Liabilities and equity in total	65,569	45,531
Market capitalization	195,021	227,532
Share price, December 31 *(DKK)*	53	59

Source: Medi-Cult

estimated at 30% to 40% for 1998. The company, which had been listed on the Oslo stock exchange since 1996, had not turned a profit in recent years.

Henrik Krogen, president of Medi-Cult, was a 42-year-old, dynamic, technically trained executive with extensive sales and marketing experience in the pharmaceutical industry. Medi-Cult employed 53 people and was fully operational, with its own R&D, patents, and manufacturing. Ten of its 53 employees were dedicated exclusively to R&D.

In addition to internal R&D, Medi-Cult also had a virtual R&D network, in which they contracted with academic institutions for particular projects. These institutions worked up new products, technologies, and documentation, which were then brought back to Medi-Cult for evaluation, testing of reproducibility, and product formulation. Medi-Cult prided itself on its partnerships with doctors, scientists, and biotechnological manufacturers throughout the world, and viewed these relationships as key to staying on the cutting edge of research in this highly competitive field. The development of IVM and its clinical success was one such example of the synergy achieved between Medi-Cult and its R&D network.

Assisted Reproductive Technologies

In 1998, about 6% of the Western population suffered from reduced fertility. On average, infertility is equally split between men and women. In most cases, the female partner is 100% healthy; however, it is usually the female, not the male partner, who undergoes treatment for infertility.

In Vitro Fertilization

The IVF method is better known as the "test tube method," though neither egg nor sperm see the inside of a test tube. The four steps in the IVF treatment are as follows: (*Refer to diagram in Exhibit 2.*)

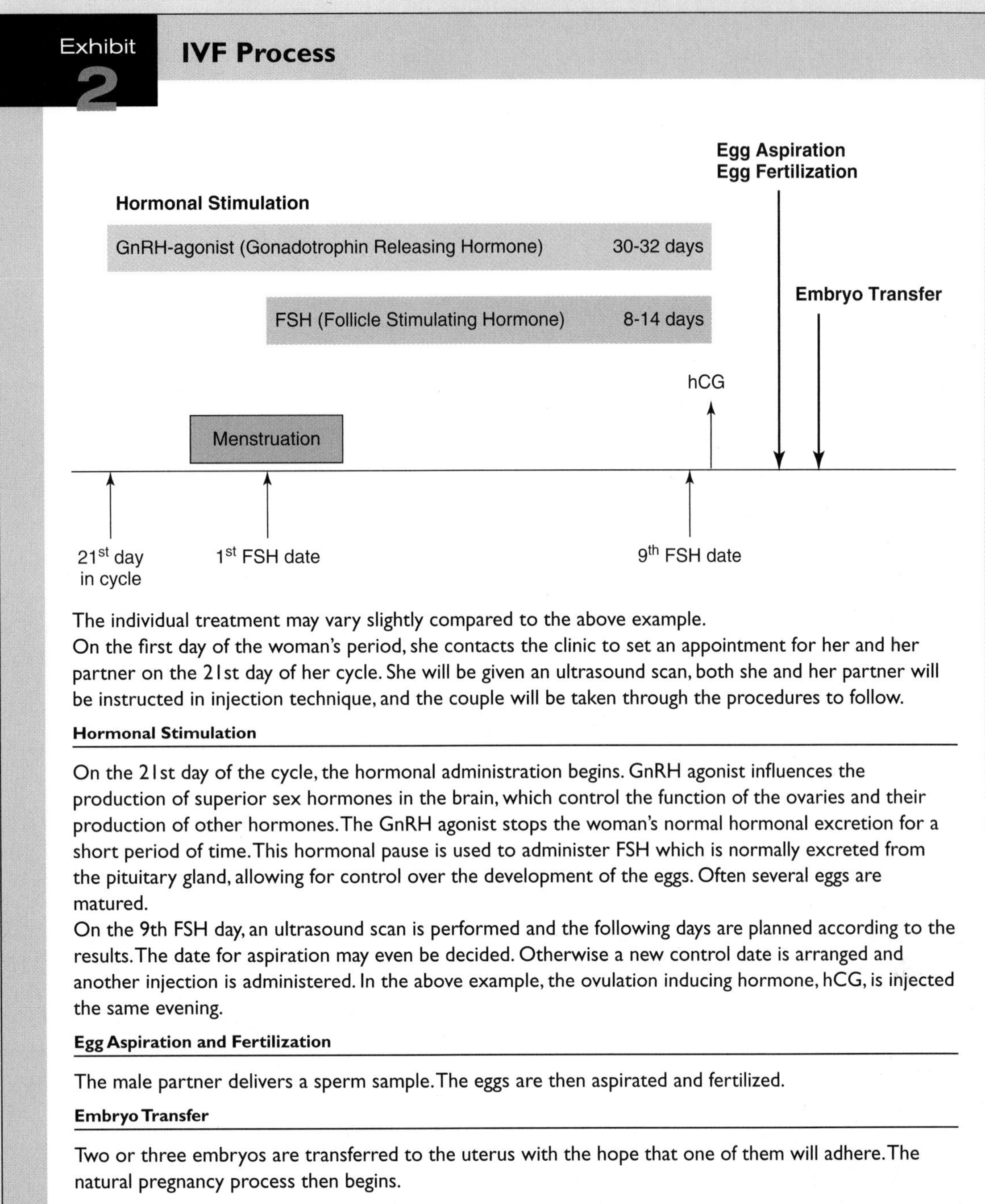

The individual treatment may vary slightly compared to the above example.

On the first day of the woman's period, she contacts the clinic to set an appointment for her and her partner on the 21st day of her cycle. She will be given an ultrasound scan, both she and her partner will be instructed in injection technique, and the couple will be taken through the procedures to follow.

Hormonal Stimulation

On the 21st day of the cycle, the hormonal administration begins. GnRH agonist influences the production of superior sex hormones in the brain, which control the function of the ovaries and their production of other hormones. The GnRH agonist stops the woman's normal hormonal excretion for a short period of time. This hormonal pause is used to administer FSH which is normally excreted from the pituitary gland, allowing for control over the development of the eggs. Often several eggs are matured.

On the 9th FSH day, an ultrasound scan is performed and the following days are planned according to the results. The date for aspiration may even be decided. Otherwise a new control date is arranged and another injection is administered. In the above example, the ovulation inducing hormone, hCG, is injected the same evening.

Egg Aspiration and Fertilization

The male partner delivers a sperm sample. The eggs are then aspirated and fertilized.

Embryo Transfer

Two or three embryos are transferred to the uterus with the hope that one of them will adhere. The natural pregnancy process then begins.

Source: Ciconia.

Step 1—Hormonal Stimulation

Only one of the 1,000 eggs a woman develops every month matures completely. Using hormone stimulation, more eggs are matured, thus increasing the chance of pregnancy. Hormonal stimulation lasts approximately 30 days and can require up to 50 self-administered injections. Some women are unable to administer the injections themselves, necessitating a daily visit to the clinic; later in the process, two daily visits are required.

The injection of these hormones is often accompanied by side effects such as general discomfort, reduced sexual desire, and extreme mood swings. About 50% of the women suffer from nausea; 10% become sick because of over-stimulation. In extreme cases, hormonal stimulation may lead to very serious, potentially life-threatening problems resulting in 2% of women requiring an average of 5 days of hospitalization. Because of the potential for side effects, all infertility patients are closely monitored during the stimulation process and have to submit bi-weekly blood samples to the clinic.

Step 2—Egg Aspiration

Egg aspiration lasts only ten minutes. During this stage, the more mature eggs are removed, examined, and placed in a nutrition fluid.

Step 3—Fertilization

After four hours in an incubator, the eggs are fertilized with the male sperm. Cell division begins 18 hours later.

Step 4—Embryo Transfer

Forty-eight hours later, the embryos are transferred to the uterus. This transfer takes just a few minutes.

The Market for In Vitro Fertilization

In 1998, the worldwide market for IVF encompassed approximately 350,000 procedures (also called cycles); according to estimates, these cycles resulted in 50,000–100,000 births. (*Refer to Exhibit 3 for details on the market.*) According to Medi-Cult, growth in the number of cycles was estimated at 5% to 10% per year. Of these cycles, 15% to 40% could be lost to non-stimulated cycles or to freezing.

The total cost for an IVF cycle varied significantly from country to country. For example, in the U.S., the total cost of the IVF treatment was \$8,000 to \$10,000, and \$4000 to \$5,000 for the rest of the world. (Table A provides a breakdown of the cycle cost for a typical patient.)

IVF is not always successful—on average, three to five attempts are made before a child is born. Because the extensive hormone treatment under the IVF method is so unpleasant and sometimes dangerous, women dislike it and often give up after the first attempt. As a result, fewer children are born because most women are unwilling to undergo IVF treatment three to five times to become pregnant.

Exhibit 3 Estimated Number of IVF Cycles/Year

Europe		
France	33,000	
Germany	30,000	
Italy	27,000	
UK	25,000	
Benelux	15,000	
Spain	13,000	
Sweden	10,000	
Denmark	7,000	
Norway	4,000	
Finland	4,000	
		168,000
North America		
USA	80,000	
Canada	10,000	
		90,000
Rest of the world		**87,000**
TOTAL CYCLES WORLDWIDE		**345,000**

Source: Medi-Cult.

Medi-Cult participated in the market by supplying the IVF media used in steps 2, 3, and 4 of the IVF method. The price of a single dose of IVF medium, sufficient for one cycle, was about \$50 per cycle. (In Table A, this price was included in the cost of IVF treatment.) Medi-Cult estimated its variable costs of production and testing

Table A Cost for IVF Cycle

	Cost of IVF Treatment (a)	Cost of Hormones[1] (b)	Lab Work (c)	Misc. Costs[2] (d)	TOTAL COST (a + b + c + d)
USA	\$4,000–\$6,000	\$3,000	\$500	\$500	\$8,000–\$10,000
Rest of the World	\$2,000–\$3,000	\$1,500	\$300	\$200	\$4,000–\$5,000

[1] The hormones are usually directly purchased by the patient at a pharmacy while the rest of the costs (IVF treatment, lab work, etc.) are billed to the patient or alternative payer by the hospital/clinic.

[2] Miscellaneous costs include additional doctor visits, ultrasound monitoring, workdays lost, and hospitalization. Note: this cost varies as hormone injections affect some women more than others.

Source: Medi-Cult.

to average approximately 30%. Medi-Cult remained the market leader in the IVF media market, despite aggressive competition from other European IVF media companies. The company was growing at 35% even though their pricing had increased 30% over the previous three years.

In Vitro Maturation and Its Development

In vitro maturation, a delicate procedure involving the collection of immature oocytes (eggs) from the ovary, used the *same* procedure as used for IVF, but without the prior hormone stimulatory regimen. Step 1 of IVF was unnecessary, but Steps 2, 3, and 4 remained the same. Once collected, the oocytes were matured outside the body (in vitro) with the help of hormones and a single dosage of the patented maturation medium developed by Medi-Cult. After two days of maturation in the laboratory, the eggs were fertilized by the partner's sperm and replaced into the woman's uterus, as with existing IVF procedures.

Since IVM eliminates the hormonal stimulation step from the IVF procedure, the cost of the hormones for patients falls by 90%. Furthermore, lab work and miscellaneous costs also drop by about 50% since there is less monitoring of patients and fewer complications. The success rate of IVM is the same as IVF; therefore, patients can also expect to undergo three to five attempts before having a child. The success of IVM depends on following both the unique clinical procedures as well as using the maturation medium developed by Medi-Cult.

Customers

Infertile Couples

In recent years, infertile couples sought out information exhaustively, and were therefore well informed about the various treatments available to assist them in having a child. Although they consulted with physicians and clinics, many couples had made up their mind beforehand about which treatment they wished to have. Since having a baby using IVF could be prohibitively expensive, the decision to undergo treatment one or more times often depended on whether medical insurance or the government would cover some or all of the expenses.

Doctors

Svend Lindenberg, a physician at Herlev Hospital in Denmark, believed that patients would choose IVM because the process was very easy for the patient to comprehend and easy to participate in, and because there was no risk of hyper-stimulation from hormones. Dr. Lindenberg also believed doctors were likely to recommend IVM because no prescriptions were required, no artificial menstrual cycles were needed, and because their patients would complain less of discomfort.

Clinics

Initially, Medi-Cult planned to select certain clinics as part of its rollout plan, since the company viewed clinics as the critical link to the market. Before Medi-Cult shared its technology with clinics, the clinics would have to sign a franchising agreement in which the clinic agreed to buy the IVM media exclusively from Medi-Cult for a predetermined period of time. The clinic would also agree not to develop its own IVM technology. Furthermore, clinics would have to agree to follow Medi-Cult protocols and quality requirements to the letter, report their results, and observe strict confidentiality.

For Medi-Cult, a potential drawback in attracting doctors and clinics was that they tended to resist signing agreements. To prevent competitors from seizing the technology and producing their own IVM media, secrecy was paramount. Dr. Lindenberg believed that doctors and clinics would still be drawn to IVM if Medi-Cult assured them that the IVM method would be continu-

Table B Cost for IVM Cycle

	Cost of IVF Treatment[1] (a)	Cost of Hormones (b)	Lab Work (c)	Misc. Costs (d)	TOTAL COST (a + b + c + d)
USA	$4,000–$6,000	$300	$250	$250	$4,800–$6,800
Rest of the World	$2,000–$3,000	$150	$150	$100	$2,400–$3,400

[1] These costs reflect the various steps of IVF treatment such as the initial doctor visit, tests, egg aspiration, fertilization, and embryo transfer which still have to be performed with the IVM. It however does not include the cost of Medi-Cult's IVM maturation medium.

Source: Medi-Cult.

ously refined, and if doctors and patients were kept educated about the process. Despite these restrictions, Dr. Lindenberg hypothesized that clinics would embrace the IVM method quickly. They would adopt the IVM method primarily because patients had a tendency to flock to clinics that were on the cutting edge, and also because there was also a certain prestige factor in being one of the first clinics to offer such an innovative technology.

Governments and Insurance Companies

Reimbursement of infertility treatments by insurance companies and governments was low because infertility patients were not considered "diseased." In the U.K., the patient had to pay almost all of the cost for infertility treatment. In contrast, the French authorities allowed four free attempts (cycles) per patient; beyond this, the patient had to pay for any additional treatments. In Denmark, infertility treatments given by private practice had to be paid out of pocket by the patient, while the first three treatments given by public clinics were free of charge, with medication and hormone costs reimbursed up to 75%. In the U.S., reimbursement was low; the amount that insurance companies were willing to pay varied from state to state, company to company, and procedure to procedure.

There was not much information available on the regulation of fertility by governments. Medi-Cult was in a difficult position because the IVM medium could not be sold without government approval, and because the cost to the patient was significantly increased if governments and insurance companies elected not to cover the costs of fertility treatment. Furthermore, there may even be pressure on Medi-Cult to keep the price of the IVM medium low so that insurance companies could move funding to other disease areas or increase the total number of couples receiving the treatment.

Competition

Medi-Cult was likely to face two different types of competition. The first type of competition would come from the large pharmaceutical companies such as Ares-Serono, Organon, Ferring, and Wyeth-Ayerst, which supplied the hormones used in IVF. At Ares-Serono, an estimated $500 million in sales revenues came from reproductive health products; at Organon, 13% of their estimated $1.1 billion in sales revenue came from infertility drugs. In Medi-Cult's estimation, these large pharmaceutical manufacturers would lose out because the IVM process significantly reduced the need for hormones. Furthermore, Medi-Cult believed that the drug companies stood to lose $200 to $300 million in new business, which was growing by 25%–50% annually. Medi-Cult suspected that upon launching IVM, these pharmaceutical giants would discredit the process, demand product approval for it, threaten withdrawal of research funds from clinics who adopt it, and stop all sponsoring of congresses for fertility physicians.

A second type of competition was likely to come from companies, which like Medi-Cult, also developed and manufactured cell culture media. Medi-Cult suspected that these biotech companies would develop their own product and clinical procedure. In Europe, for example, it is not possible to patent a process, although it is possible to patent a maturation medium. Medi-Cult worried that competitors would break Medi-Cult's IVM medium patent by using molecular modeling (also known as reverse engineering). At any rate, Medi-Cult expected to have a 2- to 3-year advantage by being the first to market since any company that wished to introduce a competing product or process would have to undertake the clinical trials and document live births.

Market Launch

Medi-Cult was considering using a hub-and-spoke approach to get to the market with the least possible delay. The central hub would consist of the Copenhagen University Institute of Human Reproductive studies, seven Danish clinics, and the Medi-Cult IVM Task Force. Secondary hubs would consist of the clinics trained at the central hub and supported by the primary spokes of information. The secondary hubs would then train tertiary centers.

The secondary training hubs would be carefully selected clinics in Norway, Sweden, Spain, Germany, France, Belgium, Italy, Israel, and the United Kingdom. These centers would be chosen based on their throughput, (i.e., above 300 cycles per year) and their willingness to enter into an agreement to operate under a Medi-Cult IVM-franchise. To expedite the IVM launch, Medi-Cult planned to recruit a business development manager and a scientific director for the special IVM Task Force.

Medi-Cult would be marketing IVM medium in the form of a single dose sufficient for one cycle. In addition, the company would be providing training, upgrading, technology development, and quality control to the clinics involved. Medi-Cult planned to produce IVM like any other IVF medium, and had calculated the cost to produce a single dose of IVM medium to be slightly more expensive than its current cost of producing IVF medium. No extra investment would be incurred by Medi-Cult in the production set-up as sufficient in-house capacity was available and the company was already producing similar products.

Exhibit 4 Results of IVM Pricing Exercise

		Potential Price Points								
		High Price			Medium Price			Low Price		
Country	Respondent	Price[1]	Volume[2]	Market Share[3]	Price	Volume	Market Share	Price	Volume	Market Share
Denmark	Kristen Krag, Int'l Sales Director	DKK 12,000	325	5.0%	DKK 10,000	500	7.0%	DKK 8,000	1,200	17.0%
France	Denis Azra, General Manager	FF 8,000	500	1.5%	FF 5,000	650	2.0%	FF 4,000	900	3.0%
UK	Lesley Hutchins, General Manager	£900	2,000	8.0%	£700	3,000	12.0%	£500	4,000	16.0%
USA	Larry Fava, General Manager	$2,200	1,200	1.5%	$1,600	1,200	1.5%	$1,000	1,200	1.5%

[1] Price for a single dosage sufficient for one cycle
[2] Estimated number of IVM cycles for the first 12 months
[3] Percentage of total number of IVF cycles within that country

Currency Exchange Rates:
US$1 = FF 5.6 (French francs)
US$1 = £0.60 (British pounds)
US$1 = DKK 6.4 (Danish krone)

Currency Exchange Rates on 01.01.99

Source: Pacific Exchange Rate Service.

Henrik Krogen's Dilemma

With IVM, we can't lose," Krogen concluded. He added, "I don't want to kill the market with a high price, but I don't want to undershoot the market either." Even though Medi-Cult was losing money, Krogen was under no pressure to set any particular price for IVM. Confident of his product, Krogen began considering his pricing options for the March 1999 launch of IVM.

Krogen knew that it would be very difficult to claim that the cost of production would justify its price. There was no tradition for pricing media at this level, and everybody would know that the cost to produce the IVM medium was insignificant, when compared to the current price for medication. But still, Krogen contemplated whether IVM should be priced according to the product's perceived value. A high launch price could signal the enhanced benefits of IVM over the existing IVF method and potentially generate greater profits. Alternatively, a low launch price could motivate faster adoption of the IVM method by clinics since they could obtain a greater share of profits.

Krogen also wondered if a single uniform price should be set worldwide, or whether the price should vary from country to country. To help make this decision, Krogen solicited from Medi-Cult managers in Denmark, France, the U.K. and the U.S. their judgments on: (a) the lowest realistic price and expected first year sales volume at that price; (b) a "medium" price and expected sales volume at that price; and (c) the highest realistic price and anticipated sales volume at that price. (*Refer to* Exhibit 4 for results.) Traditionally, drug prices had differed widely across countries, resulting in some shipment of products from low to high price countries. However, with the introduction of the Euro on January 1, 1999, market analysts expected greater harmonization of prices within Europe.

Krogen felt that the pricing strategy also needed to address the question of the appropriate long-term evolution of prices. One option was to keep real inflation-adjusted prices stable over time as this enhanced the legitimacy of the initial launch price. Alternatively, if Krogen opted for a high initial price, he could lower prices as competition materialized—or, if he selected a low initial price, he could increase prices as uncertainties about the new IVM method faded and the Medi-Cult method became the established industry standard. In the latter case, for example, "improved" versions could be launched by Medi-Cult at higher prices.

Last but not least, the reaction from the big pharmaceutical companies also had to be considered since the increased use of IVM would translate into losses of revenue for the drug companies.

There were many unanswered questions, but one thing Krogen knew for sure: infertile couples would place a high value on his product because it was easy to use, safer than the current IVF method, and would help them achieve their ultimate dream—to have a child.

Samsung: From Cheap to WOW!

Ten years ago, Samsung was a financially strapped, struggling company known primarily for its cheap microwaves and TVs.

Today, it is one of the best performing and most respected companies in the world. Samsung ranks 20th on the 2005 *Business Week/Interbrand* list of The Top 100 Global Brands—ahead of Sony (once the undisputed leader in consumer electronics, No. 28) and Motorola (once the leader in cellular phones, No. 78).[1] It ranks 12th on Boston Consulting Group's list of the most innovative companies in the world. According to BCG, Samsung "catches the pulse of the consumer; [offers] good designs; understand emotion...."[2] The story of Samsung's journey from cheap to WOW! is nowhere more evident than in the cell phone market.

According to company lore, Samsung's transformation began with a defective product. In 1995, Kun-Hee Lee, the chairman and son of the Samsung Group's founder, presented company cell phones to friends and key workers. He soon began receiving complaints that the phones didn't work. Embarrassed, he ordered the entire inventory be destroyed. Two thousand employees were assembled to watch as 150,000 wireless handsets, cordless phones, and fax machines—totaling $50 million—were hammered into pieces and thrown into a bonfire. "A defect is a cancer," Lee told his workers.[3]

To reposition Samsung as a top-end producer of high-quality digital products required a complete overhaul of the company. For this job, Lee tapped Jong-Yong Yun as president and CEO, urging him to "change everything except your spouse and children."[4] Yun, a Samsung veteran who had risen through the company's ranks, may have seemed an unlikely candidate to lead the painful restructuring. But he rose to the challenge. He laid off 24,000 workers (a third of the company's workforce), sold $2 billion in non-core businesses that were losing money, cut costs, and shook up the company's rigid management structure.[5] At the same time, he invested heavily in technology, product design, and human resources—hiring 300 U.S.-educated MBA graduates and 700 PhD-level engineers.[6]

The reforms were painful for the company, but Yun's personality and sense of humor helped him win support from employees. He is, by all accounts, an unimposing man with a down-to-earth style. As one employee put it, Yun "is like your uncle from the country. You feel comfortable with him."[7] Unlike many corporate leaders who have overseen successful turnarounds, he does not brag about Samsung's success or make bold predictions about its future. Yet, Yun can be a tough-as-nails boss, when results are needed. And he doesn't believe in letting Samsung rest on its laurels. "I'm the chaos-maker," says Yun. "I have tried to encourage a sense of crisis to drive change. We instilled in management a sense that we could go bankrupt any day."[8]

Even as Samsung's fortune has shifted, Yun does not let his managers forget the lessons learned in the bleak days in the mid-1990s. "We must not lose the sense of crisis that helped us change.... When everything goes smoothly is the time when things go wrong."[9] Given Samsung's recent performance, Mr. Yun must be very worried indeed.

Samsung's Ascendancy

The second half of the 1990s was a period of explosive growth in the cell phone industry. As technology improved, prices fell and phones shrank in size. The market evolved from techies who had to have the latest gadget, to soccer moms who appreciated the added security, to teenagers who carried phones as a fashion accessory. By the end of the decade, the cell phone had become the purview of the masses—the cord had been cut, and freedom rang.

During this period, it was the handset manufacturers who drove the market. Motorola reigned as the global leader, primarily due to its dominance in the U.S.; Nokia captured the number two position, due to its popularity in the European market. Together, the two companies controlled more than half of the world market, with the rest divided by a number of very capable and aggressive competitors, including Sony, Ericsson, and Siemens.

Manufacturers weren't the only players in the industry; demand for cell phones was also driven by the service providers or carriers. In the U.S., the major carriers included the long-distance companies, the "Baby Bells," as well as other regional companies. In Europe, each country was dominated by its own carrier, such as Vodafone in the U.K., T-Mobile in Germany, and Orange in France. It was the technology of the service providers that affected the consumers' ability to send and receive calls and voicemail—at that time, the only functions of a cell phone. So as consumer demand began to grow in the mid-1990s, the carriers were forced to invest heavily in digital equipment to improve their ability to handle more traffic and provide better customer service.

And it was this shift technology that changed the dynamics between the leading handset manufacturers. Motorola—whose advantage had been in analog—was slow to adopt digital technology. Nokia was faster to meet the technical needs of the U.S. carriers, since digital technology was already the standard in Europe. In 1998, Nokia unseated Motorola as the global market leader in handsets. Motorola's slip in the cell phone market set in motion a series of events which sent the company into a seemingly uncontrollable, downward spiral. Within five years, Motorola would drop from a 33% share of the global market to 14%, while Nokia rose from 22% to 35%.[10]

Even as the handset manufacturers dueled with one other, the industry was shifting beneath them. The burst in the technology bubble in 2000, coupled with the ensuring recession, hit the technology industry hard. Demand flattened. Service providers—desperate to distribute their investment cost over more consumers—expanded into each others' regions and gobbled up smaller competitors. With each acquisition, their customer base grew—making the carriers more important at a time when manufacturers were desperate to unload inventory. As a consequence, power shifted away from the manufacturers and to the carriers.

With increasing competition between fewer carriers, the service providers needed to differentiate themselves. To do so, they started making greater demands on the handset manufacturers. It began with little things—a case cover or an opening screen—but soon the demands expanded into something far more important, namely the look and feel of the phone itself. Vodafone wanted Vodafone's name on the phone—above Nokia's, and it wanted features that would distinguish its service from competitors.

To say that the handset manufacturers were reluctant to accommodate these demands would be an understatement. Most balked at prominently displaying the carrier's name; it was after all, *their* phone. But the carriers' demands for distinctive features were even more worrisome. If the handset manufacturers responded to requests from each carrier in the U.S., Europe, and Asia, the number of product variations would increase exponentially. And with each variation, production costs would increase.

More importantly, the handset manufacturers realized this was a battle for the consumer's mind. Every company in the technology sector had watched as IBM and its fellow denizens of hardware had lost the battle of the PC to Microsoft. Hardware had become commoditized with razor-thin margins, while software raked in the profits. The cell phone makers, particularly Nokia, had no intention of history repeating itself in their sector. With its comfortable lead in the market, Nokia decided it *wouldn't* respond to the carrier's demands. Motorola—in serious financial trouble by this point—*couldn't* respond.

Samsung did.

Samsung entered the U.S. market in 1997 with a silver, clamshell model priced at $149.[11] It was a successful debut, but gaining traction in such a competitive space wasn't easy. So Samsung took another tactic: they sought out the service providers and "bent over backward" to meet their needs. Within five years, Samsung had climbed from nowhere to a distant fourth behind Nokia, Motorola, and Siemens.

It wasn't until 2002—with the introduction of the color screen and the camera phone—that Samsung broke into the top tier of handset makers. These innovations were already a hit in Asia. But both Nokia and Motorola were skeptical that these features would be popular in Europe or the U.S., given the high price points required to cover the cost of the phones. Seeing an opportunity, Samsung jumped in; they approached T-Mobile about offering a camera phone for the Christmas season. After reaching an agreement in April, Samsung assembled 80 designers and engineers from its chip, telecom, display, computing, and manufacturing operations to develop a prototype. Once a working model had been developed, the company flew 30 engineers to Seattle to field-test the phones for T-Mobile servers and networks.[12] By November, the phones were rolling off the production line.

The phone Samsung developed, the V250, had an innovative lens that swiveled 270 degrees and wirelessly transmitted photos. It sold for $350. Even so, sales were higher than anyone—with the possible exception of Samsung—expected. T-Mobile reported sales of 300,000 units a month.[13] Overall, it had been a very good year for Samsung: global sales had increased 51%, and by year-end, the average price of a Samsung phone was $230, compared to $198 at the beginning of the year.[14]

When Nokia and Motorola finally committed to product development, they were too far behind to catch up. Both companies missed the all-important Christmas selling season. When Nokia and Motorola got their phones to market in 2003, sales had slowed and prices had plummeted. Nokia's sales were practically flat with an average selling price of $154; Motorola's sales rose only 4%, with an average selling price of $147.[15]

Samsung had captured the most lucrative portion of the market. More importantly, Samsung had made its name as the most innovative company in the handset market. By mid-2003, Samsung was in a neck-and-neck race with Motorola for number two in the global market, with Nokia maintaining a comfortable lead. But the race was far from over.

Staying Laser-Focused

Samsung had found its niche by focusing on innovative products for the high-end market. And it continued to flawlessly execute the strategy. Samsung was the first to introduce voice-activated phones and handsets with MP3 players. It introduced camera phones with better resolution than many digital cameras. In 2004, Samsung launched 40 new handset models in the U.S.; 130 models worldwide. Samsung refreshed its entire product lineup every nine months, compared to the 12 to 17 months required by Motorola.[16] "We believe in creating the wave, not riding it," says Ki Tae Lee, head of Samsung's handset business.[17]

Samsung's secret weapon, to some extent, is the South Korean market itself. After the foreign exchange crisis of 1997 in which thousands of people were thrown out of work, the South Korean government committed to supporting high-tech industries by enabling consumers. Due to investments by the South Korean government, fully 70% of homes are now wired for broadband.[18] Apartment blocks display government notices by the front door certifying the Internet connection speed.

But staying connected to the Internet doesn't tether consumers to their homes. In South Korea, connection is only as far away as the cell phone, which practically everyone carries. (Three-quarters of the South Korean population have a cell phone;[19] 20% buy a new cell phone every seven months.[20]) To the country's tech-savvy youth, cell phones are largely interchangeable with computers. Text messaging, for example, is more ubiquitous than e-mail. "You would exchange e-mails with your boss, not your friends," explains one twenty-something consumer.[21]

Simple text messages are no longer major revenue earners for South Korean service providers. So the carriers are looking for more complex data services—watching movies, activating home appliances, online banking services. According to one industry insider, "There is a future, not too far away, when the only thing you will need to leave home with is your mobile phone, because it will be your wallet and your key and all the things it already is."[22] Samsung already sells a phone in South Korea that allows users to download and view up to 30 minutes of video and watch live TV for a fixed monthly fee. Its video-on-demand phone sells for $583.

Surviving in this demanding environment requires constant innovation—and a crisis mentality. Samsung can go from new product concept to rollout in five months, compared to the 14 months it took just six years ago.[23] To achieve this, Samsung relies on its Value Innovation Program (VIP), which is "best described as an invitation-only, round-the-clock assembly line for ideas and profits where Samsung's top researchers, engineers, and designers come to solve their grittiest problems."[24] Team members are constantly reminded that speed equals success, that every overlooked detail or missed deadline takes the product one step closer to being a commodity. As one team leader puts it, "When people are told they have to come here, they know they have to come up with results in a very, very short time." Another adds, "This is not a prison, but it's not a volunteer job either."[25]

While engineers struggle with technical problems, design is not overlooked or undervalued. Fashion is a big part of Samsung's strategy—as is the design team that drives new products. In the early 1990s, Samsung had just 20 designers; now it has design centers in London, Tokyo, San Francisco, and Seoul. "That's where you find the guys with green hair and pony tails," says David Steel, vice president of marketing for Samson's digital media business. "We've given our designers a lot of influence within the company."[26] And the designers have delivered by connecting the phone's functions to consumers' emotions. From the "lady's phone," small with red lacquer finish engraved with a gold rose, to the decidedly masculine titanium slider phone, Samsung's phones are designed to elicit a "WOW!" reaction from consumers.

Innovation and design is then balanced with durability and quality. Lee, the head of the handset business, conducts his own product test when a prototype reaches his office: he throws the model across his office into a wall. "Amid fury, a bad conversation on the phone could trigger some people to throw the handset, and that got me thinking about designing a handset that would not hurt people who are accidentally hit," he explains. "I lose sleep over these things."[27]

Just as Samsung's product strategy mixes function with emotion, so does its marketing program. Samsung keeps its ear to the ground with detailers who visit stores which carry Samsung products.[28] The detailers monitor stock levels, display conformance, and competitor's products and pricing. Collected data are transmitted via the Internet to Samsung's customer relationship management (CRM) system, where the information is then disseminated to those responsible for addressing the problem. As a result, the company is better able to match product supply with retail demand on a daily basis. In addition, the detailers talk to consumers, gathering qualitative input on demand for new features and functions, even whole new products. This real-time connection to consumers gives the company a daily read on the market and helps it plot its future direction. And the information is shared with the retailers in order to gain their support for the products through their promotions and displays.

While Samsung's monitoring of the channel ensures that consumers are engaged at the point-of-purchase, the company is also effective in generating product excitement with prominent tie-ins and sponsorships. From *The Matrix* to music videos with Britney Spears and Madonna, from the Guggenheim Museum to its own flagship store in Manhattan, from the Olympic Games to the World Cyber Games, Samsung is there. While many of these venues are selected for their cache with the general public and as a means of building brand equity, others yield different rewards. The annual World Cyber Games, for example, is where "e-athletes" from more than 50 nations compete for prize money and medals in video and online games. While less visible to the consumer market, it is events like this that allow Samsung to connect with and learn from key players in the market. "One of the important things we do is reach out to the early adopter. When you start working with early adopters, and you ask what they are looking for in products, you learn how to position products you bring to market," according to Peter Weedfald, senior vice president of Samsung Electronics for North America.[29]

What's Next...

While global sales of cell phones grew 32% in 2003 and 55% in 2004, Samsung predicts a slowing to 15% growth in 2005 and a drop to 6% to 7% in 2006.[30] Asia, Europe, and the U.S. now depend almost entirely on the replacement market. Future growth from first-time buyers will come from markets like China, India, and Latin America. As one analyst observed, "We tend to forget that four billion people have never made a phone call."[31]

Lowering the price of a phone by just $20 in many countries could increase its affordability by 43%. A phone costing $30 would take less than a month's average income; at $50, it would take 1.4 month's income.[32] Motorola has already waded into the market by selling phones for $46 in India. As mature markets become ever more competitive, other handset manufacturers may find that what is good for first-time phone buyers may be good for sales.

Should Samsung follow Motorola's lead? Or would this create a crisis of strategy that even Jong-Yong Yun, Samsung's chaos-maker, would rather avoid?

Notes

1. Robert Berner and David Kiley (2005), "Global Brands," *Business Week*, August 1: 61.
2. Bruce Nussbaum (2005), "How to Build Innovative Companies," *Business Week*, August 1: 61.
3. Peter Lewis (2005), "A Perpetual Crisis Machine," *Fortune*, September 19: 58.
4. Ibid.
5. Cliff Edwards, N.J. Moon Ihlwan, Pete Engardio (2003), "The Samsung Way," *Business Week*, June 16: 56.
6. ... (2003), "South Korea Company: Reign of the 'Chaos-Maker,'" *EIU Views Wire*, March 13.
7. John Burton (2000), "Quick Turnaround Artist: Profile Yun Jong-Yong, President, Samsung Electronics," *Financial Times*, March 27:14.
8. ..., "South Korea Company: Reign of the 'Chaos-Maker.'"
9. Ibid.
10. Andrea Petersen (2001), "Softer Sell: Once-Mighty Motorola Stumbled When It Began to Act that Way," *Wall Street Journal*, May 18: A1.
11. Edwards et al., "The Samsung Way."
12. Ibid.
13. Ibid.
14. David Pringle, Jesse Drucker, Evan Ramstad (2003), "World Circuit: Cellphone Makers Pay a Heavy Toll for Missing Fads," *Wall Street Journal*, Oct. 30: A1.
15. Edwards et al., "The Samsung Way."
16. Ibid.
17. Hae-Won Choi (2004), "Upscale Phones Ring Up Sales for Samsung," *Wall Street Journal*, April 15: B1.
18. Edwards et al., "The Samsung Way."
19. ... (2005), "Survey: Man's Best Friend," *The Economist*, April 2: 8.
20. Edwards et al., "The Samsung Way."
21. ..., "Survey: Man's Best Friend."
22. Ibid.
23. Edwards et al., "The Samsung Way."
24. Peter Lewis (2005), "A Perpetual Crisis Machine," *Fortune*, September 19, 58.
25. Ibid.
26. Andrew Ward (2004), "The 1997 Asian Crisis Forced Samsung to Switch its Focus from Cheap Consumer Electronics to the Top End of the Market," *Financial Times*, September 6: 15.
27. Hae-Won Choi, "Upscale Phones Ring Up Sales for Samsung."
28. Richard O'Connor (2004), "Secrets of the Masters," *Supply Chain Management Review*, January/February: 42.
29. Kamau High (2004), "Why Tournaments Win Sponsorship Deal," *Financial Times*, October 21:12.
30. Yun-Hee Kim (2005), "Samsung Expects Cellphone Growth to Slow Next Year," *Wall Street Journal*, August 30: B5.
31. Rebecca Buckman (2005), "Cellphone Game Rings In New Niche: Ultracheap," *Wall Street Journal*, August 18: B4.
32. Ibid.

Branding: The Asian Dilemma

By the turn of the 21st century, when the global airlines industry was struggling with dwindling revenues, it was only Singapore Airlines that posted huge profits. The reason behind such a success was the airline's commitment to strategic branding. The Singapore Airlines brand and the embedded icon of the Singapore Girl were the major drivers of the company's financial value. Asian companies, towards the end of the 20th century, started realising the need for strategic branding to get on with the dynamic market changes in the form of reduced trade barriers which thus increased competition, and increased number of look-alikes in the marketplace. However, a lack of branding knowledge, expensive branding exercises, and the prejudice of the domestic consumers against them discouraged the Asian companies. Nevertheless, as always, there have been some success stories.

What's in a Name?

The South Korean consumer electronics and home appliance maker, Samsung, was an Original-Equipment Manufacturing (OEM) company in the late 1980s. By the late 1990s, the company chose to reposition its image by building its own brand and established a global marketing operations unit in 1998. In 2003, Samsung was ranked 25th among the 'Top 100 Global Brands,' according to a study conducted by *Business Week* [Exhibit 1]. That year, the Samsung brand was worth $10.85 billion, a 31% growth from the previous year's $8.3 billion.[1] Samsung was in fact following the path laid by Japan's Sony and Canon, who started selling their own brands in the 1980s. Though these companies gave Asia the taste of branding, they could not help Asia re-create such stories. The Singapore Managing Director of Interbrand, Andy Milligan, said, "The desire for OEMs to build brands may be great, but the knowledge of how to do it is poor."[2]

Asians' desire for branding was however justified. With the rapid increase in the number of look-alike products in the market place, there was a need to survive and stand out from the crowd. Branding satisfied these needs by helping companies make products that had personalities, values, and distinct faces. Assistant General Manager of Winfat Industrial Company (OEM from Hong Kong), Raymond Leung, said, "…I can see the need to survive pushing more OEMs towards creating their own products. Branding, although further down the road, is part of the process."[3] With dwindling margins in the commodity business, branding was seen to enable businesses to command a premium on their products and thus increase their margins. The premium was sought on the other hand for having created a stronger and long-lasting relationship with the customers.

Experts also observed that businesses making money were vital for the stability of a country's economy. The reasons for businesses losing money could not be overemphasised when it was opined that in the late 1990s Southeast Asian financial crisis was considered not a financial problem, or a political problem, or even a monetary problem, but a branding problem.[4] In fact, it was opined that recessions were the best times to invest in branding, "when consumers most likely change their purchasing behaviour", said Mike Sherman of McKinsey and Company. The Singapore arm of Interbrand, the U.S.-based brand consultancy, also advised businesses to take to international brand building in order to be less vulnerable during such downturns. Few like Pacific Corp., Cheoy Lee, and Haier seemed to have paid heed to the advice.

Amore Pacific (Pacific), the South Korean cosmetics manufacturer, with the launch of Lolita Lempicka per-

This case was written by P. Venkatesh, under the direction of Sumit Kumar Chaudhuri, ICFAI Business School Case Development Centre. It is intended to be used as the basis for class discussion rather than to illustrate either effective or ineffective handling of a management situation. This case was compiled from published sources.

Distributed and Printed by IBS-CDC, India
www.ibscdc.org

Exhibit 1

The Global Brand Scorecard

Rank	Brand Name	2003 Brand Value* ($ billion)	Rank	Brand Name	2003 Brand Value* ($ billion)
1	Coca-Cola	70.45	26	Morgan Stanley	10.69
2	Microsoft	65.17	27	Merrill Lynch	10.52
3	IBM	51.77	28	Pfizer	10.46
4	GE	42.34	29	Dell	10.37
5	Intel	31.11	30	Merck	9.41
6	Nokia	29.44	31	JPMorgan	9.12
7	Disney	28.04	32	Nintendo	8.19
8	McDonald's	24.70	33	Nike	8.17
9	Marlboro	22.18	34	Kodak	7.83
10	Mercedes	21.37	35	SAP	7.71
11	Toyota	20.78	36	Gap	7.69
12	Hewlett-Packard	19.86	37	HSBC	7.57
13	Citibank	18.57	38	Kellogg's	7.44
14	Ford	17.07	39	Canon	7.19
15	American Express	16.83	40	Heinz	7.10
16	Gillette	15.98	41	Goldman Sachs	7.04
17	Cisco	15.79	42	Volkswagen	6.94
18	Honda	15.63	43	IKEA	6.92
19	BMW	15.11	44	Harley-Davidson	6.78
20	Sony	13.15	45	Louis Vuitton	6.71
21	Nescafe	12.34	46	MTV	6.28
22	Budweiser	11.89	47	L'Oréal	5.60
23	Pepsi	11.78	48	Xerox	5.58
24	Oracle	11.26	49	KFC	5.58
25	Samsung	10.85	50	Apple	5.55

Compiled by ICFAI Business School Case Development Centre from: "The 100 Top Brands", *Business Week*, August 4th 2003, pages 72-78

* A note on the valuation of the brands

Business Week used the Interbrand's method that valuates the brands the same way analysts valuate other assets: on the basis of how much the brand is likely to earn in the future. Those projected profits are then discounted to a present value based on how risky the projected earnings are—that is, the likelihood that they will, in fact, materialise.

Compiled by ICFAI Business School Case Development Centre.

fume in 1997 became the top-10 seller in France.[5] With its domestic market dominance with brands like Laneige, IOPE, Hera and Sulwhasoo, Pacific's year-on-year profit rose by 27% in 2001.[6] Pacific further wanted to consolidate its position in the global arena, as the manager at Pacific's international division, Lee Sang Woo, said, "We have a dream. We want to become a strong brand in the global beauty industry".[7] For achieving this dream, Pacific had a two-pronged strategy. Focusing on the high-end fragrances in Europe, Pacific's operations in France made its products locally and marketed them under the licenses with famous fashion designers. In the rest of the world, Pacific did its own marketing. Particularly in China, Pacific planned to make mid-range cosmetics under its flagship Laneige brand, as an alternative to the more expensive Western products.

Cheoy Lee, a family-run ship-making enterprise based in Hong Kong has been a well-known name among those who could afford a deluxe craft. The more than a century-and-quarter-old enterprise that focused on making expensive sailboats, moved up the value chain in the late 1990s to make million-dollar-plus yachts. The reason for Cheoy Lee's growth to become a well-known name was its sheer quality. The yachts typically had high-grade fittings. Sheets of plywood imported from Israel were converted to furniture and the Italian marble into elegant tabletops and bathroom counters. Cheoy Lee mostly built boats on orders, each vessel designed according to the customer's specifications. Cheoy Lee's vessels have been among the most anticipated displays at the annual Fort Lauderdale, U.S., boat show, the premier trade fair for the yachting industry.

Established in 1984, China-based Haier Group Company (Haier) has been the leading manufacturer of air conditioners, refrigerators, and washing machines. It became a popular brand in the Chinese market by 1991. After having consolidated its position in its domestic market, Haier planned to go global, eyeing the developed American and European markets. By the turn of the 21st century, Haier had manufacturing units in over 13 countries, and became China's first truly global manufacturer. In 2002, Haier clocked worldwide sales of $8.5 billion, an 18% rise from the previous year.[8] Haier, however, faced the challenge of overcoming its image as a low-cost, low-quality producer, which even the Japanese faced in the 1970s, and the Taiwanese and the Koreans in the 1980s. The Asia-Pacific managing director of international brand consultants, Landor Associates, Michael Ip, said, "They [Japanese, Taiwanese, and Koreans] overcame [the stigma] because they were able to deliver on quality. So far, Haier seems to have the technology."[9] It was opined that, if Haier could succeed in the global arena with its technology, it would instill confidence in the other Asian companies to follow suit.

Proud to Be Asian

Nevertheless, Asian companies have not been able to overcome the perception their own markets had of them. The Asian consumer's affection for imported brands and the "West is Best" notion had caused the failure of Asian brands against the global brands. Any attempt to copy a global brand or to brand an Asian brand as 'foreign' only led to 'disastrous failures.'[10] Experts observed that, to be successful, Asian companies could brand effectively with Asian characteristics as a differentiating and a positive factor. The attribute of a product as being 'Asian' seemed to be catching on in the global arena when the U.S. companies were successful in branding the local products like 'Thai Jasmine rice' in the U.S., while Thailand was stuck with thinking of the product as a commodity. A good example of a company taking advantage of the Asian origin has been Cerebos Pacific Ltd.

The Singapore-based Cerebos Pacific Ltd (Cerebos)'s 'Asian Home Gourmet' (AHG)[11] brand included a range of spice pastes made from fresh herbs and spices, which were the high-quality convenience products that allowed consumers prepare different foods in a variety of Asian styles. Operating in a commodity market, AHG had to convince Asian (let alone global) consumers that it was different and better. Taking the challenge head on, AHG chose to express Asian values, in relation to food, to build the brand personality.

In Asia, the link between food and family values has been very strong. Cooking food in Asia has not been considered as an act, but as a way of expressing emotions that were seldom expressed outwardly. So when Asians cook meals for their families, it has been more an expression of love. When they cook for friends, it has been a gesture of respect and happiness for that friendship, and when they cook for their beloved, there has been an ingredient of romance. As the strategic planning director of Bartle, Bogle and Hegarty (BBH), Guy Murphy, said, "In Asia, food is a proxy for showing emotion. While people the world over have an emotional relationship with food, that relationship appears to be most intense in the Asian region."[12]

The campaign devised by BBH brought together the brand personality and Asian values with a punch line, "Recipes made with love". The television commercials portrayed animated ingredients like chilies intertwining with affection and a family of herbs holding hands. The product description said, "Our spice pastes are made from fresh herbs and spices. You can use them to create any one of a range of authentic Asian dishes. All you have to add is one important ingredient. A little of yourself".[13]

The Changing Mindset

> "The way we made money in the past was by saving money, by cutting costs. Now we have to make money by spending money, by investing in our brand."[14]
>
> —Eric Yu
> *CFO at BenQ*

In the new millennium, there was a fundamental rethinking regarding branding in Asia. Businesses started to consider branding as essential to their future health. This rethinking was based on a simple logic that was fundamental to branding. From the customers' point of view, the brands promised quality and consistency, often reinforcing a personality that customers could associate with. The consequent customer loyalty promised continued revenue streams, enabling the companies to charge a premium on their products. Though the 'ends' of branding were easily understood, the 'means,' however, remained elusive to the Asian businesses. One reason cited for this lack of branding expertise was the kind of executives that occupied the top positions in the Asian corporates. Traditionally, senior executives of Asian companies have been recruited from within the ranks of the organisation and these people happened to be from technology and/or financial backgrounds. Thus, the Asian companies lacked people with in-depth marketing and branding skills compared to Western companies. This led to the Asian companies losing strategic focus on branding. Asian companies each year churned out $ 85 billion[15] worth of goods adorned with the Western logos, instead of their own.

On the one hand, the Asian companies realised the potential of brands, while, on the other they did not have the expertise to tap that potential. Eyeing this gap, and with a view to bridging it, brand-development agencies sprang up in Asia, clinching some big contracts in Asia in the early 2000s. Noteworthy among the contracts were WPP Group's Landor Associates' contract with Taiwanese computer maker 'BenQ' and Indonesian cars-to-property conglomerate 'Astra International', and Interpublic Group's FutureBrand contract with China's largest computer-maker, 'Legend Group', to develop the new name 'Lenovo.'[16] "Asian manufacturers are the real companies of the future. They have almost all the parameters to become brands—they just don't know how to do it,"[17] said Philippe Starck, the Chief Vision Officer at 'The Key,' a Hong Kong-based designing and marketing consultancy.

To be successful in branding, however, was not guaranteed; as Rupert Purser, managing director of Hong Kong operations of Brand Finance (consultancy), said, "Building a brand can be very hit and miss. It takes a lot of time and money and there's no guarantee of success."[18] This seemed to be one of the major reasons for Asian companies to buy already established brands. For example, in 1999, Zindart, a Hong Kong-based contract manufacturer of die-cast toys acquired the brand 'Corgi Classics,' a famous brand in Britain for die-cast scale model collectibles. Another Hong Kong-based company, Shriro, an international distributor and marketer of other companies' brands[19] acquired Sweden's Hasselblad[20] brand of camera equipment in 2003.

Miles to Go...

"Asia has a long way to go in developing brands of international stature."[21]

—Kim Faulkner
Managing Director of Interbrand, Singapore.

Over the last two decades of the 20th century, Asian companies dramatically changed from cheap, low-quality manufacturers to providers of superior technology and high quality products. With their well-educated and competent workforce, R&D capabilities, rare passion for technology gadgets, and growing infrastructure, Asian companies were well equipped to position themselves in the global arena. From product marketers in the 1980s, the Asian market evolved in the early 2000s as integrated brand marketers (Exhibit 2). This evolution called for a commitment from the Asian companies to move up the value chain through strategic branding. This also required branding to be viewed not as a cost on the profit and loss statement, but as an investment on the balance sheet.

Nevertheless, high cost of advertisement and overdependence on brand seemed to be the major reasons for Asian companies to shy away from branding. Playing on price seemed prudent at least in the OEM business, as Debora Chatwin, managing director at Enterprise IG,

Exhibit 2 **Evolution of Brand Marketing**

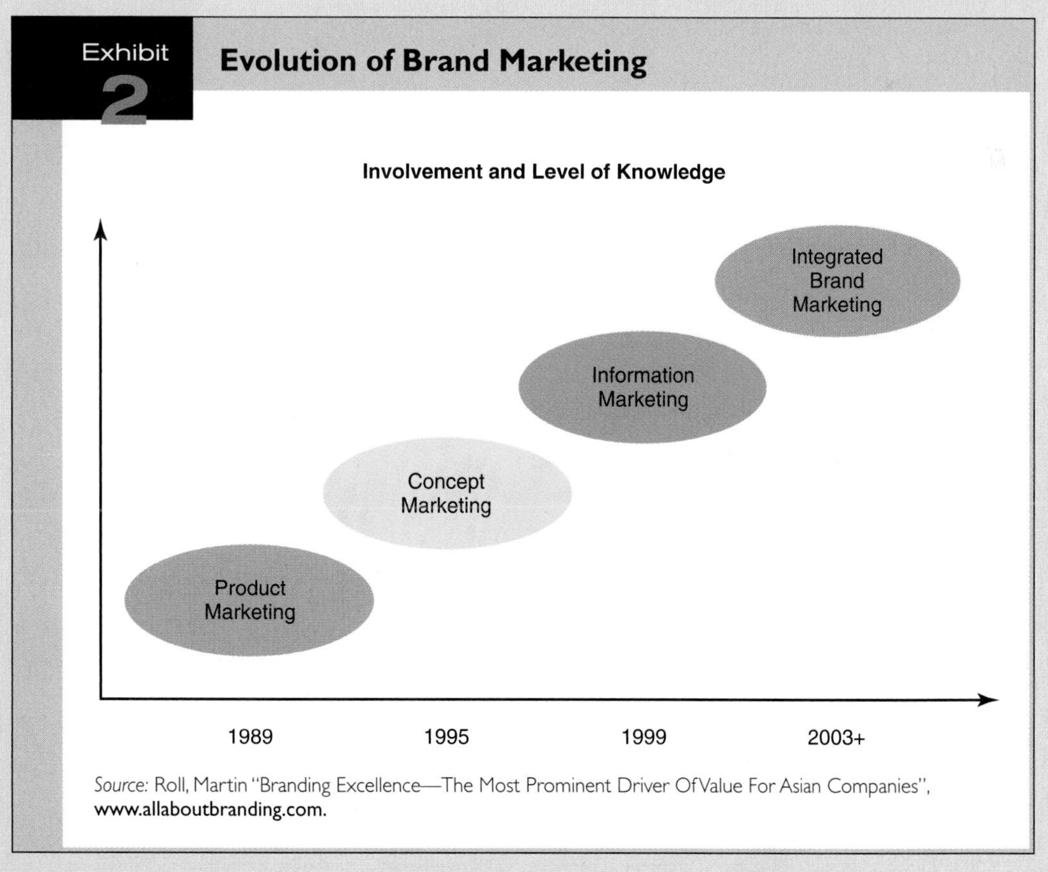

Source: Roll, Martin "Branding Excellence—The Most Prominent Driver Of Value For Asian Companies", www.allaboutbranding.com.

said, "The problem with the OEM business is that a lot of companies can manufacture the same goods, so the deciding factor over which company wins the contract is usually price."[22]

Meanwhile, China's leading computer-maker, Lenovo, made preparations to become an international Olympic sponsor for the 2006 Winter Games in Turin and the 2008 Summer Games in Beijing. By joining the Olympic sponsorship club with elite global brands like Coca-Cola, McDonald's, Panasonic, and Visa, the chief executive Yang Yuanqing was hopeful to 'demonstrate its technology and products to the world, while promoting social values and pursuing its corporate objectives.'[23] BenQ also signed a multi-million dollar contract in November 2003 for sponsoring Euro 2004.[24]

"Asian culture has always valued the long-term aspects in almost any matter. Let this unique strength influence the Asian branding efforts in the years to come."[25]

Notes

1. Lue, Annabel "Branding Key for Global Market", **www.taipeitimes.com,** September 24th 2003.
2. Fowler, Geoffrey A. "From No Name To Brand Name", **www.feer.com,** April 8th 2004.
3. Eng, Dennis "OEMs Urged to Break the Mould", **www.thestandard.com.hk,** April 5th 2004.
4. "Brands – the Key to Future", **www.iamawiz.com.**
5. "What's In a Name", www.asiaweek.com, October 5th 2001.
6. Ibid.
7. Ibid.
8. Wu, Yibing "China's Refrigerator Magnate", **www.mckinseyquarterly.com,** 2003.
9. "What's In a Name", op.cit.
10. "Being Asian – A Competitive Branding Advantage", **www.apmforum.com**, October 17th 2002.
11. Home Gourmet was the holding company of Asian Home Gourmet Pvt. Ltd (AHG), a company that started business as a distributor of edible oil for Socoil Corporation of Malaysia before diversifying into production of seasoning paste. AHG was later acquired by Singapore-based Cerebos Pacific Limited.
12. "Asian Home Gourmet", **www.brandingasia.com.**
13. Ibid.
14. Wood, Justin "Brand and Deliver", **www.cfo.com,** March 30th 2004.
15. "From No Name To Brand Name", op.cit.
16. Lenovo spent millions to secure its place as an international Olympics sponsor for the 2006 Winter Games and the 2008 Summer Games.
17. "From No Name To Brand Name", op.cit.
18. "Brand and Deliver", op.cit.
19. The brands included Arjo Wiggins, BASF, Bobcat, Casio, Conqueror, Epson, Frisk, Hasselblad, Head, Liebherr, Lindt, Mitsubishi Forklift, Moreschi, Moulinex, Neil Pryde, Petrof, Pioneer, Ricola, Rockford Fosgate, Samsung, See's Candies, Welch's and Zero Halliburton.
20. Hasselblad 500EL/70 camera was used in the historic Apollo 11 mission of NASA in 1969.
21. Mackay, Angela "THE GAME OF THE NAME", **www.cfoasia.com,** November 1999.
22. "What's in a Name?", op.cit.
23. "China Set to Leap into the World of Super Brands", **http://busines-times.asia1.com.sg,** April 3rd 2004.
24. Soccer Championship Held in Portugal between June 12th and July 4th 2004.
25. Roll, Martin "Branding Excellence—The Most Prominent Driver Of Value For Asian Companies", **www.allaboutbranding.com.**

Part 5

The Implementation of Global Marketing Strategy

Chapter

Global marketing strategies are valueless if they cannot be carried out in practice. Two key aspects of strategy implementation are discussed in this part: (1) the organization and management of foreign market operations and (2) international negotiations. Various organizational and control options are available to the firm operating abroad. These are highlighted, from the points of view of both large and small firms. The ultimate success of marketing strategies frequently depends on skillful cross-cultural negotiations and the achievement of a signed contract. The problems of international negotiations are discussed, and guidelines for the successful conduct of negotiations are put forward.

Chapter 15

Marketing Organization, Implementation, and Control

The Global MARKETPLACE 15.1

Procter & Gamble: Organization 2005

Globalization is at the heart of Procter & Gamble's restructuring of its organization, code-named Organization 2005. Organization 2005 recognizes that there is a big difference between selling products in 140 countries around the world and truly planning and managing lines of business on a global basis.

There are five key elements to Organization 2005:

- *Global Business Units (GBUs).* P&G moved from business units based on geographic regions to three GBUs based on product lines. This will drive greater innovation and speed by centring global strategy and profit responsibility on brands, rather than on geographics.
- *Market Development Organizations (MDOs).* The company established seven MDO regions that will tailor global programs to local markets and develop marketing strategies to build P&G's entire business based on superior local consumer and customer knowledge.
- *Global Business Services (GBS).* GBS brings business activities such as accounting, human resource systems, order management, and information technology into a single global organization to provide these services to all P&G business units at best-in-class quality, cost, and speed. They will be in the following locations: Americas (San José, Costa Rica); Europe, Middle East, Africa (Newcastle, United Kingdom); and Asia (Manila, Philippines).
- *Corporate Functions.* P&G has re-defined the role of corporate staff. Most have moved into new business units, with the remaining staff re-focused on developing cutting-edge new knowledge and serving corporate needs. For example, the company decentralized its 3,600-person information technology department so that 97 percent of its members now work in P&G's individual product, market, and business teams or are part of GBS, which provides shared services such as infrastructure to P&G units. The remaining 3 percent are still in corporate IT. In addition, 54 "change agents" have been assigned to work across the four GBUs to lead cultural and business change by helping teams work together more effectively through greater use of IT—in particular, real-time collaboration tools. Future plans have called for some of these functions to be outsourced.
- *Culture.* Changes to P&G's culture should create an environment that produces bolder, mind-stretching goals and plans; bigger innovations; and greater speed. For example, the reward system has been redesigned to better link executive compensation with new business goals and results.

In 2004, P&G re-balanced and re-focused its GBUs to create units of about the same size. Health, Baby, and Family Care; Household Care; and Beauty Care each command $17 billion in worldwide sales. MDOs, GBS,

The New Procter & Gamble

Global Business Units	Market Development Organizations	Global Business Services	Corporate Functions
• Health, Baby, and Family Care • Household Care • Beauty Care	• North America • Latin America • Western Europe • Central Eastern Europe/ Middle East/Africa • ASEAN/India/Australia • Northeast Asia • Greater China	• Global Enabling Team • Regional Leadership Team • Global Process Owners	• Customer Business Development • Finance & Accounting • IT • Legal • Product Supply • R&D • Human Resources • Marketing • Consumer & Market Knowledge

and Corporate Functions were combined into Global Operations.

How the new organization works can be highlighted with an example. The GBUs define the equity, or what a brand stands for. The Pantene brand, for example, gives a customer healthy, shiny hair, and a Pantene Team within the Health, Baby, and Family Care GBU is charged with building on this. It starts with product initiatives or upgrades, which ideally would be launched simultaneously around the world. It includes a marketing campaign that communicates the same fundamental benefit around the world, and it includes manufacturing the product against global formula and package specifications. The MDOs then ensure Pantene excels in their region. In the United States, this could mean focusing on Club Stores, which might entail partnering with the GBU to develop large packaging that the outlet demands to maximize value for their shoppers. Conversely, the focus in Latin America might be to develop the smallest possible package (such as a sachet), as consumers in that region want to minimize their out-of-pocket costs. The outcome should be the same overall brand equity, but very different executions by region. The GBS Center in Costa Rica would be providing support for both the U.S. and Latin America MDOs in this example (and for any other brand business team from these regions). Some of the services would include accounting, employee benefits and payroll, order management and product logistics, and systems operations. Those working directly on the business teams would likely determine the amount of Corporate Function (CF) support. Each function would want to ensure that they are capitalizing on the latest thinking or methodologies for each discipline. In this capacity, think of CF as a consulting group ready to provide service if called upon.

In the past, when a product was introduced, it might have taken years for it to be available worldwide, since management in each region was responsible for the product's launch there, including everything from test marketing to getting products onto retailers' shelves. Collaborative technologies, including chat rooms on the company's

© Dibyangshu Sarkar/AFP/Getty Images

intranet, are transforming the company's conservative culture to one that encourages employees to be candid, test boundaries, and take chances.

As with any change of consequence, challenges arose as well. The projected $2 billion in savings also resulted in 9,600 layoffs. Furthermore, many positions had new reporting structures and even new locations. More than half of the executives at the various levels are in new jobs. Physical transfers were significant as well; for example, 1,000 people were moved to Geneva from around Europe and another 200 to Singapore from various Asian locations. Furthermore, the changed reporting structures raised concerns as well; for example, Household Care reports to Brussels. Personnel transferred to MDOs suddenly had no brands to manage and had to think across borders. The change from a U.S.-centric company to a global one was a substantial demand in a short period of time and has required adjustments by those affected and in the timetables set.

Sources: "It Was a No-Brainer," *Fortune*, February 21, 2005, 96–102; *Procter & Gamble 2004 Annual Report*, 11; "P&G Profits by Paradox," *Advertising Age*, February 24, 2004, 18–19, 31; Sonoo Singh, "P&G Opens Up Its Doors and Its Ears," *Marketing Week*, February 13, 2003, 21; Jack Neff, "Does P&G Still Matter?" *Advertising Age*, September 25, 2000, 48–56; "Rallying the Troops at P&G," *The Wall Street Journal*, August 31, 2000, B1, B4; "P&G Jump-Starts Corporate Change," *Internetweek*, November 1, 1999, 30; "All around the World," *Traffic World*, October 11, 1999, 22–24; "Organization 2005 Drive for Accelerated Growth Enters Next Phase," P&G News Releases, June 9, 1999, 1–5; and "Procter & Gamble Moves Forward with Reorganization," *Chemical Market Reporter*, February 1, 1999, 12. See also **http://www.pg.com.**

As companies evolve from purely domestic entities to multinationals, their organizational structure and control systems must change to reflect new strategies. With growth comes diversity in terms of products and services, geographic markets, and personnel, leading to a set of challenges for the company. Two critical issues are basic to addressing these challenges: (1) the type of organization that provides the best framework for developing worldwide strategies, while at the same time maintaining flexibility with respect to individual markets and operations, and (2) the type and degree of control to be exercised from headquarters to maximize total effort. Organizational structures and control systems have to be adjusted as market conditions change, as seen in The Global Marketplace 15.1. While some units are charged with the development of strong global brands, others are charged with local adaptation and creating synergies across programs.

This chapter will focus on the advantages and disadvantages of the organizational structures available, as well as their appropriateness at various stages of internationalization. A determining factor is where decision-making authority within the organizational structures will be placed. The roles of different entities of the organization need to be defined, including how to achieve collaboration among these units for the benefit of the entire global organization. The chapter will also outline the need for devising a control system to oversee the global operations of the company, emphasizing the control instruments needed in addition to those used in domestic business, as well as the control strategies of multinational corporations. The appropriateness and eventual cost of the various control approaches will vary as the firm expands its global operations. Overall, the objective of the chapter is to study intra-organizational relationships in the firm's attempt to optimize competitive response in areas most critical to its business.

Organizational Structure

The basic functions of an organization are to provide (1) a route and locus of decision making and coordination, and (2) a system for reporting and communications. Increasingly, the coordination and communication dimensions have to include learning from the global marketplace through the company's different units.[1] These networks are typically depicted in the organizational chart.

Organizational Designs

The basic configurations of global organizations correspond to those of purely domestic ones; the greater the degree of internationalization, the more complex the structures can become. The core building block is the individual company operating in its particular market. However, these individual companies need to work together for maximum effectiveness—thus, the need for organizational design. The types of structures that companies use to manage foreign activities can be divided into three categories based on the degree of internationalization:

1. *Little or no formal organizational recognition of international activities of the firm.* This category ranges from domestic operations handling an occasional international transaction on an ad hoc basis to separate export departments.
2. *International division.* Firms in this category recognize the ever-growing importance of international involvement.
3. *Global organizations.* These can be structured by product, area, function, process, or customer.

Hybrid structures may exist as well, in which one market may be structured by product, another by area. Matrix organizations have emerged in large multinational corporations to combine product, regional, and functional expertise. As worldwide competition has increased dramatically in many industries, the latest organizational response is networked global organizations in which heavy flows of technology, personnel, and communication take place between strategically interdependent units, to establish greater global integration. The ability to identify and disseminate best practices throughout the organization is an important competitive advantage for global companies. For example, a U.S. automaker found that in the face of distinctive challenges presented by the local environment, Brazilian engineers developed superior seals, which the company then incorporated in all its models worldwide.[2] The increasing enthusiasm for outsourcing has put new demands on managing relationships with independent partners. Boeing, for example, holds a partners' council meeting every six weeks, and has set up a network that makes it possible for designers (both at Boeing and suppliers) to work on the same up-to-the-minute database. Virtual meetings with colleagues in different time zones take place throughout the day.[3]

Little or No Formal Organization

In the very early stages of international involvement, domestic operations assume responsibility for international marketing activities. The share of international operations in the sales and profits of the corporation is initially so minor that no organizational adjustment takes place. No consolidation of information or authority over international sales is undertaken or is necessary. Transactions are conducted on a case-by-case basis either by the resident expert or quite often with the help of facilitating agents, such as freight forwarders.

As demand from the international marketplace grows and interest within the firm expands, the organizational structure will reflect it. An export department appears as a separate entity. This may be an outside export management company—that is, an independent company that becomes the de facto export department of the firm. This is an indirect approach to international involvement, in that very little experience is accumulated within the firm itself. Alternatively, a firm may establish its own export department, hiring a few seasoned individuals to take full responsibility for international activities. Organizationally, the department may be a sub-department of marketing (as shown in Exhibit 15.1) or may have equal ranking with the various functional departments. This choice will depend on the importance assigned to international activities by the firm. Because the export department is the first real step for internationalizing the organizational structure, it should be a full-fledged marketing organization and not merely a sales organization; that is, it should have the resources for market research and market-development activities (such as trade show participation).

Licensing is the international entry mode for some firms. Responsibility for licensing may be assigned to the R & D function despite its importance to the overall global strategy of the firm. A formal liaison among the export, marketing, production, and R & D functions should be formed for the maximum utilization of licensing.[4] A separate manager should be appointed if licensing becomes a major activity for the firm.

As the firm becomes more involved in foreign markets, the export department structure will become obsolete. The firm may then undertake joint ventures or direct foreign investment, both of which require those involved to have functional experience. The firm therefore typically establishes an international division.

Some firms that acquire foreign production facilities pass through an additional stage, in which foreign subsidiaries report directly to the president or to a manager specifically assigned this duty. However, the amount of coordination and control that is required quickly establishes the need for a more formal international organization in the firm.

It is worth stressing here that smaller, nimbler firms operating internationally, of which many Canadian examples could be cited, will frequently avail themselves of numerous business networking opportunities to expedite their internationalization. At home, working with customers, suppliers, complementary businesses, research institutes, and government agencies helps even the smallest firm to appreciate the benefits of working with others. As foreign markets are penetrated, this experience can be built on. As we saw in the Clinotech case (see Chapter 12), distributors not only facilitate overseas sales, they also afford access to the *distributor's* network of contacts. This in turn can bring various benefits—access to new technology and markets, new product ideas, improved quality. Also, there is the possibility of graduating to a grander scale of global networks. Smaller firms are learning that by collaborating with others they are able to achieve international success "that they would never achieve on their own."[5] The way in which Canadian SMEs utilize networks and partnerships to expand their

Exhibit 15.1 The Export Department Structure (TAL Apparel)

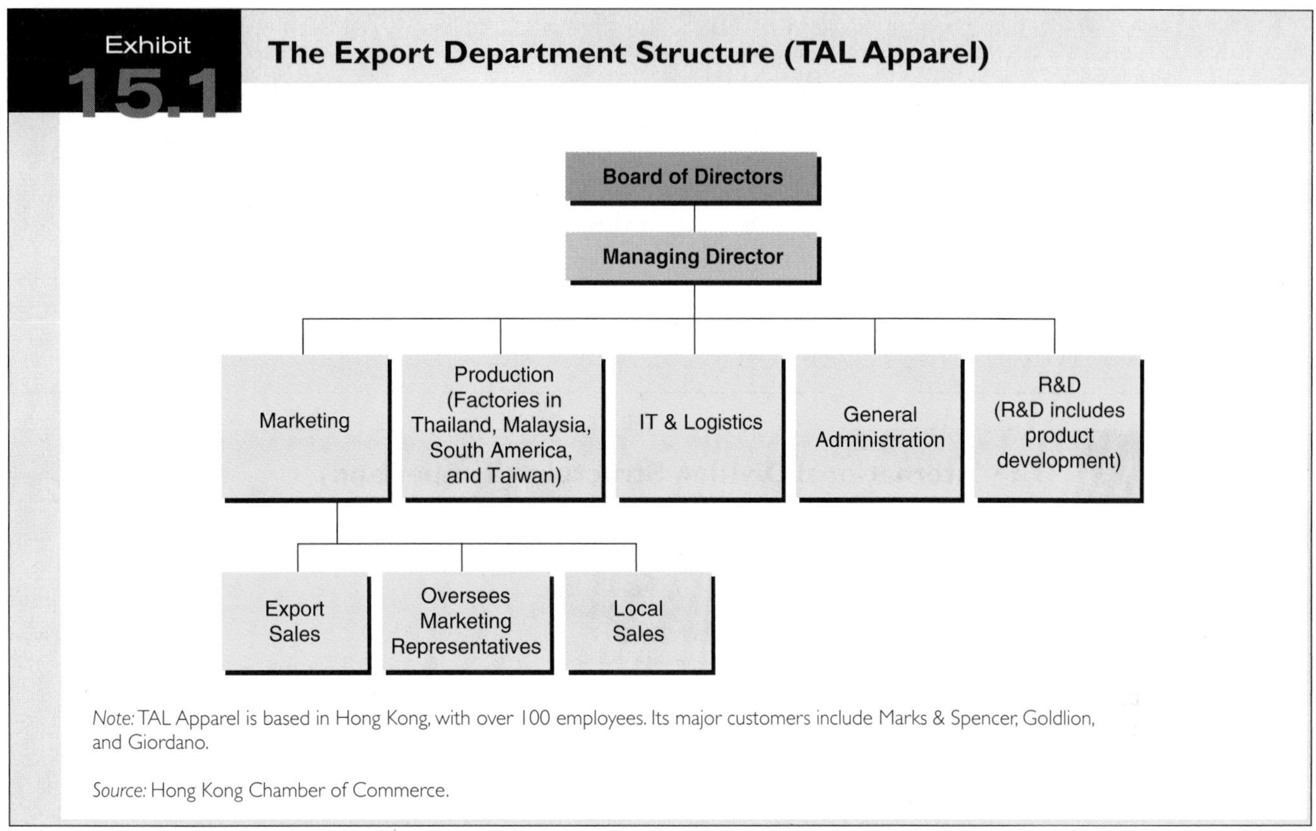

Note: TAL Apparel is based in Hong Kong, with over 100 employees. Its major customers include Marks & Spencer, Goldlion, and Giordano.

Source: Hong Kong Chamber of Commerce.

global horizons, while lacking the formality of structures found in multinational enterprises (MNEs), is worthy of increasing attention.

The International Division

The international division centralizes in one entity, with or without separate incorporation, all of the responsibility for international activities, as illustrated in Exhibit 15.2. The approach aims to eliminate a possible bias against international operations that may exist if domestic divisions are allowed to independently serve international customers. In some cases, international markets have been found to be treated as secondary to domestic markets. The international division concentrates international expertise, information flows concerning foreign market opportunities, and authority over international activities. However, manufacturing and other related functions remain with the domestic divisions in order to take advantage of economies of scale.

To avoid situations in which the international division is at a disadvantage in competing for production, personnel, and corporate services, corporations need to coordinate between domestic and international operations. Coordination can be achieved through a joint staff or by requiring domestic and international divisions to interact in strategic planning and to submit the plans to headquarters. Further, many corporations require and encourage frequent interaction between domestic and international personnel to discuss common challenges in areas such as product planning. Coordination is also important because domestic operations may be organized along product or functional lines, whereas international divisions are geographically oriented.

International divisions best serve firms with few products that do not vary significantly in terms of their environmental sensitivity, and when international sales and profits are still quite insignificant compared with those of the domestic divisions.[5] Companies may outgrow their international divisions as their international sales grow in significance, diversity, and complexity. European companies used international divisions far less than their U.S. counterparts due to the relatively small size of their domestic markets.

In More Detail 15.1

FROM INTERNATIONAL TO GLOBAL ORGANIZATION

Royal Dutch Shell or Philips would have never grown to their current prominence by relying on the Dutch market alone. While international divisions were still popular among U.S. companies in the 1980s and 1990s, globalization of markets and the increased share of overseas sales have made international divisions less suitable than global structures.[7] For example, Loctite, a leading marketer of sealants, adhesives, and coatings, moved from having an international division to being a global structure in which the company is managed by market channel (e.g., industrial automotive and electronics industry), to enable Loctite employees to synergize efforts and expertise worldwide.[8]

Exhibit 15.2 **The International Division Structure (Timberland)**

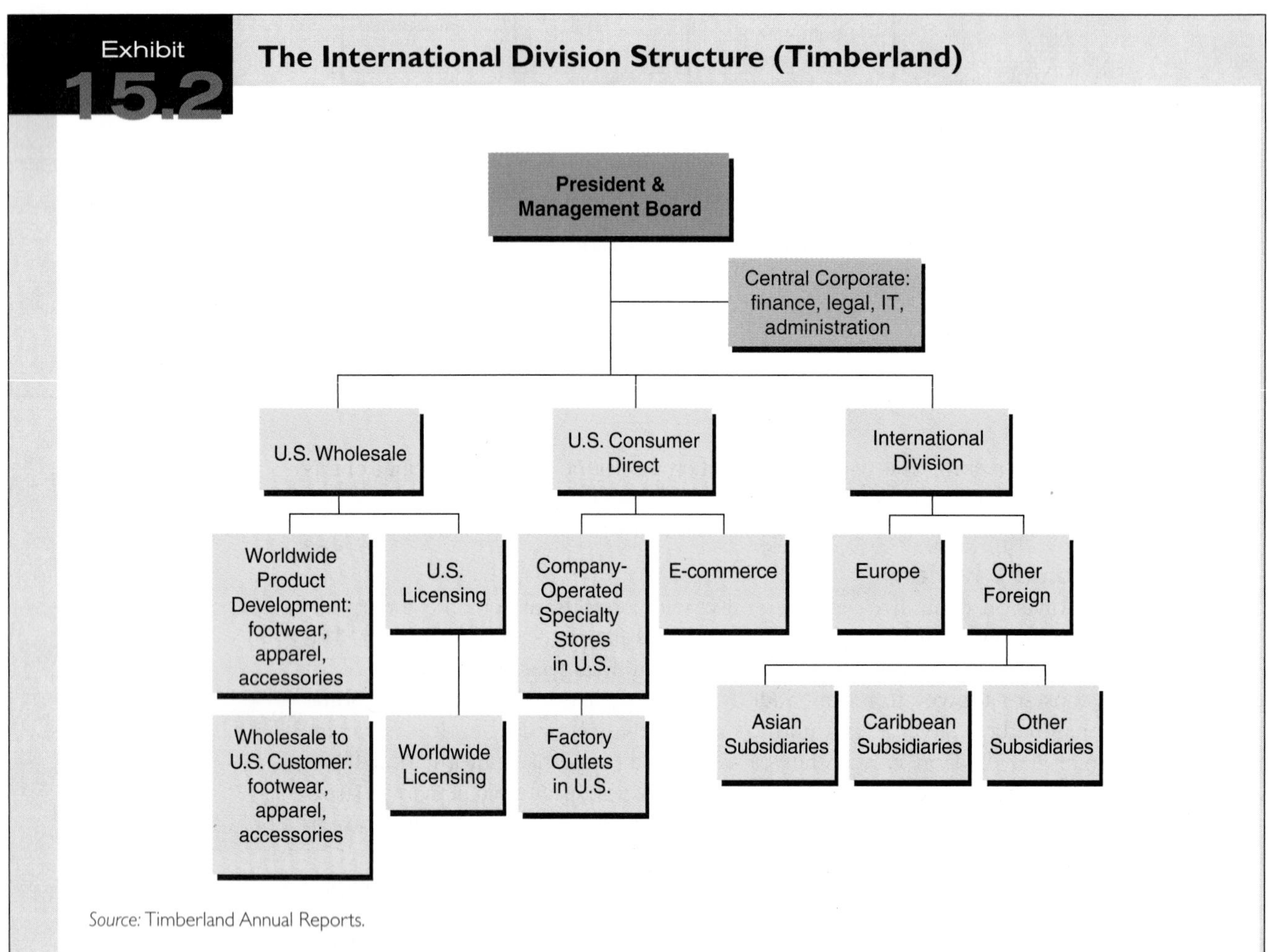

Source: Timberland Annual Reports.

Global Organizational Structures

Global structures have grown out of competitive necessity. In many industries, competition is on a global basis, with the result that companies must have a high degree of reactive capability. Five basic types of global structures are available:

1. Global product structure, in which product divisions are responsible for all manufacture and marketing worldwide
2. Global area structure, in which geographic divisions are responsible for all manufacture and marketing in their respective areas
3. Global functional structure, in which the functional areas (such as production, marketing, finance, and personnel) are responsible for the worldwide operations of their own functional areas

4. Global customer structure, in which operations are structured based on distinct worldwide customer groups
5. Mixed—or hybrid—structure, which may combine the other alternatives

Product Structure

The **product structure** is the one that is most used by multinational corporations.[9] This approach gives worldwide responsibility to strategic business units for the marketing of their product lines, as shown in Exhibit 15.3. Most consumer product firms utilize some form of this approach, mainly because of the diversity of their products. One of the major benefits of the approach is improved cost efficiency through centralization of manufacturing facilities. This is crucial in industries in which competitive position is determined by world market share, which in turn is often determined by the degree to which manufacturing is rationalized.[10] Adaptation to this approach may cause problems because it is usually accompanied by consolidation of operations and plant closings.

Another benefit is the ability to balance the functional inputs needed by a product and to react quickly to product-specific problems in the marketplace. Even smaller brands receive individual attention. Product-specific attention is important because products vary in terms of the adaptation they need for different foreign markets. All in all, the product approach ideally brings about the development of a global strategic focus in response to global competition.

At the same time, this structure fragments international expertise within the firm because a central pool of international experience no longer exists. The structure assumes that managers will have adequate regional experience or advice to allow them to make balanced decisions. Coordination of activities among the various product groups operating

Exhibit 15.3 The Global Product Structure (Kodak)

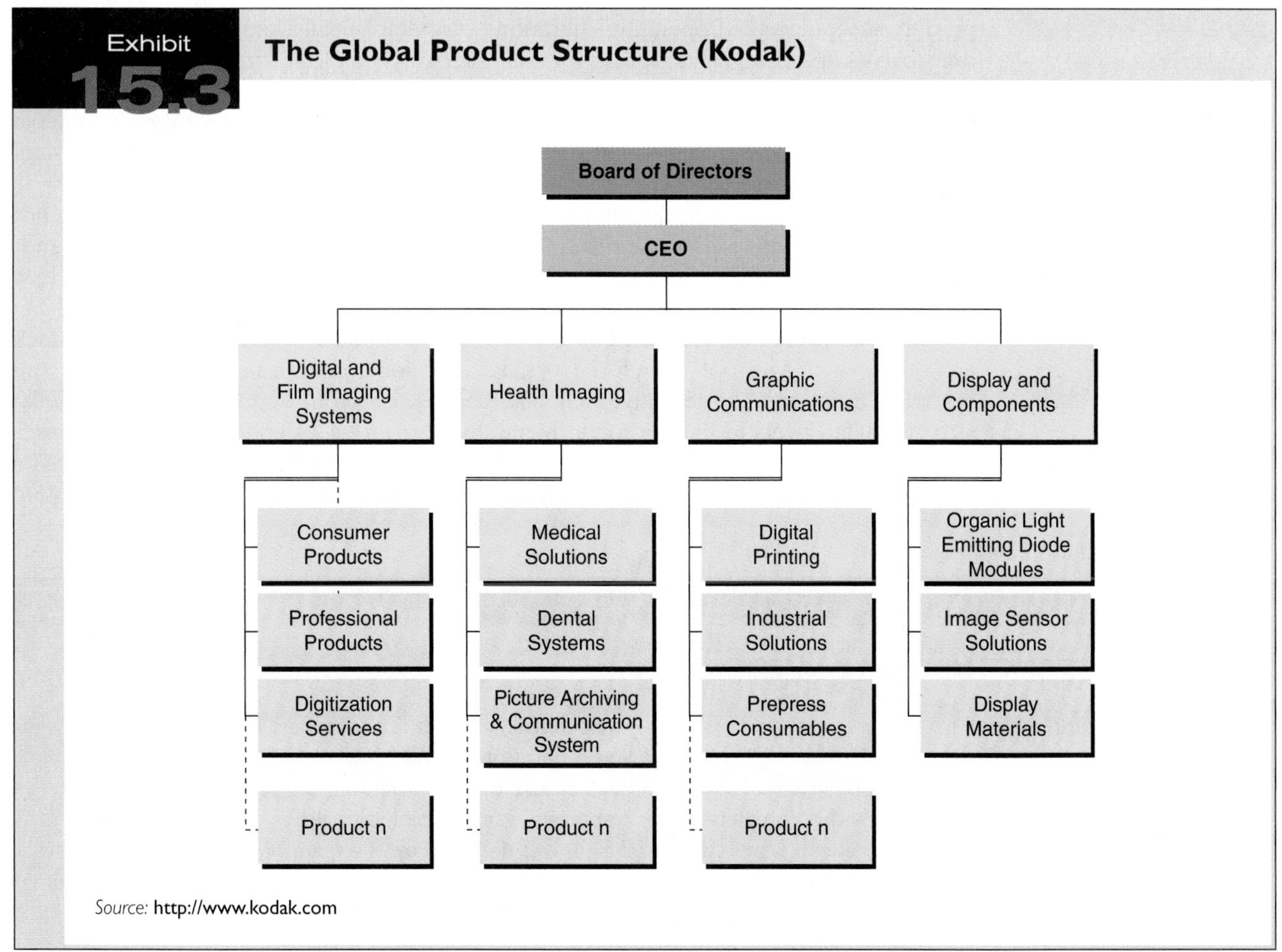

Source: http://www.kodak.com

in the same markets is crucial to avoid unnecessary duplication of basic tasks. For some of these tasks, such as market research, special staff functions may be created and then hired by the product divisions when needed. If product managers lack an appreciation for the global dimension, they may focus their attention on only the larger markets, often with emphasis on the domestic markets, and fail to take the long-term view.

Area Structure

The second most frequently adopted approach is the **area structure**, illustrated in Exhibit 15.4. The firm is organized on the basis of geographical areas; for example, operations may be divided into those dealing with North America, the Far East, Latin America, and Europe. Regional aggregation may play a major role in this structuring; for example, many multinational corporations have located their European headquarters in Brussels, where the EU has its headquarters.

The inevitability of a North American trading bloc led to the creation of the Campbell Soup Company's North American division, which replaced the U.S. operation as the power centre of the company. Organizational changes were also made at 3M as a result of NAFTA, with the focus on three concepts: simplification, linkage, and empowerment. This means, for example, that new-product launches are coordinated throughout North America, with standardization of as many elements as is feasible and prudent. The driver of the choice can also be cultural similarity, such as in the case of Asia, or historic connections between countries, such as in the case of combining Europe with the Middle East and Africa. As new markets emerge, they may first be delegated to an established country organization for guidance with the ultimate objective of having them be equal partners with others in the organization.

The area approach follows the marketing concept most closely because individual areas and markets are given concentrated attention. If market conditions with respect to product acceptance and operating conditions vary dramatically, the area approach is the one to choose. Companies opting for this alternative typically have relatively narrow product lines with similar end uses and end users. However, expertise is most needed in adapting the product and its marketing to local market conditions. Once again, to avoid duplication of effort in product management and in functional areas, staff specialists—for product categories, for example—may be used.

Without appropriate coordination from the staff, essential information and experience may not be transferred from one regional entity to another. Also, if the company expands in terms of product lines, and if end markets begin to diversify, the area structure may become inappropriate.

Some marketers may feel that going into a global product structure may be too much too quickly and will opt, therefore, to have a regional organization for planning and reporting purposes. The objective may also be to keep profit or sales centres of similar size at similar levels in the corporate hierarchy. If a group of countries has small sales compared with other country operations, they can be consolidated into a region. The benefits of a regional operation and regional headquarters are more efficient coordination

In More Detail 15.2

PRODUCT STRUCTURES IN PRACTICE

Black & Decker rationalized many of its operations in its worldwide competitive effort against Makita, the Japanese power-tool manufacturer. Similarly, Goodyear reorganized itself into a single global organization with a complete business team approach for tires and general products. The move was largely prompted by tightening worldwide competition.[11] In a similar move, Ford merged its large and culturally distinct European and North American auto operations by vehicle platform type to make more efficient use of its engineering and product development resources against rapidly globalizing rivals.[12] The Ford Fusion was designed by one team of engineers for worldwide markets.

Exhibit 15.4 **The Global Area Structure (Honda)**

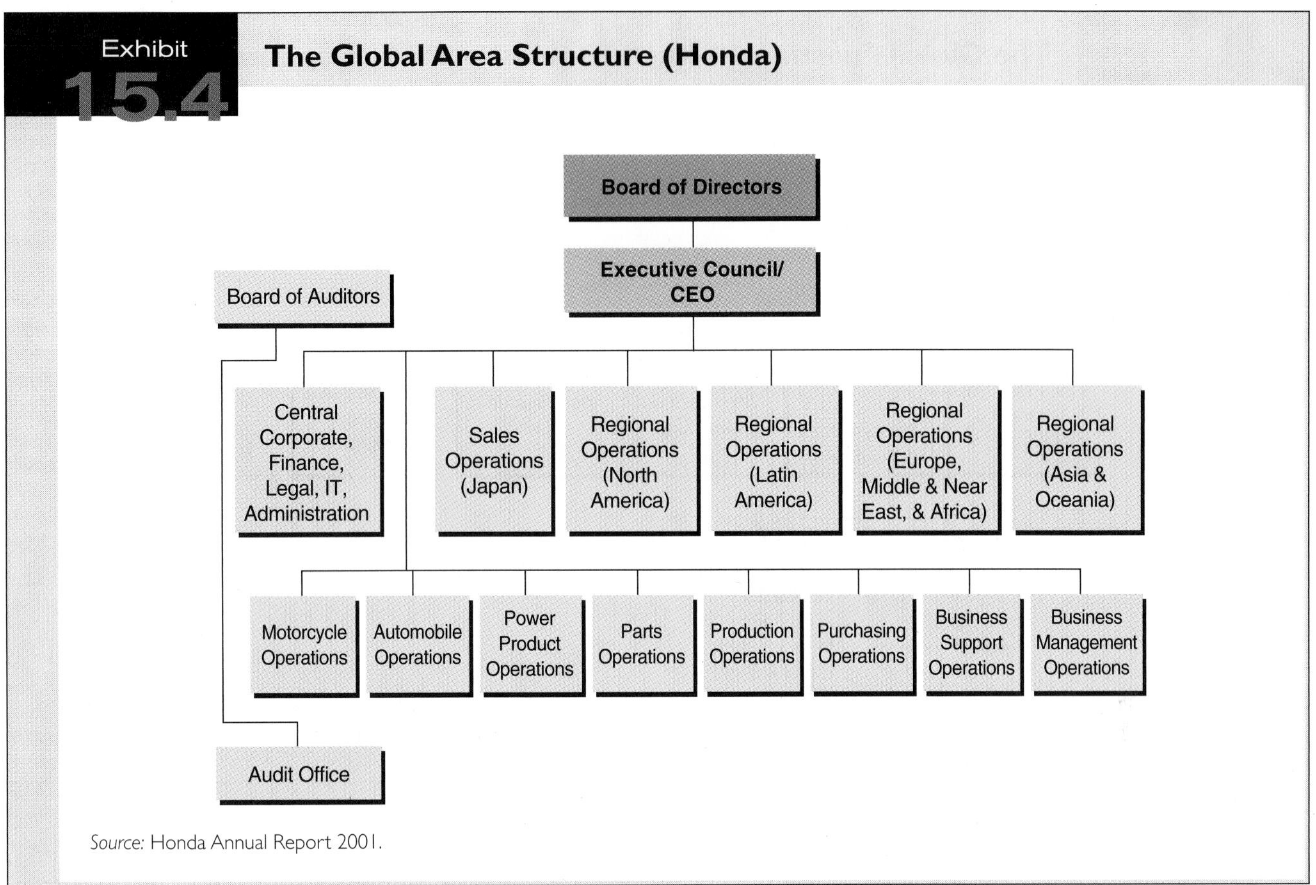

Source: Honda Annual Report 2001.

of programs across the region (as opposed to globally), a management more sensitized to country-market operations in the region, and the ability for the region's voice to be heard more clearly at global headquarters (as compared to what an individual, especially smaller, country operation could achieve).[13]

Functional Structure

Of all the approaches, the **functional structure** is the most simple from the administrative viewpoint because it emphasizes the basic tasks of the firm—for example, manufacturing, sales, and R&D. This approach, illustrated in Exhibit 15.5, works best when both products and customers are relatively few and similar in nature. Because coordination is typically the key problem, staff functions have been created to interact between the functional areas. Otherwise, the company's marketing and regional expertise may not be exploited to the fullest extent.

A variation of this approach is one that uses processes as a basis for structure. The **process structure** is common in the energy and mining industries, where one corporate entity may be in charge of exploration worldwide and another may be responsible for the actual mining operation.

Customer Structure

Firms may also organize their operations using the **customer structure**, especially if the customer groups they serve are dramatically different—for example, consumers versus businesses versus governments. Catering to these diverse groups may require the concentration of specialists in particular divisions. The product may be the same, but the buying processes of the various customer groups may differ. Governmental buying is characterized by bidding, in which price plays a larger role than when businesses are the buyers. However, products and solutions are increasingly developed around capabilities, such as networked communications, that can be used by more than one service

Exhibit 15.5 **The Global Functional Structure (NetLogic Microsystems)**

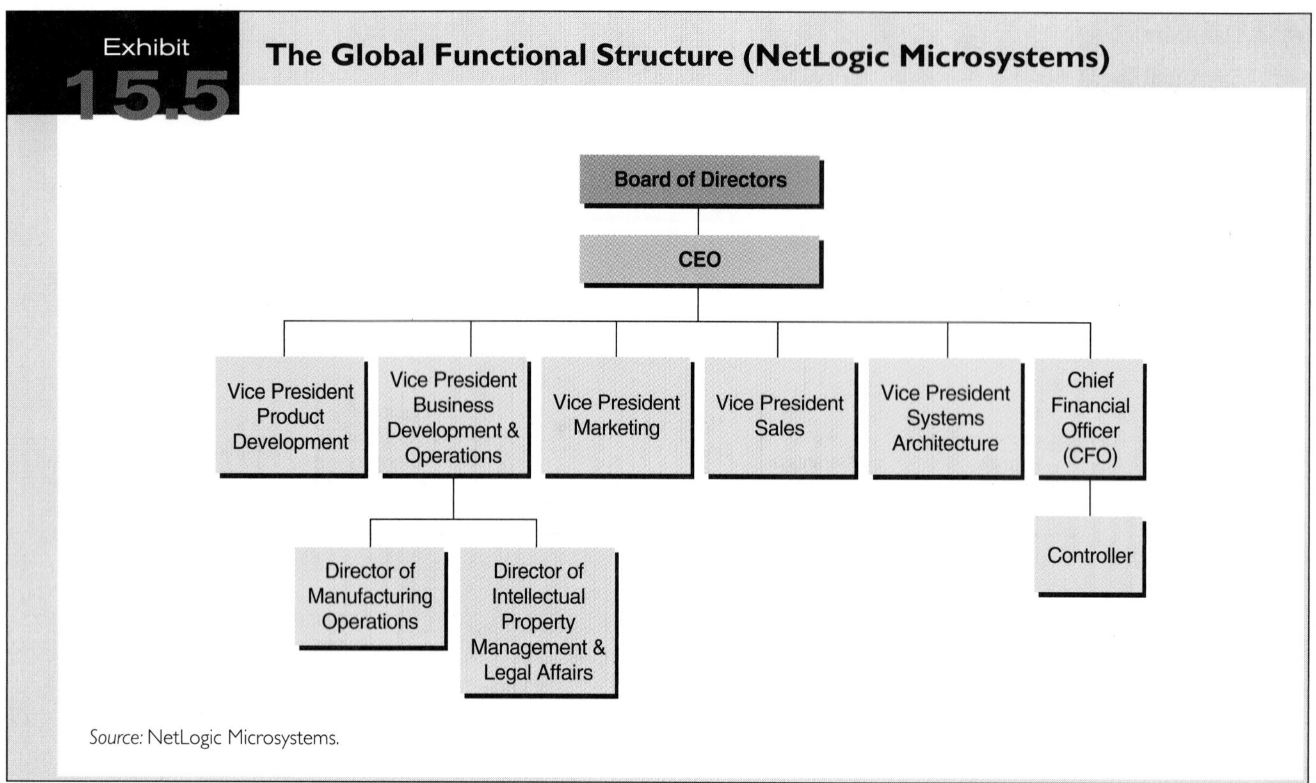

Source: NetLogic Microsystems.

or agency.[14] Similarly, in financial institutions, it is important to know whether customers who signed up for one service are already customers for other services being provided by the institution.[15]

Mixed Structure

Mixed, or hybrid, organizations also exist. A **mixed structure**, such as the one in Exhibit 15.6, combines two or more organizational dimensions simultaneously. It permits attention to be focused on products, areas, or functions, as needed. This approach may occur in a transitionary period after a merger or an acquisition, or it may come about because of a unique customer group or product line (such as military hardware). It may also provide a useful structure before the implementation of the matrix structure.[16]

Organization structures are, of course, never as clear-cut and simple as they have been presented here. Whatever the basic format, inputs are needed for product, area, and function. One alternative, for example, might be an initial product structure that would eventually have regional groupings. Another alternative might be an initial area structure with eventual product groupings. However, in the long term, coordination and control across such structures become tedious.

Matrix Structure

Many multinational corporations—in an attempt to facilitate planning, organizing, and controlling interdependent businesses, critical resources, strategies, and geographic regions—have adopted the **matrix structure**.[17] Business is driven by a worldwide business unit (e.g., photographic products or commercial and information systems) and implemented by a geographic unit (e.g., Europe or Latin America). The geographical units, as well as their country subsidiaries, serve as the "glue" between autonomous product operations.

Organizational matrices integrate the various approaches already discussed, as the Philips example in Exhibit 15.7 illustrates. The product divisions (which are then divided into 60 product groups) have rationalized manufacturing to provide products for continent-

Exhibit 15.6 **The Global Mixed Structure (DaimlerChrysler)**

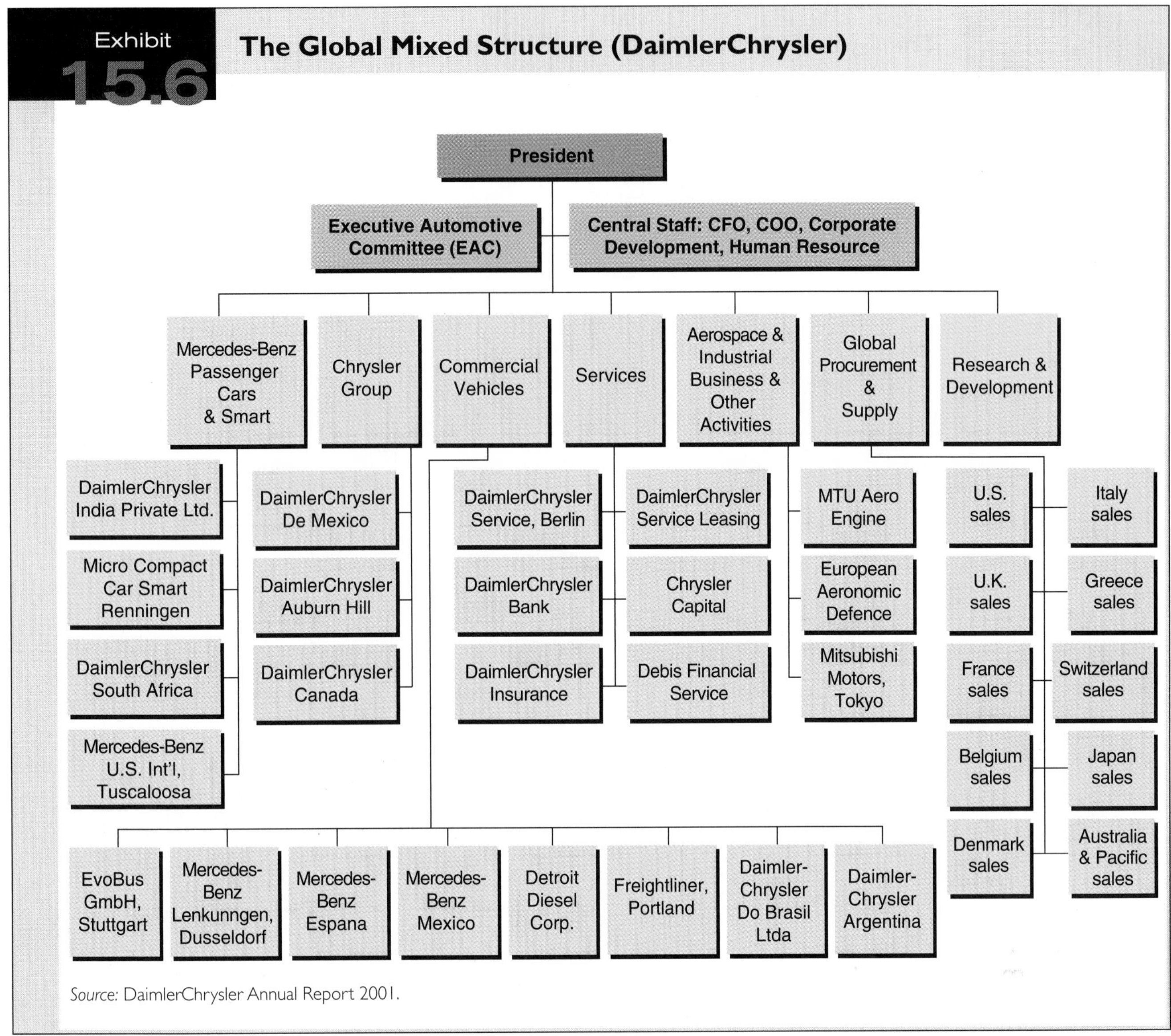

Source: DaimlerChrysler Annual Report 2001.

wide markets rather than lines of products for individual markets. These product groups adjust to changing market conditions; for example, the components division has been slated to be merged into the other divisions due to lack of stand-alone profitability.[18] Philips has three general types of country organizations: In "key" markets, such as the United States, France, and Japan, product divisions manage their own marketing as well as manufacturing. In "local business" countries, such as Nigeria and Peru, the organizations function as importers from product divisions, and if manufacturing occurs, it is purely for the local market. In "large" markets, such as Brazil, Spain, and Taiwan, a hybrid arrangement is used depending on the size and situation.

The product divisions and the national subsidiaries interact in a matrix-like configuration, with the product divisions responsible for the globalization dimension and the national subsidiaries responsible for local representation and coordination of common areas of interest, such as recruiting. The matrix structure manager has functional, product, and resource managers reporting to him or her. The approach is based on team building and multiple command, each team specializing in its own area of expertise. It provides a mechanism for cooperation among country managers, business managers, and functional managers on a worldwide basis through increased communication, control, and attention to balance in the organization.

Exhibit 15.7 **The Global Matrix Structure (Philips)**

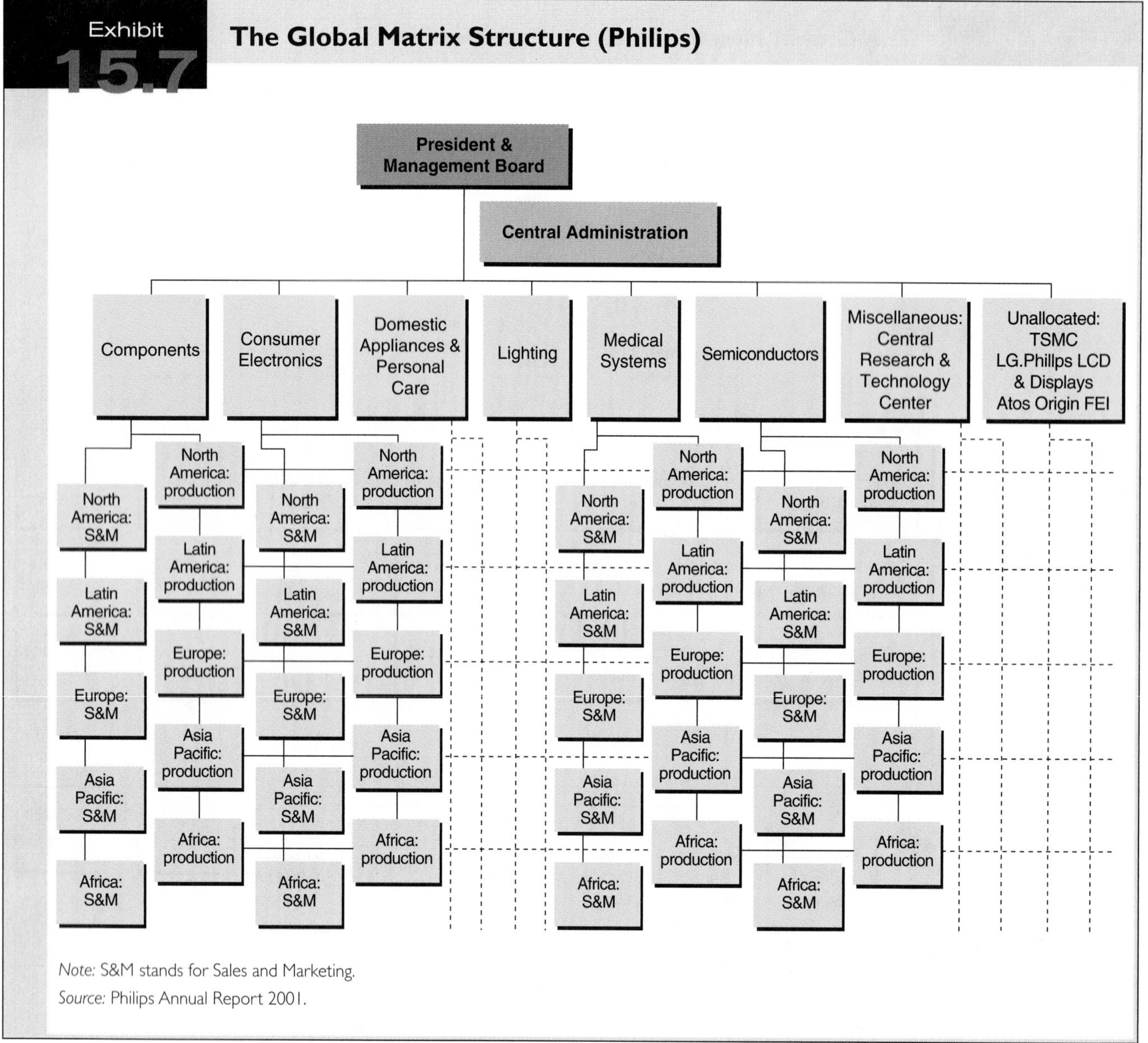

Note: S&M stands for Sales and Marketing.

Source: Philips Annual Report 2001.

The matrices used vary according to the number of dimensions needed. For example, Dow Chemical's matrix is three-dimensional, consisting of six geographic areas, three major functions (marketing, manufacturing, and research), and more than 70 products. The matrix approach helps cut through enormous organizational complexities by building in a provision for cooperation among business managers, functional managers, and strategy managers. However, the matrix requires sensitive, well-trained middle managers who can cope with problems that arise from reporting to two bosses—for example, a product-line manager and an area manager. Every management unit may have some sort of multidimensional reporting relationship, which may cross functional, regional, or operational lines. On a regional basis, group managers in Europe, for example, report administratively to a vice president of operations for Europe. But functionally, they report to group vice presidents at global headquarters.

Many companies have found the matrix structure problematic. The dual reporting channel easily causes conflict; complex issues are forced into a two-dimensional decision framework; and even minor issues may have to be resolved through committee discussion.[19] Ideally, managers should solve problems themselves through formal and informal communication; however, physical and psychic distance often make that impossible.

Especially when competitive conditions require quick reaction, the matrix, with its inherent complexity, may actually lower the reaction speed of the company. As a result, authority has started to shift in many organizations from area to product, although the matrix may still officially be used. At the same time, approaches to increase collaboration have been focused on, as seen in The Global Marketplace 15.2.

Evolution of Organizational Structures

Companies develop new structures in stages as their product diversity develops and the share of foreign sales increases.[20] At the first stage are autonomous subsidiaries reporting directly to top management, followed by the establishment of an international division. With increases in product diversity and in the importance of the foreign marketplace, companies develop global structures to coordinate subsidiary operations and rationalize worldwide production. As global corporations have faced pressures to adapt to local market conditions while trying to rationalize production and globalize competitive reaction,

The Global MARKETPLACE 15.2

Beyond the Matrix

Royal Philips Electronics of the Netherlands is one of the world's biggest electronics companies, as well as the largest in Europe, with 160,900 employees in over 60 countries and sales in 2004 of $36 billion. In the past 60 years, it has had 3 major phases of changes in its organizational structure.

Philips Electronics Ltd.

The company was one of the earliest champions of the matrix structure. After World War II, the organizational structure consisted of both national organizations and product divisions. Every division in a given country would report to the head of Philips in that country but also to the division's head at headquarters. This network was loosely held together by coordinating committees designed to resolve any conflicts between the basic reporting structures.

By the 1990s, environmental complexities had rendered the structure inefficient. Accountability and credit were difficult to assign and require. For example, who was to be held responsible for the profit-and-loss account—the country manager or the product head? The subsequent reorganization created a number of units with worldwide responsibility for groups of the company's businesses (e.g., consumer electronics and lighting products). The national offices became subservient to these units, built around products and based at headquarters.

In the last two years, changes have been made that are not necessarily evident in organizational charts. For example, a chief marketing officer has been appointed to help counter criticism of technology and new-product bias at the expense of customer orientation. Under an initiative called "One Philips," the company has introduced a number of low-key changes. Employees are encouraged to work on cross-cultural and cross-functional teams. New awards have been instituted for employees who have created value for the company by collaborating with others outside of their immediate units. Transfers across geographic entities as well as product units are expected as an explicit requirement for advancement. Top executives at Philips have argued that up to 80 percent of the desired changes will come about through readjustment of attitudes, the rest from using appropriate incentives, most of them not directly monetary. To accelerate these changes, Philips brought together its top 1,000 managers for a series of workshops designed to find ways to cut through organizational barriers.

Sources: "The Matrix Master," *The Economist*, January 21, 2006, 4. See also http://www.philips.com.

Exhibit 15.8 **Evolution of International Structures**

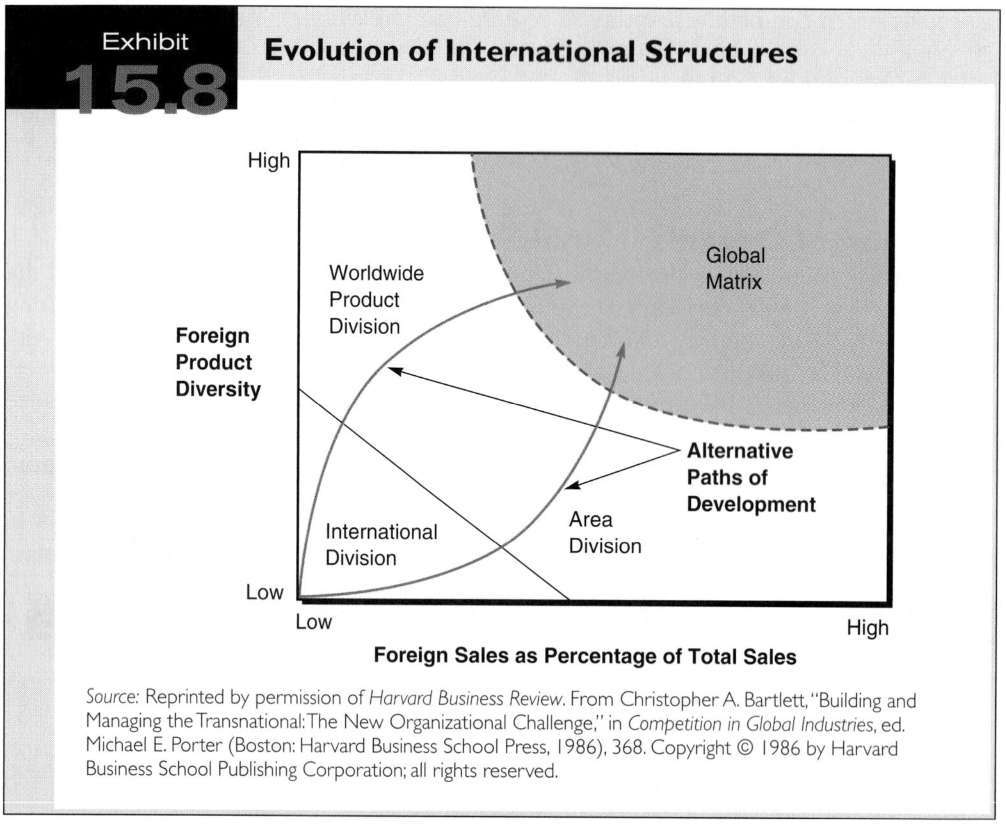

Source: Reprinted by permission of *Harvard Business Review*. From Christopher A. Bartlett, "Building and Managing the Transnational: The New Organizational Challenge," in *Competition in Global Industries*, ed. Michael E. Porter (Boston: Harvard Business School Press, 1986), 368. Copyright © 1986 by Harvard Business School Publishing Corporation; all rights reserved.

many have opted for the matrix structure. Ideally, the matrix structure probably allows a corporation to best meet the challenges of global markets—to be global and local, big and small, decentralized with centralized reporting—by allowing the optimizing of businesses globally and maximizing performance in every country of operation.[21] The evolutionary process is summarized in Exhibit 15.8.

Whatever the choice of organizational arrangement may be, the challenge of people having to work in silos remains. Employee knowledge tends to be fragmented with one unit's experience and know-how inaccessible to other units. Therefore, the wheel gets reinvented at considerable cost to the company and frustration to those charged with tasks. Information technology can be used to synchronize knowledge across even the most complicated and diverse organizations.[22] At Procter & Gamble, for example, brand managers have use of a standardized, worldwide ad-testing system that allows them access to every ad the company has ever run, providing examples for the needs that may have to be met at a particular time. Once knowledge transfer is established, what may be needed is a form of organization in which individuals and teams decide for themselves what to do, but are accountable for the results.[23]

Implementation

Organizational structures provide the frameworks for carrying out marketing decision making. However, for marketing to be effective, a series of organizational initiatives are needed to develop marketing strategy to its full potential; that is, secure implementation of such strategies at the national level and across markets.[24]

Locus of Decision Making

Organizational structures themselves do not indicate where the authority for decision making and control rests within the organization, nor will they reveal the level of coordination between units. Once a suitable form of structure has been found, it has to be made to work by finding a balance between the centre and the country organizations.

If subsidiaries are granted a high degree of autonomy, the result is termed **decentralization**. In decentralized systems, controls are relatively loose and simple, and the flows between headquarters and subsidiaries are mainly financial; that is, each subsidiary operates as a profit centre. On the other hand, if controls are tight and if strategic decision making is concentrated at headquarters, the result is termed **centralization**. Firms are typically neither totally centralized nor totally decentralized. Some functions, such as finance, lend themselves to more centralized decision making, whereas other functions, such as promotional decisions, lend themselves to far less. Research and development is typically centralized in terms of both decision making and location, especially when basic research work is involved. Partly because of governmental pressures, some companies have added R & D functions on a regional or local basis. In many cases, however, variations in decision making are product- and market-based; for example in Unilever's new organization launched in 2005, managers of global business units are responsible for brand management and product development, and managers of regional market development organizations are responsible for sales, trade marketing, and media choices.[25]

Allowing maximum flexibility at the country-market level takes advantage of the fact that subsidiary management knows its market and can react to changes quickly. Problems of motivation and acceptance are avoided when decision makers are also the implementers of the strategy. On the other hand, many marketers faced with global competitive threats and opportunities have adopted global strategy formulation, which by definition requires some degree of centralization. What has emerged as a result can be called **coordinated decentralization**. This means that overall corporate strategy is provided from headquarters, but subsidiaries are free to implement it within the range established in consultation between headquarters and the subsidiaries.

However, moving into this new mode may raise significant challenges. Among these systemic difficulties is a lack of widespread commitment to dismantling traditional national structures, driven by an inadequate understanding of the larger, global forces at work. Power barriers—especially if the personal roles of national managers are under threat of being consolidated into regional organizations—can lead to proposals being challenged without valid reason. Finally, some organizational initiatives (such as multicultural teams or corporate chat rooms) may be jeopardized by the fact that people do not have the necessary skills (e.g., language ability) or that an infrastructure (e.g., intranet) may not exist in an appropriate format.[26]

One particular case is of special interest. Organizationally, the forces of globalization are changing the country manager's role significantly. With profit-and-loss responsibility, oversight of multiple functions, and the benefit of distance from headquarters, country managers enjoyed considerable decision-making autonomy as well as entrepreneurial initiative. Today, however, many companies have to emphasize the product dimension of the product-geography matrix, which means that the power has to shift at least to some extent from country managers to worldwide strategic business-unit and product-line managers. Many of the previously local decisions are now subordinated to global strategic moves. However, regional and local brands still require an effective local management component. Therefore, the future country manager will have to have diverse skills (such as government relations and managing entrepreneurial teamwork) and wear many hats in balancing the needs of the operation for which the manager is directly responsible with those of the entire region or strategic business unit.[27] To emphasize the importance of the global/regional dimension in the country manager's portfolio, many companies have tied the country manager's compensation to the way the company performs globally or regionally, not just in the market for which the manager is responsible.

Factors Affecting Structure and Decision Making

The organizational structure and locus of decision making in multinational corporations are determined by a number of factors. They include (1) the degree of involvement in international operations, (2) the business(es) in which the firm is engaged (in terms, for example, of products marketed), (3) the size and importance of the markets, and (4) the human resource capability of the firm.[28]

The effect of the degree of involvement on structure and decision making was discussed earlier in the chapter. With low degrees of involvement by the parent company, subsidiaries can enjoy high degrees of autonomy as long as they meet their profit targets. The same situation can occur in even the most globally involved companies, but within a different framework. As an example, consider Philips USA, which generates one-third of the company's worldwide sales. Even more important, it serves a market that is on the leading edge of digital media development. Therefore, it enjoys an independent status in terms of local policy setting and managerial practices but is nevertheless within the parent company's planning and control system.

The firm's country of origin and the political history of the area can also affect organizational structure and decision making. For example, Swiss-based Nestlé, with only 1 to 2 percent of its sales in the small domestic market, has traditionally had a highly decentralized organization. Moreover, events of the past 100 years, particularly during World Wars I and II, have often forced subsidiaries of European-based companies to act independently in order to survive.

The type and variety of products marketed will have an effect on organizational decisions. Companies that market consumer products typically have product organizations with high degrees of decentralization, allowing for maximum local flexibility. On the other hand, companies that market technologically sophisticated products, such as General Electric's turbines, display centralized organizations with worldwide product responsibilities.

Going global has recently meant transferring world headquarters of important business units abroad. For example, Philips has moved headquarters of several of its global business units to the United States, including taking its Digital Video Group, Optimal Storage, and Flat Panel Display activities to Silicon Valley.

Apart from situations that require the development of an area structure, the characteristics of certain markets or regions may require separate arrangements for the firm. Upon entry, AT&T China was made the only one of 20 divisions in the world to be based on geography rather than on product or service line. Furthermore, it was the only one to report directly to the CEO.[29]

The human factor in any organization is critical. Managers both at headquarters and in the subsidiaries must bridge the physical and psychic distances separating them. If subsidiaries have competent managers who rarely need to consult headquarters about their problems, they may be granted high degrees of autonomy. In the case of global organizations, subsidiary management must understand the corporate culture, because subsidiaries must sometimes make decisions that meet the long-term objectives of the firm as a whole but that are not optimal for the local market.

The Networked Global Organization

No international structure is ideal, and some have challenged the wisdom of even looking for an ideal one. They have called attention to new processes that would, in a given structure, develop new perspectives and attitudes to reflect and respond to complex demands of the opposite forces of global integration and local responsiveness. Rather than a question of which structural alternative is best, the question is thus one of how best to take into account the different perspectives of various corporate entities when making decisions. In structural terms, nothing may change. As a matter of fact, Philips still has its basic matrix structure, yet major changes have occurred in internal relations. The basic change was from a decentralized federation model to a networked global organization; the effects are depicted in Exhibit 15.9. This approach allows for the internal **glocalization** of strategic planning and implementation.[30]

Companies that have adopted the approach have incorporated the following three dimensions into their organizations: (1) the development and communication of a clear corporate vision, (2) the effective management of human resource tools to broaden individual perspectives and develop identification with corporate goals, and (3) the integration of individual thinking and activities into the broad corporate agenda.[31] The first dimension relates to a clear and consistent long-term corporate mission that guides individuals wher-

Exhibit 15.9 **The Networked Global Organization**

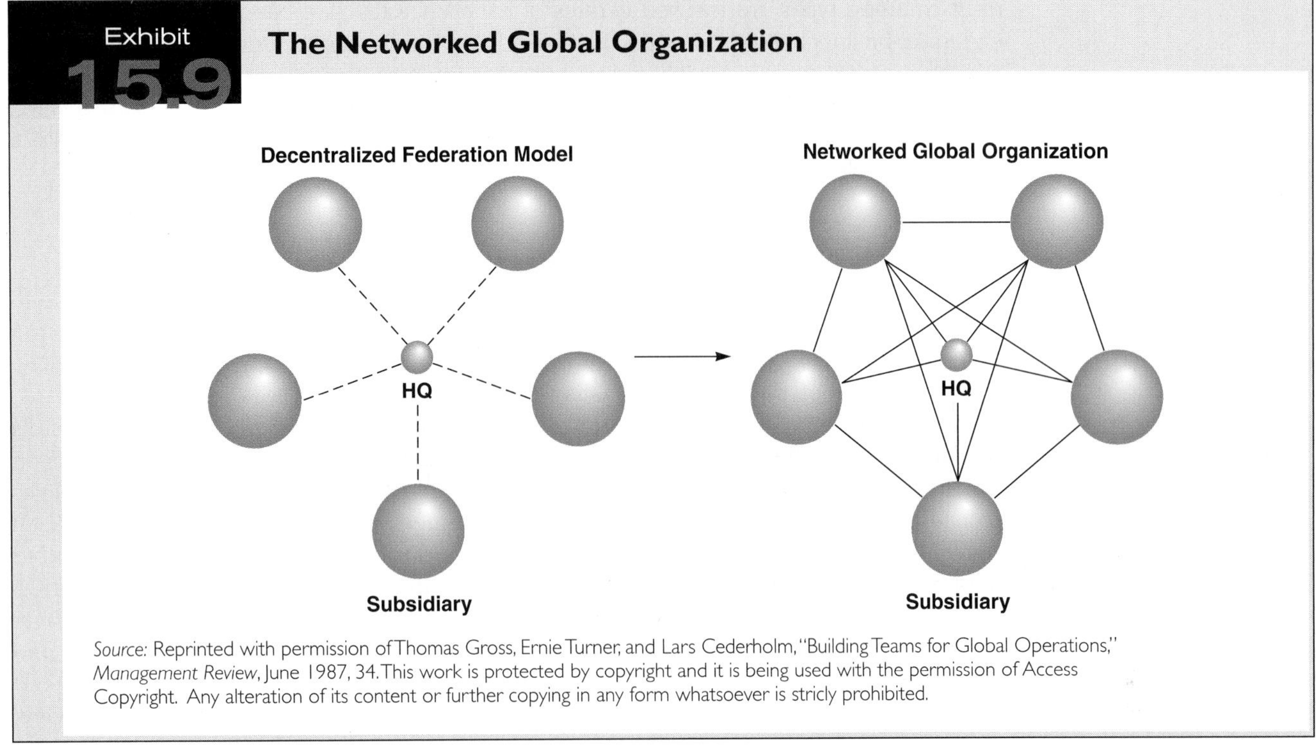

Source: Reprinted with permission of Thomas Gross, Ernie Turner, and Lars Cederholm, "Building Teams for Global Operations," *Management Review*, June 1987, 34. This work is protected by copyright and it is being used with the permission of Access Copyright. Any alteration of its content or further copying in any form whatsoever is stricly prohibited.

ever they may work in the organization. IBM has established three values for the 21st century: dedication to every client's success, innovation that matters (for the company and the world), and trust and personal responsibility in all relationships.[32] The second dimension relates both to developing global managers who can find opportunities in spite of environmental challenges and to creating a global perspective among country managers. The last dimension refers to tackling the "not-invented-here" syndrome to co-opt possibly isolated, even adversarial managers into the corporate agenda.

For example, in an area structure, units (such as Europe and North America) may operate quite independently, sharing little expertise and information with the others. While they are supposed to build links to headquarters and other units, they may actually be building walls. To tackle this problem, Nissan established four management committees, meeting once a month, to supervise regional operations. Each committee includes representatives of the major functions (e.g., manufacturing, marketing, and finance), and the committees (for Japan, Europe, the United States, and general overseas markets) are chaired by Nissan executive vice presidents based in Japan. The CEO attends the committee meetings periodically but regularly.[33]

The network avoids the problems of duplication of effort, inefficiency, and resistance to ideas developed elsewhere by giving subsidiaries the latitude, encouragement, and tools to pursue local business development within the framework of the global strategy. Headquarters considers each unit as a source of ideas, skills, capabilities, and knowledge that can be utilized for the benefit of the entire organization. This means that the subsidiaries must be upgraded from the role of implementation and adaptation to that of contribution and partnership in the development and execution of worldwide strategies. Efficient plants may be converted into international production centres, innovative R & D units may become centres of excellence (and thus role models), and leading subsidiary groups may be given a leadership role in developing new strategy for the entire corporation.

Centres of excellence can emerge in three formats: charismatic, focused, or virtual. Charismatic centres of excellence are individuals who are internationally recognized for their expertise in a function or an area. Using an expert working in a mentoring relationship, the objective is primarily to build a capability in the firm that has previously been lacking. The most common types are focused centres of excellence that are based on a single area of expertise, be it technological or product-based. The centre has an identifiable location from which members provide advice and training. In virtual centres of excellence, the core individuals live and work around the world and keep in touch through electronic means and meetings. The knowledge of dispersed individuals is brought together, integrated into a coherent whole, and disseminated throughout the firm.[34]

Promoting Internal Cooperation

The global marketing entity in today's environment can be successful only if it is able to move intellectual capital within the organization, that is, take ideas and move them around faster and faster.[35]

One of the tools for moving ideas is teaching. For example, at Ford Motor Company, teaching has taken three distinct forms, as is shown in Exhibit 15.10. Ford's approach is similar to those undertaken at many leading global marketing companies. The focus is on teachable points of view: that is, an explanation of what a person knows and believes about what it takes to succeed in his or her business.[36] For example, GE's Jack Welch coined the term "boundarylessness" to describe the way people can act without regard to status or functional loyalty and look for better ideas from anywhere. Top leadership of GE spends considerable time at training centres interacting with up-and-comers from all over the company. Each training class is given a real, current company problem to solve, and the reports can be career makers (or breakers).[37]

A number of benefits arise from this approach. A powerful teachable point of view can reach the entire company within a reasonable period by having students become teachers themselves. At PepsiCo, the CEO passed his teachable point on to 110 executives, who then passed it on to 20,000 people within 18 months. Second, participants in teaching situations are encouraged to maintain the international networks they develop during the sessions.

Teachers do not necessarily need to be top managers. When General Electric launched a massive effort to embrace e-commerce, many managers found that they knew little about the Internet. Following a London-based manager's idea to have an Internet mentor, GE encourages all managers to have one for a period of training each week.[38]

Another method to promote internal cooperation for global marketing implementation is the use of international teams or councils. In the case of a new product or program, an international team of managers may be assembled to develop strategy. Although final direction may come from headquarters, the input has included information on local conditions, and implementation of the strategy is enhanced because local managers were involved from the beginning. This approach has worked even in cases that, superficially, would seem impossible because of market differences. Both Procter & Gamble and Henkel have successfully introduced pan-European brands for which strategy was developed by European strategy teams. These teams consisted of local managers and staff personnel to smooth eventual implementation and to avoid unnecessarily long and disruptive discussion about the fit of a new product to individual markets.

On a broader and longer-term basis, companies use councils to share **best practice**, an idea that may have saved money or time, or a process that is more efficient than existing ones. Most professionals at the leading global marketing companies are members of multiple councils.

While technology has made teamwork of this kind possible wherever the individual participants may be, technology alone may not bring about the desired results; "high-tech" approaches inherently mean "low touch," sometimes at the expense of results. Human relationships are still paramount.[39] A common purpose is what binds team members to a particular task, and can only be achieved through trust, attainable through face-to-face meetings.

The term *network* also implies two-way communications between headquarters and subsidiaries and between subsidiaries themselves. This translates into intercultural communication efforts focused on developing relationships.[40] While this communication can take the form of newsletters or regular and periodic meetings of appropriate personnel,

In More Detail 15.3

WORKING TOGETHER AT BOEING

At the start of its 777 project, Boeing brought members of the design team from a dozen different countries to Everett, Washington, giving them the opportunity to work together for up to 18 months. Beyond learning to function effectively within the company's project management system, they also shared experiences that, in turn, engendered a level of trust between individuals that later enabled them to overcome obstacles raised by physical separation. The result was a design and launch in 40 percent less time than for comparable projects.

Exhibit 15.10

Teaching Programs at Ford Motor Co.

Program	Participants	Teachers	Components
Capstone	24 senior executives at a time	The leadership team	• Conducted once a year • About 20 days of teaching and discussion • Teams given six months to solve major strategic challenges • 360-degree feedback • Community service
Business Leadership Initiative	All Ford salaried employees—100,000 by 2002	The participants' managers	• Three days of teaching and discussion • Teams assigned to 100-day projects • Community service • 360-degree feedback • Exercises contrasting old and new Ford
Executive Partnering	Promising young managers	The leadership team	• Eight weeks shadowing seven senior executives
Let's Chat about the Business	Everyone who receives e-mail at Ford—about 100,000 employees	CEO	• Weekly e-mails describing Ford's new approach to business
Customer-Driven Six-Sigma	1,900 full-time employees awarded "Black Belt" in 2001	The leadership team	• 5 days of intensive instruction • "Learn-by-doing" model • Teams assigned multiple problem-solving projects

Sources: Ford Motor Company Annual Report 2004 and *Corporate Citizenship Report,* **http://www.ford.com** (accessed November 25, 2002); and Suzy Wetlaufer, "Driving Change: An Interview with Ford Motor Company's Jacques Nasser," *Harvard Business Review* 77 (March–April 1999): 76–88.

new technologies are allowing marketers to link far-flung entities and eliminate traditional barriers of time and distance. **Intranets** integrate a company's information assets into a single and accessible system using Internet-based technologies such as e-mail, newsgroups, and the World Wide Web. For example, employees at Levi Strauss & Co. can join an electronic discussion group with colleagues around the world, watch the latest Levi's commercials, or comment on the latest marketing program or plan. IBM has opened an online suggestion box called "Think Place" where ideas are logged for all to see and improve upon.[41] Of the first 4,500 to appear in 2005, 300 were implemented. In many companies, the annual videotaped greeting from management has been replaced by regular and frequent e-mails (called e-briefs at GE). The benefits of intranets are (1) increased productivity, in that there is no longer lag time between an idea and the information needed to implement it; (2) enhanced knowledge capital that is constantly updated and upgraded; (3) facilitated teamwork, enabling online communication at insignificant expense; and (4) incorporation of best practice at a moment's notice by allowing marketing managers and sales personnel to make to-the-minute decisions anywhere in the world.

The technology is increasingly available to create a culture of collaboration both within companies and with pertinent outside constituents.[42]

As the discussion indicates, the networked approach is not a structural adaptation but a procedural one that requires a change in management mentality. Adjustment is primarily in the coordination and control functions of the firm. While there is still considerable disagreement as to which of the approaches works, some measures have been shown to correlate with success, as seen in The Global Marketplace 15.3.

The Role of Country Organizations

Country organizations should be treated as a source of supply as much as they are considered a source of demand. Quite often, however, headquarters managers see their role as the coordinators of key decisions and controllers of resources and perceive subsidiaries as implementers and adapters of global strategy in their respective local markets. Furthermore, all country organizations may be seen as the same. This view severely limits the utilization of the firm's resources, by not using country organizations as resources and by depriving country managers of possibilities of exercising their creativity.[43]

The role that a particular country organization can play depends naturally on that market's overall strategic importance as well as the competencies of its organization. From these criteria, four different roles emerge (see Exhibit 15.11).

The role of **strategic leader** can be played by a highly competent national subsidiary located in a strategically critical market. The country organization serves as a partner of headquarters in developing and implementing strategy. For example, a strategic leader market may have products designed specifically with it in mind. Nissan's Z-cars have always been designated primarily for the U.S. market, starting with the 240Z in the 1970s to the 350Z introduced in 2002.[44]

A **contributor** is a country organization with a distinctive competence, such as product development or regional expertise. Increasingly, country organizations are the source of new products. These range from IBM's breakthroughs in superconductivity research, generated in its Zurich lab, to low-end innovations like Procter & Gamble's liquid Tide, made with a fabric-softening compound developed in Europe. Similarly, country organizations may be assigned as worldwide centres of excellence for a particular product category, for example, ABB Strömberg in Finland for electric drives, a category for which it is a recognized world leader.[45] Similarly, companies such as Carrier, IBM, and Hewlett-Packard use their units in Finland to penetrate the Russian market.[46]

The critical mass for the international marketing effort is provided by **implementers**. These country organizations may exist in smaller, less-established markets in which corporate commitment to market development is less. The presence in these markets is typically through a sales organization. Although most entities fill this role, it should not be slighted: implementers provide the opportunity to capture economies of scale and scope that are the basis of a global strategy.

The **black hole** is a situation that the global marketer has to work out of. A company may be in a "black hole" situation because it has read the market incorrectly (for example, Philips focused its marketing efforts in the North American market on less-expensive items instead of the upmarket products that have made the company's reputation worldwide)[47] or because government may restrict its activities (for example, Citibank being restricted in terms of activities and geography in China). If possible, the marketer can use strategic alliances or acquisitions to change its competitive position. Whirlpool established itself in the European Union by acquiring Philips' white goods operation and has used joint ventures to penetrate the Chinese market. If governmental regulations hinder the scale of operations, the firm may use its presence in a major market as an observation post to keep up with developments before a major thrust for entry is executed (for example, with China's WTO membership, the financial services sector should start opening up).

Depending on the role, the relationship between headquarters and the country organization will vary from loose control based mostly on support to tighter control in making sure strategies are implemented appropriately. Yet in each of these cases, it is imperative

The Global MARKETPLACE 15.3

Characteristics of Success

A survey of chief executive officers of 43 leading U.S. consumer companies, made by McKinsey & Co., sheds light on organizational features that distinguish internationally successful companies. Companies were classified as more or less successful compared to their specific industry average, using international sales and profit growth over a 5-year period as the most important indicators of success.

The survey results indicate certain distinctive traits that are correlated with high performance in international markets. The following are moves that companies can make to enhance prospects for international success:

- Differentiate treatment of international subsidiaries.
- Let product managers in subsidiaries report to the country general manager.
- Have a worldwide management development program.
- Make international experience a condition for promotion to top management.
- Have a more multinational management group.
- Support international managers with global electronic networking capabilities.
- Manage cross-border acquisitions particularly well.
- Have overseas R & D centres.
- Remain open to organizational change and continuous self-renewal.

In general, successful companies coordinate their international decision making globally, with more central direction than less successful competitors, as seen in the following graph. This difference is most marked in brand positioning, package design, and price setting. The one notable exception is an increasing tendency to decentralize product development.

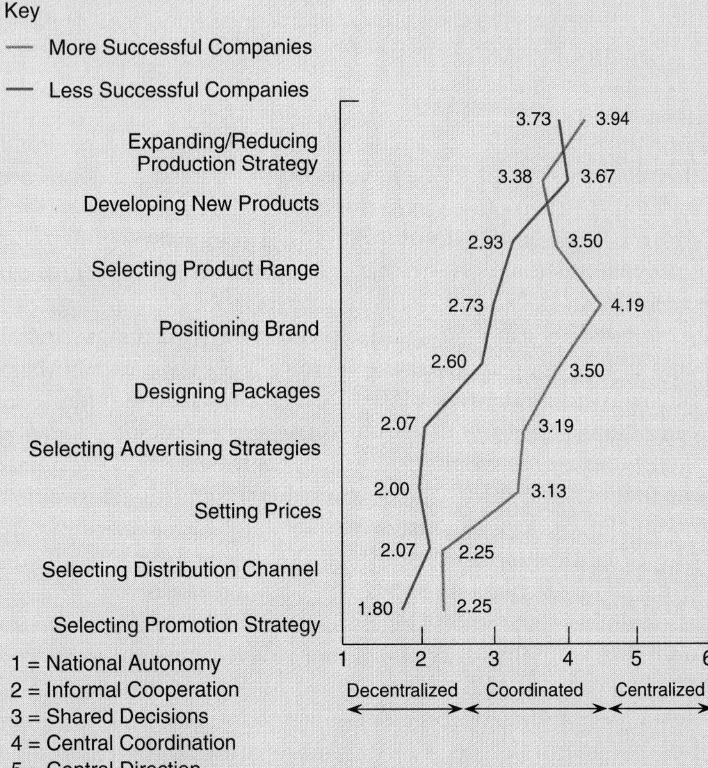

Source: Adapted from Ingo Theuerkauf, David Ernst, and Amir Mahini, "Think Local, Organize ...?" in *Best Practices in International Business*, ed. Michael R. Czinkota and Ilkka A. Ronkainen (Mason, OH: South-Western, 2001), 249–55.

Exhibit 15.11 Roles for Country Organizations

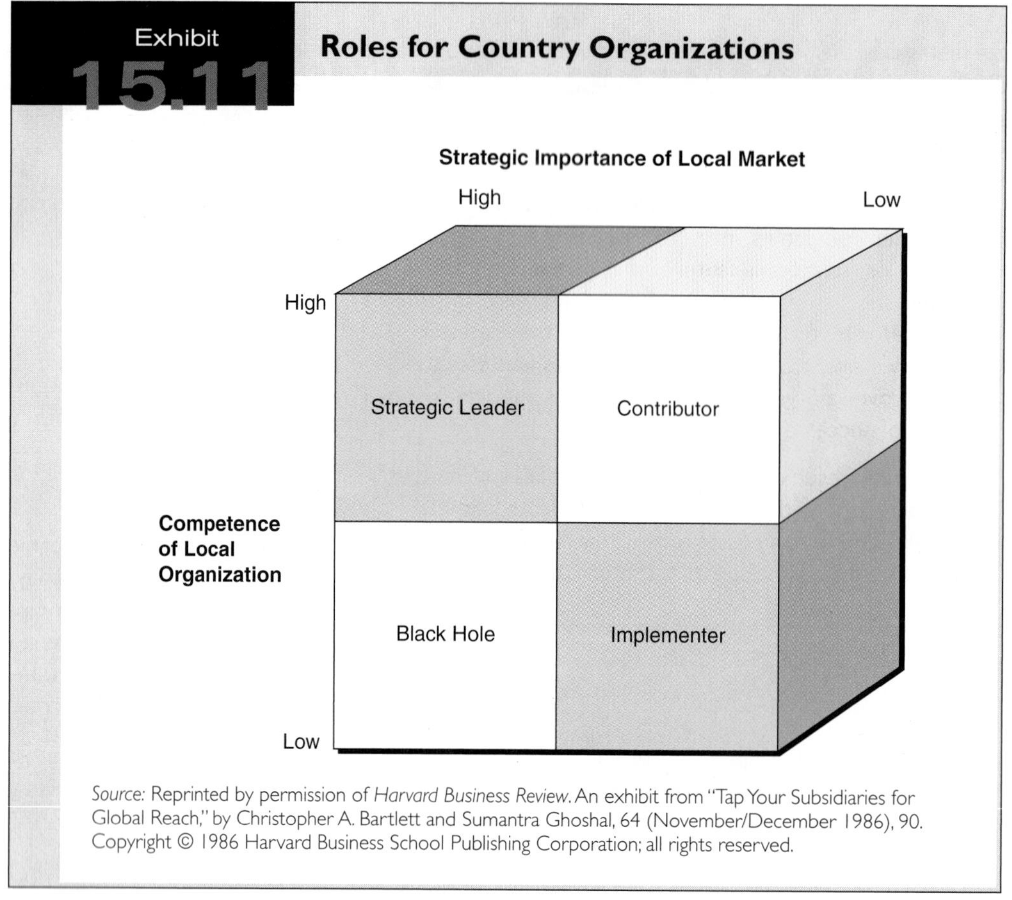

Source: Reprinted by permission of *Harvard Business Review*. An exhibit from "Tap Your Subsidiaries for Global Reach," by Christopher A. Bartlett and Sumantra Ghoshal, 64 (November/December 1986), 90. Copyright © 1986 Harvard Business School Publishing Corporation; all rights reserved.

that country organizations have enough operating independence to cater to local needs and to provide motivation to the country managers. For example, an implementer should provide input in the development of a regional or global strategy or program. Strategy formulation should ensure that appropriate implementation can be achieved at the country level.

Good ideas can, and should, come from any country organization. To take full advantage of this, individuals at the country level have to feel that they have the authority to pursue ideas in the first place and that they can see their concepts through to commercialization.[48] In some cases, this may mean that subsidiaries are allowed to experiment with projects that would not be seen as feasible by headquarters. For example, developing products for small-scale power generation using renewable resources may not generate interest in Honeywell's major markets and subsidiaries but may well be something that one of its developing-country subsidiaries should investigate. In other words, multinational or large company subsidiaries should not be thought of as solely passive receivers of capabilities and knowledge transferred from headquarters, but as active agents in their own right in the process of capability development.

However, it would be too simple to believe that conflict within the organization will never arise. Problems to be encountered are basically those deriving from devolving control of some policy decisions to subsidiaries, to the extent that this is thought necessary by the central management. It will hardly be surprising if a local company sees things from its own point of view rather than from the global viewpoint of the headquarters. In extreme cases, the subsidiary may be tempted to conduct its affairs almost like an independent company, only to find that decisions that made sense in its own context are frustrated by decisions by central management. The more successful a company is in eliminating the disadvantages of its foreign origin, the more vulnerable it becomes to the possible conflict of interest between the various national subsidiaries, which may be more ready to regard each other as rivals than as branches of the same company.

Another possible area of conflict *within* the company can arise from international human resource management issues such as promotion prospects, status, and salary. Are the key posts in the subsidiary reserved for nationals of the home country? If not, are the key posts in the headquarters likely to be reserved for nationals of the home country? What level of return position can expatriate managers expect? Is it one at least equivalent to the one they left?

One study examined the expatriate management practices of four Canadian multinationals in order to determine how close Canadian practices conformed to the "best practices" described in the international human resource management literature.[49] Results indicated that Canadian companies do not neglect expatriate management practices, but they do not fully implement them either, thus potentially adding to headquarters/subsidiary difficulties. For example, it was found that on-the-job cross-cultural training is a largely informal process: those expatriates who chose to have it were expected to find a mentor on their own. This in turn raises the question of the extent to which companies are relying on their foreign-based managers to be proactive in the management of their own careers, an area of uncertainty not likely to promote harmonious or predictable behaviours.

In a perfect world, head office/subsidiary conflict might be totally eliminated. But in reality some disagreements are bound to arise. Clear policy decisions on the issue of centralization versus decentralization will obviously help to avoid unnecessary disagreements, but it will not always be easy to specify precisely which policy decisions should be reserved for the home company and which should be devolved to the subsidiary. Any decision affecting the capital structure of the overseas companies (and, with it, control of the subsidiary) properly belongs at the centre. As to budgeting, while the subsidiary will likely draw up its own document, ultimate approval of the detailed plan should be with the home company, if only as a recognition of where the ultimate authority lies. But moving beyond these areas to issues such as hiring personnel, establishing specialized local capabilities, and formulating product and advertising strategies, decisions will depend as much on the product and intimate knowledge of local conditions as on head office policy.

Indeed, it may be increasingly irrelevant to attempt the classification of subsidiaries according to their specific "role" in the MNE. This is because single subsidiaries are more and more the site of several development and diffusion processes in their value-creating activities, processes that are recognized to be "embedded" in their host countries' knowledge development systems. Such processes are dedicated to evolving specific firm advantages (SFAs). Subsidiary initiatives are critical because they may strongly contribute to effective resource deployment within the MNE framework as a whole; as such, a modern view of the subsidiary in the MNE context can be summed up as follows:

> The framework developed reconfirms the perspective of the MNE as a differentiated network of dispersed operations, with a configuration of competences and capabilities that cannot be controlled fully through hierarchical decisions about foreign direct investment (FDI) taken by corporate headquarters.[50]

Canada and the Emerging Nations

As has frequently been stated here, Canada's main trading relationships are with the U.S.; therefore its main subsidiary operations are located in that country. However, Canadian companies continue to seek penetration of other markets, notably the BRIC countries (Brazil, Russia, India, and China), and are strongly encouraged in this direction by government agencies.[51] Setting up and operating a subsidiary in Brazil or India may seem a daunting task, and of course it is one that is not without difficulties. But the sheer numbers of companies establishing themselves in such countries suggest that any obstacles can be overcome if the company is determined enough. In the case of China, since 1995 almost 400 of the Fortune 500 MNEs have invested in that country, and most have at least one subsidiary there.[52] Larger Canadian companies working in the global market are most likely to be "China ready," but it has been suggested that most Canadian businesses are "ill-prepared to respond to the challenges and opportunities of an ascendant China."[53] Why?

Rather than speak in terms of management indifference or risk aversion, it might be better to stress something else. On the basis of research on European MNEs, it has been noted that the vast majority of European firms among the largest 500 firms worldwide have most of their sales in their home regions. The main implication for managers is therefore "to forget about the need for a global strategy."[54] Also, it is likely that SMEs in that region are "even more local." A similar argument has been made in connection with Canadian MNEs, most of which are described as regional rather than global.[55] Companies choosing to remain focused on local markets should not be judged adversely without taking this viewpoint into account. Moreover, experience suggests that when Canadian companies do elect to set up subsidiaries, their managerial skills, including the handling of expatriate management problems and headquarters/subsidiary relations, are likely to conform largely to global best practice.

Control

The function of the organizational structure is to provide a framework in which objectives can be met. A set of instruments and processes is needed, however, to influence the behaviour and performance of organization members to meet the goals. Controls focus on actions to verify and correct actions that differ from established plans. Compliance needs to be secured from subordinates through various means of coordinating specialized and interdependent parts of the organization.[56] Within an organization, control serves as an integrating mechanism. Controls are designed to reduce uncertainty, increase predictability, and ensure that behaviours originating in separate parts of the organization are compatible and in support of common organizational goals despite physical, psychic, and temporal distances.

The critical issue is the same as with organizational structure: what is the ideal amount of control? On the one hand, headquarters needs information to ensure that global activities contribute maximum benefit to the overall organization. On the other hand, controls should not be construed as a code of law and allowed to stifle local initiative.

This section will focus on the design and functions of control instruments available for the global marketer, along with an assessment of their appropriateness. Emphasis will be placed on the degree of formality of controls used.

Types of Controls

Most organizations display some administrative flexibility, as demonstrated by variations in the application of management directives, corporate objectives, or measurement systems. A distinction should be made, however, between variations that have emerged by design and those that are the result of autonomy. The one is the result of management decision, whereas the other has typically grown without central direction and is based on emerging practices. In both instances, some type of control will be exercised. Here, we are concerned only with controls that are the result of headquarters initiative rather than consequences of tolerated practices. Firms that wait for self-emerging controls often find that such an orientation may lead to rapid international growth but may eventually result in problems in areas of product-line performance, program coordination, and strategic planning.[57]

Whatever the system, it is important in today's competitive environment to have internal benchmarking. Benchmarking relays organizational learning and sharing of best practices throughout the corporate system to avoid the costs of reinventing solutions that have already been discovered. A description of the knowledge transfer process by which this occurs is provided in The Global Marketplace 15.4.

Three critical features are necessary in sharing best practice. First, there needs to be a device for organizational memory. For example, at Xerox, contributors to solutions can send their ideas to an electronic library where they are indexed and provided to potential adopters in the corporate family. Second, best practice must be updated and adjusted to new situations. For example, best practice adopted by the company's Chinese office will

The Global MARKETPLACE 15.4

International Best Practice Exchange

As growing competitive pressures challenge many global firms, strategies to improve the transfer of best practice across geographically dispersed units and time zones becomes critical. The premise is that a company with the same product range targeting the same markets pan-regionally should be able to use knowledge gained in one market throughout the organization. The fact is, however, that companies use only 20 percent of their most precious resource—knowledge, in the form of technical information, market data, internal know-how, and processes and procedures. Trying to transfer best practices internationally amplifies the problem even more. However, a corporate environment that creates informal cooperation in addition to the more formal, builds the necessary trust—and subsequently the critical mass—to share knowledge.

Copier maker Xerox (formerly Rank Xerox), with over 60 subsidiaries, is working hard to make better use of the knowledge, company-wide. A 35-person group identified nine practices that could be applicable throughout the group. These ranged from the way the Australian subsidiary retains customers to Italy's method of gathering competitive intelligence to a procedure for handling new major accounts in Spain. These practices were thought to be easier to "sell" to other operating companies, were considered easy to implement, and would provide a good return on investment.

Three countries were much quicker in introducing new products successfully than others. In the case of France, this was related to the training given to employees. The subsidiary gave its sales staff three days of hands-on practice, including competitive benchmarking. Before they attended the course, salespeople were given reading materials and were tested when they arrived. Those remaining were evaluated again at the end of the course, and performance reports were sent to their managers.

The difficult task is to achieve buy-in from the other country organizations. Six months might be spent in making detailed presentations of the best practices to all the companies and an additional three years helping them implement the needed changes. It is imperative that the country manager is behind the proposal in each subsidiary's case. However, implementation cannot be left to the country organizations after the concept has been presented. This may result in the dilution of both time and urgency and in possible country-specific customization that negates comparisons and jeopardizes the success of the change.

With time, these projects become codified into programs. Focus 500 allows the company's top 500 executives to share information on their interactions with customers and industry partners. Project Library details costs, resources, and cycle times of more than 2,000 projects, making it a vital resource in assuring Six Sigma in project management. PROFIT allows salespeople to submit hot selling tips—with cash incentives for doing so.

Sources: Philip Evans and Bob Wolf, "Collaboration Rules," *Harvard Business Review* 83 (July–August 2005): 96–104; Kristine Ellis, "Sharing Best Practices Globally," *Training*, July 2001, 34–38; Michael McGann, "Chase Harnesses Data with Lotus Notes," *Bank Systems and Technology* 34 (May 1997): 38; "Rank Xerox Aims at Sharing Knowledge," *Crossborder Monitor*, September 18, 1996, 8; and "World-Wise: Effective Networking Distinguishes These 25 Global Companies," *Computerworld*, August 26, 1996, 7. See also *Xerox Online Fact Book*, available at **http://www.xerox.com.**

be modified and customized, and this learning should then become part of the database. Finally, best practice must be legitimized. This calls for a shared understanding that exchanging knowledge across units is valued in the organization and that these systems are important mechanisms for knowledge exchange. An assessment of how effectively employees share information with colleagues and utilize the databases can also be included in employee performance evaluations.

In the design of the control system, a major decision concerns the object of control. Two major objects are typically identified: output and behaviour.[58] Output controls consist of balance sheets, sales data, production data, product-line growth, and performance reviews of personnel. Measures of output are accumulated at regular intervals and forwarded from the foreign operation to headquarters, where they are evaluated and critiqued based on comparisons to the plan or budget. Behavioural controls require the exertion of influence over behaviour after, or ideally before, it leads to action. This influence can be achieved, for example, by providing sales manuals to subsidiary personnel or by fitting new employees into the corporate culture.

Exhibit 15.12

Comparison of Bureaucratic and Cultural Control Mechanisms

	Type of Control		
Object of Control	Pure Bureaucratic/ Formalized Control	Pure Cultural Control	Characteristics of Control
Output	Formal performance reports	Shared norms of performance	HQ sets short-term performance target and requires frequent reports from subsidiaries
Behaviour	Company policies, manuals	Shared philosophy of management	Active participation of HQ in strategy formulation of subsidiaries

Sources: Peter J. Kidger, "Management Structure in Multinational Enterprises: Responding to Globalization," *Employee Relations*, August 2001, 69–85; and B.R. Baliga and Alfred M. Jaeger, "Multinational Corporations: Control Systems and Delegation Issues," *Journal of International Business Studies* 15 (Fall 1984): 28.

To institute either of these measures, corporate officials must decide on instruments of control. The general alternatives are bureaucratic/formalized control or cultural control. **Bureaucratic controls** consist of a limited and explicit set of regulations and rules that outline desired levels of performance. **Cultural controls**, on the other hand, are much less formal and are the result of shared beliefs and expectations among the members of an organization. A comparison of the two types of controls and their objectives is provided in Exhibit 15.12. It can be argued that instilling the marketing approach (i.e., customer orientation) will have to rely more on behavioural dimensions since an approach focused on outputs may put undue pressure on short-term profits.[59]

Bureaucratic/Formalized Control

The elements of bureaucratic/formalized controls are (1) an international budget and planning system, (2) the functional reporting system, and (3) policy manuals used to direct functional performance. **Budgets** are short-term guidelines in such areas as investment, cash, and personnel, whereas **plans** refer to formalized long-range programs with more than a one-year horizon. The budgeting and planning process is the major control instrument in headquarters–subsidiary relationships. Although systems and their execution vary, the objective is to achieve the best fit possible with the objectives and characteristics of the firm and its environment.

The budgetary period is typically one year because budgets are tied to the accounting systems of the company. The budget system is used for four main purposes: (1) allocation of funds among subsidiaries; (2) planning and coordination of global production capacity and supplies; (3) evaluation of subsidiary performance; and (4) communication and information exchange among subsidiaries, product organizations, and corporate headquarters.[60] Long-range plans, on the other hand, extend over periods of 2 to 10 years, and their content is more qualitative and judgmental in nature than that of budgets. Shorter periods, such as 2 years, are the norm because of the uncertainty of diverse foreign environments.

Although firms strive for uniformity, this may be comparable to trying to design a suit to fit the average person. The budget and planning processes themselves are formalized in terms of the schedules to be followed.

Control can also be seen as a mechanism to secure cooperation of local units. For example, while a company may grant substantial autonomy to a country organization in terms of strategies, headquarters may use allocation of production volume as a powerful tool to ensure compliance. Some of the ways for headquarters to gain cooperation of country organizations are summarized in Exhibit 15.13. Some of the methods used are formal, such as approval of strategic plans and personnel selection, while some are more informal, including personal contact and relationships as well as international networking.[61]

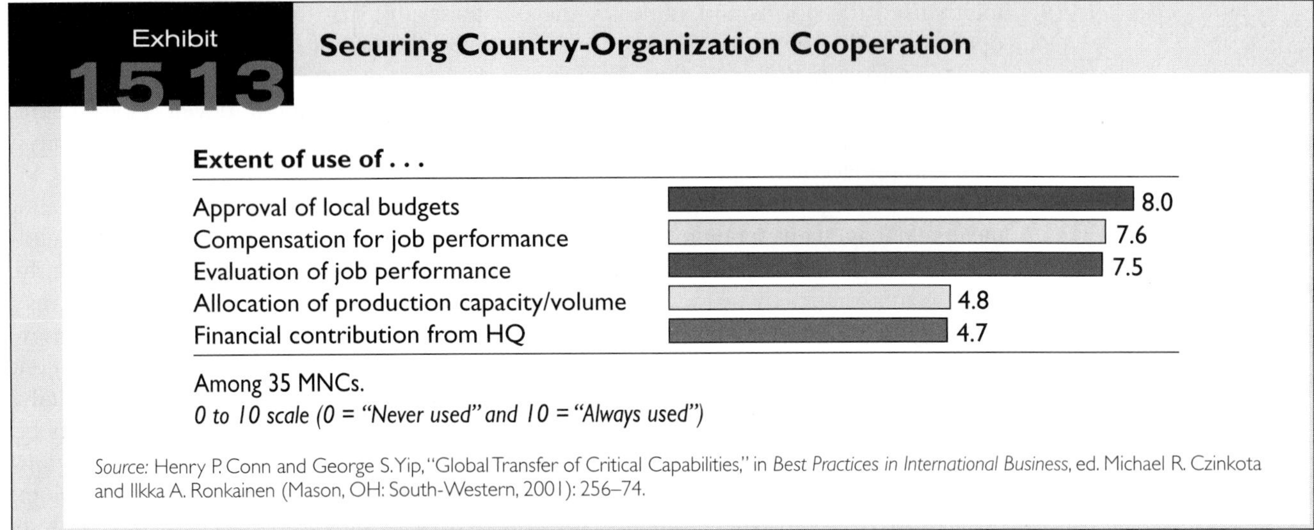
Exhibit 15.13 Securing Country-Organization Cooperation

Extent of use of . . .	
Approval of local budgets	8.0
Compensation for job performance	7.6
Evaluation of job performance	7.5
Allocation of production capacity/volume	4.8
Financial contribution from HQ	4.7

Among 35 MNCs.
0 to 10 scale (0 = "Never used" and 10 = "Always used")

Source: Henry P. Conn and George S. Yip, "Global Transfer of Critical Capabilities," in *Best Practices in International Business*, ed. Michael R. Czinkota and Ilkka A. Ronkainen (Mason, OH: South-Western, 2001): 256–74.

Since the frequency and types of reports to be furnished by subsidiaries are likely to increase due to globalization, it is essential that subsidiaries see the rationale for the often time-consuming task. Two approaches, used in tandem, can facilitate the process: participation and feedback. Involving the preparers of reports in their ultimate use serves to avoid the perception at subsidiary levels that reports are "art for art's sake." When this is not possible, feedback about results and consequences is an alternative. Through this process, communication is also enhanced.

On the behavioural front, headquarters may want to guide the way in which subsidiaries make decisions and implement agreed-upon strategies. U.S.-based multinational companies, relying heavily on manuals for all major functions, tend to be far more formalized than their Japanese and European counterparts.[62] The manuals are for functions such as personnel policies for recruitment, training, motivation, and dismissal. The use of policy manuals as a control instrument correlates with the level of reports required from subsidiaries.

Cultural Control

In countries other than the United States, less emphasis is placed on formal controls, which are viewed as rigid and too quantitatively oriented. Rather, the emphasis is on corporate values and culture, and evaluations are based on the extent to which an individual or entity fits in. Cultural controls require an extensive socialization process, and informal, personal interaction is central to the process. Considerable resources must be spent to train the individual to share the corporate culture, that is, "the way things are done at the company."[63] To build common vision and values, managers spend a substantial amount of their first months at Matsushita in what the company calls "cultural and spiritual training." They study the company credo, the "Seven Spirits of Matsushita," and the philosophy of the founder, Konosuke Matsushita. Then they learn how to translate these internalized lessons into daily behaviour and operational decisions. Although more prevalent in Japanese organizations, many Western entities have similar programs, for example, Philips's "organization cohesion training" and Unilever's "indoctrination." This corporate acculturation will be critical to achieve the acceptance of possible transfers of best practice within the organization.[64]

The primary instruments of cultural control are the careful selection and training of corporate personnel and the institution of self-control. The choice of cultural controls rather than bureaucratic controls can be justified if the company enjoys a low turnover rate. Cultural controls are thus applied, for example, when companies offer lifetime or long-term employment, as many Japanese firms do.

In selecting home-country nationals and, to some extent, third-country nationals, global companies are exercising cultural control. They assume that these managers have already internalized the norms and values of the company and that they tend to run a country operation with a more global view. In some cases, the use of headquarters personnel to ensure uniformity in decision making may be advisable. Expatriates are used in subsidiaries not only for control purposes but also for initiating change and to develop local talent. Companies control the efforts of management specifically through compensation, promotion, and replacement policies.

When the expatriate corps is small, headquarters can exercise control through other means. Management training programs for overseas managers as well as visits to headquarters will indoctrinate individuals to the company's way of doing things. Similarly, visits to subsidiaries by headquarters teams will promote a sense of belonging. These may be on a formal basis, as for a strategy audit, or less formal—for example, to launch a new product. Some innovative global marketers assemble temporary teams of their best talent to build local skills. IBM, for example, drafted 50 engineers from its facilities in Italy, Japan, New York, and North Carolina to run three-week to six-month training courses on all operations carried on at its Shenzhen facility in China. After the trainers left the country, they stayed in touch by e-mail, so whenever the Chinese managers have a problem, they know they can reach someone for help. The continuation of support has been as important as the training itself.[65]

Corporations rarely use one pure control mechanism. Rather, emphasis is placed on both quantitative and qualitative measures. Corporations are likely, however, to place different levels of emphasis on the types of performance measures and on the way the measures are taken. To generate global buy-in, annual bonuses have shifted away from the employee's individual unit and toward the company as a whole. This sends a strong signal in favour of collaboration across all boundaries. Other similar approaches to motivate and generate changes in thinking exist. At BP, for example, individual performance assessments exclude the effects of price of oil and foreign exchange because they are outside of the employee's control.[66]

Exercising Control

Within most corporations, different functional areas are subject to different guidelines. The reason is that each function is subject to different constraints and varying degrees of those constraints. For example, marketing as a function has traditionally been seen as incorporating many more behavioural dimensions than does manufacturing or finance. As a result, many multinational corporations employ control systems that are responsive to the needs of the function. Yet such differentiation is sometimes based less on appropriateness than on personality. One researcher hypothesized that manufacturing subsidiaries are controlled more intensively than sales subsidiaries because production more readily lends itself to centralized direction, and technicians and engineers adhere more firmly to standards and regulations than do salespeople.[67]

Similarly, the degree of control imposed will vary by subsidiary characteristics, including its location. For example, since Malaysia is an emerging economy in which managerial talent is in short supply, headquarters may want to participate more in all facets of decision making. If a country-market witnesses economic or political turmoil, controls may also be tightened to ensure the management of risk.[68]

In their global operations, U.S.-based multinational corporations place major emphasis on obtaining quantitative data. Although this allows for good centralized comparisons against standards and benchmarks, or cross-comparisons between different corporate units, several drawbacks are associated with the undertaking. In the international environment, new dimensions—such as inflation, differing rates of taxation, and exchange rate fluctuations—may distort the performance evaluation of any given individual or organizational unit.

For the global corporation, measuring whether a business unit in a particular country is earning a superior return on investment relative to risk may be irrelevant to the contribution an investment may make worldwide or to the long-term results of the firm. In the short term, the return may even be negative.[69] Therefore, the control mechanism may quite inappropriately indicate reward or punishment. Standardizing the information received may be difficult if the environment fluctuates and requires frequent and major adaptations. Further complicating the issue is the fact that, although quantitative information may be collected monthly, or at least quarterly, environmental data may be acquired annually or "now and then," especially when crisis seems to loom on the horizon.

To design a control system that is acceptable not only to headquarters but also to the organization and individuals abroad, a firm must take great care to use only relevant data. Major concerns, therefore, are the data collection process and the analysis and utilization of data. Evaluators need management information systems that provide for maximum comparability and equity in administering controls. The more behaviourally based and culture-oriented controls are, the more care needs to be taken.

In designing a control system, management must consider the costs of establishing and maintaining it and weigh the costs against the benefits to be gained. Any control system will require investment in a management structure and in systems design. As an example, consider the costs associated with cultural controls: personal interaction, use of expatriates, and training programs are all quite expensive. Yet these expenses may be justified in savings through lower employee turnover, an extensive worldwide information system, and a potentially improved control system.[70] Moreover, the impact goes beyond the administrative component. If controls are erroneous or too time-consuming, they can slow or misguide the strategy implementation process and thus the overall capability of the firm. The result will be lost opportunity or, worse, increased threats. In addition, time spent on reporting takes time away from other tasks. If reports are seen as marginally useful, the motivation to prepare them will be low. A parsimonious design is therefore imperative. The control system should collect all the information required and trigger all the intervention necessary but should not create a situation that resembles the pulling of strings by a puppeteer.

The impact of the environment must also be taken into account when designing controls. First, the control system should measure only dimensions over which the organization has control. Rewards or sanctions make little sense if they are based on dimensions that may be relevant for overall corporate performance but over which no influence can be exerted, for example, price controls. Neglecting the factor of individual performance capability would send wrong signals and severely impede the motivation of personnel. Second, control systems should harmonize with local regulations and customs. In some cases, however, corporate behavioural controls have to be exercised against local customs even though overall operations may be affected negatively. This type of situation occurs, for example, when a subsidiary operates in markets where unauthorized facilitating payments are a common business practice.

Corporations are faced with major challenges to implement appropriate and adequate control systems in today's business environment. With an increase in local (government) demands for a share in the control of companies established, controls can become tedious, especially if the multinational company is a minority partner. Even in a merger, such as the one between Daimler-Benz and Chrysler (though later dissolved)—or in a new entity formed by two companies, as when Toyota and GM formed NUMMI—the backgrounds of the partners may be sufficiently different to cause problems in terms of the controls.

Summary

The structures and control mechanisms needed to operate globally define relationships between the firm's headquarters and subsidiaries and provide the channels through which these relationships develop. The most fundamental test of organizational design is whether there is a fit with the company's overall marketing strategy and whether it reflects the strengths of the entities within the organization.[71]

International firms can choose from a variety of organizational structures, ranging from a domestic operation that handles ad hoc export orders to a full-fledged global organization. The choice will depend primarily on the degree of internationalization of the firm, the diversity of international activities, and the relative importance of product, area, function, and customer variables in the process. Whatever the choice of structure may be, implementation of the planned strategies is a critical factor determining success. Companies typically realize only 60 percent of their strategies' potential value due to factors such as organizational silos and culture blocking execution.[72] To close the strategy-to-performance gap, the buy-in of all units is necessary. Of these, the primary one is the use of subsidiaries as resources, not merely as implementers of headquarters' strategy.

The control function is of increasing importance because of the high variability in performance that results from divergent local environments, and the need to reconcile local objectives with the corporate goal of synergism. It is important to grant autonomy to country organizations so that they can be responsive to local market needs, but it is equally important to ensure close cooperation between units.

Control can be exercised through bureaucratic means, emphasizing formal reporting and evaluation of benchmark data. It can also be exercised through a cultural control process in which norms and values are understood by individuals and entities that compose the corporation. U.S. firms typically rely more on bureaucratic controls, whereas multinational corporations headquartered in other countries frequently control operations abroad through informal means and rely less on stringent measures.

The execution of controls requires great sensitivity to behavioural dimensions and to the environment. The measurements used must be appropriate and must reflect actual performance rather than marketplace vagaries. Entities should be measured only on factors over which they have some degree of control.

Key Terms

area structure (p. 556)
best practice (p. 566)
black hole (p. 568)
budgets (p. 574)
bureaucratic controls (p. 574)
centralization (p. 563)
contributor (p. 568)
coordinated decentralization (p. 563)
cultural controls (p. 574)
customer structure (p. 557)
decentralization (p. 563)
functional structure (p. 557)
glocalization (p. 564)
implementer (p. 568)
intranets (p. 567)
matrix structure (p. 558)
mixed structure (p. 558)
plans (p. 574)
process structure (p. 557)
product structure (p. 555)
strategic leader (p. 568)

Questions for Discussion

1. Firms differ—often substantially—in their organizational structures, even within the same industry. What accounts for these differences in their approaches?
2. Discuss the benefits gained in adopting a matrix approach in terms of organizational structure.
3. What changes in the firm and/or in the environment might cause a firm to abandon the functional approach?
4. Is there more to the "not-invented-here" syndrome than simply hurt feelings on the part of those who believe they are being dictated to by headquarters?
5. How can systems that are built for global knowledge transfer be used as control tools?
6. "Implementers are the most important country organizations in terms of buy-in for effective global marketing strategy implementation." Comment.

Internet Exercises

1. Improving internal communications is an objective for networked global organizations. Using the website of the Lotus Development Corporation **(http://www.lotus.com)** and its section on case studies, outline how marketers have used the Lotus Domino Express to interactively share information.
2. Using company and product information available on its website, determine why Siemens **(http://www.siemens.com/index.jsp)** has opted for global product/business structures for its organization.

Recommended Readings

Bartlett, Christopher, and Sumantra Ghoshal. *Managing across Borders*. Cambridge, MA: Harvard Business School Press, 1998.

Bartlett, Christopher, and Sumantra Ghoshal. *Transnational Management: Text, Cases, and Readings in Cross-Border Management.* New York: McGraw-Hill, 2000.

Cairncross, Frances. *The Company of the Future.* Cambridge, MA: Harvard Business School Press, 2002.

Chisholm, Rupert F. *Developing Network Organizations: Learning from Practice and Theory.* Boston: Addison-Wesley, 1997.

Doz, Yves, Jose Santos, and Peter Williamson. *From Global to Metanational: How Companies Win in the Knowledge Economy.* Cambridge, MA: Harvard Business School Press, 2001.

Galbraith, Jay R. *Designing Organizations: An Executive Guide to Strategy, Structure, and Process Revised.* New York: Jossey-Bass, 2001.

Ghoshal, Sumantra, and Christopher Bartlett. *The Individualized Corporation: A Fundamentally New Approach to Management.* New York: Harper Business, 1999.

Govindarajan, Vijay, Anil K. Gupta, and C.K. Prahalad. *The Quest for Global Dominance: Transforming Global Presence into Global Competitive Advantage.* New York: Jossey-Bass, 2001.

Govindarajan, Vijay, and Robert Newton. *Management Control Systems.* New York: McGraw-Hill/Irwin, 2000.

Kluge, Jurgen, Wolfram Stein, and Thomas Licht. *Knowledge Unplugged: The McKinsey & Company Global Survey on Knowledge Management.* London: Palgrave Macmillan, 2002.

McCall, Morgan W., and George P. Hollenbeck. *Developing Global Executives.* Cambridge, MA: Harvard Business School Press, 2002.

Pasternak, Bruce A., and Albert J. Viscio. *The Centerless Corporation: A New Model for Transforming our Organization for Growth and Prosperity.* New York: Simon and Schuster, 1998.

Pfeffer, Jeffrey, and Robert I. Sutton. *The Knowing-Doing Gap: How Smart Companies Turn Knowledge into Action.* Cambridge, MA: Harvard Business School Press, 1999.

Stewart, Thomas A. *The Wealth of Knowledge: Intellectual Capital and the Twenty-first Century Organization.* New York: Doubleday, 2001.

Notes

1. Lawrence M. Fischer, "Thought Leader," *Strategy and Business* 7 (4th quarter, 2002): 115–23.
2. Robert J. Flanagan, "Knowledge Management in Global Organizations in the 21st Century," *HR Magazine* 44, no. 11 (1999): 54–55.
3. "Partners in Wealth," *The Economist*, January 21, 2006, 16–17.
4. Michael Z. Brooke, *International Management: A Review of Strategies and Operations* (London: Hutchinson, 1986), 173–74; and "Running a Licensing Department," *Business International*, June 13, 1988, 177–78.
5. Sylvie Chetty and Colin Campbell-Hunt, "Explosive International Growth and Problems of Success amongst Small to Medium-sized Firms," *International Small Business Journal* 21, no. 1: 5–27.
6. Jay R. Galbraith, *Designing the Global Corporation* (New York: Jossey-Bass, 2000), chap. 3.
7. William H. Davidson and Philippe C. Haspeslagh, "Shaping a Global Product Organization," *Harvard Business Review* 59 (March–April 1982): 69–76.
8. See **http://www.loctite.com.**
9. See, for example, Samuel Humes, *Managing the Multinational: Confronting the Global–Local Dilemma* (London: Prentice Hall, 1993), chap. 1.
10. Vijay Govindarajan, Anil K. Gupta, and C.K. Prahalad, *The Quest for Global Dominance: Transforming Global Presence into Global Competitive Advantage* (New York: Jossey-Bass, 2001), chaps. 1 and 2.
11. "How Goodyear Sharpened Organization and Production for a Tough World Market," *Business International*, January 16, 1989, 11–14.
12. Michael J. Mol, *Ford Mondeo: A Model T World Car?* (Hershey, PA: Idea Group Publishing, 2002), 1–21.
13. Philippe Lasserre, "Regional Headquarters: The Spearhead for Asia Pacific Markets," *Long Range Planning* 29 (February 1996): 30–37; and John D. Daniels, "Bridging National and Global Marketing Strategies through Regional Operations," *International Marketing Review* 4 (Autumn 1987): 29–44.
14. "Boeing's Defense Unit to Divide Its Operations into 3 Segments," *The Wall Street Journal*, January 28, 2006, A5.
15. "The New Organization," *The Economist*, January 21, 2006, 3–5.
16. Daniel Robey, *Designing Organizations: A Macro Perspective* (Homewood, IL: Irwin, 1982), 327.
17. Christopher A. Bartlett and Sumantra Ghoshal, *Managing across Borders* (Cambridge, MA: Harvard Business School Press, 2002), chap. 10.
18. Spencer Chin, "Philips Shores Up the Dike," *EBN*, October 14, 2002, 4.
19. Milton Harris and Artur Raviv, "Organization Design," *Management Science* 48 (July 2002): 852–65.
20. John P. Workman Jr., Christian Homburg, and Kjell Gruner, "Marketing Organization: Framework of Dimensions and Determinants," *Journal of Marketing* 62 (July 1998): 21–41; and John U. Farley, "Looking Ahead at the Marketplace: It's Global and It's Changing," in *Reflections on the Futures of Marketing*, ed. Donald R. Lehman and Katherine E. Jocz (Cambridge, MA: Marketing Science Institute, 1995), 15–35.
21. William Taylor, "The Logic of Global Business," *Harvard Business Review* 68 (March–April 1990): 91–105.
22. Mohanbir Sawhney, "Don't Homogenize, Synchronize," *Harvard Business Review* 79 (July–August 2001): 100–108.
23. Gerard Fairtlough, *The Three Ways of Getting Things Done* (London: Triarchy Press, 2005), chaps. 3 and 4.
24. Ilkka A. Ronkainen, "Thinking Globally, Implementing Successfully," *International Marketing Review* 13, no. 3 (1996): 4–6.
25. Jack Neff, "Unilever Reorganization Shifts P&L Responsibility," *Advertising Age*, February 28, 2005, 13; "Despite Revamp, Unwieldy Unilever Falls Behind Rivals," *The Wall Street Journal*, January 3, 2005, A1, A5.
26. Russell Eisenstat, Nathaniel Foote, Jay Galbraith, and Danny Miller, "Beyond the Business Unit," *The McKinsey Quarterly* 37, no. 1 (2001): 180–95.
27. "Country Managers," *Business Europe*, October 16, 2002, 3; John A. Quelch and Helen Bloom, "The Return of the Country Man-

ager," *The McKinsey Quarterly* 33, no. 2 (1996): 31–43; and Jon I. Martinez and John A. Quelch, "Country Managers: The Next Generation," *International Marketing Review* 13, no. 3 (1996): 43–55.

28. Rodman Drake and Lee M. Caudill, "Management of the Large Multinational: Trends and Future Challenges," *Business Horizons* 24 (May–June 1981): 83–91.
29. Joe Studwell, *The China Dream* (New York: Atlantic Monthly Press, 2002), 104–5.
30. Goran Svensson, "'Glocalization' of Business Activities: A 'Glocal Strategy' Approach," *Management Decision 39, no. 1 (2001): 6–13.*
31. Christopher A. Bartlett and Sumantra Ghoshal, "Matrix Management: Not a Structure, a Frame of Mind," *Harvard Business Review* 68 (July–August 1990): 138–45.
32. "Big and No Longer Blue," *The Economist,* January 21, 2006, 15; and "Beyond Blue," *Business Week,* April 18, 2005, 68–76.
33. Carlos Ghosn, "Saving the Business without Losing the Company," *Harvard Business Review* 80 (January 2002): 37–45.
34. Karl Moore and Julian Birkinshaw, "Managing Knowledge in Global Service Firms," *Academy of Management Executive* 12, no. 4 (1998): 81–92.
35. Julian Birkinshaw and Tony Sheehan, "Managing the Knowledge Life Cycle," *Sloan Management Review* 44 (Fall 2002): 75–83.
36. Noel Tichy, "The Teachable Point of View: A Primer," *Harvard Business Review* 77 (March–April 1999): 82–83.
37. "See Jack. See Jack Run Europe," *Fortune,* September 27, 1999, 127–36.
38. "GE Mentoring Program Turns Underlings into Teachers of the Web," *The Wall Street Journal,* February 15, 2000, B1, B16.
39. Richard Benson-Armer and Tsun-Yan Hsieh, "Teamwork across Time and Space," *The McKinsey Quarterly* 33, no. 4 (1997): 18–27.
40. David A. Griffith and Michael G. Harvey, "An Intercultural Communication Model for Use in Global Interorganizational Networks," *Journal of International Marketing* 9, no. 3 (2001): 87–103.
41. "Internet Software Poses Big Threat to Notes, IBM's Stake in Lotus," *The Wall Street Journal,* November 7, 1995, A1–5.
42. Linda S. Sanford and Dave Taylor, *Let Go to Grow* (Englewood Cliffs, NJ: Prentice-Hall, 2005), chap. 1.
43. Christopher A. Bartlett and Sumantra Ghoshal, "Tap Your Subsidiaries for Global Reach," *Harvard Business Review* 64 (November–December 1986): 87–94.
44. "The Zen of Nissan," *Business Week,* July 22, 2002, 46–49.
45. "Percy Barnevik's Global Crusade," *Business Week Enterprise* 1993, 204–11.
46. Michael D. White, "The Finnish Springboard," *World Trade,* January 1999, 48–49.
47. "A European Electronics Giant Races to Undo Mistakes in the U.S.," *The Wall Street Journal,* January 7, 2004, A1, A10.
48. Julian Birkinshaw and Neil Hood, "Unleash Innovation in Foreign Subsidiaries," *Harvard Business Review* 79 (March 2001): 131–37; and Julian Birkinshaw and Nick Fry, "Subsidiary Initiatives to Develop New Markets," *Sloan Management Review* 39 (Spring 1998): 51–61.
49. Sharon Leiba O'Sullivan, Steven H. Appelbaum, and Corinne Abikhzer, "Expatriate Management "Best Practices" in Canadian MNCs: A Multiple Case Study," *Career Development International* 7, no. 2 (2002): 79–95.
50. Alan M. Rugman and Alain Verbeke, "Subsidiary-Specific Advantages in Multinational Enterprises," *Strategic Management Journal* 22 (2001): 237–50.
51. "Doing Business in Emerging Markets," BDC; **http://www.bdc.ca/en/my_project/Projects/articles/exporting_emergingmarkets.htm?cooki** (accessed May 26, 2007).
52. Jifu Wang and Jinghua Zhao, "Strategic Perspective: MNC Subsidiaries in China," IABR (Business) and TLC (Teaching) Conference Proceedings (Mazatlan, Mexico, 2007).
53. Asia Pacific Foundation of Canada News Release, December 7, 2006, **http://www.asiapacific.ca/about/pressreleases/2006/CMEsurvey_7dec06.cfm.**
54. Alan M. Rugman and Simon Collinson, "Multinational Enterprises in the New Europe: Are They Really Global?" *Organizational Dynamics* 34, no. 3 (2005): 258–72.
55. Karl Moore and Alan Rugman, "Canadian Multinationals are Regional, Not Global," *Options Politiques* (August 2003): 44–46.
56. Vijay Govindarajan and Robert Newton, *Management Control Systems* (New York: McGraw-Hill Irwin, 2000), chap. 1.
57. Anil Gupta and Vijay Govindarajan, "Organizing for Knowledge within MNCs," *International Business Review* 3, no. 4 (1994): 443–57.
58. William G. Ouchi, "The Relationship between Organizational Structure and Organizational Control," *Administrative Science Quarterly* 22 (March 1977): 95–112.
59. Cheryl Nakata, "Activating the Marketing Concept in a Global Context," *International Marketing Review* 19, no. 1 (2002): 39–64.
60. Laurent Leksell, *Headquarters-Subsidiary Relationships in Multinational Corporations* (Stockholm, SE: Stockholm School of Economics, 1981), chap. 5.
61. Henry P. Conn and George S. Yip, "Global Transfer of Critical Capabilities," *Business Horizons* 38 (January/February 1997): 22–31.
62. Arant R. Negandhi and Martin Welge, *Beyond Theory Z* (Greenwich, CT: JAI Press, 1984), 16.
63. Richard Pascale, "Fitting New Employees into the Company Culture," *Fortune,* May 28, 1994, 28–40.
64. Michael R. Czinkota and Ilkka A. Ronkainen, "International Business and Trade in the Next Decade: Report from a Delphi Study," *Journal of International Business Studies* 28, no. 4 (1997): 676–94.
65. Tsun-Yan Hsieh, Johanne La Voie, and Robert A. P. Samek, "Think Global, Hire Local," *The McKinsey Quarterly* 35, no. 4 (1999): 92–101.
66. "Thinking for a Living," *The Economist,* January 21, 2006, 9–12.
67. R.J. Alsegg, *Control Relationships between American Corporations and Their European Subsidiaries,* AMA Research Study No. 107 (New York: American Management Association, 1971), 7.
68. Ron Edwards, Adlina Ahmad, and Simon Moss, "Subsidiary Autonomy: The Case of Multinational Subsidiaries in Malaysia," *Journal of International Business Studies* 33, no. 1 (2002): 183–91.
69. John J. Dyment, "Strategies and Management Controls for Global Corporations," *Journal of Business Strategy* 7 (Spring 1987): 20–26.
70. Alfred M. Jaeger, "The Transfer of Organizational Culture Overseas: An Approach to Control in the Multinational Corporation," *Journal of International Business Studies* 14 (Fall 1983): 91–106.
71. Michael Goold and Andrew Campbell, "Do You Have a Well-Designed Organization?" *Harvard Business Review* 80 (March 2002): 117–24.
72. Michael C. Mankins and Richard Steele, "Turning Great Strategy into Great Performance," *Harvard Business Review* 83 (July–August 2005): 65–72.

Chapter 16

International Negotiations

The Global MARKETPLACE 16.1

The Art of Negotiation

Nation-states and firms do not make deals; individuals do that for them. In most cases, successful deals are a result of multiple negotiations for which preparation must be extensive, particularly in understanding cross-cultural differences. Imbedded in these differences are national culture, organizational factors, and the personality traits of the individuals carrying out the negotiations. Understanding one's counterpart may not suffice; understanding one's own cultural "baggage" may be critical as well.

One such interaction occurred between representatives of Atacs Products, Inc.—a Seattle-based supplier of aircraft repair systems—and Aviation Transactions Conseils, which stocks those supplies, in Juilly, France, during an international trade exhibition in Seattle.

Terry Cooney, Atacs's sales manager, discovered a mutual interest during a chance meeting with ATC's president, Pierre-Jean Back, and sales manager Patrick Naumann. Cooney then arranged a more formal meeting, and they reconvened with Andrew Thibault, an interpreter.

Cooney began his presentation—speaking slowly and clearly, but without condescension—on technical fronts. During the product demonstration for a heat-sensitive device, Cooney took care to speak in terms of ambient temperature in Bordeaux instead of just saying "72 degrees." And Naumann understood English well enough to laugh at Cooney's references to misuse of the product causing "permanently curly hair." Throughout the presentation, Thibault softly translated, primarily for Back's benefit. Occasionally, the demonstration slowed if either had a question. After the demonstration, Cooney explained Atacs's stance on foreign distributors. "If you start losing business," he joked, "I'm in the Irish mafia."

He mentioned several sales techniques, whom to contact, and the latitude of offers ATC would be able to make to customers. Naumann and Back conferred in French, and then Thibault presented Back's objection: what would prevent Atacs from ending its agreement once ATC had nurtured the territory?

Cooney said he didn't "know how to overcome" that objection. Then, force of personality began to transcend language. "I can be the biggest (expletive) you ever met," Cooney said, "but I'm honest. I don't even cheat in tennis against my sons."

Cooney closed with two more appeals, posed vehemently yet calmly. One mentioned the amount of dollars it could cost ATC not to accept the arrangement. The other: "If you place an order, you still have 90 days for payment, unless the dollar drops against the franc. Then we'll give you 120 days." They all laughed at that remark, but ATC's representatives still did not agree. Cooney said, "That's all I've got to say."

After the meeting, Back said in an interview, "I'm not suspicious of this gentleman, in particular, but it's the general manner of doing business in the American way. In general, when working with Americans, when things are going fine, there's no problem. But when the market starts to go down, Americans tend to bail out. Good business relationships take time to develop.... You know that relations are really good when there are problems with money and they'll still allow you to operate.

"However, I would not trust a large American company. There's such a turnover rate in employees that from one day to another it changes completely, so it's really hard to have continuous relations. The best prospects for American businesses to operate in France [are] with small businesses because there's a more personal relationship."

It would have been useful for Cooney to know about the French as negotiating partners. U.S.-centric references should be avoided, especially self-congratulatory ones, which are perceived as arrogant. Any notion of superiority or the attitude that "We are Number 1" can rub a French businessperson the wrong way. U.S. speakers often try to export baseball, football, or golf metaphors they use at home but that are mostly unknown abroad. However, if one is speaking in France or to the French, relating sports metaphors to World Cup soccer (and especially to the French success in 1998) is appropriate. Throughout the preliminary and middle stages of negotiating, the French manager will judge counterparts carefully on their intellectual skills and their ability to react quickly and with authority. In many ways, the French still embrace the art of diplomatic negotiation invented in France in the 14th century. As one French manager put it, "Sometimes I am more impressed by brilliant savvy than by a well-reasoned argument." Because French education stresses mathematics and logic, doing business is a highly intellectual process for French managers. One study found that the style of French negotiators was the most aggressive of 13 diverse cultural groups analyzed.

Sources: Bill Hory, "Building International Relationships," *World Trade*, November 2002, 47–49; "Splitting the Difference," *Global Business*, July 2000, 50; Raymond Saner, Lichia Yiu, and Mikael Sondergaard, "Business Diplomacy Management: A Core Competency for Global Companies," *Academy of Management Executive*, February 1, 2000, 80–92; Sherrie Zhan, "Trade Shows Mean Big Business," *World Trade*, September 1999, 88; John L. Graham, "Vis-à-Vis International Business Negotiations," in *International Business Negotiations*, ed. Jean-Claude D. Usunier and Pervez N. Ghauri (London: The Dryden Press, 1996), chap. 7; "Negotiating in Europe," *Hemispheres*, July 1994, 43–47; David Jacobson, "Marketers Swap More Than Goodwill at Trade Show," *Business Marketing* 75 (September 1990): 48–51; and **http://www.atacs.com.**

Effective communications are particularly important in international marketing because of the geographic and psychological distances that separate a firm from its intermediaries and customers. Although there are different forms of communication—advertising, publicity, sales promotion—this chapter is concerned with face-to-face, buyer–seller negotiations, which are perhaps the most fundamental marketing process.[1] While technological advances (for example fax, videoconferencing, and the Internet) may have made buyer–seller negotiations more efficient, the fundamental process and its purpose have remained unchanged. Face-to-face contact is still necessary for two basic reasons. The first is the need for detailed discussion and explanation, and the second is the need to establish the rapport that forms the basis of lasting business relationships. Technology will then provide support in the maintenance of the relationship.

For negotiations to work successfully, a relationship between the negotiating partners has to be established from the beginning and deepened over time. The majority of communications in negotiations is verbal, but nonverbal communications and the concept of silent languages must also be considered. This is because these often create challenges for the international marketer, as seen in The Global Marketplace 16.1.

After emphasizing the importance of negotiations in global marketing, this chapter discusses the key steps in the negotiation process. Then the chapter focuses on the influences of culture on global negotiations, including discussion of such factors as religion, values, and ethics. Preparing for global negotiations, perhaps involving the creation of negotiating teams, is shown to demand a knowledge of these and other factors, and an empathy with them. But negotiation must also pay attention to "hard" issues such as price bargaining and ensuring that the firm's profitability objectives are respected. The chapter concludes with a summary of some key guidelines for effective negotiation practice at an international level.

The Importance of Negotiations in Global Marketing

Because of growing interdependencies in the global marketing arena and the increasing pressures on firms to "think globally," it is vital for marketers to hone their negotiating skills, especially in cross-cultural terms. The phrase "cultural sensitivity" is hackneyed and overworked, yet in its absence negotiators can potentially run into serious difficulties at any point in perhaps a long period of negotiation. The final prize of a successful outcome, including the securing of an important contract, may be entirely lost for this reason alone, not to be saved by the quality or price features of the proposal.

In addition, various developments on the world stage will impose greater challenges to negotiation skills. For example, we are increasingly seeing the formation of different types of cooperative agreements among entities in various parts of the world. Among these are co-production arrangements, joint research and development, and co-marketing, many of which are set up on a project basis. Negotiators will have to be adept at dealing with these new forms of collaborative arrangements. Moreover, new challenges for negotiators keep emerging as a result of fundamental and rapid changes in the political and economics systems in many countries around the world, and changes in their economic fortunes. Such changes present more challenges and opportunities for doing business in these countries, for example, the rapid growth in democracy, especially among the more developed countries (though authoritarian regimes of one sort or another still persist), and the emergence of China as a major economic power. Negotiators need to understand the full implications of such developments and operate within the contexts of evolving political, economic, and societal frameworks.

A further challenge to negotiators is the growing participation of ethnic minorities and women in professional and managerial ranks in many industrialized nations. The approach to business by ethnic minorities may be significantly different from that favoured by Canadian negotiators because the former may still adhere to values and attitudes that are part of their ancestors' cultural heritage. Negotiators need to be sensitive to any differences at work in the negotiation and adjust their styles appropriately.

Good negotiating skills are necessary at almost every phase of a firm's operations in the international arena. At an early stage, the SME needs good skills to negotiate initial contracts or to finalize arrangements with key foreign distributors. As business develops, the company sales force will find itself in need of these skills in any number of settings, for example, negotiating sales service terms or negotiating final deals. The firm may ultimately contemplate manufacturing and marketing its products and services abroad, but before it can do so it must negotiate with the host government and host-country partner (in the event of a cooperative agreement) for the terms and conditions of the entry and/or collaboration. Even after an agreement has been reached, negotiations are still necessary to resolve differences that may arise between the partners throughout the relationship to maintain amicable coexistence. As Canada's international trade expands, the need for negotiating competence will only increase. When international marketers travel abroad to do business, they are frequently shocked to discover the extent to which the many variables of foreign behaviour and custom complicate their efforts.[2] This means that global marketers have to adjust their approaches to establishing rapport, information exchange, persuasion, and concession making if they are to be successful in dealing with their clients and partners, such as intermediaries.[3]

The two biggest dangers faced in international negotiations are **parochialism** and **stereotyping**. Parochialism, that is, having a very narrow or limited outlook, can lead to the misleading perception that the Western business model is the only valid one. This, in turn, leads to stereotyping, which is adopting generalized views, both positive and negative, about how people will behave. For example, a positive stereotype has a clear influence on decisions to explore business options, whereas a negative stereotype may lead to a request to use a low-risk payment system, such as a letter of credit.[4] The level of adjustment in a negotiation depends on the degree of cultural familiarity the parties have and their ability to use that familiarity effectively.[5] For example, in negotiating with the Chinese, an ideal team would include a non-Chinese who understands the culture and an ethnic-Chinese individual. Together, the two can play "good guy–bad guy" roles and resist unreasonable demands.[6] If neither party is familiar with the counterpart's culture, outside facilitators should be employed.

With the increased use of the Internet, the question arises as to its use in international negotiations. Using the e-dimension does allow the exporter to overcome distances, minimize social barriers (e.g., age, gender, status), obtain instant feedback, negotiate from a home base, and do so with a number of parties simultaneously. However, it cannot be used in isolation given the critical role of building trust in negotiations. Additionally, its extensive use may restrict much of the interaction to focusing mostly on price. The Internet is effective in the exchange of information and for possible clarification during the course of the process.[7] It should be noted that technology is only gradually making its way to such employment; lack of the necessary tools and mindset may challenge the Internet's use for this purpose.

Stages of the Negotiating Process

The process of international business negotiations can be divided into five stages: the offer, informal meetings, strategy formulation, negotiations, and implementation.[8] The stage that is emphasized and the length of the overall process will vary dramatically by culture. The negotiation process can be a short one, with the stages collapsing into one session, or a prolonged endeavour taking weeks or longer. The differences between northern and southern Europe highlight this.[9]

Exhibit 16.1 **The Deal Is Cemented with a Handshake**

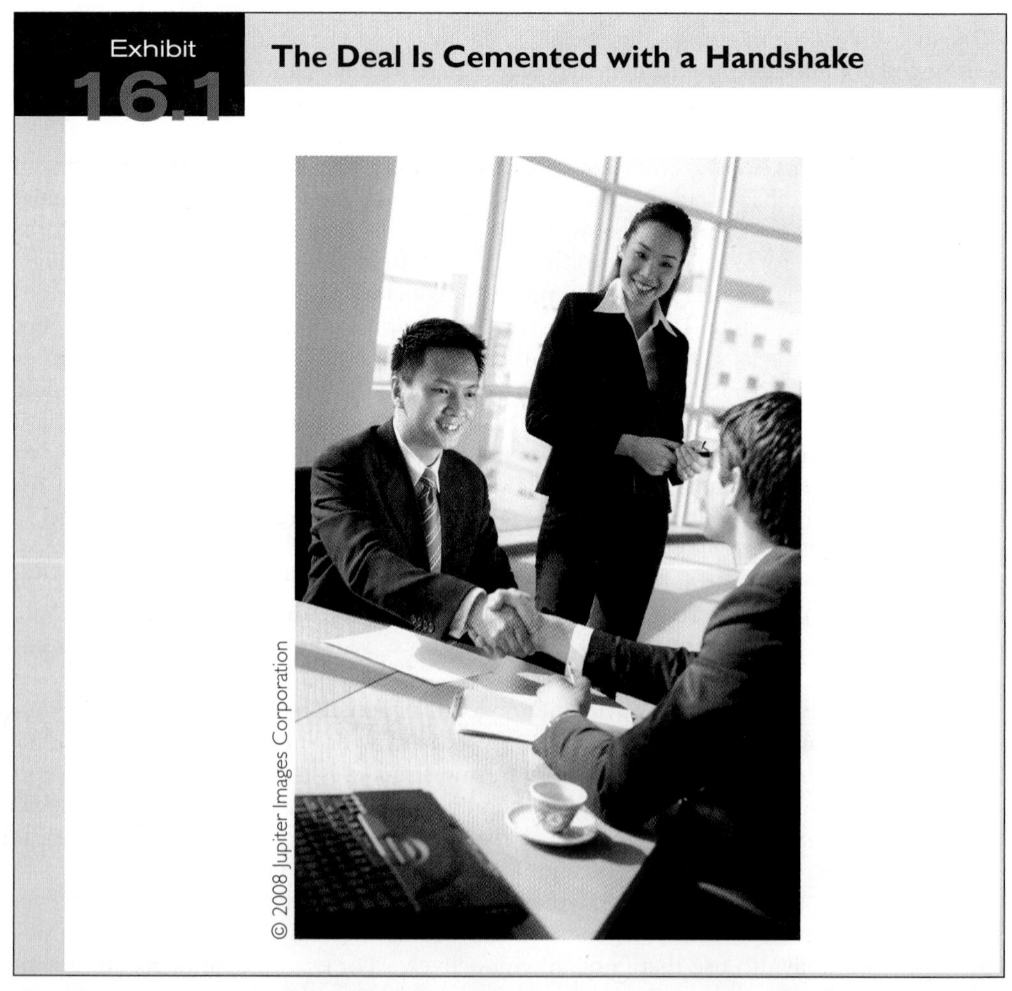

The offer stage allows the two parties to assess each other's needs and degree of commitment. The initiation of the process and its progress are determined to a great extent by background factors of the parties (such as objectives) and the overall atmosphere (for example, a spirit of cooperativeness). After the buyer has received the offer, the parties meet to discuss the terms and get acquainted. In many parts of the world (Asia, the Middle East, southern Europe, and Latin America), informal meetings may often make or break the deal. Foreign buyers may want to ascertain that they are doing business with someone who is sympathetic and whom they can trust. Price may not be seen as the critical variable driving buying decisions.[10]

Both parties have to formulate strategies for formal negotiations. This means not only careful review and assessment of all the factors affecting the deal to be negotiated but also preparation for the actual give-and-take of the negotiations. Thus Canadian negotiators may be happier with the outcome if it maximizes joint gain, while Hong Kong Chinese negotiators may be more satisfied when they achieve outcome parity. This suggests that cultural values (e.g., harmonious relationships for the Chinese) create the environment in which negotiation tactics are selected.[11] Thus, managers should consciously and carefully consider competitive behaviours of clients and partners.

The actual face-to-face negotiations and the approach used in them will depend on the cultural background and business traditions prevailing in different countries. The most commonly used are the **competitive and collaborative approaches**.[12] In a competitive strategy, the negotiator is concerned mainly about a favourable outcome at the expense of the other party, while in the collaborative approach the focus is on mutual needs, especially in the long term.

Exhibit 16.2 **One International Business School Sees Culture as the Key Factor in Understanding Globalization**

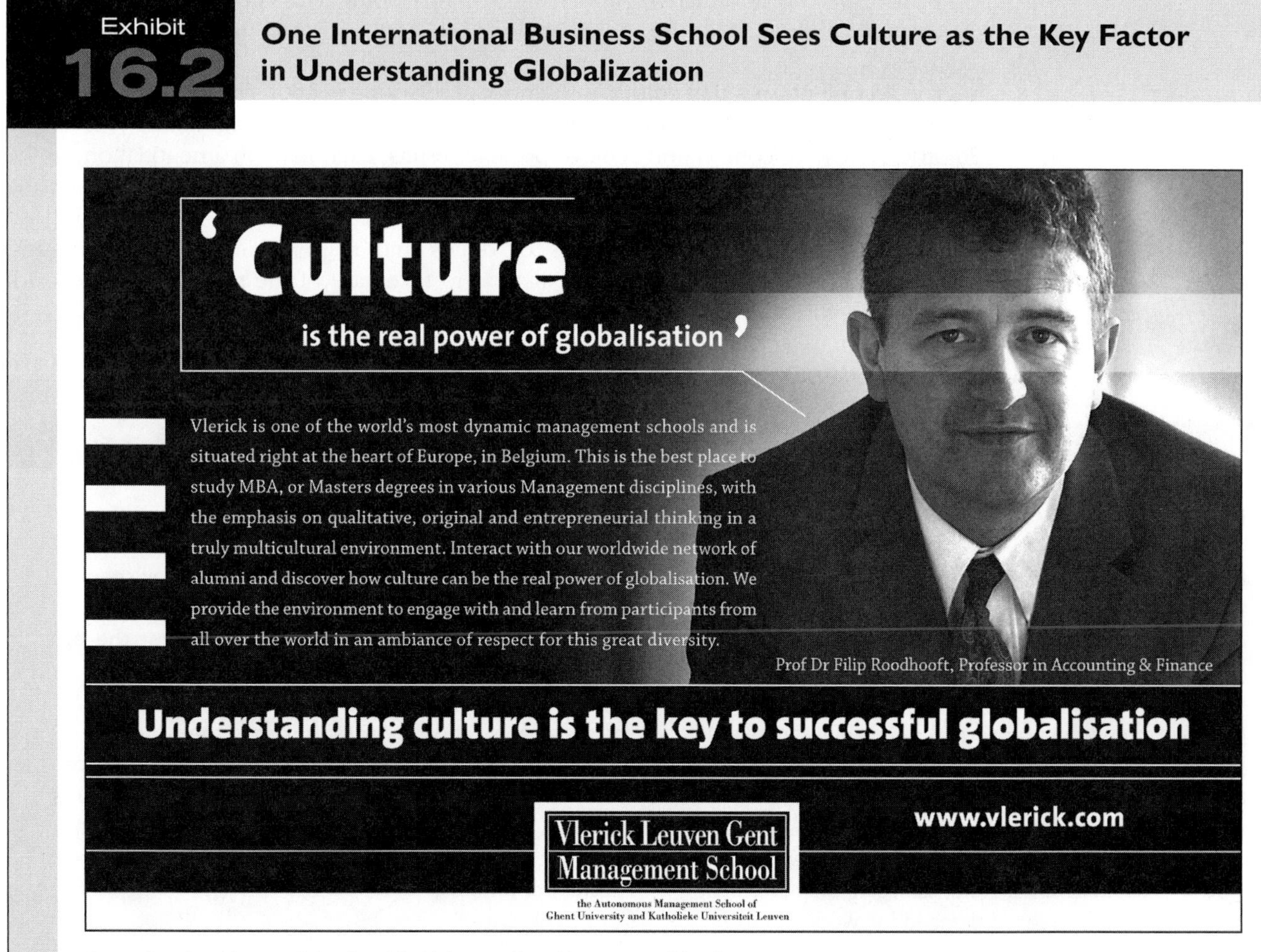

Source: Reprinted by permission from Vlerick Leuven Gent Management School.

The choice of location for the negotiations plays a role in the outcome as well. Many negotiators prefer a neutral site. This may not always work, for reasons of resources or parties' perceptions of the importance of the deal. The host does enjoy many advantages, such as lower psychological risk due to familiar surroundings. Guests may run the risk of cultural shock and being away from professional and personal support systems. These pressures are multiplied if the host chooses to manipulate the situation with delays or additional demands. In addition, visiting a partner, present or potential, shows commitment to the effort.[13]

Negotiator characteristics (e.g., gender, race, or age) may work for or against the negotiator in certain cultures. It is challenging to overcome stereotypes, but well-prepared negotiators can overcome these obstacles or even make them work to their advantage. For example, a female negotiator may use her uniqueness in male-dominated societies to gain better access to decision makers.[14]

The Influence of Culture on Global Negotiations

Culture is a key contributor to our understanding of globalization (see Exhibit 16.2). In Chapter 3 we dwelt on its pervasive role in global marketing. This impact is felt not only at a general level in terms of global strategy, but also at specific levels such as that of international negotiations.

Culture can affect negotiations in at least three specific ways.[15] Firstly, it influences how people process and interpret information. Secondly, it affects peoples' perception of what is reasonable and acceptable and hence the positions they will take during negotiations, and finally, it results in differences in negotiating styles.

With respect to information processing, the first point, The Global Marketplace 16.2 gives an example of how the same situation can be interpreted differently by different cultures.[16]

The second point is that culture influences people's perceptions of what is reasonable, right, and acceptable. This in turn affects the choice of strategies negotiators will pursue in order to resolve conflict and achieve positive results. Each party in a negotiation can be expected to insist on its rights—the right to higher wages, for example. In Japan, on the other hand, the notion of "right" is more problematic because of the historic predisposition to define relationships in terms of duties and responsibilities. Following this, management is seen as having the obligation to take care of the work force, the work force having the duty to work hard to fulfill organizational goals.[17]

The Global MARKETPLACE 16.2

How the Japanese See Things

In Japan, there are two types of logic: linear logic (similar to Greek Aristotelian logic) and indirection. Indirection can be illustrated by the Japanese saying "When the wind blows, it is good for the makers of wooden tubs." The logic of this is approximately as follows: when it is windy, people become sad; to overcome their melancholy, they play a samisen (stringed instrument), the strings of which are made of catgut; to make the samisen, people kill cats, which results in a depletion of the feline population and leads to a proliferation of mice; the mice gnaw at the wooden tubs that store grain, damaging them, resulting ultimately in an increased demand for wooden tubs.

This explains the saying. Although the logic may seem convoluted and incomprehensible from a Western perspective, it highlights two significant points: first, the Japanese preoccupation with long-term implications of actions; and second, their ability to see relationships between apparently unrelated systems, the wind blowing and the demand for wooden tubs. Differences in logical systems explain how two people from different cultures can view the same situation—an objective reality—and arrive at totally different interpretations of what had occurred.

The Global MARKETPLACE 16.3

A Majestic Misstep in Thailand

A Toronto telecommunications company targeted Southeast Asia as a promising new market for its services. The company successfully established a joint-venture partnership in Malaysia and had its sights set on Thailand's emerging market. A team of senior executives from the firm travelled to Bangkok for a series of meetings with a potential joint-venture partner—a prominent, respected, and well-connected local company. The first day of meetings proceeded well, and the Thai hosts invited the Canadians to a reception and dinner.

During the reception, the senior Canadian executive made an offhand remark about the Thai royal family. His Thai counterpart smiled politely and soon excused himself from the conversation. Over the evening, the Canadian sensed that something in the manner of his Thai host had changed but could not understand why. This sense persisted over the next day of meetings, where the Thais seemed more reserved and formal. The Canadian team, baffled by this turn of events, returned home with little more than a vague commitment for future discussions. No discussions or agreement occurred, and, over the ensuing months, the Canadian company found doors in Thailand closed, not only with the Thai company with whom they had hoped to form a partnership, but with other Thai firms they approached.

What happened?

- Canadian culture tolerates criticism of our monarchy and senior status figures.
- Thais deeply respect status and hierarchy, and they revere their monarchy.
- The Canadian executive's lack of knowledge of, and insensitivity to, the status of the royal family resulted in him inadvertently insulting his host.
- The close-knit nature of Thai society resulted in the story of the Canadian firm's cultural blunder becoming well known in Bangkok's business community, closing doors to other potential opportunities.

Source: Industry Canada, "Service Industries—The Cross-Marketing Edge." Created 2005–2006, Updated 2006–04–16, available at **http://www.strategis.ic.gc.ca.** Reproduced with the permission of the Minister of Public Works and Government Services, 2008.

Thirdly, cultural differences result in contrasts in decision-making and **negotiating styles**. For example, in Southeast Asian countries, Western negotiators may find more delays in decision making than they are accustomed to elsewhere, an inclination to avoid direct confrontation, and the use of silence at particular points in the negotiation. Further examples of such contrasting styles are given later in the chapter.

The way in which cultural impacts are felt can be discussed in terms of particular aspects of culture, for example, language or religion. In general, human beings deal with situations based on cultural codes and reactions to cues from others. Language, dress, mannerisms, and interactions may appear similar in other cultures but may mean something very different. Interpreting cues from a Canadian perspective may result in behaviour that is inappropriate or offensive in other cultures, as is seen in The Global Marketplace 16.3. This may undermine or destroy the chances for success. Knowing the subtleties of marketing one's product or service in another country can provide what can be termed a cross-cultural advantage. In the following section, we discuss some key cultural elements that affect negotiation success.

Verbal Communications (Language)

Strange though it is to say, it is important first of all for the negotiator to choose the correct language. For example, businesspeople who do not speak Portuguese, the official language of Brazil, are cautioned to speak English instead, not Spanish.[18] Brazilians consider themselves distinct from other Latin Americans.

Even with excellent fluency or interpretation skills in the chosen language, **verbal communications** can still cause difficulty. Semantics or word meanings differ across cultures. For example, the phrase "makes business sense" has virtually no meaning in Russia.

Word connotations may also vary. The Japanese word *hai* ("yes") may mean "I'm listening," not "I agree." Tone is also a potential source of misunderstanding. Some cultures use formal, polite tones; others are more offhand.

In light of the potential for miscommunication, some commonsense tactics are advisable: rephrasing important points to ensure understanding; asking open-ended questions to obtain information; summarizing what you have said or believe you have heard; acknowledging others who are accommodating you by speaking in a second language; clarifying vague or indirect answers (for example, a "yes" that sounds like a "no").

It may be necessary to include a bilingual member in the negotiating team, if one can be found. Such a member, while not actively involved in the translations, can correct mistakes as they occur. Misunderstandings because of poor interpretation services impede the progress of negotiations and may completely disrupt them because the perspectives of both sides cannot be presented accurately. In addition to simple interpretation, a bilingual person from within the partner's culture can also interpret any nonverbal messages for the rest of the team.

In general, it might be a good gesture to deliver the first comments in the local language to break the ice. The use of interpreters allows the negotiator longer response time and a more careful articulation of arguments. If English is being used, a native speaker should avoid both jargon and idiomatic expressions, avoid complex sentences, and speak slowly and enunciate clearly.[19]

Nonverbal Communications

Nonverbal communications have the ability to produce potentially disastrous results in international business. Gestures, speech volume, facial expressions, posture, and physical contact convey different messages in different cultures. To negotiate effectively abroad, a marketer needs to read correctly all types of communication. In some countries, silence speaks volumes. Canadian businesspeople may interpret inaction and silence as a negative sign. Finns may sit through a meeting expressionless, hands folded and not moving much. This may be off-putting to the Canadian negotiator who is more accustomed to some kind of positive, demonstrable response. But there is nothing necessarily negative about this. Difficult though it may be to accept, this behaviour should be interpreted as showing respect to the speaker with their focused, dedicated listening.[20]

In Japan, vagueness in responses in negotiations is sometimes accompanied by prolonged periods of silence. In that country, the maxim that "silence is golden" still holds true and may stem from the Japanese desire to avoid **confrontation**, which is deeply ingrained in individuals from childhood.[21] Westerners, on the other hand, including Canadians, may feel uncomfortable and have the urge to say something. At these crucial junctures, the dangers of committing tactical errors are greatest. On the other hand, Canadian negotiators should be wary of the tactic of using silence to fluster the partner in order to get a price reduction or a sweetening of the deal.

Effective nonverbal communication involves knowing the ground rules, being an active listener (and watcher), and taking an open-minded approach. Other recommendations that might be made include avoiding judging nonverbal behaviours by Canadian standards; watching body language for clues when others are speaking; being alert for feedback such as annoyance, surprise, irritation, or a change in demeanour when you are speaking; and avoiding any imitation of nonverbal behaviour in the belief that this will increase rapport.

Dress and Etiquette

Trivial though dress and etiquette may seem when considered in tandem with weightier issues under negotiation, they are nonetheless a potential source of relationship-wrecking gaffes. Dress is important because it contributes to image credibility. This is based on the audience's appreciation of the status and respect created by the negotiator's physical appearance. Predictably, this varies greatly across cultures.

Consider, too, the area of correct etiquette, especially important for the negotiator when meetings are being arranged. In China, for example, the best advice for successfully getting through a business meeting is to "go with the flow."[22] In the case of negotiations in Hong Kong, the larger the local firm, the further in advance meetings should be scheduled. One piece of advice is to send, prior to arrival, a list of all delegates attending, in ranking order, with titles next to each name.[23] Because the Hong Kong team may well be seated and waiting for the Canadian team's arrival, it is sensible to enter the room in hierarchical order and sit across from the Hong Kong person who holds the same position of equal status to your own. Social conversation will normally start the meeting until the group spokesperson, usually a high-ranking officer, moves the talk to business. Because group consensus is the norm in decision making, and private post-meeting discussion is usual, the Canadian negotiators should not expect a "reading" at the first meeting.

In contrast to these niceties, a much more matter-of-fact approach is to be expected in, for example, Australia, where words are taken at face value and directness is highly valued. Canadian negotiators need to be familiar with whatever variations in etiquette are typical for individual foreign countries.

Ethics

In marketing, the test of what ought to be done is a conflicting one. On the one hand, there is the economic necessity for achieving business goals and generating revenues, and on the other, there is the code of behaviour that is held to be correct by the host society at large. Normal practices in a given foreign country will be based on that country's ethics, and these host-country practices may conflict with the company's domestic practices or beliefs. For example, the practice of patent infringement and product pirating, though not necessarily pervasive in China, are less likely to be found in Canada.

The Global Marketplace 16.4 illustrates one ethical dilemma—gift-giving.[24] But other problems abound. Indeed, ethical considerations enter into virtually all aspects of both domestic and global marketing, to a greater or lesser extent. This is not to say that unethical behaviour is widespread, only that ethical dimensions are quite ubiquitous and can arise at any point in the marketing and negotiating process. Nor can Western or Canadian companies be exempted from "blame," if this word can be used. Consider, for example, the packaging consultant who designs a package so as to give a deceptive idea of size; the artist or copywriter whose product advertising plays on peoples' gullibility; the salesman's "strong-arm" tactics, and so on. All these practices, and many more, can be considered unethical and can be found readily enough in Western business practice.

The Global MARKETPLACE 16.4

Should You Give a Gift?

Firms operating abroad are not necessarily expected to adhere to the national norms of a host society, but behavioural differences may nonetheless put strain on a manager's ethical codes. For example, using gifts and flattery to gain business advantages will seem unethical to many Canadians. But in many countries, especially in Asia, failure to bring a small gift may not only be considered a breach of etiquette but also be interpreted as indicating a lack of interest in the relationship. The difference may be explained by the fact that most Westerners are conditioned to express gratitude verbally, and most Asians, particularly Chinese, are conditioned to express appreciation tangibly, such as with gifts. Giving gifts or payments to government officials may be particularly perplexing to Canadians, such gifts or payments being customary in many places to obtain government services or contracts. On the other hand, with the passage of time, it is undeniable that many firms have come to look on these payments as simply "the cost of doing business" in the foreign country, and therefore they "pay up" accordingly. The practice will remain an ethical problem for some people in the company, but less so for others. Is it unethical to pay what may in effect be a bribe, in order to achieve the desirable outcomes of new business, profits, and continued employment for workers? These are difficult questions, and they can only be answered within the context of the individual's ethical standards and expectations.

In the negotiating situation, therefore, unless both sides send their most inexperienced representatives (which is of course not likely), there will be plentiful knowledge, on both sides, of the business practices of the other, including perceptions of ethical standards. In other words, it is not simply a matter of the Canadian company trying to understand and adjust to the foreign partner's practices and outlook; it is also a matter of trying to anticipate how the partner will perceive those of the Canadian company. Once an ethical standard has been decided upon, it must become the common approach to be taken by all members of the negotiating team. In this way, consistency of action across all members will be achieved.

Values

In Chapter 3 we discussed the concept of cultural values. It is not difficult to see how an understanding of such values, beliefs, assumptions, and superstitions will provide important insights into a foreign country's goals, priorities, and motivations. Such information is difficult to access and interpret but is nonetheless essential. For example, a Canadian negotiator who knows that the Japanese value **harmony** would avoid aggressive or confrontational behaviour. An architect working in China would understand the importance of accommodating feng shui, the belief that a building's layout affects the lives of those who live and work within it. Sensitivity to such values and beliefs must be seen as part of the arsenal of the overseas negotiator.

Religion

We discussed world religion in Chapter 3. Here we can note that, as far as Canadians are concerned, they often take for granted a pluralistic society with different groups competing for recognition and benefits. Religion is considered just one aspect of life, albeit a very important one to many. Relying on the separation of church and state, Canadians pursue many secular aspects of human activity with no particular heed to religious decrees and guidelines. In other countries, however, religion may be the foundation of government and a dominant business factor that influences the type of negotiating behaviour to be expected. In dealing with some Muslim countries, for example, the Canadian negotiator will encounter explanations, excuses, options, and proposals that give almost a metaphysical dimension to everyday matters. At the simplest level, Canadian executives must respect Islamic legal holidays and bear in mind that these are as important as Christmas or Passover are in the West.

Preparing for Global Negotiations

Preparing for an actual negotiation abroad can potentially involve the negotiating team in endless amounts of preparatory work. Virtually anything that can throw light on likely behaviour is fair game for study—cultural values, religion, ethical standards, local customs, and so on. In addition, however, Canadian negotiators need to be familiar with their own culture to give a backdrop for making comparisons with cultures greatly different from their own. It is also important to find out as much as possible about the probable negotiating tactics to be encountered (use of silence, long delays) so that appropriate strategies can be set. Read The Global Marketplace 16.5 for a highly practical account of negotiating in China.

There are five key guidelines for the intending negotiator:

1. Know your own culture.
2. Know the negotiating partner's culture.
3. Know the negotiating partner's negotiation tactics.
4. Determine the composition of the negotiating team.
5. Pay attention to contract details.

Know Your Own Culture

The idea of Canadian values is frequently heard in political discussions and when Canada as a country embarks on an international venture of one sort of another, for example, involvement in Afghanistan. That other countries do not necessarily share these values is

The Global MARKETPLACE 16.5

Practical Advice for Negotiating with Chinese Partners: "Where You Stand Depends on Where You Sit"

When Whiting Corporation, a heavy-equipment producer based in Welland, Ontario, decided to establish a manufacturing plant as a joint venture in China, Rudi Kroeker, president and CEO of the company, found that his ability to negotiate was critical to the success and even survival of the Chinese venture. As a result of hard experience, Mr. Kroeker learned a number of highly practical lessons about negotiating successfully in that country.

1. *Use a principled or interest-based negotiation approach.* By this Mr. Kroeker means that negotiators should use the same principles no matter where they are in the world, because people will not agree unless their best interests are being served. Therefore, understanding and doing one's best to cater to these interests should underlie negotiating approaches everywhere. According to Roger Fisher and Scott Brown (see Sources, below) all people in varying degrees need consistency in the way they relate their perceptions and beliefs. There is a great deal of truth to the adage "Where you stand depends on where you sit," meaning that when people are further apart (in terms of culture, role, or just distance) the contrast between their perceptions will be greater, and each will find it more difficult to appreciate how the other sees things.
2. *Only use interpreters with an appropriate corporate rank.* Whiting's interpreter was called "Chief Representative, China Operations, North America Metallurgical Group (China) Inc., Specialty Steel Division" (equivalent to a general manager or vice president). The municipality of Tongxiang in China, where the plant is located, used a "Director." Whiting also had a Canadian lawyer as a peripheral advisor and occasional interlocutor who was qualified in both British Columbia and China.
3. *Avoid using a person with low social standing as an interpreter.* This diminishes the importance and credibility of the message to the level of the messenger's station in society. According to Mr. Kroeker, you are better served by a poor, inaccurate translation from a highly ranked interpreter than an accurate translation from a clerical-level person. Mr. Kroeker recalls the president of Bao Steel walking out on the chairman of Praxair Inc. because the chairman brought his secretary to translate. The secretary had a Canadian MBA; the problem was her rank.
4. *Pay careful attention to the concept of "losing face."* Although this concept can be explained to Westerners, Mr. Kroeker's experience is that it is never "charismatically understood" by them. In his experience, it can result in a lifelong obsession for the destruction of the person who offended you across generations. The West has no parallel for such depth of emotion. Ultimately, both for Asians and North Americans, "losing face is better than losing shirt."
5. *When the negotiation is at an impasse, walk away.* Here Mr. Kroeker's advice is very direct: explain why their position is not a principled one; point out what they are doing and object to it; set a deadline for the day that you will leave and don't deviate from it for any reason. In his experience, the Chinese have government-trained negotiators who seem to use every one of the dirty tricks of the "hard bargainer," such as yelling and shouting, good cop/bad cop, having you face the sunlight, and floating trial balloons. Tell them it is unproductive, Mr. Kroeker says, and that it is making you uncomfortable. Be prepared to walk away. Don't fall in love with the deal, because this will make you less inclined to walk away.
6. *After the job is booked, be fully committed.* In this connection, Mr. Kroeker makes a point not well known in the West: when a problem comes up later (e.g., a violation of the contract terms that is not their fault), in Asia they will work on the problem to figure out the best course of action to put things right. They do not go back to the contract and look for loopholes, as tends to happen in the West. There is less of a tendency to immediately end up in court, and they are prepared to make compromises to solve the problem.

Let us give the last word to Mr. Kroeker. He has found negotiating to be not only extremely challenging but also a process that is at times baffling in its complexity; yet it *is* possible to succeed. As he says, "It's like the way I see a kabuki dance: beautiful, impossible to understand, and not necessary to understand to get the result."

Sources: "'Where You Stand Depends on Where You Sit': Principled Negotiation Meets the Challenge in China," *Common Ground: Conflict Resolution News*, (Spring 2002); and Roger Fisher and Scott Brown, *Getting Together: Building Relationships as We Negotiate*, (New York: Penguin Books, 1989).

now well known. It is also likely that, when pressed, many Canadians will probably not be able to enunciate these values in a detailed way. Yet possessing this knowledge, broadened to include what might be called Canada's "cultural characteristics," is vital for the intending negotiator, and might include at least the following:[25]

- individual is more important than group
- explicit communicators
- future-oriented: time is valuable
- prefer to control nature, not be controlled by it
- action-oriented
- value privacy and personal space
- individual worth is determined by what we do, not who we are
- moderate respect for rank and authority
- written contracts are important
- often prefer to get down to business relatively quickly

In preparing for the negotiation, the businessperson needs to think carefully about how to handle completely different viewpoints and behaviour, for example, how to handle great respect for rank and titles, excessive time-wasting and socializing, use of unfamiliar nonverbal communications, and so on.

Know the Negotiating Partner's Culture

In Chapter 3 and in this chapter we have already discussed various aspects of the cultures of foreign countries. This knowledge must now be sharpened and focused for a specific, upcoming negotiation in a designated country. The company will also be gathering competitive intelligence about the market, establishing pricing, or trying to determine customer need profiles. But this must be augmented by cultural knowledge to help determine the value and role of the product or service in another country. During the preparation stage, in short, thorough research is needed.[26]

In addition to the various cultural factors we have already reviewed, the following need attention before the negotiator leaves Canada:

- *Traditions and customs.* For newcomers, status relations and business procedures must be carefully considered with the help of consultants or local representatives. For example, in highly structured societies, such as Korea, great respect is paid to age and position.[27] It is prudent to use informal communication to let counterparts know, or ask them about, any prestigious degrees, honours, or accomplishments by those who will be facing one another in negotiations. What seem like simple rituals can cause problems. No first encounter in Asia is complete without an exchange of business cards. Both hands should be used to present and receive cards, and respect should be shown by reading them carefully.[28] One side should be translated into the language of the host country.
- *Social institutions.* Social structures influence the behaviour of people. For example, in Latin America, where family is the most important social group, negotiators need to recognize that family connections may take precedence over business, including the negotiation itself. Nepotism, the granting of special favours to a relative, may be seen in Latin America as justifiable because it fulfills an obligation. The Canadian businessperson is likely to take a less benevolent view of such a practice. The institution of monarchy may be taken very seriously in some countries. Treating this lightly may offend the host and bring an early termination to the negation, as shown in The Global Marketplace 16.3.
- *History and geography.* Historical and geographical factors, together with other influences, can strongly influence the development of a country's national character or self-image—a people's idea of itself—which in turn colours their ideas of how they ought to behave. In the case of Australia, a harsh geography (the bush; the outback; vast, unforgiving desert terrain) created a frontier mentality that promoted nationalism and an individualist outlook.[29] The loneliness and hardships of outback life historically taught the value of cooperation ("mate-

ship") and brought a more communitarian or collectivist outlook. Other aspects of the country's history (origins as a dumping ground for English convicts; struggle for independence and nationhood) have also promoted a strong nationalism. Ideas of national character are often romanticized or exaggerated, of course: Crocodile Dundee is hardly representative of the modern, 21st-century Australian. But historical roots run deep and should be understood by visitors. Similarly, with knowledge of the history and topography of Finland and Sweden, and allowing for possible exaggeration, one might find common characteristics such as shyness, lack of emotion, conflict avoidance, and even melancholy and dourness.

- *Regional differences.* Canadians are familiar with strong regional differences that influence how business is done in their own country. The granting of nation status to Quebec ("within a united Canada") is illustration enough, though one might add the distinctiveness of Western Canada and Atlantic Canada. Such differences are, not surprisingly, evident in other countries too. For example, the United States **Tri-State** area, consisting of New Jersey, Connecticut, and southern New York State (including New York City) is one of Canada's best markets for a huge range of commodities, products, and services.[30] This region is home to 16 percent of all U.S. Fortune 500 companies and almost 25 percent of all major U.S. corporations. The region's population is nearly as big as Canada's, and its GDP is 34 percent higher. Indeed, if the region were a country, it would be Canada's third-largest export market after the United States as a whole, with Michigan coming second. Doing business in the Tri-State is likely to provide sharp contrasts compared with the prairie states or the South.
- *Ethnic background and caste systems.* In a similar manner to Canada, other countries have social and ethnic groups, some more powerful and prominent than others, with varying values and social standing. As members of these groups are likely to be encountered in the negotiating situation, it is as well to be familiar with them. In Nigeria, for example, there are more than 200 ethnic groups, of which the dominant ones, distinguished by different languages, are the mainly Muslim Fulani in the north, the mainly Christian Yoruba in the south and west, and the mainly Christian Ibo in the east. Tensions between Christians and Muslims at times flare up into open violence, as occurred in 2004. Many of Nigeria's military dictators have been from the north, leading to the complaint by Yoruba people that the north benefits from government patronage. There is therefore a perception of an unequal distribution of wealth and influence between the ethnic groups. Also, the Nigerian caste system ostracizes the lower-caste groups from the rest of their communities.
- *Popular culture.* International success in sports such as swimming and golf is a source of great pride to Australians. Soccer is followed at an almost fanatical level in Brazil and Portugal. Cinema stars achieve cult status in India. To enter a discussion with limited or no knowledge of these is undesirable and will be perceived as a lack of interest in the country. Relationships are cemented not just by the terms of the deal but also by genuine interest in the other's culture, at different levels. Social skills and knowledge are also desirable. The Canadian in Shanghai who is not flustered by the prospect of a 15-course meal, dishes like shark-fin soup, and using chopsticks, has an advantage with Chinese hosts.

Know the Negotiating Partner's Negotiation Tactics

As part of preparatory research, the Canadian negotiator needs to think carefully about *what* is being negotiated, as well as the individuals involved in the negotiation, if that information can be obtained in advance. For example, matters to be negotiated could be setting up a joint-venture arrangement, agreeing on the contract terms for a new distributor, or winning a sales contract against heavy local competition. The nature of the task at hand will influence the type of tactics chosen. The individuals making up the partner negotiating team should also be investigated. This might involve prior discussions with specific individuals, without compromising the integrity of the upcoming negotiation, of course. The company may already be doing business with the other organization and will therefore be familiar with key individuals. In the absence of this knowledge, questions should be asked of other companies familiar with the partner, or perhaps an in-depth investigation of the partner will be felt necessary.

Of key importance is the determination of authority limits. Negotiators from North America and Europe are often expected to have full authority when they negotiate in the Far East, although their local counterparts seldom if ever do. Announcing that the negotiators do not have the final authority to conclude the contract may be perceived negatively; however, if it is used as a tactic to probe the motives of the buyer, it can be quite effective. It is important to verify who does have that authority and what challenges may be faced in getting the final decision. In negotiating in Russia, for example, where there is a movement toward bringing back under state control once-privatized companies in industries such as engineering and mining, the global marketer will have to ascertain who actually has final decision-making authority—the central, provincial, or local government—especially if permits are needed.

The gathering of information helps the negotiator to develop a game plan that assists him or her in identifying aspects of the situation that can be used to advantage later. As we saw earlier in the chapter, such a game plan involves choosing between a *competitive* and a *collaborative* strategy, tempered of course by the dictates of various cross-cultural factors.[31] According to one writer, a competitive strategy entails concealment and seeking concessions, while a cooperative strategy entails (1) offering concessions in the hope that reciprocation will take place and (2) disclosing information about goals, priorities, and limits.[32] These two strategies are sometimes referred to as the "hard" approach and the "soft" approach. A collaborative strategy is more appropriate when one negotiator trusts the other to some extent and when there is a likelihood that a mutually beneficial exchange—a win-win outcome—is possible. On the other hand, a competitive strategy is more appropriate when a negotiator believes that the partner team will try exploitative tactics.

Determine the Composition of the Negotiating Team

As far as the negotiating team is concerned, two key issues are (1) the size of the team and (2) how to negotiate as a team.

Team Size

Using specialists will strengthen the team substantially and allow for all points of view to be given proper attention. Further, observation of negotiations can be valuable training experience for less-experienced participants. Whereas Western teams may average two to four people, a Chinese negotiating team may consist of up to 10 people.[33] A study of how U.S. purchasing professionals conduct negotiations abroad revealed that while the vast majority believed a small team (two to five individuals) was ideal, they also said their teams were often outnumbered by their international counterparts.[34] Even if there are intra-group disagreements during the negotiations, it is critical to show one face to the counterparts and handle issues within the team privately, outside the formal negotiations.

Particular attention to the size and composition of the negotiating team should be given in the following circumstances:[35]

- Complex negotiations that require a diversity of knowledge, abilities, or expertise. Here it may be necessary to add people with specialized skills or expertise (e.g., design engineers).
- Negotiations that include significant potential for especially creative solutions. Research suggests that effective teams generate more integrative and creative solutions than sole negotiators. In negotiating a sales-promotion contract, for example, different members from the advertising department might be included (e.g., creative copywriters).
- Negotiations where different internal constituencies should be represented at the table. In some government negotiations conducted internationally, it is helpful to have members of the executive and legislative branches present, as both must ultimately approve the deal.
- Environments where a large team will be perceived as reflecting strength and going it alone will be perceived as a weakness.

How to Negotiate as a Team

The first requirement is to determine the personnel who will add value to the team and to secure their services with their commitment to devote the time and effort needed to make the negotiation a success. The second requirement is to ensure that the team will work cohesively, avoiding conflicting signals or inadvertently working at cross-purposes. Effective team negotiations require a great deal of coordination before the negotiation is actually begun, along with a thorough grasp of the strategy to be followed. Finally, it is important to prepare individuals for the roles each is to play. There should be a team leader, with someone else being the substantive expert or the "numbers person." Team members should also have a clear prior knowledge of how and where they should engage in the negotiation itself, not leaving this to chance or based on "follow the leader."

Pay Attention to Contract Details

Export Development Canada gives a timely warning not to get too excited about obtaining an overseas order: it is important to remain clear-headed about getting the terms and conditions of the deal right. Some aspects of the deal might go wrong later, so this protects the company's interests in the future. The Global Marketplace 16.6 pursues this theme through a paper reproduced from EDC publications.

The Meaning of Agreements

Eventually the negotiation will reach what is hoped will be a successful conclusion. However, what constitutes a final agreement will vary from one market to another. In many parts of the world, legal contracts are still not needed; as a matter of fact, reference to legal counsel may indicate that the relationship is in trouble. For the Chinese, the written agreement exists mostly for the convenience of their Western partners and represents an agenda on which to base the development of the relationship.[36]

When a verbal agreement is reached, it is critical that both parties leave with a clear understanding of what they have agreed to. In the case of large-scale projects, details must be explored and spelled out. In contracts that call for cooperative efforts, the responsibilities of each partner must be clearly specified. Otherwise, obligations that were anticipated to be the duty of one contracting party may result in costs to another. For example, foreign principal contractors may be held responsible for delays that have been caused by the inability of local subcontractors (whose use might be a requisite of the client) to deliver on schedule.

The Global Marketplace 16.6 gives some "do's and don'ts" and some "how to's" of contract negotiation abroad. This is a reminder that, despite the importance of cultural factors, some very "hard" issues need to be thought about in overseas negotiations. It is one thing to have determined how to work well with a negotiating partner, another to be sure that you have an absolutely solid, reliable contract backing you up, in particular one that meets the firm's profit and other objectives. This can be illustrated by citing the case of distributor contracts, the most common type for Canadian companies beginning their international expansion (see In More Detail 16.1: The Case of Distributors' Contracts). (Other contracts are important too, of course, for example, licensing and joint-venture contracts, the latter illustrating the hard issues mentioned above. For instance, the company considering a joint venture needs to balance carefully the precise areas of responsibility of each party and be careful not to give away more than intended. Moreover, it will be necessary to determine the value of one's own assets and the assets of the potential partner as a basis for assessing how to increase one's assets' value in the negotiation).

Success Factors in Global Negotiations

Based on the material discussed in this chapter, it should be clear that successful negotiation outcomes will depend on a variety of factors, for example, cultural sensitivity, good preparation, knowledge of the country, clear company objectives, knowledge of the Canadian culture, and so on. Success will also flow from the successful implementation of sound strategy and tactics, exemplified below. The list that follows does not claim to be exhaustive, nor does it attempt an importance ranking, but a 10-point checklist of success factors might be built along the following lines:

1. Study the contextual environments, that is, the political, economic, institutional-legal, and cultural systems that can affect the process and outcome of negotiations. Be ready to study in detail the elements of the country's culture that will most influence the negotia-

The Global MARKETPLACE 16.6

Don't Contract Yourself into a Corner

by **Suzanne Morris,** *Vice-President, Small Business Services, Export Development Canada*

In the excitement of getting a new order from a foreign customer, it is important to remain clear-headed about getting the terms and conditions of the deal right. This will protect your interests if some aspect of the deal goes wrong later on. So, whether you negotiate directly with your buyer, or hire a local representative, be sure to fully understand all elements of the contract of sale and identify any aspects that might affect your business in the future.

At a minimum, the following key terms should be spelled out:

- the legal entities entering into the contract
- the contract's period of validity, completion date, and other related conditions
- the goods or services to be provided, their purchase price, and payment terms
- any warranty and/or maintenance terms and conditions
- the party responsible for obtaining any import/export licences
- any performance security requirements such as bank letters of guarantee or surety bonds
- any remedies available if the buyer defaults or cancels
- the provisions for independent mediation or arbitration to resolve disputes, and the jurisdiction where this would take place

Obviously all parties to the contract have to sign it. If possible, before you do so, have the document reviewed by a lawyer who understands the laws of your buyer's country.

Whether you are selling in industrialized or developing markets, here are some contract precautions to bear in mind.

Leave some wiggle room: While signing a contract usually ends the negotiations in Canada, in some countries this simply means that you and the buyer have agreed to a framework to do business. Some concessions may still be considered "negotiable" by the foreign buyer. If you don't realize this, you may end up including all that you can afford to give in the contract, while the buyer is still expecting some added benefits. A reputable local representative can help you to avoid such problems and allow you to leave some room to manoeuvre. You should also ensure that the party who is responsible for payment signs the contract—not just an agent working on the buyer's behalf. Otherwise, you would have no written evidence that the buyer owes you the money and you could have trouble getting paid.

Setting the payment terms: Small-to-medium-sized exporters often obtain a down payment of at least 15 percent of the contract amount, either on signing or within 30 days after signing. The balance is normally paid on shipment of goods or completion of services. There are many variations of this, and you'll have to decide what you can accept. When making the decision, consider their experience with the buyer and market, and your working capital requirements. While offering payment terms can make your business more competitive, it can also leave you cash strapped and at risk of not getting paid. Accounts receivable insurance may be able to help with some of your cash requirements and protect against credit losses if the buyer can't or won't pay you.

Bonding without breaking: In some industry sectors, such as construction and engineering, foreign buyers require exporters to provide financial security to back their commitments at both the contract's bid and performance stage. This security can be an on-demand bank letter of guarantee, a standby letter of credit, or a surety performance bond. In all cases, suppliers should make sure the contract clearly stipulates their performance obligations and the conditions under which their buyer can make a valid call for non-performance. Contract bonding and insurance programs can help you obtain the required bonds or guarantees without restricting your working capital, by providing support to your bank or surety company that issues these products.

These and other contract precautions will help ensure that your export experience is rewarding and trouble-free.

Source: Toby Herscovitch, Export Development Canada, "Don't Contract Yourself into a Corner," *EDC Publications* (January 2005). Reprinted with permission.

In More Detail 16.1

THE CASE OF DISTIBUTORS' CONTRACTS

In the case of distributors' contracts, generally the manufacturer or service provider will provide the initial contract, which may of course be drawn up deliberately to reflect the manufacturer's best interests. If this is so, the distributor can be expected to object and try to remove or alter at least some of the contract provisions. The manufacturer or service provider may adopt different strategies for approaching the negotiating situation and resolving differences. For example, it may be decided to make an offer at the outset and remain firm on it throughout. Another strategy involves delaying tactics, the objective being to "wear down" one's opponent. However, it is more likely that the negotiation will involve some kind of compromise on both sides.

Here is an approach favoured by some companies when negotiating distributor contracts:

1. Start fairly aggressively, taking a position strongly favouring your company.
2. Negotiate away items of little concern.
3. Hold strongly to items of particular concern.

The decision whether to initiate a contract negotiation at all will depend critically on whether the envisaged relationship is judged likely to yield the benefits that the service provider wants. Price issues, including the margin to be enjoyed by the distributor, are critical, because these will determine profitability levels. The manufacturer needs to work through two key issues: what is the lowest acceptable price to the company, and what is the lowest price and margin the distributor is likely to accept? Then it can be decided which price range should be proposed to initiate the negotiation.

The firm's negotiating stance with respect to price will reflect their price objectives. For example, the objective may be rapid cost recovery because the foreign market is thought to be volatile. The negotiator might then hold firm for a higher than usual price. Or the objective may be a "satisfactory" rate of return on capital (more flexible bargaining position), or a desire for speedy market share improvement (low price bargaining position). None of this background need be revealed to the prospective distributor, of course, but one can see how much work and strategic thinking will be needed as a precursor to the negotiation.

It is vital to recognize how detailed a distributor contract can be. It is little wonder that much experience and qualified legal help are needed to perform the task successfully. Understanding the theoretical steps to follow can only be a beginning. Among the items that will typically be negotiated are the following:

- price level and margins
- warranties
- claims against the company
- sales promotion
- distributor performance targets
- after-market support
- safety standards
- handling customer complaints
- confidentiality of company information
- use of trademarks
- termination of contract (rights of parties)

Disagreement—major or minor—can arise at any point. For example, the manufacturer may favour a one-year initial term, the distributor two; the manufacturer may favour 30 days notice of price changes, the distributor 90 days, and so on. Decisions on the extent of exclusivity, if any, can also be contentious. This again emphasizes the need for a legal input to the negotiation, which many Canadian SMEs may not be able to provide readily. However, the existence of many competent law firms in the country able to conduct this type of work eases the situation.

tion: verbal and nonverbal communication, the country's ethical standards, values, and religion.

2. Prepare meticulously for the negotiation, gathering as much information as possible about the negotiating partner, including motives and criteria. Build and nurture relationships with the partner, particularly the key decision makers.
3. Pay close attention to the membership of the negotiating team. Recognize that some negotiations call for a larger team than others. Where possible, include a bilingual member on the team. Make sure that all important areas of expertise are represented on the team.

4. Establish your negotiating strategy in advance.
5. Strategically prepare the roles each team member is to play. Someone should take the lead. Another member might be the substantive expert or the "numbers" person. Decide how and where team members should engage during the negotiation. Do not play follow the leader.
6. Avoid insisting on answers and an outcome because this may be seen as a threat by negotiating partners abroad. In some markets, negotiations are seen as a means of establishing long-term commercial relations, not as an event with winners and losers. Confrontations are to be avoided because minds cannot be changed at the negotiation table; this has to be done informally. Face is an important concept throughout the Far East.
7. Avoid concessions until all issues have been discussed, so as to preclude the possibility of granting unnecessary benefits to the negotiation partners. Concessions traditionally come at the end of bargaining. This is especially true in terms of price negotiations. If price is agreed on too quickly, the counterpart may want to insist on too many inclusions for that price.
8. Do not forget to study apparently trivial things, such as the country's popular culture (attitudes to sport, film stars, national pastimes).
9. Listen, be observant, be flexible, ask probing questions, and be patient—allow matters to progress at their own pace.
10. Above all, know yourself and your heritage.

Summary

One-on-one negotiations are important because of growing interdependencies in the global marketing arena, and because of the increased pressure on firms to think globally. Good negotiation skills are needed at almost every phase of a firm's international operations, and the resulting need for negotiating competence will increase as Canada's global trade expands.

The two main dangers faced by international negotiators are parochialism (seeing things mainly from one's own or a country's point of view) and stereotyping (making positive or negative generalizations about individuals or groups). In a face-to-face situation, what is needed is sensitivity to others' points of view and a willingness to adjust behaviour to establish a productive rapport. Employing the Internet for negotiation tasks is a growing trend, but its use has limitations because the face-to-face aspect is missing and trust is therefore difficult to build.

The process of international negotiation can be divided into a series of stages, the length of each varying greatly by culture. In the actual negotiating situation, the approach used will depend on the cultural background and business traditions prevailing in different countries, as well as the strategy it is decided to adopt. Cultural factors influence negotiations through different cultural elements such as verbal and nonverbal communications, dress and etiquette, ethical standards, values, and religion.

Preparing to negotiate involves a four-stage process: knowing your culture, knowing the partner's culture, knowing the partner's likely tactics, and determining the composition of the negotiating team. Contract negotiation including price bargaining is a complex undertaking that will likely demand assistance from legal specialists. Successful negotiation depends on a number of factors that are summarized at the conclusion of the chapter.

Key Terms

competitive and collaborative approaches (p. 585)
confrontation (p. 588)
harmony (p. 590)
negotiating styles (p. 587)
nonverbal communications (p. 588)
parochialism (p. 583)
stereotyping (p. 583)
Tri-State (p. 593)
verbal communications (p. 587)

Questions for Discussion

1. Discuss the opinion that because nonverbal communications by negotiating partners cannot be dealt with directly, they should be ignored.
2. Give your opinion of the following statement: "Lack of foreign-language skills puts Canadian negotiators at a disadvantage."

3. You arrive to conduct a negotiation in Shanghai and discover you are outnumbered three to one. In addition to its regional vice president, the other side includes a technical expert and an administrative assistant whose sole purpose is to take notes. What should you do? What will you do in future?
4. What are the main ways in which culture influences the conduct of a negotiation?
5. Why is knowledge of a country's geography and history important to a negotiator?
6. Some people believe that in negotiations you should "go with the flow." Yet others advocate a careful determination of what strategy to follow. Can you reconcile these points of view?

Internet Exercises

1. One way to improve your negotiating skills is to understand how foreign people perceive Canadians. Go to **http://international.monster.ca/8880_en-CA_p1.asp** and read the article "Canadian Business Culture." Do you think the writer fairly represents how Canadian people actually behave?
2. A Canadian construction company is concerned about the possible impact of corrupt practices on their international contracts. The chief executive officer wants to establish a series of guidelines to help the company identify and deal with potential or real problems. You are asked to provide some input. Go to **http://www.transparency.org** and follow the links to the International Version of the Anti-Corruption Handbook. Consult the section at the end of the handbook dealing with possible actions that companies can take. Prepare a list of key factors for the company's consideration.

Recommended Readings

Agarwall, Milind R., Cavusgil, S. Tamer, and Pervez N. Ghauri. *Doing Business in Emerging Markets: Entry and Negotiation Strategies.* New York: Sage Publications, 2002.

Ambler, Tim, and Morgen Witzel. *Doing Business in China.* 2nd ed. London: RoutledgeCurzon, 2004.

Brake, T., D. Medina Walker, and T. Walker. *Doing Business Internationally: The Guide to Cross-Cultural Success.* Burr Ridge, IL: Irwin Professional Publishing, 1995.

Centre for Intercultural Learning E-thologies, **http://www.e-thologies.com/default.asp** (a collection of general and cultural information on countries around the world).

Ghauri, Pervez N., and Jean-Claude Usunier. *International Business Negotiations.* 2nd ed. Boston: Pergamon, 2003.

Hooker, John, *Working across Cultures.* Stanford, CA: Stanford Business Books, 2003.

Morrison, Terri, Wayne A. Conaway, and George A. Borden. *Kiss, Bow or Shake Hands: How to Do Business in 60 Countries.* Holbrook, MA: Bob Adams, 1994.

O'Hara-Devereaux, Mary, and Robert Johansen. *Globalwork: Bridging Distance, Culture, and Time.* San Francisco: Jossey-Bass, 1994.

Salacuse, Jeswald W. *The Global Negotiator: Making, Managing and Mending Deals Around the World in the 21st Century.* London: Palgrave Macmillan, 2003.

Notes

1. John L. Graham and Persa Economou, "Introduction to the Symposium on International Business Negotiations," *Journal of International Business Studies* 29, no. 4 (1998): 661–63.
2. Terence Brake, Danielle Walker, and Thomas Walker, *Doing Business Internationally: The Guide to Cross-Cultural Success* (New York: McGraw-Hill Trade, 1994), chaps. 1 and 2.
3. Courtney Fingan, "Table Manners," *Global Business*, July 2000, 48–52.
4. Nurit Zaidman, "Stereotypes of International Managers: Content and Impact on Business Interactions," *Group and Organization Management* 25 (March 2000): 45–66.
5. Stephen E. Weiss, "Negotiating with the Romans: Part I," *Sloan Management Review* 36 (Spring 1994): 85–99.
6. Arnold Pachtman, "Getting to 'Hao!'" *International Business*, July–August 1998, 24–26.
7. Claude Cellich, "FAQ ... About Business Negotiations on the Internet," *International Trade Forum* 15, no. 1 (2001): 10–11.
8. Pervez N. Ghauri, "Guidelines for International Business Negotiations," *International Marketing Review* 4 (Autumn 1986): 72–82.
9. "Negotiating in Europe," *Hemispheres*, July 1994, 43–47.

10. Virginia J. Rehberg, "Kuwait: Reality Sets In," *Export Today* 7 (December 1991): 56–58.

11. Catherine H. Tinsley and Madan M. Pillutla, "Negotiating in the United States and Hong Kong," *Journal of International Business Studies* 29, no. 4 (1998): 711–28.

12. Claude Cellich, "Negotiations for Export Business: Elements for Success," *International Trade Forum* 9, no. 4 (1995): 20–27.

13. Jackie Mayfield, Milton Mayfield, Drew Martin, and Paul Herbig, "How Location Impacts International Business Negotiations," *Review of Business* 19 (Winter 1998): 21–24.

14. "'Stay-at-Home' Careers?" *Global Business,* January 2001, 62.

15. Rosalie L. Tung, "International Business Negotiations," in *International Encyclopedia of Business and Management,* ed. Malcolm Warner (London: Thomson International Business Press, 1996), 3:2281–97.

16. E.T. Hall and M. Hall, *Hidden Differences: Doing Business with the Japanese* (Garden City, NY: Anchor Press, 1987).

17. R.J. Ballon, "Japan: The Government-Business Relationship," in *Strategic Management in the United States and Japan: A Comparative Analysis,* ed. R.L. Tung (Cambridge, MA: Ballinger, 1986).

18. Dale Morris, "Gearing up in Brazil," *Exportwise,* Fall 2006, 16–21.

19. Kathy Schmidt, "How to Speak So You're Open to Interpretation," *Presentations* 13 (December 1999): 126–27.

20. Richard D. Lewis, *When Cultures Collide* (London: Nicholas Brealey Publishing, 2000), chap. 17.

21. H.F. Van Zandt, "How to Negotiate in Japan," *Harvard Business Review* 25 (November–December 1970): 45–56.

22. Ann Marie Sabath, *International Business Etiquette,* **http://www.worldroom.com** (accessed November 24, 2006).

23. Sabath, op. cit.

24. Boye de Mente, *Chinese Etiquette and Ethics in Business* (Lincolnwood, IL: NTC, 1989).

25. Industry Canada, *The Cross-Cultural Marketing Edge,* **http://www.strategis.ic.gc.ca** (accessed October 20, 2006).

26. B.A. Ramundo, *Effective Negotiation: A Guide to Dialogue Management and Control* (New York: Quorum Books, 1992).

27. Frank L. Acuff, "Just Call Me Mr. Ishmael," *Export Today* 11 (July 1995): 14–15.

28. Andrea Kirby, "Doing Business in Asia," *Credit Management,* October 2002, 24–25.

29. Robert Hughes, *The Fatal Shore* (New York: Alfred A. Knopf, 1987).

30. Dennis Jones and Sandi Jones, "New York and the Tri-State Area," *Exportwise,* Fall 2006, 26–27.

31. J. Hayes, *Interpersonal Skills: Goal-Directed Behaviour at Work* (London: Routledge, 1991).

32. Hayes, op. cit.

33. Sally Stewart and Charles F. Keown, "Talking with the Dragon: Negotiating in the People's Republic of China," *Columbia Journal of World Business* 24 (Fall 1989): 68–72.

34. Hokey Min and William P. Galle, "International Negotiation Strategies of U.S. Purchasing Professionals," *International Journal of Purchasing and Materials Management* 29 (Summer 1993): 41–53.

35. Marty Latz, "Negotiating as a Team Requires Strategic Planning," *The Business Journal of Phoenix,* May 6, 2005, 1–3.

36. Y.H. Wong and Thomas K. Leung, *Guanxi: Relationship Marketing in a Chinese Context* (Binghampton, NY: Haworth Press, 2001), chap. 3.

Importing Industry Specific Software: How American Are Canadians?

In 1997, Gudrun Curri, the Registrar at Dalhousie University in Halifax, Nova Scotia, Canada stared out of the window of her office watching students on the lawn playing frisbee. She had just been informed that the implementation problem first identified at the last meeting with the software vendor had been confirmed. The Student Information System (SIS) from SCT, a major US educational software company, did not allow a student to register in year-based and term-based courses in the same registration period. As many students in the Faculties of Arts and Social Sciences and of Science took both types of courses at the same time, Curri knew that this was a crucial issue for the teaching faculty of the University with the potential to jeopardize the entire SIS implementation project. Time to resolve the issue was also running out as the current system was not Y2K compliant. In other words, it would not operate beyond December 31, 1999. Moreover, the former VP-Academic, who had been the academic sponsor of the project, had left the university and an interim replacement had been appointed.

Background

Dalhousie University is one of the oldest universities in Canada. It provides a wide range of programmes from undergraduate and professional to doctoral level in a dozen faculties. Over 12,500 students are enrolled in 182 academic programmes taught by over 1500 full- and part-time faculty members and supported by 1200 administrative and clerical staff. The university's alumni, who play professional and community leadership roles across Canada, are over 60,000 strong.

This case has been prepared by Dr. Gudrun Curri with the assistance of Virginia Lee, Director, Business Process and Integration, both of Dalhousie University, as a basis for classroom discussion rather than to illustrate effective or ineffective handling of an administrative situation. The financial assistance of the Trade, Education and Skills Development funding program under the Atlantic Trade and Investment Partnership is gratefully acknowledged.

In 1993, the Administrative Computing Services Group at Dalhousie began to rewrite its home-grown SIS to be Y2K compliant. The new system was scheduled to be completed within 18 months and was intended to take advantage of new technologies. Everyone was very excited at the opportunity. By the beginning of 1995, it was determined that the plan was too optimistic. Dalhousie did not have the technical resources needed to complete a project of this magnitude on time. At this point Dalhousie attempted to partner with another university to develop a system that could be used by both institutions. This initiative was also unsuccessful.

After these two failed attempts to develop a new student information system in-house, the Vice-President Finance and Administration in 1995 charged the Executive Director of University Computing and Information Services (UCIS), who was responsible for Administrative Computing, to investigate the comparative benefits of buying or building a Y2K compliant student information system. The Executive Director, working with the Registrar, the Directors of Finance, Human Resources, and Alumni Services devoted the next twelve months to investigating the relative merits of developing a stand-alone SIS or acquiring a system suite which would service all four units, a U.S. approach to integrated university information management.

Despite considerable objections from the Finance Department which had only recently undergone a major system upgrade, the Vice-President Finance and Administration accepted the recommendation of this group that it would be in the long-term best interest of the university to adopt an integrated approach for all its administrative systems rather than to replace its SIS with a stand-alone system. As a result, the scope, the risk, the significance, and the cost of the project increased significantly because the implementation now included SIS, Finance, Human Resources, and Alumni Development modules. Since the current SIS was the only system known to be not Y2K compliant, its replacement was therefore most urgent. Curri, as custodian of the SIS, was charged with the task of implementing the new SIS software module in accordance with Dalhousie's academic rules and processes.

Shortly after the build-or-buy investigation began, Dalhousie University joined the Consortium of Halifax Universities to explore the possibility of sharing one common administrative information system. A Selection Committee was established with representatives from each institution for each module to determine if different software requirements existed among the institutions and how and whether they could be accommodated. As part of the SIS review by the Selection Committee, Curri raised with her registrarial colleagues Dalhousie's concern about anticipated opposition from faculty members to changing current procedures for the purpose of meeting new system requirements. There is a strong conviction among academics that systems should not dictate process and that academic concerns alone should determine the rules on GPA, Dean's list, entrance and in-course scholarships, degree structure, etc. On the other hand, the then Vice-President Academic, who was the academic sponsor of the project, felt that the introduction of the new system would be a good opportunity for Dalhousie University to simplify many of its academic and business processes using the introduction of new technology to drive change. It was understood that the Vice-President Academic would champion the process of review and reform of academic regulations and processes in the face of possible opposition from faculty members.

The Selection Process

In 1996, with the assistance of a national Canadian consulting firm, Deloitte and Touche, two U.S. software vendors, SCT and Datatel, were identified as offering integrated administrative information system suites that appeared to meet most of the common requirements for SIS, Finance, Human Resources, and Alumni. Each institution reviewed the suites paying special attention to the modules in terms of its own requirements. As both products were similar with respect to meeting the basic requirements of the institutions, site visits to the U.S. headquarters of both vendors were arranged.

Due to the way Dalhousie, like most other Canadian universities, delivered academic programs to students, it had a list of questions regarding the SIS module that were critical in the selection decision. Specifically, Curri asked *How does the software handle student registrations of courses/classes with different durations? Can students register by term? By year?* The SCT consultant answered without hesitation, *Yes, you can register students for each of these, as well as by weeks, even days.*

Having attended many American Registrars' conferences over the years, Curri knew that students in U.S. universities typically registered for one semester at a time (four or three months) whereas students in most Canadian universities register for the full academic year. During one academic year a student can register for eight month courses and/or for four month courses. Unlike the US universities, where the length of courses is uniform within programmes, courses in Canadian universities may differ in length within the same program. When Curri asked the question, she wanted to make sure that a student could enroll in both types of courses at the same time. From her Canadian perspective, Curri had not perceived a need to add the phrase 'within the same academic year' because to her that was a given. Nor did it occur to her to use the American term 'semester' because, throughout the negotiation process with SCT, common terminology had not been an issue. It appeared that both parties were speaking the same language. The consultant's assurance and the fact that two other Canadian universities had previously selected the product gave additional confidence in the product's ability to accommodate simultaneous registration in courses of different duration.

As part of the due diligence process, the SIS subcommittee of the Selection Committee consulted both these Canadian universities and learned that one had abandoned the Banner project and the other had implemented it but had customized many of its processes. A site visit to the latter was arranged but the issue of students registering in courses of different lengths did not surface in the discussions about customization.

Upon completion of the selection process, the committee summarized its findings:

> The task of determining which of the two systems satisfies our needs better is not easy. While there have been a number of communications with vendors, site visits, teleconference and video conference calls with other institutions using the software, specifically identifying which product 'gives a better fit' to our institution is difficult. Both products offer roughly the same features and it is estimated that either system would satisfy roughly 80% of requirements.
>
> In today's marketplace, the ease of access to information is paramount. We need to associate ourselves with a vendor who has vision for the future, who is looking at higher education from the perspective of the future student market, new methods of class delivery, ease of access by students, faculty and staff, and the latest technologies. We believe SCT has this progressive nature, has shown it in their product today and their aims for the future.

The Purchase Decision

In late 1996, members of the University Consortium discussed the Selection Committee's report but could not agree on a recommendation to purchase SCT Banner.

However, Dalhousie was facing the Y2K deadline for its SIS and could not afford to wait for the Consortium to arrive at a joint decision.

Dalhousie concluded that it needed a robust system that could handle many different faculties, schools, programmes and academic terms. According to SCT, its product, Banner, met these requirements although it did not offer all functionalities currently in use at Dalhousie. Moreover, SCT stated that it was committed to enter the Canadian Market in a serious way and that it would do whatever was necessary to achieve its goal.

Using the evaluation results of the Dalhousie team, the university decided to capitalize on the opportunity to force the re-engineering of academic administration processes in order to take advantage of the efficiencies of new technology. In December 1996, following a high-level overview presentation to the Faculties by the vendor, Dalhousie made the decision to purchase SCT Banner and to implement it without customization.

The Implementation Plan

With little time to spare and following SCT's advice during a half day workshop which had been reduced, at the insistence of the university executive, from the original three days, the broad-based Project Steering Committee was charged with overall planning and implementation. As the current SIS was not Y2K compliant and therefore most at risk, the committee agreed that the student information system module had top priority. Curri was instructed to proceed with the planning, analysis, and implementation of the functional processes provided by the new system.

In June 1997, the University President announced the implementation plan for Banner at a special meeting of Deans, Directors, and Chairs. He explained that the current SIS would not function effective January 1, 2000 and the university had decided that, to save time and cost, it would buy a proven U.S. product rather than build one. He outlined the advantages of buying an integrated administrative information system that had been successfully implemented in many U.S. colleges and universities and urged all faculties, schools and departments to participate fully. He emphasized the need for changing current procedures, which were often cumbersome, error prone, and costly to maintain.

He described the implementation schedule and process. He concluded with a vision of Dalhousie as a leader in adopting new technology to provide better service to students, faculty, and administration.

The Crisis

Having reviewed the events of the last four years, Curri came back to the following questions: Why did the academic term issue come up now when SCT had confirmed that there was no problem with students registering in courses of different length? Why did Deloitte and Touche, a Canadian consulting company, not identify this problem in its search for possible software products in the U.S.? Did the vendor lie to me? Why did I not pick up on the fact that SCT and I were not speaking the same language although we were using the same terminology/words? Did I focus too much on the new technology and not enough on Dalhousie's academic requirements and culture? Was I too sure that the university would use technology to make major changes to become more efficient in its administrative academic processes? What did I miss despite over 20 years registrarial experience in two major Canadian universities?

Curri requested an emergency meeting with the Project Steering Committee to discuss the crisis and to start searching for solutions. With only 18 months left to install and test the new SIS in order to admit and register students for the 1999/2000 academic year, she knew a solution had to be found fast. Moreover, because Dalhousie had decided to implement an off-the-shelf product, she was not sure if a technical solution was feasible in the time available. What was the likelihood that faculty members would accept teaching their year-long courses as two-term courses because the new information system could not handle the former? Little did Curri anticipate that within a matter of weeks the crisis would be exacerbated by the departure of the Vice-President Academic, the champion of re-engineering academic business processes, and the appointment of an interim acting Vice-President Academic. The problem Curri was facing would not be easily solved. There was much at stake for the university in terms of its academic culture and legal reporting requirements. Reviewing all the events leading to this moment, Curri concluded that, when importing software from the U.S., performing due diligence is as much a cultural and language issue as a technical one.

Teleflex Canada: A Culture of Innovation

Teleflex Canada, a division of Teleflex Inc., manufactured a range of products, including marine hydraulic steering systems, trim components for marine propulsion, heating equipment for both the truck and bus industries, a range of proprietary fluid controls, and field cookstoves for the U.S. Army. Over the past 30 years, Teleflex Canada grew from sales of a few million dollars to more than $160 million in 2004. The company has a reputation as a world leader in the design and manufacture of hydraulic and thermal technology products. Within Teleflex Canada there was a consensus that continual innovation in product design, manufacturing, and marketing was critical to the success of the organization.

In 2005, Teleflex Canada executives were faced with various questions: Would size inhibit the ability to innovate? Would increased corporate centralization at Teleflex Inc. impact Teleflex Canada's ability to respond quickly to new market opportunities? At the Teleflex Inc. corporate level, different questions were being asked: Could the culture of innovation in Teleflex Canada be transferred to other parts of the company? What was the appropriate level of corporate support and control necessary to foster innovation and high performance at Teleflex Canada and at other Teleflex business units?

Teleflex Inc.

Teleflex Inc., a diversified manufacturing company, was headquartered in Limerick, Pennsylvania, just outside Philadelphia. The company had three principal business segments: Commercial, Medical, and Aerospace.

Commercial

The Commercial segment manufactured various products for automotive, marine, and industrial markets, including manual and automatic gearshift systems; transmission guide controls; mechanical and hydraulic steering systems; vehicle pedal systems; heavy-duty cables; hoisting and rigging equipment for oil drilling and other industrial markets; mobile auxiliary power units used for heating and climate control in heavy-duty trucks, industrial vehicles, and locomotives; and fluid management products for automobiles and pleasure boats.

Medical

The Medical segment manufactured health care supply and surgical devices including anesthesiology devices, sutures, ligation solutions, chest drainage systems, and high-quality surgical and orthopedic instruments.

Aerospace

The Aerospace segment manufactured products for the commercial and military aerospace, power generation, and industrial turbine machinery markets. Aerospace businesses provided repair products and services for flight and ground-based turbine engines; manufactured precision-machined components and cargo-handling systems; and provided advanced engine surface treatments. Products in the Commercial segment were generally produced in higher unit volumes than that of the company's other two segments.

In the fiscal year ended December 31, 2004, Teleflex's consolidated sales were $2.49 billion, with 48% coming from the Commercial segment, while Medical and Aerospace represented 30% and 22%, respectively. With approximately 21,000 employees and major operations in more than 70 locations worldwide, Teleflex Inc. operations were highly decentralized, with dozens of small profit centers and a corporate office consisting of a few senior executives and support staff. A few years ago, a major effort was begun to redefine Teleflex as a unified operating company that shared people, products, and processes across divisions and business units. The objective of the reorganization was to establish some common operational standards to improve productivity. Not surprisingly, in a company where autonomy had always been the hallmark of business unit activity, increased efforts at standardization, consolidation, and sharing resources were met with some managerial resistance at the business unit level.

Teleflex Canada

Teleflex Canada, based in Richmond, British Columbia, in the metropolitan Vancouver area, had been one of the best performing business units within Teleflex for several decades. Through internal development, licensing, and acquisition, its growth rate averaged 20% per year for 25 years. Total sales in 2004 were about $160 million. Teleflex Canada designed and produced a variety of products utilizing hydraulic and thermal technologies.

Marine and Industrial Hydraulic Systems

Teleflex Canada was created in 1974 when Teleflex Inc. purchased part of Capilano Engineering, a small machine shop in Vancouver that was developing hydraulic steering systems for boats. At that time, another Teleflex unit was producing marine steering systems with mechanical cable steering. Teleflex management knew that as marine engines got larger and more powerful, mechanical steering would become obsolete because it could no longer provide the necessary comfort and safety.

Teleflex Canada's hydraulic steering systems—SeaStar, SeaStar Pro, and BayStar—were designed to enable more comfortable control of pleasure boats. These products fundamentally changed the marine steering industry. In 2004 Teleflex Canada sold more than 100,000 SeaStar systems, an increase of more than 30% over the previous year (retail prices for the higher-end products ranged from about $1,200 to $1,500 per system, while lower-end systems were about $250). The company had an estimated 95% market share in North America and 50% share in markets outside the continent. Teleflex Canada's steering products were usually among the highest-priced products available in the marketplace.

The marine steering industry had two main market segments. One segment included stern drive engine companies like Volvo Penta that would purchase a private label steering system and integrate it with their engine to provide a complete steering and controls package to boat builders. A second segment was the marine distribution and dealer network that sold Teleflex-branded products to boat companies and individual boat owners. Sales of marine products were split almost equally between original equipment manufacturers like Volvo Penta and aftermarket dealers.

In addition to steering systems, Teleflex Canada also produced components for marine engine companies like Bombardier and Volvo Penta. These products were referred to as industrial actuation systems.

Energy

Teleflex Canada was successful in applying its boat-based technology to the needs of other markets. In 1985 Teleflex Canada began licensing an engine governor technology for large diesel trucks. In 1990 an auxiliary heater business for large trucks and buses was purchased from Cummins, which led to the development of the ProHeat vehicle heater product line. The heater technology was adapted in 1997 to create cookstoves, called modern burner units (MBUs), for use in army field kitchens. A major contract was signed with the U.S. military for the production of MBUs. By 1999 Teleflex was producing 10,000 MBUs per year for military purposes.

Innovation, Technology, and Product Development

Teleflex Canada innovation focused on product and market development that solved customer problems or created new markets. Much of Teleflex Canada's success has come about because a demand was identified for new products in niche markets that were ready for a change in technology. As explained by a Teleflex Canada executive:

> Our fundamental belief is that we don't use any technology that is not proven. We call ourselves product developers. We will not develop any technology that cannot be robust and highly reliable with a low repair requirement. We take existing technology and tweak it to make it better.... We usually don't invent anything radically new (although sometimes new technology had to be invented to solve a customer's problem). We are a company that has been innovative in applications engineering. We focus on products we know we can sell because we are close to the market and know the customers.... Innovation at Teleflex Canada involves three questions:
>
> 1. How do we exploit existing technology?
> 2. How do we develop reliable and robust products from that technology?
> 3. How do we penetrate and dominate some market niche with that product?
>
> For example, we are looking for new areas where we can use electro-hydraulic applications. There are other markets where this technology could work, such as dental chairs and hospital beds or suspensions systems for lawn and garden equipment. These are markets that will pay a premium for a customer-built system using hydraulics.

The next sections discuss some products development activities at Teleflex Canada.

SeaStar Development

When Teleflex Inc. acquired Capilano Engineering, the intent was to expand into new markets. At that time, the company was producing a heavy-duty commercial hydraulic steering system. In 1978 Teleflex Canada introduced Syten, the world's first low-cost hydraulic system for the mass pleasure-boat market. Cost was a big factor because Syten competed against low-priced mechanical steering systems. Unfortunately, Syten's plastic parts deteriorated when used beyond their mechanical capability, leading to unsatisfied customers and a risk that Teleflex Canada would lose its position in hydraulic steering. At that time, Teleflex Canada had about 10% of the hydraulic steering market (the largest competitor had a share of about 80%).

Teleflex Canada developed a new hydraulic steering system called SeaStar, which was introduced in 1984. SeaStar became the leading product on the market. In 1989 the new SeaStar was introduced. The mandate for the development team was smaller size to expand the potential market, lower cost, and better performance. Using some patented technology (a floating spigot), the new Seastar was 30% cheaper to produce, 18% more efficient, and sold at the same price as the older model. In 1993 Seastar Pro was introduced and was very successful in the Bass boat market where performance was the primary purchase criterion. BayStar, introduced in 2002 for the lower-end market, was very successful (although it cannibalized sales of a mechanical steering system produced by another Teleflex division).

Again, a Teleflex Canada executive explains:

> To regain our reputation in the marketplace, we had to come out with an overkill approach with the product. We developed a much more sophisticated and rugged all-metal system, which became SeaStar. This decision involved heated internal debates because the development costs were substantial. This required a lot of trust from Bim Black (Teleflex Inc. Chairman and former CEO). He was willing to take some risk in the investment. These were a lot of skeptics. But, the hydraulics technology was well-proven and being used in automotive systems. We were applying existing technology to a customized marketplace. From a technology perspective, the risk was not high. From a market point of view, we knew that our current line of cables (from another Teleflex Inc. business unit) was not going to satisfy customers as boat engines got bigger and more difficult to steer.
>
> We have 35 patents but the technology was not earth-shattering. The marketplace wanted higher horsepower and more comfort, and we were able to convince people to change to hydraulics.... Harold (Copping, Teleflex Canada President at the time) kept a nice fence between corporate and Teleflex Canada. And, we were small enough to fall under the radar screen at corporate. For example, we were able to order some tooling without approval.
>
> When the development of SeaStar was done, the marine industry was going through a downturn. Our competitors were laying off engineers and trying to survive. We kept our engineers developing products. When we came out of the downturn, we had new products that allowed us to grow.
>
> There are two keys to the success of SeaStar over the years. One, we always kept innovating. Our competitors would copy our designs and in about six months we would have a better product on the market. Since our products were 30% to 40% better than the competition we could keep our margins up. As time went on, the performance gap narrowed. But, because we built scale economies through our size and innovated in manufacturing, we have the lowest cost. So, we have the lowest cost and the best performing product. Two, a lot of our success is through innovation on the shop floor to ensure that we had a cost-effective product. The corporation pushed us to use more advanced machine tools and to be more analytical. SeaStar involved innovation in technology, product development, marketing, and manufacturing processes that were developed at the shop floor level. The product designs were enhanced because of the manufacturing processes, some of which must be kept in-house because they are proprietary.
>
> Also, having a good product is only part of the story. You also need to sell the product. To me, selling is like being a farmer. You go out and spread some seeds, water them daily, and eventually they come to fruition. I always fought corporate—they kept telling me to close the deal. I was very patient. I was very generous with our product. I would give away our product and let them try it. I am out there constantly talking with customers, looking at the competition.
>
> Our competitors are getting better, but our market share makes it difficult for other companies to compete on cost. We continue to focus on being the best and never giving any customers an excuse to go looking elsewhere.... One day, all boats will steer as comfortably as cars. That has been my passion. To make that happen. I have never deviated from it.

Energy Product Development

ProHeat, an auxiliary power and climate control system for trucks and buses, was introduced in 1992.

> To get into heaters we bought a product line from Cummins Engine. Cummins was not successful with the product so we bought the remaining inventory. This got our foot in the door, and it is much easier to start a business when you have something to sell. When we did the deal with Cummins, we had already concluded that the product [the truck heater] was not any good. We did the deal anyway because it got us into a new market that we thought we could serve better with new products.
>
> We never actually produced any of the Cummins products, but we learned a lot about the market. There was a clear demand for a product that could be used to heat trucks and was more fuel-efficient than leaving the engine idling. We were able to figure out the type of product innovation

that was necessary and spent about two years bringing the product to market. The first truck heater was ProHeat in 1992. Once we had some success in the Canadian market, we looked to the U.S. market. We needed a different product because of air conditioning. Teleflex usually doesn't like to start from scratch so we looked around for a possible acquisition. We bought a small company in Ontario that had a product. That allowed us to get into the market.

We then took the truck heater to the transit bus market. We started talking to different city bus companies and were able to adapt our technology for the bus market. These were not huge leaps, and to us they seemed very obvious. We never say build it and they will come. We try to get the order first and then build the product. We start by selling concepts along with our credibility in the market.

The development of the truck heater, along with several other products, including a heater for tents used by the military, provided Teleflex Canada with a solid base of experience in combustion technology. This led to the development of the military cookstove called the MBU. The MBU used the same combustion technology as the truck heater and could be used as a block heater, passenger heat source, barbecue, or oven.

The MBU project started with an inventor who had built a prototype stove. The inventor was able to convince the U.S. Army to put the project out for bid on the specifications he had developed in his prototype. Harold Copping described how the military cookstove project got started:

We understood the military market. When we did our licensing deal for the tent heater, we had an understanding that we would not develop a cookstove. Eventually, we agreed to license the technology for the cookstove. I visited the military and made sure the funding was in place. I knew the U.S. Army liked the design, and I saw a huge opportunity for Teleflex. I saw this as a chance to back a winner and take a gamble. We put together a team of some of our best people to develop a working prototype. It was not a big risk because I knew that we had very good burner technology and I knew the Army liked the people and the design. We were in their good books because we had had great success with previous projects for them. We spent $500,000 and it worked out well. Our people improved the inventor's design and made it manufacturable and safer.

Another Teleflex executive added the following comments about product development:

To make these programs work, it started at the very top of Teleflex Inc. There were skunk works going on, but they were tolerated. When we were trying to diversity the business, Harold protected us from the operations mentality. For each of the key projects, we put a dedicated team together whose priority was not operations. For several programs we moved engineers out of the building to off-site locations. We wanted these engineers to worry about the development project, not the stuff that was in production. We wanted their full attention on the product development. There has to be a wall between development and existing operations. The next challenge is how to reintegrate the new business into operations and try to avoid the us-and-them attitude. Operations people like stability, and design engineers like change.

You need a focused team that says "our mission is to capture this market." In other groups in Teleflex, there is not the same acceptance about product development teams that may take years to bring a product to market. They ask: how can you justify that over the next quarter?

Teleflex Canada Culture

Harold Copping describes some of the characteristics of the Teleflex Canada culture:

I joined the company two years after the acquisition [by Teleflex Inc.]. My strength was an ability to recognize the strengths of other people. I cared a lot about people enjoying their work and doing interesting jobs. We had one person who was a mechanical genius but very difficult to work with. He was a great source of innovation in improved manufacturing methods and quality. He had a very temperamental personality, and in the early days there were fisticuffs on the shop floor and all kinds of things that should not happen. I protected him because I recognized how much he could do. We had another engineer who was brilliant and could think out of the box. He was off the wall and I had to protect him on two occasions against his bosses. I believed something good was going to come out of this guy [he is still at Teleflex Canada].

Right from the beginning, there was a nucleus of very good people in Teleflex Canada in terms of inventive creativity and willingness to solve problems and make things happen. There was some adversity that forced us to work together, such as vast quantities of products being returned by customers [the first innovative hydraulic steering system]. This helped me understand who contributed to solutions and who didn't. It also allowed me to play on the theme that if we did not do this right, the corporation will take it away from us. This was our chance to show them that we could manufacture in Vancouver.

We had discipline but we also had freedoms. We allowed a pretty free rein on innovation, and at the same time were adding systems and standardization. I tried to build the organization around a spirit of independence and risk-taking with a passionate group of people. I wanted the organization to work around the innovative people even if they were eccentric and hard to work with. Enthusiasm and passion are variables that are not measurable. I maintain that one degree of passion is worth 10 degrees of efficiency. All of our customers could sense the enthusiasm. People really cared at Teleflex Canada.

We had a culture of admiration for people with innovative engineering talent. We were also strongly motivated to never be second-class. There were drivers in the marketplace that pushed us to excel, and there was a constant focus on continuous improvement.

You have to create an identity and differentiation that is different from the rest of the corporation. If you lose the identity, you become an employee. You don't have the nice feeling of being part of a cause and a culture that you understand. Therefore, there has to be some symbolism around the identity and also some competition with other divisions of Teleflex. We tried to identify threats so that people would be scared and there would never be complacency. We used threats to draw people together. Some of our greatest successes came about when there was a lot of adversity because of customer problems or breakdowns.

Other managers echoed Harold Copping's views:

Harold was able to maintain a chemistry between the group of individuals that had to make it happen. That is easier when you are a small company. Harold surrounded himself with people who were passionate about what they believed in. If there was a common denominator, it was passion to be the best and the most successful. If you did not believe in this, you were gone. We were almost competing with each other but still working together as a team. The chemistry was as good as it could have been.

Everybody can question anyone about technical details. We have always had a culture that allows people to question everything. Everyone realizes that they are in a position where they could be questioned. We all have egos, but people have to check them at the door at Teleflex Canada. Harold knew that if you put people on too high a pedestal, it can cost you money.... Harold was the president, but he did not have his own parking space. People related to that. He did not try to be better than anyone.

We had some people who were unorthodox but were real technical geniuses. We also had some managers who were eternal optimists. If you have a negative attitude, it will kill entrepreneurial thinking.

Managerial commitment to Teleflex Canada was another key element in the company culture, as indicated by the following statement:

After the reorganization in May 2004, we realized there were a few businesses that were in serious trouble. The first company I was asked to visit was in Ontario. Within the first few hours of discussion, I discovered that the fundamental issue was the uncontrolled financial expense relative to a declining market. I was asked to run the company as general manager for the next 3 to 4 months. This was not the best time from a personal perspective: I was in the middle of building a new house (acting as general contractor) and had a number of personal issues involving the sale of my current house and dealing with the planned move of my family.

I spoke to my wife and family the next day, and we both agreed that the need for me to work in Ontario was greater than the need for me to continue as general contractor for the house. She rearranged her work schedule, and my parents stepped in to help get the kids to their various activities. On May 30, 2004, I took the red-eye from Vancouver and went straight into work on arrival in Toronto. For the next 8 months I flew out every Sunday night, spent long hours at work from Monday to Thursday, and flew back for the weekend. Even the weekend we moved into our new house, I flew back on Friday, moved into the house, and flew out on Sunday. I appreciated the opportunity Teleflex Canada had provided me over the past few years, and this was my way of showing them how dedicated I was to the company's success.

Teleflex Inc. and Teleflex Canada

Harold Copping described the relationship between Teleflex Canada and Teleflex Inc.:

I was running a remote subsidiary in a decentralized company. That was a huge advantage. From the very outset, I had a feeling of positive support from corporate and a feeling that I was controlling my own destiny. I tried to help the staff understand that it was really up to us, and I tried to create a culture where we controlled our own destiny.

The relationship was not "control by corporate." It was "help being available from corporate." We had people available from corporate to help teach us about quality and engineering. I always felt that I could choose to see the corporate resources that were available to me. If I could use local resources cost effectively, I did so. I pushed back when someone tried to force corporate resources on me ... Access to the corporation definitely played a role in our progress. [Chairman] Bim [Black] fostered a climate of cross-pollination between divisional and general managers by holding interesting meetings, although as the company got bigger there were fewer meetings. These meetings were very good in helping us know where to go and who to call. I used to find an excuse to visit other Teleflex facilities.

There was enough interaction and influence from corporate to allow people to create successful business relationships [with other parts of Teleflex Inc.]. Since they were not forced by corporate, only the viable relationships occurred. If we could help each other, we did. The attitude was based on open markets.... There were many benefits to being part of a large corporation. It was a nice environment to be in. As we got bigger, we were increasingly under the microscope.

We did not know the word core competence at the time. By the early 1980s we began to think that we were not really limited to the marine market. We were small enough and far enough away from corporate that nobody really cared what we did. We could explore new opportunities without being unduly restrained. As long as we were making money and growing, we had a lot of latitude. Nobody restricted me—freedom was a big factor.

Pull-Through Strategy

Rather than designing products and then looking for channels through which to sell them, Teleflex Canada focused on end users. Executives described this strategy as a pull-through strategy:

Our strategy in the truck business is pull-through. The reason why the truck companies [OEM manufacturers] put our ProHeat product on the truck is because the customer [the truck fleet operators] wanted it. The same thing happens with SeaStar. The boat builders buy it from us but the customer [the boat buyer] demands it.

A pull-through strategy is pragmatic. I can call on OEMs all day long but if no end users are asking for the product, we won't sell anything. We still have to negotiate with OEMs, but they don't get to make the call. It is the fleet customer who says we want ProHeat. We are trying to keep our products from becoming commodities, where the OEMs only care about price. They never ask for better—they only ask for cheaper. A lot of companies are confused about who their customers really are. The OEM is not the customer; the OEM is the channel. The customer is the person who will actually use the product.

The SeaStar technology was developed for a market that was prepared to pay a premium for higher comfort. People have asked, "why don't you leverage this technology into high volume sectors like automotive?" The problem with those markets is that the pricing pressures are intense and the volumes are much higher. We build about a half-million steering systems per year. Plus, we see automotive as more of a commodity market. Marine customers are using surplus funds to buy their products. Nobody has to own a boat. Boats are not a commodity, and we can demand a higher premium in the marine market. We have never entered another steering market.

We want to move boats closer to car steering comfort levels. Our next level of product innovation is to take comfort to a new level through power steering. We thought we would sell 2,000 power steering systems this year and it looks like we will sell 20,000. The boat builders initially resisted the shift to power steering. We gave the boat builders the new systems to try. Our philosophy is not to sell to the boat builders; we want them to buy it from us.

It does not matter what the technology is. The market will decide. Everybody is willing to pay a fair price for fair value.... We always try to be a few steps ahead of our customers. For example, we have an expensive power steering system for 60- to 100-foot luxury yachts. It is a very technical product and there are varying levels of expertise within the boat building companies. We believe that if we want to capture a bigger share of the market, we will have to simplify the technology and make it "bubba-proof." That is what we strive for: how do we make our product better and easier for our customers to use. Since our competitors are followers they cannot think like this.

The Future

As Teleflex Canada executives looked towards the future, they were faced with various issues, such as the degree of vertical integration, the relationship with Teleflex Inc., managing the size of the organization, and the future for new product development.

Vertical Integration

Teleflex Canada had always been vertically integrated. There was a consensus that, in the future, there would be less vertical integration.

All our customers want us to be as cost-effective as possible. In the past we were incredibly vertically integrated. For example, when we started with ProHeat, we needed various parts, like flame sensor, a compressor, a blower, and a water pump. Nobody built any of these parts to our specs, so we developed them ourselves from scratch. What are we doing developing a flame sensor? There are companies out there who should be able to do these things better than us. We spent a lot of money doing a lot of things, and we would have been better served if we had had the option to look outside. We developed some stuff that we had no business developing. As a general rule, we will buy technology rather than develop technology. We will develop new products. That is not the way we got here, but it is the way we need to go.

We have developed a strategic plan that involves core and non-core capabilities. We went through all our manufacturing processes and asked what is really core from process and intellectual property points of view. We have to protect intellectual property. We identified about 80% of our manufacturing processes as non-core.

We are going to try to shift from a manufacturer to an integrator and a tester. We will only fabricate what is considered absolutely core for protecting our manufacturing and quality processes and our intellectual property. Everything else is up for grabs. If we cannot be competitive here, the work will go elsewhere. We will be going through a rapid change. We want to focus on marketing, sales, product development and engineering, prototyping, final assembly, and testing. Fabrication and subassembly may go elsewhere. We want to be an OEM or a tier 1 player.

Not everyone was in complete agreement that the shift from manufacturer to integrator and tester was the basis for a unique strategy. According to one manager:

Every company in the world is trying to be an early adopter with low-cost manufacturing and outsourcing of non-core activities. That is not a strategy—that is good business practice. If you lose the ability to innovate on the production floor, you lose some of the ability to lower costs. That is my fear with off-shore production. Also, how are we going to protect key product designs and innovation when we spread work out to partners?

Relationships with Teleflex Inc.

Within all of Teleflex Inc. there was an ongoing debate about the merits of centralization and unified operating processes. Within Teleflex Canada, this debate was particularly relevant given the history of the subsidiary (i.e., 3,000 miles from headquarters) and its successful innovations:

The bigger area of conflict from a corporate unified perspective involves market and product development, who owns it, and how do we keep the innovation happening.

With more centralization going on, how do you make sure you don't kill the entrepreneurialism? Everybody knows that if you go completely centralized, you totally lose the innovation. What we have agreed on is that product development has to stay close to the market. There has to be some consolidation at a group level but not at a corporate level. We are creating centers of excellence such as hydraulics and power generation.

I understand the need for centralization. I also understand that the centralization pendulum usually swings too far. As far as the centralization of patent attorneys, this will take away from our ability to get prompt intellectual property. We will get it, but it will be slower. It is critical to understand your intellectual property before you spend too much time in development. Centralization of HR may also affect us. For example, corporate edicts about raises may make it hard to keep engineers, since Vancouver is such a hot tech area.

If you take away all of the divisional autonomy, you cripple the divisions. Before, purchases for $25,000 or less could be approved at the division. Now everything has to go corporate. Unless you are yelling or screaming, it can be a two- or three-month process to get approval. Because of Sarbanes-Oxley, things have to be done in a specific way. Too many rules will take away someone's incentive to stick their neck out and try something different. The old environment is gone, but we will make it happen somehow.

Managing Size

Teleflex Canada had grown rapidly over the past three decades. Size has brought a variety of challenges, as the following comments demonstrate:

We went from $4.5 million when I started to $160 million today. Every time we made a big jump in revenue, there were benefits and downsides. Getting big can be a problem, which is one reason Harold split the company into three divisions—he saw that we were getting too big.

The problem with growth is that as you get bigger, it gets more difficult to manage and control. Then you get to a point where the corporation becomes huge and the latest flavor of the month comes in, like "go to China for your raw materials." Now the buzz word is "cut costs, cut costs." If all we focus on is cutting costs, we will stifle the entrepreneurialism, and that is the beginning of the end. Once you stifle entrepreneurialism, passion, and creativity, you become like any other corporation. Margins will drop because you cannot be fast and innovative. You slowly start losing. We are on the edge.

As we get bigger we have to follow more processes, sign more forms; and by the time you get done, it is too late. It is not how big you are that makes you successful—it is how fast you are to market. In efforts to consolidate, we are risking our fast response time. When we were smaller, I could get things done in 24 hours. Now it takes forever.

We have always been known as a company that solved customer problems. We were very good at getting to the root cause of the problem. When a customer calls us, we take care of them. This got us a lot of respect and market share, and this was not the way our competitors did it. As we get bigger we may not be able to react quickly enough.

To keep our edge, we need to keep up with technology, move fast, and make sure quality does not suffer as we experiment with offshore sourcing. Basically, we need to continue to deliver what we promise. Do not take cost-cutting to the point where it affects what you have promised your customers.

One way we are trying to deal with size is with the Virtual Development Center. We are leaving too many opportunities on the table. This Center will be a small group that acts as an interface between the customers and the divisions. The Center will have two main objectives: one, to make sure the customers get proper focus from the people best qualified to deal with their problems; and two, to make sure the development project goes to the appropriate division.... Our goal is to provide a customer with a conceptual design in 7 days and a prototype within 30 days. In a way, we are trying to break free of the shackles of size by responding quickly to customers. Once we have a customer, we will put the product into the appropriate division to develop it, make it manufacturable, optimize it, etc.

There is a limit to how big the firm can get and still be innovative and entrepreneurial. It is easier with smaller groups. Once an organization gets over 150 people, it should be subdivided. You need to strike the right balance between operational efficiency, serving the customer well, and maintaining a spirit of identity.... Balancing operational efficiency with subdividing the organization is more of a challenge because there are tradeoffs. When people work together in subunits and depend on each other for overall success, politics is minimized. The challenges are to work with people and stay connected with people at every single level. If people believe that they succeed together and make things happen together, they will have some job security and will reap some rewards. It is much easier to excite people about a portion of the business rather than the whole business.

Forward Thinking: New Product Development and New Technologies

New product development was central to the success of Teleflex Canada and central to continued growth. Executives were generally confident that the organization would continue to develop and exploit existing technologies. Some comments about the marine area are as follows:

I don't see an issue with product development. The bigger challenge is dealing with new technologies. The risk is that our existing products get replaced by new technologies in which we have no expertise. Take steering systems. We know that hydraulics will go away eventually, and the market will demand more comfort at lower prices. The boat builders may integrate steering into their outboards. Most stern drive engine steering uses a cable with a power steering system.

We will have to reduce costs and develop more robust designs for larger outboard engines. There will be new technologies that replace hydraulic steering. Electro over hydraulic with programmable tension and torque levels is the next generation and will come out soon. The next shift will be to electro-mechanical actuation or steer-by-wire, which is disruptive technology. We believe we can bring this to market, and we had the foresight to realize that we were going to become an electronics company. Five years ago we engaged a local university professor—an expert in fault tolerant systems—to work with us privately on steer-by-wire. Corporate and other engineers did not know we were doing this. We scavenged the money where we could and eventually bought an equity stake in an offshoot company owned by the university and the professor. When corporate found out what we were doing, they saw that it made sense and gave us steer-by-wire responsibility for the corporation. We are going to be ready with a steer-by-wire product when the world is ready for the technology.

We are also trying to develop new products for boats. We know that we will lose market share when hydraulic steering goes away. We also know that the engine companies want to integrate steering with their engines. We need to be forward-looking and help our customers sell their products. We need to make sure we are the company that the engine manufacturer wants as the integrator. Our plan is to develop new business with Yamaha, Bombardier, and other engine companies.

Conclusion

Teleflex Canada had provided a high margin contribution to the Teleflex corporation for many years. Would success breed complacency and stagnation? Or, would Teleflex Canada continue to grow, innovate, and develop new products? According to one executive:

> We can't get fat and lazy, because that will be the beginning of the end. We have to continue to solve our customers' problems and make their lives easier. As long as we do what we promise and don't get arrogant, we will be fine. If we start acting like an 800-pound gorilla, customers will find a way to deal with us. We need to work with our customers and make their lives easier. It is a fine line and you need to know where the line is. Most of our boat builders are entrepreneurs; there are no barriers to entry in the boat business. This helps keep the automotive mentality out of this industry.

Part 6

Looking Ahead

Global marketers constantly face global change. Recently the pace of change has been accelerating, resulting in more severe impacts. Because of growing real-time access to knowledge of customers, suppliers, and competitors, communications in the global marketplace are increasingly instantaneous. The world is, in effect, becoming flat. Moreover, a nation's political stability can be totally disrupted in a few months. This part discusses possible future developments in the international environment, highlighting the implications of these changes for global marketing strategy, and offers suggestions for a creative response. The implications for career choice in global marketing are also emphasized.

Chapter 17

The Future of Global Marketing

The Global MARKETPLACE 17.1

Marketing Overseas: Excellent for Career Advancement

Overseas experience is beneficial and lucrative not only to companies that have gone international, but also to the marketing employees in those companies. In an increasingly internationalized world, job opportunities for marketers have become global. Companies are forced to meet a variety of consumer preferences, which are mainly attributed to different cultural and societal values. One way in which companies can attain a better understanding of others' cultural values is through the overseas experience of personnel.

Working overseas provides an opportunity to see how people live, to study how other countries market products and services, and to understand and gauge political and economic situations in other countries. This experience can be a great way to build a résumé and climb the corporate ladder. For example, Ian Cook joined New York–based Colgate-Palmolive Company in its London office in 1976. Since then he has worked in marketing positions around the world, including in the Philippines and in the Nordic countries, with a total of 19 years of overseas experience. Today, Cook is the president of Colgate-Palmolive North America, proving that overseas experience leads to career advancement.

Another example is Henry "Hank" McKinnell, a Canadian born in Victoria, British Columbia. After receiving a PhD in business from Stanford University, Hank gave up a chance to join Pfizer to do consulting work instead. Thereafter he describes his career path as "unusual." Although he did ultimately join Pfizer, he spent 14 years working for the company in various foreign divisions (including President of Pfizer, Asia) spending no time either in Canada itself or at head office. Yet Hank was appointed CEO and chairman of the company in 2001, and gives much credit for his success to the "great respect for diversity" he acquired in foreign countries.

Overseas experience does not have to be through corporate transfers. It may be possible to find work abroad independently. For example, Beth Rehman, currently an account executive at TSI Communications Worldwide in New York, decided shortly after college to work in France and landed a six-month internship with Saatchi Healthcom in Paris. After getting married, Rehman went back to Paris for 18 months and worked as a marketer for a high-tech public-relations firm, Rumeur Publique. Her corporate career has shown that career advancement can be achieved transferring from firm to firm.

With more companies expanding into the world market, it is becoming a requirement for those in senior executive–level positions in multinational corporations to have had prior overseas experience. Today, with more and more companies engaged in international business, it is necessary and, as an added incentive, gives marketing employees the edge for career advancement.

Sources: Lisa Bertagnolli, "Marketing Overseas Excellent for Career," *Marketing News*, June 4, 2001, 4, 6; and Zena Olijnyk, "Henry 'Hank' McKinnell," *Canadian Business*, March, 2005.

Global marketers are constantly faced with global change. This is not a new situation, nor one to be feared, because change provides the opportunity for the emergence of new market positions. Recognizing the importance of change and adapting creatively to new situations are the daily bread of marketing professionals and offer a chance for advancement, as The Global Marketplace 17.1 shows.

Recently, however, changes are occurring more frequently and more rapidly, and they are having a more severe impact. Due to growing real-time access to knowledge about and for customers, suppliers, and competitors, the international marketing environment is increasingly characterized by high speed bordering on instantaneity.[1] In consequence, the past has lost much of its value as a predictor of the future. What occurs today may be not only altered but completely overturned or reversed in the future. For example, new technologies can alter ways of doing business. As a result, some countries can find that their major export industries, highly competitive for decades, can lose their international edge within a very short time. The political balance of some countries may be quickly upset when simmering problems erupt into open disturbances such as street rioting (e.g., Pakistan and Myanmar in late 2007). In all, global marketers today face complex and rapidly changing economic and political conditions.

This chapter will discuss possible future developments in the international marketing environment, highlight the implications of these changes for global marketing management, and offer suggestions for a creative response. The chapter will also explore the meaning of strategic changes to the reader, with particular emphasis on career choice and career path alternatives in global marketing.

The Global Marketing Environment

Internationally, the political and economic environment is undergoing a substantial transformation, influencing the individual countries and country groupings that marketers target. Global marketers need familiarity with these changes because successful marketing always depends on knowledge of the market. The problem is that the global scene, with its rapid change and volatility, presents us with intimidating amounts of information—at times seemingly distant from conventional marketing—to absorb. Yet this study cannot be escaped if marketers are to evolve truly responsive strategies.

In this section we will look at the changes influencing countries and regions under four main headings:

1. Planned versus market economies
2. The North–South relationship
3. The Asia-Pacific region and China
4. The BRIC countries

Planned versus Market Economies

The second half of the last century was shaped by the political, economic, and military competition between the United States and the Soviet Union, which resulted in the creation of two virtually separate economic systems. This key adversarial posture has now largely disappeared, with market-based economic thinking emerging as the front-runner. Virtually all of the former centrally planned economies are undergoing a transition with the goal of becoming market oriented.

International marketing has made important contributions to this transition process. Trade and investment have offered the populace in these nations a new perspective, new choices, new jobs, and new alternatives for marketing their products and services. At the same time, the bringing together of two separate economic and business systems has resulted in new, and sometimes devastating competition, a loss of government-ordained trade relationships, and substantial dislocations and pain during the adjustment process.

Over the next few years the countries of Eastern and Central Europe will continue to be attractive for international investment not simply because of low labour costs, low-priced input factors, and unused production capacities, but also because countries in the region are becoming richer and their companies and financial markets better governed. This attractiveness will translate into growing investment from Western Europe for reasons of geographic proximity and attractive outsourcing opportunities.[2] Even these investment flows, however, are likely to take place only selectively, resulting in unbalanced economic conditions in the region.

Economic growth has varied widely across the so-called transition countries since 1989, Central Europe generally having performed better than Southeastern Europe, which in turn has outperformed Russia, Ukraine, and the other members of the Commonwealth of Independent States (CIS).[3] Firms and governments outside of Western Europe will likely continue their reluctance to invest in Eastern Europe, but this reluctance will diminish as the region continues to develop economically and achieves growing stability. What aversion exists is not driven by any fear of a revival of Communism, or fear of economic and political turbulence, but because of the availability of attractive investment alternatives elsewhere, for example, China and India.

Although Russia and the other nations of the former Soviet Union have faced difficulties in the past, and many still persist, the next decade should, taking an optimistic view, see some easing of these. Foreign investment in Russia has grown, as has outward investment from Russia into other countries, as Russian companies look for business opportunities

Exhibit 17.1 **Busy Russian Markets Add Up to Canadian Opportunities**

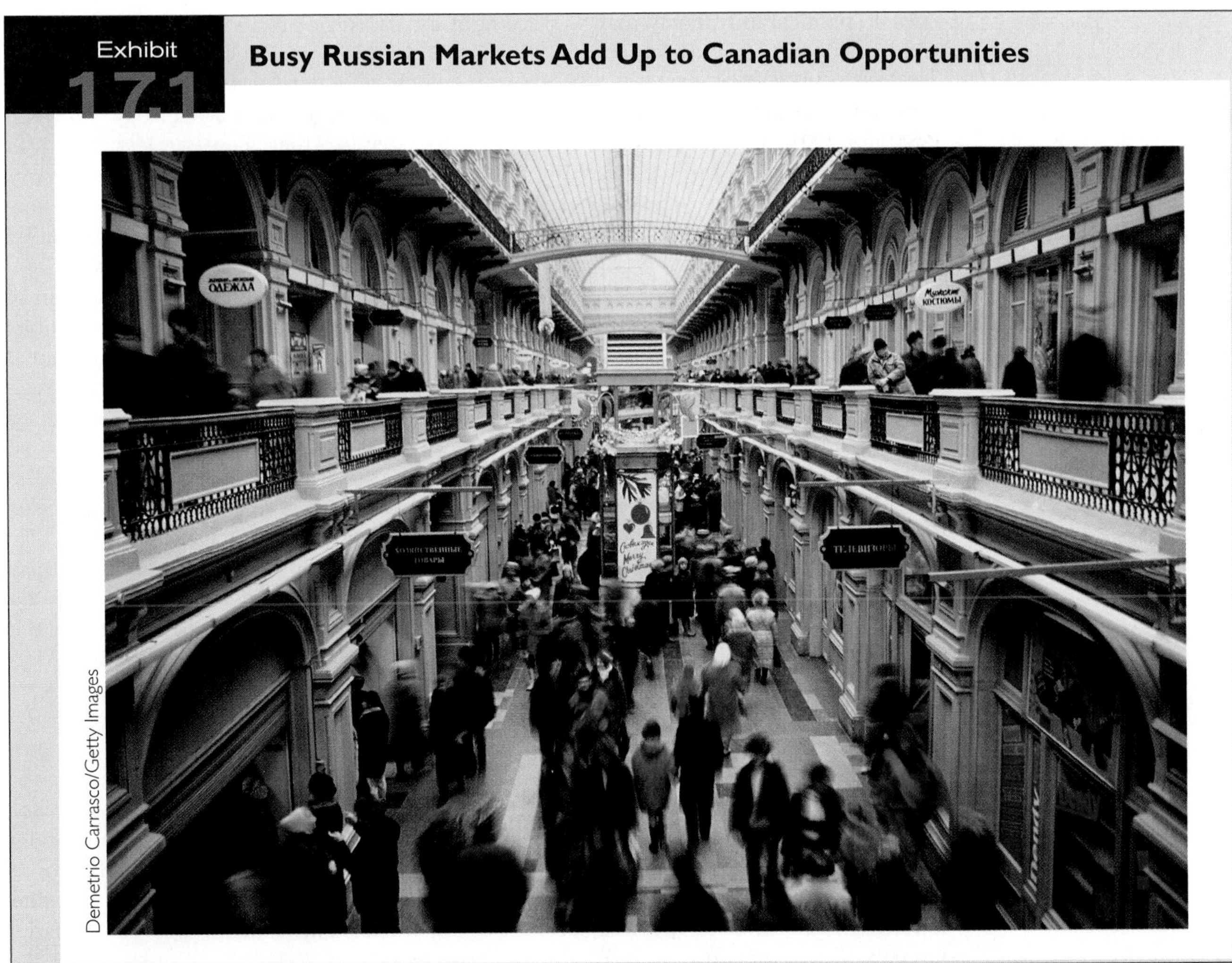

Demetrio Carrasco/Getty Images

abroad.[4] A major challenge for Russia is to continue the diversification of its economy to avoid over-dependence on high commodity prices for growth, which, however, has propelled the country's GDP from $200 billion in 1999 to $960 billion in 2006.[5] Paradoxically, this growth has somewhat cooled Russian interest in joining the WTO, because exports of oil and gas, which account for approximately 50 percent of exports, are not affected by protectionist measures. But the fact that the country is seeking entry into the WTO, allied with the successful conclusion of bilateral negotiations with the U.S., suggests that formal membership will be achieved, leading to more systematic trade relations with other countries. The investment in new car manufacturing in Russia by Magna International suggests the kinds of relationships that will increasingly occur in future. However, smooth sailing is not guaranteed given the protracted negotiation period and the on-again, off-again attitude by Moscow to WTO membership.

Overall, many business activities will be subject to regional economic and political instability, increasing the risk to international partners. Progress toward the institution of market-based economies may be halted or even reversed as large population segments are exposed to growing hardship during the transformation process. It will be important to develop institutions and processes internally that assure domestic and foreign investors that there will be protection from public and private corruption and respect for property rights and contractual arrangements.

The North–South Relationship

The distinction between developed and less-developed countries (LDCs) is unlikely to change. The ongoing disparity between developed and developing nations is likely to be based, in part, on continuing debt burdens and problems with satisfying basic needs. As a result, political uncertainty may well result in increased polarization between the haves and have-nots, with growing potential for political and economic conflict. Demands for political solutions for economic problems are likely to increase. About one-fifth of the Earth's population, or 1.1 billion people, currently live on less that $1 per day. Between 1981 and 2001, the percentage of people in sub-Saharan Africa living on less than $1 a day increased by 93 percent, from 164 million to 316 million.[6] Some countries may consider migration as a key solution to population-growth problems, yet many emigrants may encounter government barriers to their migration. There may well be more investment by firms bringing their labour-intensive manufacturing operations to these countries.

The fact that many countries, particularly in Africa, seem left out from the expansion of international prosperity is partly due to prevailing uncertainty and productivity limitations that have made firms reluctant to expand into these areas. Where there is a substantial increase in stability, accompanied by local institutions desiring peace and economic development, the international production expansion might well extend to the less-developed nations. Today's trickle of investment and purchasing in poorer countries could well become a torrent from firms in search of new opportunities. Those concerned with enforcing the peace in regions that might breed terrorists would be well served to consider such peace as a key instrument for the economic growth and prosperity in disadvantaged nations.[7]

An emphasis on education, training and the development of a supportive infrastructure are crucial, since that is where the investments and jobs go.[8] It is not enough to expect a rising tide to raise all boats. There must also be significant effort expended to ensure the seaworthiness of the boat, the functioning of its sails, and the capability of its crew. Market-oriented performance will be critical to success in the longer run.

The issue of **environmental protection** will also be a major force shaping the relationship between the developed and the developing world. What approach shall we take? And who pays? For example, simply designating large areas of land as out-of-bounds for development will be difficult to accept for nations that intend to pursue all options for further economic progress. Corporations in turn recognize that by being environmentally responsible, a company can build trust and improve its image—therefore becoming more competitive. For example, in the early 1990s, the first annual corporate environmental report was published; now over 2,000 companies a year publish such reports.[9] In Canada, more than 100 companies were producing these reports by 2004.[10]

No one model will dictate the ultimate shape of relations between rich and poor countries. However, in light of divergent trends by different groups, different scenarios are possible: for example, confrontation or isolation. For the sake of continued growth in trade, it can be hoped that a third route—cooperation—will be favoured.

The Asia-Pacific Region and China

The Asia Pacific region is likely to regain its growth in the next decade. For the industrialized nations, this development will offer a significant opportunity for exports and investment, but not all countries will benefit equally. The richest country (in per capita terms), Singapore, is more than 50 times as rich as the poorest, Cambodia. The nations in the region are likely to continue their collaboration. Predictions that this would not lead to the formation of a bloc similar to the European Union or NAFTA have turned out to be false. The first East Asian summit of regional leaders in Kuala Lumpur in December 14, 2005, has been described as a "historic event."[11] This is because it goes beyond narrow geographical definitions of ethnic/racial identity in attempting to lay the groundwork for a new regional institution. This will include Japan, South Korea, China, India, Australia, and New Zealand. How the new bloc will evolve is uncertain, but discussions have featured use of the term "East Asian Community" which recalls the supra-national European Community. The Global Marketplace 17.2 describes some events leading up to the creation of the new summit.

In light of China's membership in the WTO, its continued emergence as a trade power is likely to be the economic event of the decade. Despite innumerable risks, experts see Chinese pragmatism prevailing. Companies already present in the market and those willing to make significant investments are likely to be the main beneficiaries of growth. Long-term commitment, willingness to transfer technology, and an ability to partner either with local firms through joint ventures or with overseas Chinese-run firms are considered crucial for success. The strategic impact of Chinese trade participation is also likely to change. Due to WTO rules, the recipients of Chinese goods will be less able to exclude them with higher tariffs or non-tariff barriers. China, in turn, is likely to assume a much higher profile in its trading activities. For example, rather than be the supplier of goods that are then marketed internationally under a Japanese or U.S. label, Chinese firms will increasingly develop their own brand names and fight for their own name recognition, customer loyalty, and market share.[12]

The BRIC Countries

Promising emerging markets are often referred to as the **BRIC countries** (Brazil, Russia, India, and China). Other promising markets also deserve mention: for example, Mexico and South Korea. We have already mentioned the rapid economic growth of China. With regard to South Korea and India, South Korea could emerge as a participant in worldwide competition, while India is considered more important for the size of its potential market. South Korean firms must still improve their ability to adopt a global mindset. In addition, the possible impact of the reunification of the Korean peninsula on the country's globalization efforts must be taken into account in the longer term.

With the considerable liberalization that took place in India during the 1990s, many expect it to offer major international marketing opportunities due to its size; its significant natural wealth; and its large, highly educated middle class. While many experts believe that political conflict (both domestic and regional), nationalism, and class structure may temper the ability of Indian companies to emerge as a worldwide competitive force, there is strong agreement that India's disproportionately large and specialized work force in engineering and computer sciences makes the nation a power to be reckoned with.

In the case of Brazil, this country continues a process of maturation, emerging as an important economic power, representing a wide range of export and investment opportunities for exporting countries. The country has opened its oil and gas sector, inviting foreign investment and engaging in joint ventures with foreign companies to secure a footing in the global supply chain. Political volatility still presents problems in the case of

The Global MARKETPLACE 17.2

Laying the Groundwork for East Asian Collaboration

The East Asia Economic Summit of 2002, held in Kuala Lumpur, Malaysia, marked the renewal of commitments by many East Asian leaders to increase regional and global integration in the near future. This commitment was to flower three years later (in 2005 in Kuala Lumpur) into discussion of a new regional institution similar to NAFTA, a historic development. Whether the effort focused upon strengthening the already existent trade bloc, ASEAN, or creating a free-trade area between the ASEAN nations and China or India, most members of the summit in 2002 agreed to prioritize the push for integration, a dream that is now becoming a reality.

The key reason for such a surge in liberal trade policy: competitiveness. The Asian nations are currently in a strong position to become global economic contenders along with a strong United States and a strengthening Europe, which they see as both potential partners and aggressive competitors. "We should push ahead with greater integration of East Asian economies. It will put us in better stead to respond to the formation of large economic blocs in Europe and the Americas," said Goh Chok Tong, prime minister of Singapore.

Prime Minister Thaksin Shinawatra of Thailand made a call for the development of stronger financial institutions, including developing an Asian bond market. Prime Minister Goh Chok Tong closed the summit by re-focusing attention on the actual institutions and processes that could be used to further the task of Asian integration. Such processes include, first, increased regional cooperation via ASEAN and neighbour states such as China and India, and subsequently, an effort to integrate globally. Finally, Prime Minister Mahathir bin Mohamad of Malaysia further underscored the need for Asians to work together, as well as the need for Asians to support efforts to join in multilateral efforts such as the World Trade Organization.

The leaders of the leading East Asian nations have made strides toward regional integration through ASEAN and have demonstrated their future commitment to a more global presence at the Kuala Lumpur summit, but commitments of current leaders will not be enough to carry East Asia into the global economy. The next generation, those young leaders of tomorrow, must demonstrate their commitment to global integration.

While the Kuala Lumpur summit stressed the goals of the traditional regional leaders, the World Economic Forum's Global Leaders for Tomorrow has created the New Asian Leaders Initiative to stress the goals of the leaders of tomorrow. Unlike modern Europe, which is marked by a noticeably aging population, Asia is home to very young societies, in which youth are taking on an increasing role in setting the regional agenda. There seems to be a growing understanding of the key role that *both* generations must play in guaranteeing the long-term viability of East Asian integration.

The role of the initiative is to "enhance the capacity of Asia's new generation of leaders ... to confront challenges and provide the leadership and vision needed in Asia." The initiative's mission statement proclaims its objective "to provide young Asian leaders with a platform where [they] can exchange ideas which will enable [them] to put forward to the current leadership of [their] respective countries the view that the voices of the younger generation should be considered when national regional policies for the future are being formulated."

The New Asian Leaders Initiative guarantees that the current commitment to global integration will not die with current leaders. The initiative proves that this commitment is not being forced from the top down, but that the next generation of leaders also supports the push for regional and global integration. By joining forces across national borders, young leaders will set a precedent for their national leaders to do the same. By joining forces early in the integration process, young leaders are ensuring that the effort will be accomplished in the long run. Events in 2005 justify this optimism.

Sources: East Asia Summit 2002, "Renewing Asia's Foundations of Growth: Building on Diversity," *World Economic Forum,* http://www.weforum.org/site/homepublic.nsf/Content/East+Asia+Economic+Summit+2002; and Barry Desker, "Why the East Asian Summit Matters," *Asia Times,* December 13, 2005.

Russia, but the country, like Brazil, is increasingly reaching beyond domestic borders and announcing joint action with foreign partners in the international market, in effect pursuing a globalization of its business. This is likely to continue. After a period of stagnation, the Mexican economy is once again growing. With low inflation rates, the country is enjoying strong economic stability. Also it is now less affected by previous economic crashes (Argentina, Brazil) and has diversified its commercial activities through several international agreements such as NAFTA.

In More Detail 17.1

SELLING MOBILE TELEPHONES AND LAPTOPS TO POORER COUNTRIES

The number of mobile telephones in use has passed the 2 billion point, according to industry statistics. Most of the next billion subscribers will have to come from the developing world, including poorer countries. This is illustrated by Africa, which leads the world in subscriber growth, with this growth exceeding 150 percent per year in some countries. The greatest barrier to wider adoption of mobile phones and other products in the developing world is cost. But the market prospects can be huge. In another case, that of laptop computers, one company targeting the education sector sees the market as global—more than 1 billion schoolchildren worldwide, if costs can be made affordable. The poorest countries—Cambodia, Senegal, Somalia—still lack income, of course, and without purchasing power demand will remain largely latent. But if initiatives such as the introduction of micro-credit—the granting of small loans to poor families to enable them to start local businesses—ultimately helps poorer economies to grow and prosper, this problem will be alleviated. It is a fairly safe prediction that forward-looking companies are increasingly aware of these issues and will act upon them. For example Digicel, a telecommunications company, is known to be performing exceptionally well in Trinidad and Tobago, and in Haiti, the poorest country in the western hemisphere.

Overall, the growth potential of these emerging economies may be threatened by uncertainty in terms of international relations and domestic policies, as well as social and political dimensions, particularly those pertaining to income distribution. Concerns also exist about infrastructural inadequacies, both physical (such as transportation) and societal (such as legal systems). These difficulties, as apparent in, for example, Latin America, stand to be eased, or at least sympathized with and allowed for, by proponents of freer trade in the Americas as a whole, to which the FTAA (Free Trade Association of the Americas) is dedicated. On balance, the consensus of experts is that growth in emerging economies as a whole will be significant. Indeed, given that the economies of the BRIC countries have been predicted to become larger than those of the G6 in the next 40 years,[13] it is not surprising that exporting countries such as Canada have singled them out for special attention. For example, Export Development Canada has developed specialized publications designed to assist Canadian exporters to penetrate them.[14]

In the future, companies will pay increasing attention even to the poorest countries. There is now much interest in marketing to subsistence economies as global firms "run out of steam" in more mature markets.

Such a divergence of values will require a major readjustment of the activities of the global corporation. A continuous scanning of newly emerging national values thus becomes imperative for the international executive.

Factors Influencing Global Marketing

In this section we will review a series of influences on the conduct of international marketing, and comment on future trends. The factors are finance, technology, trade, and population.

The Global Financial Environment

The U.S. dollar will remain one of the major international currencies with little probability of gold returning to its former status in the near future. However, a looming concern in the international financial environment is the international debt load of the United States. Both domestically and internationally, the United States is incurring debt that would have been inconceivable only a few decades ago. The United States entered the new century with an international debt burden of more than $2 trillion. This debt level makes the United States the largest debtor nation in the world, owing more to other nations than all the developing nations combined. In light of ongoing trade deficits at the time, it was projected by some in 2001 that this net negative investment position might grow to $4 trillion by 2005. In reality, by 2005 the actual figure had more than doubled to almost $9 trillion, and it shows no sign of slackening.[15] Others argue against an unsustainable scenario, believing that there are special mitigating circumstances which let the U.S. tolerate this burden, such as the fact that most of the debts are denominated in U.S. dollars and that, even at such a large debt volume, U.S. debt-service requirements are only a relatively small portion of GNP. Yet this accumulation of foreign debt may very well introduce entirely new dimensions into the international business relationships of individuals and nations. Once debt has reached a certain level, the creditor as well as the debtor is hostage to the loans. A comparison with Canada's performance can be made by consulting the information provided in Chapter 2. For example, it will be noted that, unlike the U.S., Canada operates a trade surplus. A comparison of data on the net negative investment position of the two countries is also illuminating. The reader will not fail to note the sheer magnitude of the U.S. numbers compared with those of Canada.

The Influence of Technology

The concept of the global village is commonly accepted today and indicates the importance of communication and technology. Worldwide, the estimated number of people online on January 4, 2006, surpassed 1 billion, up from 45 million in 1995 and 420 million in 2000.[16] The 2-billion-users milestone is expected to be reached by 2011. The United States continues to lead with nearly 200 million Internet users at year-end 2005. However, the online audience in the U.S. and Canada represents less than a quarter of Internet users in the world, whereas 10 years ago it accounted for two-thirds of the global audience.[17] The two most populous countries, China and India, are now sharing the top four places in Internet use with Japan. Other populous countries such as Brazil, Russia, and India can now be counted among the top 15. Internet user penetration is now in the 65 percent to 75 percent range for the leading countries, and future growth is limited. The penetration rate for developing countries is in the 10 percent to 20 percent range, and therefore there is more room to grow. Nonetheless, there is a wide digital gap around the globe because in some nations, such as Yemen, 220,000 users or fewer are hooked up to the Internet.[18]

For both consumer services and business-to-business relations, the Internet is democratizing global business. It has made it easier for new global retail brands (e.g., **amazon.com** and **CDnow.com**) to emerge. The Internet is also helping specialists such as Australia's high-sensitivity hearing aids manufacturer Cochlear to reach target customers around the world without having to invest in a distribution network in each country. The ability to reach a worldwide audience economically via the Internet spells success for niche marketers who could never make money by just servicing their niches in the domestic market. The Internet also allows customers, especially those in emerging markets, to access global brands at more competitive prices than those offered by exclusive national distributors.[19]

Starting a New Business

This will be much easier, allowing a far greater number of suppliers to enter a market. Small and medium-sized enterprises, as well as large multinational corporations, will now be full participants in the global marketplace. Businesses in developing countries can now overcome many of the obstacles of infrastructure and transport that limited their economic potential in the past. The global services economy will be a knowledge-based economy, and its most precious resource will be information and ideas. Unlike the classical factors of production—land, labour, capital, and enterprise—information and knowledge are not bound to any region or country but are almost infinitely mobile and infinitely capable of expansion.[20] This wide availability, of course, also brings new risks to firms. For example, unlike in the past, today one complaint can easily be developed into millions of complaints by e-mail.[21] Consequently, firms are subject to much more scrutiny and customer response on an international level.

Changes in Technology

These changes also make available vast amounts of data worldwide. Therefore the management of information becomes as important as the information itself. The premium will be on the organization, maintenance, and use of huge, current, and accurate databases covering customers, vendors, regulations, and standards. Knowledge distribution experts will form an entire new profession with two distinct specializations: *knowledge focusers* will be in charge of ensuring that the right kind of information is provided; *knowledge erasers* will concentrate on weeding out old or outdated data, in order to limit capacity constraints of information storage and to delete corporate information that may lead to future interpretation problems. Due to rising public concerns about the dissemination of information, the role of privacy experts will also be on the increase.

High Technology

High technology will be one of the more volatile and controversial areas of economic activity globally. Developments in biotechnology are already transforming agriculture, medicine, and chemistry. Chemically engineered foods, patient-specific pharmaceuticals, gene therapy, and even genetically engineered organs are on the horizon. Innovations such as these will change what we eat, how we treat illness, and how we evolve as a civilization.[22] Canada is on the leading edge of many such technologies. However, skepticism of technological innovations is rampant. In many instances, people are opposed to such changes due to religious or cultural reasons, or simply because they do not want to be exposed to such "artificial" products. Achieving agreement on what constitutes safe products and procedures, or what is natural and what is not, will constitute one of the great areas of debate in the years to come. Firms and their managers must remain keenly aware of popular perceptions and misperceptions and of government regulations in order to remain successful participants in markets.

Marshalling Funds

Even firms and countries that are at the leading edge of technology will find it increasingly difficult to marshal the funds necessary for further advancements. For example, investments in semiconductor technology are measured in billions rather than millions of dollars and do not bring any assurance of success. Not to engage in the race, however, will mean falling behind quickly in all areas of manufacturing when virtually every industrial and consumer product is "smart" due to its chip technology.

Technology Sharing

To spread the necessary financial commitments and to reduce the risk of permanent losses by participants in the race, firms will increasingly share technology provided that payment is made for shared information. In addition, industry consolidation, cooperative agreements, joint ventures, and strategic partnering will proliferate. Concurrently, governments will increase their spending on research and development and will promote techno-nationalism through the creation of more sources of technological innovation within their boundaries. Government-sponsored collaborative research ventures are likely to increase across industries and country groupings. However, difficulties may emerge when global firms threaten to internationalize rapidly and neutralize any gains from such regionalized research ventures.

Trade and Protectionism

The formation of the WTO concluded a lengthy and sometimes acrimonious round of global trade negotiations. However, key disagreements among major trading partners are likely to persist. Ongoing major imbalances in trade flows will tempt nations to apply their own national trade remedies, particularly in the anti-dumping field. Even though WTO rules permit retaliation against unfair trade practices, such action would only result in an ever-increasing spiral of adverse trade relations.

Exhibit 17.2 **Rapid Telecom Growth in Pakistan**

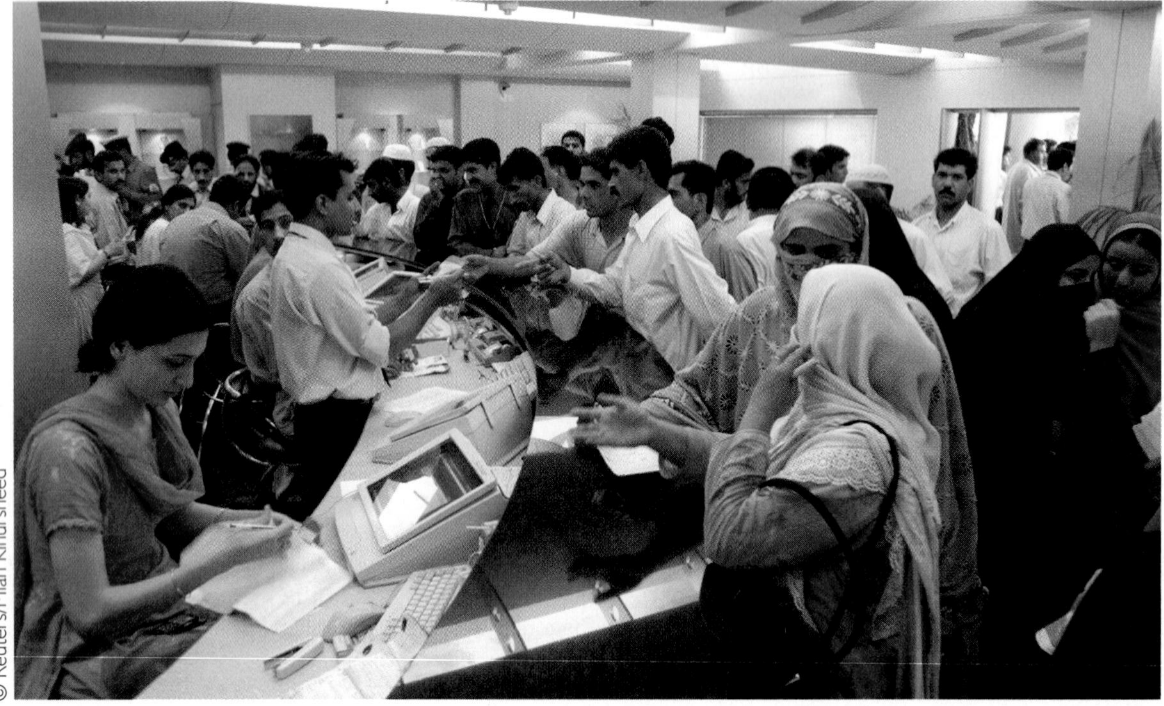

© Reuters/Mian Kihursheed

A key question will be whether nations and their citizens are willing to abrogate some of their sovereignty even during difficult economic times. An affirmative answer will strengthen the multilateral trade system and enhance the flow of trade. However, if key trading nations resort to the development of insidious non-tariff barriers, unilateral actions, and bilateral negotiations, protectionism will increase on a global scale and the volume of international trade is likely to decline. The danger is real. Popular support for international trade agreements appears to be on the wane. Public demonstrations during WTO meetings, including protest marches in Hong Kong in 2005 and in Montreal in 2007, indicate that there is much ambivalence by individuals and non-governmental organizations about trade. Here international business experts are, or should be, the guardians who separate fact from fiction in international trade policy discussions. Qualified not by weight of office but by expertise, international business experts, including marketers, are the indirect guarantors of and guides toward free and open markets. Without their input and impact, public apathy and ignorance may well result in missteps in trade policy.[23]

International trade relations also will be shaped by new participants whose market entry will restructure the composition of global trade. For example, new players with exceptionally large productive potential, such as the People's Republic of China and Central Europe, will substantially alter world trade flows. And while both governments and firms will be required to change many trade policies and practices as a result, they will also benefit in terms of market opportunities and sourcing alternatives.

Population and Immigration

The population discrepancy between less-developed nations and the industrialized countries will continue to increase. In the industrialized world, population growth will become a national priority, given the fact that in many countries, particularly in Western Europe, the population is shrinking rather than increasing. This shrinkage may lead to labour shortages and to major societal difficulties when a dwindling number of workers has to provide for a growing elderly population. As The Global Marketplace 17.3 shows, large-scale migration flows may well be an important alternative to the dangers of a population decline. However, as is also shown, migrants do return to their own countries; in Canada, an outflow "back home" of immigrants originally from China, Hong Kong, and India is being seen. These immigrants originally entered Canada as foreign investors and are now leaving, having made money and developed their marketing expertise in North America. Any loss of capital, entrepreneurial skill, and employment-generating business is bound to be a concern for the federal government.

In the developing world, **population stabilization** will continue to be one of the major challenges of governmental policy. In spite of well-intentioned economic planning, continued rapid increases in population will make it more difficult to ensure that the pace

The Global MARKETPLACE 17.3

Migration: A Double Blessing

An estimated 2.5 percent of the world's population, or 150 million people, had migrated from their mother country by the start of the new millennium. A variety of reasons, both push and pull factors, cause migrants to settle in a foreign country. Push factors include human rights violations, political oppression, economic hardships, crime, and violence; pull factors include economic opportunities, political freedom, physical safety, and security.

International migration holds benefits for both the sending country and the receiving country. For the receiving country, migrants, whether skilled or unskilled, provide a larger pool of labourers. When labour shortages occur, foreign workers are especially valued because they may meet the demand of a specific sector, for example, information technology or seasonal agriculture.

The recent surge of migration from Latin America to the United States can be used to illustrate the benefits that migration may bring to both the sending and receiving country. Fifteen million Latin Americans are now living in the United States, allowing the American economy to expand without worrying about labour shortages, as do many other countries.

Migrants also help the United States by raising fertility rates, preventing population decline and correcting uneven age-distribution in the population. In industrialized countries such as the United States and Europe, the fertility rate, or average number of children born per woman, is below replacement level. Not only does this lead to a decrease in the labour force, it also reduces the ratio of working-age people to retired people and increases the burden of retirement. Migrants increase the population of the United States directly; they also increase the population indirectly by raising the fertility rate. The higher fertility rate of Latinos at 3.0 children per woman will raise the fertility rate of the United States, increasing births and reducing the aging problem.

On the other hand, sending countries also benefit from migration. Remittance, or sending money back to one's home country, is one of the primary ways in which migrants help their home country. The Federal Reserve in Chicago estimates that in 2000, recorded remittances in the form of cheques or money transfers from the United States totaled $20 billion. In many countries, remittances even exceed foreign investment, exports, or foreign aid and serve as the main source of support for many families. While the majority of remittances are used to provide survival necessities such as food and health care, the impact of remittances spent in the form of investments is just as valuable and extensive by creating jobs.

Migrants may also improve their home country by returning with skills and connections acquired in the United States. Some migrants contribute to the development of their mother country by starting joint ventures. In 1992, Colombia created a network of expatriate researchers and engineers from 30 countries. Other migrants help by using their position in the United States to persuade multinational firms to invest in their home country. Still others, such as Bolivian native Virginia Sanchez, a New York banker, encourage the Bolivian-American Chamber of Commerce to assist Bolivian emigrants to ease their adjustment in the United States.

Sources: "Half a Billion Americans?" *The Economist*, August 24, 2002; Susan Martin, "Heavy Traffic: International Migration in an Era of Globalization," *The Brookings Review*, Fall 2001, 41–44; *ABI/Inform Global*, September 6, 2002; and Kenneth Tom, "Making the Most of an Exodus," *The Economist*, February 23, 2002.

Exhibit 17.3

The 10 Largest Urban Areas in the World, 2002

Area	Population (millions)
Tokyo (Japan)	35.1
New York (U.S.A.)	21.7
Seoul (South Korea)	21.4
Mexico City (Mexico)	21.0
São Paulo (Brazil)	19.9
Bombay (India)	18.4
Osaka (Japan)	18.1
Delhi (India)	17.5
Los Angeles (U.S.A.)	16.9

Source: Thomas Brinkhoff, "The Principal Agglomerations around the World," **http://www.citypopulation.de** (accessed December 6, 2002).

of economic development exceeds population growth. This task becomes even more complex when we consider that within countries with high population increases, large migration flows take place from rural to urban areas.[24] The increasing number of mega-cities of more than 8 million inhabitants illustrates the change. In 1950, only two cities, London and New York, were that size. In 2015, the projected number of mega-cities is 36—with 30 of them in the developing world and most (22) in Asia. Exhibit 17.3 shows the 10 largest urban areas in 2002.

Urbanization is taking place at different speeds on different continents. In North America, the number of city dwellers overtook the rural population before 1940. In Europe, this happened after 1950 and in Latin America, at the beginning of the 1960s. Today, these three continents are almost equally urbanized; 75 percent of Europeans and Latin Americans are city dwellers and 77 percent of North Americans, according to UN estimates. A similar process is occurring in Africa and Asia, which are still mainly rural. Their proportion of city dwellers rose from 25 percent in 1975 to a little more than 37 percent in 2001.[25] The turning point, when the figure will top 50 percent, is predicted to occur around 2025. Such movements and concentrations of people are likely to place significant stress on economic activity and the provision of services but will also make it easier for marketers to direct their activities toward customers. Of key concern in some countries is **population balance**. In some countries, for example, girls of marriageable age are in such short supply that some parents are offering a "bride price" to families of prospective mates for their sons.[26]

Another problem of many less-developed countries is an **expectation–reality gap** felt by their population. Because the persistence of unfulfilled expectations fosters discontent, these countries must close the gap. This can be accomplished either by improving economic reality—that is, offering more goods at lower prices and increasing the general standard of living—or by reducing the expectations. Although nations will attempt to improve the living standards of their people, substantial efforts to reduce expectations also appear quite likely. These efforts may require the use of de-marketing techniques on a national level.

Government Policy

A worldwide trend exists toward increased management of trade by governments. International trade activity now affects domestic policy more than in the past. Governments, in their desire to structure their domestic economic activity, will feel forced to intervene more frequently in international markets. For example, trade flows can cause major structural shifts in employment with subsequent downstream effects. Changes in automobile production will also affect the steel and plastics industries, as well as auto-parts suppliers such as those in Canada; similarly, shifts in the sourcing of textiles will affect the cotton industry. As a result, changes in international trade will require many industries to restructure their activities and their employment because of productivity gains and competitive pressures.

Yet such restructuring is not necessarily negative. For example, in 1999 in Canada, farm employment as a main job fell 6 percent from 1998. In 2000 it dropped a further 13 percent. This was followed by a further decline in 2001, so that by the end of the year farm employment was 313,000—a drop of 26 percent in 3 years, and the largest drop in 35 years.[27] As the number of farms in Canada has declined, farm labour productivity has increased with new farms and machinery investment. This enhanced productivity together with improvements in competitiveness translates into a more economical allocation of scarce labour resources to other sectors of the economy, for example to transportation and manufacturing.

Government Attitudes

Governments cannot be expected, for the sake of the theoretical ideal of "free trade," to sit back and watch the effects of deindustrialization on their countries. In this context, one frequently hears reference to the "hollowing out" of Canadian industry. The most that can be expected is that they will permit an open-market orientation, subject to the needs of domestic policy. Even an open-market orientation will be maintained only if governments can provide reasonable assurances to their firms and citizens that this openness applies not only to their own markets but to foreign markets as well. Therefore, unfair trade practices, such as governmental subsidization, dumping, and industrial targeting, will be examined more closely, and retaliation for such activities will be increasingly swift and harsh. For example, the softwood lumber dispute between Canada and the United States demonstrated the Canadian government's unwillingness to accept the level of duties imposed by the U.S.

Increasingly, governments will attempt to coordinate policies that affect the global marketing environment. At the same time, governments will find it more difficult to achieve a consensus. In the Western world, the period from 1945 to 1990 was characterized by a commonality of purpose. The common defence against the Communist enemy relegated trade relations to second place and provided a bond that encouraged collaboration. With the common threat gone, however, the bonds have also been diminished, if not dissolved, and the priority of economic performance has increased. Unless a new key jointness of purpose can be found by governments, collaborative approaches will become increasingly difficult.

Governmental policymakers must understand the global repercussions of domestic legislation. For example, in Canada the imposition of special levies (such as a penalty or surcharge on pollution-emitting industries, to support Kyoto or other targets) will need to be carefully considered in light of its repercussions on the global competitiveness of industry.

Policymakers also need a better understanding of the nature of the global trade issues confronting them. Most countries today face both short-term and long-term trade problems. Trade balance issues, for example, are short-term in nature, whereas competitiveness issues are much more long-term. All too often, however, short-term issues are attacked with long-term trade policy mechanisms, and vice versa. In the United States, for example, the desire to "level the international playing field" by negotiating a further opening of Japan's market to foreign corporations will have only a minor immediate effect on that country's trade surplus or the U.S. trade deficit.[28] Yet it is the expectation and hope of many in both the public and the private sectors that such immediate changes will occur. For the sake of the credibility of policymakers, it therefore becomes increasingly imperative to identify precisely the nature of the problem, to design and use policy measures that are appropriate for its resolution, and to communicate the hoped-for results. Of course, the level-playing-field concept will underlie the overall competitive approach of many countries, for example, Canada's broad position with regard to agri-foods.[29]

In More Detail 17.2

PICKING WINNERS AND LOSERS

The Canadian government, in common with others who support the general principle of free trade, are cautious to provide direct subsidization of companies and industrial sectors (though there are clear exceptions, for example aerospace and agriculture). Governments may also be loath to be cast in the role of choosing winners and losers in the competitive race. This does not prevent requests for help, as by the Canadian automakers hurt by the high Canadian dollar and other factors. Governments reluctant to provide direct financial help can respond in other ways, for example by providing research and development assistance. Such an approach is relevant to automakers now forced by global competition to become high-tech manufacturers, for example by installing better robotics systems. The future will see redoubled efforts by governments to develop industrial strategies that reconcile the demands of freer trade with pleas for more help.

In the years to come, governments will be faced with an accelerating technological race and with emerging problems that seem insurmountable by individual firms alone, such as pollution of the environment and global warming. Other problems might also be mentioned. For example, product standardization will continue in the future as a result of market and competitive pressures (notwithstanding the innovative efforts of Canadian firms), but enforcing world standards presents acute problems, for example, in the case of defective toys imported from China. Greater harmonization of customs regulations can also be expected in the future, but stalled WTO negotiations point to great future difficulties in this area. Lastly, world currencies present their own difficulties, for example, the concern of Western governments about what is considered the artificially low value of the yuan, to say nothing of the impact on Canadian manufacturing of the rising dollar.

As a result of such problems it seems likely that the concepts of administrative guidance and **government–corporate collaboration** will increasingly become part of the policy behaviour of governments heretofore pledged to believe only in the invisible hand of the free market. Governments can be expected to offer a variety of supporting postures toward the global marketer. The global marketer in turn will have to spend more time and effort dealing with governments and with macro rather than micro issues. (For further comments on this issue with special reference to the Canadian situation, see the last section of this chapter).

The Future of Global Marketing Management

Global marketing continues to be seen as a key contributor to Canada's overall economic performance. In this section we will review some future prospects for global marketing using the marketing mix framework: research, product policies, global communications, distribution trends, and pricing policies.

As an introduction, let us note that markets and marketing were affected in a major way by the terrorist attacks of September 11, 2001. Because this particular assault was focused on the United States, the country's sense of stability, feeling of security, and attitudes toward the world were profoundly changed in a few hours. However, the emotional reaction was immediate and felt throughout the world, and the economic impact of the terrorist attacks continues.

Directly or indirectly, virtually all global business activities have been affected by these events. Overall consumer demand went into shock worldwide, and in some industries, particularly those pertaining to luxury goods, it declined precipitously. The marginal customers who had gradually become important to many industries dropped out in droves as they hunkered down to observe everyone else's reactions. Airlines, airports, concession stands, hotels, and travel agents experienced massive dislocations. Findings from one large-scale study, carried out at Georgetown University, specifically comment on how the terrorist attacks are likely to affect global marketing.[30]

One conclusion of the study was the observation that countries are more willing to collaborate with one another. The agreement to a new round of trade talks, reached at the end of the WTO's 2001 meeting in Doha, support this view. Several highly controversial issues, such as agricultural subsidies, dumping regulations, property rights, and investment rules were placed on the table in spite of dire predictions by trade-policy naysayers.

Mutual respect and collaboration have opened the road toward progress, but the fact that the Doha round was halted in July 2006 after major powers disagreed on sensitive political issues, especially the call for dismantling agricultural protection, shows that the road ahead will still present difficulties. Yet four years after the Georgetown University study, the resilience of world trade is not in doubt. Overall merchandise trade growth increased by almost 9 percent in 2005, admittedly a lower growth rate compared with an almost 12 percent increase in 2004.[31] But global concern with terrorism remains widespread, and the fallout of 9/11 is still being contended with in various forms, for example, the much greater emphasis placed on security by the U.S., which influences Canada's cross-border transactions with its largest trading partner.

Research and Planning

Focus on the customer will remain a major factor in marketing. The global marketer must continue to serve customers well. At the same time, governmental demands will increasingly intrude in the worldwide marketing arena. This means that the global marketing manager will have to take general governmental concerns much more into account when planning a marketing strategy. In light of a greater security focus, firms now concentrate more on where to sell, what to sell, and to whom to sell, rather than just selling wherever possible. Managers are developing an appreciation for the type and degree of risk exposure in certain regions of the world. Leading risk factors include the policies of home and host governments, exchange rate fluctuations, and economic turmoil.

More firms are developing trade portfolios that allocate effort and limits in different regions of the world. These portfolios are intended to achieve two goals: 1) limit dependence on any region or customer in order to reduce a firm's exposure to conflict or unexpected interruptions, and 2) systematically develop markets to balance existing exposure, to diversify a firm's risk, and to offer a fallback position.

Exporting, for its part, permits a broader and quicker coverage of world markets with the ability to respond to changes. Risks are lower, but costs tend to be higher because of transshipment and transaction expenses. Even though an export orientation is seen to be less risky, many firms are not as aggressive as they used to be in seeking new business or new accounts. A new desire to deal with old, established customers, "people whom we

In More Detail 17.3

THE GLOBAL MARKETER'S CATCH-22

Global marketers face a catch-22 situation. On the one hand they must base their decisions upon comprehensive marketing research and other information. Without this the company is "flying blind." On the other hand, market knowledge and modern research techniques alone will not guarantee a source of market advantage because these are available widely to competitors. What is the company to do? One answer is self-evident and yet demands extraordinary commitment and hard work: simply be the best in one's chosen market. This is illustrated by the Canadian company Extreme CCTV, located in Burnaby, British Columbia, which in a short space of years has emerged as a leading innovator in the design and manufacture of advanced infrared illuminators and precision-engineered video surveillance products. Founded by UBC engineering graduates, the company has won international product achievement awards every year since breaking into the United States security market in 1997, and now exports all over the world. This has been the result of extraordinary attention to performance excellence, and an unwavering insistence on innovation as a way of company life. This will lay the foundation for growth in the future.

know and with whom we have developed a feeling of trust," has emerged. An export approach appears to be the preferred method of new market entry these days. It may remain the principal tool of international expansion for firms new to the global market or those highly concerned about international risk.

The diverging needs of foreign consumers will result in more available niches in which firms can create a distinct global competence, an art that many Canadian SMEs have mastered. This points toward increased specialization and segmentation. Firms will attempt to fill very narrow and specific demands or to resolve very specific problems for their worldwide customers. Identifying and filling these niches will be easier in the future because of the greater availability of international research tools and information. At the same time, the greater availability of information will make it tougher to compete, since many more competitors will become active globally.

Public outrage can depress sales or block permits for new facilities, while public approval of a company's association with good causes can create customer and public goodwill and even allay local concerns about foreign companies. In Canada, Lululemon Athletica Inc., a Vancouver-based athletic-wear company, supports rower Silken Laumann's Active Kids Movement, which promotes unstructured play by children. EDS, a large systems-integration company, has run a Global Volunteer Day (GVD) since 1993; in India, the new relationships and positive aura created by GVD were a main factor in successful market entry. These activities bear no resemblance to traditional charity; they apply a company's skills and innovation processes to increase quality of life.[32] The result is new opportunities for both customers and firms.

Global marketers will therefore be torn in many directions. In order to provide results that are acceptable to governments, customers, and the societies they serve, they must walk a fine line, balancing the public and the private good.

Reputation management, or the strategy of building reputation as a corporate asset, is likely to gain prominence in the years ahead as pressure on corporations to be good corporate citizens grows.[33] Globally, the acceptance of market thinking can only work if accompanied by managerial and corporate virtue, vision, and veracity. Unless the world can believe in what firms and managers say and do, it will be nearly impossible to forge a global commitment between those doing the marketing and those being marketed to. It is therefore of vital interest to the proponents of globalization to ensure that corruption, bribery, lack of transparency, and the misleading of stakeholders are relegated to the scrapheap of history. Perhaps the WTO should take steps to ensure a commitment to long-term thinking and truthfulness on the part of global marketers.[34]

Product Policies

One key issue affecting product planning will be environmental concerns. Major public attention paid to the natural environment, environmental pollution, and global warming will provide many new product opportunities and affect existing products to a large degree. For example, manufacturers will increasingly be expected to take responsibility for their products from cradle to grave and to be intimately involved in product disposal and recycling. Although some consumers show a growing interest in truly "natural" products, even if they are less convenient, consumers in most industrialized nations will require products that are environmentally friendly but at the same time do not require too much compromise on performance and value. Management is likely to resist the additional business cost and taxes required for environmental protection, at least until investors and other constituent groups assure executives that environmental concern is acceptable even if it cuts into profit.

Greater Speed of Product Introductions

Worldwide introduction of products will occur much more rapidly in the future. Already, **international product life cycles** have accelerated substantially. Whereas product introduction could previously be spread out over several years, firms now must prepare for product life cycles that can be measured in months or even weeks.[35] As a result, firms must design products and plan even their domestic marketing strategies with the international product cycle in mind. Product introduction will grow more complex, more expensive, and more risky, yet the rewards to be reaped from a successful product will have to be accumulated more quickly.

Early incorporation of the global dimension into product planning, however, does not point toward increased standardization. On the contrary, companies will have to be ready to deliver more mass customization. Customers are no longer satisfied with simply having a product: they want it to precisely meet their needs and preferences. **Mass customization** requires working with existing product technology, often in modular form, to create specific product bundles for a particular customer.

Factor Endowment Advantages

These advantages have a significant impact on the decisions of global marketers. Given the acceleration of product life cycles, nations with low production costs will be able to replicate products more quickly and cheaply. Countries such as China, India, and the Philippines offer large pools of skilled people at labour rates much lower than those in Europe, Japan, or Canada. All this talent also results in a much wider dissemination of technological creativity, a factor that will affect the innovative capability of firms. For example, nearly half of all the U.S. patents granted in 2002 were awarded to foreign entities. This indicates that firms need to make such foreign know-how part of their production strategies, or they need to develop consistent comparative advantages in production technology in order to stay ahead of the game. Similarly, workers engaged in the production process must attempt, through training and skill enhancement, to stay ahead of foreign workers who are willing to charge less for their time.

Trend Toward Strategic Alliances

An increase will occur in the trend toward strategic alliances, or partnering, permitting the formation of collaborative arrangements between firms. These alliances will enable firms to take risks that they could not afford to take alone, facilitate technological advancement, and ensure continued global market access. These partners do not need to be large in order to make a major contribution. Depending on the type of product, very small firms can serve as coordinating subcontractors and collaborate in product and service development, production, and distribution.

Production Management

On the production management side, security concerns now make it imperative to identify and manage one's dependence on global inputs. Industrial customers, in particular, are often seen as pushing for local sourcing. A domestic source simply provides a greater feeling of comfort. A sales manager in Ontario, for example, may find that his customers feel more at home with goods made in an Oshawa plant rather than with those that come from Argentina, Greece, or Venezuela. Interruptions in supply and related issues are valid concerns, but, rightly or wrongly, deeply seated psychological factors are more likely at work. Some firms also report a new meaning associated with the *made-in* dimension in country-of-origin labelling. In the past, this dimension was viewed as enhancing products, as with perfumes made in France or cars made in Germany. Lately, the made-in dimension of some countries may create an exclusionary context by making both industrial customers and consumers reject products from specific regions. As a result, negative effects may result from geographic proximity to terrorists, as has been claimed by some about textile imports from Pakistan.

The bottom line still matters. After all, money needs to be made, and global marketing tends to be quite profitable. However, the issue of dependability of supplies is raised at many senior-management meetings, and a premium is now associated with having a known and long-term supplier. In the future, foreign suppliers may have to be recommended by existing customers or partners and be able to cope with contingencies before their products are even considered.

Trends in Global Communications

Advances in worldwide communications will have a profound impact on the global marketer. Entire industries are becoming more footloose in their operations; that is, they are less tied to their current location in their interaction with markets. Most affected by these advances will be members of the services industry. By easily bridging distances, service providers will mainly be concerned about the right to operate rather than the right to establish themselves in the global arena. Communications for worldwide operations, for example, could be located in Africa or Asia and not impair global corporate activities.

For manufacturers, staff in different countries not only can talk together but also can share pictures and data on their computer screens. These simultaneous interactions with different parts of the world will strengthen research and development efforts. Faster knowledge transfer will allow for the concentration of product expertise, increased division of labour, and a proliferation of global operations.

Distribution Trends

Innovative distribution approaches will determine new ways of serving markets. For example, television through QVC has already created a $3.9 billion shopping mall available in more than 125.6 million homes worldwide.[36] Over time, self-sustaining consumer–distributor relationships will emerge. The link to distribution systems will also be crucial to global marketers on the business-to-business level. As large retailers develop sophisticated inventory tracking and reordering systems, only the firms able to interact with such systems will remain eligible suppliers. Therefore, firms need to create their own distribution systems that are able to respond to information technology requirements around the globe.

Impact of the New Security Environment

Companies have already accepted that the global pipeline has slowed down and that customary steps will now take longer in the new security environment. But the structure of the pipeline and the scrutiny given to the materials going through the pipeline have become important. Firms that had developed elaborate just-in-time delivery systems for their global supplies were severely affected by the border and port closures immediately following the attacks of September 11, 2001. These firms and their service providers continue to be affected by increased security measures. Firms are also focusing more on internal security and the need to demonstrate externally how much more security-oriented they have become. In many instances, government authorities require evidence of threat-reduction efforts to speed shipments along. Also, insurance companies have increased their premiums substantially for firms that are exposed to increased risk.

Carriers with sophisticated hub-and-spoke systems have discovered that transshipments between the different spokes may add to delays because of the time needed to re-scrutinize packages. Firms with a just-in-time system are also exploring alternative management strategies, such as shifting international shipments from air to sea. More dramatically, some firms are considering replacing international shipments with domestic ones, in which truck transport would replace trans-border movement altogether and eliminate the use of vulnerable ports. Future scenarios also accommodate the effects of substantial and long-term interruptions of supplies or operations. Still, any actual move away from existing just-in-time systems is likely to be minor unless new large-scale interruptions occur. See The Global Marketplace 17.4 for further evidence of future change in the logistics area.

Continued Vulnerability to Attack

Many positions have been created in the corporate security field, focusing on new production sites, alternative distribution methods, server mobility, and new linkages with customers. In some instances, key customers have been involved in the development of emergency procedures to keep operations going.

In spite of these measures, however, vulnerability to attack continues to be high. For example, 43 percent of all the maritime containers that arrived in the United States in 2001 came through the ports of Los Angeles and Long Beach. There are no required security

The Global MARKETPLACE 17.4

Towards Paperless Trading?

Considering Canada/U.S. trade, what is referred to as the 49th parallel is in fact a boundary stretching almost 9000 kilometers between the two countries with some 130 crossing locations where freight can be exchanged. However, one critical crossing site is not to be found in the atlas—the so-called "electronic border," which is becoming increasingly significant in the clearance of imported and exported goods. More and more of the essential paperwork between the two countries is being carried out electronically, and computer-to-computer linkups with Canadian and U.S. customs is in many ways a model that other countries might emulate.

Whether intercountry trading in general will eventually evolve towards a paperless basis is a moot question. Certainly if this could be accomplished, various advantages would follow: both exporters and importers would benefit from reduced costs of shipping goods across borders, lower communications and paper-handling charges, fewer errors and faster receipts of payments, reduced trade finance charges, and lower inventories. Considerable savings would also accrue to banks, insurers, carriers, and governments in administering cross-border transactions. In addition, SMEs would find expanded opportunities as traditional impediments (e.g., cost and complexity of compliance with export/import regulations) became less pressing.

Governments such as those of Canada and the U.S., with strong cross-agency co-ordination mechanisms, are likely to make the most progress in removing regulations and institutional barriers to paperless trading, even if security concerns seem at times to frustrate this objective. However, other countries, for example members of APEC (Asia-Pacific Economic Council), are also making progress towards this end.

But the obstacles should not be overlooked. Governments will not easily remove mandatory requirements for paper-based documents in international trade. Also consider the antiquity of some of the documents in current use: the letter of credit and bill of lading, for example, were first invented in the 16th century, and despite technological developments in the recent past, are still basic to trade today. Any new system developed officially or by specialist software organizations must be easily assimilated into long-established and familiar workflows and practices.

Another challenge is driving adoption of new methods among a wide range of players who provide or utilize documents in any given transaction—exporters, banks, purchasers, shipping lines, logistics companies, sales agents, inspection services, and so on. If one link is missing, the value of a unified system is compromised. Despite these difficulties the future is highly likely to see a continued effort by all parties to reduce and perhaps ultimately eliminate documentation hurdles in international trade.

Sources: Herscovitch, Toby, "Wide Range: Cutting the Cost of Crossing Borders," *Exportwise,* (Winter 2006); *Paperless Trading: Benefits to APEC,* Foreign Affairs and Trade, Ministry of Foreign Trade and Economic Cooperation, Commonwealth of Australia, 2001, **www.dfat.gov.au/publications/paperless/index.html**; *Paperless Trade,* Global Facilitation Partnership for Transportation and Trade, The United Nations Trade Facilitation Network, January 30, 2008, **www.gfptt.org/entities/TopicProfile.aspx?name=paperless.**

standards governing the loading or transport of an inter-modal container. Most are "sealed" with a 50-cent lead tag. An explosive device in a single container might well gridlock the entire flow and loading systems.[37]

Pricing Policies

Many products, as they become distributed more widely throughout the world, will take on commodity characteristics, as semiconductors did in the 1980s. Therefore, small price differentials per unit may become crucial in making international sales. For new products and technologies, firms will increasingly be forced to engage in **forward pricing** by distributing development cost over the anticipated volume of sales. This task will be difficult and controversial because demand levels for totally new products are impossible to predict accurately. As a result, firms will be open to charges of dumping.

Even for consumer products, price competition will be substantial. Because of the increased dissemination of technology, the firm that introduces a product will not be able to justify higher prices for long; domestically produced products will soon be of similar

In More Detail 17.4

SHORT- VS. LONG-TERM PRICING PROBLEMS

The appreciation of the Canadian currency to parity with the U.S. dollar has led companies to ponder the question of whether this should be treated as a short- or long-term phenomenon. In the short term, different strategies are possible. One approach is to shift the focus from pricing to benefits and features, that is, product differentiation. Another is to choose distributors who agree to adopt aggressive pricing. Alternatively, the firm may simply lower prices. If these and other approaches do not yield results, perhaps there is no simple answer in the short term. The freight, duty, taxes, and related costs may simply make the Canadian product totally noncompetitive in the U.S. (or other) markets. Therefore in the longer term firms may have to consider relatively more expensive and risky options. These will help to reduce costs. Options include partial manufacturing (export the product partially finished), local assembly (ship components for assembly in the foreign market), licensing, and foreign manufacturing. In formulating their future global strategies, Canadian firms will need to review these options in tandem with their judgements of longer-term currency movements.

quality. As a result, exchange-rate movements may play more significant roles in maintaining the competitiveness of the global firm. Firms can be expected to prevail on their government to manage the country's currency to maintain a favourable exchange rate, though not always successfully, as evidenced in 2007 by the rise in the Canadian currency to parity with the U.S. dollar and the resulting pressures on manufacturers. Technology also allows much closer interaction on pricing between producer and customer.

The success of electronic commerce providers such as eBay (**http://www.ebay.com**) and Priceline (**http://www.priceline.com**) demonstrates how auctioning and bidding, alone or in competition with others, offers new perspectives on the global price mechanism. Government management of trade will continue to influence international pricing in other ways. Through subsidization, targeting, and government contracts, nations will attempt to stimulate their global competitiveness. Because of the price sensitivity of many products, the global marketer will be forced to identify such unfair practices quickly, communicate them to his or her government, and insist on either similar benefits or government negotiation of an internationally level playing field.

Concurrently, however, global marketers will continue to differentiate themselves in the market on a non-price basis. Major efforts will be undertaken to appeal to the market via services, quality, or other special aspects rather than on price alone. By accomplishing such an objective successfully, a firm can buy itself freedom from short-term fluctuations in its business relationships.

Careers in Global Marketing

The reader of this book, it is hoped, has learned about the intricacies, complexities, and thrills of global marketing. Of course, a career in global marketing does not consist only of jet-setting travel between Rome, London, and Paris. It is hard work and requires knowledge and expertise. Globalists need to be well versed in the specific business functions and may wish to work at summer internships abroad, take language courses, and travel not simply for pleasure but to observe business operations overseas and to gain a greater understanding of different peoples and cultures. Taking on and successfully completing an international assignment is seen by managers as crucial for the development of professional, managerial, and intercultural skills and is highly likely to affect career advancement.[38]

Further Training

One option for the student on the road to more global involvement is to obtain further in-depth training by enrolling in graduate business school programs that specialize in international business education. But this is not the only educational route. Two- or three-year college international business programs are also extremely valuable, and indeed are admired for their pragmatic approach. There many excellent colleges of this sort in Canada. A substantial number of universities in Canada, the U.S., and around the world specialize in training global managers. According to the Institute of International Education, the number of U.S. students studying for a degree at universities abroad rose to almost 206,000 students in 2006. Furthermore, American students increasingly go abroad for business and economics degrees, not just for a semester or two. At the same time, business and management are the most popular fields of study for the 564,766 international students at American universities.[39] A review of college catalogues and of materials from groups such as the Academy of International Business will be useful here. Not all international students will travel abroad in order to obtain management degrees, of course, and some countries will favour "home-grown" graduates, at least for first degrees.

In the case of other countries, about 4 percent of Australian students study abroad, and with regard to the European Union, some 8 percent of students go on short-term exchanges. However, less than 1 percent of Canadian postsecondary students have an opportunity to work abroad. According to the Association of Universities and Colleges of Canada, this gap can be explained by a relative lack of federal funding, although other factors are also at work, such as fee levels and travels costs. On a per capita basis, Canada spends 80 cents, Australia the equivalent of $9.07, Germany $3.02, and the U.S. $4.70 on federal international scholarships and exchange programs. This places Canada far behind other OECD countries in terms of sending students abroad to gain international experience and knowledge, a disturbing state of affairs.[40]

In addition, as the world becomes more global, more organizations are able to assist students interested in studying abroad or in gathering foreign work experience. Apart from individual universities and their programs for study abroad, many nonprofit institutions stand ready to help and to provide informative materials. For those ready to enter or rejoin the "real world," different employment opportunities need to be evaluated.

Employment with Large Firms

One career alternative in global marketing is to work for a large multinational corporation, though the variety of choice is smaller in some countries (e.g., Canada) than in others (e.g., the United States). These firms constantly search for personnel to help them in their global operations. For example, a Procter & Gamble recruiting advertisement published in a university's student newspaper is reproduced in Exhibit 17.4.

Many multinational firms, while seeking specialized knowledge such as languages, expect employees to be firmly grounded in the practice and management of business. Rarely, if ever, will a firm hire a new employee at the starting level and immediately place him or her in a post of international responsibility. Usually, a new employee is expected to become thoroughly familiar with the company's internal operations before being considered for an international position. The reason a manager is sent abroad is that the company expects him or her to reflect the corporate spirit, to be tightly wed to the corporate culture, and to be able to communicate well with both local and corporate management personnel. In this liaison position, the manager will have to be exceptionally sensitive to both headquarters and local operations. As an intermediary, the expatriate must be empathetic and understanding yet fully prepared to implement the goals set by headquarters.

As noted in Chapter 14, it is very expensive for companies to send an employee overseas. Typically, the annual cost of maintaining a manager abroad is about three times the cost of hiring a local manager. Companies want to be sure that the expenditure is worth the benefit they will receive, even though certainty is never possible.

Even if a position opens up in international operations, there is some truth in the saying that the best place to be in global business is on the same floor as the chairperson at headquarters. Employees of firms that have taken the international route often come back to headquarters to find only a few positions available for them. Such encounters lead, of course, to organizational difficulties, as well as to financial pressures and family problems, all of which may add up to significant executive stress. Because family reentry angst is one reason 25 percent of expatriates quit within a year of their return, companies are paying increasing attention to the spouses and children of employees. For example, about 15 percent of Fortune 500 firms offer support for children of employees relocated abroad.[41]

Exhibit 17.4 Advertisement Recruiting New Graduates for Employment in International Operations

EN BUSCA DE SU TALENTO

Procter & Gamble
División de Peru/Latino America

¤ Más de 40 productos de consumo en Latino America como Pampers, Ace, Ariel, Crest, Head & Shoulders, Camay y Vicks.

¤El area tiene el mayor volumen de ventas entre todas las divisiones Internacionales de P&G.

¤Oportunidades de desarrollar una carrera profesional en areas como Mercadeo, Finanzas, Computación, Ventas, etc.

Buscamos individuos con Talento, Empuje, Liderazgo, y continuo afán de superación para posiciones permanentes o practicas de verano en Peru, Puerto Rico, México, Colombia, Venezuela, Brazil, Chile, etc.

Es muy importante que envies tu RESUME pronto ya que estaremos visitando tu Universidad en la primera semana de Noviembre.

¿QUE DEBES HACER?
Envia tu resume tan pronto como sea posible a la atencion de Ms. Cynthia Huddleston (MBA Career Services) antes del 18 de Octubre.

Source: The Procter & Gamble Company. Used by permission.

Employment with SMEs

A second alternative is to begin work in a small or medium-sized firm, an option that will be commonly chosen by Canadian employees. Very often, these firms have only recently developed an international outlook, and the new employee will arrive on the "ground floor." Initial involvement will normally be in the export field—evaluating potential foreign customers, preparing quotes, and dealing with mundane activities such as shipping and transportation. With a very limited budget, the export manager will only occasionally visit foreign markets to discuss marketing strategy with foreign distributors. Most of the work will be done by e-mail, fax, or telephone. The hours are often long because of the need to reach contacts overseas, for example, during business hours in Hong Kong. Yet the possibilities for implementing creative business methods are virtually limitless, and the contribution made by the successful export manager will be visible in the firm's growing export volume.

Alternatively, international work in a small firm may involve importing—finding new low-cost sources for domestically sourced products. Decisions often must be based on limited information, and the import manager is faced with many uncertainties. Often, things do not work out as planned. Shipments are delayed, letters of credit are cancelled, and products almost never arrive in exactly the form and shape anticipated. Yet the problems are always new and offer an ongoing challenge.

As a training ground for global marketing activities, there is probably no better place than a smaller firm. Ideally, the person with some experience may find work with an export-training or export-management company, resolving other people's problems and concentrating virtually exclusively on the international arena.

Self-Employment

A third alternative is to hang up a consultant's shingle or to establish a trading firm. Many companies are in dire need of help for their international marketing effort and are quite prepared to part with a portion of their profits to receive it. Yet in-depth knowledge and broad experience are required to make a major contribution to a company's international marketing endeavour or to run a trading firm successfully. Specialized services that might be offered by a consultant include international market research, international strategic planning, or, particularly desirable, beginning-to-end assistance in international market entry or international marketing negotiations.

The up-front costs of offering such a service are substantial and are not covered by turnover but rather have to be covered by profits. Yet the rewards are there. For an international marketing expert, the hourly billable rate typically is as high as $400 for experienced principals and $150 for staff. Whenever international travel is required, overseas activities are often billed at the daily rate of $3,000 plus expenses. The latter can add up quickly, as the cost-per-diem map in Exhibit 17.5 shows. When trading on one's own, income and risk can be limitless. Even at these relatively high rates, solid groundwork must be completed before all the overhead is paid. The advantage is the opportunity to become a true global entrepreneur. Consultants and owners of trading firms will work at a higher degree of risk than employees, but with the opportunity for higher rewards.

Opportunities for Women

As firms become more and more involved in global business activities, the need for skilled global managers is growing. Concurrent with this increase in business activity is the ever-growing presence and managerial role of women in global business.

Research conducted during the mid 1980s[42] indicated that women held 3.3 percent of the overseas positions in U.S. business firms. Five years prior to that time, almost no women were global managers in either expatriate or professional travel status. Thus, the 3.3 percent figure represented a significant increase. By 2000, 13 percent of expatriates in U.S. corporations were women.[43] The reason for the low participation of women in global management roles seems to have been the assumption that because of their subservient role in Japan, Latin America, and the Middle East, neither local nor expatriate women would be allowed to succeed as managers. The error is that expatriates are not seen as local women, but rather as "foreigners who happen to be women," thus solving many of the problems that would be encountered by a local woman manager.

There appear to be some distinct advantages for a woman in a management position overseas. Among them are the advantages of added visibility and increased access to

Exhibit 17.5

The Cost Per Diem in the World's Major Business Cities (in U.S. dollars)

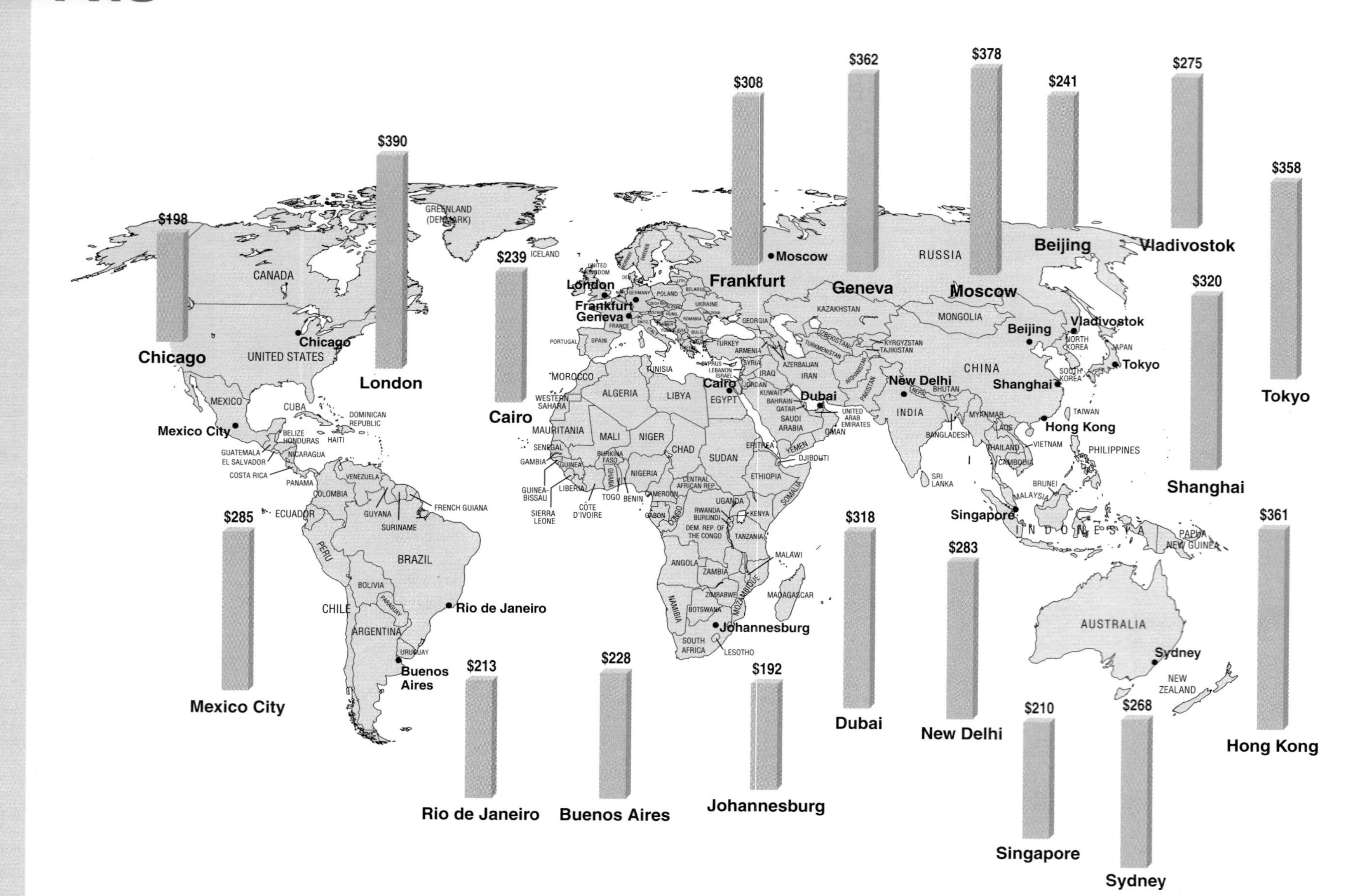

Source: U.S. Department of State, January 2006, **http://www.state.gov/travel** (accessed December 6, 2002).

clients. Clients tend to assume that "expatriate women must be excellent, or else their companies would not have sent them."

It also appears that companies that are larger in terms of sales, assets, income, and employees send more women overseas than smaller organizations. Further, the number of women expatriates is not evenly distributed among industry groups. Industry groups that utilize greater numbers or percentages of women expatriates include banking, electronics, petroleum, publishing, diversified corporations, pharmaceuticals, and retailing and apparel.

For the future, it is anticipated that the upward trend previously cited reflects increased participation of women in global management roles.

Canada and the "New" International Competition

Only a few years ago, it seemed a safe bet to predict that multinational companies would dominate world markets and that huge emerging markets such as China and India would present endless market opportunities (but also challenges). While accepting that those countries would eventually become "economic powerhouses" in their own right by developing their industries, few would have imagined that eventually new emerging-market companies would actually challenge the supremacy of entrenched multinationals.

In fact this is now happening. In the words of one source, "While globalization has opened new markets to rich-world companies, it has also given birth to a pack of fast-moving, sharp-toothed new multinationals that is emerging from the poor world."[44] Let us conclude this chapter by looking a little more closely at the implications of this development for the future of Canadian global marketers.

This newer challenge will not confront multinationals alone, but will also eventually have an impact on any Canadian company active in global markets, as "Indian and Chinese firms are now starting to give their rich-world rivals a run for their money."[45] This is hardly good news for SMEs of all kinds who have tended to view large emerging markets as arenas awaiting the plucking, the main requirement being a willingness to seek out the business. To illustrate the vitality of the new competition, in 2007, Indian firms, led by Hindalco and Tata Steel, have bought some 34 foreign companies for a combined $10.7 billion. Also, Indian IT-service companies such as Infosys, Tata Consulting Services, and Wipro are increasingly challenging established firms such Accenture and even IBM. Brazilian and Russian multinationals are also emerging.

These are early days, of course. The emerging companies still cannot match the established firms in terms of market reach and power, although they can claim great agility. These companies will also find it difficult to match the array of non-price and service-style benefits (e.g., quality assurance, relationship marketing, customer-service skills, reliability reputation) that established firms can offer. But the newer firms are here and are developing rapidly, leaving existing companies to ask if their accustomed sources of market advantage are about to change drastically, and what to do about it. This dilemma is bound to confront Canadian firms in the next several years.

What Can Be Done?

It is not too fanciful to anticipate that firms will need to contemplate radical and far-reaching changes in their approach to global marketing—in fact, to develop new business models. This is the view of the president and chief executive officer of IBM.[46] In his opinion, MNEs have passed through three main stages. Firstly was the "international model," whereby firms were based in their home country but sold goods through overseas sales offices. Secondly came the classic multinational firm, in which the parent company created smaller versions of itself in countries throughout the world. Now, thirdly, we are beginning to see the emergence of the "globally integrated enterprise," in which the firm shapes its strategy, management, and operations as a single global entity, putting people and jobs anywhere in the world, wherever the jobs are performed best at lowest cost. IBM, for example, has over 50,000 employees in India, and its head of procurement has been relocated to Shenzen in China.

The president of IBM concedes that the company transformation will be the work of a generation. But the writing is on the wall now for Canadian companies. What might they do? Though Canada is not heavily populated by MNEs, those that do exist need to ask the same fundamental question that IBM is asking—how are our competitive advantages to be sustained in the new environment? It seems that only a sweeping rethinking of marketing and other strategies, in which all conventional wisdom is challenged, will meet the situation.

Canada's SMEs are right to point out that they are not multinationals. But it would make little sense to ignore the growing severity of competition and the newer sources from which it is coming. For many SMEs, the cultivation of a specialized market niche will be the chosen route. Innovative new products developed through intensive R & D and incorporating breakthrough technologies will provide the needed market advantage. Encouraging such an approach is a deliberate plank of government strategy—to propel Canada into the position of a leading-edge, technology-driven economy, with a variety of official agencies providing help, support, and finance. Canadian innovation has been described as a "kaleidoscope of technological breakthroughs."[47] Niches where significant advances have been made include space technology (e.g., Canadarm2), geomatics (Canada is a world leader), and bio-security. Worldwide markets seem secured by Canadian ingenuity—or are they?

No matter how advanced the product, others can catch up. Also, there is much more to global marketing than the product offering, important though that is. An old marketing adage says that if you build a better mousetrap, the world will beat a path to your door. But firms have learned that without proper attention to marketing, as developed in this book, the world will not beat this path. There is no doubt that Canadian global marketers have attracted their fair share of criticism. There have been complaints that companies have made a poor show of penetrating new markets such as China. Popular business publications take firms to task for a lack of spirit and determination in making inroads abroad, and for showing too much timidity and reluctance to develop newer Canadian MNEs.[48] And of course these charges are vigorously denied, especially by those familiar with the international achievements of Canadian business.

The Role of the Government

A critical point arises: if indeed some companies could do more internationally, what should the role of the government be as we move into this super-competitive era? Direct support and encouragement through various agencies in Canada will continue and will be intensified in future, even if the help itself, paradoxically, is sometimes criticized. Why criticized? Because something that is offered for free is often thought to be without value. This is fundamentally why critics are quick to suggest that services have a low rate of usage among eligible companies and that their availability is not even widely known. To the extent that this is true, government support agencies in future need to pay attention to their own marketing strategies, including promotion, so that maximum benefit is delivered.

At a deeper level, one school of thought sees government engagement in industry as "interference" and would like to see officialdom taken "off the backs" of business. Canada is one of the world's leading free trading countries, but this is accompanied by central policies that some believe are contradictory. Consider for example such "signs" in the Canadian economy as relatively low productivity, a growing gap in real incomes between Canada and the U.S., relatively high personal and business taxes, and a fondness for regulation and government control. Some observers take the view that a reduction in tax burdens, fewer regulations, leaving more decisions in the hands of consumers, and other measures, will lead to a more vibrant economy conducive to entrepreneurship and business growth. In this model, companies would become less dependent on the state and more self-reliant, and therefore better able and more inclined to take on future competitive challenges internationally.

However, it is not the purpose of this book to advocate one government policy or another, only to note that the future competitive prospects of Canadian industry will depend not solely on a willingness to make difficult strategic decisions, including marketing ones, but also on what stance the central government takes. This intermingling of business enterprise and official activities will be a key theme running through global marketing in the future and will do much to condition competitive success.

Summary

This chapter has provided an overview of the global changes facing global marketers and the alternative managerial responses to these changes. Global marketing is a complex and difficult activity, yet it affords many challenges and opportunities. In the chapter we dealt with these issues under five major headings. Firstly, we looked at the global market environment from the viewpoint of how countries and country groupings are changing. We compared developing versus developed countries and planned versus free economies, and we paid special attention to Southeast Asia and the BRIC countries. Secondly, we examined a series of factors influencing global marketing: finance, technology, trade, and population. We noted various changes occurring in these areas and the resulting impact on global marketing. Thirdly, we reviewed likely future trends in marketing management, and we conducted this review under marketing mix headings: research and planning, product policies, communications, distribution, and pricing policies. Fourthly, we discussed the question of careers in global marketing and spelled out several of the key routes to such careers. Lastly, we discussed newer competitive forces emerging in the global marketplace and the likely impact of these on Canadian global marketers.

Key Terms

BRIC countries (p. 619)
environmental protection (p. 618)
expectation–reality gap (p. 626)
forward pricing (p. 633)
government–corporate collaboration (p. 628)
international product life cycles (p. 630)
mass customization (p. 631)
population balance (p. 626)
population stabilization (p. 625)
reputation management (p. 630)

Questions for Discussion

1. For many developing countries, debt repayment and trade are closely interlinked. What does protectionism mean to them?
2. Explain why global companies will increasingly attempt to market their products to subsistence economies. What special marketing problems will be presented by targeting these markets?
3. How do security concerns change the way international markets do business?
4. How do you expect global competition to change in the future? If Canadian products are advanced technologically, will this be a sufficient protection from rivals?
5. Some people argue that in the next decade a successful corporate marketing strategy must take into account the promotion of the public good (such as contributing to reducing environmental pollution and global warming). Do you agree with this and why?
6. What do you think are the qualifications needed to successfully locate a good job in global marketing in the next decade?

Internet Exercises

1. Using the website of Living Abroad (**http://www.livingabroad.com**), research several international schools that may interest you. What are the site's most interesting links to other websites concerning international issues? Why are you particularly interested in them?
2. The website **http://www.overseasjobs.com** provides valuable information for those interested in jobs overseas. What skills do international employers seem to value most? Peruse the job listings and find several jobs that might interest you. Also, take a look at the profiles of several international companies that you might be interested in working for. What characteristics do the international firms listed here possess?

Recommended Readings

Adler, Nancy. *From Boston to Beijing.* Cincinnati, OH: South-Western College Publishing, 2002.

Buckley, Peter, and Mark Casson. *The Future of the Multinational Enterprise.* New York: Palgrave Macmillan, 2002.

Clifford, Mark, and Supachai Panitchpadki. *China and the WTO: Changing China, Changing World Trade.* Singapore: John Wiley & Sons, 2002.

Condon, Bradly. *NAFTA, WTO, and Global Business Strategy: How Aids, Trade and Terrorism Affect Our Economic Future.* Westport, CT: Quorum Books, 2002.

Cornelius, Peter, and Klaus Schwab, eds. *The Global Competitiveness Report 2002–2003.* Oxford: Oxford University Press, 2002.

Czinkota, Michael R., and Ilkka A. Ronkainen, eds. *Best Practices in International Marketing.* Mason, OH: Thomson, 2002.

Friedman, Thomas L. *The Lexus and the Olive Tree.* Wilmington, NC: Anchor Books, 2000.

Gilpin, Robert. *The Challenge of Global Capitalism: The World Economy in the 21st Century.* Princeton, NJ: Princeton University Press, 2002.

Hollenbeck, George P., and Morgan W. McCall Jr. *Developing Global Executives.* Boston: Harvard Business School Press, 2002.

Omae, Kenichi. *The Invisible Continent: Four Strategic Imperatives of the New Economy.* New York: Harperbusiness, 2001.

Notes

1. William Lazer and Eric H. Shaw, "Global Marketing Management: At the Dawn of the New Millennium," *Journal of International Marketing* 8, no. 1 (2000): 65–77.
2. Reiner Springer and Michael R. Czinkota, "Marketing's Contribution to the Transformation of Central and Eastern Europe," *Thunderbird International Business Review* 41, no. 1 (1999): 29–48.
3. "What Drives Growth in the Transition Countries?" *European Bank for Reconstruction and Development,* November 2006, **http://www.ebrd.com** (accessed December 21, 2006).
4. "Russian Business Makes Up for Lost Time," *RIA Novosti,* December 14, 2006, **http://en.rian.ru/analysis/20061214/56910499.html** (accessed December 24, 2006).
5. Andrea Aslund, "Russia's WTO Accession," Peter G. Peterson Institute for International Economics, Testimony at the Hearing on European Union Economic and Trade Relations with Russia, Committee on International Trade, European Parliament, Brussels, November 21, 2006.
6. World Resources Institute, *World Resources 2005: The Wealth of the Poor: Managing Ecosystems to Fight Poverty* (Washington, DC: WRI, 2005).
7. Michael R. Czinkota, Ilkka A. Ronkainen, and Bob Donath, *Mastering Global Markets* (Cincinnati, OH: Thomson, 2003).
8. "Business and Political Leaders Discuss Digital Divide," *World Economic Forum,* Davos, **http://www.weforum.org/**.
9. "The Corporation and the Public: Open for Inspection," *World Economic Forum,* January 27, 2001, **http://www.weforum.org/**.
10. Environment Canada, *Corporate Environmental Innovation: Corporation Sustainability Reporting,* **http://www.ec.gc.ca** (accessed December 21, 2006).
11. Barry Desker, "Why the East Asian Summit Matters," *Asia Times,* December 13, 2005; Christopher Lockwood, "The Club that Excludes America: The Significance of the Inaugural East Asia Summit," *The Economist: The World in 2006* (Economist Publications, 2006).
12. Michael R. Czinkota, Ilkka A. Ronkainen, and Bob Donath, *Mastering Global Markets* (Cincinnati, OH: Thomson, 2003).
13. Goldman Sachs, Global Economics Paper No. 99: *Dreaming with BRICs: the Path to 2050,* October 2003.
14. Export Development Canada, *Discover New Markets,* 2006, **http://www.edc.ca/english/publications_8927.htm** (accessed December 20, 2006).
15. CIA, *The World Factbook 2006,* United States, **https://www.cia.gov?cia/publications/factbook/print/us.html/** (accessed July 1, 2007).
16. *Computer Industry Almanac,* **http://www.c-i-a.com/pr032102.htm** (accessed December 21, 2006).
17. *Comscore* Press Release May 4, 2006, **http://www.comscore.com/press/release.asp?press=849** (accessed December 21, 2006).
18. *CIA World Factbook,* **http://www.cia.gov/cia/publications/factbook/index.html** (accessed December 5, 2002).
19. John Quelch, "Global Village People," *WorldLink Magazine,* January–February 1999.
20. Renato Ruggiero, "The New Frontier," *WorldLink Magazine,* January–February 1998.
21. Minoru Makihara, Co-Chairman of the Annual Meeting of the World Economic Forum, Davos 2001, **http://www.weforum.org/**.
22. Polly Campbell, "Trend Watch 2001," *The Edward Lowe Report,* January 2001, 1–3.
23. Michael R. Czinkota, "The Policy Gap in International Marketing," *Journal of International Marketing* 8, no. 1 (2000): 99–111.
24. Murray Weidenbaum, "All the World's a Stage," *Management Review,* October 1999, 42–48.
25. UN Population Division, *World Urbanization Prospects,* **http://www.un.org/esa/population** (accessed December 10, 2002).
26. John Lancaster, "The Desperate Bachelors," *The Washington Post,* December 2, 2002, A1, A17.
27. Statistics Canada, "Farmers Leaving the Field," *Perspectives on Labour and Income* 3, no. 2 (February 2002).
28. Michael R. Czinkota and Masaaki Kotabe, "The Role of Japanese Distribution Strategies," in *Japanese Distribution Strategy,* ed. M.R. Czinkota and M. Kotabe (London: Business Press, 2000), 6–16.
29. Agriculture and Agri-Food Canada, *Levelling the International Playing Field for Canadians: Reaching a Milestone in WTO Agricultural Negotiations,* **http://www.agr.gc.ca/**.
30. Michael R. Czinkota, "From Bowling Alone to Standing Together," *Marketing Management,* March–April 2002, 12–16.
31. The World Bank, *Rapid Growth: Prospects for the Global Economy,* May 30, 2006.

32. Rosabeth Moss Kanter, "Six Strategic Challenges," *WorldLink Magazine*, January–February 1998.

33. "The Corporation and the Public: Open for Inspection," World Economic Forum, **http://www.weforum.org/**.

34. Michael R. Czinkota, "Success of Globalization Rests on Good Business Reputations," *The Japan Times*, October 12, 2002, 9.

35. Michael R. Czinkota and Masaaki Kotabe, "Product Development the Japanese Way," in *Trends in International Business: Critical Perspectives*, ed. M. Czinkota and Masaaki Kotabe (Oxford: Blackwell Business, 1998), 153–58.

36. Business Overview of QVC, Inc., **http://www.qvc.com** (accessed December 6, 2002).

37. Gary Hart and Warren B. Rudman (Stephen E. Flynn, Project Director), *America Still Unprepared—America Still in Danger* (New York: Council on Foreign Relations, December 6, 2002).

38. Gunter K. Stahl, Edwin L. Miller, and Rosalie L. Tung, "Toward the Boundaryless Career: A Closer Look at the Expatriate Career Concept and the Perceived Implications of an International Assignment," *Journal of World Business* 37 (2002): 216–27.

39. Institute of International Education, *Open Doors*, November 18, 2002, **http://www.iie.org**.

40. Association of Universities and Colleges of Canada, *Reality Check* 1, no. 2 (January 2003). A series of fact-based essays dispelling common myths about Canadian universities.

41. Joann S. Lublin, "To Smooth a Transfer Abroad, a New Focus on Kids," *The Wall Street Journal*, January 26, 1999, B1, B14.

42. Nancy J. Adler, "Women in International Management: Where Are They?" *Californian Management Review* 26, no. 4 (1984): 78–89.

43. "U.S. Women in Global Business Face Glass Borders," *Catalyst Perspective*, November 2000, **http://www.catalystwomen.org/**.

44. "Globalisation's Offspring: How the New Multinationals are Remaking the Old," *The Economist*, April 7–13, 2007, 11.

45. "Globalisation's Offspring," op. cit.

46. "Globalisation's Offspring," op. cit.

47. "Why Trade Matters: Canadian Innovation: The Power of Ingenuity," Foreign Affairs and International Trade Canada, **http://www.dfait-maeci.gc.ca/tna-nac/stories117-en.asp**.

48. Andrea Mandel-Campbell, *Why Mexicans Don't Drink Molson: Rescuing Canadian Business from the Suds of Global Obscurity* (Toronto: Douglas and McIntyre, 2007).

Glossary

A

absolute advantage An economic principle stating that a country should specialize in the production of that which it can produce more efficiently than its prospective trading partners and should trade with those countries for all other products it wishes to consume.

acculturation Adjusting and adapting to a specific culture other than one's own.

activity objectives Objectives based on activities carried out, such as number of sales calls made. *See also* results objectives.

adaptive selling Selling by salespersons in which they adapt or modify their behaviour to suit individual buyer circumstances rather than using a "canned" or more mechanical approach.

ad valorem tariff A tax on an imported product that is imposed by a domestic government and assessed as a percentage of its market value.

agents Intermediaries for the distribution of goods who earn a commission on sales. *See also* distributors.

ambush marketing The unauthorized use of an event without the permission of the event owner (e.g., an advertising campaign that suggests a sponsorship relationship).

anti-dumping duty A duty imposed on imports alleged to be "dumped"—or sold at less than fair market value—on a domestic marketplace.

anti-dumping laws Laws prohibiting below-cost sales of products.

area structure An approach to organization based on geographical areas.

area studies Environmental briefings and cultural orientation programs; factual preparation for living or working in another culture.

arm's-length price A basis for intra-company transfer pricing; the price that unrelated parties would have arrived at for the same transaction.

autarky A term used to describe the absence of international trade.

B

backward innovation Simplifying a product or service due to lack of purchasing power or usage conditions.

balance of payments An accounting statement that summarizes economic transactions between one country and other countries with which it does business.

balance of trade A term used to describe the difference between a country's exports and imports.

banker's acceptance A method of payment for exported goods: when a time draft, with a specified term of maturity, is drawn on and accepted by a bank, it becomes a banker's acceptance, which is sold in the short-term money market. *See also* documentary collection; discounting.

barriers to entry Obstacles to trade created by governments and market conditions.

barter Exchange of goods for other goods of equal value.

best practice An idea that has saved money or time, or a process that is more efficient than existing ones; usually established by councils appointed by a company.

bilateral negotiations Trade agreements carried out mainly between two nations.

bill of lading A document that acknowledges receipt of the goods, represents the basic contract between the shipper and the carrier, and serves as evidence of title to the goods for collection by the purchaser; required for export.

black hole A situation that the international marketer has to work his or her way out of; a company may be in a "black hole" because it has read the market incorrectly or because government has restricted its activities.

boycotts Refusing to purchase from or trade with a company because of political or ideological differences.

brain drain Foreign direct investors attracting the best and brightest employees from a domestic firm; said to deprive domestic firms of talent.

brand Name, term, symbol, sign, or design used by a firm to differentiate its offerings from those of its competitors.

BRIC countries An acronym used to describe four significant emerging markets: Brazil, Russia, India, and China.

budgets Short-term financial guidelines in such areas as investment, cash, and personnel. *See also* plans.

bulk service Ocean-freight service that mainly provides contractual services for individual voyages for prolonged periods of time.

bureaucratic controls A limited and explicit set of regulations and rules that outline desired levels of performance. *See also* cultural controls.

buyback A form of countertrade; a compensation arrangement whereby one party agrees to supply technology or equipment that enables the other party to produce goods with which the price of the supplied technology or equipment is repaid.

C

cash in advance A method of payment for exported goods; the most favourable term to the exporter; not widely used, except for smaller, custom orders, first-time transactions, or situations in which the exporter has reason to doubt the importer's ability to pay.

cause-related marketing Marketing that links a company or brand with a cause, such as environmental protection or children's health.

centralization When a firm maintains tight controls and strategic decision making is concentrated at headquarters. *See also* coordinated decentralization.

certificate of origin A document required by certain countries to ensure correct tariffs are paid.

change agent The introduction into a culture of new products, ideas, or practices that may lead to changes in consumption.

channel design Refers to decisions made by the firm with respect to the length and width of the channel that the firm will utilize to reach its final consumers.

clearing arrangements Clearing accounts for deposit and withdrawal of results of countertrade activities.

code law A comprehensive set of written statutes; countries with code law try to spell out all possible legal rules explicitly; based on Roman law and found in a majority of nations.

commercial risk Term referring primarily to an overseas buyer suspected of insolvency or protracted payment default.

common law Based on tradition; depends less on written statutes and codes than on precedent and custom.

common market Goods and services, including labour, capital, and technology, are freely exchanged among member countries; restrictions are removed on immigration and cross-border investment; member countries adopt common trade policies with non-members.

comparative advantage An economic principle that states that a country should specialize in the production and export of products it can produce relatively more efficiently and import all other products; according to this principle, a country still benefits from international trade even when it does not have an absolute advantage.

competitive and collaborative approaches Two contrasting views of approaches to global negotiating: the former emphasizes "hard" bargaining, in which the negotiator might try to exact concessions, while the latter emphasizes "soft" bargaining, in which concessions might be offered in the hope of reciprocation and the establishment of mutual benefits.

compound tariffs Tariffs that have both ad valorem and specific components.

computer-aided design (CAD) A combination of hardware and software that allows for the design of products.

concentration A market expansion policy characterized by focusing on and developing a small number of markets. *See also* diversification.

confiscation Transfer of ownership from a foreign firm to the host country without compensation to the owner.

confrontation The use of aggressive or coercive behaviour by a negotiator to try to force a one-sided outcome from a negotiating partner.

consignment selling A method of payment that allows the importer to defer payment until the imported goods are actually sold.

construct validity A term used to describe a measurement instrument that in fact measures the phenomenon that the market researcher sets out to measure.

consular invoice A document required by certain countries for data collection purposes in order to track exports and imports.

consumer ethnocentrism The purchase of goods and services for cultural or nationalist reasons rather than for more customary reasons such as price. An extreme form of ethnocentrism in which the purchase of foreign products is viewed as unpatriotic or even morally wrong.

consumer patriotism Preference for domestically produced goods and services over foreign ones.

container ships Cargo vessels that carry standardized containers, which greatly facilitate the loading and unloading of cargo and inter-modal transfers.

contender A local company whose assets are transferable, allowing it to compete head-on with established global players worldwide.

content analysis A research technique investigating the content of communication in a society; for example, counting the number of times preselected words, themes, symbols, or pictures appear in a given medium.

contributor A role of a country organization; a subsidiary with a distinctive competence, such as product development or regional expertise.

convergent validity A form of construct validity in which the same results are obtained when a construct is measured in two different ways.

coordinated decentralization Overall corporate strategy is provided from headquarters (centralized decision making) but subsidiaries are free to implement it within the range established in consultation between headquarters and the subsidiaries.

corporate image advertising An umbrella marketing communications plan to make the company itself be correctly understood or perceived more positively.

cost-plus method A pricing strategy based on the true cost of a product (inclusive of domestic and foreign marketing costs).

counterpurchase A form of countertrade that is a parallel barter agreement: the participating parties sign two separate contracts that specify goods and services to be exchanged (some cash may be exchanged to compensate for differences in value).

countertrade Transactions in which purchases are tied to sales and sales to purchases.

countervailing duties A duty imposed on imports alleged to be priced at less than fair market value, due to subsidization of an industry by a foreign government.

country similarity theory A theory that states that countries should be expected to trade most intensely with other countries with similar levels of per capita income and less intensely with countries with dissimilar levels of per capita income; also known as the Linder theory.

cross-subsidization The use of resources accumulated in one part of the world to compete for market share in another part of the world.

cultural controls Informal rules and regulations that are the result of shared beliefs and expectations among the members of an organization. *See also* bureaucratic controls.

cultural convergence The growing similarity of attitudes and behaviours across cultures.

cultural diversity The wide range of unique cultures in countries around the world.

cultural knowledge Broad, multifaceted knowledge acquired through living in a certain culture.

cultural literacy The acquisition of detailed knowledge of the culture of the target market that enables a person to function effectively in that culture.

cultural universals Characteristics common to all cultures, such as body adornments, courtship, etiquette, family gestures, joking, mealtimes, music, personal names, status differentiation, and so on.

culture An integrated system of learned behaviour patterns that are distinguishing characteristics of members of any given society.

currency variation Changes in exchange rates; can affect the purchases and profitability of the international firm.

customer involvement The degree of participation of the recipient in the production of a service.

customer relationship management An attempt by a company to develop deeper, stronger relations with customers; for example, an exporter's strategy to increase perceived attention to the foreign customer through call-centre technologies, customer-service departments, and the company's website.

customer structure An approach to organization that is based on the customer groups that are served—for example, consumers versus businesses versus governments.

customs broker An agent for an importer with authority to clear inbound goods through customs and ship them on to their destination.

customs union Nation members of customs unions agree to set aside trade barriers and also establish common trade policies with non-member nations.

D

database marketing Promotional tool combining telemarketing with data on the purchasing habits of a customer; allows the creation of an individual relationship with each customer or prospect.

dealer interference A strategy to combat parallel distribution in which grey products are tracked down in the importing country and the offending dealer is asked to destroy the products.

debt problem Developing countries can be burdened with loans from international sources or other countries, which can crush a nation's buying power and force imports down and exports up to meet interest payments.

decentralization When a firm grants its subsidiaries a high degree of autonomy; controls are relatively loose and simple. *See also* coordinated decentralization.

defender A local company that has assets that give it a competitive advantage only in its home market.

Delphi forecasting A forecasting technique in which the judgments of a number of experts who cannot come together physically are solicited using two or more rounds of a structured questionnaire; the technique seeks to arrive at a consensus forecast by providing experts with controlled statistical feedback between successive rounds of questionnaire administration.

demand interference A strategy to combat parallel distribution in which advertisements are rolled out that educate the consumer about the benefits of dealing with authorized dealers and the dangers of dealing with grey-market dealers.

density Weight-to-volume ratio of goods; high-density goods are more likely to be shipped as airfreight rather than ocean freight.

direct exporters Exporting firms that transact directly with intermediaries in foreign countries.

direct exporting A distribution channel in which the marketer takes direct responsibility for its products abroad by either selling directly to the foreign customer or finding a representative in the foreign country to sell its products in the market. *See also* indirect exporting.

direct exports Dealing directly with a foreign entity in the foreign market (e.g., an agent or a distributor) rather than through another domestic company. *See also* indirect exports.

discounting When a time draft (a method of payment for exported goods with a specified term of maturity) is drawn on and accepted by a bank, it may be converted into cash by the exporter by discounting; the draft is sold to a bank at a discount from face value. *See also* banker's acceptance.

discretionary product adaptation Conforming a product or service to meet prevailing social, economic, and climactic conditions in the market.

discriminant validity A form of construct validity; refers to whether or not the construct is different from other concepts.

discriminatory regulations Rules and laws that impose larger operating costs on foreign firms than on local competitors, that provide subsidies to local firms only, or that deny competitive opportunities to foreign suppliers; non-discriminatory regulations may be inconvenient and may hamper business operations, but they offer less opportunity for international criticism.

distribution culture Existing channel structures and philosophies for the distribution of goods.

distributors Intermediaries who purchase goods for resale through their own channels. *See also* agents.

diversification A market expansion policy characterized by growth in a relatively large number of markets. *See also* concentration.

documentary collection A method of payment for exported goods: the seller ships the goods, and the shipping documents and the draft demanding payment are presented to the importer through a bank acting as the seller's agent; the draft, also known as the bill of exchange, may be a sight draft or a time draft.

dodger A local company that sells out to a global player or becomes part of an alliance.

domestication Gaining control over the assets of a foreign firm by demanding partial transfer of ownership and management responsibility to the host country.

draft A method of payment for exported goods that is similar to a personal cheque; an order by one party to pay another; documentary drafts must be accompanied by specified shipping documents, while clean drafts do not require documentation; also known as the bill of exchange. *See also* documentary collection.

dual pricing Differentiation of domestic and export prices.

dual-use items Goods that are useful for both military and civilian purposes.

duty drawbacks A refund of up to 99 percent of duties paid on imports when they are re-exported or incorporated into articles that are subsequently exported within five years of the importation.

E

economic union Integration of economic policies among member countries; monetary policies, taxation, and government spending are harmonized.

economies of scale A production condition where an increase in the quantity of the product results in a decrease of the production cost per unit.

economies of scope The reduction in cost per unit as the firm spreads its total costs (production, marketing, and R & D) over a larger number of brands, product lines, or target markets.

efficiency seekers Firms that attempt to obtain the most economic sources of production in their foreign direct investment strategy.

embargo Governmental action that terminates the free flow of trade in goods, services, or ideas; imposed for adversarial and political purposes.

encultured A situation in which a person has learned the "right" way to function in a particular culture.

environmental protection A major force shaping the relationship between the developed and developing world; being environmentally responsible may help a company to build trust and improve its image, but may be contradictory to a developing nation's need to expand into undeveloped areas and exploit its resources.

estimation by analogy An approach to forecasting in which the researcher first establishes a relationship between the foreign-market demand to be estimated and a factor (such as population size) that is to be used in the estimation; once the correlation between the demand and the factor has been established, the foreign-market demand in question is estimated from the known situation.

ethnocentric Characterized by the belief that one's own culture is superior to other cultures.

European Union Effective January 1, 1994; formed by the ratification of the Maastricht Treaty; set the foundation for economic and monetary union among member countries and the establishment of a common currency, the euro.

expectation–reality gap Divergence between hoped-for and achieved conditions, frequently experienced with the standard of living in less-developed nations; countries must either lower expectations or make more goods available at lower prices.

experiential knowledge Knowledge acquired only by being involved in a culture other than one's own.

experimental exporter A stage in which a domestic firm chooses to engage in limited export, usually to countries that are "psychologically close," without yet having evaluated whether and how an international strategy makes sense.

exploratory stage A stage in which a firm begins to explore the feasibility of exporting or otherwise engaging in international trade.

export adaptation An experienced export firm with the ability to adjust its activities to keep pace with changing exchange rates, tariffs, and other variables in the international market.

export control systems Governmental policy designed to deny or at least delay the acquisition of strategically important goods by adversaries.

export embargo A government action that prohibits the export of goods and services to a specific country or group of countries for political rather than economic reasons.

export promotion Measures such as subsidies, trade missions, and the provision of foreign market intelligence, introduced to enhance exporting activity at the company, industry, or national level.

export tariff A tax imposed by the domestic government on a product that is being exported.

expropriation Seizure of foreign assets by a government with payment of compensation to the owners.

extender A company that is able to exploit its success at home as a platform for expansion elsewhere; this calls for markets or segments that are similar in terms of customer preferences.

F

factor mobility The loosening of restrictions on the trade of capital, labour, and technology among nations.

factoring A trade financing method; companies known as factoring houses may purchase an exporter's receivables for a discounted price; factors also provide the exporter with a complete financial package combining credit protection, accounts-receivable bookkeeping, and collection services.

factual information Objective knowledge of a culture obtained from others through communication, research, and education.

fade-in/fade-out strategy A brand changeover strategy in which the global brand is associated with the local brand for a specified period of time, after which the local brand is dropped.

field experience The placement of a trainee in a different cultural environment for a limited time; for example, the trainee lives with a host family of the nationality to which the trainee will be assigned.

financial incentives Special funding legislated by governments to attract foreign investments.

fiscal incentives Special funding legislated by governments to attract foreign investments.

forced distribution tests A group of consumers reports on new products they encounter in normal retail outlets. *See also* laboratory test markets; microtest marketing.

foreign direct investment Capital funds that flow from abroad; company is held by non-citizens; foreign ownership is typically undertaken for longer-term participation in an economic activity.

foreign exchange licence A licence that may be required by certain countries for an importer to secure the needed hard currency to pay for an import shipment; the exporter has to provide the importer with the data needed to obtain these licences from governmental authorities and should make sure that the importer has indeed secured the documents.

foreign production The final stage in the process of internationalization in which companies establish full-fledged manufacturing operations in a foreign country, investing in plant and equipment and maintaining a complement of production and management staff.

foreign sales subsidiary A stage in the process of internationalization in which the firm establishes a dedicated sales force to handle marketing operations in the foreign country.

foreign trade zones Geographic areas in a country within which foreign companies receive preferential treatment of their imported raw materials and exports of their finished products.

forewarn A brand changeover strategy in which the firm informs consumers in advance that their local brand will soon be known by its global name

forfaiting A trade financing technique; the importer pays the exporter with bills of exchange or promissory notes guaranteed by a leading bank in the importer's country; the exporter can sell these to a third party at a discount from their face value for immediate cash.

Fortress Europe Term expressing the fear that unified European nations will raise barriers to trade with other nations, including setting rules about domestic content and restricting imports.

forward exchange market A method used to counter challenges in currency movements; the exporter enters into an agreement for a rate at which the exporter will buy the foreign currency at a future date; the rate is expressed as either a premium or a discount on the current spot rate.

forward pricing Distributing development costs over the anticipated volume of future sales of a product.

free trade area The least restrictive and loosest form of economic integration among nations; goods and services are freely traded among member countries.

Free Trade Area of the Americas (FTAA) A proposed free trade zone reaching from Point Barrow, Alaska, to Patagonia.

functional lubrication Bribes that are not imposed by individual greed, but that serve to "grease the wheels" of bureaucratic processes; amounts tend to be small, the "express fee" is standardized, and the money is passed along to the party in charge of processing a document.

functional structure An approach to organization that emphasizes the basic tasks of the firm—for example, manufacturing, sales, and research and development.

futures A method used to counter problems of currency movements; in the currency futures market, for example, a buyer agrees to buy futures on the British pound sterling, which implies an obligation to buy in the future at a pre-specified price. *See also* option.

G

geocentric A global pricing strategy in which the firm establishes a minimum floor price below which the product cannot be sold by its subsidiaries in any country. Managers are, however, allowed to add a country markup to better reflect demand and competitive conditions in their national markets.

global account management Account programs extended across countries, typically for the most important customers, to build relationships.

globalization The increased integration of the world's economies.

global marketing The planning, coordination, and integration of marketing activities across multiple country markets.

global media Media vehicles that have target audiences on at least three continents.

glocalization Building in organizational flexibility to allow for local/regional adjustments in global strategic planning and implementation; uniformity is sought in strategic elements such as positioning of a product; care is taken to localize tactical elements, such as distribution.

glocal marketing A strategic orientation that reflects the need for balance between global marketing, with its focus on standardization, and local marketing, with its focus on adaptation to country differences.

government–corporate collaboration Cooperation between policymakers and business executives; on the rise due to the accelerating technological race and emerging key concerns such as environmental pollution and global warming.

grey-market goods Goods that enter the marketplace through distribution channels uncontrolled by the goods' producers or in ways not desired by the goods' manufacturers.

Group of Five Five industrialized nations regarded as economic superpowers: the United States, Britain, France, Germany, and Japan.

Group of Seven Seven industrialized nations regarded as economic superpowers: the United States, Britain, France, Germany, Japan, Italy, and Canada.

Group of Ten Ten industrialized nations regarded as economic superpowers: the United States, Britain, France, Germany, Japan, Italy, Canada, the Netherlands, Belgium, and Sweden.

H

harmony A pleasing combination of circumstances; in a cross-cultural negotiation, describes the inclination of some countries (e.g., Japan) to avoid confrontation, thereby giving strategy clues to the negotiating partner.

high context cultures Cultures in which the context is at least as important as what is actually said; for example, Japan and Saudi Arabia have cultures in which what is not said can carry more meaning than what is said.

household All the persons, both related and unrelated, who occupy a housing unit.

I

implementer A role of a country organization; although implementers are usually placed in smaller, less-developed countries, they provide the opportunity to capture economies of scale and scope that are the basis of a global strategy.

import licence A licence that may be required by certain countries for particular types or amounts of imported goods.

import substitution A policy that requires a nation to produce goods that were formerly imported.

import tariffs A tax imposed by the domestic government on a product that is being imported.

Incoterms Internationally accepted standard definitions for terms of sale, covering variable methods of transportation and delivery between country of origin and country of destination; set by the International Chamber of Commerce (ICC) since 1936.

indirect exporters Exporting firms that transact with an intermediary in their home country; this intermediary, in turn, makes the firm's products available to intermediaries in a foreign country.

indirect exporting A distribution channel that requires dealing with another domestic firm that acts as a sales intermediary for the marketer, often taking over the international side of the marketer's operations. *See also* direct exporting.

indirect exports Relying on a third party (e.g., an export management company) to perform exporting tasks. *See also* direct exports.

infant industry Relatively new firms are sometimes seen as deserving of protection, which allows the industry to "grow up" before having to compete with "adult" global industries.

inflation The increase in consumer prices compared with a previous period.

innate exporters Start-up exporters; firms founded for the express purpose of marketing abroad; also described as "born global."

intangibility The quality of not being able to be seen, touched, or held; a key difference between goods and services.

integrated distribution An export marketing strategy in which the marketer makes an investment in the foreign market for the purpose of selling its products.

integrated exports An export marketing strategy in which the marketer takes direct responsibility for its products abroad by either selling directly to the foreign customer or finding a local representative to sell its products in the market.

integrated marketing communications Coordinating various promotional strategies according to target market and product characteristics, the size of budget, the type of international involvement, and control considerations.

intellectual property rights Safeguarding rights by providing the originators of an idea or process with a proprietary compensation, at least, in order to encourage quick dissemination of innovations.

intermediaries Independent distributors of goods, operating primarily at a local level. *See also* distributors; agents.

international comparative research Research carried out between nations, particularly those with similar environments, where the impact of uncontrollable macro variables is limited.

international freight forwarder An agent who provides services in moving cargo to an overseas destination.

internationalization The process by which firms become gradually more engaged in global markets.

international marketing The process of planning and conducting transactions across national borders to create exchanges that satisfy the objectives of individuals and organizations.

international product life cycles The length of market viability of a product; cycles are shorter than in previous decades, and firms must now prepare for product introductions over months, or even weeks, rather than spread out over several years.

interpretive knowledge Knowledge that requires comprehensive fact finding and preparation, as well as an ability to appreciate the nuances of different cultural traits and patterns.

intranets Company networks that integrate a company's information assets into a single and accessible system using Internet-based technologies such as e-mail, newsgroups, and the World Wide Web.

L

laboratory test markets Participants are exposed to a product and their reactions measured in a controlled environment. *See also* microtest marketing; forced distribution tests.

labour theory of value An economic principle that states that commodities should be valued in terms of the amount of labour embodied in their production.

lead-lag analysis A forecasting technique in which the researcher uses time series data from one country to project sales in other countries. The approach is based on the assumption that the fundamental drivers of demand are the same in both countries and that only time separates them.

lead users Companies, organizations, or individuals who are ahead of trends or have needs that go beyond what is available at the present time.

Leontief statistic The metric $(K/L)_m/(K/L)_x$, where $(K/L)_x$ is the capital-to-labour ratio for exports and $(K/L)_m$ is the capital-to-labour ratio for imports.

letter of credit A method of payment for exported goods; an instrument issued by a bank at the request of a buyer: the bank promises to pay a specified amount of money on presentation of documents stipulated in the letter of credit (usually the bill of lading, consular invoice, and a description of the goods).

licensing An agreement in which one firm (the licensor) permits another firm (the licensee) to use its intellectual property in exchange for compensation designated as a royalty.

liner service Ocean-freight service that offers regular scheduled passage on established routes.

local assembly A stage in the process of internationalization in which a firm sources components in its home country and assembles and markets the final product in a foreign country.

localized The modification of a product to enable it to function or be saleable in some foreign markets.

low context cultures Cultures in which most information is contained explicitly in words; for example, North American cultures.

low-pressure selling Selling by salespersons that avoids coercion, relying instead on a more indirect approach based on questioning the buyer and obtaining agreement through logical argument.

M

management contract An agreement where the supplier brings together a package of skills that will provide for the ongoing operation of the client's facilities.

mandatory product adaptation Conforming a product or service to meet prevailing legal and regulatory conditions in the market.

maquiladora A Mexican plant that makes goods and parts or processes food for export to the United States.

marginal cost method A pricing strategy that considers only the direct cost of producing and selling products for export as the floor beneath which prices cannot be set; overhead costs are disregarded, allowing an exporter to lower prices to be competitive in markets that otherwise might not be accessed.

market-differentiated pricing Export pricing based on the dynamic, changing conditions of each marketplace.

market pricing Determining the initial price of a product by comparison to competitors' prices.

market seekers Firms that search for better opportunities for entry and expansion in their foreign direct investment strategy.

marketspace The virtual marketplace where buyers and sellers transact online.

market transparency Clarity of the offering made to the customer; transparency in service delivery is often difficult to ensure, because services may be customized to individual needs.

mass customization Manufacturing that meets customers' growing desires for products that precisely meet their needs and preferences; requires working with existing technology, often in modular form, to produce large quantities of base products that are then adapted and refined.

master franchising system A system wherein foreign partners are selected and awarded the franchising rights to territory that they, in turn, can subfranchise.

materials management The timely movement of raw materials, parts, and supplies into and through a firm.

matrix structure An approach to organization based on the coordination of product and geographic dimensions of planning and implementing strategy.

mercantilism An economic doctrine that holds that a nation's wealth is measured by its stock of precious metals (specie).

microtest marketing A panel of consumers is exposed to new products through a retail grocery operated by a research agency. *See also* laboratory test markets; forced distribution tests.

missionary selling Selling by salespersons intended to build goodwill, perform promotional services, and provide information and other services for the customers; order solicitation is not expected.

mixed structure An approach to organization that combines one or more possible structures (*see also* product, functional, process, and customer structures); also called a hybrid structure.

modes of entry Institutional arrangements used by firms to enter foreign markets.

monopolistic competition A market structure under which firms produce differentiated products and consumer brand loyalty is possible.

multi-domestic marketing A strategic orientation in which a firm develops and implements a unique marketing strategy for each country in which it does business with little or no coordination of operations between countries.

multilateral negotiations Trade agreements carried out among a number of nations.

N

naive rule An approach in which a firm uses the same entry mode irrespective of the foreign market that is to be penetrated.

national security Protecting the welfare—economic, cultural, or military—of a nation's people; tariffs, barriers to entry, and other obstacles to trade often are established to ensure such protection.

negotiating styles The use of culturally unique or distinctive approaches to negotiating; for example, avoiding direct confrontation or using long periods of silence, as might be expected in some Southeast Asian countries.

new trade theory A theory of international trade that is based on the concepts of monopolistic competition and economies of scale.

nomological validity A form of construct validity; refers to whether or not the construct is related to some other external criterion.

non-discriminatory regulations Rules and laws that may be inconvenient and hamper business operations, but that are imposed in an evenhanded manner, without discriminating between local and foreign suppliers.

non-financial incentives Support such as guaranteed government purchases, special protection from competition through tariffs, import quotas, and local content requirements designed to attract foreign investments.

non-tariff barriers Barriers to trade that are more subtle than tariff barriers; for example, these barriers may be government or private-sector "buy domestic" campaigns, preferential treatment of domestic bidders over foreign bidders, or the establishment of standards that are not common to foreign goods or services.

nonverbal communications The use during negotiations of non-speech communications such as body language, signals, or facial gestures.

not-invented-here (NIH) syndrome Local resistance or decline in morale caused by the perception that headquarters is not sensitive to local needs.

O

offset A form of countertrade; industrial compensation mandated by governments when purchasing defence-related goods and services in order to equalize the effect of the purchase on the balance of payments.

open account A method of payment, also known as open terms; an exporter selling on open account removes both real and psychological barriers to importing, but no written evidence of the debt exists and there is no guarantee of payment.

operating risk Exposing ongoing operations of a firm to political risk in another nation.

opportunity costs Costs resulting from the foreclosure of other sources of profit, such as exports or direct investment; for example, when licensing eliminates options.

option A method used to counter challenges in currency movements; gives the holder the right to buy or sell foreign currency at a pre-specified price on or up to a pre-specified date. *See also* futures.

order-mindedness An attitude of salespeople recognizing that obtaining an order from the customer is a key objective of their activities; in the absence of this attitude, salespeople may develop good relationships with customers but fail to obtain any business for their company.

outcome The result of meeting objectives that seek to generate awareness, evoke a positive attitude, or increase purchases.

over-invest In the initial acquisition process, buying more land, space, and equipment than is needed immediately to accommodate future growth.

ownership risk Exposing property and life to political risk in another nation.

own intensity preference The proposition that a country has a preference for products that are produced with the factor that is most abundant in that country.

P

parallel importation Authentic and legitimately manufactured trademark items that are produced and purchased abroad but imported or diverted to the markets by bypassing designated channels; also called grey market.

parochialism Derived from the word *parish,* describing a very narrow outlook; can lead to misleading perceptions (e.g., that all countries should follow Western-oriented business practices).

partially interested exporter A firm that becomes involved in a very limited way in global trade, by choosing to respond to unsolicited overseas orders or otherwise responding to international market stimuli.

penetration pricing Introducing a product at an initial low price to generate sales volume and achieve high market share.

perishability The rapidity with which a service or good loses value or becomes worthless; for example, unused capacity in the form of an empty seat on an airplane quickly becomes non-saleable.

physical distribution The movement of a firm's finished product to its customers.

Physical Quality of Life Index (PQLI) A composite measure of the level of welfare in a country, including life expectancy, infant mortality, and adult literacy rates.

plans Formalized long-range financial programs with more than a one-year horizon. *See also* budgets.

political risk The risk of loss when investing in a given country caused by changes in the country's political structure or policies, such as tax laws, tariffs, expropriation of assets, or restriction in repatriation of profits; a factor beyond the control of an exporter or importer; for example, a foreign buyer may be willing to pay, but the local government may delay methods of payment.

political union Unification of policies among member nations and establishment of common institutions.

polycentric A global pricing strategy in which the firm sets prices in each country market independent of head office involvement.

population balance The proportion of male to female children in a population; in many countries, male heirs are preferred, and the result of technologies that can predict the sex of a child has been that populations are skewed toward males, resulting in a gender inequality.

population stabilization Reducing sharp population growth; important in determining and predicting the standard of living (measured by dividing a nation's GDP by its population).

positioning The presentation of a product or service to evoke a positive and differentiated mental image in the consumers' perception.

pragmatic rule An approach in which a firm focuses on always selecting the mode of entry that minimizes its exposure to risk in the particular transaction.

pre-approach Essential market research and other information gathering about a customer that is performed by a salesperson prior to making a sales call to determine the best method of approaching individual customers.

predatory dumping Dumping—or selling goods overseas for less than in the exporter's home market or at a price below the cost of production, or both—that is termed "predatory" because it is used deliberately to increase the exporter's market share and undermine domestic industries.

pretest The administration of a survey instrument to a sample of a population in order to identify problems with the survey instrument.

price controls Government regulations that set maximum or minimum prices; governmental imposition of limits on price changes.

price elasticity of consumer demand Adjusting prices to current conditions: for example, a status-conscious market that insists on products with established reputations will be inelastic, allowing for more pricing freedom than a price-conscious market.

price escalation The higher cost of a product resulting from the costs of exporting and marketing in a foreign country.

primary research Market research undertaken with primary data.

process structure An approach to organization that uses processes as a basis for structure; common in the energy and mining industries, where one entity may be in charge of exploration worldwide and another may be responsible for the actual mining operation.

product placement Creating brand awareness by arranging to have a product shown or used in visual media such as movies, television, games, or websites.

product structure An approach to organization that gives worldwide responsibility to strategic business units for the marketing of their product lines.

profit repatriation Transfer of business gains from a local market to another country by the foreign direct investor.

promotional mix The tools an international marketer has available to form a total communications program for use in a targeted market: advertising, personal selling, publicity, sales promotion, and sponsorship.

prospecting The search by salespeople for potential customers and the process of determining which among them are the most promising sources of sales orders.

protectionism Measures adopted by national governments to unduly restrict trade and foreign investment.

proxy variable A substitute for a variable that one cannot directly measure.

psychological distance Perceived distance from a firm to a foreign market, caused by cultural variables, legal factors, and other societal norms; a market that is geographically close may seem to be psychologically distant.

pull strategies Promotional strategies in a targeted market relying primarily on mass communication tools, mainly advertising; appropriate for consumer-oriented products with large target audiences and long channels of distribution.

purchasing power parities (PPPs) A measure of how many units of currency are needed in one country to buy the amount of goods and services that one unit of currency will buy in another country.

push strategies Promotional strategies in a targeted market relying primarily on personal selling; higher cost per contact, but appropriate for selling where there are shorter channels of distribution and smaller target populations.

Q

qualitative data Data are gathered to better understand situations, behavioural patterns, and underlying dimensions.

quantitative data Data are amassed to assess statistical significance; surveys are appropriate research instruments.

quota A quantitative restriction on the volume of a product that can be imported into a country over a specified time period; a form of non-tariff barrier used by countries to restrict free trade and protect domestic industries.

quota systems Control of imports through quantitative restraints.

R

R & D consortia Companies that collaborate in long-term research and development projects to create technologies without the threat of antitrust suits.

R & D costs Costs resulting from the research and development of licensed technology.

realism check A step in the analysis of data in which the researcher determines what facts may have inadvertently skewed the responses; for example, if Italian responders report that very little pasta is consumed in Italy, the researcher may find that the responders were distinguishing between store-bought and homemade pasta.

reference groups Persons or groups that significantly influence an individual's attitude and behaviour.

relationship selling Building ties to customers based on the salesperson's attention and commitment to customer needs over time; the focus is on satisfied long-term customers, not one-time sales.

reliability The vagaries of nature can impose delays on transportation services; these delays tend to be shorter in absolute time for air shipments, which are considered more predictable.

reputation management The strategy of building a corporate reputation for virtue, vision, and veracity, the attributes of a good corporate citizen.

research consortia Joint industry efforts in the research and development of new products to combat the high costs and risks of innovation; often supported by governments.

research specifications In the centralized approach to coordinating international marketing, specifications such as focus, thrust, and design are directed by the home office to the local country operations for implementation.

resource-based view A concept of the company and of strategic planning that focuses on the individual resources and capabilities of the organization as the drivers of strategy rather than on the needs of the market or the strategies common to all companies in the industry.

resource seekers Firms that search for either natural resources or human resources in their foreign direct investment strategy.

results objectives Objectives based on results achieved (e.g., the number and value of sales orders obtained by a salesperson). *See also* activity objectives.

S

safety-valve activity The use of overseas sales as a way to balance inventories or compensate for overproduction in the short term.

sales-force automation (SFA) The application of technology to help improve selling efficiency, for example, by eliminating paperwork and order processing, solving customer problems on the spot, and saving time; often implemented globally to support customer relations management (CRM).

sales management objectives Objectives set by sales management for the total sales force and for each salesperson, serving as performance standards for evaluating the sales force. *See also* activity objectives; results objectives.

secondary research Market research undertaken with secondary data.

self-reference criterion The unconscious reference to one's own cultural values in comparison to other cultures.

seminar missions Promotional event in which 8 to 10 firms are invited to participate in a 1- to 4-day forum; a soft-sell approach aimed at expanding sales abroad.

sensitivity training An approach based on the assumption that understanding and accepting oneself is critical to understanding a person from another culture.

service capacity Ability to supply service on demand, including the planning of backup during peak periods; similar to an inventory of goods.

service consistency Uniformity or standardization in the offering of a service; unlike products, services are often subject to individual influences and the need to customize to satisfy unique customer interactions.

shipper's declaration for dangerous goods A document required for shipments such as corrosives, flammables, and poisons.

shipper's export declaration A document that states proper authorization for export and serves as a means for governmental data collection efforts.

Single European Act Ratified in 1987 by 12 European countries to free the exchange of goods, services, capital, and people among member countries.

skimming Offering a product at an initial high price to achieve the highest possible sales contribution in a short time period; as more market segments are identified, the price is gradually lowered.

social stratification The division of a particular population into classes.

sogoshosha Large Japanese trading companies, such as Sumitomo, Mitsubishi, Mutsui, and C. Itoh.

solo exhibitions Promotional events, generally limited to one or a few product themes and held only when market conditions warrant them; aimed at expanding sales abroad.

special drawing rights An international reserve asset introduced by the IMF in 1969.

specie-flow mechanism An economic principle that states that the accumulation of specie (stock of precious metals) by one country via a trade surplus will lead to an increase in the money supply and force an increase in wages and prices.

specific tariff A product tax that is imposed by a domestic government and assessed as a dollar amount added to the market value of each unit of the product which enters, leaves, or is transshipped through the country.

sprinkler strategy An approach to foreign market expansion in which the firm enters a number of unrelated markets simultaneously or within a short time period.

standard worldwide price A price-setting strategy in which a product is offered at the same price regardless of the geography of the buyer.

stereotyping The adoption of oversimplified ideas, both positive and negative, of the typical characteristics of countries or groups (e.g., that all salespersons use dubious techniques, or all Canadians are tolerant and caring).

strategic alliance A special form of joint venture consisting of an arrangement between two or more companies with a common business objective; more than the traditional customer–vendor relationship, but less than an outright acquisition.

strategic attack A strategy to combat parallel distribution in which a firm create stronger reasons (e.g., price incentives) for consumers to patronize authorized dealers instead of grey traders.

strategic leader A role of a country organization; a highly competent national subsidiary located in a strategically critical market.

strategy rule An approach in which a firm systematically analyzes each entry mode and applies a common evaluative metric, such as the potential to maximize net profit contribution.

summary axing A brand changeover strategy in which the local brand is simply dropped and the global brand simultaneously introduced.

supply interference A strategy to combat parallel distribution whereby a firm attempts to build a better relationship with its distributors in order to encourage them to better screen orders and tighten procedures for dealing with surplus inventory.

switch-trading Credits in a clearing account (established for countertrading) can be sold or transferred to a third party.

systems concept One of three major concepts of the logistics of international management, based on the notion that materials-flow activities within and outside the firm are so extensive and complex that they can be considered only in the context of their interaction. *See also* total cost concept; tradeoff concept.

T

tariff An import control mechanism that raises prices through the placement of a tax.

telemarketing Promotional tool that is growing worldwide as customers become more accustomed to calling toll-free numbers and more willing to receive calls from marketers.

theocracy A legal perspective that holds faith and belief as its key focus and is a mix of societal, legal, and spiritual guidelines.

total cost concept One of three major concepts of the logistics of international management, in which cost is used as a basis for measurement; the purpose of the total cost concept is to minimize the firm's overall logistics cost by implementing the systems concept appropriately. *See also* systems concept; tradeoff concept.

trade deficits Occur when a country imports more goods and services than it exports.

trade missions A promotional event aimed at expanding sales abroad; may be a country-specific, industry-organized, or government-approved event. *See also* seminar missions.

trade sanctions Governmental actions that inhibit the free flow of trade in goods, services, or ideas, imposed for adversarial and political purposes.

trademark licensing The ownership of the name or logo of a designer, literary character, sports team, or movie star, for example, which can be used on merchandise.

tradeoff concept One of three major concepts of the logistics of international management; recognizes that linkages within logistics systems lead to interactions; for example, locating a warehouse near the customer may reduce the cost of transportation, but requires investment in a new warehouse. *See also* systems concept; total cost concept.

tramp service Ocean-freight service that is available for irregular routes and is scheduled only on demand.

transaction-costs approach A characterization of the firm that emphasizes the costs incurred in making an economic exchange (e.g., search and information costs; bargaining costs); for example, direct or indirect exports involve different levels of transactions costs, which will influence the choice of entry mode.

transfer costs Costs incurred in negotiating licensing agreements; all variable costs resulting from transfer of a technology to a licensee, and all ongoing costs of maintaining the agreement.

transfer risk Exposing the transfer of funds to political risk across international borders.

transit tariff A tax imposed by a domestic government on a product that is being transshipped from one country to another.

translation–back-translation Reducing problems in the wording of questions by translating the question into a foreign language and having a second translator return the foreign text to the researcher's native language.

transportation modes Choices among airfreight and ocean freight, pipeline, rail, and trucking.

triad The megamarkets of North America, Europe, and the Asia-Pacific region.

Tri-State The populous region of the United States comprising New Jersey, Connecticut, and southern New York State (including New York City). The population of this area is close to that of Canada and is considered a substantial market for Canadian goods and services.

turnkey operation A complete operational system, including the skills investment sufficient to allow unassisted maintenance and operation of the system following its completion.

U

unintentional dumping Dumping—or selling goods overseas for less than in the exporter's home market or at a price below the cost of production, or both—that is termed "unintentional" because the lower price is due to currency fluctuations.

urbanization Descriptions of urbanization range from densely populated cities to built-up areas to small towns with proclaimed legal limits.

V

value-added tax (VAT) A tax on the value added to goods and services charged as a percentage of the price at each stage in the production and distribution chain.

verbal communications The use of the spoken word in communications; issues facing the negotiator include choosing the right language, fluency in the negotiating partner's language, and problems associated with semantics or word meaning. *See also* nonverbal communications.

video/catalogue exhibitions Promotional tools coordinating product presentations from several companies in one catalogue or video; aimed at expanding sales abroad.

virtual trade shows Electronic promotional tools enabling exporters to promote their products and services over the Internet and to have an electronic presence without actually attending an overseas trade show; aimed at expanding sales abroad.

W

waterfall strategy An approach to foreign market expansion in which the firm gradually moves its products and services into overseas markets; given success in the home market, the firm gradually begins marketing activities in psychologically close markets, then to other mature but high-growth markets, and finally to riskier developing country markets.

Web-based research Surveys and other data collection techniques that are administered using the resources of the Internet.

Z

zero-sum game A situation in which one party must lose in order for another to win.

Index

A

B

C

D

N

T